Multiprocessor Performance Measurement and Evaluation

Laxmi N. Bhuyan

Xiaodong Zhang

IEEE Computer Society Press
Los Alamitos, California

Washington • Brussels • Tokyo

Library of Congress Cataloging-in-Publication Data

Multiprocessor performance measurement and evaluation / [edited by]
Laxmi N. Bhuyan, Xiaodong Zhang.
     p.   cm.
  Includes bibliographical references.
  ISBN 0-8186-6522-X. — ISBN 0-8186-6521-1 (fiche)
  1. Multiprocessors—Evaluation. I. Bhuyan, Laxmi N.   II. Zhang, Xiaodong.
QA76.9.E94M84   1995
    004' .35 — dc20
                                                        94-21718
                                                          CIP

IEEE Computer Society Press
10662 Los Vaqueros Circle
P.O. Box 3014
Los Alamitos, CA 90720-1264

IEEE Computer Society Press Order Number 6522-01
Library of Congress Number 94-21718
IEEE Catalog Number EH0409-3
ISBN 0-8186-6522-X (case)
ISBN 0-8186-6521-1 (microfiche)

Additional copies may be ordered from:

IEEE Computer Society Press	IEEE Service Center	IEEE Computer Society	IEEE Computer Society
Customer Service Center	445 Hoes Lane	13, Avenue de l'Aquilon	Ooshima Building
10662 Los Vaqueros Circle	P.O. Box 1331	B-1200 Brussels	2-19-1 Minami-Aoyama
P.O. Box 3014	Piscataway, NJ 08855-1331	BELGIUM	Minato-ku, Tokyo 107
Los Alamitos, CA 90720-1264	Tel: +1-908-981-1393	Tel: +32-2-770-2198	JAPAN
Tel: +1-714-821-8380	Fax: +1-908-981-9667	Fax: +32-2-770-8505	Tel: +81-3-3408-3118
Fax: +1-714-821-4641			Fax: +81-3-3408-3553
Email: cs.books@computer.org			

Technical Editor: Mukesh Singhal
Editorial production by Lisa O'Conner
Cover by BookMasters, Inc.
Printed in the United States of America by Braun-Brumfield, Inc.

 The Institute of Electrical and Electronics Engineers, Inc.

Contents

Chapter 3: Performance of Large-Scale Shared-Memory Multiprocessor Systems

Preface

The quantitative evaluation of computer performance is important during the entire life cycle of a computer system, from design to application to future design. Parallel computers can be divided broadly into two categories: *single-instruction, multiple-data* (SIMD) and *multiple-instruction, multiple-data* (MIMD) computers. The focus of this book is on MIMD computers, also known as *multiprocessors* and *multicomputers*. As commercial multiprocessors proliferate in the marketplace, there is an increasing need to understand their relative performance when executing various applications. The challenge faced in computer performance evaluation is that the development of the required performance evaluation methods keep pace with the explosion of multiprocessor architecture designs. To meet the challenge requires an understanding of performance evaluation techniques that are particularly applicable to multiprocessors. The purpose of this book is to provide an up-to-date and comprehensive study in this area.

The present commercially available MIMD computers are divided into two categories: *shared-memory* and *message-passing* architectures. The shared-memory model uses a global shared memory that can be accessed by all the processors through an interconnection network. This global memory can be either a physical memory bank or a single address memory space connected by a set of distributed-memory modules. Communication among the processors is accomplished through reading from and writing to the global shared memory. In the simplest implementation of the shared-memory model, called a *bus-based shared-memory multiprocessor*, processors and shared-memory modules are connected by a single bus. Representative systems of this type are the Sequent Symmetry and the Encore Multimax. However, the bus-based shared-memory architectures are not scalable to connect a large number of processors, because the single bus forms a communication bottleneck. An effective approach to building a large-scale shared-memory system is to connect processors and shared-memory modules using a more complex interconnection network, such as a multistage interconnection network or a hierarchical ring network. The most promising direction for research and development in multiprocessor architecture is to use a shared address space where the physical memory is distributed. Examples of large-scale distributed shared-memory systems are the BBN Butterfly systems, the Stanford DASH prototype, the Kendall Square Research KSR systems, and the Cray T3D shared-memory systems.

In the message-passing model, there is no shared memory, but rather each processor has its own local memory. Processors communicate through an interconnection network consisting of direct communication links connecting certain pairs of processors. Since each node of the system is a complete computer system, with a processor, a memory, an I/O system, and an operating system, the message-passing model is also called a *multicomputer*. The most commonly used interconnection topologies are the hypercube and the two-dimensional (2D) mesh. For example, Intel iPSC/1, iPSC/2, and iPSC/860 and *n*-cube multicomputers are all connected in a hypercube topology, whereas the Intel Paragon, the most recent multicomputer, uses a 2D-mesh topology. The Connection Machine CM-5 employs the fat-tree network structure. The papers in this book present performance evaluation and measurement for large-scale shared-memory and message-passing parallel-computer systems, with experiments on many of the above-mentioned architectures.

Computer evaluation methods are generally divided into three main areas: *performance measurement, analytic performance modeling*, and *performance simulation*. Performance measurement is conducted on an existing computer system to identify current performance bottlenecks, correct them, and identify and prevent potential future performance problems. The advantage of performance measurement over performance modeling is that performance measurement obtains the performance of the *real* system, whereas performance modeling obtains the performance of a *model* of the system. Many important factors may be present in a system that affect performance and are difficult to capture in an analytic or simulation model. Disadvantages of performance measurement include its need for a real running system and for measurement instrumentation design. In addition, measurement results sometimes may not represent the general performance of a system, may cause large instrumentation overhead, and may not provide complete information for future architectural designs. Along with performance measurement, analytic modeling may be required in order to predict more effectively system performance during design and development of architectures.

Analytic modeling has been successfully applied to studying the performance of proposed future computer architectures and systems. Analytic models are extremely cost-effective compared to performance measurement, because they are based on efficient solutions to mathematical equations. However, analytic models cannot capture all of the detailed performance factors, because certain simplifying assumptions must be made regarding the structure of the model. Performance simulation provides a powerful tool to model extremely complex systems, whereas analytic models have limitations in capturing detailed factors. Analytic models also have difficulties accurately capturing the dynamic behavior of executions of parallel algorithms. Furthermore, whereas analytic models typically provide only mean values, simulations can provide estimates of distributions and many other variations. In addition, dynamic behavior can be studied using simulation, while analytic models usually can be used only to study steady-state behavior. The problem with the simulation approach is that it is expensive and time-consuming.

Increasingly, graphical visualizations are becoming useful and powerful tools for understanding and explaining complex tasks of parallel executions. Computer visualization software has become a common and standard system environment in workstations and many parallel computers, allowing us to track multiple complex visual patterns and to easily spot anomalies in these patterns. Therefore, computer visualization is an important tool to aid all aspects of performance evaluation of parallel computing.

In summary, measurement, modeling, simulation, and visualization of system performance are of great practical importance to the design of multiprocessor architectures, the development of system software, and the implementation of parallel algorithms. Readers can learn real applications of computer evaluation methods on different types of MIMD multiprocessor systems from the papers in this book. Also, we have included here some discussions of visualization as part of performance evaluation techniques.

This book is organized into four chapters, each including five to 10 papers. A bibliography is appended at the end of each chapter introduction to provide a list of further materials for the interested reader. To evaluate the performance of any system, a thorough knowledge of the system and its operation is essential. This book presents various parallel architectures existing in the marketplace. Multiprocessor organizations are explained in terms of their interconnections, cache memory organizations, and operational principles. The efficiency of the programming environment is important to parallel-system performance evaluation. Chapter 1 presents an overview of multiprocessor architectures, operating systems, programming software, and languages. Chapter 2 introduces techniques for multiprocessor performance evaluation based on measurement, analysis, simulation, and visualization. Examples and applicability of these techniques for general multiprocessor systems are discussed. The final two chapters present performance measurement and evaluation for large-scale shared-memory (Chapter 3) and message-passing (Chapter 4) MIMD parallel-computer systems.

Laxmi N. Bhuyan and Xiaodong Zhang
September 1994

Chapter 1
Multiprocessor Architectures, Operating Systems, and Programming Environment

In the last few years, we have seen an explosion in the interest and availability of parallel computers and a corresponding expansion in applications programming activity. Parallel processing applies a simple idea: Computing a job can be divided into several tasks that may be executed in parallel. In multiprocessing, all these tasks execute independently on different processors. Therefore, the following three basic problems are identified in multiprocessing:

- the *partitioning problem*, which is to partition a program into tasks, at least parts of which can be executed concurrently;
- the *scheduling problem*, which is to assign each task to a processor for execution; and
- the *synchronization problem*, which is to ensure an order of execution that leads to correct results.

The partitioning problem is concerned with developing parallel programs at the user's and compiler's levels. Scheduling and synchronization problems should be handled efficiently by the operating systems supporting parallel architectures. Furthermore, parallel-computer performance is affected by the programming environment where users develop, execute, and tune the parallel programs.

In order to write a parallel-application program, a programmer must know the parallel algorithms for the application, the languages to be used for implementing the algorithms, and the architectures and systems upon which the application programs will be run. This is a challenge for parallel programming. A parallel-programming environment is a coordinated collection of languages and tools that support programming on parallel computers. An efficient parallel-programming environment should provide the following support to the programmer:

- the languages and other related facilities to express parallelism of applications explicitly and efficiently and
- the tools to provide easy and effective views for debugging programs, for tuning, and for predicting program performance.

A good programming environment should not require that application programmers learn a great deal about machine-dependent programming techniques, compiler transformations, and the impact of architecture on efficiency. Unfortunately, such a parallel-programming environment has not yet become available. Current developers of application programs have to make tremendous efforts to tune their programs for high performance on different types of architectures.

This chapter discusses three major issues in parallel processing: parallel architectures, operating systems, and the programming environment. The first paper, by Bell, gives a comprehensive survey of parallel-computer architectures and applications. The survey's primary emphasis is the recent development and the near-future potential of parallel-computing research and development. The second paper studies operating systems for parallel architectures, with Black presenting a real implementation of process scheduling in the Mach operating system. Efficient parallelization and execution of large-scale applications will require a good operating environment.

A lot of work needs be done to improve the current programming environment for parallel computing. We selected the next three papers to give an overview of some of the currently available tools and languages. The first of these papers, by Karp, gives an introduction to the expression of parallel algorithms in a programming language with support of parallel-computing primitives. The parallel algorithms are implemented in shared-memory and message-passing programming models. Several examples of programming code are presented in the paper. The PVM (Parallel Virtual Machine) is a popular programming library that allows work to be distributed and executed in parallel without using special-purpose hardware and software. PVM has been widely used on the workstation-based network environment for large-scale scientific computation. The paper written by Beguelin et al. (the PVM group) describes a set of programming, debugging, and performance visualization tools like PVM for distributed computing across a heterogeneous network of computers as a single source. Finally, we introduce a parallel-compiler paper written by Hiranandani, Kennedy, and Tseng, which presents techniques for efficiently compiling Fortran D programs on distributed-memory multicomputers.

Bibliography

Accetta, M., "Mach: A New Kernel Foundation for Unix Development," *Proc. Summer 1986 Usenix Conf.*, Usenix, Sunset Beach, Calif., 1986, pp. 93–112.

Agrawal, D.P., *Tutorial on Advanced Computer Architecture*, IEEE CS Press, Los Alamitos, Calif., 1986.

Almasi, G.S., and A. Gottlieb, *Highly Parallel Computing*, Benjamin/Cummings Pub. Co., Inc., Menlo Park, Calif., 1989.

Bhuyan, L.N., ed., *Computer*, Vol. 20, No. 6, June 1987 (special issue on interconnection networks).

Carle, A., et al., "A Practical Environment for Scientific Programming," *Computer*, Vol. 20, No. 11, Nov. 1987, pp. 75–89.

Carriero, A.S., and D. Gelernter, "Linda and Friends," *Computer*, Vol. 19, No. 8, Aug. 1986, pp. 26–34.

Chandy, K.M., and J. Misra, *Parallel Program Design*, Addison-Wesley Pub. Co., Reading, Mass., 1988.

Corbato, F.J., "On Building Systems That Will Fail," *Comm. ACM*, Vol. 34, No. 6, June 1991, pp. 72–81.

Dongarra, J., et al., "A Tool to Aid in the Design, Implementation, and Understanding of Matrix Algorithms for Parallel Processors," *J. Parallel and Distributed Computing*, Vol. 9, No. 2, 1990, pp. 185–202.

Duncan, R., "A Survey of Parallel Computer Architectures," *Computer*, Vol. 23, No. 2, Feb. 1990, pp. 5–16.

Feitelson, D.G., and L. Rudolph, "Distributed Hierarchical Control for Parallel Processing," *Computer*, Vol. 23, No. 5, May 1990, pp. 65–77.

Gehringer, E., et al., "A Survey of Commercial Parallel Processors," *ACM SIGARCH Computer Architecture News*, Sept. 1988, pp. 75–107.

Geist, G.A., and V.S. Sunderam, "Experiences with Network-Based Concurrent Computation on the PVM System," *Concurrency Practice and Experience*, Vol. 4, No. 4, 1992, pp. 293–311.

Gelernter, D., A. Nicolau, and D. Padua, eds., *Languages and Compilers for Parallel Computing*, MIT Press, Cambridge, Mass., 1990.

Hennessy, J.L., and D.A. Patterson, *Computer Architecture: A Quantitative Approach*, Morgan Kaufmann Pub., San Mateo, Calif., 1990.

Hwang, K., *Advanced Computer Architectures*, McGraw-Hill, Inc., New York, N.Y., 1993.

Johnson, T., and T. Durham, *Parallel Processing: The Challenge of New Computer Architectures*, Ovum, Inc., 1986.

Jordan, H., "The Force," in *The Characteristics of Parallel Algorithms*, L. Jamieson, D. Gannon, and R. Douglass, eds., MIT Press, Cambridge, Mass., 1987, pp. 395–436.

Kallstrom, M., and S.S. Thakkar, "Programming Three Parallel Computers," *IEEE Software*, Vol. 5, No. 1, Jan. 1988, pp. 11–22.

Lipovski, G.J., and M. Malek, *Parallel Computing: Theory and Comparisons*, John Wiley & Sons, Inc., New York, N.Y., 1987.

Pancake, C.M., "Software Support for Parallel Computing: Where Are We Headed?," *Comm. ACM*, Vol. 34, No. 11, Nov. 1991, pp. 53–64.

Patton, P.C., "Multiprocessors: Architecture and Applications," *Computer*, Vol. 18, No. 6, June 1985, pp. 29–40.

Pease, D., et al., "PAWS: A Performance Evaluation Tool for Parallel Computing Systems," *Computer*, Vol. 24, No. 1, Jan. 1991, pp. 18–29.

Reilly, M.H., *A Performance Monitor for Parallel Programs*, Academic Press, Inc., New York, N.Y., 1990.

Rosing, M., et al., "The DINO Parallel Programming Language," *J. Parallel and Distributed Computing*, Vol. 13, 1991, pp. 30–42.

Siegel, H.J., *Interconnection Networks for Large-Scale Parallel Processing: Theory and Case Studies*, Lexington Books, 1985.

Simmons, M., R. Koskela, and I. Bucher, eds., *Instrumentation for Future Parallel Computing Systems*, ACM Press, New York, N.Y., 1990.

Stumm, M., and S. Zhou, "Algorithms Implementing Distributed Shared Memory," *Computer*, Vol. 23, No. 5, May 1990, pp. 54–64.

Sunderam, V.S., "PVM: A Framework for Parallel Distributed Computing," *Concurrency Practice and Experience*, Vol. 2, 1990, pp. 315–339.

Tanenbaum, A.S., *Modern Operating Systems*, Prentice-Hall, Inc., Englewood Cliffs, N.J., 1992.

Tanenbaum, A.S., M.F. Kaashoek, and H.E. Bal, "Parallel Programming Using Shared Objects and Broadcasting," *Computer*, Vol. 25, No. 8, Aug. 1992, pp. 10–19.

Treleaven, P.C., "Parallel Architecture Overview," *Parallel Computing*, Vol. 8, 1988, pp. 59–70.

Young, M., et al., "The Duality of Memory and Communication in the Implementation of a Multiprocessor Operating System," *Proc. 11th Symp. Operating System Principles*, 1987, pp. 63–76.

Zorpette, G., "The Power of Parallelism," *IEEE Spectrum*, Vol. 29, No. 9, Sept. 1992, pp. 28–33.

Gordon Bell

ULTRACOMPUTERS
A Teraflop Before Its Time

The quest for the Teraflops Supercomputer to operate at a peak speed of 10^{12} floating-point operations per sec is almost a decade old, and only one three-year computer generation from being fulfilled. The acceleration of its development would require an ultracomputer. First-generation, ultracomputers are networked computers using switches that interconnect thousands of computers to form a multicomputer, and cost $50 to $300 million in 1992. These scalable computers are also classified as massively parallel, since they can be configured to have more than 1,000 processing elements in 1992. Unfortunately, such computers are specialized since only highly parallel, coarse-grained applications, requiring algorithm and program development, can exploit them. Government purchase of such computers would be foolish, since waiting three years will allow computers with a peak speed of a teraflop to be purchased at supercomputer prices ($30 million), due to advancements in semiconductors and the intense competition resulting in "commodity supercomputing." More important, substantially better computers will be available in 1995 in the supercomputer price range if the funding that would be wasted in buying such computers is instead spent on training and software to exploit their power.

In 1989 I described the situation in high-performance computers in science and engineering, including several parallel architectures that could deliver teraflop power by 1995, but with no price constraint [2]. I predicted either of two alternatives: SIMDs with thousands of processing elements or multicomputers with 1,000+ interconnected, independent computers, could achieve this goal. A shared-memory multiprocessor looked infeasible then. Traditional, multiple vector processor supercomputers such as Crays would simply not evolve to a teraflop until 2000. Here is what happened.

1. During 1992, NEC's four-processor SX3 is the fastest computer, delivering 90% of its peak 22Gflops for the Linpeak benchmark, and Cray's 16-processor YMP C90 provides the greatest throughput for supercomputing workloads.

2. The SIMD hardware approach that enabled Thinking Machines to start up in 1983 and obtain DARPA funding was abandoned because it was only suitable for a few, very large-scale problems, barely multiprogrammed, and uneconomical for workloads. It is unclear whether large SIMDs are "generation"-scalable, and they are clearly not "size"-scalable. The main result of the CM2 computer was 10Gflop-level of performance for large-scale problems.

3. Ultracomputer-sized, scalable multicomputers (smC) were introduced by Intel and Thinking Machines, using "Killer" CMOS, 32-bit microprocessors. These product introductions join multicomputers from companies such as Alliant, AT&T, IBM, Intel, Meiko, Mercury, NCUBE, Parsytec, and Transtech. At least Convex, Cray, Fujitsu, IBM, and NEC are working on new-generation smCs that use 64-bit processors. By 1995, this score of efforts, together with the evolution of fast, LAN-connected workstations will create "commodity supercomputing." The author advocates workstation clusters formed by interconnecting high-speed workstations via new high-speed, low-overhead switches, in lieu of special-purpose multicomputers.

4. Kendall Square Research introduced their KSR 1 scalable, shared-memory multiprocessors (smP) with 1,088 64-bit microprocessors. It provides a sequentially consistent memory and programming model, proving that smPs are feasible. The KSR breakthrough that permits scalability to allow it to become an ultracomputer is based on a distributed, memory scheme, ALLCACHE™ that eliminates physical memory addressing. The ALLCACHE design is a confluence of cache and virtual memory concepts that exploit locality required by scalable, distributed computing. Work is not bound to a particular memory, but moves dynamically to the processors requiring the data. A multiprocessor provides the greatest and most flexible ability for workload since any processor can be deployed on either scalar or parallel (e.g., vector) applications, and is general-purpose, being equally useful for scientific and commercial processing, including transaction processing, databases, real time, and command and control. The KSR machine is most likely the blueprint for future scalable, massively parallel computers.

Figure 1 shows the evolution of supers (four- to five-year gestation) and micro-based scalable computers (three-year gestation). In 1992, petaflop (10^{15} flops) ultracomputers, costing a half-billion dollars do not look feasible by 2001. Denning and Tichy [7] argue that significant scientific problems exist to be solved, but a new approach may be needed to build such a machine. I concur, based on results to date, technology evolution, and lack of user training.

The teraflop quest is fueled by the massive (gigabuck-level) High Performance Computing and Communications Program (HPCC, 1992) budget and DARPA's military-like, tactical focus on teraflops and massive parallelism with greater than 1,000 processing elements. The teraflops boundary is no different than advances that created electronic calculators (kiloflops), Cray computers (megaflops), and last-generation vector supercomputers (Gflops). Vector processing required new algorithms and new programs, and massively parallel systems will also require new algorithms and programs. With slogans such as "industrial competitiveness," the teraflop goal is fundable—even though competitiveness and teraflops are difficult to link. Thus, HPCC is a bureaucrat's dream. Gigabuck programs that accelerate evolution are certain to trade off efficacy, balanced computing, programmability, users, and the long term. Already, government-sponsored architectures and selected purchasing have eliminated benchmarking and utility (e.g., lacking mass storage) concerns as DARPA focus narrowed on the teraflop. Central purchase of an ultracomputer for a vocal minority wastes resources, since no economy of scale exists, and potential users are not likely to find or justify problems that effectively utilize such a machine without a few years of use on smaller machines.

Worlton describes the potential risk of massive parallelism in terms of the "bandwagon effect," where we make the biggest mistakes in managing technology [23]. The article defines "bandwagon" as "a propaganda device by which the purported acceptance of an idea, product or the like by a large number of people is claimed in order to win further public acceptance." He describes a massively parallel bandwagon drawn by vendors, computer science researchers, and bureaucrats who gain power by increased funding. Innovators and early adopters are the riders. The bandwagon's four flat tires are caused by the lack of systems software, skilled programmers, guide-

posts (heuristics about design and use), and parallelizable applications.

The irony of the teraflops quest is that programming may not change very much even though virtually all programs must be rewritten to exploit the very high degree of parallelism required for efficient operation of the coarse-grained, scalable computers. Scientists and engineers will use just another dialect of Fortran that supports data parallelism.

All computers, including true supers, use basically the same, evolving, programming model for exploiting parallelism: SPMD, a single program, multiple data spread across a single address space that supports Fortran [16]. In fact, a strong movement is directed toward the standardization of High Performance Fortran (HPF) using parallel data structures to simplify programming. With SPMD, the same program is made available to each processor in the system. Shared memory multiprocessors simply share a copy in common memory and each computer of a multicomputer is given a copy of the program. Processors are synchronized at the end of parallel work units (e.g., outermost DO loop). Multicomputers, however, have several sources of software overhead due to communication being message-passing instead of direct, memory reference. With SPMD and microprocessors with 64-bit addressing, multicomputers will evolve to be the multiprocessors they simulate by 1995. Thus, the mainline, general-purpose computer is almost certain to be the shared memory, multiprocessor after 1995.

The article will first describe supercomputing evolution and the importance of size-, generation-, and problem-scalability to break the evolutionary performance and price barriers. A discussion about measuring progress will follow. A taxonomy of alternatives will be given to explain the motivation for the multiprocessor continuing to be

the mainline, followed by specific industrial options that illustrate real trade-offs. The final sections describe computer design research activities and the roles of computer and computational science, and government.

Evolution to the Ultracomputer: A Scalable Supercomputer

Machine scalability allows the $30 million price barrier to be broken for a single computer so that for several hundred million dollars' or a teraflop's worth of networked computers, the ultracomputer, can be assembled. Until 1992, a super-

---

Figure 1. Performance (Gflops) of Cray and NEC supercomputers, and Cray, Intel, and Thinking Machines scalable computers vs. introduction date

computer was defined both as the most powerful central computer for a range of numerically intense computation (i.e., scalar and vector processing), with very large data sets, and costing about $30 million. The notion of machine or "size" scalability, permitting computers of arbitrary and almost unlimited size, together with finding large-scale problems that run effectively have been key to the teraflop race [10]. This is a corollary of the Turing test: People selling computers must be smarter than their computers. No matter how difficult a computer is to use or how poorly it performs on real workloads, given enough time, someone may find a problem for which the computer performs well. The problem owner extols the machine to perpetuate government funding.

In 1988, the Cray YMP/8 delivered a peak of 2.8 Gflops. By 1991,

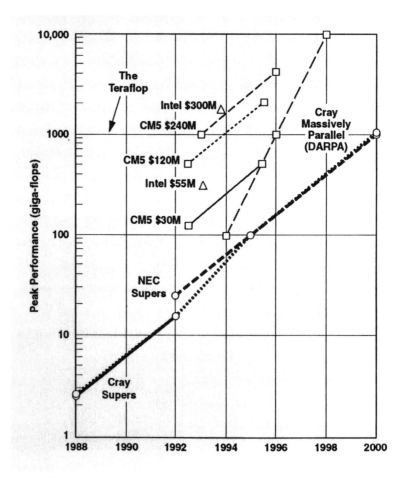

the Intel Touchstone Delta (672 node multicomputer) and the Thinking Machines CM2 (2K processing element SIMD), both began to supply an order of magnitude more peak power (20 gigaflops) than supercomputers. In supercomputing, peak or advertising power is the maximum performance that the manufacturer guarantees no program will exceed. Benchmark kernels such as matrix operations run at near peak speed on the Cray YMP. Multicomputers require O(25,000) matrices to operate effectively (e.g., 14 Gflops from a peak of 20), and adding processors does not help. For O(1,000) matrices that are typical of super-computer applications, smCs with several thousand processing elements deliver negligible performance.

Supers 1992 to 1995

By mid-1992 a completely new generation of computers have been introduced. Understanding a new generation and redesigning it to be less flawed takes at least three years. Understanding this generation should make it possible to build the next-generation supercomputer class machine, that would reach a teraflop of peak power for a few, large-scale applications by the end of 1995.

Table 1 shows six alternatives for high-performance computing, ranging from two traditional supers, one smP, and three "commodity supers" or smCs, including 1,000 workstations. Three metrics characterize a computer's performance and workload abilities. Linpeak is the operation rate for solving a system of linear equations and is the best case for a highly parallel application. Solving systems of linear equations is at the root of many scientific and engineering applications. Large, well-programmed applications typically run at one-fourth to one-half this rate. Linpack $1K \times 1K$ is typical of problems solved on supercomputers in

Table 1a.
Physical Characteristics of 1992 Supercomputing Alternatives

Machine	Proc's #	Clk MHz	Peak Gflops	Price $M	Mp.size GB	I/O.Bw GB
Traditional supercomputers						
Cray C90	16	250	16	30	2(16)**	13.6
NEC SX3 (R series)	4	400	25.6	25	8(64)	5.4
Scalable Multiprocessors						
KSR 1	1088	20	43.5	30	34.8	15.3
Scalable Multicomputers						
Intel Paragon§	4096	50	300	55	128	?
TMC CM5†	Cc+Cio+1024	33	128	30	32+	?
Workstations						
DEC alpha	1024	150	150	20	32	100

*Author's estimate
**Fast access blocked, secondary memory
§Available: Q1 1993. Four processors form a multiprocessor node; a fifth processor handles communication.
†Cc := control computer; Cio := i/o computers;

Table 1b.
Workload Characteristics of 1992 Supercomputing Alternatives

Machine	Streams #jobs	Linpeak Gflops(size)	Lin1K Gflops	LFKWorkload Mflops
Traditional supercomputers				
Cray C90	16	13.7(4K)	9.7	16 × 44
NEC SX3 (345 MHz clock)	4	20(6K)	13.4	4 × 39
Scalable multiprocessors				
KSR 1	1088		513(32Proc.)	1088 × 6.6
Scalable multicomputers				
Intel Paragon	1024	13.9(25K)/.5K	?	1K × 6*
TMC CM5	≤32 Cc's	70*	32 × ?	≤32 × 6*
LAN-connected workstations				
DEC Alpha	1024		64	1K × 15

*Author's estimate
Unavailable from manufacturer

1992. The Livermore Fortran Kernels (LFK) harmonic mean for 24 loops and 3 sizes, is used to characterize a numerical computer's ability, and is the worst-case rating for a computer as it represents an untuned workload.

New-generation, traditional or "true" multiple vector processor supercomputers have been delivered by Cray and NEC that provide one-fourth to one-eighth the peak power of the smCs to be delivered in 1992. "True" supercomputers use the Cray design formula: ECL circuits and dense packaging technology to reduce size, allow the fastest clock; one or more pipelined vector units with each processor provide peak processing for a Fortran program; and multiple vector processors communicate via a switch to a common, shared memory to handle large workloads and parallel processing. Because of the dense physical packaging of high-power chips and relatively low density of the 100,000 gate ECL chips, the inherent cost per operation for a supercomputer is roughly 500 to 1,000 peak flops/$ or 4 to 10 times greater than simply packaged, 2 million transistor "killer" CMOS microprocessors that go into leading edge workstations (5,000 peak flops/$). True supercomputers are not in the teraflops race, even though they are certain to provide most of the supercomputing capacity until 1995.

Intel has continued the pure multicomputer path by introducing its third generation, Paragon with up to 4K Intel i860 microprocessor based nodes, each with a peak of 4×75 Mflops for delivery in early 1993. Intel is offering a 6K node, $300 million, special ultracomputer for delivery in late 1993 that would provide 1.8 peak teraflops or 6K peak flop/$.

In October 1991, Thinking Machines Corp. (TMC) announced its first-generation multicomputer consisting of Sun servers controlling up to 16K Sparc microprocessor-based computational nodes, each with four connected vector

processors to be delivered in 1992. The CM5 workload ability of a few Sun servers is small compared to a true supercomputer and to begin to balance the computer for general utility would require several disks at each node. The expected performance for both supercomputer-sized problems and a workload means that the machine is fundamentally special-purpose for highly parallel jobs. The CM5 provides 4,300 peak flops/$.

In both the Paragon and CM5 it is likely that the most cost-effective use will be with small clusters of a few (e.g., 32) processors.

1995 Supers: Vectors, Scalable Multicomputers or Multiprocessors

Traditional or "true" supercomputers have a significant advantage in being able to deliver the computational power during this decade because they have evolved for four, four-year generations for almost 20 years,[1] and have an installed software-based, programming paradigm, trained programmers, and wider applicability inherent in finer granularity. The KSR-1 scalable multiprocessor runs traditional, fine-grained supercomputer Fortran programs, and has extraordinary single-processor scalar and commercial (e.g., transaction processing) throughput.

The smCs are unlikely to be alternatives for general-purpose computing or supercomputing because they do not deliver significant power for scalar- and finer-grained applications that characterize a supercomputer workload. For example, the entire set of accounts using the Intel smC at Cal Tech is less than 200, or roughly the number of users that simultaneously use a large super. Burton Smith [20] defines a general-purpose computer as: 1. Reasonably fast execution of any algorithm that performs well on another machine. Any kind

---

[1]Cray 1 (1975), Cray IS (1978), Cray XMP-2, 4 (1982, 1984), Cray YMP-8 (1988), and Cray C-90 (1992)

of parallelism should be exploitable. 2. Providing a machine-independent programming environment. Software should be no harder to transport than to any other computer. 3. A storage hierarchy performance consistent with computational capability. The computer should not be I/O bound to any greater extent than another computer.

Whether traditional supercomputers or massively parallel computers provide more computing, measured in flops/month by 1995 is the object of a bet between the author and Danny Hillis of Thinking Machines [11]. Scalable multicomputers (smCs) are applicable to coarse-grained, highly parallel codes and someone must invent new algorithms and write new programs. Universities are rewarded with grants, papers, and the production of knowledge. Hence, they are a key to utilizing coarse-grained, parallel computers. With pressure to aid industry, the Department of Energy laboratories see massive parallelism as a way to maintain staffs. On the other hand, organizations concerned with cost-effectiveness, simply cannot afford the effort unless they obtain uniquely competitive capabilities.

Already, the shared, virtual memory has been invented to aid in the programming of multicomputers. These machines are certain to evolve to multiprocessors with the next generation. Therefore, the mainline of computing will continue to be an evolution of the shared memory multiprocessor just as it has been since the mid-1960s [4]. In 1995, users should be able to buy a scalable parallel multiprocessor for 25K peak flops/$, and a teraflop computer would sell for about $40 million.

Measuring Progress
Supercomputer users and buyers need to be especially cautious when evaluating performance claims for supercomputers. Bailey's [1] twelve ways to obfuscate are:

1. Quote 32-bit performance results as 64-bit performance

2. Present inner kernel performance as application performance, neglect I/O

3. Employ assembly, micro-code and low-level code

4. Scale up problem size to avoid performance drop-off when using large numbers of processors with overhead or inter-communication delays or limits

5. Quote performance results extrapolated to a full system based on one processor

6. Compare results against unoptimized, scalar Cray code

7. Compare direct run-time with old code on an obsolete system (e.g., Cray 1)

8. Quote additional operations that are required when using a parallel, often obsolete, algorithm

9. Quote processor utilization, speedup, or Mflops/$ and ignore performance

10. Mutilate the algorithm to match the architecture, and give meaningless results

11. Compare results using a loaded vs. dedicated system

12. If all else fails, show pictures and videos

Each year a prize administered by the ACM and IEEE Supercomputing Committees awards a prize to reward practical progress in parallelism, encourage improvements, and demonstrate the utility of parallel processors [9]. Various prize categories recognize program speedup through parallelism, absolute performance, performance/price, and parallel compiler advances. The first four years of prizes are given in Table 2.

The 1987 prize for parallelism was won by a team at Sandia National Laboratory using a 1K node NCUBE and solving three problems. The team extrapolated that with more memory, the problem could be scaled up to reduce overhead, and a factor of 1,000 (vs. 600) speedup could be achieved. An NCAR Atmospheric Model running on the Cray XMP had the highest performance. In 1989 and 1990, a CM2 (SIMD with 2K processing elements) operated at the highest speed and the computation was done with 32-bit floating point numbers. The problems solved were 4 to 16 times larger than would ordinarily have been solved with modified problems requiring additional operations [1].

Benchmarking

The benchmarking process has been a key to understanding computer performance until the teraflop started and peak performance replaced reality as a selection criterion. Computer performance for an installation can be estimated by looking at various benchmarks of similar programs, and collections of benchmarks that represent a workload [5]. Benchmarks can be synthetic (e.g., Dhrystones and Whetstones), kernels that represent real code (e.g., Livermore Loops, National Aerody-

Scalability

The perception that a computer can grow forever has always been a design goal (e.g., IBM System/360 [c1964] provided a 100:1 range, and VAX existed at a range of 1,000:1 over its lifetime). Ideally, one would start with a single computer and buy more components as needed to provide size scalability. Similarly, when new processor technology increased performance, one would add new-generation computers in a generations-scalable fashion. Ordinary workstations provide some size and generation scalability, but are LAN-limited. By providing suitable high-speed switching, workstation clusters can supply parallel computing power and are an alternative to scalable multicomputers. Problem scalability is the ability of a problem, algorithm, or program to exist at a range of sizes so it can be used efficiently and correctly on a given, scalable computer.

Worlton [23] discusses Amdahl's law and the need for a very large fraction, F, of a given program to be parallel, when using a large number of processors, N to obtain high efficiency, $E(F,N)$.

$$E(F,N) = 1 / (F + N \times (1 - F))$$

Thus, scaling up slow processors is a losing proposition for a given fraction of parallelism.

For an efficiency of 50%, requires $1 - F = 1 / (N - 1)$; for 1,000 processors F must be 0.999 parallel.

Size Scalability: Locality Is the Key

Size scalability has become an academic topic [12, 20]. Size scalability simply means that a very large computer such as the ultracomputer can be built. Typical definitions fails to recognize cost, efficiency, and whether such a large-scale computer is practical (affordable) in a reasonable time scale. For example, a cross-point switch is supposedly not scalable because the switching area grows $O(n2)$ even though switch cost may be insignificant. Much supercomputer cost is the processor-memory switch, and scaling is accomplished by having different switch/cabinets for different size computers. For example, Cray Research, Intel, and Thinking Machines all build active switches into their cabinets into which computing elements are plugged. The CM5 and KSR computers require switching cabinets when going beyond the first levels of their hierarchies. KSR interconnects processors using a near zero cost ring, since each node just connects to its next neighbor. No computers are truly scalable in a linear fashion.

A size-scalable computer is designed from a small number

namic Simulation), numerical libraries (e.g., Linpack for matrix solvers, FFT), or full applications (e.g., SPEC for workstations, Illinois's Perfect Club, Los Alamos Benchmarks). No matter what measure is used to understand a computer, the only way to understand how a computer will perform is to benchmark the computer with the applications to be used. This also measures the mean time before answers (mtba), a most important measure of computers productivity.

Several Livermore Loop metrics, using a range of three vector lengths for the 24 loops, are useful: the arithmetic mean typifying the best applications (.97 vector ops), the arithmetic mean for optimized applications (.89 vector ops), geometric mean for tuned workload (.74 vector ops), harmonic mean for untuned workload (.45 vector ops), and harmonic mean compiled as a scalar for an all-scalar operation (no vector ops). Three Linpack mea-

surements are important: Linpack 100 × 100, Linpack 1,000 × 1,000 for typical supercomputing applications, and Linpeak (for an unconstrained sized matrix). Linpeak is the only benchmark that is run effectively on a large multicomputer. Massive multicomputers can rarely run an existing supercomputer program (i.e., the dusty deck programs) without a new algorithm or new program. In fact, the best benchmark for any computer is whether a manufacturer can and is

of basic components, with no single bottleneck component, so the computer can be incrementally expanded over its designed scaling range, delivering linear incremental performance for a well-defined set of applications. The components include computers, processors or processing elements, memories, switches, and cabinets. For example, since the highly parallel computers are interconnected by switches, the bandwidth of the switch should increase linearly with processing power. It is clear that a balanced, general-purpose teraflop computer is not feasible based on I/O considerations. For example, if I/O requirements increase with performance as in a general-purpose computer, then roughly 0.1 terabytes/sec or 20,000 5MB/sec disks operating in parallel would be needed to balance the computer (about one bit of data transferred for every flop). Emitting video from a computer for direct visualization is one way to effectively utilize the I/O bandwidth and reduce mass storage.

The key to size scalability is a belief in spatial and temporal locality, since very large systems have inherently longer latencies than small, central systems. All supercomputers are predicated to some degree on locality (i.e., once a datum is accessed a near physical neighbor will be accessed [spatial]

and the same datum will be repeatedly accessed [temporal]). Locality of program execution is the phenomenon that allowed the first one-level store computer, Atlas to be built. This led to the understanding of paging, virtual memory, and working sets that are predicated on locality [6]. Caches exploit spatial and temporal locality automatically. Large register arrays, including vector registers are mechanisms for a compiler to exploit and control locality.

In 1989, building computers that scaled economically over a very wide range of implementations looked impractical because of the enormous interconnection bandwidth requirements. The Cray YMP 8 and CM2 scaled over a range of eight (eight processors in the Cray, and 8K to 64K processing elements in the CM2). The Cray C-90 scaling range is 16, and other implementations of the Cray architecture increase the performance range a factor of 5. Also, four C90s can be interconnected providing 64 peak Gflops. The CM5 scaling range is 32 for 1,024 computers and KSR 1 has a range of 128 (8 to 1,088) processor-memory pairs. The CM5 scaling range extends to 512 with 16K computers as a $480 million ultracomputer. In practical terms, a scalable computer is one that can exist at the largest size an organization (including a country) will ever buy.

Generation (time) Scalability
Generation (time) scalability is as important as size scalability, since the basic microprocessor nodes become obsolete every three years. Furthermore, the time to find an algorithm and write a program is long, requiring significant investment that needs to be preserved. A generation-scalable computer can be implemented in a new technology, and thus take advantage of increased circuit and packaging technologies. Since CMOS evolves rapidly, the interconnection bandwidth must grow at the same rate as processing speed and memory. For example, it is irrelevant to have a design that can exploit "next-generation" microprocessor nodes without increasing the switch bandwidth and decreasing the overhead and latency proportionally. All characteristics of a computer must scale proportionally: processing speed, memory speed and sizes, interconnect bandwidth and latency, I/O, and software overhead in order to be useful for a given application.

Problem Scalability: Key to Performance
Problem scalability defines whether an application is feasible on a computer with given granularity characteristics. In practical terms, problem scalability means that a program can be made large enough to operate efficiently

willing to benchmark a user's programs.

Two factors make benchmarking parallel systems difficult: problem scalability (or size) and the number of processors or job streams. The maximum output is the perfectly parallel workload case in which every processor is allowed to run a given-size program independently and the uniprocessor work-rate is multiplied by the number of processors. Similarly, the minimum wall clock time should be when all processors are used in parallel. Thus, performance is a surface of varying problem size (scale) and the number of processors in a cluster.

The Commercial Alternatives

The quest generated by the HPCC Program and the challenge of parallelism has attracted almost every computer company lashing together microprocessors (e.g., Inmos Transputers, Intel i860s, and Sparcs) to provide commodity, multicomputer supercomputing in every price range from PCs to ultracomputers. In addition, traditional supercomputer evolution will continue well into the twenty-first century. The main fuel for growth is the continued evolution of "killer" CMOS microprocessors and the resulting workstations.

on a computer with a given granularity. Problems such as Monte Carlo simulation and "ray tracing" are "perfectly parallel" since their threads of computation almost never come together. Obtaining parallelism (i.e., performance) has turned out to be possible with new algorithms and new codes. Problem granularity (operations on a grid point/data required from adjacent grid points) must be greater than a machine's granularity (node operation rate/node-to-node communication data-rate) in order for a computer to be effective. Several kinds of messages must pass among distributed computer nodes: a priori messages that a compiler can generate to ensure that data is available to a node before it is needed; computer address data, requiring messages for both address and data; and various broadcast and synchronization information. For example, message-passing and random access references are sufficiently large to render today's multicomputers, ineffective for classical benchmarks such as the Livermore kernels. Denning and Tichy [7] discuss the effects of problem scalability and granularity on performance.

In the case of models of physical structures, as the problem size is scaled up by increasing the grid points, the work or potential parallelism and memory increases at least

$O(n^3)$, where n is the problem dimension. The communication with other cells only grows as $O(n^2)$. Thus, communication overhead can often be reduced or ignored compared to the computation if a problem can be made large enough (i.e., get enough grid points) to still fit in primary memory of a distributed node. For example, in solving LaPlace's equation computation is $7 n^3$ (the time to average the neighboring points) and on a distributed memory computer, the communication is $6 n^2$, where n is the problem dimension. Thus, a 100Mflop computer intercommunicating at 1 Megaword per sec is balanced when the computation time of $.07 n^3$ microsec equals the communication time of $6 n^2$ microsec. That is, n must be larger than 86, to hold the 3d array of 640K points or just 5MB. About 1 microsec, however, is required to send or receive a word on multicomputers, representing an opportunity cost of 2×100 operations. For a problem that would fill a 32MB memory, n is about 160. This size problem requires 0.3 sec of computation and 2×0.15 sec of send and receive time in which the processor is idle. The iteration time is 0.6 seconds, resulting in a computation rate of 50Mflops with only 0.15 sec of communication link time, and smaller problems would run more slowly. Since the memory is full, the problem cannot be

further scaled to increase efficiency.

For some problems, scaling a problem may produce no better results than a coarser grain, and less costly solution. Another risk of problem-scaling is to exacerbate the limited I/O capability. For example, the $25K \times 25K$ matrix that Intel's Delta used for a 15Gflop matrix multiply takes 5GB of memory, and 500 sec to load using 10MB disks. The matrix multiply time is ≈ 2000 sec. In contrast, a C90 achieves peak power on a $4K \times 4K$ matrix that takes only 10 sec to compute and 128MB to store. Contrast this structure with computers connected via Ethernet, which has a total bandwidth of 1 million words per sec for all nodes, and message-passing overheads of at least 1,000 microsec (100,000 operations on a 100Mflop computer). However, given a large enough problem and enough memory per node, even such a collection of workstations can be scaled to have a long enough grain to be effective for solving the preceding problem.

Figure 2 shows the structure of a basic unit of multithreaded computation independent of whether it is run on a SIMD, multiprocessor or multicomputer, or has distributed or shared components. Hockney and Jesshope [14] formulated models that predict performance as a function of a computer's characteristics and

Traditional or "True" Supercomputer Manufacturer's Response

In 1989 the author estimated that several traditional supers would be announced this year by U.S. companies. Cray Research and NEC have announced products, and Fujitsu has announced its intent to enter the U.S. supercomputer market. Seymour Cray formed Cray Computer. Supercomputer Systems Inc. lacks a product, and DARPA's Tera Computer Company is in the design phase. Germany's Suprenum project was stopped. The French Advanced Computer Research Institute (ACRI) was started. Numerous Japanese multicomputer projects are underway. Supercomputers are on a purely evolutionary path driven by increasing clock speed, pipelines, and processors. Clock increases in speed do not exceed a factor of two every five years (about 14%). In 1984, a committee projected the Cray 3 would operate in 1986. In 1989, the 128-processor Cray 4 was projected to operate at 1GHz. in 1992. In 1992, the 16-processor Cray 3, projected to operate at 500MHz, was stopped. NEC has pioneered exceptional vector speeds, retaining the title of the world's fastest vector processor. The NEC vector processor uses 16 parallel pipelines and performs

problem parallelism. The computation starts with a sequential thread (1), followed by supervisory scheduling (2), where the processors begin threads of computation (3), followed by inter-computer messages that update variables among the nodes when the computer has a distributed memory (4), and finally synchronize prior to beginning the next unit of parallel work (5). The communication overhead period (3) inherent in distributed memory structures is usually distributed throughout the computation and possibly completely overlapped. Message-passing overhead (send and receive calls) in multicomputers can be reduced by specialized hardware operating parallel with computation. Communication bandwidth limits granularity, since a certain amount of data has to be transferred with other nodes in order to complete a computational grain. Message-passing calls and synchronization (5) are nonproductive.

The Paragon should be able to operate on relatively smaller-grained problems than a CM5, since hardware granularity (node operation rate per internode communication rate) appears to be lower. The CM5 requires a problem-grain length of at least 102 operations per word transferred (128Mflops/10/8Mwords per sec); this means that for every word transmitted to another node, at least 102 operations

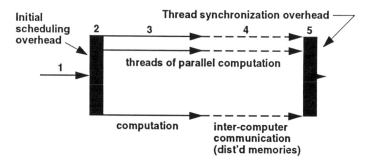

Figure 2. Structure of multithreaded, parallel computation

have to be carried out in order to avoid waiting for data. Paragon is projected to be 3 operations per word. To reduce this effective grain size, the problem just has to be scaled up to "bundle" a large number of computational grid points within a physical node to reduce internode communication. Very large-grained problems typically have several thousand operations per grain in order to reduce all overheads.

Additionally, the message-passing time is lost time that also limits system performance. Assuming the operating system is not involved in passing a message, David Culler, at Berkeley has measured 3.3 microsec for a CM5 to send and receive a message plus 1.0 microsec per word sent or received. During this lost time of 2 microsec, 256 operations could have been carried out. Paragon attempts to reduce the message-passing overhead and increase the bandwidth by having a separate processor and block transfer hardware manage message transfers.

In a distributed memory multiprocessor no messages are explicitly passed; however, hardware processes messages and caches data. Multiprocessors avoid several sources of software overhead inherent in 1992 multicomputers: converting the addresses of each 32-bit computer into a single, >32-bit global address; deciding in which computer to locate data, including the possibility of relocating and renaming data dynamically— i.e., controlling locality by simulating caches; passing messages containing variables that other nodes need just in time for another computer to use; and passing computed addresses and data when random access of memory is required. ∎

operations at a 6.4Gflop rate. Fujitsu's supercomputer provides two, 2.5Gflop vector units shared by four scalar processors. Every four- or five years the number of processors is doubled, providing a gain of 18% per year. The C90 increased the clock frequency by 50% to 250MHz, doubled the number of pipelines and the number of processors over the YMP. Figure 1 projects a 1995 Cray supercomputer that will operate at 100Gflops using a double-speed clock, twice the number of processors, and twice the number of pipelines.

In most production environments, throughput is the measure

and the C-90 clearly wins, since it has a factor of four times the number of processors of either Fujitsu or NEC. In an environment where a small number of production programs are run, additional processors with scalar capability may be of little use. Environments that run only a few coarse-grained codes can potentially use smCs for large-grained problems.

The traditional supercomputer market does not look toward high growth because it provides neither the most cost-effective solution for simpler scalar programs, nor the peak power for massively parallel

applications. Scalar codes run most cost-effectively on workstations, while very parallel code may be run on massively parallel computers, provided the granularity is high and the cost of writing the new code is low. Despite these factors, I believe traditional supercomputers will be introduced in 2000.

"Killer" CMOS Micros for Building Scalable Computers
Progress toward the affordable teraflop using "killer" CMOS micros is determined by advances in microprocessor speeds. The projection [2] that microprocessors would improve at a 60%-per-year rate,

Table 2.
Gordon Bell Prize Winners

Year	Peformance Gflops	Price/Performance Gflops/$1 million	Speed-up
1987	0.45	0.03	600
1988	1.0	0.05	800
1989	6.0	0.5	1100
1990	14.0	2.0	1800

Table 3.
Contemporary Microprocessor Performance

Micro	Year	Clock (MHz)	I-Spec	f-Spec (Specmarks*)	Spec	Linpack	Lapeak (Mflops)	LFK(hm)	Pk
DEC VAX780	78.2	5*	1	1	1	0.15		0.16	1
DEC Alpha	92.2	200			150†		85†	20†	200†
Fujitsu-VP	92.4	50				>50	95	12.5	108
HP PA	92.2	100	—	—	138	56	67	—	200
HP PA	91.1	66	52	78	102	24		13.3	66
IBM RS6000	91.2	42	33	120	72	27	70	14.5	83
Intel 486 PC	91.3	50	28	15	19	2.0	—	1.8	
MIPS R3000	88.3	25			18	4.2	7	3.6	8
MIPS R4000	92.2	100**	60	77	70	17.5	36	11.5	50
SUN Sparc 2	91.3	40	22	27	25	4.1	—	—	—
1995 Micro	95	200–400			300				400–800

*CISC architecture. A comparable RISC architecture would operate at approx. 2MHz.
**External clock rate is 50MHz.
†Estimate

Tera Taxonomy

The taxonomy of the tera candidates, shown in Figure 3, includes only shared-memory multiprocessors and various multicomputers (MIMDs) . A superscalar or extra long word RISC, a vector processor, and a processor with thousands of processing elements are just SIMD processors, since they all have a single instruction stream.

Distributed (Boudoir) vs. Centralized (Dance Hall) Computing: Locality Beliefs

Two attributes structure the taxonomy: multiprocessors vs. multicomputers; and scalability using a physically distributed vs. a central memory. Scalability measures whether it is practical to construct ultracomputers. A memory is either centralized in a pool, "dance hall" (processors—switch—memories); or distributed with each processor enabling scalability, "boudoir" (processor-memory]—switch), and is the key to scalability. Switches bottleneck overall performance and limit system size in every computer; thus the switch is the determinant of a computer's scalability. Switches such as the CM5 has, allow a very large network of computers to be put together just as an arbitrary number of workstations or telephones can be interconnected. Although large switches permit arbitrary peak power, the cost is problem granularity, mean time before applications, and limited applicability.

Multiprocessors vs. Multicomputers

The hardware distinction between multiprocessors and multicomputers is whether the system has and maintains a single address space and a single coherent memory and whether explicit messages are required to access memory on other computing nodes as shown in the programming view in Figure 4. The question is similar to RISC vs. CISC, since multicom-

Figure 3. Taxonomy of multiprocessors and multicomputers

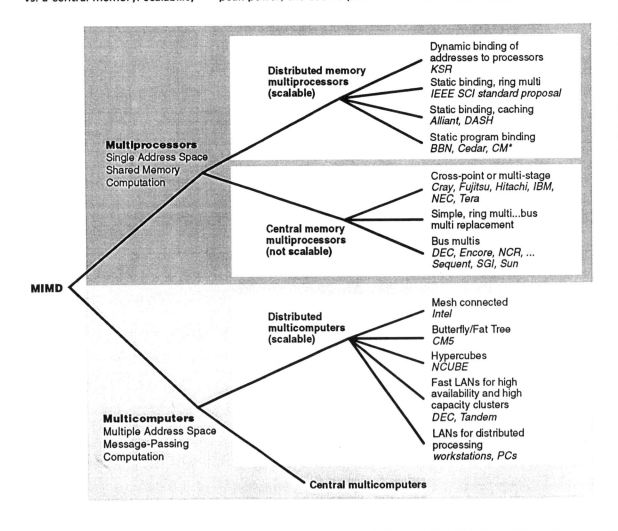

Figure 4. Programming views of shared-memory multiprocessor and distributed multicomputer

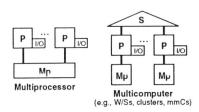

Multiprocessor

Multicomputer
(e.g., W/Ss, clusters, mmCs)

puter operating systems are evolving to carry out the functions (e.g., address construction, caching, message-passing for data access) that multiprocessor hardware provides. The differences are:

1. Multiprocessors have a single address space supported by hardware. Each computer of a multicomputer has its own address space. Software forms a common, global address space as a concatenation of a computer's node number and the computer node's address to support the SPMD program model.
2. Multiprocessors have a single, uniformly accessible memory and are managed by and provide a single, timeshared operating system programming environment (i.e., Unix). Multicomputers are a collection of independent, interconnected computers under control of a LAN connected, distributed workstation-like operating system. Each computer has a copy or kernel of the operating system.

3. A multiprocessor has a common work queue that any processor may access and be applied to. In a multicomputer, work (programs and their data) is distributed among the computers, usually on a static basis. As the load on the computers or clusters change, work may have to be moved.

Any node in a multiprocessor may run any size job from its shared, virtual memory. In mul-

ticomputers, a job's size is limited by a node's memory size, and a computer is incapable of or ineffective at running a collection of large, scalar programs that typify perfectly parallel applications such as digital simulation.

4. Multiprocessors communicate data implicitly by directly accessing a common memory. Multicomputers explicitly pass messages that may or may not be hidden from the user by hardware and the compiler.

When a multiprocessor is used for parallel processing, data and programs are equally accessible to all processors. Programs and their data must be allocated among computers in order to minimize message passing overhead. To minimize message-passing data may also have to be moved and renamed as in a virtual memory system.

5. Multiprocessors provide a single, sequentially consistent memory and program model. Since message-passing is used to move data in multicomputers, different copies of variables may reside in various computer nodes at one time.
6. Distributed memory multiprocessors have an automatic mechanism, caching, to implicitly control locality. As a datum is accessed it is automatically moved to another processor's memory. With multicomputers every nonlocal access requires software for address translation, message-passing access, and memory management to deal with copies of data.
7. Multiprocessors provide the most efficient support for message-passing applications because messages are passed by passing pointers as in uniprocessors. Multicomputers require moving data.
8. A multiprocessor is inherently general-purpose, since any collection of small to large

and sequential-to-parallel programs can be operated on at any time. A multicomputer operates best on a very large, parallel program which is run to completion. If any of the nodes lack a facility that must be obtained in other nodes, bottlenecks can occur when accessing other nodes.

Because of the general-purposeness, scalable multiprocessors can be applied to real time, command and control, commercial transaction processing and database management. Multicomputers are not general-purpose in terms of either applications or job size mix.

Latency Inherent with Performance: There's No Free Lunch

Each computer represents a trade-off to deal with the increased latency inherent in building a large computer requiring high bandwidth. In the case of multiprocessors, data is in a shared memory that is delayed by switching (dance hall) or in another distributed processor-memory pair (boudoir). Similarly, in a multicomputer, explicit messages must be sent to another computer. The alternatives represent trade-offs among such issues as how to and where to deal with latency, the degree of locality, and the degree of problem granularity. These architectural alternatives represent different beliefs about application locality:

1. SIMDs: Put processing elements with memory, do operations fast, allocate data to minimize communication with other nodes, send data when required and wait when parts of the computation need to share data. (CM1 . . . CM2) Thinking Machines abandoned SIMD since only one very-large-scale parallel job could be run at a given time, making it cost-ineffective and non-general-purpose. Also, SIMDs have negligible scalar perfor-

mance, making them useless for anything but massively parallel, coarse-granularity applications.

2. Multivector processor supercomputers: Use vector processors to move more data (a vector) in one instruction, overlap instructions, and join operations of several instructions together in a single pipeline (chaining). The vector registers hide the latency that comes with bandwidth. Employ programmed controlled buffer memories to further cache data (Crays, Fujitsu, Hitachi, NEC)

3. Distributed multiprocessors Caching, pre-fetching, and post-storing are used to hide latency. Programs and data migrate to a processor-memory node on demand. Hardware automatically replicates data in local nodes using caches and maintains memory coherence. (KSR, DASH, T*, Alewife)

4. Multicomputers: Couple processors and memories to form cost-effective computer nodes. Place the same program in all nodes and allocate data across all computers to minimize moving data. When data movement is required in nonperfectly parallel programs, the compiler generates messages to transfer data to other nodes. Build mechanisms to broadcast data and recombine results (TMC and Intel)

5. Multistream (or multithreaded), multiprocessors: Provide a constant, but long latency path between physical processors and memory. Build multi-instruction stream processors whereby one physical processor acts as many separate processors. Pre-fetch and post-store data to cover the long, constant latency. This processor can be used in all the preceding computers (Tera, T*, Alewife)

The Species
The specific distributed multicomputers of Figure 3 are seg-

mented by interconnection bandwidth. LAN-connected workstations have the lowest bandwidth, but in the future could provide a significant amount of computing power by utilizing various parallel computing environments such as Linda, Parasoft's Express, or the Parallel Virtual Machine (PVM). Since 1975 Tandem has been using clusters of computers for redundancy and increased capacity; DEC introduced VAX clusters in 1982. Seitz (Cal Tech) pioneered the multicomputer for supercomputing, and Intel has built three generations based on much of this work. Many companies offer multicomputers using Transputers or Intel i860 processors for practical and pedagogical use.

Two alternative interconnect switches are used for nonscalable multiprocessors. A single bus, Figure 5 is the simplest way to build a multiple microprocessor or "multi" [2]. With the evolution of microprocessors to support "multis" any computer from the simplest PC can easily become a multiprocessor. Multis are limited by the capability of the bus that is formed on printed wiring, and hence is not capable of significant size or generation scalability. In the future, the bus will be replaced by a ring, providing the essential features of a bus, but scales with size and generation (i.e., clock speed since a chip only drives a neighbor), as shown in Figure 6. The bandwidth for a "ring multi" increases as the number of nodes increase (using multiple tokens) at the expense of increased latency (to be hidden by a cache).

Mainframes and supers use cross-points and multistage networks to interconnect processors and memories (Figure 7). Since up to three memory accesses may be required to execute a statement such as A = B + C in order to compute

Figure 5. Bus "multi" (e.g., DEC, Sequent, SGI, Sun)

Figure 6. Ring "multi" (e.g., IEEE SCI)

Figure 7. Multiple vector processor supercomputers (e.g., Cray, Fujitsu, Hitachi, NEC)

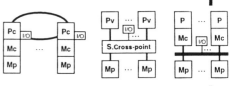

one flop, it is easy to see why the switch connecting processors and memory limits a computer. As a switch is increased in size and bandwidth, latency and grain increase. Worse yet, scalar performance decreases.

Three scalable multiprocessors were built as research efforts beginning with CMU's Cm*. The single address space was used to eliminate message-passing and to simplify the naming and allocation of memory. All required programs to be located in particular nodes and suffered from the same flaw on which multicomputers are predicated. Stanford's DASH binds programs statically to nodes, but uses caching to reduce latency when a remote node requires data. This reduces or eliminates the need for perfect data-to-node assignment. Nevertheless, over long-term use, it is imperative to move data permanently to the computing node requiring the data.

The KSR smP to be described solves the data-to-node assignment problem inherent in a distributed memory mP by providing hardware that controls the automatic migration of memory to any that may need it. KSR's breakthrough occurred by conceptually eliminating physical addresses and making the memory into a cache so that information could be automatically moved to a processor when needed. ∎

providing a quadrupling of performance each three years still appears to be possible for the next few years (Table 3). The quadrupling has its basis in Moore's Law stating that semiconductor density would quadruple every three years. This explains memory-chip-size-evolution. Memory size can grow proportionally with processor performance, even though the memory bandwidth is not keeping up. Since clock speed only improves at 25% per year (a doubling in three years), the additional speed must come from architectural features (e.g., superscalar or wider words, larger cache memories, and vector processing).

The leading edge microprocessors described at the 1992 International Solid State Circuits Conference included: a microprocessor based on Digital's Alpha architecture with a 150- or 200MHz clock rate; and the Fujitsu 108 (64)|216 (32-bit) Mflop Vector Processor chip that works with Sparc chips. Using the Fujitsu chip with a microprocessor would provide the best performance for traditional supercomputer-oriented problems. Perhaps the most important improvement to enhance massive parallelism is the 64-bit address enabling a computer to have a large global address space. With 64-bit addresses and substantially faster networks, some of the limitations of message-passing multicomputers can be overcome.

In 1995, $20,000 distributed computing node microprocessors with peak speeds of 400 to 800 Mflops can provide 20,000 to 40,000 flops/$. For example, such chips are a factor of 12 to 25 times faster than the vector processor chips used in the CM5 and would be 4.5 to 9 times most cost-effective. Both ECL and GaAs are unlikely runners in the teraflop race since CMOS improves so constantly in speed and density. Given the need for large on-chip cache memories and the additional time and cost penalties for external caches, it is likely that CMOS will be the semiconductor technology for scalable computers.

Not Just Another Workstation: A Proposal for Having Both High-Performance Workstations and Massive Parallelism

Workstations are the purest and simplest computer structure able to exploit microprocessors since they contain little more than a processor, memory, CRT, network connection, and i/o logic. Furthermore, their inherent CRTs solve a significant part of the i/o problem. A given workstation or server node (usually just a workstation without a CRT, but with large memory and a large collection of disks) can also become a multicomputer.

Nielsen of Lawrence Livermore National Laboratory (LLNL) has outlined a strategy for transitioning to massively parallel computing [18]. LLNL has made the observation that is spends about three times as much on workstations that are only 15% utilized, as it does on supercomputers. By 1995, microprocessor-based workstations could reach a peak of 500Mflops, providing 25,000 flops per dollar or 10 times the projected cost-effectiveness of a super. This would mean that inherent in its spending, LLNL would have about 25 times more unused peak power in its workstations than it has in its central supercomputer or specialized massively parallel computer.

The difficult part of using workstations as a scalable multicomputer (smC) is the low-bandwidth communication links that limit their applicability to long-grained problems. Given that every workstation environment is likely to have far greater power than a central super, however, the result should clearly justify the effort. An IEEE standard, the Scalable Coherent Interface or SCI, is being implemented to interconnect computers as a single, shared-memory multiprocessor. SCI uses a ring, such as KSR, to interconnect the computers. A distributed directory tracks data as copies migrate to the appropriate computer node. Companies such as Convex are exploring the SCI for interconnecting HP's micros as an alternative and preferred mini-super that can also address the supercomputing market.

A cluster of workstations interconnected at speeds comparable to Thinking Machines's CM5, would be advantageous in terms of power, cost-effectiveness, and administration compared with LAN-connected workstations and supercomputers. Such a computer would have to be centralized in order to have low latency. Unlike traditional timeshared facilities, however, processors could be dedicated to individuals to provide guaranteed service. With the advent of HDTV, low-cost video can be distributed directly to the desktop, and as a byproduct users would have video conferencing.

smPs: Scalable Multiprocessors

The Kendall Square Research KSR 1. The Kendall Square Research KSR 1 is a size-and-generation-scalable, shared-memory multiprocessor computer. It is formed as a hierarchy of interconnected "ring multis:" Scalability is achieved by connecting 32 processors to form a "ring multi" operating at oneGB/sec (128 million accesses per sec). Interconnection bandwidth within a ring scales linearly, since every ring slot may contain a transaction. Thus, a ring has roughly the capacity of a typical cross-point switch found in a supercomputer room that interconnects 8 to 16, 100MB/sec HIPPI channels. The KSR 1 uses a two-level hierarchy to interconnect 34 rings (1,088 processors), and is therefore massive. The ring design supports an arbitrary number of levels, permitting ultras to be built.

Each node is comprised of a primary cache, acting as a 32MB primary memory, and a 64-bit superscalar processor with roughly the same performance as an IBM RS6000 operating at the same clock-rate. The superscalar proces-

sors containing 64 floating-point and 32 fixed-point registers of 64 bits is designed for both scalar and vector operations. For example, 16 elements can be pre-fetched at one time. A processor also has a 0.5MB sub-cache supplying 20 million accesses per sec to the processor (computational efficiency of 0.5). A processor operates at 20MHz. and is fabricated in 1.2 micron CMOS. The processor, *sans* caches, contains 3.9 million transistors in 6 types of 12 custom chips. Three-quarters of each processor consists of the Search Engine responsible for migrating data to and from other nodes, for maintaining memory coherence throughout the system, using distributed directories, and ring control.

The KSR 1 is significant because it provides size- (including I/O) and generation-scalable smP in which every node is identical; an efficient environment for both arbitrary workloads (from transaction processing to timesharing and batch) and sequential to parallel processing through a large, hardware-supported address space with an unlimited number of processors; a strictly sequential consistent programming model; and dynamic management of memory through hardware migration and replication of data throughout the distributed, processor memory nodes, using its Allcache mechanism.

With sequential consistency, every processor returns the latest value of a written value, and results of an execution on multiple processors appear as some interleaving of operations of individual nodes when executed on a multithreaded machine. With Allcache, an address becomes a name and this name automatically migrates throughout the system and is associated with a processor in a cache-like fashion as needed. Copies of a given cell are made by the hardware and sent to other nodes to reduce access time. A processor can pre-fetch data into a local cache and post-store data for other cells. The hardware is designed to exploit spatial and tempo-

ral locality. For example, in the SPMD programming model, copies of the program move dynamically and are cached in each of the operating nodes' primary and processor caches. Data such as elements of a matrix move to the nodes as required simply by accessing the data, and the processor has instructions that pre-fetch data to the processor's registers. When a processor writes to an address, all cells are updated and memory coherence is maintained. Data movement occurs in sub-pages of 128 bytes (16 words) of its 16K pages.

Every known form of parallelism is supported via KSR's Mach-based operating system. Multiple users may run multiple sessions, comprising multiple applications, comprising multiple processes (each with independent address spaces), each of which may comprise multiple threads of control running simultaneously sharing a common address space. Message-passing is supported by pointer-passing in the shared memory to avoid data copying and enhance performance.

KSR also provides a commercial programming environment for transaction processing that accesses relational databases in parallel with unlimited scalability, as an alternative to multicomputers formed from multiprocessor mainframes. A 1K-node system provides almost two orders of magnitude more processing power, primary memory, I/O bandwidth, and mass storage capacity than a multiprocessor mainframe. For example, unlike the typical tera-candidates, a 1,088-node system can be configured with 15.3 terabytes of disk memory, providing 500 times the capacity of its main memory. The 32- and 320-node systems are projected to deliver over 1,000 and 10,000 transactions per sec, respectively, giving it over a hundred times the throughput of a multiprocessor mainframe.

smCs: Scalable Multicomputers for "Commodity Supercomputing"
Multicomputer performance and

applicability are determined by the number of nodes and concurrent job streams, the node and system performance, I/O bandwidth, and the communication network bandwidth, delay, and overhead time. Table 1 gives the computational and workload parameters, but for a multicomputer operated as a SPMD, the communications network is quite likely the determinant for application performance.

Intel Paragon: A Homogeneous Multicomputer. This is shown in Figure 8. A given node consists of five i860 microprocessors: four carry out computation as a shared-memory multiprocessor operating at a peak of 300Mflops rate, and the fifth handles communication with the message-passing network. Each processor has a small cache, and the data-rate to primary memory is 50 million accesses per sec, supporting a computational intensity of 0.67 for highly select problems. The message-passing processor and the fast 2D mesh topology provide the very high, full-duplex data-rate among the nodes of 200MB/sec. The mesh provides primitives to support synchronization and broadcasting.

Paragon is formed as a collection of nodes controlled by the OSF1 (Mach) operating system with micro kernels that support message-passing among the nodes. Each node can be dynamically configured to be a service processor for general-purpose timesharing, or part of a parallel-processing partition, or an

Figure 8. Intel Paragon multicomputer

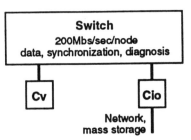

I/O computer because it attaches to a particular device. A variety of programming models are provided, corresponding to the evolution toward a multiprocessor. Two basic forms of parallelism are supported: SPMD using a shared virtual memory and MIMD. With SPMD, a single, partition-wide, shared virtual memory space is created across a number of computers, using a layer of software. Memory consistency is maintained on a page basis. With MIMD a program is optimized to provide the highest performance within a node using vector processing, for example. Messages are explicitly passed among the nodes. Each node can have its own virtual memory.

CM5: A Multicomputer Designed to Operate as a Collection of SIMDs. The CM5 is shown in Figure 9 consisting of 1 to 32 Sun server control computers, Cc, (for a 1K-node system), on which user programs run; the computational computers, Cv, with vector units; Sun-based I/O server nodes, Cio; and a switch to interconnect the elements. The system is divided into a number of independent partitions with at least 32 Cv's that are managed by one Cc. A given partitioning is likely to be static for a relatively long time (e.g., work shift to days). The Sun servers and I/O computers run variants of Sun O/S, providing a familiar user-operating environment together with all the networking, file systems, and

graphical user interfaces. Both the SPMD and message-passing programming models are supported. Each of the computational nodes, Cv, can send messages directly to Cio's, but other system calls must be processed in the Cc.

The computational nodes are Sparc micros that control four independent vector processors that operate independently on 8MB memories. A node is a message-passing multicomputer in which the Sparc moves data within the four 8MB memories. Memory data is accessed by the four vector units at 16Maccess per sec (Maps) each, providing memory bandwidth for a computational intensity of 0.5. Conceptually, the machine is treated as an evolution of the SIMD CM2 that had 2K floating-point processing elements connected by a message-passing hypercube. Thus, a 1K-node CM5 has 4K processing element, and message-passing among the 4 vector units and other nodes is controlled by the Sparc processors. The common program resides in each of the nodes. Note that using Fujitsu Vector Processing chips instead of the four CM5 vector chips would increase peak performance by a factor of 3.3, making the 1995 teraflop peak achievable at the expense of a well-balanced machine.

Computational intensity is the number of memory accesses per flop required for an operation(s) of a program. Thus depending on the computational intensity of the operations, speed will vary greatly. For example, the computational intensity of the expression $A = B + C$ is 3, since 3 accesses are required for every flop, giving a peak rate of 21Mflops from a peak of 128. A C90 provides 1.5Maps per 1Mflops, or a 16-processor system is capable of operating at 8Gflops.

The switch has three parts: diagnosis and reconfiguration; data message-passing; and control. The data network operates at 5MB/sec full duplex. A number of control messages are possible, and all proc-

essors use the network. Control network messages include broadcasting (e.g., sending a scalar or vector) to all nodes unless it abstains, results recombining (network carries out arithmetic and logical operations on data supplied by each node), and global signaling, synchronization for controlling parallel programs. The switch is wired into each cabinet that holds the 256 vector computers.

A Score of Multicomputers. Cray Research has a DARPA contract to supply a machine capable of peak teraflop operation by 1995, and a sustained teraflop by 1997 using DEC Alpha microprocessors. Convex has announced it is working on a massively parallel computer, using HP's microprocessor as its base. IBM has several multicomputer systems that it may productize based on RS6000 workstations. Japanese manufacturers are building multicomputers, for example, using a comparatively small number (100s) of fast computers (i.e., 1Gflop) interconnected via very high-speed networks in a small space.

A number of multicomputers have been built using the Inmos Transputer and Intel i860 (e.g., Transtech Parallel Systems). Mercury couples 32, 40MHz. i860s and rates the configuration at 2.5Gflops for signal processing, simulation, imaging, and seismic analysis. Meiko's 62-node multicomputer has a peak of 2.5Gflops and delivered 1.3Gflops for Linpeak, or approximately half its peak on a O(8500) matrix [8]. Parsytec GC consists of 64 16K nodes, delivering a peak of 400Glops. The nCUBE 2 system has up to 8K nodes with up to 64MB per node.

Multicomputers are also built for specific tasks. IBM's Power Visualizer uses several i860s to do visualization transformations and rendering. AT&T DSP3 Parallel Processor provides up to 2.56Gflops, formed with 128 signal-processing nodes. The DSP3 is used for such tasks as signal- and image-processing, and

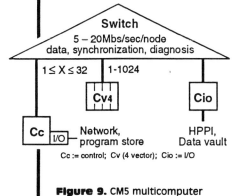

Figure 9. CM5 multicomputer

speech recognition. The DARPA-Intel iWarp™ developed with CMU is being used for a variety of signal- and image-processing applications that are typically connected to workstations. An iWarp node provides only 10Mflops (or 20Mflops for 32-bit precision) and 0.5 to 16MB of memory per node. Each node can communicate at up to 320MB per sec on 8 links.

The Teradata/NCR/AT&T systems are used for database retrieval and transaction-processing in a commercial environment. The system is connected by a tree-structured switch, and the hundreds of Intel 486 leaf nodes processors handle applications, communications, or disk access. A system can process over 1,000 transactions per sec working with a single database, or roughly four times the performance of a multiprocessor mainframe.

Programming Environments to Support Parallelism
Although the spectacular increases in performance derived from microprocessors are noteworthy, perhaps the greatest breakthrough has come in software environments such as Linda, the Parallel Virtual Machine (PVM), and Parasoft's Express that permit users to structure and control a collection of processes to operate in parallel on independent computers using message passing. Of course, user interface software, debuggers, performance-monitoring, and many other tools are part of these basic parallel environments.

Several programming models and environments are used to control parallelism. For multiprocessors, small degrees of parallelism are supported through such mechanisms as multitasking and Unix™ pipes in an explicit or direct user control fashion. Linda extends this model to manage the creation and distribution of independent processes for parallel execution in a shared address space. Medium (10 to 100) and high degrees of parallelism (1,000) for a single job can be

carried out in either an explicit message-passing or implicit fashion. The most straightforward implicit method is the SPMD model for hosting Fortran across a number of computers. A Fortran 90 translator should enable multiple workstations to be used in parallel on a single program in a language evolutionary fashion. Furthermore, a program written in this fashion can be used equally effectively across a number of different environments from supercomputers to workstation networks. Alternatively, a new language, having more inherent parallelism, such as dataflow may evolve. Fortran will adopt it.

Research Computers
Much of university computer architecture research is aimed at scalable, shared-memory multiprocessors (e.g., [20]) and supported by DARPA. In 1991, MITI sponsored the first conference on shared-memory multiprocessors in Tokyo, to increase international understanding. It brought together research results from 10 universities (eight U.S, two Japanese), and four industrial labs (three U.S., one Japanese). This work includes, directory schemes to efficiently "track" cached data as it is moved among the distributed processor-memory pairs, performance analysis, interconnection schemes, multithreaded processors, and compilers.

Researchers at the University of California, Berkeley are using a 64-node CM5 to explore various programming models and languages including dataflow. Early work includes a library to allow the computer to simulate a shared memory multiprocessor. An equally important part of Berkeley's research is the Sequoia 2000 project being done in collaboration with NASA and DEC that focuses on real-time data acquisition of 2 terabytes of data per day, secondary and tertiary memories, and very large databases requiring multiple accesses.

Seitz at Cal Tech, developed the

first multicomputer (interconnected via a hypercube network) and went on to develop high-bandwidth grid networks that use wormhole routing. The basic switch technology is being used in a variety of multiprocessor and multicomputers including Intel and Cray.

The CEDAR project at the University of Illinois is in the completion phase, and scores of papers describe the design, measurements, and the problem of compiling for scalable multiprocessors. Unfortunately, CEDAR was built on the now defunct Alliant Multiprocessor.

MIT has continued researching multiple machine designs. The Monsoon dataflow computer became operational with 16, 5Mflop nodes and demonstrates scalability and implicit parallelism using a dataflow language. The next dataflow processor design, T* is multithreaded to absorb network latency. The J-machine is a simple multicomputer designed for message-passing and low-overhead system calls. The J-machine, like the original RISC designs, places hardware functions in software to simplify the processor design. A J-machine, with sufficient software, carries out message-passing functions to enable shared-memory multiprocessing. Alewife, like Stanford's DASH is a distributed multiple multithreaded processor that is interconnected via a grid switch. Additional efforts are aimed at switches and packaging, including a 3D interconnection scheme.

Rice University continues to lead compiler research in universities and was responsible for the HPF Forum. HPF is a successor to Fortran D (data parallelism) that was initially posited for all high-performance machines (SIMDs, vector multiprocessors, and multicomputers). The challenge in multicomputers is initial data allocation, control of memory copies, and avoiding latency and overhead when passing messages.

Stanford's DASH is a scalable multiprocessor with up to 64 pro-

Role of Computer and Computational Science

A recent panel of computer and computational scientists described their reservations about the progress in parallel computing, expressing concerns about training and people interested in computational science, machine availability, and lack of standards caused by too many programming models [19]. They compared progress to the difficulty in learning to use vector processors. A recent study by the IEEE Technical Committee on Supercomputing (IEEE 1992) showed that out of approximately 8,000 users of the NSF Supercomputer centers, less than 100 computer science and about 200 electrical engineering users used a negligible amount of the resources. With today's parallel computers that are an artifact of massive federal funding, however, computer science has been slowly attracted to helping understand fundamentals.

In 1987, as assistant director of computing at NSF, I urged the computer science community to become involved in parallelism by using and understanding the plethora of computers that can be applied to computational science [2]. This would entail understanding applications, including solving problems using new parallel structures, writing texts, training students, and carrying out research. Today, much computer science research is devoted to some form of parallelism. Making significant contributions in parallelism requires understanding and solving problems that are usually numerically intensive. Numerical analysis is not part of the computer science core curriculum. In a similar fashion, the results of supercomputing often require visualization (also not part of the curriculum). Visualization also changes the nature of I/O and mass storage. Now, I suggest the following:

1. Collaborating with scientists and engineers on real problems using real computers. This enhances the training of computational scientists who understand and enrich computer science.
2. Training and understanding using traditional, uniprocessor supercomputers and shared-memory multiprocessors that provide fine granularity. If code runs poorly on a super or a shared-memory multiprocessor, it is certain to run poorly on a distributed multicomputer.
3. Installing, teaching, and using environments composed of existing workstations that have very long granularity. These can and must be dealt with using programming environments such as Linda or PVM.

Attaching SIMDs and multicomputers to workstations for specialized problems.

4. Progressing to problems and algorithms that can tolerate the latencies inherent in multicomputers.
5. Designing benchmarks and workloads typifying new programs and computers to enhance understanding. Collaborating on computers that are being designed, and making them run well is much more important than producing any more computers.

We must thoroughly understand the machines we have by using and measuring them on a range of real problems. The goal should be to look at a problem / program / algorithm and know *a priori* how an application will run, based on the computer / compiler as measured by its various parameters. Making a parallel application run effectively is an *ad hoc* art. ∎

cessors arranged in a grid of 4 × 4 nodes. Each node consists of a four-processor Silicon Graphics multiprocessor that is roughly equivalent to a uniprocessor with an attached vector unit. DASH demonstrated linear speedups for a wide range of algorithms, and is used for compiler research. Some applications have reached over 100Mflops for 16 processors, which is about the speed a four-vector processor system of comparable speed achieves. Since the system is relatively slow, it is unclear which principles have applicability for competitive computers.

DARPA has funded Tera Computer to start-up. Tera, a second-generation HEP, is to have 256 128-instruction stream processors or 32K processors and operate in 1995. With a multiple instruction stream or multithreaded processor, any time a processor has to wait for a memory access, the next instruction stream is started. Each processor is built using very fast gate arrays (e.g., GaAs) to operate at 400MHz. The expected latency to memory is between 40 and 100 ticks, but since each processor can issue multiple requests, a single physical processor appears to support 16 threads (or virtual processors). Thus, a processor appears to have access to a constant, zero latency memory. Since a processor is time-shared, it is comparatively slow and likely to be unusable for scalar tasks, and is hardly a general-purpose computer according to Smith's definition [21]. The physical processors connect to 512 memory units, 256 I/O cache units (i.e., slower memories used for buffering I/O), and I/O processors through a 4K-node interconnection network. In order to avoid the "dance hall" label, the network has four times more nodes than are required by the components. Tera's approach has been to design a computer that supports a parallelizing compiler.

Summary and Conclusions

In 1989 I projected that supercom-

puters would reach a teraflop by 1995 using either a SIMD or multicomputer approach, but neglected to mention the price. By mid-1992, scalable multicomputers have improved by a factor of 5 to 10 to reach 100 ± 20 Gflops at a supercomputer price level, and the SIMD approach was dropped. Scalable multicomputers also break through the $30 million supercomputer barrier to create a teraflop ultracomputer ($50 to 400 million), and are not recommended buys. In 1995 semiconductor gains should increase performance by a factor of four and competition should reduce the price a factor of two to supercomputer levels as projected in Figure 1. Given the number of applications and state of training, waiting for the teraflop at the supercomputer price level is recommended.

Multiprocessors have been the mainline of computing because they are general-purpose and can handle a variety of applications from transaction-processing to time-sharing, that are highly sequential to highly parallel. KSR demonstrated that massive, scalable

Government Policy: Why We Don't Need "State" Computer Architectures

In January 1992, the President signed a law authorizing the spending of $1 billion for various agencies to comply with the HPCC Act. The law provides for building a National Research and Education Network (NREN), as well as work on parallel computing, algorithms, and computer science education. The HPCC Report (OSTP, 1992) outlines the role of the various agencies (DARPA, DOC, DOE, EPA, NIH/NLM, and NSF) in computing systems, software technology and algorithms, the network, and basic research and human resources. The report outlines a variety of grand challenges in science and engineering, ranging from weather and climate prediction and global change, to astronomy, semiconductors, superconductors, speech, and vision. According to the report's budget, DARPA has two-thirds of the budget, or over $100 million in 1992 for high-performance computing systems. Other agencies have the grand challenge problems. Undoubtedly, the most important aspect of the program will be training and the network. So far, the architectures and companies resulting from this massive funding have been less than spectacular, which confirms my opinion that DARPA should not directly fund the development of computers at companies.

DARPA has a long and successful record of sponsoring university research that creates companies and products such as MIPS, Sun, and Sparc in cases where no products or technology existed. It fostered AI, graphics, operating systems, packet switching, speech understanding, time-sharing, VLSI design, and workstations at universities. Supercomputing, including using a massive (>1000) number of processors is a commercial area that has been developed by industry and does not require the selection or support of particular architectures or companies. DARPA's role in the development of massive parallelism can be terminated because it has been picked up by industry. Almost a dozen companies are building multicomputers that compete with DARPA's incestuous product divisions (Cray, Intel, Tera, and Thinking Machines). The situation of funding the design and purchase of a computer is not a healthy one.

I know of no successful products developed by funding company product development, including the vast array of military computers. DARPA funded Burroughs to build the unsuccessful Illiac IV in the late 1960s, a 64-processor SIMD. ARPA funded BBN to provide the first switching computers for ARPAnet. BBN was successful for almost a decade during which it had a technology monopoly as the government paid for product development and bought and tested its products. In 1992, BBN is a minor supplier in a flourishing communications market. Similarly, BBN's government-funded computer development that was initiated by DARPA folded in 1991. The several hundred million dollars of funds that went into a couple of massively parallel computers this last decade could have been used to provide substantially more computing power to real users. By way of contrast, NSF spends about $60 million annually to support four supercomputing centers. Funding to create a monopoly company only inhibits the development of technology and products at other companies. Product development contracts and purchase orders have not created lasting companies, and are not likely to in the future. Companies funded in an incestuous fashion simply cannot stand up to a "real" market, and will not be able to compete internationally. A large fraction of the market is reduced or eliminated when government funds and buys its own designs, closing the early adopter and innovator government markets to privately financed computer companies. Furthermore, once started, DARPA-funded companies require continued funding to remain healthy . . . just as the defense contractors that are being downsized.

22

distributed, shared-memory multi-processors (smPs) are feasible. Multicomputers from the score of companies combining computers will evolve to multiprocessors just to reduce overhead in simulating a single-memory address space, memory access, and supporting efficient multiprogramming. Next-generation multicomputers are likely to resemble BBN's distrib-uted memory computers as they evolve to become multiprocessors.

Important gains in parallelism have come from software environments that allow networks of computers to be applied to a single job. Thus every laboratory containing fast workstations has or will have its own supercomputer for highly parallel applications. The rapid in-crease in microprocessor power ensures that the workstation will perform at near super speed for sequential applications. LAN environments can provide significant supercomputing for highly parallel applications by 1995. It is critical for companies to provide fast, low-overhead switches that will allow users to configure multicomputers composed of less than 100 high-

By taking over computer design through funding and purchasing, users do not benchmark or understand the machines they are given or forced to use. At a time when gigabucks for teraflops may induce brain damage, it is critical to consider all the factors of an architecture and especially the mean time before answers. In the future, government laboratories are likely to be measured on their ability to replicate and transfer results, and having programs that run well across a variety of machines is more important than exploiting the latest fad. When government support for the HPCC program ends, it is the market rather than a bureaucrat's dream of an architecture or industry, that determines economics.

At the Sid Fernbach Memorial Symposium, February 1992, speakers reiterated the policy that Fernbach used, as head of computation at Lawrence Livermore National Laboratory, to help supercomputing come into existence: be a knowledgeable, demanding, tolerant, and helpful customer. Department of Energy laboratories purchased, not funded the development of early computers by providing needs specifications.

Following is a suggested policy to support development of high-performance computing:

1. The concept of the ultracomputer is so artificial and deleterious to the com-puter industry that buying a single ultra should be discouraged. An affordable teraflop will come by 1995. Let evolution work to produce better computers that are balanced and usable, not aimed at a single, peak number.
2. Support users to purchase machines that can be justified for specific programs at various agencies and organizations that have "grand challenge" problems. Contracts would be open bid, and benchmarks that characterize the user workload would be required. The reestablishment of benchmarking would cause reality to replace hope as a buying criteria.

Allow universities to choose the computers they buy. Don't control the purchasing or the design of computers from Washington (funding agency, Congress). Given the specialized nature and high cost of a supercomputer or ultracomputer, users (e.g., weapons designers) who can justify them from tool and experiment budgets should simply buy them.

3. Encourage collaboration. Any company should be free to work with a laboratory project to produce technology, prototype, or product. Fund university projects (not their codevelopers) where a codeveloping company is capable of or likely to be able to take the product to market.

Encourage laboratories to obtain clustered computers based on workstation nodes providing more than an order of magnitude more peak power than supers. Such machines would provide the same power as scalable multicomputers, but in addition, dedicated power for visualization and video conferencing.
4. Do not fund computer development *per se*. Industry has always been able to fund good ideas. There is really no effective way to select the "right" winner from Washington. Once started, funding becomes an ongoing government responsibility and right for startups: get the money and do it. In the case of large companies: if the technology is worth funding, fund it. A company only takes government money to build a computer if the project is not worthwhile, and they are supporting its staff.
5. Encourage the use of computers in universities vs. designing more computers by people who have never used or built a computer. The world is drowning in computers that absorb programmers trying to realize peak performance.
6. Eliminate funding by congressional-directed centers even though this might work. Chose centers based on competence.
7. In the very unlikely event that no one is building the appropriate computer and a special one must be funded for clear military need, build a few prototypes (≤ 2), open the process to all bidders without the usual military procurement hassles. ∎

performance workstations, because these are likely to provide the most cost-effective and useful computing environments.

A petaflop (10^{15} floating-point operations per sec) at less than $500 million level is likely to be beyond 2001. By 2001, semiconductor gains provide an increase factor of 16 over 1995 computers. Better packaging and lower price margins through competition could provide another increase factor of two or three. The extra increase factor of 20 for a petaflop is unclear. Based on today's results and rationales, a petaflop before its time is as bad an investment as the teraflop before its time. Evolution and market forces are just fine . . . if we will just let them work.

Acknowledgments

The author would like to thank Peter Denning and other reviewers for their helpful suggestions in the editing process. These individuals provided performance data and helpful insight: David Culler (University of California, Berkeley), Charles Grassl (Cray Research), Justin Rattner (Intel), Ron Jonas and Ruby Lee (HP), Chani Pangali (Kendall Square Research), Frank MacMahon (Lawrence Livermore National Laboratories), John Mashey (MIPS), Tadashi Watanabe (NEC), Jack Dongarra (Oak Ridge National Laboratory and University of Tenn.), Mike Humphrey (Silicon Graphics Inc.), Burton Smith (Tera Computer), David Douglas and John Mucci (Thinking Machines Corp.), and Jack Worlton (Worlton & Assoc.) C

References

1. Bailey, D.H. Twelve ways to fool the masses when giving performance result on parallel computers. *Supercomput. Rev.* (Aug. 1991), 54–55.
2. Bell, G. The future of high performance computers in science and engineering. *Commun. ACM 32*, 9 (Sept. 1989), 1091–1101.
3. Bell, G. 11 rules of supercomputer design. University Video Communications Videotape, vol. III, Stanford Calif., 1989.
4. Bell, G. Three decades of multiprocessors. CMU Computer Science: 25th Anniversary Commemorative R. Rashid, Ed. ACM Press, Addison-Wesley, Reading, Mass., 1991, pp. 3–27.
5. Berry, M., Cybenko, G., and Larson, J. Scientific benchmark characterizations. *Parallel Comput. 17*, (1991), 1173–1194.
6. Denning, P.J. Working sets past and present. *IEEE Trans. Softw. Eng. SE-6* (Jan. 1980), 64–84.
7. Denning, P.J. and Tichy, W. Highly parallel computation. *Science 250*, xx (Nov. 30, 1990), 1217–1222.
8. Dongarra, J.J. Performance of various computers using standard linear equation software. University of Tennesse and Oak Ridge National Laboratory, CS-89-85, Jan. 13, 1992.
9. Dongarra, J.J., Karp, Miura, K. and Simon, H.D. Gordon Bell Prize Lectures. In *Proceedings Supercomputing 91* (1991), pp 328–337.
10. Gustafson, J.L., Montry, G.R. and Benner, R.E. Development of parallel methods for a 1024 processor hypercube. *SIAM J. Sci. Stat. Comput. 9*, 4 (July 1988), 609–638.
11. Hennessy, J.L. and Patterson, D.A. *Computer Architecture: A Quantitative Approach.* Morgan Kaufman, San Mateo, Calif., 1990.
12. Hill, M.D. What is scalability? *Computer Architecture News 18*, 4 (Dec. 1990), 18–21.
13. Hillis, D. and Steele, G. The CM5, University Video Communications, Two videotapes, vol. IV, Stanford Calif., 1992.
14. Hockney R.W. and Jesshope, C.R. *Parallel Computers 2*, Adam Hilger, Bristol, 1988.
15. IEEE Computer Society Technical Committee on Supercomputing Applications. NSF Supercomputer Centers Study, Feb. 1992.
16. Li, K. and Schafer, R. A hypercube shared virtual memory system. *1989 International Conference on Parallel Systems,*
17. Office of Science and Technology Policy (OSTP). Grand challenges 1993: High performance computing and communications, A report by the Committee on Physical, Mathematical, and Engineering Sciences of the Federal Coordinating Council for Science, Engineering, and Technology in the Office of Science and Technology Policy, National Science Foundation, 1992.
18. Nielsen, D.E. A stategy for smoothly transitioning to massively parallel computing. *Energy and Tech. Rev.* (Nov. 1991), 20–31.
19. Pancake, C.M. Software support for parallel computing: Where are we headed? *Commun. ACM 34.*, 11 (Nov. 1991), 52–66.
20. Scott, S.L. A cache coherence mechanism for scalable, shared-memory multiprocessors. In *Proceedings of the International Symposium of Shared Memory Multiprocessing Information Processing Society of Japan,* (Tokyo, Apr., 1991) 49–59.
21. Smith, B. The end of architecture. *Comput. Architecture News 18.*, 4 (Dec. 1990), 10–17.
22. Watanabe, The NEC SX3 Supercomputer, University Video Communications, Videotape, Stanford Calif., 1992.
23. Worlton, J. A critique of "massively" parallel computing. Worlton & Associates Tech. Rep. 41, Salt Lake City Utah, May 1992.
24. Worlton, J. The MPP Bandwagon. *Supercomput. Rev.*, To be published.

CR Categories and Subject Descriptors: B.0 [**Hardware**]: General; C.0 [**Computer Systems Organization**]: General—*instruction set design (e.g., RISC, CISC);* J.1 [**Computer Applications**]: Administrative Data Processing—*government, system architectures*

General Terms: Design, Management
Additional Key Words and Phrases: Government policy, parallel processing, scientific programming

About the Author:
GORDON BELL is a computer industry consultant. He has been vice president of R&D at Digital Equipment Corp., a founder of various companies, and was the first assistant director of the NSF Computing Directorate. From 1966 to 1972 he was a professor of computer science at Carnegie Mellon University. In 1991 Bell won the National Medal of Technology and in 1992 was awarded the IEEE's Von Neumann Medal. **Author's Present Address:** 450 Old Oak Court, Los Altos, CA 94022

Scheduling Support for Concurrency and Parallelism in the Mach Operating System

David L. Black

Carnegie Mellon University

Significant changes in the use of multiprocessors require new support from operating system schedulers. Originally, multiprocessors increased throughput by running several applications at once, but no individual application ran faster. This use is giving way to parallel programming, which reduces the runtime of individual applications.

Parallel-programming models and languages often anticipate dedicated use of processors or an entire multiprocessor, but few machines are used in this fashion. Most modern general-purpose multiprocessors run a time-sharing operating system such as Unix. The shared-use model of these systems conflicts with the dedicated-use model of many programs, but the conflict is seldom resolved by restricting multiprocessor use to one application at a time.

Another impact on schedulers comes from the increased use of concurrency. The *application parallelism* for a multiprocessor application is the actual degree of parallel execution achieved, while *application concurrency* is the maximum degree of parallel execution that could be achieved with unlimited processors. For example, an application consisting of 10 independent processes running on a six-processor multiprocessor has an applica-

> **Traditional time-sharing schedulers are inadequate for parallel and concurrent programs, which require new techniques such as processor allocation and handoff scheduling.**

tion parallelism of six, based on the six processors, and an application concurrency of 10, because it could use up to 10 processors. Application concurrency beyond hardware parallelism can improve hardware use; if one portion of the application blocks (for example, a disk or network operation), other portions can still proceed. The use of concurrency can also sim-plify programming of concurrent applications by capturing the state of ongoing interactions in local variables of executing entities instead of in a state table.

Application parallelism and concurrency complicate two areas of scheduling: making effective use of the processing resources available to individual applications and dividing processing resources among competing applications. The problem of scheduling within applications seldom arises for serial applications because they can often be scheduled independently with little impact on overall performance. In contrast, the medium- to fine-grain interactions of parallel and concurrent programs may require scheduling portions of these programs together to achieve acceptable performance. Parallel applications that require a fixed number of processors complicate scheduling across applications. They make division of machine time more difficult and may introduce situations for which a fair-sharing policy is inappropriate. For example, an application configured for a fixed numbers of processors may be unable to cope efficiently with fewer processors.

At Carnegie Mellon University, developing the Mach operating system[1] for uniprocessors and multiprocessors produced some new approaches to scheduling. Mach provides flexible memory manage-

0-8186-6522-X/95 $4.00 © 1990 IEEE

ment and sharing, multiple *threads* (control locus, program counter, registers) within a single address space or *task* for concurrency and parallelism, and a network-transparent communication subsystem. This communication subsystem is called the IPC (interprocess communication) subsystem for historical reasons; all communication in Mach is actually between tasks. The Mach kernel incorporates compatibility code derived from 4.3BSD Unix[2] that provides complete binary compatibility. Mach runs on a variety of uniprocessor and multiprocessor architectures, including the DEC VAX, Sun 3, IBM RP3, and Encore Multimax. Mach is available and supported as a product by a number of hardware vendors, including Next, Encore, and Omron. It is also the base technology for the OSF/1 operating system from the Open Software Foundation.

This article concentrates on the shared use of general-purpose uniprocessors and shared-memory multiprocessors, emphasizing support for common uniform-memory-access architectures that have all memory equidistant from all processors in terms of access time. This work is also applicable to nonuniform-memory-acc s machines, whose memory access times depend on the physical distance between the processor and the accessed memory, but it does not provide a complete solution to load-balancing problems for this class of machine.

Time-sharing scheduling

A major goal of time-sharing schedulers is allocating resources so that competing applications receive approximately equal portions of processor time. The "approximately equal" notion applies over periods of a few seconds to ensure interactive response in the presence of computation-bound jobs. In practice, this requires tracking processor usage and using the information in scheduling decisions. The simplest use, a decreasing-priority scheduler, continuously decreases a process' priority as it uses processor time and favors higher priority processes. Multics[3] used such a scheduler and discovered its major disadvantage: on a heavily loaded system with many short-lived jobs, the priority of a lengthy job can decrease until little or no further processor time is available to it. The automatic priority depression of lengthy jobs in some versions

of Unix also exhibits this drawback.

To avoid the problem of permanently depressed priorities, it is necessary to elevate them in some manner. The two major elevation methodologies are event-based elevation and processor usage aging. Event-based elevation deliberately favors interactive response over computation-bound jobs. It elevates process priority through such events such as I/O completion. Elevations associated with events of interest must be determined in some manner, such as tuning under expected workloads to produce desired behavior. This methodology, used by VAX/VMS,[4] assumes that jobs are either distinctly computation-bound or distinctly interactive and that interactive jobs are more important. Users whose interactive work consumes large amounts of processor time may not do well under this methodology. Such applications may not generate enough priority-raising events to offset the priority decreases caused by processor usage. Also, under this methodology, it may be necessary to retune priority elevations in response to workload or hardware changes.

Under the second priority-elevation methodology, processor usage aging, a scheduler elevates priorities by gradually forgetting about past processor usage, usually in an exponential fashion. For example, usage from one minute ago is half as costly as use within the past minute, usage from two minutes ago is half again as costly, and so on. As a result, the scheduler's measure of usage is an exponentially weighted average over the lifetime of a process. A simple exponential average is not desirable; it has the unexpected side effect of raising priorities when system load rises. This happens because, under higher loads, each process gets a smaller share of the processor, so its usage average drops, causing its priority to rise. These elevated priorities can degrade system response under heavy loads because no process accumulates enough usage to drop its priority. The 4.3BSD version of Unix solves this problem by making the aging rate depend on the load factor. Aging is slower in the presence of a higher load, which keeps priorities in approximately the same range.[2] An alternative technique uses an overload factor to alter the rate at which usage accumulates. Under this technique, the usage accumulated by the scheduler is the actual usage multiplied by a factor based on the system load.

For a multiprocessor scheduler, the concept of fair sharing is strongly inter-

twined with that of load balancing. The goal of load balancing is to spread the system's computational load evenly among the available processors over time. For example, if three similar jobs are running on a two-processor system, each should average two-thirds of a processor. This often requires the scheduler to shuffle processes among processors to keep the load balanced. An important trade-off between load balancing and overhead is that optimal load balancing causes high scheduler overhead due to frequent context switches for load balancing. A uniprocessor time-sharing scheduler encounters similar issues in minimizing the number of context switches used to implement fair sharing.

Mach scheduler

The Mach operating system splits the usual process notion into task and thread abstractions, but the Mach time-sharing scheduler only schedules threads. The knowledge that two threads occur in the same task can be used to optimize the context switch between them but is not used to select which threads run. Favoring threads on this basis may not improve performance, depending on the hardware and application involved. It can also be detrimental to usage and load balancing because this favoritism may conflict with decisions needed to accomplish balancing.

Data structures. The primary data structure used by the Mach scheduler is the *run queue*, a priority queue of runnable threads implemented by an array of doubly linked queues. Mach uses 32 queues, so four priorities from the Unix range of 0 to 127 map to each queue. (More recent Mach kernels use a priority range of 0 to 31 so that queues and priorities correspond.) Lower priorities correspond to higher numbers and vice versa.

A hint is maintained that indicates the probable location of the highest priority thread. The highest priority thread cannot be at a higher priority than the hint, but it may be at a lower priority. This allows the search for the highest priority thread to start from the hint, potentially avoiding the search of a dozen or more queues because the highest possible priority for most user threads is 50 to match Unix.

Each run queue also contains a mutual exclusion lock and a count of threads currently enqueued. The count optimizes testing for emptiness by replacing a scan of the individual queues with a comparison of the counter to zero. This eliminates the need to hold the run queue lock when the run queue is empty, thereby reducing potential contention for this important lock. The use of a single lock assumes that clock interrupts on the processors of a multiprocessor are not synchronized. Significant contention can be expected in the synchronized case; thus, a shared global run queue may not be appropriate.

Figure 1 shows a run queue with three threads. The queues containing the threads are doubly linked, but, for clarity, only the forward links are shown. The hint is 2, indicating that queues 0 and 1 are empty and can be skipped in a search for the highest priority thread.

When a new thread is needed for execution, each processor consults the appropriate run queues. The kernel maintains a *local run queue* for each processor and a shared *global run queue*. The local run queue is used by threads that have been temporarily bound to a specific processor for one of two reasons: (1) Although most of the Unix compatibility code in current Mach kernels has been parallelized,[5] threads executing in the unparallelized portion are temporarily bound to a single, designated *master processor*; (2) interrupts that invoke Unix compatibility code are also restricted to this processor. The remaining use of the local run queues is by the processor allocation operation described in the section entitled "Processor allocation."

Mach is self-scheduling in that, instead of having threads assigned by a centralized dispatcher, individual processors consult the run queues when they need a new thread to run. A processor examines the local run queue first to give bound threads absolute preference over unbound threads. This precaution avoids bottlenecks by maximizing throughput of the unparallelized Unix compatibility code[6] and improves processor allocation performance by preempting other operations. If the local queue is empty, the processor examines the global run queue. In either case, it dequeues and runs the highest priority thread. If both queues are empty, the processor becomes idle.

Special mechanisms are used for idle processors. Most uniprocessor systems execute the idle loop by borrowing the kernel stack of the most recently run thread or process. On a multiprocessor this can be disastrous. If the thread resumes execution on another processor, the two processors will corrupt the thread's kernel stack.

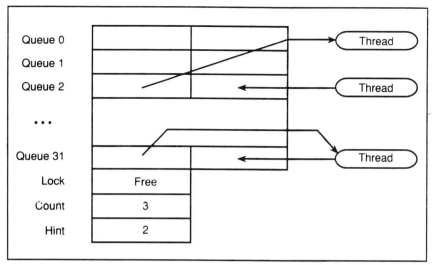

Figure 1. Mach run-queue structure.

To avoid stack corruption, Mach uses a dedicated *idle thread* for each processor. Idle processors are dispatched by a mechanism that bypasses the run queues. Threads that become runnable are matched with idle processors. The idle thread on each processor picks up the corresponding new thread and context switches directly to it, gaining performance by bypassing the run queues. This mechanism is one example of a general technique, called handoff scheduling, that context switches directly to a new thread without searching for it on a run queue.

Priority calculations. Thread priorities consist of a base priority plus an offset derived from recent processor usage. The base priority is set low enough to allow internal kernel threads, which perform critical kernel functions such as pageout, to run at higher priorities than user threads. The offset derived from usage is weighted by a load factor to preserve system responsiveness under load. If an adequate hardware source of time stamps exists, such as a 32-bit microsecond counter, the scheduler can be configured to base usage calculations on time stamps from this counter. This configuration eliminates the inaccuracies and distortions caused by statistical usage calculations (see Wendorf[6] for details).

Mach uses the overload factor technique for processor usage aging. Aging overhead is distributed by making each thread responsible for aging its processor usage. Clock interrupts and events that unblock a thread cause it to check its local

copy of a counter against a global value that is incremented once a second. If these values differ, the thread ages its usage by a factor of 5/8 for each unit of difference. This results in each thread's accumulated usage being multiplied by 5/8 once a second. This figure was chosen for efficiency (two shifts and an add can implement multiplication by 5/8) and to produce behavior similar to other time-sharing systems. (The number used by 4.3BSD Unix depends on load; it varies from 1/2 to 2/3 for the 0.5 to 1.0 range.) The Mach scheduler uses a load factor of the number of runnable threads divided by the number of processors with a minimum factor of 1. This factor is calculated as an exponential average to smooth the impact of abrupt load changes.

The scheduling algorithm requires all threads to check their copy of the counter on a regular basis. The clock interrupt handler performs the check for running threads, and threads that are not running defer the check until they become runnable. Runnable threads with low priorities may spend long periods on a run queue while higher priority threads monopolize the processor. Such threads would run if they could check their copy of the counter and age their usage, but their low-priority positions prevent them from running to perform the check. To avoid such "starvation," an internal kernel thread scans the run queues every two seconds to age and elevate any threads caught in that situation. The two-second period, selected on the basis of experience with versions that exhibited starvation, produces acceptable behavior.

Managing context switches. The scheduler uses time quanta to minimize the number of context switches it causes. When a processor begins running a thread, that thread is assigned a time quantum. Periodic clock interrupts (every 10 to 100 milliseconds) decrement this quantum, and a rescheduling check occurs when the quantum expires if the thread is still running. This rescheduling check causes a context switch if there is another runnable thread of equal or higher priority; otherwise, the original thread continues running with a new quantum. The context switch mechanism uses an asynchronous system trap (AST) to avoid context switches in interrupt service routines. An AST is a general mechanism that allows an interrupt service routine to force the current thread to trap into the kernel from user mode. ASTs may be directly supported in hardware, implemented entirely in software, or a combination of the two. Priority reductions due to processor usage accumulated during a thread's first quantum do not cause context switches. This feature reduces the number of context switches for load and usage balancing by extending the time period between context switches.

Context switches also preempt lower priority threads when higher priority threads become runnable. On a uniprocessor, where an AST is requested as part of making the higher priority thread runnable, preemption occurs immediately. On a multiprocessor, if another processor must notice the presence of a higher priority thread on a run queue, preemption can take up to one clock-interrupt period. Mach doesn't use interprocessor interrupts for preemption; they haven't been necessary to achieve acceptable time-sharing behavior. Consequently, the scheduler doesn't maintain data structures that permit efficient identification of the lowest priority processor. However, as Mach evolves to support real-time applications, the addition of interprocessor interrupts for preemption is likely.

Programming models

Application programming models can introduce concurrency beyond hardware parallelism at two levels. An operating system can introduce concurrency by multiplexing Unix processes, Mach threads, or other independently schedulable entities (called *virtual processors*) onto hardware processors. A user-level library or language runtime can introduce

Table 1. Programming models for parallel and concurrent programming.

Relationship	Model
MR = VP = PP	Pure parallelism
MR ≥ VP = PP	User concurrency
MR = VP ≥ PP	System concurrency
MR ≥ VP ≥ PP	Dual concurrency

further concurrency by multiplexing language-level entities onto the VPs. Called *multiroutines*, these entities can be thought of as multiprocessor generalizations of coroutines. Special cases of multiroutines include coroutines (only one virtual processor) and the common programming notion of multiple threads (one virtual processor per multiroutine) found in many systems, including the Mach Cthreads library.[7] Multiroutines and virtual processors can be identified in almost any parallel programming language implementation or environment. One example is an Ada runtime on Unix, which would use Unix processes as its virtual processors and Ada tasks as its multiroutines. The Mach Cthreads library uses Mach threads as its virtual processors and Cthreads as its multiroutines.

Parallel and concurrent programming models can be classified by the relationships among the multiroutines (MRs), virtual processors (VPs), and physical processors (PPs) they support (see Table 1). For *pure parallelism* models, the programmer's notion of concurrency is identical to the hardware parallelism. Compiler-generated code for parallel execution of loop bodies is a common example. *User concurrency* models introduce additional concurrency at the user level. An example would be programs based on a queue of user-defined tasks dequeued and executed in parallel by virtual processors. A *coroutine* model is a user concurrency model with exactly one physical processor and hence one virtual processor. *System concurrency* models, used by most multithreading packages and many parallel language runtime systems, introduce additional concurrency only at the system level. *Dual concurrency* models, a relatively new class, introduce concurrency at both the system and user levels. The programming model for an application depends on both the programming language or library and how it is used. For example, pure parallelism applications can be writ-

ten with a system concurrency library or language by creating only as many virtual processors as physical processors.

Fine-grain applications, which execute tens to hundreds of instructions between interactions with other multiroutines, cannot use system concurrency models. They require models with corresponding virtual and physical processors in which every virtual processor is always executing. This assumption is designed into the models' synchronization primitives, such as spin locks, and performance suffers if it is violated. Hence, programs using these models require dedicated physical processors. (Coroutine models, which use only one physical processor, are an exception.) The major disadvantage of these models is inefficient implementation of blocking system operations including page faults. Blocking a virtual processor in the operating system also blocks a physical processor, which wastes time when the physical processor is dedicated to the application.

The remaining model classes support blocking operations efficiently, but their potentially large synchronization overheads make them inappropriate for fine-grain applications. Their blocking operations are efficient because system concurrency can make an additional virtual processor available to use time relinquished by a blocked virtual processor. The blocking nature of synchronization in languages such as Ada and programming paradigms like message passing forces the use of models from these classes. The need for dedicated processors in these models is application dependent rather than inherent to the model. Applications for which parallel execution is important may need dedicated processors, while others may not. Communication or synchronization with nonexecuting virtual processors can be expensive because the operating system might not understand which processors are involved. Operating system support for such synchronization and communication can improve performance. But, even with this support, synchronization can consume hundreds of instructions, making these models inappropriate for fine-grain parallel applications.

Scheduling concurrency support

Applications using more virtual than physical processors can benefit from user input to scheduling decisions. Users may have application-specific information about which virtual processors should or should not be running. The Mach scheduler is implemented in the operating system kernel but accepts user hints. These hints consist of local information involving the hint's thread, and possibly one other, so that users can avoid maintaining overall status information on their applications. The hints are based on two pieces of scheduling information that may be available when a thread attempts to communicate or synchronize with another thread that is not running. The first thread may be unable to make further progress until the communication or synchronization is complete, and it may know the identity of the thread that will complete the operation. For example, in a synchronization based on a message exchange, the initiating thread must block, and the identity of the thread that will reply to the message is often known.

The Mach scheduler accepts and uses two classes of hints: discouragement and handoff. A new primitive, thread_switch, allows simultaneous hints from both classes.

• *Discouragement hints*, which can be mild, strong, or absolute, indicate that the current thread should not run. Mild hints suggest giving up the processor to any other thread if possible. Strong hints go one step further and temporarily depress priority. Absolute hints block for a specified period.

• *Handoff hints* indicate that a specific thread should run instead of the current one.

Discouragement hints are useful for optimizing shared-memory synchronization in applications employing system concurrency. The lock holder's identity is not recorded by the common test-and-set instructions used to implement shared memory locks, making a handoff hint impossible. A mild discouragement hint yields the processor in the hope that the lock's holder will run. This can cause problems if more than one thread is yielding. They may yield to each other, with the result that no useful computation occurs. This situation can occur if the time-sharing scheduler gives the yielding threads higher usage-based priorities than the thread(s) they are waiting for. Absolute discouragement prevents this problem by blocking the threads, but the available time resolution based on clock interrupts is usually too coarse for medium- to fine-grain synchronization. Strong discouragement is a compromise that avoids the

weaknesses of the other alternatives. Strong discouragement causes the scheduler to favor threads doing useful work, without the overhead of actually blocking those unable to proceed. A thread that issues a strong discouragement hint may explicitly cancel it when the desired event occurs; otherwise, the hint expires at a timeout supplied with the hint.

The second class of hint, handoff scheduling, directly "hands off" the processor to the specified thread, bypassing the internal scheduler mechanisms. Handoff scheduling may designate a thread within the same task or a different task on the same host to run next. A shared memory lock based on a compare-and-swap instruction can identify the target thread, or its identity may be available from the application's structure; for example, if a buffer is empty and only one thread fills it, then that thread should be run. One promising use of this technique addresses the "priority inversion" problem, where a low-priority thread holds a lock needed by a high-priority thread. The high-priority thread can detect this situation and hand the processor to the low-priority thread. When used from outside the kernel, handoff scheduling removes the specified thread from its run queue and runs it, avoiding a run queue search. Mach's message-passing subsystem also uses handoff scheduling inside the kernel to immediately run the recipient of a message. Use inside the kernel aids performance by avoiding the run queue entirely.

Performance. Two experiments — performed on an Encore Multimax with NS32332 processors having a speed of approximately 2 MIPS — have shown that scheduling hints benefit performance.

Synchronization hints. The first experiment investigated the use of hints for synchronizing with a thread that is not running. It used a multithreaded test program that synchronized with randomly selected threads. A shared variable contained a

thread number. That thread replaced it with another randomly chosen thread number, which then replaced it with another randomly chosen thread number, and so on. This program was restricted to a single processor, so it repeatedly synchronized with a nonexecuting thread. Threads not targeted for synchronization could use a scheduling hint to encourage the operating system to run the target.

Table 2 shows the elapsed time per synchronization in microseconds for different scheduling hints and numbers of threads as mean ± standard deviation. The mild discouragement hint exhibits two different behaviors. If all threads are at the same usage-based priority, the mild-ok line applies, and synchronization occurs quickly. If some of the threads are at different priorities, the mild-bad line applies, and the time per synchronization not only increases but exhibits pronounced variability. The mild-bad data is shown as ranges because the distributions are skewed toward higher frequencies at lower values. Multiple runs of the same test exhibit both behaviors unpredictably. This is strong evidence that, in many cases, mild discouragement is is not an appropriate scheduling hint. Strong discouragement is an appropriate alternative. Its behavior is far more stable, and its performance is better than most bad cases of mild discouragement. The synshronization times from the five-thread test cases for all hints is slightly better than expected, based on the other results. This is probably because the number of threads is a divisor of the 10-Hertz clock frequency that drives the scheduler, so stable behavior is more likely. Absolute discouragement was not tested because it would result in times on the order of 100 milliseconds per synchronization, given the hardware clock-interrupt frequency of 10 Hertz.

The results show the benefits of scheduling hints. Running the program without scheduling hints yields times of one-half to one second per synchronization, demonstrating the potential performance pen-

Table 2. Synchronization experiment results (in microseconds).

Threads	3	4	5	6	7
Mild-ok	467 ± 3	633 ± 3	817 ± 6	973 ± 12	1,160 ± 19
Mild-bad	578 - 1,224	1,128 - 4,427	3.9 - 7.5 ms	8 - 607 ms	138 - 487 ms
Strong	897 ± 6	1,215 ± 9	1,434 ± 11	1,825 ± 10	2,130 ± 18
Handoff	413 ± 3	418 ± 5	417 ± 3	421 ± 4	428 ± 4

Table 3. Message-passing handoff results (in microseconds).

Messages	Remote Procedure Call		One-way	
Idle processor?	No	Yes	No	Yes
No Handoff	1,914 ± 11	1,630 ± 6	857 ± 5	432 ± 3
Handoff	1,848 ± 8	1,628 ± 7	861 ± 10	429 ± 4

alties for ignoring the problem. If the threads are at the same priority, context switching is effective; however, if that is not the case, priority inversions cause poor results. Strong discouragement performs predictably but is slower than the best cases of mild discouragement because of the timeout costs associated with priority depressions. These costs also account for the increasing difference between the strong and mild-ok results as the number of threads increases. Handoff scheduling performs the best and is significantly faster than sending a message, since no time is spent formatting and transporting the message or blocking to wait for it. These results suggest that system-concurrent applications require strong-discouragement support and that handoff scheduling is effective if the required information is available. These are worst-case results, but they do indicate the relative performance of the hints.

IPC handoff scheduling. The second experiment concerned the performance benefits of using handoff scheduling in the kernel. It used a message-passing exerciser to measure the performance impact of handoff scheduling in Mach's network-transparent communication subsystem, the IPC. The experiment involved exchanging messages between two threads in a task on both single and multiple processor configurations. The key difference between the uniprocessor and multiprocessor experiments is the availability of an idle processor to run the recipient thread. Hence, the uniprocessor results are also applicable to multiprocessors when no idle processors are available. The experiment was run for both unidirectional and bidirectional (remote procedure call (RPC)) message exchanges.

Table 3 shows the results in microseconds of elapsed time per exchange as mean ± standard deviation. The time differences are statistically significant only for RPCs without idle processors. The RPC case with idle processors benefits from a hand-

off in the dispatching code (see "Mach Scheduler, Data Structures," above). This handoff was not disabled for these experiments. It is not specific to the IPC system, and disabling it requires scheduler modifications that impact the critical-context switch path. One-way message exchanges do not gain performance from handoff scheduling for two reasons. First, in the absence of handoff scheduling, a sender can queue multiple messages before context switching to the receiver. Second, on a multiprocessor, the sender and receiver can run in parallel with complete overlap.

Based on these results, Mach is configured to use handoff scheduling for RPC when no idle processor is available. Current Mach kernels can hand off only once per RPC because the RPC send half is implemented separately. Thus, the sender hands off to the receiver before the sender is queued for the reply. When the reply comes back, no thread is queued and no handoff takes place. The Mach IPC system is being redesigned to incorporate a bidirectional message primitive that can hand off in both directions. Similar functionality exists in other systems, such as the Topaz operating system developed at DEC's Systems Research Center for the Firefly.[8]

Alternatively, scheduling hints could be combined into higher level kernel synchronization primitives, such as semaphores or condition variables. Higher level primitives can provide a cleaner interface, by hiding more scheduler details, and can simplify the implementation of a library or language runtime that uses them. The disadvantages are that languages and libraries must use these primitives to influence the scheduler, and the primitives may be specialized toward some languages or classes of applications. This specialization can impact performance if the primitives are not a good match to the programming language or model. The Topaz system uses this approach, but specialization is not an issue in that environment because most programming is done in Modula-2+.[8]

Processor allocation

Gang scheduling, which guarantees simultaneous scheduling of an application's components, is one use for processor allocation in multiprocessor operating systems. It is necessary for fine-grain parallel applications whose performance severely degrades when any part of the application is not running, but it is also applicable to other classes of parallel programs. The need for gang scheduling is widely recognized, and implementations exist on a variety of multiprocessors. This section describes the design and implementation of Mach's processor allocation facility.

Design. Because Mach supports a multitude of applications, languages, and programming models on a variety of multiprocessor architectures, flexibility is the driving factor in the design of its processor allocation facility. This flexibility has several aspects.

• The facility should be capable of allocating processors to applications written in different languages with different programming models. Binding threads to individual processors is not sufficient because applications that use system concurrency need to bind a pool of threads to a pool of processors. Such *pool binding* improves performance by allowing any thread to run on a processor vacated by a blocked thread.

• The facility should be adaptable to the different multiprocessor architectures that can run Mach. In particular, it should support uniform-memory access (UMA) and nonuniform-memory-access (NUMA) architectures without major changes to the kernel interface.

• The facility should accommodate different policies — sure to exist at various installations — concerning who can allocate how many processors, when, and for how long. Changes to these policies should not require rebuilding the kernel.

• Finally, the facility should offer applications complete control over which threads execute on which processors, but it should not force implementation on applications not wanting this degree of control.

Mach's processor allocation facility meets these goals by dividing the responsibility for processor allocation among the three components shown in Figure 2:

• kernel, performs allocation mechanisms only;

- server, implements allocation policy;
- application, requests processors from server and uses them. Can control their use if desired.

The server must be privileged, to gain direct control over processors. As the component most affected by changes in usage policies or hardware configuration, the server is designed to be much easier to replace or reconfigure than the kernel. The design assumes that processors will be dedicated to applications for seconds or longer, rather than milliseconds, to amortize the overhead of crossing boundaries among components. The application-to-server interface is not specified because it will be affected by changes in usage policy and hardware architecture. Some servers may require applications to provide authentication information to establish their right to use certain processors, while other servers may require information describing the location of requested processors in a NUMA architecture. The kernel interface does not change from machine to machine, but some calls return machine-dependent information.

The allocation facility adds two new objects to the Mach kernel interface, the *processor* and the *processor set*. Processor objects correspond to and manipulate physical processors. Processor set objects are independent entities to which threads and processors can be assigned.

Processors only execute threads assigned to the same processor set and vice-versa, and every processor and thread is always assigned to a processor set. If a processor set has no assigned processors, then threads assigned to it are suspended. Assignments are initialized by an inheritance mechanism. Each task is also assigned to a processor set, but this assignment is used only to initialize the assignment of threads created in that task. In turn, each task inherits its initial assignment from its parent upon creation, and the first task in the system is initially assigned to the *default processor set*. Thus, in the absence of explicit assignments, every thread and task in the system inherits the first task's assignment to the default processor set. All processors are initially assigned to the default processor set, and at least one processor must always be assigned to it so that internal kernel threads and important daemons can be run.

Processors and processor sets are represented by Mach ports. Because access to a port requires a kernel-managed capability for that port, or *port right*, entities other

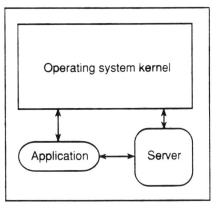

Figure 2. Processor allocation components.

than the appropriate server and/or application lack the required port right(s) and cannot interfere with allocations. Processor sets also have a name port for identification and status queries, but this port cannot be used to manipulate the processor set.

Responsibility for the allocation and use of dedicated processors is divided among the application, server, and kernel. The application controls the assignment of tasks and threads to processor sets. The server controls the assignment of processors to processor sets. The kernel does whatever the application and server ask it to do.

Here's how an application might allocate six processors for its use:

(1) **Application ⇒ Kernel** Create processor set.
(2) **Application ⇒ Server** Request six processors for processor set.
(3) **Application ⇒ Kernel** Assign threads to processor set.
(4) **Server ⇒ Kernel** Assign processors to processor set.
(5) **Application** Use processors.
(6) **Application ⇒ Server** Finished with processors (optional).
(7) **Server ⇒ Kernel** Reassign processors.

This example illustrates three important features of the allocation facility.

- The application creates the processor set and uses it as the basis of its communication with the server, freeing the server from dependence on the internal structure of the application.
- Only one processor set is used. The scheduling algorithms, described earlier, function within each processor set, and if the task in this example contains six or fewer threads, there will be no context

switches to shuffle the threads among the allocated processors.

- The server does not need the application's cooperation to remove processors from it. The server retains complete control over the processors at all times because it retains the access rights to the processor objects. Removing processors without the application's cooperation should not be necessary for well-behaved applications, but it can be useful for a runaway application that has exceeded its allocated time.

This design meets its flexibility goals. It supports different programming models and languages; it can assign processors to individual processor sets or to one or more common sets that match application requirements. Assigning one processor to each of several processor sets gives the application complete control over which threads run on which processors.

Isolating scheduling policy in a server simplifies changes for different hardware architectures and site-specific usage policies. NUMA machines can use this allocation facility to match processor sets to clusters of processors with identical memory access characteristics. This disables the kernel scheduler's load balancing between clusters, which is a minimum requirement for scheduling on NUMA machines. The facility does not replace the disabled load balancing, but, by design, the kernel interface makes sufficient information available for a user-mode implementation of a NUMA load balancer.

Implementation. Kernel implementation of processor sets extends the Mach time-sharing scheduler. The data structure for each processor set contains a run queue that is used as the global run queue for processors assigned to the set. A list of idle processors is also maintained on a per-processor-set basis because a processor can only run threads assigned to its current set. The processor-set data structure also heads individual linked lists that are threaded through the data structures of assigned tasks, threads, and processors so that these entities can be found and reassigned when the processor set is terminated. In addition, the data structure contains state information required to run the time-sharing scheduling algorithm, the identities of ports that represent the set, and a mutual-exclusion lock to control access to the data structure. Thread assignment suspends the thread involved so that it can remain suspended if assigned to a processor set with no processors. Interprocessor interrupts are used for thread and processor assignment as needed.

Table 4 shows times required by basic operations in the processor allocation system as mean ± standard deviation in microseconds. The "self" and "other" cases of thread assignment correspond to a thread assigning itself and a thread assigning another thread.

Special techniques manage processor-to-processor set relationships. Code in a critical scheduler path reads a processor's assignment as part of finding a thread to run on that processor. To optimize this common case against infrequent assignment changes, each processor can change only its own assignment. This restriction avoids the need for a mutual-exclusion lock because a processor cannot look for a new thread and change its assignment simultaneously. The cost to the assignment operation is that it must temporarily bind a thread to the processor while changing the assignment. An internal kernel thread, the *action thread*, serves this purpose. Current kernels use only one action thread but are designed to accommodate more. The processor assignment interface lets a server avoid synchronizing with each assignment's completion, so a server thread can exercise the parallelism available from multiple action threads.

Gang-scheduling server. To demonstrate the utility of this work, we implemented a simple processor-allocation server for gang scheduling. The server is a batch scheduler for processors that schedules requests on a greedy first-come, first-served basis, subject to the number of available processors. The server is configured for a maximum allocation of 75 percent of the machine for, at most, 15 minutes at a time.

The server implementation uses two threads: one to manage processors and another to communicate with applications. The primary interaction between the threads is via operations on shared data structures describing the requests, but the interaction thread sends a message to the processor thread when an immediate change in processor assignment is needed. One such situation is the receipt of an allocation request that can be satisfied immediately.

Library routines are available to hide the server interfaces, so an application can make a single call indicating how many processors it wants for how many seconds. This routine contacts the server, arranges

Table 4. Allocation operation performance.

Operation	Time (μs)
Create processor set	2,250 ± 50
Assign processor	4,772 ± 28
Assign thread (self)	1,558 ± 25
Assign thread (other)	2,624 ± 185

the allocation, and returns when the server has begun assigning the requested processors. The routine takes about 35 milliseconds to allocate one processor plus about 5 milliseconds per additional processor. This overhead is acceptable, given expected allocations of tens of seconds to tens of minutes.

At Carnegie Mellon University, researchers and students in an undergraduate parallel programming course have successfully used this server and library interface in measuring the performance of parallel programs. The server removed most of the usual administrative obstacles to obtaining dedicated machine time. In addition, it demonstrated the utility of implementing policy in a separate server; server crashes did not crash the operating system.

Many extensions and changes to the policy implemented in the cpu_server are possible. Since it is a batch scheduler, techniques originally developed for batch scheduling of memory, such as assigning higher priority to shorter requests, are applicable. In addition, the server could be extended to allow some users higher or absolute priority in allocating processors or to allow allocation of more processors during light usage periods. Finally, the server could be entirely replaced by a server that implements a different scheduling policy. One promising new policy is to vary the number of processors available to applications according to overall demand. A server with this policy would tell applications to reconfigure when it changes the number of processors available. Researchers at Stanford are pursuing this approach and have implemented such a server under Mach with good initial results.[9]

Related work

Previous work[10,11] on *policy mechanism separation* proposed separating the scheduler into two pieces, with mechanisms implemented in the operating system and policy decisions made by a user-mode *policy module*. This work, which considered only the problem of scheduling within applications, encountered two problems.

The first problem was the overhead of crossing the boundary between the operating system and an application to access a policy module. Crossing the boundary required operating-system implementation of short-term policy, which, to the detriment of the policy modules, made it more efficient to delay long-term policy decisions.

The second difficulty, revealed through experience with the resulting systems, was that most applications did not use the available flexibility. One reason for this lies in the inherent complexity of policy modules; most nontrivial instances require an intricate scheduler implementation.[10,11]

Our use of policy/mechanism separation avoids both problems. Processor allocation decisions are infrequent enough to effectively amortize boundary crossing costs, and the complex policy implementation resides in a server that is implemented once for a system rather than in a module that must be customized to each application.

Another body of related work concerns coscheduling, a multiprocessor scheduling policy that attempts simultaneous scheduling of an application's components but makes no guarantee of success. This policy was originally proposed for medium-grain, parallel message-passing applications with hundreds to thousands of instructions between interactions. Such applications benefit from coscheduling but achieve reasonable performance without it.

The major work on coscheduling was done for the Medusa operating system on Cm*.[11] It is not directly applicable to current multiprocessors because the techniques depend on synchronized clocks and a memory structure that precludes short-term load balancing. In contrast, the uniform shared-memory machines that are our primary interest do need short-term load balancing and do not have synchronized clocks.

The Alliant Concentrix scheduler, described by Jacobs,[12] is an alternative approach to processor allocation and control. This scheduler supports a fixed number of scheduling classes and uses a *scheduling vector* for each processor to indicate which classes should be searched for work in what order. Each processor cycles through a set of scheduling vectors based on time durations associated with each vector, typically fractions of a second. Processes are assigned to scheduling classes by their characteristics or a system call available to privileged users and applications. This scheduler is oriented toward dividing processors among statically defined classes of applications over short periods of time. This contrasts with Mach's orientation of dedicating processors to applications over longer periods of time. Mach's processor sets can be created dynamically in contrast to Concentrix's fixed number of scheduling classes. Scheduling servers could be implemented by reserving some scheduling classes for their exclusive use, but the static class and vector definitions appear to restrict the flexibility available in forming processor sets. The Concentrix scheduler also enforces a more restrictive version of gang scheduling in which a blocking operation by any thread blocks the entire gang. This limits it to applications not using system concurrency and makes parallel handling of blocking operations, such as I/O and page faults, all but impossible.

Many parallel and concurrent applications cannot be scheduled acceptably by traditional time-sharing means. Dedicated processors are required to obtain acceptable performance from some parallel applications. For concurrent applications, communication and synchronization performance can be improved by taking advantage of application-specific scheduling information. Mach's scheduler has been enhanced to meet these challenges.

Mach allows concurrent programs to provide handoff and discouragement hints to influence scheduling decisions. Of these two, handoff hints are more effective; naming the next thread to run bypasses much of the scheduler logic that normally makes this decision. These hints are based on local information that is easy to obtain and provide to the scheduler. Using local information and hints avoids the overhead and complexity drawbacks of previous work based on application-specific policy modules.

Obtaining and scheduling dedicated processors is supported by Mach's processor allocation and control facilities. The Mach kernel implements only allocation mechanisms; policy decisions are made by a privileged server that is much easier to reconfigure or replace than the kernel. This provides a wide degree of flexibility to implement allocation policies and accommodate different multiprocessor architectures. This design also accommodates applications based on different programming models.

Code to implement the Mach features described in this article will be available from several sources. Future Mach releases from Carnegie Mellon University and Mt. Xinu are expected to support these features, but the current 2.5 and 2.6 MSD releases do not. These features are a part of the OSF/1 operating system from the Open Software Foundation and are or will be available in some vendor versions of Mach (for example, Encore's Mach for the Multimax). ∎

Acknowledgments

The initial design of the run queue structure is due to Avadis Tevanian, Jr., and is similar to structures used in various versions of Unix. The initial implementation of handoff scheduling for kernel use was done by Richard Rashid. The author would like to thank all members of the Mach project for making this research possible and *Computer*'s referees and editors for suggestions that greatly improved the structure and presentation of this article.

This research was sponsored by the Defense Advanced Research Projects Agency (DOD), monitored by the Space and Naval Warfare Systems Command under Contract N00039-87-C-0251. However, the views and conclusions contained in this article are those of the author and should not be interpreted as representing official policies, either expressed or implied, of DARPA or the US government.

References

1. R.F. Rashid, "Threads of a New System," *Unix Review*, Vol. 4, Aug. 1986, pp. 37-49.

2. S.J. Leffler et al., *Design and Implementation of the 4.3BSD Unix Operating System*, Addison-Wesley, Reading, Mass., 1989.

3. E.I. Organick, *The Multics System: An Examination of Its Structure*, MIT Press, Cambridge, Mass., 1972.

4. L.J. Kenah and S.F. Bate, *VAX/VMS Internals and Data Structures*, Digital Press, Maynard, Mass., 1984.

5. A. Langerman et al., "A Highly-Parallelized Mach-based Vnode Filesystem," *Proc.*
Winter 1990 Usenix Conf., Jan. 1990, pp 297-312.

6. J.W. Wendorf, "Operating System/Application Concurrency in Tightly Coupled Multiple-Processor Systems," PhD thesis, Tech. Rep. CMU-CS-88-117, Carnegie Mellon University, Computer Science Dept., Pittsburgh, 1987.

7. E.C. Cooper and R.P. Draves, "C Threads," Tech. Rep. CMU-CS-88-154, Carnegie Mellon University, Computer Science Dept., Pittsburgh, 1988.

8. C.P. Thacker, L.C. Stewart, and J.E.H. Satterwaithe, "Firefly, A Multiprocessor Workstation," *IEEE Trans. Computers*, Vol. 37, No. 8, Aug. 1988, pp. 909-920.

9. A. Tucker and A. Gupta, "Process Control and Scheduling Issues for Multiprogrammed Shared Memory Multiprocessors," *Proc. 12th ACM Symp. Operating Systems Principles*, Dec. 1989, pp. 159-166.

10. W.A. Wulf, R. Levin, and S.P. Harbison, *Hydra/C.mmp: An Experimental Computer System*, McGraw-Hill, New York, 1981.

11. E.F. Gehringer, D.P. Siewiorek, and Z. Segall, *Parallel Processing: The Cm* Experience*, Digital Press, Maynard, Mass., 1987.

12. H. Jacobs, "A User-Tunable Multiple Processor Scheduler," *Proc. Winter 1986 Usenix Conf.*, Jan. 1986, pp. 183-191.

David L. Black is a graduate student and PhD candidate in the School of Computer Science at Carnegie Mellon University, where he has worked on the design and implementation of the Mach operating system since 1986. His research interests are in operating systems, with emphasis on multiprocessor and scheduling issues.

Black received BA and MA degrees in mathematics and the BSE degree in computer science and engineering from the University of Pennsylvania in 1983. He received the MS degree in computer science from Carnegie Mellon University in 1985. He is a member of the ACM, IEEE, the Computer Society, and several honorary societies.

Readers may contact Black at Carnegie Mellon University, School of Computer Science, Pittsburgh, PA 15213 or, by e-mail, at david.black@cs.cmu.edu.

Programming
for
Parallelism

Alan H. Karp

IBM Palo Alto Scientific Center

The state of the art of parallel programming and what a sorry state that art is in.

In the last few years we have seen an explosion in the interest in and availability of parallel processors[1] and a corresponding expansion in applications programming activity. Clearly, applications programmers need tools to express the parallelism, either in the form of subroutine libraries or language extensions. There has been no shortage of providers of such tools.[2-7] These tools allow the applications programmer to express the parallelism explicitly. There are also projects underway to provide automatic parallelization of sequential code.[8-10]

While this article presents language extensions in use at the end of 1985, it is not comprehensive. I will concentrate on the following aspects of the problem:

• Scientific programming: Characterized by a high degree of floating-point computation, usually coded in Fortran. The discussion is not relevant to logic programming such as AI applications expressed in Lisp or Prolog.

• General-purpose machines: Machines capable of running a wide variety of applications with reasonable efficiency. In special-purpose machines such as image, signal, and array processors, and systolic arrays the algorithms are coded into the hardware. Even general-purpose array processors rarely exhibit the parallelism of interest here.

• MIMD processors: Multiple-instruction, multiple-data machines, not vector processors, which are single-instruction, multiple-data (SIMD) machines. I treat the vector unit, if available, in much the way I treat the floating-point multiplier, as another functional

unit. I will not discuss parallel SIMD machines here, like the Illiac IV,[11] ICL DAP,[12] MPP,[13] and Connection Machine.[14] Nor will I discuss microinstruction machines. For example, each processor in a systolic array[15] is not a complete computer in the sense that an entire application cannot be run on it.

• Moderately parallel systems: No more than tens of processors. The tools described leave it up to the programmer to distribute the work, even to the extent of having a different program running on each processor. Massively parallel systems of the order of a thousand or more processors are quite different. At this time there are no general-purpose, MIMD machines in this class that are widely available, so no one has experience programming them.

• Fortran: The most commonly used language for scientific computers. Since most of the work to date has been done in Fortran, and because most scientific programmers are familiar with it, I use Fortran for all the examples. It is possible to use these constructs in other languages, but "modern" languages like Pascal and Ada that attempt to eliminate side effects are quite different. Side effects represented by Fortran COMMON data present important advantages and problems for the application programmer.

• Explicitly declared parallelism: Parallelism controlled by the programmer. I describe a style in which the programmer controls the parallelism. Even though great strides have been made in automatic parallelization, the only automatic system available to date[10] is limited to individual

0-8186-6522-X/95 $4.00 © 1987 IEEE

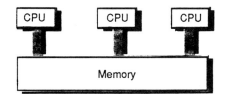

Figure 1. Schematic of a shared memory system.

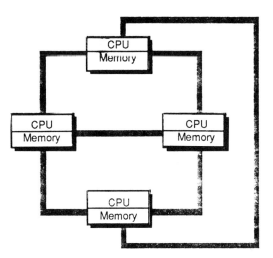

Figure 2. Schematic of a fully interconnected message passing system.

loops. Parallelism at a larger granularity must still be specified by the programmer.

Rather than enumerate all possible ways of describing a particular type of parallelism, I use generic notation. This notation indicates how the parallelism is described without worrying about details of implementation. For example, I will not discuss locks, semaphores, and monitors that can be used to implement the constructs I describe. Actual implementations are, and must be, somewhat more complicated than those described here.

Taxonomy

A common myth is that the programmer does not need to understand the hardware being used. Like all myths, it contains a grain of truth. However, when performance becomes critical, programmers have used their knowledge of paging, cache size, vector lengths, and so forth to tune their programs.

The situation is worse for parallel processors than for uniprocessors because of the wider variety of architectures. Although a number of efforts are being made to write portable programs for parallel processors,[7,16] some algorithms will run poorly on certain architectures. In addition, the coding style used will frequently depend on the type of parallelism in the hardware.

Rather than attempt a complete taxonomy, I restrict the classification to those aspects that affect coding style. I put all systems into one of three classes: shared memory, message passing, or hybrid. While I don't expect such a simple scheme to describe the variety of machines possible, it is sufficient to demonstrate the variety of programming styles used.

It is common to distinguish between processes and processors. A process is a running program; a processor is a computer. In many operating systems it is possible to have many processes running on one processor. For the remainder of this article, I ignore this distinction and assume each processor has only one process. Such an assumption is reasonable for scientific codes running on a stand-alone parallel processor.

Shared memory. A shared memory machine has a single global memory accessible to all processors. The simplest configuration is shown in Figure 1. Each processor may have some local memory, such as registers as on the Cray X-MP,[17] or the cache on the IBM 3090,[18] but I assume the operating system presents to the user the image of totally shared memory. For example, although the cache on the IBM 3090 is local to a processor, cross-cache validation makes the cache transparent to the user. The user need not worry that a piece of data is in the cache of the wrong processor, since the operating system makes sure that the correct value is delivered. In fact, the programmer is not allowed to explicitly use the cache in any way, making the system look like it has a single, global memory.

Other types of shared memory organizations are possible. For example, the Alliant FX/8[10] has several processors run out of a common cache. A completely different approach was taken by the NYU Ultra machine.[19] Although the memory is distributed, the system fits my definition of a shared memory machine because any processor module can be connected to any memory module.

A key feature of shared memory systems is that the access time to a piece of data is independent of the processor making the request. If the code running on two processors can be swapped without affecting performance, the system has a true, shared memory. This is not to say that there is no memory contention. Such issues as page faults and memory bank conflicts still affect performance, just as in uniprocessors. Clearly, the aggregate memory bandwidth will limit the number of processors that can be accommodated on the system.

Message passing. Message passing systems are configured so that some memory is local to each processor but none is globally accessible. The only way for the application to share data among processors is for the programmer to explicitly code commands to move data from one node to another. The time it takes for a processor to access data depends on its distance from the processor that currently has the data in its local memory. Therefore, in contrast to the shared memory systems, the performance of an algorithm will depend on how well the location of data matches up with its use.

Figure 2 shows a fully interconnected message passing system, with each processor having a direct connection to every other processor. Such a scheme is impractical when there are a large number of processors. Therefore, designers of message passing systems are forced to pick less dense wirings. The particular choice made has an important influence on the algorithms to be run on the machine. An algorithm designed for one machine can perform very badly on a different machine.

A large number of connection schemes have been used.[20] The simplest approach is to connect the machines in a ring with each processor talking to its two nearest neighbors. In such a machine, it takes a time proportional to the number of processors to send data to each processor.

A machine with a denser wiring is a mesh machine in which the processors are connected in a two-dimensional grid. Each processor talks to its north, south, east, and west neighbors. If there are p processors in the machine, it takes time proportional to $\sqrt{p}$ to send data to each processor.

An even denser wiring is provided by a hypercube interconnection, one of today's most popular designs.[21-23] Each processor is assigned a binary id number $0 \leq n \leq 2^d - 1$, where d is called the *dimension* of the cube. Two processors are connected through a port if their identification numbers differ only in the corresponding bit in the id number. Thus, processor 0000 is connected to processor 1000 through the left-most communications port of each processor. The machine is called a hypercube because the connection scheme can be pictured as a cube for $d = 3$. Each node is placed at a corner and the direct links become the edges of the cube. The advantage of this configuration is that the largest distance between processors is proportional to $\log_2 p$.

There exists a very simple connection system with a maximum distance of two from any processor to any other processor: a star connection. In such a configuration, a central processor connects to every other machine. Because of the large amount of traffic that the center machine must handle, it often differs from the rest of the processors.[24] Although the maximum distance between processors is independent of p, the processor in the middle must be able to handle all the traffic generated, which limits the number of processors in such a system.

Hybrid. Hybrid systems have some of the properties of shared memory systems and some of the properties of message passing. As illustrated in Figure 3, all memory is local to a given processor, but the operating system makes the machine look like it has a single, global memory. Thus, programs are written as if for a shared memory system. However, data must be laid out as if for a message passing system if the best performance is to be obtained, since the access time depends on the distance between the owner of the data and

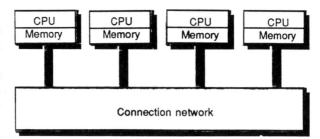

Figure 3. Schematic of a hybrid machine.

the requester. The IBM RP3,[25] BBN Butterfly,[26] and Cedar[27] are examples of hybrid machines.

As far as the programmer is concerned, hybrid systems are coded like shared memory systems. Even the bugs in programs are the same as for shared memory. However, the performance considerations resemble those of message passing machines. Fortunately, the penalties for poor data layout are often considerably smaller on hybrid systems. Message passing systems typically take hundreds to thousands of machine cycles to deliver a message, while hybrid systems deliver data from a remote memory in tens of cycles. Even so, data layout is key to algorithm performance, and the aggregate communications speed is a limit on the number of processors that can be accommodated.

Comments on taxonomy. While Hockney[28] was careful to distinguish architecture from function, I am more interested in the programmer's view of the system. Such a view necessarily mixes the actual hardware with the picture of the machine presented by the available software. For example, a group of processors sharing a common memory would be classified as a message passing system if the software tools only used the shared memory for message buffers. However, a clever programmer who managed to use these buffers to share data would think of the machine as a shared memory system.

My classification scheme also includes questions of performance, something intentionally left out of other taxonomies. In particular, the principal difference between a hybrid and a shared memory system is one of performance. A programmer interested only in correct operation can treat a hybrid system as if it were a shared memory system. This approach is reasonable if the penalty for accessing data out of the local memory is small. However, the programmer must be aware of the details of the hardware implementation in

order to produce efficient code. Even a factor of two delay in getting data can seriously degrade performance.

Software tools

Parallel processing hardware does the programmer no good without a means of describing the parallelism to the system. In large measure, the type of parallelism selected by the programmer depends as much on the software tools as on the underlying hardware. This section describes some of the tools that can be used to make a program run on several processors.

Message passing. Message passing systems need only two basic functions added to the standard language support, SEND and RECEIVE. Of course, most implementations include a variety of mode setting and query functions not discussed here.

SEND is used to send a message containing data from one processor to another. There are actually two forms of SEND. One continues processing immediately on dispatching the message; the other waits to make sure the message has arrived (but not necessarily been read into the memory of the recipient). The latter is called a *blocked* SEND and the former, an *unblocked* SEND. At a minimum, the arguments include a destination, the message length, and an array containing the message. Other arguments often used are a status word, a port address or routing information, and a flag to indicate whether or not to wait for an acknowledgment.

In general, a blocked SEND is used only in the presence of unreliable communications. For example, if the processors do not maintain message queues, a message will be rejected until the previous message has been received. If it is important that all messages be sent in a particular order, a

```
      parallel do 10 I=1,3          parallel case
         IF (I.EQ.1) THEN               ....
            .....                         parallel
         ELSE IF (I.EQ.2) THEN            ....
            .....                         parallel
         ELSE IF (I.EQ.3) THEN            ....
            .....                    end parallel case
         ENDIF
   10 CONTINUE
```

Figure 4. PARALLEL CASE code.

blocked SEND must be used. (I assume that the operating system will continually try to transmit a rejected message from a blocked SEND.)

A RECEIVE is used to read a message sent from another processor. It can also be blocked or unblocked. At a minimum, the arguments include an array to contain the message and the length of this array. Other options frequently used are the processor id of the sender or the input port to be read, a status flag, and an indication of whether or not to send an acknowledgment.

Both blocked and unblocked modes are needed. If the algorithm requires a specific piece of data from another processor, the programmer codes a blocked RECEIVE. The receiver then waits for the data to arrive. Unfortunately, blocked RECEIVE can lead to a deadlock in which two processors are waiting for data from each other.

Unblocked RECEIVE has two uses. The most common use is to implement a global receive, in which the processor needs to receive messages on several input ports but the order doesn't matter. If the port id is an argument to the RECEIVE, an unblocked RECEIVE allows the program to continually test the input ports and read the data as it arrives. This requirement could be met by providing a RECEIVE FROM ANY construct.

The other use for unblocked RECEIVE is asynchronous input. Here the program continually checks the input port for a message. If there is no message, one piece of work is done; if there is a message, a different piece of work is done. In general, such a scheme is useful for load balancing. If the message carries data needed by high priority work, it is still possible to do low priority work until the data arrives. If a blocked RECEIVE were used, the processor would be idle until the message arrived.

Shared memory. For a number of reasons, the language extensions needed by shared memory systems are much more extensive than those for message passing machines. First, there is the need to distinguish which data is private to each processor and which is known to all processors. Second, because data is shared, synchronization is needed to prevent out-of-sequence access to memory. Primarily, though, the shared memory allows an entirely different style of programming that has several modes of operation, each requiring a different set of language extensions.

There are two commonly used ways to divide up the work in a shared memory system. In the fork-join style, a process will spawn subprocesses, a FORK, and wait for them to finish, a JOIN. In the SPMD (single program, multiple data) style, each processor runs the same program but executes different code depending on its processor id or data in shared memory.

Both fork-join and SPMD programs need a means to restrict access to code. A *critical section* contains code that gets executed by all processors one at a time. It is usually used for reduction operations such as summing into a global variable. A *serial section* is code to be executed by only one processor and skipped by all others. It is usually used to initialize global data.

Synchronization is also needed. In message passing systems a blocked RECEIVE synchronizes; in fork-join, the JOIN serves this purpose. In SPMD programming, other constructs are needed. A *barrier* is a point in the code where all processors wait for the last one to arrive. A barrier is dangerous because a processor might branch around it, which causes all the other processors to wait until the program terminates. Another way of synchronizing is the WAIT UNTIL construct. Here each processor continually checks shared memory to see if some particular condition is met. In contrast to the barrier where the processors wait at a specific line of code, each processor can WAIT UNTIL the

same condition is met from different parts of the program. One common use is to wait until an input or output operation finishes before continuing the computation.

Probably the most common SPMD construct is the PARALLEL DO. Since the cost of sharing data is very small in shared memory systems, programmers often parallelize their code at the DO-loop level. If all iterations of a loop are independent, each processor can run a different subset of the loop index range as long as each value of the index gets used exactly once.

Two mechanisms are used to distribute the work in the loop to the processors. A *self-scheduled* PARALLEL DO works by giving the first value of the loop index to the first processor to arrive, the second index to the second processor, and so forth. A processor that reaches the end of the loop returns to the top to get more work. A *prescheduled* PARALLEL DO works by partitioning the loop ahead of time so that each processor will do a certain set of loop indices, no matter how long each one takes.

Self-scheduled PARALLEL DO provides for automatic load balancing, since processors get more to do as soon as they have finished with their work. However, assuring that each processor gets a unique value of the loop index forces some synchronization not needed for prescheduled loops.

The choice between self- and prescheduled loops depends on both the application and the hardware. If the work is naturally load balanced, and the synchronization cost is high, then prescheduling is preferred. If the amount of work depends on the loop index or if the synchronization cost is low, then self-scheduling will perform better.

Another useful construct is the PARALLEL CASE. Its structure is similar to a standard CASE statement available in several languages. It differs from the usual definition in that all cases get executed in parallel. It can be implemented with a PARALLEL DO, but PARALLEL CASE leads to more readable code as shown in Figure 4.

Simple problem

The best way to get a feel for what the programming tools described in the previous section imply is to look at a simple example, summing a list of 1,000,000 numbers. Actually, this problem is nontrivial if the best performance is to be achieved, and numerous algorithms have been proposed.[12] Since we are interested

37

in coding style, I will discuss only the simplest method.

Figure 5 shows a program that could be run on a uniprocessor. The main program reads in the numbers to be summed, calls a subroutine to do the arithmetic, and prints the result. The subroutine initializes the sum, adds the numbers, and returns. I have separated the work in this way to illustrate several of the coding styles.

A simple notation has been used in the sample codes. Code shown in uppercase is standard Fortran; code in lowercase represents language extensions. While these codes have not been run, a desk check has been done.

Shared memory. One of the first things tried on a parallel processor was the fork-join approach shown in Figure 6a. We can see how the constructs introduced in "Software tools" are used to get the program running on more than one processor. First, we declare the shared data GLOBAL. Each processor will have a private copy of any variable not explicitly declared as shared. In order to divide up the work equally, we need to know how many processors are available. It is common practice to code all programs independently of the number of processors. This convention not only enhances the portability of the code, but makes it easier to debug on a single processor. I assume the system will provide the number of processors through the system variable NPROCS.

Work is divided among the processors using the CREATE function. Each time a CREATE statement is executed, a task is generated that runs the indicated subroutine, here SUMSUB. Each task works on a different part of the array, as indicated by A(IS). It is important that the address of A(IS) be computed before the CREATE is completed. If we rely on the created task to fetch the address of A(IS) from shared memory, we may find that the main routine has changed it before the created task gets started.

Once the main program has finished distributing the work, it does the remaining part of the job. When the main program reaches the JOIN statement, it waits until all other tasks have completed, at which time the result can be printed.

All the computational work is done in the subroutine SUMSUB. Here we see the use of a serial section and a critical section. Since SUM is a global variable, we could get wrong results if all processors were allowed to initialize the variable so we use

```
      PARAMETER ( N = 1000000 )
      DIMENSION A(N)
      READ (*) A
      CALL SUMSUB (SUM,A,N)
      WRITE(*) SUM
      END
C
      SUBROUTINE SUMSUB (SUM,A,N)
      DIMENSION A(N)
      SUM = 0.0
      DO 10 I = 1, N
          SUM = SUM + A(I)
   10 CONTINUE
      RETURN
      END
```

Figure 5. Uniprocessor version.

```
      PARAMETER ( N = 1000000 )
      global A(N), SUM, N
      READ (*) A
      INC = (N+nprocs-1)/nprocs
      IS = 1
      DO 10 J = 1, nprocs-1
          create ( 'SUMSUB', SUM, A(IS), INC)
          IS = IS + INC
   10 CONTINUE
      CALL SUMSUB ( SUM, A(IS), N-IS+1 )
      join
      WRITE (*) SUM
      END
C
      SUBROUTINE SUMSUB ( SUM, A, N )
      DIMENSION A(N)
      serial section
      SUM = 0.0
      end serial section
      DO 10 I = 1, N
      critical section
          SUM = SUM + A(I)
      end critical section
   10 CONTINUE
      RETURN
      END
(a)
```

```
      SUBROUTINE SUMSUB (SUM,A,N)
      DIMENSION A(N)
      serial section
          SUM = 0.0
      end serial section
      SUMLOC = 0.0
      DO 10 I = 1, N
          SUMLOC = SUMLOC + A(I)
   10 CONTINUE
      critical section
          SUM = SUM + SUMLOC
      end critical section
      RETURN
      END
(b)
```

Figure 6. Fork-join (a) and fork-join with good performance (b).

```
      PARAMETER ( N = 1000000 )
      DIMENSION A(N)
      READ (*) A
      INC = (N+nprocs-1)/nprocs
      IS = 1
      DO 10 J = 1, nprocs-1
          send ( J, 'INC:1, A(IS):INC' )
          IS = IS + INC
   10 CONTINUE
      CALL SUMSUB ( SUM, A(IS), N-IS+1 )
      DO 20 J = 1, nprocs-1
          receive from any ( 'SUMJ:1' )
          SUM = SUM + SUMJ
   20 CONTINUE
      WRITE (*) SUM
      END
  (a)
```

```
      PARAMETER (N = 1000000,INCR=(N+nprocs-1)/nprocs)
      DIMENSION A(INCR)
      receive ( 0, 'INC:1, A:INC' )
      CALL SUMSUB ( SUM, A, INC )
      send ( 0, 'SUM:1' )
      END
  (b)
```

```
      PARAMETER ( N = 1000000 )
      DIMENSION A(N)
      INC = (N+nprocs-1)/nprocs
      IF ( procid .EQ. 0 ) THEN
          READ (*) A
          IS = 1
          DO 10 J = 1, nprocs-1
              send ( J, 'A(IS):INC' )
              IS = IS + INC
   10     CONTINUE
          CALL SUMSUB ( SUM, A(IS), N-IS+1 )
          DO 20 J = 1, nprocs-1
              receive from any ( 'SUMJ:1' )
              SUM = SUM + SUMJ
   20     CONTINUE
          WRITE (*) SUM
      ELSE
          receive ( 0, 'A:INC' )
          CALL SUMSUB ( SUM, A, INC )
          send ( 0, 'SUM:1' )
      ENDIF
      END
  (c)
```

Figure 7. Message passing code for processor 0 (a), message passing code for processors other than 0 (b), and message passing for SPMD code (c).

a serial section. We could have set SUM = 0 in the main routine, but perhaps we don't want to rely on the user remembering to initialize. (The real reason is that I didn't want to pass up the opportunity to illustrate a serial section.)

We need the critical section in the loop because SUM is a global variable. If processor 1 and processor 2 each fetch the old value, add their respective contributions, and store the new value, the program will produce an incorrect result. The critical section guarantees that only one processor can update the global variable SUM at any instant.

Even though the code in Figure 6a will produce correct results, it suffers from what is called a *performance bug*; it runs much slower than it should. The reason is the critical section within the loop. Since only one processor is allowed to update the value at any time, only one addition can be done at a time. Therefore, we have lost almost all the possible parallelism in the code. The code in Figure 6a will run slower than the uniprocessor version because of the synchronization overhead incurred at the critical section.

The code in Figure 6b, where we sum the data into a local variable, will perform much better. Since each processor has its own copy of SUMLOC, all the arithmetic in the loop can be done in parallel. At the end of the loop each processor adds its contribution to the global sum in a critical section. Now the critical section is encountered only once per processor instead of once per addition.

This routine has a curious kind of side effect. Fortran programmers are used to calling subroutines and having the values of variables in the calling sequence and in COMMON changed. Normally though, except for knowing the data types of the variables in the calling sequence and COMMON, the person writing the subroutine need not know what is happening in the calling routine. Such is not the case here. The person writing SUMSUB must know that SUM is a global variable. The absence of any such indication within the subroutine is a serious problem for debugging and maintenance.

Message passing. The coding style on a message passing system is quite different from that used on a shared memory system for two main reasons. First, data must be explicitly moved from the memory of one processor to the memory of another. Second, there is often no master processor to spawn tasks as in Figure 6a. This second difference is due in part to the distributed memory. For a master processor to create tasks, code would have to be physically moved from the master processor to each slave. The communications cost of such a transfer makes this approach impractical. Therefore, it is usual to load the code for each processor once at the start of the job. Figure 7a shows the program that runs on processor 0, and Figure 7b shows the code running on all other processors.

Processor 0 reads the data and distributes it using the SEND command. The arguments can be interpreted as saying

SEND a message to processor J consisting of one word starting at the address of INC and INC words starting at the address of A(IS).

Next, processor 0 calls SUMSUB to add up the rest of the numbers. After that is done, it goes into a loop to get the partial sums from the other processors. The RECEIVE

FROM ANY says to read one word from any processor into SUMJ. Once all partial sums have been received, the total is printed.

All the other processors run the program shown in Figure 7b. As soon as the data arrives at the communications port of a processor waiting at a RECEIVE, it can copy the data into its local memory and proceed. Each receives a message from processor 0 consisting of one word to be stored as INC and INC words to be stored into array A. Each then calls a version of SUMSUB identical to that in Figure 5. On return from SUMSUB, each processor sends its contribution to processor 0 and exits. Since this is the main routine on these processors, the job terminates. In order to compute more than one sum, the programmer would have to code a loop with an appropriate termination condition.

Another way to manage the code in such an environment is to program in the single program, multiple data style. When coded this way, each processor runs the same code unless a processor-dependent control is used. An example of SPMD programming is shown in Figure 7c.

At the start of the job, each processor is in the same state except for a unique identifier, the PROCID. Each processor first computes its own copy of INC. On reaching the first IF statement, all processors but number 0 skip immediately to the RECEIVE where they wait for data to arrive. Processor 0 reads the data and distributes it using the SEND command. On finishing with SUMSUB, each processor (other than processor 0) sends its contribution to processor 0 and exits. Processor 0 sums the partial sums and prints the result.

Notice that the main routine is somewhat more complicated than the shared memory version. To compensate for this complexity, SUMSUB is much simpler and independent of the architecture of the machine. In addition, there are no problems of data dependence, and all synchronization is handled by the SEND and RECEIVE commands. However, this example does not require any global synchronization, which would be more complicated than on a shared memory system.

Several features of this code affect the elapsed time needed to run the program. First, there is the cost of communication. There will be some overhead in routing the data through the interconnection network in addition to the time taken to physically move the data. This overhead may be a small part of the communication cost of sending a long list of array values, but it is

```
PARAMETER ( N = 1000000 )
global A(N), SUM, N, JSYNC
DATA JSYNC/0/
IF ( procid .EQ. 0 ) THEN
    READ (*) A
    SUM = 0.0
    JSYNC = 1
ENDIF
INC = (N+nprocs-1)/nprocs
IS = INC*procid
INCR = MIN ( INC, N-IS )
wait-until ( JSYNC .NE. 0 )
CALL SUMSUB (SUM,A(IS+1),INCR)
barrier
IF ( procid .EQ. 0 ) WRITE (*) SUM
END
```

Figure 8. SPMD code.

certain to dominate the cost of sending the partial sums back to processor 0. Second, there is the problem of load balancing. It is conceivable that some of the processors will have completed their work before the last one has received all its data. We say the load balancing is poor because some processors are idle while useful work remains to be done.

SPMD shared memory. The SPMD coding style is not limited to message passing systems.[6,29,30] Figure 8 shows how SPMD could be used on a shared memory system. Subroutine SUMSUB is identical to that in Figure 6b.

As with the previous shared memory example, some of the data must explicitly be declared GLOBAL. As with the message passing example, all processors but number 0 skip the code that reads the data. However, we do not have the SEND-RECEIVE mechanism to synchronize the processors so we use the WAIT UNTIL. The WAIT UNTIL construct is an example of *event* synchronization. In this example, each processor continually checks global variable JSYNC until it takes on a value different from 0. On some systems the memory location containing JSYNC will be a *hot spot*. Special hardware is often needed to prevent such hot spots from degrading system performance.[19,25,31]

While they are waiting for JSYNC to be set, all processors compute their own copies of the local variables INC, INCR, and IS. While these variables could be made global and computed in a serial section, the overhead in any extra synchronizations and additional memory contention would outweigh any possible savings.

Once JSYNC = 1, the waiting proces-

sors call SUMSUB. Next, we synchronize with a barrier to prevent processor 0 from writing SUM until all processors have finished adding their contributions. As soon as the last processor reaches the barrier, they all continue processing.

Realistic problem

While a simple problem like summing a series of numbers would appear to be a trivial task, we have seen that there are some subtle points to consider on a parallel processor. In this section, we will look at these points again with a nontrivial problem, solving systems of linear equations.

We want to solve the system of equations $\mathbf{A}\ \mathbf{x} = \mathbf{b}$. The best method for general, dense matrices is Gaussian elimination to perform an LU decomposition followed by a forward elimination and a backward substitution. The procedure is

(1) Use Gaussian elimination to find two triangular matrices L and U such that $\mathbf{A} = \mathbf{LU}$.
(2) Solve the lower triangular linear system $\mathbf{L}\ \mathbf{y} = \mathbf{b}$ by forward elimination.
(3) Solve the upper triangular linear system $\mathbf{U}\ \mathbf{x} = \mathbf{y}$ by back substitution.

The time needed to factor a matrix of order N into its LU components is proportional to N^3, while the time for the forward elimination and back substitution only increases as N^2. For matrices with $N > 100$, the LU decomposition accounts for over 90 percent of the execution time. Therefore, I discuss only the factorization step.

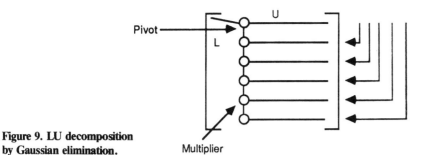

Figure 9. LU decomposition by Gaussian elimination.

```
      SUBROUTINE FACTOR(A,N,IPVT,INFO)
      DIMENSION A(N,N),IPVT(N)
      INFO = 0
      DO 20 K = 1, N-1
         IPVT(K) = ISAMAX(N-K+1,A(K,K),1) + K - 1
         CALL SSWAP (N-K+1,A(K,K),N,A(IPVT(K),K),N)
         IF ( A(K,K) .EQ. 0.0 ) THEN
            INFO = K
         ELSE
            T = -1.0/A(K,K)
            CALL SSCAL (N-K,T,A(K+1,K),1)
            DO 10 J = K+1, N
               CALL SAXPY(N-K,A(K,J),A(K+1,K),1,A(K+1,J),1)
10          CONTINUE
         ENDIF
20    CONTINUE
      IF ( A(N,N) .EQ. 0.0 ) INFO = N
      RETURN
      END
```

Figure 10. LU decomposition.

Figure 9 illustrates the decomposition process. The following procedure is used for each column in turn:

(1) Search the elements on or below the diagonal of the current column.

(2) Interchange rows to move the largest of these elements to the diagonal. This new diagonal element is called the *pivot*.

(3) Divide the elements below the diagonal by the pivot to produce a set of *multipliers*.

(4) Multiply the part of the pivot row to the right of the diagonal times each multiplier and subtract the product from the corresponding part of each row.

The code in Figure 10 embodies the LU decomposition algorithm. It is nearly identical to SGEFA from Linpack and calls several subroutines from the BLAS.[32] As used here they mean

ISAMAX: Search elements K to N of column K and return the index of the element having the largest magnitude.

SSWAP: Interchange elements K to N of rows K and IPVT(K).

SSCAL: Multiply elements K+1 to N of column K by T.

SAXPY: Multiply elements K+1 to N of column K by A(K,J) and add the result to the corresponding elements of column J.

The arguments in the calling sequence are

A: the matrix to be factored;
N: the order of the matrix;
IPVT: an array to save the order of interchanges needed for pivoting; and
INFO: a flag that indicates if a pivot is identically zero.

Shared memory. Figure 11a shows the FACTOR routine as it might be coded on a shared memory system using the fork-join approach. Assume that the arrays A and IPVT have been declared global by the calling routine. There are only two differences between the sample codes in Figures 10 and 11a. Figure 11a uses a CREATE

function instead of a CALL to routine SAXPY, and a JOIN to synchronize the processes. Nothing else changes.

This program creates a task for each column to be processed. This approach is inefficient if there are fewer processors than columns due to the unavoidable overhead in starting the tasks. A better approach is shown in Figure 11b, where we divide the work up equally among the available processors. The additional argument in SAXPY tells each processor the number of columns to process.

Programming this problem SPMD on a shared memory system is slightly more complicated, as shown in Figure 12a. First, we need to assume that A and IPVT have both been declared global by the calling routine. We need one serial section to find the pivot and interchange rows. The barrier assures that none of the processors tests A(K,K) before the pivot step is complete. Next, everyone else waits at the second barrier while a processor scales the subdiagonal part of the current column. Finally, we have a PARALLEL DO. The WAIT UNTIL ensures that the next column has been computed before the search for the pivot element begins.

This example illustrates one of the disadvantages of SPMD programming. In general, synchronization must be done before most program branches. Not only does this requirement introduce extra overhead, but it is a source of potential errors. In practice, the extra overhead is small because most of the processors go immediately to the synchronization point. In addition, errors are made that involve skipping barriers in the program. These errors are easier to find than most because processors end up at a barrier waiting for a processor that never shows up. The programmer has available the exact location where the processors are waiting, which helps in finding the error.

It is also possible to provide a PRESCHEDULED DO. One way of prescheduling a loop is shown in Figure 12b. The PARALLEL DO has been replaced by a conventional DO that depends on the processor id and the number of processors. Each processor entering the loop is guaranteed to get a unique value of J, and each value of J will be taken by some processor.

Message passing. When discussing the shared memory implementations of LU decomposition, we assumed the data was already in shared memory. We cannot

41

```
      SUBROUTINE FACTOR(A,N,IPVT,INFO)
      DIMENSION A(N,N), IPVT(N)
      INFO = 0
      DO 20 K = 1, N-1
         IPVT(K) = ISAMAX(N-K+1,A(K,K),1)+K-1
         CALL SSWAP (N-K+1,A(K,K),N,
     *               A(IPVT(K),K),N)
         IF ( A(K,K) .EQ. 0.0 ) THEN
            INFO = K
         ELSE
            T = -1.0/A(K,K)
            CALL SSCAL (N-K,T,A(K+1,K),1)
            DO 10 J = K+1, N
               create('SAXPY',N-K,A(K,J),
     *                 A(K+1,K),1,A(K+1,J),1)
10          CONTINUE
            join
         ENDIF
20    CONTINUE
      IF ( A(N,N) .EQ. 0.0 ) INFO = N
      RETURN
      END

   (a)
```

```
      SUBROUTINE FACTOR(A,N,IPVT,INFO)
      DIMENSION A(N,N), IPVT(N)
      INFO = 0
      DO 20 K = 1, N-1
         IPVT(K) = ISAMAX(N-K+1,A(K,K),1)+K - 1
         CALL SSWAP (N-K+1,A(K,K),N,
     *               A(IPVT(K),K),N)
         IF ( A(K,K) .EQ. 0.0 ) THEN
            INFO = K
         ELSE
            T = -1.0/A(K,K)
            CALL SSCAL (N-K,T,A(K+1,K),1)
            NC = (N-K+nprocs-1)/nprocs
            J = 1
            DO 10 I = 1, nprocs
               NC = MIN ( NC, N-K-J+1 )
               create('SAXPY',NC,N-K,A(K,J),
     *                 A(K+1,K),1,A(K+1,J),1)
               J = J + NC
10          CONTINUE
            join
         ENDIF
20    CONTINUE
      IF ( A(N,N) .EQ  0.0 ) INFO = N
      RETURN
   (b) END
```

Figure 11. Fork-join LU, one processor per column (a) and fork-join LU, several columns per process (b).

ignore the step of getting the data into memory on a message passing system. Figure 13a shows one way of distributing the data to the contributing processors.

We have used the trick of having processor 0 send data to itself. Notice that the columns of the matrix are distributed to the processors much as one would deal cards in a bridge game: processor 0 gets columns $1, p+1, 2p+1, ...$; processor 1 gets columns $2, p+2, 2p+2, ...$; and so forth. If instead we gave processor 0 the first group of columns, processor 1 the next set, and so forth, we would get very poor load balancing. Referring to Figure 9 shows that after the first group of columns had been reduced, processor 0 would have no more work to do. Eventually, only one processor would be doing all the work.

In Figure 13b we see how the work is distributed. We have included additional arguments in the calling sequence: M, the number of columns to be held by each processor, and W, a work array used to hold the pivot column sent from another processor. On entering the DO 20 loop in routine FACTOR, the processor that owns the current pivot column finds the index of the maximum and scales the column. It then broadcasts the index of the pivot and the multipliers to all other processors. As soon as one of the other processors receives

```
      SUBROUTINE FACTOR(A,N,IPVT,INFO)
      DIMENSION A(N,N), IPVT(N)
      global JSYNC
      INFO = 0
      DO 20 K = 1, N-1
         serial section
            IPVT(K) = ISAMAX(N-K+1,A(K,K),1) + K - 1
            CALL SSWAP (N-K+1,A(K,K),N,A(IPVT(K),K),N)
         end serial section
         barrier
         IF ( A(K,K) .EQ. 0.0 ) THEN
            INFO = K
         ELSE
            serial section
               T = -1.0/A(K,K)
               CALL SSCAL (N-K,T,A(K+1,K),1)
               JSYNC = 0
            end serial section
            barrier
            parallel do 10 J = K+1, N
               CALL SAXPY (N-K,A(K,J),A(K+1,K),1,A(K+1,J),1)
               JSYNC = J
10          CONTINUE
            wait until ( JSYNC .GE. K+1 )
         ENDIF
20    CONTINUE
      IF ( A(N,N) .EQ. 0.0 ) INFO = N
      RETURN
   (a) END
```

```
         ---
         DO 10 J = K+1+procid, N, nprocs
            CALL SAXPY (N-K,A(K,J),A(K+1,K),1,A(K+1,J),1)
10       CONTINUE
   (b)  ---
```

Figure 12. SPMD LU decomposition (a) and SPMD LU decomposition, prescheduled DO (b).

its data, it does the row interchange and forms the appropriate linear combinations for the columns it owns.

There is no need for a barrier at the end of the loop. Any processor that finishes early will quickly find itself at the RECEIVE waiting for the new pivot column to send the required data. If the owner of the pivot column finishes first, it immediately starts work on finding the pivot and producing the multipliers. The RECEIVE command guarantees the needed synchronization.

Hybrid systems. Hybrid systems are programmed like shared memory systems, but have data access delays like message passing systems. These delays are usually much smaller than on message passing systems, but they can be significant. For example, the design of the IBM RP3[25] calls for local data to be delivered in two machine cyles while remote data will take 10 machine cycles to reach the functional unit.

Although the code in Figure 12a could be used on a hybrid system, there is a potential performance bug. Assume the data is distributed among the processors as done for the message passing system. A single processor will own the column containing the pivot and the multipliers. As coded, the first processor to reach the serial section will search for the pivot, and another will form the multipliers. If the processor performing these tasks is not the owner of the data, the program will run slower than it should.

The hybrid system may not need to explicitly move the data if the operating system can be directed to map the data as needed. One way to achieve this end without direct support from the operating system or the compiler is shown in Figure 14. Here we assume the data is read into the memory local to processor 0 and that A is declared global in the calling routine.

The matrix gets distributed to the other processors by being copied into a local variable, AL. Two work arrays, one local and one global, are used to move the multipliers between the local memories of the processors. First, the owner of the current column copies the multipliers from its private memory, AL, into the global work array W. After the barrier, each processor copies the global work array into its local work array, WL. This approach saves time since the multipliers are used many times in the DO 20 loop. At the end of the factorization, the entire matrix gets reassembled in the DO 40 loop. An undesirable side effect of this approach is that memory is wasted because two copies of the array are needed.

Clearly, this code for the hybrid system is more complex and harder to debug than either the shared memory or message passing versions. Note, however, that this complication is needed only to improve performance. The program in Figure 12a will run correctly on a hybrid system. If the ratio of the access times for local and

```
      PARAMETER ( N=1000, M=(N+nprocs-1)/nprocs )
      DIMENSION A(N,M), IPVT(N), COL(N), W(N), IP(N)
      IF ( procid .EQ. 0 ) THEN
         DO 10 I = 0, N-1
            READ (*) COL
            ICOL = MOD(I,nprocs)
            send ( ICOL, 'COL:N' )
10       CONTINUE
      ENDIF
      DO 20 K = 1, M
         receive ( 0, 'A(1,K):N' )
20    CONTINUE
      CALL FACTOR ( A, N, M, IP, W, IN )
      IF ( procid .EQ. 0 ) THEN
         DO 40 K = 0, nprocs-1
            receive ( K, 'INFO:1, IP:N' )
            IN = MAX (IN,INFO)
            DO 30 J = 0, N-1
               IF (MOD(J,nprocs).EQ.K) IPVT(J)=IP(J)
30          CONTINUE
40       CONTINUE
      ENDIF
      RETURN
      END
```
(a)

```
      SUBROUTINE FACTOR ( A, N, M, IP, W, IN )
      DIMENSION A(N,M), IP(N), W(N)
      IN = 0
      IC = 1
      DO 20 K = 1, N-1
         IT = MOD(K-1,nprocs)
         IF ( procid .EQ. IT ) THEN
            L = ISAMAX(N-K+1,A(K,IC),1) + K - 1
            IF ( A(L,IC) .EQ. 0.0 ) THEN
               IN = K
            ELSE
               T = -1.0/A(L,IC)
               CALL SSCAL (N-K,T,A(K+1,IC),1)
            ENDIF
            send (*, 'IN:1, L:1, A(K+1,IC):N-K' )
         ENDIF
         receive ( IT, 'IN:1, L:1, W(K+1):N-K' )
         IP(K) = L
         CALL SSWAP (M-IC+1,A(K,IC),N,A(L,IC),N)
         IF ( procid .EQ. IT ) IC = IC + 1
         IF ( IN .NE. K ) THEN
            DO 10 J = IC, M
               CALL SAXPY (N-K,A(K,J),W(K+1),1,A(K+1,J),1)
10          CONTINUE
         ENDIF
20    CONTINUE
      IT = MOD(N-1,nprocs)
      IF ( A(N,M) .EQ. 0.0 .AND. procid .EQ. IT ) IN = N
      send ( 0, 'IN:1, IP:N' )
      RETURN
      END
```
(b)

Figure 13. Message passing data distribution (a) and message passing computation (b).

remote data is near unity, there will be no need to worry about the location of the data.

Published examples

Solving systems of linear equations is an important part of many applications and often accounts for a large part of the computer time. Because the algorithm can be written in a very compact program, it is commonly used as an example.[33,34]

This section presents four versions of this algorithm that illustrate some of the parallel processing constructs used. These programs are based on subroutine SGEFA from Linpack.[32] Liberties were taken with the published codes to make them more readable and more like my examples. The reader is referred to the cited publications for the full programs.

VM/EPEX. I wrote the first example, Figure 15, to show SPMD programming using the VM/EPEX software available for use within IBM for experimental purposes.[6] VM/EPEX works with the VM/CMS operating system using unprotected shared segments to provide a shared memory area. Each processor is a distinct virtual machine, and all synchronization is handled by semaphores in shared memory.

Although the hardware can have one, two, or four processors, the software makes it possible to simulate any number of processors. VM/EPEX comes with a preprocessor that scans a source file for constructs beginning with @. These constructs get converted into in-line code and calls to subroutines that provide the required functions.

The VM/EPEX code is very similar to the code in Figure 12a. The @SHARED in the example is translated into COMMON and marked for loading into the shared memory. The construct is equivalent to declaring the variables A, IPVT, and N to be GLOBAL. @SERIAL BEGIN PROCESS = 1 defines a serial section to be executed by the processor with PROCID = 1. It is terminated with @SERIAL END WAIT, which is equivalent to the END SERIAL SECTION followed by a barrier. The @DO is a self-scheduled, PARALLEL DO terminated by the @ENDDO WAIT. Again, the WAIT is equivalent to putting a barrier following the loop. The option CHUNK is used to reduce the overhead in assigning loop indi-

```
      SUBROUTINE FACTOR(A,AL,N,M,IP,W,WL,IN)
      DIMENSION A(N,N),AL(N,M),IP(N),W(N),WL(N)
      global L, PIVOT, W
      INFO = 0
      IC = 0
      DO 10 K = procid, N, nprocs
         IC = IC + 1
         CALL SCOPY (N,A(1,K),1,AL(1,IC),1)
   10 CONTINUE
      IC = 1
      DO 30 K = 1, N-1
         IT = MOD(K-1,nprocs)
         IF ( procid .EQ. IT ) THEN
            IP(K) = ISAMAX (N-K+1,AL(K,IC),N) + K - 1
            L = IP(K)
            PIVOT - AL(L,IC)
         ENDIF
         barrier
         CALL SSWAP ( M-IC+1, AL(K,IC), N, AL(L,IC), N )
         IF ( PIVOT .EQ. 0.0 ) THEN
            IN = K
         ELSE
            IF ( procid .EQ. IT ) THEN
               T = -1.0/PIVOT
               CALL SSCAL (N-K,T,AL(K,IC),1)
               CALL SCOPY (N-K,AL(K+1,IC),1,W(K+1),1)
               IC = IC + 1
            ENDIF
            barrier
            CALL SCOPY (N-K,W(K+1),1,WL(K+1),1)
            DO 20 J = IC, M
               CALL SAXPY(N-K,AL(K,J),WL(K+1),1,AL(K+1,J),1)
   20       CONTINUE
         ENDIF
   30 CONTINUE
      IC = 0
      DO 40 K = procid, N, nprocs
         IC = IC + 1
         CALL SCOPY (N,AL(1,IC),1,A(1,K),1)
   40 CONTINUE
      IF ( A(N,N) .EQ. 0.0 ) IN = N
      RETURN
      END
```

Figure 14. SPMD LU decomposition of a hybrid.

```
      SUBROUTINE DGEFA(LDA,INFO)
      @SHARED/ARRAY/A(100,100),IPVT(100),N
      INFO = 0
      DO 60 K = 1, N-1
         @SERIAL BEGIN PROCESS = 1
            L = ISAMAX(N-K+1,A(K,K),1)+K-1
            IPVT(K) = L
            IF (A(L,K) .EQ. 0.0D0) THEN
               INFO = K
            ELSE
               T = -1.0D0/A(L,K)
               CALL SSCAL(N-K+1,T,A(K+1,K),1)
            ENDIF
         @SERIAL END WAIT
         L = IPVT(K)
         IF ( A(L,K) .NE. 0.D0 ) THEN
            CALL SSWAP ( N-K+1, A(L,K), N, A(K,K), N )
            @DO 30 J = K+1, N, CHUNK = 10
               CALL SAXPY(N-K,A(K,J),A(K+1,K),1,A(K+1,J),1)
   30       @ENDDO WAIT
         ELSE
            INFO = K
         ENDIF
   60 CONTINUE
      IPVT(N) = N
      IF (A(N,N) .EQ. 0.0D0) INFO = N
      END
```

Figure 15. VM/EPEX code.

```
        forcesub SGEFA(LDA,INFO) of NPROC on NPEM ident ME
          global A(1000,1000), IPVT(1000), N, INFO
      end header
      INFO = 0
      DO 50 K = 1, N-1
          barrier
              L = ISAMAX ( N-K+1, A(K,K), 1 ) + K - 1
          end barrier
          IF ( A(L,K) .EQ. 0.0 ) THEN
              INFO = K
          ELSE
              barrier
                  IPVT(K) = L
                  CALL SSWAP (N-K+1,A(K,K),N,A(IPVT(K),K),N)
                  T = -1.0/A(K,K)
                  CALL SSCAL (N-K,T,A(K+1,K),1)
              end barrier
              selfsched DO 40 J = K+1, N
                  CALL SAXPY (N-K,A(K,J),A(K+1,K),1,A(K+1,J),1)
   40         end selfsched DO
          ENDIF
   50 CONTINUE
      END
```

Figure 16. Force code.

```
      REAL S
      do parallel ( I = 1, N )
          begin
              REAL T
              ...
          end
      end parallel
```

Figure 17. BEGIN-END code.

```
      PARAMETER (ND=100)
      DIMENSION A(ND,ND), TEMP(ND)
      READ (5,*) N
      CALL SETRNG(A,N,N)
      CALL SETRNG(TEMP,N)
      DO 20 IC = 1, N-1
          CMAX = MAX(A(IC:N,IC))
          IMAX   = LOCMAX(A(IC:N,IC))
          TEMP = A(IMAX,:)
          A(IMAX,:) = A(IC,:)
          A(IC,:) = TEMP
          do parallel (JR=IC+1,N)
              begin
                  A(IC,JR) = A(IC,JR)/CMAX
                  do parallel (K = IC+1:N)
                      A(JR,K) = A(JR,K) - A(IC,K)*A(JR,IC)
                  end parallel
              end
          end parallel
   20 CONTINUE
      END
```

Figure 18. Protran code.

ces to processors. Here it tells the system to give each processor 10 values of the loop index each time they get work. Because of the synchronization needed to get unique loop indices, the reduction in elapsed time is significant.

The Force. This example, Figure 16, shows the SPMD programming style using the Force.[2] The basic concept of the Force is very similar to that of VM/EPEX although they were developed independently. I have modified the published code to make it closer to the examples shown earlier. As published, the program does both the search for the pivot element and the scaling of the pivot column in parallel. Since these steps represent only a small part of the work if the matrix is large, I have chosen to do them on a single processor.

A Force subroutine has a header that indicates how many processes, NPROC, are to be run on how many processors, NPEM, and the local variable used to store the process id, ME. The header also contains the declaration of global data. Like VM/EPEX, COMMON is used to implement data sharing.

The Force uses a generalized concept of a barrier. All processes stop at the barrier until the last one has arrived. That process then executes the code up to the END BARRIER. Once the first process has reached this point, all processes continue executing at the line following the END BARRIER. Thus, this construct is equivalent to our serial section bracketed by our BARRIER. If there is no code between BARRIER and END BARRIER, then this construct is equivalent to our BARRIER. The SELFSCHED DO is equivalent to our PARALLEL DO.

Protran. A collection of problems has been put together to test language extensions to support vector and parallel processors.[35] One of these extensions to Fortran was developed by IMSL, Inc., and is called Protran.[36] In addition to vector and matrix operations, it has a number of problem solving statements. Extensions include some that make the language look more like the proposed Fortran 8X array extensions[37] and others that add parallel processing constructs.

The parallel processing constructs added to Protran are DO PARALLEL, CRITICAL, and BEGIN-END. The first two extensions do not need further explanation. Since this language is intended for use on shared memory systems, the BEGIN-

END is the only way of providing private data among processors operating within a DO PARALLEL. Although the sample code presented does not need any local variables, if needed they can be declared within the scope of the BEGIN-END. In the example of Figure 17, each processor executing the DO PARALLEL has the same value of S and a distinct value of T. In addition, T does not exist outside the BEGIN-END.

In the Protran version of the factorization code shown in Figure 18, routine SETRNG is used to set up a dope vector containing the lengths of the arrays being used. These lengths need not be the same as the dimensions of the arrays. This code also shows several of the array extensions proposed for Fortran 8X.

Note the use of a nested DO PARALLEL. It is left to the compiler to decide what work can be done in parallel. For example, the inner DO PARALLEL cannot be started until the column scaling is complete. Depending on the hardware, the scaling could be done on one processor or distributed over processors. In this case, we let the compiler contain the knowledge of the hardware instead of the programmer. Such a procedure puts more pressure on compiler writers, but leads to more portable code.

Hypercube. The code presented in Figure 19 is part of the Linpack library being written for the iPSC,[21] a hypercube message passing system marketed by Intel Corporation. It is quite similar to the program shown in Figure 13b as subroutine FACTOR. Although the distribution of the data is not shown, a scheme similar to that shown in Figure 13a could be used.

Each node of the hypercube runs the same subroutine, so this code is an example of SPMD programming. In this system, both the number of processors, IP, and the process id, ID, are passed through the argument list. The GSEND routine is similar to the SEND(*,... construct used in Figure 13b. GSEND also contains code to receive the data. Thus, all data routing and synchronization is handled in this routine. If the program were moved to a different message passing system, all that need be changed is GSEND.

T he point of parallel processing is to reduce the elapsed time to complete the job. If the program that

```
      SUBROUTINE PGEFA(A,LDA,N,M,IP,CID,ID,IPVT,BUF)
      DIMENSION A(LDA,M), BUF(N), IPVT(M)
      L = 1
      DO 20 K = 1, N
         IR = MOD(K-1,IP)
         IF ( IR .EQ. ID ) THEN
            KP = ISAMAX ( N-K+1, A(K,L), 1 ) + K + 1
            IF ( A(KP,L) .EQ. 0.D0 ) KP = 0
            IPVT(L) = KP
            IF( KP .NE. 0 ) THEN
               T = -1.0/A(K,L)
               CALL SSCAL ( N-K, T, A(K+1,L) , 1 )
            ENDIF
            CALL SCOPY(N-K,A(K+1,L),1,BUF,1)
            BUF(N-K+1) = KP
            L = L + 1
         ENDIF
         CALL GSEND(ID,IR,K,IP,CID,BUF,N-K+1)
         KP = BUF(N-K+1)
         IF ( KP .NE. 0 ) THEN
            CALL SSWAP ( M-L+1, A(IPVT(K),L),N,A(K,L),N )
            DO 10 J = L, M
               CALL SAXPY(N-K,A(K,L),BUF,1,A(K+1,J),1)
10          CONTINUE
         ENDIF
20    CONTINUE
      END
```

Figure 19. iPSC code.

sums 1,000,000 numbers were run on a 1-Mflop uniprocessor, it would finish in about one second. The time the program takes on a parallel processor will depend on the coding style, the architecture of the machine, and the hardware implementation. However, run on 10 processors each capable of 1 Mflop, the job will certainly take longer than 0.1 seconds to complete. The job of the system designers, compiler and library writers, and application programmers is to get the actual time for the job as close as possible to the ideal.

I have identified three classes of parallel architectures: shared memory, message passing, and hybrid. I have also illustrated two programming styles: fork-join and SPMD. Each programming style can be used on each of the parallel architectures depending on the tools provided to the applications programmer.

Algorithms are easy to design for shared memory systems. One simply puts the data in memory as if running on a uniprocessor. On the other hand, programs are hard to debug. An error usually involves picking up wrong data from a global variable. The processor then continues computing, with the bad data producing an erroneous final result. There is no indication of when the error occurred.

Message passing systems are different. Algorithm design is hard because the data must be distributed so that communications traffic is minimized. Debugging is easier than in shared memory systems because errors normally cause the system to stop at the point of the error. Thus, the programmer knows the complete state of the machine at the point where the error occurred. This is not to say that debugging is easy. There are many times where it is very hard to track down the cause of the error, but at least the programmer knows where to start looking.

Hybrid systems are the worst of both worlds. Errors are hard to find because they are the same ones made on shared memory systems. In addition, care is needed in organizing the data in order to reduce the amount of data to be moved. All is not lost, however, since hybrid systems may be easier to build than either shared memory or message passing systems.

From these comments we see that data organization is the key to parallel algorithms even on shared memory systems. Unfortunately, Fortran programmers have such simple data structures available to them, just scalars and arrays, that we tend to concentrate on program flow. It will take some retraining to get Fortran programmers to plan their data first and their program flow later.

The importance of data management is also a problem for people writing automatic parallelization compilers. To date, our compiler technology has been directed toward optimizing control flow. Such features as common expression elimination, code movement, and dependence analysis for vectorization have been used for many years. Even today, when hierarchical memories make program performance a function of data organization, no compiler in existence changes the data addresses specified by the programmer to improve performance. If such compilers are to be successful, particularly on message passing and hybrid systems, a new kind of analysis will have to be developed. This analysis will have to match the data structures to the executable code in order to minimize memory traffic.

A more fundamental problem on shared memory systems arises when the parallelism is nested. Most parallel processors allow only a single level of parallelism, which greatly simplifies the data sharing specification. In these systems, a master process is allowed to spawn subprocesses, but the subprocesses may not themselves spawn processes. Alternatively, all processors run the same code as their peers. In both cases, data is either known to all processes or is private.

The situation is more complicated when a subprocess is allowed to spawn subprocesses of its own. Consider a parallel job currently running two subprocesses that each call a library routine to work on some private data. If the library routine spawns subprocesses of its own, a simple global/local dichotomy for the data will not suffice. Each of the library routine invocations must share a different set of data among its subprocesses. Clearly, some form of scoping of the global data is required. The data scoping rules in such block-structured languages as Algol and PL/I provide a useful model, but to date no systems have addressed this issue.

As I stated in the introduction, my goal was to present the state of the art of parallel programming. I believe I have shown what a sorry state that art is in. We are just beginning to define the appropriate set of language extensions. Much more work is needed in compiler-assisted dependence analysis and in developing debugging tools.□

Acknowledgments

I would like to thank an anonymous referee for suggesting important improvements to the organization of this paper.

References

1. J.J. Dongarra and I.S. Duff, "Advanced Computer Architectures," Mathematics and Computer Science Div. Report TM-57, Argonne National Laboratory, Argonne, Ill., 1985.

2. H.F. Jordan, "Structuring Parallel Algorithms in an MIMD, Shared Memory Environment," Report Number CSDG 84-2, Dept. of Electrical and Computer Engineering, University of Colorado, 1984.

3. P. Mehrotra and J. Van Rosendale, "The BLAZE Language: A Parallel Language for Scientific Programming," ICASE Report Number 85-29, NASA Langley Research Center, Langley, Va., 1985.

4. S. Shin et al., "Parallel Computation on the Loosely Coupled Array of Processors: A Guide to the Preprocessor," IBM Report # KGN-42, Kingston, N.Y., 1985.

5. T.W. Pratt, "PISCES: An Environment for Parallel Scientific Computation," ICASE Report Number 85-12, NASA Langley Research Center, Langley, Va., 1985.

6. F. Darema-Rogers et al., "An Environment for Parallel Execution," IBM Research Report #11225, Yorktown Heights, N.Y., 1985.

7. E.L. Lusk and R.A. Overbeek, "Implementation of Monitors with Macros: A Programming Aid for the HEP and Other Parallel Processors," Report Number ANL-83-97, Argonne National Laboratory, Argonne, Ill., 1983.

8. D. Kuck, "High Speed Multiprocessing and Compilation Techniques," IEEE Trans. on Computers, C-29, Piscataway, N.J., 1980, pp. 763-776.

9. J.R. Allen and K. Kennedy, "PFC: A Program to Convert Fortran to Parallel Form," Proc. IBM Conf. Parallel Computers in Scientific Computations, Rome, Italy, 1982. Also published in Supercomputers: Design and Applications, K. Hwang, ed., IEEE Computer Society Press, Silver Spring, Md., 1984.

10. R. Perron and C. Mundie, "The Architecture of the Alliant FX/8 Computer," Digest of Papers, Compcon, Spring 86, A.G. Bell, ed., IEEE Computer Society Press, Washington, D.C., 1986.

11. G.H. Barnes et al., "The Illiac IV Computer," C-17, IEEE Trans. on Computers, Piscataway, N.J., 1968, pp. 746-757.

12. R.W. Hockney and C.R. Jesshope, Parallel Computers, Adam Hilger, Ltd., Bristol, 1981.

13. K.E. Batcher, "Design of a Massively Parallel Processor," IEEE Trans. on Computers, C-29, Piscataway, N.J., 1980, pp. 836-340. Also published in Supercomputers: Design and Applications, K. Hwang, ed., IEEE Computer Society Press, Silver Spring, Md., 1984.

14. W.D. Hillis, The Connection Machine, MIT Press, Cambridge, Mass., 1985.

15. S.Y. Kung, "On Supercomputing with Systolic/Wavefront Array Processors," Proc. IEEE, Vol. 72, Piscataway, N.J., 1984, pp. 867-884. Also published in Supercomputers: Design and Applications, K. Hwang, ed., IEEE Computer Society Press, Silver Spring, Md., 1984.

16. J.J. Dongarra, B.T. Smith, and D.C. Sorensen, "Algorithm Design for Different Computer Architectures," in "New Directions for Advanced Computer Architectures," Report Number ANL/MCS-TM-32, Argonne National Laboratory, Argonne, Ill., 1984.

17. J.L. Larson, "An Introduction to Multitasking on the Cray X-MP-2 Multiprocessor," Computer, July 1984, pp. 62-69.

18. IBM Corp., "IBM 3090 System Summary—Engineering/Scientific," announcement letter 185-120, 1985.

19. A. Gottlieb et al., "The NYU Ultracomputer—Designing an MIMD Shared Memory Parallel Computer," IEEE Trans. on Computers, C-32, Piscataway, N.J., 1983, pp. 175-189. Also published in Supercomputers: Design and Applications, K. Hwang, ed., IEEE Computer Society Press, Silver Spring, Md., 1984.

20. T. Feng, "A Survey of Interconnection Networks," Computer, Dec. 1981, pp. 12-27. Also published in Supercomputers: Design and Applications, K. Hwang, ed., IEEE Computer Society Press, Silver Spring, Md., 1984.

21. J. Rattner, "Concurrent Processing: A New Direction in Scientific Computing," AFIPS Conference Proc., 54, AFIPS Press, Reston, Va., 1985, pp. 159-166.

22. C.L. Seitz, "The Cosmic Cube," Comm. ACM, 28, New York, N.Y., 1985, pp. 22-33.

23. J.F. Palmer, "A VLSI Parallel Computer," Digest of Papers, Compcon, Spring 86, A.G. Bell, ed., IEEE Computer Society Press, Washington, D.C., 1986.

24. E. Clementi and D. Logan, "Parallel Processing with the Loosely Coupled Array of Processors System," IBM Report # KGN-43, Kingston, N.Y., 1985.

25. G.F. Pfister et al., "The IBM Research Parallel Processor Prototype (RP3)," Int'l Conf. Parallel Processing, IEEE Computer Society Press, Washington, D.C., 1985.

26. W. Crowther et al., "Performance Measurements on a 128-node Butterfly Parallel Processor," Int'l Conf. Parallel Processing Proc., IEEE Computer Society Press, Washington, D.C., 1985, pp. 531-535.

27. D. Gajski et al., "CEDAR," Digest of Papers, Compcon, Spring 86, A.G. Bell, ed., IEEE Computer Society Press, Washington, D.C., 1986.

28. R.W. Hockney, "MIMD Computing in the USA—1984," Parallel Computing, Vol. 2, 1985, pp. 119-136.

29. H.F. Jordan, "Parallel Computation with the Force," Report Number 85-45, ICASE, NASA Langley, Hampton, Va., 1985.

30. M. Booth and K. Misegades, "Microtasking: A New Way to Harness Multiproces-

sors," *Cray Channels*, Summer 1986, pp. 24-27.

31. R. Rettberg and R. Thomas, "Contention Is No Obstacle to Shared-Memory Multiprocessing," *Comm. ACM*, Vol. 29, New York, N.Y., 1986, pp. 1202-1212.

32. J.J. Dongarra et al., *Linpack Users' Guide*, Society of Industrial and Applied Mathematics, Philadelphia, 1979.

33. J.J. Dongarra, F.G. Gustavson, and A.H. Karp, "Implementing Linear Algebra Algorithms for Dense Matrices on a Vector Pipeline Machine," *SIAM Review*, Vol. 26, 1984, pp. 91-112.

34. J.J. Dongarra, "Performance of Various Computers using Standard Linear Equations Software in a FORTRAN Environment," Mathematics and Computer Science Div. Report TM-23, Argonne National Laboratory, Argonne, Ill., 1986.

35. J.R. Rice, "Problems to Test Parallel and Vector Languages," Report Number CSD-TR 516, Dept. of Computer Sciences, Purdue University, W. Lafayette, Ind., 1985.

36. J.R. Rice, *Numerical Methods, Software and Analysis*, McGraw-Hill, New York, 1983.

37. G. Paul, "Vectran and the Proposed Vector/Array Extensions to ANSI Fortran for Scientific and Engineering Computation," *Proc. IBM Conference on Parallel Computers in Scientific Computations*, Rome, Italy, 1982. Also published in *Supercomputers: Design and Applications*, K. Hwang, ed., IEEE Computer Society Press, Silver Spring, Md., 1984.

Alan Karp is a staff member at IBM's Palo Alto Scientific Center. He has worked on problems of radiative transfer in moving stellar matter and in planetary atmospheres, hydrodynamics problems in pulsating stars and in enhanced oil recovery, and numerical methods for parallel processors. He is currently studying the interface between programmers and parallel processors, with special attention to debugging parallel algorithms.

Karp received his PhD in astronomy from the University of Maryland in 1974. He has served on the editorial boards of the *Journal of Quantitative Spectroscopy and Radiative Transfer* and the *Journal of Transport Theory and Statistical Physics*.

Readers may write to Karp at the IBM Scientific Center, 1530 Page Mill Road, Palo Alto, CA 94304.

Visualization and Debugging in a Heterogeneous Environment

Adam Beguelin, Carnegie Mellon University and Pittsburgh Supercomputing Center

Jack Dongarra, University of Tennessee and Oak Ridge National Laboratory

Al Geist, Oak Ridge National Laboratory

Vaidy Sunderam, Emory University

A monitoring tool and a graphical interface working on top of the PVM software can help programmers make better use of heterogeneous networks of computers.

The emergence of a wide variety of commercially available parallel computers has created a software dilemma. Will it be possible to design general-purpose software that is both efficient and portable across these new parallel computers? Moreover, will it be possible to provide programming environments sophisticated enough for explicit parallel programming to exploit the performance of these new machines? For many computational problems, the design, implementation, and understanding of efficient parallel algorithms can be a formidable challenge. Additional issues of synchronization and multiple-task coordination make efficient parallel programs more difficult to write and understand than efficient sequential programs. Parallel programs are often less portable than serial codes because their structure may depend critically on the hardware's specific architectural features (such as how it handles data sharing, memory access, synchronization, and process creation).

The computing requirements of many current and future applications, ranging from scientific computational problems in the material and physical sciences to simulation, engineering design, and circuit analysis, are best served by concurrent processing. Multiprocessors can frequently address the computational requirements of these high-performance applications, but other aspects of concurrent computing are not adequately addressed when conventional parallel processors are used.

For instance, software aspects, including program development methods, scalable programs, profiling tools, and support systems, require significant development. While hardware and architectural advances in parallelism have been rapid, the software infrastructure has not kept pace, resulting in unsystematic and ad hoc approaches to the implementation of concurrent applications. In recent years, several research groups have focused on various aspects of this shortcoming, producing significant developments in programming paradigms, data partitioning, algorithms, languages, and scheduling.

Heterogeneous networks of computers ranging from workstations to supercomputers are becoming commonplace in high-performance computing. Until recently, each computing resource on the network remained a separate unit, but now hundreds of institutions worldwide are using the Parallel Virtual Machine[1] soft-

Reprinted from *Computer*, Vol. 26, No. 6, June 1993, pp. 88–95.

0-8186-6522-X/95 $4.00 © 1993 IEEE

PVM: Heterogeneous distributed computing

PVM (Parallel Virtual Machine) is a software package being developed by Oak Ridge National Laboratory, the University of Tennessee, and Emory University. It enables a heterogeneous collection of Unix computers linked by a network to function as a single large parallel computer. Thus, large computational problems can be solved by the aggregate power and memory of many computers.

PVM supplies the functions to start tasks and lets the computers communicate and synchronize with each other. It survives the failure of one or more connected computers and supplies functions for users to make their applications fault tolerant. Users can write applications in Fortran or C and parallelize them by calling simple PVM message-passing routines such as pvm_send() and pvm_recv(). By sending and receiving messages, application subtasks can cooperate to solve a problem in parallel.

PVM lets subtasks exploit the type of computer best suited for finding their solution. Thus some subtasks may run on a vector supercomputer and others on a parallel computer or powerful workstation. PVM applications can be run transparently across a wide variety of architectures; PVM automatically handles all message conversion required if linked computers use different data representations. Participating computers can be distributed anywhere in the world and linked by a variety of networks.

The PVM source code and user's guide are available by electronic mail. The software is easy to install. The source has been tested on Sun, DEC, IBM, HP, Silicon Graphics Iris, Data General, and Next workstations, as well as parallel computers by Sequent, Alliant, Intel, Thinking Machines, BBN, Cray, Convex, IBM, and KSR. In addition, Cray Research, Convex, IBM, Silicon Graphics, and DEC supply and support PVM software optimized for their systems.

PVM is an enabling technology. Hundreds of sites around the world already use PVM as a cost-effective way to solve important scientific, industrial, and medical problems. PVM users include petroleum, aerospace, chemical, pharmaceutical, computer, medical, automotive, and environmental cleanup companies. Department of Energy and NASA laboratories use PVM for research, and numerous universities around the US use it for both research and teaching.

The software described in this article is freely distributed to researchers and educators, allowing them to harness their distributed computation power into comprehensive virtual machines. PVM and Hence are available by sending electronic mail to netlib@ornl.gov containing the line "send index from pvm3" or "send index from hence." Instructions on how to receive the various parts of the PVM and Hence systems will be sent by return mail.

Xab is also available from netlib. The index from pvm explains how to obtain this software. PVM problems or questions can be sent to pvm@msr.epm.ornl.gov for a quick and friendly reply.

---

ware package to develop truly heterogeneous programs utilizing multiple computer systems to solve applications (see sidebar). We designed PVM with heterogeneity and portability as primary goals. It lets machines with different architectures and floating-point representations work together on a single computational task.

In the development of heterogeneous concurrent applications for heterogeneous target environments, coarse-grained subtask partitioning and processor allocation are critical. Additionally, program module construction, specification of interdependencies and synchronization, and management of multiple objects for different architectures are tedious, error-prone activities. To address these issues and to provide at least partial solutions, we developed Xab and Hence, two packages that work on top of PVM to aid in the use, programming, and analysis of parallel computers.

Xab (X Window Analysis and Debugging) is a tool for runtime monitoring of PVM programs. Using Xab, programmers can easily instrument and monitor PVM programs by simply relinking to the Xab libraries. Xab is itself a PVM program, so it is very portable. However, making it peacefully coincide with the programs it monitors is problematic.

Hence (Heterogeneous Network Computing Environment) is an environment for the development of high-level programming techniques for the type of concurrent virtual machines provided by PVM. Its goal is to simplify the task (and thus reduce the chance of error) of programming a heterogeneous network of computers, while still providing the programmer with access to the high performance available from such configurations. There are several systems with goals similar to those of Hence. The Code system[2] and Paralex[3] both allow graph-based high-level specifications of parallel programs. Code includes tools that can map the specification into several different parallel languages or libraries such as Ada or C with shared-memory extensions. Paralex directly maps its specifications into C with calls to the Isis library.[4]

PVM

With PVM, users can exploit the aggregate power of distributed workstations and supercomputers to solve the computational Grand Challenges.

Users view PVM as a loosely coupled distributed-memory computer programmed in C or Fortran with message-passing extensions. The hardware that constitutes a user's personal PVM may be any Unix-based network-accessible machine on which the user has a valid login.

We have tested the software with combinations of the following machines: Sun3, Sparcstation, MicroVAX, DECstation, IBM RS/6000, HP-9000, Silicon Graphics Iris, Next, Sequent Symmetry, Alliant FX, IBM 3090, Intel iPSC/860, Thinking Machines CM-2 and CM-5, KSR-1, Convex, Cray Y-MP, Fujitsu VP-2000, DEC Alpha, Intel Paragon, and Cray C90. In addition, users can port PVM to new architectures by simply modifying a generic "makefile" supplied with the source and recompiling.

Using PVM, users can configure their own parallel virtual computers, which can overlap with other users' virtual computers. Configuring a personal parallel virtual computer involves simply listing the names of the machines in a file that is read when PVM is started. Several different physical networks can coexist inside a virtual machine. For example, a local Ethernet, a Hippi (High-Performance Parallel Interface), and a

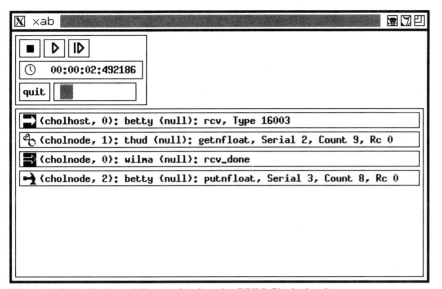

Figure 1. Xab display while monitoring the PVM Cholesky demo.

fiber-optic network can all be part of a user's virtual machine. Each user can have only one virtual machine active at a time; however, since PVM is multitasking, several applications can run simultaneously on a parallel virtual machine.

The PVM package is small (approximately 1 Mbyte) and easy to install. It needs to be installed only once on each machine to be accessible to all users. Moreover, installation does not require special privileges on any machines, so any user can do it.

Application programs that use PVM are composed of subtasks at a moderately coarse level of granularity. The subtasks can be generic serial codes or specific to a particular machine. In PVM, the user may access computational resources at three different levels:

- the *transparent* mode, in which subtasks are automatically located at the most appropriate sites,
- the *architecture-dependent* mode, in which the user can indicate specific architectures on which particular subtasks are to execute, and
- the *machine-specific* mode, in which the user can specify a particular machine.

Such flexibility lets different subtasks of a heterogeneous application exploit particular strengths of individual machines on the network.

The PVM programming interface requires that programmers explicitly type all message data. PVM performs machine-independent data conversions when required, thus letting machines with different integer and floating-point representations pass data. Applications

access PVM resources via a library of standard interface routines. These routines allow the initiation and termination of processes across the network, as well as communication and synchronization among processes.

Application programs under PVM can possess arbitrary control and dependency structures. In other words, at any point in the execution of a concurrent application, the existing processes can have arbitrary relationships with each other and, further, any process can communicate or synchronize with any other.

While PVM is a very popular system for programming heterogeneous networks of computers, it is not the only system of this type. The p4 system[5] from Argonne National Laboratory, Express[6] from Parasoft, and Linda[7] from Scientific Computing Associates provide functionality similar to that of PVM.

Monitoring, debugging, and performance tuning

Tools should help programmers write and debug applications and tune their performance. With small-scale changes based on analysis of execution profiles, communication patterns, and load imbalances, programmers can improve concurrent application performance by an order of magnitude. Previous research in visualization focused on homogeneous parallel processing for both shared- and distributed-memory machines.[8] Our work focuses on visualization and debugging for networks of heterogeneous computers. Xab and Hence provide tools

to help users with the complex task of understanding a program's behavior for both correctness and performance.

Xab. While PVM provides a solid programming base, it does not give users many options for analyzing or debugging PVM programs. To help in the development of PVM programs, Xab, a runtime monitoring tool, gives users direct feedback about the PVM functions their programs are performing. Xab has three parts: an Xab library to which the user links applications, a PVM process called *abmon* that quietly receives tracing messages from the library routines, and a display process called *xab* that is a graphical X Window display of the trace events.

Real-time monitoring is particularly apropos in a heterogeneous multiprogramming environment where differences in computation and communication speeds result from both heterogeneity and external CPU and network loads. Monitoring gives the user insight into program behavior in such an environment.

Xab monitors a PVM program by instrumenting calls to the PVM library. The instrumented calls generate events displayed during program execution.

A Fortran program normally accesses the PVM user routines via the libfpvm library that comes with PVM. Fortran programs use Xab by simply linking to libxpvm in place of libfpvm. With C, the procedure is slightly more complicated. The programmer must add the include file xab.h to source files that call PVM routines and then recompile the modified source files. This include file contains macros that replace the normal PVM routines with calls to the Xab library. Both Fortran and C programs must be linked with the Xab library, called *libab*.

Event messages. The Xab libraries call the normal PVM functions for the user, but they also send PVM messages to a special monitoring process called *abmon*.

Xab event messages generally contain an event type, a time stamp (in microseconds), and event-specific information. The event type indicates which PVM call is being invoked. In some cases, a PVM call may generate two events. For instance, the PVM barrier function generates an event before and after the barrier call. This lets the user see when barriers are initiated and completed. The time stamp in the event message is the time of day on the machine executing the PVM call. The clocks on various machines involved in a computation may not be synchronized, so Xab does not rely on synchronized clocks. Events are simply displayed as they arrive.

Although future versions of Xab may use the time stamps, it is not always necessary to synchronize machine clocks. For instance, it may be informative to know how long processes wait at a particular program barrier. Xab could use the time stamps from barrier events to display this information, independent of relative machine clock synchronization. The event-specific information in an Xab message varies for different PVM routines. For the event generated at the start of a barrier, it is the name of the barrier and the number of processes that must reach the barrier before continuing. Other event messages contain similar event-specific information.

Besides the event messages, Xab also inserts one additional piece of information into user messages. Each message is given a serial number, prepended to the user's message buffer so that every message can be uniquely identified by its source process and serial number. Currently, we are exploring the usefulness of adding pseudo time stamps to Xab. Pseudo time stamps combine real clocks and logical clocks.

Monitoring processes. The abmon process receives event messages from the instrumented PVM calls and formats them into human-readable form. The abmon program must be running before the user's program starts, since it needs to receive event messages from the instrumented calls. The formatted event messages can be either written to a file or sent to the Xab display program. Just as an astronomer on Earth observes events that have traveled various distances, the abmon process observes events relative to its position in the virtual machine. When abmon formats events, it also adds its own perspective within the virtual machine by placing local time stamps into the event record. To discern its perspective, abmon may use the additional time stamps to ascertain how long it takes events to propagate from a user process to the monitor process.

The display process takes events formatted by abmon and displays them in a window, as shown in Figure 1. Xab supports two modes of event playback: continuous play or single step. When the user presses the play button, the events are displayed in real time. The slider controls the playback speed in continuous-play mode. Users can stop playback at any time by pressing the stop button. The single-step button will show only the next event.

The following command line executes Xab, displaying the events in real time and saving them in a file for later review:

% abmon | tee evfile | xab

The abmon program reads event messages and writes them to standard output. The Unix command tee copies the events to the file evfile and also passes them to xab via the pipe. The Xab program actually opens a window and displays the events.

Timeliness versus message traffic. Every user call to the PVM library uses the method for sending Xab monitor messages described in the previous section. This approach generates an inordinately large number of messages. There is a trade-off between the number of messages and the timeliness of the event display. If events are buffered and sent to the monitor after every n events, then the event display becomes more asynchronous as n grows. In fact,

when n reaches the number of events in the program, the monitor provides post-mortem rather than real-time information. Since the display lags behind the program state, users cannot detect certain problems in program behavior. (We give an example in the next section.) Another factor that must be considered is the memory required to store events before sending them to the monitor. Xab immediately dispatches events. As a result, it adds little, in terms of memory requirements, to the PVM processes it monitors. We are exploring the possibility of allowing the user to dynamically alter the event flow. This extension requires the addition of bidirectional data exchanges to the one-way dataflow currently used for Xab's monitoring.

An example. An example program that comes with PVM 2.4 is a distributed-matrix decomposition program based on a Cholesky factorization of the matrix. The window in Figure 1 is the Xab display in progress for this program. The host process, (cholhost, 0), is blocked on a receive. Process (cholnode, 0) has just received a message. The node process (cholnode, 1) is extracting data from a message buffer, while (cholnode, 2) is placing eight floats into a message buffer.

As shown in Figure 2, an advantage of Xab's real-time display is its ability to

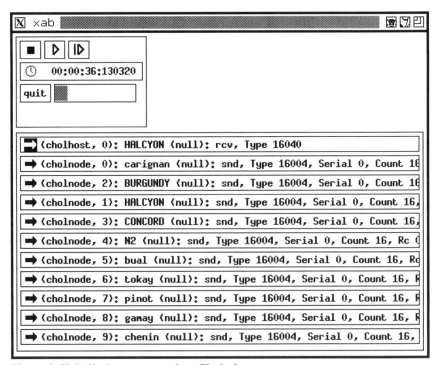

Figure 2. Xab displays an error in a Cholesky program.

detect errors in a dynamic environment. The same Cholesky example contains a deliberately introduced error. The host is waiting for a message of type 16040, while all the cholnode processes are sending messages of type 16004; thus the program has blocked indefinitely. In this case, postmortem monitoring would not work: The program would not complete and therefore would never flush the events for display.

Several research projects focus on displaying events generated by distributed-memory parallel programs, notably ParaGraph,[9] Pablo,[10] Upshot,[11] and Bee.[12] Currently, Xab events are stored in Xab's own ASCII-based format. Because of ParaGraph's wide availability, we provide a program that converts Xab event files to a ParaGraph-compatible format. The ParaGraph tool provides a rich set of displays for visualizing message-passing parallel programs. Figure 3 shows a ParaGraph visualization of the PVM Cholesky program with one host process and two slave processes.

There are several differences between the ParaGraph and the Xab displays. ParaGraph provides a variety of views but is limited to postmortem visualization. Xab currently has a limited display facility but can operate in real time. The ParaGraph trace events must be in temporal order. Xab simply displays events as they arrive. ParaGraph was developed originally for multicomputers that did not support multitasking.

Hence. In developing software, the programmer often designs the initial definitions and specifications graphically; flowcharts and dependency graphs are well-known examples. Designers can visualize the problem's overall structure far more easily from these graphical representations than from textual specifications. Such a representation enhances the quality of the resulting software. However, to be executed, these descriptions must be converted to program form, typically manifested as source code; that is, the graphical representations must be translated to operational programs. The graphical depiction of a concurrent application and strategies for its successful execution

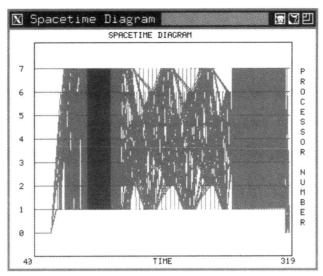

Figure 3. ParaGraph views of the Cholesky program.

on a heterogeneous network are the two fundamental inputs to the Hence environment.

With the Hence graphics interface implemented on a workstation, a user can develop a parallel program as a computational graph; the nodes in the graph represent the computations to be performed and the arcs represent the dependencies between the computations. From this graphical representation, Hence can generate a lower level portable program, which when executed will perform the computations specified by the graph in an order consistent with the dependencies specified. This programming environment allows for a high-level description of the parallel algorithm and, when the high-level description is translated into a common programming language, permits portable program execution. Thus the algorithm developer has an abstract model of computation that can bind effectively to a wide variety of parallel processors. We confined specific machine intrinsics to the tool's internal workings to provide a common user interface to various parallel processors.

Another problem facing the developers of algorithms and software for parallel computers is performance analysis of the resulting programs. Performance bugs are often far more difficult to detect and overcome than the synchronization and data-dependency bugs normally associated with parallel programs. We have developed a fairly sophisticated postprocessing performance-analysis tool for the Hence graphics programming interface. This tool is quite useful in understanding the execution flow and processor utili-

zation in a parallel program.

Hence gives the programmer a higher level environment for using heterogeneous networks. The Hence philosophy of parallel programming is to have the programmer explicitly specify the parallelism of a computation and to automate, as much as possible, the tasks of writing, compiling, executing, debugging, and analyzing the parallel computation. Central to Hence is an X Window interface that the programmer uses to perform these functions (see Figure 4).

The Hence environment contains a compose tool that lets the user explicitly specify parallelism by drawing a graph of the parallel application. (If an X Window interface is not available, the user can input textual graph descriptions.)

Each node in a Hence graph represents a procedure written in either Fortran or C. The procedure can be a subroutine from an established library or a special-purpose subroutine supplied by the user. Arcs between nodes represent data dependency and control flow. A dependency arc from one node to another represents the fact that the arc's tail node must run before its head. Data is sent to a node from its ancestors in the graph (usually its parents).

In addition to simple nodes, four types of control constructs are available in the Hence graph language. The first represents looping, the second conditional dependency, the third a fan-out to a variable number of identical subgraphs, and the fourth pipelining. The graph can contain loops around subgraphs that execute a variable number of times on the basis of the expression in the loop construct. Using a conditional construct, Hence can execute or bypass a section of the graph on the basis of an expression evaluated at runtime. A variable fan-out (and subsequent fan-in) construct is available while composing the graph. The fan-out's width is specified as an expression evaluated at runtime. This construct is similar to a *parallel-do* construct found in several parallel Fortrans. In pipelined sections, when a node finishes with one set of input data, it reruns with the next piece of pipelined data.

Once users specify the dynamic graph,

they use a configuration tool in the Hence environment to specify the configuration of machines that will compose the parallel virtual machine. The configuration tool also helps users set up a cost matrix that determines which machine can perform which task and gives priority to certain machines. Hence uses this cost matrix at runtime to determine the most effective machine on which to execute a particular procedure in the graph.

The Hence environment also contains a build tool to perform three tasks. First, by analyzing the graph, Hence automatically generates the parallel program using PVM calls for all the communication and synchronization required by the application. Second, by knowing the desired PVM configuration, Hence automatically compiles the node procedures for the various heterogeneous architectures. Finally, the build tool installs the executable modules on the particular machines in the PVM configuration.

The execute tool in the Hence environment starts the requested virtual machine and begins application execution. During execution, Hence automatically maps procedures to machines in the heterogeneous network on the basis of the cost matrix and the Hence graph. Trace and scheduling information saved during execution can be displayed in real time or replayed later.

The Hence environment has a trace tool that enables visualization of the parallel run. The trace tool is X Window based and consists of three windows. One window shows a representation of the network and machines underlying PVM. This display illuminates icons of the active machines with different colors, depending on whether they are computing or communicating. Under each icon is a list of the node procedures mapped to this machine at any given instant. The second window displays the user's graph of the application, which changes dynamically to show the actual paths and parameters taken during a run. The nodes in the graph change colors to indicate the various activities in each procedure. The third window shows a histogram of processor utilization. Figure 5 on the next page shows a snapshot of the trace tool in action.

In addition to discovering mistakes in the graph specification, this representation helps expose more subtle aspects of the executing program, such as load balancing and network speeds. For example, the graph produced by Hence shows noticeable differences from the abstract user-specified graph. The Hence graph may expose inherent serial bottlenecks in the algorithm or a problem

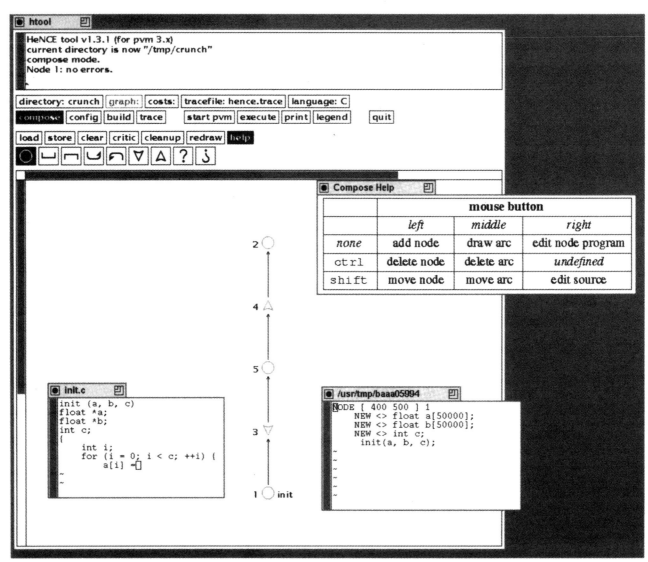

Figure 4. Composing a parallel program in the Hence environment.

with various networks used by the computation.

Our goals here are simple: to be able to schedule and trace the execution flow within an application and to understand where bottlenecks occur. In the past, users have monitored performance using a timing routine. This approach has a number of limitations in the parallel setting. We want an animation of runtime behavior that visualizes the parallel parts in execution as the application is running. We would like to know what performance issues arise during execution and what bottlenecks develop, and to see where programming errors cause a parallel program to get into trouble.

A main advantage of sequential debuggers is that they show the point of failure. In fact, many programmers resort to debuggers only when they are mystified about the point of failure, for example, dividing by zero or dereferencing a null pointer. In a parallel program there may be multiple failures; or, perhaps more perplexing, one part of the program may crash while other parts continue executing for some time. An advantage of the Hence trace display is that its two-dimensional display can inform the programmer of such problems. If part of a Hence program fails and other parts continue to execute, the trace tool displays the program node failure but continues to display the progress of other program nodes as they execute.

The trace animation is also important in performance tuning. Almost all the machines used with Hence are multitasking, and this leads to unpredictable execution-time profiles. The trace animation provided by Hence shows the programmer in real time how the program is progressing. From this animation, a programmer can analyze a program's behavior and tune it to better match the execution environment. For instance, a scientist using a network of

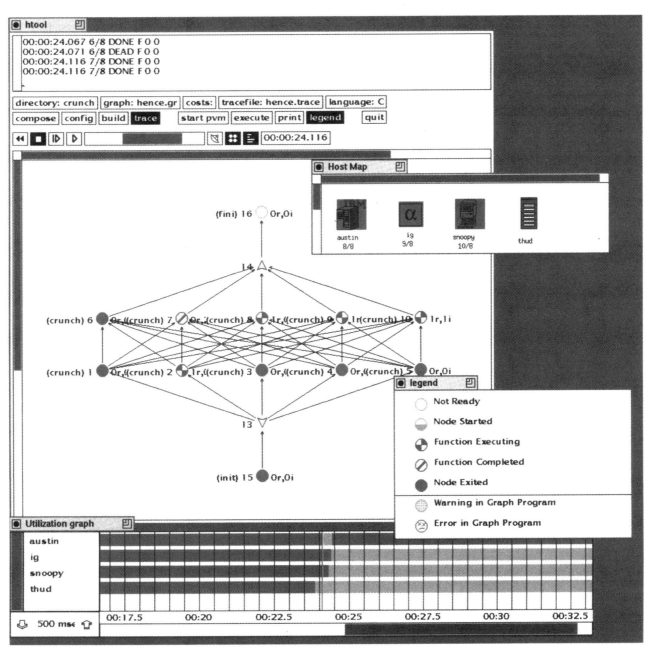

Figure 5. Tracing a parallel program in Hence.

55

workstations along with a Cray supercomputer may realize that during certain periods of the day it is more productive to map fewer processes to the Cray because it is heavily loaded. The Hence trace tools make this kind of information intuitively obvious. Moreover, Hence mapping is easily adjusted via the cost matrix. The user's program need not be recompiled during tuning.

The Hence tool evolved naturally as we programmed various parallel machines. We were motivated primarily by the lack of uniformity and the limited capabilities offered by vendors for explicit parallel programming. Our experience with Hence has been encouraging. We do not view it as a "solution" to the software problem we face in parallel programming. However, we think it will be useful in the short term, and perhaps it will have some influence on the development of a long-term solution.

The focus of our work is to provide a paradigm and graphical support tools for programming a heterogeneous network of computers as a single resource. PVM and its auxiliary tools Xab and Hence help the user effectively use a heterogeneous computer network to solve scientific applications.

PVM, Xab, and Hence are active research projects and continue to evolve. Many of Hence's features will find their way into tools like Xab that eventually will fit directly into the PVM framework. We have already built prototype systems that are in use today.

There is a critical need for standards and tools for today's high-performance computer systems. By building prototype tools as outlined here and listening to users' feedback, we hope to provide an easy-to-use, portable system for heterogeneous computing. Many significant research issues about this approach to parallel programming remain. ∎

Acknowledgments

We thank Robert Manchek, Keith Moore, and James Plank for their contributions to PVM, Xab, and Hence. This work was supported in part by the Applied Mathematical Sciences subprogram of the Office of Energy Research, US Department of Energy, under contract DE-AC05-84OR21400, and in part by the National Science Foundation Science and Technology Center Cooperative Agreement No. CCR-8809615.

References

1. G.A. Geist and V.S. Sunderam, "Experiences with Network-Based Concurrent Computing on the PVM System," *Concurrency: Practice and Experience*, Vol. 4, No. 4, June 1992, pp. 293-311.

2. J.C. Browne, M. Azam, and S. Sobek, "CODE: A Unified Approach to Parallel Programming," *IEEE Software*, Vol. 6, No. 4, July 1989, pp. 10-18.

3. O. Babaoglu et al., "Paralex: An Environment for Parallel Programming in Distributed Systems," *Proc. 1992 Int'l Conf. Supercomputing*, ACM Press, New York, July 1992, pp. 178-187.

4. K.P. Birman and T.A. Joseph, "Reliable Communication in the Presence of Failures," *ACM Trans. Computer Systems*, Vol. 5, No. 1, Feb. 1987, pp. 47-76.

5. E. Lusk et al., *Portable Programs for Parallel Processors*, Holt, Rinehart, and Winston, New York, 1987.

6. J. Flower, A. Kolawa, and S. Bharadwaj, "The Express Way to Distributed Processing," *Supercomputing Review*, May 1991, pp. 54-55.

7. N. Carriero and D. Gelernter, "How to Write Parallel Programs: A Guide to the Perplexed," *ACM Computing Surveys*, Sept. 1989, pp. 323-357.

8. M. Simmons and R. Koskela, *Performance Instrumentation and Visualization*, ACM Press, New York, 1990.

9. M. Heath and J. Etheridge, "Visualizing the Performance of Parallel Programs," *IEEE Software*, Vol. 8, No. 5, Sept. 1991, pp. 29-39.

10. D.A. Reed et al., "Scalable Performance Environments for Parallel Systems," *Proc. Sixth Distributed-Memory Computing Conf.*, Q. Stout and M. Wolfe, eds., IEEE CS Press, Los Alamitos, Calif., Order No. 2290, 1991, pp. 562-569.

11. V. Herrarte and E. Lusk, "Studying Parallel Program Behavior with Upshot," Tech. Report ANL-91/15, Argonne Nat'l Laboratory, Mathematics and Computer Science Division, Aug. 1991.

12. B. Bruegge, "A Portable Platform for Distributed-Event Environments," *ACM SIGPlan Notices*, Vol. 26, No. 12, Dec. 1991, pp. 184-193.

Adam Beguelin holds a joint appointment at Carnegie Mellon University's school of computer science and the Pittsburgh Supercomputing Center. His primary interests are the design and development of programming tools and environments for high-performance parallel and distributed computing.

Beguelin received his PhD in computer science from the University of Colorado.

Jack Dongarra holds a joint appointment as professor of computer science at the University of Tennessee and as distinguished scientist in the Mathematical Sciences Section at Oak Ridge National Laboratory. He specializes in numerical algorithms in linear algebra, parallel computing, use of advanced computer architectures, programming methodology, and tools for parallel computers. He was involved in the design and implementation of the software packages Eispack, Linpack, Blas, Lapack, and PVM/Hence.

Al Geist leads the computer science group in the Mathematical Sciences Section at Oak Ridge National Laboratory. His research interests are parallel and distributed processing, scientific computing, and high-performance numerical software.

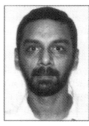

Vaidy Sunderam is a professor in the Department of Mathematics and Computer Science at Emory University. His research interests include parallel and distributed processing, particularly high-performance concurrent computing in heterogeneous networked environments.

Sunderam received a PhD in computer science from the University of Kent in Canterbury, England, in 1986.

Questions regarding this article can be directed to Al Geist at Oak Ridge National Laboratory, PO Box 2008, Oak Ridge, TN 37831-3153; Internet, pvm@msr.epm.ornl.gov.

Seema Hiranandani, Ken Kennedy
Chau-Wen Tseng

COMPILING FORTRAN D

for MIMD Distributed-Memory Machines

arallel computing represents the only plausible way to continue to increase the computational power available to scientists and engineers. Parallel computers, however, are not likely to be widely successful until they are easy to program. A major component in the success of vector supercomputers is the ability of scientists to write Fortran programs in a "vectorizable" style and expect vectorizing compilers to automatically produce efficient code [8, 35]. The resulting programs are easily maintained, debugged, and ported across different vector machines.

Compare this with the current situation for programming parallel machines. Scientists wishing to use such machines must rewrite their programs in an extension of Fortran that explicitly reflects the architecture of the underlying machine. *Multiple-instruction, multiple-data* (MIMD) shared-memory machines such as the Cray Research Y-MP C90 are programmed with explicit synchronization and parallel loops found in Parallel Computing Forum (PCF) Fortran [24]. *Single-instruction, multiple-data* (SIMD) machines such as the Thinking Machines CM-2 are programmed using parallel array constructs found in Fortran 90 [3].

MIMD distributed-memory machines such as the Intel Paragon provide the most difficult programming model. Users must write message-passing Fortran 77 programs that deal with separate address spaces, synchronizing processors, and communicating data using messages. The process is time-consuming, tedious, and error-prone. Significant increases in source code size are not only common but expected.

Because parallel programs are extremely machine-specific, scientists are discouraged from utilizing

parallel machines because they risk losing their investment whenever the program changes or a new architecture arrives. We propose to solve this problem by developing the compiler technology needed to establish a machine-independent programming model. It must be easy to use, yet perform with acceptable efficiency on different parallel architectures, at least for data-parallel scientific codes.

The question is whether any existing Fortran dialect suffices. Parallel Computing Fortran is undesirable because it is easy to inadvertently write programs with data races that produce indeterminate results. Message-passing Fortran 77 is portable, but difficult to use. Fortran 90 is promising, but may not be sufficiently flexible. What all these languages lack is a way to specify the decomposition and placement of data in the program.

We find that selecting a data decomposition is one of the most important intellectual steps in developing data-parallel scientific codes. Though many techniques have been developed for automatic data decomposition, we feel that the compiler will not be able to choose an efficient data decomposition for all programs. To be successful, the compiler needs additional information not present in vanilla Fortran. Most parallel programming languages, however, provide no support for data decomposition [27].

For these reasons, we have developed an enhanced version of Fortran that introduces data decomposition specifications. We call the extended language Fortran D, where "D" suggests data, decomposition, or distribution. As shown in Figure 1, we believe that if a Fortran D program is written in a data-parallel programming style with reasonable data decompositions, it can be implemented efficiently on a variety of parallel architectures. We should note that our goal in designing Fortran D is not to support the most general data decompositions possible. Instead, our intent is to provide data decompositions that are both powerful enough to express data parallelism in scientific programs, and simple enough to permit the compiler to produce efficient programs.

An essential part of the research program is demonstrating a compiler technology capable of achieving both expressive power and efficiency in the generated code. To that end, we have embarked on a program to implement Fortran D for several different architectures. The most mature implementation, which we have been pursuing for over two years, is for MIMD distributed-memory machines. In this article we describe the design of that compiler. Its goal is to automate the task of deriving node programs based on the data decomposition. For these machines, it is particularly important to reduce both communication and load imbalance. We present a code generation strategy based on the concept of *data dependence* [23] that unifies and extends previous techniques.

The remainder of this article presents the data decomposition specifications in Fortran D, basic compiler analysis and code generation algorithms, and compiler optimizations to reduce communication

cost and exploit pipeline parallelism. We conclude with a comparison to related work and a description of the current status of the compiler.

Fortran D Language

The data decomposition problem can be approached by considering the two levels of parallelism in data-parallel applications. First, there is the question of how arrays should be *aligned* with respect to one another, both within and across array dimensions. We call this the *problem mapping* induced by the structure of the underlying computation. It represents the minimal requirements for reducing data movement for the program given an unlimited number of processors, and is largely independent of any machine considerations. The alignment of arrays in the program depends on the natural fine-grained parallelism defined by individual members of data arrays.

Second, there is the question of how arrays should be *distributed* onto the actual parallel machine. We call this the *machine mapping* caused by translating the problem onto the finite resources of the machine. It is affected by the topology, communication mechanisms, size of local memory, and number of processors in the underlying machine. The distribution of arrays in the program depends on the coarse-grained parallelism defined by the physical parallel machine.

Fortran D provides data decomposition specifications for these two levels of parallelism using DECOMPOSITION, ALIGN, and DISTRIBUTE statements. A decomposition is an abstract problem or index domain; it does not require any storage. Each element of a decomposition represents a unit of computation. The DECOMPOSITION statement declares the name, dimensionality, and size of a decomposition for later use.

The ALIGN statement is used to map arrays onto decompositions. Arrays mapped to the same decomposition are automatically aligned

with one another. Alignment can take place either within or across dimensions. The alignment of arrays to decompositions is specified by placeholders in the subscript expressions of both the array and decomposition. Perfect alignment results if no subscripts are used. In the following example,

REAL A(N,N)
DECOMPOSITION D(N,N)
ALIGN A(I,J) with D(J−2,I+3)

D is declared to be a 2D decomposition of size $N \times N$. Array A is then aligned with respect to D with the dimensions permuted and offsets specified within each dimension.

After arrays have been aligned with a decomposition, the DISTRIBUTE statement maps the decomposition to the finite resources of the physical machine. Distributions are specified by assigning an independent *attribute* to each dimension of a decomposition. Predefined attributes are BLOCK, CYCLIC, and BLOCK_CYCLIC. The symbol ":" marks dimensions that are not distributed. Choosing the distribution for a decomposition maps all arrays aligned with the decomposition to the machine. Scalars and unaligned arrays are replicated (*i.e.*, owned by all processors).

In the following example, distributing decomposition D by (:,BLOCK) results in a column partition of arrays aligned with D. Distributing D by (CYCLIC,:) partitions the rows of D in a round-robin fashion among processors. These sample data alignment and distributions are shown in Figure 2.

DECOMPOSITION D(N,N)
DISTRIBUTE D(:,BLOCK)
DISTRIBUTE D(CYCLIC,:)

Note that data distribution does not subsume alignment. For instance, the DISTRIBUTE statement alone cannot specify that one 2D array be mapped with the transpose of another.

Many previous researchers have supplied data decomposition extensions [7, 22, 28, 30, 32, 37]. Because its goal is to support both SIMD and MIMD architectures, Fortran D is the first language to implement both alignment and distribution specifications. Fortran D also provides a FORALL loop, irregular data distribution, and dynamic data decomposition (i.e., changing the alignment or distribution of a decomposition at any point in the program). The complete language is described in detail elsewhere [10].

Fortran D Compiler

The two major steps in writing a data-parallel program are selecting a data decomposition and using it to derive node programs with explicit data movement. We leave the task of selecting a data decomposition to the user or to automatic tools. The Fortran D compiler automates the second step by generating node programs with explicit communication for a given data decomposition.

The main goal of the compiler is to exploit parallelism and reduce communication cost. It translates a Fortran D program into a *single-program, multiple-data* (SPMD) program with explicit message-passing that executes directly on the nodes of the distributed-memory machine. The compiler partitions the program using the *owner computes* rule, by which each processor computes values of data it owns [7, 28, 37]. The compiler is subdivided into three major phases—program analysis, program optimization, and code generation. The structure of the compiler is shown in Figure 3.

Program Analysis

Dependence Analysis. Dependence analysis is the compile-time analysis of control flow and memory accesses to determine a statement execution order that preserves the meaning of the original program. A *data dependence* between the two references R_1 and R_2 indicates that they read or write a common memory location in a way that requires their execution order to be maintained [23]. We call R_1 the *source* and R_2 the *sink* of the dependence if R_1 must be executed before R_2. If R_1 is a write and R_2 is a read, we call the result a *true* (or *flow*) dependence.

Dependences may be either loop-independent or loop-carried. *Loop-independent* dependences occur on the same loop iteration;

loop-carried dependences occur on different iterations of a particular loop. The *level* of a loop-carried dependence is the depth of the loop carrying the dependence [1]. Loop-independent dependences have infinite depth. The number of loop iterations separating the source and sink of the loop-carried dependence may be characterized by a dependence *distance* or *direction* [34].

Dependence analysis is vital to shared-memory vectorizing and parallelizing compilers. We show that it is also highly useful for guiding compiler optimizations for distributed-memory machines. The prototype Fortran D compiler is being developed in the context of the ParaScope programming environment and incorporates the analysis capabilities described in the following paragraphs [6, 21].

Scalar dataflow analysis. Control flow, control dependence, and live range information are computed during the scalar dataflow analysis

Figure 1. Fortran dialects and machine architectures

Figure 2. Fortran D data decomposition specifications

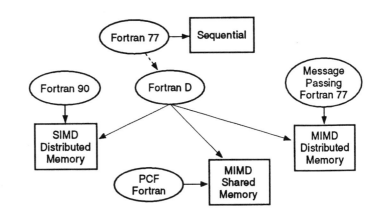

DECOMPOSITION D(N,N)

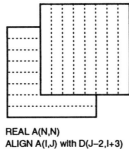

REAL A(N,N)
ALIGN A(I,J) with D(J−2,I+3)

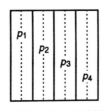

DISTRIBUTE D(:,BLOCK)

DISTRIBUTE D(CYCLIC,:)

phase. In addition, scalar and array variables are labeled *private* with respect to a loop if their values are used only within the current loop iteration; this is useful for eliminating unnecessary computation and communication.

Symbolic analysis. Constant propagation, auxiliary induction variable elimination, expression folding, and loop invariant expression recognition are performed during the symbolic analysis phase of the Fortran D compiler. The goal of symbolic analysis is to provide a simplified program representation for the Fortran D compiler that improves program analysis and optimization. Consider the following example:

```
do i = 1,n-1
    F(i) = F(i)/B(n)
enddo
```

If constant propagation is able to produce a constant value for n, or if n is identified as a loop-invariant expression, the Fortran D compiler can communicate $B(n)$ with an efficient *broadcast* preceding the loop.

Symbolic analysis also recognizes *reductions,* operations such as SUM, MIN, or MAX that are both commutative and associative. Once identified, reductions may be executed locally in parallel and the results combined efficiently using collective communication routines. Reduction operations are tagged during symbolic analysis for later use.

Dependence testing. Dependence testing determines the existence of data dependences between array references by examining their subscript expressions. Dependences found are characterized by their dependence level, as well as by distance and direction vectors. This information is used to guide subsequent compiler analysis and optimization.

Data Decomposition Analysis. The Fortran D compiler requires a new type of program analysis to generate the proper program—it must

1. Program analysis
  (a) Dependence analysis
  (b) Data decomposition analysis
  (c) Partitioning analysis
  (d) Communication analysis
2. Program optimization
  (a) Message vectorization
  (b) Collective communications
  (c) Run-time processing
  (d) Pipelined computations
3. Code generation
  (a) Program partitioning
  (b) Message generation
  (c) Storage management

Figure 3. Fortran D compiler structure

determine the data decomposition for each reference to a distributed array.

Reaching decomposition. Because data access patterns may change between program phases, Fortran D provides dynamic data decomposition by permitting executable ALIGN and DISTRIBUTE statements to be inserted at any point in a program. This complicates the job of the Fortran D compiler, since it must know the decomposition of each array.

We define *reaching decompositions* to be the set of decomposition specifications that may reach an array reference aligned with the decomposition; it may be calculated in a manner similar to *reaching definitions.* The Fortran D compiler will apply both intra- and interprocedural analysis to calculate reaching decompositions for each reference to a distributed array. If multiple decompositions reach a procedure, runtime or node-splitting techniques such as *cloning* may be required to generate the proper code for the program.

Partitioning Analysis. After data-decomposition analysis is performed, the program-partitioning analysis phase of the Fortran D compiler divides the overall data and computation among processors. This is accomplished by first partitioning all arrays onto processors, then using the owner computes rule to derive the functional decomposition of the program. We begin with some useful definitions.

Iteration and index sets, RSDs. An *iteration set* is simply a set of loop iterations—it describes a section of the work space. An *index set* is a set of locations in an array—it describes a section of the data space. In many cases, the Fortran D compiler can construct iteration or index sets using *regular section descriptors* (RSDs), a compact representation of rectangular sections (with some constant step) and their higher dimension analogs [14]. The union and intersection of RSDs can be calculated inexpensively, making them highly useful for the Fortran D compiler.

In this article we will write RSDs as $[l_i:u_i:s_i, \ldots]$, where l_i, u_i, and s_i indicate the lower bound, upper bound, and the step of the ith dimension of the RSD, respectively. A default unit step is assumed if not explicitly stated. In loop nests or multidimensional arrays, the leftmost dimension of the RSD corresponds to the outermost loop or the leftmost array dimension. The other dimensions are listed in order.

Global vs. local indices. Because the Fortran D compiler creates SPMD node programs, all processors must possess the same array declarations. This forces all processors to adapt *local indices.* Figure 4 is an example illustrating the program and the node program produced when array A is block-distributed across four processors.

The local indices for A on each processor are all [1:25], even though the equivalent global indices for A are [1:25], [26:50], [51:75], and [76:100] on processors 1 through 4, respectively. A similar conversion of loop indices may also occur, with the global loop indices [1:100] translated to the local loop indices [1:25].

Local index sets. As the first step in partitioning analysis, the Fortran D compiler uses the Fortran D statements associated with the reaching decomposition to calculate the *local index set* of each array—the local array section owned by every processor. This creates the data partition used in the program.

We demonstrate the analysis required to partition the Jacobi code shown in Figure 5. For this and all future examples we will be compiling for a four-processor machine. In the example, both arrays A and B are aligned identically with decomposition D, so they have the same distribution as D. Because the first dimension of D is local and the second dimension is block-distributed, the local index set for both A and B on each processor (in local indices) is [1:100,1:25].

Local iteration sets. Once the local index set for each array has been calculated, the Fortran D compiler uses it to derive the functional decomposition of the program. We define the *local iteration set* of a reference R on a processor to be the set of loop iterations that cause R to access data owned by the processor. It can be calculated by applying the inverse of the array subscript functions to the local index set of R, then intersecting the result with the iteration set of the enclosing loops.

The calculation of local index and iteration sets is vital to the partitioning analysis of the Fortran D compiler. When applying the owner computes rule, the set of loop iterations on which a processor must execute an assignment statement is exactly the local iteration set of the left-hand side (*lhs*). The Fortran D compiler can thus partition the computation by assigning iteration sets to each statement based on its *lhs*.

To demonstrate the algorithm, we will calculate the local iteration set for the assignment statement S_1 in the Jacobi example. Remember that the local index set of A is [1:100,1:25]. First we apply to it the inverse of the subscript functions of the *lhs*, $A(i, j)$. This yields the unbounded local iteration set [:,1:25,1:100]. The first entry is ":"

since all iterations of the k loop access local elements of A. The inverse subscript functions cause the j and i loops to be mapped to [1:25] and [1:100], respectively.

Next we intersect the unbounded iteration set with the actual bounds of the enclosing loops, since these are the only iterations that actually exist. The iteration set of the loop nest (in global indices) is [1:*time*,2:99,2:99]. Converting it into local indices for each processor and performing the intersection yields the following local iteration sets for each processor (in local indices):

$Proc(1) =$
    $[1 : time, 2 : 25, 2 : 99]$
$Proc(2 : 3) =$
    $[1 : time, 1 : 25, 2 : 99]$
$Proc(4) =$
    $[1 : time, 1 : 24, 2 : 99]$

Similar analysis produces the same local iteration sets for statement S_2. Note how the local indices calculated for the local index set of each array have been used to derive the local indices for the local iteration set. The calculation of local index and iteration sets is described in greater detail elsewhere [17].

Handling boundary conditions. Because alignment and distribution specifications in Fortran D are fairly simple, local index sets and their derived iteration sets may usually be calculated at compile time. In fact, in most regular computations local index and iteration sets are identical for every processor except for boundary conditions. When boundary conditions for each array dimension or loop are independent, as in the Jacobi example, the Fortran D compiler can store each boundary condition separately. This avoids the need to calculate and store a different result for each processor.

We may summarize independent boundary conditions for iteration or index sets as *pre*, *mid*, and *post* sets for each loop or array dimension. The mid-set describes the interior uniform case. The pre- and

post- iteration sets describe the boundary conditions encountered and their positions. These sets are represented in the Fortran D compiler by *augmented* iteration sets. Instead of a single section, each dimension of the augmented iteration set contains three component sections for the pre-, mid-, and post-sets as well as their positions.

Because boundary conditions for iteration and index sets can be handled in the same manner, we will restrict our discussion to an example case for iteration sets. When partitioning the Jacobi example, the *pre-*, *mid-*, and *post*-iteration sets are calculated by the Fortran D compiler as illustrated in Figure 6.

In the *augmented* RSD representing the pre-, mid-, and post-iteration sets, "@" indicates the position for each pre- or post-set. If an interior processor is causing a boundary condition, processors between it and the edge will not be assigned loop iterations. A pre- or post-iteration set may also be empty if that boundary condition does not exist.

The iteration set for each processor is calculated by taking the Cartesian product of the pre-, mid-, and post-iteration sets for each dimension of the augmented iteration set. Unfortunately, not all boundary conditions may be succinctly represented by augmented iteration sets. In the worst case the Fortran D compiler is forced to derive and store an individual index or iteration set for each processor.

Private variables and reductions. Statements performing assignments to scalar and replicated array variables present a special challenge for the Fortran D compiler. Naive application of the *owner computes* rule would cause every processor to execute the assignment on all iterations. The assignment, however, can often be partitioned because its value is used only in the current loop iteration. These cases are readily recognized, since the variable being assigned will have been labeled *private* during dependence analysis.

To partition statement S, the Fortran D compiler calculates the union of the iteration sets of all statements that use S. These statements can be identified by tracking all true dependence edges with S as its source. This union becomes the iteration set for S. The process is simplified if the iteration sets are calculated in reverse order for statements in each loop nest.

For instance, consider the loop in Figure 7. Because QA is a replicated scalar, the *owner computes* rule would assign all loop iterations as the iteration set for statement S_1. Since the only use of QA occurs in the same loop iteration, it is classified as a private variable. The Fortran D compiler can thus assign S_1 the same iteration set as S_2, the only statement containing a true dependence with S_1 as its source.

In other cases, a statement or group of statements will be marked during dependence analysis as performing a *reduction*. To parallelize the reduction, an iteration set that partitions the computation across processors should be selected. To reduce data movement, the Fortran D compiler may partition the computation using the local iteration set of a variable on the right-hand side (*rhs*). Communication will later be inserted to accumulate the partial results.

Communication Analysis. Once partitioning analysis determines how data and work are partitioned across processors, communication analysis determines which variable references cause nonlocal data accesses.

Computing nonlocal index sets. In this phase, all *rhs* references to distributed arrays are examined. For each *rhs*, the Fortran D compiler constructs the index set accessed by each processor. The index set is computed by applying the subscript functions of the *rhs* to the local iteration set assigned to the statement. The local index set is subtracted from the resulting RSD to check whether the reference accesses

nonlocal array locations. If only local accesses occur, the *rhs* reference may be discarded. Otherwise the RSD representing the *nonlocal index set* accessed by the *rhs* is retained.

If boundary conditions exist for the local iteration set of the statement, the Fortran D compiler must compute the index set for each group of processors assigned different iteration sets. In the worst case the index set for each processor must be calculated separately.

We show how index sets are computed for the Jacobi example. We first consider the four *rhs* references to B in statement S_1. The iteration set boundary conditions cause processors to be separated into three groups. The group of interior processors, $Proc(2:3)$, have the local iteration set [1:*time*,1:25,2:99]. This derives the following index sets:

$$B(i, j - 1) = [2:99, 0:24]$$
$$B(i - 1, j) = [1:98, 1:25]$$
$$B(i + 1, j) = [3:100, 1:25]$$
$$B(i, j + 1) = [2:99, 2:26]$$

Since the local index set for B is [1:100,1:25], $B(i - 1, j)$ and $B(i + 1, j)$ cause only local accesses and may be ignored. However, $B(i, j - 1)$ and $B(i, j + 1)$ access nonlocal locations [2:99,0] and [2:99,26], respectively. Both references are marked and their nonlocal index sets stored.

Computing the index sets using the local iteration sets for the other two group, $Proc(1)$ and $Proc(4)$, does not yield additional nonlocal references. Examination of the index sets for the *rhs* reference to $A(i, j)$ in statement S_2 show that only local accesses occur.

Program Optimization

The program optimization phase of the Fortran D compiler utilizes the results of program analysis to improve program performance. Its two primary goals are to exploit parallelism and reduce communication overhead. Most computations are fully data-parallel; parallelism is discovered and utilized during partitioning analysis. More

advanced optimizations are required to exploit parallelism for *pipeline computations*. We defer their discussion to the subsection "Parallelism Optimizations."

In this section we concentrate on optimizations to reduce communication overhead. It is particularly useful to consider *cross-processor* dependences—dependences whose endpoints are executed by different processors.

Message Vectorization. A naive but workable algorithm known as *run-time resolution* inserts guarded *send*

Figure 4. Converting global to local indices

Figure 5. Jacobi

Figure 6. Augmented iteration set for Jacobi

Figure 7. Livermore Kernel 23

```
{* Original program *}    {* SPMD node program *}
REAL A(100)               REAL A(25)
do i = 1, 100             do i = 1, 25
   A(i) = 0.0                A(i) = 0.0
enddo                     enddo
```

```
REAL A(100,100), B(100,100)
DECOMPOSITION D(100,100)
ALIGN A, B with D
DISTRIBUTE D(:,BLOCK)
do k = 1,time
   do j = 2,99
      do i = 2,99
S₁       A(i,j) = (B(i,j-1)+B(i-1,j)+
                   B(i+1,j)+B(i,j+1))/4
      enddo
   enddo
   do j = 2,99
      do i = 2,99
S₂       B(i,j) = A(i,j)
      enddo
   enddo
enddo
```

$$\left[1{:}time, \left\{ \begin{array}{l} pre = [2{:}25] \, @p_1 \\ mid = [1{:}25] \\ post = [1{:}24] \, @p_4 \end{array} \right\}, 2{:}99 \right]$$

```
do l = 1,time
   do j = 2,6
      do k = 2,n
S₁       QA = ZA(k,j+1)*ZR(k,j) +...
S₂       ZA(k,j) = ZA(k,j)+.175*(QA-ZA(k,j))
      enddo
   enddo
enddo
```

and/or *recv* operations directly preceding each nonlocal reference [7, 28, 37]. Unfortunately, this simple approach generates many small messages that prove extremely inefficient due to communication overhead [18, 28].

The most basic communication optimization performed by the Fortran D compiler is *message vectorization*. It uses the level of loop-carried data dependences to calculate whether communication may be legally performed at outer loops. This replaces many small messages with one large message, reducing both message start-up cost and latency.

Algorithm. We use the following algorithm from Balasundaram et al. and Gerndt to calculate the appropriate loop level to insert messages for nonlocal references [4, 12]. We define the *commlevel* for loop-carried dependences to be the level of the dependence. For loop-independent dependences we define it to be the level of the deepest loop common to both the source and sink of the dependence.

To vectorize messages for a *rhs* reference R with a nonlocal index set, we examine all cross-processor true dependences with R as the sink. The deepest commlevel of all such dependences determines the loop level at which the message may be vectorized. If the deepest commlevel is for a dependence carried by loop L, we insert a message tag for R marked *carried* at the header for loop L. This tag indicates that nonlocal data accessed by R must be communicated between iterations of loop L.

Otherwise, the deepest commlevel is for a loop-independent dependence with loop L as the deepest loop enclosing both the source and sink. We insert a tag for R marked *independent* at the header of the next deeper loop enclosing R at level $L + 1$, or at R itself if no such loop exists. This tag indicates that nonlocal data accessed by R must be communicated at this point on each iteration of loop L. Additionally,

the Fortran D compiler may move this tag to any statement in loop L between the source and the sink of the dependence in order to combine messages arising from different references.

Example 1: Jacobi. We illustrate the message vectorization algorithm with three examples. First we examine the Jacobi code in Figure 5. In the communication analysis phase, we have already determined that for the given data decomposition only the *rhs* references $B(i, j - 1)$ and $B(i, j + 1)$ from S_1 access nonlocal locations. The only cross-processor true dependences incident on these references are from the definition to B in S_2. These dependences are carried on the k loop, so we insert their tags (labeled *carried*) at the header of the k loop. The code generation phase will later insert messages for those references inside the k loop.

Example 2: Successive over-relaxation (SOR). In the code for SOR in Figure 8, communication analysis discovers that the *rhs* references $A(i + 1, j)$ and $A(i - 1, j)$ have nonlocal index sets. Since dependence analysis shows that the reference $A(i + 1, j)$ has a cross-processor true dependence carried on the k loop, we insert its tag (labeled *carried*) at the k loop header. The deepest loop-carried true dependence for reference $A(i - 1, j)$ is carried on the i loop, so we insert its tag (also labeled *carried*) at the i loop header.

Example 3: Red-black SOR. In the code in Figure 9, communication analysis discovers that all *rhs* references except $V(i, j)$ possess nonlocal index sets. Dependence analysis, however, shows that the only cross-processor true dependences incident on the *rhs* references for statements S_1 and S_2 are carried on the k loop from S_3 and S_4. The tags for these references (labeled as carried) are inserted at the header of the k loop. During the code generation phase they will generate messages at the beginning of the k loop.

For statements S_3 and S_4, de-

pendence analysis shows that the only cross-processor true dependences incident on their *rhs* references are loop-independent dependences from S_1 and S_2. Their commlevel is set to the k loop because it is the deepest loop enclosing both the source and sink of these dependences. We insert tags (labeled independent) for all *rhs* references in S_3 at its enclosing j loop, since it is the next loop deeper than k enclosing S_3. Similar analysis causes us to insert tags (labeled independent) for all *rhs* references in S_4 at its enclosing j loop.

Communication Selection. Message vectorization determines where communication should be inserted, but the Fortran D compiler also needs to select an efficient communication mechanism. We do this by comparing the subscript expression of each distributed dimension in the *rhs* with its aligned dimension in the *lhs* reference.

Consider the example shown in Figure 10. Message vectorization determines that communication can be extracted from both the i and j loops. The arrays A and B are aligned identically and both dimensions are distributed, so we need to compare the first dimensions with each other, then the second.

In S_1, the aligned dimensions of both the *lhs* and *rhs* references contain constant offsets to the same loop index variable. For these *stencil computations* involving shifts, individual calls to *send* and *recv* primitives are very efficient. This is the case for the Jacobi, SOR, and Red-black SOR examples previously discussed.

Collective Communication. More complicated subscript expressions indicate the need for *collective communication* [25]. For example, the loop-invariant subscript for $B(c, j)$ in S_2 can be efficiently communicated using *broadcast*. Collective communication is also useful in performing transposes for differing alignments between *lhs* and *rhs* references, or accumulating partial results for reductions. Collective communication is selected because these communication patterns are not well-described by individual messages, and can be performed significantly faster using special-purpose routines. For these cases the Fortran D compiler applies techniques pioneered by Li and Chen [25].

Run-time Processing. A third type of communication is needed to communicate the values needed by $B(f(i), j)$ in S_3. Because f is an irregular function (e.g., an index array), the Fortran D compiler cannot precisely determine at compile time what communication is required. However, *inspectors* and *executors* may be created during code generation to combine messages at run-time [22, 26].

Additional Optimizations. The Fortran D compiler also performs other communication optimizations. *Message coalescing* combines messages for different references to the same array. *Message aggregation* combines messages from different arrays to the same processor, at the expense of copying them to a single contiguous buffer.

A number of optimizations seek to hide communication overhead by overlapping messages with computation. *Message pipelining* attempts to hide message transit time by separating *send* and *recv* primitives for element messages; *vector message pipelining* does the same for vectorized messages. *Iteration reordering* extracts local loop iterations to increase the amount of computation that can be overlapped. *Nonblocking messages* rely on architectural support to hide or eliminate message copy times. These optimizations are discussed in detail elsewhere [18, 22, 28].

Communication may also be optimized by considering interactions between all the loop nests in the program. Intra- and inter-procedural dataflow analysis of array sections can show that an assignment to a variable is *live* at a point in the program if there are no intervening assignments to that variable. This array kill information may be used to eliminate or combine redundant messages. Relaxing the owner computes rule may also improve communication.

Code Generation

Once program analysis and optimization is complete, the code generation phase of the Fortran D compiler utilizes information concerning local index and iteration sets, RSDs, and collective communication to create the actual SPMD node program.

Program Partitioning. The Fortran D compiler partitions data by reducing array bounds so that each processor allocates storage only for locally owned data. In addition, the compiler must modify the program to ensure that each processor only executes a statement on loop iterations in its local iteration set.

Loop bounds reduction and *guard introduction* are the two program transformations used to instantiate the computation partition. The Fortran D compiler first reduces the loop bounds so that each processor only executes iterations in the union of local iteration sets for all statements in the loop. It then inserts code to calculate boundary conditions, as shown the bounds generated for the *j* loop in Figure 11.

With multiple statements in the loop, the local iteration set of a statement may be a subset of the reduced loop bounds. For these statements the compiler needs to add explicit guards based on membership tests for the local iteration set of the statement [7, 17, 28, 37].

Message Generation: The Fortran D compiler uses information calculated in the communications analysis and optimization phases to guide message generation. Nonblocking *sends* and blocking *receives* are inserted for the following types of messages:

Loop-independent messages. For messages tagged at loop headers for loop-independent cross-processor dependences, the Fortran D compiler inserts calls to *send* and *recv* primitives preceding the loop header. For messages tagged at individual references, the

---

Figure 8. Successive Over-Relaxation (SOR)

Figure 9. Red-black SOR

Figure 10. Communication selection example

```
REAL A(100,100)
DECOMPOSITION D(100,100)
ALIGN A, B with D
DISTRIBUTE D(BLOCK,:)
do k = 1,time
  do j = 2,99
    do i = 2,99
      A(i,j) = (ω/4)*(A(i,j-1)+A(i-1,j)+
        A(i+1,j)+A(i,j+1))+(1-ω)*A(i,j)
    enddo
  enddo
enddo
```

```
REAL V(N,N)
DECOMPOSITION D(N,N)
ALIGN V with D
DISTRIBUTE D(BLOCK,BLOCK)
do k = 1,time
  {*compute red points*}
  do j = 3,N-1,2
    do i = 3,N-1,2
S₁    V(i,j) = (ω/4)*(V(i,j-1)+V(i-1,j)+
        V(i,j+1)+V(i+1,j))+(1-ω)*V(i,j)
    enddo
  enddo
  do j = 2,N-1,2
    do i = 2,N-1,2
S₂    V(i,j) = (ω/4)*(V(i,j-1)+V(i-1,j)+
        V(i,j+1)+V(i+1,j))+(1-ω)*V(i,j)
    enddo
  enddo
  {*compute black points*}
  do j = 3,N-1,2
    do i = 2,N-1,2
S₃    V(i,j) = (ω/4)*(V(i,j-1)+V(i-1,j)+
        V(i,j+1)+V(i+1,j))+(1-ω)*V(i,j)
    enddo
  enddo
  do j = 2,N-1,2
    do i = 3,N-1,2
S₄    V(i,j) = (ω/4)*(V(i,j-1)+V(i-1,j)+
        V(i,j+1)+V(i+1,j))+(1-ω)*V(i,j)
    enddo
  enddo
enddo
```

```
DECOMPOSITION D(N,N)
ALIGN A, B WITH D
DISTRIBUTE D(BLOCK,BLOCK)
do j = 2,N
  do i = 2,N
S₁    A(i,j) = B(i,j-1)+B(i-1,j)
S₂    A(i,j) = B(c,j)+B(j,i)
S₃    A(i,j) = B(f(i),j)
  enddo
enddo
```

Fortran D compiler inserts *send* and *recv* in the body of the loop preceding the reference. All messages are guarded so that the owners execute *send* and recipients execute *recv*. To calculate the data that must be sent, the Fortran D compiler builds the RSD for the reference at the loop level that the message is generated. This represents data sent on each loop iteration. This strategy is used to generate messages preceding the loop nests enclosing S_3 and S_4 for Red-black SOR in Figure 9.

Loop-carried messages. The situation is more complex for messages representing loop-carried dependences. To calculate the data that must be communicated, we build the RSD for each *rhs* reference at the level of the loop L carrying the dependence. If iterations of L are executed by all processors, the Fortran D compiler inserts calls to *send* and *recv* primitives inside the loop header for L, at the beginning of the loop body. If the iterations of L are partitioned across processors, loop-carried messages represent data synchronization. The compiler inserts calls to *recv* preceding loop L, since they occur before the local iterations of L. Similarly, calls to *send* are inserted after L, since they are executed after the local iterations of L.

We illustrate message generation for two examples. For the Jacobi

---

Figure 11. Generated Jacobi

Figure 12. Generated SOR

```
REAL A(100,25), B(100,0:26)
if (P_local = 1) lb_1 = 2 else lb_1 = 1
if (P_local = 4) ub_1 = 24 else ub_1 = 25
do k = 1,time
   if (P_local > 1) send(B(2:99,1), P_left)
   if (P_local < 4) send(B(2:99,25), P_right)
   if (P_local < 4) recv(B(2:99,26), P_right)
   if (P_local > 1) recv(B(2:99,0), P_left)
   do j = lb_1,ub_1
      do i = 2,99
         A(i,j) = (B(i,j-1)+B(i-1,j)+
                  B(i+1,j)+B(i,j+1))/4
      enddo
   enddo
   do j = lb_1,ub_1
      do i = 2,99
         B(i,j) = A(i,j)
      enddo
   enddo
enddo
```

```
REAL A(0:26,100)
if (P_local = 1) lb_2 = 2 else lb_2 = 1
if (P_local = 4) ub_2 = 24 else ub_2 = 25
do k = 1,time
   if (P_local > 1) send(A(1,2:99), P_left)
   if (P_local < 4) recv(A(26,2:99), P_right)
   do j = 2,99
      if (P_local > 1) recv(A(0,j), P_left)
      do i = lb_2, ub_2
         A(i,j) = (ω/4)*(A(i,j-1)+A(i-1,j)+
                  A(i+1,j)+A(i,j+1))+(1-ω)*A(i,j)
      enddo
      if (P_local < 4) send(A(25,j), P_right)
   enddo
enddo
```

code in Figure 5, recall that the k loop carries true dependences for the *rhs* references in S_1. These messages were tagged at the k loop header as carried. We first compute RSDs for the data that need to be communicated. Boundary conditions cause three RSDs to be generated for each *rhs* reference. Below are the RSDs for the reference $B(i, j + 1)$ at the k loop level.

$Proc(1) = [2 : 99, 3 : 26]$
$Proc(2 : 3) = [2 : 99, 2 : 26]$
$Proc(4) = [2 : 99, 2 : 25]$

We subtract the local index set from these RSDs to determine the RSDs for the nonlocal index set. The nonlocal RSDs for $Proc(1)$ and $Proc(2:3)$ are both $[2:99, 26]$ and therefore combined. The RSD for $Proc(4)$ consists of only local data and is discarded.

The sending processor is determined by computing the owners of the section $[2:99, 26]$ @ $Proc(1:3)$, resulting in $Proc(2:4)$ sending data to their left processors. To compute the data that must be sent, we translate the local indices of the receiving processors to that of the sending processors, obtaining the section $[2:99, 26-25] = [2:99, 1]$. Since loop k is executed by all processors, the messages are inserted at the beginning of the loop body. Messages for $B(i, j - 1)$ are calculated in a similar manner. The communication generated is shown in Figure 11.

Now consider the SOR code depicted in Figure 8. Dependences for $A(i + 1, j)$ are carried on the k loop, causing vectorized messages to be inserted at the beginning of the k loop body as in Jacobi. The communication generated for $A(i - 1, j)$ is more complicated. Boundary conditions and dependences carried by the i loop cause the following three RSDs to be generated at the level of the i loop.

$Proc(1) = [1 : 24, j]$
$Proc(2 :) = [0 : 24, j]$
$Proc(4) = [0 : 23, j]$

The local index set is subtracted from these RSDs to determine the

RSDs for the nonlocal index set, producing the empty set for *Proc*(1). The nonlocal RSDs for both *Proc*(2:3) and *Proc*(4) are [0, *j*] and are combined. This shows that processors 2 through 4 require data from their left neighbor. Iterations of the *i* loop are partitioned, alerting the Fortran D compiler that the *send* for $A(i - 1, j)$ occurs after the last local *i* loop iteration, and the *recv* occurs before the first local *i* loop iteration. It thus inserts the *recv* before the *i* loop and the *send* after the *i* loop, resulting in the code shown in Figure 12.

Collective Communication. During communication optimization, opportunities for reductions and collective communication have been marked separately. Instead of individual calls to *send* and *recv*, the Fortran D compiler inserts calls to the appropriate collective communication routines. Additional communication is also appended following loops containing reductions to accumulate the local results of each reduction.

Run-time Processing. Run-time processing is applied to computations whose nonlocal data requirements are not known at compile time. An *inspector* [26] is constructed to preprocess the loop body at runtime to determine what nonlocal data will be accessed. This in effect calculates the *receive* index set for each processor. A global transpose operation between processors is then used to calculate the *send* index sets. Finally, an *executor* is built to actually communicate the data and perform the computation.

An inspector is the most general way to generate *send* and *receive* sets for references without loop-carried true dependences. Despite the expense of additional communication, experimental evidence from several systems shows that it can improve performance by grouping communication to access nonlocal data outside of the loop nest, especially if the information generated may be reused on later iterations [22, 26].

The inspector strategy is not applicable for unanalyzable references causing loop-carried true dependences. In this case the Fortran D compiler inserts guards to resolve the needed communication and program execution using run-time resolution [7, 28, 37].

Storage Management. One of the major responsibilities of the Fortran D compiler is to select and manage storage for all nonlocal array references. There are three different storage schemes.

Overlaps. Overlaps are expansions of local array sections to accommodate neighboring nonlocal elements [12]. For programs with high locality of reference, overlaps are useful for generating clean code. They are, however, permanent and specific to each array, and thus may require more storage.

Buffers. Buffers avoid the contiguous and permanent nature of overlaps. They are useful when storage for nonlocal data must be reused, or when the nonlocal area is bounded in size but not near the local array section.

Hash tables. Hash tables may be used when the set of nonlocal elements accessed is sparse, as for many irregular computations. They also provide a quick look-up mechanism for arbitrary sets of nonlocal values [19].

The extent of all RSDs representing nonlocal accesses produced during message generation are examined to select the appropriate storage type for each array. If overlaps have been selected, array declarations are modified to take into account storage for nonlocal data. For instance, array declarations in the generated code in Figures 11 and 12 have been extended for overlap regions. If buffers are used, additional buffer array declarations are inserted. Finally, all nonlocal array references in the program are modified to reflect the actual data location selected.

Parallelism Optimizations

This section describes how the For-
tran D compiler exploits parallelism found in *pipelined computations*. We begin by describing some program transformations.

Program Transformations. Shared-memory parallelizing compilers apply program transformations to expose or enhance parallelism in scientific codes, using dependence information to determine their legality and profitability [1, 21, 23, 34]. Program transformations are also useful for distributed-memory compilers. The legality of each transformation is determined in exactly the same manner, since the same execution order must be preserved to retain the meaning of the original program. However, their profitability criteria are now totally different.

Loop Distribution. Loop distribution separates independent statements inside a single loop into multiple loops with identical headers. Loop distribution may be applied only if the statements are not involved in a recurrence and the direction of existing loop-carried dependences are not reversed in the resulting loops [21, 23]. It can separate statements in loop nests with different local iteration sets, avoiding the need to evaluate guards at runtime. Loop distribution may also separate the source and sink of loop-carried or loop-independent cross-processor dependences, allowing individual messages to be combined into a single vector message.

Loop Fusion. Loop fusion combines multiple loops with identical headers into a single loop. It is legal if the direction of existing dependences are not reversed after fusion [23, 34]. Loop fusion can improve data locality, but its main use is to enable loop interchange and stripmining.

Loop Interchange. Loop interchange swaps adjacent loop headers to alter the traversal order of the iteration space. It may be applied only if the source and sink of each dependence are not reversed in the resulting program. This may be de-

INPUT:
    Loop nest $\{L_1,..., L_n\}$ with index variables $\{I_1,..., I_n\}$
    List of all loop-carried true dependences
    Data decomposition of all distributed arrays in loop nest

OUTPUT:
    Loops = Set of cross-processor loops

ALGORITHM:
    Loops ← ∅
    for each loop-carried true dependence between
            references $A(f_1,..., f_m)$ and $A(g_1,..., g_m)$ **do**
        for each distributed dimension k of A **do**
            $\{* f_k$ and g_k are subscripts in dimension k *$\}$
            if $f_k \neq g_k$ **or** f_k is not of form $\alpha I_j + \beta$ **then**
                for each index variable I_j in either f_k or g_k **do**
                    if L_j encloses both references to A **then**
                        Loops ← *Loops* ∪ $\{L_j\}$
                    endif
                endfor
            endif
        endfor
    endfor

Figure 13. Finding cross-processor loops

termined by examining the distance or direction vector associated with each dependence [1, 34].

Strip Mining. Strip mining increases the step size of an existing loop and adds an additional inner loop. The legality of strip-mining followed by loop interchange is determined in the same manner as for *unroll-and-jam* [21]. The Fortran D compiler may apply strip mining in order to reduce storage requirements for computations. It may also be used with loop interchange to help exploit pipeline parallelism, as discussed in the following subsection.

Pipelined Computations. In *loosely synchronous* computations all processors execute SPMD programs in a loose lockstep, alternating between phases of local computation and synchronous global communication [11]. These problems achieve good load balance because all processors are utilized during the computation phase. For instance, Jacobi and Red-black SOR are loosely synchronous. The Fortran D compilation strategy presented so far is well-suited to compiling such programs, since it identifies and inserts efficient vector or collective com-

munication at appropriate points in the program.

A different class of computations, however, contain loop-carried cross-processor data dependences that sequentialize computations over distributed array dimensions. Synchronization is required and processors are forced to remain idle at various points in the computation, resulting in poor load balance. We call these computations, such as SOR, *pipelined.* They present opportunities for optimization to exploit partial parallelism through pipelining, enabling processors to overlap computation with one another (hence the name).

Cross-Processor Loops. The Fortran D compiler identifies pipelined computations using *cross-processor* loops. We classify loops in numeric computations as either time-bound or space-bound. *Time-bound* loops correspond to time steps in the computation, with each iteration accessing much or all of the data space. They are usually outermost loops that need to be executed sequentially. In comparison, *space-bound* loops iterate over the data space, with each iteration accessing part of each array. These loops are usually parallel in data-parallel computations, but may be sequential if they cause a computation *wavefront* to sweep

across the data space.

The Fortran D compiler labels loops as *cross-processor* if they are sequential space-bound loops causing computation wavefronts that cross processor boundaries (i.e., sweep over the distributed dimensions of the data space). Cross-processor loops may be calculated by considering all pairs of array references that cause loop-carried true dependences. If nonidentical subscript expressions occur in a distributed dimension of the array, index variables appearing in the subscript expressions belong to cross-processor loops. The algorithm for calculating cross-processor loops is shown in Figure 13. In most cases, cross-processor loops are loops carrying true dependences whose iterations have been partitioned across processors.

Figure 14 illustrates cross-processor dependences and loops. We denote cross-processor loops as do∗. All loops in the example are space-bound loops that sweep the data space. In Loop 1, the i loop is cross-processor because the computation wavefront sweeps the i dimension across processors. There are no cross-processor loops in Loop 2 because the computation wavefront is internalized and does not cross processor boundaries. In Loop 3 both the i and j loops are cross-processor because the computation wavefront sweeps across processors in both dimensions.

These examples make it clear how cross-processor loops may be used to classify computations. Computations such as Loop 2 that do not possess cross-processor loops are loosely synchronous, since all processors may execute in parallel. Computations such as Loops 1 and 3 that do possess cross-processor loops are pipelined, since processors must wait in turn for computation to be completed.

Exploiting Pipeline Parallelism. Parallelism may be exploited in pipelined computations through *message pipelining*—sending a message when its value is first computed, rather than waiting until its value is needed [28]. Rogers and Pingali applied this optimization to a Gauss-Seidel computation (a special case of SOR) that is distributed cyclically. More sophisticated approaches, however, are usually required.

Figure 15 illustrates the tradeoffs between communication and parallelism that must be considered when compiling pipelined computations. It presents the program text, data space traversal order, and a processor trace for three versions of the computation. In the processor trace, elapsed time proceeds from left to right. The computation for each processor is represented as a solid line, and messages are shown as dashed lines between processors.

In the original program execution order, message vectorization minimizes communication overhead but sequentializes the computation. Applying message pipelin-

Figure 14. Examples of cross-processor dependencies and loops

Figure 15. Examples of pipelined computations

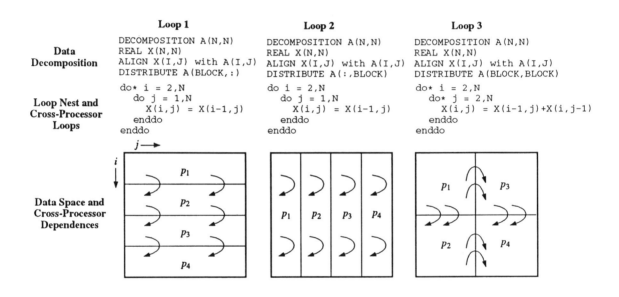

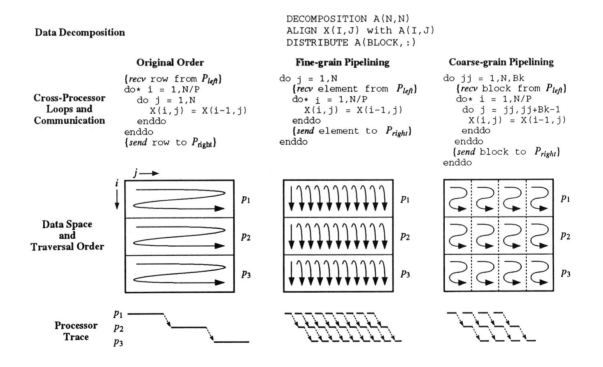

ing alone is insufficient, since only the computation for the last row will be pipelined. The key observation is that for some pipelined computations, the program execution order must also be changed. We present two optimizations to exploit pipeline parallelism. *Fine-grain pipelining* interchanges cross-processor loops as deeply as possible to maximize parallelism. This is a major improvement over sequentialized computation, but incurs the most communication overhead since a message is sent for every nonlocal array element.

Coarse-grained pipelining uses strip mining and loop interchange to adjust the granularity of pipelining. A message is sent for each block of nonlocal data, decreasing communication overhead at the expense of some parallelism. Selecting an efficient block size depends on the data decomposition, processor topology, and ratio of communication to computation cost for the underlying machine. A detailed algorithm is presented elsewhere [18]. Empirical results show that exploiting pipeline parallelism is important for common scientific computations such as tridiagonal solvers.

Related Work
We view the Fortran D compiler as a second-generation distributed-memory compiler that integrates and extends analysis and optimization techniques from many other research projects. It is related to other distributed-memory compilation systems such as AL [33], CM FORTRAN [32], C* [29], DATAPARALLEL C [13], DINO [30], MIMDIZER [15], PANDORE [2], PARAGON [9], and SPOT [31], but mostly builds on the following research projects.

SUPERB is a semiautomatic parallelization tool that supports arbitrary user-specified contiguous BLOCK distributions [12, 37]. It originated *overlaps* as a means to both specify and store nonlocal data accesses. *Exsr* statements are inserted in the program to communi-

cate overlap regions. Data dependence information is then used to apply *loop distribution* and vectorize these statements, resulting in vectorized messages. SUPERB also performs interprocedural analysis and code generation.

Callahan and Kennedy propose distributed-memory compilation techniques based on data dependence [7]. User-defined distribution functions are used to specify the data decomposition for Fortran programs. The compiler inserts *load* and *store* statements to handle data movement, then applies numerous program transformations to optimize guards and messages.

ID NOUVEAU is a functional language enhanced with BLOCK and CYCLIC distributions [28]. Initially, *send* and *receive* statements are inserted to communicate each nonlocal array access. *Message vectorization* is applied to combine messages for previously written array elements. *Loop jamming (fusion)* and *strip mining* are used when writing array elements. Analysis is considerably simplified through the use of write-once arrays called *I-structures*. Global *accumulate* (reduction) operations are supported. Unlike other systems, program partitioning produces distinct programs for each node processor.

CRYSTAL is a high-level functional language compiled to distributed-memory machines using both automatic data decomposition and communication generation [25]. Program analysis and optimization are different because they target a purely functional language. CRYSTAL pioneered the strategy of identifying collective communication opportunities used in the Fortran D compiler.

ASPAR is a Fortran compiler that performs simple dependence analysis using *A-lists* to detect parallel loops [20]. Loop iterations are then partitioned and used to automatically derive data decompositions. A *micro-stencil* based on the computation is used to generate a *macro-stencil*, identifying communication requirements. Collective

communications are also generated.

KALI is the first compiler that supports both regular and irregular computations on MIMD distributed-memory machines [22]. Since dependence analysis is not provided, programmers must declare all parallel loops. Instead of deriving a parallel program from the data decomposition, KALI requires that the programmer explicitly partition loop iterations onto processors using an *on clause*.

ARF is a compiler that automatically generates *inspector* and *executor* loops for run-time preprocessing of programs with BLOCK, CYCLIC, and user-defined irregular distributions [36]. It was motivated by PARTI, a set of runtime library routines that support irregular computations on MIMD distributed-memory machines. PARTI is the first to propose and implement user-defined irregular distributions [26] and a hashed cache for nonlocal values [19].

Comparison with Fortran D
The Fortran D compiler integrates more compiler optimizations than the first-generation research systems described, and in addition possesses two main advantages. First, dependence analysis enables the compiler to exploit parallelism without relying on single-assignment semantics (e.g., CRYSTAL, ID NOUVEAU) or explicitly parallel programs (e.g., KALI, ARF). Precise analysis also allows the compiler to perform more optimizations. Most systems vectorize messages by extracting communication out of parallel regions, but systems such as SUPERB or Fortran D can also vectorize messages in sequential regions such as those found in SOR.

Second, the Fortran D compiler performs its analysis up front and uses the results to drive code generation, unlike transformation-based systems (e.g., Callahan and Kennedy, ID NOUVEAU, SUPERB) that begin by inserting guards and element-wise messages, then apply program transformations and partial evaluation in order to produce more efficient code. This approach is simpler and provides greater flexibility. For instance, the Fortran D compiler may apply program transformations without the possibility of introducing deadlock due to message-reordering.

Conclusions

A usable yet efficient machine-independent parallel programming model is needed to make large-scale parallel machines useful for scientific programmers. We believe that Fortran D, a version of Fortran enhanced with data decompositions, provides such a portable data-parallel programming model. Its success will depend on the effectiveness of the compiler, as well as environmental support for automatic data decomposition and static performance estimation [4, 5, 16].

The current prototype of the Fortran D compiler performs message vectorization, collective communication, fine-grained pipelining, and several other optimizations for block-distributed arrays. Though significant work remains to implement other optimizations presented in this article, preliminary results lead us to believe the Fortran D compiler will generate efficient code for a large class of data-parallel programs with only minimal user effort.

Acknowledgments

The authors wish to thank Vasanth Balasundaram, Geoffrey Fox, Marina Kalem, and Ulrich Kremer for inspiring many of the ideas in this work. We are also grateful to the ParaScope and Fortran D research groups for their assistance in implementing the Fortran D compiler. This research was supported by the Center for Research on Parallel Computation, a National Science Foundation Science and Technology Center. ◖

References

1. Allen, J.R. and Kennedy, K. Automatic translation of Fortran programs to vector form. *ACM Trans. Prog. Lang. Syst. 9*, 4 (Oct. 1987), 491–542.
2. André, F., Pazat, J. and Thomas, H. Pandore: A system to manage data distribution. In *Proceedings of the 1990 ACM International Conference on Supercomputing.* June 1990, Amsterdam, The Netherlands.
3. ANSI X3J3/s8.115. Fortran 90. June 1990.
4. Balasundaram, V., Fox, G., Kennedy, K. and Kremer, U. An interactive environment for data partitioning and distribution. In *Proceedings of the 5th Distributed Memory Computing Conference.* (Apr. 1990, Charleston, S.C.).
5. Balasundaram, V., Fox, G., Kennedy, K. and Kremer, U. A static performance estimator to guide data partitioning decisions. In *Proceedings of the Third ACM SIGPLAN Symposium on Principles and Practice of Parallel Programming.* (Apr. 1991, Williamsburg, Va.).
6. Callahan, D., Cooper, K., Hood, R., Kennedy, K. and Torczon, L. ParaScope: A parallel programming environment. *Int. J. Supercomput. App. 2*, 4 (Winter 1988), 84–99.
7. Callahan, D. and Kennedy, K. Compiling programs for distributed-memory multiprocessors. *J. Supercomput. 2* (Oct. 1988), 151–169.
8. Callahan, D., Kennedy, K. and Kremer, U. A dynamic study of vectorization in PFC. Tech. Rep. TR89-97, Dept. of Computer Science, Rice University, July 1989.
9. Chase, C., Cheung, A., Reeves, A. and Smith, M. Paragon: A parallel programming environment for scientific applications using communication structures. In *Proceedings of the 1991 International Conference on Parallel Processing* (Aug. 1991, St. Charles, Il.).
10. Fox, G., Hiranandani, S., Kennedy, K., Koelbel, C., Kremer, U., Tseng, C. and Wu, M. Fortran D language specification. Tech. Rep. TR 90-141, Dept. of Computer Science, Rice University, Dec. 1990.
11. Fox, G., Johnson, M., Lyzenga, G., Otto, S., Salmon, J. and Walker, D. *Solving Problems on Concurrent Processors,* volume 1. Prentice-Hall, Englewood Cliffs, N.J. 1988.
12. Gerndt, M. Updating distributed variables in local computations. *Concurrency: Practice & Experience 2,* 3 (Sept. 1990), 171–193.
13. Hatcher, P., Quinn, M., Lapadula, A., Seevers, B., Anderson, R. and Jones, R. Data-parallel programming on MIMD computers. *IEEE Trans. Para. Distrib. Syst. 2*, 3 (July 1991), 377–383.
14. Havlak, P. and Kennedy, K. An implementation of interprocedural bounded regular section analysis. *IEEE Trans. Para. Distrib. Syst. 2*, 3 (July 1991), 350–360.
15. Hill, R. MIMDizer: A new tool for parallelization. *Supercomput. Rev. 3*, 4 (Apr. 1990), 26–28.
16. Hiranandani, S., Kennedy, K., Koelbel, C., Kremer, U. and Tseng, C. An overview of the Fortran D programming system. *Languages and Compilers for Parallel Computing, Fourth International Workshop.* (Santa Clara, Calif.) Springer-Verlag, 1992.
17. Hiranandani, S., Kennedy, K. and Tseng, C. Compiler support for machine-independent parallel programming in Fortran D. In J. Saltz and P. Mehrotra, Ed., *Languages, Compilers, and Run-Time Environments for Distributed Memory Machines.* North-Holland, Amsterdam, 1992.
18. Hiranandani, S., Kennedy, K. and Tseng, C. Evaluation of compiler optimizations for Fortran D on MIMD distributed-memory machines. In *Proceedings of the 1992 ACM International Conference on Supercomputing,* (July 1992, Washington, DC).
19. Hiranandani, S., Saltz, J., Mehrotra, P. and Berryman, H. Performance of hashed cache data migration schemes on multicomputers. *J. Para. Distrib. Comput. 12*, 4 (Aug. 1991), 415–422.
20. Ikudome, K., Fox, G., Kolawa, A. and Flowers, J. An automatic and symbolic parallelization system for distributed memory parallel computers. In *Proceedings of the 5th Distributed Memory Computing Conference,* (Apr. 1990, Charleston, S.C.).
21. Kennedy, K., McKinley, K.S. and Tseng, C. Analysis and transformation in the ParaScope Editor. In *Proceedings of the 1991 ACM International Conference on Supercomputing,* (June 1991, Cologne, Germany).
22. Koelbel, C. and Mehrotra, P. Compiling global name space parallel loops for distributed execution. *IEEE Trans. Para. Distrib. Syst. 2*, 4 (Oct. 1991), 440–451.
23. Kuck, D., Kuhn, R., Padua, D.,

Leasure, B. and Wolfe, M.J. Dependence graphs and compiler optimizations. In *Conference Record of the Eighth Annual ACM Symposium on the Principles of Programming Languages.* (Jan. 1981, Williamsburg, Va.).

24. Leasure, B., Ed. *PCF Fortran: Language Definition, version 3.1.* The Parallel Computing Forum, Champaign, Il, Aug. 1990.

25. Li, J. and Chen, M. Compiling communication-efficient programs for massively parallel machines. *IEEE Trans. Para. Distrib. Syst. 2*, 3 (July 1991), 361–376.

26. Mirchandaney, R., Saltz, J., Smith, R., Nicol, D. and Crowley, K. Principles of runtime support for parallel processors. In *Proceedings of the Second International Conference on Supercomputing.* (July 1988, St. Malo, France).

27. Pancake, C. and Bergmark, D. Do parallel languages respond to the needs of scientific programmers? *IEEE Comput. 23*, 12 (Dec. 1990), 13–23.

28. Rogers, A. Pingali, K. Process decomposition through locality of reference. In *Proceedings of the SIGPLAN '89 Conference on Program Language Design and Implementation,* (June 1989, Portland, Ore.).

29. Rose, J., Steele, Jr., G. C*: An extended C language for data parallel programming. In L. Kartashev and S. Kartashev, Eds., *Proceedings of the Second International Conference on Supercomputing,* (May 1987, Santa Clara, Calif.).

30. Rosing, M., Schnabel, R. and Weaver, R. The DINO parallel programming language. *J Para. Distrib. Comput. 13*, 1 (Sept. 1991), 30–42.

31. Socha, D. Compiling single-point iterative programs for distributed memory computers. In *Proceedings of the 5th Distributed Memory Computing Conference,* (Apr. 1990, Charleston, S.C.).

32. Thinking Machines Corporation, Cambridge, Mass. *CM Fortran Reference Manual,* version 5.2-0.6 edition, Sept. 1989.

33. Tseng, P.-S. A parallelizing compiler for distributed memory parallel computers. In *Proceedings of the SIGPLAN '90 Conference on Program Language Design and Implementation,* (June 1990, White Plains, N.Y.).

34. Wolfe, M.J. *Optimizing Supercompilers for Supercomputers.* The MIT Press, Cambridge, Mass., 1989.

35. Wolfe, M.J. Semi-automatic domain decomposition. In *Proceedings of the 4th Conference on Hypercube Concurrent Computers and Applications,* (Mar. 1989, Monterey, Calif.).

36. Wu, J., Saltz, J., Hiranandani, S. and Berryman, H. Runtime compilation methods for multicomputers. In *Proceedings of the 1991 International Conference on Parallel Processing,* (Aug. 1991, St. Charles, Il.).

37. Zima, H., Bast, H.-J. and Gerndt, M. SUPERB: A tool for semi-automatic MIMD/SIMD parallelization. *Parallel Computing, 6* (1988), 1–18.

CR Categories and Subject Descriptors: C.1.2 [**Processor Architectures**]: Multiple Data Stream Architectures (Multiprocessors) — *multiple-instruction-stream, multiple-data-stream processors (MIMD), parallel processors;* D.1.3 [**Software**]: Programming Techniques—*concurrent programming;* D.3.2 [**Programming Languages**]: Language Constructs—*concurrent programming structures;* D.3.4 [**Programming Languages**]: Processors—*code generation, compilers, optimization, preprocessors*

General Terms: Languages, Performance

Additional Key Words and Phrases: concurrent languages; distributed languages; distributed programming; Fortran D; parallel languages; parallel programming

About the Authors:
SEEMA HIRANANDANI is a researcher at the Center for Research on Parallel Computation at Rice University. Current research interests include compilation techniques for distributed-memory multiprocessors and runtime support for irregular computations.

KEN KENNEDY is Noah Harding Professor of computer science at the Computer Science Department at Rice University and director of the Center for Research on Parallel Computation, a National Science Foundation Science and Technolgoy Center. Current research interests include extending techniques developed for automatic vectorization to programming tools for parallel computer systems and high-performance microprocessors.

CHAU-WEN TSENG is a doctoral candidate in the Computer Science Department at Rice University. Current research interests include parallel and distributed systems, optimizing and parallelizing compilers.

Authors' Present Address: Department of Computer Science, Rice University, Houston, TX 77251-1892; email: {seema, ken, tseng}@rice.edu

Chapter 2
Performance Evaluation Techniques

Computer performance may be obtained from the computer system itself by measurement or from an analytic model or by simulation. Measurement is important in performance evaluation to gather real-time system information under various work loads and computing environments. The most important steps of performance measurement are the following:

- decide what to measure,
- construct the basic metrics and select the measurement tools, and
- design the experiments and select the benchmarks.

An analytic model of a computer system is a mathematical representation of the system, consisting of a certain amount of organized information about it under certain assumptions. The deeper our knowledge of a system is, the more precise a model of it we may develop and the easier and more successful the performance evaluation is likely to be. Simulation is an evaluation technique that represents a model of the behavior of a system in the time domain. A simulator, constructed on a computer, is viewed as a system, because it reproduces not only the time behavior of the modeled system but also its structure and organization. Simulation is a key technology for experimental architecture design, especially in the complex area of multiprocessors. An important usage of simulation is to simulate only part of an architecture, such as cache/memory systems. Competitive simulation tools can improve the decision making in a design and shorten the decision path.

The measurement, modeling, and simulation of system performance are of great practical importance to the design of parallel architectures, the development of system software, and the implementation of parallel algorithms. In summary, there are trade-offs in choosing which technique to use — measurement, modeling, or simulation. While measurements are accurate, they require instrumentation of a real system. Analytic models are very efficient but may suffer from not being able to capture accurately all the effects. Simulations can be arbitrarily accurate but suffer from inefficiency, are time-consuming, and yield possibly insufficient results for architecture designs.

Using visualization tools to aid debugging and parallel programming has become very important. As computer graphics provide an easy user interface on various workstations and parallel machines, performance visualization has also become a standard evaluation presentation. This chapter gives an overview of the basic metrics for evaluating, modeling, measuring, and visualizing multiprocessor performance.

The well-known Amdahl's Law gives a simple model showing the general shape of the execution time as a function of the number of processes for an imperfectly parallelized program. This model can be viewed as separating a program into a perfectly parallelized time section and a strictly sequential time section. From this simple model, one can derive two important measures of performance: *speedup* and *efficiency*. The first paper, by Eager, Zahorjan, and Lazowska, investigates — through analytic models and simulations — the trade-off between the speedup and the efficiency that is inherent in a software system. The short paper by Gustafson argues why, in practice, some application programs can achieve higher speedups on parallel machines than the speedups predicted by Amdahl's Law. Also, the paper proposes a new concept of scaled speedup. The next paper, by Nelson, Towsley, and Tantawi, describes a queuing theoretic approach for evaluating parallel systems by considering a parallel job as a bulk of tasks. Also, the paper derives performance results for various scheduling schemes in a parallel system.

Parallel-computing *scalability* may not yet have a commonly accepted definition. However, in scientific computations, people are more interested in knowing if there is a corresponding increase in the performance of a computation as the size of the computing problem and the size of the parallel machine are both increased. The scalability metric proposed in the paper by Grama, Gupta, and Kumar evaluates the performance of an algorithm-machine combination through modeling an isoefficiency function. The isospeed metric proposed in Sun and Rover's paper is a practical metric for a quantitative measurement of the scalability.

The next paper, by Karp and Flatt, applies experimental approaches to performance evaluation. This method is called *benchmarking* of systems, which is to compose a benchmark kernel and a collection of representative application programs. The paper presents a new metric for measuring the performance of parallel algorithms running on parallel architectures and gives the measured performance results by the new metric on various parallel architectures.

The following three papers introduce performance evaluation for architecture design through simulation methods. In evaluating multiprocessor memory and cache system performance, *address tracing* is a powerful method that records sequences of memory and cache addresses referenced by processors during execution. The first of these three papers, by Stunkel, Janssens, and Fuchs, surveys several new address-tracing techniques for both shared-memory and message-passing parallel computers. *Trace-driven simulation* is a more general simulation technique, where one or more application programs are executed, and a complete trace is collected from each. Trace-driven simulation produces the most realistic results, because its inputs are derived from actual programs rather than from statistical models. However, perturbations to the trace data caused by the trace process may affect the simulation results. Another important technique, called *execution-driven simulation*, allows more accurate simulation. This simulation provides detailed performance measurements for an application program and shows how it interacts with the target architecture by interpreting execution operations instruction by instruction. In addition, execution-driven simulation ensures accurate ordering of program events and permits accurate simulation of interconnection network and memory contention and application code process interactions. However, this type of simulation, often computationally intensive, requires a large memory space. The second of the three simulation papers mentioned above is by Davis, Goldschmidt, and Hennessy. It presents a software simulation and tracing system called *Tango*. Tango supports trace-driven simulation, but users have the option of using execution-driven simulation. Finally, the paper by Reinhardt et al. presents the Wisconsin Wind Tunnel simulator, which runs a parallel shared-memory program on a parallel computer (CM-5) and uses execution-driven, distributed, discrete-event simulation to calculate accurately the program execution time.

The need for development of debugging and visualization tools using available window-based graphics tools is critical to the performance evaluation of multiprocessors. The last paper in this chapter, by Heath and Etheridge, overviews the ParaGraph, a performance visualization tool currently run on the Intel hypercube multicomputers. It may be pointed out here that the paper by Beguelin et al. included in Chapter 1 presents a monitoring tool and graphical interface working on top of the PVM software.

Bibliography

Archibald, J., and J.-L. Baer, "Cache Coherence Protocols: Evaluation Using a Multiprocessor Simulation Model," *ACM Trans. Computer Systems*, Vol. 4, Nov. 1986, pp. 273–298.

Berry, M., G. Cybenko, and J. Larson, "Scientific Benchmark Characterizations," *Parallel Computing*, Vol. 17, 1991, pp. 1173–1194.

Brorsson, M., et al., "The CacheMire Test Bench — A Flexible and Effective Approach for Simulation of Multiprocessors," *Proc. 26th Ann. Simulation Symp.*, IEEE CS Press, Los Alamitos, Calif., 1993, pp. 41–49.

Casavant, T., ed., *J. Parallel and Distributed Computing*, Vol. 18, No. 2, 1993 (special issue on tools and methods for visualization of parallel systems and computations).

Cybenko, G., "Supercomputer Performance Trends and the PERFECT Benchmarks," *Supercomputing Rev.*, Apr. 1991, pp. 53–60.

Gelenbe, E., *Multiprocessor Performance*, John Wiley & Sons, Inc., New York, N.Y., 1989.

Ghosal, D., and L.N. Bhuyan, "Performance Evaluation of a Dataflow Architecture," *IEEE Trans. Computers*, Vol. 39, No. 5, May 1990, pp. 615–627.

Goldberg, A.J., and J.L. Hennessy, "Mtool: An Integrated System for Performance Debugging Shared Memory Multiprocessor Applications," *IEEE Trans. Parallel and Distributed Systems*, Vol. 4, No. 1, Jan. 1993, pp. 28–40.

Heidelberger, P., and S.S. Lavenberg, "Computer Performance Evaluation Mothodology," *IEEE Trans. Computers*, Vol. C-35, No. 12, Dec. 1984, pp. 1195–1220.

Jain, R., *The Art of Computer Systems Performance Analysis*, John Wiley & Sons, Inc., New York, N.Y., 1991.

Jiang, H., L.N. Bhuyan, and D. Ghosal, "Approximate Analysis of Multiprocessing Task Graphs," *Proc. 1990 Int'l Conf. Parallel Processing, Vol. III: Algorithms and Applications*, Penn State Press, University Park, Pa., 1990, pp. III-228–III-235.

Koldinger, E.J., S.J. Eggers, and H.M. Levy, "On the Validity of Trace-Driven Simulation for Multiprocessors," *Proc. 18th Ann. Int'l Symp. Computer Architecture*, ACM Press, New York, N.Y., 1991, pp. 244–253.

Madala, S., and J.B. Sinclair, "Performance of Synchronous Parallel Algorithms with Regular Structures," *IEEE Trans. Parallel and Distributed Systems*, Vol. 2, No. 1, Jan. 1991, pp. 105–116.

Mak, V.M., and S.F. Lundstrom, "Predicting Performance of Parallel Computations," *IEEE Trans. Parallel and Distributed Systems*, Vol. 1, No. 3, July 1990, pp. 257–270.

Marson, M.A., G. Balbo, and G. Conte, *Performance Models of Multiprocessor Systems*, MIT Press, Cambridge, Mass., 1986.

Singh, J.P., W.D. Weber, and A. Gupta, "SPLASH: Stanford Parallel Applications for Shared-Memory," *ACM Computer Architecture News*, Vol. 20, No. 1, Mar. 1992, pp. 5–44.

Sun, X.-H., and L. Ni, "Scalable Problems and Memory-Bounded Speedup," *J. Parallel and Distributed Computing*, Vol. 19, Sept. 1993, pp. 27–37.

Thomasian, A., and P.F. Bay, "Analytical Queueing Network Models for Parallel Processing of Task Systems," *IEEE Trans. Computers*, Vol. C-35, No. 12, Dec. 1986, pp. 1045–1054.

Worley, P., "The Effects of Time Constraints on Scaled Speedup," *SIAM J. Scientific and Statistical Computing*, Vol. 11, No. 5, 1990, pp. 838–858.

Yang, Q., L.N. Bhuyan, and B.C. Liu, "Analysis and Comparison of Cache Coherence Protocols for a Packet Switched Multiprocessor," *IEEE Trans. Computers*, Vol. 38, No. 8, Aug. 1989, pp. 1143–1153.

Zhang, X., Y. Yan, and K. He, "Evaluation and Measurement of Multiprocessor Latency Patterns," *Proc. 8th Int'l Parallel Processing Symp.*, IEEE CS Press, Los Alamitos, Calif., 1994, pp. 845–852.

Zhang, X., Y. Yan, and K. He, "Latency Metric: An Experimental Method for Measuring and Evaluating Program and Architecture Scalability," *J. Parallel and Distributed Computing*, Vol. 22, No. 3, 1994, pp. 392–410.

Speedup Versus Efficiency in Parallel Systems

DEREK L. EAGER, MEMBER, IEEE, JOHN ZAHORJAN, AND EDWARD D. LAZOWSKA

Abstract—If a software system can be structured as a collection of largely independent subtasks, significant reductions in elapsed time can be realized by executing these subtasks in parallel on multiple processors. This effect, known as *speedup*, typically increases (up to some limit) with the number of processors dedicated to the problem.

Along with an increase in speedup comes a decrease in *efficiency*: as more processors are devoted to the execution of a software system, the total amount of processor idle time can be expected to increase, due to factors such as contention, communication, and software structure.

This paper investigates the tradeoff between speedup and efficiency that is *inherent* to a software system. We show the extent to which this tradeoff is determined by the *average parallelism* of the software system, as contrasted to other, more detailed, characterizations. We bound the extent to which both speedup and efficiency can simultaneously be poor: we show that for any software system and any number of processors, the sum of the average processor utilization (i.e., efficiency) and the attained fraction of the maximum possible speedup must exceed one. We give bounds on speedup and efficiency, and on the incremental benefit and cost of allocating additional processors. We give an explicit formulation, as well as bounds, for the location of the "knee" of the execution time–efficiency profile, where the benefit per unit cost is maximized.

Index Terms—Bounds on performance, computer system performance analysis, parallel computing, parallel software, parallel software structure, performance.

I. INTRODUCTION

EXPLOITING parallelism is an increasingly common approach to improving the performance of computer systems. In terms of hardware, this typically means providing multiple, simultaneously active processors. In terms of software, this typically means structuring a program as a set of largely independent subtasks.

In the sequential world, the performance of a system usually can be adequately characterized in terms of the instruction rate of the single processor and the execution time requirement of the software on a processor of unit rate (which we refer to as its *service demand*). In the parallel world, things are considerably more complex. In the hardware domain, we must

Manuscript received September 13, 1986; revised September 17, 1987. This work was supported by the National Science Foundation under Grants DCR-8302383, DCR-8352098, CCR-8619663, and CCR-8703049, the Natural Sciences and Engineering Research Council of Canada, the Naval Ocean Systems Center, U S WEST Advanced Technologies, the Washington Technology Center, and Digital Equipment Corporation (the Systems Research Center and the External Research Program).

D. L. Eager is with the Department of Computational Science, University of Saskatchewan, Saskatoon, Sask., Canada S7N 0W0.

J. Zahorjan and E. D. Lazowska are with the Department of Computer Science, University of Washington, Seattle, WA 98195.

IEEE Log Number 8825678.

be concerned not only with the instruction rate of a processor, but also with factors such as the number of processors. In the software domain, we must be concerned not only with service demands, but also with factors such as the structure of the software.

In evaluating a parallel system, two performance measures of particular interest are *speedup* and *efficiency*. Speedup is defined for each number of processors n as the ratio of the elapsed time when executing a program on a single processor (the single processor *execution time*) to the execution time when n processors are available. In the notation that we shall use throughout this paper,

$$S(n) = \frac{T_1}{T_n}.$$

Efficiency is defined as the average utilization of the n allocated processors. Ignoring I/O, the efficiency of a single processor system is 1. Speedup in this case is of course 1. In general, the relationship between efficiency and speedup is given by

$$E(n) = \frac{S(n)}{n}.$$

If efficiency remains at 1 as processors are added, we have *linear* speedup. (Technically, for speedup to be linear requires only that $S(n) = \alpha n$ for some constant α, $0 < \alpha \le 1$, but we will use the stricter definition $\alpha = 1$ throughout.) This is the ideal case, as improvements in speedup can be obtained at no cost in efficiency. Linear speedup is not achievable, in general, because of contention for shared resources, the time required to communicate between processors and between processes, and the inability to structure the software so that an arbitrary number of processors can be kept usefully busy. Minsky and Papert noted evidence that the "typical" speedup has the form $S(n) = \log n$ [15]; other studies have provided evidence that much larger "typical" speedups can be attained [12].

Although the idea of speeding up computations through parallelism has existed for more than a century [11], general purpose systems based on multiple (five or more) processors have only recently become common (e.g., commercial machines by Sequent, Encore, Alliant, and BBN, and limited-edition machines such as IBM's RP3 and DEC's Firefly). The existence of such systems has stimulated widespread research activity: algorithm work concerned with parallel solutions in many problem domains, compiler work concerned with parallelizing code, architecture work concerned with how best

0-8186-6522-X/95 $4.00 © 1989 IEEE

to interconnect processors, etc. Obviously, results in these areas play a critical role in improving the speedup and efficiency properties of parallel systems.

This paper takes a more abstract view. Rather than studying specific implementations and implementation problems, we study the *tradeoff* between speedup and efficiency that is *inherent* to a software system. Furthermore, we do not do this in the context of a specific software structure (e.g., as was done by Heidelberger and Trivedi [8] and by Fayolle, King, and Mitrani [5]); instead, we derive relationships that can be very broadly applied. We are interested both in fundamental issues concerning the properties of this tradeoff, and in practical issues that might arise in considering specific software systems. Among the fundamental issues that we address are the following.

• To what extent is the speedup–efficiency tradeoff determined by the *average parallelism* of a software system, as contrasted to other, more detailed characterizations?

• How "bad" can speedup and efficiency *simultaneously* become?

• What is the nature of the "knee" of the execution time–efficiency profile, where the benefit (increase in speedup) per unit cost (decrease in efficiency) is maximized? For example, what guarantees can be made regarding speedup and efficiency values at the knee?

Among the practical issues related to specific software systems that we consider are the following.

• To achieve a given speedup, what efficiency penalty must be paid?

• What speedup advantage will result when increasing the number of processors by some factor, and what efficiency penalty will accompany it?

• What number of processors yields the knee of the execution time–efficiency profile?

Our objective is to address these questions by obtaining *bounds* on performance—bounds expressed in terms of the average parallelism measure of software structure. It should be clear that, given complete information regarding a specific software structure, precise answers (rather than bounds) could be obtained for many of these questions. There are two reasons, though, why bounds expressed in terms of one or a small number of parameters may be more desirable than precise solutions that require complete information.

• It is unlikely in practice that complete information will be available. For most software systems, parallelism will depend to some extent on the (unknown or varying) data that would be supplied as inputs. The volume of information required will in many cases be prohibitive.

• It often is the case that bounds based on simple characterizations yield more insight than exact answers utilizing complete information.

The results that we seek are in the spirit of the results of Chen [2], and, more widely known, in the spirit of Amdahl's law, which states that if a fraction f of a computation is inherently sequential, then the speedup $S(n)$ is bounded above by $1/(f + (1 - f)/n)$ [1]. (Precisely, f is defined to be the ratio of the service demand of sequential parts of the computation to the service demand of the entire computation.)

This is a simple upper bound on speedup that is expressed in terms of a single-parameter characterization of the software (f) and a single-parameter characterization of the hardware (n). It provides considerably more insight than more detailed alternatives, such as a table displaying exact speedup values computed for a number of specific software structures running on a number of specific hardware structures.

In Section II, we describe our models of parallel software and of its execution, and the average parallelism measure that we use to characterize this software. Of special interest:

• We show that there are four equivalent definitions of average parallelism.

• We show that the number of available processors n and the average parallelism of the software structure A provide complementary *hardware* and *software* upper bounds on speedup.

In Section III, we develop lower bounds on speedup and efficiency in terms of n and A, and apply these bounds to answer a number of the questions posed above. Specifically:

• We obtain lower bounds on the speedup and efficiency with n processors. These bounds apply to *any* work-conserving scheduling discipline, and are the best obtainable bounds (Theorem 1).

• Restricting ourselves to the processor sharing scheduling discipline, we show that, although tighter bounds can be obtained, they require information about the software structure in addition to the average parallelism (Theorem 2).

• We show that for any work-conserving scheduling discipline, any software structure, and any number of processors, the sum of the attained efficiency and the attained fraction of the maximum possible speedup must always exceed 1. In other words, we show that a low efficiency is guaranteed to "buy" a high relative speedup (Corollary 1.1).

• We bound efficiency in terms of the average parallelism and the speedup; in other words, we determine the efficiency penalty that must be paid to achieve some target speedup (Corollary 1.2).

• We show that average parallelism is a good characterization of the software structure. We do so in two ways. First, we show that a specific speedup estimate derived from only n and A can be in error by at most 34 percent. (Corollary 1.3). Then, we show that only a slight improvement in our bounds can be achieved by using some additional information, specifically the fraction of work that is inherently sequential (Corollaries 2.1 and 2.2).

In Section IV, we consider the incremental cost/benefit of adding processors. For an increase from n to kn processors, we obtain both upper and lower bounds on the increase in speedup and the decrease in efficiency. These bounds are expressed in terms of k, n, and A (Theorem 3).

Finally, in Section V, we study questions concerning the knee of the execution time–efficiency profile.

• We show that this profile has a unique knee, and obtain an exact expression for the number of processors that attains this knee—an expression that requires complete information concerning the software structure (rather than simply the average parallelism) (Theorem 4).

• We show that when this number of processors is allocated,

the attained speedup is *at least* 50 percent of the maximum possible and the efficiency is *at least* 50 percent (Theorem 5).

• We obtain a bound for this "optimal" number of processors in terms of the average parallelism, A (Theorem 6).

• We show that when the number of available processors is equal to the average parallelism, the guarantees regarding speedup and efficiency are identical to those at the knee (Theorem 7).

II. THE SYSTEM MODEL AND THE AVERAGE PARALLELISM MEASURE

In Section II-A, we outline the graph model of parallel software that we will use, as well as our model of execution. The former model reflects our goal of fundamental and generally applicable insights, and incorporates only those aspects common to all parallel software systems. The latter model reflects, in addition, our focus on the parallelism inherent to a software system, and makes an assumption of "ideal hardware." In Section II-B, we describe the average parallelism measure that we use to characterize software parallelism.

A. The System Model

We represent the software component of the system using a traditional graph model (e.g., [6]). In this model, a software system is represented by an acyclic directed graph. Each vertex of the graph corresponds to a "subtask" of the software system. Each subtask has an associated processor service demand. Precedence constraints may exist among the subtasks; for example, the initiation of a subtask may require data that are available only after the termination of some other subtask. These precedence constraints are modeled by the arcs of the graph: an arc from vertex A to vertex B means that subtask B cannot begin execution until subtask A completes execution. (It would be incorrect to think that a subtask in this model necessarily corresponds directly to a process or to some other operating system or programming language construct. Rather, a subtask corresponds to an "independent unit of sequential work." A single process might be represented by several such units, for example, with the precedence constraints representing synchronization requirements achieved by some communication primitive.) Fig. 1 illustrates a software structure graph that might arise from an algorithm such as Quicksort; service demands appear within the vertices.

The hardware component of the system is modeled as some number n of identical processors, each of unit speed. We assume that n is constant throughout the execution. In practice, n might be determined by either hardware or software. If the entire computer is devoted to a single task, the number of available processors is fixed by the hardware. If the computer is multiprogrammed, the operating system may choose to allocate a fixed subset of the processors to each task during its execution. Some of the questions that we consider in this paper are more relevant in one of these contexts than in the other. For example, questions regarding the knee of the execution time–efficiency profile are most relevant to the multiprogramming context, in which there is considerable

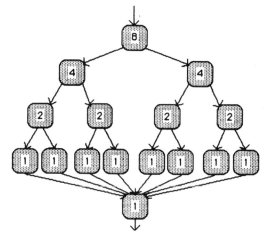

Fig. 1. Graph representation of an example software system.

freedom in determining the number of processors allocated to each software system.

It is possible that at various points during execution, the number of runnable subtasks will exceed the number of available processors. A scheduling algorithm then is required to decide which subtasks should be run. Some of our results will be established for any scheduling discipline that is work-conserving [9]. (A work-conserving discipline is one that never leaves idle a subtask that is eligible for execution when there is a processor available.) Other results will consider a specific discipline, *processor sharing*. Under this discipline, if k subtasks are eligible for execution and there are n available processors ($n < k$), each subtask receives service at a rate that is n/k times the rate at which it would receive service if a processor were dedicated to it.

In closing this section, we should specifically discuss the representation of overheads in our execution model. The principal focus of this paper is the influence of software structure on parallel program performance. Overheads such as those due to interconnection network topologies, memory contention, and locking are of course another important influence on performance, but are not our principal focus. These overheads are represented by including them in the service demands of the various subtasks in the graph. This is a common approach in computer system performance analysis. The implicit assumption is that these overheads are *fixed*—that they do not vary with the number of processors dedicated to the computation nor with the schedule used.

B. The Average Parallelism Measure

The graph representation of a parallel software system contains complete information about the parallelism inherent in that system. We argued in Section I that this representation is too detailed to be practical or yield insight. We seek a simpler characterization that still captures the essential behavior of the software.

An example of such a characterization is the one used by Amdahl [1]: the fraction f of a computation that is inherently sequential. For our work, we have chosen to use a different, fairly common (e.g., [7]), and intuitively appealing measure:

average parallelism. Average parallelism can be rigorously defined in four equivalent ways.

1) the average number of processors that are busy during the execution time of the software system in question, given an unbounded number of available processors;

2) the speedup, given an unbounded number of available processors,

3) the ratio of the total service required by the computation (the sum of the service demands of the subtasks) to the length of a longest path in the subtask graph (the length of a path is the sum of the service demands of its subtasks), and

4) the intersection point of the *hardware bound* and the *software bound* on speedup (these will be defined shortly).

The equivalence of these four definitions is not entirely obvious. Recall that speedup with n processors, $S(n)$, is defined as the ratio of the execution time when only a single processor is available to the execution time when n processors are available. Since the former is equal to the total service demand, and the ratio of the total service demand to the execution time gives the average number of busy processors, definition 2) is equivalent to definition 1).

If an unbounded number of processors is available, the execution time of a software system is simply the total service demand along some longest path. Hence, from the definition of speedup, definition 3) is equivalent to definition 2).

There are two simple upper bounds on speedup. The *hardware bound* reflects the limitation imposed by the hardware, and is given by the number n of available processors. This bound can be achieved only if all n processors can be kept busy all of the time. The *software bound* reflects the limitation imposed by the software, and is derived by noting that, no matter how many processors are available to a system, the execution time must be at least as long as the length of a longest path. Hence, the speedup is at most the ratio of the total service demand to the length of a longest path. The hardware and software bounds, and the actual speedup function, are depicted in Fig. 2 for the example software system whose directed graph representation is shown in Fig. 1.

The intersection point of the hardware and software bounds on speedup is significant: when additional processors are allocated, it is certain that there is not enough parallelism in the software to keep all of the processors busy all of the time. This intersection point is the point where n (the hardware bound) is identical to the ratio of the total service demand to the length of the longest path (the software bound). Thus, definition 4) is equivalent to definition 3), and all four definitions are now shown to be equivalent.

We note that the hardware and software bounds on speedup are analogous to (and have an identical form as) the *Asymptotic Bound Analysis (ABA)* bounds on system throughput in a queueing network model of a computer system in which a number of identical, independent processes compete for service at a collection of system resources [4], [16]. There is a simple mapping between the two problem domains, with the number of independent processes in the ABA model corresponding to the number of processors in our model, and the bottleneck service demand in the ABA model corresponding to

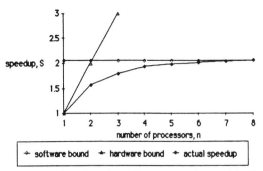

Fig. 2. Upper bounds and actual speedup for the graph in Fig. 1.

the length of a longest path in the directed graph representing the software system in our model. A similar mapping was employed by Kumar and Gonsalves [13] for performance models of software containing critical sections.

It is natural to ask how to determine the average parallelism of a particular software system. There are analytic approaches (considering the graph representation of the system) and experimental approaches (running the software with a sufficient number of processors). As with Amdahl's simple measure, though, the important issue is not how the measure is determined, but rather that once it has been determined, it provides a succinct characterization of the inherent parallelism of the software system. As the remainder of this paper will show, there is a considerable amount of information built into this measure.

III. LOWER BOUNDS ON SPEEDUP AND EFFICIENCY, AND APPLICATIONS OF THESE BOUNDS

In Section II, we showed the upper bounds on speedup that are established by hardware and by software. There are corresponding upper bounds on efficiency, since the average processor utilization (efficiency) can be computed as the speedup divided by the number of available processors.

In this section, we derive lower bounds on speedup and efficiency, and apply these bounds to a number of questions regarding the speedup–efficiency tradeoff.

A. Lower Bounds on Speedup and Efficiency

Theorem 1: Let A denote the average parallelism of a software structure, $S(n)$ denote the speedup with n processors, and $E(n)$ denote the efficiency with n processors. For any work-conserving scheduling discipline

$$S(n) \geq \frac{nA}{n+A-1}$$

and

$$E(n) \geq \frac{A}{n+A-1}.$$

These bounds can be attained.

Proof: Because speedup and efficiency are related in a simple way, it suffices to show the speedup result. Consider an arbitrary software structure with average parallelism A. Let T_∞ denote the elapsed time of its execution given an unlimited number of processors. It follows from the definition of average parallelism that the total processor busy time accumulated during such an execution (summed over all n processors) is $T_\infty A$.

Now, suppose that this software structure is executed using n processors and some arbitrary work-conserving scheduling discipline. Since the discipline is work-conserving, it follows that the total busy time (summed over all processors) is, as before, $T_\infty A$. The execution time is then given by $(T_\infty A + I(n))/n$, where $I(n)$ denotes the total idle time (summed over all processors) that is accumulated during this execution. From the definition of speedup, noting that the sequential execution time is $T_\infty A$, we then have $S(n) = nA/(A + I(n)/T_\infty)$.

To establish the desired result, we only need to show that $I(n) \le T_\infty(n - 1)$. To this end, define $\omega(t)$ to be the portion of the original software structure graph that has not completed execution at time t. $\omega(t)$ includes those tasks that have not yet been initiated, and those tasks that have been initiated but not yet completed. The service demand of each task in $\omega(t)$ is its original service demand diminished by the amount of service (if any) already provided to the task. (The precedence arcs in $\omega(t)$ are identical to those in the original graph.)

Define $L(t)$ to be the length (i.e., the total service demand) of a longest path within $\omega(t)$. Note that the value of $L(t)$ varies from T_∞ (at the start of the execution) to zero (at the end of the execution). If, at some time t, $L(t)$ is *not* decreasing, there must be some task at the head of a longest path in $\omega(t)$ that is not being executed. Since no precedence constraints prevent the execution of such a task, and since the scheduling discipline is work-conserving, it must be the case that there are no idle processors at time t. Thus, processors can be idle only during those periods of time when $L(t)$ is decreasing. Since $L(t)$ decreases (linearly) for a total length of time T_∞, and since at most $n - 1$ processors can be idle at any point in time, the total idle time $I(n)$ is at most $T_\infty(n - 1)$, which establishes the result.

We show that the speedup bound can be attained by means of an example. Consider first-come-first-served scheduling, and a software system that consists of a subtask that, upon completion, enables $kn + 1$ additional subtasks, where kn is some multiple of n that is greater than A. If we constrain the service times of each of the $kn + 1$ additional subtasks to be identical, the service time of the first subtask can be derived as $T_\infty(kn + 1 - A)/kn$, and that of each of the remaining subtasks as $T_\infty(A - 1)/kn$. The speedup is then given by

$$S(n) = \frac{(kn+1)T_\infty \dfrac{A-1}{kn} + T_\infty \dfrac{kn+1-A}{kn}}{T_\infty \dfrac{kn+1-A}{kn} + (k+1)T_\infty \dfrac{A-1}{kn}}$$

This reduces to the speedup given in the theorem.   Q.E.D.

Note that if $n \ll A$, $S(n) \to n$, and if $n \gg A$, $S(n) \to A$. Fig. 3 adds the lower bound of this theorem to the upper bounds displayed in Fig. 2. Bear in mind that the bounds of this theorem apply to *any* work-conserving scheduling discipline. No matter how poorly designed such a discipline may be, or how baroque a software structure is presented, the

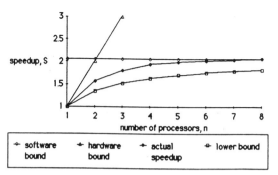

Fig. 3. Lower bound added to Fig. 2.

behavior of the software system can be no worse than the stated bounds. Furthermore, these are the best such bounds obtainable, since for any choice of A and n there exists a choice of work-conserving discipline and software structure such that the system performance is no better than that given by the bounds.

Because Theorem 1 is concerned with the worst case over the entire space of work-conserving disciplines, it is possible that the bound does not give a reasonable indication of the performance to be expected of "rational" scheduling disciplines. Theorem 2 specializes the results to the case of processor sharing scheduling, an idealization of round-robin scheduling. We find that, although a tighter bound can in fact be obtained, this requires not only that we consider a specific scheduling discipline, but also that we provide additional information about the software structure, specifically, the maximum parallelism.

Theorem 2: Let A denote the average parallelism, $m_{\max}$ denote the maximum parallelism (the maximum number of processors that are simultaneously busy when an unlimited number are available), $S(n)$ denote the speedup with n processors, and $E(n)$ denote the efficiency with n processors. With processor sharing scheduling

$$S(n) \ge \min\left(A, \frac{nA}{n+A-1-\dfrac{(n-1)(A-1)}{m_{\max}-1}}\right)$$

and

$$E(n) \ge \min\left(\frac{A}{n}, \frac{A}{n+A-1-\dfrac{(n-1)(A-1)}{m_{\max}-1}}\right)$$

These bounds can be attained. (The min function is necessary only to take care of the extreme case in which $n > m_{\max}$.)

Proof: Consult the Appendix.

A key point is that if we have no information about the maximum parallelism, i.e., if the maximum parallelism can be arbitrarily high, then these bounds reduce to those given in Theorem 1.

B. Applications

1) How "Bad" Can Speedup and Efficiency Simultaneously Become?: Typically, as we make additional processors available to a software system, increases in speedup are obtained at the expense of decreases in efficiency. It is natural to wonder if a low efficiency is guaranteed to "buy" a high speedup, or whether a poor choice of scheduling discipline and/or an inappropriate number of available processors might result in both low efficiency and low speedup. Corollary 1.1 offers reassurance in this regard.

Corollary 1.1: For any work-conserving scheduling discipline, any software structure, and any number of processors, the sum of the attained efficiency and the attained fraction of the maximum possible speedup must always exceed 1, i.e., $E(n) + S(n)/A > 1$.

Proof: From Theorem 1, $S(n)/A \geq n/(n + A - 1)$ and $E(n) \geq A/(n + A - 1)$. Thus, $S(n)/A + E(n) \geq (n + A)/(n + A - 1) > 1$.   Q.E.D.

Thus, an average processor utilization (efficiency) of 20 percent, for example, implies an attained speedup of more than 80 percent of the maximum possible.

2) To Achieve a Given Speedup, What Efficiency Penalty Must be Paid?: Here, we wish to obtain bounds on efficiency, given that sufficient processors have been made available to attain some target speedup S. (Clearly, S can be at most the maximum possible speedup, as given by the average parallelism A.)

Corollary 1.2: For any nonsequential program structure (that is, any structure with $A > 1$) and any work-conserving scheduling discipline, $E(n) \geq (A - S(n))/(A - 1)$.

Proof: From Theorem 1, $S(n) \geq nA/(n + A - 1)$, so $n \leq S(n)(A - 1)/(A - S(n))$, and thus $S(n)/n = E(n) \geq (A - S(n))/(A - 1)$.   Q.E.D.

Note that for small values of S, the efficiency penalty is guaranteed to be small. However, as S approaches the maximum possible speedup A, the efficiency may, in the worst case, degrade linearly to arbitrarily low values. This agrees with our intuition regarding the likely effect of trying to exploit all of the possible parallelism in a system by dedicating large numbers of processors.

3) To What Extent is the Speedup-Efficiency Tradeoff Determined by Average Parallelism?: We address this issue by answering two related questions. First, how tightly can speedup be bounded using only the average parallelism of a software system and the number of available processors? Second, how much additional information regarding speedup is provided by knowledge of 1) the maximum parallelism, or 2) the fraction of the total work that is inherently sequential? We consider only speedup, since efficiency is easily derived once the speedup is known.

Fig. 3 illustrated, for a specific software structure, the actual speedup function $S(n)$, the upper bounds established by software (A) and hardware (n), and the lower bound of Theorem 1 ($nA/(n + A - 1)$). We will measure the "tightness" of these bounds in the general case by determining the maximum possible error in an estimate of the speedup function that is computed by a particular averaging of the bounds.

Corollary 1.3: For any work-conserving scheduling discipline, the speedup estimate

$$\hat{S}(n) = 2 \times \frac{\min(n, A)\dfrac{nA}{n+A-1}}{\min(n, A) + \dfrac{nA}{n+A-1}}$$

has a relative error of less than 34 percent, i.e., $|\hat{S}(n) - S(n)|/S(n) < 0.34$.

Proof: It is straightforward to show that the relative error in this estimate is maximized when the true speedup attains either the lower or the upper speedup bound. Therefore, the relative error is at most

$$\frac{\min(n, A) - \dfrac{nA}{n+A-1}}{\min(n, A) + \dfrac{nA}{n+A-1}}$$

which is maximized at $n = A$ and is thus strictly less than 34 percent.   Q.E.D.

Thus, knowing only the average parallelism and the number of available processors, a speedup estimate can be computed that is guaranteed to have a relative error of less than 34 percent.

This result indicates that at most a modest benefit can be had by considering measures of software parallelism more detailed than average parallelism. Nonetheless, we will briefly examine two such measures that have a reasonable likelihood of being known or reliably estimated in practice: the maximum parallelism and the fraction of the total work that is inherently sequential. (Another reasonable characteristic to consider might be the fraction of the total work that is accomplished with the (known) maximum parallelism. The additional benefit of this information is, however, very similar in nature to that of the fraction of the total work that is inherently sequential, and we do not treat it explicitly here. We consider other measures, such as the variance in parallelism or the percentiles of parallelism, to be too detailed for practical use.)

Knowledge of the maximum parallelism can be used to tighten only the lower bound on speedup. The extent of this improvement is illustrated in Theorem 2 for the processor sharing scheduling discipline. If m_{max} (the maximum parallelism) is large, the benefit of knowing its value is minimal—one might just as well assume that it is unbounded. If m_{max} is small, the speedup bound is considerably tightened. (Of course, m_{max} must be at least as large as A.) For intermediate values, the benefit of knowing m_{max} is maximized when n is close to A, which corresponds to the region of greatest uncertainty in speedup when only the average parallelism is known. For example, suppose that $n = A$ and that $m_{max} = kA$ for some integer k. Then knowledge of m_{max} tightens (increases) the speedup lower bound by a factor of approximately $2k/(2k - 1)$.

Knowledge of the fraction f of work that is inherently sequential (recall that this is defined to be the ratio of the service demand of the sequential parts of the computation to the total service demand of the computation) can be used to tighten both the upper and the lower bounds on speedup. The extent of these improvements will be illustrated for the processor sharing scheduling discipline, using the following two corollaries to Theorem 2. We first consider the improvement in the lower bound.

Corollary 2.1: Let A denote the average parallelism, f denote the fraction of work that is inherently sequential, and

$S(n)$ denote the speedup with n processors. With processor sharing scheduling and $n \geq 2$

$$S(n) \geq \frac{nA}{n+A-1-(1-fA)} .$$

(fA will always be between 0 and 1.)

Proof: Consult the Appendix.

Comparing this bound to that given in Theorem 1 (or, equivalently, to that given in Theorem 2 when m_{max} is unknown), we note that for reasonably large n or A, knowledge of f provides negligible improvement in the speedup lower bound.

We next consider the improvement in the upper bound presented in Section II, $\min(n, A)$.

Corollary 2.2: Let A denote the average parallelism, f denote the fraction of work that is inherently sequential, and $S(n)$ denote the speedup with n processors. With processor sharing scheduling

$$S(n) \leq \min\left(\frac{n}{1+f(n-1)} , A \right) .$$

Proof: Consult the Appendix.

(Note that the first term of this bound is identical to the bound given by Amdahl.)

Comparison with the bound from Section II shows that for small f, the improvement is negligible. As f approaches 1 the improvement increases, and, in fact, the new upper bound approaches the lower bound given by Theorem 1. For fixed f and A, the improvement is maximized when n is closest to A, which corresponds to the region of greatest uncertainty in speedup when only the average parallelism is known.

In summary, the average parallelism of a software system does, to a considerable extent, determine the associated speedup–efficiency tradeoff. Knowing only the average parallelism and the number of processors, a speedup estimate can be derived that has a relative error of less than 34 percent. Knowledge of other system characteristics such as the maximum parallelism m_{max} or the fraction f of work that is inherently sequential is of limited benefit: these measures yield useful information only when they indicate a severe constraint on parallelism, for example, a large value of f or a small value of m_{max}.

IV. Incremental Cost and Benefit of Adding Processors

In this section, we study the cost (decreased efficiency) and benefit (increased speedup) that will result when increasing by some factor the number of processors allocated to a software system. Theorem 3 addresses these questions by providing bounds expressed in terms of average parallelism.

Theorem 3: With processor sharing scheduling, an increase in the number of processors from n to kn (n, $k \geq 1$) affects speedup as follows:

$$\max\left(1, \frac{kA}{(k-1)n+A} \right)$$

$$\leq \frac{S(kn)}{S(n)} \leq \min\left(1+(A-1)\frac{k-1}{kn-1} , k \right) .$$

Correspondingly, efficiency is affected as follows:

$$\max\left(\frac{1}{k}, \frac{A}{(k-1)n+A} \right)$$

$$\leq \frac{E(kn)}{E(n)} \leq \min\left(\frac{1}{k}+(A-1)\frac{1-\frac{1}{k}}{kn-1} , 1 \right) .$$

These bounds can be attained.

Proof: Consult the Appendix.

A number of observations can be made regarding these bounds. We first show that they are consistent with earlier bounds, and then consider the insight that they provide regarding system behavior. Since the efficiency bounds are so closely related to the speedup bounds, we discuss only the latter directly.

For $n = 1$, Theorem 3 provides bounds on speedup with k processors, since the factor by which speedup increases is equal to the speedup itself. These bounds correspond exactly to those given in Section II (the upper bounds established by hardware and by software) and in Section III (the lower bound of Theorem 1). Also, note that when $k \rightarrow \infty$ (with fixed n, A), the resulting speedup must be the maximum possible speedup, A, and that therefore the bounds on the change in speedup can be used to bound the original speedup with n processors. The upper bound on the change in speedup reduces to $(n + A - 1)/n$ in this case, and the lower bound reduces to $\max(1, A/n)$. Since A is the resulting speedup, the original speedup with n processors is bounded below by $nA/(n + A - 1)$ and above by $\min(n, A)$, again corresponding exactly to the bounds given in Sections II and III.

Consider now the system behavior as the number of processors is increased, for various initial numbers of processors. For n and kn that are small relative to A, the lower bound on the factor by which speedup increases guarantees a speedup close to linear in the number of processors. For example, with $n = A/9$, doubling the number of processors will cause an increase in speedup of at least 80 percent. As n increases beyond A, the upper bound on the factor by which speedup may increase approaches the lower bound of 1 quickly. For example, suppose that initially we use A processors, and that A is large. If we then double the number of processors from A to $2A$, speedup will increase by at most 50 percent. If we double the number of processors again (from $2A$ to $4A$), speedup will increase by at most 25 percent. In general, at the ith doubling, speedup will increase by at most $1/2i \times 100$ percent.

As we have seen several times before, the greatest uncertainty arises when the number of processors is close to the average parallelism A. For example, with $n = 2/3\,A$ (and large A), doubling the number of processors could increase speedup by anywhere from 20 to 75 percent.

V. The Knee of the Execution Time–Efficiency Profile

Profiles that plot a measure of "benefit" against a measure of "cost" arise naturally in many areas; for example, the throughput–delay profile in computer-communication system design [10] and the lifetime curve in memory management [3]. The concept of the *knee* of such a profile [3] (or, alternatively, the point of "maximum power" [10]) is a fundamental one. The knee is the point where the benefit per unit cost is maximized, and, intuitively, represents an optimal system operating point.

In this section, we investigate an important cost-benefit tradeoff in parallel systems: the *execution time-efficiency profile*. There are two equivalent views that motivate this tradeoff. In the first of these, we view efficiency as an indication of benefit (the higher the efficiency, the higher the benefit), and execution time as an indication of cost (the higher the execution time, the higher the cost). The implied system objective is to achieve efficient usage of each processor, while taking into account the cost to users in the form of increased task execution times. Since efficiency is closely related to the "per-processor throughput," this view is analogous to that motivating the throughput-delay profile in computer-communication network design.

The second, equivalent view has a somewhat different implied objective. Here, execution time is taken as an indication of benefit (the lower the execution time, the higher the benefit), and efficiency is taken as an indication of cost (the lower the efficiency, the higher the cost). The implied objective is to achieve low task execution times, while taking into account the "opportunity cost" of low efficiency. (In a multiprogramming environment, a low efficiency implies that processors could have been more appropriately allocated to a different task.)

The execution time-efficiency profile, motivated by each of these views, is a graph in which execution time is given on the y-axis and efficiency on the x-axis. Each point represents the combination of execution time and efficiency achieved by some particular number of processors. The knee of the profile occurs where the ratio of efficiency to execution time, $E(n)/T_n$ (T_n is the execution time when n processors are allocated), is maximized. As an example, Fig. 4 shows the profile for the software system whose graph representation and speedup function are given in Figs. 1 and 2, respectively. The knee is indicated by the arrow.

It is important to be able to compute, or at least estimate, the number of processors that yields the knee. In a multiprogramming environment, for example, this would represent the appropriate allocation of processors to each job.

In Section V-A, we show how to find the location of the knee for an arbitrary software system, assuming complete information about that system. Previously, the location of the knee had been found efficiently only for very regular structures (e.g., [14]). Using our new formulation for the location of the knee, we show several properties regarding speedup and efficiency that will hold if the number of processors allocated is the number that attains the knee.

The approach in Section V-A requires complete information. In Section V-B, we bound the location of the knee in terms of average parallelism. Interestingly, the average parallelism itself is essentially at the midpoint of these bounds. Thus, choosing to allocate a number of processors equal to the average parallelism measure is appropriate, in the sense that it

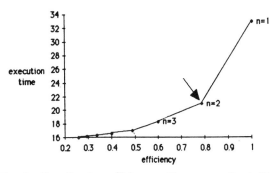

Fig. 4. Execution time-efficiency profile corresponding to Fig. 1.

yields a point on the execution time-efficiency profile relatively close to the knee. We show several properties regarding speedup and efficiency that will hold if the number of processors allocated is identical to the average parallelism A, and compare these properties with those that hold at the knee.

A. The Exact Location of the Knee

In Theorem 4, we show that the execution time-efficiency profile for any software system must have a knee (a point where the ratio of efficiency to execution time is maximized), we show that this knee must be unique, and we give the location of the knee. Here, as in all of Section V, we assume processor sharing scheduling, and allow a nonintegral number of processors n. (Results that allow a nonintegral number of processors are in some sense "more general" than those for an integral number of processors. The nonintegral results can easily be specialized to integers. A nonintegral number of processors can be viewed as resulting from the sharing of a processor between two jobs in a multiprogrammed parallel environment.)

Theorem 4: Let p_m denote the proportion of time that m processors are simultaneously busy when an unlimited number are available, and let m_{max} denote the maximum parallelism (the maximum number of processors that are simultaneously busy when an unlimited number are available). Under the processor sharing discipline, the execution time-efficiency profile for any software system has a unique knee. The number of processors that attains the knee, i.e., that maximizes $E(n)/T_n$, is given by

$$n = \frac{\sum_{m=\lfloor n \rfloor + 1}^{m_{max}} p_m m}{\sum_{m=1}^{\lfloor n \rfloor} p_m}$$

if this equation has a solution, and by the unique integer n satisfying

$$\frac{\sum_{m=n+1}^{m_{max}} p_m m}{\sum_{m=1}^{n} p_m} \leq n \leq \frac{\sum_{m=n}^{m_{max}} p_m m}{\sum_{m=1}^{n-1} p_m}$$

otherwise.

Proof: Consult the Appendix.

As noted earlier, the knee of the execution time–efficiency profile intuitively represents a good system operating point. We now consider what guarantees are possible. Measures of interest include the *attained speedup* $S(n)$ in comparison with the maximum achievable speedup $S(m_{max})$, the *efficiency* $E(n)$, the *utilization of the kth last processor* for various values of k, and the *utilization of the kth additional processor* for various values of k. These last two quantities require some explanation (during which, for simplicity, we will assume an integral number of processors).

The utilization of the kth last processor indicates whether or not the number n of available processors is too large, and is defined as follows. Processors are numbered from 1 to n. If the number of subtasks s that are eligible for execution at a particular instant is less than n, then only processors 1 to s are utilized (even if physically this would require preempting a subtask executing on a higher numbered processor and rescheduling it on a lower numbered processor). Given this dispatching rule, the utilization of the kth last processor is defined as the average utilization of processor $n - k + 1$. Note that all processors numbered from 1 to $n - k$ must have utilizations greater than or equal to this value, and that all processors numbered from $n - k + 2$ to n must have utilizations that are less than or equal to this value.

The utilization of the kth additional processor indicates whether or not the number n of available processors is large enough. As above, processors are numbered from 1 to n. Using the dispatching rule just described, the utilization of the kth additional processor is defined as the utilization of the $n + k$th processor when the number of available processors is increased to $n + k$. Note that this utilization will be less than or equal to that of all other processors, in particular processors $n + 1$ to $n + k - 1$.

Let the number of processors that yields the knee be denoted by K. In Theorem 5, we give bounds on the attained speedup in comparison with the maximum possible speedup, the efficiency, the utilization of the kth last processor, and the utilization of the kth additional processor, for a number of available processors equal to K. For these last two quantities we fix k to be 1—we consider only the utilization of the last processor and the utilization of a single additional processor.

Theorem 5: Under the processor sharing discipline, when the number of available processors is equal to K (achieving the knee of the execution time–efficiency profile), the attained speedup is *at least* 50 percent of the maximum possible, the efficiency is *at least* 50 percent, the utilization of the last processor is *at least* 50 percent, and the utilization of a single additional processor is *no more than* 50 percent. These bounds can be attained in the limit as $A \to \infty$.

Proof: Consult the Appendix.

Intuitively, Theorem 5 shows that the conflicting goals of high efficiency and large speedup are being "perfectly balanced" when we choose to operate at the knee of the execution time–efficiency profile. An efficiency of at least 50 percent is guaranteed, as is a speedup of at least 50 percent of the maximum possible. All of the current processors are utilized at least 50 percent, but if another processor were introduced it would be utilized no more than 50 percent.

B. Bounds on the Location of the Knee

The results of the previous section allow the location of the knee to be determined precisely, but require complete information concerning the software system (in particular, the proportions p_m). We now bound the location of the knee in terms of average parallelism. These bounds indicate the close correspondence between the average parallelism A and the knee location K.

Theorem 6: Under the processor sharing discipline, the number of processors K that yields the knee of the execution time–efficiency profile must satisfy

$$\frac{A}{2} \leq K \leq 2A - 1.$$

When integers, these bounds on K can be attained.

Proof: Consult the Appendix.

Theorem 6 shows that the number of processors that yields the knee is at most a factor of two different from the average parallelism. This suggests that it might be reasonable to use the average parallelism itself as an approximation to the knee location. The reasonableness of this approximation depends on how the properties given in Theorem 5 are affected by using A rather than K processors. This concern is addressed in Theorem 7, where for clarity we consider only integral A.

Theorem 7: Under the processor sharing discipline, when the number of available processors is chosen to equal the average parallelism A, the attained speedup is *at least* 50 percent of the maximum possible, the efficiency is *at least* 50 percent, the utilization of the kth last processor ($k < A$) is *at least* $k/(k + A)$, and the utilization of the kth additional processor is *no more than* $(A - 1)/(A + k - 1)$. These bounds can be attained.

Proof: Consult the Appendix.

Theorem 7 shows that when the number of available processors is equal to the average parallelism, the guarantees regarding speedup and efficiency are *identical* to those at the knee—speedup and efficiency each must be within 50 percent of their maximum values. However, in contrast to the situation at the knee, there are no guarantees as to whether the number of processors is actually somewhat too large (implying that nearly the same speedup could be achieved with fewer processors), or somewhat too small (implying that increases in speedup could be achieved with a slight increase in the number of processors).

VI. Conclusions

In 1967, Amdahl gave a simple bound on the speedup that could be obtained by parallel processing as a function of the fraction of sequential code in a computation. This bound has proven useful in shaping our understanding of parallel systems because it strikes a useful balance between simplicity and precision.

In this paper, we have investigated the tradeoff between execution time speedup and processor efficiency that arises from the inherent characteristics of parallel software systems. Like Amdahl, our goal is to find bounds on performance that can be expressed as functions of simple measures of the parallel system, and that provide insight into the behavior of these systems. Using average parallelism as our characterization, we have shown that speedup and efficiency cannot simultaneously be low, regardless of scheduling discipline or software structure. This indicates that parallel software systems are "robust," in the sense that very poor, anomalous behavior cannot exist. We have also shown that average parallelism provides a great deal of information about the system, in the sense that incrementally more information allows one to tighten the performance bounds only marginally.

Finally, we have examined questions related to the construction and management of parallel systems. Our results bound the efficiency cost and speedup benefit possible by altering the number of allocated processors. The knee of the execution time–efficiency profile has been investigated, a concept with application to multiprogrammed multiprocessors with static processor allocation. We use an explicit formulation of the knee location to show that this location is well approximated by the average parallelism, and to derive bounds on the speedup and efficiency values that are attained at the knee.

It is clear that for any particular problem, all measures of interest can be computed exactly (within our model) from the full specification of the software structure graph. Our intention has been to show formally that a vastly simpler characterization of the software provides considerable information about how the system will behave, and to use this characterization to develop simple relationships that enhance our understanding of the tradeoffs inherent in the design and use of parallel systems.

APPENDIX

Theorem 2: Let A denote the average parallelism, m_{max} denote the maximum parallelism (the maximum number of processors that are simultaneously busy when an unlimited number are available), $S(n)$ denote the speedup with n processors, and $E(n)$ denote the efficiency with n processors. With processor sharing scheduling

$$S(n) \geq \min \left(A, \frac{nA}{n + A - 1 - \frac{(n-1)(A-1)}{m_{max} - 1}} \right)$$

and

$$E(n) \geq \min \left(\frac{A}{n}, \frac{A}{n + A - 1 - \frac{(n-1)(A-1)}{m_{max} - 1}} \right).$$

These bounds can be attained.

Proof: In an execution of a software system using processor sharing and n processors, subtasks are executed in the same groupings as in an execution with an unbounded number of processors. The only difference is that the length of those periods during which the number m of executing subtasks exceeds n is inflated by a factor of m/n. This observation yields the following expression for the execution time under processor sharing, where p_m denotes the propor-

tion of time that m processors are simultaneously busy when an unlimited number are available.

$$T_n = T_\infty \left(\sum_{m=1}^{n} p_m + \sum_{m=n+1}^{m_{max}} p_m \frac{m}{n} \right). \tag{1}$$

To establish the bound on speedup (from which the bound on efficiency directly follows), we first show that the above expression attains its maximum value when p_1 and $p_{m_{max}}$ are the only nonzero proportions, under the constraint of a fixed average parallelism A. For suppose that $p_k > 0$ for some k such that $1 < k < m_{max}$. We can reduce p_k to zero, increase p_1 by $p_k(m_{max} - k)/(m_{max} - 1)$, and increase $p_{m_{max}}$ by $p_k(k - 1)/(m_{max} - 1)$, while keeping A fixed and ensuring that the proportions still sum to one. It is easily verified that this change does not decrease the value of (1): note that

$$\text{for } m_{max} > n \geq k, \ p_k \frac{m_{max} - k}{m_{max} - 1} + p_k \frac{k-1}{m_{max} - 1} \frac{m_{max}}{n} \geq p_k$$

$$\text{for } m_{max} \geq k > n, \ p_k \frac{m_{max} - k}{m_{max} - 1} + p_k \frac{k-1}{m_{max} - 1} \frac{m_{max}}{n} \geq p_k \frac{k}{n}$$

$$\text{for } n \geq m_{max} \geq k, \ p_k \frac{m_{max} - k}{m_{max} - 1} + p_k \frac{k-1}{m_{max} - 1} \geq p_k.$$

Hence, (1) attains its maximum value when p_1 and $p_{m_{max}}$ are the only nonzero proportions.

From the constraints $p_1 + p_{m_{max}} = 1$ and $p_1 + p_{m_{max}} m_{max} = A$, p_1 and $p_{m_{max}}$ can be derived as $(m_{max} - A)/(m_{max} - 1)$ and $(A - 1)/(m_{max} - 1)$, respectively. Substitution in (1) yields, after simplification

$$T_n = T_\infty \left(1 + \frac{A-1}{n} - \frac{n-1}{n} \frac{A-1}{m_{max} - 1} \right)$$

if $n < m_{max}$, and T_∞ otherwise. From the definition of speedup, and the fact that the execution time with only a single processor is $T_\infty A$, this establishes the desired result.

The above proof also shows that the bounds can be attained: we need only consider a software system in which some portion is sequential, and the remainder has a fixed parallelism m_{max}. Q.E.D.

Corollary 2.1: Let A denote the average parallelism, f denote the fraction of work that is inherently sequential, and $S(n)$ denote the speedup with n processors. With processor sharing scheduling and $n \geq 2$

$$S(n) \geq \frac{nA}{n + A - 1 - (1 - fA)}.$$

(fA will always be between 0 and 1.)

Proof: For the processor sharing discipline, the execution time T_n is given by (1). Note that, in our notation, $f = T_\infty p_1 / T_\infty A = p_1 / A$.

Using (1), it is straightforward to show that T_n attains its maximum value when p_2 and $p_{m_{max}}$ ($m_{max} > 2$) are the only other nonzero proportions, under the constraint of fixed p_1 and A. For suppose that $p_k > 0$ for some k such that $2 < k <$

m_{max}. We can reduce p_k to zero, increase p_2 by $p_k (m_{max} - k)/(m_{max} - 2)$, and increase $p_{m_{max}}$ by $p_k k - 2/(m_{max} - 2)$, while keeping p_1 and A fixed and ensuring that the proportions still sum to one. It is easily verified that this change does not decrease the value of (1), hence T_n attains its maximum value when p_2 and $p_{m_{max}}$ are the only other nonzero proportions.

From the constraints $p_1 + p_2 + p_{m_{max}} = 1$ and $p_1 + p_2 2 + p_{m_{max}} m_{max} = A$, $p_{m_{max}}$ and p_2 can be derived as $((A - 1) - (1 - p_1))/(m_{max} - 2)$ and $((m_{max} - 1)(1 - p_1) - (A - 1))/(m_{max} - 2)$, respectively. Assuming that $n \geq 2$, substitution in (1) yields, after simplification,

$$T_n = T_\infty \left(1 + \frac{(A-1)-(1-p_1)}{n} - \frac{n-2}{n} \frac{(A-1)-(1-p_1)}{m_{max}-2} \right)$$

if $n < m_{max}$, and T_∞ otherwise. This yields

$$S(n) \geq \frac{nA}{n+A-1-(1-p_1)}$$

which is equivalent to

$$S(n) \geq \frac{nA}{n+A-1-(1-fA)} .$$

Q.E.D.

Corollary 2.2: Let A denote the average parallelism, f denote the fraction of work that is inherently sequential, and $S(n)$ denote the speedup with n processors. With processor sharing scheduling

$$S(n) \leq \min\left(\frac{n}{1+f(n-1)}, A \right) .$$

Proof: For simplicity we will restrict our attention to integral A. (The bound actually is unnecessarily weak for nonintegral A, but the possible improvement is so minor for reasonably large A that we ignore it.) We similarly assume that $(A - p_1)/(1 - p_1)$ is integral. It is then straightforward to show that (1) is minimized when p_1 and $p_{(A-p_1)/(1-p_1)}$ are the only nonzero proportions, under the constraint of fixed A and p_1. The resulting speedup can then be shown to be $\min(n/(1 + p_1/A(n - 1)), A)$, or $\min(n/(1 + f(n - 1)), A)$.

Q.E.D.

Theorem 3: With processor sharing scheduling, an increase in the number of processors from n to kn ($n, k \geq 1$) affects speedup as follows:

$$\max\left(1, \frac{kA}{(k-1)n+A} \right)$$

$$\leq \frac{S(kn)}{S(n)} \leq \min\left(1 + (A-1) \frac{k-1}{kn-1}, k \right). \quad (2)$$

Correspondingly, efficiency is affected as follows:

$$\max\left(\frac{1}{k}, \frac{A}{(k-1)n+A} \right)$$

$$\leq \frac{E(kn)}{E(n)} \leq \min\left(\frac{1}{k} + (A-1) \frac{1-\frac{1}{k}}{kn-1}, 1 \right).$$

These bounds can be attained.

Proof: The claims regarding the change in efficiency follow directly from those regarding the change in speedup, since efficiency (average processor utilization) is just speedup divided by the number of processors. Therefore, only the claims regarding the change in speedup will be considered.

An increase in the number of processors from n to kn increases speedup by a factor equal to

$$\frac{S(kn)}{S(n)} = \frac{\sum_{m=1}^{n} p_m + \sum_{m=n+1}^{m_{max}} p_m \frac{m}{n}}{\sum_{m=1}^{kn} p_m + \sum_{m=kn+1}^{m_{max}} p_m \frac{m}{kn}} . \quad (3)$$

It is easy to show that this expression is no less than 1 and no more than k. Thus, it is only necessary to consider the second lower bound and the first upper bound in expression (2). Noting that the second lower bound is effective only for $n < A$, and that the first upper bound is effective only for $kn > A$, we need only consider these two bounds for $n < A$ and $kn > A$, respectively.

We can restrict attention to those cases in which all of the proportions p_i for $n + 1 \leq i \leq kn - 1$ are zero. For suppose that some p_i in this range is greater than zero. We can reduce p_i to zero, increase p_n by $p_i (kn - i)/(kn - n)$, and increase p_{kn} by $p_i (i - n)/(kn - n)$, while keeping A fixed and ensuring that the proportions still sum to one. It is easily verified that the value of expression (3) is not affected by this change.

If all p_i for $i \geq kn$ are also zero, the speedup does not change with the increase in the number of processors, and the theorem holds. Assume, therefore, that the p_i for $n + 1 \leq i \leq kn - 1$ are zero, but that there is at least one p_i for $i \geq kn$ that is greater than zero. The following expression is then equivalent to expression (3)

$$\frac{S(kn)}{S(n)} = \frac{\dfrac{\sum_{m=1}^{n} p_m}{\sum_{m=kn}^{m_{max}} p_m m} + \dfrac{1}{n}}{\dfrac{\sum_{m=1}^{n} p_m}{\sum_{m=kn}^{m_{max}} p_m m} + \dfrac{1}{kn}} . \quad (4)$$

Expression (4) is minimized when the ratio of sums in this expression is maximized. Under the assumption that $n < A$, we apply a technical lemma, stated and proved as Lemma 3.1 below, with $l = n$ and $j = kn - n$, to show that the ratio of sums is bounded above by $1/(A - n)$. Thus, for $n < A$

$$\frac{\dfrac{1}{A-n}+\dfrac{1}{n}}{\dfrac{1}{A-n}+\dfrac{1}{kn}} \leq \frac{S(kn)}{S(n)} .$$

Simplification yields the second lower bound in (2), establishing the desired lower bound on the change in speedup.

For $n \geq A$, the lower bound is attained by any software system that does not attain a parallelism of greater than n during its execution. For $n < A$, it can be easily checked that the bound is attained in the limit as $m_{\max} \to \infty$ by a software system whose execution consists of two phases: one during which its parallelism is n, and a second during which its parallelism is $m_{\max}$.

Expression (4) is maximized when the ratio of sums in the expression is minimized. Assuming that $kn > A$, Lemma 3.1 applied with $l = n$ and $j = kn - n$ shows that the ratio of sums is bounded below by $(kn - A)/(kn(A - 1))$. Thus,

$$\frac{\dfrac{kn-A}{kn(A-1)}+\dfrac{1}{n}}{\dfrac{kn-A}{kn(A-1)}+\dfrac{1}{kn}} \geq \frac{S(kn)}{S(n)} .$$

Simplification yields the first upper bound in (2), establishing the desired upper bound on the change in speedup.

For $kn \leq A$, the upper bound is attained by a software system with constant parallelism A. For $kn > A$, it can be easily checked that the bound is attained by a software system whose execution consists of two phases: one during which execution is sequential, and one during which the parallelism is equal to kn. Q.E.D.

Lemma 3.1: For any positive integers l, j such that $p_i = 0$ for $l < i < l + j$,

$$\frac{1}{A-l} \geq \frac{\displaystyle\sum_{m=1}^{l} p_m}{\displaystyle\sum_{m=l+j}^{m_{\max}} p_m m}$$

for $l < A$, and

$$\frac{\displaystyle\sum_{m=1}^{l} p_m}{\displaystyle\sum_{m=l+j}^{m_{\max}} p_m m} \geq \frac{l+j-A}{(l+j)(A-1)}$$

for $l + j > A$.

Proof: To establish the upper bound on the ratio of sums, note that, for $l < A$,

$$\frac{\displaystyle\sum_{m=1}^{l} p_m}{A-l\displaystyle\sum_{m=1}^{l} p_m} \geq \frac{\displaystyle\sum_{m=1}^{l} p_m}{\displaystyle\sum_{m=l+j}^{m_{\max}} p_m m} .$$

The upper bound then results from the fact that $\sum_{m=1}^{l} p_m < 1$.

To establish the lower bound on the ratio of sums, it must be shown that the ratio of sums is minimized when p_1 and p_{l+j} are the only nonzero proportions (given that $p_i = 0$ for $l < i < l + j$). This can be shown in two steps. First, it can be shown that the value of the ratio is not increased when the proportions p_i for $1 < i \leq l$ are reduced to zero by increasing p_1 and p_{l+j} (while keeping A fixed, and ensuring that the proportions still

sum to one). Second, it can be shown that the value of the ratio is not increased when the proportions p_i for $i > l + j$ are reduced to zero by correspondingly increasing p_{l+j} and decreasing p_1. (This is possible since $l + j > A$.) Solving for p_1 and p_{l+j} in terms of A yields the stated lower bound. Q.E.D.

Theorem 4: Let p_m denote the proportion of time that m processors are simultaneously busy when an unlimited number are available, and let $m_{\max}$ denote the maximum parallelism (the maximum number of processors that are simultaneously busy when an unlimited number are available). Under the processor sharing discipline, the execution time–efficiency profile for any software system has a unique knee. The number of processors that attains the knee, i.e., that maximizes $E(n)/T_n$, is given by

$$n = \frac{\displaystyle\sum_{m=\lfloor n \rfloor + 1}^{m_{\max}} p_m m}{\displaystyle\sum_{m=1}^{\lfloor n \rfloor} p_m} \tag{5}$$

if this equation has a solution; otherwise, it is given by the unique integer n satisfying

$$\frac{\displaystyle\sum_{m=n+1}^{m_{\max}} p_m m}{\displaystyle\sum_{m=1}^{n} p_m} \leq n \leq \frac{\displaystyle\sum_{m=n}^{m_{\max}} p_m m}{\displaystyle\sum_{m=1}^{n-1} p_m} . \tag{6}$$

Proof: A knee of the execution time–efficiency profile occurs at a point at which the ratio of efficiency (average processor utilization) to execution time is maximized. Since $E(n)/T_n = S(n)/(nT_n) = T_1/(nT_n^2)$, maximizing $E(n)/T_n$ is equivalent to minimizing $\sqrt{n}T_n$. By (1), this is equivalent to minimizing the following function of n:

$$\sqrt{n}\sum_{m=1}^{\lfloor n \rfloor} p_m + \frac{1}{\sqrt{n}}\sum_{m=\lfloor n \rfloor + 1}^{m_{\max}} p_m m. \tag{7}$$

Note that function (7) is a continuous function of n that tends to infinity for $n \to \infty$ and also for $n \to 0$, and that is equal to 1 for $n = 1$. Hence, function (7) has a minimum, showing existence of the knee.

To show uniqueness, it is first necessary to define the derivative of function (7). At nonintegral points, the standard definition applies. At integral points, we define the derivative to be the right derivative. Note that at nonintegral points, the derivative is a continuous function, but that at the integral points there may be discontinuities.

Uniqueness is then shown in two steps. First, we show that there is at most a single nonintegral point at which the derivative of function (7) is zero, and that this point, should it exist, is a minimum of function (7). Second, we show that there is at most a single integral point at which the derivative changes sign, and that this point, should it exist, is a minimum of function (7). Since it is easy to see that both points cannot exist simultaneously, these two facts are sufficient to show uniqueness.

The derivative of function (7) is given by

$$\frac{1}{2\sqrt{n}} \sum_{m=1}^{\lfloor n \rfloor} p_m - \frac{1}{2n\sqrt{n}} \sum_{m=\lfloor n \rfloor+1}^{m_{max}} p_m m$$

which is zero at each point n satisfying

$$n = \frac{\displaystyle\sum_{m=\lfloor n \rfloor+1}^{m_{max}} p_m m}{\displaystyle\sum_{m=1}^{\lfloor n \rfloor} p_m} \tag{8}$$

Since the left-hand side of this equation is a strictly increasing function of n, while the right-hand side is a nonincreasing function of n, the equation can have at most one solution. Therefore, there is at most a single point at which the derivative of function (7) is zero. It is straightforward to verify that the second derivative of function (7) is positive at this point. (If the point is an integer, the second derivative is defined as the right second derivative.) If the point is nonintegral, this implies that the point must be a minimum of function (7).

Now, suppose that there is an integer n at which the derivative of function (7) changes sign. If the sign changes from positive to negative, it must be the case that

$$\frac{1}{2\sqrt{n}} \sum_{m=1}^{n-1} p_m - \frac{1}{2n\sqrt{n}} \sum_{m=n}^{m_{max}} p_m m \geq 0$$

and

$$\frac{1}{2\sqrt{n}} \sum_{m=1}^{n} p_m - \frac{1}{2n\sqrt{n}} \sum_{m=n+1}^{m_{max}} p_m m \leq 0$$

implying that

$$n \geq \frac{\displaystyle\sum_{m=n}^{m_{max}} p_m m}{\displaystyle\sum_{m=1}^{n-1} p_m}$$

and

$$n \leq \frac{\displaystyle\sum_{m=n+1}^{m_{max}} p_m m}{\displaystyle\sum_{m=1}^{n} p_m}$$

These last two relations can be satisfied simultaneously only if both are equalities. In this case, however, it it easy to verify that the derivative must be positive over the interval $(n, n + 1)$, in contradiction to our assumption that the derivative changes sign from positive to negative at n.

If there is an integer n at which the derivative of function (7) changes sign, the sign must therefore change from negative to

positive, yielding

$$\frac{1}{2\sqrt{n}} \sum_{m=1}^{n-1} p_m - \frac{1}{2n\sqrt{n}} \sum_{m=n}^{m_{max}} p_m m \leq 0$$

and

$$\frac{1}{2\sqrt{n}} \sum_{m=1}^{n} p_m - \frac{1}{2n\sqrt{n}} \sum_{m=n+1}^{m_{max}} p_m m \geq 0.$$

These relations imply that

$$n \leq \frac{\displaystyle\sum_{m=n}^{m_{max}} p_m m}{\displaystyle\sum_{m=1}^{n-1} p_m} \tag{9}$$

and

$$n \geq \frac{\displaystyle\sum_{m=n+1}^{m_{max}} p_m m}{\displaystyle\sum_{m=1}^{n} p_m} \tag{10}$$

From relation (10), it follows that

$$n + 1 > \frac{\displaystyle\sum_{m=n+1}^{m_{max}} p_m m}{\displaystyle\sum_{m=1}^{n} p_m}$$

Since the right-hand side of relation (9) is a nonincreasing function of n, this last relation implies that no integer larger than n can satisfy relation (9). Similarly, it can be shown that no integer smaller than n can satisfy relation (10). Therefore, there must be at most one integer at which the derivative of function (7) changes sign, and this sign change must be from negative to positive, implying that the point is a minimum of function (7).

We have now shown that there exists a unique knee. The location of the knee was determined in the proof of uniqueness [(8) for a nonintegral knee, and relations (9) and (10) for an integral knee], and matches that given in the theorem statement. (Note that if (5) has an integral solution, this solution also satisfies relation (6).)   Q.E.D.

Theorem 5: Under the processor sharing discipline, when the number of available processors is equal to K (achieving the knee of the execution time–efficiency profile), the attained speedup is *at least* 50 percent of the maximum possible, the efficiency is *at least* 50 percent, the utilization of the last processor is *at least* 50 percent, and the utilization of a single additional processor is *no more than* 50 percent. These bounds can be attained in the limit as $A \rightarrow \infty$.

Proof: Consider first the attained speedup. The execution time with K processors is given by

$$T_\infty \left(\sum_{m=1}^{\lfloor K \rfloor} p_m + \sum_{m=\lfloor K \rfloor+1}^{m_{max}} p_m \frac{m}{K} \right)$$

Since, from (5) and relation (6), $K \geq \sum_{m=\lfloor K \rfloor+1}^{m_{\max}} p_m m$, it follows that the execution time with K processors can be at most $2T_\infty$. Therefore, the attained speedup with K processors is at least equal to 50 percent of the maximum possible speedup. It is straightforward to verify that this bound is attained in the limit as $A \to \infty$ by a software system whose execution consists of two phases; a first phase during which execution is sequential, and a second phase during which the parallelism is equal to A^2 (for integer A). (Note that K tends to A in this case.)

Since efficiency is the average processor utilization, if we can show that the utilization of the last processor is at least 50 percent, then this will also show that the efficiency is at least 50 percent. The utilization of the last processor is given by

$$\frac{\sum\limits_{m=\lceil K \rceil}^{m_{\max}} p_m \frac{m}{K}}{\sum\limits_{m=\lceil K \rceil}^{m_{\max}} p_m \frac{m}{K} + \sum\limits_{m=1}^{\lceil K \rceil-1} p_m}.$$

Since, from (5) and (6),

$$K \leq \frac{\sum\limits_{m=\lceil K \rceil}^{m_{\max}} p_m m}{\sum\limits_{m=1}^{\lceil K \rceil-1} p_m}$$

the utilization of the last processor is at least 50 percent. This bound can be attained in the limit as $A \to \infty$, since, in fact, it is possible for the efficiency as well to drop to 50 percent in the limit. This occurs for a software system of the same structure as that which attains the lower bound on speedup, as described earlier.

The utilization of a single additional processor is the final quantity of interest. Since $K < \lfloor K \rfloor + 1$, this utilization is bounded above by

$$\frac{\sum\limits_{m=\lfloor K \rfloor+1}^{m_{\max}} p_m \frac{m}{K}}{\sum\limits_{m=\lfloor K \rfloor+1}^{m_{\max}} p_m \frac{m}{K} + \sum\limits_{m=1}^{\lfloor K \rfloor} p_m}.$$

Since, from (5) and (6),

$$K \geq \frac{\sum\limits_{m=\lfloor K \rfloor+1}^{m_{\max}} p_m m}{\sum\limits_{m=1}^{\lfloor K \rfloor} p_m}$$

the utilization of a single additional processor is bounded above by 50 percent. This bound is attained in the limit as $A \to \infty$ by a software system of the same structure as that which attains the lower bound on speedup, as described earlier.   Q.E.D.

Theorem 6: Under the processor sharing discipline, the number of processors K that yields the knee of the execution time–efficiency profile must satisfy

$$\frac{A}{2} \leq K \leq 2A - 1. \tag{11}$$

When integers, these bounds on K can be attained.

Proof: Equation (5) and relation (6) yield

$$\frac{\sum\limits_{m=\lfloor K \rfloor+1}^{m_{\max}} p_m m}{\sum\limits_{m=1}^{\lfloor K \rfloor} p_m} \leq K \leq \frac{\sum\limits_{m=\lceil K \rceil}^{m_{\max}} p_m m}{\sum\limits_{m=1}^{\lceil K \rceil-1} p_m}. \tag{12}$$

Lemma 3.1 with $l = \lfloor K \rfloor$ and $j = 1$ implies, for $\lfloor K \rfloor < A$, that

$$A - \lfloor K \rfloor \leq \frac{\sum\limits_{m=\lfloor K \rfloor+1}^{m_{\max}} p_m m}{\sum\limits_{m=1}^{\lfloor K \rfloor} p_m}.$$

The same lemma with $l = \lceil K \rceil - 1$ and $j = 1$ implies, for $\lceil K \rceil > A$, that

$$\frac{\sum\limits_{m=\lceil K \rceil}^{m_{\max}} p_m m}{\sum\limits_{m=1}^{\lceil K \rceil-1} p_m} \leq \frac{\lceil K \rceil(A-1)}{\lceil K \rceil - A}.$$

In conjunction with relation (12), these last two relations imply that

$$A - \lfloor K \rfloor \leq K$$

for $\lfloor K \rfloor < A$ and

$$K \leq \frac{\lceil K \rceil(A-1)}{\lceil K \rceil - A}$$

for $\lceil K \rceil > A$, which in turn yields (with the same constraints on K),

$$A - K \leq K$$

and

$$K \leq \frac{K(A-1)}{K-A}.$$

Simplification yields the bounds given in relation (11).

For $A/2$ an integer, it is straightforward to verify that the lower bound on K is attained in the limit as $m_{\max} \to \infty$ by a software system whose execution consists of two phases: one in which the parallelism is $A/2$, and a second in which the parallelism is $m_{\max}$. For $2A - 1$ an integer, the upper bound on K is attained by a software system whose execution consists of two phases: one in which execution is sequential, and a second in which the parallelism is $2A - 1$.   Q.E.D.

Theorem 7: Under the processor sharing discipline, when the number of available processors is chosen to equal the average parallelism A, the attained speedup is *at least* 50 percent of the maximum possible, the efficiency is *at least* 50 percent, the utilization of the kth last processor ($k < A$) is *at least* $k/(k + A)$, and the utilization of the kth additional processor is *no more than* $(A - 1)/(A + k - 1)$. These bounds can be attained.

Proof: We assume that A is integral here. The claims regarding speedup and efficiency follow from Theorem 1 (Section III) with n substituted for by A. Only the claims regarding the utilizations of the kth last and the kth additional processors need be considered further.

The utilization of the kth last processor is given by

$$\frac{\displaystyle\sum_{m=A-k+1}^{A-1} p_m + \sum_{m=A}^{m_{\max}} p_m \frac{m}{A}}{\displaystyle\sum_{m=1}^{A-1} p_m + \sum_{m=A}^{m_{\max}} p_m \frac{m}{A}}.$$

It is straightforward to show that the value of this expression does not increase when p_j for $A - k < j < A$ is reduced to zero by correspondingly increasing p_{A-k} and p_A. Therefore, the utilization of the kth last processor is bounded below by

$$\frac{\dfrac{1}{A}}{\dfrac{\displaystyle\sum_{m=1}^{A-k} p_m}{\displaystyle\sum_{m=A}^{m_{\max}} p_m m} + \dfrac{1}{A}}.$$

Lemma 3.1 applied with $l = A - k$ and $j = k$ yields a lower bound on this latter expression of

$$\frac{\dfrac{1}{A}}{\dfrac{1}{k} + \dfrac{1}{A}}.$$

Simplification produces the desired result.

It is straightforward to verify that the lower bound on the utilization of the kth last processor is attained in the limit as $m_{\max} \to \infty$ by a software system whose execution consists of two phases: one in which the parallelism is $A - k$, and a second in which the parallelism is $m_{\max}$.

The utilization of the kth additional processor is given by

$$\frac{\displaystyle\sum_{m=A+k}^{m_{\max}} p_m \frac{m}{A+k}}{\displaystyle\sum_{m=1}^{A+k-1} p_m + \sum_{m=A+k}^{m_{\max}} p_m \frac{m}{A+k}}$$

which is equal to

$$\frac{\dfrac{1}{A+k}}{\dfrac{\displaystyle\sum_{m=1}^{A+k-1} p_m}{\displaystyle\sum_{m=A+k}^{m_{\max}} p_m m} + \dfrac{1}{A+k}}.$$

Lemma 3.1 applied with $l = A + k - 1$ and $j = 1$ yields an upper bound on this latter expression of

$$\frac{\dfrac{1}{A+k}}{\dfrac{k}{(A+k)(A-1)} + \dfrac{1}{A+k}}.$$

Simplification produces the desired result.

It is straightforward to verify that the upper bound on the utilization of the kth additional processor is attained by a software sytem whose execution consists of two phases: one in which execution is sequential, and a second in which the parallelism is $A + k$.   Q.E.D.

ACKNOWLEDGMENT

J.-L. Baer, S. Owicki, K. Sevcik, and two anonymous referees offered helpful comments on earlier versions of this paper.

REFERENCES

[1] G. M. Amdahl, "Validity of the single processor approach to achieving large-scale computing capabilities," in *Proc. AFIPS*, vol. 30, 1967, pp. 483–485.
[2] T. C. Chen, "Overlap and pipeline processing," in *Introduction to Computer Architecture*, H. Stone, Ed. SRA, 1975, pp. 375–431.
[3] P. J. Denning, "Working sets past and present," *IEEE Trans. Software Eng.*, vol. SE-6, no. 1, pp. 64–84, 1980.
[4] P. J. Denning and J. P. Buzen, "The operational analysis of queueing network models," *Comput. Surveys*, vol. 10, no. 3, pp. 225–261, 1978.
[5] G. Fayolle, P. J. B. King, and I. Mitrani, "On the execution of programs by many processors," in *Proc. 9th Int. Symp. Comput. Perform. Modeling, Measurement Eval.* 1983, pp. 217–228.
[6] R. L. Graham, "Bounds for certain multiprocessing anomalies," *Bell Syst. Tech. J.*, vol. 45, pp. 1563–1581, 1966.
[7] J. R. Gurd, C. C. Kirkham, and I. Watson, "The Manchester prototype dataflow computer," *Commun. ACM*, vol. 28, no. 1, pp. 34–52, 1985.
[8] P. Heidelberger and K. S. Trivedi, "Queueing network models for parallel processing with asynchronous tasks," *IEEE Trans. Comput.*, vol. C-31, no. 11, pp. 1099–1109, 1982.
[9] L. Kleinrock, *Queueing Systems: Vol. 2, Computer Applications*. New York: Wiley, 1976.
[10] ——, "Power and deterministic rules of thumb for probabilistic problems in computer communications," in *Proc. Int. Conf. Commun.*, 1979, pp. 43.1.1–43.1.10.
[11] D. J. Kuck, "A survey of parallel machine organization and programming," *ACM Comput. Surveys*, vol. 9, no. 1, pp. 29–59, 1977.
[12] D. J. Kuck et al., "The effects of program restructuring, algorithm change and architecture choice on program parallelism," in *Proc. Int. Conf. Parallel Processing*, 1984, pp. 129–138.
[13] B. Kumar and T. A. Gonsalves, "Modelling and analysis of distributed software systems," in *Proc. 7th ACM Symp. Oper. Syst. Principles*, 1979, pp. 2–8.

[14] K. C-Y. Kung, "Concurrency in parallel processing systems," UCLA CSD Rep. 840039, Comput. Sci. Dep. Univ. of California, Los Angeles, 1984.

[15] M. Minsky and S. Papert, "On some associative, parallel and analog computations," in *Associative Information Technologies*, E. J. Jacks, Ed. New York: Elsevier North Holland, 1971.

[16] R. R. Muntz and J.W.-N. Wong, "Asymptotic properties of closed queueing network models," in *Proc. 8th Princeton Conf. Inform. Sci. Syst.*, 1974, pp. 348-352.

John Zahorjan received the Sc.B. degree from Brown University, Providence, RI, in 1975, and the M.Sc. and Ph.D. degrees in computer science from the University of Toronto, Toronto, Ont., Canada, in 1976 and 1980, respectively.

Presently, he is Associate Professor of Computer Science at the University of Washington, Seattle. His active research interests include computer system performance modeling and evaluation, the performance of parallel and distributed systems, naming and location in distributed systems, and load sharing in distributed and parallel systems. He is the author of papers in these areas and co-author of the text *Quantitative System Performance: Computer System Analysis Using Queueing Network Models*.

Dr. Zahorjan a member of the board of SIGMETRICS (the ACM special interest group concerned with computer system performance), and a member of IFIP Working Group 7.3 on Computer System Modeling.

Derek L. Eager (M'87) received the B.Sc. degree in computer science from the University of Regina, Regina, Sask., Canada, in 1979, and the M.Sc. and Ph.D. degrees in computer science from the University of Toronto, Toronto, Ont., Canada, in 1981 and 1984, respectively.

He is currently an Associate Professor in the Department of Computational Science at the University of Saskatchewan, Saskatoon, Sask., Canada. His research interests are in the areas of performance modeling and distributed and parallel systems.

Edward D. Lazowska, photograph and biography are not available.

REEVALUATING AMDAHL'S LAW

JOHN L. GUSTAFSON

At Sandia National Laboratories, we are currently engaged in research involving massively parallel processing. There is considerable skepticism regarding the viability of massive parallelism; the skepticism centers around *Amdahl's law*, an argument put forth by Gene Amdahl in 1967 [1] that even when the fraction of serial work in a given problem is small, say, *s*, the maximum speedup obtainable from even an infinite number of parallel processors is only $1/s$. We now have timing results for a 1024-processor system that demonstrate that the assumptions underlying Amdahl's 1967 argument are inappropriate for the current approach to massive ensemble parallelism.

If N is the number of processors, s is the amount of time spent (by a serial processor) on serial parts of a program, and p is the amount of time spent (by a serial processor) on parts of the program that can be done in parallel, then Amdahl's law says that speedup is given by

$$Speedup = (s + p)/(s + p/N)$$

$$= 1/(s + p/N),$$

where we have set total time $s + p = 1$ for algebraic simplicity. For $N = 1024$ this is an unforgivingly steep function of s near $s = 0$ (see Figure 1).

The steepness of the graph near $s = 0$ (approximately $-N^2$) implies that very few problems will experience even a 100-fold speedup. Yet, for three very practical applications ($s = 0.4$–0.8 percent) used at Sandia, we have achieved speedup factors on a 1024-processor hypercube that we believe are unprecedented [2]: *1021* for beam stress analysis using conjugate gradients, *1020* for baffled surface wave simulation using explicit finite dif-

ferences, and *1016* for unstable fluid flow using flux-corrected transport. How can this be, when Amdahl's argument would predict otherwise?

The expression and graph both contain the implicit assumption that p is independent of N, which *is virtually never the case*. One does not take a fixed-sized problem and run it on various numbers of processors

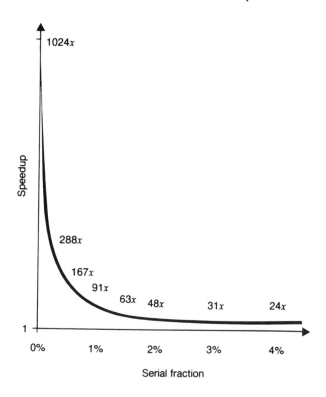

FIGURE 1. Speedup under Amdahl's Law

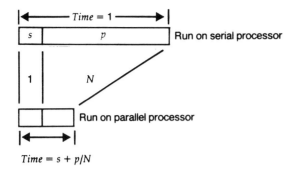

FIGURE 2a. Fixed-Sized Model for *Speedup* $= 1/(s + p/N)$

$$Scaled\ speedup = (s + p \times N)/(s + p)$$
$$= s + p \times N$$
$$= N + (1 - N) \times s.$$

In contrast with Figure 1, this function is simply a *line*, and one with a much more moderate slope: $1 - N$. It is thus much easier to achieve efficient parallel performance than is implied by Amdahl's paradigm. The two approaches, fixed sized and scaled sized, are contrasted and summarized in Figure 2a and b.

Our work to date shows that it is *not* an insurmountable task to extract very high efficiency from a massively parallel ensemble, for the reasons presented here. We feel that it is important for the computing

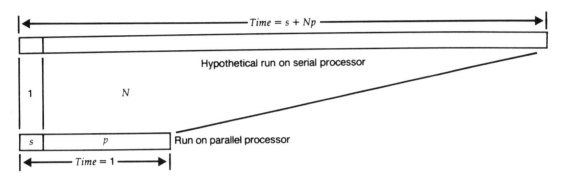

FIGURE 2b. Scaled-Sized Model for *Speedup* $= s + Np$

except when doing academic research; in practice, *the problem size scales with the number of processors.* When given a more powerful processor, the problem generally expands to make use of the increased facilities. Users have control over such things as grid resolution, number of time steps, difference operator complexity, and other parameters that are usually adjusted to allow the program to be run in some desired amount of time. Hence, it may be most realistic to assume *run time*, not *problem size*, is constant.

As a first approximation, we have found that it is the *parallel* or *vector* part of a program that scales with the problem size. Times for vector start-up, program loading, serial bottlenecks, and I/O that make up the *s* component of the run do *not* grow with problem size. When we double the number of degrees of freedom in a physical simulation, we double the number of processors. But this means that, as a first approximation, the amount of work that can be done in parallel *varies linearly with the number of processors.* For the three applications mentioned above, we found that the parallel portion scaled by factors of 1023.9969, 1023.9965, and 1023.9965. If we use *s* and *p* to represent serial and parallel time spent on the *parallel* system, then a serial processor would require time $s + p \times N$ to perform the task. This reasoning gives an alternative to Amdahl's law suggested by E. Barsis at Sandia:

research community to overcome the "mental block" against massive parallelism imposed by a misuse of Amdahl's speedup formula; speedup should be measured by scaling the problem to the number of processors, not by fixing problem size. We expect to extend our success to a broader range of applications and even larger values for *N*.

REFERENCES
1. Amdahl, G.M. Validity of the single-processor approach to achieving large scale computing capabilities. In *AFIPS Conference Proceedings*, vol. 30 (Atlantic City, N.J., Apr. 18–20). AFIPS Press, Reston, Va., 1967, pp. 483–485.
2. Benner, R.E., Gustafson, J.L., and Montry, R.E. Development and analysis of scientific application programs on a 1024-processor hypercube. SAND 88-0317, Sandia National Laboratories, Albuquerque, N.M., Feb. 1988.

CR Categories and Subject Descriptors: C.1.2 [**Processor Architectures**]: Multiple Data Stream Architectures (Multiprocessors)—*parallel processors*
General Terms: Theory
Additional Key Words and Phrases: Amdahl's law, massively parallel processing, speedup

Author's Present Address: John L. Gustafson, Sandia National Laboratories, Albuquerque, NM 87185.

Performance Analysis of Parallel Processing Systems

RANDOLPH NELSON, DON TOWSLEY, MEMBER, IEEE, AND ASSER N. TANTAWI, MEMBER, IEEE

Abstract—A bulk arrival $M^X/M/c$ queueing system is used to model a centralized parallel processing system with job splitting. In such a system, jobs wait in a central queue, which is accessible by all the processors, and are split into independent tasks that can be executed on separate processors. The job response time consists of three components: queueing delay, service time, and synchronization delay. An expression for the mean job response time is obtained for this centralized parallel processing system. Centralized and distributed parallel processing systems (with and without job splitting) are considered and their performances compared. Furthermore, the effects of parallelism and overheads due to job splitting are investigated.

Index Terms—Bulk arrival queues, fork/join queues, job splitting, modeling and analysis, parallel processing, synchronization delay.

I. Introduction

PERFORMANCE modeling of parallel processing systems must take into account the job structure and the system structure. The *job structure* describes the precedence relationships among the various components, called tasks, of the job and is usually given by a task graph model. A simple job structure is a fork/join one where a job consists of a set of independent tasks. For such a structure, a job is considered completed only when all of its tasks are completed. The *system structure* is modeled by a queueing system consisting of a system of queues and a set of servers. Generally speaking, we may have either a central queue which is accessible by all the processors or a distributed queue where each processor serves its own queue. A queue may hold jobs or tasks depending on whether jobs are split into tasks before entering the queue or not. We index the tasks composing a job by their order of departure and define the time between the departure of the first and last task to be the *synchronization delay* of that job. The job response time, which includes this synchronization delay, is hard to obtain even for simple system structures [1], [3]–[5]. In the nonsplitting case, the analysis is much easier since all tasks from the same job are executed sequentially on the same processor.

Spies and Geilenkeuser [6] study a related system. They consider multiple processors serving jobs that arrive according to a Poisson process. Each job consists initially of a single task. Upon completion, each task generates zero or more additional tasks that require further processing. Hence a job is represented by a tree precedence graph where control flows from the root to the leaves. The statistics of the number of tasks in the system are derived under the assumption that task service times are independent and identically distributed exponential random variables. However, no results are reported regarding the job response time characteristics.

In this paper, we model a parallel processing system with a central queue and job splitting as a bulk arrival $M^X/M/c$ queueing system where customers and bulks correspond to tasks and jobs, respectively. Such a system has been studied in [2], [7] and an expression for the mean response time of a random customer is obtained. However, since we are interested in the time that a job spends in the system, including the synchronization delay, we must evaluate the bulk response time rather than simply the customer response time.

In Section II we describe the queueing system under consideration. The job response time is the sum of the job waiting time and the job service time. In Section III we analyze the bulk queueing system and obtain an expression for the mean job waiting time. The mean job service time is given by a set of recurrence equations. In Section IV we consider queueing models of a wide range of parallel processing systems covering systems with centralized and distributed queues as well as with and without job splitting. In these models we assume that jobs consist of fork/join task graphs in which each task has the same distribution of service which is assumed to be exponential. These are simplifying assumptions and are made so the resultant queueing systems are mathematically tractable. In real systems jobs could consist of an arbitrary task graph and could have very different task service distributions. We believe, however, that fundamental performance characteristics are captured by our models and that the relationships found by comparing their relative response time, in Section V, continue to hold under less restrictive assumptions. Other characteristics that we study in Section V include the effects of parallelism on response time and the overhead delays due to job splitting.

II. Model Description

We consider a system of c identical servers that serve a single queue. Jobs enter the system according to a Poisson process with parameter λ. Each job consists of one or more tasks that can be processed independently of each other. Specifically, let X be a random variable (r.v.) that

Manuscript received March 31, 1987; revised September 30, 1987. The work of D. Towsley was supported in part by the National Science Foundation under Contract ECS8406402.

R. Nelson and A. N. Tantawi are with the IBM Thomas J. Watson Research Center, Yorktown Heights, NY 10598.

D. Towsley is with the Department of Computer and Information Science, University of Massachusetts, Amherst, MA 01003.

IEEE Log Number 8819727.

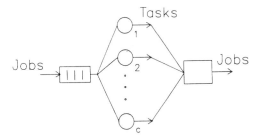
Fig. 1. Queueing model.

denotes the number of tasks within a job. We assume that X has probability distribution $\alpha_i = P[X = i]$, $i = 1, 2, \cdots$ and probability generating function (p.g.f.) $X(z) = \sum_{i=1}^{\infty} \alpha_i z^i$. The service time required by a task is assumed to be an exponential r.v. with parameter μ and is independent of the service requirements of all other tasks.

We are interested in the steady state behavior of this system. In particular, we focus on the response time of a random job, i.e., the interval of time measured from the arrival of a job until the service completion of the *last task* associated with that job. One can envision the system as consisting of a queue for tasks awaiting service, c servers, and a waiting area for tasks that have completed service but are awaiting the completion of the last task associated with a job (Fig. 1). All of the tasks within a job depart this last waiting area when all have completed their service. Denote this response time as T. Last, we assume that jobs are scheduled into service in a first-come first-serve manner. Tasks within a single job are scheduled in random order.

III. ANALYSIS

As described, this system is modeled as a continuous time, discrete state Markov process. We obtain the statistics for the response time of a job by decomposing the problem into two parts each of which can be handled in a simple manner. Specifically, the response time T of a random job can be expressed as the sum of two terms: $T = W + S$. The first term W is the *job waiting time* and corresponds to the time that the job waits in the queue before the first of its tasks is scheduled. If the job arrives to a system where one or more of the servers are idle then $W = 0$, otherwise $W > 0$. The second term S is the *job service time* and corresponds to the time required to process all of the tasks associated with the job once the first task is scheduled. The mean response time is given by

$$E[T] = E[W] + E[S]. \tag{1}$$

The statistics for W can be obtained by studying the bulk arrival $M^X/M/c$ queue that underlies the parallel processing system of interest to us. Specifically, W in our system corresponds to the time that a bulk of customers in the $M^X/M/c$ must wait before the first customer begins service. Section III-A focuses on this random variable. The statistics of the job service time are obtained in Section III-B. Unfortunately, we are unable to obtain closed form expressions for these statistics, but must numerically solve a set of recurrence relations.

A. Mean Job Waiting Time

In this section, we analyze the behavior of the $M^X/M/c$ queue. This provides us with the statistics for W, the time that a job waits in the queue of the parallel processing system. The queue length distribution for the bulk arrival $M^X/M/c$ queue will also be used to obtain the service time statistics in the parallel processing system. We shall use the following terminology. The bulk arrival system processes *tasks*. Tasks that arrive simultaneously form a *group of tasks*. The reader should note that a job in the parallel processing system corresponds to a group of tasks in the bulk arrival system. In addition to the notation introduced in the previous Section, we define N to be a random variable denoting the steady state number of tasks in the system. N has distribution $\pi_i = P[N = i]$, $i = 0, 1, \cdots$, and p.g.f. $\Pi(z) = \sum_{i=0}^{\infty} \pi_i z^i$. The steady state queue length distribution, π_i, $i = 0, 1, \cdots$ satisfies the following difference equations,

$$\lambda \pi_0 = \mu \pi_1, \tag{2}$$

$$(\lambda + i\mu) \pi_i = \lambda \sum_{k=0}^{i-1} \pi_k \alpha_{i-k} + (i + 1) \mu \pi_{i+1},$$
$$0 < i < c, \tag{3}$$

$$(\lambda + c\mu) \pi_i = \lambda \sum_{k=0}^{i-1} \pi_k \alpha_{i-k} + c\mu \pi_{i+1}, \quad i \geq c. \tag{4}$$

By multiplying both sides of each of the above equations by z^i and summing, we obtain

$$(\lambda + c\mu) \Pi(z) - \sum_{i=0}^{c-1} \mu(c - i) \pi_i z^i$$

$$= \lambda \sum_{i=1}^{\infty} z^i \sum_{k=0}^{i-1} \pi_k \alpha_{i-k} + \sum_{i=1}^{c-1} i\mu \pi_i z^{i-1}$$

$$+ \sum_{i=c}^{\infty} c\mu \pi_i z^{i-1}.$$

By defining $A(z) = \sum_{i=0}^{c-1} (c - i) \pi_i z^i$ and substituting it into the above equation, we finally obtain

$$\Pi(z) = A(z) \mu(z - 1) / [\lambda z(1 - X(z)) + c\mu(z - 1)]. \tag{5}$$

By taking the limit of the above equation as z goes to 1, we get $\Pi(1) = A(1) \mu / [c\mu - \lambda E[X]]$, which, as $\Pi(1) = 1$, yields $A(1) = (c\mu - \lambda E[X])/\mu$. The above expression along with (2) and (3) can be used to obtain an expression for $\Pi(z)$. The moment generating properties of the p.g.f. allow us to obtain the expected number of tasks in the system, i.e., $E[N] = d\Pi(z)/dz \big|_{z=1}$. Let Q be an r.v. that denotes the number of tasks in the queue awaiting service; then we have

$$E[Q] = E[N] - c + \sum_{i=0}^{c-1} (c - i) \pi_i$$

$$= E[N] - c + A(1).$$

The mean job waiting time $E[W]$ in the original parallel processing system corresponds to the average time that a group of tasks waits in the $M^X/M/c$ queue before the first job enters a server. $E[W]$ is therefore given by

$$E[W] = (E[Q] + P[N \geq c])/(c\mu). \qquad (6)$$

This completes our discussion of the bulk arrival $M^X/M/c$ queue.

B. Mean Job Service Time

In this section we determine the value of the mean job service time $E[S]$ for a random job. The analysis is simplified if we condition the job service time on the number of processors that can be initially scheduled (i.e., at the time that the first task is scheduled) and on the total number of tasks that must be completed (including those in service).

Let $s_{i,n}$, $(0 < i \leq \min\{c, n\}, 1 \leq n < \infty)$, be the mean job service time given that there are n tasks to be executed and that i tasks are initially scheduled to servers. The quantity $s_{i,n}$ satisfies the following equations,

$$s_{1,1} = 1/\mu,$$

$$s_{n,n} = s_{n-1,n-1} + 1/(n\mu) = H_n/\mu,$$

$$1 \leq n \leq c,$$

$$s_{c,n} = 1/(c\mu) + s_{c,n-1} = (n-c)/(c\mu) + H_c/\mu,$$

$$n > c,$$

$$s_{i,n} = 1/(c\mu) + is_{i,n-1}/c + (c-i)s_{i+1,n}/c,$$

$$1 \leq i < \min\{c, n\},$$

where $H_n = \sum_{k=1}^n 1/k$ is the harmonic series.

The number of servers available when the job is first scheduled is related to the number of idle servers at job arrival time. If the job arrives when all servers are busy, $N \geq c$, then exactly one server will be available when the first task is scheduled. If there are one or more idle servers at the time that the job arrives, $N < c$, then the job is scheduled immediately and will initially schedule $\min\{X, c - N\}$ servers at that time. Consequently, removal of the conditioning on the number of servers initially available yields

$$E[S \mid X = n] = \sum_{i=0}^{c-1} \pi_i s_{\min\{n, c-i\}, n}$$

$$+ \left(1 - \sum_{i=0}^{c-1} \pi_i\right) s_{1,n}, \qquad 1 \leq n.$$

Removal of the conditioning on the number of tasks in a job yields

$$E[S] = \sum_{i=0}^{c-1} \pi_i \sum_{n=1}^{\infty} s_{\min\{n, c-i\}, n} \alpha_n$$

$$+ \left(1 - \sum_{i=0}^{c-1} \pi_i\right) \sum_{n=1}^{\infty} s_{1,n} \alpha_n. \qquad (7)$$

The mean job response time $E[T]$ is obtained by substituting (6) and (7) into (1).

As an example, we consider a special case where the number of tasks in a job is a geometric r.v., i.e., $P[X = n] = p^{n-1}(1 - p)$, $n > 0$. We shall focus on deriving the expected service time, $E[S]$. The following analysis is made possible by the memoryless property of the geometric distribution. Let s_i, $0 < i \leq c$, be the mean service time of a job given that i tasks are initially scheduled to i processors and that it contains *at least one* task in the queue. This conditional expectation satisfies the following equations,

$$s_i = 1/(c\mu) + (1 - p)\left(\frac{i}{c} H_i + \frac{c - i}{c} H_{i+1}\right)\bigg/\mu$$

$$+ p\left(\frac{i}{c} s_i + \frac{c - i}{c} s_{i+1}\right), \qquad 0 < i < c,$$

$$s_c = 1/(c\mu) + (1 - p) H_c/\mu + ps_c$$

$$= 1/((1 - p)c\mu) + H_c/\mu, \qquad i = c.$$

By substitution into (7) we obtain

$$E[S] = \sum_{i=0}^{c-1} \pi_i \left(\sum_{n=1}^{c-i} p^{n-1}(1 - p) H_n/\mu + p^{c-i+1}s_{c-i}\right)$$

$$+ \left(1 - \sum_{i=0}^{c-1} \pi_i\right)[(1 - p)/\mu + ps_1]. \qquad (8)$$

IV. PARALLEL PROCESSING MODELS

In the remainder of this paper we consider the following question. How should one architect a system that processes an arrival stream of jobs composed of independent tasks on a system consisting of c identical processors. Since the queueing system analyzed in the previous section is just one way to architect a parallel processing system, we find it to be of more interest in this section to expand the class of architectures that we consider.

In Fig. 2 we present four models of parallel processing systems: distributed/splitting (D/S), distributed/no splitting (D/NS), centralized/splitting (C/S), and centralized/no splitting (C/NS). In each of these systems there are c processors, jobs are assumed to consist of set of tasks that are independent and have exponentially distributed service requirements, and arrivals of jobs are assumed to come from a Poisson point source with intensity λ. The systems differ in the way jobs queue for the processors and in the way jobs are scheduled on the processors. The queueing of jobs for processors is *distributed* if each processor has its own queue, and is *centralized* if there is a common queue for all the processors. The scheduling of jobs on the processors is *no splitting* if the entire set of tasks composing that job are scheduled to run sequentially on the same processor once the job is scheduled. On the other hand, the scheduling is *splitting* if the tasks of a job are scheduled so that they can be run independently and potentially in parallel on different processors. In the splitting case a job is completed only when 'll of its tasks have

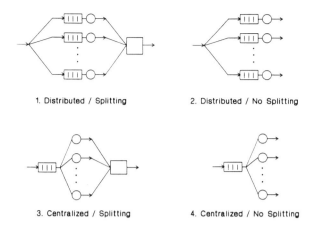

1. Distributed / Splitting   2. Distributed / No Splitting

3. Centralized / Splitting   4. Centralized / No Splitting

Fig. 2. Parallel processing models.

finished execution. This is known as a *join* operation. We distinguish this case in the figures by showing a "waiting" box after the processors in the ./S systems.

In our study we compare the mean response time of jobs in each of the systems for differing values of the number of processors, number of tasks per job, server utilization, and certain overheads associated with splitting up a job. The $M^X/M/c$ system studied in the previous section corresponds to the C/S system. In this system, as processors become free they serve the first task in the queue. D/. systems are studied in [5]. We use the approximate analysis of the D/S system and the exact analysis of the D/NS system that are given in that paper. For systems with 32 processors or less, the relative error in the approximation for the D/S system was found to be less than 5 percent. The approximation for the D/S system given in [5] requires that the number of tasks per job equals the number of processors, each task is scheduled on a different processor. In the D/NS system, jobs are assigned to processors with equal probabilities. The approximation we use for the mean job response time for the C/NS system is found in [8]. Although an extensive error analysis for this system over all parameter ranges has not been carried out, the largest relative error for the $M/E_2/10$ system reported in [8] is about 0.1 percent.

V. RESULTS

In this section we present the results of our investigations into the performance of the four parallel processing systems described in Section IV. We ran four different experiments to compare and contrast the performance of the different systems. The performance metric we use in these comparisons is the mean job response time and, for comparative purposes, often plot the ratio of mean job response times for the different systems. We plot the curves in this section as a function of the utilization of each server in the system given by $\rho = \lambda E[X]/c\mu$. We compare systems for a common ρ since this corresponds to viewing each system under an equal load. Experiment 1 is a comparison of the mean job response times for the four systems to determine their relative performance for different utilizations. In experiment 2 we quantify the ef-

fects of executing the tasks of a job in a parallel, rather than sequential, manner. In experiment 3 we consider a system which has two types of jobs: edit jobs and batch jobs. Edit job are assumed to consist of a single task whereas batch jobs may consist of many tasks. With the idea that the response time of edit jobs might be severely increased by the existence of batch jobs on the same system, we consider the effects of partitioning the processors of the system so that edit and batch jobs are run on different sets of processors. Finally, in experiment 4, we investigate the effects of including overhead resulting from the splitting of jobs into tasks.

A. A Comparison of Parallel Processing Systems

In this section we compare the mean job response time for the four parallel processing systems described in Section IV to determine their relative performance over different utilizations. In Fig. 3 we plot the mean job response time for the four different systems for a system consisting of $c = 8$ processors and where jobs are assumed to consist of exactly 8 tasks.

The figure contains several interesting comparisons. For any server utilization ρ, we note that the ./S systems yield lower mean job response times than the ./NS systems. This implies that, in the absence of overhead associated with splitting jobs up into tasks, it is better to run the tasks of a job in parallel and incur a synchronization delay than it is to avoid this delay and run tasks sequentially on the same processor. This same observation, for the D/. systems, was made in [5]. The intuition behind this observation lies in the fact that in the splitting case work is spread in smaller increments over all the processors. Intuitively, it is more likely in the no splitting case for a set of processors to be idle when others are busy processing larger, unsplit jobs, than it is in the splitting case. In comparing distributed and centralized systems as shown in Fig. 3 we see that the C/S system has a better performance than that of the D/S system. Once again the same observation explains this effect, namely one is more likely to find idle processors even when there is work available for processing in the distributed system than in the centralized system.

From Fig. 3 we conclude that, for all utilizations, the C/S system has the least mean job response time, the D/NS system the greatest, and that the D/S system has a lower response time than the D/NS system. These qualitative relationships are not actually surprising and could have been anticipated from basic queueing considerations. What could not have been so easily predicted, however, is the relationship between the D/S and C/NS systems. The relationship between the mean job response time for these systems, as shown in Fig. 3, depends on the utilization of the system. Specifically, we see that for $\rho < 0.7$ the D/S system has a lower mean job response time than the C/NS system and that the roles are reversed for higher utilizations. Evidently the parallelism found in splitting up jobs into tasks in the D/S system reduces the mean job response time for low to moderate utilizations

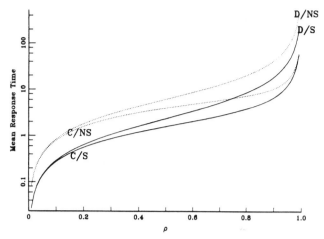

Fig. 3. Comparison of four systems, $C = 8$, $\lambda = 1$.

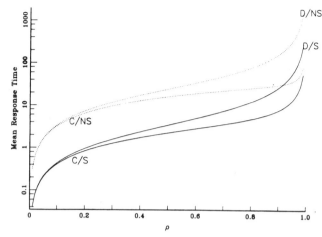

Fig. 4. Comparison of four systems, $C = 32$, $\lambda = 1$.

so that its mean job response time is lower than in the C/NS system. For high utilizations, however, the synchronization delay incurred in the D/S system becomes an increasing factor in the overall mean job response time and, as shown in the figure, grows sufficiently so that the C/NS system, which suffers no such delay, yields a lower mean job response time.

In Fig. 4 we plot the same set of curves for the case of $c = 32$ and jobs consisting of 32 tasks. Observe the similarity between this figure and Fig. 3. The point at which the C/NS system has a lower mean job response time than the D/S system increases to $\rho = 0.9$. This can be explained by the fact that with 32 processors there is an increased opportunity for parallelism in processing tasks in the D/S system than with 8 processors.

The relative performances of the D/S and C/NS systems to that of the system with the minimal mean job response time, the C/S system, are compared and plotted in Fig. 5. We have eliminated the D/NS system from consideration because of its poor performance. There are two sets of curves in Fig. 5. In the first set, we investigate the effects of splitting jobs into tasks for a centralized queueing structure. The top two curves in the figure are the ratios of the mean job response times for the C/NS system to the C/S system for varying utilizations with $c = 8$ and $c = 32$. As before, we assume that a job consists of the same number of tasks as processors. For centralized systems, these curves show that for low utilizations it is very important to split jobs into tasks. This importance decreases with increasing utilization and, at very heavy traffic, both systems perform similarly. These relationships can best be explained by considering each system for low utilizations. Assume in such a case that an arriving job finds no jobs in the queue and thus the mean job response time is simply the service time for the job. In the splitting case, the work of the job is distributed over all the processors whereas in the no splitting case all of the work is performed by one processor. Clearly the splitting case will be faster than the no splitting case and as the system approaches saturation, and queueing delay becomes a larger component of the total job response time,

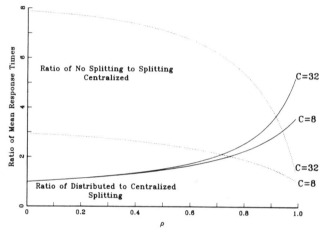

Fig. 5. Ratio of mean response times, $\lambda = 1$.

this effect becomes less important. These effects will be analyzed more fully in experiment 2.

In the second set of curves in Fig. 5 we evaluate the effect of the queueing structure on the mean job response time. In this case we plot the ratio of the mean job response times for the D/S system to that of the C/S system. In this case it is evident from the figure that keeping jobs in a central queue becomes more important as the utilization of the system increases. This follows from the fact that, because of the differences in the queueing structures for these systems, the synchronization time for tasks in the C/S system is lower than that for the D/S system.

B. The Effect of Parallelism

Having established that the C/S system yields the least mean job response time over all utilizations, we now use it as a touchstone for further experiments. In the second set of experiments we explore the effect of parallelism on the mean job response time by comparing the performance of the C/NS system to that of the C/S system. In Fig. 6 we plot the ratio of mean job response times for the C/NS system to that of the C/S system for various utilizations as a function of c. We assume that each job consists of 8 tasks. As noted in the last part of experiment

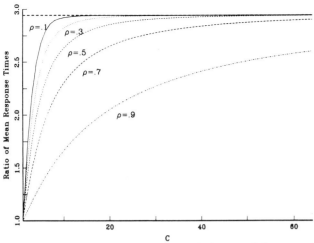

Fig. 6. Ratio of mean response times, no splitting to splitting, centralized.

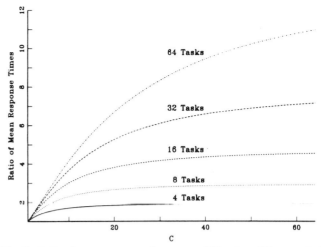

Fig. 7. Ratio of mean response times, no splitting to splitting, centralized.

1, when c is fixed, the performance improvement obtained from splitting jobs into tasks decreases with increasing utilization. For a fixed utilization, however, this performance improvement increases with c. This arises from the fact that as c increases, the chance for processing tasks of the same job in parallel increases. As seen in Fig. 6, for all utilizations all curves increase asymptotically to the solid line on the top of the figure. To derive the value of this asymptote consider the ratio of the mean job response times for low utilizations. This will effectively be the ratio of the two service times, or $8/(\Sigma_{j=1}^{8} 1/j) = 2.943$. As c increases, for a fixed processor utilization, the probability that a job arrives and has all of its tasks scheduled simultaneously increases to one. Thus, as the number of processors grows to infinity and for any fixed processor utilization, the ratio of the mean job response times reaches the above value.

In Fig. 7 we investigate the effects of parallelism as we vary the number of tasks per job. The utilization is fixed at $\rho = 0.7$. As just noted, as c approaches infinity the ratio of the mean job response times reaches the limit $X/(\Sigma_{j=1}^{X} 1/j)$, where X is the number of tasks in a job. For a fixed c, it is interesting to note that the ratio of mean job response times increases with increasing X. Thus breaking up jobs into a large number of smaller pieces is beneficial to a parallel processing system. Naturally this conclusion is only valid if one ignores any overhead incurred with splitting jobs up into pieces. We investigate the phenomena of including overhead associated with this process in experiment 4.

C. Processor Partitioning

In this set of experiments we assume that there are two classes of jobs each with different processing requirements. *Edit* jobs are assumed to consist of simple operations that have no inherent parallelism and thus consist of only one task. *Batch* jobs, on the other hand, are assumed to be inherently parallel and can be broken up into tasks. All tasks from either class are assumed to have the same service requirements. It is not at all clear that two such

divergently differing job classes should be executed on the same system since edit jobs could potentially suffer a poor performance because of the presence of the more computationally bound batch jobs. Furthermore, the existence of the edit jobs on the system could decrease the parallelism available to the batch jobs and thus increase their response time. In order to investigate the interaction of these two classes of jobs, we compare the performance of a combined system to that of a partitioned system. We refer to the C/S system, where both classes share the processors, as a combined system. A partitioned system is a system where processors are partitioned into two sets, one set for each class. We assume that batch jobs consist of 16 tasks, that there are $c = 16$ processors, and that in the partitioned system K, $1 \le K \le c$, processors are allocated to edit jobs and $c - K$ processors are allocated to batch jobs. Our performance metric is the ratio of mean response times for each class of jobs of the partitioned system to that of the combined system. For either class, a ratio greater than (less than) 1 indicates that in the partitioned system that class of jobs has a greater (lesser) mean response time than that obtained in the combined system. We should note here that our comparison assumes that jobs in either system are processed FCFS. We expect a real system to use some scheduling discipline that, in general, gives priority to the edit class of jobs.

In Fig. 8 we assume that edit jobs compose 50 percent of the job stream and plot the ratio of mean job response times in the partitioned system to that of the combined system as a function of utilization, for different values of K. These curves reveal a very interesting phenomena that can arise in a parallel processing system. Specifically, one sees that when one processor is allocated to the edit jobs, $K = 1$, the mean response time for *both* edit and batch jobs increases. In other words, both classes are negatively influenced by partitioning the system in this manner. Improvement to edits jobs, at the cost of increasing the mean response time of batch jobs, results only when the number of processors allocated to edit jobs increases to 2, as shown in the figure. Clearly, for $K > 2$ the performance

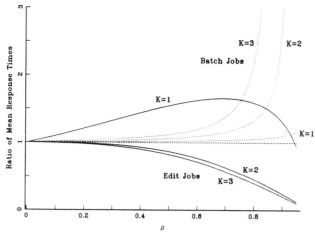

Fig. 8. Comparing combined system to partitioned system, 50 percent edit jobs.

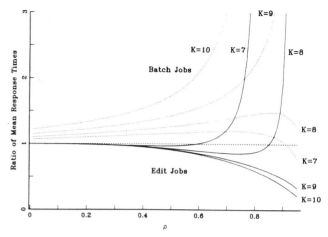

Fig. 9. Comparing combined system to partitioned system, 95 percent edit jobs.

of the edit jobs improves as seen in the figure. As the relative arrival rate of edit jobs increases, as shown in Fig. 9 where the proportion of edit jobs is 95 percent, we see that more processors must be allocated to edit jobs before their mean response time is decreased. As shown in the figure, nine processors are required to decrease the mean job response time over all utilizations. Once again there are regions over which the mean response times of both job classes increase in the partitioned system. For parallel processing systems, these considerations suggest that it is desirable to have a controllable boundary for processor partitioning. We should observe here that since there are regions over which both classes of jobs have their mean response time increased in the partitioned system, one might hope to find regions over which both classes had their mean response time *decreased*. Looking for such a region is a vain pursuit, however, as one might expect upon reflection.

D. Effect of Overhead

So far, we have ignored any costs associated with splitting jobs up into separately executable tasks. Such costs may arise from data dependencies between tasks of the same job. To model these costs we associate with each task an increase in service requirement that depends upon the number of tasks per job. Specifically we will assume that the average service requirement for a task of a job consisting of X tasks, is given by $1/X + H$, where H is the overhead cost. Each job thus requires a total of one unit of processing time in the absence of overhead. The tradeoff we investigate in this set of experiments concerns breaking up a job into a number of tasks. As noted in discussing Fig. 7, if $H = 0$, for a given c and processor utilization, the mean job response time decreases with X. This is no longer true if there is overhead associated with splitting jobs into tasks since increasing the number of tasks of a job also results in higher service times.

In Fig. 10 we plot the mean job response time for the C/S system for different arrival rates λ as a function of X. We assume that $H = 0.1$, which may correspond to an overhead of 10 percent of the total service required by a

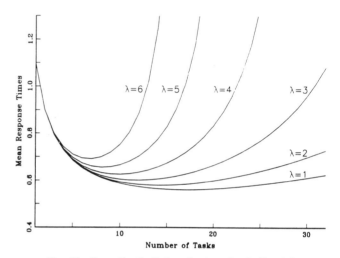

Fig. 10. Centralized/splitting, fixed overhead, $H = 0.1$.

job per task. The convex nature of the curves arises from the tradeoff just mentioned, namely that increasing the number of tasks at first initially decreases the mean job response time until a certain point after which the overhead costs predominate and the mean job response time increases. The optimal number of tasks, as shown by the lowest point on these curves, decreases as the arrival rate increases. Note that, as the system becomes more heavily loaded, queueing effects, which are increased because of the existence of overhead, become more predominant. This also explains why the curves become steeper with increasing λ.

In Fig. 11 we show, on the same scale as in Fig. 10, the effects of increasing the overhead to $H = 0.2$. Each curve increases due to the effect of the increased load on the system and similarly the optimal values of X also decrease from that shown in Fig. 10. When the overhead becomes a substantial portion of the service requirement of a task, for example if $H = 1$, than it is no longer advisable, for any arrival rate, to split jobs up into tasks. For this case, parallelism is too expensive and for a real system could correspond to jobs which have strong data dependencies.

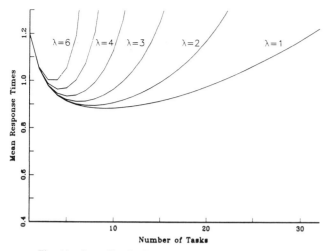

Fig. 11. Centralized/splitting, fixed overhead, $H = 0.2$.

VI. CONCLUSION

We have analyzed the bulk arrival $M^X/M/c$ queueing system and obtained an expression for the mean job response time in centralized parallel processing systems with job splitting into independent tasks.

To compare this system with other parallel processing systems, the following four systems are considered: distributed/splitting, distributed/no splitting, centralized/splitting, and centralized/no splitting. For all values of utilization ρ and similar queueing structures, our results show that the splitting systems yield lower mean job response time than the no splitting systems. This follows from the fact that, in the splitting case, work is distributed over all the processors. For any ρ, the lowest (highest) mean job response time is achieved by the C/S system (the D/NS system). The relative performance of the D/S system and the C/NS system depends on the value of ρ. For small ρ, the parallelism achieved by splitting jobs into parallel tasks in the D/S system reduces its mean job response time as compared to the C/NS system, where tasks of the same job are executed sequentially. However, for high ρ, the C/NS system has lower mean job response time than the D/S system. This is due to the long synchronization delay incurred in the D/S system at high utilizations.

The effect of parallelism on the performance of parallel processing systems is studied by comparing the performance of the C/NS system to that of the C/S system. The performance improvement obtained by splitting jobs into tasks is found to decrease with increasing utilization. For a fixed number of processors and fixed ρ, we find that by increasing the number of tasks per job, i.e., higher parallelism, the mean job response time of the C/NS system relative to that of the C/S system increases. By considering an overhead delay associated with splitting jobs into independent tasks, we observe that the mean job response time is a convex function of the number of tasks, and thus, for a given arrival rate, there exists a unique optimum number of tasks per job.

We also consider problems associated with partitioning the processors into two sets, each dedicated to one of two classes of jobs: edit jobs and batch jobs. We analyzed an example where the mean job response time for both classes of jobs *increases* if one processor is strictly allocated to edit jobs. Improvement to edit jobs, at a cost of increasing the mean job response time of batch jobs, results only when the number of processors allocated to edit jobs is increased to two. This, and other results, suggest that it is desirable for parallel processing systems to have a controllable boundary for processor partitioning.

Lastly we comment on the effect of some of our assumptions on the relative performance of the four parallel processing models studied in the paper. Although we do not have an analysis for the case in which task service times are generally distributed, we believe that the synchronization time, and thus the response time, increases with the variance of service time. Intuitively this follows from the fact that for a large service variation there is a greater probability of a job waiting a long time for a large task to finish execution. Since tasks in real systems are bounded and, in some cases, tend to have less variation than that of an exponential distribution, we believe the analysis for the splitting cases found in the paper is pessimistic for some systems. This suggests that, for these systems, the relative performance of splitting to nonsplitting would be better than that given in this paper. Acting against this, however, is the fact that there are some overheads associated with splitting jobs into, perhaps dependent, tasks that have not been modeled. As these overheads grow, it is clear that the nonsplitting models perform relatively better.

REFERENCES

[1] F. Baccelli and A. M. Makowski, "Simple computable bounds for the fork-join queue," presented at the Johns Hopkins Conf. Inform. Sci., Johns Hopkins Univ., 1985.
[2] M. L. Chaudhry and J. G. C. Templeton, *A First Course in Bulk Queues.* New York: Wiley, 1983.
[3] L. Flatto, "Two parallel queues created by arrivals with two demands II," *SIAM J. Appl. Math.*, vol. 45, pp. 861–878, Oct. 1985.
[4] L. Flatto and S. Hahn, "Two parallel queues created by arrivals and with two demands I," *SIAM J. Appl. Math.*, vol. 44, pp. 1041–1053, Oct. 1984.
[5] R. Nelson and A. N. Tantawi, "Approximate analysis of fork/join synchronization in parallel queues," IBM Res. Rep. RC11481, Oct. 1985; also *IEEE Trans. Comput.*, to be published.
[6] P. P. Spies and W. J. Geilenkeuser, "Queueing systems serving task families," in *Performance '83*, A. K. Agrawala and S. K. Tripathi, Eds., 1983, pp. 187–201.
[7] D. D. Yao, "Some results for the queues $M^X/M/c$ and $GI^X/G/c$," *Oper. Res. Lett.*, vol. 4, pp. 79–83, July 1985.
[8] ——, "Refining the diffusion approximation for the $M/G/m$ queue," *Oper. Res.*, vol. 33, pp. 1266–1277, Nov. 1985.

Randolph Nelson received the B.S. degree in physics from Rutgers University, New Brunswick, NJ, the M.S. degree in mathematics from Arizona State University, Tempe, and the Ph.D. degree in computer science from the University of California, Los Angeles. At UCLA his main research interests were in computer communication systems with a special emphasis on multihop packet radio networks.

Since 1982 he has been employed as a Research Staff Member at the IBM Thomas J. Watson Research Center, Yorktown Heights, NY. His current research interests are concerned with performance evaluation of computer systems.

Don Towsley (M'78) received the B.A. degree in physics and the Ph.D. degree in computer sciences from the University of Texas at Austin in 1971 and 1975, respectively.

From 1976 to 1985 he was a member of the faculty of the Department of Electrical and Computer Engineering at the University of Massachusetts, Amherst, where he achieved the rank of Associate Professor. He is currently an Associate Professor of Computer and Information Science at the University of Massachusetts. During 1982–1983, he was a Visiting Scientist at the IBM Thomas J. Watson Research Center, Yorktown Heights, NY. His research interests are in computer networks, distributed computer systems, and performance evaluation.

Dr. Towsley is currently an Associate Editor of *Networks* and IEEE TRANSACTIONS ON COMMUNICATIONS. He is also a member of the Association for Computing Machinery and the Operations Research Society of America.

Asser N. Tantawi (M'87) received the B.S. and M.S. degrees in computer science from Alexandria University, Alexandria, Egypt, and the Ph.D. degree in computer science from Rutgers University, New Brunswick, NJ.

He joined the IBM Thomas J. Watson Research Center, Yorktown Heights, NY, in 1982, as a Research Staff Member, where he is currently associated with the Systems Analysis Group of the Department of Computer Sciences. His fields of interest include performance modeling, queueing theory, load balancing, parallel processing and reliability modeling.

Dr. Tantawi is a member of the Association for Computing Machinery and the Operations Research Society of America. He has served as an ACM National Lecturer since 1984.

Isoefficiency: Measuring the Scalability of Parallel Algorithms and Architectures

Ananth Y. Grama, Anshul Gupta, and Vipin Kumar
University of Minnesota

Reprinted from *IEEE Parallel & Distributed Technology*, Vol. 1, No. 3, Aug. 1993, pp. 12–21. Copyright © 1993 by The Institute of Electrical and Electronics Engineers, Inc. All rights reserved.

Isoefficiency analysis helps us determine the best algorithm/architecture combination for a particular problem without explicitly analyzing all possible combinations under all possible conditions.

An earlier version of this article appeared as "Analyzing Performance of Large-Scale Parallel Systems" by Anshul Gupta and Vipin Kumar on pp. 144-153 of the *Proceedings of the 26th Hawaii International Conference on System Sciences*, published in 1993 by IEEE Computer Society Press, Los Alamitos, Calif.

The fastest sequential algorithm for a given problem is the best sequential algorithm. But determining the best parallel algorithm is considerably more complicated. A parallel algorithm that solves a problem well using a fixed number of processors on a particular architecture may perform poorly if either of these parameters changes. Analyzing the performance of a given parallel algorithm/architecture calls for a comprehensive method that accounts for scalability: the system's ability to increase speedup as the number of processors increases.

The isoefficiency function is one of many parallel performance metrics that measure scalability.[1-6] It relates problem size to the number of processors required to maintain a system's efficiency, and it lets us determine scalability with respect to the number of processors, their speed, and the communication bandwidth of the interconnection network. The isoefficiency function also succinctly captures the characteristics of a particular algorithm/architecture combination in a single expression, letting us compare various combinations for a range of problem sizes and numbers of processors. Thus, we can determine the best combination for a problem without explicitly analyzing all possible combinations under all possible conditions. (The sidebar on page 14 defines many basic concepts of scalability analysis and presents an example that is revisited throughout the article.)

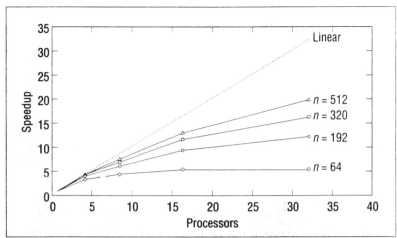

Figure 1. Speedup versus number of processors for adding a list of numbers on a hypercube.

Scalable parallel systems

The number of processors limits a parallel system's speedup: The speedup for a single processor is one, but if more are used, the speedup is usually less than the number of processors.

Let's again consider the example in the sidebar. Figure 1 shows the speedup for a few values of n on up to 32 processors; Table 1 shows the corresponding efficiencies. The speedup does not increase linearly with the number of processors; instead, it tends to saturate. In other words, the efficiency drops as the number of processors increases. This is true for all parallel systems, and is often referred to as Amdahl's law. But the figure and table also show a higher speedup (efficiency) as the problem size increases on the same number of processors.

If increasing the number of processors reduces efficiency, and increasing the problem size increases efficiency, we should be able to keep efficiency constant by increasing both simultaneously. For example, the table shows that the efficiency of adding 64 numbers on a four-processor hypercube is 0.80. When we increase p to eight and n to 192, the efficiency remains 0.80, as it does when we further increase p to 16 and n to 512. Many parallel systems behave in this way. We call them *scalable* parallel systems.

The isoefficiency function

A natural question at this point is: At what rate should we increase the problem size with respect to the number of processors to keep the efficiency fixed? The answer varies depending on the system.

In the sidebar, we noted that the sequential execution time T_1 equals the problem size W multiplied by the cost of executing each operation (t_c). Making this substitution in the efficiency equation gives us

$$E = \frac{1}{1 + \frac{T_0}{W t_c}}$$

If the problem size W is constant while p increases, then the efficiency decreases because the total overhead T_0 increases with p. If W increases while p is constant, then, for scalable parallel systems, the efficiency increases because T_0 grows slower than $\Theta(W)$ (that is, slower than all functions with the same growth rate as W). We can maintain the efficiency for these parallel systems at

Table 1. Efficiency as a function of n and p for adding n numbers on p-processor hypercubes.

	$p = 1$	$p = 4$	$p = 8$	$p = 16$	$p = 32$
$n = 64$	1.0	.80	.57	.33	.17
$n = 192$	1.0	.92	.80	.60	.38
$n = 320$	1.0	.95	.87	.71	.50
$n = 512$	1.0	.97	.91	.80	.62

a desired value (between 0 and 1) by increasing p, provided W also increases. For different parallel systems, we must increase W at different rates with respect to p to maintain a fixed efficiency. For example, W might need to grow as an exponential function of p. Such systems are poorly scalable: It is difficult to obtain good speedups for a large number of processors on such systems unless the problem size is enormous. On the other hand, if W needs to grow only linearly with respect to p, then the system is highly scalable: Its speedups increase linearly with respect to the number of processors for problem sizes increasing at reasonable rates.

For scalable parallel systems, we can maintain efficiency at a desired value ($0 < E < 1$) if T_0/W is constant:

$$E = \frac{1}{1 + \frac{T_0}{W t_c}}$$

$$\frac{T_0}{W} = t_c \left(\frac{1 - E}{E} \right)$$

$$W = \frac{1}{t_c} \left(\frac{E}{1 - E} \right) T_0$$

If $K = E/(t_c(1 - E))$ is a constant that depends on the efficiency, then we can reduce the last equation to

$$W = K T_0$$

Definitions and assumptions

A parallel algorithm cannot be evaluated apart from the architecture it is implemented on, so we define a *parallel system* as the combination of a parallel algorithm and a parallel architecture. The time taken by an algorithm to execute on a single processor is its *sequential execution time*, T_1. The execution time of the corresponding parallel algorithm on p identical processors is its *parallel execution time*, T_P.

During execution, a parallel algorithm incurs overhead due to idling, communication, contention over shared data structures, and so on. The total time spent by all processors doing work that is not done by the sequential algorithm is the *total overhead*, T_o. In general, T_o is a function of the problem size and the number of processors. The total time spent by all processors is pT_P, and the total overhead is T_o, so

$$pT_P = T_1 + T_o$$

or

$$T_P = \frac{T_1 + T_o}{p}$$

A parallel system's speedup S is the ratio of sequential execution time to parallel execution time:

$$S = \frac{T_1}{T_P} = \frac{pT_1}{T_1 + T_o}$$

Its efficiency E is the ratio of the speedup to the number of processors used:

$$
\begin{aligned}
E &= \frac{S}{p} \\
&= \frac{T_1}{T_1 + T_o} \\
&= \frac{1}{1 + \frac{T_0}{T_1}}
\end{aligned}
$$

For certain parallel algorithm/architecture combinations, T_o can be negative, implying that the speedup on p processors could exceed p. This phenomenon is called *superlinear speedup*. A parallel system might exhibit such behavior if its memory is hierarchical and if access time increases (in discrete steps) with the memory used by the program. In this case, the effective computation speed of a large program could be slower on a serial processor than on a parallel computer using similar processors. This is because a sequential algorithm using M bytes of memory will use only M/p bytes on each processor of a p-processor parallel computer. Cache and virtual memory effects could reduce the serial processor's effective computation rate. (To simplify this article, we'll assume that T_o is nonnegative.)

PROBLEM SIZE

One way to express problem size is as a parameter of the input size. For example, for any matrix problem involving $n \times n$ matrices, the problem size could be n. But this definition allows problem size to be interpreted differently for different problems: For example, doubling the input size results in an eight-fold increase in serial execution time for matrix multiplication but only a four-fold increase for matrix addition.

A better definition would not lead to such varying interpretations; doubling the problem size would always lead to twice as much computation. Therefore, we express problem size in terms of the total number of basic operations in the problem: The problem size for $n \times n$ matrix multiplication is $\Theta(n^3)$, while that for the addition of two $n \times n$ matrices is $\Theta(n^2)$ (where $\Theta(x)$ is the set of all functions that have the same growth rate as x). To keep the problem size unique for

---

Through algebraic manipulations, we can use this equation to obtain W as a function of p. This function dictates how W must grow to maintain a fixed efficiency as p increases. This is the system's *isoefficiency function*. It determines the ease with which the system yields speedup in proportion to the number of processors. A small isoefficiency function implies that small increments in the problem size are sufficient to use an increasing number of processors efficiently; hence, the system is highly scalable. Conversely, a large isoefficiency function indicates a poorly scalable parallel system. Furthermore, the isoefficiency function does not exist for some parallel systems, because their efficiency cannot be kept constant as p increases, no matter how fast the problem size increases.

For the equation above, if we substitute the value of T_o from the example in the sidebar, we get $W = 2Kp \log p$. Thus, this system's isoefficiency function is $\Theta(p \log p)$. If the number of processors increases from p to p', the problem size (in this case n) must increase by a factor of $(p' \log p')/(p \log p)$ to maintain the same efficiency. In other words, increasing the number of processors by a factor of p'/p requires n to be increased by a factor of $(p' \log p')/(p \log p)$ to increase the speedup by a factor of p'/p.

In this simple example of adding n numbers, the communication overhead is a function of only p. But a typical overhead function can have several terms of different orders of magnitude with respect to both the problem size and the number of processors, making it impossible (or at least cumbersome) to obtain the isoefficiency function as a closed form function of p.

Consider a parallel system for which

$$T_o = p^{3/2} + p^{3/4} W^{3/4}$$

The equation $W = KT_o$ becomes

$$W = Kp^{3/2} + Kp^{3/4} W^{3/4}$$

For this system, it is difficult to solve for W in terms of p. However, since the condition for constant efficiency is that the ratio of T_o and W remains fixed, then if p and W increase, the efficiency will not drop if none of the terms of T_o grows faster than W. We thus balance each term of T_o against W to compute the corresponding isoa given problem, we define it as the number of operations the best sequential algorithm executes to solve the problem on a single processor. For some problems, the best algorithm is not known; for others, the generally best algorithm may perform worse than others for particular instances of the problem. In these cases, we can use the number of operations in the serial algorithm that is considered best for each instance. For example, for matrix multiplication, the simple $\Theta(n^3)$ algorithm is often the algorithm of choice, even though Strassen's algorithm has a better asymptotic complexity. We will use the symbol W to denote problem size. If the cost of executing each operation is t_c, then $T_1 = Wt_c$.

AN EXAMPLE
If we add n numbers on a sequential machine, the number of operations — and hence the problem size W — equals n. If each addition takes time t_c, then the sequential execution time T_1 equals nt_c. (This is an approximation for large values of n; in reality, W is $n - 1$, and T_1 is $(n - 1)t_c$.)

Now consider a parallel algorithm for adding n numbers using a p-processor

hypercube (Figure A shows this algorithm for $n = 16$ and $p = 4$). Each processor is allocated n/p numbers. In the first step, each processor locally adds its n/p numbers in $\Theta(n/p)$ time. The problem is now reduced to adding the p partial sums on p processors, which can be done by propagating and adding the partial sums. A single step consists of one addition and one nearest-neighbor communication of a partial sum (typically a single word). If we assume that it takes one unit of time to add two numbers, and one unit of time to communicate a number between two processors, then n/p time is spent adding the n/p local numbers at each processor. After the local addition, the p partial sums are added in $\log p$ steps, each consisting of one addition and one communication. Thus, the total parallel execution time T_P is $n/p + 2 \log p$.

So, of the $n/p + 2 \log p$ time units that each processor spends in parallel execution, n/p time is spent performing

Figure A. Adding 16 numbers on a four-processor hypercube.

useful work. The remaining $2 \log p$ units of time per processor contribute to a total overhead of

$$T_o = 2p \log p$$

The speedup S and efficiency E are

$$S = \frac{T_1}{T_P} = \frac{n}{\frac{n}{p} + 2p \log p}$$

$$E = \frac{S}{p} = \frac{n}{n + 2p \log p}$$

efficiency function. The term that causes the problem size to grow fastest with respect to p determines the system's overall isoefficiency function. Solving for the first term in the above equation gives us

$$W = Kp^{3/2} = \Theta(p^{3/2})$$

Solving for the second term gives us

$$W = Kp^{3/4}W^{3/4}$$
$$W^{1/4} = Kp^{3/4}$$
$$W = K^4p^3 = \Theta(p^3)$$

So if the problem size grows as $\Theta(p^{3/2})$ and $\Theta(p^3)$, respectively, for the first two terms of T_o, then efficiency will not decrease as p increases The isoefficiency function for this system is therefore $\Theta(p^3)$, which is the higher rate. If W grows as $\Theta(p^3)$, then T_o will remain of the same order as W.

OPTIMIZING COST
A parallel system is *cost-optimal* if the product of the number of processors and the parallel execution time is

proportional to the execution time of the best serial algorithm on a single processor:

$$pT_P \propto W$$

In the sidebar, we noted that $pT_P = T_1 + T_o$, so

$$T_1 + T_o \propto W$$

Since $T_1 = Wt_c$, we have

$$Wt_c + T_o \propto W$$
$$W \propto T_o$$

This suggests that a parallel system is cost-optimal if its overhead function and the problem size are of the same order of magnitude. This is exactly the condition required to maintain a fixed efficiency while increasing the number of processors. So, conforming to the isoefficiency relation between W and p keeps a parallel system cost-optimal as it is scaled up.

How small can an isoefficiency function be, and what is an ideally scalable parallel system? If a problem consists of W basic operations, then a cost-optimal system can use no more than W processors. If the problem size grows at a rate slower than $\Theta(p)$ as the number of processors increases, then the number of processors will eventually exceed W. Even in an ideal parallel system with no communication or other overhead, the efficiency will drop because the processors exceeding W will have no work to do. So, the problem size has to increase at least as fast as $\Theta(p)$ to maintain a constant efficiency; hence $\Theta(p)$ is the lower bound on the isoefficiency function. It follows that the isoefficiency function of an ideally scalable parallel system is $\Theta(p)$.

DEGREE OF CONCURRENCY

The lower bound of $\Theta(p)$ is imposed on the isoefficiency function by the algorithm's *degree of concurrency*: the maximum number of tasks that can be executed simultaneously in a problem of size W. This measure is independent of the architecture. If $C(W)$ is an algorithm's degree of concurrency, then given a problem of size W, at most $C(W)$ processors can be employed effectively. For example, using Gaussian elimination to solve a system of n equations with n variables, the total amount of computation is $\Theta(n^3)$. However, the n variables have to be eliminated one after the other, and eliminating each variable requires $\Theta(n^2)$ computations. Thus, at most $\Theta(n^2)$ processors can be kept busy at a time.

Now if $W = \Theta(n^3)$ for this problem, then the degree of concurrency is $\Theta(W^{2/3})$. Given a problem of size W, at most $\Theta(W^{2/3})$ processors can be used, so given p processors, the size of the problem should be at least $\Theta(p^{3/2})$ in order to use all the processors. Thus, the isoefficiency function of this computation due to concurrency is $\Theta(p^{3/2})$.

The isoefficiency function due to concurrency is optimal — $\Theta(p)$ — only if the algorithm's degree of concurrency is $\Theta(W)$. If it is less than $\Theta(W)$, then the isoefficiency function due to concurrency is worse (greater) than $\Theta(p)$. In such cases, the system's overall isoefficiency function is the maximum of the isoefficiency functions due to concurrency, communication, and other overhead.

Isoefficiency analysis

Isoefficiency analysis lets us test a program's performance on a few processors and then predict its performance on a larger number of processors. It also lets us study system behavior when other hardware parameters change, such as processor and communication speeds.

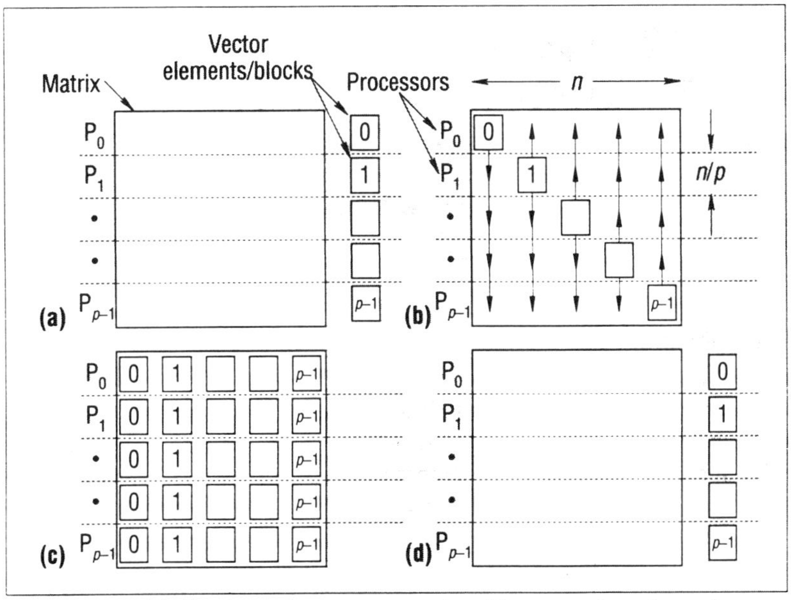

COMPARING ALGORITHMS

We often must compare the performance of two parallel algorithms for a large number of processors. The isoefficiency function gives us the tool to do so. The algorithm with the smaller isoefficiency function yields better performance as the number of processors increases.

Consider the problem of multiplying an $n \times n$ matrix with an $n \times 1$ vector. The number of basic operations (the problem size W) for this matrix-vector product is n^2. If the time taken by a single addition and multiplication operation together is t_c, then the sequential execution time of this algorithm is $n^2 t_c$ (that is, $T_1 = n^2 t_c$).

Figure 2 illustrates a parallel version of this algorithm based on a striped partitioning of the matrix and the vector. Each processor is assigned n/p rows of the matrix and n/p elements of

Figure 2. Multiplication of an $n \times n$ matrix with an $n \times 1$ vector using "rowwise" striped data partitioning.

the vector. Since the multiplication requires the vector to be multiplied with each row of the matrix, every processor needs the entire vector. To accomplish this, each processor broadcasts its n/p elements of the vector to every other processor (this is called an *all-to-all broadcast*). Each processor then has the vector available locally and n/p rows of the matrix. Using these, it computes the dot products locally, giving it n/p elements of the resulting vector.

Let's now analyze this algorithm on a hypercube. The all-to-all broadcast can be performed in $t_s \log p + t_w n(p-1)/p$ (t_s is the startup time of the communication network, and t_w is the per-word transfer time).[7] For large values of p we can approximate this as $t_s \log p + t_w n$. Assuming that an addition/multiplication pair takes t_c units of time, each processor spends $t_c n^2/p$ units of time in multiplying its n/p rows with the vector. Thus, the parallel execution time of this procedure is

$$T_P = t_c(n^2/p) + t_s \log p + t_w n$$

The speedup and efficiency are

$$S = \frac{p}{1 + \frac{p(t_s \log p + t_w n)}{t_c n^2}}$$

$$E = \frac{1}{1 + \frac{t_s p \log p + t_w np}{t_c n^2}}$$

Using the relation $T_o = pT_P - T_1$, the total overhead is

$$T_o = t_s p \log p + t_w np$$

Now we can determine the isoefficiency function. Rewriting the equation $W = KT_o$ using only the first term of T_o gives the isoefficiency term due to the message startup time:

$$W = Kt_s p \log p$$

Similarly, we can balance the second term of T_o (due to per-word transfer time) against the problem size W:

$$n^2 = Kt_w np$$

$$n = Kt_w p$$

$$W = n^2 = K^2 t_w^2 p^2$$

From the equations for both terms, we can infer that the problem size needs to increase with the number of

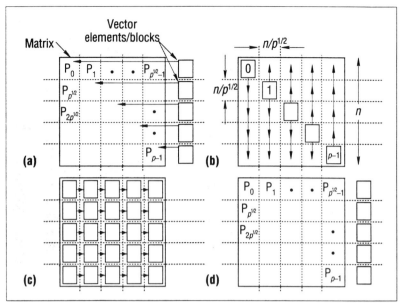

Figure 3. Matrix-vector multiplication using checkerboard partitioning.

processors at an overall rate of $\Theta(p^2)$ to maintain a fixed efficiency.

Another example

Now instead of partitioning the matrix into stripes, let's use *checkerboard partitioning*: divide it into p squares, each of dimensions $(n/\sqrt{p}) \times (n/\sqrt{p})$.[7] Figure 3 shows the algorithm.

The vector is distributed along the last column of the mesh. In the first step, all processors of the last column send their $n/\sqrt{p}$ elements of the vector to the diagonal processor of their respective rows (Figure 3a). Then the processors perform a columnwise one-to-all broadcast of the $n/\sqrt{p}$ elements (Figure 3b). The vector is then aligned along the rows of the matrix. Each processor performs n^2/p multiplications and locally adds the $n/\sqrt{p}$ sets of products. Each processor now has $n/\sqrt{p}$ partial sums that need to be accumulated along each row to obtain the product vector (Figure 3c). The last step is a single-node accumulation of the $n/\sqrt{p}$ values in each row, with the last processor of the row as the destination (Figure 3d).

On a hypercube with store-and-forward routing, the first step can be performed in at most $t_s + t_w(n/\sqrt{p}) \log \sqrt{p}$ time.[7] The second step can be performed in $(t_s + t_w n/\sqrt{p}) \log \sqrt{p}$ time. If a multiplication and an addition are assumed to take t_c units of time, then each processor spends about $t_c n^2/p$ time performing computation. If the product vector must be placed in the last column (like the starting vector), then a single-node accumulation of vector components of size $n/\sqrt{p}$ must be performed in each row. Ignoring the time needed to perform additions during this step, the accumulation can be performed with a communication time of $(t_s + t_w n/\sqrt{p}) \log \sqrt{p}$. The total parallel execution time is

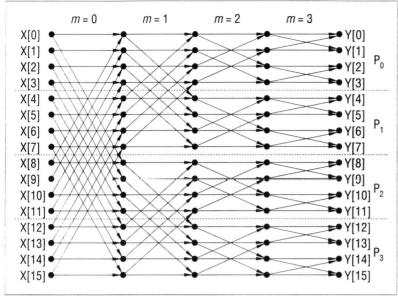

Figure 4. A 16-point fast Fourier transform on four processors. P_i is processor i and m is the iteration number.

an n-point, single-dimensional, unordered, radix-2 fast Fourier transform.[7,8] The sequential complexity of this algorithm is $\Theta(n \log n)$. We'll use a parallel version based on the binary exchange method for a d-dimensional ($p = 2^d$) hypercube (see Figure 4). We partition the vectors into blocks of n/p contiguous elements ($n = 2^r$) and assign one block to each processor. In the mapping shown in Figure 4, the vector elements on different processors are combined during the first d iterations while the pairs of elements combined during the last $(r - d)$ iterations reside on the same processors. Hence, this algorithm involves interprocessor communication only during $d = \log p$ of the $\log n$ iterations. Each communication operation exchanges n/p words of data, so communication time over the entire algorithm is $(t_s + t_w n/p) \log p$. During each iteration, a processor updates n/p elements of vector R. If a complex multiplication and addition take time t_c, then the parallel execution time is

$$T_P = t_c(n/p) \log n + t_s \log p + t_w(n/p) \log p$$

The total overhead T_o is

$$T_o = t_s p \log p + t_w n \log p$$

We know that the problem size for an n-point fast Fourier transform is

$$W = n \log n$$

Using the same method as in the previous subsection, we can now determine the system's isoefficiency by equating the problem size with each term in the total overhead. For the first term (t_s), $W \propto t_s p \log p$, which corresponds to an isoefficiency function of $\Theta(p \log p)$. We can similarly determine the isoefficiency for the second term (t_w):

$$n \log n = K t_w n \log p$$
$$\log n = K t_w \log p$$
$$n = p^{K \frac{t_w}{t_c}}$$
$$n \log n = K t_w p^{K t_w} \log p$$

$$W = \frac{E}{1 - E} \frac{t_w}{t_c} p^{\frac{E}{1-E} \frac{t_w}{t_c}} \log p$$

For this last equation, if $t_w E/(t_c(1 - E))$ is less than 1, then

---

$$T_P = t_c(n^2/p) + t_s + 2t_s \log \sqrt{p} + 3t_w(n/\sqrt{p}) \log \sqrt{p}$$

We can approximate this as

$$T_P = t_c(n^2/p) + t_s \log p + (3/2)t_w(n/\sqrt{p}) \log p$$

So, the total overhead T_o is

$$T_o = t_s p \log p + (3/2)t_w n \sqrt{p} \log p$$

As before, we equate each term of T_o with the problem size W. For the isoefficiency due to t_s, we get $W \propto K t_s p \log p$. For isoefficiency due to t_w, we get

$$n^2 t_c = K(3/2) t_w n \sqrt{p} \log p$$
$$n = K(3/2)(t_w/t_c)\sqrt{p} \log p$$
$$n^2 = K^2(9/4)(t_w^2/t_c^2) p \log^2 p$$

The isoefficiency due to t_w is $\Theta(p \log^2 p)$, which is also the overall isoefficiency, since it dominates the $\Theta(p \log p)$ term due to t_s.

Based on this and the previous example, the isoefficiency function of the stripe-based algorithm is $\Theta(p^2)$, which is higher than the $\Theta(p \log^2 p)$ of the checkerboard-based algorithm. This implies that the stripe-based version is less scalable; as the number of processors increases, it requires much larger problem sizes to yield the same efficiencies as the checkerboard-based version.

MACHINE-SPECIFIC PARAMETERS

Changing processor and communication speeds affects the scalability of some parallel systems only moderately; it affects others significantly. Isoefficiency analysis can help predict the effects of changes in such machine-specific parameters.

Consider the Cooley-Tukey algorithm for computing

W's rate of growth is less than $\Theta(p \log p)$, so the overall isoefficiency function is $\Theta(p \log p)$. But if $t_w E/(t_c(1 - E))$ is greater than 1, then the overall isoefficiency function is greater than $\Theta(p \log p)$. The isoefficiency function depends on the relative values of $E/(1 - E)$, t_w, and t_c. Thus, this algorithm is unique in that the isoefficiency function is a function not only of the desired efficiency, but also of the hardware-dependent parameters. In fact, the efficiency corresponding to $t_w E/(t_c(1 - E)) = 1$ — that is, $E/(1 - E) = t_c/t_w$, or $E = t_c/(t_c + t_w)$ — acts as a threshold value for efficiency. For a hypercube, efficiencies up to this value can be obtained easily. But much higher efficiencies can be obtained only if the problem size is extremely large.

Let's examine the effect of the value of $t_w E/(t_c(1 - E))$ on the isoefficiency function. If $t_w = t_c$, then the isoefficiency function is $E/(1 - E)p^{E/(1 - E)} \log p$. Now for $E/(1 - E) \leq 1$ (that is, $E \leq 0.5$), the overall isoefficiency is $\Theta(p \log p)$, but for $E > 0.5$ it is much worse. For instance, if $E = 0.9$, then $E/(1 - E) = 9$ and the isoefficiency function is $\Theta(p^9 \log p)$. Now if $t_w = 2t_c$ and the threshold efficiency is 0.33, then the isoefficiency function for $E = 0.33$ is $\Theta(p \log p)$, for $E = 0.5$ it is $\Theta(p^2 \log p)$, and for $E = 0.9$ it is $\Theta(p^{18} \log p)$.

These examples show that the efficiency we can obtain for reasonable problem sizes is limited by the ratio of the CPU speed to the hypercube's communication bandwidth. We can raise this limit by increasing the bandwidth, but making the CPU faster without improving the bandwidth lowers this threshold. In other words, this algorithm performs poorly on a hypercube whose communication and computation speeds are not balanced. However, the algorithm is fairly scalable on a balanced hypercube with an overall isoefficiency function of $\Theta(p \log p)$, and good efficiencies can be expected for a reasonably large number of processors.

CONCURRENCY

Some parallel algorithms that seem attractive because of their low overhead have limited concurrency, making them perform poorly as the number of processors grows. Isoefficiency analysis can capture this effect.

> **Some parallel algorithms that seem attractive because of their low overhead have limited concurrency, making them perform poorly as the number of processors grows. Isoefficiency analysis can capture this effect.**

Consider Dijkstra's all-pairs shortest-path problem for a dense graph with n vertices.[7,9] The problem involves finding the shortest path between each pair of vertices. The best-known serial algorithm takes $\Theta(n^3)$ time. We can also solve this problem by executing one instance of the single-source shortest-path algorithm for each of the n vertices. The latter algorithm determines the shortest path from one vertex to every other vertex in the graph. Its sequential complexity is $\Theta(n^2)$.

We can derive a simple parallel version of this algorithm by executing a single-source shortest-path problem independently on each of n processors. Since each of these computations is independent of the others, the parallel algorithm requires no communication, making it seem that it is the best possible algorithm. But the algorithm can use at most n processors ($p = n$), and since the problem size W is $\Theta(n^3)$, W must grow at least as $\Theta(p^3)$ to use more processors. So the overall isoefficiency is relatively high; other algorithms with better isoefficiencies are available.

CONTENTION FOR SHARED DATA STRUCTURES

An algorithm can have low communication overhead and high concurrency, but still have overhead from contention over shared data structures. Such overhead is difficult to model, making it difficult to compute the parallel execution time. However, we can still use isoefficiency analysis to determine the scalability.

Consider an application that solves discrete optimization problems by performing a depth-first search of large unstructured trees. Some parallel algorithms solve this problem by using a dynamic load-balancing strategy.[10,11] All work is initially assigned to one processor. An idle processor P_i selects a processor P_a using some selection criterion and sends it a work request. If processor P_a has no work, it responds with a reject message; otherwise, it partitions its work into two parts and sends one part to P_i (as long as the work is larger than some minimum size). This process continues until all processors exhaust the available work.

One selection criterion — *global round robin* — maintains a global pointer G at one of the processors. This pointer initially points to the first processor. When an idle processor needs to select P_a, it reads the current value of G, and requests work from P_G. The pointer is incremented by one (modulo p) before the next request is processed. The pointer distributes the work requests evenly over the processors.

The nondeterministic nature of this algorithm makes it impossible to estimate the exact parallel execution time beforehand. We can, however, set an upper bound on the communication cost.[7,10] Under certain assumptions,[10] the upper bound on the number of communications is $O(p \log W)$ (that is, it is of the same order or smaller than $p \log W$). If each communication takes $O(\log p)$ time, then the total overhead from the communication of work is bounded by $O(p \log p \log W)$. As before, we can equate this term with the problem size to derive the isoefficiency due to communication overhead:

$$W \propto O(p \log p \log W)$$

If we take the W on the right hand side of this expression, put the *value* of W in its place, and ignore the double log terms, then the isoefficiency due to communication overhead is $O(p \log^2 p)$.

But this term does not specify the system's overall isoefficiency because the algorithm also has overhead due to contention: Only one processor can access the global variable at a time; others must wait. So, we must also analyze the system's isoefficiency due to contention.

The global variable is accessed a total of $O(p \log W)$ times (for the read and increment operations). If the processors are used efficiently, then the total execution time is $\Theta(W/p)$. If there is no contention while solving a problem of size W on p processors, then W/p is much greater than the total time during which the shared variable is accessed. Now, as we increase the number of processors, the total execution time (W/p) decreases, but the number of times the shared variable is accessed increases. At some point, the shared variable access becomes a bottleneck, and the overall execution time cannot be reduced further. We can eliminate this bottleneck by increasing W at a rate such that the ratio between W/p and $O(p \log W)$ remains the same. Equating W/p and $O(p \log W)$ and then simplifying yields an isoefficiency of $O(p^2 \log p)$. Thus, since the isoefficiency due to contention dominates the isoefficiency due to communication, the overall isoefficiency is $O(p^2 \log p)$. (It has been shown elsewhere that dynamic load-balancing schemes with better isoefficiency functions outperform those with poorer isoefficiency functions.[10])

The isoefficiency metric is useful when we want performance to increase at a linear rate with the number of processors: If the problem size grows at the rate specified by the isoefficiency function, then the system's speedup is linear. In some cases, though, we might not want (or be able) to increase the problem size at the rate specified by the isoefficiency function; if the problem size grows at a smaller rate, then the speedup is sublinear.

For a given growth rate, we can use the speedup curve as a scalability metric. If the problem size increases at a linear rate with the number of processors, the curve shows *scaled speedup*.[2] The growth rate can also be constrained by the computer's memory, in which case the problem size increases at the fastest rate allowed by the available memory.[2,4,6]

In many situations, the growth rate is dictated by the time available to solve the problem, in which case the problem size increases with the number of processors in such a way that the run time remains constant.[2,4,6] We can also keep the problem size fixed and use the speedup curve as a scalability metric.[12]

There are interesting relationships between isoefficiency and some of these metrics. If the isoefficiency function is greater than $\Theta(p)$, then the problem size for a scalable parallel system cannot increase indefinitely while maintaining a fixed execution time, no matter how many processors are used.[1,12] Also, for a class of parallel systems, the isoefficiency function specifies the relationship between the problem size's growth rate and the number of processors on which the problem executes in minimum time.[12] ▨

ACKNOWLEDGMENTS

This work was supported by Army Research Office grant 28408-MA-SDI to the University of Minnesota, and by the Army High Performance Computing Research Center at the University of Minnesota. We also thank Daniel Challou and Tom Nurkkala for their help in preparing this article.

REFERENCES

1. V. Kumar and A. Gupta, "Analyzing Scalability of Parallel Algorithms and Architectures," Tech. Report 91-18, Computer Science Dept., Univ. of Minnesota, Minneapolis, 1991.

2. J.L. Gustafson, "Reevaluating Amdahl's Law," *Comm. ACM*, Vol. 31, No. 5, 1988, pp. 532-533.

3. J.L. Gustafson, "The Consequences of Fixed-Time Performance Measurement," *Proc. 25th Hawaii Int'l Conf. System Sciences*, Vol.

III, IEEE Computer Soc. Press, Los Alamitos, Calif., 1992, pp. 113-124.

4. X.-H. Sun and L.M. Ni, "Another View of Parallel Speedup," *Proc. Supercomputing '90*, IEEE Computer Soc. Press, Los Alamitos, Calif., 1990, pp. 324-333.

5. X.-H. Sun and D.T. Rover, "Scalability of Parallel Algorithm-Machine Combinations," Tech. Report IS-5057, Ames Lab., Iowa State Univ., 1991.

6. P.H. Worley, "The Effect of Time Constraints on Scaled Speedup," *SIAM J. Scientific and Statistical Computing*, Vol. 11, No. 5, Sept. 1990, pp. 838-858.

7. V. Kumar et al., *Introduction to Parallel Computing: Algorithm Design and Analysis*, Benjamin/Cummings, Redwood City, Calif., to be published (1994).

8. A. Gupta and V. Kumar, "The Scalability of FFT on Parallel Computers," *IEEE Trans. Parallel and Distributed Systems*, Vol. 4, No. 7, July 1993.

9. V. Kumar and V. Singh, "Scalability of Parallel Algorithms for the All-Pairs Shortest-Path Problem," *J. Parallel and Distributed Computing*, Vol. 13, No. 2, Oct. 1991, pp. 124-138.

10. V. Kumar, A. Grama, and V.N. Rao, "Scalable Load-Balancing Techniques for Parallel Computers," Tech. Report 91-55, Computer Science Dept., Univ. of Minnesota, Minneapolis, 1991.

11. V. Kumar and V.N. Rao, "Parallel Depth-First Search, Part II: Analysis," *Int'l J. Parallel Programming*, Vol. 16, No. 6, Dec. 1987, pp. 501-519.

12. A. Gupta and V. Kumar, "Performance Properties of Large-Scale Parallel Systems," to appear in *J. Parallel and Distributed Computing*, Nov. 1993.

Anath Y. Grama is a doctoral candidate in computer science at the University of Minnesota. His research interests include the design and analysis of scalable parallel algorithms, and architecture-independent parallel programming. He received his MS in computer engineering from Wayne State University, Detroit, in 1990, and his BE in computer science from the University of Roorkee, India, in 1989.

Anshul Gupta is a doctoral candidate in computer science at the University of Minnesota. His research interests include parallel algorithms, scientific computing, and scalability and performance evaluation of parallel and distributed systems. He received his B.Tech. degree in computer science from the Indian Institute of Technology, New Delhi, in 1988.

Vipin Kumar is an associate professor in the Department of Computer Science at the University of Minnesota. His research interests include parallel processing and artificial intelligence. He is coeditor of *Search in Artificial Intelligence, Parallel Algorithms for Machine Intelligence and Vision*, and *Introduction to Parallel Computing*. Kumar received his PhD in computer science from the University of Maryland, College Park, in 1982; his ME in electronics engineering from Philips International Institute, Eindhoven, The Netherlands, in 1979; and his BE in electronics and communication engineering from the University of Roorkee, India, in 1977. He is a senior member of IEEE, and a member of ACM and the American Association for Artificial Intelligence.

The authors can be reached at the department of Computer Science, 200 Union St. SE, University of Minnesota, Minneapolis, MN 55455; Internet: kumar, ananth, or agupta@cs.umn.edu

Scalability of Parallel Algorithm–Machine Combinations

Xian-He Sun and Diane T. Rover

Abstract—Scalability has become an important consideration in parallel algorithm and machine designs. The word *scalable*, or *scalability*, has been widely and often used in the parallel processing community. However, there is no adequate, commonly accepted definition of scalability available. Scalabilities of computer systems and programs are difficult to quantify, evaluate, and compare. In this paper, scalability is formally defined for algorithm–machine combinations. A practical method is proposed to provide a quantitative measurement of the scalability. The relation between the newly proposed scalability and other existing parallel performance metrics is studied. A harmony between speedup and scalability has been observed. Theoretical results show that a large class of algorithm–machine combinations is scalable and the scalability can be predicted through premeasured machine parameters. Two algorithms have been studied on an nCUBE 2 multicomputer and on a MasPar MP-1 computer. These case studies have shown how scalabilities can be measured, computed, and predicted. Performance instrumentation and visualization tools also have been used and developed to understand the scalability related behavior.

Index Terms—Scalable high performance computing, performance metrics, performance evaluation of parallel algorithms and machines, scalability, scientific computation, visualization.

I. INTRODUCTION

IN 1988, researchers at Sandia National Laboratory achieved speedup greater than 1000 on a 1024-processor multicomputer [1], [2]. The Sandia work [1] is based on the *scaled up* principle: problem size increases with the size of the given computer system. Three applications, in wave mechanics, fluid dynamics, and beam-strain analysis, were implemented on a hypercube architecture multicomputer [1]. The implementation results show that when the problem size is scaled up with the system size the speedup increases linearly with the system size. Each of these applications provides an ideal situation. For massively parallel computing, we would like the performance to increase linearly with the system size. In general, because of design restrictions and physical limitations, the efficiency provided by a given computer for a given algorithm will decrease when the system size is increased. Problem size in general has to be increased to achieve a linear increase of performance. The ratio of system size and problem size increases is closely related to the computation and communication patterns of the application, and to the hardware support of the underlying architecture.

The word *scalable*, or *scalability*, has been widely used in practice to describe how the system size and problem size will influence the performance of parallel machines and algorithms. Scalability is an important issue in parallel processing. It measures the ability of a parallel architecture to support parallel processing at different machine sizes, and measures the inherent parallelism of a parallel algorithm. Scalability can be used to predict the performance of large system and problem sizes based on the performance of small system and problem sizes. It suggests which computer systems could be built with more processors and which algorithms might be more suitable for larger computer systems. Despite the fact that scalability is important and has been widely used in practice, there is no adequate, commonly accepted definition of scalability available. Indeed, scalabilities of computer systems and programs are difficult to quantify, evaluate, and compare. Intensive research has been conducted in this area during recent years [3]. Some metrics have been proposed to measure the scalability of algorithms and computer systems [4], [5], and a formal definition for the scalability of parallel machines also has been proposed [6]. Although these proposed metrics provide ways to measure some special properties of algorithms and architectures, each has certain deficiencies for measuring the scalability of an algorithm-machine combination. In this paper, the *isospeed* metric is proposed. Based on the new metric, the scalability of a parallel algorithm-machine combination is formally defined. The validity of the new definitions is discussed and studied. Three approaches for obtaining the scalability of an algorithm-machine combination are proposed, implemented, and compared. A scalability analysis is applied to actual algorithms. In addition to analytical results, the scalability of these algorithms is experimentally measured on an nCUBE 2 multicomputer and on a MasPar MP-1 data parallel computer. The analytical and experimental results show that the newly defined scalability metric provides a unique quantitative measurement to describe the behavior of a parallel algorithm-machine combination as sizes are varied, which cannot be provided by any other performance metric.

The remainder of this paper is organized as follows. In Section II we present a historical background and the requirements of scalability. The isospeed metric and formal definitions of scalable and scalability are proposed in Section

Manuscript received August 13, 1991; revised June 1, 1993. This work was supported in part by the Applied Mathematical Sciences Program of Ames Laboratory, which is operated for the U.S. Department of Energy under Contract W-7405-ENG-82 while the authors were with Ames Laboratory, Iowa State University, Ames, IA, and in part by the National Aeronautics and Space Administration under NASA Contract NAS1-19480.

X.-E. Sun was with ICASE, NASA Langley Research Center, Hampton, VA 23681–0001, USA. He is now with the Department of Computer Science, Louisiana State University, Baton Rouge, LA 70803, USA.

D. T. Rover is with the Department of Electrical Engineering, Michigan State University, East Lansing, MI 48824–1226, USA.

IEEE Log Number 9216782.

113

0-8186-6522-X/95 $4.00 © 1994 IEEE

III. The relationships between scalability and execution time and between scalability and speedup are studied. Performance prediction is considered. A formula based on scalability is derived for a large class of algorithm-machine combinations. In Section IV, three approaches to obtain scalabilities are proposed. The *Burg* algorithm [7], which is a popular and computationally efficient signal processing procedure, is studied in detail to illustrate the concept of scalability and to compare the three approaches for obtaining scalabilities. The behavior and scalability of a more complicated program, solving a radiosity application [8], is also visualized and studied in Section IV. This visualization approach provides a unique way to reveal characteristics which correspond to the scalability of an algorithm-machine combination. The scalability of the two algorithms are measured on the nCUBE 2 and MasPar MP-1 parallel computers. The observed results are compared, and the influence of hardware design on scalability are discussed. Section V gives the conclusion and comments.

For the purpose of this study, we assume the underlying parallel machine is homogeneous, i.e., all processors are identical. The isospeed scalability proposed in this paper can be applied to any machine architecture. However, the scalability prediction of heterogeneous computing would be more sophisticated than that of homogeneous computing studied here.

II. BACKGROUND AND PRELIMINARY

Scalability has been used in practice as a property that describes the demand for proportionate changes in performance with adjustments in system size. So, a simple, intuitive definition of scalability might be given as follows.

Definition 1: Scalability is a property which exhibits performance linearly proportional to the number of processors employed.

While Definition 1 is very understandable and acceptable, it does not provide enough information. Two questions remain open. First, what performance metric should be chosen to measure the scalability? Second, having selected a metric, how should it be measured? Since *speedup* is one of the most commonly used metrics for parallel processing, and the Sandia work has shown a linear increasing of speedup, speedup seems to be a natural choice. If we choose speedup as the metric, then we need to decide how to measure the speedup. There are three known notions of speedup, *fixed-size speedup*, *fixed-time speedup*, and *memory-bounded speedup* [9], [10]. Fixed-size speedup fixes the problem size and emphasizes how fast a problem can be solved. Amdahl's law [11] is based on the fixed-size speedup model. Therefore, fixed-size speedup is bounded by the reciprocal of the serial fraction of the algorithm. This hard performance limitation implies that fixed-sized speedup is inadequate [6]. Fixed-time speedup argues that parallel computers are designed for otherwise intractably large problems. It fixes the execution time and emphasizes how much more work can be done with parallel processing within the same time. Memory-bounded speedup assumes that a physical limitation of the machine, its memory capacity, is the primary constraint on larger problem sizes. It allows memory capacity to increase linearly with the number of processors available. Both fixed-time and memory-bounded speedup are forms of scaled speedup. Each allows problem size to increase with the system size. The difference between the two speedups is that fixed-time speedup uses execution time to limit the problem size, and memory-bounded speedup uses the memory capacity to limit the problem size. The term "scaled speedup" is used for memory-bounded speedup by many authors [1], [6].

In general, operational complexity increases faster than storage complexity for a given application. Thus, memory-bounded speedup typically yields higher performance than fixed-time speedup. Unfortunately, even with the most liberal speedup, i.e., memory-bounded speedup, no parallel program can possibly exhibit speedup which is linearly proportional to the number of processors available unless the program contains no sequential portion (see [9], [15], and [6]). Speedup is defined to measure the performance gain of parallel processing. It compares the parallel performance over the sequential performance. Operating on a scaled problem size, sequential execution could be impossible or could be very slow, and, therefore, yield a very high speedup. Speedup is a tool for analysis, not the goal of parallel processing. It is not an acceptable metric for representing scalability.

To measure the scalability of parallel algorithms, Kumar *et al.* [4] proposed the *isoefficiency* concept. Isoefficiency fixes the efficiency and measures how much work must be increased to keep the efficiency unchanged. An *isoefficiency function*, $f(N)$, is defined to measure the scalability of parallel algorithms, where N is the number of processors and $f(N)$ is the amount of work needed to maintain the efficiency. The value of $f(N)$ could be arbitrarily large. *Efficiency* is defined as speedup divided by N. So, constant efficiency means that speedup increases linearly with system size. Thus, Kumar *et al.* still use speedup as the performance metric. The significant improvement of their work is its independence of any of the notions of the three speedup models. By using an isoefficiency function, they allow the problem size to increase without bound to attain the requisite efficiency. This approach not only lets algorithms meet the isoefficiency requirement on a given architecture but also prescribes a quantitative measurement. Although the isoefficiency approach is more advanced than the speedup approaches, it is deficient because of its inherent ties to parallel speedup.

Nussbaum and Agarwal [6] proposed a definition of scalability of parallel machines. They define the scalability of a parallel machine, $\Psi(W)$, where W is the problem size, as the best speedup of the given architecture over the best speedup of an ideal parallel machine. This definition of $\Psi(W)$ still relies on speedup as the performance metric; however it measures the speedup differently. It determines the best speedup over the number of processors used, given an unbounded number of processors. While $\Psi(W)$ provides a way to evaluate the design of an architecture, what it represents is the ratio of the best possible performance of the given architecture to the best possible performance of an ideal architecture. In other words, it gives the achieved design efficiency of the architecture. Observe that a given architecture could achieve its best performance at N equals 10, and the ideal architecture could achieve its best performance at N equals 100. $\Psi(W)$ does not give us any information on how increases in system size will influence algorithm performance. Because of this, it does not match our intuitive understanding of scalability (see Definition 1).

To develop a good definition, we must identify the essential characteristics of scalability. First, based on the intuitive Definition 1, scalability should provide information about how the system size will influence the performance. Can the performance be scaled up with the system size? And, what price must we pay to achieve this scaled performance? Scalability should be a function of the variation of system size.

Second, in general, scalability is a function of the pair of parallel algorithm and machine. Both algorithms and architectures have parallel overhead, and when large system size is employed, the overhead may significantly degrade performance. The sources of degradation are sometimes specified with respect to algorithm and architecture. The commonly considered algorithmic degradation is *uneven allocation*, or *load imbalance* [9]. The commonly considered architecture degradation is *communication cost* which contains the communication latency and other delay incurred by interprocessor communication. These two degradations cannot be clearly separated. On the one hand, the communication delay will influence the achieved degree of parallelism of a given algorithm. On the other hand, unless we have synchronous communication, the communication cost will vary with the inherent degree of parallelism of a given algorithm, even for algorithms with the same communication requirement. With some simplified assumptions, we could distinguish between algorithmic scalability and architectural scalability. For instance, we could use idealized parallel machines and algorithms [5], [6]. However, in general, when we talk of algorithm scalability, we mean the algorithm's scalability with respect to a given architecture. If the architecture represents a large class of architectures, then the algorithm scalability is a general scalability suitable for the class of architectures. Similarly, architecture scalability is a scalability with respect to a given algorithm unless this algorithm represents a class of algorithms. Scalability is an inherent property of algorithms, architectures, and their combinations. Scalability should first be considered for algorithm-machine combinations. Algorithm scalability and architecture scalability could then be defined based on the scalability of the algorithm-machine combination.

Third, scalability should be a *meaningful* and *quantitative* performance metric that can be evaluated and compared. Its meaning should be driven by the motivations and goals of parallel processing. Its value must be calculated by a method that is consistent with the meaning we assign to scalability.

We do not consider physical constraints of the hardware. If the performance cannot scale up with the system size, we say that the machine, or the algorithm-machine combination, is unscalable even if it achieves the best performance using today's technology. Distinguishing such performance degradations will motivate the need for new technologies. For instance, constrained by the three dimensionality of space and today's technologies, systems having more processors

require longer wires for interprocessor connection. Therefore, the communication cost will increase at least logarithmically with the system size for a large class of algorithms. This degradation has spurred the development of new technologies, e.g., optical communication, for the next generation parallel machines.

III. DEFINITION AND ANALYSIS

There are three main driving forces behind parallel processing: faster execution time; solving otherwise intractably large problems; and providing a better system cost-performance ratio. If we focus on the first two factors, then the performance that we seek from parallel processing involves both execution time and problem size. What we seek from parallel processing is *speed*, where speed is defined as work divided by time. For scientific applications, work is generally measured as floating point operations performed. A parallel algorithm may increase parallelism by sacrificing mathematical efficiency. For this reason, the floating point operations count of parallel processing is usually based on a conventional sequential algorithm. Problem size sometimes has been referred to as a parameter which determines the floating point operations, e.g., the order of a matrix. For this study, we will use the term work and problem size interchangeably without distinction. While we agree with others that this measure of work is less than adequate in some contexts, we measure work in terms of floating point operations in this study because of its prevalence. Our objective here is to define *scalability* not *work*. The scalability metric we define is not biased toward any particular work measure and can adopt a better work measure when one is developed. With speed as a goal, we seek the power to solve problems of some magnitude in a reasonably short amount of time. Speed is a quantity that ideally would increase linearly with system size. So, it is consistent with the scalability property proposed in Definition 1. Based on this reasoning, we propose the isospeed approach.

Definition 2: The `average unit speed` is the achieved speed of the given computing system divided by N, the number of processors.

We refer to average unit speed as *average speed* when the context is clear. Saying that the speed of a computing system is linearly proportional to the system size is the same as saying that the average speed is a constant number independent of system size. Using average speed, following Definition 1, we give the following definition for any algorithm-machine combination in which the parallel machine is homogeneous.

Definition 3: An `algorithm-machine combination` is `scalable` if the achieved average speed of the algorithm on the given machine can remain constant with increasing numbers of processors, provided the problem size can be increased with the system size.

By Definition 3, scalability is expressed in terms of system size. In general, increasing the problem size will increase the computation/overhead ratio, and therefore, increase the speed. This is especially true for parallel processing where the computation/communication ratio increases with problem size for most algorithms. For a large class of algorithm-machine combinations, the average speed can be maintained by increasing problem size (see case studies in Section IV). The necessary problem size increase varies with algorithms, machines, and their combination. This variation provides a quantitative measurement for scalability. Let W be the amount of work of an algorithm when N processors are employed in a machine, and let W' be the amount of work of the algorithm when $N' > N$ processors are employed to maintain the average speed, then we define the *scalability from system size N to system size N'* of the algorithm-machine combination as follows.

$$\psi(N, N') = \frac{N'W}{NW'}. \tag{1}$$

The work W' is determined by the isospeed (or, to be accurate, the iso-average-speed) constraint. In the ideal situation, we have trivial parallelism, or the local computation model [12]. There is no communication necessary and work is replicated on each processor. In this case, $W' = \frac{N'W}{N}$ and $\psi(N, N') = 1$. In general, $W' > \frac{N'W}{N}$ and $\psi(N, N') < 1$. The initial work W is a problem size which can achieve the initial speed. It is determined by the average speed constraint. To have a unique scalability for an algorithm-machine combination, we need to define the initial average speed uniquely for each algorithm-machine pair. Borrowing the asymptotic performance idea from Hockney [13], we define the asymptotic average unit speed of an algorithm-machine combination, r_∞, as the maximum speed reached by the single processor execution of the algorithm on the machine when problem size goes to infinity. The initial average speed is a fraction of the asymptotic speed. Following the $n_{1/2}$ defined in [13], we choose the initial average speed, $r_{1/2}$, as half of the asymptotic speed.

When $N = 1$, we denote $\psi(N, N')$ by $\psi(N')$. Recall that speed is equal to work divided by time, and average speed is equal to speed divided by the number of processors. Let T_N, $T_{N'}$ be the execution time when N and N' processors are employed, respectively; then when the average speeds are the same, we have

$$\frac{W}{NT_N} = \frac{W'}{N'T_{N'}}$$
$$\frac{N'W}{NW'} = \frac{T_N}{T_{N'}},$$

and

$$\psi(N, N') = \frac{T_N}{T_{N'}}. \tag{2}$$

When N equals one,

$$\begin{aligned}\psi(N') &= \frac{T_1}{T_{N'}} \\ &= \frac{sequential\ execution\ time\ with\ problem\ size\ W}{parallel\ execution\ time\ with\ problem\ size\ W'}.\end{aligned} \tag{3}$$

Equation (3) has a representation similar to the traditional definition of speedup. The difference is that in traditional speedup the problem size is fixed and in scalability the speed is fixed. Speedup measures the performance gain of

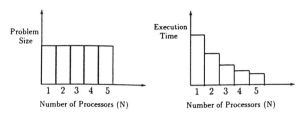

Fig. 1. Traditional speedup: Fix problem size, measure execution time.

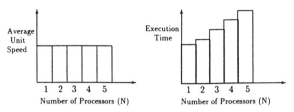

Fig. 2. Scalability: Fix average speed, measure execution time.

parallel processing versus sequential processing (see Fig. 1). Scalability measures the performance degradation of larger parallel systems versus smaller parallel systems (see Fig. 2). From (3), we can see the harmony and discord between speedup and scalability.

- Both speedup and scalability depend on the initial status (initial problem size and number of processors) and the "distance", i.e., the incremental change in the number of processors. In general, as "distance" increases, the speedup will increase and the scalability will decrease.
- Both speedup and scalability are dimensionless quantities, unlike performance metrics such as execution time or speed. However, each relates to these dimensioned performance metrics in some way. Speedup provides the variation ratio of the chosen dimensioned performance metric when the system size is increased. Scalability indicates the ability of the system to maintain the chosen dimensioned performance metric when the system size is increased.

Traditionally, speedup has been defined as sequential execution time over parallel execution time. A generalized speedup was recently introduced by Gustafson and Sun [14]. The relationship between generalized speedup and traditional speedup has been studied in [14]. The generalized speedup is defined as

$$Generalized\ speedup = \frac{parallel\ speed}{sequential\ speed}. \tag{4}$$

If generalized speedup is used and assuming the sequential speed is independent of problem size (which is not true in general), then two implementations have the same efficiency if and only if they have the same average speed. In this case, the isospeed approach is the same as the isoefficiency approach.

In general, sequential execution speed varies with problem size. Overhead exists, and achieved speed rarely matches peak speed. Excluding any virtual memory effects, it is likely that increasing the problem size will increase the sequential execution speed. We use $\mu(W)$ to represent the sequential execution speed when W amount of work is done. When N processors are used concurrently, the parallel execution time can be divided into two parts, $T_N = t_{cN} + t_{oN}$, where t_{cN} (c stands for computing) is the computation time, and t_{oN} (o stands for overhead) is the cumulative time spent on communication, synchronization and other overhead caused by parallel processing. The following theorem shows that a large class of algorithm-machine combinations is scalable and the scalability can be calculated from precomputed parameters.

Theorem 1: If an algorithm has a balanced load on each processor, its communication cost is independent of problem size, and the single processor speed of the underlying machine increases with work load, then the algorithm-machine combination is scalable and the scalability

$$\psi(N, N') = \frac{t_{cN}}{t_{oN'}}\left[1 - \frac{\mu(W/N)}{\mu(W'/N')}\right] + \frac{t_{oN}}{t_{oN'}}. \quad (5)$$

Proof: If N processors are used to implement W amount of work, and W' is the amount of work required to maintain the average unit speed when $N' > N$ processors are employed, then we have

$$\frac{W}{NT_N} = \frac{W'}{N'T_{N'}}$$

$$\frac{W}{N(t_{cN} + t_{oN})} = \frac{W'}{N'(t_{cN'} + t_{oN'})}.$$

Since the work is distributed evenly among all processors,

$$\frac{W}{N(\frac{W}{N\mu(W/N)} + t_{oN})} = \frac{W'}{N'(\frac{W'}{N'\mu(W'/N')} + t_{oN'})}$$

$$\left(\frac{1}{\mu(W/N)} - \frac{1}{\mu(W'/N')}\right) + \frac{Nt_{oN}}{W} = \frac{N't_{oN'}}{W'}. \quad (6)$$

Since $\left(\frac{1}{\mu(W/N)} - \frac{1}{\mu(W'/N')}\right) + \frac{Nt_{oN}}{W} > 0$ and $t_{oN'}$ is independent of problem size, by (6), the algorithm-machine combination is scalable and the amount of work required to maintain the average unit speed is

$$W' = \frac{N't_{oN'}}{\left(\frac{1}{\mu(W/N)} - \frac{1}{\mu(W'/N')}\right) + \frac{Nt_{oN}}{W}}. \quad (7)$$

In this case

$$\psi(N, N') = \frac{N'W}{NW'} = \frac{W[(\frac{1}{\mu(W/N)} - \frac{1}{\mu(W'/N')}) + \frac{Nt_{oN}}{W}]}{Nt_{oN'}}$$

$$= \frac{(\frac{W}{\mu(W/N)} - \frac{W}{\mu(W'/N')}) + Nt_{oN}}{Nt_{oN'}}$$

$$= \frac{t_{oN}}{t_{oN'}} + \frac{1}{t_{oN'}}\left[t_{cN} - t_{cN}\frac{\mu(W/N)}{\mu(W'/N')}\right].$$

Therefore,

$$\psi(N, N') = \frac{t_{cN}}{t_{oN'}}\left[1 - \frac{\mu(W/N)}{\mu(W'/N')}\right] + \frac{t_{oN}}{t_{oN'}}. \quad (8)$$

□

Based on the proof of Theorem 1, we can see that the conditions "communication cost is independent of problem size" and "single processor speed of the underlying machine increases with work load" are only used to guarantee Equation (7) having a feasible solution. Replacing the two conditions by (7), we have the following.

Theorem 2: If an algorithm has a balanced load on each processor, and the equation

$$W' = \frac{N't_{oN'}(W')}{\left(\frac{1}{\mu(W/N)} - \frac{1}{\mu(W'/N')}\right) + \frac{Nt_{oN}(W)}{W}}$$

has a positive solution for any positive number W, then the algorithm-machine combination is scalable and the scalability

$$\psi(N, N') = \frac{t_{cN}(W)}{t_{oN'}(W')}\left[1 - \frac{\mu(W/N)}{\mu(W'/N')}\right] + \frac{t_{oN}(W)}{t_{oN'}(W')}. \quad (9)$$

While its condition is more difficult to verify, Theorem 2 has a weaker condition than Theorem 1. The following corollary was used in our case studies.

Corollary 1: Under the assumptions of Theorem 1 (or of Theorem 2), if the communication cost goes to infinity as the system size goes to infinity, then for any fixed N, $\lim_{N' \to \infty} \psi(N, N') = 0$.

Proof: By Theorem 1,

$$\psi(N, N') = \frac{t_{cN}(W)}{t_{oN'}(W')}\left[1 - \frac{\mu(W/N)}{\mu(W'/N')}\right] + \frac{t_{oN}(W)}{t_{oN'}(W')}.$$

By the definition of asymptotic speed r_∞, $\mu(W'/N') < r_\infty$. Therefore,

$$1 - \frac{\mu(W/N)}{\mu(W'/N')} < 1 - \frac{\mu(W/N)}{r_\infty},$$

$$0 \le \psi(N, N') \le \frac{t_{cN}(W)}{t_{oN'}(W')}\left[1 - \frac{\mu(W/N)}{r_\infty}\right] + \frac{t_{oN}(W)}{t_{oN'}(W')}.$$

Since $t_{oN'} \to \infty$, when $N' \to \infty$, we have

$$\lim_{N' \to \infty}\left(\frac{t_{cN}(W)}{t_{oN'}(W')}\left[1 - \frac{\mu(W/N)}{r_\infty}\right] + \frac{t_{oN}(W)}{t_{oN'}(W')}\right) = 0.$$

Thus,

$$\lim_{N' \to \infty} \psi(N, N') = 0$$

for any fixed N. □

In Theorem 1 and Theorem 2, we do not consider the physical limitations of the underlying machine. We assume that the target architecture has adequate memory capacity to sustain problem size increases. This assumption may not be generally applicable. If the memory capacity of a machine becomes a factor, the condition $W' \le W_0$ (or $\frac{W'}{N'} \le W_0$ for distributed memory multiprocessors), for some constant number W_0, should be included in the theorems. In general the scalability of an algorithm-machine combination is constrained by memory and communication requirements. That is, certain combinations of problem and system sizes can result in memory bound or communication bound program execution. Fig. 3 diagrams the general scalability space of algorithm-machine combinations.

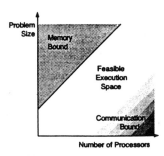

Fig. 3. Problem-ensemble space.

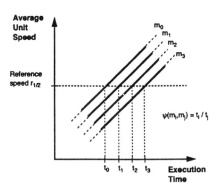

Fig. 4. Illustration of approach 2.

IV. CASE STUDIES: MEASUREMENT AND VISUALIZATION

In this section, we present four case studies that illustrate the preceding definitions relating to scalability and show how the scalability could be measured, computed, and predicted. Each case study involves a parallel program having a structure that is to some extent scalable on the parallel machine. That is, each is executable over a range of problem sizes on small scale to large scale system sizes. In each case, we briefly describe the algorithm-machine combination, do a scalability analysis, and highlight program characteristics via performance visualization.

The two programs under study are: the Burg algorithm and the modified SLALOM benchmark program. The Burg program is a linear signal processing procedure for fitting an autoregressive model to a time series data set [7]. Time (and work, measured as the number of floating point operations performed) varies linearly with the number of data points in the series; storage also varies linearly. SLALOM (Scalable Language-independent Ames Laboratory One-minute Measurement) [15] is a program designed as a scalable computer benchmark. It solves a radiosity problem by calculating the equilibrium radiation given off by a coupled set of diffuse surfaces that emit and absorb radiation. The surfaces are decomposed into patches, which are the basis for a radiosity matrix. The core computation of SLALOM is solving the radiosity matrix by Gaussian elimination, resulting in at most order n^3 time (or work) and order n^2 storage, where n is the number of patches.

The two machines under study are: the nCUBE 2 computer and the MasPar MP-1 computer. The nCUBE 2 is a distributed memory message-passing MIMD computer with a hypercube interconnection topology. Each node is a 32-bit custom CISC processor having a minimum of one megabyte of memory and operating at 20 megahertz clock rate. To contrast, while double-precision multiply and add require 6 clocks and 7 clocks, respectively, message overhead consumes approximately 1600 clocks. At the beginning of this study, we used a 64-node system in our laboratory (now, 128 nodes). The largest installed system has 1024 nodes. The MasPar MP-1 is a distributed memory massively parallel SIMD computer with a high-speed two-dimensional toroidal mesh topology. A control unit issues instructions at 12.5 megahertz clock rate. Each processing element in the array is a 4-bit custom load/store processor having a minimum of 16 kilobytes of memory. While double-precision multiply and add require

530 and 180 clocks, respectively, the mesh network overhead is approximately 12–30 clocks. We used an 8192-processor system in our laboratory. The system now has been upgraded to 16384 processors.

A. Calculation of Scalability

Three different approaches to obtain the scalabilities of an algorithm-machine combination have been noticed and compared in our study.

1) The scalability can be *measured* in software by a control program that invokes the application program and searches for the run having the desired fixed average unit speed.
2) The scalability can be *computed* by first finding the relation between average unit speed and execution time (or work) and then using Equation 2 (or Equation 1).
3) The scalability can be *predicted* by deriving a general scalability formula.

The first approach is the most direct and accurate. It is easy to understand and implement. The only point requiring mention is that we do not include redundant work (extra work added for parallel processing) in the work calculation. The second approach provides more information than the first approach. It shows the influence of initial speed. If we assume the derived relation remains true for larger system size and problem size or if we can predict the relation for large system and problem size based on the performance of small system and problem size, it also can be used to predict scalability. A graphical method of calculating scalability based on approach 2 is shown in Fig. 4. The method uses a set of measured data to find the relation between average unit speed and execution time. One curve (relation) is plotted for each machine size, with execution time on the horizontal axis and average unit speed on the vertical axis. Execution time varies as the problem size is varied. The third approach is the simplest one if a formula can be derived. However, in general, a formula may not be available or only can be found under certain simplified conditions.

In the sample plot of Fig. 4, four curves are drawn, one per machine size (typically m_0 is the smallest size), in order to illustrate approach 2. Each curve is generated by measuring average unit speed and execution time for runs of increasing problem size. The maximum average unit speed is calculated by taking the asymptotic limit of average unit speed with

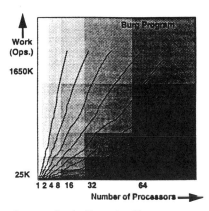

Fig. 5. Isospeed curves for the Burg algorithm.

TABLE I
COMPUTED SCALABILITY OF BURG-nCUBE COMBINATION (APPROACH 2)

$\psi(N, N')$	1	2	4	8	16	32	64	128
1	1.00	0.441	0.296	0.215	0.188	0.157	0.136	0.121
2		1.00	0.670	0.488	0.426	0.357	0.308	0.274
4			1.00	0.728	0.635	0.532	0.460	0.408
8				1.00	0.827	0.693	0.599	0.531
16					1.00	0.837	0.724	0.642
32						1.00	0.865	0.767
64							1.00	0.887
128								1.00

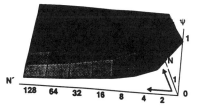

Fig. 6. Variation in scalability: Three-dimensional surface plot of computed scalability for the Burg-nCUBE combination (see Table I).

respect to time as time (or work) approaches infinity. The constant average unit speed used as the reference point could be any fraction of this maximum: we choose half of the maximum of single processor execution in our study. This reference speed is marked in the figure with the horizontal dashed line. The intersection of this speed line with each curve determines the program execution time delivering that speed. The ratios of these times, as defined in Section 3, yields a set of scalability numbers. The relative horizontal time positions indicate time (or work) variation and provide visual cues for the scalabilities.

The Burg-nCUBE combination is used to compare the three approaches.

B. Burg-nCUBE Combination

The Burg program employs a block decomposition form of data parallelism on the nCUBE 2 computer. Each processor does a number of calculations dependent primarily on its block size, and so for evenly distributed data there is a balanced load. The main loop of the Burg program can be approximately divided into three phases [7]: 1) a linear shift operation to align arrays, followed by local array calculations; 2) a global sum operation; and 3) local array update calculations. The number of communication steps required for the linear shift operation is constant, and the number for the global sum is logarithmic with respect to machine size. Communication in the Burg algorithm is independent of problem size. The Burg algorithm fits the conditions of Theorem 1 well.

The measured isospeed (i.e., constant average unit speed) curves are shown in the contour plot of Fig. 5. Each curve represents system size-problem size combinations that yield approximately equal average speed per processor. The desired average unit speed used as the reference point for calculating scalabilities corresponds to a curve within this contour plot. Considering Definition 3, we can see that the Burg algorithm is scalable: a constant average speed can be identified as system size increases. The background shading indicates the value of the average speed, where lighter shading corresponds to relatively higher speeds.

Selecting the isospeed corresponding to half of the asymptotic speed and applying approach 2, we derive a set of scalabilities, listed in Table I. The asymptotic speed calcu-

lated for this algorithm-machine combination is 1.7 MFLOPS (millions of floating point operations per second), giving a reference speed of 0.85 MFLOPS. As in Fig. 4, a set of average unit speed (as a function of time) curves is plotted based on measured data, and from this, a set of times is obtained. The execution times (in milliseconds) used to compute the scalabilities are shown in Table II. The variation in scalability can be shown pictorially by representing the tabular data (of Table I) as a three-dimensional surface plot, as in Fig. 6. The table rows and columns map to two dimensions, and scalability, to the third dimension. Higher scalability values also are represented by darker shading for emphasis. This plot portrays the range and trends of algorithm-machine scalabilities at a glance.

Another useful pictorial representation of the tabular data is shown in Fig. 7. A set of curves is drawn, one curve per machine size N (or per row of Table I). Scalability ψ is on the vertical axis, and machine size N' (columns of Table I) is on the horizontal axis. The variation in scalability is shown for 1) each initial machine size with respect to larger machine sizes (i.e., N with respect to N') and 2) increasing initial machine sizes N.

The average unit speed requirement makes the execution time unique for each system size. Notice that by the definition of scalability (1) $\psi(N, N'') = \psi(N, N') * \psi(N', N'')$ for any $0 < N < N' < N''$. The scalability matrix of Table I can be abbreviated as a vector array as shown in Table III. All the scalabilities in Table I can be computed directly from the scalabilities in Table III.

By Theorem 1, the scalability of the Burg algorithm also can be predicted via (5). In hypercube multicomputers, message transfer time between two adjacent processors can be expressed as $\alpha + \beta S$, where α is the communication latency, β is the transmission time per byte, and S is the number of bytes in the message. We have measured $\alpha = 130$ (microsecond) and $\beta = 0.5$ (microsecond) for our nCUBE 2 multicomputer. Substituting the communication cost of the Burg algorithm

TABLE II
TIME VARIATION OF BURG-nCUBE COMBINATION

system size	1	2	4	8	16	32	64	128
Time	0.004029	0.00913	0.01362	0.01774	0.02144	0.02561	0.0296	0.03338

TABLE III
COMPUTED SCALABILITY OF BURG-nCUBE COMBINATION (APPROACH 2)

$\psi(1,2)$	$\psi(2,4)$	$\psi(4,8)$	$\psi(8,16)$	$\psi(16,32)$	$\psi(32,64)$	$\psi(64,128)$
0.441	0.670	0.728	0.827	0.837	0.865	0.887

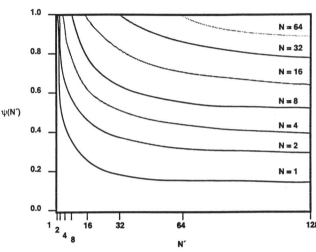

Fig. 7. Variation in scalability: Interpolated plot of $\psi(N')$ for each N (see Table I).

TABLE IV
PREDICTED SCALABILITY OF BURG-nCUBE COMBINATION (APPROACH 3)

$\psi(N,N')$	1	2	4	8	16	32	64	128
1	1.00	0.410	0.336	0.281	0.238	0.207	0.182	0.162
2		1.00	0.743	0.581	0.478	0.405	0.352	0.311
4			1.00	0.783	0.643	0.545	0.474	0.419
8				1.00	0.826	0.691	0.589	0.536
16					1.00	0.837	0.713	0.652
32						1.00	0.852	0.769
64							1.00	0.885
128								1.00

TABLE V
MEASURED SCALABILITY OF BURG-nCUBE COMBINATION (APPROACH 1)

$\psi(N,N')$	1	2	4	8	16	32	64	128
1	1.00	0.451	0.319	0.240	0.193	0.161	0.138	0.121
2		1.00	0.707	0.533	0.427	0.357	0.306	0.269
4			1.00	0.753	0.604	0.504	0.433	0.380
8				1.00	0.802	0.670	0.575	0.504
16					1.00	0.835	0.717	0.629
32						1.00	0.859	0.753
64							1.00	0.876
128								1.00

into (5), we have

$$\psi(N, N') = \frac{t_c N}{[\alpha + 4\beta] + \log(N')[\alpha + 8\beta]}\left[1 - \frac{\mu(W/N)}{\mu(W'/N')}\right]$$
$$+ \frac{[\alpha + 4\beta] + \log(N)[\alpha + 8\beta]}{[\alpha + 4\beta] + \log(N')[\alpha + 8\beta]}. \qquad (10)$$

The set of predicted scalabilities obtained by applying approach 3 and the prediction formula from (10) is shown in Table IV. Finally, the set of directly measured scalabilities obtained by applying approach 1 is given in Table V.

Compared to the measured scalability of Table V, both the predicted scalability of Table IV and the computed scalability of Table I provide good approximations for the Burg-nCUBE combination. The predicted scalability tends to be slightly higher than the measured scalability due to the fact that in the actual algorithm, in addition to the communication cost $\alpha + \beta S$, extra operations are involved to prepare variables for communication. For the computed scalability, its function fitting method has included this extra cost in the fitting function.

Taking advantage of the fitting function method used for the computed scalability, we can predict the performance of a larger system based on the performance of smaller systems. For example, the predicted execution time for a 128-node system, based on the computed execution times calculated for systems up to 64 nodes, is 0.03409 sec. (only $\approx$ 2% greater than the number listed in Table II). Using this time with the others yields the following scalabilities for $N < 128$

and $N' = 128$: 0.118, 0.269, 0.400, 0.520, 0.629, 0.751, and 0.868. Comparing these numbers with the rightmost column of Table IV, which is the scalability predicted by approach 3, we observe that they more closely approximate the actual numbers in the rightmost column of Table V, which is the measured scalability. Here, prediction via computed values from approach 2 is better than prediction via approach 3. Whereas approach 2 uses all the information available, approach 3 only uses the single node execution information.

The communication cost of the Burg-nCUBE combination increases slowly with the system size. If $N' - N = constant$, the second term of Equation (10), the ratio of communication, will increase with N and approaches 1 as N approaches infinity. As N grows, the Burg-nCUBE combination should exhibit better scalability. This is confirmed by the measured results (see Table V).

Another trend observed via the measured results can be explained analytically. Note in Table V the lower scalabilities for small N and large N'. This is consistent with Corollary 1 in Section III, which says that as N' grows for fixed N, scalability should approach zero. How fast it approaches zero depends on the computation time versus communication time ratio of the system and on the initial system size. Since this ratio is small for the nCUBE 2 (e.g., 7 clock cycles/1600 clock

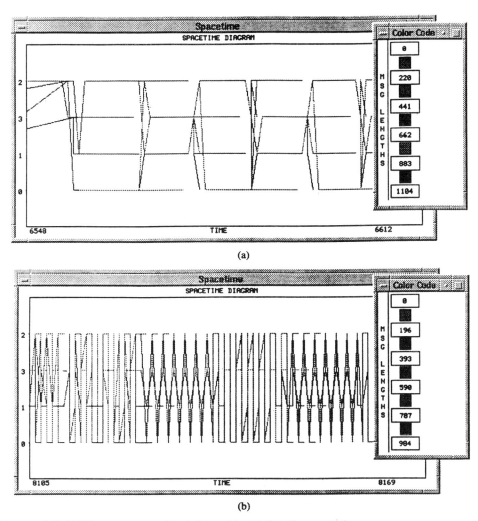

Fig. 8. Spacetime diagrams of SLALOM program execution during matrix solution (4 processors).

cycles), the reduction in scalability for small initial system sizes is steep. That is, despite increasing slowly with system size, communication cost can be relatively high compared to time spent in computation. The effort (in terms of increasing problem size) needed to offset the overhead and to reach the isospeed is then considerable.

C. SLALOM-nCUBE Combination

The SLALOM program does not satisfy the condition of Theorem 1. Thus, approach 3 for calculating scalability is not applicable. Results from applying approaches 1 and 2 are presented in this section. Tables VI and VII give sets of computed and measured scalabilities for the SLALOM-nCUBE combination, respectively. This version of SLALOM for the nCUBE computer only executes on "square" hypercubes (hence the N and N' used in the tables). The asymptotic speed calculated for the SLALOM-nCUBE combination is 1.5 MFLOPS, giving a reference speed of 0.75 MFLOPS.

The SLALOM algorithm has a more complex structure than the Burg algorithm. The computed scalability of the SLALOM-nCUBE combination does not match the measured scalability as closely as in the Burg-nCUBE combination. Performance instrumentation and visualization tools are es-

TABLE VI
COMPUTED SCALABILITY OF SLALOM-nCUBE COMBINATION (APPROACH 2)

$\psi(N, N')$	1	4	16	64
1	1.00	0.65	0.54	0.38
4		1.00	0.83	0.59
16			1.00	0.71
64				1.00

TABLE VII
MEASURED SCALABILITY OF SLALOM-nCUBE COMBINATION (APPROACH 1)

$\psi(N, N')$	1	4	16	64
1	1.00	0.625	0.504	0.344
4		1.00	0.806	0.549
16			1.00	0.681
64				1.00

pecially useful for these more complex cases. The tools—by capturing and depicting the dynamic behavior of parallel program execution—can contribute to and expand our perception of scalability. We applied the PICL (Portable Instrumented Communication Library) [16] and ParaGraph [17] toolset to the SLALOM-nCUBE combination for this purpose. PICL produces an execution trace during an actual run of an in-

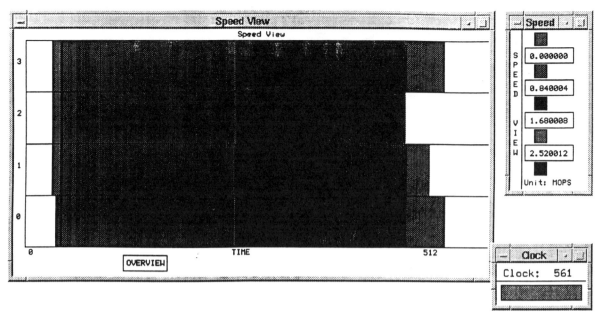

Fig. 9. Average speed chart and clock for SLALOM program execution (4 processors).

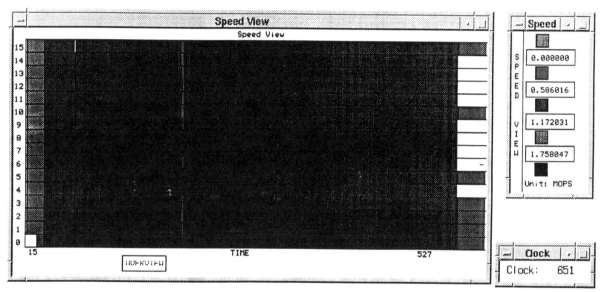

Fig. 10. Average speed chart and clock for SLALOM program execution (16 processors).

strumented program, and ParaGraph replays this trace using multiple views. Each was developed by researchers at Oak Ridge National Laboratory and is available via *netlib*. We selected appropriate views in ParaGraph to depict scalability-related information. Because scalability involves a comparison based on constant average unit speed, we compare views under those conditions. Two of these views are the Spacetime Diagram and the Average Speed Chart.

The Spacetime Diagram, supplied with ParaGraph, is patterned after the diagrams that are used in physics to depict interactions between particles. Processor activity is indicated by horizontal lines, one for each processor, while messages between processors are depicted by slanted lines between the sending and receiving processor activity lines, indicating the times at which each message was sent and received.

A blank horizontal line indicates that a processor is idle waiting to receive a message. The color of a slanted line represents the relative size of the message in bytes. The Spacetime Diagram presents the structure of communication for the algorithm-machine combination. Comparing multiple Spacetime Diagram views, we observe how problem size and/or system size variations affect the structure. We can detect communication dependencies on problem size or system size, uniformities, periodicities, etc., all of which can influence scalability.

The structure of the SLALOM program is complicated. It contains different phases which have totally different computation and communication structures. Fig. 8 shows Spacetime Diagrams for one part of SLALOM, the core computation of matrix solution. Fig. 8(a) depicts the beginning of the

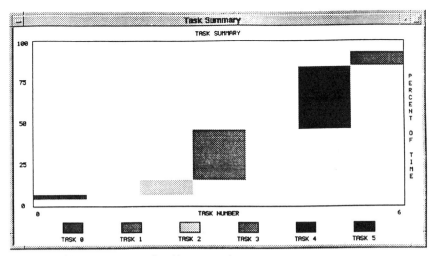

Fig. 11. Task summary view of SLALOM program execution (4 processors).

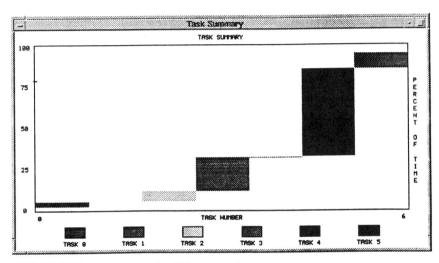

Fig. 12. Task summary view of SLALOM program execution (16 processors).

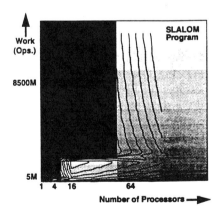

Fig. 13. Isospeed curves for SLALOM program.

factoring algorithm, and Fig. 8(b), the backsolving algorithm. The communication requirement is high, and it depends on both system size and problem size.

The Average Speed Chart, a view we designed and integrated into ParaGraph, depicts the speed of individual processors by a horizontal bar chart as a function of time. The color of each bar indicates the average speed (in MFLOPS) of the corresponding processor during each user-defined phase. The Average Speed Chart demonstrates that the isospeed conditions of scalability are being met and graphically displays the execution times for comparative analysis. Execution times for phases of the algorithm as well as the whole algorithm are shown.

Figs. 9 and 10 show Average Speed Charts for two complete runs of the SLALOM program. In each case, an average unit speed of 0.75 MFLOPS is achieved. Fig. 9 corresponds to a run using 4 nodes, and Fig. 10, 16 nodes. Problem sizes are 276 patches and 490 patches, respectively. SLALOM's core computation part comprises the widest shaded bar in each chart. Clock views, displaying simulated execution time, are also shown in the figures. An estimate of the scalability, $\psi(4, 16)$, can be obtained by reading the Clocks and taking the ratio of total execution times, $T_4 / T_{16} = 561/651 = 0.862$. (Note that the times are in Paragraph's simulated time units, which are related to real time units based on factors internal to Paragraph and entered by the user.)

From the idle processors in Fig. 8 and the non-uniform processor profiles in Fig. 10, we can see that the SLALOM

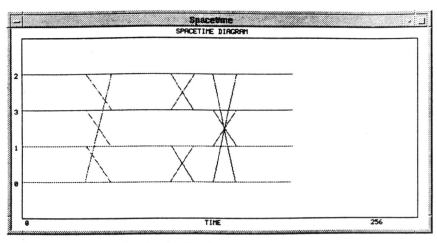

Fig. 14. Spacetime diagram of Burg program execution, first iteration (4 processors).

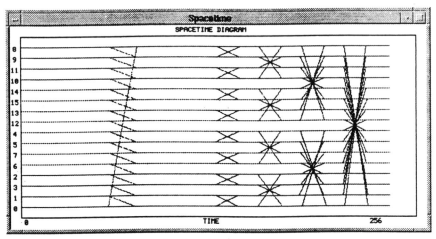

Fig. 15. Spacetime diagram of Burg program execution, first iteration (16 processors).

program has noticeable load imbalance degradation. Comparing Fig. 9 with Fig. 10, we can also see that the ratio of the execution time of each phase to the total execution time varies with system size. This variation makes the scalability of a SLALOM-nCUBE combination (or a SLALOM-MasPar combination) unpredictable with present analytical methods. The variation is specifically shown in the Task Summary views of Figs. 11 and 12 (4 and 16 node cases, respectively). These views show the percent of total execution time spent in each task, or phase, of the program. The tasks are identified with numbers (circularly) on the horizontal axis, and the slice of time taken by each task is displayed on the vertical axis. Seven tasks are delineated within SLALOM.

Fig. 13 shows the isospeed curves of SLALOM-nCUBE combinations. Comparing Fig. 13 with Fig. 5, we can see that for the domain under study these isospeed curves have a more complicated structure, including sharp turning points and peaks.

To contrast the SLALOM and Burg algorithms further, consider selected Paragraph views of Burg-nCUBE combinations. Figs. 14 and 15 show Spacetime Diagrams for two executions of the Burg algorithm. Fig. 14 corresponds to a run using 4 nodes, and Fig. 15, 16 nodes. Problem sizes are 440 data points and 2880 data points, respectively. In each case, an average

unit speed of 0.85 MFLOPS is achieved. From these figures we can see that the Burg algorithm has only two communication patterns, and each is neatly structured. The first is independent of system size, and the second has a number of communication steps which increases logarithmically with system size (two send-receive pairwise exchanges in Fig. 14 and four pairwise exchanges in Fig. 15). Observe that no processors ever wait to receive a message; the load is evenly distributed.

Figs. 16 and 17 show Average Speed Charts and Clocks for the two executions of the Burg algorithm corresponding to Figs. 14 and 15, respectively. An estimate of the scalability, $\psi(4, 16)$, via reading the Clocks, is $T_4 / T_{16} = 195/301 = 0.648$. The three phases of the algorithm (see Section 4.2) are delineated within these Average Speed Charts. Taking note of the Speed Legends in the figures and comparing the two combinations, we see that the "phase speeds" (i.e., the speeds of processors during the same phase) are approximately equal. Differences in speed are due mainly to instrumentation artifact. We can also see that the ratio of the execution time of each phase to the total execution time is approximately unchanged. This means that the scalabilities of the parts (i.e., the phases) are equal to the scalabilities of the whole. This can be shown analytically. As the Burg-nCUBE combination scales, so does each particular phase of the algorithm.

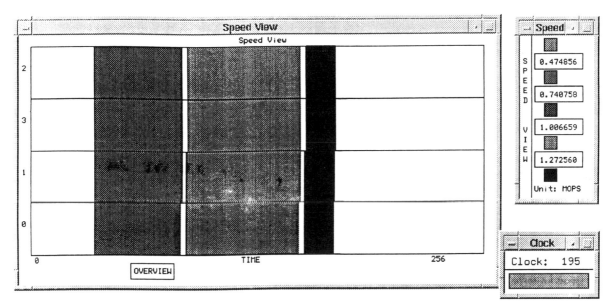

Fig. 16. Average speed chart and clock for Burg program execution, first iteration (4 processors).

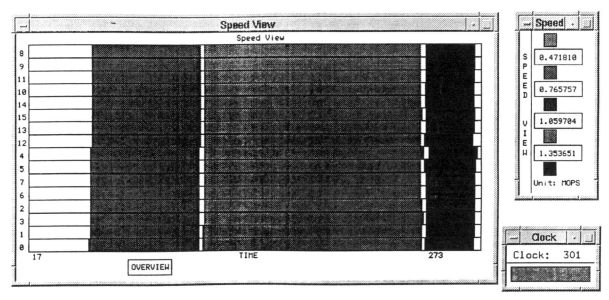

Fig. 17. Average speed chart and clock for Burg program execution, first iteration (16 processors).

The nice properties of the Burg algorithm make its scalability predictable. However, many practical algorithms behave like the SLALOM program in terms of having load imbalance degradation and communication cost varying with problem size. It is difficult to derive a general scalability formula for these algorithms. Performance measurement and visualization provide a feasible way to analyze and estimate the scalability of these algorithms.

D. Burg-Maspar and Slalom-Maspar Combinations

Next, we consider the scalability of the Burg and SLALOM programs on the MasPar computer. The Burg program employs a scattered decomposition form of data parallelism on the MasPar MP-1 computer [7]. The program has exhibited superior performance on the MasPar computer [7]. Machine sizes

for this study include 1024 (or 1 K), 2048, 4096, and 8192 processors. The set of computed scalabilities (approach 2) for the Burg-MasPar combination is given in Table VIII. The asymptotic average unit speed calculated for the Burg–MasPar combination is 41 KFLOPS, giving a reference speed of 20.5 KFLOPS. The times used to compute the scalabilities are listed in Table IX. It is clear that while this scalability does vary similar to the Burg-nCUBE combination scalability, it is initially higher and decreases at a much slower rate. The more gradual decline is due to the larger computation to communication ratio of the MasPar system (e.g., 180 clock cycles / 30 clock cycles). Comparing the scalabilities of the Burg-nCUBE and the Burg–MasPar combinations, we can see the influence of the computing/communication ratio on scalability.

TABLE VIII
COMPUTED SCALABILITY OF BURG–MASPAR COMBINATION (APPROACH 2)

$\psi(N, N')$	1 K	2 K	4 K	8 K
1 K	1.00	0.93	0.89	0.83
2 K		1.00	0.95	0.90
4 K			1.00	0.94
8 K				1.00

TABLE IX
TIME VARIATION OF BURG–MASPAR COMBINATION (SECONDS)

system size	1 K	2 K	4 K	8 K
Time	0.0135	0.0145	0.0152	0.0162

TABLE X
COMPUTED SCALABILITY OF SLALOM–MASPAR COMBINATION (APPROACH 2)

$\psi(N, N')$	1 K	2 K	4 K	8 K
1 K	1.00	0.74	0.75	0.34
2 K		1.00	1.02	0.46
4 K			1.00	0.46
8 K				1.00

TABLE XI
TIME VARIATION OF SLALOM–MASPAR COMBINATION (SECONDS)

system size	1 K	2 K	4 K	8 K
Time	8.42	11.37	11.20	24.60

Since the validation of Theorem 1 is only dependent on the parallel algorithm's properties, (5) also could be used for predicting the scalability of the Burg–MasPar combination.

Table X gives the computed scalabilities of the SLALOM–MasPar combination. The asymptotic average unit speed calculated for this combination is 18 KFLOPS, giving a reference speed of 9 KFLOPS. Table XI lists the times used to compute the scalabilities. Recall that the MasPar computer has a two-dimensional toroidal mesh connection. When 1-K processors or 4-K processors are used, the underlying machine topology is a 32×32 or 64×64 square mesh, respectively. When 2-K processors or 8-K processors are used, the connection topology is a 32×64 or 64×128 rectangular mesh, respectively. As previously noted, the core computation of SLALOM is solving a dense $n \times n$ matrix by Gaussian elimination. The work load is imbalanced during the core computation. When the underlying machine connection is non-symmetric—as for 2-K and 8-K processors—the load imbalance is magnified and leads to lower performance (relative to the symmetric configuration). This, for example, accounts for the $\psi(2 \text{ K}, 4 \text{ K})$ value in Table XI, which is the scalability of a square machine with respect to a rectangular one. The SLALOM–MasPar combination has shown how the scalability could be influenced by the shape of the machine configuration. More work is needed in this area.

V. CONCLUSION

As more and more people accept massively-parallel computing as a practical approach for achieving high performance, more and more people start using the word *scalable*. The term has a reputation as a nice property of parallel machines and algorithms. However, with the lack of a clear definition, it is impossible to compare scalability over algorithms, architectures, and algorithm-machine combinations. We all know that scalability is the *ability to scale*, i.e., the ability to adjust according to a proportion (Webster's Dictionary definition). But, adjust what? to what proportion? These are the complicated parts which had not been clearly defined and often lead to confusion. In our study, the scalability of algorithm-machine combinations is carefully defined and a quantitative measurement is proposed. We adjust the problem size (or equivalently execution time) with the system size and proportion the adjustment to obtain a fixed average unit processor speed. We have shown that all three quantities, system size,

problem size (work), and speed, are inter-related. Their relation reflects the inherent parallel degradations of the algorithm and architecture under consideration, and provides the scalability information of the algorithm-machine combination. Scalability is a metric which reveals aspects of the performance which are not easily discerned from other metrics. Scalability itself is not a measurement of parallel processing gain. It is a factor that contributes to the ability of a system to deliver the expected performance. It has valid uses for predicting the behavior of large scale computations.

The scalability variation of algorithm-machine combinations is also carefully studied. Scalability formulas have been derived for a relatively large class of algorithm-machine combinations. Three different approaches have been proposed to measure, compute, and predict scalability. Two algorithms have been investigated on an nCUBE 2 multicomputer and on a MasPar MP-1 parallel computer. The first algorithm, the Burg algorithm, has a nice structure. It satisfies the preconditions of our theoretical results. The experimental results match our theoretical results closely. The second algorithm, the SLALOM algorithm, has a more sophisticated structure. It has load imbalance degradation and a complicated communication pattern. It contains several computing phases. Each phase has a different speed and the relative duration of each phase varies with the system size. The SLALOM algorithm represents another class of algorithms. These algorithms have an intricate system size, problem size, and speed relation. There is no easy way to derive a satisfiable scalability formula for this type of algorithm. To overcome the lack of theoretical guidelines, performance instrumentation and visualization tools for multicomputers are used and developed to observe the algorithm behavior. Our experience shows that visualization provides an accurate and perceptible indication of the full-scale behavior of a parallel algorithm-machine combination.

ACKNOWLEDGMENT

We are indebted to several individuals at Ames Laboratory for their help with this research. In particular, J. Gustafson offered thoughtful discussion about the concept of scalability. J. Kim implemented our custom views for Paragraph. M. Carter provided assistance with the systems, especially to gather the performance data.

REFERENCES

[1] J. Gustafson, G. Montry, and R. Benner, "Development of parallel methods for a 1024-processor hypercube," *SIAM J. SSTC*, vol. 9, July 1988.

[2] J. Gustafson, "Reevaluating Amdahl's law," *Commun. ACM*, vol. 31, pp. 532–533, May 1988.

[3] V. Kumar and A. Gupta, "Analysis of scalability of parallel algorithms and architectures: A survey," in *Proc. Int. Conf. on Supercomputing*, June 1991.

[4] V. Kumar and V. Singh, "Scalability of parallel algorithms for the all-pairs shortest path problem: A summary of results," in *Proc. of Conf. on Parallel Processing*, Chicago, IL, 1990, pp. III 136–140.

[5] M. Willebeek-LeMair, A. P. Reeves, and C. H. Ning, "Characterization of multicomputer system: a transfer ration approach," in *Proc. Int. Conf. on Parallel Processing*, Chicago, IL, 1990, pp. II 171–178.

[6] D. Nussbaum and A. Agarwal, "Scalability of parallel machines," *Commun. the ACM*, vol. 34, no. 3, pp. 57–61, 1991.

[7] D. Rover, V. Tsai, Y. Chow, and J. Gustafson, "Signal processing algorithms on parallel architectures: A performance update," *J. Parallel Distrib. Computing*, vol. 13, pp. 237–245, Nov. 1991.

[8] C. Goral, K. Torrance, D. Greenberg, and B. Battaile, "Modeling the interaction of light between diffuse surfaces," *Comput. Graphics*, vol. 18, pp. 213–222, July 1984.

[9] X.-H. Sun and L. Ni, "Another view on parallel speedup," in *Proc. of Supercomputing'90*, NY, 1990, pp. 324–333.

[10] ——, "Scalable problems and memory-bounded speedup," *J. Parallel Distrib. Computing*, vol. 19, pp. 27–37, Sept. 1993.

[11] G. Amdahl, "Validity of the single-processor approach to achieving large scale computing capabilities," in *Proc. AFIPS Conf.*, 1967, pp. 483–485.

[12] X.-H. Sun, L. Ni, F. Salam, and S. Guo, "Compute-exchange computation for solving power flow problems: The model and application," in *Proc. 4th SIAM Conf. Parallel Processing for Scientific Computing*, 1989, pp. 198–203.

[13] R. W. Hockney, "Parametrization of computer performance," *Parellel Computing*, vol. 5, 1987.

[14] X.-H. Sun and J. Gustafson, "Toward a better parallel performance metric," *Parallel Computing*, vol. 17, Dec. 1991.

[15] J. Gustafson, D. Rover, S. Elbert, and M. Carter, "The design of a scalable, fixed-time computer benchmark," *J. Parallel Distrib. Computing*, vol. 11, Aug. 1991.

[16] G. Geist, M. Heath, B. Peyton, and P. Worley, "A machine-independent communication library," in *Proc. 4th Conf. Hypercubes, Concurrent Computers, and Applications*, 1989, pp. 565–568.

[17] M. T. Heath and J. A. Etheridge, "Visualizing the performance of parallel programs," *IEEE Software*, vol. 8, pp. 29–39, Sept. 1991.

Xian-He Sun received the B.S. degree in mathematics from Beijing Normal University, Beijing, China, the M.S. degree in mathematics and M.S. and Ph.D. degrees in computer science from Michigan State University.

After graduating from Michigan State, he joined the Ames Laboratory, operated for the Department of Energy by Iowa State University. During the year 1991-92, he was a visiting faculty member at Clemson University. He is currently a staff scientist at ICASE, NASA Langley Research Center. His research interests include parallel processing, parallel numerical algorithms, performance evaluation, and database systems.

Dr. Sun is a Guest Editor for the special issue of *Journal of Parallel and Distributed Computing* on Analyzing Scalability of Parallel Algorithms and Architectures. He is a member of the IEEE Computer Society and the Association for Computing Machinery.

Diane T. Rover received the B.S. degree in computer science in 1984, the M.S. degree in computer engineering in 1986, and the Ph.D. degree in computer engineering in 1989, all from Iowa State University.

From 1985 to 1988, she was awarded an IBM Graduate Fellowship. In 1986, she was an intern with McDonnell Douglas Corp. and in 1987, she was with the IBM Thomas J. Watson Research Center. Under a DOE Postdoctoral Fellowship from 1989 to 1991, she was a researcher in the Scalable Computing Laboratory at the Ames Laboratory. She is currently an Assistant Professor in the Department of Electrical Engineering at Michigan State University. Her research interests include parallel processing, computer architecture, reconfigurable hardware, and performance evaluation, instrumentation, and visualization.

With colleagues at the Ames Laboratory, Dr. Rover received an R&D 100 Award for the development of the Slalom benchmark. She is a member of the Program Committee for Supercomputing '94. She is a member of the IEEE Computer Society, ACM ASEE, and the Society of Women Engineers.

Measuring Parallel Processor Performance

Many metrics are used for measuring the performance of a parallel algorithm running on a parallel processor. This article introduces a new metric that has some advantages over the others. Its use is illustrated with data from the Linpack benchmark report and the winners of the Gordon Bell Award.

Alan H. Karp and Horace P. Flatt

There are many ways to measure the performance of a parallel algorithm running on a parallel processor. The most commonly used measurements are the elapsed time, price/performance, the speed-up, and the efficiency. This article defines another metric which reveals aspects of the performance that are not easily discerned from the other metrics.

The elapsed time to run a particular job on a given machine is the most important metric. A Cray Y-MP/1 solves the order 1,000 linear system in 2.17 seconds compared to 445 seconds for a Sequent Balance 21000 with 30 processors [2]. If you can afford the Cray and you spend most of your time factoring large matrices, then you should buy a Cray.

Price/performance of a parallel system is simply the elapsed time for a program divided by the cost of the machine that ran the job. It is important if there are a group of machines that are "fast enough." Given a fixed amount of money, it may be to your advantage to buy a number of slow machines rather than one fast machine. This is particularly true if you have many jobs to run and a limited budget. In the previous example, the Sequent Balance is a superior price/performer than the Cray if it costs less than 0.5 percent as much. On the other hand, if you can't wait 7 minutes for the answer, the Sequent is not a good buy even if it wins in price/performance.

These two measurements are used to help you decide what machine to buy. Once you have bought the machine, speed-up and efficiency are the measurements often used to let you know how effectively you are using it.

The speed-up is generally measured by running the same program on a varying number of processors. The speed-up is then the elapsed time needed by 1 processor divided by the time needed on p processors, $s = T(1)/T(p)$. (Of course, the correct time for the uniprocessor run would be the time for the best serial algorithm, but almost nobody bothers to write two programs.) If you are interested in studying algorithms for

parallel processors, and system A gives a higher speed-up than system B for the same program, then you would say that system A provides better support for parallelizing this program than does system B.

An example of such support is the presence of more processors. A Sequent with 30 processors will almost certainly produce a higher speed-up than a Cray with only 8 processors.

The issue of efficiency is related to that of price/performance. It is usually defined as

$$e = \frac{T(1)}{pT(p)} = \frac{s}{p}. \tag{1}$$

Efficiency close to unity means that you are using your hardware effectively; low efficiency means that you are wasting resources. As a practical matter, you may buy a system with 100 processors that each takes 100 times longer than you are willing to wait to solve your problem. If you can code your problem to run at high efficiency, you'll be happy. Of course, if you have 200 processors, you may not be unhappy with 50 percent efficiency, particularly if the 200 processors cost less than other machines that you can use.

Each of these metrics has disadvantages. In fact, there is important information that cannot be obtained even by looking at all of them. It is obvious that adding processors should reduce the elapsed time, but by how much? That is where speed-up comes in. Speed-up close to linear is good news, but how close to linear is good enough? Well, efficiency will tell you how close you are getting to the best your hardware can do, but if your efficiency is not particularly high, why? The new metric defined in the following section is intended to answer these questions.

NEW METRIC

We will now derive our new metric, the experimentally determined serial fraction, and show why it is useful. We will start with Amdahl's Law [1] which in its simplest form says that

$$T(p) = T_s + \frac{T_p}{p}, \qquad (2)$$

where T_s is the time taken by the part of the program that must be run serially and T_p is the time in the parallelizable part. Obviously, $T(1) = T_s + T_p$. If we define the fraction serial, $f = T_s/T(1)$ then equation (2) can be written as

$$T(p) = T(1)f + \frac{T(1)(1 - f)}{p}, \qquad (3)$$

or, in terms of the speed-up s

$$\frac{1}{s} = f + \frac{1 - f}{p}. \qquad (4)$$

We can now solve for the serial fraction, namely

$$f = \frac{1/s - 1/p}{1 - 1/p}. \qquad (5)$$

The experimentally determined serial fraction is our new metric. While this quantity is mentioned in a large percentage of papers on parallel algorithms, it is virtually never used as a diagnostic tool the way speed-up and efficiency are. It is our purpose to correct this situation.

The value of f is useful because equation (2) is incomplete. First, it assumes that all processors compute for the same amount of time, i.e., the work is perfectly load balanced. If some processors take longer than others, the measured speed-up will be reduced giving a larger measured serial fraction. Second, there is a term missing that represents the overhead of synchronizing processors.

Load-balancing effects are likely to result in an irregular change in f as p increases. For example, if you have 12 pieces of work to do that take the same amount of time, you will have perfect load balancing for 2, 3, 4, 6, and 12 processors, but less than perfect load balancing for other values of p. Since a larger load imbalance results in a larger increase in f, you can identify problems not apparent from speed-up or efficiency.

The overhead of synchronizing processors is a monotonically increasing function of p, typically assumed to increase either linearly in p or as log p. Since increasing overhead decreases the speed-up, this effect results in a smooth increase in the serial fraction f as p increases. Smoothly increasing f is a warning that the granularity of the parallel tasks is too fine.

A third effect is the potential reduction of vector lengths for certain parallelizations of a particular algorithm. Vector processor performance normally increases as vector length increases except for vector lengths slightly larger than the length of the vector registers. If the parallelization breaks up long vectors into shorter vectors, the time to execute the job can increase. This effect then also leads to a smooth increase in the measured serial fraction as the number of processors increases. However, large jobs usually have very long vectors, vector processors usually have only a few processors (the Intel iPSC-VX is an exception), and there are usually parallelizations that keep the vector lengths fixed. Thus, the reduction in vector length is rarely a problem and can often be avoided entirely.

In order to see the advantage of the serial fraction over the other metrics, look at Table I which is extracted from Table 2 of the Linpack report [2]. The Cray Y-MP shows speed-ups ranging from 1.95 to 6.96. Is that good? Even if you look at the efficiency, which ranges from 0.975 to 0.870, you still don't know. Why does the efficiency fall so rapidly? Is there a lot of overhead when using 8 processors? The serial fraction, f, answers the question; the serial fraction is nearly constant for all values of p. The loss of efficiency is due to the limited parallelism of the program.

The single data point for the Sequent Balance reveals that f performs better as a metric as the number of processors grows. The efficiency of the 30 processor Sequent is only 83 percent. Is that good? Yes, it is since the serial fraction is only 0.007.

The data for the Alliant FX/40 shows something different. Here the speed-up ranges from 1.90 to 3.22 and the efficiency from 0.950 to 0.805. Although neither of these measurements tells much, the fact that f ranges from 0.053 to 0.080 does; there is some overhead that is increasing as the number of processors grows. We can't tell what this overhead is due to—synchronization cost, memory contention, or what—but at least we know it is there. The effect on the FX/80 is much smaller although there is a slight increase in f, especially for fewer than 5 processors.

Even relatively subtle effects can be seen. The IBM 3090 has a serial fraction under 0.007 for 2 and 3 processors, but over 0.011 for 4 or more. Here the reason is most likely due to the machine configuration; each set of 3 processors is in a single frame and shares a memory management unit. Overhead increases slightly when two of these units must coordinate their activities. This effect also shows up on the 3090-280S which has two processors in two frames. Its run has twice the serial fraction as does the run on the 3090-200S. None of the other metrics would have revealed this effect.

Another subtle effect shows up on the Convex. The 4 processor C-240 shows a smaller serial fraction than does the 2 processor C-220. Since the same code was presumably run on both machines, the actual serial fraction must be the same. How can the measured value decrease? This appears to be similar to the "superlinear" speed-ups reported on some machines. As in those cases, adding processors adds cache and memory bandwidth which reduces overhead. Perhaps that is the case here.

Care must be used when comparing different machines. For example, the serial fraction on the Cray is 3 times larger than on the Sequent. Is the Cray really that inefficient? The answer is no. Since almost all the parallel work can be vectorized, the Cray spends relatively less time in the parallel part of the code than does the Sequent which has no vector unit. Since the parallelizable part speeds up more than the serial part which

Table I. Summary of Linpack report Table 2

Computer	p	Time(sec)	s	e	f
Cray Y-MP/8	1	2.17	—	—	—
Cray Y-MP/8	2	1.11	1.95	0.975	0.024
Cray Y-MP/8	3	0.754	2.88	0.960	0.021
Cray Y-MP/8	4	0.577	3.76	0.940	0.021
Cray Y-MP/8	8	0.312	6.96	0.870	0.021
IBM 3090-180S VF	1	7.27	—	—	—
IBM 3090-200S VF	2	3.64	2.00	1.000	0.002
IBM 3090-280S VF	2	3.65	1.99	0.995	0.004
IBM 3090-300S VF	3	2.46	2.96	0.987	0.007
IBM 3090-400S VF	4	1.89	3.85	0.963	0.013
IBM 3090-500S VF	5	1.52	4.78	0.956	0.011
IBM 3090-600S VF	6	1.29	5.64	0.940	0.012
Alliant FX/40	1	66.1	—	—	—
Alliant FX/40	2	34.8	1.90	0.950	0.053
Alliant FX/40	3	24.9	2.65	0.883	0.066
Alliant FX/40	4	20.5	3.22	0.805	0.080
Alliant FX/80	1	57.7	—	—	—
Alliant FX/80	2	29.8	1.94	0.970	0.032
Alliant FX/80	3	20.7	2.79	0.930	0.038
Alliant FX/80	4	16.2	3.56	0.890	0.041
Alliant FX/80	5	13.6	4.24	0.848	0.045
Alliant FX/80	6	11.8	4.89	0.815	0.046
Alliant FX/80	7	10.6	5.44	0.777	0.048
Alliant FX/80	8	9.64	5.99	0.749	0.048
Sequent	1	11111	—	—	—
Sequent	30	445	25.0	0.833	0.007
Convex C-210	1	15	—	—	—
Convex C-220	2	7.98	1.88	0.940	0.064
Convex C-240	4	4.03	3.72	0.930	0.025

Note: p=#processors, s=speed-up, e=efficiency, f=serial fraction

has less vector content, the fraction of the time spent in serial code is increased.

The Linpack benchmark report measures the performance of a computational kernel running on machines with no more than 30 processors. The results in Table II are taken from the work of the winners of the Gordon Bell Award [5]. Three applications are shown with maximum speed-ups of 639, 519, and 351 and efficiencies ranging from 0.9965 to 0.3430. We know this is good work since they won the award, but how good a job did they do? The serial fraction ranges from 0.00051 to 0.0019 indicating that they did a very good job, indeed.

The serial fraction reveals an interesting point. On all three problems, there is a significant reduction in the serial fraction in going from 4 to 16 processors (from 16 to 64 for the wave motion problem). As with the Convex results, these numbers indicate something akin to "superlinear" speed-up. Perhaps the 4-processor run sends longer messages than does the 16-processor run, and these longer messages are too long for the system to handle efficiently. At any rate, the serial fraction has pointed up an inconsistency that needs further study.

SCALED SPEED-UP

All the analysis presented so far refers to problems of fixed size. Gustafson [4] has argued that this is not how parallel processors are used. He argues that users will increase their problem size to keep the elapsed time of the run more or less constant. As the problem size grows, we should find the fraction of the time spent executing serial code decreases, leading us to predict a decrease in the measured serial fraction.

If we assume that the serial time and overhead are independent of problem size, neither of which is fully justified, [3]

$$T(p, k) = T_s + \frac{kT_p}{p}, \qquad (6)$$

where $T(p, k)$ is the time to run the program on p processors for a problem needing k times more arithmetic. Here k is the scaling factor and $k = 1$ when $p = 1$. Flatt [3] points out that the scaling factor k must count arithmetic, not some more convenient measure such as memory size.

Our definition of speed-up must now account for the additional arithmetic that must be done to solve our

Table II. Summary of Bell Award winning performance

p	s	e	f
	Wave Motion		
4	3.986	0.9965	0.0012
16	15.86	0.9913	0.00097
64	62.01	0.9689	0.00051
256	226.2	0.8836	0.00052
1024	639.0	0.6240	0.00059
	Fluid Dynamics		
4	3.959	0.9898	0.0035
16	15.47	0.9669	0.0023
64	58.53	0.9145	0.0015
256	201.6	0.7875	0.0011
1024	519.1	0.5069	0.00095
	Beam Stress		
4	3.954	0.9885	0.0039
16	15.46	0.9663	0.0023
64	57.46	0.8978	0.0018
256	177.5	0.6934	0.0017
1024	351.2	0.3430	0.0019

Note: p=#processors, s=speed-up, e=efficiency, f=serial fraction

larger problem. We can use

$$s_k = \frac{kT(1, 1)}{T(p, k)}. \qquad (7)$$

The scaled efficiency is then $e_k = s_k/p$, and the scaled serial fraction becomes

$$f_k = \frac{1/s_k - 1/p}{1 - 1/p}. \qquad (8)$$

By our previous definitions we see that $f = kf_k$ which under ideal circumstances would remain constant as p increases.

The scaled results are shown in Table III. Although these runs take constant time as the problem size grows, the larger problems were run with shorter time steps. A better scaling would be one in which the time integration is continued to a specific value.

If the run time were still held constant, the problems would scale more slowly than linearly in p. In these examples, the Courant condition limits the step size which means that the correct scaling would be $k = \sqrt{p}$. The scaling chosen for the problems of Table III is $k = p$.

As predicted [3], the efficiency decreases, barely, as p increases even for scaled problems. The scaled serial fraction, on the other hand, decreases smoothly. This fact tells us that the decreasing efficiency is not caused by a growing serial fraction. Instead it tells us the problem size is not growing fast enough to completely counter the loss of efficiency as more processors are added.

The variation in f_k as the problem size grows makes it difficult to interpret. If we allow for the fact that ideally the increase in the problem size does not affect the serial work, we again have a metric that should remain constant as the problem size grows. Table III shows how kf_k varies with problem size. We see that this quantity grows slowly for the wave motion problem, but that there is virtually no increase for the fluid dynamics problem. These results indicate that the serial work increases for the wave motion problem as the problem size grows but not for the fluid dynamics problem. The irregular behavior of kf_k for the beam stress problem warrants further study.

SUMMARY

We have shown that the measured serial fraction, f, provides information not revealed by other commonly used metrics. The metric, properly defined, may also be useful if the problem size is allowed to increase with the number of processors.

What makes the experimentally determined serial fraction such a good diagnostic tool of potential per-

Table III. Bell Award scaled problems. $k=p$

p	s_k	e_k	f_k	kf_k
		Wave Motion		
4	3.998	0.9995	0.00013	0.00053
16	15.95	0.9969	0.00020	0.0032
64	63.61	0.9939	0.000097	0.0062
256	254.1	0.9926	0.000029	0.0074
1024	1014	0.9902	0.0000098	0.010
		Fluid Dynamics		
4	3.992	0.9980	0.00067	0.0027
16	15.96	0.9975	0.00015	0.0024
64	63.82	0.9972	0.000046	0.0029
256	255.2	0.9969	0.000013	0.0033
1024	1020	0.9961	0.0000033	0.0034
		Beam Stress		
4	4.001	1.000	0.0	0.0
16	16.00	1.000	0.000021	0.00034
64	63.96	0.9994	0.000015	0.00098
256	255.8	0.9992	0.0000038	0.00096
1024	1023	0.9990	0.0000012	0.0013

Note: p=#processors, s_k=scaled speed-up, e_k=scaled efficiency, f_k=scaled serial fraction

formance problems? While elapsed time, speed-up, and efficiency vary as the number of processors increases, the serial fraction would remain constant in an ideal system. Small variations from perfect behavior are much easier to detect from something that should be constant than from something that varies. Since kf_k for scaled problems shares this property, it, too, is a useful tool.

Ignoring the fact that p takes on only integer values makes it easy to show that

$$\frac{d}{dp}\frac{1}{e} = f \qquad (9)$$

if we ignore the overhead and assume that the serial fraction is independent of p. Thus, we see that the serial fraction is a measure of the rate of change of the efficiency. Even in the ideal case, $1/e$ increases linearly as the number of processors increases. Any deviation of $1/e$ from linearity is a sign of lost parallelism. The fraction serial is a particularly convenient measure of this deviation from linearity.

The case of problem sizes that grow as the number of processors is increased is only slightly more complicated. In this case

$$\frac{d}{dp}\frac{1}{e_k} = f_k + (p-1)\frac{df_k}{dp} = \frac{f}{k}\left(1 - \frac{p-1}{k}\frac{dk}{dp}\right). \qquad (10)$$

If $k = 1$, i.e., there is no scaling, equation (10) reduces to equation (9). If $k = p$, then $1/e$ has a slope of f/p^2 which is a very slow loss of efficiency. Other scalings lie between these two curves.

It is easy to read too much into the numerical values. When the efficiency is near unity, $1/s$ is close to $1/p$ which leads to a loss of precision when subtracting in the numerator of equation (5). If care is not taken, variations may appear that are mere round-off noise. All entries in the tables were computed from

$$f = 1 - \frac{1 - 1/s}{1 - 1/p}. \qquad (11)$$

Since both s and p are considerably greater than unity and neither $1/s$ nor $1/p$ is near the precision of the floating point arithmetic, there is only one place where precision can be lost. Rounding the result to the significance of the reported times guarantees that the results are accurate. Similarly,

$$f_k = 1 - \frac{1 - 1/s_k}{1 - 1/p} \qquad (12)$$

is used for the scaled serial fraction.

Although our numerical examples come from rather simple cases, one of us (Alan Karp) has successfully used this metric to find a performance bug in one of his applications. Noting an irregularity in the behavior of f led him to examine the way the IBM Parallel Fortran prototype compiler was splitting up the work in the loops. Due to an oversight, the compiler truncated the result of dividing the number of loop iterations by the number of processors. This error meant that one processor had to do one extra pass to finish the work in the loop. For some values of p this remainder was small; for others, it was large. The solution was to increase his problem size from 350, which gives perfect load balancing on his six-processor IBM 3090-600S only for 2 and 5 processors, to 360 which always balances perfectly. (This error was reported to the IBM Parallel Fortran compiler group.)

REFERENCES
1. Amdahl, G.M. Validity of the single processor approach to achieving large scale computer capabilities. In *Proceedings of AFIPS Spring Joint Computer Conference, 30*. Atlantic City, NJ, 1967.
2. Dongarra, J.J. Performance of various computers using standard linear equation software. Report CS-89-85, Computer Science Department, Univ. Tennessee, Knoxville, October 12, 1989.
3. Flatt, H.P., and Kennedy, K. Performance of parallel processors. *Parallel Comput. 12*. (Oct. 1989), 1–20.
4. Gustafson, J.L. Reevaluating Amdahl's Law. *Commun. ACM 31*, 5 (May 1988), 532–533.
5. Gustafson, J.L., and Montry, G.R., and Brenner, R.E. Development of parallel methods for a 1024-processor hypercube. *SIAM Sci. Stat. Comp. 9*, (July 1988), 609–638.

CR Categories and Subject Descriptors: C.1.2 [**Processor Architectures**]: Multiple Data Stream Architectures (Multiprocessors)—*parallel processors*; C.4 [**Computer Systems Organization**]: Performance of Systems—*measurement techniques*
General Terms: Measurement, Performance
Additional Key Words and Phrases: Parallel performance

ABOUT THE AUTHORS:

ALAN KARP is a staff member at IBM's Palo Alto Scientific Center. He has worked on problems of radiative transfer in moving stellar matter and in planetary atmospheres, hydrodynamics problems in pulsating stars and in enhanced oil recovery, and numerical methods for parallel processors. He is currently studying the interface between programmers and parallel processors with special attention to debugging parallel algorithms.

HORACE P. FLATT is manager of IBM's Palo Alto Scientific Center. He received a Ph.D. in mathematics from Rice University in 1958, subsequently becoming manager of the applied mathematics group of Atomics International, Inc. He joined IBM in 1961 and has primarily worked in management assignments in applied research in computer systems and applications. Authors' Present Address: IBM Scientific Center, 1530 Page Mill Road, Palo Alto, CA 94304.

Address Tracing for Parallel Machines

Craig B. Stunkel, IBM T.J. Watson Research Center

Bob Janssens and W. Kent Fuchs

University of Illinois at Urbana-Champaign

A ddress traces, the records of sequences of memory addresses referenced by processors during execution, are widely used by designers and researchers to assess performance issues related to computer processors and their memory systems. Parallel processors raise a multitude of issues regarding accessing memory and sharing data efficiently among processors. Parallel processors also exacerbate the difficulties in collecting address traces. This critical survey examines address-tracing techniques from the perspective of parallel processing systems and evaluates existing-tracing methods for a number of criteria.

Event traces are used by computer system designers and researchers in two principal ways. One method, known as trace-driven simulation, uses a trace as input to a simulation model of a selected part of a computer system. The other method, analytical modeling, often analyzes traces to extract parameters for analytical (mathematically tractable) models of the system. Using traces in either modeling method enables designers to predict the effect of changing selected parts of the computer system without building actual hardware prototypes to test these changes.

An address trace is useful in several

This survey of recently implemented approaches to address tracing highlights the issues specific to collection of traces for both shared and distributed memory parallel computers.

areas of computer system performance evaluation. Evaluation of memory systems is the most common usage, especially for systems employing on-chip or off-chip memory caches. Shared-memory multiprocessors create unique cache performance issues. The caches in these systems must remain coherent; memory reads must not return stale data, necessitating invalida-

tion of selected cache data or write broadcasting to all caches.

Adequate cache performance is vital to shared-memory systems, since cache misses cause accesses to a global memory that is often much slower than a typical uniprocessor main memory. Other issues that can be assessed with the aid of address traces include interconnection networks for global memory, memory paging strategies, processor instruction mixes and branching characteristics, and validation of results from analytical models.

Address-tracing metrics

In this survey, we examine parallel system address-tracing methods based on several metrics. Since quantitatively comparing many of these metrics is impossible, the observations are largely qualitative.

Accuracy of captured traces. Performance monitoring may change some aspect of a processor's execution, thereby changing the observed performance data. Because address tracing attempts to capture performance data at a fine level of detail (mem-

Reprinted from *Computer*, Vol. 24, No. 1, Jan. 1991, pp. 31–38.

0-8186-6522-X/95 $4.00 © 1991 IEEE

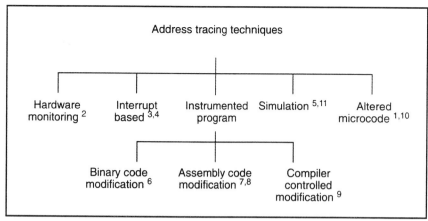

Figure 1. A taxonomy of address-tracing techniques.

ory requests can occur in a significant percentage of processor cycles) the measurement-disturbing problem is nontrivial, particularly for parallel computers.

The often complex interaction between processors in a parallel system can be easily perturbed by tracing overhead. This interaction is most pronounced in shared-memory parallel systems, for which out-of-order accesses to shared memory potentially change the sequence of execution for one or more processors. In parallel message-passing distributed-memory systems, the change in execution time caused by address-tracing overhead may change the order in which messages are received, and may change the sequence of instruction execution.

Speed of trace capture. The speed at which memory reference addresses can be captured affects the size of traces that one is willing to generate. As processor caches grow larger, the corresponding cache simulation models require longer address traces to accurately estimate cache performance.

Applicability to a wide variety of systems. Particular tracing methods may possess superior characteristics and yet be incompatible with a given processor architecture or an implementation of that architecture.

Completeness of address traces. A trace may be fragmented if only a limited number of references can be captured before a trace-processing phase interrupts the address generation. Depending on the usage of the traces, such a fragmentation may degrade the accuracy of performance studies

that rely on such traces. Another form of fragmentation occurs when a tracing process can only record a subset of the addresses generated by a processor.

Operating system references and multiprogrammed workloads. Many existing tracing systems can only capture user-code addresses and omit operating system references. Performance studies for caches have demonstrated the errors inherent in ignoring system references.[1] An increasing number of systems can support multiprogrammed workloads. Some cache performance studies simulate the effect of multiprogramming by interleaving traces at regular intervals, but obtaining more valid traces containing the actual interleaving of separate user programs (as well as system references) is desirable.

Address-trace collection methods

Address-trace collection methods can be classified into five general categories, as illustrated in Figure 1. This section introduces and examines these techniques according to the comparison metrics presented in the previous section.

Hardware-captured traces. Hardware monitors directly record processor memory requests sent to off-chip caches or main memory.[2] This monitoring captures both user and operating system references, as well as multiprogrammed streams of references. These captured references are typically physical memory addresses, which are often desirable for cache simulation

studies, but which are not as useful as virtual addresses for evaluating processor performance issues. With advances in chip technology, most new microprocessors incorporate on-chip caches, which allow some memory references to be handled internally. These memory references are thus not traceable.

Complexity, cost, and lack of flexibility are the primary limitations of this approach. Because of limited memory and bandwidth, hardware monitors often cannot capture the whole trace and settle for isolated collections of contiguous references or counts of events, rather than a listing of the events themselves. To collect trace information for every processor in a parallel system, either the tracing hardware increases in complexity with the number of processors, or the traces are gathered one processor at a time via a number of different executions of the same workload.

Since current (and likely future) parallel processors are often constructed from the highest performance microprocessors available, the trend toward on-chip caches in these processors will limit the effectiveness of hardware-based tracing techniques. The completeness of the trace is also likely to be a problem due to trace fragmentation from limited storage buffers.

Interrupt-based traces. Since hardware-based tracing techniques are difficult to adapt to tracing parallel processors, software-based techniques have received widespread attention. Some computer systems provide the capability of interrupting the execution of a program after each instruction.[3] As shown in Figure 2, each tracing interrupt transfers control to an operating system or user-code routine that calculates address references based on the instruction found at the current user program counter.

Since operating system routines typically disable interrupts, the operating system execution usually cannot be traced. The need to interrupt each instruction slows down the program execution considerably (typically from a hundred to a thousand times slower). Still, many current parallel processors are built using processors that facilitate interrupts after every instruction. Eggers and Katz[4] recorded traces on a bus-based shared-memory machine via interrupts.

Simulation-based traces. Simulation can also provide user traces and can simultaneously model the execution time of a processor; this can facilitate modeling the interaction between different processors. Simulation is typically slower than interrupt-based traces, however, since the simulator must model much of the real hardware, including the actual ALU operations, flag setting, instruction fetching, and main memory accesses. Simulation has been used to synthesize traces for shared-memory multiprocessors.[5]

Simulation offers the potential for highly accurate traces — even involving complex parallel systems — and is widely applicable to different architectures. Simulation could conceivably collect operating system references as well, although we are not aware of tracing systems with this property. The speed of trace collection is the slowest of any tracing methodology, and this has been a prime deterrent to its widespread use.

Altered microcode-based traces. Address tracing using microcode (ATUM) is a technique that enables the capture of full address traces for multiprogrammed user-code and operating system activity.[1] It is also fast, with a slow-down factor of 20 reported. The attractiveness of this approach is tempered by obstacles to implementing microcode alteration on existing and future parallel processors. The main difficulty is that the processors in commercial parallel systems tend to be one-chip microprocessors. In addition, the processors either do not use microcode or contain their microcode in ROM.

Instrumented program-based traces. These methods directly modify the executable code (application and/or operating system) to be traced. This code modification need not depend upon any special hardware features nor any extensive emulation capability. Thus, it has recently received considerable attention. Methods of this genre must be capable of ascertaining any virtual address changes that are side effects of the program modification itself.

In this approach, the program is split into units called basic blocks, which are sets of machine-level instructions that always execute in sequence (in the absence of any interrupts). Each basic block is analyzed to extract instruction and operand address-reference information. The virtual addresses for some references cannot be determined before the actual program execution. For these references, extra instructions are added to save runtime information (usually register contents) that aids in virtual address calculations. At the beginning of each basic block, a branch to

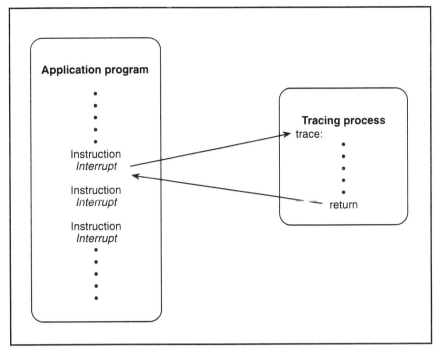

Figure 2. Interrupt-based tracing: sequence of execution.

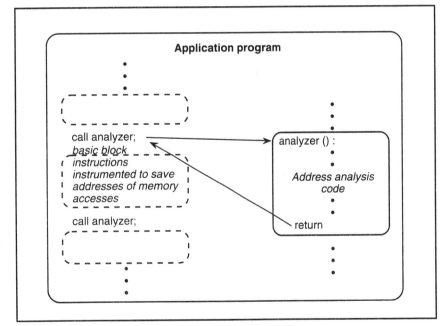

Figure 3. Instrumented program-based tracing: sequence of execution.

an address analyzer is inserted, as illustrated in Figure 3.

There are several conceivable strategies for program modification. For example, depending on processor architecture, it may be possible to directly modify the binary code in an executable file. Direct modifi-

cation of binary code is only possible when the binary code can be precisely disassembled to analyze the machine instructions. Precise disassembly is hindered or impossible in many systems due to addresses embedded in the machine code. These embedded addresses support indirect ad-

135

Table 1. Summary of evaluation of general address-tracing techniques.

Metric	Hardware Monitoring	Interrupt-Based	Simulation	Altered Microcode	Instrumented Program
Accuracy*	High	Medium-high	Low-high	Medium-high	Medium-high
Speed	1×	100×	1,000×	10×	10×
Applicability	Low	Medium	High	Low	High
Trace Completeness	Low	High	High	High	High
System Tracing	Yes	No	Possible	Yes	Possible
Multiprogram Tracing	Yes	No	Possible	Yes	Possible
Virtual/Physical Address	Physical	Virtual	Virtual	Both	Virtual

* Dependent on actual implementation.

dressing via memory locations, but cannot be distinguished from actual instructions by a disassembler. Recently, Borg, Kessler, and Wall introduced a direct binary-code modification approach for a RISC (reduced instruction-set computer) microprocessor.[6] The MIPS Corporation offers Pixie, a performance analysis tool that incorporates tracing via a similar direct binary-code modification.

The TRAPEDS (trace-producing execution-driven simulation)[7] and MPtrace[8] methods use a different program modification strategy aimed at a more general set of architectures. These techniques modify machine code at the assembly-source-code level. By bypassing the disassembly requirement, the techniques are applicable to any type of processor, regardless of the addressing modes. However, it is sometimes difficult to obtain the assembly language source for system-provided routines.

At a slightly higher level, researchers are now developing compiler-based, machine-code-modification techniques. These approaches attempt to produce similar types of tracing modifications using the compiler's knowledge of the program's assembly language structure.[9]

Summarizing the suitability of address-tracing techniques. Table 1 (similar to the table in Agarwal, Sites, and Horowitz[1]) summarizes the discussion of this section. Although hardware-based and microcode-based tracing possess several superior tracing characteristics, they have limited applicability for current and future parallel processors. Interrupt-based tracing is suitable for parallel processors, but offers few advantages over simulation-based and instrumented program-based techniques. It

cannot trace operating system references and has slow trace generation. For these reasons, the most common techniques for collecting complete address traces on future parallel processors likely will be simulation based or instrumented-program based.

Address tracing on shared-memory multiprocessors

Shared-memory multiprocessors present unique problems to the implementation of address tracing. The generated traces usually contain some distortions, since complete simulation of the fine-grained interaction between processors is too costly, regardless of the method used to generate the individual processor traces.

Trace validity. A shared-memory multiprocessor-address trace is a time-ordered list of accesses by all processors. A trace collection method introduces distortion if the address trace collected differs from that which would have been collected on an uninstrumented system. Distortion can be tolerated as long as it does not affect the validity of the resulting trace. The nondeterminism of shared-memory computer systems causes the behavior of any program to vary across executions with the same input. Validity can be described as the degree to which the set of possible behaviors reflected by a trace for an instrumented program differs from the set of possible behaviors of that program on an uninstrumented system. In general, a trace can be considered valid if its effect is similar to that which might have been seen in an

uninstrumented system under the same input. Unfortunately, validity as defined above is almost always impossible to measure and varies with the behavior the trace is intended to reflect. Therefore, a trace generation method designer will attempt to minimize distortion and thereby hopefully maximize validity.

Categories of trace distortion. As illustrated with examples in Figure 4, trace distortion can be classified into three categories: execution-pattern distortion, wait-time distortion, and access-order distortion.

Execution-pattern distortion occurs in dynamically scheduled tasks, when reordering of accesses to synchronization points modifies the actual pattern of execution of the traced program(s). Programming models that use fine-grained lightweight threads are especially susceptible to execution-pattern distortion. In environments where the validity of the trace may be affected by execution-pattern distortion, keeping the time dilation due to instrumentation to a minimum is essential. An alternate strategy is to attempt to preserve the relative timing by slowing down the whole system, including the thread or task scheduler.

Even if a trace does not suffer from execution-pattern distortion, it may still contain wait-time distortion. This distortion occurs when the instrumentation modifies the number of iterations of an idle loop while a process is waiting at a synchronization point. The amount of wait time at synchronization points will vary with features of the particular machine, such as the type of cache and interconnection network. Therefore, reimplementing synchronization as part of the trace-driven simulator is often desirable. This requires that the trace generator include a record of the synchronization events in the trace. The trace-driven simulator can then ignore synchronization accesses in the trace and use its own synchronization primitives. Since all idle waiting is determined after the trace has been generated, any amount of wait-time distortion can be tolerated in the trace.

The finest grain distortion that can be introduced by tracing is access-order distortion. The behavior of a multiprocessor is determined by the exact order of all memory accesses. A distortion as small as an interchange in time of two accesses can change the performance of the memory system. Fortunately, access-order distortion usually does not significantly affect the validity of a multiprocessor trace. The only accesses affected are those to shared variables that are not ordered by synchronization points, which the programming model usually assumes to occur in any unspecified order.

Dealing with distortion. There are two ways in which an implementation of a trace generation method can reduce the effects of distortion. First, it can attempt to minimize the amount of its interference in the normal execution of the application being traced. Second, if the interference is large enough to cause distortion, it can supply relative timing information in the trace to aid the trace-driven simulator in recreating a valid trace. In this case, the multiprocessor trace can consist of separate trace files for each processor, which are interleaved by the simulator. Most implementations use a combination of these two techniques.

ATUM-2,[10] the bus-based multiprocessor version of the ATUM[1] microcode-based address-tracing technique, does not supply relative timing information in the trace. Addresses generated by processors are all stored in a single buffer, with memory access conflicts resolved by the common system bus. The microcode modifications to implement tracing and the extra interference caused by the contention for the buffer affect the timing of the processors, potentially introducing distortion. However, the effect on timing is relatively uniform across all user and system processors.

By instrumenting the program, rather than the microcode, flexibility is gained in reducing distortion. Compiler flow-analysis techniques can be used to reduce the number of instrumentation points in the program. Synchronization information can be included in the trace. The amount of instrumentation can be varied, depending on the intended application. MPtrace[8] is a pro-

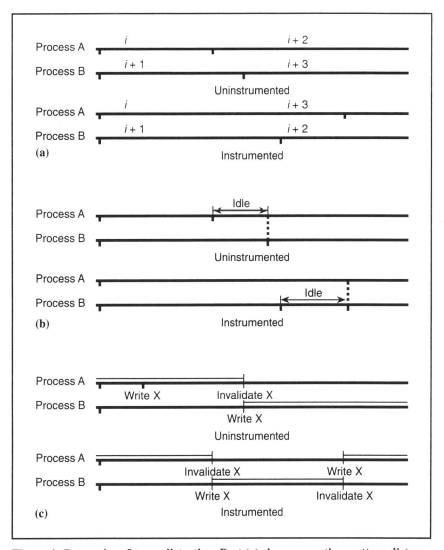

(a)
Uninstrumented
Instrumented

(b)
Uninstrumented
Instrumented

(c)
Uninstrumented
Instrumented

Figure 4. Categories of trace distortion. Part (a) shows execution-pattern distortion: A self-scheduled loop running on two processors. The scheduling of iteration $i+2$ and $i+3$ is interchanged in the instrumented program, resulting in a modified trace. Part (b) shows wait-time distortion: In the instrumented program, Process B reaches the barrier first, resulting in a modification of the number of memory accesses in the idle loops of processes A and B. Part (c) shows access-order distortion: Coherence protocol is invalidation-based, with Process A initially owning cache line X. In the instrumented program, the write to X in cache A occurs after the write to X in cache B, causing an extra invalidation.

gram instrumentation-based tracing tool implemented on the Sequent Symmetry multiprocessor in a lightweight thread environment. It generates a separate trace file, which includes synchronization information, for each processor. The trace is reinterleaved during simulation, eliminating wait-time distortion.

Tracing methods that employ simulation to generate the per-processor address traces are most prone to distortion. PSIMUL[5] is such a method. The simulator is itself a parallel program, having a process for every processor used by the application being traced. Much potential exists for execution-pattern distortion, especially since the simulator is usually run on a uniprocessor. Therefore, only programs that use the SPMD (single program, multiple data) programming model, which only uses static scheduling, can be traced. All synchronization points are marked, and the traces are interleaved during postprocessing.

In the hybrid instrumentation/simulation method called Tango,[11] traces are gathered on a uniprocessor, as in PSIMUL,

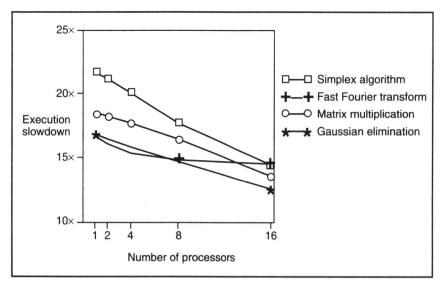

Figure 5. Execution slowdown for TRAPEDS trace-address-generation only.

and can be fed directly into a trace-driven simulator. The tracing software allows the user to specify the events to trace, and the memory and synchronization models to use in the simulation. This flexible environment allows the simulation to be tailored to a user's requirements of simulation cost and allowable distortion.

Trace storage and utilization. Trace data tends to be generated faster than the I/O system can store it. In shared-memory systems, there are usually few I/O channels compared to the number of processors, exacerbating the problem. The memory management necessary to overcome this bottleneck can affect the completeness and validity of the trace. Approaches to resolving this problem include buffering of address traces, concurrent simulation with tracing, trace compression, and trace sampling.[12]

In the ATUM system, tracing is controlled by a high-level program that executes a special patched instruction. When the trace buffer fills up, the program stops tracing and dumps the buffer to disk. No attempt is made to halt execution when the trace buffer needs to be emptied, so the trace consists of noncontiguous samples of the size of the buffer.

The MPtrace system overlaps tracing and I/O, but when more than two processors are traced, the trace buffers fill up faster than they can be emptied. In its current implementation, MPtrace associates one thread with each processor and threads do not migrate. During execution, threads pull buffers from a common pool,

fill them with trace data, and place them in a buffer queue. A number of writer threads, executing on separate processors so they do not cause distortion, remove buffers from the queue, write the buffers to disk, and recycle them. When all buffers are filled, execution stalls until they have all been written to disk.

To avoid writes to disk altogether, trace-driven simulation can be performed during generation.[7] Tango offers the capability of feeding the trace directly into a memory simulator. TRAPEDS (see the next section) consumes traces on-the-fly for distributed-memory multicomputers.[7] In these systems, trace consumption can still be a bottleneck, making it necessary for execution to stall while the traces are processed.

Applicability of tracing methods. The selection of a tracing method depends largely on the intended use of the traces. Currently, only the ATUM-2 traces can capture operating system and multiprogramming behavior. They are well suited for studies of interference between processes and process migration. Program instrumentation-based tracers have more difficulty tracing migrating processes, requiring modification of the process scheduler.[8]

Traces generated by program instrumentation or simulation techniques, however, have an advantage over ATUM-2 when synchronization affects performance. There is no way to compensate for the wait-time distortion in ATUM-2 traces, causing the validity of the synchronization

sections to be in question. In the other methods, the synchronization sections are marked and the postprocessor can resimulate synchronization to eliminate any distortion.

The usefulness of the ATUM method is also limited by its dependence on a specific system; most multiprocessors do not have writable microcode. Program instrumentation methods, on the other hand, can be applied to any multiprocessor system. However, a large part of the instrumentation code (about 25 percent in MPtrace) may have to be rewritten to port an implementation to a new machine. In contrast, pure simulation-based approaches are the most portable, as long as they do not rely on the underlying operating system.

Address tracing on distributed memory machines

In this section, we focus on distributed memory (multicomputer) address-tracing problems and present possible solutions. Each processor in a multicomputer system accesses a separate address space, which greatly simplifies the trace collection process. However, because software-based tracing methods slow down the execution of programs, interaction between processors (via messages) can conceivably occur in a different order than in the original code, creating execution pattern distortion. The tracing software need not concern itself with out-of-order execution between these message interactions. Thus, access order distortion does not occur in multicomputers.

Modeling interprocessor communication. On existing multicomputers, messages are passed using send and receive routines. Several approaches with varying levels of accuracy and implementation difficulty can be used for controlling these message-passing routines in an attempt to maintain the original ordering of messages. In order of increasing complexity, the approaches are:

(1) Make no attempt to regulate message ordering. This approach assumes that the ordering of messages will not be affected by tracing or that the effect of tracing will be unimportant to trace characteristics. Many programs are written with fixed communication sequences. In contrast, many message passing systems allow asynchronous messages and accept mes-

sages based on type, not origin. A fixed message ordering model, therefore, is likely unrealistic for programs with general communications requirements.

(2) Simulate message ordering using execution-time information generated by the tracing technique. In the most complex scenario, this approach would involve full distributed simulation. One drawback is that the simulated message interaction is based on another simulation (execution-time simulation) that reduces the accuracy of the message reordering.

(3) Collect the sequence of messages produced by a normal execution and use the sequence to control the ordering of messages in the traced modified execution. This is the method chosen for the TRAPEDS implementation. It guarantees that messages will be received in the original order with no extra guidance from the user, and its success does not depend on the accuracy of a simulated elapsed time.

Idle time. For multicomputers, passing messages can create idle wait time during message reception. Any operating system addresses generated during these idle times should be treated differently from other generated addresses. For example, the cache hits or misses associated with a tight idle loop have no impact on the overall execution time, while the cache hit rate in nonidling code does affect execution time. Including the idle time hits could also be misleading in forming estimates of operating system behavior. Besides idle loops, other parts of a program execution have no effect on total execution time. One example is the code immediately preceding a message receive routine when that routine results in an idle wait loop.

Trace storage and utilization. Current multicomputers have poor I/O performance relative to their computing power. Attempting to save streams of trace data concurrently for multiple processors rapidly slows current systems. As an example, in the TRAPEDS implementation on the iPSC/2 hypercube, when trace addresses were generated but not saved, the traced execution ran two orders of magnitude faster than when traces were stored to disk. To illustrate this, Figure 5 shows a plot of the execution slowdown for generating but not saving addresses. Execution slowdown due to TRAPEDS is less than 30× for execution on a single node. As the number of nodes increases, the slowdown factor decreases. This occurs because, for traced programs, the time spent in the computa-

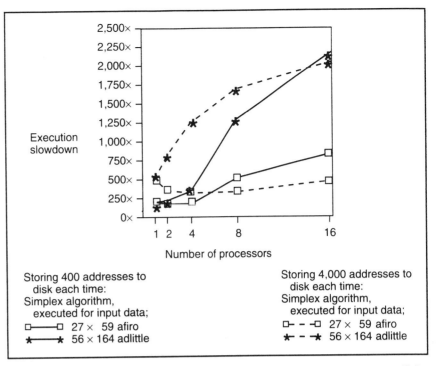

Figure 6. Execution slowdown for generating addresses and storing them to disk files.

tional phases of the execution grows much larger, but the time spent in communication phases (handled by special routing hardware) remains about the same.

When the generated traces were stored to disk on the iPSC/2 hypercube, the execution slowdown climbed to about 2,000 times, as depicted in Figure 6. Moreover, because all disk writes on this system must pass through a single host node, this cost rapidly increases as the number of nodes increases. Hence, all simulations performed with TRAPEDS traces are currently conducted on the fly. Traces are not stored, but are fed immediately to a simulation routine.

Although hardware monitoring and microcode-based methods each possess superior characteristics for a subset of the metrics proposed in this survey, the trends in parallel processor design make it difficult to apply these methods to future generations of machines.

The most successful methods of reducing address-trace distortion rely on identifying synchronization points and simulating the processor execution by counting the number of cycles between synchronization points. Indeed, as the complexity of interaction in parallel systems continues to

grow, simulation will become an increasingly necessary element of successful tracing implementations. The most promising address-tracing solutions will likely be hybrid techniques that instrument programs and simulate execution time. ∎

Acknowledgments

This research was supported in part by the National Aeronautics and Space Administration under Contract NASA NAG 1-613, by SDIO/IST, and managed by the Office of Naval Research under contract N00014-88-K-0656, and by a Shell Doctoral Fellowship.

References

1. A. Agarwal, R.L. Sites, and M. Horowitz, "ATUM: A New Technique for Capturing Address Traces Using Microcode," *Proc. 13th Int'l Symp. Computer Architecture*, 1986, pp. 119-127.

2. D.W. Clark, "Cache Performance in the VAX 11/780," *ACM Trans. Computer Systems*, Vol. 1, No. 1, Feb. 1983, pp. 24-37.

3. C.A. Wiecek, "A Case Study of VAX 11 Instruction Set Usage for Compiler Execution," *Proc. Symp. Architectural Support for Programming Languages and Operating Systems*, 1982, pp. 177-184.

4. S.J. Eggers and R.H. Katz, "A Characterization of Sharing in Parallel Programs and its Application to Coherency Protocol Evaluation," *Proc. 15th Int'l Symp. Computer Architecture*, 1988, IEEE CS Press, Los Alamitos, Calif. Order No. 861, pp. 373-382.

5. K. So et al., "PSIMUL — A System for Parallel Execution of Parallel Programs," in *Performance Evaluation of Supercomputers*, J.L. Martin, ed., Elsevier Science Publishers B.V., North Holland, 1988, pp. 187-213.

6. A. Borg, R.E. Kessler, and D.W. Wall, "Generation and Analysis of Very Long Address Traces," *Proc. 17th Int'l Symp. Computer Architecture*, May 1990, IEEE CS Press, Los Alamitos, Calif. Order No. 2047, pp. 270-279.

7. C.B. Stunkel and W.K. Fuchs, "TRAPEDS: Producing Traces for Multicomputers Via Execution-Driven Simulation," *Proc. ACM SIGMetrics Int'l Conf. Measurement and Modeling of Computer Systems*, 1989, pp. 70-78.

8. S.J. Eggers et al., "Techniques for Efficient In-Line Tracing on a Shared-Memory Multiprocessor," *Proc. ACM SIGMetrics Int'l Conf. Measurement and Modeling of Computer Systems*, 1990, pp. 37-47.

9. J.R. Larus, "Abstract Execution: A Technique for Efficiently Tracing Programs," tech. report, Computer Sciences Dept., Univ. of Wisconsin at Madison, 1990.

10. R.L. Sites and A. Agarwal, "Multiprocessor Cache Analysis Using ATUM," *Proc. 15th Int'l Symp. Computer Architecture*, 1988, IEEE CS Press, Los Alamitos, Calif. Order No. 861, pp. 186-195.

11. S.R. Goldschmidt and H. Davis, "Tango Introduction and Tutorial," Tech. Report CSL-TR-90-410, Computer Systems Laboratory, Stanford Univ., Stanford, Calif., Jan. 1990.

12. S. Laha, J.H. Patel, and R.K. Iyer, "Accurate Low-Cost Methods for Performance Evaluation of Cache Memory Systems," *IEEE Trans. Computers*, Vol. 37, No. 11, Nov. 1988, pp. 1,325-1,336.

Bob Janssens is a candidate for MS and PhD degrees in electrical engineering at the University of Illinois at Urbana-Champaign. His research interests include computer architecture, parallel processing, and fault-tolerant computing.

Janssens received a BS degree from the University of Illinois at Urbana-Champaign in 1987. He is a student member of the IEEE, the IEEE Computer Society, and the ACM.

Craig B. Stunkel is a research staff member at IBM's T.J. Watson Research Center, Yorktown Heights, N.Y. His research interests include parallel architectures, algorithms, and performance analysis.

Stunkel received BS and MS degrees in electrical engineering in 1982 and 1983, respectively, from Oklahoma State University, and a PhD in electrical engineering in 1990 from the University of Illinois at Urbana-Champaign, where he was a Shell Doctoral Fellow. He is a member of the IEEE Computer Society and the ACM.

W. Kent Fuchs is an associate professor in the departments of Electrical and Computer Engineering and Computer Science, and in the Coordinated Science Laboratory at the University of Illinois at Urbana-Champaign. His research interests include parallel computing and VLSI system design, with an emphasis on reliable computation. He received the Best Article Award in the simulation and test category at the 1986 IEEE/ACM Design Automation Conference; the Incentives for Excellence Faculty Award of the College of Engineering, University of Illinois, and Digital Equipment Corporation in 1986-1988; and the Xerox Faculty Award for Excellence in Research in 1987. In 1990, he was appointed a fellow of the Center for Advanced Studies at the University of Illinois.

Fuchs received the BSE degree in electrical engineering from Duke University in 1977, the MS degree in electrical engineering from the University of Illinois at Urbana-Champaign in 1982, the MDiv degree from Trinity Evangelical Divinity School, Deerfield, Ill., in 1984, and the PhD in electrical engineering from the University of Illinois in 1985. He is a senior member of the IEEE Computer Society.

Readers can contact Stunkel at the IBM T.J. Watson Research Center, PO Box 218, Yorktown Heights, NY 10598. Janssens and Fuchs can be reached at the Center for Reliable and High-Performance Computing, Coordinated Science Lab, University of Illinois at Urbana-Champaign, 1101 W. Springfield Ave., Urbana, IL 61801.

MULTIPROCESSOR SIMULATION AND TRACING USING TANGO

Helen Davis, Stephen R. Goldschmidt, John Hennessy
Computer Systems Laboratory
Stanford University, CA 94305

Abstract— Tango is a software simulation and tracing system used to obtain data for evaluating parallel programs and multiprocessor systems. The system provides a simulated multiprocessor environment by multiplexing application processes onto a single processor. The user application is compiled into a simulation system that is customized to meet the accuracy and efficiency requirements for a particular set of experiments. Tango supports *trace-driven* simulation, but users also have the option of using *execution-driven* simulation. Unlike trace-driven simulation, execution-driven simulation ensures accurate ordering of program events and permits accurate simulation of contention and process interactions. Tango avoids costly instruction interpretation and emulation by directly executing user application code whenever possible. Simulation time is also greatly reduced by allowing the user to focus on the program operations of primary interest, such as shared data references or synchronization operations. The system is currently being used in a wide range of investigations, from algorithm studies to detailed hardware evaluations.

1 Introduction

The enormous performance potential of multiprocessing has motivated studies in parallel algorithms and multiprocessor architectures. Unfortunately, the complexity of these systems makes analytical modeling of their behavior difficult at best. Under these circumstances, simulation can play an important role in the design and analysis of both hardware and software systems. In addition to guiding the development and verification of analytical models, simulation can also help identify system bottlenecks, determine resource requirements, and predict the performance of unavailable hardware. The latter capability is particularly important in parallel hardware and software research, since we need to evaluate hardware designs and understand the behavior of applications running on novel systems with more processors than are currently available to us. This paper describes Tango, a software simulation system developed to support these studies by providing data for evaluating parallel programs and multiprocessor systems.

Tango provides a simulated multiprocessor environment and can be used to gather execution statistics or generate traces of synchronization events and data references. An efficient compiled simulation system is produced by augmenting the application to perform monitoring and simulation tasks. During the simulation, the augmented application processes are time-multiplexed to run on a uniprocessor in a way that ensures memory and synchronization operations are executed in the correct order.

Many previous simulators lack generality and flexibility for supporting a variety of studies. This is because trade-offs must be made between a system's efficiency, accuracy, and generality. For example, many systems designed to support accurate hardware evaluations are too inefficient to be used in general algorithm studies; conversely, systems that efficiently support algorithm studies will often not provide the accuracy required when evaluating hardware design choices. Thus, performance trade-offs result in systems that offer only a single level of accuracy and therefore support only a small set of studies.

We believe that simulation accuracy and costs should be determined by the information desired by the user, not what the system happens to offer. As a result of this "pay for what you need" philosophy, Tango provides an unusually flexible interface for program monitoring and memory system simulation. The user may monitor all data references, shared data references, or synchronization operations and any user-defined events. A variety of memory models may be incorporated so that the most efficient memory simulation for a set of experiments may be used. Additional efficiency is gained by predicting operation delays at compile time whenever possible and only performing complex timing simulations at run time when necessary. As we will see, the simulation cost for an application may vary by several orders of magnitude, depending on the program operations under study and the complexity of the memory system simulation.

The following section considers general techniques that have been used to gather information about program execution, and the basic approach taken in the design of Tango. Section 3 describes how the functional and timing behavior of an application is simulated, and how an application is compiled into a customized simulation system. In Section 4 we describe experiences using Tango and in in Section 5 we investigate simulation overhead in Tango.

2 Measurement Techniques

There are two basic approaches to gathering execution information: monitoring and simulation. Monitoring is a technique in which observations of execution on an existing machine are made. Monitoring may be done with special hardware [4, 5, 21], modified microcode [2], software systems that "single-step" the program (much as debuggers do) [12, 25], or by modifying the application or software system to be self-instrumenting and gather information "on-the-fly" during its execution [1, 9, 13, 18, 21, 22, 24, 28]. Monitoring is attractive because it can be efficient and system implementations can be relatively simple. The accuracy of monitoring systems depends on how much they perturb system behavior. Several types of program distortions that result when using various monitoring techniques are discussed by Agarwal in [2]. While accurate monitoring can be useful for studying *existing* machines, extrapolating results to proposed dissimilar machines is problematic. In particular, we would like to study systems with more processors than are currently available to us which have novel network and memory systems. In these cases, it is particularly difficult to assure that results obtained from simple monitoring of an existing machine can accurately be used in studies of proposed architectures.

High flexibility is provided by software systems that simulate the behavior of a target system. In this case, software running on an available host machine is used to emulate the program execution on some target machine. Interpreting and emulating every instruction is complex and time consuming, requiring hundreds or thousands of times longer than running an application directly [2, 12]. However, it is often possible to avoid costly emulation of many instructions by executing them directly on an available host machine. This is most easily done when the host and target machines have similar instruc-

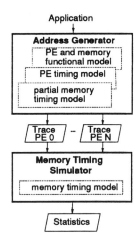

Figure 1: Structure of a trace-driven multiprocessor simulator.

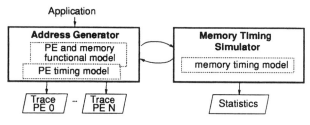

Figure 2: Structure of Tango, an execution-driven simulator.

tion set architectures [1]. In this case, emulation is only required for novel target machine instructions and to determine the latency of operations that have delays that cannot be determined at compile time. This simulation approach is very attractive for multiprocessor studies since they often use conventional processing elements with novel memory systems. In these studies, most instructions are directly executed and detailed emulation is only required for memory references and any proposed new instructions. By using this simulation approach, Tango is able to efficiently support a wide range of multiprocessing studies. In the remainder of this section we discuss two alternative simulation techniques, *trace-driven* and *execution-driven* simulation, which are both supported by Tango and gain efficiency by directly executing application code.

2.1 Trace-Driven Simulation

One common way to structure a simulation system is to use *trace-driven simulation*, which decomposes the simulation system into two components: an address generator and memory/network timing simulator. The generator produces a trace of a program's interesting execution events; the timing simulator emulates the target system in enough detail to estimate the timing the program would have on the target machine. Trace-driven simulators have been used in several multiprocessor studies. Tango supports trace-driven simulation by optionally producing a log of all the program events of primary interest; Section 3.5 describes how traces are generated by Tango.

The most difficult issue in trace-driven multiprocessor simulation is that of assuring accuracy. Many parallel programs are nondeterministic: the execution path through the program, the order of traced events, and even the latency of operations may depend on the precise timing of events. For example, which process next acquires a lock may depend on the relative execution rates of processes. This means that the address generator must assume some timing values for processor and memory operations, but notice these assumed values will not accurately account for contention or target system architectural details. In general, a later trace-driven simulator can adjust timing values but cannot change the execution path through the program. Therefore, the accuracy of the timing simulation will be limited by any inaccuracy in the timing assumptions made by the address generator. Perhaps an even more critical problem is that it isn't always possible to reasonably bound the consequences of any introduced error. So, although trace-driven simulation is sometimes useful, more work needs to be done to determine when it can be used, and the ramifications of any introduced errors [17].

2.2 Execution-Driven Simulation

Execution-driven simulation is an alternative to trace-driven simulation that allows more accurate simulation. As described by Covington et al. [8], execution-driven simulation systems interleave the execution of the application with the simulation of the target system architecture. Sequences of application instructions are directly executed until a branch or label is encountered, or the program performs some globally visible operation (such as sending a message). At that time, simulation code updates simulated time by either a simple increment or by performing a more detailed emulation of the target architecture. As the application continues execution, the correct ordering of program events can be ensured since simulation times are known. So, unlike trace-driven simulation, execution-driven simulation permits very accurate simulation of contention and interactions among processes.

In trace-driven simulation, the memory simulator is a postprocessor that only provides *timing* information. When execution-driven simulation is used, the user may choose to also simulate *data values* in the memory simulator. This makes the memory simulator more complex, but may be necessary to achieve accuracy in some studies, such as those involving novel synchronization primitives or memory models with weak consistency. In general, the memory simulator only needs to manage data values in very detailed studies in which a single variable may have multiple simultaneous values distributed throughout the hardware system.

Figure 2 shows how Tango is configured to support execution-driven simulation. The simulation system is partitioned into two modules that share memory and interact during execution: an address generator that simulates processing element (PE) operations, and a memory simulator that simulates memory operations. In the simplest case, the memory simulator is a subroutine that is called whenever memory operations are encountered in the execution stream by the address generator. Alternatively, the memory simulator may be a separate process with its own internal state. This reduces the size of application processes, simplifies accessing shared data, and allows easier simulation of interactions between references. When a separate process is used, the address generator and the memory simulator interact in a co-routine fashion: when the address generator encounters a memory operation, it issues the operation to the memory simulator; the memory simulator simulates forward until some memory operation completes, or immediately before the next memory operation to be issued by the address generator. Notice that whenever Tango uses execution-driven simulation, the address generator makes *no* assumptions about the timing of memory operations – it always calls the memory simulator for accurate memory timing information.

The basic concept of execution-driven simulation has been discussed elsewhere [3, 6, 8, 10, 11, 14, 27]; we extend the published work in several ways. First, in the following section, we present a more detailed implementation description so that the reader can better evaluate the execution-driven approach and the accompanying implementation trade-offs. Previous work has focused on a single set of events to be studied; using Tango we show that allowing users to choose the set of events to be studied simplifies simulation ex-

---

[1][7] and [14] discuss techniques that can be used to allow simulation of a machine with a different instruction set.

periments and increases performance. Lastly, we present performance measurements. Previously published work generally reports only a few observed program slow-downs, or no performance measurements at all. As we will see in Section 5, program slow-down depends as much on the (unreported) program characteristics and the architecture being simulated as it does on the cost of managing the execution-driven simulation. The complexity of the memory system being simulated dramatically affects the overall simulation time as demonstrated in [11]. We focus on the overhead and trade-offs associated with managing the execution-driven simulation itself and on monitoring only the necessary events, rather than the cost of simulating the memory system. We thoroughly analyze the separate sources of overhead in Tango, and explain the overhead variation that is seen across different benchmarks, memory architectures, and numbers of processors.

3 Tango Implementation

This section describes our computing environment and the implementation of Tango. While the details of our environment are not relevant here, we do assume that user synchronization operations are explicit, and that the operating system supports shared memory.

3.1 Environment

Our applications are written in C or Fortran using macros developed at the Argonne National Laboratory (ANL) [20]. The macros present a variety of abstractions that the programmer can use, such as locks, barriers, distributed loops, and messages. The macros are implemented using UNIX processes and semaphores; this makes the macro package very portable, however, switching between processes is very expensive. Currently our applications all use a shared memory programming model, although our system can be used to study applications written using a message passing model.

Our implementation is designed to run under an operating system that provides support for shared memory and semaphores. Currently Tango is running on the MIPS M/120 and the SGI 4D/240S under System V, and on the DECstation 3100 under Ultrix. The number of application processes is limited by the number of processes and semaphores the system allows; our systems currently restrict the number of application processes to less than 256.

3.2 Program Operations of Interest

In multiprocessing studies, it is the parallel aspects of the computation that are of the greatest interest. These can often be studied by focusing on *global operations* – shared data, message, and synchronization operations that are visible to more than one process. *Private operations*, which are visible to a single process, are generally relevant only with respect to how they impact the timing of global operations.

Because of their importance in many investigations, Tango allows users to efficiently focus on global operations. In some detailed studies it may be necessary to consider the impact of local data operations on memory or network performance, and so Tango also allows simulating local data operations in detail. Users independently specify which type of events are to be monitored, issued to the memory simulator, and ensured to be interleaved correctly among processes. So, for example, a user may choose to trace synchronization operations while performing a detailed memory simulation of all references and maintaining global ordering only at shared references.

In Tango, the application code is augmented to perform simulation and monitoring functions at selected events. Since synchronization operations are explicit and implemented in a separate macro library, the synchronization source code can be easily modified without changing the application code itself. Data references cannot always be inferred statically in high-level languages, and so the assembly language of the application is augmented to call simulation and monitoring routines at these points. Accesses to shared and private data are distinguished at compile time in the case of accesses to static data and the stack. References to dynamically allocated shared and private data are differentiated at runtime using addresses; Tango routines are conditionally called at runtime for these accesses.

A faithful simulation must represent both the functional execution and also the progression of time of an application on some target system. The following sections explain how these tasks are performed in Tango. We then describe Tango event monitoring and how the user application is automatically augmented during compilation to create a compiled simulator.

3.3 Functional Simulation

A simulation process is created for each process in the application, and is assumed to be associated with a unique processor in the target multiprocessor system [2]. We simulate the functional behavior of a process by compiling the associated application code and executing it on an available machine. Novel target machine instructions, such as proposed synchronization primitives that do not exist on the available machine are implemented in libraries. Generally, program data values are managed entirely in the original application code although users may select to simulate memory data values in a memory simulator. Running compiled application code in this manner is simpler and much more efficient than using a software interpreter which emulates every instruction.

The compiled application processes are multiplexed to run in a way that preserves the ordering and timing of the events of interest with respect to the target system's simulated global time. Since we assume that a process executing between events of interest is not affected by any other process, preserving the order of events can be done by rescheduling processes immediately before these events. Thus, no operation under study is executed until it is known to be the next event of interest. The multiplexing of processes is implemented by a distributed scheduler: each application process is augmented to reschedule itself before each event of interest. Distributed scheduling avoids the extra context switches and overhead associated with repeatedly calling a centralized scheduler.

High level synchronization operations are simulated differently in various architectural models. Libraries for synchronization abstractions can be written using target machine primitives. In this case, the libraries are executed as application code, and the synchronization primitives may be issued into memory system simulator, just like memory references. Alternatively, synchronization abstractions can be simulated by a modified version of the ANL macros. If a memory system simulator is being used, the process issues a pseudo operation into the memory simulator whenever a process first reaches a synchronization abstraction. This ensures that the synchronization abstraction is executed in the correct order with respect to simulated memory operations. If a memory simulator is not used, reschedule operations inserted into the macros maintain correct ordering among synchronization operations.

3.4 Timing Simulation

In Tango, the progression of time is simulated, and the actual time to perform the simulation does not affect reported times. Simulating time with a global system clock would be complex and slow because all processes must be strictly synchronized. Instead, Tango

---

[2]Support has been added to Tango to allow simulations of multiprogrammed systems or applications running with more processes than processors. However, to simplify our discussion we omit these issues from this paper.

associates a software clock with each process that represents its simulated time.

During simulation, the individual process clocks do not run in lock-step, but instead are loosely synchronized while maintaining the correct global ordering of the operations of interest. As mentioned before, options allow the user to specify a set of operation types for which accurate global ordering is ensured. The strictest, and most costly, option is to synchronize the process clocks at all data references and synchronization operations. This is only necessary for detailed simulations in which the complete data cache must be simulated in detail. Under a frequently used second option, the process clocks are kept within one global operation of each other, differing only by the duration of sequences of exclusively private computation. For higher simulation efficiency, a third option assures only that clocks be within one synchronization event of each other. This option is most useful when studying synchronization. It can also be used when using programming models in which processes communicate only through messages or explicit synchronization operations, or when trading-off some accuracy for faster simulation.

A process clock is updated in each program basic block, at simulated memory references, and at synchronization points. The target PE is assumed to have a basic instruction set architecture that can be approximated by the architecture of the machine used to run simulations. Each assembly language instruction of the *available* machine is assigned a default delay corresponding to the latency of the target machine. During the compilation process, the application assembly language code is augmented to update the process's clock by the known latency of each basic block. When a delay is not known at compile time, a routine is called to perform the necessary calculation or simulation. Synchronization wait times, during which a process is delayed due to contention or a dependency on another process, are not known at compile time, and so they are determined at run-time.

3.5 Monitoring Simulation Events

Tango provides simple tracing and also a general monitoring interface. The general interface is is very similar to the memory system simulator interface and is used to monitor events as the program executes. An incorporated monitor may also interface to the memory system simulator to allow data specific to a particular memory hardware system to be gathered and displayed. Simple monitors may consist of functions to process trace information during simulation to avoid storage of trace data. More complex monitors may run concurrently with the simulation system and provide information to user interface tools, such as run-time performance display tools.

The implementation of an execution-driven simulation system requires modifying the application code. As a result, the addresses accessed by the application will not be identical to those that would have been produced during execution on the target system. TRAPEDS is an execution-driven address generator for multicomputers, and [27] describes the added complexity of maintaining original application addresses in that system.

3.6 Compilation into a Tango Simulator

The user written application source code is only modified if the user wishes to selectively disable tracing or simulation. A shell script is used to simplify the process of compiling a simulation and specifying simulation options. The compilation process consists of the five steps: macro expansion, compilation into assembly language, assembly code augmentation, assembly, and linkage. The first step is to expand the macros which provide machine and synchronization abstractions. An extended macro library is used; it implements synchronization primitives in terms of the target machine primitives, calls the monitor and/or memory simulator at synchronization events, provides user macros to control simulation and tracing, and declares

routines and structures used by Tango. The output of the macro expansion is a C or Fortran source file, and a standard compiler is used to produce an assembly language file from this source. An added augmentation step inserts assembler code to increment virtual time for each process, and to call monitoring and memory simulation routines at data references. The standard assembler is used to convert the augmented code into an object module. The final step is to link the object modules of the modified program with the memory simulator and Tango support routines.

In addition to the Tango macro library and run-time libraries, two parameter files are used as input to the simulator. The *CPU Parameters* file is read during the augmentation step, and contains timing values for each operation provided by the host machine. The *Memory Parameters* file is read during simulation, and contains synchronization operation latencies and other parameters needed by the memory simulator.

4   Using Tango

We have found that initial experiments by designers tend to use very simple memory models, both for increased efficiency and also so that results are as architecturally independent as possible. Later experiments, by both hardware and software designers, incorporate more realistic and more specific architectural features. Hardware designers become interested in greater accuracy and more detailed design comparisons; software designers become interested in more realistic performance predictions and in understanding the impact of architectural features on program performance. These more detailed experiments can be prohibitively slow unless the user is allowed to customize the memory/network simulation to provide higher accuracy only where it is required. To illustrate the flexibility and use of Tango, this section briefly describes different ways that Tango has been used in a few research efforts.

4.1   Architecture and Hardware Evaluation

A current focus of research at Stanford is distributed shared-memory organizations and scalable cache consistency mechanisms. This effort includes the development of the DASH architecture [19], which consists of small clusters of processors connected together by an interconnection network. Several DASH simulators of varying complexity and accuracy have been developed and run with Tango. The most accurate, and expensive, simulator mimics the behavior of the hardware at the register-transfer-level. This detailed simulator has been valuable in verifying the DASH design, and in evaluating general design options involving distributed shared-memory multiprocessors and directory based cache coherence. For example, in [15] the authors evaluate the effectiveness of coherent caches, multiple-context CPUs, relaxed memory consistency, and data prefetching as latency hiding techniques. In design verification simulations, the memory simulator not only provided accurate timing values, but it also simulated the state of memory data values to ensure that the consistency protocol and hardware design were implemented correctly. By incorporating accurately detailed memory simulators into Tango, reliable simulations could be performed and accurate comparisons and verifications could be made.

4.2   Program Characterization

Tango simulations have been used to identify performance attributes intrinsic to application algorithms, and also to study detailed program behavior on a specific proposed system. For instance, in exploring parallel logic simulation, Soule and Gupta were initially interested in determining how much parallelism could be potentially exploited by various extensions to the Chandy-Misra algorithm [26]. In this experiment, characteristics inherent to the algorithm were of interest. The Tango simulations did not incorporate a separate memory simulator; instead, constant latencies for memory and synchronization operations were incorporated at compile time. This resulted in extremely efficient simulation and avoided introducing unnecessary architectural dependencies into the results.

The realized performance of parallel programs is often highly dependent on multiprocessor hardware features. In studying large sparse systems of equations, Rothberg et al. measured processor utilization and found most of the performance loss in a previously proposed algorithm was due to servicing cache misses [23]. They proposed an extension to the algorithm that executes fewer memory operations and produces fewer cache misses. However, the proposed scheme resulted in more load imbalance due to an increase in the task grain size. The trade-off between better memory system behavior and additional load imbalance could only be demonstrated by assuming some specific memory features of a target multiprocessor system. For their studies they used Tango and a simplified memory simulator for the DASH architecture. Since they were very interested in cache and memory performance, they simulated the finite caches and delays associated with the distributed memory structure. Measurements showed that the network bandwidth utilization was low and so, for simplicity and to increase the speed of simulations, they ignored the details of the network architecture and its contention. A flexible memory simulation interface permitted these algorithm designers to focus on issues most critical to performance.

4.3 System Software

Tango has been used in research of software techniques to improve program performance, such as automatic data placement, prefetching, language design, and scheduling policies. Here we discuss one study that considered several different multiprogramming scheduling strategies.

In [16] the authors evaluate the impact of operating system scheduling policies and synchronization methods on program performance. They decided to simulate a simple bus-based multiprocessor and to ignore any bus contention. This was because they felt that scheduling strategies for simple uniform-memory access multiprocessors are not yet well understood, and so making the architecture more complex would confuse results. They showed that multiplexing processes can significantly increase lock wait times when simple busy waiting is used. To demonstrate the benefits of blocking synchronization primitives, they modified the Tango synchronization macro library to yield the processor at busy locks and measured the resulting performance gains. Performance degradation can also result from worsening cache performance, since a process's cached data can be displaced when another process is switched in to run. This effect was measured by including a simple cache model in the memory simulator and measuring cache miss rates while simulating various scheduling algorithms. By incorporating alternative synchronization primitives and the desired simple memory hierarchy into Tango, these researchers were able to isolate and compare the performance impact of the proposed scheduling algorithms. These examples reveal the importance of modularity and flexibility; users need to be able to customize their simulations to meet the needs of individual experiments.

5 Tango Performance

This section investigates the performance of the Tango system and sources of simulation overhead. Although we have not yet tuned Tango to optimize its efficiency, the level of performance currently achieved by the system demonstrates the viability of our approach. As we shall see, simulation times depend primarily on the complexity of the memory system simulation, the type of events simulated at

run time, and the application's synchronization and data reference characteristics.

Measurements reported in this paper were taken on a DECstation 3100 workstation running Ultrix 2.0. The Ultrix `rusage()` facility was used to measure execution times.

5.1 Applications

The complete execution of three programs were simulated to illustrate simulation performance of Tango. Table 1 shows the basic characteristics of the programs. The number of processes simulated is generally limited to thirty in the data presented here, although we present some data for 90 processes.

Pthor is a compiled logic-level circuit simulator [26]. It uses the Chandy-Misra simulation algorithm to avoid reliance on a single global time, and uses a separate task queue for each process. The test problem is a small circuit with 56 gates and latches.

Mincut is a graph bisection algorithm using simulated annealing. The quality of the resulting partition depends somewhat on the number of processes, as does the number of accepted moves. The test problem is a 500-node graph with an average degree of eleven.

Mp3d is a three-dimensional rarified flow model; the algorithm simulates individual particles moving and colliding in three-dimensional space. For these experiments, Mp3d is run with 10,000 particles in an empty 288-cell space array for five time steps.

5.2 Memory Simulators

As described in Section 2.2, the memory system simulator incorporated into Tango may be implemented as either a subroutine or as a separate process. In our measurements, we compare the minimum overhead associated with these two interfaces. To put Tango overheads into perspective, we also evaluate the cost of simulating with a subroutine-style simulator of a proposed architecture.

The *Multiple-Issue* memory simulator uses the most general, and expensive, simulator interface. The simulation code runs as a separate UNIX process, and the application processes block each time the simulator is invoked. Simulated operations are issued in the correct global order, and concurrent operations are issued to the memory simulator together. The interface is intended to be used for detailed simulations that require accurate simulation of the interactions between multiple outstanding references. However, we use a very simple model of constant latencies for references to isolate the overhead associated with Tango from that of the memory simulator.

A second memory simulator, the *Single-Issue* simulator, is used to determine the overhead associated with the subroutine-style memory simulator interface. This memory simulator is intended to demonstrate the Tango overhead that might occur in studies that do not consider the effects of contention very accurately. For this reason, the global order of synchronization operations is maintained, but the global order of memory data operations is not. This means that processes are rescheduled only for synchronization operations. Like the Multiple-Issue simulator, the Single-Issue simulator implements constant latencies.

The third memory simulator, called *Hyphen*, [3] uses the same simple Tango interface as the Single-Issue simulator, but has a more realistic memory timing model. The simulator models a grid of processing nodes in which each node is a bus-based multiprocessor. This model simulates two levels of caching at each processor, and accounts for bus contention in an inexact fashion that requires correct global ordering of all simulated operations. As a result, processes are rescheduled at both synchronization and data references. The Hyphen simulator is not intended for very accurate hardware design

---

[3]Hyphen simulates a simplified model of the DASH architecture described in [19].

Table 1: Application characteristics.

Application	Source Lines	Uniprocessor Run-Time (ms)	Instructions Executed ($\times 10^6$)	Operations as a % of Instructions Executed			
				Synchronization Operations	Shared Data References	Private Data References	Total
Mincut	462	640.	47.8	1.28	9.	25.5	35.7
Mp3d	1530	2410.	10.1	0.00071	20.6	3.3	23.9
Pthor	8000	272.	0.397	0.83	16.9	26.2	43.8

evaluations, but it is being used for detailed studies of program behavior. Results from this model should indicate the costs associated with a reasonably accurate, but low cost, memory system simulator.

In all three models, synchronization is simulated by a general default mechanism. The operations are simulated by ANL macros (see Section 3.3), but the memory simulator is still called at significant events, so that the memory simulator may provide any desired additional latency. For locks, the request, acquire, and release phases are each issued to the memory simulator as separate events. When a process must block due to contention at a lock, additional block and release events are issued to the memory simulator. For barriers, the entry and exit of each process is treated as a separate event. In more customized simulation systems, synchronization operations would be be handled in either the macros or the memory simulator, rather than both.

5.3 Sources of Overhead

To run under Tango, the applications have been augmented to multiplex processes, simulate time, and optionally log events. Each of these activities adds to the cost of simulation.

Multiplexing application processes onto a uniprocessor requires scheduling at each event for which correct global ordering must be guaranteed. When large numbers of processes are being simulated, almost every call to the scheduler results in a context switch. The cost of these required context switches dominate the cost of scheduling. Tango is implemented using UNIX system semaphores and processes, and so the cost of a context switch requires about 180-250 microseconds.

Each process updates its virtual clock at the beginning of each basic block to account for delays that are known at compile time. This typically requires five assembly language instructions, so if each basic block has five to ten instructions, these updates should produce a slowdown factor of 1.5 to 2.

The remaining application code consists of synchronization or memory operations that must be simulated at run time. Invoking the simulator requires about 70 instructions when a subroutine-style simulator is used, but a context switch is required when the simulator runs on a separate process. If the simulator is only called at shared data references, there is an overhead of about a dozen instructions per memory reference to distinguish shared data references from private data references. In addition to this intrinsic Tango overhead, there is the cost of the memory timing simulation itself, which varies considerably, depending on its complexity.

Because Tango supports efficient execution-driven simulation, trace files are rarely needed. Using buffered UNIX writes to a local disk, writing 12-byte record requires about 31 microseconds.

Augmenting the program and linking in Tango libraries increases the size of executables, as shown in Table 2. The increase in size depends on the memory model used, the static frequency of instrumented operations, and the average basic block size. The increase is typically a factor of 2 to 3 for the applications studied. Program size does not affect simulation results, but it will degrade simulation performance by increasing the amount of memory swapping.

Table 2: Relative increase in object code size under Tango.

Events Simulated	Memory Model	Mp3d (82 Kbytes)	Mincut (63 Kbytes)
Synchronization	Single-Issue	1.90	1.87
	Multiple-Issue	2.01	2.01
	Hyphen	2.10	2.14
Synchronization and Shared References	Single-Issue	2.60	1.94
	Multiple-Issue	2.71	2.08
	Hyphen	2.80	2.21
Synchronization and All References	Single-Issue	3.25	2.14
	Multiple-Issue	3.36	2.28
	Hyphen	3.51	2.41

5.4 Program Measurements

To evaluate Tango's performance, we compared the execution time of the sample applications run directly on a uniprocessor (without Tango) to the time required to run the same applications for simulation using various Tango options. Each application was run from start to finish, including initialization code.

5.4.1 Simulation Event Overhead

Most of the overhead in Tango is associated with evaluating events that must be simulated at run time by invoking the memory simulator. To understand the nature of this overhead, we measured the average cost per simulated event. Figures 3, 4, and 5 show the average overhead per operation when simulating only global events, that is, shared data and synchronization operations. In the graphs, solid curves represent the observed Tango costs, computed by subtracting the uniprocessor run times from the Tango run times and dividing by the number of events simulated. However, since much of the overhead is due to the high cost of process context switches, we made an attempt to compensate for this by subtracting 180 microseconds per Tango-induced context switch; these adjusted overheads are shown by the dashed curves.

When the simulator is implemented as a separate process, as with the Multiple-Issue model (Figure 3), two context switches are required each time the simulator is invoked, one to enter the simulator and one to exit. Rescheduling may also cause context switches, and occurs at both synchronization events and simulated data references. Rescheduling requires a context switch whenever the current process is ahead of another process. Thus, as the number of processors simulated increases, there is an increase in the likelihood that a context switch will be required. This results in an initial rise in the number of context switches. Eventually there is a context switch for each operation, and the overhead reaches a maximum. Notice, however, that the total observed overhead soon begins to *decrease* as more processors are simulated. This is because, with the Multiple-Issue model, concurrent memory operations are issued to the memory simulator in a single invocation; as the number of processors is increased, more operations are issued in parallel and

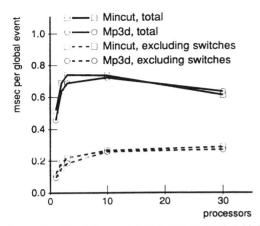

Figure 3: Simulation overhead per event for *Multiple-Issue* simulator at global events.

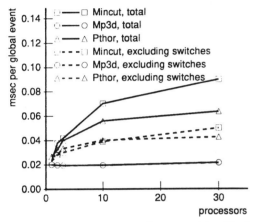

Figure 4: Simulation overhead per event for *Single-Issue* simulator at global events.

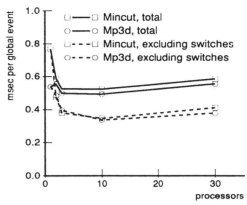

Figure 5: Simulation overhead per event for *Hyphen* simulator at global events.

so there are fewer memory system simulator invocations. If the cost of process context switches is omitted, the computational overhead can be seen to level off.

With the Single-Issue simulator, the three applications exhibit similar overheads when simulating a single process, as shown in Figure 4. However, as the number of processes simulated increases, Mp3d shows little increase in cost, while the overhead grows for the other applications. Two factors contribute to this rise in costs. First, some of the rise occurs because there is increasing lock contention and the cost of simulating locks is higher when there is contention in our default system [4]. This increase in simulation costs accounts for much of the increase in overhead for Mincut, since it contains a lock that quickly becomes a point of high contention. A second factor that contributes to higher average overhead the Mincut program is an increase in the number of synchronization events. Since memory operations do not require a context switch, they are much faster to simulate than synchronization operations. Due to non-determinism in Mincut, the number of synchronization events increases by a factor of two (from 0.6 million operations with one processor to almost 1.2 million operations with 10 processors); this increases the average cost of simulating global events.

When using the Single-Issue simulator, the total overhead is only

3% - 14% of that found using the Multiple-Issue model. This is primarily because there are many fewer context switches during the simulation, since context switches are not necessary when invoking the the Single-Issue simulator and rescheduling is performed only at synchronization points and not at memory references. Even though the Single-Issue simulator is much more efficient than the Multiple-Issue simulator, we have found implementing the memory simulator as a separate process useful for all of our detailed hardware simulators. It allows complex memory simulations to be more easily incorporated into Tango. For each of these hardware simulators, simulation costs are overwhelmingly dominated by the memory system simulator, so the overheads intrinsic to Tango are less important. The larger overhead for the Multiple-Issue model makes it evident that, although this interface is convenient for hardware design evaluations, it is also worthwhile for Tango to provide the low-cost interface for other studies.

Figure 5 shows the overhead per event for the Hyphen model. The simulation overhead first decreases as processors are added and then begins to rise. This is because the cost of simulating bus contention depends on the number of simulation cycles and the amount of activity simulated in each cycle. Initially, the number of simulated cycles decreases significantly due to program speedup. With more processors, extra work in simulating each event begins to dominate the savings in reducing the cycle count. The shape of the overhead curve is similar to that observed for our hardware simulators which simulate in a more detailed, cycle-by-cycle fashion.

The Hyphen model, unlike the Single-Issue model, must reschedule on every shared data event, so it suffers more significant overhead due to context switches. However, even allowing for context switches, the Hyphen model runs about 10 times slower than the Single-Issue model, despite their using the same interface. This confirms that Tango overheads are small relative to the costs of even a simplified simulator for a complex memory system.

When looking over the graphs for the three different models, the most important feature is that when more than a few processors are simulated, the simulation overhead does not increase significantly as more processors are simulated. Generally, the growth in cost is less than 10% as the number of processors is increased from 10 to 30. The largest increase, 28%, was seen when simulating the Mincut program with the Single-Issue memory model. As we described earlier, this larger rise is due an increasing amount of contention and synchronization in the application. The general leveling-off of simulation costs indicates that simulation costs become relatively independent of the number of processors simulated, so we can expect to use Tango to efficiently simulate many processors.

---

[4]In the default system used for our measurements, synchronization primitives are implemented by macros rather than in the memory system. Using this approach, additional context switches occur when a process must block to wait for a lock.

5.4.2 Program Slow-down

In the previous section we considered the simulation overhead per event. The *frequency* of simulated events also strongly affects the elapsed time for a simulation. Figure 6 shows the observed slow-down as the number of simulated processors is varied for Mincut, and Figure 7 shows the slow-down for Mp3d. To make the graphs more comparable, the timing values have been normalized relative to the uniprocessor times for each application without Tango.

In looking at Figure 6, we see that the slow-down when simulating Mincut with 30 processors has a wide range, from less than 700 to over 18,000. In many multiprocessor studies, local references are of little interest, since performance is determined primarily by the global operations. For Mincut, 74% of the data references are to private data, so omitting these events cuts costs by 31%-64%, depending on the memory model used. Similarly, if the user focuses on synchronization behavior, savings of 44%-91% are achieved.

Much lower simulation costs were observed when simulating Mp3d, as shown in Figure 7. When simulating 30 processors, even the most expensive Mp3d simulation has less slowdown than the fastest Mincut simulation. This is primarily because Mincut performs synchronization much more frequently, which is expensive to simulate in the default configuration. The maximum simulation cost for Mincut is also higher because it has more frequent data references (35% of instruction reference data in Mincut, while less than 24% do in Mp3d). As with Mincut, there is a large range of slowdowns observed for Mp3d, depending on the memory model used and the types of events simulated. Since there are very few synchronization operations, both memory models perform very well simulating synchronization operations only. In Mp3d, there is little performance benefit in omitting the simulation of private data references, since fewer than 4% of the instructions reference private data.

As these two examples illustrate, simulation times vary tremendously, depending largely on an application's synchronization and data reference characteristics. Programs written in dissimilar languages and programming styles are expected to perform differently. In many cases, simulation times can be reduced if the memory simulator can be implemented as a subroutine, or detailed simulations can be limited to just shared data references or synchronization operations. The large range of observed simulation costs make it clear that simulation tools need to provide flexible user interfaces so that users can avoid unnecessarily high simulation times.

6   Conclusions

We have found Tango very helpful in a variety of research areas, including studies in multiple-context CPUs, cache directory organizations, consistency protocols, synchronization, data sharing behavior, algorithms, prefetching, parallel languages, and scheduling. Tango accurately supports this wide range of studies by allowing users to incorporate a memory simulator that meets accuracy requirements as efficiently as possible. When simulating non-deterministic programs, trace-driven simulators may yield incorrect results. Tango gives users the option of using execution-driven simulation, which ensures accurate ordering of program events. A general monitoring interface allows users to specify the amount of information to be monitored and to monitor interesting program events at run time. By customizing the simulation system at compile time to meet the needs of the user, Tango does not sacrifice efficiency or accuracy for generality, but instead offers a general purpose system built on a "pay for what you need" principle.

Tango simulation overheads were found to vary by several orders of magnitude, depending primarily on the complexity of the memory simulation, the type of operations under study, and the application's synchronization and data reference characteristics. As Tango is used to simulate more processors, the simulation cost initially rises, but

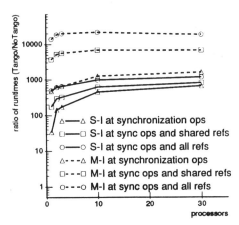

Figure 6: Relative simulation times for Mincut using the Single-Issue Model (S-I) and the Multiple-Issue Model (M-I).

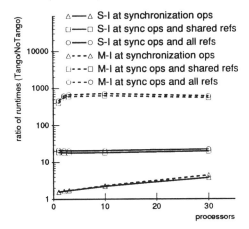

Figure 7: Relative simulation times for Mp3d using the Single-Issue Model (S-I) and the Multiple-Issue Model (M-I).

then levels off. This is encouraging, since it indicates that simulation costs become relatively independent of the number of processors, allowing Tango to be used to simulate systems with many more processors than are currently available to us.

We currently find that users' memory system simulations dominate the simulation cost in almost all of our experiments. However, the execution time of Tango itself is not insignificant, and there are still several attractive avenues for improving Tango performance. Obvious performance could be gained by porting Tango to a light-weight threads environment. Parallel simulations of independent events would allow Tango to take advantage of multiprocessors that support fine-grain parallelism. If simulation accuracy can be compromised somewhat, it might be possible to significantly increase simulation performance; the interesting open question is how to measure the accuracy sacrificed for increased efficiency. A parallel and more optimized successor to Tango is under development. When running on a uniprocessor and ordering all memory references, it is currently about 30 times faster than the initial Tango prototype discussed in this paper. This new parallel Tango will be used to explore simulation techniques on large scale multiprocessors and to investigate the trade-offs between accuracy and performance.

7 Acknowledgments

Helpful discussions throughout this work with Mark Horowitz, Michael Powell, Greg Nelson, Anoop Gupta, Richard Simoni, and Neil Wilhelm are appreciated. Applications were developed and generously made available to us by Jonathan Rose, Larry Soule, and Jeff McDonald. We also appreciate comments on drafts of this paper made by Richard Simoni, Josep Torrellas, and Margaret Martonosi. This work was supported in part by fellowships provided by the Hertz Foundation and Xerox, and in part by DARPA contract N00014-87-K-0828; this support is gratefully acknowledged.

References

[1] W. Abu-Sufah and A. Y. Kwok. Performance Prediction Tools for CEDAR: A Multiprocessor Supercomputer. In *Proceedings of the 12th Annual Int'l Symposium on Computer Architecture*, pages 406–413. ACM-IEEE, 1985.

[2] A. Agarwal, R. L. Sites, and M. Horowitz. ATUM: A New Technique for Capturing Address Traces Using Microcode. In *Proceedings of the 13th Annual Int'l Symposium on Computer Architecture*. ACM-IEEE, Jun 1986. Published as Vol. 14, No. 2, of Computer Architecture News.

[3] Anita Borg, R. E. Kessler, Georgia Lazana, and David W. Wall. Long Address Traces from RISC Machines: Generation and Analysis. Technical Report 89/14, DEC Western Research Laboratory, Sept 1989.

[4] T.A. Cargill and B.N. Locanthi. Cheap Hardware Support for Software Debugging and Profiling. In *Proceedings of the Second Int'l Conf. on Architectural Support for Programming Languages and Operating Systems*. ACM-IEEE, Oct 1987.

[5] Robert J. Carpenter. Performance Measurement Instrumentation for Multiprocssor Computers. Technical Report NBSIR 87-3627, Institute for Computer Sciences and Technology, National Bureau of Standards, Aug 1987.

[6] Ding-Kai Chen. MaxPar: An Execution Driven Simulator for Studying Parallel Sytems. Technical Report CSRD 917 and UILU-ENG-89-8013, University of Illinois, Oct 1989.

[7] R.G. Covington, J.R. Jump, and J.B. Sinclair. Cross-Profiling as an Efficient Technique in Simulating Parallel Computer Systems. In *Proceedings of the IEEE 13th Annual International Computer Software and Applications Conference*. IEEE, Sep 1989.

[8] R.G. Covington, S. Madala, V. Mehta, J.R. Jump, and J.B. Sinclair. The Rice Parallel Processing Testbed. In *Proceedings of the 1988 ACM SIGMETRICS Conf. on Measurement and Modeling of Computer Systems*. ACM, May 1988.

[9] Helen Davis and John Hennessy. Characterizing the Synchronization Behavior of Parallel Programs. In *Proceedings of the ACM/SIGPLAN PPEALS Parallel Programming: Experience with Applications, Languages and Systems*. ACM, July 1988.

[10] Michel Dubois, Faye' A. Briggs, Indira Patil, and Meera Balakrishnan. Trace-Driven Simulations of Parallel and Distributed Algorithms in Multiprocessors. In *Proc. 1986 Int'l Conference on Parallel Processing*, pages 909–915, Aug 1986.

[11] S. Dwarkadas, J.R. Jump, and J.B. Sinclair. Efficient Simulation of Cache Memories. In *Proc. 1989 Winter Computer Simulation Conference*, pages 1032–1041, Dec 1989.

[12] S. J. Eggers. Simulation Analysis of Data Sharing in Shared Memory Multiprocessors. Technical Report UCB/CSD 89/501, University of California, Berkeley, 1989.

[13] Susan J. Eggers, David R. Keppel, Eric J. Koldinger, and Henry M. Levy. Techniques for Efficient Inline Tracing on a Shared-Memory Multiprocessor. In *Proceedings of the 1990 ACM SIGMETRICS Conference on Measurement and Modeling of Computer Systems*. ACM, May 1990.

[14] Richard M. Fujimoto. The Simon Simulation and Development System. In *Proc. 1985 Summer Computer Simulation Conference*, pages 123–128, July 1985.

[15] Anoop Gupta, John Hennessy, Kourosh Gharachorloo, Todd Mowry, and Wolf-Dietrich Weber. Comparative Evaluation of Latency Reducing and Tolerating Techniques. In *Proceedings of the 18th Annual Int'l Symposium on Computer Architecture*. ACM-IEEE, May 1991. To appear.

[16] Anoop Gupta, Andrew Tucker, and Shigeru Urushibara. The Impact of Operating System Scheduling Policies and Synchronization Methods on the Performance of Parallel Applications. In *Proceedings of the ACM SIGMETRICS Conf. on Measurements and Modeling of Computer Systems*. ACM, May 1991. To appear.

[17] Mark A. Holliday and Carla S. Ellis. Accuracy of Memory Reference Traces of Parallel Computation in Trace-Driven Simulation. Technical Report CS-1990-8, Duke University, May 1990.

[18] Teemu Kerola and Herb Schwetman. Monit: A Performance Monitoring Tool for Parallel and Pseudo-Parallel Programs. In *Proceedings of the ACM SIGMETRICS Conf. on Measurements and Modeling of Computer Systems*. ACM, May 1987.

[19] D. Lenoski, K. Gharachorloo, J. Laudon, A. Gupta, J. Hennessy, M. Horowitz, and M. Lam. Design of scalable shared-memory multiprocessors: The DASH approach. *COMPCON 90*, 1990.

[20] Lusk, Overbeek, and et al. *Portable Programs for Parallel Processors*. Holt, Rinehart and Winston, Inc., 1987.

[21] Allen D. Malony, Daniel A. Reed, Ruth A. Aydt James W. Arendt, Dominique Grabas, and Brian K. Totty. An Integrated Performance Data Collection, Analysis, and Visualization System. Technical Report TTR11, University of Illinois at Urbana-Champaign, March 1989.

[22] Barton P. Miller, Morgan Clark, Steven Kierstead, and Sek-See Lim. IPS-2: The Second Generation of a Parallel Program Measurement System. Technical Report WISCCS 783, University of Wisconsin-Madison, 1988.

[23] Edward Rothberg and Anoop Gupta. A Comparative Evaluation of Nodal and Supernodal Parallel Sparse Matrix Factorization: Detailed Simulation Results. Technical Report CSL-TR-90-416, Stanford University, Feb 1990.

[24] Zary Segall and Larry Rudolph. PIE: A Programming and Instrumentation Environment for Parallel Processing. *IEEE Software*, pages 22–37, Nov 1985.

[25] K. So, F. Darema-Rogers, D. George, V. A. Norton, and G. F. Pfister. PSIMUL – A System For Parallel Simulations of the Execution of Parallel Programs. Technical Report RC11674, IBM, Oct 1987.

[26] Larry Soule and Anoop Gupta. Parallel Distributed-Time Logic Simulation. *IEEE Design & Test of Computers*, pages 32–48, Dec 1989.

[27] C. Stunkel and W. Fuchs. TRAPEDS: Producing Traces for Multicomputers Via Execution Driven Simulation. In *International Conference on Measurement and Modeling of Computer Systems*, 1989.

[28] Pen-Chung Yew, Alexander Veidenbaum, and Hoichi Cheong. Chief: a Parallel Simulation Environment for Parallel Systems. Technical Report CSRD 915, University of Illinois at Urbana-Champaign, Aug 1989.

The Wisconsin Wind Tunnel:
Virtual Prototyping of Parallel Computers*

Steven K. Reinhardt, Mark D. Hill, James R. Larus,
Alvin R. Lebeck, James C. Lewis, and David A. Wood
Computer Sciences Department
University of Wisconsin–Madison
1210 West Dayton Street
Madison, WI 53706 USA
wwt@cs.wisc.edu

Abstract

We have developed a new technique for evaluating cache coherent, shared-memory computers. The Wisconsin Wind Tunnel (WWT) runs a parallel shared-memory program on a parallel computer (CM-5) and uses execution-driven, distributed, discrete-event simulation to accurately calculate program execution time. WWT is a virtual prototype that exploits similarities between the system under design (the target) and an existing evaluation platform (the host). The host directly executes all target program instructions and memory references that hit in the target cache. WWT's shared memory uses the CM-5 memory's error-correcting code (ECC) as valid bits for a fine-grained extension of shared virtual memory. Only memory references that miss in the target cache trap to WWT, which simulates a cache-coherence protocol. WWT correctly interleaves target machine events and calculates target program execution time. WWT runs on parallel computers with greater speed and memory capacity than uniprocessors. WWT's simulation time decreases as target system size increases for fixed-size problems and holds roughly constant as the target system and problem scale.

---

*This work is supported in part by NSF PYI Awards CCR-9157366 and MIPS-8957278, NSF Grant CCR-9101035, Univ. of Wisconsin Graduate School Grant, Wisconsin Alumni Research Foundation Fellowship and donations from A.T.&T. Bell Laboratories and Digital Equipment Corporation. Our Thinking Machines CM-5 was purchased through NSF Institutional Infrastructure Grant No. CDA-9024618 with matching funding from the Univ. of Wisconsin Graduate School.

1 Introduction

The architecture of a parallel computer is a specification of an interface between software and hardware. The complex interactions in a system of this type are best studied by running and measuring real applications. Paper studies, analytic models, and simulations of abstract workloads can uncover architectural flaws. Nevertheless, running real applications and system software can expose software and hardware problems that other techniques cannot find and encourages improvements through successive refinement [9].

The two well-known methods for evaluating parallel computer architectures with real workloads are execution-driven simulation and hardware prototyping. Call the computer under study the *target machine* and the existing computer used to perform the evaluation the *host machine*. With execution-driven simulation, researchers write a host machine program, called a *simulator*, that interprets a target machine program, mimics the operation of the target machine, and estimates its performance [9]. By contrast, with hardware prototyping, researchers build a copy (or a few copies) of the target system, execute target programs, and measure their performance [20].

Execution-driven simulation and hardware prototyping offer largely complementary advantages and disadvantages. Simulators can be constructed relatively quickly, can be modified easily, and can compare radically different alternatives. However, simulators often are too slow and run on machines without enough memory to simulate realistic workloads and system parameters. Parallel target machines exacerbate the deficiencies of execution-driven simulation, since a single host must simulate many processors. A uniprocessor workstation host with 128 megabytes of memory, for example, cannot simulate even 64 processors with 4 megabytes each. Hardware prototypes, on the other hand, run fast enough to execute real work-

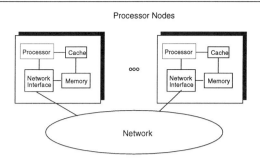

Processor Nodes

Figure 1: Organization of a parallel computer. Many parallel computers are composed of processor nodes, each of which contains a CPU, cache, and local memory. The nodes are connected by an interconnection network (e.g., a 2D mesh or fat tree).

loads, but are expensive, require years to construct, and are difficult to modify.

Our evaluation method combines the advantages and mitigates the disadvantages of execution-driven simulation and hardware prototyping by exploiting the commonality in parallel computers. The common hardware base (see Figure 1) consists of a collection of processing nodes connected by a fast network. Each node contains a processor, memory module, network interface, and often a cache. Of course, computers differ in network topologies; processor architectures; and, most important, in the primitives built on the base hardware. For example, although interconnection networks exchange messages, some machines expose this facility (e.g., Intel Paragon) while others use it to construct a shared-memory abstraction (e.g., Kendall Square KSR-1).

A new approach to exploiting this commonality underlies our system for evaluating cache-coherent, shared-memory computers. The Wisconsin Wind Tunnel (WWT) runs a parallel shared-memory program on a parallel message-passing computer (a CM-5) and concurrently calculates the program's execution time on the proposed system. We call WWT a *virtual prototype* because it exploits similarities between the system under design (the target) and an existing evaluation platform (the host). In WWT, the host directly executes all target instructions and memory references that hit in the target cache. *Direct execution* means that the host hardware executes target program operations—for example, a floating-point multiply instruction runs as a floating-point multiply [5, 6, 9, 11]. Simulation is only necessary for target operations that a host machine does not support. Direct execution runs orders of magnitude faster than software simulation [9].

A unique aspect of WWT is that it directly executes memory references that hit in a target cache. Other direct-execution simulators test for a cache hit before every memory reference. WWT uses the CM-5 memory's error-correcting code (ECC) as valid bits to build a fine-grained extension of Li's shared virtual memory [21]. Only the memory references that miss in the target cache trap to WWT, which simulates a cache coherence protocol by explicitly sending messages.

WWT, like uniprocessor execution-driven simulators, correctly interleaves target machine events and calculates target program execution times. Because WWT runs on a parallel computer, it requires two new techniques to integrate distributed simulation on a parallel computer with direct execution of target processes. First, WWT manages target node interactions by dividing execution into lock-step quanta to ensure all events originating on a remote node that affect a node in the current quantum are known at the beginning of the quantum. Second, WWT orders all events on a node for the current quantum and directly executes the process up to its next event.

The key contributions of this work are the development and demonstration of the two techniques necessary to build virtual prototypes of parallel, cache-coherent, shared-memory computers. The first technique is fine-grained shared virtual memory, which enables shared-memory programs to run efficiently on non-shared-memory computers (Section 3). The second technique is the integration of direct execution and distributed, discrete-event simulation, which together efficiently run a parallel shared-memory program and accurately compute its execution time (Section 4). Section 5 compares WWT with a uniprocessor simulation system (Stanford's Tango/Dixie) simulating the Stanford DASH multiprocessor. Section 6 describes related work, Section 7 describes extensions and future work. Section 8 presents our conclusions.

2 Background

This section provides background by briefly reviewing machines that we want to simulate (Section 2.1), important characteristics of the host machine (Section 2.2), and simulation techniques (Section 2.3).

2.1 Cache-Coherent, Shared-Memory Target Machines

Figure 1 illustrates the essential features of a target machine. It has N processors, where N currently cannot exceed the number of host processors (however, see Section 7). To permit high-bandwidth access, memory is divided into N memory modules, each of which is physically adjacent to a processor. A processor, memory module, cache, and network interface form a processing node. Nodes are connected by an interconnection network that delivers point-to-point messages.

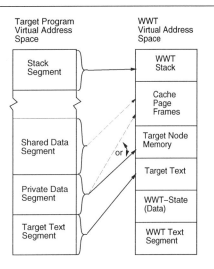

Figure 2: The target program's address space is shown on the left. The virtual prototype's (WWT) address space (right) is a separate SPARC context. The arrows show how WWT maps target data into its address space. Dashed lines indicate that a mapping exists only for pages containing cached blocks. The mappings are logical and implemented with virtual address aliases to common physical pages.

The target machine supports shared memory by allowing all processors to address a single virtual address space. The current target programs are single-program-multiple-data (SPMD) shared-memory programs that run one process per node. Each process's virtual address space contains four segments—text (code), private data, shared data, and stack—as illustrated on the left side of Figure 2. All processes identically map the shared-data segment. Other segments are mapped to physically local memory, so distinct processes access different private locations. Shared data is interleaved by placing successive pages ($\geq$ 4K bytes) on successive nodes.

To reduce average memory latency, each cache holds blocks ($\geq$ 32 bytes) recently referenced by its processor. A processor node handles a cache miss by sending a message to the referenced block's home node and receiving the block's contents in a reply message. Processors use a directory protocol to keep cache and memory blocks coherent [1]. Typically, a directory is distributed so a directory entry and memory block reside on the same node. The directory protocol determines the contents of a directory entry and the messages used to maintain coherence.

We assume that the execution time for each instruction is fixed. Instruction fetches and stack references require no cycles beyond the basic instruction time. Other memory locations are cached in a node's cache. A cache hit requires no additional cycles, while a cache miss invokes a coherence protocol that sends messages, accesses a directory entry, etc. All messages and cache or directory transitions have a cost. A cache or directory processes messages in first-come-first-serve (FCFS) order. Queuing delay is included in the cache miss cost. Network topology and contention are ignored, and the latency of all messages is fixed at T cycles.

2.2 TMC CM-5 Host

The host platform for WWT is a Thinking Machines CM-5 [33]. The architecture supports from 32 to 16,384 processing nodes. Each node contains a SPARC processor, cache, memory management unit (MMU), custom vector/memory controller units, up to 128 MB of memory, and a custom network interface. Nodes are connected by two user-accessible networks. The data network allows a program to send short (five-word) point-to-point messages, but does not guarantee order of arrival. The control network performs fast barriers, broadcasts, and parallel prefix computations. WWT does not use the vector units.

2.3 Distributed, Discrete-Event Simulation

In *discrete-event simulation*, the target system (sometimes called the *physical system*) is modeled by a set of state variables that make discrete transitions in response to events [12]. A uniprocessor host computer performs discrete-event simulation by removing the first event from an event list (ordered by target time), processing the event to change the system state, and scheduling zero or more events. *Distributed, discrete-event simulation* partitions the target system's state and event lists among the multiple processing nodes of a parallel host system. Generally, each node processes events in a manner similar to a uniprocessor and sends messages to other nodes to schedule events that affect remote state. The fundamental difficulty is to determine the next event. The first event in the local event list may not be the event that should be processed first, because a message may subsequently arrive with an event from an earlier target time.

Aggressive distributed, discrete-event simulation algorithms optimistically process the local event list and exchange information that causes rollbacks of prematurely-processed events. By contrast, *conservative* algorithms ensure causality by exchanging information to determine when the first item in the local list can be processed safely. A node processes its first event only when no node will subsequently send an earlier event. Section 4.1 describes WWT's conservative technique and Section 6 compares it with related algorithms.

3   Parallel Direct Execution of Shared-Memory Programs

This section describes how WWT directly executes shared-memory programs on the CM-5. The next section provides details of the performance calculation. Non-shared-memory machines, such as the CM-5, do not provide hardware mechanisms to handle cache misses on remote memory references. WWT simulates this mechanism with a software trap handler that is invoked on target cache misses. Our approach is a fine-grained extension of Li's shared virtual memory. With this technique, WWT directly executes all instructions and all memory references that hit in the target cache. Only target cache misses require simulation.

Li's *shared virtual memory (SVM)* [21] implements shared memory on a distributed-memory system. Pages local to a processor are mapped into the processor's virtual address space. A remote page is left unmapped so a reference to it causes a page fault, which invokes system software to obtain the page.

Although SVM allows direct execution of memory references, sharing is limited to page granularity (typically 4K bytes), which is much larger than target cache blocks (e.g., 128 bytes). WWT refines SVM to support fine-grained sharing by logically adding a valid bit to every 32 bytes in the host pages underlying the target cache. An access to an invalid block traps and software simulates a cache coherence protocol that obtains the block. The CM-5 does not provide memory valid bits, but it does provide precise interrupts on double-bit error correcting code (ECC) errors. WWT marks invalid blocks with a bad ECC value, which causes a trap on loads and stores.

WWT target programs are SPARC binaries that run directly on the CM-5's SPARC processors. As described in Section 2.1, each target process sees the virtual address space illustrated on the left side of Figure 2. WWT runs in a different SPARC context. The right side of Figure 2 illustrates WWT's virtual address space, all of which is mapped to local memory. The text segment holds WWT code and the stack segment contains WWT's and the target program's stack. WWT's data is divided into four regions: WWT-state, target text, target node memory, and cache page frames (CPFs). WWT-state holds WWT-specific data structures. Target text is a copy of the target program. Target node memory holds all data that resides in the target node's local memory module and is logically equivalent to the target node's physical memory.[1] Finally, WWT uses CPFs to model the target node's cache, as explained below.

To understand how WWT models a cache, let's follow the steps (under a simple cache coherence protocol) when a memory reference misses in the cache. Initially, the target's private and shared data segments are unmapped so the first reference to a page generates a fault that the CM-5 passes to WWT. This reference would be a cache miss on the target shared-memory machine. WWT regains control on all cache misses so it can simulate the target cache.

Assume for a moment that the target cache's block size equals the host page size (4K bytes). In this case, WWT handles a cache miss in a similar manner as shared virtual memory (SVM) [21]. Upon a cache miss, WWT allocates a page from the pool of CPFs and changes the target's page tables so the faulting address maps to the CPF. WWT then simulates the target cache-coherence protocol by sending messages to other processors to obtain the referenced block and update directory information. Finally, WWT writes the block to the allocated page and resumes the target program. Subsequent references to the same block execute directly. WWT removes a block from the cache—either because of cache replacement or a coherence message—by unmapping the CPF and returning the block's data to its home memory module. As a further refinement, we simulate a translation lookaside buffer (TLB) by selectively unmapping CPFs.

Cache blocks in foreseeable systems will be much smaller than 4K bytes, so WWT simulates multiple blocks per host page. WWT logically adds a valid bit to each block in a mapped CPF page. On a target cache miss to a previously unrefenced page, WWT maps the page into a CPF (as above), writes the block's data into a valid block, and marks as invalid all other blocks on the page. Subsequent references to these blocks cause an "invalid" trap that WWT

---

[1] WWT can model machines in which private and shared data is stored in the same cache—by storing private data in CPFs—or stored separately—by mapping private data to target node memory.

services similarly.

Since the CM-5, like most machines, does not provide valid bits, we synthesize them from existing hardware. We divide the CPF pages into blocks of the same size as those in the CM-5's SPARC cache (32 bytes). WWT marks a block invalid by using a CM-5 diagnostic mode to change the error correcting codes (ECC) for the block's memory double-words to invalid values that cause a double-bit ECC error. By running the CM-5's SPARC cache in write-back mode, all target memory references appear to the memory controller as 32-byte cache fills. A cache fill of a valid block loads the data into the SPARC cache. An invalid block incurs a double-bit ECC error, which causes the memory controller to interrupt the processor and transfer control to WWT.

Target cache blocks larger than 32 bytes are easily handled by having WWT manipulate aligned groups of 32-byte blocks. Read-only blocks require setting the block's page protection to read-only, which causes protection violations on writes. Regrettably, protection must be read-only if any block in a page is read-only. A write to another, writable block in the page causes a protection violation, but WWT determines that the write is permissible and completes it.

Conservative users may be surprised to learn that WWT's use of ECC bits has little effect on the CM-5's standard ECC coverage. Most memory is outside the CPFs and unaffected by our use of the ECC bits. Valid blocks within the CPFs have valid ECC. On an ECC error, WWT checks a block's validity. If the block is invalid, WWT simulates a cache miss. Otherwise, WWT signals a true ECC error. However, a bit error could make an invalid block appear valid. Writing invalid ECC codes in the two double words in a block ensures that two single-bit errors are necessary to cause this problem.

4 Calculating Performance

The discussion above described how WWT accurately and efficiently mimics the functionality of a cache-coherent, shared-memory computer. Functional simulation without performance metrics, however, is insufficient to study and compare computer architectures. A program's running time is the single most important metric in determining how well the program runs on a computer. This section describes how WWT computes a program's execution time on a target machine.

WWT adds logical clocks to target processes, protocol messages, directory hardware, etc. to enable WWT to model latencies, dependencies, and queuing.

The result is an event-driven simulation of a parallel target machine that runs on a parallel host machine. WWT differs from other distributed, discrete-event simulators [12] because its workload is an executing program. Driving a simulation from an executing target program requires new techniques because of the frequency with which the program modifies the target machine's state. By contrast, a queuing network simulation only modifies target state on job arrival and departure. Treating every instruction execution as an event would be prohibitively costly and would forfeit the benefits of the efficient functional simulation described above.

WWT uses two techniques to combine the distributed simulation of a parallel computer with direct execution. First, WWT manages interprocessor interactions by dividing program execution into lock-step quanta to ensure all events originating on a remote node that affect a node in the current quantum are known at the quantum's beginning. Second, WWT orders all events on a node for the current quantum and directly executes the process up to its next event. These two techniques result in an efficient simulation that delivers accurate, reproducible results without approximations. Section 4.1 describes how WWT simulates interactions among processor nodes. Section 4.2 shows how WWT integrates direct-execution of target programs with discrete-event simulation.

4.1 Inter-Node Simulation

In this section, we ignore the details of WWT's processor simulation. From this perspective, WWT performs a distributed, discrete-event simulation that exploits characteristics of the target and host machines. First, rollback is impractical because directly executed programs can modify any part of a target processor's state (e.g., registers and memory). Second, determining the local time of nodes that could possibly send an event is expensive because any target node can communicate with any other target node. Third, our host system hardware (the CM-5) does not guarantee that messages from one host node to another node arrive in order. However, the CM-5 does provide hardware support for efficient reductions.

WWT coordinates simulation of processor nodes by breaking the target program's execution into lock-step quanta Q target machine instruction cycles long. Every quantum ends with a CM-5 reduction that ensures all outstanding messages containing events are received. Setting $Q \leq T$ (where T is the minimum latency of the target machine's interconnection network) guarantees that at the beginning of a quantum, a host node has received all remotely-generated events that could affect the target node in the quantum, because:

- all messages containing events that originated during the previous quantum have been delivered, and

- all events produced during the current quantum cannot affect target state on other nodes during this quantum.

We choose this approach because it avoids rollbacks, makes good use of the efficient CM-5 reductions, and tolerates unordered data messages. In practice, the technique works well, as the numbers in Section 5 demonstrate. Section 6 discusses how the technique relates to other distributed, discrete-event simulation algorithms.

4.2 Node Simulation

This section explains how WWT coordinates direct program execution with the distributed, discrete-event simulation. On each host node, WWT runs the target program up to the first event, processes the event, and continues running the program up to the next event or until the quantum expires. If the local program produces events (e.g., cache misses), they are easily added to the event list.

WWT directly executes many instructions consecutively by identifying the points in a program at which events can interact with the program and only checking for a pending event at these points. Instructions that do not access memory only affect a processor's local state and neither cause nor are directly affected by shared-memory events. These instructions execute directly. A memory reference produces an event when it misses in the target machine's cache. Fortunately, fine-grained shared virtual memory (Section 3) efficiently identifies these memory references and returns control to WWT. Finally, shared-memory references can interact with events caused by other processor nodes. For example, another processor can steal a cache block from the local node. These events must be carefully coordinated so state changes occur at the correct point with respect to the local program's execution. Because WWT knows all non-local events at the beginning of a quantum, it runs the program up to the first event, changes the cache or directory state as dictated by the event, and continues the program.

Each WWT host node performs the discrete-event simulation of a target node by repeatedly processing the first event in the local event list and performing an appropriate action. Target machine coherence protocol messages are sent via CM-5 data messages. WWT

timestamps each message with its sending time plus T (to model the target network latency). When a data message is received, WWT inserts its event on the local event list. WWT also schedules a quantum-expiration event every Q target cycles. This event causes a host node to wait for all other nodes to reach a barrier and all data messages to reach their destination. WWT uses the CM-5's fast reductions to determine when all messages are delivered.

WWT currently processes requests on a target directory at the request's arrival time rather than enqueuing the request until its service time. This optimization, advocated by Ayani [3], is possible because the directory uses first-come-first-serve queuing in which an event is unaffected by events that arrive after it. The optimization is important because directory service and completion events need not be enqueued and the running program is interrupted less often. WWT processes external requests on a target cache in the same fashion as directory requests.

— Initialization not shown
while (simulation not complete) **do**
  begin
    while (time (cpu) $\geq$ time (event_queue.head)) **do**
      begin
        — Process interprocessor events that occur
        — before the next instruction execution.
        — Remember: quantum expiration is event.
        first_event = dequeue (event_queue);
        process_event (first_event);
      end

    — Run the target program up to the next event,
    — $\Delta_{permitted}$ cycles in the future.
    $\Delta_{permitted}$ = time (first_event) - time (cpu);
    — Δ_{actual} is the actual time that the program ran.
    Δ_{actual} = run_program ($\Delta_{permitted}$);
    time (cpu) = time (cpu) + Δ_{actual};
  end

Figure 3: WWT's event loop.

Figure 3 shows WWT's event processing loop. The routine *run_program* runs the target program and returns control to WWT at the first target cache miss or before the first memory reference that executes at or after $\Delta_{permitted}$ cycles. The program need not stop precisely at $\Delta_{permitted}$ cycles, because additional instructions that do not reference memory cannot interact with external events. The function returns the amount of time that the program actually ran (Δ_{actual}). On a cache miss, $0 \leq \Delta_{actual} \leq \Delta_{permitted}$, so the cache miss occurs before the first event in the local event list. If the memory access references the local memory module, its event is inserted before the former (and still unprocessed) first event and the loop continues. If the miss references a remote memory module, WWT sends a message, suspends the program, and processes the event list since the response to the message cannot arrive until the next quantum.

run_program returns control of the host processor to the target program. WWT ensures that the target program always returns before the next event by using a modified version of *qpt* [4] to add quick tests to the target program's binary executable. Before resuming the target program, WWT sets a counter in a global register to $\Delta_{permitted}$. Conceptually after each instruction, the instrumented target program decrements the counter by the instruction's static cycle cost. For memory references, this cost assumes a cache hit. On a cache miss, WWT regains control and accounts for the miss penalty. To improve performance, the cycle counter is actually decremented only before non-private references and at the end of basic blocks. The instrumented program only tests the counter before non-private references. If the counter is negative, the program returns control to WWT, which processes the next event before executing the memory reference. The decrement and test each require a single instruction and consequently do not greatly affect the program's execution time.

5 A Comparison

To improve upon direct-execution uniprocessor simulators, WWT must obtain results of comparable accuracy and run large parallel programs more quickly. This section shows that WWT produces results similar to Stanford's Tango/Dixie, a direct-execution uniprocessor simulator. It also shows how WWT scales to simulate large target systems more effectively than a uniprocessor simulator.

5.1 Validation

WWT is a complex system for modeling complex software and hardware systems. To build confidence in WWT, we compared it against an existing simulator—a process that is often optimistically called *validation*. The similar—though not identical, for reasons discussed below—results increased our confidence in WWT. Even so, the process did not prove WWT correct, because testing never proves software to be correct. The validation only showed that the two systems produced similar results. It did

Name	Application	Input Data Set	Size (lines)
cholesky	Sparse matrix cholesky factorization	bcsstk14	1888
mp3d	Hypersonic flow simulation	10000 mols 20 iter	1607
tomcatv	Parallel SPEC benchmark	128×128 10 iter	404

Table 1: Applications used in validation.

These three benchmarks, two from the SPLASH benchmark suite [29] and a parallelized version of a SPEC benchmark [31], were chosen because they make little use of the math libraries. We could not simulate these libraries with Tango, because we did not have MIPS math library sources.

not demonstrate that either system correctly modeled a real computer.

We compared WWT against *Dixie*, a Tango-based simulation of the DASH multiprocessor [26]. Tango is a direct-execution simulation system that runs on a uniprocessor MIPS-based workstation. Tango instruments a target program's assembly code with additional code that computes instruction execution times and calls the simulator before loads and stores. The Dixie memory system simulation models the DASH prototype hardware [20]. Together, Dixie and Tango execute parallel shared-memory programs and estimate system performance.

Our original intent was to perform a black box comparison by writing our own DASH simulator for WWT (WWT/DASH) from only published details and reproducing DASH performance results. Unfortunately, this goal proved impossible because of myriad unpublished, subtle, and detailed design choices that significantly affect shared-memory system performance. For example, differences in memory allocation (e.g., in *malloc* and *sbrk*) resulted in a nearly 100% discrepancy in cache performance.

Instead, we "opened the black box" and modified both WWT/DASH and Tango/Dixie until they modeled similar systems. We made most changes to our description of DASH. The principal exception was the memory hierarchy. The DASH multiprocessor has a four-level memory hierarchy: primary cache, write buffer, secondary cache, and remote access cache. To reduce the complexity of our DASH simulation, we disabled most levels of the hierarchy and simulated a system with a single direct-mapped cache, no clusters, and $T = 100$ cycles to send a coherence protocol message.

During the validation, we found several major dif-

Application	Proc	Message Counts			Simulated Cycles		
		WWT	T/D	Diff.	WWT	T/D	Diff.
cholesky	4	1253504	1259467	-0.47%	103379891	107713586	-4.02%
cholesky	8	1756122	1747374	0.50%	93356751	99380412	-6.06%
cholesky	16	2197179	2220362	-1.04%	87566479	94468953	-7.31%
mp3d	4	2823164	2799511	0.84%	95464151	104226210	-8.41%
mp3d	8	3276119	3267250	0.27%	64579958	68684983	-5.98%
mp3d	16	3778487	3769719	0.23%	47764673	49901197	-4.28%
tomcatv	4	332995	332181	0.25%	52214338	43086273	21.19%
tomcatv	8	330091	328362	0.53%	26468922	22029613	20.15%
tomcatv	16	197397	195722	0.86%	12606286	9991406	26.17%

Table 2: Results of Validation.

WWT/DASH (WWT) and Tango/Dixie (T/D) are very close in message counts. The percent difference ($100\% \times (WWT - T/D)/T/D$) is less than 1.1% in all cases. The simulated cycle counts—execution times—are not as close since the two host systems have different instruction sets, different compilers, and use different instrumentation. Both systems are simulating direct-mapped, 64K byte caches with 32-byte blocks.

ferences in the way that WWT and Tango/Dixie manage memory. First, Tango/Dixie does not simulate a translation lookaside buffer (TLB), while WWT does. For large virtual address spaces and large data sets, TLB performance can be important. To minimize this difference, we simulated a very large, fully-associative TLB in WWT. Second, because Tango shares the same address space as an application program, Tango's data structures are intermixed with the application's private data. In WWT, an application has its own address space. This difference caused non-trivial differences in cache performance. To remedy it, we ensured that both simulators cached only shared data and allocated shared data contiguously.

After making these changes, we ran the three parallel benchmarks listed in Table 1. Table 2 summarizes the simulated message and target cycle counts. We simulated target systems with 4–16 processors, because Tango/Dixie could not handle larger systems on our workstations. The message counts are close, with less than 1.1% deviation in all cases. The estimated cycle counts—target execution times—are not quite as close. Some deviation is unavoidable because Tango/Dixie runs on a MIPS, while WWT runs on a SPARC. Cmelik et al. showed that programs on these architectures typically perform within 10% for similar compilers [8]. To minimize instruction set differences, we assumed all instructions execute in a single cycle. A problem, however, is that Tango/Dixie counts instructions in compiler-generated assembly code. Because the MIPS assembler expands pseudo-instructions, assembly code differs from executed binary code. This was particu-

larly important for *Tomcatv*, whose inner loop expanded from 969 pseudo-instructions to 1394 binary instructions (on the SPARC, the inner loop takes 1329 binary instructions). Despite these differences, the cycles counts for *MP3D* and *Cholesky* are within 10%. *Tomcatv's* differences are 20-26%, due to the large assembler expansion. Finally, Tango/Dixie did not measure the math library routines, whose sources were unavailable. WWT, because it instruments and runs executables, measures all code in a program.

5.2 Performance Evaluation

Another goal of WWT is to simulate programs faster than direct-execution uniprocessor simulators such as Tango/Dixie. It is tempting to compare directly the performance of Tango/Dixie and WWT/DASH. For at least three reasons, this comparison is not meaningful. First, the Dixie memory system simulator models the DASH implementation more completely than WWT/DASH. In particular, although we disabled the effects of Dixie's four-level memory hierarchy, much of the code still executed. Second, isolating the effect of different instruction sets, compilers and operating systems is difficult. Third, WWT/DASH is newer than Tango/Dixie. Unreleased versions of Tango/Dixie might perform better.

For these reasons, we focus on how performance changes as we increase the number of processors in a target system, both without and with changing the program's size. The WWT numbers were collected on a 64-processor CM-5 running pre-release (beta) CMOST 7.2 S4.

Consider first the simulation time when the num-

Application	Procs	WWT			Tango/Dixie		
		Time (sec.)	Rate (cyc./sec.)	Slowdown (host/target)	Time (sec.)	Rate (cyc./sec.)	Slowdown (host/target)
cholesky	4	586	176416	187	5659	19034	2101
cholesky	8	353	264466	124	8474	11727	3410
cholesky	16	236	371044	88	16695	5658	7068
cholesky	32	182	469111	70	n/a	n/a	n/a
cholesky	64	168	504118	65	n/a	n/a	n/a
mp3d	4	725	131674	250	3891	26786	1493
mp3d	8	322	200558	164	4048	16967	2357
mp3d	16	179	266841	123	4601	10845	3688
mp3d	32	114	335560	98	n/a	n/a	n/a
mp3d	64	79	414663	79	n/a	n/a	n/a
tomcatv	4	114	458020	72	2705	15928	2511
tomcatv	8	58	456360	72	2902	7591	5269
tomcatv	16	20	630314	52	3039	3287	12166
tomcatv	32	13	533214	61	n/a	n/a	n/a
tomcatv	64	14	304765	108	n/a	n/a	n/a

Table 3: WWT/DASH and Tango/Dixie simulation speed and slowdown.

This table shows simulation time, the number of target cycles simulated per second, and the host cycles required to simulate each target cycle. WWT runs on 33-Mhz SPARCs in a CM-5. Tango/Dixie runs on a 40-Mhz DECstation 5000/240. Results for Tango/Dixie with 32 and 64 processors are unavailable (n/a), because we could not run Tango/Dixie on these target systems on our workstations.

ber of processors in a target system increases and the program's size is fixed. Uniprocessor simulators are, at best, unaffected by the change since the program, at best, performs the same operations on more target processors. In practice, additional context switching overhead and host TLB and cache contention increase simulation time. Since WWT runs on a parallel host, we increase the number of host nodes (up to the size of the host) as the target system grows. Consequently, WWT's simulation time should decrease, rather than increase, because each target (and host) node performs fewer operations. Table 3 and Figure 4a clearly demonstrate this behavior. For *MP3D* and *Tomcatv*, Tango/Dixie's execution time increases slightly from 4 to 16 processors. WWT's elapsed time decreases nearly linearly for *MP3D* and *Tomcatv* as the target system size increases. In *Cholesky*, moreover, processes spin on a shared variable, which increases the number of target instructions executed as the number of target processors increases. Since Tango/Dixie simulates all processors serially, its execution time triples from 4 to 16 processors. WWT's elapsed time again decreases.

The advantage of WWT is more striking for scaled speedup. Gustafson [14] and others have argued that parallel speedup is uninteresting: give scientists a larger machine and they will solve larger problems

in the same amount of time. This argument calls for scaling a problem's size approximately linearly with the number of processor nodes. On uniprocessor simulators, like Tango/Dixie, scaling a problem increases simulation time at least linearly. On WWT, as illustrated in Figure 4b, simulation time increases much more slowly.

6 Related Work

WWT is a tool for evaluating large-scale, parallel computer system software and hardware. The two closely-related methods for studying large-scale parallel computers are hardware prototyping and software simulation. The methods are not mutually-exclusive as simulation usually precedes prototyping.

Stanford DASH [20], MIT Alewife [7], and MIT J-Machine [10] are projects that built hardware prototypes. WWT offers at least four advantages over hardware prototyping. First, WWT ran programs after two months, ran large applications four months later (instead of multiple years), and produced accurate cycle counts in two more months. Second, WWT modules can be modified in days or weeks (instead of months or years). Third, WWT can be built in a university without the infrastructure for hardware development. Finally, WWT can be distributed to

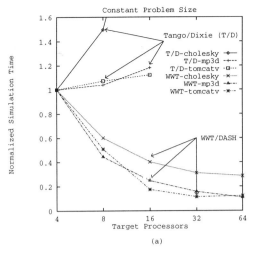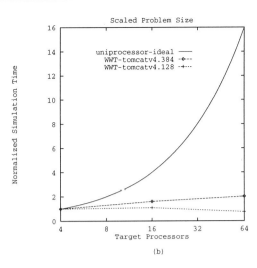

Figure 4: Normalized simulation time vs target system size.

This figure plots the relative simulation times as the target system size increases for both constant problem size (a) and scaled (linearly with target system size) problem size (b). Each curve is normalized against the respective simulator time for 4 processors. For constant problem size, Tango/Dixie's simulation time increases with target system size, while WWT's time decreases nearly linearly. For scaled problem size, WWT's simulation time increases slowly, while the simulation time on a uniprocessor host must increase at least linearly (exponentially on this semi-log plot). The tomcatv4.128 line corresponds to 4, 16, and 64 processors and 128×128, 256×256, and 512×512 matrices, respectively. The tomcatv4.384 line corresponds to 4, 16, and 64 processors and 384×384, 768×768, and 1536×1536 matrices, respectively.

other sites.

The disadvantages of WWT include not providing participants with experience in building actual hardware and the ever-present question as to how closely a simulation reflects the actual system. Of course, even academic hardware prototypes are not completely realistic, because of constraints on infrastructure, money, and availability of experienced designers.

An alternative to hardware prototyping is software simulation. MIT Proteus [6], Berkeley FAST [5], Rice Parallel Processing Testbed [9], and Stanford Tango [11] are simulation systems that simulate parallel machines by running actual programs (as opposed to distribution-driven or trace-driven workloads). All use direct execution and run on a uniprocessor host. WWT improves on these systems by extending direct execution to all target operations except shared-memory references that *miss* and by running on a parallel host with gigabytes of main memory. These differences enable WWT to evaluate larger and more realistic workloads including real applications, data sets, and system software.

A disadvantage of WWT with respect to uniprocessor simulators is the high cost of WWT's host. Never-

theless, WWT provides two advantages. First, it can perform more realistic evaluations, because the CM-5 provides more main memory than can be placed on most workstations (and this memory accounts for a significant fraction of the CM-5's cost). Second, it facilitates successive refinement of software and hardware by providing a much faster response time.

Other researchers [12, 16, 18, 24, 25, 3, 28, 27] have studied simulation systems for parallel hosts. These systems perform a discrete-event simulation of a parallel target using a discrete-event workload. These systems and WWT exploit the parallel host by avoiding a fine-grained global simulation clock that advances in lock-step.

The key advance of WWT over these systems is that WWT supports dynamic execution of target program binaries. As discussed by Covington, et al. [9], execution-driven simulation of computer systems produces more detailed results than either distribution- or trace-driven simulation. To the best of our knowledge, all other distributed, discrete-event simulation systems simulate queuing networks or computer systems with stochastic workload models, not real programs.

WWT's method for coordinating nodes for the execution time calculation is a conservative, synchronous method. *Synchronous* algorithms use the target times of some or all neighboring nodes to ensure causality [3, 24, 28, 27]. The difference between the target times of two nodes is called *lag* and the minimum target time for one node to affect another is called *distance*. Synchronous algorithms ensure the lag between each pair of nodes is always less than the distance.

WWT ensures that lag is less than distance with barriers at fixed target intervals smaller than the minimum distance between any two target nodes. Our approach is closely related to the methods of Ayani, Lubachevsky and Nicol. Ayani uses barriers, but runs on a shared-memory host machine and simulates at most one event per node per barrier. Lubachevsky [24] repeatedly broadcasts the time of the slowest node (to maintain a bounded lag), but allows the lag to be greater than the distance between some nodes. Nicol [27] uses barriers at variable intervals. After each barrier, nodes cooperate to determine the next barrier time. WWT eliminates this phase by using a fixed time between barriers.

Konas and Yew and Lin et al. perform parallel simulations of multiprocessors, but neither system directly executes target programs. Konas and Yew [18, 19] use distribution-driven workloads and simulation algorithms that rely on a shared-memory host. Lin et al. [22] use trace-driven workloads in which the trace and interactions among processors are unaffected by a memory-reference miss (as if a cache hit and miss take the same time). WWT models reference times more accurately to compute target execution time and allows memory system behavior to affect program execution.

Finally, WWT allocates cache page frames in 4K-byte blocks, but usually uses smaller blocks ($\geq$ 32 bytes) for data transfers and coherence. The IBM 360/85 cache [23] used different block sizes for allocation and transfer. Goodman [13] discusses the use of different block sizes for allocation, transfer, and coherence. These ideas are also used more recently by Tamir [32] and Kendall Square [17].

7   Extensions and Future Work

Currently, WWT is a novel simulator of cache-coherent, shared-memory computers that runs on a Thinking Machines CM-5. We believe that virtual prototyping is very general concept and can be used to model *any* target system and to extend WWT to run on other hosts. The primary issue is how efficiently a specific target feature can be modeled. As an example, WWT could easily support message-passing programs. This only requires a library of message-passing primitives that use WWT timestamps to compute message latency. A more expensive change would enable WWT to model interconnection network topology and contention. WWT could charge a minimum latency determined by network topology and add a stochastic contention penalty. Finally, WWT could, at great cost, model contention exactly by using CM-5 nodes to simulate network routing.

WWT can model most target node features. Instruction set extensions—e.g., a `compare-and-swap` instruction—are implemented by existing instructions (either in-line, in a call, or with a simulator trap). *qpt* models the instruction's performance by charging an assumed cycle count. *qpt* can also form the basis of a binary-to-binary translator that permits non-SPARC instruction sets [30]. This technique could model a dynamic pipeline of arbitrary complexity. At some point, however, the complexity of translating an instruction set outweights the benefits of direct execution and an instruction simulator is a better alternative.

Fine-grained shared-virtual memory efficiently simulates caches that use pseudo-random replacement. A second-level cache can be simulated during the traps for level-one cache misses. Algorithms that cause state changes on some cache hits, such as LRU replacement, require a full address trace, which *qpt* can provide.

Currently, WWT runs one target node on a host node. Future versions will run multiple target nodes on a host node, which will permit evaluation of larger systems. WWT will use a separate context (i.e., virtual address space) for each target node. During a quantum, a host node will run each target node, in turn, for Q cycles. Causality is preserved because the communication latency of the target nodes running on a host node is still $T \geq Q$ cycles. In addition, we could switch contexts more frequently when modeling a target system with low intracluster communication latency. Finally, this improvement will enable us to simulate multithreaded architectures that context switch frequently.

WWT could run on machines besides a CM-5. The key CM-5 features exploited by WWT are precise interrupts on ECC errors, fast user-level messages, and efficient reductions. Without the ECC mechanism, fine-grained shared virtual memory could be implemented with memory tag bits (e.g., Tera [2]). On a machine with neither mechanism, *qpt* can add additional code to a program to directly test if a shared-memory reference will miss, as in Tango/Dixie. The performance of this approach relative to the ECC mechanism depends on its overhead on cache hits, since the cost of a cache miss dwarfs the tests and traps.

WWT can run on machines without the CM-5's fast user-level messages and reductions. High latency messages will slow WWT's execution. On a shared-memory host, WWT could directly write to remote event lists to add events. Again, the efficiency depends how quickly the host's memory system perform these accesses. WWT quanta end with a reduction that completes when all outstanding messages are received. A barrier would suffice on a machine that has another mechanism for ensuring that remote events are scheduled (e.g., shared memory). On machines without barrier or reduction hardware, WWT could use software reductions and barriers, or the system could be radically changed to use another distributed, discrete-event simulation technique.

This paper contains some results for a simulation of a shared-memory machine similar to Stanford DASH. We are using WWT to compare existing and new cache-coherence protocols. WWT facilitates these studies, because it clearly separates the modules that specify a target machine's cache coherence protocol and the rest of WWT. To date, WWT runs DASH [20], $Dir_i NB$ for $i = 1 \dots N$ [1], $Dir_i B$ for $i = 0 \dots N$ [1], and $Dir_1 SW$ variants [15, 34].

8 Conclusions

This paper describes the Wisconsin Wind Tunnel (WWT)—a system for evaluating cache-coherent, shared-memory computers on a Thinking Machines CM-5. WWT runs parallel shared-memory binaries and concurrently calculates the programs' execution times on the target hardware with a distributed, discrete-event simulation. The non-shared-memory host directly executes all target instructions and memory references that hit in the target cache. WWT's shared memory uses the CM-5 memory's error-correcting code (ECC) as valid bits to build a fine-grained extension of Li's shared virtual memory.

WWT calculates target program execution times on the parallel host with a distributed, discrete-event simulation algorithm. WWT manages the interactions among target nodes by dividing execution into lock-step quanta that ensure all events originating on a remote node that affect a node in the current quantum are known at the quantum's beginning. On each node, WWT orders all events in a quantum and directly executes the process up to the next event.

We showed that WWT produces results that are close to Tango/Dixie for a Stanford DASH-like system. Finally, we examined how WWT's performance scales as target systems increase in size. WWT's execution time decreases for fixed-size problems running on larger target systems and increases slowly as problems are scaled to run on larger systems. Neither result is surprising, because WWT uses the processors and memory of a parallel host. Nevertheless, they demonstrate that WWT can support evaluations of much more realistic parallel workloads than previously possible without building hardware.

Acknowledgements

Dave Douglas, Danny Hillis, Roger Lee, and Steve Swartz of Thinking Machines provided invaluable advice and assistance in building WWT. Satish Chandra, Glen Ecklund, Shubhendu Mukherjee, Subbarao Palacharla, and Timothy Schimke helped develop WWT and applications. Richard Fujimoto and David Nicol provided readings in distributed, discrete-event simulation. Sarita Adve, Richard Fujimoto, Stephen Goldschmidt, Rahmat Hyder, Alain Kägi, Edward Lazowska, David Nicol, and John Zahorjan provided helpful comments that greatly improved this paper.

We would also like to acknowledge the invaluable assistance provided by the Stanford DASH project. Helen Davis, Kourosh Gharachorloo, Stephen Goldschmidt, Anoop Gupta, John Hennessy, and Todd Mowry wrote and generously provided Tango and Dixie. Singh *et al.* [29] wrote and distributed the SPLASH benchmarks.

References

[1] Anant Agarwal, Richard Simoni, Mark Horowitz, and John Hennessy. An Evaluation of Directory Schemes for Cache Coherence. In *Proceedings of the 15th Annual International Symposium on Computer Architecture*, pages 280–289, 1988.

[2] Robert Alverson, David Callahan, Daniel Cummings, Brian Koblenz, Allan Porterfield, and Burton Smith. The Tera Computer System. In *Proceedings of the 1990 International Conference on Supercomputing*, pages 1–6, June 1990.

[3] Rassul Ayani. A Parallel Simulation Scheme Based on the Distance Between Objects. In *Proceedings of the SCS Multiconference on Distributed Simulation*, pages 113–118, March 1989.

[4] Thomas Ball and James R. Larus. Optimally Profiling and Tracing Programs. In *Conference Record of the Nineteenth Annual ACM Symposium on Principles of Programming Languages*, pages 59–70, January 1992.

[5] Bob Boothe. Fast Accurate Simulation of Large Shared Memory Multiprocessors. Technical Report CSD 92/682, Computer Science Division (EECS), University of California at Berkeley, January 1992.

[6] Eric A. Brewer, Chrysanthos N Dellarocas, Adrian Colbrook, and William Weihl. PROTEUS: A High-Performance Parallel-Architecture Simulator. Technical Report MIT/LCS/TR-516, MIT Laboratory for Computer Science, September 1991.

[7] David Chaiken, John Kubiatowics, and Anant Agarwal. LimitLESS Directories: A Scalable Cache Coherence Scheme. In *Proceedings of the Fourth International Conference on Architectural Support for Programming Languages and Operating Systems (ASPLOS IV)*, pages 224–234, April 1991.

[8] Robert F. Cmelik, Shing I. Kong, David R. Ditzel, and Edmund J. Kelly. An Analysis of MIPS and SPARC Instruction Set Utilization on the SPEC Benchmarks. In *Proceedings of the Fourth International Conference on Architectural Support for Programming Languages and Operating Systems (ASPLOS IV)*, pages 290–302, April 1991.

[9] R.C. Covington, S. Madala, V. Mehta, J.R. Jump, and J.B. Sinclair. The Rice Parallel Processing Testbed. In *Proceedings of the 1988 ACM SIGMETRICS Conference on Measurement and Modeling of Computer Systems*, pages 4–11, May 1988.

[10] William J. Dally, Andrew Chien, Stuart Fiske, Waldemar Horwat, John Keen, Michael Larivee, Rich Nuth, Scott Wills, Paul Carrick, and Greg Flyer. The J-Machine: A Fine-Grain Concurrent Computer. In G. X. Ritter, editor, *Proc. Information Processing 89*. Elsevier North-Holland, Inc., 1989.

[11] Helen Davis, Stephen R. Goldschmidt, and John Hennessy. Multiprocessor Simulation and Tracing Using Tango. In *Proceedings of the 1991 International Conference on Parallel Processing (Vol. II Software)*, pages II99–107, August 1991.

[12] Richard M. Fujimoto. Parallel Discrete Event Simulation. *Communications of the ACM*, 33(10):30–53, October 1990.

[13] James R. Goodman. Coherency for Multiprocessor Virtual Address Caches. In *Proceedings of the Second International Conference on Architectural Support for Programming Languages and Operating Systems (ASPLOS II)*, pages 408–419, October 1987.

[14] John L. Gustafson. Reevaluating Amdahl's Law. *Communications of the ACM*, 31(5):532–533, May 1988.

[15] Mark D. Hill, James R. Larus, Steven K. Reinhardt, and David A. Wood. Cooperative Shared Memory: Software and Hardware for Scalable Multiprocessors. In *Proceedings of the Fifth International Conference on Architectural Support for Programming Languages and Operating Systems (ASPLOS V)*, pages 262–273, October 1992.

[16] David R. Jefferson. Virtual Time. *ACM Transactions on Programming Languages and Systems*, 7(3):404–425, July 1985.

[17] Kendall Square Research. Kendall Square Research Technical Summary, 1992.

[18] Pavlos Konas and Pen-Chung Yew. Parallel Discrete Event Simulation on Shared-Memory Multiprocessors. In *Proc. of the 24th Annual Simulation Symposium*, pages 134–148, April 1991.

[19] Pavlos Konas and Pen-Chung Yew. Synchronous Parallel Discrete Event Simulation on Shared-Memory Multiprocessors. In *Proceedings of 6th Workshop on Parallel and Distributed Simulation*, pages 12–21, January 1992.

[20] Daniel Lenoski, James Laudon, Kourosh Gharachorloo, Wolf-Dietrich Weber, Anoop Gupta, John Hennessy, Mark Horowitz, and Monica Lam. The Stanford DASH Multiprocessor. *IEEE Computer*, 25(3):63–79, March 1992.

[21] Kai Li and Paul Hudak. Memory Coherence in Shared Virtual Memory Systems. *ACM Transactions on Computer Systems*, 7(4):321–359, November 1989.

[22] Y.-B. Lin, J.-L. Baer, and E. D. Lazowska. Tailoring a Parallel Trace-Driven Simulation Technique to Specific Multiprocessor Cache Coherence Protocols. Technical Report 88-01-02, Department of Computer Science, University of Washington, March 1988.

[23] J. S. Liptay. Structural Aspects of the System/360 Model 85, Part II: The Cache. *IBM Systems Journal*, 7(1):15–21, 1968.

[24] Boris D. Lubachevsky. Efficient Distributed Event-Driven Simulations of Multiple-Loop Networks. *Communications of the ACM*, 32(2):111–123, January 1989.

[25] Jayadev Misra. Distributed-Discrete Event Simulation. *ACM Computing Surveys*, 18(1):39–65, March 1986.

[26] Todd Mowry and Anoop Gupta. Tolerating Latency Through Software-Controlled Prefetching in Shared-Memory Multiprocessors. *Journal of Parallel and Distributed Computing*, 12:87–106, June 1991.

[27] David Nicol. Conservative Parallel Simulation of Priority Class Queueing Networks. *IEEE Transactions on Parallel and Distributed Systems*, 3(3):398–412, May 1992.

[28] David M. Nicol. Performance Bounds on Parallel Self-Initiating Discrete-Event Simulations. *ACM Transactions on Modeling and Computer Simulation*, 1(1):24–50, January 1991.

[29] Jaswinder Pal Singh, Wolf-Dietrich Weber, and Anoop Gupta. SPLASH: Stanford Parallel Applications for Shared Memory. *Computer Architecture News*, 20(1):5–44, March 1992.

[30] Richard L. Sites, Anton Chernoff, Matthew B. Kirk, Maurice P. Marks, and Scott G. Robinson. Binary Translation. *Communications of the ACM*, 36(2):69–81, February 1993.

[31] SPEC. SPEC Benchmark Suite Release 1.0, Winter 1990.

[32] Yuval Tamir and G. Janakiraman. Hierarchical Coherency Management for Shared Virtual Memory Multicomputers. *Journal of Parallel and Distributed Computing*, 15(4):408–419, August 1992.

[33] Thinking Machines Corporation. The Connection Machine CM-5 Technical Summary, 1991.

[34] David A. Wood, Satish Chandra, Babak Falsafi, Mark D. Hill, James R. Larus, Alvin R. Lebeck, James C. Lewis, Shubhendu S. Mukherjee, Subbarao Palacharla, and Steven K. Reinhardt. Mechanisms for Cooperative Shared Memory. In *Proceedings of the 20th Annual International Symposium on Computer Architecture*, pages 156–168, May 1993.

Visualizing the Performance of Parallel Programs

MICHAEL T. HEATH, *University of Illinois*
JENNIFER A. ETHERIDGE, *Oak Ridge National Laboratory*

◆ ParaGraph animates trace information from actual runs to depict behavior and provides graphical performance summaries. It provides 25 perspectives on the same data, lending insight that might otherwise be missed.

Graphical visualization aids human comprehension of complex phenomena and large volumes of data. The behavior of parallel programs on advanced architectures is often extremely complex, and monitoring the performance of such programs can generate vast quantities of data. So it seems natural to use visualization to gain insight into the behavior of parallel programs so we can better understand them and improve their performance.

We have developed ParaGraph, a software tool that provides a detailed, dynamic, graphical animation of the behavior of message-passing parallel programs and graphical summaries of their performance.

GRAPHICAL SIMULATION

For lack of a better term, we use "sim-ulation" to mean graphical animation. By "simulation," we do not mean to suggest that there is anything artificial about the programs or their behavior as ParaGraph portrays them. ParaGraph displays the behavior and performance of real parallel programs running on real parallel computers to solve real problems. In effect, ParaGraph provides a visual replay of the events that actually occurred when a parallel program was run on a parallel machine.

To date, ParaGraph has been used only for post-processing trace files created during execution and saved for later study. But its design does not rule out the possibility that data could arrive at the graphical workstation as the program executes.

However, there are major impediments to genuine real-time performance visualization. With the current generation of distributed-memory parallel architec-

0-8186-6522-X/95 $4.00 © 1991 IEEE

tures, it is difficult to extract performance data from the processors and send it to the outside world during execution without significantly perturbing the program being monitored. Also, the network bandwidth between the processors and the workstation and the drawing speed of the workstation are usually inadequate to handle the very high data-transmission rates that a real-time display requires. Finally, humans would be hard pressed to digest a detailed graphical depiction unfolding in real time. One of ParaGraph's strengths is that it lets you replay the same execution trace data repeatedly.

Some performance-visualization packages treat the trace file of events saved after a program executes as a static, immutable object to be studied by various analytical or statistical means. Such packages provide graphical tools designed for visual browsing of the performance data from various perspectives using scroll bars and the like.

ParaGraph adopts a more dynamic approach whose conceptual basis is algorithm animation. We see the trace file as a script to be played out, visually reenacting the original live action to provide insight into a program's dynamic behavior.

Both the static and dynamic approaches have advantages and disadvantages. Algorithm animation is good at capturing a sense of motion and change, but it is difficult to control the simulation's apparent speed. The static browser approach gives the user fine control over the speed at which the data are viewed (time can even move backward), but it does not provide an intuitive feeling for dynamic behavior.

Design goals. We wanted ParaGraph to be easy to understand, easy to use, and portable.

Easy to understand. The whole point of visualization is to aid understanding, so it is imperative that the visual displays be as intuitively meaningful as possible. The charts and diagrams should be aesthetically appealing and the information they convey should be self-evident. A diagram is not likely to be useful if it requires an extensive explanation, so the information

it conveys should either be immediately obvious or easily remembered once learned.

The display's colors should reinforce the meaning of graphical objects and be consistent across views. Above all, the system must provide many visual perspectives, because no single view is likely to provide full insight into the behavior and data associated with parallel-program execution. ParaGraph provides more than 20 displays or views based on the same underlying trace data.

Easy to use. Software tools should relieve tedium, not promote it. We use color and animation to make ParaGraph painless, even entertaining, to use. ParaGraph has an interactive, mouse- and menu-oriented user interface so its features are easily invoked and customized.

Another important factor in ease of use is that the object under study (the parallel program) need not be modified extensively to obtain the visualization data. ParaGraph's input are trace files produced by the Portable Instrumented Communication Library,[1] which lets users produce trace data automatically.

Portability. Portability is important in two senses. First, the graphics package itself should be portable. ParaGraph is based on X Windows, and thus runs on many vendors' workstations. Although it is most effective in color, it also works on monochrome and grayscale monitors — it detects automatically which monitor type is in use.

Second, the package must be able to display execution behavior from different parallel architectures and parallel-programming paradigms. ParaGraph inherits a high degree of such portability from PICL, which runs on parallel architectures from many different vendors (including Cogent, Intel, N-Cube, and Symult).

On the other hand, many of

ParaGraph's displays are based on the message-passing paradigm, so it does not support programs explicitly based on shared-memory constructs.

PARAGRAPH FEATURES

ParaGraph is distinguished from other visualization systems[2] in:

♦ The number of displays it provides. While other packages provide multiple views, none we know of provides the variety of perspectives ParaGraph does. Some of ParaGraph's displays are original; others have been inspired by similar displays in other packages.

♦ Its portability among architectures and displays. ParaGraph is applicable to any parallel architecture having message passing as its programming paradigm, and ParaGraph itself is based on X Windows.

♦ The intuitive appeal and aesthetic quality of its displays, which we hope reach a new, higher standard. Of course, how successful we've been is in the eye of the beholder.

♦ Its ease of use, attributable both to its interactive, graphical interface and to its use of PICL to provide the trace data without requiring the user to instrument the program under study.

♦ Its extensibility. ParaGraph lets users add new displays of their own design to the views already provided.

An indication of how successful we've been in making ParaGraph easy to use and understand is the fact that many users have obtained an early version from Netlib on Internet during the last year, built the program, and used it effectively without the benefit of any documentation except a one-page Readme file.[3]

Relationship to PICL. PICL runs on several message-passing parallel architectures.[1] As its name implies, it provides both portability and instrumentation for programs that use its communication facilities to

> The whole point of visualization is to aid understanding, so it is imperative that the visual displays be as intuitively meaningful as possible.

pass messages among processors.

On request, PICL provides a trace file that records important execution events (like sending and receiving messages). The trace file contains one event record per line, and each event record comprises an integer set that specifies the event type, time stamp, processor number, message length, and other similar information.

ParaGraph has a producer-consumer relationship with PICL: ParaGraph consumes the trace data PICL produces. Using PICL instead of a machine's native parallel-programming interface gives the user portability, instrumentation, and the ability to use ParaGraph to analyze behavior and performance.

These benefits are essentially "free" in that once you've implemented a parallel program using PICL, you don't have to change the source code to move it to a new machine (provided PICL is available on the new machine), and little or no effort is required to instrument the program for performance analysis.

On the other hand, because ParaGraph's dependence on PICL is solely for input data, ParaGraph could work equally well with any data source that has the same format and semantics. So other message-passing systems can be instrumented to produce trace data in ParaGraph's format, and ParaGraph's input routine can be adapted to different input formats. Indeed, ParaGraph has been used with communication systems other than PICL.

Clock synchronization. For meaningful simulation, the event's time stamps should be as accurate and consistent across processors as possible. This is not necessarily easy when each processor has its own clock with its own starting time and runs at its own rate. Also, the clock's resolution may be inadequate to resolve events precisely.

Poor clock resolution and/or synchronization can lead to what we call *tachyons* in the trace file — messages that appear to be received before they are sent (a tachyon is a hypothetical particle that travels faster than light). Tachyons confuse ParaGraph, because much of its logic depends on pairing sends and receives.

Because this possibility will invalidate some ParaGraph displays, PICL goes to considerable lengths to synchronize processor clocks and adjust for potential clock drift, so time stamps are as consistent and meaningful as possible. On some machines, PICL actually provides higher clock resolution than the system was supplied with.

Overhead. Collecting trace data can add to overhead. PICL tries to minimize tracing perturbation by saving trace data in each processor's local memory, downloading them to disk only after the program has finished execution. Nevertheless, monitoring inevitably introduces extra overhead: In PICL, the clock calls necessary to determine the time stamps for the event records, plus other minor overhead, add a fixed amount (independent of message size) to the cost of sending each message.

Thus, the overhead added is a function of the frequency and volume of communication traffic; it also varies from machine to machine. In general, we believe that this perturbation is small enough that the program's behavior is not altered fundamentally. In our experience, the lessons we learn from the visual study of instrumented runs always improve the performance of uninstrumented runs.

USING PARAGRAPH

ParaGraph supports command-line options that specify a host name for remote display across a network, forced monochrome display mode (useful if black-and-white hard copies are to be made from a color screen), or a trace-file name. You can also specify (or change) the trace-file name during execution by typing the file name in an options menu. ParaGraph preprocesses the input trace file to determine some parameters (like time

> Because ParaGraph's dependence on PICL is solely for input data, ParaGraph could work equally well with any data source that has the same format and semantics.

scale and number of processors) automatically, before the simulation begins; the user can override most of these values.

Interface. The initial ParaGraph display is a main menu of buttons with which you control the execution and select submenus. Submenus include those for three display types, or families (utilization, communication, and tasks), for miscellaneous displays, and for options and parameters.

You can select as many displays as will fit on the screen, and you can resize displays within reason. It is difficult to pay close attention to many displays at once, but it is useful to have several simultaneous displays for comparison and selective scrutiny.

After selecting the displays, you press start to begin the graphical simulation of the parallel program based on the trace file you specified. The animation proceeds to the end of the trace file, but you can interrupt it with a pause/resume button. For even more detailed study, the step button provides a single-step mode that processes the trace file one event at a time.

You can also single out a time interval by specifying a starting and stopping time (the defaults are the beginning and ending of the trace file), or you can have the simulation stop at each occurrence of some event. And you can restart the entire animation at any time by simply pressing the start button.

Some ParaGraph displays change in place as events occur, representing execution time from the original run with simulation time in the replay. Other displays represent execution time in the original run with one space dimension on the screen, scrolling (by a user-controllable amount) as simulation time progresses, in effect providing a moving window for viewing a static picture. No matter which time representation is used, all displays are updated simultaneously and synchronized with each other.

Speed. The relationship between simulation speed and execution speed is necessarily imprecise. The speed of the graphical simulation is determined primarily by the drawing speed of the workstation, which in turn is a function of the number and complexity of displays that have been selected. There is no way to make the simulation speed uniformly proportional to the original execution speed.

For the most part, ParaGraph simply processes the event records and draws the resulting displays as fast as it can. If there are gaps between consecutive time stamps, ParaGraph fills them in with a spin loop so there is at least a rough (if not uniform) correspondence between simulation time and execution time. Fortunately, close correspondence does not seem to be critical in visual performance analysis. What's most important is that the graphical replay preserve the correct relative order of events. Moreover, the figures of merit ParaGraph produces are based on actual time stamps, not simulation speed.

Because ParaGraph's speed is determined primarily by the workstation's drawing speed, the number of displays you select can speed it up or slow it down. ParaGraph's speed is also affected by the displays' complexity and the type and amount of scrolling used.

When ParaGraph provided only a few displays, it included parameterized delay loops to slow the drawing in case it moved too quickly for the eye to follow. But as we added more displays this ceased to be a problem, so we dispensed with the delay loops. Now users sometimes complain that the simulation is too slow rather than too fast, since most like to have many displays open. You can always resort to single-step mode if you want to study program behavior very closely.

SOFTWARE DESIGN

ParaGraph is an interactive, event-driven program. Its basic structure is that of an event loop and a large switch that selects actions based on each event's nature. Menu selections determine ParaGraph's execution behavior, both statically (initial display selection, options, and parameter values) and dynamically (pause/resume, single-step mode).

ParaGraph has two event queues: a queue of X events produced by the user (mouse clicks, key presses, window exposures) and a queue of trace events produced by the program under study. ParaGraph must alternate between these queues to provide both a dynamic depiction of the program and responsive user interaction.

The X-event queue must be checked frequently enough to provide good responsiveness, but not so frequently as to degrade drawing speed. The trace-event queue must be processed as rapidly as possible while the simulation is active, but it need not be checked at all if the next possible event must be an X event (as happens before a simulation starts, after it finishes, when it is in single-step mode, or when it has been paused and can be resumed only by the user).

So ParaGraph's alternation between queues is not strict. Because not all event records PICL produces are of interest to ParaGraph, it fast-forwards through such uninteresting records before it rechecks the X-event queue. Also, ParaGraph checks the X-event queue with both blocking and nonblocking calls, depending on the circumstances, so workstation resources are not consumed unnecessarily when the simulation is inactive.

DISPLAYS

Printed illustrations obviously cannot convey ParaGraph's dynamism, but we must be content with snapshots. Due to space limitations, we cannot illustrate all 25 displays, so we selected the most useful and interesting ones from a typical ParaGraph session. For clarity and simplicity, the examples use only a few processors. With one noted exception, all of the views shown can display at least 128 processors and most of them can display up to 512 processors. The figures reproduced here were produced from trace files made on an Intel iPSC/2 hypercube.

The parallel program illustrated in most of the figures is a common computation in scientific computing: the solution of a large sparse system of linear equations by Cholesky factorization. (See our technical report for details of the parallel algorithm used here.[4])

In the example, the sparse matrix of the linear system arises from a 15×15 square grid, so the matrix is of order 225. The nodes of the grid, and hence the rows and columns of the matrix, are ordered by nested dissection, which is a type of domain decomposition that leads to a typical divide-and-conquer parallel algorithm for the factorization.

In the example, each of the eight processors first computes the portion of the factorization corresponding to the interior of its own part of the grid, which it can do independent of the other processors. However, eventually the processors reach a point where interprocessor communication is required to supply boundary data from neighboring grid portions before computations can proceed. The processors team up in four pairs, then in two sets of four, and finally all eight together, as they work their way up the elimination tree and communicate across higher level boundaries.

Most of the displays fall into one of three categories — utilization, communication, and task information — although some contain more than one type of information and a few do not fit these categories at all.

Utilization displays. Figure 1 shows processor-utilization displays, which show how effectively processors are used and how evenly the computational work is distributed among them.

> With one noted exception, all of the views shown can display at least 128 processors and most of them can display up to 512 processors.

166

Processor count. The utilization-count display (top-left window in Figure 1) shows the total number of processors in each of three states — busy, overhead, and idle — as a function of time. The number of processors is on the vertical axis and time is on the horizontal axis, which scrolls as necessary as the simulation proceeds.

The color scheme is borrowed from traffic signals: green (go) for busy, yellow (caution) for overhead, and red (stop) for idle. Along the vertical axis we show green at the bottom, yellow in the middle, and red at the top.

ParaGraph categorizes a processor as idle if it has suspended execution awaiting a message that has not yet arrived or if it has ceased execution at the end of the run, overhead if it is executing in the communication subsystem but not awaiting a message, and busy if it is executing some portion of the program other than the communication subsystem.

Because these three categories are mutually exclusive and exhaustive, the total height of the composite is always equal to the total number of processors. Ideally, we would like to interpret busy as meaning that a processor is doing useful work, overhead as meaning that a processor is doing work that would be unnecessary in a serial program, and idle as meaning that a processor is doing nothing. Unfortunately, the monitoring required to make such a determination would almost certainly be nonportable and/or excessively intrusive. So busy time may well include redundant work or other work that would not be necessary in a serial program, because our monitor detects only that overhead associated with communication.

However, we find that in practice these definitions are quite adequate to illustrate the effectiveness of parallel programs. In Figure 1, the perfectly parallel initial phase of the divide-and-conquer algorithm for sparse-matrix factorization corresponds to the all-green portion at the far left, before subsequent communication causes processor use to decline.

Gantt chart. This display (bottom-left window in Figure 1), patterned after graphical charts used in industrial management,[5]

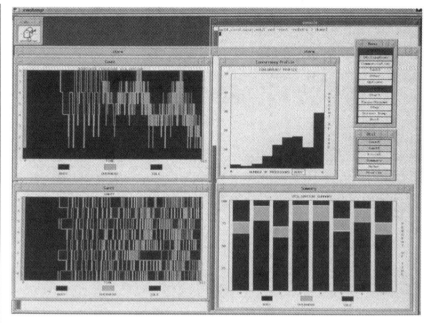

Figure 1. *Processor-utilization displays. Top row, from left: count of processors in each of three states; percentage of time a certain number of processors were in a given state. Bottom row, from left: activity of individual processors over time; percentage of time each processor spent in each state.*

depicts the activity of individual processors with a horizontal bar chart in which the color of each bar indicates the busy/overhead/idle status of the corresponding processor as a function of time, again using the traffic-signal color scheme.

Processor number is on the vertical axis; time on the horizontal axis, which scrolls as necessary as the simulation proceeds. The Gantt chart provides the same information as the utilization-count display, but by individual processor instead of by aggregate. As Figure 1 shows, the utilization-count display is simply the Gantt chart with the green sunk to the bottom, the red floated to the top, and the yellow sandwiched in between.

Summary. The utlization-summary display (bottom-right window in Figure 1) shows the percent of time over the entire run that each processor spent in each of the three states (busy, overhead, and idle). The percentage is shown on the vertical axis; the processor number on the horizontal axis. This display also uses the traffic-light color scheme.

In addition to a visual impression of overall program efficiency, this display gives a visual indication of the load balance across processors. In the sparse-matrix example shown in Figure 1, four of the processors are assigned the four corners of the grid, while the other four are assigned central portions of the grid, leading to a load imbalance that is clearly visible.

Concurrency profile. This display (top-right window in Figure 1) shows the percentage of time that a certain number of processors were in a given state. The percentage of time is shown on the vertical axis; the number of processors on the horizontal axis. The profile for each possible state is shown separately; the user can cycle through the three states by clicking on a subwindow.

The actual concurrency profile for real programs shown by this display is usually in marked contrast to the idealized conditions that are the basis for Amdahl's Law, which assumes that at any given time the computational work is either strictly serial or fully parallel. Figure 1 shows the busy profile for the sparse-matrix example; the

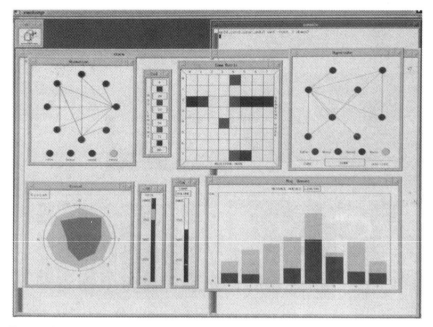

Figure 2. *Communication and utilization displays. Top row, from left: logical connectivity of multiprocessors; message length; matrix of message size, duration, and pattern; node layouts that correspond to networks embedded in a hypercube. Bottom row, from left: geometric depiction of an individual processor's use and overall load balance; percentage of maximum number of processors in each of three states; current communication volume as a percentage of the maximum; size of each processor's incoming message queue.*

idle and overhead profiles are not shown.

Utilization meter. This display (bottom-center window in Figure 2) uses a colored vertical bar, with the traffic-light color scheme, to indicate the percentage of the maximum number of processors that are currently in each of the three states.

The visual effect, shown in Figure 2, is similar to a thermometer. This display provides essentially the same information as the utilization-count display, but saves screen space because it changes in place rather than scrolling with time.

Kiviat diagram. This display (bottom-left window in Figure 2), adapted from related graphs used in other types of performance evaluation,[6-7] gives a geometric depiction of individual processor's usage and the overall load balance across processors.

As Figure 2 shows, each processor is represented as a spoke on a wheel. The recent average fractional usage of each processor determines a point on its spoke, with the hub of the wheel representing

zero (completely idle) and the outer rim representing one (completely busy).

Taken together, the points for all the processors determine the vertices of a polygon whose size and shape illustrate both processor use and load balance. Low usage concentrates the polygon near the center, while high usage causes the polygon to lie near the perimeter. Poor load balance across processors causes it to be strongly skewed or asymmetric. Any change in load balance is clearly shown: With many ring-oriented algorithms, for example, the moving polygon has the appearance of a rotating camshaft as the heavier workload moves around the ring.

In Figure 2, current usage is shown in dark shading, and the "high-water mark" thus far has a lighter shading. The current usage is a moving average over a user-specified time, because instantaneous usage would always be either zero or one for each processor.

Communication displays. Interprocessor-communication displays are helpful in de-

termining communication frequency, volume, and overall pattern, and whether there is congestion in the message queues.

Message queues. This display (bottom-right window in Figure 2) depicts the size of the each processor's incoming-message queue with a vertical bar whose height varies with time as messages are sent, buffered, and received. The processor number is shown on the horizontal axis.

You can set the queue size to be measured either by the number of messages or by their total length in bytes. A processor's input queue size is incremented each time a message is sent to that processor, and decremented each time the user process on that processor receives a message. On most message-passing parallel systems, transmission time between processors is negligible compared to the overhead in handling messages, so the time between send and receive events is a reasonable approximation of the time a message actually spends in the destination processor's input queue.

Depending on their types, messages may not be received in the same order in which they arrive for queuing, so queues may grow and shrink in complicated ways. As before, dark shading depicts the current queue size on each processor, and lighter shading the high-water mark.

This display gives a pictorial indication of whether there is communication congestion (if messages are accumulating in the input queue) or if messages are being consumed at about the same rate as they arrive. Of course, it is best if messages arrive slightly before they are actually needed, so the receiving processor does not become idle. But a large backlog of incoming messages can consume excessive buffer space, so a happy medium is desirable. In the example shown in Figure 2, processor 2 has no messages in its input queue, the other processors all have messages awaiting receipt by their user processes, and no queue is at its maximum size so far.

Communication matrix. In this display (top-center window in Figure 2), messages are represented by squares in a two-dimensional array whose rows and columns correspond to each message's sending and receiving processor. During simulation, each message is depicted by coloring the appropriate square when the message is sent and erasing it when the message is received.

The square's color indicates message size in bytes, as given in a separate color-code display. Thus, this display shows message size, duration, and overall pattern. The nodes can be ordered along the axes in either natural or Gray code order; your choice will strongly affect the communication pattern. At the end of the simulation, this display shows the cumulative communication volume for the entire run between each pair of processors.

Animation. In this display (top-left window in Figure 2), the multiprocessor is represented by a graph whose nodes (numbered circles) represent processors, and whose arcs (lines between circles) represent communication links.

Each node's status (busy, idle, sending, and receiving) is indicated by its color, so the circles are like the multiprocessor's front-panel lights. An arc is drawn between the source and destination processors when a message is sent, and erased when the message is received. So both node color and graph connectivity change as simulation proceeds.

The small circles are arranged in a large circle merely for convenience in drawing straight lines between processor pairs without intersecting any other processors; this arrangement is not meant to suggest that the underlying architecture is a ring. The nodes can be ordered around the circle in either natural or Gray code order; again, your choice will strongly affect the communication pattern.

The arcs represent the logical, rather than physical, connectivity of the multiprocessor network, and possible routing of messages through intervening nodes is not depicted unless the program being visualized does such forwarding explicitly.

Various combinations of states are possible for the sending and receiving processors. As Figure 2 shows, the processors on both ends of a message line can be busy,

one having already sent the message and resumed computing, while the other has not yet stopped computing to receive it. At the end of a simulation, this display shows a summary of all logical communication links used in the run.

Hypercube. This display (top-right window in Figure 2) is similar to the animation display, except it provides additional node layouts to exhibit more clearly communication patterns that correspond to the various networks that can be embedded in a hypercube. The layouts provided include ring, ring of rings, web, cube, lateral cubes, nested cubes, mesh, linear, tree, tesseract (four-dimensional cube), and polytope arrangements.

This display does not require that a machine's interconnection network be a hypercube — it highlights the hypercube structure merely as a matter of interest. The scheme for coloring nodes and drawing arcs is the same as the animation display, except that curved arcs are often used to avoid, as much as possible, intersecting intermediate nodes.

To help the user of a hypercube determine if the network's physical connectivity is honored by the program's communication, message arcs corresponding to genuine physical hypercube links are drawn in a different color from message arcs along virtual links that do not exist in a hypercube and therefore entail indirect routing through intervening processors.

In Figure 2, the message between nodes 2 and 7 must travel over a virtual link by being forwarded through an intermediate processor, whereas the message between nodes 2 and 6 travels directly over the physical link between those two processors. As in the animation display, at the conclusion of the simulation a summary of all logical communication links used during the run is shown. Unfortunately, the

method used to draw the hypercube display does not scale up to large numbers of processors, and it is limited to displaying at most 16 processors.

Communication meter. This display (bottom-center window in Figure 2) uses a vertical bar to indicate the current communication volume as a percentage of the maximum. This display provides essentially the same information as the communication traffic display, but saves screen space by changing in place rather than scrolling with time. Conceptually, this thermometer-like display is similar to the utilization-meter display, and the two are interesting to observe side by side.

Communication traffic. This display (top-left window in Figure 3) is a simple plot of the total communication traffic in the interconnection network (including message buffers) as a function of time. The curve plotted is the total length or number of messages sent but not yet received. It can be expressed by message count or by volume in bytes.

The communication traffic can also be either the aggregate over all processors or just the messages pending for any individual processor. Message volume or count is shown on the vertical axis; time on the horizontal axis, which scrolls as necessary. Figure 3 shows the successively higher peaks in communication traffic for the sparse-matrix example as the program encounters higher level grid separators.

Space-time diagram. Patterned after diagrams used in relativity theory, this display (top-right window in Figure 3) depicts interactions among processors through space and time. This diagram has been used by Leslie Lamport to describe the order of events in a distributed system.[8] The same pictorial concept was used over a century

> The layouts provided include ring, ring of rings, web, cube, lateral cubes, nested cubes, mesh, linear, tree, tesseract (four-dimensional cube), and polytope arrangements.

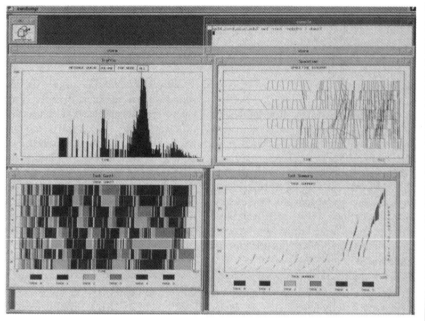

Figure 3. *Communication and task displays. Top row, from left: plot of total communication traffic over time; interactions among processors through space and time. Bottom row, from left: each processor's task activity over time; duration of each task as a percentage of total execution time.*

ago to prepare graphical railway schedules.[9]

In our adaptation of the space-time diagram, processor number is on the vertical axis, time on the horizontal, which scrolls as necessary. Processor activity (busy or idle) is indicated by horizontal lines, one for each processor, with the line drawn solid if the corresponding processor is busy (or doing overhead), and blank if the processor is idle.

Messages between processors are depicted by slanted lines between the sending and receiving processor activity lines, indicating the times at which each message was sent and received. These sending and receiving times are from user process to user process (not simply the physical transmission time), and hence the slopes of the resulting lines give a visual indication of how soon a piece of data produced by one processor is needed by the receiving processor. The communication lines are color-coded to indicate the sizes of the messages being transmitted.

The space-time diagram shown in Figure 3 clearly shows the divide-and-conquer nature of the sparse-matrix example. The eight processors initially work inde-

pendently, then combine in successively larger groups as they move up the elimination tree. The space-time diagram is one of the most informative of all the displays, because it depicts both individual processor utilization and all message traffic in full detail. For example, it can easily be seen which message wakes up an idle processor that was blocked. Unfortunately, this fine level of detail does not scale up beyond about 128 processors, as the diagram becomes extremely cluttered.

Task displays. The displays thus far have depicted a number of important aspects that help detect performance bottlenecks. However, they contain no information about where in the parallel program the behavior occurs.

To remedy this situation, we considered several automated approaches to providing such information (such as picking up line numbers in the source code from the compiler), but all of these involved nasty practical difficulties. So we reluctantly made an exception to our rule that the ParaGraph user need do nothing to instrument the program under study.

We developed several new task displays that use information provided by the user and PICL to depict the portion of the program that is executing. The user defines tasks within a program by using special PICL routines to mark the beginning and end of each task and assign it a task number.

The scope of what is meant by a task is left entirely to the user: A task can be a single line of code, a loop, an entire subroutine, or any other unit of work that is meaningful. For example, in matrix factorization you might define the computation of each column to be a task and assign the column number as the task number. You need to define tasks only if you want to view the task displays. If the trace file contains no event records that define tasks, the task displays will simply be blank.

Tasks can be nested, but if they are they should be properly bracketed by matching task begin and end records. Note also that more than one processor can be assigned the same task (or, more accurately, each processor can be assigned its own portion of the same task); indeed, the model we have in mind is that all processors collaborate on each task, rather than that each task is assigned to a single processor. In many contexts, such as the matrix example mentioned above, there is a natural ordering and corresponding numbering of the tasks in a parallel program.

In most of the task displays described here, task numbers are color-coded. Because the number of tasks is likely to be larger than the number of colors that can be easily distinguished, ParaGraph recycles colors to depict successive task numbers. We use one of six basic colors for indicating each task, with the choice of color given by the task number modulo six. In the sparse-matrix example, we defined the factorization computation of each column to be a separate task, with the column number as task number, for a total of 225 tasks.

Task Gantt. This display (bottom-left window in Figure 3) depicts the task activity of individual processors with a horizontal bar chart in which the color of each bar indicates the current task being executed by the corresponding processor as a function of time. Processor number is on the vertical axis; time on the horizontal axis, which scrolls as necessary.

You can compare this display with the utilization Gantt chart to correlate a processor's busy-overhead-idle status with its task. Comparing Figure 3 with Figure 1 shows that for the sparse-matrix example the longer tasks tend to be caused by extended idle periods within the task while the processor awaits needed data, rather than by a heavier work load for that processor.

Task summary. This display (bottom-right window in Figure 3) indicates the duration of each task (from earliest beginning to last completion by any processor) as a percentage of the overall execution time and also places the duration interval of each task within the overall execution interval of the program. The percentage of the total execution time is shown on the vertical axis, the task number on the horizontal axis. As Figure 3 shows, this display provides another striking depiction of the divide-and-conquer sparse-matrix example, with the 8-4-2-1 sequence clearly visible.

Other task displays, not shown here, include task count, which shows the number of processors that are executing a given task at a given time, and task status, which indicates whether a task has yet to begin, is currently in progress, or has been completed.

Other displays. Some displays either do not fit into a category or cut across more than one category.

Critical path. Similar to the space-time diagram, this display (top window in Figure 4) uses a different color coding to highlight the longest serial thread in a parallel computation.

As Figure 4 shows, the processor and message lines along the critical path are shown in red, while all other processor and message lines are in light blue. This display helps identify performance bottlenecks and tune the parallel program by focusing on the part of the computation that is limiting performance. Any improvement in performance must necessarily shorten the longest serial thread run-

ning through the computation, so this is the first place to look for potential algorithm improvements.

Phase portrait. Patterned after phase portraits used in differential equations and classical mechanics to depict the relationship between two variables that depend on some independent variable, these displays (bottom-left and bottom-right windows in Figure 4) illustrate the relationship over time between communication and processor use.

At any point in time, the percentage of processors in the busy state and the percentage of the maximum volume of communication in transit together define a single point in a two-dimensional plane. This point changes with time as communication and processor use vary, thereby tracing out a trajectory in the plane that is plotted in this display, with communication and use on the two axes.

Because the overhead and potential idleness due to communication inhibit processor use, you expect communication and use generally to have an inverse relationship. Thus the phase trajectory should tend to lie along a diagonal. This display

reveals repetitive or periodic behavior, which tends to show up in the phase portrait as an orbit pattern.

The bottom-left window of Figure 4 shows two distinct computation phases, each of which exhibits a high degree of periodic behavior. By setting task numbers, you can color-code the trajectory to highlight either major phases in a computation or individual orbits. For example, the two phases shown in Figure 4 are matrix factorization (blue) and triangular solution (green) in solving a system of linear equations, and in the bottom-right window each separately colored orbit is a different dimension of a fast Fourier transform.

Other displays not shown here include processor status, which is a comprehensive display that attempts to capture detailed information about processor use, communication, and tasks in a compact format that scales up well to very large numbers of processors; clock, which provides both digital and analog clock readings during simulation; trace, a textual display of an annotated version of each trace event as it is read from the trace file (useful primarily in single-step mode for debug-

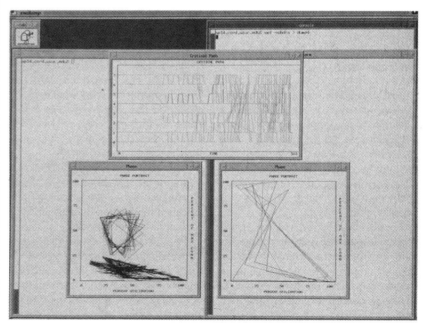

Figure 4. Miscellaneous displays. Top: space-time diagram with longest serial thread highlighted. Bottom: two phase portraits that illustrate the relationship between communication and processor use over time.

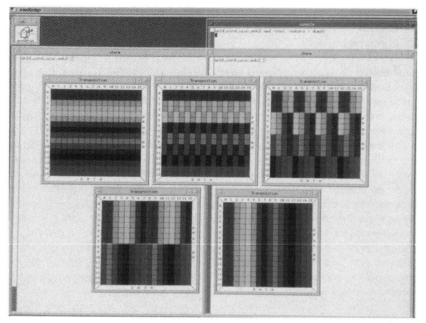

Figure 5. *Successive snapshots of an application-specific display showing several stages of recursive matrix transposition.*

ging or other detailed study on an event-by-event basis); and statistical summary, a textual display of numerical values for various statistics summarizing processor use and communication, both for individual processors and processor aggregates (useful in preparing tables and graphs that require exact numerical quantities for printed reports or for analytical performance modeling).

Application-specific displays. All the displays shown so far are generic — they are applicable to any parallel program based on message-passing. In general, this wide applicability is a virtue, but knowledge of the application often lets you design a special-purpose display that reveals greater detail or insight than generic displays would permit.

For example, if you are studying a parallel-sorting algorithm, generic displays can show which processors communicate and the communication volume, but not which specific data items are being exchanged among processors. Obviously, ParaGraph cannot provide such application-specific displays, but it is extensible so users can add application-specific displays of their own de-

sign that they can add to the menu and view along with the generic displays.

ParaGraph contains calls at appropriate points to application-specific routines for the initialization, data input, event handling, and drawing of displays. If the user does not supply these routines, dummy "stub" routines are instead linked into ParaGraph when the executable module is built. When an application-specific display has been linked into ParaGraph and the resulting module is executed, the user-supplied display is given access to all of the event records in the trace file that ParaGraph reads and can use them in any manner it chooses.

The events generated by PICL may suffice for the application-specific display. Or you can insert additional events during execution to supply additional data for the application-specific display.

PICL's tracemarks event is perhaps the most useful for this purpose, because it lets users insert into the trace file time-stamped records containing arbitrary lists of integers, which might be used to provide loop indices, array indices, memory addresses, or other information that would let the application-specific display

convey more fully and precisely the program's activity in the context of the particular application.

Unfortunately, writing the necessary routines to support an application-specific display is a decidedly nontrivial task that requires a general knowledge of X Windows programming. But at least the user of this capability can concentrate on only those portions of the graphics programming that are relevant to his application, taking advantage of ParaGraph's supporting infrastructure to provide all of the other necessary facilities to drive and control the overall graphical simulation and provide a meaningful context in which to view the application-specific information.

To help users who want to develop application-specific displays, we have developed several prototype displays to depict parallel-sorting algorithms, matrix transposition, and various other matrix computations. These example routines are distributed along with the source code for ParaGraph. Figure 5 shows successive snapshots of an application-specific display for matrix transposition that is driven by event records that indicate which data items are being exchanged among the processors.

FUTURE WORK

ParaGraph is a reasonably mature tool, although we intend to add more displays as helpful new perspectives are devised. There are a few minor technical points about ParaGraph that could stand improvement. It would be nice to have more explicit control over simulation speed. The contents of many displays are lost if the window is obscured and then reexposed. This inability to repair or redraw windows, short of rerunning the simulation from the beginning, was a deliberate design decision based on a desire to conserve the substantial amount of memory that would be required to save the contents of all windows for possible restoration. Nevertheless, this "feature" can be annoying at times and should eventually be fixed.

A more serious limitation of ParaGraph in its current form is the number of processors that can be depicted effectively. A few of the current displays are simply too detailed to scale up beyond about 128 processors and still be comprehensible. Most of the displays scale up well to a level of 512 or 1,024 processors on a normal-sized workstation screen, but at this point they are down to representing each processor by a single pixel (or pixel line), and hence cannot be scaled any further in their current form.

To visualize programs for massively parallel architectures that have thousands of processors, we must either devise new displays that scale up to this level, or adapt the existing displays by aggregating or selecting information. For example, the current displays could depict processor clusters or subsets (cross sections).

It is fairly easy to imagine how graphics technology might be adapted to meet the needs of visualizing massively parallel computations, but it is much less obvious how to handle the vast volume of trace data that would result from monitoring thousands of processors. It is already difficult to store and process the trace data collected from long runs even with the modest numbers of processors currently supported by PICL and ParaGraph. To go beyond the present level will almost certainly require some degree of behavior abstraction, both in the data and in its graphical presentation. We simply cannot afford to continue to record or display all communication events when they become so voluminous.

Unfortunately, many of ParaGraph's displays depend critically on the availability of data on each individual event. Thus, the development of new visual displays and new data abstractions must proceed in tandem so the monitoring facility will produce data that can be visually displayed in a meaningful way.

Source code for ParaGraph, as well as sample trace files for demonstrating its use, are available for free over Internet's Netlib software-distribution service.[3] To receive detailed instructions for obtaining ParaGraph, send an electronic mail message to netlib@ornl.gov containing the text "send index from paragraph." ♦

ACKNOWLEDGMENTS

The detailed implementation of ParaGraph has been done almost entirely by undergraduate students on research internships at Oak Ridge National Laboratory. The software's overall structure and the conceptual designs of the individual displays were developed by Heath. The bulk of the programming was done by Etheridge while she was an undergraduate student, first at Roanoke College and later at the University of Tennessee.

Loretta Auvil, then an undergraduate at Alderson Broaddus College, developed the Hypercube display, and Michelle Hribar, then an undergraduate at Albion College, developed the first two application-specific displays (to illustrate parallel sorting and matrix transposition) as extensions to ParaGraph. In each case these undergraduates began their work on ParaGraph without any prior knowledge of Unix, C, computer graphics, workstations, or X Windows, and within a single term each was contributing to the sophisticated software described here. ParaGraph's development has been an interesting educational experiment that has provided a useful tool for the performance analysis of parallel programs.

This research was supported by the Applied Mathematical Sciences Research Program, Office of Energy Research, US Energy Dept. under contract DE-AC05-84OR21400 with Martin Marietta Energy Systems.

REFERENCES

1. G.A. Geist et al., *PICL: A Portable Instrumented Communication Library, C Reference Manual*, Tech. Report ORNL/TM-11130, Oak Ridge Nat'l Lab., Oak Ridge, Tenn., 1990.
2. M.T. Heath and J.A. Etheridge, *Visualizing Performance of Parallel Programs*, Tech. Report ORNL/TM-11813, Oak Ridge Nat'l Lab., Oak Ridge, Tenn., 1991.
3. J.J. Dongarra and E. Grosse. "Distribution of Mathematical Software via Electronic Mail," *Comm. ACM*, May 1987, pp. 403-407.
4. M.T. Heath, E. Ng, and B.W. Peyton, "Parallel Algorithms for Sparse Linear Systems," *SIAM Review*, Sept. 1991, pp. 420-460.
5. H.L. Gantt, "Organizing for Work," *Industrial Management*, Aug. 1919, pp. 89-93.
6. K. Kolence and P. Kiviat, "Software Unit Profiles and Kiviat Figures," *Performance Evaluation Rev.*, Sept. 1973, pp. 2-12.
7. M.F. Morris, "Kiviat Graphs: Conventions and Figures of Merit," *Performance Evaluation Rev.*, Oct. 1974, pp. 2-8.
8. L. Lamport, "Time, Clocks, and the Ordering of Events in a Distributed System, *Comm. ACM*, July 1978, pp. 558-565.
9. E.R. Tufte, *The Visual Display of Quantitative Information*, Graphics Press, Cheshire, Conn., 1983.

Michael T. Heath is a computer science professor and research scientist at the National Center for Supercomputing Applications at the University of Illinois at Urbana-Champaign. He was a senior research-staff member and computer science group leader in the Mathematical Sciences Section at Oak Ridge National Laboratory. His research interests are in large-scale scientific computing on parallel computers, numerical linear algebra, and performance visualization.

Heath received a PhD in computer science from Stanford University.

Jennifer A. Etheridge is a technical research associate in the mathematical sciences section at Oak Ridge National Laboratory. Her current interests are in computer graphics and visualization.

Etheridge received a BS in mathematics from the University of Tennessee at Knoxville.

Address questions about this article to Heath at the National Center for Supercomputing Applications, 4157 Beckman Institute, University of Illinois, 405 Mathews Ave., Urbana, IL 61801-2300; Internet heath@ncsa.uiuc.edu.

Chapter 3
Performance of Large-Scale
Shared-Memory Multiprocessor Systems

The simplest way to construct a multiprocessor is to connect the processors on a shared bus that provides a shared global memory. Many of the commercially available shared-memory multiprocessors belong to the category of multiprocessors constructed in this way. Some examples are the Sequent Balance, the Sequent Symmetry, and the Encore Multimax. The bus-based shared-memory multiprocessor system is cost-effective and provides an easy programming model to the users. However, since the bus provides a low bandwidth for memory accesses, this type of architecture can support only a small number of processors.

In order to build large-scale shared-memory multiprocessor systems, the large shared address space must be constructed through a distributed-memory organization. A scalable interconnection network is used to connect a processor and its local memory with all other processors and their memory modules. Besides being able to support a large number of processors, the distributed-memory systems have other unique features. First, each processor in the system has nonuniform memory access times to different memory modules, depending on their physical location. Therefore, choices for placement and movement of data as the computation proceeds can have a significant effect on the overall performance of the applications. Thus, a user has to program carefully to handle efficiently issues like locality, granularity, and scheduling in order to achieve high performance. Second, this type of architecture can support a multicomputer environment in which data sharing and communication are conducted by message passing through the network.

In a multiprocessor, each processor may have a cache memory that enables the processors to reduce their use of the shared memory and limit the effects of memory latency and network contention on performance. However, a local cache generates a complex cache coherence problem to maintain data coherence among various copies of a shared block, which may reside in multiple local caches and in the shared memory. A cache coherence protocol must be implemented to ensure that each processor sees a consistent view of the datum. These protocols may degrade shared-memory computing performance by requiring expensive, nonlocal operations to invalidate or update shared data in remote caches and in the shared memory. Besides cache coherence, factors such as network contention, synchronization, resource scheduling, and multiprogramming also affect performance of a shared-memory multiprocessor.

Parallel-computing performance on large shared-memory architectures depends to a large extent on the structure of the interconnection network and the efficiency of the memory/cache management systems. The choice of interconnection networks to connect processor nodes to other nodes can make NUMA times vary drastically, depending upon the particular memory access patterns. Some examples of interconnection networks to build large-scale shared-memory multiprocessors are multistage interconnection networks used in the BBN Butterfly systems, hierarchical ring structures used in the Kendall Square Research KSR systems, and torus networks used in the Cray T3D systems. In large NUMA architectures, the memory system organization also affects communication latency. A shared-memory architecture can be classified into the following two categories in terms of memory organization, data migration, and coherence:

(1) *NUMA*. NUMA architecture can be divided into three types. The first type has no local caches at all (an example is the BBN GP1000). The second type is a cache-based

NUMA, where each processor node consists of a high-performance processor, an associated cache, and a designated portion of the global shared memory. However, the system disallows caching of shared data in order to avoid the cache coherence problem (an example is the BBN TC2000). The University of Illinois Cedar multiprocessor project also belongs to this category. In the third type of NUMA multiprocessor, the cache coherence is maintained by a directory-based, write-invalidate cache coherence protocol. Examples of such a system are the Stanford DASH and other systems being developed in many ongoing research projects.

(2) *COMA*. COMA stands for *cache-only memory architecture*. As in NUMA, each processor node has a high-performance processor, a cache, and a designated portion of the global shared memory. The difference is that, in COMA, there is no home location for a data block and the memory associated with each node is assumed to act as a large cache. Consistency among cache/memory blocks in the system is maintained using a write-invalidate protocol. A COMA system allows transparent migration and replication of data items to the nodes where they are referenced. Examples of such systems are the Kendall Square Research KSR1 system and the Swedish Institute of Computer Science's Data Diffusion Machine (DDM).

This chapter is concerned mainly with the performance evaluation and measurement results for various large-scale shared-memory architectures. Performance of large-scale multiprocessor systems depends mainly on the performance of the interconnection network and of the system support, such as cache coherence protocols, synchronization schemes, and others. The first paper, by Bhuyan, Yang, and Agrawal, presents a tutorial on analytic techniques to evaluate interconnection network performance. The performance evaluation of a MIN is emphasized because it is highly suitable for building large-scale systems. For example, the Cedar parallel system is a MIN-based shared-memory research prototype at the University of Illinois. The second paper, by Kuck et al., gives a comprehensive and comparative performance evaluation of the Cedar system.

Synchronization is an important issue in parallel processing on a shared-memory multiprocessor system when a shared critical section can be processed exclusively only by a single processor. This problem requires some method to ensure mutually exclusive access to the logically atomic operations on the shared critical section. The paper by Dubois, Scheurich, and Briggs addresses the issues of establishing synchronization processes, maintaining data coherence, and ordering events in shared-memory multiprocessors from the hardware design level up to the programming language level. Mellor-Crummey and Scott's paper further studies algorithms and performance for scalable synchronization on large shared-memory multiprocessors.

Cache coherence protocols dynamically maintain the consistency of the data in each cache. Many strategies can be used in maintaining the data consistency; however, an inefficient strategy can cause a significant amount of overhead and will increase the execution time. In their paper, Chaiken et al. present an overview of different directory-based cache coherence protocols and compare them using simulations. The paper by Lenoski et al. addresses the design and performance of the Stanford DASH shared-memory multiprocessor, which implements a directory-based cache coherence protocol.

The hierarchical ring structure is another important network for building large-scale shared-memory multiprocessors. The basic structure of a hierarchical ring network is the slotted ring, where the ring bandwidth is divided into a number of slots circulating continuously through the ring. The Kendall Square Research KSR1 system is a commercially available ring-based shared-memory system based on COMA. The paper by Rosti et al. presents performance results and programming experiences from using the poststore technique to improve program efficiency on the KSR1. The paper by Hagersten, Landin, and Haridi also describes a COMA architecture, DDM, developed at the Swedish Institute of Computer Science. The next paper, by Stenström, Joe, and Gupta, presents a comparative performance evaluation of cache-coherent NUMA and COMA architectures.

The distributed shared-memory model implements a shared-memory environment on top of a message-passing multicomputer architecture. This type of system not only provides users a single address space for easy programming but also provides another direction for building large and scalable shared-memory multiprocessors. The last paper, by Zhou et al., studies the design, implementation, and performance of a distributed shared-memory system.

Bibliography

Agrawal, A., and A. Gupta, "Memory Reference Characteristics of Multiprocessor Applications under Mach," *Proc. ACM SIGMETRICS*, ACM, New York, N.Y., 1988, pp. 215–225.

Barroso, L.A., and M. Dubois, "The Performance of Cache-Coherent Ring-Based Multiprocessors," *Proc. 20th Ann. Int'l Symp. Computer Architecture*, IEEE CS Press, Los Alamitos, Calif., 1993, pp. 268–277.

Bell, C.G., "Multis: A New Class of Multiprocessor Computers," *Science*, Vol. 228, 1985, pp. 462–466.

Bhuyan, L.N., "An Analysis of Processor-Memory Interconnection Networks," *IEEE Trans. Computers*, Vol. C-34, No. 3, Mar. 1985, pp. 279–283.

Bhuyan, L.N., and D.P. Agrawal, "Design and Performance of Generalized Interconnection Networks," *IEEE Trans. Computers*, Vol. C-32, No. 12, Dec. 1983, pp. 1081–1089.

Bodin, F., et al., "Performance Evaluation and Prediction for Parallel Algorithms on the BBN GP1000," *Proc. 1990 ACM Int'l Conf. Supercomputing*, ACM Press, New York, N.Y., 1990, pp. 401–413.

Cheriton, D.R., H.A. Goosen, and P.D. Boyd, "Paradigm: A Highly Scalable Shared-Memory Multicomputer Architecture," *Computer*, Vol. 24, No. 2, Feb. 1991, pp. 33–46.

Dubois, M., and C. Scheurich, "Memory Access Dependencies in Shared-Memory Multiprocessors," *IEEE Trans. Software Eng.*, Vol. 16, No. 6, June 1990, pp. 660–673.

Eagers, S.J., and R.H. Katz, "The Effect of Sharing on the Cache and Bus Performance of Parallel Programs," *Proc. 3rd Int'l Conf. Architectural Support Programming Languages and Operating Systems (ASPLOS-III)*, ACM, New York, N.Y., 1989, pp. 257–270.

Graunke, G., and S. Thakkar, "Synchronization Algorithms for Shared Memory Multiprocessors," *Computer*, Vol. 23, No. 6, June 1990, pp. 60–69.

Gupta, A., and W. Weber, "Cache Invalidation Patterns in Shared-Memory Multiprocessors," *IEEE Trans. Computers*, Vol. 41, No. 7, July 1992, pp. 794–810.

Jiang, H., L.N. Bhuyan, and J.K. Muppala, "MVAMIN: Mean Value Analysis Algorithms for Multistage Interconnection Networks," *J. Parallel and Distributed Computing*, Vol. 12, July 1991, pp. 189–201.

Kruskal, C.P., and M. Snir, "The Performance of Multistage Interconnection Networks for Multiprocessors," *IEEE Trans. Computers*, Vol. C-32, No. 12, Dec. 1983, pp. 1091–1098.

LaRowe, R.P., Jr., and C.S. Ellis, "Experimental Comparison of Memory Management Policies for NUMA Multiprocessors," *ACM Trans. Computer Systems*, Vol. 9, No. 4, 1991, pp. 319–363.

Lilja, D.J., "Cache Coherence in Large-Scale Shared-Memory Multiprocessors: Issues and Comparisons," *ACM Computing Surveys*, Vol. 25, No. 3, 1993, pp. 303–338.

Mudge, T.N., J.P. Hayes, and D.C. Winsor, "Multiple Bus Architectures," *Computer*, Vol. 20, No. 6, June 1987, pp. 42–49.

Nanda, A.K., and L.N. Bhuyan, "Design and Analysis of Cache Coherent Multistage Interconnection Networks," *IEEE Trans. Computers*, Vol. 42, No. 4, Apr. 1993, pp. 458–470.

Pfister, G.F., et al., "The IBM Research Parallel Processor Prototype (RP3): Introduction and Architecture," *Proc. 1985 Int'l Conf. Parallel Processing*, IEEE CS Press, Los Alamitos, Calif., 1985, pp. 764–771.

Rettberg, R.D., et al., "The Monarch Parallel Processor Hardware Design," *Computer*, Vol. 23, No. 4, Apr. 1990, pp. 18–30.

Scott, S.L., and J.R. Goodman, "Pruning-Cache Directories for Large-Scale Multiprocessors," *IEEE Trans. Parallel and Distributed Systems*, Vol. 4, No. 5, May 1993, pp. 520–534.

Stenström, P., "A Survey of Cache Coherence Schemes for Multiprocessors," *Computer*, Vol. 23, No. 6, June 1990, pp. 12–24.

Thakkar, S., et al, "Scalable Shared-Memory Multiprocessor Architectures," *Computer*, Vol. 23, No. 6, June 1990, pp. 71–83.

Thomas, R.H., and W. Crowther, "The Uniform System: An Approach to Runtime Support for Large Scale Shared Memory Parallel Processors," *Proc. 1988 Int'l Conf. Parallel Processing, Vol. II: Software*, Penn State Press, University Park, Pa., 1988, pp. 245–254.

Vranesic, Z.G., et al. "Hector: A Hierarchically Structured Shared-Memory Multiprocessor," *Computer*, Vol. 24, No. 1, Jan. 1991, pp. 72–79.

Yang, Q., G. Thangadurai, and L.N. Bhuyan, "Design of an Adaptive Cache Coherence Protocol for Large-Scale Multiprocessors," *IEEE Trans. Parallel and Distributed Systems*, Vol. 3, No. 3, May 1992, pp. 281–293.

Zhang, X., "Performance Measurement and Modeling to Evaluate Various Effects on a Shared-Memory Multiprocessor," *IEEE Trans. Software Eng.*, Vol. 17, No. 1, Jan. 1991, pp. 87–93.

Zhang, X., and X. Qin, "Performance Prediction and Evaluation for a NUMA Multiprocessor," *IEEE Trans. Software Eng.*, Vol. 17, No. 10, Oct. 1991, pp. 1059–1068.

Zhang, X., R. Castañeda, and E.W. Chan, "Spin-Lock Synchronization on the Butterfly and KSR1," *IEEE Parallel & Distributed Technology*, Vol. 2, No. 1, Spring 1994, pp. 51–63.

Performance of Multiprocessor Interconnection Networks

Laxmi N. Bhuyan, University of Southwestern Louisiana

Qing Yang, University of Rhode Island

Dharma P. Agrawal, North Carolina State University

With device characteristics approaching physical limits, parallel or distributed processing has been widely advocated as a promising approach for building high performance computing systems. The continued impetus in research in these areas arises from two factors: (a) the technological development in the area of VLSI chips and (b) the observation that significant exploitable software parallelism is inherent in many scientific and engineering applications.

To exploit this parallelism efficiently, a parallel/distributed system must be designed to considerably reduce the communication overhead between the processors. The communication architecture of the system might support one application well but might prove inefficient for others.

Therefore, we need to take a general approach, independent of the application, while designing the communication system or the interconnection network (IN) of a general-purpose parallel/distributed system. The IN must be efficient, reliable, and cost effective. A complete interconnection, such as a crossbar, might be cost prohibitive, but a shared-bus interconnection might be inefficient and unreliable. Thus, present research is directed to designing INs whose cost and performance lie somewhere between the two extremes.

> **Multiprocessor designers need analytical techniques to evaluate network performance. This article presents a tutorial on these evaluation tools to guide designers through the design process.**

Ongoing research in the area of parallel and distributed processing suggests a number of promising INs. Because of the high cost involved in hardware implementation or software simulation of these INs, performance evaluation of these networks needs to be carried out through analytical techniques so that we can make a choice between various alternatives. A mathematical model makes it possible to study the efficiency of the IN in terms of various design parameters used as inputs to a model. Therefore, the intent of this article is to provide a tutorial on the subject of performance evaluation of multiprocessor interconnection networks to guide system designers in their design process.

A classification of parallel/distributed systems. We can divide general-purpose parallel/distributed computer systems into two categories: multiprocessors and multicomputers. The main difference between them lies in the level at which interactions between the processors occur.

A multiprocessor must permit all processors to directly share the main memory. All the processors address a common main memory space. In a multicomputer, however, each processor has its own memory space, and sharing between the processors occurs at a higher level as with a complete file or data set. A processor cannot directly access another processor's local memory.

Multiprocessors can be further divided as tightly coupled and loosely coupled. In a tightly coupled system, the main memory is situated at a central location so that the access time from any processor to the

Reprinted from *Computer*, Vol. 22, No. 2, Feb. 1989, pp. 25–37.

0-8186-6522-X/95 $4.00 © 1989 IEEE

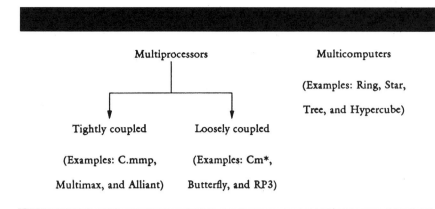

Figure 1. A classification of parallel/distributed systems.

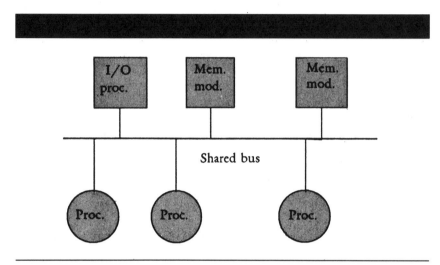

Figure 2. A single shared bus structure.

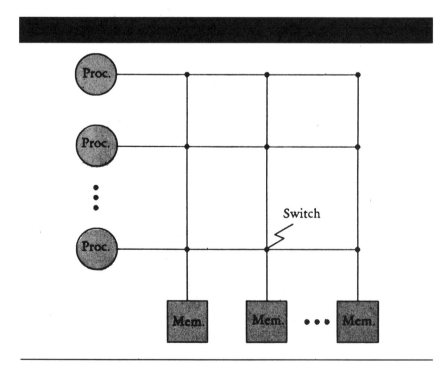

Figure 3. A crossbar interconnection network.

memory is the same. In addition to this central memory (also called main memory, shared memory, global memory, etc.), each processor might consist of some local memory or cache. The C.mmp of Carnegie Mellon University, the Multimax of Encore Computer, the FX of Alliant, and the Balance series of Sequent Corp. are examples of such tightly coupled multiprocessors.

In a loosely coupled system, the main memory is partitioned and attached to the processors, although the processors share the same memory address space. A processor can directly address a remote memory, but the access time is much higher compared to a local memory access. As a result, partitioning and allocation of program segments and data play a crucial role in the overall performance of an application program. The Cm* of CMU, the Butterfly machine of BBN Laboratories, and the RP3 of IBM are examples of such architectures.

As mentioned previously, the memory in a multicomputer is not shared. The interaction between the processors relies on message passing between the source and destination processors (nodes). The message passes over a link that directly connects two nodes and might have to pass through several such nodes in a store-and-forward manner before it reaches its destination. Therefore, each interaction involves a lot of communication overhead, and only those applications that need less interprocessor communication are well suited to multicomputers.

The multicomputers are usually based on topologies such as ring, tree, star, hypercube, etc. Hypercube machines such as Intel's iPSC are commercially available. Based on the description above, a classification of parallel/distributed computers appears in Figure 1. The classification does not include array and pipelined computers and local area networks. This is because array or pipelined computers are part of parallel processing but not distributed processing and, similarly, LANs are part of distributed processing but not parallel processing.

Essentially, our classification is valid for multiple instruction stream, multiple data stream computers. This article will concentrate solely on multiprocessor INs. A discussion of the performance of multicomputer interconnection networks can be found in Reed and Grunwald.[1]

Multiprocessor IN topologies. A multiprocessor organization is defined in terms of the IN used. The performance of a multiprocessor rests primarily on the design of its IN. A shared-bus interconnection, shown in Figure 2, is the least complex and most popular among manufacturers. The Multimax and Alliant are examples of such multiprocessors. The shared bus does not allow more than one transfer between the processors and memories at a time. A large number of processors means a long wait for the bus.

On the other hand, a crossbar, as used in C.mmp and depicted in Figure 3, supports all possible distinct connections between the processors and memories simultaneously. Unfortunately, the cost of such a network is $O(NM)$ for connecting N inputs and M outputs. For a system with hundreds of processors and memories, the cost of such an IN is prohibitively high.

In terms of cost and performance, multistage interconnection networks (MINs) and multiple-bus networks achieve a reasonable balance between those of a shared bus and crossbar. MINs and multiple-bus networks are depicted in Figures 4 and 5, respectively, and will be described in later sections. Then, we will investigate the performance of these networks. A shared bus is essentially a special type of multiple-bus IN with the number of buses equal to one.

Classification of INs

An IN is a complex connection of switches and links that permits data communication between the processors and memories. Depending on the timing philosophy, switching mode, and control strategy, each set of topologically equivalent networks can have different operational characteristics giving rise to different system behaviors. These operational characteristics also necessitate different methodologies to be used in IN performance evaluation.

Timing philosophy. Timing philosophy is one of the most important attributes characterizing a communication system. Basically, there are two types of possible timing schemes in a system: synchronous and asynchronous.

Synchronous control techniques are well understood and widely used in computer system designs. They are characterized by the existence of a central, global clock that broadcasts clock signals to all devices in a system so that the entire system operates in a lock-step fashion.

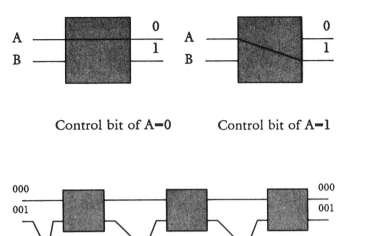

(a)

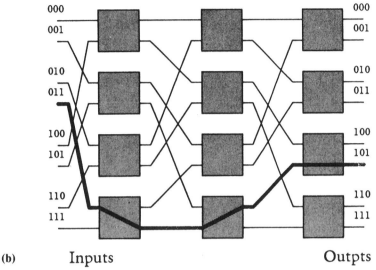

(b)

Figure 4. Operation of a 2×2 switch in 4a, and an 8×8 omega network in 4b.

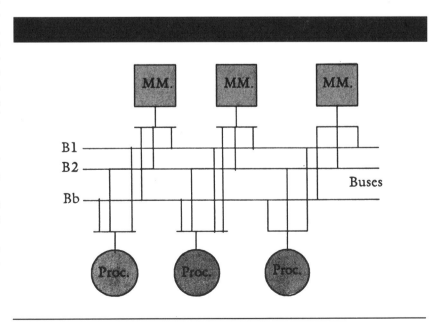

Figure 5. A multiple-bus multiprocessor system.

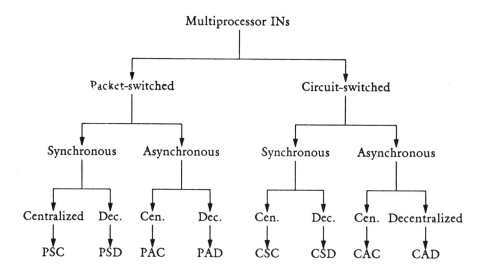

Figure 6. A classification of multiprocessor interconnection networks.

Asynchronous techniques, on the other hand, operate without a global clock. The communications among operational units in the system are performed by means of interlock hand shaking. As a result, they have good expandability and modularity, but are difficult to design.

Switching methodology. There are basically two major switching methodologies: packet switching and circuit switching. In packet switching, a message is broken into small packets transmitted through the network in a "store-and-forward" mode. Thus, a packet experiences a random delay at each switching point, depending on the traffic in the network along its path to the destination.

Conversely, circuit switching actually establishes a physical path between a source and a destination. A time delay is needed when the path is being established. Once the path is completed, it is held for the entire data transmission. In general, circuit switching is much more suitable for long messages, and packet switching is more efficient for short messages.

Control strategy. Control strategy mainly concerns the way control signals direct the dataflow generated in a network. In a centralized control scheme, all the control signals come from a single source. Obviously, the central controller creates a system bottleneck and directly affects the performance and reliability of the entire system. The design of this central con-

troller must be very complex to retain good system performance. These drawbacks can be avoided through the use of distributed control strategies in which a small controller is associated with each component of the system. In multiprocessor applications, control of crossbar networks is usually centralized and control of MINs is usually decentralized. Multiple-bus IN control can be either centralized or decentralized.

Based on the operational characteristics above, INs can be classified into eight different categories for a given topology. The detailed classification scheme is shown in Figure 6. For example, PSC means a packet-switched, synchronous, centrally controlled IN. Together with the topology, these three operational characteristics define an IN. We will examine the performance models of the INs based on this classification scheme.

Basic terminologies for performance evaluation

Before we describe performance analyses of different INs, we need to define several terms. Many performance parameters are applicable for INs. Memory *bandwidth* (BW) is the most common performance parameter used in analyzing a synchronous IN in a multiprocessor. It is defined as the mean number of active memory modules in a transfer cycle of the IN. In this case, the term "active" means a processor is successfully performing

memory operation (either read or write) in that memory module. BW also takes into account the memory access conflicts caused by the random nature of the processors' requests.

Another parameter often used in synchronous analysis, *probability of acceptance* (P_A), is defined as the ratio of expected bandwidth to the expected number of requests generated per cycle.

In asynchronous operation, the *throughput* (Thr) of a network is defined as the average number of packets delivered by the network in unit time. In a multiprocessor IN, throughput is the mean number of memory access completions per unit time.

Processor utilization (P_u) is also used as a performance measure and is defined as the expected value of the percentage of time a processor is active. A processor is said to be active when it is doing internal computation without accessing the global memory. Processing power is a simple extension of P_u, which is the sum of processor utilizations over the number of processors.

Other performance parameters can be easily related to the parameters above by applying Little's Law.[2] Moreover, P_u, BW, and Thr can also be related as

$$P_u = \frac{BW}{N\lambda T}$$

$$P_u = \frac{Thr}{\lambda}$$

where N is the number of processors, T is the time taken for a memory read or write operation, and λ is the memory request rate.

Analytical modeling is a cost effective technique used to study the performance of a computer system. However, any real system is too complex to be modeled exactly.

To make an analytical model tractable, certain approximation assumptions are necessary. Most of the IN analyses assume identical processors and a *uniform reference model*. The URM implies that, when a processor makes a memory request to the global memory, the request will be directed to any one of M memory modules with the same probability $1/M$. That is, the destination address of a memory request is uniformly distributed among M memory modules. This assumption provides us with the symmetric property, significantly simplifying the modeling.

If the memory system is M-way interleaved, this assumption also represents the program behavior reasonably accurately. When the main memory is not interleaved, there is a locality of reference and a favorite memory assumption[3] is more accurate.

The *request rate* of a processor identifies how often a processor accesses global memory. This indirectly reflects the average execution time of an instruction.

In synchronous systems, the request rate can be specified by a probability that a processor generates a memory request at the beginning of a cycle. In asynchronous systems, on the other hand, a memory request could be generated at any instant in time since there is no global clock. However, an exponential thinking time for a processor is commonly assumed, which means that the duration between the completion of a request and generation of the next request to the global memory is an exponentially distributed random variable.

The *request independence assumption* (also called Strecker's approximation[4]) in a synchronous system analysis states that a memory request generated in a cycle is independent of the requests of the previous cycles. In reality, this is not true because a request that was rejected in the previous cycle will be resubmitted in the current cycle. However, as we shall see, this assumption simplifies the analysis to a great extent while keeping the results reasonably accurate.

Performance of crossbar interconnection networks

A crossbar interconnection network is an array of individually operated contact pairs in which there is one pair for each input-output combination, as shown in Figure 3. A crossbar network with N inputs and M outputs is referred to as an $N \times M$ crossbar. As long as there is no memory interference among a set of memory requests generated by the processors (that is, no two or more processors request the same memory module), all connections can be established at the same time. Thus, all memory accesses can proceed simultaneously.

But this capability comes at a high switching cost, which is $(O(NM))$. Although the crossbar network can provide all simultaneous connections, memory bandwidth is much less than its actual capacity. This reduction is due to the memory interference caused by the random nature of the memory requests in a multiprocessor environment. Therefore, the performance analysis of a crossbar network becomes the analysis of memory interference.

The literature[5] contains a number of memory interference models for centralized, synchronous, and circuit-switched crossbar systems. In most of these models, system operations are approximated by stochastic processes as follows: At the beginning of the system cycle, a processor selects a memory module at random and makes a request to access that module with some probability p. If more than one request is made to the same memory module, the memory controller will choose one at random, and the rejected processors will retry in the next cycle. The behavior of the processors is considered independent and statistically identical, as is the behavior of the memory modules.

Bhandarkar[4] studied the memory interference problem in detail in which several discrete Markov chain models were developed. In these models, a memory module is characterized by its cycle time t_c, which consists of an access time t_a, followed by a rewrite time t_w. Processor behavior is modeled as an ordered sequence, consisting of a memory request followed by a certain amount of execution time t_p. The processing time t_p is measured from the time data were obtained from the previous request to the time the next request is issued to the memory.

In real systems, the processor can start execution when the memory is in its rewrite cycle. So, when $t_w = t_p$, the situation would be equivalent to the case where the processor generates a memory request at the beginning of each memory cycle. In this study, an exact model for the case $t_p = t_w$ and with URM was presented. However, the model becomes very unwieldy for a large number of processors and memory modules.

The complexity of the memory interference model is simplified if one assumes that a blocked processor discards the request and generates a new independent request at the start of the next cycle (request independence assumption). For a system with N processors and M memory modules, if a processor generates a request with probability p in a cycle directed to each memory with equal probability (URM), then the memory bandwidth is given by Strecker[4] as

$$BW = M\left(1 - \left(1 - \frac{p}{M}\right)^N\right) \qquad (1)$$

A simple explanation of this formula is as follows: Since p/M is the probability that a processor requests a particular memory module, $[1 - (p/M)]^N$ is the probability that none of the N processors requests the memory module in a particular cycle. Subtracting this term from 1 gives the probability that at least one request to this memory is issued. Multiplying by M yields the expected number of distinct memory modules being requested in a cycle and hence the bandwidth. The maximum percentage of error with this approximation is limited to 8 percent for $M/N > 0.75$.[4] As a result, this simple formula, Equation 1, is widely used for predicting the performance of crossbar networks. The accuracy can be further increased by a "rate adjustment" technique[6] where the input request rate is adjusted upward to take into account the resubmission of rejected requests. Yen[6] provides a comparison of various memory interference models for synchronous crossbars.

The model described above assumes a URM. However, as mentioned previously, the distribution of memory requests in real systems depends on program behavior, and such distributions are not necessarily uniform. Bhuyan[3] has examined this nonuniform reference problem by introducing the concept of favorite memory of a processor. The memory module requested most often by a processor is

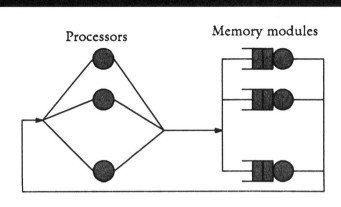

Figure 7. A queueing model for asynchronous crossbar multiprocessors.

called the favorite memory of the processor. Let m represent the probability with which a processor addresses its favorite memory given that the processor generates a request in a cycle. Then, the memory bandwidth for an $N \times N$ crossbar-based multiprocessor is given by

$$BW = N[1-(1-pm)(1-p\frac{1-m}{N-1})^{N-1}] \quad (2)$$

Solutions for favorite memory cases are also provided for $M \leq N$ and $M \geq N$.[7] By substituting $m = 1/M$, the analysis reduces to that of URM (Equation 1).

In the descriptions above, we have considered only circuit-switched and synchronous systems. The analysis of asynchronous circuit-switched systems can be done by assuming a random period of processor thinking time and memory access time. The processors are then modeled by a set of delay servers and memory modules by a set of first-come, first-serve (FCFS) queues, as shown in Figure 7. This figure depicts a well-known closed queueing network in performance evalu-ation, and efficient algorithms to solve this network exist.[2]

Because the crossbar network is a single-staged network (that is, every input and output is connected by a single switching element), packet switching makes no difference from circuit switching from a performance point of view. Similarly, two control strategies result in the same system behavior. Thus, we need not consider them separately. Table 1 summarizes the different analytical techniques of the crossbar system and their accuracy, work-load representations, performance metrics, and computational costs.

Analyses of multistage interconnection networks

As stated previously, the cost of a crossbar network is too high to be practical for building large multiprocessor systems. As an alternative to the crossbar network, multistage interconnection networks (MINs) have assumed importance in recent times. The main advantage of these networks is their cost-effectiveness. They allow a rich subset of one to one and simultaneous mappings of processors to memory modules, while reducing the hardware cost to $O(N\log N)$ in contrast to $O(N^2)$ for crossbar networks.

An $N \times N$ MIN connects N processors to N memories. For N a power of two, it employs $\log_2 N$ stages of 2×2 switches with $N/2$ switches per stage. Each switch has two inputs and two outputs. The connection between an input and an output is established depending on a control bit c provided by the input. When $c = 0$, the input is connected to the upper output, and when $c = 1$, it is connected to the lower output, as shown in Figure 4a.

An omega network[5,8], shown in Figure 4b, is characterized by a perfect shuffle interconnection preceding every stage of switches. The requesting processor generates a tag that is the binary representation of the destination. The connection of a switch at the ith stage is then accomplished by the ith bit of this binary tag counted from the most significant bit.

The connection between input 3 and output 5 (101_2) is shown by a bold line in Figure 4b. This self-routing property of a MIN avoids the need for a central controller, making it very suitable for multiprocessors. Thus, the performance discussions presented in this section will concentrate solely on the decentralized control scheme.

Many significant MINs, such as Banyan, generalized cube, base line, etc.,[8] have been proposed. However, most of these networks are similar except for the interconnection between the adjacent stages.

The switch size in an MIN need not be restricted to 2×2. In fact, the Butterfly parallel processor connects N inputs to N

Table 1. Summary of crossbar analyses.

	Synchronous crossbar		Asynchronous crossbar
Analysis technique	Discrete Marcov chain[4]	Probabilistic with independence assumption[3,4]	Queueing network[2]
Workload representation	Request rate	Probability of request	Think time
Performance parameters	BW or P_A	BW or P_A	P_u or P_W
Accuracy	Exact	Good	Exact
Computational cost	Very high	Low (closed form formula)	Moderate

outputs using 4×4 crossbar switches and $\log_4 N$ stages with $N/4$ switches per stage. A delta network can connect $M = a^n$ inputs to $N = b^n$ outputs through n stages of $a \times b$ crossbar switches.[9] The generalized shuffle network (GSN) is capable of connecting any $M = m_1 * m_2 * \ldots * m_r$ inputs to $N = n_1 * n_2 * \ldots * n_r$ outputs through r stages of switches.[7] The ith stage employs $m_i \times n_i$ crossbar switches and is preceded by a generalized shuffle interconnection that is essentially a superset of the omega and delta interconnections. This is the most generalized version of an MIN that allows different input and output sizes, and all the other networks can be obtained by choosing the m_is and n_is, appropriately. For example, when $m_i = a$, $n_i = b$ for all is, it is a delta network; $m_i = n_i = 2$ for all is gives an omega network; $r = 1$ gives a crossbar; and $M = M * 1$ and $N = 1 * N$ provides a shared-bus connection.

The advantages of MINs were widely recognized by researchers, and a lot of research projects started at universities and industries. Examples of university projects include TRAC (the Texas Reconfigurable Array Computer) at the University of Texas at Austin, Pasm (partitionable single instruction, multiple data [SIMD], multiple instruction, multiple data [MIMD]) at Purdue University, Ultra-Computer at New York University, and Cedar at the University of Illinois at Urbana-Champaign. RP3 is a notable industry project at IBM, and Butterfly is a successfully marketed product by BBN Laboratories.

As these projects were starting, a serious drawback of the MINs surfaced. There is only one path from an input to an output. It was necessary to incorporate some fault-tolerance into these networks so that at least a single fault in a switch or a link could be tolerated. This has given rise to an abundance of research during the past few years devoted to the design and evaluation of fault-tolerant MINs. Adams[10] contains a survey and comparison of such fault-tolerant networks. The evaluation techniques for basic MINs are explained below, but can be extended to fault-tolerant MINs.

Patel[9] suggested a probabilistic approach to analyze the delta network based on URM and the request independence assumption. Assume a delta network of size $a^n \times b^n$ constructed from $a \times b$ crossbar modules. Each stage of the delta network is controlled by a distinct destination digit (in base b) for setting of

individual $a \times b$ switches. Since the destinations are independent and uniformly distributed, the requests at any $a \times b$ modules are independent and uniformly distributed over b different destinations. In addition, the switches at a particular stage behave similarly. Therefore, Equation 1 can be applied to any switching element in the delta network.

The expected number of requests that pass to the b outputs is obtained by setting $N = a$ and $M = b$ in Equation 1. Dividing this number by b gives us the probability of request on any of the b output lines of an $a \times b$ switch as a function of its input probability. Since the output of a stage is the input of the next stage, one can recursively evaluate the output probability of any stage starting at stage 1. If p_i is the probability that there is a request at the output of a switch at stage i, then

$$p_i = 1 - (1 - \frac{P_{i-1}}{b})^a \qquad (3)$$

for $1 \leq i \leq n$. In particular, the output probability of the final stage determines the bandwidth of a delta network, that is, $BW = p_n b^n$. This analytical technique has been widely used to evaluate various MINs.

Bhuyan[3] extended the analysis to favorite-memory cases. For $N \times N$ networks, with $N = a^n$, the processors are defined to be connected to their favorite memories when all the switches are straight connected, that is, input i of a switch is connected to the output i of the switch. In an omega network memory, MM_j becomes the favorite memory of processor P_j. Let q_{i-1} be the probability that there is a favorite request to the input at stage i. In an $N \times N$ ($N = a^n$) delta network,

$$p_i = 1 - (1 - p_{i-1} q_{i-1})(1 - p_{i-1} \frac{1 - q_{i-1}}{a - 1}) \qquad (4)$$

About six other equations are needed to determine q_{i-1} at stage i[3] and, finally, $BW = Np_n$. The analyses above[3,9] are valid for synchronous packet-switched MINs provided that (a) packets are generated only at the beginning of the network cycle and (b) switches do not have buffers (are unbuffered) so that packets are randomly chosen in case of conflicts and unsuccessful packets are lost.

The above analyses presented a recurrence relation for the performance of unbuffered networks, but not a closed-form solution. Kruskal and Snir[11] obtained an asymptotic expression for the output request probability of a stage for an

unbuffered delta network. Let p_m denote the probability that there is a packet on any particular input at the mth stage of a square MIN composed of $k \times k$ switches. Through some algebraic manipulations, Kruskal and Snir[11] approximated the asymptotic formula for p_m as

$$p_m = \frac{2k}{(k-1)m + \frac{2k}{p}} \qquad (5)$$

where p is the probability of request generation by a processor. From this expression, one can see that the probability that a message is not deleted is inversely proportional to the number of stages in the network. The solution for an unbuffered network by Kruskal and Snir has been shown to be a strict upper bound in the throughput of a delta network. For buffered networks, Kruskal and Snir assume an infinite buffer associated with each output of a switching element. In each cycle, a random number of packets join an output queue without any packet being lost. This random number has a Bernoulli distribution, since all incoming packets from the inputs of the switch have an equal probability (for URM) of going to that output. The average transit time through the network can be derived by means of the $M/G/1$ queueing formula.[11]

Dias and Jump[12] have studied buffered delta networks by means of petri nets, which were introduced first as a useful graphical tool for the precise description of the system operations and as a modeling technique that permits easy evaluation of the performance of small systems.

These graph models have recently become very popular for the representation of distributed computing systems because of their ability to clearly describe concurrency, conflicts, and synchronization of tasks. However, the complexity of petri nets increases exponentially with the increase in system size. With this modeling technique, 14 distinguishable states of a (2×2) switch exist with a single buffer between stages.[12] The state transition tables and the probabilities in each state are derived. The steady state throughput and turnaround time (network delay) are obtained by iterating through use of the transition tables and probability equations. The results of analysis and simulation indicate that buffering produces a considerable improvement in the performance of these networks.

All the analyses above pertain to synchronous circuit-switched or packet-switched environments. For large MINs,

Table 2. Summary of MINs analyses.

	Synchronous MIN without buffer	Synchronous MIN with infinite buffers	Synchronous MIN with finite buffers	Asynchronous MIN with finite buffers
Analysis technique	Probabilistic with independence assumption[3,9]	$M/G/1$ queue with infinite buffers[11]	Petri net[12]	Multiple chain MVA[5]
Workload representation	Request rate	Request rate	Processor think time	Processor think time
Performance parameters	BW or P_A	Queueing delay or transit time	Throughput or turn-around time	Throughput or response time
Accuracy	Good	Fair	Good	Good
Computation cost	Low for recurrence solutions	Closed form formula	High	Moderate

controlling the network operation from a central global clock is difficult. Hence, asynchronous designs should be considered for large multiprocessor systems.

The second disadvantage with the above analyses is that they do not incorporate the waiting time of a processor for completion of the memory access, but assume continuous Poisson arrival at the input side.

The third disadvantage is the assumption of uniform or favorite memory access. Memory reference patterns are highly program dependent and could be arbitrary.

To overcome these drawbacks, we have recently developed[5] a closed queueing network model and mean value analysis (MVA)[2] for the MINs under asynchronous packet-switched operation. Modeling asynchronous circuit-switched MINs seems very difficult because of the simultaneous possession of switches and links by unsuccessful requests. Table 2 lists the different analyses of MINs described in this section.

Performance analyses of multiple-bus systems

Most commercial systems containing more than one processor employ a single shared bus as shown in Figure 2. This interconnection scheme is well known as being inexpensive and easy to implement. But when the system size is large, a single bus becomes a severe system bottleneck.

A natural extension is to employ several buses instead of a single one to increase the bandwidth and fault tolerance at moderate cost. Recently, the multiple-bus interconnection scheme has drawn considerable attention from many computer scientists and engineers. In an $N \times M \times B$ multiple-bus multiprocessor system, all the N processors and M memory modules are connected to all the B buses.

Unlike a crossbar or multistage network, the multiple-bus configuration offers high reliability, availability, and easy incremental system growth. Higher reliability is obvious because, in case of a bus failure, $(B-1)$ distinct paths still exist between a processor and a memory. However, when the number of buses is less than the number of memory modules or the number of processors, bus contention can arise. As a result, the performance analysis of a multiple-bus system involves modeling the effects of bus conflicts and memory interference.

Many researchers have studied the performance of synchronous, circuit-switched, and centrally controlled multiple-bus multiprocessor systems through analysis and simulation.[5,13] The memory bandwidth of the system increases with an increase in the number of buses. But, for all practical purposes, a few buses might be sufficient.

In a synchronous system, all the events occur at the beginning of a system cycle. Therefore, the system can be modeled by means of a discrete Markov process. Bhuyan has developed a combinatorial and probabilistic approach to derive an equation for the BW of such multiple-bus multiprocessor systems.[5,13] His analysis is based on the URM and request independence assumptions.

With these assumptions in mind for a given set of memory requests, knowing the number of ways in which the requests are distributed among the memory modules is easy. In addition, one can determine the number of ways by which the given requests are addressed to M memory modules such that x memory modules are requested and $M - x$ of them are idle.

For each value of x, Bhuyan defines a state. The BW can be computed by multiplying the probability of being in a state with the number of busy memory modules in that state. If the number of buses in a system is less than the number of memory modules, the number of busy memory modules in a cycle would be upper bounded by the number of buses. The bandwidth for an $N \times M \times B$ system is given by

$$
\begin{aligned}
BW = M &\left\{ 1 - \left(1 - \frac{p}{M}\right)^N \right\} \\
&- \sum_{y=B+1}^{N} \binom{N}{y} p^y (1-p)^{N-y} \quad (6) \\
&\times \sum_{x=B+1}^{t_y} \frac{(x-B)x! \binom{M}{x} S(y,x)}{M^y}
\end{aligned}
$$

where, $x!$ is the factorial x, $t_y = min(y,M)$, p is the probability of request of a processor, $\binom{N}{y}$ is the binomial coefficient, and $S(y,x)$ is the Stirling number of the second kind defined as

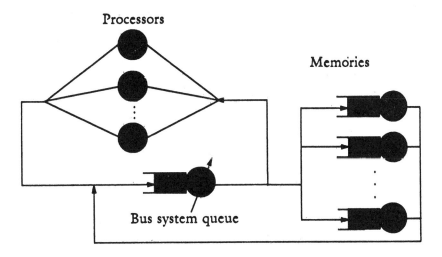

Figure 8. A queueing network model for asynchronous multiple-bus systems.

$$x! \; S(y,x) \; = \; \sum_{i=0}^{x} (-1)^i \binom{x}{i} (x-i)^y$$

The numerical results obtained from this equation are quite close to simulation results. Mudge[13] contains a detailed review and comparison of various analyses on synchronous circuit-switched multiple-bus systems.

In asynchronous systems, memory request generation and memory access completion can occur at any point in time since there is no synchronization by a clock. Therefore, the system can be modeled with a continuous stochastic process. Each shared resource, such as a bus or a memory module, is considered a queueing service center.

Because of circuit switching, the processor that issues a memory request holds a system bus while accessing the main memory. Thus, two system resources, bus and memory, are simultaneously held by a memory operation. This simultaneous resource possession phenomenon makes the analysis nontrivial.

One study[14] uses the *flow equivalence* technique to approximately solve the queueing network. The bus and memory subsystem, called aggregate, is replaced by a single flow equivalent service center (FESC).[2] The model has been compared with simulation results, and the agreement is quite good over a wide range of bus load.[14]

All the studies above consider only centrally controlled, circuit-switched

multiple-bus systems. In circuit switching, a device will occupy the bus for the entire duration of data communication once the device is granted use of a bus.

For instance, a processor in a read operation will occupy the bus during the time it is sending a request, performing a memory operation, and receiving the requested data. The result will be the waste of a significant fraction of bus bandwidth because of a mismatch between the speeds of the processing unit, the bus, and the memory unit.

All these facts serve to demonstrate the attractiveness of the packet-switching approach. Encore's Multimax is an example of a multiprocessor employing a packet-switched shared bus between processors and memories.

Yang studied[15] packet-switched multiple-bus systems where analytical models were developed for both synchronous and asynchronous timings. In the synchronous case, both centralized and decentralized controlled schemes are treated equally, since all the events in the system occur at the beginning of a cycle regardless of the control strategies used. A discrete probabilistic approach is applied to analyze such systems.

The model has been based on a decomposition technique that considers simple analysis of a set of single-server queues. The consequence of the analysis is an equation consisting of one unknown variable, P_u, processor utilization; it can be solved by using a standard numerical method.

For an asynchronous case, the queueing

network is shown in Figure 8. Processors in the system are modeled as delay servers, and memory modules are modeled as FCFS servers. The bus system is modeled as an FESC[2] representing B buses with a single (centralized) queue.

The routing of a packet in the network can be described as follows: A request packet generated by a processor is first put in the central server queue, waiting for an available bus. After it gains access to a bus, the packet joins one of the M memory queues. The memory module that finishes the service of a request again puts the response packet in the central server queue. From there, the response packet gets back to the requesting processor through a bus. To this point, the packet finishes one rotation through the network, and the processor resumes its background activity. The model can be solved using any standard product-form algorithm, considering the bus system queue as a load-dependent server.[2]

In the case of a decentralized control, the actual implementation can be either token bus or daisy chain bus. Due to the lack of central controller, the analysis of decentralized packet-switching multiple-bus systems is very complicated. The FCFS service discipline is not valid for bus system queue in this case. The service discipline depends on the position of tokens with respect to the positions of requesting devices.

The exact solution for such a system seems infeasible, but one method for approximating the behavior of the system is to use hierarchical modeling tech-

Table 3. Summary of multiple-bus analyses.

	Circuit-switched synchronous	Circuit-switched asynchronous	Packet-switched synchronous	Packet-switched asynchronous
Analysis technique	Probabilistic with independence assumption[5,13]	Queue network with infinite buffers[14]	Probabilistic queueing analysis[15]	Queueing network with FESC[15]
Workload representation	Request rate	Processor think time	Request rate	Processor think time
Performance parameters	BW or P_A	Throughput or P_u	P_u	Throughput or P_u
Accuracy	Fair	Good	Good	Fair
Computation cost	Low	Moderate	Low, but iteration	Moderate

Table 4. Summary of hardware features of the three INs.

	Crossbar	MINs	Multiple-bus
No. switches or connections	$N*M$	$N\log N$	$B*(N+M)$
Load of buses	N	1	B
No. of wires	M	N	B
Arbiter	M 1-of-N arbiters	$N\log N$ 1-of-2 arbiters	1 B-of-M and M 1-of-N arbiters
Fault-tolerant and expansion	Fair	Poor, but fair with additional hardware	Good

niques.[15] As in the previous case, the bus system is represented by FESC (Figure 8) with the service rate obtained by shorting out the processors and the memory modules. The model is then solved by using the mean value analysis algorithm.[2]

Numerical results obtained from the models have shown that packet switching reduces the communication bottleneck of shared bus systems.[15] Table 3 summarizes analyses of different categories of multiple-bus systems.

Comparison and discussions

As indicated in the previous sections, the three types of interconnection networks possess different hardware features and different system performances. In this section, we will look into these differences

quantitatively. In particular, we will compare the hardware cost and system performance of the three interconnection networks.

Table 4 lists selective hardware features of the three networks. As we already know, the number of switching elements used in an $N \times M$ crossbar is $N \times M$ in contrast to $N\log N$ of MINs. The number of connections necessary in an $N \times M \times B$ multiple-bus system is proportional to $B(N + M)$. Since each bus in the multiple-bus system needs to drive $N + M$ modules, the bus load is proportional to $N + M$, while the bus load of an MIN is one due to the one-to-one connection.

All three of these networks require certain types of arbiters to resolve the request conflicts. In a crossbar network, M N-users 1-server arbiters are necessary, each of which selects one of up to N outstanding requests for a memory during a mem-

ory cycle. The MINs, on the other hand, require two 2-user 1-server arbiters for each switching element for $(N/2)\log_2 N$ switches.

In a multiple-bus system, an M-users B-servers arbiter is needed to assign the B buses to the outstanding requests. Once a bus is granted to a memory, only one of the processors that requests the memory can proceed while the others, if any, are delayed. This choice is implemented by an N-users 1-server arbiter. Thus, a multiple-bus system requires $M + 1$ arbiters, one arbiter of the M-users B-servers type and M arbiters of the N-users 1-server type.

Expandability and reliability are two other very important hardware features. In this context, a multiple-bus system shows its advantages over the other two because of its reconfigurability and multiple-data paths between every processor and memory. It can still operate in a

Prob. of Acceptance (P_A)

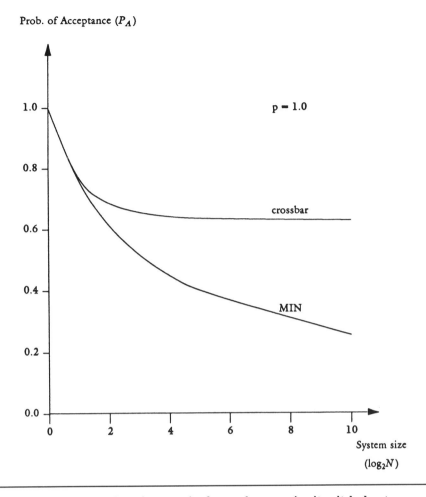

Figure 9. Probability of acceptance as a function of system size for synchronous circuit-switched systems.

degraded mode after the failure of a subset of the buses.

A lot of research has gone into the reconfigurable and fault-tolerant MINs.[10] The fault-tolerance of a MIN can be realized by adding additional hardware such as extra stages or duplicated data paths. It is easier to reconfigure a crossbar than an MIN. In case of a fault, a particular row or a column in Figure 3 can be removed and the network can operate in a degraded mode.

Next, we'll consider the performance of the three interconnection networks based on the analytical models described in the previous sections. Figure 9 shows the probability of a memory request being accepted, $P_A = BW/p \cdot N$, as a function of system size for synchronous circuit-switched systems with $p = 1.0$.

Two curves, one for crossbar and one for MIN, are plotted according to Equation 1 and Equation 3, respectively. The difference between the two curves increases as the system size grows. The probability of acceptance in the crossbar system remains constant when the system size becomes very large. However, in the case of MIN, P_A keeps decreasing as the system size increases.

Figure 10 shows the memory bandwidth of 16×16 synchronous circuit-switched multiprocessor systems. The horizontal axis represents a processor's probability of request. As we can see, the single bus performs worse since it gets saturated very quickly and the BW can never exceed 1. The BW increases as the number of buses increases, as shown in the figure.

Figure 11 shows the comparison of synchronous packet-switched networks. In this figure, processor utilizations are plotted against the probability of request for a 16×16 multiprocessor. Processor cycle times, bus transfer delay, as well as the total ideal packet transfer time between an input and an output of an MIN are assumed to be fixed at the system cycle time. The memory access time is assumed to take four system cycles (similar to Encore's Multimax) for all three systems. During a memory access, the processor that issued the memory request remains idle until the memory access is finished.

The memory request rate of a processor as seen by an interconnection network is adjusted[6] in plotting the processor utilization in Figure 11. The performance difference between various networks is not as pronounced as in Figure 10. This is due to the packet-switched operation of the INs. Additionally, a multiple-bus-based multiprocessor system with only four buses can achieve almost the same performance as that of the crossbar system while reducing the hardware cost significantly.

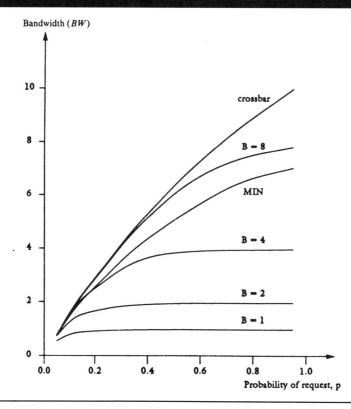

Figure 10. Memory bandwidth as a function of probability of request for 16 × 16 synchronous circuit-switched systems.

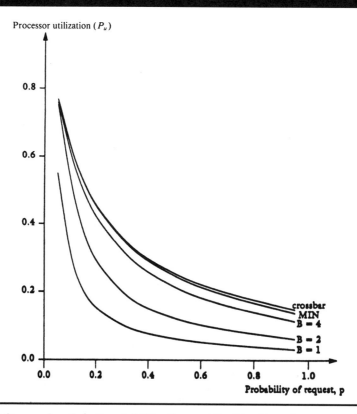

Figure 11. Processor utilization as a function of probability of request for 16 × 16 synchronous packet-switched systems.

All the comparisons above apply to synchronous systems based on system cycle. We have intentionally avoided comparing asynchronous systems because their performance is so dependent on the input parameters that choosing the wrong parameters might give rise to the wrong conclusions. However, the analytical techniques that can be applied to evaluate those systems are given in this article. The information provided here is useful for predicting the approximate performance of an IN structure before its design and implementation. Further references and a more detailed survey on the performance evaluation of multiprocessor INs can be found in Bhuyan.[5]

It seems that enough research has already been done in evaluating INs in isolation. We strongly feel that more work is needed at the system level that includes the IN as a major component. For example, evaluation of multiprocessor systems with prefetching, bulk data read or write, and solving cache coherence with INs shows promise for future research.

Similarly, task (application) level modeling on multiprocessor architectures might produce some good insight into the trade-offs between computation versus communication, low versus large granularity, static versus dynamic scheduling, etc.

Finally, some actual measurements (traces) should be obtained on real multiprocessors and applied to the analytical models as their input parameters. □

Acknowledgments

Bhuyan's research was supported by National Science Foundation grant No. MIP-8807761 and by a grant from the Louisiana Board of Regents. Agrawal's research was partly supported by US Army Research Office contract No. DAAG 29-85-K-0236.

References

1. D.A. Reed and D.C. Grunwald, "The Performance of Multicomputer Interconnection Networks," *Computer,* Vol. 20, No. 6, June 1987, pp. 63-73.
2. E.D. Lazowska et al., *Quantitative System Performance—Computer System Analysis Using Queueing Network Models,* Prentice Hall, Englewood Cliffs, N.J., 1984.
3. L.N. Bhuyan, "An Analysis of Processor-Memory Interconnection Networks," *IEEE Trans. Computers,* Vol. C-34, No. 3, Mar. 1985, pp. 279-283.
4. D.P. Bhandarkar, "Analysis of Memory Interference in Multiprocessors," *IEEE Trans. Computers,* Vol. C-24, Sept. 1975, pp. 897-908.
5. L.N. Bhuyan, "Performance Evaluation of Multiprocessor Interconnection Networks," *Tutorial Note,* ACM SIGMetrics Conf., May 1988.
6. D.W. Yen, J.H. Patel, and E.S. Davidson, "Memory Interference in Synchronous Multiprocessor Systems," *IEEE Trans. Computers,* Vol. C-31, Nov. 1982, pp. 1,116-1,121.
7. L.N. Bhuyan and D.P. Agrawal, "Design and Performance of Generalized Interconnection Networks," *IEEE Trans. Computers,* Vol. C-32, Dec. 1983, pp. 1,081-1,090.
8. Tse-Yun Feng, "A Survey of Interconnection Networks," *Computer,* Vol. 14, No. 12, Dec. 1981, pp. 12-27.
9. J.H. Patel, "Performance of Processor-Memory Interconnections for Multiprocessors," *IEEE Trans. Computers,* Vol. C-30, Oct. 1981, pp. 771-780.
10. G.B. Adams III, D.P. Agrawal, and H.J. Siegel, "A Survey and Comparison of Fault-Tolerant Multistage Interconnection Networks," *Computer,* Vol. 20, No. 6, June 1987, pp. 14-27.
11. C.P. Kruskal and M. Snir, "The Performance of Multistage Interconnection Networks for Multiprocessors," *IEEE Trans. Computers,* Vol. C-32, Dec. 1983, pp. 1,091-1,098.
12. D.M. Dias and J.R. Jump, "Analysis and Simulation of Buffered Delta Networks," *IEEE Trans. Computers,* Vol. C-30, Apr. 1981, pp. 273-282.
13. T.N. Mudge et al., "Analysis of Multiple-Bus Interconnection Networks," *J. Parallel and Distributed Computing,* Vol. 3, No. 3, Sept. 1986, pp. 328-343.
14. D. Towsley, "Approximate Models of Multiple Bus Multiprocessor Systems," *IEEE Trans. Computers,* Vol. C-35, Mar. 1986, pp. 220-228.
15. Q. Yang, L.N. Bhuyan, and R. Pavaskar, "Performance Analysis of Packet-Switched Multiple-Bus Multiprocessor Systems," *Proc. 8th Real-Time System Symp.,* Dec. 1987, CS Press, Los Alamitos, Calif., pp. 170-178.

Laxmi N. Bhuyan is an associate professor at the Center for Advanced Computer Studies at the University of Southwestern Louisiana in Lafayette. His research interests include parallel and distributed computer architecture, performance and reliability evaluation, and local area networks.

Bhuyan received BS and MS degrees in electrical engineering from the Regional Engineering College, Rourkela under Sambalpur University in India. He received a PhD in computer engineering from Wayne State University in Detroit in 1982. Bhuyan is a senior member of the IEEE, a distinguished visitor of the IEEE Computer Society, and served as guest editor of the *Computer* issue on interconnection networks in June 1987.

Qing Yang is an assistant professor in the Department of Electrical Engineering at the University of Rhode Island. His research interests include parallel and distributed computer systems, design of digital systems, performance evaluation, and local area networks.

Yang received a BSc degree in computer science from Huazhong University of Science and Technology in China in 1982 and an MASc in electrical engineering from the University of Toronto in 1985. He received a PhD in computer engineering from the Center for Advanced Computer Studies, University of Southwestern Louisiana. Yang is a member of the IEEE Computer Society.

Dharma P. Agrawal is a professor of electrical and computer engineering at North Carolina State University in Raleigh. He is the group leader for the B_Hive multicomputer project at NCSU. His research interests include both software and hardware aspects of parallel and distributed processing, computer architecture, and fault tolerant computing.

Agrawal received the BE degree from Ravishankar University in India, the ME degree from the University of Roorkee in India, and the DScTech degree in 1975 from the Federal Institute of Technology in Switzerland. He is the author of the tutorial text *Advanced Computer Architecture* published by the IEEE Computer Society; a member of the *Computer* Editorial Board; an editor of the *Journal of Parallel and Distributed Computing* and the *International Journal on High-Speed Computing*; a fellow of the IEEE; a member of the IEEE Computer Society; and a recipient of the society's Certificate of Appreciation.

Readers may write to Bhuyan at the Center for Advanced Computer Studies, University of Southwestern Louisiana, Lafayette, LA 70504-4330.

The Cedar System and an Initial Performance Study*

D. Kuck, E. Davidson,† D. Lawrie,† A. Sameh
C.-Q Zhu,† A. Veidenbaum, J. Konicek, P. Yew,
K. Gallivan, W. Jalby,† H. Wijshoff,† R. Bramley,† U.M. Yang
P. Emrath, D. Padua, R. Eigenmann, J. Hoeflinger, G. Jaxon,† Z. Li,†
T. Murphy, J. Andrews, S. Turner

Center for Supercomputing Research and Development
University of Illinois
Urbana, IL, 61801

Abstract

In this paper, we give an overview of the Cedar mutliprocessor and present recent performance results. These include the performance of some computational kernels and the Perfect Benchmarks® . We also present a methodology for judging parallel system performance and apply this methodology to Cedar, Cray YMP-8, and Thinking Machines CM-5.

1 Introduction

Tremendous progress in VLSI technology today has made it possible to build large-scale parallel systems with dazzling peak performances. Several such systems have even been commercialized over the last 5 years. However, the goal of building a general-purpose large-scale parallel system remains quite elusive. Many of the systems still have very little software support and are very difficult to program. The sustainable performance from various real applications running on those machines remains erratic and unpredictable. These phenomena show that we still do not know how to build parallel machines, how to program such machines, or how to characterize the performance of such machines for writing good application codes. The difficulties stem from the fact that in order to build a large-scale parallel machines that can deliver

"practical parallelism," we need to understand the interactions among system architecture, system software and parallel application codes.

The Cedar project brought together a group of people in the areas of computer architecture, parallelizing compilers, operating systems, and parallel algorithms/applications to help solve the real problems associated with building a "complete" parallel system, and to study the effects of interaction among these components on such a machine [GKLS83, KDLS86]. The machine has been in full operation since late 1990. The Cedar experience includes the architecture, compiler, OS, and application perspectives and this paper attempts to summarize these for the architecture community.

We describe the machine organization in Section 2, concentrating on the unique aspects of Cedar. Programming and compilation for Cedar are discussed in Section 3. Performance measurements of the systems and the interpretation of those results are presented in Section 4.

2 The Organization of Cedar

Cedar is a cluster-based shared memory multiprocessor. The system consists of four clusters connected through two unidirectional interconnection networks to a globally shared memory (Fig. 1). Each cluster is a slightly modified Alliant FX/8 system with eight processors. In this section we first summarize the features of these clusters and then describe the unique features of Cedar. For a more detailed overall description of Cedar see [KTVZ91].

*This research was supported by the Department of Energy under Grant No. DE-FG02-85ER25001 and by the National Science Foundation under Grants No. US NSF-MIP-8410110 and NSF-MIP-89-20891, IBM Corporation, and the State of Illinois.

†Affiliated with CSRD for a portion of the project.

Reprinted from *Proc. 20th Ann. Int'l Symp. Computer Architecture*, IEEE CS Press, Los Alamitos, Calif., 1993, pp. 213–223. Copyright © 1993 by The Institute of Electrical and Electronics Engineers, Inc. All rights reserved.

0-8186-6522-X/95 $4.00 © 1993 IEEE

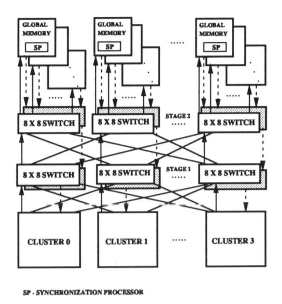

SP - SYNCHRONIZATION PROCESSOR

Figure 1: Cedar Architecture

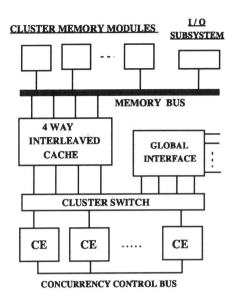

Figure 2: Cluster Architecture

Alliant clusters The organization of an Alliant FX/8 cluster is shown in Figure 2. Each Alliant FX/8 contains 8 *computational elements* (CEs). The CEs are connected to a 4-way interleaved *shared cache* which in turn is connected to an interleaved cluster memory. The FX/8 also includes *interactive processors* (IPs) and IP caches. IPs perform input/output and various other tasks.

The CE is a pipelined implementation of the 68020 instruction set augmented with vector instructions. The CE instruction cycle is 170ns. The vector unit implements 64-bit floating-point as well as integer operations. Vector instructions can have a register-memory format with one memory operand. The vector unit contains eight 32-word registers. The peak performance of each CE is 11.8 Mflops on 64-bit vector operations.

Each CE is connected to a *concurrency control bus* designed to support efficient execution of parallel loops. Concurrency control instructions implement fast fork, join and synchronization operations. For example: concurrent start is a single instruction that "spreads" the iterations of a parallel loop from one to all the CEs in a cluster by broadcasting the program counter and setting up private, per processor stacks. The whole cluster is thus "gang-scheduled." CEs within a cluster can then "self-schedule" iterations of the parallel loop among themselves.

Each Alliant FX/8 has 32MB of cluster memory. All references to data in cluster memory first check the 512KB physically addressed shared cache. Cache line

size is 32 bytes. The cache is write-back and lockup-free, allowing each CE to have two outstanding cache misses. Writes do not stall a CE. The cache bandwidth is eight 64-bit words per instruction cycle, sufficient to supply one input stream to a vector instruction in each processor. This equals 48MB/sec per processor or 384MB/sec per cluster. The cluster memory bandwidth is half of that or 192MB/sec.

Memory Hierarchy The Cedar memory hierarchy consists of 64MB of shared global memory and four cluster memories with caches. It supports a virtual memory system with a 4KB page size. The physical address space is divided into two equal halves: cluster memory is in the lower half and shared memory is in the upper half. Global memory is directly addressable and shared by all CEs. Cluster memory is only accessible to the CEs within that cluster. Data can be moved between cluster and global shared memory only via explicit moves under software control. It can be said that cluster memories form a distributed memory system in addition to the global shared memory. Coherence between multiple copies of globally shared data residing in cluster memory is maintained in software. The global memory system is weakly ordered. Global memory is double-word (8byte) interleaved and aligned. The peak global memory bandwidth is 768MB/sec or 24MB/sec per processor.

Global Network The Cedar network was designed to support simultaneous vector loads/stores from global memory by all processors. It is a multistage shuffle-exchange network as shown in Figure 1. The network is self-routing, buffered and packet-switched. Routing is based on the tag control scheme proposed in [Lawr75], and provides a unique path between any pair of input/output ports. Each network packet consists of one to four 64-bit words, the first word containing routing and control information and the memory address. The network is constructed with 8×8 crossbar switches with 64-bit wide data paths. A two word queue is used on each crossbar input and output port and flow control between stages prevents queue overflow. The network bandwidth is 768MB/sec for the entire system or 24MB/sec per processor, which matches the global memory bandwidth.

Data Prefetch The Cedar *data prefetch unit* (PFU) is designed to mask the long global memory latency and to overcome the limit of two outstanding requests per Alliant CE. Each CE has its own individual PFU. Each PFU supports one vector load from global memory. A PFU is "armed" by giving it the length, the stride and the mask of the vector to be fetched. It is then "fired" by the physical address of the first word to be fetched. This starting address can be supplied by a special prefetch instruction or by the first address of a vector load. In the former case the prefetch is completely autonomous and can be overlapped with computation or cluster memory accesses. In the latter case it is only overlapped with the current vector instruction. When a prefetch crosses a page boundary the PFU suspends until the processor supplies the first address in the new page because only physical addresses are available to the PFU. In the absence of page crossings the PFU issues up to 512 requests without pausing. The data returns to a 512-word prefetch buffer which is invalidated when another prefetch is started. It is possible to keep prefetched data in that buffer and reuse it from there. Data can enter the prefetch buffer from the global network out of order due to memory and network conflicts. A full/empty bit per word allows the CE both to access the buffer without waiting for the prefetch to be complete and to get the data in same order as requested.

Memory-based Synchronization requires read-modify-write operations on global memory. However, given multistage interconnection networks it is impossible to provide standard lock cycles and very inefficient to perform multiple memory accesses for synchronization. Cedar implements a set of indivisible synchronization instructions in each memory module. These include Test-And-Set and Cedar synchronization instructions based on [ZhYe87], which are performed by a special processor in each memory module. Cedar synchronization instructions implement Test-And-Operate, where Test is any relational operation on 32-bit data (e.g. $\geq$) and Operate is a Read, Write, Add, Subtract, or Logical operation on 32-bit data. Synchronization instructions are accessible from a CE via memory-mapped instructions initiated by a Test-And-Set to a global memory address.

Performance monitoring The Cedar approach to performance monitoring relies on external hardware to collect time-stamped event traces and histograms of various hardware signals. The event tracers can each collect 1M events and the histogrammers have 64K 32-bit counters. These can be cascaded to capture more events. Each of the major Cedar units has several important signals available for external monitoring. Any other accessible hardware signal can also be monitored. Software tools start and stop the experiments and move the data collected by the performance hardware to workstations for analysis. It is also possible to post events to the performance hardware from programs executing on Cedar, which allows software event tracing.

3   Programming Cedar

Cedar programs can be written using the CEDAR FORTRAN language, Xylem assembler or C. All of these make use of the abstractions provided by the Xylem kernel [EABM91] which links the four separate operating systems in Alliant clusters into the Cedar OS. Xylem exports virtual memory, scheduling, and file system services for Cedar.

A program for Cedar can be written using explicit parallelism and memory hierarchy placement directives. Parallelism can be in the form of DOALL loops or concurrent tasks. Alternatively, programs written in Fortran 77 can be translated automatically into CEDAR FORTRAN by the "Parallelizing Restructurer". The overall compilation and program execution process is simple and identical to the same process on a single-processor workstation. Writing programs that extract all of Cedar performance is a more challenging task.

The CEDAR FORTRAN language is a dialect of FORTRAN77 that includes parallel and vector extensions. CEDAR FORTRAN is translated into ALLIANT FORTRAN and Alliant's compiler performs code generation. Programming in FORTRAN77 provides a simpler user interface and better portability, although sometimes at the expense of performance.

CEDAR FORTRAN offers an application programmer explicit access to all the key features of the

194

Cedar system: the memory hierarchy, the prefetching capability from global memory, the global memory synchronization hardware, and cluster features including concurrency control. This access is supported by language extensions and run-time library functions. The CEDAR FORTRAN language extensions and compilation for Cedar are described next. CEDAR FORTRAN is fully described in [Hoef91] and description of the Cedar Compiler project can be found in [EHJL91, EHLP91, EHJP92].

3.1 Fortran Extensions

Parallel Loops A programmer can express parallelism using DOALL loop constructs. A DOALL is a loop in which iterations are independent and therefore can be executed in parallel. Several flavors of DOALLs are provided in order to better control load balancing, data placement, and scheduling overhead. These include CDOALL, SDOALL, and XDOALL which will be described below.

Data Placement and Sharing Data can be placed in either cluster or shared global memory on Cedar. A user can control this using a GLOBAL attribute. Variable placement is in cluster memory by default. A variable can also be declared inside a parallel loop. The loop-local declaration of a variable makes a private copy for each processor which is placed in cluster memory.

3.2 Compilation for Cedar

Parallel Loops XDOALL makes use of all the processors in the machine and schedules each iteration on a processor. The processors get started, terminated, and scheduled through functions of the run-time library. Since these operations work through the global memory there is a typical loop startup latency of 90 μs and fetching the next iteration takes about 30 μs. The second type of parallel loop is the SDOALL which schedules each iteration on an entire cluster. Each iteration starts executing on one processor of the cluster. The other processors in the cluster remain idle until a CDOALL is executed within the body of the SDOALL. The CDOALL makes use of the concurrency control bus to schedule loops on all processors in a cluster and can typically start in a few microseconds. The XDOALL has more scheduling flexibility but also higher overhead. An SDOALL/CDOALL nest has a lower scheduling cost due to the use of the concurrency control bus. Both SDOALL and XDOALL loops

can be statically scheduled or self-scheduled via runtime library options. CDOALL loops are used to exploit the faster loop control and shared cluster memory and cache in a cluster. Data that is private to an SDOALL iteration but shared by all cluster processors will be placed in the cluster memory.

Data Prefetching The compiler backend inserts an explicit prefetch instruction, of length 32 words or less, before each vector operation which has a global memory operand. The compiler then attempts to float the prefetch instructions in order to overlap prefetch operations with computation. This rarely succeeds and thus most of the time prefetch is started immediately before the vector instruction. More aggressive methods are being investigated [GoGV90].

Data privatization CEDAR FORTRAN uses data declared local to a loop in place of scalar and array expansion. In all Perfect programs we have found loop-local data placement to be an important factor in reducing data access latencies. In addition to loop-local declaration, data can be localized by partitioning and distributing them to the cluster memories. Subsequent loops can operate on these data by distributing iterations to clusters according to the data partitions. CEDAR FORTRAN supports this by scheduling iterations of successive SDOALLs on the same clusters.

Global Synchronization The Cedar synchronization instructions have been mainly used in the implementation of the runtime library, where they have proven useful to control loop self-scheduling. They are also available to a Fortran programmer via run-time library routines.

3.3 Program Restructuring

The parallelizing compiler project has two parts. In the first phase we retargeted an early copy of KAP restructurer to Cedar (KAP from KAI as released in 1988) and evaluated its performance. In the second phase we searched for restructuring techniques that improved the performance of real application programs significantly. We did these experiments by manually restructuring the suite of Perfect Benchmarks® programs, using techniques that may be automated in an eventual implementation of the parallelizer. The results are summarized in Table 3.

The table lists speed improvements over the serial execution time of two versions of the Perfect programs. The results in column "Compiled by Kap/Cedar" show that with the original compiler most programs have very limited performance improvement. This happened even though we set compiler options according to the Perfect Benchmarks rules. Specifically, in a few cases program execution was confined to a single cluster to avoid intercluster overhead.

The *Automatable* column presents the performance of the programs to which we applied compiler transformations by hand. The name automatable is somewhat optimistic because we have not yet implemented these transformations in an actual parallelizer. However we believe that most of the applied transformations are realizable. These transformations include array privatization, parallel reductions, advanced induction variable substitution, runtime data dependence tests, balanced stripmining, and parallelization in the presence of SAVE and RETURN statements. Many of these transformations require advanced symbolic and interprocedural analysis methods. The transformations have been described in more detail in [EHLP91, EHJL91, EHJP92]

4   Cedar Performance

Examples of Cedar performance are discussed in this section. Given the complexity of the Cedar architecture, compilers, OS, and of the codes themselves it is very difficult to isolate the performance effects of various architectural features at the level of full codes. Therefore, we start by considering data from well-understood algorithms and kernels which are much smaller and can be modified easily to explore the system. We continue with the performance of the Perfect codes achieved via automated and automatable restructuring transformations. Next we comment on the performance improvements possible for some of the codes when algorithmic and architectural knowledge is used to transform the codes in nonautomatable ways. Finally, we present a methodology for judging parallel system performance and apply this methodology to Cedar, Cray YMP-8, and Thinking Machines CM-5.

4.1   Memory System Performance

The effect of the memory system on performance can be demonstrated by considering three versions of a matrix primitive which computes a rank-64 update to an $n \times n$ matrix. For all versions the matrices reside in global memory. The difference between the versions lies in the mode of access of the data and the transfer of subblocks to cluster cache. Specifically: in the GM/no-pref version all vector accesses are to global

memory and do not use prefetching, the GM/pref version is identical with the exception that prefetching is used and the GM/cache version transfers a submatrix to a cached work array in each cluster and all vector accesses are made to the work array. All versions chain two operations per memory request.

The performance difference for a matrix of size $n = 1K$ (see Table 1) between the three versions is solely due to memory latency. The table shows megaflops achieved for the three versions. The performance of the GM/no-pref version is determined by the 13 cycle latency of the global memory and the two outstanding requests allowed per CE, and is typical of codes that cannot effectively exploit prefetching in their global accesses. The aggressive use of prefetch can mitigate this latency effectively for up to 16 CEs. The GM/pref version demonstrates this with performance improvement factors of 3.5 and 2.9 on 8 and 16 CEs respectively. For three and four clusters, the effectiveness of prefetching is reduced and improvements of only 2.2 and 1.9 are observed. To achieve a significant fraction of the 376 MFLOPS absolute peak performance (or the 274 MFLOPS effective peak due to unavoidable vector startup) the caches in each cluster must be used. The GM/cache version achieves improvements over GM/no-pref that range from 3.5 on one cluster (identical to the effect of prefetch) to 3.8 on four clusters. The 32 CE observed performance yields 74 % efficiency compared to the effective peak and is consistent with the observed maximum bandwidth of memory system characterization benchmarks [GJTV91].

	1 cl.	2 cl.	3 cl.	4 cl.
GM/no pref	14.5	29.0	43.0	55.0
GM/pref	50.0	84.0	96.0	104.0
GM/Cache	52.0	104.0	152.0	208.0

Table 1: MFLOPS for rank-64 update on Cedar

To explore the cause of the degradation of the effectiveness of prefetch for more than two clusters we analyze the performance of four computational kernels using the hardware performance monitor. We consider a vector load (VL), a tridiagonal matrix-vector multiply (TM), the rank-64 update of a matrix (RK), and a simple conjugate gradient algorithm (CG) to show directly the behavior of the global memory and networks in Table 2. The codes use 8, 16, and 32 processors, global data only, and prefetching. The RK kernel prefetches blocks of 256 words and aggressively overlaps it with computation, the other codes use compiler-generated 32-word prefetches. The metrics used are first word Latency and Interarrival time between the remaining words in the block, in instruction cycles. These are measured for every prefetch request by recording when an address from the prefetch unit is issued to the forward network and when each datum returns to the prefetch buffer via the reverse networks from memory. Minimal Latency is 8 cycles and minimal Interarrival time is 1 cycle. The cycles needed to move data between the CE and prefetch buffer complete the 13 cycle latency mentioned above. Monitoring these times required access to internal hardware signals and is not possible on all processors. As a result, we monitored all requests of a single processor and compared repeated experiments for consistency. The results of all experiments were within 10% of each other.

	Prefetch Speedup			Latency (cycles)			Interarrival (cycles)		
# CEs	8	16	32	8	16	32	8	16	32
TM	2.1	2.0	1.5	9.4	10.2	14.2	1.1	1.2	2.1
CG	2.4	2.2	1.5	9.4	10.3	15.1	1.1	1.2	2.1
VF	1.8	1.7	1.5	9.6	11.0	16.7	1.2	1.4	2.2
RK	3.4	2.9	1.8	12.9	15.3	18.3	1.2	1.8	3.2

Table 2: Global memory performance

The results in Table 2 show that global memory degradation due to contention causes the reduction in the effectiveness of prefetching as the number of CEs used increases. For one cluster both the latency and interarrival time are near their minimums. RK degrades most quickly due to the fact that it uses the longest prefetch block and overlaps all operations with memory accesses. VF is also dominated by memory accesses but degrades less quickly due to the smaller prefetch block which reduces access intensity. The TM and CG kernels suffer approximately the same degradation and are affected less than the others due to the presence of register-register vector operations which reduce the demand on the memory system. We have shown via detailed simulations that this degradation is not inherent in the type of network used but is a result of specific implementation constraints [Turn93].

4.2 Cedar Performance Using the Perfect Codes

All the results presented in this section were collected in single-user mode to avoid the nondeterminism of multiprogramming. The results are shown in Table 3 and have speed improvements versus uniprocessor scalar versions of the same codes. Comparison of automatic restructuring with automatable transformations was given is Section 3.3.

Effect of Cedar Features. The results for the versions derived from automatable transformations in Table 3 assume the use of compiler-generated prefetch and Cedar synchronization in the runtime library. "Slowdown" with respect to "Automatable" results for some of these codes when Cedar synchronization is not used for loop scheduling is due to parallel loops with relatively small granularity requiring low-overhead self-scheduling support, e.g., DYFESM and OCEAN. "Slowdown" without the use of prefetching (given with respect to "No Synchronization" results) for many of the codes is typically due to one of two reasons. The first is a domination of scalar accesses, e.g., TRACK. The second is the presence of a large amount of short-lived loop-local data that is placed in cluster memory. The automatable version of the code DYFESM benefits significantly from prefetch due to the large number of vector fetches from global memory on a small number of processors (due to the limited parallelism available).

Hand Optimization. It is possible to improve the execution time of the Perfect codes using knowledge of their main algorithms and of Cedar.[1] Table 4 contains the execution times for these updated codes. Some of the codes were analyzed resulting in changes that ranged in complexity from a simple modification of I/O (BDNA) to a complete rewriting (TRFD).

The execution time for BDNA is reduced to 70 secs. by simply replacing formatted with unformatted I/O. Careful consideration of ARC2D reveals a substantial number of unnecessary computations. Primarily due to their elimination but also due to aggressive data distribution into cluster memory the execution time is reduced to 68 secs. [BrBo91]. If a hand-coded parallel random number generator is used, QCD can be improved to yield a speed improvement of 20.8 rather than the 1.8 reported for the automatable code.

FLO52, DYFESM, and TRFD require more elaborate analyses and modifications. Four of the five major

---

[1] We use prefetch but not Cedar synchronization.

Program	Compiled by Kap/Cedar time (Improvement)	Auto. transforms time (Improvement)	W/o Cedar Synchronization time (% slowdown)	W/o prefetch time (% slowdown)	MFLOPS (YMP-8/Cedar)
ADM	689 (1.2)	73 (10.8)	81 (11%)	83 (2%)	6.9 (3.4)
ARC2D	218 (13.5)	141 (20.8)	141 (0%)	157 (11%)	13.1 (34.2)
BDNA	502 (1.9)	111 (8.7)	118 (6%)	122 (3%)	8.2 (18.4)
DYFESM	167 (3.9)	60 (11.0)	67 (12%)	100 (49%)	9.2 (6.5)
FLO52	100 (9.0)	63 (14.3)	64 (1%)	79 (23%)	8.7 (37.8)
MDG	3200 (1.3)	182 (22.7)	202 (11%)	202 (0%)	18.9 (1.1)
MG3D [a]	7929 (1.5)	348 (35.2)	346 (0%)	350 (1%)	31.7 (3.6)
OCEAN	2158 (1.4)	148 (19.8)	174 (18%)	187 (7%)	11.2 (7.4)
QCD	369 (1.1)	239 (1.8)	239 (0%)	246 (3%)	1.1 (11.8)
SPEC77	973 (2.4)	156 (15.2)	156 (0%)	165 (6%)	11.9 (4.8)
SPICE	95.1 (1.02)	NA	NA	NA	0.5 (11.4)
TRACK	126 (1.1)	26 (5.3)	28 (8%)	28 (0%)	3.1 (2.7)
TRFD	273 (3.2)	21 (41.1)	21 (0%)	21 (0%)	20.5 (2.8)

[a]This version of MG3D includes the elimination of file I/O.

Table 3: Cedar execution time, megaflops, and speed improvement for Perfect Benchmarks

Code	Time	Improvement
ARC2D	68	2.1
BDNA	70	1.7
DYFESM	31	2.2
FLO52	33	1.9
SPICE	26	3.7
TRFD	7.5	2.8
QCD	21	11.4

Table 4: Execution times (secs.) for manually altered Perfect Codes and improvement over automatable w/ prefetch and w/o Cedar synchronization

routines in FLO52 require a series of multicluster barriers. Unfortunately, the associated synchronization overhead degrades performance for problems that are not sufficiently large, e.g., the Perfect data set. Analysis of the algorithms reveals that by introducing a small amount of redundancy, we can transform the sequence of multicluster barriers into a single multicluster barrier and four independent sequences of barriers that can exploit the concurrency control hardware in each cluster. This along with eliminating several recurrences in the remaining major routine results in an execution time of 33 secs.

The major problem with DYFESM is the very small problem size used in the benchmark. If some of the data structures are reshaped and certain key kernels are reimplemented, aggressively using Cedar's prefetch unit via Xylem assembler, the execution time drops to around 40 secs. If we change the algorithm used in the code and exploit the hierarchical SDOALL/CDOALL control structure an execution time of 31 secs. results [YaGa93].

The execution time of TRFD was reduced to 11.5 secs. by implementing high performance kernels to efficiently exploit the clusters' caches and vector registers [AnGa93]. The improved version was shown to have almost four times the number of page faults relative to the one-cluster version and was spending close to 50% of the time in virtual memory activity. The extra faults are TLB miss faults as each additional cluster of a multicluster version first accesses pages for which a valid PTE exists in global memory. Based on analysis of the virtual memory performance of Cedar, [MaEG92], a distributed memory version of the code was developed to mitigate this problem and yielded a final execution time of 7.5 secs.

SPICE also benefits significantly from algorithmic attention. After considering all of the major phases of the application and developing new approaches where needed the time is reduced to approximately 26 secs.

4.3 Judging Parallelism

In this section we present a performance evaluation methodology for parallel systems. We will cast this discussion in general terms and will compare initial Cedar performance data to commercially available systems. However, our goal is not to argue that system X is better than system Y, but rather to shed light on how to understand performance and thereby to make parallel processing a practical real-world technology in the future. We first define five practical parallelism tests, then some performance metrics, and finally discuss acceptable performance levels.

The Practical Parallelism Tests

Practical parallelism has not yet been demonstrated; in fact, no standard definition of it exists. It seems clear that there should be "laboratory level" and "commercial level" criteria for judging practical parallelism, and we will now propose five criteria that form a Practical Parallelism Test.

At the laboratory level, we will use as our criterion for the success of parallelism,

The Fundamental Principle of Parallel Processing (FPPP): Clock speed is interchangeable with parallelism while (A) maintaining delivered performance, that is (B) stable over a certain class of computations.

There are really three statements in the FPPP: first, the well-established point that high peak speeds are possible through parallelism, and then two important constraints that we shall use as Practical Parallelism Tests (PPT's) 1 and 2.

Practical Parallelism Test 1. Delivered Performance: The parallel system delivers performance, as measured in speedup or computational rate, for a useful set of codes.

Practical Parallelism Test 2. Stable Performance: The performance demonstrated in Test 1 is within a specified stability range as the computations vary with respect to certain program structures, data structures, and data sizes.

Next we discuss two additional tests that must be met if one has demonstrated the FPPP and wants to use it in a commercially viable product.

Practical Parallelism Test 3. Portability and Programmability: The computer system is easy to port codes to and to program, for many applications.

Practical Parallelism Test 4. Code and Architecture Scalability: The computer system effectively runs each code/data size on a range of processor counts, and each code's data size can be scaled up or down on a given architecture.

Finally, if the first system is a success and the company is to survive over time, the system must demonstrate:

Practical Parallelism Test 5. Technology and Scalable Reimplementability: The system architecture must be capable of being reimplemented (scaled up) with much larger processor counts in the current technology or in new, faster or less expensive technologies as they emerge.

In what follows, we will expand these ideas and illustrate methods by which we can observe the PPT's and track progress toward satisfying them over time. Despite the great enthusiasm for parallel processing today, not even the Fundamental Principle of Parallel Processing has been demonstrated generally. Substantial amounts of work will be required before the remaining three PPT's are passed.

For at least twenty years we have used speedup and efficiency as abstract measures of performance. In addition, we now define stability, St, on P processors of an ensemble of computations over K codes as follows:

$$St(P, N_i, K, e) = \frac{min\ performance(K, e)}{max\ performance(K, e)},$$

where N_i is the problem size of i-th code, and e computations are excluded from the ensemble because their results are outliers from the ensemble (and each code may have a different number of data sets). Instability, In, is defined as the inverse of Stability. The traditional megaflops (millions of floating-point operations per second) are used as our rate measure. We avoid debating how to define floating-point operation counts by simply using the floating-point counts obtained from the Cray Hardware Performance Monitor.

Acceptable Performance Levels Given a speedup we are confronted with the question of "how good is good?" We should answer this using some function of the total number of processors P. Most people experienced with running a variety of real codes on parallel machines would be pleased if they could achieve some fraction of P or even $P/\log P$, especially as P grows to hundreds or thousands of processors. Note that in terms of the 10X/7 years performance improvement achieved over the history of supercomputing, which has mainly been due to hardware speed increases, such a 1000 processor machine would provide about 15 equivalent years of electronics-advancement speed improvement. Thus, if we knew how to build machines that met all five of the PPT's, $O(P/\log P)$ would be a good performance level. For this discussion, we shall use $P/2$ and $P/2\log P$, for $P \geq 8$, as levels that denote **high performance** and **acceptable performance**, respectively. We refer to speedups in the three bands defined by these two levels as high, intermediate, or unacceptable.

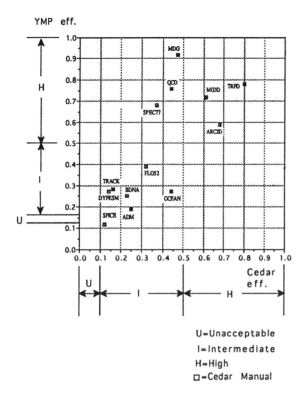

YMP eff.

U=Unacceptable
I=Intermediate
H=High
□=Cedar Manual

Figure 3: Cray YMP/8 vs. Cedar Efficiency

Applying the Methodology

In this section we apply the ideas of the previous section by using the first four PPT's to analyze Cedar and compare it to other systems.

Practical Parallelism Test 1 is the easiest of the PPT's to meet, and has been demonstrated many times by showing that one code or another runs well on a parallel machine. Figure 3 shows a scatter plot of Cray YMP/8 vs. Cedar efficiencies for the manually optimized Perfect codes. The 8-processor YMP has about half high and half intermediate levels of performance, while the 32-processor Cedar has about one-quarter high and three-quarters intermediate. Note that the YMP has one unacceptable performance, while Cedar has none. We conclude from this that both the Cray YMP and Cedar are on the average acceptable, delivering intermediate parallel performance and thus pass PPT1 for the Perfect codes.

Practical Parallelism Test 2 is much more difficult to meet than PPT1, as it requires that a whole set of programs runs well on some parallel machine. To show the world that it really is a practical system, a parallel machine should be demonstrated on a wide range of program structures, data structures and data sizes. What stability range can one expect on

supercomputers in general, and, at the other extreme, what could one expect on workstations? For the past 20 years, from the VAX 780 through various modern workstations (Sun SPARC2, IBM RS6000), an instability of about 5 has been common for the Perfect benchmarks. Users are evidently not concerned with such computational rate variations on workstations, so we will define a system as **stable** if $\frac{1}{6} \leq St(K, e)$, for small e, and as unstable, otherwise. However, if on some architecture, the computational rate varied by substantially more, the net effect could be noticed by many users.

Table 5 shows that Cedar and the Cray YMP/8 both have terrible instabilities for their baseline-automatable computations. This is generally caused by several very poor performers (e.g., SPICE) and several very high performers. So we are led to examining the number of exceptions required to achieve workstation-level stability. We find that two exceptions are sufficient on the Cray 1 and Cedar, whereas the YMP needs six – about half of the Perfect codes. Thus, the YMP cannot be judged as passing PPT2 for the Perfect codes, i.e., it is unstable, while the other two systems do pass with two exceptions.

	$In(13, 0)$	$In(13, 2)$	$In(13, 6)$
Cedar	63.4	5.8	–
Cray 1 [a]	10.9	4.6	–
YMP/8	75.3	29.0	5.3

[a]with modern compiler

Table 5: Instability for Perfect codes

It may be regarded as absurd to invoke a test that can be passed by ignoring codes that give top performance. On the other hand, consider two points. First, it can be argued that if a few codes have very high performance, then users should expect that (eventually) all codes will perform well, as is the case with workstations. Secondly, the Perfect codes have relatively small data sizes and stability is a measure that can focus us on the class of codes that are well matched to the system, so varying the data size and observing stability would be instructive. Both of these points indicate that the general purpose abilities of a system are related to its stability.

Practical Parallelism Test 3 Automatic compilation will go a long way towards portability and programmability of parallel systems. Our discussion of PPT3 will thus center on the performance levels that can be obtained by using compilers on parallel systems. As we discussed earlier, fully automatic compilation is not yet available on Cedar. However, we have developed several compiler enhancements that have not yet been implemented but have been applied manually to the Perfect codes. These "automatable" results are reported together with automatic results for CRAY YMP/8 in Table 6 . We conclude from this that the state of today's compiler art indicates that acceptable levels for the Perfect codes may be reached in the next few years. Thus, we can expect PPT3 to be passed by parallel systems in the near future.

Performance Level	Cedar	Cray YMP
High $(E_p \geq .5)$	1 Codes	0 Codes
Intermediate $(E_p \geq 1/2 \log P)$	9 Codes	6 Codes
Unacceptable $(E_p < 1/2 \log P)$	3 Codes	7 Codes

Table 6: Restructuring Efficiency

Absolute Performance: Cray YMP/8 vs. Cedar The previous discussion has ignored absolute performance in terms of time or megaflops. Table 3 shows the megaflops generated by Cedar automatable versions [Add1], as well as Cray YMP/8 baseline compiler MFLOPS to Cedar MFLOPS ratios. The harmonic mean for the MFLOPS on the YMP/8 is 23.7, 7.4 times that of Cedar. It should be remembered that the ratios of clock speeds of the two systems is 170ns/6ns = 28.33.

Practical Parallelism Test 4 Parallel system performance can vary widely as a function of both the number of processors used and the size of the problems being solved. We shall use the High and Intermediate efficiency (see Table 6) and stability range of $.5 \leq St(P, N, 1, 0) \leq 1$ as acceptability criteria. The system is scalable in a range of processor counts and problem sizes where these criteria are satisfied. We are being more restrictive here than we were in PPT 2. This is reasonable because one should expect less variation in performance when varying data size alone than when varying data size as well as program and data structures, as is done across any benchmark suite. Furthermore, based on a number of measurements (not shown here) an Instability of 2 seems reasonable to expect on workstations as data size varies.

It is difficult to vary the problem sizes and col-

lect scalability information for the Perfect codes, so we drop to the level of algorithm studies here, and use the Thinking Machines, Inc. CM-5 for comparison because it has a larger number of processors than CRAY YMP/8. The performance of a conjugate gradient (CG) iterative linear system solver was measured on Cedar while varying the number of processors from 2 to 32. This computation involves 5-diagonal matrix-vector products as well as vector and reduction operations of size N, $1K \leq N \leq 172K$. Cedar exhibits scalable high performance for matrices larger than something between 10K and 16K, and on up to the largest problems run. Cedar exhibits scalable intermediate performance for smaller matrices, evidently ranging well below the smallest actual runs of $N = 1K$. No unacceptable performance was observed in the data that was gathered.

In [FWPS92], a number of linear algebra experiments are reported on the CM-5. For comparison, we quote data for matrix-vector products with bandwidths 3 and 11. The CM-5 used does not have floating-point accelerators. For problem sizes run, $16K \leq N \leq 256K$, high performance was not achieved relative to 32, 256, or 512 processors. The communication structure of the CM-5 evidently causes these performance difficulties [FWPS92]. The CM-5 exhibits scalable intermediate performance with these three processor counts for problems evidently smaller than 16K for bandwidth 11 and evidently much smaller problems for bandwidth 3. No unacceptable performance was observed in the ranges reported.

Thus we conclude that, for these problems and for the number of processors studied, CM-5 is scalable with intermediate performance, while for up to 32 processors Cedar is scalable with high performance for many problem sizes and with intermediate performane for debugging sized runs.

Absolute Performance: The 32-processor Cedar delivers between 34 and 48 MFLOPS as the CG problem size ranges from 10K to 172K. On the banded matrix-vector product, the 32-processor CM-5 delivers between 28 and 32 MFLOPS for BW=3 and between 58 and 67 MFLOPS for BW=11, as the problem sizes range from 16K to 256K. Thus, the per-processor MFLOPS of the two systems on these problems are roughly equivalent.

We are in the process of collecting detailed simulation data for various computations on scaled-up Cedar-like systems. This takes us into the realm of PPT 5 which we shall not deal with further, in this paper.

Acknowledgments.

We acknowledge the contributions of D. Gajski, R. Downing, T. Tilton, M. Haney, R. McGrath, R. Barton, M. Sharma, D. Lavery, A. Malony, M. Farmwald, S. Midkiff, M. Guzzi, V. Guarna, C. Polychronopoulos, L. Harrison and T. Beck.

References

[Add1]   CSRD Staff. *Perfect Report 2: Addendum 1.* Center for Supercomputing Research and Development, University of Illinois, 1991.

[AnGa93] J. Andrews and K. Gallivan. *Analysis of a Cedar Implementation of* TRFD, CSRD Report in preparation, University of Illinois.

[BrBo91] R. Bramley and J. Bordner. *Sequential Optimization and Data Distribution for* ARC2D *on the Cedar Hierarchical Multiprocessor,* CSRD Report No. 1128, University of Illinois, 1991.

[EABM91] Emrath, P., et al. *The Xylem Operating System.* Procs. of ICPP'91, vol. 1, pg. 67-70, 1991.

[EHJL91] Eigenmann, et al. *Restructuring Fortran Programs for Cedar.* Procs. of ICPP'91, vol. 1, pp. 57-66, 1991.

[EHJP92] Eigenmann, et al. *The Cedar Fortran Project.* CSRD Report No. 1262, University of Illinois, 1992.

[EHLP91] Eigenmann, et al. *Experience in the automatic Parallelization of Four Perfect-Benchmark Programs.* Proceedings of the Fourth Workshop on Languages and Compilers for Parallel Computing, pp. 65-83, 1991.

[FWPS92] Ferng, W., et al. *Basic Sparse Matrix Computations on Massively Parallel Computers.* AHPCRC Preprint 92-084, University of Minnesota, July, 1992.

[GJTV91] K. Gallivan, et al. *Preliminary Performance Analysis of the Cedar Multiprocessor Memory System.* Proc. 1991 ICPP, Vol. I, pp. 71-75, 1991.

[GJWY93] K. Gallivan, et al. *Comments on a Cedar Implementation of* FLO52, CSRD Report in preparation, University of Illinois.

[GKLS83] Gajski, D., et al. *CEDAR – a Large Scale Multiprocessor,* Procs. 1983 ICPP, pp. 524-529, 1983.

[GoGV90] Gornish, E., et al. *Compiler-directed Data Prefetching in Multiprocessors with Memory Hierarchies.* Procs. ICS'90, Amsterdam, The Netherlands, vol. 1, pp. 342-353, 1990.

[Hoef91] Hoeflinger, J. *Cedar Fortran Programmer's Handbook.* Center for Supercomputing Research and Development, University of Illinois, 1991.

[KDLS86] Kuck, D., et al. *Parallel Supercomputing Today and the Cedar Approach,* Science, vol. 231, pp. 967-974, Feb. 28, 1986.

[KTVZ91] Konicek, J., et al. *The Organization of the Cedar System.* Procs. ICPP'91, vol. 1, pg. 49-56, 1991.

[Lawr75] Lawrie, D., *Access and Alignment of Data in an Array Processor.* IEEE Trans. on Computers, vol. C-24, no. 12, pp. 1145-1155, Dec. 1975.

[MaEG92] B. Marsolf, P. Emrath, and K. Gallivan. *Investigation of the Page Fault Performance of Cedar,* CSRD Report No. 1263, University of Illinois, 1992.

[Turn93] S. Turner. *Performance Analysis of Interconnection Networks,* PhD Thesis in preparation, 1993.

[YaGa93] U. M. Yang and K. Gallivan. *Analysis of a Cedar Implementation of* DYFESM, CSRD Report No. 1284, University of Illinois, 1993.

[ZhYe87] Zhu, C-Q. and Yew, P-C., *A Scheme to Enforce Data Dependence on Large Multiprocessor Systems.* IEEE Transactions on Software Engineering, vol. SE-13, no. 6, pp. 726-739, June 1987.

Synchronization, Coherence, and Event Ordering in Multiprocessors

Michel Dubois and Christoph Scheurich

Computer Research Institute, University of Southern California

Fayé A. Briggs

Sun Microsystems

Multiprocessors, especially those constructed of relatively low-cost microprocessors, offer a cost-effective solution to the continually increasing need for computing power and speed. These systems can be designed either to maximize the throughput of many jobs or to speed up the execution of a single job; they are respectively called *throughput-oriented* and *speedup-oriented multiprocessors*. In the first type of system, jobs are distinct from each other and execute as if they were running on different uniprocessors. In the second type an application is partitioned into a set of cooperating processes, and these processes interact while executing concurrently on different processors. The partitioning of a job into cooperating processes is called *multitasking*[1]* or *multithreading*. In both systems global resources must be managed correctly and efficiently by the operating system. The problems addressed in this article apply to both throughput-

*Multitasking is not restricted to multiprocessor systems; in this article, however, we confine our discussion, with no loss of generality, to multitasking multiprocessors.

> **Efficient multiprocessing depends on a harmonious blend of synchronization, coherence, and event ordering in a system that provides the user with a simple logical model of concurrency behavior.**

and speedup-oriented multiprocessor systems, either at the user level or the operating-system level.

Multitasked multiprocessors are capable of efficiently executing the many cooperating numerical or nonnumerical tasks that comprise a large application. In general, the speedup provided by multitasking reduces the turnaround time of a job and therefore ultimately improves the user's productivity. For applications such as real-time processing, CAD/CAM, and simulations, multitasking is crucial because the multiprocessor structure improves the execution speed of a given algorithm within a time constraint that is ordinarily impossible to meet on a single processor employing available technology.

Designing and programming multiprocessor systems correctly and efficiently pose complex problems. Synchronizing processes, maintaining data coherence, and ordering events in a multiprocessor are issues that must be addressed from the hardware design level up to the programming language level. The goal of this article is not only to review these problems in some depth but also to show that in the design of multiprocessors these problems are intricately related. The definitions and concepts presented here provide a solid foundation on which to reason about the logical properties of a specific multiproces-

Reprinted from *Computer*, Vol. 21, No. 2, Feb. 1988, pp. 9–21.

0-8186-6522-X/95 $4.00 © 1988 IEEE

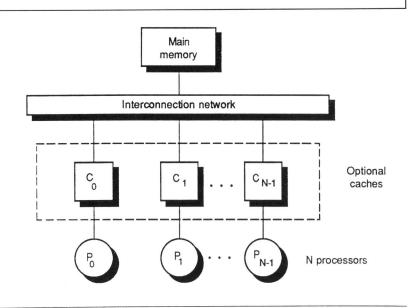

Figure 1. A shared-memory multiprocessor with optional private caches. The interconnection network may be either a simple bus or a complex network.

sor and to demonstrate that the hardware adheres to the logical model expected by the programmer. This foundation aids in understanding complex but useful architectures such as multiprocessors with private caches or with recombining interconnection networks (Figure 1).[2] Other important issues, such as scheduling and partitioning, have been addressed in a previous survey article.[3] Readers who are not familiar with the concept of cache memory should consult the survey by Smith.[4]

Basic definitions

The instruction set of a multiprocessor usually contains basic instructions that are used to implement synchronization and communication between cooperating processes. These instructions are usually supported by special-purpose hardware. Some primary hardware functions are necessary to guarantee correct interprocess communication and synchronization, while other, secondary hardware functions simplify the design of parallel applications and operating systems. The notions of synchronization and communication are difficult to separate because communication

primitives can be used to implement synchronization protocols, and vice versa. In general, *communication* refers to the exchange of data between different processes. Usually, one or several sender processes transmit data to one or several receiver processes. Interprocess communication is mostly the result of explicit directives in the program. For example, parameters passed to a coroutine and results returned by such a coroutine constitute interprocess communications. *Synchronization* is a special form of communication, in which the data are control information. Synchronization serves the dual purpose of enforcing the correct sequencing of processes and ensuring the mutually exclusive access to certain shared writable data. For example, synchronization primitives can be used to

(1) Control a producer process and a consumer process such that the consumer process never reads stale data and the producer process never overwrites data that have not yet been read by the consumer process.

(2) Protect the data in a database such that concurrent write accesses to the same record in the database are not allowed. (Such accesses can lead to the loss of one or more updates if two processes first read the data in sequence and then write the

updated data back to memory in sequence.)

In shared-memory multiprocessor systems, communication and synchronization are usually implemented through the controlled sharing of data in memory.

A second issue addressed in this article is *memory coherence*, a system's ability to execute memory operations correctly. Censier and Feautrier define a coherent memory scheme as follows: "A memory scheme is coherent if the value returned on a Load instruction is always the value given by the latest Store instruction with the same address."[5] This definition has been useful in the design of cache coherence mechanisms.[4] As it stands, however, the definition is difficult to interpret in the context of a multiprocessor, in which data accesses may be buffered and may not be atomic. Accesses are buffered if multiple accesses can be queued before reaching their destination, such as main memory or caches. An access by processor i on a variable X is atomic if no other processor is allowed to access any copy of X while the access by processor i is in progress. It has been shown that memory accesses need not be atomic at the hardware level for correct execution of concurrent programs.[6,7] Correctness of execution depends on the expected behavior of the machine. Two major classes of logical machine behavior have been identified because they are common in existing multiprocessor systems: the *strongly ordered* and the *weakly ordered* models of behavior.[7] The hardware of the machine must enforce these models by proper ordering of storage accesses and execution of synchronization and communication primitives. This leads to the third issue, the *ordering of events*.

The strictest logical model for the ordering of events is called *sequential consistency*, defined by Lamport. In a multiprocessor *sequential consistency* refers to the allowable sequence of execution of instructions within the same process and among different concurrent processes. Lamport defines the term more rigorously: "[A system is sequentially consistent if] the result of any execution is the same as if the operations of all the processors were executed in some sequential order, and the operations of each individual processor appear in this sequence in the order specified by its program."[8]

Since the only way that two concurrent processors can affect each other's execution is through the sharing of writable data and the sending of interrupt signals, it is the order of these events that really matters. In systems that are sequentially consistent we say that events are strongly ordered.

However, if we look at many systems (transaction systems, for example), it becomes clear that sequential consistency is often violated in favor of a weaker condition. In many machines it is often implicitly assumed that the programmer should make no assumption about the order in which the events that a process generates are observed by other processes between two explicit synchronization points. Accesses to shared writable data should be executed in a mutually exclusive manner, controlled by synchronizing variables. Accesses to synchronizing variables can be detected by the machine hardware at execution time. Strong ordering of accesses to these synchronizing variables and restoration of coherence at synchronization points are therefore the only restrictions that must be upheld. In such systems we say that events are weakly ordered. Weak ordering may result in more efficient systems, but the implementation problems remain the same as for strong ordering: strong ordering must still be enforced for synchronizing variables (rather than for all shared writable data).

We can infer from this discussion that synchronization, coherence, and ordering of events are closely related issues in the design of multiprocessors.

```
       {Processor 1:}
       A:=0
       .
       .
       A:=1                     /* event S1(A) */
LAB1:  If (B=1) goto LAB1       /* event L1(B) */
       <critical section>
       A:=0

       {Processor 2:}
       B:=0
       .
       .
       B:=1                     /* event S2(B) */
LAB2:  If (A=1) goto LAB2       /* event L2(A) */
       <critical section>
       B:=0
```

Figure 2. Synchronization protocol using two shared variables, *A* and *B*.

Communication and synchronization

Communication and synchronization are two facets of the same basic problem: how to design concurrent software that is correct and reliable, especially when the processes interact by exchanging control and data information. Multiprocessor systems usually include various mechanisms to deal with the various granules of synchronizable resources. Usually, low-level and simple primitives are implemented directly by the hardware. These primitives are the basic mechanisms that enforce mutual exclusion for more complex mechanisms implemented in microcode or software.

Hardware-level synchronization mechanisms. All multiprocessors include hardware mechanisms to enforce atomic operations. The most primitive memory operations in a machine are Loads and Stores. With atomic Loads and Stores complex synchronization protocols can be built. Figure 2 depicts a simple protocol. Before a processor can enter its critical section, it sets its control variable (*A* for processor 1 and *B* for processor 2) to 1. Hence, for both processors to be in their critical sections concurrently, both *A* and *B* must equal 1. But this is not possible, since a processor cannot enter its critical section if the other processor's control variable equals 1. Therefore, the two processors cannot execute their respective critical sections concurrently. This simple protocol can be deadlocked, but the problem can be remedied.[8] Such protocols are hard to design, understand, and prove correct, and in many cases they are inefficient.

More sophisticated synchronization primitives are usually implemented in hardware. If the primitive is simple enough, the controller of the memory bank can execute the primitive at the memory in the same way it executes a Load or a Store, at the added cost of a more complex memory controller. This is typically the case for the Test&Set and the Full/Empty bit primitives described below. Interprocessor interrupts are also possible hardware mechanisms for synchronization and communication. To send a message to another process currently running on a different processor, a process can send an interrupt to that processor to notify the destination process.

A common set of synchronization primitives consists of Test&Set(lock) and Reset(lock). The semantics of Test&Set and Reset are

```
TEST&SET(lock)
  { temp ← lock; lock ← 1;
    return temp; }
RESET(lock)
  { lock ← 0; }
```

The microcode or software will usually repeat the Test&Set until the returned value is 0. Synchronization at this level implies some form of busy waiting, which ties up a processor in an idle loop and increases the memory bus traffic and contention. The type of lock that relies on busy waiting is called a *spin-lock*.

To avoid spinning, interprocessor interrupts are used. A lock that relies on interrupts instead of spinning is called a *suspend-lock* (also called *sleep-lock* in the C.mmp[1]). This lock is similar to the spin-lock in the sense that a process does not relinquish the processor while it is waiting on a suspend-lock. However, whenever it fails to obtain the lock, it records its status in one field of the lock and disables all interrupts except interprocessor interrupts. When a process frees the lock, it signals all waiting processors through an interprocessor interrupt. This mechanism prevents the excessive interconnection traffic caused by busy waiting but still consumes processor cycles. Spin-locks and suspend-locks can be based on primitives similar to Test&Set, such as Compare&Swap.

The Compare&Swap(r1,r2,w) primitive is a synchronization primitive in the IBM 370 architecture; r1 and r2 are two machine registers, and w points to a memory location. The success of the Compare&Swap is indicated by the flag z. The semantics of the Compare&Swap instruction are

```
COMPARE&SWAP(r1,r2,w)
    { temp ← w; if (temp = r1)
      then {w ← r2; z ← 1;}
      else {r1 ← temp; z ← 0;}
    }
```

Test&Set and Compare&Swap are also called *read-modify-write* (RMW) primitives. A common performance problem associated with these basic synchronization primitives is the complexity of locking protocols. If N processes attempt to access a critical section at the same time, the memory system must execute N basic lock operations, one after the other, even if at most one process is successful. The NYU Ultracomputer[2] and the RP3 multiprocessor[9] use the Fetch&Add(x,a) primitive, where x is a shared-memory word and a is an increment. When a single processor executes the Fetch&Add on x, the semantics are

```
FETCH&ADD(x,a)
    { temp ← x; x ← temp + a;
      return temp; }
```

The implementation of the Fetch&Add primitive on the Ultracomputer is such that the complexity of an N-way synchronization on the same memory word is independent of N. The execution of this primitive is distributed in the interconnection network between the processors and the memory module. If N processes attempt to Fetch&Add the same memory word simultaneously, the memory is updated only once, by adding the sum of the N increments, and a unique value is returned to each of the N processes. The returned values correspond to an arbitrary serialization of the N requests. From the processor and memory point of view, the result is similar to a sequential execution of N Fetch&Adds, but it is performed in one operation. Consequently, the

Fetch&Add primitive is extremely effective in accessing sequentially allocated queue structures and in the forking of processes with identical code that operate on different data segments. For example, the following high-level parallel Fortran statement[10] can be executed in parallel by P processors if there is no dependency between iterations of the loop:

```
DOALL N = 1 to 100
    < code using N >
ENDDO
```

Each processor executes a Fetch&Add on N before working on a specific iteration of the loop. Each processor will return a unique value of N, which can be used in the code segment. The code for each processor is as follows (N is initially loaded with the value 1):

```
n ← FETCH&ADD (N,1)
while (n ≤ 100) do
    { < code using N >
      n ← FETCH&ADD (N,1);
    }
```

In the HEP (Heterogeneous Element Processor) system, shared-memory words are tagged as *empty* or *full*. Loads of such words succeed only after the word is updated and tagged as full. After a successful Load, the tag can be reset to empty. Similarly, the Store on a full memory word can be prevented until the word has been read and the tag cleared. These mechanisms can be used to synchronize processes, since a process can be made to wait on an empty memory word until some other process fills it. This system also relies on busy waiting, and memory cycles are wasted on each trial. Each processor in the HEP is a multistream pipeline, and several process contexts are present in each processor at any time. A different process can immediately be activated when an attempt to synchronize fails. Very few processor cycles are wasted on synchronization. However, the burden of managing the tags is left to the programmer or the compiler. A more complex tagging scheme is advocated for the Cedar machine.[3]

Software-level synchronization mechanisms. Two approaches to synchronization are popular in multiprocessor operating systems: semaphores and message passing. We will discuss message passing in the next section. Operations on semaphores are P and V. A binary semaphore has the values 0 or 1, which signal acquisition and blocking, respectively. A counting semaphore can take any integer

value greater than or equal to 0. The semantics of the P and V operations are

```
P(s)
    { if (s > 0) then
        s ← (s − 1);
        else
      { Block the process and append it
        to the waiting list for s;
        Resume the highest priority pro-
        cess in the READY LIST;}
    }
```

```
V(s)
    { if (waiting list for s empty) then
        s ← (s + 1);
        else
      { Remove the highest priority pro-
        cess blocked for s;
        Append it to the READY LIST;}
    }
```

In these two algorithms shared lists are consulted and modified (namely, the Ready List* and the waiting list for s). These accesses as well as the test and modification of s have to be protected by spin-locks, suspend-locks, or Fetch&Adds associated with semaphore s and with the lists. In practice, P and V are processor instructions or microcoded routines, or they are operating system calls to the process manager. The process manager is the part of the system kernel controlling process creation, activation, and deletion, as well as management of the locks. Because the process manager can be called from different processors at the same time, its associated data structures must be protected. Semaphores are particularly well adapted for synchronization. Unlike spin-locks and suspend-locks, semaphores are not wasteful of processor cycles while a process is waiting, but their invocations require more overhead. Note that locks are still necessary to implement semaphores.

Another synchronization primitive implemented in software or microcode is Barrier, used to "join" a number of parallel processes. All processes synchronizing at a barrier must reach the barrier before any one of them can continue. Barriers can be defined as follows after the task counter Count has been initialized to zero:

```
BARRIER(N)
    { count : = count + 1;
      if (count ≥ N) then
      { Resume all processes on barrier
        queue;
```

---

*The Ready List is a data structure containing the descriptors of processes that are runable.

Table 1. Synchronization, communication, and coherence in various multiprocessors.

Multiprocessor	Number of processors	CPU architecture	Hardware primitives	Cache	Coherence scheme
IBM 3081	≤ 4	IBM 370	Compare&Swap (CS, CDS), Test&Set (TS)	Write-back	Central table
Synapse N + 1*	≤ 32	Motorola 68000	Compare&Swap (CAS), Test&Set (TAS)	Write-back	Distributed table/ bus watching
Denelcor HEP*	100s	Custom	Full/empty bit	No cache	
IBM RP3†	100s	IBM ROMP	Fetch&Op (e.g., Fetch&Add)	Write-back	No shared writable data in cache
NYU Ultracomputer†	100s		Fetch&Add	Write-back	No shared writable data in cache
Encore Multimax	≤ 20	National Semiconductor 32032	Test&Set ("interlocked" instructions)	Write-through (two processors share each cache)	Bus watching
Sequent Balance 8000	≤ 12	National Semiconductor 32032	Test&Set (spin-lock using lock cache and bus watching)	Write-through	Bus watching

*Commercial machines no longer in production.
†Experimental prototype.

Reset count; }
   else
  Block task and place in barrier
  queue;
}

The first N-1 tasks to execute Barrier would be blocked. Upon execution of Barrier by the Nth task, all N tasks are ready to resume. In the HEP each task that is blocked spin-locks on a Full/Empty bit. The Nth task that crosses the barrier writes into the tagged memory location and thereby wakes up all the blocked tasks. This technique is very efficient for executing parallel, iterative algorithms common in numerical applications.

Interprocess communication. In a shared-memory multiprocessor, interprocess communication can be as simple as one processor writing to a particular memory location and another processor reading that memory location. However, since these activities occur asynchronously, communication is in most cases implemented by synchronization mechanisms. The reading process must be informed at what time the message to be read is valid, and the writing process must know at what time it is allowed to write to a particular memory location without destroying a message yet to be read by another process. Therefore, communication is often implemented by mutually exclusive accesses to mailboxes. Mailboxes are configured and maintained in shared memory by software or microcode.

Message-based communication can be synchronous or asynchronous. In a synchronous system the sender transmits a message to a receiving process and waits until the receiving process responds with an acknowledgment that the message has been received. Symmetrically, the receiver waits for a message and then sends an acknowledgment. The sender resumes execution only when it is confirmed that the message has been received. In asynchronous systems the sending process does not wait for the receiving process to receive the message. If the receiver is not ready to receive the message at its time of arrival, the message may be buffered or simply lost. Buffering can be provided in hardware or, more appropriately, in mailboxes in shared memory.

A summary of synchronization and communication primitives for different processors is given in Table 1.

Coherence in multiprocessors

Coherence problems exist at various levels of multiprocessors. Inconsistencies (i.e., contradictory information) can occur between adjacent levels or within the same level of a memory hierarchy. For example, in a cache-based system with write-back caches, cache and main memory may contain inconsistent copies of data.[4] Multiple caches conceivably could possess different copies of the same memory block because one of the processors has modified its copy. Generally, this condition is not allowable.

In some cases data inconsistencies do not affect the correct execution of a program (for example, inconsistencies between memory and write-back caches may be tolerated). In the following paragraphs we identify the cases for which data

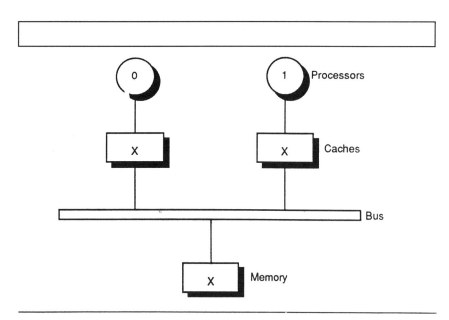

Figure 3. Cache configuration after a Load on X by processors 0 and 1. Copies in both caches are consistent.

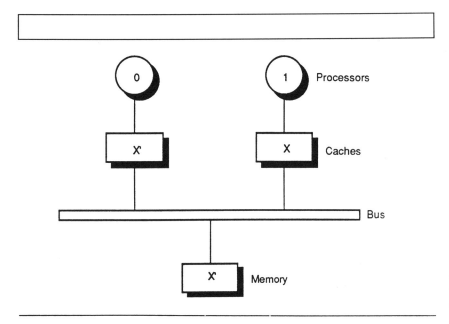

Figure 4. Cache configuration after a Store on X by processor 0 (write-through cache). The copies are inconsistent.

inconsistencies pose a problem and discuss various solutions.

Conditions for coherence. Data coherence problems do not exist in multiprocessors that maintain only a single copy of data. For example, consider a shared-memory multiprocessor in which each CPU does not have a private memory or cache (Figure 1 without optional caches). If Loads, Stores, and RMW cycles are atomic, then data elements are accessed and modified in indivisible operations. Each access to an element applies to the latest copy. Simultaneous accesses to the same element of data are serialized by the hardware.

Cache coherence problems exist in multiprocessors with private caches (Figure 1 with optional caches) and are caused by three factors: sharing of writable data, process migration, and I/O activity. To illustrate the effects of these three factors, we use a two-processor architecture with private caches (Figures 3-5). We assume that an element X is referenced by the CPUs. Let $L_j(X)$ and $S_j(X)$ denote a Load and a Store by processor j for element X in memory, respectively. If the caches do not contain copies of X initially, a Load of X by the two CPUs results in consistent copies of X, as shown in Figure 3. Next, if one of the processors performs a Store to X, then the copies of X in the caches become inconsistent. A Load by the other processor will not return the latest value. Depending on the memory update policy used in the cache, the cache level may also be inconsistent with respect to main memory. A write-through policy maintains consistency between main memory and cache. However, a write-back policy does not maintain such consistency at the time of the Store; memory is updated eventually when the modified data in the cache are replaced or invalidated. Figures 4 and 5 depict the states of the caches and memory for write-through and write-back policies, respectively.

Consistency problems also occur because of the I/O configuration in a system with caches. In Figure 6 the I/O processor (IOP) is attached to the bus, as is most commonly done. If the current state of the system is reached by an $L_0(X)$ and $S_0(X)$ sequence, a modified copy of X in cache 0 and main memory will not have been updated in the case of write-back caches. A subsequent I/O Load of X by the IOP returns a "stale" value of X as contained in memory. To solve the consistency problem in this configuration, the I/O processor must participate in the cache coherence protocol on the bus. The configuration in Figure 7 shows the IOPs sharing the caches with the CPUs. In this case I/O consistency is maintained if cache-to-cache consistency is also maintained; an obvious disadvantage of this scheme is the likely increase of cache perturbations and poor locality of I/O data, which will result in high miss ratios.

Some systems allow processes to migrate—i.e., to be scheduled in different processors during their lifetime—in order to balance the work load among the processors. If this feature is used in conjunction with private caches, data inconsistencies can result. For example, process A, which runs on CPU_0, may alter data contained in its cache by executing $S_0(X)$ before it is suspended. If process A migrates to CPU_1 before memory has been updated with the most recent value of X, process A may subsequently Load the stale value of X contained in memory.

It is obvious that a mere write-through policy will not maintain consistency in the system, since the write does not automatically update the possible copies of the data contained in the other caches. In fact, write-through is neither necessary nor sufficient for coherence.

Solutions to the cache coherence problem. Approaches to maintaining coherence in multiprocessors range from simple architectural principles that make incoherence impossible to complex memory coherence schemes that maintain coherence "on the fly" only when necessary. Here we list these approaches from least to most complex:

(1) A simple architectural technique is to disallow private caches and have only shared caches that are associated with the main memory modules. Every data access is made to the shared cache. A network interconnects the processors to the shared cache modules.

(2) For performance considerations it is desirable to attach a private cache to each CPU. Data inconsistency can be prevented by not caching shared writable data; such data are called *noncachable*. Examples of shared writable data are locks, shared data structures such as process queues, and any

other data protected by critical sections. Instructions and other data can be copied into caches as usual. Such items are referred to as *cachable*. The compiler must tag data as either cachable or noncachable. The hardware must adhere to the meaning of the tags. This technique, apparently

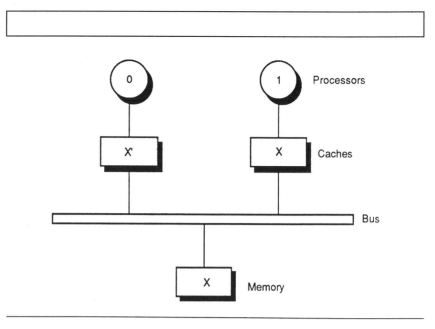

Figure 5. Same as Figure 4 but with write-back cache. The copies are inconsistent.

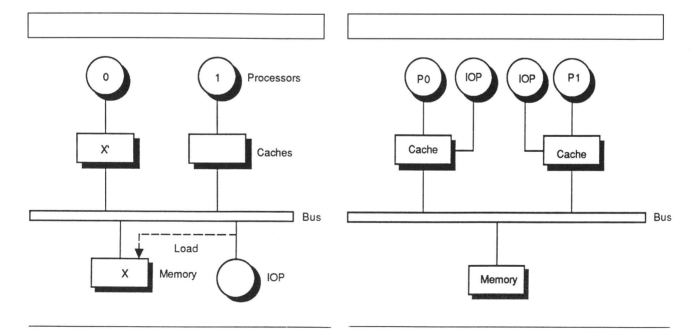

Figure 6. IOPs are attached to the bus and bypass the cache.　**Figure 7. IOPs are attached to the caches.**

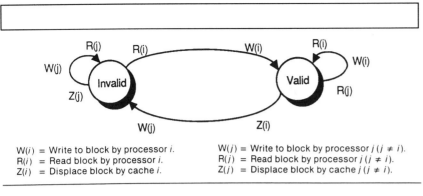

W(i) = Write to block by processor i.
R(i) = Read block by processor i.
Z(i) = Displace block by cache i.

W(j) = Write to block by processor j (j ≠ i).
R(j) = Read block by processor j (j ≠ i).
Z(j) = Displace block by cache j (j ≠ i).

Figure 8. State diagram for a given block in cache *i* for a write-through coherence protocol.

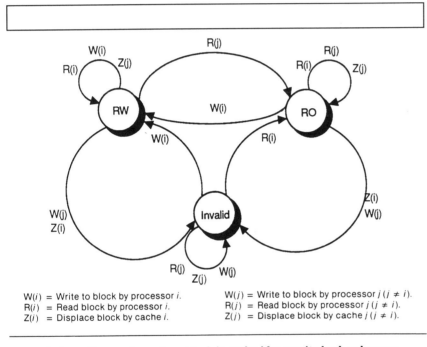

W(i) = Write to block by processor i.
R(i) = Read block by processor i.
Z(i) = Displace block by cache i.

W(j) = Write to block by processor j (j ≠ i).
R(j) = Read block by processor j (j ≠ i).
Z(j) = Displace block by cache j (j ≠ i).

Figure 9. State diagram for a given block in cache *i* for a write-back coherence protocol.

simple in principle, must rely on the detection within each CPU that a block is cachable or not. Such a detection can be made in a virtual memory environment by tagging each page. The tag is stored in entries in the CPU's translation buffers. Translation buffers (TBs) are similar to caches, but they store virtual-to-physical address translations.

(3) If all shared writable data are declared noncachable, the performance may be degraded appreciably. If accesses to shared writable data always occur in critical sections, then such data can be cached. Only the locks that protect the critical sections must remain noncachable. However, to maintain data consistency, all data modified in the critical section must be invalidated in the cache when the critical section is exited. This operation is often referred to as a *cache flush*. The flushing operation ensures that no stale data remain in the cache at the next access to the critical section. If another cache accesses the data via the acquisition of the lock, consistency is maintained. This scheme is adequate for transaction-processing systems in which a shared record is acquired,

updated in a critical section, and subsequently released. It works for write-through caches; for write-back caches, the design is more complex.

(4) A scheme allowing shared writable data to exist in multiple caches employs a centralized global table[5] and is used in many mainframe multiprocessor systems, such as the IBM 308x. The table stores the status of memory blocks so that coherence enforcement signals, called *cache cross-interrogates* (XI), can be generated on the basis of the block status. To maintain consistency, XI signals with the associated block address are propagated to the other caches either to invalidate or to change the state of the copies of the referenced block. An arbitrary number of caches can contain a copy of a block, provided that all the copies are identical. We refer to such a copy as a *read-only copy* (RO). To modify a block present in its cache, the processor must own the block with read and write access. When a block is copied from memory into cache, the block is tagged as exclusive (EX) if the cache is the only cache that has a copy of the block. A block is owned exclusively with read and write (RW) access when it has been modified. Only one processor can own an RW copy of a block at any time. The state IN (invalid) signals that the block has been invalidated.

The centralized table is usually located in the storage control element, which may also incorporate a crossbar switch that connects the CPUs to the main memory. To limit the accesses to the global table, local status flags can be provided in the cache directories for the blocks that reside in the cache. Depending on the status of the local flags and the type of request, the processor is allowed to proceed or is required to consult the global table.

(5) In bus-oriented multiprocessors the table that records the status of each block can be efficiently distributed among processors. The distributed-table scheme takes advantage of the broadcasting capability of the bus. Typically, consistency between the caches is maintained by a bus-watching mechanism, often called a *snoopy cache controller*, which implements a cache coherence protocol on the bus. In a simple scheme for write-through caches, all the snoopy controllers watch the bus for Stores. If a Store is made to a location cached in remote caches, then the copies of the block in remote caches are either invalidated or updated. This scheme also maintains coherence with I/O activity. Figure 8 depicts a state diagram of the block state changes depending on

the access type and the previous state of the block. A similar scheme was applied in the Sequent Balance 8000 multiprocessor, which can be configured with up to 12 processors.

The efficiency of the hardware that maintains coherence on the fly is vital. Recognizing that the Store traffic may contribute to bus congestion in a write-through system, Goodman proposed a scheme called *write-once*, in which the initial Store to a block copy in the cache also updates memory.[11] This Store also invalidates matching entries in remote caches, thereby ensuring that the writing processor has the only cached copy. Furthermore, Stores can be performed in the cache at the cache speed. Subsequent updates of the modified block are made in the cache only. A CPU or IOP Load is serviced by the unit (a cache or the memory) that has the latest copy of the block.

Multiprocessors with write-back caches rely on an ownership protocol. When the memory owns a block, caches can contain only RO copies of the block. Before a block is modified, ownership for exclusive access must first be obtained by a read-private bus transaction, which is broadcast to the caches and memory. If a modified block copy exists in another cache, memory must first be updated, the copy invalidated, and ownership transferred to the requesting cache. Figure 9 diagrams memory block state transitions brought about by processor actions. The first commercial multiprocessor with write-back caches was the Synapse N + 1.

Variants of the cache coherence bus protocols have been proposed. One scheme, proposed for the Spur project at the University of California, Berkeley, combines compile-time tagging of shared and private data and the ownership protocol. In another system, the Xerox Dragon multiprocessor, a write is always broadcast to other caches and main memory is updated only on replacement. These bus protocols are described and their performances compared in an article by Archibald and Baer.[12]

Advantages and disadvantages. Although scheme 1 provides coherence while being transparent to the user and the operating system, it does not reduce memory conflicts but only the memory access latency. Shared caches, by necessity, contradict the rule that processors and caches should be as close together as possible. I/O accesses must be serviced via the shared caches to maintain coherence.

> **Tagging shared writable data fails to alleviate the coherence problem caused by I/O accesses.**

There are a number of disadvantages associated with scheme 2, which tags data as cachable or noncachable. The major one is the nontransparency of the multiprocessor architecture to the user or the compiler. The user must declare data elements as shared or nonshared if a concurrent language such as Ada, Modula-2, or Concurrent Pascal is used.[13] Alternatively, a multiprocessing compiler, such as Parafrase,[10] can classify data as shared or nonshared automatically. The efficiency of these approaches depends respectively on the ability of the language to specify data structures (or parts thereof) that are shared and writable and of the compiler to detect the subset of shared writable data. Since in practical implementations a whole page must be declared as cachable or not, internal fragmentation may result, or more data than the shared writable data may become noncachable.

Tagging shared writable data also fails to alleviate the coherence problem caused by I/O accesses. Either caches must be flushed before I/O is allowed to proceed, or all data subject to I/O must be tagged as noncachable as well. Depending on the frequency of I/O operations, both approaches reduce the overall hit rate of the caches and hence the speedup obtained by using caches.

Another common drawback of tagging shared writable data rather than maintaining coherence on the fly is the inefficiency caused by process migration. Caches must be flushed before each migration or process migration must be disallowed at the cost of limiting scheduling flexibility.

Scheme 3—flushing caches only when synchronization variables are accessed—has performance problems. In practice the whole cache has to be flushed, or else the data accessed in a critical section must be tagged in the cache. I/O must also be preceded by cache flushing. Note that the programmer must be aware that coherence is restored only at synchronization points.

Scheme 3 appears to be attractive only for small caches.

Scheme 4 solves the problems caused by I/O accesses and process migration. However, a global table that must be accessed by all cache controllers can become a bottleneck, even when XIs are filtered by hardware. But the main problem of this coherence scheme is the distance between the processors and the global table. As processors become faster, the access latency of the table becomes a limiting factor of system performance; in particular, when cache access times are very fast, the time penalty for a miss (*miss penalty*) must be minimized.

By distributing the table among the caches, the last scheme partly solves the problems of table access contention and latency. However, the complexity of the bus interface unit is increased because it has to "watch" the bus. Furthermore, since the scheme relies on a broadcast bus, the number of processors that can be interconnected is limited by the bus bandwidth.

Ping-pong effect. In systems with caches employing scheme 4 or 5, the execution of synchronization primitives, such as atomic read-modify-write memory cycles, can create additional access penalties. If two or more processors are spinning on a lock, RMW cycles that cause the lock variable to bounce repeatedly from one cache to another are generated. This can be aggravated by clustering different locks into a given block of memory. However, if RMW operations are implemented carefully, spin-locks can be efficient.

Let us illustrate the ping-pong problem by an example and discuss techniques for reducing system performance degradations. In this example we will assume the use of the Test&Set(lock) instruction; however, the problem can occur with other primitives. The traditional segment of code executed to acquire access to a critical section via a spin-lock is the following:

while (TEST&SET(lock) = 1) **do** nothing;
  /* spin-lock with RMW cycles */
  < execute critical section >
RESET(lock);
  /* exit critical section */

Assume that each processor has a private write-back cache and that three or more processors attempt to access the critical section concurrently. If processor P_0 succeeds in acquiring the lock, the other processors (P_1 and P_2) will spin-lock and cause the modified lock variable to be invalidated in the other processors' caches for each access to the lock. As a result of the invalidation of the modified lock variable, the block is transferred to the requesting cache—a significant penalty. The modification is a result of the writing in the last part of the RMW memory cycle.

One technique for avoiding the ping-pong effect is to use the following segment of code in place of the while statement in the previous code segment:

repeat
    while (LOAD(lock) = 1) **do** nothing;
    /* spin without modification */
until (TEST&SET(lock) = 0);

In this segment of code the lock is first loaded to test its status. If available, a Test&Set is used to attempt acquisition. However, while a processor is attempting to acquire the lock, it "spins" locally in its cache, repeating the execution of a tight loop made of a Load followed by a Test. This spinning causes no invalidation traffic on the bus. On a subsequent release of the lock, the processors contend for the lock, and only one of them will succeed. The ping-pong problem is solved; spin-locks can therefore be implemented efficiently in cache-based systems.

Ping-ponging also occurs for shared writable variables. A typical example is the index N in the Doall loop described earlier, in the section on hardware-level synchronization mechanisms. Unless the implementation of Fetch&Add is carefully designed, accesses to the index N create a "hot spot,"[9] which in a cache-based system results in intense ping-ponging between the caches. The careful implementation of synchronization primitives and the creation of hot spots in cache-based systems are research topics that deserve more attention.

Strong and weak ordering of events

The mapping of an algorithm as conceived and understood by a human programmer into a list of machine instructions that correctly implement that algorithm is a complex process. Once the translation has been accomplished, however, it is relatively easy in the case of a uniprocessor to understand what modifications of the machine code can be made without altering the outcome of the execution. A compiler, for example, can resequence instructions to boost performance, or the processor itself can execute instructions

---

> **Local dependency checking is necessary, but it may not preserve the intended outcome of a concurrent execution.**

---

out of order if it is pipelined. This is allowable in uniprocessors, provided that hardware mechanisms (interlocks) exist to check data and control dependencies between instructions to be executed concurrently or out of program order.

If a processor is a part of a multiprocessor that executes a concurrent program, then such local dependency checking is still necessary but may not be sufficient to preserve the intended outcome of a concurrent execution. Maintaining correctness and predictability of the execution of concurrent programs is more complex for three reasons:

(1) The order in which instructions belonging to different instruction streams are executed is not fixed in a concurrent program. If no synchronization among instruction streams exists, then a very large number of different instruction interleavings is possible.

(2) If for performance reasons the order of execution of instructions belonging to the same instruction stream is different from the order implied by the program, then an even larger number of instruction interleavings is possible.

(3) If accesses are not atomic (for example, if multiple copies of the same data exist), as is the case in a cache-based system, and if not all copies are updated at the same time, then different processors can individually observe different interleavings during the same execution. In this case the total number of possible execution instantiations of a program becomes still larger.

To illustrate the possible types of interleavings, we examine the following three program segments to be executed concurrently by three processors (initially $A = B = C = 0$, and we assume that a Print statement reads both variables indivisibly during the same cycle):

P1	P2	P3
a: $A \leftarrow 1$	c: $B \leftarrow 1$	e: $C \leftarrow 1$
b: Print BC	d: Print AC	f: Print AB

If the outputs of the processors are concatenated in the order P1, P2, and P3, then the output forms a six-tuple. There are 64 possible output combinations. For example, if processors execute instructions in program order, then the execution interleaving a,b,c,d,e,f is possible and would yield the output 001011. Likewise, the interleaving a,c,e,b,d,f is possible and would yield the output 111111. If processors are allowed to execute instructions out of program order, assuming that no data dependencies exist among reordered instructions, then the interleaving b,d,f,e,a,c is possible and would yield the output 000000. Note that this outcome is not possible if processors execute instructions in program order only.

Of the 720 (6!) possible execution interleavings, 90 preserve the individual program order. We have already pointed out that of the 90 program-order interleavings not all six-tuple combinations can result (i.e., 000000 is not possible). The question remains whether out of the 720 non-program-order interleavings all six-tuple combinations can result. So far we have assumed that the memory system of the example multiprocessor is access atomic; this means that memory updates affect all processors at the same time. In a cache-based system such as depicted in Figure 1, this may not be the case; such a system can be nonatomic if an invalidation does not reach all caches at the same time.

In an atomic system it is easy to show that, indeed, not all six-tuple combinations are possible, even if processors need not adhere to program order. For example, the outcome 011001 implies the following: Processor P1 observes that C has been updated and B has not been updated yet. This implies that P3 must have executed statement e before P2 executed statement c. Processor P2 observes that A has been updated before C has been updated. This implies that P1 must have executed statement a before P3 executed statement e. Processor P3 observes that B has been updated but A has not been updated. This implies that P2 must have executed statement c before P1 executed statement a. Hence, e occurred before c, a occurred before e, and c occurred before a. Since this ordering is plainly impossible, we can conclude that in an atomic system, the outcome 011001 cannot occur.

The above conclusion does not hold true

in a nonatomic multiprocessor. Let us assume that the actual execution interleaving of instructions is a,c,e,b,d,f. Let us further assume the following sequence of events: When P1 executes b, P1's own copy of B has not been updated, but P1's own copy of C has been updated. Hence, P1 prints the tuple 01. When P2 executes d, P2's own copy of A has been updated, but P2's own copy of C has not been updated. Hence, P2 prints the tuple 10. When P3 executes f, P3's own copy of A has not been updated, but P3's own copy of B has been updated. Hence, P3 prints the tuple 01. The resulting six-tuple is indeed 011001. Note that all instructions were *executed* in program order, but other processors did not *observe* them in program order.

We might ask ourselves whether a multiprocessor functions incorrectly if it is capable of generating any or all of the above-mentioned six-tuple outputs. This question does not have a definitive answer; rather the answer depends on the expectations of the programmer. A programmer who expects a system to behave in a sequentially consistent manner will perceive the system to behave incorrectly if it allows its processors to execute accesses out of program order. The programmer will likely find that synchronization protocols using shared variables will not function. The difficulty of concurrent programming and parallel architectures stems from the effort to disallow all interleavings that will result in incorrect outcomes while not being overly restrictive.

Systems with atomic accesses. We have shown in an earlier work[14] that a necessary and sufficient condition for a system with atomic memory accesses to be sequentially consistent (the strongest condition for logical behavior) is that memory accesses must be performed in the order intended by the programmer—i.e., in program order. (A Load is considered performed at a point in time when the issuing of a Store from any processor to the same address cannot affect the value returned by the Load. Similarly, a Store on X by processor i is considered performed at a point in time when an issued Load from any processor to the same address cannot return a value of X preceding the Store.) In a system where such a condition holds, we say that storage accesses are *strongly ordered*.

In a system without caches a memory access is performed when it reaches the memory system or at any point in time

when the order of all preceding accesses to memory has become fixed. For example, if accesses are queued in a FIFO (first in, first out) buffer at the memory, then an access is performed once it is latched in the buffer. When a private cache is added to each processor, Stores can also be atomic in the case of a bus system because of the simultaneous broadcast capability of the buses; in such systems the invalidations generated by a Store and the Load requests broadcast by a processor are latched simultaneously by all the controllers (including possibly the memory controllers). As soon as each controller has taken the proper action on the invalidation, the access can be considered performed.

Buffering of access requests and invalidations also become possible if the rules governing sequential consistency are carefully observed. With extensive buffering at all levels, and provided that the interconnection and the memory system have sufficient bandwidth, the efficiency of all processors may be very high, even if the memory access latency is large compared to the processor cycle time. Two articles present more detailed discussions of the buffering of accesses and invalidations in cache-based multiprocessors.[7,15]

In a weakly ordered system the condition of strong ordering is relaxed to include accesses to synchronization variables only. Synchronization variables must be hardware-recognizable to enforce the specific conditions of strong ordering on them. Moreover, before a lock access can proceed, all previous accesses to nonsynchronization data must be allowed to "settle." This means that all shared memory accesses made before the lock operation was encountered must be completed before the lock operation can proceed. In systems that synchronize very infrequently, the relaxation of strong ordering

to weak ordering of data accesses can result in greater efficiency. For example, if the interconnection network is buffered and packet-switched, the interface between the processor and the network can send global memory requests only one at a time to the memory if strong ordering is to be enforced. The reason for this is that in such a network the access time is variable and unpredictable because of conflicts; in many cases waiting for an acknowledgment from the memory controller is the only way to ensure that global accesses are performed in program order. In the case of weak ordering the interface can send the next global access directly after the current global access has been latched in the first stage of the interconnection network, resulting in better processor efficiency. However, the frequency of lock operations will be higher in a program designed for a weakly ordered system.

Systems with nonatomic accesses. In a multiprocessor system with nonatomic accesses, it has been shown that the previous condition for strong ordering of storage accesses (and sequential consistency) is not sufficient.[14]

Example 1. In a system with a recombining network[2] the network can provide for access short-circuiting, which combines Loads and Stores to the same address within the network, before the Store reaches its destination memory module. For the parallel program in Figure 10—$S_i(X)$ and $L_i(X)$ represent global accesses "Store into location X by processor i" and "Load from location X by processor i," respectively—such short-circuiting can result in the following sequence of events:

(1) Processor 1 issues a command to store a value at memory location A.

Processor 1	Processor 2	Processor 3
.	.	.
.	.	.
$S_1(A)$	$L_2(A)$	$L_3(B)$
	$S_2(B)$	$L_3(A)$
.	.	.
.	.	.

Figure 10. Concurrent program for three processors accessing shared variables.

(2) Processor 2 reads the value written by processor 1 "on the fly" before A is updated.

(3) Because of the successful read of A in step 2, processor 2 issues a command to write a value at memory location B.

(4) Processor 3 reads the value written by processor 2; it reflects the updated B.

(5) Processor 3 reads memory location A and an old value for A is returned because the write to A by processor 1 has not propagated to A yet.

Each processor performs instructions in the order specified by the programmer, but sequential consistency is violated. Processor 2 implies that step 1 has been completed by processor 1 when it initiates step 3. In step 4 processor 3 recognizes that implication by successfully reading B. But when processor 3 then reads A, it does not find the implied new value but rather the old value. Consequently, processor 3 observes an effect of step 1 before it is capable of observing step 1 itself.

Example 2. In a cache-based system where memory accesses and invalidations are propagated one by one through a packet-switched (but not recombining) network, the same problem as in the previous example may occur. Initially, all processors have an RO copy of A in their cache.

(1) Processor 1 issues a command to store a value at memory location A. Invalidations are sent to each processor with a copy of A in its cache. (For simplicity we assume that the size of a cache block is one word.)

(2) Processor 2 reads the value of A as updated by processor 1, because the invalidation has reached its cache; processor 1 writes the data back to main memory and forwards a copy to processor 2.

(3) Because of the successful read of A in step 2, processor 2 issues a command to write a value at memory location B, sending invalidations for copies of B.

(4) Processor 3 reads the value written by processor 2; it reflects the updated B, because the associated invalidations have propagated to processor 3.

(5) Processor 3 reads memory location A and an old value for A is returned because the invalidation for A caused by processor 1 has not yet propagated to the third processor's cache.

Again each processor executes all instructions in program order. Furthermore, a processor does not proceed to issue memory accesses before all previous invalidations broadcast by the processor have been acknowledged. Yet the same problem occurs as in the previous example; sequential consistency is violated. This is the case because invalidations are essentially memory accesses. Because invalidations are not atomic, the system is not strongly ordered.

User interface

The discussion in this article shows that the issues of synchronization, communication, coherence, and ordering of events in multiprocessors are intricately related and that design decisions must be based on the environment for which the machine is destined. Coherence depends on synchronization in some coherence protocols because the user has to be aware that synchronization points are the only points in time at which coherence is restored. Strict ordering of events may be enforced all the time (strong ordering) or at synchronization points only (weak ordering).

At the user level most features of the physical (hardware) architecture are not visible. The instruction set of each processor and the virtual memory are the most important system features visible to the programs. Depending on the features of the physical architecture that are visible to the programmer, the task of programming the machine may be more difficult, and it may be more difficult to share the machine among different users.

Nontransparent coherence or ordering schemes. A sophisticated compiler may succeed in efficiently detecting and tagging the shared writable data to avoid the coherence problem. Such a compiler may also be able to make efficient use of synchronization primitives provided at different levels. The compiler may be aware of access ordering on a specific machine and generate code accordingly. It is not clear that compiler technology will improve to a point where efficient code can be generated for these different options.

If a program is written in a high-level concurrent language, the facility to specify shared writable data may not exist in the language, in which case we must still rely on the compiler for detecting the minimum set of data to tag as noncachable. It should be emphasized that perfectly legal programs in concurrent languages that allow the sharing of data, generally will not execute correctly in a system where events are weakly ordered.

User access to synchronization primitives. Programmers of concurrent applications may have in their repertoires different hardware- or software-controlled synchronization primitives. For performance reasons it may be advisable to let basic hardware-level synchronization instructions be directly accessible to users, who know their applications and can tailor the synchronization algorithm to their own needs. The basic drawback of such a policy is the increased possibility of deadlocks, resulting from programming errors or processor failure. Spin-locks and suspend-locks consume processor cycles and bus cycles. Therefore, such locks should never be held for a long time. Ideally, a processor should not be interruptible during the time that it owns a lock; for example, one or several processors may spin forever on a lock if the process that "owns" the lock has to be aborted because of an exception. In a virtual-machine environment the user process does not have any control over the interruptibility of the processor, and thus a process can be preempted while it is owning a lock. This will result in unnecessary, resource-consuming spinning from all other processes attempting to obtain the lock.

A solution to this problem is the taskforce scheduling strategy,[1] in which all active processes of a multitask are always scheduled and preempted together. Another solution is the implementation of some kind of time-out on spinning. The drastic solution to all these problems is to involve the operating system in every synchronization or communication, so that it can include these mechanisms in its scheduling policy to maximize performance.

Making a multiprocessor function correctly can be a simple or an extremely difficult task. Basic synchronization mechanisms can be primitive or complex, wasteful of processor cycles or highly efficient. In any case the underlying hardware must support the basic assumptions of the logical model expected by the user. In a strongly ordered system such an assumption usually is that the system behaves in a sequentially consistent manner.

Increased transparency comes at the cost of efficiency and increased hardware complexity. But traditional and significant advantages such as the ability to protect users against themselves and other users, ease of programming, portability of programs, and efficient management of shared resources by multiple users are strong arguments for the designers of general-purpose computers to accept the hardware complexity and the negative effect on performance. The designers of general-purpose machines will probably prefer coherence enforcement on the fly in hardware, strong ordering of memory accesses, and restricted access to synchronization primitives by the user.

On the other hand, for machines with limited access by sophisticated users, such as supercomputers and experimental multiprocessor systems, the performance of each individual task may be of prime importance, and the increased cost of transparency may not be justified.

The challenge of the future lies in the ability to control interprocess communication and synchronization in systems without rigid structures. Efficient multiprocessing will be provided by systems in which synchronization, coherence, and logical ordering of events are carefully analyzed and blended together harmoniously in the context of efficient hardware implementations. It is necessary, however, to provide the programmer with a simple logical model of concurrency behavior. When multiprocessors do not conform to the concept of a single logical model, but rather must be viewed as a dynamic pool of processing, storage, and connection resources, the control in software over communication and synchronization becomes a truly formidable task. The concepts of strong and weak ordering as defined in this article correspond to two widely accepted models of multiprocessor behavior, and we believe that future designs will conform to one of the two models.□

Acknowledgment

Through many technical discussions, William Collier of IBM Poughkeepsie helped shape the content of this article.

References

1. A.K. Jones and P. Schwarz, "Experience Using Multiprocessor Systems—A Status Report," *Computing Surveys*, June 1980, pp. 121-165.

2. A. Gottlieb et al., "The NYU Ultracomputer—Designing an MIMD Shared Memory Parallel Computer," *IEEE Trans. Computers*, Feb. 1983, pp. 175-189.

3. D. Gajski and J.-K. Peir, "Essential Issues in Multiprocessor Systems," *Computer*, June 1985, pp. 9-27.

4. A.J. Smith, "Cache Memories," *Computing Surveys*, Sept. 1982, pp. 473-530.

5. L.M. Censier and P. Feautrier, "A New Solution to Coherence Problems in Multicache Systems," *IEEE Trans. Computers*, Dec. 1978, pp. 1112-1118.

6. W.W. Collier, "Architectures for Systems of Parallel Processes," IBM Technical Report TR 00.3253, Poughkeepsie, N.Y., Jan. 1984.

7. M. Dubois, C. Scheurich, and F. Briggs, "Memory Access Buffering In Multiprocessors," *Proc. 13th Int'l Symp. Computer Architecture*, June 1986, pp. 434-442.

8. L. Lamport, "How to Make a Multiprocessor Computer That Correctly Executes Multiprocess Programs," *IEEE Trans. Computers*, Sept. 1979, pp. 690-691.

9. G.F. Pfister et al., "The IBM Research Parallel Processor Prototype (RP3): Introduction and Architecture," *Proc. 1985 Parallel Processing Conf.*, pp. 764-771.

10. D.A. Padua, D.J. Kuck, and D.H. Lawrie, "High-Speed Multiprocessors and Compilation Techniques," *IEEE Trans. Computers*, Sept. 1980, pp. 763-776.

11. J.R. Goodman, "Using Cache Memory to Reduce Processor-Memory Traffic," *Proc. 10th Int'l Symp. Computer Architecture*, June 1983, Stockholm, Sweden, pp. 124-131.

12. J. Archibald and J.-L. Baer, "Cache Coherence Protocols: Evaluation Using a Multiprocessor Simulation Model," *ACM Trans. Computer Systems*, Nov. 1986, pp. 273-298.

13. G.R. Andrews and F.B. Schneider, "Concepts and Notations for Concurrent Programming," *Computing Surveys*, Mar. 1983, pp. 3-43.

14. M. Dubois and C. Scheurich, "Dependency and Hazard Resolution in Multiprocessors," Univ. of Southern Calif. Technical Report CRI 86-20.

15. C. Scheurich and M. Dubois, "Correct Memory Operation of Cache-Based Multiprocessors," *Proc. 14th Int'l Symp. Computer Architecture*, June 1987, pp. 234-243.

Michel Dubois has been an assistant professor in the Department of Electrical Engineering of the University of Southern California since 1984. Before that, he was a research engineer at the Central Research Laboratory of Thomson-CSF in Orsay, France. His main interests are computer architecture and parallel processing with an emphasis on high-performance multiprocessor systems. He has published more than 30 technical papers on multiprocessor architectures, performance, and algorithms, and he served on the program committee of the 1987 Architecture Symposium.

Dubois holds a PhD from Purdue University, an MS from the University of Minnesota, and an engineering degree from the Faculté Polytechnique de Mons in Belgium, all in electrical engineering. He is a member of the ACM and the Computer Society of the IEEE.

Christoph Scheurich is a doctoral student and research assistant in the Department of Electrical Engineering-Systems at USC. He received the BSEE in 1981 from the University of the Pacific, Stockton, California, and the MS degree in computer engineering in 1985 from USC. His current interests lie in computer architecture, specifically the design and implementation of multiprocessor memory systems.

Scheurich is a student member of the ACM and the Computer Society of the IEEE.

Fayé A. Briggs is in the Advanced Development Group at Sun Microsystems. He was an associate professor of electrical and computer engineering at Rice University, and prior to that he was on the faculty of Purdue University. He has also served as a consultant to IBM, TI, and Sun. His current research interests are multiprocessor and vector architectures, their compilers, operating systems, and performance. He has published more than 35 technical papers in these areas and is the coauthor of *Computer Architecture and Parallel Processing* (McGraw-Hill).

Briggs has a PhD from the University of Illinois and an MS from Stanford University, both in electrical engineering.

Readers may write to the authors c/o Michel Dubois, Dept. of Electrical Engineering, University of Southern California, University Park, Los Angeles, CA 90089-0781.

Algorithms for Scalable Synchronization on Shared-Memory Multiprocessors

JOHN M. MELLOR-CRUMMEY
Rice University

and

MICHAEL L. SCOTT
University of Rochester

Busy-wait techniques are heavily used for mutual exclusion and barrier synchronization in shared-memory parallel programs. Unfortunately, typical implementations of busy-waiting tend to produce large amounts of memory and interconnect contention, introducing performance bottlenecks that become markedly more pronounced as applications scale. We argue that this problem is not fundamental, and that one can in fact construct busy-wait synchronization algorithms that induce no memory or interconnect contention. The key to these algorithms is for every processor to spin on separate *locally-accessible* flag variables, and for some other processor to terminate the spin with a single remote write operation at an appropriate time. Flag variables may be locally-accessible as a result of coherent caching, or by virtue of allocation in the local portion of physically distributed shared memory.

We present a new scalable algorithm for spin locks that generates $O(1)$ remote references per lock acquisition, independent of the number of processors attempting to acquire the lock. Our algorithm provides reasonable latency in the absence of contention, requires only a constant amount of space per lock, and requires no hardware support other than a swap-with-memory instruction. We also present a new scalable barrier algorithm that generates $O(1)$ remote references per processor reaching the barrier, and observe that two previously-known barriers can likewise be cast in a form that spins only on locally-accessible flag variables. None of these barrier algorithms requires hardware support beyond the usual atomicity of memory reads and writes.

We compare the performance of our scalable algorithms with other software approaches to busy-wait synchronization on both a Sequent Symmetry and a BBN Butterfly. Our principal conclusion is that *contention due to synchronization need not be a problem in large-scale shared-memory multiprocessors*. The existence of scalable algorithms greatly weakens the case for costly special-purpose hardware support for synchronization, and provides a case against so-called "dance hall" architectures, in which shared memory locations are equally far from all processors.

This paper was funded in part by the National Science Foundation under Cooperative Agreement CCR-8809615 and under Institutional Infrastructure grant CDA-8822724.

Authors' Addresses: J. M. Mellor-Crummey, Center for Research on Parallel Computation, Rice University, P.O. Box 1892, Houston, TX 77251-1892. M. L. Scott, Computer Science Department, University of Rochester, Rochester, NY 14627.

Categories and Subject Descriptors: B.3.2 [**Memory Structures**]: Design Styles—*cache memories, shared memories*; C.1.2 [**Processor Architecture**]: Multiple Data Stream Architectures (Multiprocessors)—*interconnection architectures, parallel processors*; C.4 [**Computer Systems Organization**]: Performance of Systems—*design studies*; D.4.1 [**Operating Systems**]: Process Management—*mutual exclusion, synchronization*; D.4.2 [**Operating Systems**]: Storage Management—*storage hierarchies*; D.4.8 [**Operating Systems**]: Performance—*measurements*

General Terms: Algorithms, Performance

Additional Key Words and Phrases: Atomic operations, barrier synchronization, contention, fetch-and-phi, locality, spin locks

---

1. INTRODUCTION

Techniques for efficiently coordinating parallel computation on MIMD, shared-memory multiprocessors are of growing interest and importance as the scale of parallel machines increases. On shared-memory machines, processors communicate by sharing data structures. To ensure the consistency of shared data structures, processors perform simple operations by using hardware-supported atomic primitives and coordinate complex operations by using synchronization constructs and conventions to protect against overlap of conflicting operations.

Synchronization constructs can be divided into two classes: *blocking* constructs that deschedule waiting processes and *busy-wait* constructs in which processes repeatedly test shared variables to determine when they may proceed. Busy-wait synchronization is fundamental to parallel programming on shared-memory multiprocessors and is preferred over scheduler-based blocking when scheduling overhead exceeds expected wait time, when processor resources are not needed for other tasks (so that the lower wake-up latency of busy waiting need not be balanced against an opportunity cost), or when scheduler-based blocking is inappropriate or impossible (for example in the kernel of an operating system).

Two of the most widely used busy-wait synchronization constructs are spin locks and barriers. Spin locks provide a means for achieving mutual exclusion (ensuring that only one processor can access a particular shared data structure at a time) and are a basic building block for synchronization constructs with richer semantics, such as semaphores and monitors. Spin locks are ubiquitously used in the implementation of parallel operating systems and application programs. Barriers provide a means of ensuring that no processes advance beyond a particular point in a computation until all have arrived at that point. They are typically used to separate "phases" of an application program. A barrier might guarantee, for example, that all processes have finished updating the values in a shared matrix in step t before any processes use the values as input in step $t + 1$.

The performance of locks and barriers is a topic of great importance. Spin locks are generally employed to protect very small critical sections, and may be executed an enormous number of times in the course of a computation. Barriers, likewise, are frequently used between brief phases of data-parallel algorithms (e.g., successive relaxation), and may be a major contributor to run time. Unfortunately, typical implementations of busy-waiting tend to produce large amounts of memory and interconnection network contention, which causes performance bottlenecks that become markedly more pronounced in larger machines and applications. As a consequence, the overhead of busy-wait synchronization is widely regarded as a serious performance problem [2, 6, 11, 14, 38, 49, 51].

When many processors busy-wait on a single synchronization variable, they create a *hot spot* that is the target of a disproportionate share of the network traffic. Pfister and Norton [38] showed that the presence of hot spots can severely degrade performance for all traffic in multistage interconnection networks, not just traffic due to synchronizing processors. As part of a larger study, Agarwal and Cherian [2] investigated the impact of synchronization on overall program performance. Their simulations of benchmarks on a cache-coherent multiprocessor indicate that memory references due to synchronization cause cache line invalidations much more often than nonsynchronization references. In simulations of the benchmarks on a 64-processor "dance hall" machine (in which each access to a shared variable traverses the processor-memory interconnection network), they observed that synchronization accounted for as much as 49 percent of total network traffic.

In response to performance concerns, the history of synchronization techniques has displayed a trend toward increasing hardware support. Early algorithms assumed only the ability to read and write individual memory locations atomically. They tended to be subtle, and costly in time and space, requiring both a large number of shared variables and a large number of operations to coordinate concurrent invocations of synchronization primitives [12, 25, 26, 36, 40]. Modern multiprocessors generally include more sophisticated atomic operations, permitting simpler and faster coordination strategies. Particularly common are various `fetch_and_`Φ operations [22] which atomically read, modify, and write a memory location. `Fetch_and_`Φ operations include `test_and_set`, `fetch_and_store` (swap), `fetch_and_add`, and `compare_and_swap`.[1]

More recently, there have been proposals for multistage interconnection networks that combine concurrent accesses to the same memory location [17, 37, 42], multistage networks that have special synchronization variables embedded in each stage of the network [21], and special-purpose cache hardware to maintain a queue of processors waiting for the same lock [14, 28, 35]. The principal purpose of these hardware primitives is to reduce the impact of busy waiting. Before adopting them it is worth considering the extent to which software techniques can achieve a similar result.

---

[1] `Fetch_and_store` exchanges a register with memory. `Compare_and_swap` compares the contents of a memory location against a given value, and sets a condition code to indicate whether they are equal. If so, it replaces the contents of the memory with a second given value.

For a wide range of shared-memory multiprocessor architectures, we contend that appropriate design of spin locks and barriers can eliminate all busy-wait contention. Specifically, by distributing data structures appropriately, we can ensure that each processor spins only on locally-accessible locations, locations that are not the target of spinning references by any other processor. All that is required in the way of hardware support is a simple set of fetch_and_Φ operations and a memory hierarchy in which each processor is able to read some portion of shared memory without using the interconnection network. On a machine with coherent caches, processors spin on locations in their caches. On a machine in which shared memory is distributed (e.g., the BBN Butterfly [8], the IBM RP3 [37], or a shared-memory hypercube [10]), processors spin only on locations in the local portion of shared memory.

The implication of our work is that efficient synchronization algorithms can be constructed *in software* for shared-memory multiprocessors of arbitrary size. Special-purpose synchronization hardware can offer only a small constant factor of additional performance for mutual exclusion, and at best a logarithmic factor for barrier synchronization.[2] In addition, the feasibility and performance of busy-waiting algorithms with local-only spinning provides a case against "dance hall" architectures in which shared memory locations are equally far from all processors.

We discuss the implementation of spin locks in Section 2, presenting both existing approaches and a new algorithm of our own design. In Section 3 we turn to the issue of barrier synchronization, explaining how existing approaches can be adapted to eliminate spinning on remote locations, and introducing a new design that achieves both a short critical path and the theoretical minimum total number of network transactions. We present performance results in Section 4 for a variety of spin lock and barrier implementations, and discuss the implications of these results for software and hardware designers. Our conclusions are summarized in Section 5.

2. SPIN LOCKS

In this section we describe a series of five implementations for a mutual-exclusion spin lock. The first four appear in the literature in one form or another. The fifth is a novel lock of our own design. Each lock can be seen as an attempt to eliminate some deficiency in the previous design. Each assumes a shared-memory environment that includes certain fetch_and_Φ operations. As noted above, a substantial body of work has also addressed mutual exclusion using more primitive read and write atomicity; the complexity of the resulting solutions is the principal motivation for the development of fetch_and_Φ primitives. Other researchers have considered mutual exclusion in the context of distributed systems [31, 39, 43, 45, 46] but the

---

[2]Hardware combining can reduce the time to achieve a barrier from $O(\log P)$ to $O(1)$ steps if processors happen to arrive at the barrier simultaneously.

characteristics of message passing are different enough from shared memory operations that solutions do not transfer from one environment to the other.

Our pseudo-code notation is meant to be more or less self explanatory. We have used line breaks to terminate statements, and indentation to indicate nesting in control constructs. The keyword `shared` indicates that a declared variable is to be shared among all processors. The declaration implies no particular physical location for the variable, but we often specify locations in comments and/or accompanying text. The keywords `processor private` indicate that each processor is to have a separate, independent copy of a declared variable. All of our atomic operations are written to take as their first argument the address of the memory location to be modified. All but `compare_and_swap` take the obvious one additional operand and return the old contents of the memory location. `Compare_and_swap (addr, old, new)` is defined as `if addr ^ != old return false; addr ^ := new; return true`. In one case (Figure 3) we have used an `atomic_add` operation whose behavior is the same as calling `fetch_and_add` and discarding the result.

2.1. The Simple `Test_and_Set` Lock

The simplest mutual exclusion lock, found in all operating system textbooks and widely used in practice, employs a polling loop to access a Boolean flag that indicates whether the lock is held. Each processor repeatedly executes a `test_and_set` instruction in an attempt to change the flag from false to true, thereby acquiring the lock. A processor releases the lock by setting it to false.

The principal shortcoming of the `test_and_set` lock is contention for the flag. Each waiting processor accesses the single shared flag as frequently as possible, using relatively expensive read-modify-write (`fetch_and_`Φ) instructions. The result is degraded performance not only of the memory bank in which the lock resides but also of the processor/memory interconnection network and, in a distributed shared-memory machine, the processor that owns the memory bank (as a result of stolen bus cycles).

`Fetch_and_`Φ instructions can be particularly expensive on cache-coherent multiprocessors since each execution of such an instruction may cause many remote invalidations. To reduce this overhead, the `test_and_set` lock can be modified to use a `test_and_set` instruction only when a previous read indicates that the `test_and_set` might succeed. This so-called test-and-test_and_set technique [44] ensures that waiting processors poll with read requests during the time that a lock is held. Once the lock becomes available, some fraction of the waiting processors detect that the lock is free and perform a `test_and_set` operation, exactly one of which succeeds, but each of which causes remote invalidations on a cache-coherent machine.

The total amount of network traffic caused by busy-waiting on a `test_and_set` lock can be reduced further by introducing delay on each processor between consecutive probes of the lock. The simplest approach employs a constant delay; more elaborate schemes use some sort of backoff on unsuccessful probes. Anderson [5] reports the best performance with exponential backoff; our experiments confirm this result. Pseudo-code for a

```
type lock = (unlocked, locked)

procedure acquire_lock (L : ^lock)
    delay : integer := 1
    while test_and_set (L) = locked     // returns old value
        pause (delay)                   // consume this many units of time
        delay := delay * 2

procedure release_lock (L : ^lock)
    lock  := unlocked
```

Fig. 1. Simple test_and_set lock with exponential backoff.

test_and_set lock with exponential backoff appears in Figure 1. Test_and_set suffices when using a backoff scheme; test-and-test_and_set is not necessary.

2.2. The Ticket Lock

In a test-and-test_and_set lock, the number of read-modify-write operations is substantially less than for a simple test_and_set lock but still potentially large. Specifically, it is possible for every waiting processor to perform a test_and_set operation every time the lock becomes available, even though only one can actually acquire the lock. We can reduce the number of fetch_and_Φ operations to one per lock acquisition with what we call a ticket lock. At the same time, we can ensure FIFO service by granting the lock to processors in the same order in which they first requested it. A ticket lock is fair in a strong sense; it eliminates the possibility of starvation.

A ticket lock consists of two counters, one containing the number of requests to acquire the lock, and the other the number of times the lock has been released. A processor acquires the lock by performing a fetch_and_in-crement operation on the request counter and waiting until the result (its *ticket*) is equal to the value of the release counter. It releases the lock by incrementing the release counter. In the terminology of Reed and Kanodia [41], a ticket lock corresponds to the busy-wait implementation of a semaphore using an eventcount and a sequencer. It can also be thought of as an optimization of a Lamport's bakery lock [24], which was designed for fault-tolerance rather than performance. Instead of spinning on the release counter, processors using a bakery lock repeatedly examine the tickets of their peers.

Though it probes with read operations only (and thus avoids the overhead of unnecessary invalidations in coherent cache machines), the ticket lock still causes substantial memory and network contention through polling of a common location. As with the test_and_set lock, this contention can be reduced by introducing delay on each processor between consecutive probes of the lock. In this case, however, exponential backoff is clearly a bad idea. Since processors acquire the lock in FIFO order, overshoot in backoff by the first processor in line will delay all others as well, causing them to back off even farther. Our experiments suggest that a reasonable delay can be determined by using information not available with a test_and_set lock: namely, the number of processors already waiting for the lock. The delay can

```
type lock = record
    next_ticket : unsigned integer := 0
    now_serving : unsigned integer := 0

procedure acquire_lock (L : ^lock)
    my_ticket : unsigned integer := fetch_and_increment (&L->next_ticket)
        // returns old value; arithmetic overflow is harmless
    loop
        pause (my_ticket - L->now_serving)
            // consume this many units of time
            // on most machines, subtraction works correctly despite overflow
        if L->now_serving = my_ticket
            return

procedure release_lock (L : ^lock)
    L->now_serving := L->now_serving + 1
```

Fig. 2. Ticket lock with proportional backoff.

be computed as the difference between a newly-obtained ticket and the current value of the release counter.

Delaying for an appropriate amount of time requires an estimate of how long it will take each processor to execute its critical section and pass the lock to its successor. If this time is known exactly, it is in principle possible to acquire the lock with only two probes, one to determine the number of processors already in line (if any), and another (if necessary) to verify that one's predecessor in line has finished with the lock. This sort of accuracy is not likely in practice, however, since critical sections do not in general take identical, constant amounts of time. Moreover, delaying proportional to the expected *average* time to hold the lock is risky: if the processors already in line average less than the expected amount, the waiting processor will delay too long and slow the entire system. A more appropriate constant of proportionality for the delay is the *minimum* time that a processor can hold the lock. Pseudo-code for a ticket lock with proportional backoff appears in Figure 2. It assumes that the new_ticket and now_serving counters are large enough to accommodate the maximum number of simultaneous requests for the lock.

2.3. Array-Based Queuing Locks

Even using a ticket lock with porportional backoff, it is not possible to obtain a lock with an expected constant number of network transactions, due to the unpredictability of the length of critical sections. Anderson [5] and Graunke and Thakkar [18] have proposed locking algorithms that achieve the constant bound on cache-coherent multiprocessors that support atomic fetch_and_increment or fetch_and_store, respectively. The trick is for each processor to use the atomic operation to obtain the address of a location on which to spin. Each processor spins on a different location, in a different cache line. Anderson's experiments indicate that his queuing lock outperforms a test_and_set lock with exponential backoff on the Sequent Symmetry when more than six

```
type lock = record
    slots : array [0..numprocs -1] of (has_lock, must_wait)
        := (has_lock, must_wait, must_wait, ..., must_wait)
        // each element of slots should lie in a different memory module
        // or cache line
    next_slot : integer := 0

// parameter my_place, below, points to a private variable
// in an enclosing scope

procedure acquire_lock (L : ^lock, my_place : ^integer)
    my_place^ := fetch_and_increment (&L->next_slot)
        // returns old value
    if my_place^ mod numprocs = 0
        atomic_add (&L->next_slot, -numprocs)
        // avoid problems with overflow; return value ignored
    my_place^ := my_place^ mod numprocs
    repeat while L->slots[my_place^] = must_wait        // spin
    L->slots[my_place^] := must_wait                    // init for next time

procedure release_lock (L : ^lock, my_place : ^integer)
    L->slots[(my_place^ + 1) mod numprocs] := has_lock
```

Fig. 3.   Anderson's array-based queuing lock.

processors are competing for access. Graunke and Thakkar's experiments indicate that their lock outperforms a test_and_set lock on the same machine when more than three processors are competing.

Pseudo-code for Anderson's lock appears in Figure 3;[3] Graunke and Thakkar's lock appears in Figure 4. The likely explanation for the better performance of Graunke and Thakkar's lock is that fetch_and_store is supported directly in hardware on the Symmetry; fetch_and_add is not. To simulate fetch_and_add, Anderson protected his queue-based lock with an outer test_and_set lock. This outer lock (not shown in Figure 3) introduces additional overhead and can cause contention when the critical section protected by the queue-based lock is shorter than the time required to acquire and release the outer lock. In this case competing processors spend their time spinning on the outer test_and_set lock rather than the queue-based lock.

Neither Anderson nor Graunke and Thakkar included the ticket lock in their experiments. In qualitative terms both the ticket lock (with proportional backoff) and the array-based queuing locks guarantee FIFO ordering of requests. Both the ticket lock and Anderson's lock use an atomic fetch_and_increment instruction. The ticket lock with porportional backoff is likely to require more network transactions on a cache-coherent multiprocessor but fewer on a multiprocessor without coherently cached shared variables. The array-based queuing locks require space *per lock* linear in the number of processors whereas the ticket lock requires only a small constant

---

[3]Anderson's original pseudo-code did not address the issue of overflow, which causes his algorithm to fail unless numprocs = 2^k. Our variant of his algorithm addresses this problem.

```
type lock = record
    slots : array [0..numprocs -1] of Boolean := true
        // each element of slots should lie in a different memory module
        // or cache line
    tail : record
        who_was_last : ^Boolean := 0
        this_means_locked : Boolean := false
        // this_means_locked is a one-bit quantity.
        // who_was_last points to an element of slots.
        // if all elements lie at even addresses, this tail "record"
        // can be made to fit in one word
processor private vpid : integer // a unique virtual processor index

procedure acquire_lock (L : ^lock)
    (who_is_ahead_of_me : ^Boolean, what_is_locked : Boolean)
        := fetch_and_store (&L->tail, (&slots[vpid], slots[vpid]))
    repeat while who_is_ahead_of_me^ = what_is_locked

procedure release_lock (L : ^lock)
    L->slots[vpid] := not L->slots[vpid]
```

Fig. 4.   Graunke and Thakkar's array-based queuing lock.

amount of space.[4] We provide quantitative comparisons of the locks' performance in Section 4.3.

2.4. A New List-Based Queuing Lock

We have devised a new mechanism called the MCS lock (after out initials) that

—guarantees FIFO ordering of lock acquisitions;
—spins on locally-accessible flag variables only;
—requires a small constant amount of space per lock; and
—works equally well (requiring only $0(1)$ network transactions per lock acquisition) on machines with and without coherent caches.

The first of these advantages is shared with the ticket lock and the array-based queuing locks, but not with the test_and_set lock. The third is shared with the test_and_set and ticket locks, but not with the array-based queuing locks. The fourth advantage is in large part a consequence of the second and is unique to the MCS lock.

Our lock was inspired by the Queue On Lock Bit (QOLB) primitive proposed for the cache controllers of the Wisconsin Multicube [14], but is implemented entirely in software. It requires an atomic fetch_and_store (swap) instruction and benefits from the availability of compare_and_swap. Without compare_and_swap, we lose the guarantee of FIFO ordering and

---

[4]At first glance, one might suspect that the flag bits of the Graunke and Thakkar lock could be allocated on a per-processor basis, rather than a per-lock basis. Once a processor releases a lock, however, it cannot use its bit for anything else until some other processor has acquired the lock it released.

```
type qnode = record
    next : ^qnode
    locked : Boolean
type lock = ^qnode

// parameter I, below, points to a qnode record allocated
// (in an enclosing scope) in shared memory locally-accessible
// to the invoking processor

procedure acquire_lock (L : ^lock, I : ^qnode)
    I->next := nil
    predecessor : ^qnode := fetch_and_store (L, I)
    if predecessor != nil      // queue was non-empty
        I->locked := true
        predecessor->next := I
        repeat while I->locked              // spin

procedure release_lock (L : ^lock, I: ^qnode)
    if I->next = nil      // no known successor
        if compare_and_swap (L, I, nil)
            return
            // compare_and_swap returns true iff it swapped
        repeat while I->next = nil          // spin
    I->next->locked := false
```

Fig. 5.   The MCS list-based queuing lock.

introduce the theoretical possibility of starvation, though lock acquisitions
are likely to remain very nearly FIFO in practice.

Pseudo-code for our lock appears in Figure 5. Every processor using the
lock allocates a qnode record containing a queue link and a Boolean flag.
Each processor employs one additional temporary variable during the ac-
quire_lock operation. Processors holding or waiting for the lock are chained
together by the links. Each processor spins on its own locally-accessible flag.
The lock itself contains a pointer to the qnode record for the processor at the
tail of the queue, or a nil if the lock is not held. Each processor in the queue
holds the address of the record for the processor behind it—the processor it
should resume after acquiring and releasing the lock. Compare_and_swap
enables a processor to determine whether it is the only processor in the
queue, and if so remove itself correctly, as a single atomic action. The spin in
acquire_lock waits for the lock to become free. The spin in release_lock
compensates for the timing window between the fetch_and_store and the
assignment to predecessor->next in acquire_lock. Both spins are local.

Figure 6, parts (a) through (e), illustrates a series of acquire_lock and
release_lock operations. The lock itself is represented by a box containing
an 'L.' The other rectangles are qnode records. A box with a slash through it
represents a nil pointer. Non-nil pointers are directed arcs. In (a), the lock is
free. In (b), processor 1 has acquired the lock. It is running (indicated by the
'R'), thus its locked flag is irrelevant (indicated by putting the 'R' in
parentheses). In (c), two more processors have entered the queue while the
lock is still held by processor 1. They are blocked spinning on their locked

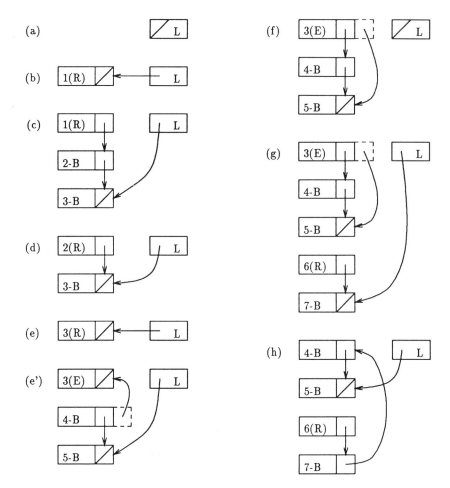

Fig. 6. Pictorial example of MCS locking protocol in the presence of competition.

flags (indicated by the 'B's.). In (d), processor 1 has completed and has changed the locked flag of processor 2 so that it is now running. In (e), processor 2 has completed, and has similarly unblocked processor 3. If no more processors enter the queue in the immediate future, the lock will return to the situation in (a) when processor 3 completes its critical section.

Alternative code for the `release_lock` operation, without `compare_and_swap`, appears in Figure 7. Like the code in Figure 5, it spins on processor-specific, locally-accessible memory locations only, requires constant space per lock, and requires only $0(1)$ network transactions regardless of whether the machine provides coherent caches. Its disadvantages are extra complexity and the loss of strict FIFO ordering.

Parts (e) through (h) of Figure 6 illustrate the subtleties of the alternative code for `release_lock`. In the original version of the lock, `compare_and_swap` ensures that updates to the tail of the queue happen atomically. There are no

```
procedure release_lock (L : ^lock, I : ^qnode)
    if I->next = nil        // no known successor
        old_tail : ^qnode := fetch_and_store (L, nil)
        if old_tail = I     // I really had no successor
            return
        // we have accidentally removed some processor(s) from the queue;
        // we need to put them back
        usurper := fetch_and_store (L, old_tail)
        repeat while I->next = nil          // wait for pointer to victim list
        if usurper != nil
            // somebody got into the queue ahead of our victims
            usurper->next := I->next        // link victims after the last usurper
        else
            I->next->locked := false
    else
        I->next->locked := false
```

Fig. 7. Code for release_lock, without compare_and_swap.

processors waiting in line if and only if the tail pointer of the queue points to the processor releasing the lock. Inspecting the processor's next pointer is solely an optimization to avoid unnecessary use of a comparatively expensive atomic instruction. Without compare_and_swap, inspection and update of the tail pointer cannot occur atomically. When processor 3 is ready to release its lock, it assumes that no other processor is in line if its next pointer is nil. In other words, it assumes that the queue looks the way it does in (e). (It could equally well make this assumption after inspecting the tail pointer and finding that it points to itself, but the next pointer is local and the tail pointer is probably not.) This assumption may be incorrect because other processors may have linked themselves into the queue between processor 3's inspection and its subsequent update of the tail. The queue may actually be in the state shown in (e'), with one or more processors in line behind processor 3, the first of which has yet to update 3's next pointer. (The 'E' in parentheses on processor 3 indicates that it is exiting its critical section; the value of its locked flag is irrelevant.)

When new processors enter the queue during this timing window, the data structure temporarily takes on the form shown in (f). The return value of processor 3's first fetch_and_store in release_lock (shown in the extra dotted box) is the tail pointer for a list of processors that have accidentally been linked out of the queue. By waiting for its next pointer to become non-nil, processor 3 obtains a head pointer for this "victim" list. It can patch the victim processors back into the queue, but before it does so additional processors ("usurpers") may enter the queue with the first of them acquiring the lock, as shown in (g). Processor 3 puts the tail of the victim list back into the tail pointer of the queue with a fetch_and_store. If the return value of this fetch_and_store is nil, processor 3 unblocks its successor. Otherwise, as shown in (h), processor 3 inserts the victim list behind the usurpers by writing its next pointer (the head of the victim list) into the next pointer of the tail of the usurper list. In either case, the structure of the queue is restored.

227

To demonstrate formal correctness of the MCS lock, we can prove mutual exclusion, deadlock freedom, and fairness for a version of the algorithm in which the entire `acquire_lock` and `release_lock` procedures comprise atomic actions that are broken only when a processor waits (in `acquire_lock`) for the lock to become available. We can then refine this algorithm through a series of correctness-preserving transformations into the code in Figure 5. The first transformation breaks the atomic action of `acquire_lock` in two and introduces auxiliary variables that indicate when a processor has modified the tail pointer of the queue to point at its qnode record, but has not yet modified its predecessor's next pointer. To preserve the correctness proof in the face of this transformation, we (1) relax the invariants on queue structure to permit a non-tail processor to have a `nil` next pointer, so long as the auxiliary variables indicate that its successor is in the timing window, and (2) introduce a spin in `release_lock` to force the processor to wait for its next pointer to be updated before using it. The second transformation uses proofs of interference freedom to move statements outside of the three atomic actions. The action containing the assignment to a predecessor's next pointer can then be executed without explicit atomicity; it inspects or modifies only one variable that is modified or inspected in any other process. The other two actions are reduced to the functionality of `fetch_and_store` and `compare_and_swap`. The details of this argument are straightforward but lengthy (they appear as an appendix to the technical report version of this paper [33]); we find the informal description and pictures above more intuitively convincing.

3. BARRIERS

Barriers have received a great deal of attention in the literature, more so even than spin locks, and the many published algorithms differ significantly in notational conventions and architectural assumptions. We present five different barriers in this section: four from the literature and one of our own design. We have modified some of the existing barriers to increase their locality of reference or otherwise improve their performance; we note where we have done so.

3.1. Centralized Barriers

In a centralized implementation of barrier synchronization, each processor updates a small amount of shared state to indicate its arrival and then polls that state to determine when all of the processors have arrived. Once all of the processors have arrived, each processor is permitted to continue past the barrier. Like the `test_and_set` spin lock, centralized barriers are of uncertain origin. Essentially equivalent algorithms have undoubtedly been invented by numerous individuals.

Most barriers are designed to be used repeatedly (to separate phases of a many-phase algorithm, for example). In the most obvious formulation, each instance of a centralized barrier begins and ends with identical values for the shared state variables. Each processor must spin twice per instance; once to

```
shared count : integer := P
shared sense : Boolean := true
processor private local_sense : Boolean := true

procedure central_barrier
    local_sense := not local_sense    // each processor toggles its own sense
    if fetch_and_decrement (&count) = 1
        count := P
        sense := local_sense          // last processor toggles global sense
    else
        repeat until sense = local_sense
```

Fig. 8.   A sense-reversing centralized barrier.

ensure that all processors have left the previous barrier and again to ensure
that all processors have arrived at the current barrier. Without the first spin,
it is possible for a processor to mistakenly pass through the current barrier
because of state information being used by processors still leaving the
previous barrier. Two barrier algorithms proposed by Tang and Yew (the
first algorithm appears in [48, Algorithm 3.1] and [49, p. 3]; the second
algorithm appears in [49, Algorithm 3.1]) suffer from this type of flaw.

We can reduce the number of references to the shared state variables and
simultaneously eliminate one of the two spinning episodes by "reversing the
sense" of the variables (and leaving them with different values) between
consecutive barriers [19].[5] The resulting code is shown in Figure 8. Arriving
processors decrement count and then wait until sense has a different value
than it did in the previous barrier. The last arriving processor resets count
and reverses sense. Consecutive barriers cannot interfere with each other
because all operations on count occur before sense is toggled to release the
waiting processors.

Lubachevsky [29] presents a similar barrier algorithm that uses two shared
counters and a processor private two-state flag. The private flag selects which
counter to use; consecutive barriers use alternate counters. Another similar
barrier can be found in library packages distributed by Sequent Corporation
for the Symmetry multiprocessor. Arriving processors read the current value
of a shared epoch number, update a shared counter, and spin until the epoch
number changes. The last arriving processor reinitializes the counter and
advances the epoch number.

The potential drawback of centralized barriers is the spinning that occurs
on a single, shared location. Because processors do not in practice arrive at a
barrier simultaneously, the number of busy-wait accesses will in general be
far above the minimum.[6] On broadcast-based cache-coherent multiprocessors,

---

[5] A similar technique appears in [4, p. 445], where it is credited to Isaac Dimitrovsky.
[6] Commenting on Tang and Yew's barrier algorithm (Algorithm 3.1 in [48]), Agarwal and
Cherian [2] show that on a machine in which contention causes memory accesses to be aborted
and retried, the expected number of memory accesses initiated by each processor to achieve a
single barrier is linear in the number of processors participating, even if processors arrive at the
barrier at approximately the same time.

these accesses may not be a problem. The shared flag or sense variable is replicated into the cache of every waiting processor, so subsequent busy-wait accesses can be satisfied without any network traffic. This shared variable is written only when the barrier is achieved, causing a single broadcast invalidation of all cached copies.[7] All busy-waiting processors then acquire the new value of the variable and are able to proceed. On machines without coherent caches, however, or on machines with directory-based caches without broadcast, busy-wait references to a shared location may generate unacceptable levels of memory and interconnect contention.

To reduce the interconnection network traffic caused by busy waiting on a barrier flag, Agarwal and Cherian [2] investigated the utility of adaptive backoff schemes. They arranged for processors to delay between successive polling operations for geometrically-increasing amounts of time. Their results indicate that in many cases such exponential backoff can substantially reduce the amount of network traffic required to achieve a barrier. However, with this reduction in network traffic often comes an increase in latency at the barrier. Processors in the midst of a long delay do not immediately notice when all other processors have arrived. Their departure from the barrier is therefore delayed, which in turn delays their arrival at subsequent barriers.

Agarwal and Cherian also note that for systems with more than 256 processors, for a range of arrival intervals and delay ratios, backoff strategies are of limited utility for barriers that spin on a single flag [2]. In such large-scale systems, the number of network accesses per processor increases sharply as collisions in the interconnection network cause processors to repeat accesses. These observations imply that centralized barrier algorithms will not scale well to large numbers of processors even when using adaptive backoff strategies. Our experiments (see Section 4.4) confirm this conclusion.

3.2. The Software Combining Tree Barrier

To reduce hot-spot contention for synchronization variables, Yew, Tzeng, and Lawrie [51] have devised a data structure known as a software combining tree. Like hardware combining in a multistage interconnection network [17], a software combining tree serves to collect multiple references to the same shared variable into a single reference whose effect is the same as the combined effect of the individual references. A shared variable that is expected to be the target of multiple concurrent accesses is represented as a tree of variables, with each node in the tree assigned to a different memory module. Processors are divided into groups, with one group assigned to each leaf of the tree. Each processor updates the state in its leaf. If it discovers that it is the last processor in its group to do so, it continues up the tree and updates its parent to reflect the collective updates to the child. Proceeding in this fashion, late-coming processors eventually propagate updates to the root of the tree.

---

[7]This differs from the situation in simple spin locks, where a waiting processor can expect to suffer an invalidation for every contending processor that acquires the lock before it.

```
type node = record
    k : integer              // fan-in of this node
    count : integer          // initialized to k
    locksense : Boolean      // initially false
    parent : ^node           // pointer to parent node; nil if root

shared nodes : array [0..P-1] of node
    // each element of nodes allocated in a different memory module or cache line
processor private sense : Boolean  := true
processor private mynode : ^node     // my group's leaf in the combining tree

procedure combining_barrier
    combining_barrier_aux (mynode)      // join the barrier
    sense := not sense                  // for next barrier

procedure combining_barrier_aux (nodepointer: ^node)
    with nodepointer^ do
        if fetch_and_decrement (&count) = 1     // last one to reach this node
            if parent != nil
                combining_barrier_aux (parent)
            count := k                      // prepare for next barrier
            locksense := not locksense      // release waiting processors
        repeat until locksense = sense
```

Fig. 9.   A software combining tree barrier with optimized wakeup.

Combining trees are presented as a general technique that can be used for several purposes. At every level of the tree, atomic instructions are used to combine the arguments to write operations or to split the results of read operations. In the context of this general framework, Tang and Yew [49] describe how software combining trees can be used to implement a barrier. Writes into one tree are used to determine that all processors have reached the barrier; reads out of a second are used to allow them to continue. Figure 9 shows an optimized version of the combining tree barrier. We have used the sense-reversing technique to avoid overlap of successive barriers without requiring two spinning episodes per barrier, and have replaced the atomic instructions of the second combining tree with simple reads, since no real information is returned.

Each processor begins at a leaf of the combining tree and decrements its leaf's count variable. The last processor to reach each node in the tree continues up to the next level. The processor that reaches the root of the tree begins a reverse wave of updates to locksense flags. As soon as it awakes, each processor retraces its path through the tree unblocking its siblings at each node along the path. Simulations by Yew, Tzeng, and Lawrie [51] show that a software combining tree can significantly decrease memory contention and prevent tree saturation (a form of network congestion that delays the response of the network to large numbers of references [38]) in multistage interconnection networks by distributing accesses across the memory modules of the machine.

231

From our point of view, the principal shortcoming of the combining tree barrier is that it requires processors to spin on memory locations that cannot be statically determined, and on which other processors also spin. On broadcast-based cache-coherent machines, processors may obtain local copies of the tree nodes on which they spin but on other machines (including the Cedar machine which Yew, Tzeng, and Lawrie simulated) processors will spin on remote locations, leading to unnecessary contention for interconnection network bandwidth. In Section 3.5 we present a new tree-based barrier algorithm in which each processor spins on its own unique location, statically determined and thus presumably locally accessible. Our algorithm uses no atomic instructions other than read and write, and performs the minimum possible number of oprations across the processor-memory interconnect.

3.3. The Dissemination Barrier

Brooks [9] has proposed a symmetric "butterfly barrier," in which processors participate as equals, performing the same operations at each step. Each processor in a butterfly barrier participates in a sequence of $\sim \log_2 P$ pairwise synchronizations. In round k (counting from zero), processor i synchronizes with processor $i \oplus 2^k$ where $\oplus$ is the exclusive or operator. If the number of processors is not a power of 2, then existing processors stand in for the missing ones, thereby participating in as many as $2 \lceil \log_2 P \rceil$ pairwise synchronizations.

Hensgen, Finkel, and Manber [19] describe a "dissemination barrier" that improves on Brooks's algorithm by employing a more efficient pattern of synchronizations and by reducing the cost of each synchronization. Their barrier takes its name from an algorithm developed to disseminate information among a set of processes. In round k, processor i signals processor $(i + 2^k) \bmod P$ (synchronization is no longer pairwise). This pattern does not require existing processes to stand in for missing ones, and therefore requires only $\lceil \log_2 P \rceil$ synchronization operations on its critical path regardless of P. Reference [19] contains a more detailed description of the synchronization pattern and a proof of its correctness.

For each signalling operation of the dissemination barrier, Hensgen, Finkel, and Manber use alternating sets of variables in consecutive barrier episodes, avoiding interference without requiring two separate spins in each operation. They also use sense reversal to avoid resetting variables after every barrier. The first change also serves to eliminate remote spinning. The authors motivate their algorithmic improvements in terms of reducing the number of instructions executed in the course of a signalling operation, but we consider the elimination of remote spinning to be an even more important benefit. The flags on which each processor spins are statically determined, and no two processors spin on the same flag. Each flag can therefore be located near the processor that reads it, leading to local-only spinning on any machine with local shared memory or coherent caches.

Figure 10 presents the dissemination barrier. The parity variable controls the use of alternating sets of flags in successive barrier episodes. On a

```
type flags = record
    myflags : array [0..1] of array [0..LogP-1] of Boolean
    partnerflags : array [0..1] of array [0..LogP-1] of ^Boolean

processor private parity : integer := 0
processor private sense : Boolean := true
processor private localflags : ^flags
shared allnodes : array [0..P-1] of flags
    // allnodes[i] is allocated in shared memory
    // locally accessible to processor i

    // on processor i, localflags points to allnodes[i]
    // initially allnodes[i].myflags[r][k] is false for all i, r, k
    // if j = (i+2^k) mod P, then for r = 0, 1:
    //     allnodes[i].partnerflags[r][k] points to allnodes[j].myflags[r][k]

procedure dissemination_barrier
    for instance : integer := 0 to LogP-1
        localflags^.partnerflags[parity][instance]^ := sense
        repeat until localflags^.myflags[parity][instance] = sense
    if parity = 1
        sense := not sense
    parity := 1 - parity
```

Fig. 10. The scalable, distributed dissemination barrier with only local spinning.

machine with distributed shared memory and without coherent caches, the shared allnodes array would be scattered statically across the memory banks of the machine, or replaced by a scattered set of variables.

3.4. Tournament Barriers

Hensgen, Finkel, and Manber [19] and Lubachevsky [30] have also devised tree-style "tournament" barriers. The processors involved in a tournament barrier begin at the leaves of a binary tree much as they would in a combining tree of fan-in two. One processor from each node continues up the tree to the next "round" of the tournament. At each stage, however, the "winning" processor is statically determined and there is no need for fetch_and_Φ instructions.

In round k (counting from zero) of Hensgen, Finkel, and Manber's barrier, processor i sets a flag awaited by processor j, where $i \equiv 2^k \pmod{2^{k+1}}$ and $j = i - 2^k$. Processor i then drops out of the tournament and busy waits on a global flag for notice that the barrier has been achieved. Processor j participates in the next round of the tournament. A complete tournament consists of $\lceil \log_2 P \rceil$ rounds. Processor 0 sets a global flag when the tournament is over.

Lubachevsky [30] presents a concurrent read, exclusive write (CREW) tournament barrier that uses a global flag for wakeup similar to that of Hensgen, Finkel, and Manber. He also presents an exclusive read, exclusive write (EREW) tournament barrier in which each processor spins on separate flags in a binary wakeup tree, similar to wakeup in a binary combining tree using Figure 9.

Because all processors busy wait on a single global flag, Hensgen, Finkel, and Manber's tournament barrier and Lubachevsky's CREW barrier are appropriate for multiprocessors that use broadcast to maintain cache consistency. They will cause heavy interconnect traffic, however, on machines that lack coherent caches or that limit the degree of cache line replication. Lubachevsky's EREW tournament could be used on any multiprocessor with coherent caches, including those that use limited-replication directory-based caching without broadcast. Unfortunately, in Lubachevsky's EREW barrier algorithm, each processor spins on a non-contiguous set of elements in an array, and no simple scattering of these elements will suffice to eliminate spinning-related network traffic on a machine without coherent caches.

By modifying Hensgen, Finkel, and Manber's tournament barrier to use a wakeup tree, we have constructed an algorithm in which each processor spins on its own set of contiguous, statically allocated flags (see Figure 11). The resulting code is able to avoid spinning across the interconnection network both on cache-coherent machines and on distributed shared memory multiprocessors. In addition to employing a wakeup tree, we have modified Hensgen, Finkel, and Manber's algorithm to use sense reversal to avoid reinitializing flag variables in each round. These same modifications have been discovered independently by Craig Lee of Aerospace Corporation [27].

Hensgen, Finkel, and Manber provide performance figures for the Sequent Balance (a bus-based, cache-coherent multiprocessor), comparing their tournament algorithm against the dissemination barrier as well as Brooks's butterfly barrier. They report that the tournament barrier outperforms the dissemination barrier when $P > 16$. The dissemination barrier requires $O(P \log P)$ network transactions, while the tournament barrier requires only $O(P)$. Beyond 16 processors, the additional factor of $\log P$ in bus traffic for the dissemination barrier dominates the higher constant of the tournament barrier. However, on scalable multiprocessors with multistage interconnection networks, many of the network transactions required by the dissemination barrier algorithm can proceed in parallel without interference.

3.5. A New Tree-Based Barrier

We have devised a new barrier algorithm that

—spins on locally-accessible flag variables only;

—requires only $O(P)$ space for P processors;

—performs the theoretical minimum number of network transactions ($2P-2$) on machines without broadcast; and

—performs $O(\log P)$ network transactions on its critical path.

To synchronize P processors, our barrier employs a pair of P-node trees. Each processor is assigned a unique tree node which is linked into an arrival tree by a parent link and into a wakeup tree by a set of child links. It is useful to think of these as separate trees because the fan-in in the arrival tree differs from the fan-out in the wakeup tree. We use a fan-in of 4 (1) because it produced the best performance in Yew, Tzeng, and Lawrie's

```
type round_t = record
    role : (winner, loser, bye, champion, dropout)
    opponent : ^Boolean
    flag : Boolean
shared rounds : array [0..P-1][0..LogP] of round_t
    // row vpid of rounds is allocated in shared memory
    // locally accessible to processor vpid
processor private sense : Boolean := true
processor private vpid : integer // a unique virtual processor index

// initially
//     rounds[i][k].flag = false for all i,k
// rounds[i][k].role =
//     winner if k > 0, i mod 2^k = 0, i + 2^(k-1) < P, and 2^k < P
//     bye if k > 0, i mod 2^k = 0, and i + 2^(k-1) >= P
//     loser if k > 0 and i mod 2^k = 2^(k-1)
//     champion if k > 0, i = 0, and 2^k >= P
//     dropout if k = 0
//     unused otherwise; value immaterial
// rounds[i][k].opponent points to
//     rounds[i-2^(k-1)][k].flag if rounds[i][k].role = loser
//     rounds[i+2^(k-1)][k].flag if rounds[i][k].role = winner or champion
//     unused otherwise; value immaterial

procedure tournament_barrier
    round : integer := 1
    loop                   // arrival
        case rounds[vpid][round].role of
            loser:
                rounds[vpid][round].opponent^ := sense
                repeat until rounds[vpid][round].flag = sense
                exit loop
            winner:
                repeat until rounds[vpid][round].flag = sense
            bye:           // do nothing
            champion:
                repeat until rounds[vpid][round].flag = sense
                rounds[vpid][round].opponent^ := sense
                exit loop
            dropout:   // impossible
        round := round + 1
    loop                   // wakeup
        round := round - 1
        case rounds[vpid][round].role of
            loser:         // impossible
            winner:
                rounds[vpid][round].opponent^ := sense
            bye:           // do nothing
            champion:      // impossible
            dropout:
                exit loop
    sense := not sense
```

Fig. 11.   A scalable, distributed tournament barrier with only local spinning.

experiments with software combining, and (2) because the ability to pack 4 bytes in a word permits an optimization on many machines in which a parent can inspect status information for all of its children simultaneously at the same cost as inspecting the status of only one. We use a fan-out of 2 because it results in the shortest critical path to resume P spinning processors for a tree of uniform degree. To see this, note that in a p-node tree with fan-out k (and approximately $\log_k p$ levels) the last processor to awaken will be the kth child of the kth child ... of the root. Because $k - 1$ other children are awoken first at each level, the last processor awakes at the end of a serial chain of approximately $k \log_k p$ awakenings, and this expression is minimized for $k = 2$.[8] A processor does not examine or modify the state of any other nodes except to signal its arrival at the barrier by setting a flag in its parent's node and, when notified by its parent that the barrier has been achieved, to notify each of its children by setting a flag in each of their nodes. Each processor spins only on state information in its own tree mode. To achieve a barrier, each processor executes the code shown in Figure 12.

Data structures for the tree barrier are initialized to that each node's parentpointer variable points to the appropriate childnotready flag in the node's parent and the childpointers variables point to the parentsense variables in each of the node's children. Child pointers of leaves and the parent pointer of the root are initialized to reference pseudo-data. The havechild flags indicate whether a parent has a particular child or not. Initially, and after each barrier episode, each node's childnotready flags are set to the value of the node's respective havechild flags.

Upon arrival at a barrier, a processor tests to see if the childnotready flag is clear for each of its children. For leaf nodes, these flags are always clear, so deadlock cannot result. After a node's associated processor sees that its childnotready flags are clear, it immediately reinitializes them for the next barrier. Since a node's children do not modify its childnotready flags again until they arrive at the next barrier, there is no potential for conflicting updates. After all of a node's children have arrived, the node's associated processor clears its childnotready flag in the node's parent. All processors other than the root then spin on their locally-accessible parentsense flag. When the root node's associated processor arrives at the barrier and notices that all of the root node's childnotready flags are clear, then all of the processors are waiting at the barrier. The processor at the root node toggles the parentsense flag in each of its children to release them from the barrier.

---

[8]Alex Schäffer and Paul Dietz have pointed out that better performance could be obtained in the wakeup tree by assigning more children to processors near the root. For example, if after processor a awakens processor b it takes them the same amount of time to prepare to awaken others, then we can cut the critical path roughly in half by having each processor i awaken processors $i + 2^j$, $i + 2^{j+1}$, $i + 2^{j+2}$, etc., where $j = \lfloor \log_2 i \rfloor$. Then with processor 0 acting as the root, after a serial chain of t awakenings there are 2^t processors active. Unfortunately, the obvious way to have a processor awaken more than a constant number of children involves a loop whose additional overhead partially negates the reduction in tree height. Experiments with this option (not presented in Section 4.4), resulted in only about a 3 percent performance improvement for $p < 80$.

```
type treenode = record
    parentsense : Boolean
    parentpointer : ^Boolean
    childpointers : array [0..1] of ^Boolean
    havechild : array [0..3] of Boolean
    childnotready : array [0..3] of Boolean
    dummy : Boolean      // pseudo-data

shared nodes : array [0..P-1] of treenode
    // nodes[vpid] is allocated in shared memory
    // locally accessible to processor vpid
processor private vpid : integer      // a unique virtual processor index
processor private sense : Boolean

// on processor i, sense is initially true
// in nodes[i]:
//     havechild[j] = true if 4*i+j < P; otherwise false
//     parentpointer = &nodes[floor((i-1)/4)].childnotready[(i-1) mod 4],
//        or &dummy if i = 0
//     childpointers[0] = &nodes[2*i+1].parentsense, or &dummy if 2*i+1 >= P
//     childpointers[1] = &nodes[2*i+2].parentsense, or &dummy if 2*i+2 >= P
//     initially childnotready = havechild and parentsense = false

procedure tree_barrier
    with nodes[vpid] do
        repeat until childnotready = {false, false, false, false}
        childnotready := havechild      // prepare for next barrier
        parentpointer^ := false         // let parent know I'm ready
        // if not root, wait until my parent signals wakeup
        if vpid != 0
            repeat until parentsense = sense
        // signal children in wakeup tree
        childpointers[0]^ := sense
        childpointers[1]^ := sense
        sense := not sense
```

Fig. 12. A scalable, distributed, tree-based barrier with only local spinning.

At each level in the tree, newly released processors release all of their children before leaving the barrier, thus ensuring that all processors are eventually released. As described earlier, consecutive barrier episodes do not interfere, since the childnotready flags used during arrival are reinitialized before wakeup occurs.

Our tree barrier achieves the theoretical lower bound on the number of network transactions needed to achieve a barrier on machines that lack broadcast and that distinguish between local and remote memory. At least $P - 1$ processors must signal their arrival to some other processor, requiring $P - 1$ network transactions, and then must be informed of wakeup, requiring another $P - 1$ network transactions. The length of the critical path in our algorithm is proportional to $\lceil \log_4 P \rceil + \lceil \log_2 P \rceil$. The first term is the time to propagate arrival up to the root and the second term is the time to propagate wakeup back down to all of the leaves. On a machine with coherent caches and unlimited replication, we could replace the wakeup

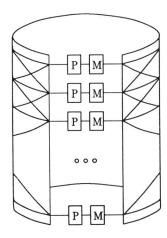

Fig. 13. The BBN Butterfly 1.

phase of our algorithm with a spin on a global flag. We explore this alternative on the Sequent Symmetry in Section 4.4.

4. PERFORMANCE MEASUREMENTS

We have measured the performance of various spin lock and barrier algorithms on the BBN Butterfly 1, a distributed shared memory multiprocessor, and the Sequent Symmetry Model B, a cache-coherent, shared-bus multiprocessor. Anyone wishing to reproduce our results or extend our work to other machines can obtain copies of our source code (assembler for the spin locks, C for the barriers) via anonymous ftp from titan.rice.edu (directory /public/scalable_synch).

4.1. Hardware Description

BBN Butterfly

The BBN Butterfly 1 is a shared-memory multiprocessor that can support up to 256 processor nodes. Each processor node contains an 8 MHz MC68000 that uses 24-bit virtual addresses and 1 to 4 megabytes of memory (one on our machine). Each processor can access its own memory directly, and can access the memory of any node through a $\log_4$-depth switching network (see Figure 13). Transactions on the network are packet-switched and nonblocking. If collisions occur at a switch node, one transaction succeeds and all of the others are aborted to be retried at a later time (in hardware) by the processors that initiated them. In the absence of contention, a remote memory reference (read) takes about $4\,\mu\text{s}$, roughly five times as long as a local reference.

The Butterfly 1 supports two 16-bit atomic operations: `fetch_and_clear_then_add` and `fetch_and_clear_then_xor`. Each operation takes three arguments: the address of the 16-bit destination operand, a 16-bit mask, and the value of the 16-bit source operand. The value of the destination operand is anded with the one's complement of the mask and then added or xored with

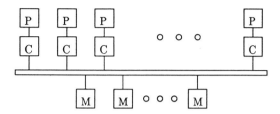

Fig. 14. The Sequent Symmetry Model B.

the source operand. The resulting value replaces the original value of the destination operand. The previous value of the destination operand is the return value for the atomic operation. Using these two primitives, one can perform a variety of atomic operations, including `fetch_and_add`, `fetch_and_store (swap)`, and `fetch_and_or` (which, like swap, can be used to perform a `test_and_set`).

Sequent Symmetry

The Sequent Symmetry Model B is a shared-bus multiprocessor that supports up to 30 processor nodes. Each processor node consists of a 16 MHz Intel 80386 processor equipped with a 64 KB two-way set-associative cache. All caches in the system are kept coherent by snooping on the bus (see Figure 14). Each cache line is accompanied by a tag that indicates whether the data is replicated in any other cache. Writes are passed through to the bus only for replicated cache lines, invalidating all other copies. Otherwise the caches are write-back.

The Symmetry provides an atomic `fetch_and_store` operation and allows various logical and arithmetic operations to be applied atomically as well. Each of these operations can be applied to any 1, 2, or 4 byte quantity. The logical and arithmetic operations do not return the previous value of the modified location; they merely update the value in place and set the processor's condition codes. The condition codes suffice in certain limited circumstances to determine the state of the memory prior to the atomic operation (e.g., to determine when the counter has reached zero in Figure 8) but the lack of a genuine return value generally makes the Symmetry's atomic instructions significantly less useful than the `fetch_and_Φ` operations of the Butterfly. Neither the Symmetry nor the Butterfly supports `compare_and_swap`.

4.2. Measurement Technique

Our results were obtained by embedding lock acquisitions or barrier episodes inside a loop and averaging over a large number of operations. In the spin lock graphs, each data point (P,T) represents the average time T to acquire and release the lock with P processors competing for access. On the Butterfly, the average is over 10^5 lock acquisitions. On the Symmetry, the average is over 10^6 lock acquisitions. For an individual test of P processors collectively executing K lock acquisitions, we required that each processor acquire and release the lock $| K/P |$ times. In the barrier graphs, each data point (P,T) represents the average time T for P processors to achieve a barrier. On both the Symmetry and the Butterfly, the average is over 10^5 barriers.

When $P = 1$ in the spin lock graphs, T represents the latency on one processor of the `acquire_lock` and `release_lock` operations in the absence of competition. When P is moderately large, T represents the time between successive lock acquisitions on competing processors. This *passing time* is smaller than the single-processor latency in almost all cases, because significant amounts of computation in `acquire_lock` prior to actual acquisition and in `release_lock` after actual release may be overlapped with work on other processors. When P is 2 or 3, T may represent either latency or passing time, depending on the relative amounts of overlapped and non-overlapped computation. In some cases (Anderson's lock, the MCS lock, and the locks incorporating backoff), the value of T for small values of P may also vary due to differences in the actual series of executed instructions, since code paths may depend on how many other processors are competing for the lock and on which operations they have so far performed. In all cases, however, the times plotted in the spin lock graphs are the numbers that "matter" for each of the values of P. Passing time is meaningless on one processor, and latency is swamped by wait time as soon as P is moderately large.[9]

Unless otherwise noted, all measurements on the Butterfly were performed with interrupts disabled. Similarly on the Symmetry, the `tmp_affinity()` system call was used to bind processes to processors for the duration of our experiments. These measures were taken to provide repeatable timing results.

4.3. Spin Locks

Figure 15 shows the performance on the Butterfly of the spin lock algorithms described in Section 2.[10] The top curve is a simple `test_and_set` lock, which displays the poorest scaling behavior.[11] As expected, a ticket lock without backoff is slightly faster, due to polling with a read instead of a `fetch_and_Φ`. We would expect a `test_and_test_and_set` lock to perform similarly. A linear least squares regression on the timings shows that the time to acquire and release the `test_and_set` lock increases 7.4 μs per additional processor. The time for a ticket lock without backoff increases 7.0 μs per processor.

---

[9]Since T may represent either latency or passing time when more than one processor is competing for a lock, it is difficult to factor out overhead due to the timing loop for timing tests with more than one processor. For consistency, we included loop overhead in all of the average times reported (both spin locks and barriers).

[10]Measurements were made for all numbers of processors; the tick marks simply differentiate between line types. Graunke and Thakkar's array-based queuing lock had not yet appeared at the time we conducted our experiments. Performance of their lock should be qualitatively identical to Anderson's lock, but with a smaller constant.

[11]We implement `test_and_set` using the hardware primitive `fetch_and_clear_then_add` with a mask that specifies to clear the lowest bit, and an addend of 1. This operation returns the old value of the lock and leaves the lowest bit in the lock set.

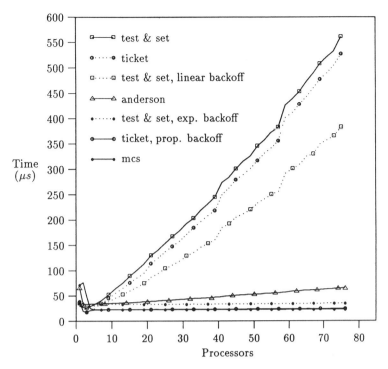

Fig. 15. Performance of spin locks on the Butterfly (empty critical section).

By analogy with the exponential backoff scheme described in Section 2, we investigated the effect of having each processor delay between polling operations for a period of time directly proportional to the number of unsuccessful test_and_set operations. This change reduces the slope of the test_and_set lock graph to 5.0 μs per processor, but performance degradation is still linear in the number of competing processors.

The time to acquire and release the test_and_set lock, the ticket lock without backoff, and the test_and_set lock with linear backoff does not actually increase linearly as more processors compete for the lock, but rather in a piecewise linear fashion. This behavior is a function of the interconnection network topology and the order in which we add processors to the test. For the tests shown in Figure 15, our Butterfly was configured as an 80 processor machine with five switch cards in the first column of the interconnection network, supporting 16 processors each. Processors were added to the test in a round robin fashion, one from each card. The breaks in the performance graph occur as each group of 20 processors is added to the test. These are the points at which we have included four more processors from each switch card, thereby filling the inputs of a 4-input, 4-output switch node on each card. Adding more processors involves a set of previously unused switch nodes. What we see in the performance graphs is that involving new switch nodes causes behavior that is qualitatively different from that

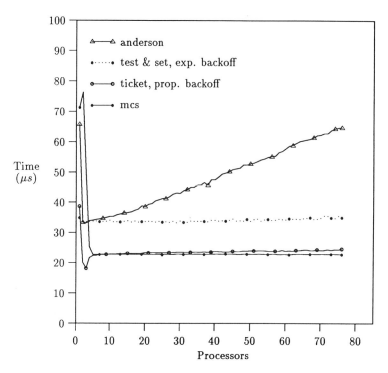

Fig. 16. Performance of selected spin locks on the Butterfly (empty critical section).

obtained by including another processor attached to a switch node already in use. This difference is likely related to the fact that additional processors attached to a switch node already in use add contention in the first level of the interconnection network, while involving new switch nodes adds contention in the second level of the network. In a fully configured machine with 256 processors attached to 16 switch cards in the first column of the interconnection network, we would expect the breaks in spin lock performance to occur every 64 processors.

Figure 16 provides an expanded view of performance results for the more scalable algorithms, whose curves are grouped together near the bottom of Figure 15. In this expanded graph, it is apparent that the time to acquire and release the lock in the single processor case is often much larger than the time required when multiple processors are competing for the lock. As noted above, parts of each acquire/release protocol can execute in parallel when multiple processors compete. What we are measuring in our trials with many processors is not the time to execute an acquire/release pair from start to finish but rather than length of time between a pair of lock acquisitions. Complicating matters is that the time required to release an MCS lock depends on whether another processor is waiting.

The top curve in Figure 16 shows the performance of Anderson's array-based queuing algorithm, modified to scatter the slots of the queue across the

242

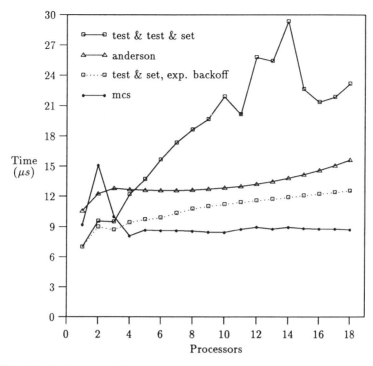

Fig. 17. Performance of spin locks on the Symmetry (empty critical section).

available processor nodes. This modification distributes traffic evenly in the interconnection network by causing each processor to spin on a location in a different memory bank. Because the Butterfly lacks coherent caches, however, and because processors spin on statically unpredictable locations, it is not in general possible with the array-based queuing locks to spin on *local* locations. Linear regression yields a slope for the performance graph of 0.4 μs per processor.

Three algorithms—the `test_and_set` lock with exponential backoff, the ticket lock with proportional backoff, and the MCS lock—all scale extremely well. Ignoring the data points below 10 processors (which helps us separate throughput under heavy competition from latency under light competition), we find slopes for these graphs of 0.025, 0.021, and 0.00025 μs per processor, respectively. Since performance does not degrade appreciably for any of these locks within the range of our tests, we would expect them to perform well even with thousands of processors competing.

Figure 17 shows performance results for several spin lock algorithms on the Symmetry. We adjusted data structures in minor ways to avoid the unnecessary invalidations that would result from placing unrelated data items in the same cache line. The test-and-test_and_set algorithm showed the poorest scaling behavior, with the time to acquire and release the lock

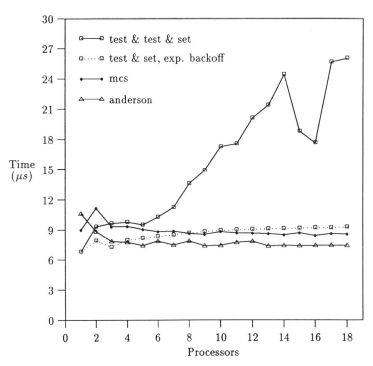

Fig. 18. Performance of spin locks on the Symmetry (small critical section).

increasing dramatically even over this small range of processors. A simple `test_and_set` would perform even worse.

Because the atomic add instruction on the Symmetry does not return the old value of its target location, implementation of the ticket lock is not possible on the Symmetry, nor is it possible to implement Anderson's lock directly. In his implementation [5], Anderson (who worked on a Symmetry) introduced an outer `test_and_set` lock with randomized backoff to protect the state of his queue.[12] This strategy is reasonable when the critical section protected by the outer lock (namely, acquisition or release of the inner lock) is substantially smaller than the critical section protected by the inner lock. This was not the case in our initial test, so the graph in Figure 17 actually results from processors contending for the *outer* lock, instead of the inner, queue-based lock. To eliminate this anomaly, we repeated our tests with a nonempty critical section, as shown in Figure 18. With a sufficiently long critical section (6.48 μs in our tests), processors have a chance to queue up on the inner lock, thereby eliminating competition for the outer lock and

---

[12]Given that he required the outer lock in any case, Anderson also replaced the `nextslot` index variable with a pointer, to save time on address arithmetic.

allowing the inner lock to eliminate bus transactions due to spinning. The time spent in the critical section has been factored out of the plotted timings.

In addition to Anderson's lock, our experiments indicate that the MCS lock and the test_and_set lock with exponential backoff also scale extremely well. All three of the scalable algorithms have comparable absolute performance. Anderson's lock has a small edge for nonempty critical sections (Graunke and Thakkar's lock would have a larger edge) but requires statically-allocated space per lock linear in the number of processors. The other two algorithms need only constant space and do not require coherent caches to work well. The test_and_set lock with exponential backoff shows a slight increasing trend and would not be expected to do as well as the others on a very large machine since it causes more network traffic.

The peak in the cost of the MCS lock on two processors reflects the lack of compare_and_swap. Some fraction of the time, a processor releasing the lock finds that its next variable is nil but then discovers that it has a successor after all when it performs its fetch_and_store on the lock's tail pointer. Entering this timing window necessitates an additional fetch_and_store to restore the state of the queue, with a consequent drop in performance. The non-empty critical sections of Figure 18 reduce the likelihood of hitting the window, thereby reducing the size of the two-processor peak. With compare_and_swap that peak would disappear altogether.

Latency and Impact on Other Operations

In addition to performance in the presence of many competing processors, an important criterion for any lock is the time it takes to acquire and release it in the absence of competition. Table I shows this measure for representative locks on the Butterfly and the Symmetry. The times for the test_and_set lock are with code in place for exponential backoff; the time for the ticket lock is with code in place for proportional backoff. The test_and_set lock is cheapest on both machines in the single processor case; it has the shortest code path. On the Butterfly, the ticket lock, Anderson's lock, and the MCS lock are 1.11, 1.88, and 2.04 times as costly, respectively. On the Symmetry, Anderson's lock and the MCS lock are 1.51 and 1.31 times as costly as the test_and_set lock.

Two factors skew the absolute numbers on the Butterfly, making them somewhat misleading. First, the atomic operations on the Butterfly are inordinately expensive in comparison to their non-atomic counterparts. Most of the latency of each of the locks is due to the cost of setting up a parameter block and executing an atomic operation. (We reuse partially-initialized parameter blocks as much as possible to minimize this cost.) The expense of atomic operations affects the performance of the MCS lock in particular since it requires at least two fetch_and_store operations (one to acquire the lock and another to release it) and possibly a third (if we hit the timing window). Second, the 16-bit atomic primitives on the Butterfly cannot manipulate 24-bit pointers atomically. To implement the MCS algorithm, we were forced to replace the pointers with indices into a replicated, statically-allocated array of pointers to qnode records.

Table I. Time for an Acquire/Release Pair in the Single Processor Case.

	test_and_set	ticket	Anderson	MCS
Butterfly	34.9 μs	38.7 μs	65.7 μs	71.3 μs
Symmetry	7.0 μs	NA	10.6 μs	9.2 μs

Table II. Increase in Network Latency (relative to that of an idle machine) on the Butterfly Caused by 60 Processors Competing for a Busy-Wait Lock.

Busy-wait Lock	Increase in network latency measured from	
	Lock node (%)	Idle node (%)
test_and_set	1420	96
test_and_set w/linear backoff	882	67
test_and_set w/exp. backoff	32	4
ticket	992	97
ticket w/prop. backoff	53	8
Anderson	75	67
MCS	4	2

Absolute performance for all of the algorithms is much better on the Symmetry than on the Butterfly. The Symmetry's clock runs twice as fast and its caches make memory in general appear significantly faster. The differences between algorithms are also smaller on the Symmetry, mainly because of the lower difference in cost between atomic and non-atomic instructions, and also because the Symmetry's 32-bit fetch_and_store instruction allows the MCS lock to use pointers. We believe the numbers on the Symmetry to be representative of actual lock costs on modern machines. Recent experience with the BBN TC2000 machine confirms this belief: single-processor latencies on this machine (a newer Butterfly architecture based on the Motorola 88000 chipset) vary from 8.1 μs for the simple test_and_set lock to 12.2 μs for the MCS lock. The single-processor latency of the MCS lock on the Symmetry is only 31 percent higher than that of the simple test_and_set lock; on the TC2000 it is 50 percent higher.

A final important measure of spin lock performance is the amount of interconnection network traffic caused by busy-waiting processors, and the impact of this traffic on other activity on the machine. In an attempt to measure these quantitites, we obtained an estimate of average network latency on the Butterfly by measuring the total time required to probe the network interface controller on each of the processor nodes during a spin lock test. Table II presents our results in the form of percentage increases over the value measured on an idle machine. In the Lock Node column, probes were made from the processor on which the lock itself resided (this processor was otherwise idle in all our tests); in the Idle Node column, probes were made from another processor not participating in the spin lock test. Values in the two columns differ markedly for both the test_and_set and ticket locks (particularly without backoff) because competition for access to the lock is focused on a central hot spot and steals network interface bandwidth from the process attempting to perform the latency measurement on the lock node. Values in the two columns are similar for Anderson's lock because its data structure (and hence its induced contention) is distributed throughout the machine. Values are both similar and low for the MCS lock because its data structure is distributed and because each processor refrains from spinning on the remote portions of that data structure.

Discussion and Recommendations

Spin lock algorithms can be evaluated on the basis of several criteria:

—scalability and induced network load,
—one-processor latency,
—space requirements,
—fairness/sensitivity to preemption, and
—implementability with given atomic operations.

The MCS lock and, on cache-coherent machines, the array-based queuing locks are the most scalable algorithms we studied. The test_and_set and ticket locks also scale well with appropriate backoff but induce more network load. The test_and_set and ticket locks have the lowest single-processor latency, but with good implementations of fetch_and_Φ instructions the MCS and Anderson locks are reasonable as well. The space needs of Anderson's lock and of the Graunke and Thakkar lock are likely to be prohibitive when a large number of locks is needed—in the internals of an operating system, for example—or when locks are being acquired and released by processes significantly more numerous than the physical processors. If the number of processes can change dynamically, then the data structures of an array-based lock must be made large enough to accommodate the maximum number of processes that may ever compete simultaneously. For the Graunke and Thakkar lock, the set of process ids must also remain fairly dense. If the maximum number of processes is underestimated the system will not work; if it is overestimated then space will be needlessly wasted.

The ticket lock, the array-based queuing locks, and the MCS lock all guarantee that processors attempting to acquire a lock will succeed in FIFO order. This guarantee of fairness is likely to be considered an advantage in many environments, but is likely to waste CPU resources if spinning processes may be preempted. (Busy-wait barriers may also waste cycles in the presence of preemption.) We can avoid this problem by coscheduling processes that share locks [34]. Alternatively (for mutual exclusion), a test_and_set lock with exponential backoff will allow latecomers to acquire the lock when processes that arrived earlier are not running. In this situation the test_and_set lock may be preferred to the FIFO alternatives. Additional mechanisms can ensure that a process is not preempted while actually holding a lock [47, 52].

All of the spin lock algorithms we have considered require some sort of fetch_and_Φ instructions. The test_and_set lock of course requires test_and_set. The ticket lock requires fetch_and_increment. The MCS lock requires fetch_and_store[13], and benefits from compare_and_swap. Anderson's lock benefits from fetch_and_add. Graunke and Thakkar's lock requires fetch_and_store.

For cases in which competition is expected, the MCS lock is clearly the implementation of choice. It provides a very short passing time, ensures FIFO ordering, scales almost perfectly, and requires only a small, constant amount of space per lock. It also induces the least amount of interconnect contention. On a machine with fast fetch_and_Φ operations (particularly if compare_and_swap is available), its one-processor latency will be competitive with all the other algorithms.

The ticket lock with proportional backoff is an attractive alternative if one-processor latency is an overriding concern, or if fetch_and_store is not available. Although our experience with it is limited to a distributed-memory multiprocessor without cache coherence, our expectation is that the ticket lock with proportional backoff would perform well on cache-coherent multiprocessors as well. The test_and_set lock with exponential backoff is an attractive alternative if preemption is possible while spinning or if neither fetch_and_store nor fetch_and_increment is available. It is significantly slower than the ticket lock with proportional backoff in the presence of heavy competition, and results in significantly more network load.

4.4. Barriers

Figure 19 shows the performance on the Butterfly of the barrier algorithms described in Section 3. The top three curves are all sense-reversing, counter-based barriers as in Figure 8, with various backoff strategies. The slowest performs no backoff. The next uses exponential backoff. We obtained the best performance with an initial delay of 10 iterations through an empty loop with a backoff base of 2. Our results suggest that it may be necessary to limit the maximum backoff in order to maintain stability. When many barriers are executed in sequence, the skew of processors arriving at the barriers appears to be magnified by the exponential backoff strategy. As the skew between arriving processors increases, processors back off farther. With a backoff base larger than 2, we had to cap the maximum delay in order for our experiments to finish. Even with a backoff base of 2, a delay cap improved performance. Our best results were obtained with a cap of $8P$ delay loop iterations.

In our final experiment with a centralized, counter-based barrier, we used a variant of the proportional delay idea employed in the ticket lock. After incrementing the barrier count to signal its arrival, each processor participating in the barrier delays a period of time proportional to the total number of participants (*not* the number yet to arrive), prior to testing the sense variable for the first time. The rationale for this strategy is to timeslice available interconnect bandwidth between the barrier participants. Since the

---

[13]It could conceivably be used with only compare_and_swap, simulating fetch_and_store in a loop, but at a significant loss in scalability.

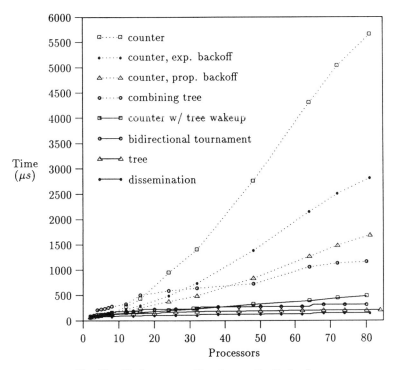

Fig. 19. Performance of barriers on the Butterfly.

Butterfly network does not provide hardware combining, at least $2P - 1$ accesses to the barrier state are required (P to signal processor arrivals, and $P - 1$ to discover that all have arrived). Each processor delays long enough for later processors to indicate their arrival and for earlier processors to notice that all have arrived. As shown in Figure 19, this strategy outperforms both the naive central barrier and the central barrier with exponential backoff. At the same time, all three counter-based algorithms lead to curves of similar shape. The time to achieve a barrier appears to increase more than linearly in the number of participants. The best of these purely centralized algorithms (the proportional backoff strategy) requires over 1.4 *ms* for an 80 processor barrier.

The fourth curve in Figure 19 is the combining tree barrier of Algorithm 8. Though this algorithm scales better than the centralized approaches (in fact, it scales roughly logarithmically with P, although the constant is large), it still spins on remote locations and encounters increasing interconnect contention as the number of processors grows.

Figure 20 provides an expanded view of performance results for the algorithms with the best performance, whose curves are grouped together near the bottom of Figure 19. The code for the upper curve uses a central counter to tally arrivals at the barrier, but employs a binary tree for wakeup, as in

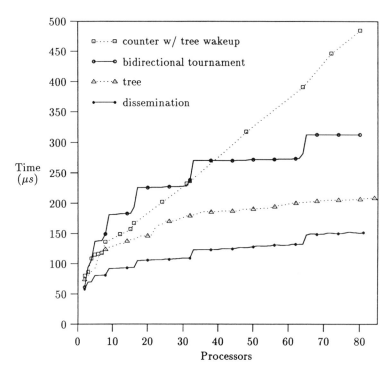

Fig. 20. Performance of selected barriers on the Butterfly.

Algorithm 11. The processor at the root of the tree spins on the central counter. Other processors spin on flags in their respective nodes of the tree. All spins are local but the tallying of arrivals is serialized. We see two distinct sections in the resulting performance curve. With fewer than 10 processors, the time for wakeup dominates and the time to achieve the barrier is roughly logarithmic in the number of participants. With more than 10 processors, the time to access the central counter dominates and the time to achieve the barrier is roughly linear in the number of participants.

The three remaining curves in Figure 20 are for the bidirectional tournament barrier, our tree barrier, and the dissemination barrier. The time to achieve a barrier with each of these algorithms scales logarithmically with the number of processors participating. The tournament and dissemination barriers proceed through $O(\lceil \log P \rceil)$ rounds of synchronization that lead to a stair-step curve. Since the Butterfly does not provide coherent caches, the tournament barrier employs a binary wakeup tree, as shown in Figure 11. It requires $2\lceil \log_2 P \rceil$ rounds of synchronization, compared to only $\lceil \log_2 P \rceil$ rounds in the dissemination barrier, resulting in a roughly two-fold difference in performance. Our tree-based barrier lies between the other two; its critical path passes information from one processor to another approximately $\log_4 P + \log_2 P$ times. The lack of clear-cut rounds in our barrier explains its

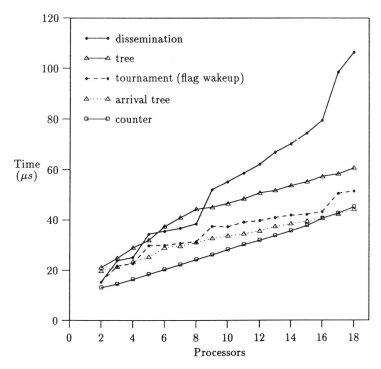

Fig. 21. Performance of barriers on the Symmetry.

smoother performance curve: each additional processor adds another level to some path through the tree, or becomes the second child of some node in the wakeup tree that is delayed slightly longer than its sibling.

Figure 21 shows the performance on the Sequent Symmetry of several different barriers. Results differ sharply from those on the Butterfly for two principal reasons. First, it is acceptable on the Symmetry for more than one processor to spin on the same location; each obtains a copy in its cache. Second, no significant advantage arises from distributing writes across the memory modules of the machine; the shared bus enforces an overall serialization. The dissemination barrier requires $0(P \log P)$ bus transactions to achieve a P-processor barrier. The other four algorithms require $0(P)$ transactions, and all perform better than the dissemination barrier for $P > 8$.

Below the maximum number of processors in our tests, the fastest barrier on the Symmetry used a centralized counter with a sense-reversing wakeup flag (from Figure 8). P bus transactions are required to tally arrivals, 1 to toggle the sense-reversing flag (invalidating all the cached copies), and $P - 1$ to effect the subsequent reloads. Our tree barrier generates $2P - 2$ writes to flag variables on which other processors are waiting, necessitating an additional $2P - 2$ reloads. By using a central sense-reversing flag for wakeup (instead of the wakeup tree), we can eliminate half of this overhead. The resulting algorithm is identified as "arrival tree" in Figure 21. Though the arrival tree barrier has a larger startup cost, its $P - 1$ writes are cheaper than the P read-modify-write operations of the centralized barrier, so its slope is lower. For large values of P, the arrival tree with wakeup flag is the best performaning barrier and should become clearly so on larger machines.

The tournament barrier on the Symmetry uses a central wakeup flag. It roughly matches the performance of the arrival tree barrier for $P = 2^i$ but is limited by the length of the execution path of the tournament champion, which grows suddenly by one each time that P exceeds a power of 2.

Discussion and Recommendations

Evaluation criteria for barriers include:

—length of critical path,
—total number of network transactions,
—space requirements, and
—implementability with given atomic operations.

Space needs are constant for the centralized barrier, linear for our tree-based barrier and for the combining tree barrier, and $O(P \log P)$ for the dissemination barrier and for all variants of Hensgen, Finkel, and Manber's tournament barrier. (Lubachevsky's EREW version of the tournament barrier is $O(P)$). With appropriate distribution of data structures, the dissemination barrier requires a total of $O(P \log P)$ network transactions. The tournament barrier and our tree-based barrier require $O(P)$. The centralized and combining tree barriers require $O(P)$ on machines with broadcast-based coherent caches and a potentially unbounded number on other machines.

On a machine in which independent network transactions can proceed in parallel, the critical path length is $O(\log P)$ for all but the centralized barrier, which is $O(P)$. On a machine that serializes network transactions (e.g., on a shared bus), this logarithmic factor will be dominated asymptotically by the linear (or greater) total number of network transactions. The centralized and combining tree barriers require an atomic increment or decrement instruction with at least a limited mechanism for determining the value of memory prior to modifications. The other barriers depend only on the atomicity of ordinary reads and writes.

The dissemination barrier appears to be the most suitable algorithm for distributed memory machines without broadcast. It has a shorter critical path than the tree and tournament barriers (by a constant factor) and is therefore faster. The class of machines for which the dissemination barrier should outperform all other algorithms includes the BBN Butterfly [8], the IBM RP3 [37], Cedar [50], the BBN Monarch [42], the NYU Ultracomputer [17], and proposed large-scale multiprocessors with directory-based cache coherence [3]. Our tree-based barrier will also perform well on these machines. It induces less network load and requires total space proportional to P rather than $P \log P$, but its critical path is longer by a factor of about 1.5. It might conceivably be preferred over the dissemination barrier when sharing the processors of the machine among more than one application, if network load proves to be a problem.

Our tree-based barrier with wakeup flag should be the fastest algorithm on large-scale multiprocessors that use broadcast to maintain cache coherence (either in snoopy cache protocols [15] or in directory-based protocols with broadcast [7]). It requires only $O(P)$ updates to shared variables in order to tally arrivals compared to $O(P \log P)$ for the dissemination barrier. Its updates are simple writes, which are cheaper than the read-modify-write operations of a centralized counter-based barrier. (Note, however, that the centralized barrier outperforms all others for modest numbers of processors.) The space needs of the tree-based barrier are lower than those of the tournament barrier ($O(P)$ instead of $O(P \log P)$), its code is simpler, and it performs slightly less local work when P is not a power of 2. Our results are consistent with those of Hensgen, Finkel, and Manber [19] who showed their tournament barrier to be faster than their dissemination barrier on the Sequent Balance multiprocessor. They did not compare their algorithms against a centralized barrier because the lack of an atomic increment instruction on the Balance precludes efficient atomic update of a counter.

The centralized barrier enjoys one additional advantage over all of the other alternatives: it adapts easily to differing numbers of processors. In an application in which the number of processors participating in a barrier changes from one barrier episode to another, the log-depth barriers will all require internal reorganization, possibly swamping any performance advantage obtained in the barrier itself. Changing the number of processors in a centralized barrier entails no more than changing a single constant.

4.5. Architectural Implications

Many different shared memory architectures have been proposed. From the point of view of synchronization, the two relevant issues seem to be (1) whether each processor can access some portion of shared memory locally (instead of through the interconnection network), and (2) whether broadcast is available for cache coherency. The first issue is crucial; it determines whether busy waiting can be eliminated as a cause of memory and interconnect contention. The second issue determines whether barrier algorithms can efficiently employ a centralized flag for wakeup.

The most scalable synchronization algorithms (the MCS spin lock and the tree, bidirectional tournament, and dissemination barriers) are designed in such a way that each processor spins on statically-determined flag variable(s) on which no other processor spins. On a distributed shared memory machine, flag variables can be allocated in the portion of the shared memory co-located with the processor that spins on them. On a cache-coherent machine, they migrate to the spinning processor's cache automatically. Provided that flag variables used for busy-waiting by different processors are in separate cache lines, network transactions are used only to update a location on which some processor is waiting (or for initial cache line loads). For the MCS spin lock, the number of network transctions per lock acquisition is constant. For the tree and tournament barriers, the number of network transactions per barrier is linear in the number of processors involved. For the dissemination barrier, the number of network transactions is $O(P \log P)$, but still $O(\log P)$ on the critical path. No network transactions are due to spinning, so interconnect contention is not a problem.

On "dance hall" machines, in which shared memory must always be accessed through a shared processor-memory interconnect, there is no way to eliminate synchronization-related interconnect contention in software. Nevertheless, the algorithms we have described are useful since they minimize memory contention and hot spots caused by synchronization. The structure of these algorithms makes it easy to assign each processor's busy-wait flag variables to a different memory bank so that the load induced by spinning will be distributed evenly throughout memory and the interconnect, rather than being concentrated in a single spot. Unfortunately, on dance hall machines the load will still consume interconnect bandwidth, degrading the performance not only of synchronization operations but also of all other activity on the machine, severely constraining scalability.

Dance hall machines include bus-based multiprocessors without coherent caches, and multistage network architectures such as Cedar [50], the BBN Monarch [42], and the NYU Ultracomputer [17]. Both Cedar and the Ultracomputer include processor-local memory, but only for private code and data. The Monarch provides a small amount of local memory as a "poor man's instruction cache." In none of these machines can local memory be modifed remotely. We consider the lack of local shared memory to be a significant architectural shortcoming; the inability to take full advantage of techniques such as those described in this paper is a strong argument against the construction of dance hall machines.

To assess the importance of local shared memory, we used our Butterfly 1 to simulate a machine in which all shared memory is accessed through the interconnection network. By flipping a bit in the segment register for the synchronization variables on which a processor spins, we can cause the processor to go out through the network to reach these variables (even though they are in its own memory), without going through the network to reach code and private data. This trick effectively flattens the two-level shared memory hierarchy of the Butterfly into a single level organization similar to that of Cedar, the Monarch, or the Ultracomputer.

Figure 22 compares the performance of the dissemination and tree barrier algorithms for one and two level memory hierarchies. All timing mesurements in the graph were made with interrupts disabled, to eliminate any effects due to timer interrupts or scheduler activity. The bottom two curves are the same as in Figures 19 and 20. The top two curves show the corresponding performance of the barrier algorithms when all accesses to shared memory are forced to go through the interconnection network. When busy-waiting accesses traverse the interconnect, the time to achieve a barrier using the tree and dissemination algorithms increases linearly with the number of processors participating. A least squares fit shows the additional cost per processor to be 27.8 μs and 9.4 μs, respectively. For an 84-processor

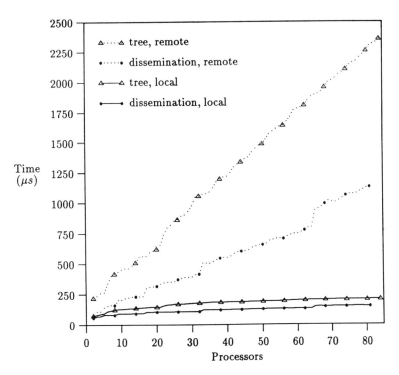

Fig. 22. Performance of tree and dissemination barriers with and without local access to shared memory.

barrier, the lack of local spinning increases the cost of the tree and dissemination barriers by factors of 11.8 and 6.8, respectively.

In a related experiment, we measured the impact on network latency of executing the dissemination or tree barriers with and without local access to shared memory. The results appear in Table III. As in Table II, we probed the network interface controller on each processor to compare network latency of an idle machine with the latency observed during a 60 processor barrier. Table III shows that when processors are able to spin on shared locations locally, average network latency increases only slightly. With only network access to shared memory, latency more than doubles.

Studies by Pfister and Norton [38] show that hot-spot contention can lead to tree saturation in multistage interconnection networks with blocking switch nodes and distributed routing control, independent of the network topology. A study by Kumar and Pfister [23] shows the onset of hot-spot contention to be rapid. Pfister and Norton argue for hardware message combining in interconnection networks to reduce the impact of hot spots. They base their argument primarily on anticipated contention for locks, noting that they know of no quantitative evidence to support or deny the value of combining for general memory traffic. Our results indicate that the cost of synchronization in a system without combining, and the impact that synchronization activity will have on overall system performance, is much less than previ-

Table III. Increase in Network Latency (relative to that of an idle machine) on the Butterfly Caused by 60 Processor Barriers Using Local and Network Polling Strategies.

Barrier	Local polling (%)	Network polling (%)
Tree	10	124
Dissemination	18	117

ously thought (provided that the architecture incorporates a shared memory hierarchy of two or more levels). Although the scalable algorithms presented in this paper are unlikely to match the performance of hardware combining, they will come close enough to provide an extremely attractive alternative to complex, expensive hardware.[14]

Other researchers have suggested building special-purpose hardware mechanisms solely for synchronization, including synchronization variables in the switching nodes of multistage interconnection networks [21] and lock queuing mechanisms in the cache controllers of cache-coherent multiprocessors [14, 28, 35]. Our results suggest that simple exploitation of a multilevel memory hierarchy, *in software*, may provide a more cost-effective means of avoiding lock-based contention.

The algorithms we present in this paper require no hardware support for synchronization other than commonly-available atomic instructions. The scalable barrier algorithms rely only on atomic read and write. The MCS spin lock algorithm uses `fetch_and_store` and maybe `compare_and_swap`. Graunke and Thakkar's lock requires `fetch_and_store`. Anderson's lock benefits from `fetch_and_increment`, and the ticket lock requires it. All of these instructions have uses other than the construction of busy-wait locks. `Fetch_and_store` and `compare_and_swap`, for example, are essential for manipulating pointers to build concurrent data structures [20, 32]. Because of their general utility, `fetch_and_`Φ instructions are substantially more attractive than special-purpose synchronization primitives. Future designs for shared memory machines should include a full set of `fetch_and_`Φ operations, including `compare_and_swap`.

Our measurements on the Sequent Symmetry indicate that special-purpose synchronization mechanisms such as the QOLB instruction [14] are unlikely to outperform our MCS lock by more than 30 percent. A QOLB lock will have higher single-processor latency than a `test_and_set` lock [14, p.68], and its performance should be essentially the same as the MCS lock when competition for a lock is high. Goodman, Vernon, and Woest suggest that a QOLB-like mechanism can be implemented at very little incremental cost (given that they are already constructing large coherent caches with multidimensional snooping). We believe that this cost must be extremely low to make it worth the effort.

---

[14] Pfister and Norton estimate that message combining will increase the size and possibly the cost of an interconnection network 6- to 32-fold. Gottlieb [16] indicates that combining networks are difficult to bit-slice.

Of course, increasing the performance of busy-wait locks and barriers is not the only possible rationale for implementing synchronization mechanisms in hardware. Recent work on weakly-consistent shared memory [1, 13, 28] has suggested the need for synchronization "fences" that provide clean points for memory semantics. Combining networks, likewise, may improve the performance of memory with bursty access patterns (caused, for example, by sharing after a barrier). We do not claim that hardware support for synchronization is unnecessary, merely that the most commonly cited rationale for it—that it is essential to reduce contention due to synchronization—is invalid.

5. SUMMARY OF RECOMMENDATIONS

We have presented a detailed comparison of new and existing algorithms for busy-wait synchronization on shared-memory multiprocessors, with a particular eye toward minimizing the network transactions that lead to contention. We introduced the MCS lock, the new tree-based barrier, and the notion of proportional backoff for the ticket lock and the centralized barrier. We demonstrated how to eliminate fetch_and_Φ operations from the wakeup phase of the combining tree barrier, presented a wakeup mechanism for the tournament barrier that uses contiguous, statically allocated flags to ensure local-only spinning, and observed that the data structures of the dissemination barrier can be distributed for local-only spinning.

The principal conclusion of our work is that memory and interconnect contention due to busy-wait synchronization in shared-memory multiprocessors need not be a problem. This conclusion runs counter to widely-held beliefs. We have presented empirical performance results for a wide variety of busy-wait algorithms on both a cache-coherent multiprocessor and a multiprocessor with distributed shared memory. These results demonstrate that appropriate algorithms using simple and widely-available atomic instructions can reduce synchronization contention effectively to zero.

For spin locks on a shared-memory multiprocessor, regardless of architectural details, we suggest:

1. If the hardware provides an efficient fetch_and_store instruction (and maybe compare_and_swap), then use the MCS lock. One-processor latency will be reasonable, and scalability will be excellent.

2. If fetch_and_store is not available, or if atomic opertions are very expensive relative to non-atomic instructions and one-processor latency is an overwhelming concern, then use the ticket lock with proportional backoff (assuming the hardware supports fetch_and_increment). The code for such a lock is typically more complicated than code for the MCS lock, and the load on the processor-memory interconnect will be higher in the presence of competition for the lock, but speed on a single processor will be slightly better and scalability will still be reasonable.

3. Use the simple lock with exponential backoff (with a cap on the maximum delay) if processes might be preempted while spinning, or if one-processor latency is an overwhelming concern and the hardware does not support

`fetch_and_increment` (assuming of course that it *does* support `test_and_set`).

For barrier synchronization we suggest:

1. On a broadcast-based cache-coherent multiprocessor (with unlimited replication), use either a centralized counter-based barrier (for modest numbers of processors), or a barrier based on our 4-ary arrival tree and a central sense-reversing wakeup flag.

2. On a multiprocessor without coherent caches, or with directory-based coherency without broadcast, use either the dissemination barrier (with data structures distributed to respect locality) or our tree-based barrier with tree wakeup. The critical path through the dissemination barrier algorithm is about a third shorter than that of the tree barrier, but the total amount of interconnect traffic is $O(P \log P)$ instead of $O(P)$. The dissemination barrier will outperform the tree barrier on machines such as the Butterfly, which allow noninterfering network transactions from many different processors to proceed in parallel.

For the designers of large-scale shared-memory multiprocessors, our results argue in favor of providing distributed memory or coherent caches, rather than dance-hall memory without coherent caches (as in Cedar, the Monarch, or the Ultracomputer). Our results also indicate that combining networks for such machines must be justified on grounds other than the reduction of synchronization overhead. We strongly suggest that future multiprocessors include a full set of `fetch_and_`Φ operations (especially `fetch_and_store` and `compare_and_swap`).

ACKNOWLEDGMENTS

Tom LeBlanc and Evangelos Markatos provided helpful comments on an early version of this paper. Comments of the referees were also very helpful.

Some of the experiments described in this paper were performed on a BBN TC2000 that is part of the Advanced Computing Research Facility, Mathematics and Computer Science Division, Argonne National Laboratory.

REFERENCES

1. ADVE, S. V., AND HILL, M. D. Weak ordering—A new definition. In *Proceedings of the International Symposium on Computer Architecture* (May 1990), 2-14.
2. AGARWAL, A., AND CHERIAN, M. Adaptive backoff synchronization techniques. In *Proceedings of the International Symposium on Computer Architecture* (May 1989), 396-406.
3. AGARWAL, A., SIMONI, R., HENNESSY, J., AND HOROWITZ, M. An evaluation of directory schemes for cache coherence. In *Proceedings of the International Symposium on Computer Architecture* (June 1988), 280-289.
4. ALMASI, G. S., AND GOTTLIEB, A. *Highly Parallel Computing.* Benjamin/Cummings, Redwood City, Calif., 1989.
5. ANDERSON, T. E. The performance of spin lock alternatives for shared-memory multiprocessors. *IEEE Trans. Parallel Distributed Syst.* 1, 1 (Jan. 1990), 6-16.
6. ANDERSON, T. E., LAZOWSKA, E. D., AND LEVY, H. M. The performance implications of thread management alternatives for shared-memory multiprocessors. *IEEE Trans. Comput.* 38, 12 (Dec. 1989), 1631-1644.

7. ARCHIBALD, J. AND BAER, J.-L. An economical solution to the cache coherence problem. In *Proceedings of the International Symposium on Computer Architecture* (1984), 355-362.

8. BBN Laboratories. Butterfly parallel processor overview. Tech. Rep. 6148, version 1, BBN Laboratories, Cambridge, Mass, Mar. 1986.

9. BROOKS, E. D., III. The butterfly barrier. *Int. J. Parallel Program. 15*, 4 (1986), 295-307.

10. BROOKS, E. D., III. The shared memory hypercube. *Parallel Comput. 6* (1988), 235-245.

11. DAVIS, H., AND HENNESSY, J. Characterizing the synchronization behavior of parallel programs. In *Proceedings of the ACM Conference on Parallel Programming: Experience with Applications, Languages and Systems* (July 1988), 198-211.

12. DIJKSTRA, E. Solution of a problem in concurrent programming and control. *Commun. ACM.* 8, 9 (Sept. 1965), 569.

13. GHARACHORLOO, K., LENOSKI, D., LAUDON, J., GIBBONS, P., GUPTA, A., AND HENNESSY, J. L. Memory consistency and event ordering in scalable shared-memory multiprocessors. In *Proceedings of the International Symposium on Computer Architecture* (May 1990), 15-26.

14. GOODMAN, J.R., VERNON, M. K., AND WOEST, P. J. Efficient synchronization primitives for large-scale cache-coherent multiprocessors. In *Proceedings of the Third International Conference on Architectural Support for Programming Languages and Operating Systems* (Apr. 1989), 64-75.

15. GOODMAN, J. R., AND WOEST, P. J. The Wisconsin Multicube: A new large-scale cache coherent multiprocessor. In *Proceedings of the International Symposium on Computer Architecture* (May 1988), 422-431.

16. GOTTLIEB, A. Scalability, combining and the NYU ultracomputer. Ohio State University Parallel Computing Workshop, Mar. 1990. Invited Lecture.

17. GOTTLIEB, A., GRISHMAN, R., KRUSKAL, C. P., McAULIFFE, K. P., RUDOLPH, L., AND SNIR, M. The NYU Ultracomputer—Designing an MIMD shared memory parallel computer. *IEEE Trans. Comput. C-32*, 2 (Feb. 1983), 175-189.

18. GRAUNKE, G., AND THAKKAR, S. Synchronization algorithms for shared-memory multiprocessors. *Computer 23*, 6 (June 1990), 60-69.

19. HENSGEN, D., FINKEL, R., AND MANBER, U. Two algorithms for barrier synchroniztion. *Int. J. Parallel Program.* 17, 1 (1988) 1-17.

20. HERLIHY, M. A methodology for implementing highly concurrent data structures. In *Proceedings of the Second ACM Symposium on Principles and Practice of Parallel Programming* (Mar. 1990), 197-206.

21. JAYASIMHA, D. N. Distributed synchronizers. In *Proceedings of the 1988 International Conference on Parallel Processing* (Aug. 1988), 23-27.

22. KRUSKAL, C.P., RUDOLPH, L., AND SNIR, M. Efficient synchronization on multiprocessors with shared memory. In *Proceedings of the Fifth ACM Symposium on Principles of Distributed Computing* (1986), 218-228.

23. KUMAR, M., AND PFISTER, G. F. The onset of hot spot contention. In *Proceedings of the 1986 International Conference on Parallel Processing* (1986), 28-34.

24. LAMPORT, L. A new solution of Dijkstra's concurrent programming problem. *Commun. ACM* 17, 8 (Aug. 1974), 453-455.

25. LAMPORT, L. The mutual exclusion problem: Part I—A theory of interprocess communication; Part II—Statement and solutions. *J. ACM* 33, 2 (Apr. 1986), 313-348.

26. LAMPORT, L. A fast mutual exclusion algorithm. *ACM Trans. Comput. Syst.* 5, 1 (Feb. 1987) 1-11.

27. LEE, C. A. Barrier synchronization over multistage interconnection networks. In *Proceedings of the Second IEEE Symposium on Parallel and Distributed Processing* (Dallas, Tex, Dec. 1990), 130-133.

28. LEE, J., AND RAMACHANDRAN, U. Synchronization with multiprocessor caches. In *Proceedings of the International Symposium on Computer Architecture* (May 1990), 27-37.

29. LUBACHEVSKY, B. An approach to automating the verification of compact parallel coordination programs. I. *Acta Inf. 21* (1984), 125-169.

30. LUBACHEVSKY, B. Synchronization barrier and related tools for shared memory parallel programming. In *Proceedings of the 1989 International Converence on Parallel Processing* (Aug. 1989), II-175-II-179.

31. MAEKAWA, M. A $\sqrt{N}$ algorithm for mutual exclusion in decentralized systems. *ACM Trans. Comput. Syst. 3*, 2 (*May* 1985), 145–159.

32. MELLOR-CRUMMEY, J. M. Concurrent queues: Practical fetch-and-Φ algorithms. Tech. Rep. 229, Computer Science Dept., Univ. of Rochester, Nov. 1987.

33. MELLOR-CRUMMEY, J. M., AND SCOTT, M. L. Algorithms for scalable synchronization on shared-memory multiprocessors. Tech. Rep. 342, Computer Science Dept., Univ. of Rochester, Apr. 1990. Also COMP TR90-114, Dept. of Computer Science, Rice Univ., May 1990.

34. OUSTERHOUT, J. K., SCELZA, D. A., AND SINDHU, P. S. Medusa: An experiment in distributed operating system structure. *Commun. ACM 23*, 2 (Feb. 1980), 92–105.

35. P1596 Working Group of the IEEE Computer Society Microprocessor Standards Committee. SCI (scalable coherent interface): An overview of extended cache-coherence protocols, Feb. 5, 1990. Draft 0.59 P1596/Part III-D.

36. PETERSON, G. L. A new solution to Lamport's concurrent programming problem using small shared variables. *ACM Trans. Program. Lang. Syst. 5*, 1 (Jan. 1983), 56–65.

37. PFISTER, G., BRANTLEY, W. C., GEORGE, D. A., HARVEY, S. L., KLEINFELDER, W. J., McAVLIFFE, K. P., MELTON, T. A., NORTON, V. A., AND WEISS, J. The IBM research parallel processor prototype (RP3): Introduction and architecture. In *Proceedings of the 1985 International Conference on Parallel Processing* (Aug. 1985), 764–771.

38. PFISTER, G., AND NORTON, V. A. "Hot spot" contention and combining in multistage interconnection networks. *IEEE Trans. Comput. C-34*, 10 (Oct. 1985), 943–948.

39. RAYMOND, K. A tree-based algorithm for distributed mutual exclusion. *ACM Trans. Comput. Syst. 7*, 1 (Feb. 1989), 61-77.

40. RAYNAL, M. *Algorithms for Mutual Exclusion*. MIT Press Series in Scientific Computation. MIT Press, Cambridge, Mass., 1986. Translated from the French by D. Beeson.

41. REED, D. P., AND KANODIA, R. K. Synchronization with eventcounts and sequencers. *Commun. ACM 22*, 2 (Feb. 1979), 115–123.

42. RETTBERG, R. D., CROWTHER, W. R., CARVEY, P. P., AND TOMLINSON, R. S. The Monarch parallel processor hardware design. *Computer 23*, 4 (Apr. 1990), 18–30.

43. RICART, G., AND AGRAWALA, A.K. An optimal algorithm for mutual exclusion in computer networks. *Commun. ACM. 24*, 1 (Jan. 1981) 9-17.

44. RUDOLPH, L., AND SEGALL, Z. Dynamic decentralized cache schemes for MIMD parallel processors. In *Proceedings of the International Symposium on Computer Architecture* (1984), 340–347.

45. SANDERS, B. A. The information structure of distributed mutual exclusion algorithms. *ACM Trans. Comput. Syst. 5*, 3 (Aug. 1987), 284–299.

46. SCHNEIDER, F. B. Synchronization in distributed programs. *ACM Trans. Program. Lang. Syst. 4*, 2 (Apr. 1982), 179–195.

47. SCOTT, M. L., LEBLANC, T. J., AND MARSH, B. D. Multi-model parallel programming in Psyche. In *Proceedings of the Second ACM Symposium on Principles and Practice of Parallel Programming* (Mar. 1990), 70–78.

48. TANG, P., AND YEW, P.-C. Processor self-scheduling for multiple-nested parallel loops. In *Proceedings of the 1986 International Conference on Parallel Processing* (Aug. 1986), 528–535.

49. TANG, P., AND YEW, P.-C. Algorithms for distributing hot-spot addressing. CSRD Rep. 617, Center for Supercomputing Research and Development, Univ. of Illinois at Urbana-Champaign, Jan. 1987.

50. YEW, P.-C. Architecture of the Cedar parallel supercomputer. CSRD Rep. 609, Center for Supercomputing Research and Development, Univ. of Illinois at Urbana-Champaign, Aug. 1986.

51. YEW, P.-C., TZENG, N.-F., AND LAWRIE, D. H. Distributing hot-spot addressing in large-scale multiprocessors. *IEEE Trans. Comput. C-36*, 4 (Apr. 1987), 388–395.

52. ZAHORIAN, J., LAZOWSKA, E. D., AND EAGER, D. L. The effect of scheduling discipline on spin overhead in shared memory parallel processors. Tech. Rep. TR-89-07-03, Computer Science Dept., Univ. of Washington, July 1989.

Received June 1990; revised January 1991; accepted January 1991

Directory-Based Cache Coherence in Large-Scale Multiprocessors

David Chaiken, Craig Fields, Kiyoshi Kurihara,

and Anant Agarwal

Massachusetts Institute of Technology

I n a shared-memory multiprocessor, the memory system provides access to the data to be processed and mechanisms for interprocess communication. The bandwidth of the memory system limits the speed of computation in current high-performance multiprocessors due to the uneven growth of processor and memory speeds. Caches are fast local memories that moderate a multiprocessor's memory-bandwidth demands by holding copies of recently used data, and provide a low-latency access path to the processor. Because of locality in the memory access patterns of multiprocessors, the cache satisfies a large fraction of the processor accesses, thereby reducing both the average memory latency and the communication bandwidth requirements imposed on the system's interconnection network.

Caches in a multiprocessing environment introduce the *cache-coherence problem*. When multiple processors maintain locally cached copies of a unique shared memory location, any local modification of the location can result in a globally inconsistent view of memory. Cache-coherence schemes prevent this problem by

This article addresses the usefulness of shared-data caches in large-scale multiprocessors, the relative merits of different coherence schemes, and system-level methods for improving directory efficiency.

maintaining a uniform state for each cached block of data.

Several of today's commercially available multiprocessors use bus-based memory systems. A bus is a convenient device for ensuring cache coherence because it

allows all processors in the system to observe ongoing memory transactions. If a bus transaction threatens the consistent state of a locally cached object, the cache controller can take such appropriate action as invalidating the local copy. Protocols that use this mechanism to ensure coherence are called *snoopy* protocols because each cache snoops on the transactions of other caches.[1]

Unfortunately, buses simply don't have the bandwidth to support a large number of processors. Bus cycle times are restricted by signal transmission times in multidrop environments and must be long enough to allow the bus to "ring out," typically a few signal propagation delays over the length of the bus. As processor speeds increase, the relative disparity between bus and processor clocks will simply become more evident.

Consequently, scalable multiprocessor systems interconnect processors using short point-to-point wires in direct or multistage networks. Communication along impedance-matched transmission line channels can occur at high speeds, providing communication bandwidth that

Reprinted from *Computer*, Vol. 23, No. 6, June 1990, pp. 49–58.

scales with the number of processors. Unlike buses, the bandwidth of these networks increases as more processors are added to the system. Unfortunately, such networks don't have a convenient snooping mechanism and don't provide an efficient broadcast capability.

In the absence of a systemwide broadcast mechanism, the cache-coherence problem can be solved with interconnection networks using some variant of directory schemes.[2] This article reviews and analyzes this class of cache-coherence protocols. We use a hybrid of trace-driven simulation and analytical methods to evaluate the performance of these schemes for several parallel applications.

The research presented in this article is part of our effort to build a high-performance large-scale multiprocessor. To that end, we are studying entire multiprocessor systems, including parallel algorithms, compilers, runtime systems, processors, caches, shared memory, and interconnection networks. We find that the best solutions to the cache-coherence problem result from a synergy between a multiprocessor's software and hardware components.

Classification of directory schemes

A cache-coherence protocol consists of the set of possible states in the local caches, the states in the shared memory, and the state transitions caused by the messages transported through the interconnection network to keep memory coherent. To simplify the protocol and the analysis, our data block size is the same for coherence and cache fetch.

A cache-coherence protocol that does not use broadcasts must store the locations of all cached copies of each block of shared data. This list of cached locations, whether centralized or distributed, is called a *directory*. A directory entry for each block of data contains a number of *pointers* to specify the locations of copies of the block. Each directory entry also contains a dirty bit to specify whether or not a unique cache has permission to write the associated block of data.

The different flavors of directory protocols fall under three primary categories: *full-map directories, limited directories,* and *chained directories.* Full-map directories[2] store enough state associated with each block in global memory so that every cache in the system can simultaneously store a copy of any block of data. That is, each directory entry contains N pointers, where N is the number of processors in the system. Such directories can be optimized to use a single bit pointer. Limited directories[3] differ from full-map directories in that they have a fixed number of pointers per entry, regardless of the number of processors in the system. Chained directories[4] emulate the full-map schemes by distributing the directory among the caches.

To analyze these directory schemes, we chose at least one protocol from each category. In each case, we tried to pick the protocol that was the least complex to implement in terms of the required hardware overhead. Our method for simplifying a protocol was to minimize the number of cache states, memory states, and types of protocol messages. All of our protocols guarantee *sequential consistency*, which Lamport[5] defined to ensure the correct execution of multiprocess programs.

Full-map directories. The full-map protocol uses directory entries with one bit per processor and a dirty bit. Each bit represents the status of the block in the corresponding processor's cache (present or absent). If the dirty bit is set, then one and only one processor's bit is set, and that processor has permission to write into the block. A cache maintains two bits of state per block. One bit indicates whether a block is valid; the other bit indicates whether a valid block may be written. The cache-coherence protocol must keep the state bits in the memory directory and those in the caches consistent.

Figure 1a illustrates three different states of a full-map directory. In the first state, location X is missing in all of the caches in the system. The second state results from three caches (C1, C2, and C3) requesting copies of location X. Three pointers (processor bits) are set in the entry to indicate the caches that have copies of the block of data. In the first two states, the dirty bit — on the left side of the directory entry — is set to clean (C), indicating that no processor has permission to write to the block of data. The third state results from cache C3 requesting write permission for the block. In this final state, the dirty bit is set to dirty (D), and there is a single pointer to the block of data in cache C3.

It is worth examining the transition from the second state to the third state in more detail. Once processor P3 issues the write to cache C3, the following events transpire:

(1) Cache C3 detects that the block containing location X is valid but that the processor does not have permission to write to the block, indicated by the block's write-permission bit in the cache.

(2) Cache C3 issues a write request to the memory module containing location X and stalls processor P3.

(3) The memory module issues invalidate requests to caches C1 and C2.

(4) Cache C1 and cache C2 receive the invalidate requests, set the appropriate bit to indicate that the block containing location X is invalid, and send acknowledgments back to the memory module.

(5) The memory module receives the acknowledgments, sets the dirty bit, clears the pointers to caches C1 and C2, and sends write permission to cache C3.

(6) Cache C3 receives the write permission message, updates the state in the cache, and reactivates processor P3.

Note that the memory module waits to receive the acknowledgments before allowing processor P3 to complete its write transaction. By waiting for acknowledgments, the protocol guarantees that the memory system ensures sequential consistency.

The full-map protocol provides a useful upper bound for the performance of centralized directory-based cache coherence. However, it is not scalable with respect to memory overhead. Assume that the amount of distributed shared memory increases linearly with the number of processors N. Because the size of the directory entry associated with each block of memory is proportional to the number of processors, the memory consumed by the directory is proportional to the size of memory ($\Theta(N)$) multiplied by the size of the directory entry ($\Theta(N)$). Thus, the total memory overhead scales as the square of the number of processors ($\Theta(N^2)$).

Limited directories. Limited directory protocols are designed to solve the directory size problem. Restricting the number of simultaneously cached copies of any particular block of data limits the growth of the directory to a constant factor. For our analysis, we selected the limited directory protocol proposed in Agarwal et al.[3]

A directory protocol can be classified as $Dir_i X$ using the notation from Agarwal et al.[3] The symbol i stands for the number of pointers, and X is NB for a scheme with no broadcast and B for one with broadcast. A full-map scheme without broadcast is represented as $Dir_N NB$. A limited directory protocol that uses $i<N$ pointers is denoted Dir_iNB. The limited directory protocol is similar to the full-map directory, except in the case when more than i caches request read copies of a particular block of data.

Figure 1b shows the situation when three caches request read copies in a memory system with a Dir_2NB protocol. In this case, we can view the two-pointer directory as a two-way set-associative cache of pointers to shared copies. When cache C3 requests a copy of location X, the memory module must invalidate the copy in either cache C1 or cache C2. This process of pointer replacement is sometimes called *eviction*. Since the directory acts as a set-associative cache, it must have a pointer replacement policy. Our protocol uses an easily implemented pseudorandom eviction policy that requires no extra memory overhead. In Figure 1b, the pointer to cache C3 replaces the pointer to cache C2.

Why might limited directories succeed? If the multiprocessor exhibits processor locality in the sense that in any given interval of time only a small subset of all the processors access a given memory word, then a limited directory is sufficient to capture this small "worker-set" of processors.

Directory pointers in a Dir_iNB protocol encode binary processor identifiers, so each pointer requires $\log_2 N$ bits of memory, where N is the number of processors in the system. Given the same assumptions as for the full-map protocol, the memory overhead of limited directory schemes grows as $\Theta(N\log N)$. These protocols are considered scalable with respect to memory overhead because the resources required to implement them grow approximately linearly with the number of processors in the system.

Dir_iB protocols allow more than i copies of each block of data to exist, but they resort to a broadcast mechanism when more than i cached copies of a block need to be invalidated. However, interconnection networks with point-to-point wires do not provide an efficient systemwide broadcast capability. In such networks, it is also difficult to determine the completion of a broadcast to ensure sequential consistency. While it is possible to limit some Dir_iB broadcasts to a subset of the system (see Agarwal et al.[3]), we restrict our evaluation of limited directories to the Dir_iNB protocols.

Chained directories. Chained directories, the third option for cache-coherence schemes that do not utilize a broadcast

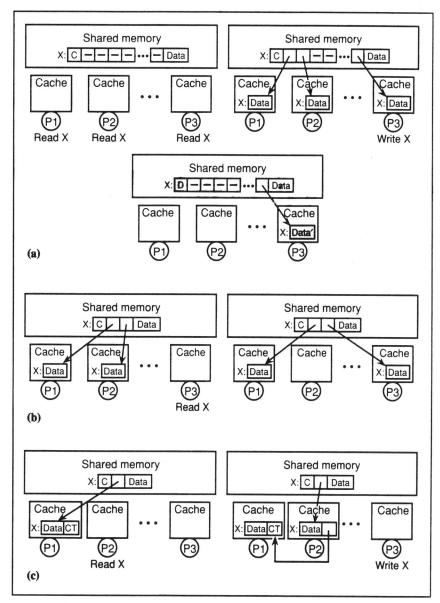

Figure 1. Three types of directory protocols: (a) three states of a full-map directory; (b) eviction in a limited directory; and (c) chained directory.

mechanism, realize the scalability of limited directories without restricting the number of shared copies of data blocks.[4] This type of cache-coherence scheme is called a *chained* scheme because it keeps track of shared copies of data by maintaining a chain of directory pointers. We investigated two chained directory schemes.

The simpler of the two schemes implements a singly linked chain, which is best described by example (see Figure 1c). Suppose there are no shared copies of location X. If processor P1 reads location X, the memory sends a copy to cache C1, along with a chain termination (CT) pointer. The memory also keeps a pointer

to cache C1. Subsequently, when processor P2 reads location X, the memory sends a copy to cache C2, along with the pointer to cache C1. The memory then keeps a pointer to cache C2. By repeating this step, all of the caches can cache a copy of location X. If processor P3 writes to location X, it is necessary to send a data invalidation message down the chain. To ensure sequential consistency, the memory module denies processor P3 write permission until the processor with the chain termination pointer acknowledges the invalidation of the chain. Perhaps this scheme should be called a *gossip* protocol (as opposed to a snoopy protocol) because information is

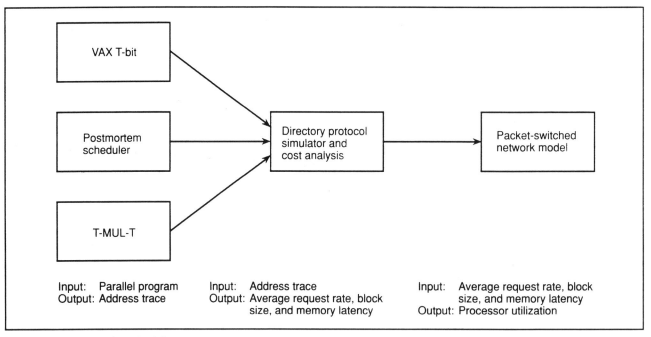

Figure 2. Diagram of methodology.

passed from individual to individual, rather than being spread by covert observation.

The possibility of cache-block replacement complicates chained directory protocols. Suppose that cache C_1 through cache C_N all have copies of location X and that location X and location Y map to the same (direct-mapped) cache line. If processor P_i reads location Y, it must first evict location X from its cache. In this situation, two possibilities exist:

(1) Send a message down the chain to cache C_{i-1} with a pointer to cache C_{i+1} and splice C_i out of the chain, or

(2) Invalidate location X in cache C_{i+1} through cache C_n.

For our evaluation, we chose the second scheme because it can be implemented by a less complex protocol than the first. In either case, sequential consistency is maintained by locking the memory location while invalidations are in progress.

Another solution to the replacement problem is to use a doubly linked chain. This scheme maintains forward and backward chain pointers for each cached copy so that the protocol does not have to traverse the chain when there is a cache replacement. The doubly linked directory optimizes the replacement condition at the cost of a larger average message block size (due to the transmission of extra directory pointers), twice the pointer memory in the caches, and a more complex coherence protocol.

Although the chained protocols are more complex than the limited directory protocols, they are still scalable in terms of the amount of memory used for the directories. The pointer sizes grow as the logarithm of the number of processors, and the number of pointers per cache or memory block is independent of the number of processors.

Caching only private data. Up to this point, we have assumed that caches are allowed to store local copies of shared variables, thus leading to the cache-consistency problem. An alternative shared memory method avoids the cache-coherence problem by disallowing caching of shared data. In our analysis, we designate this scheme by saying it only caches private data. This scheme caches private data, shared data that is read-only, and instructions, while references to modifiable shared data bypass the cache. In practice, shared variables must be statically identified to use this scheme.

Methodology

What is a good performance metric for comparing the various cache-coherence schemes? To evaluate the performance of the memory system, which includes the cache, the memory, and the interconnection network, we determine the contribution of the memory system to the time needed to run a program on the system. Our analysis computes the *processor utilization*, or the fraction of time that each processor does useful work. One minus the utilization yields the fraction of processor cycles wasted due to memory system delays. The actual system speedup equals the number of processors multiplied by the processor utilization. This metric has been used in other studies of multiprocessor cache and network performance.[6]

In a multiprocessor, processor utilization (and therefore system speedup) is affected by the frequency of memory references and the latency of the memory system. The latency (T) of a message through the interconnection network depends on several factors, including the network topology and speed, the number of processors in the system, the frequency and size of the messages, and the memory access latency. The cache-coherence protocol determines the request rate, message size, and memory latency. To compute processor utilization, we need to use detailed models of cache-coherence protocols and interconnection networks.

Figure 2 shows an overview of our analysis process. Multiprocessor address traces generated using three tracing methods at Stanford University, IBM, and MIT are run on a cache and directory simulator that counts the occurrences of different types of protocol transactions. A cost is assigned to each of these transaction types to compute the average processor request rate, the average network message block size, and the average memory latency per transaction. From these parameters, a model of a packet-switched, pipelined, multistage interconnection network calculates the average processor utilization.

Getting multiprocessor address trace data. The address traces represent a wide range of parallel algorithms written in three different programming languages. The programs traced at Stanford were written in C; at IBM, in Fortran; and at MIT, in Mul-T,[7] a variant of Multilisp. The implementation of the trace collector differs for each of the programming environments. Each tracing system can theoretically obtain address traces for an arbitrary number of processors, enabling a study of the behavior of cache-coherent machines much larger than any built to date. Table 1 summarizes general characteristics of the traces. We will compare the relative performance of the various coherence schemes individually for each application.

The SA-TSP, MP3D, P-Thor, and LocusRoute traces were gathered via the Trap-Bit method using 16 processors. SA-TSP uses simulated annealing to solve the traveling salesman problem. MP3D is a 3D particle simulator for rarified flow. P-Thor is a parallel logic simulator. LocusRoute is a global router for VLSI standard cells. Weber and Gupta[8] provide a detailed description of the applications.

Trap-bit (T-bit) tracing for multiprocessors is an extension of single-processor trap-bit tracing. In the single processor implementation, the processor traps after each instruction if the trap bit is set, allowing interpretation of the trapped instruction and emission of the corresponding memory addresses. Multiprocessor T-bit tracing extends this method by scheduling a new process on every trapped instruction. Once a process undergoes a trap, the trace mechanism performs several tasks. It records the corresponding memory addresses, saves the processor state of the trapped process, and schedules another process from its list of processes, typically in a round-robin fashion.

The Weather, Simple, and fast Fourier transform traces were derived using the postmortem scheduling method at IBM. The Weather application partitions the atmosphere around the globe into a three-

Table 1. Summary of trace statistics, with length values in millions of references to memory.

Source	Language	Processors	Application	Length
VAX T-bit	C	16	P-Thor	7.09
			MP3D	7.38
			LocusRoute	7.05
			SA-TSP	7.11
Postmortem scheduler	Fortran	64	FFT	7.44
			Weather	31.76
			Simple	27.03
T-Mul-T	Mul-T	64	Speech	11.77

dimensional grid and uses finite-difference methods to solve a set of partial differential equations describing the state of the system. Simple models the behavior of fluids and employs finite difference methods to solve equations describing hydrodynamic behavior. FFT is a radix-2 fast Fourier transform.

Postmortem scheduling is a technique that generates a parallel trace from a uniprocessor execution trace of a parallel application. The uniprocessor trace is a task trace with embedded synchronization information that can be scheduled, after execution (*postmortem*), into a parallel trace that obeys the synchronization constraints. This type of trace generation uses only one processor to produce the trace and to perform the postmortem scheduling. So, the number of processes is limited only by the application's synchronization constraints and by the number of parallel tasks in the single processor trace.

The Speech trace was generated by a compiler-aided tracing scheme. The application comprises the lexical decoding stage of a phonetically based spoken language understanding system developed by the MIT Spoken Language Systems Group. The Speech application uses a dictionary of about 300 words represented by a 3,500-node directed graph. The input to the lexical decoder is another directed graph representing possible sequences of phonemes in the given utterance. The application uses a modified Viterbi search algorithm to find the best match between paths through the two graphs.

In a compiler-based tracing scheme, code inserted into the instruction stream of a program at compile time records the addresses of memory references as a side effect of normal execution. Our compiler-aided multiprocessor trace implementation is T-Mul-T, a modification of the Mul-

T programming environment that can be used to generate memory address traces for programs running on an arbitrary number of processors. Instructions are not currently traced in T-Mul-T. We assume that all instructions hit in the cache and, for processor utilization computation, an instruction reference is associated with each data reference. We make these assumptions only for the Speech application, because the other traces include instructions.

The trace gathering techniques also differ in their treatment of private data locations, which must be identified for the scheme that only caches private data. The private references are identified statically (at compile time) in the Fortran traces and are identified dynamically by postprocessing the other traces. Since static methods must be more conservative than dynamic methods when partitioning private and shared data, the performance that we predict for the private data caching scheme on the C and Mul-T applications is slightly optimistic. In practice, the nontrivial problem of static data partitioning makes it difficult to implement schemes that cache only private data.

Simulating a cache-coherence strategy. For each memory reference in a trace, our cache and directory simulator determines the effects on the state of the corresponding block in the cache and the shared memory. This state consists of the cache tags and directory pointers used to maintain cache coherence. In the simulation, the network provides no feedback to the cache or memory modules. Assume all side effects from each memory transaction (entry in the trace) are stored simultaneously. While this simulation strategy does not accurately model the state of the memory system on a cycle-by-cycle basis,

Table 2. Simulation parameter defaults for the cache, directory, and network.

Type of Parameter	Name	Default Value
Cache/Directory	Cache size	256 Kbytes
	Cache-block size	16 bytes
	Cache associativity	Direct mapped
	Cache-update policy	Write back
	Directory pointer replace policy	Random
Network	Network message header size	16 bits
	Network switch size	4×4
	Network channel width	16 bits
	Processor cycle time	$2 \times$ network switch cycle time
	Memory address size	32 bits
	Base memory access time	$6 \times$ network switch cycle time

it does produce accurate counts of each type of protocol transaction over the length of a correct execution of a parallel program.

However, since we assume that all side effects of any transaction occur simultaneously, we do not model the difference between sequential and concurrent operations. This inaccuracy particularly affects the analysis of chained directory schemes. Specifically, when a shared write is performed in a system that uses a chained directory scheme, the copies of the written location must be invalidated in sequence, while a centralized directory scheme may send the invalidations in parallel and keep track of the number of outstanding acknowledgments. Thus, the minimum latency for shared writes to clean cache blocks is greater for the distributed schemes than for the centralized schemes.

Analyzing the trade-offs between centralized and distributed schemes requires a much more detailed simulation. While it is possible to accurately model the memory system on a cycle-by-cycle basis, such a simulation requires much higher overhead than our simulations in terms of both programming time and simulation runtime. Our MIT research group is running experiments on a simulator for an entire multiprocessor system. Simulations of the entire system run approximately 100 times slower than the trace-driven simulations used for this article. Variants of coherence schemes are harder to implement in the detailed simulator than in the trace-driven environment. To investigate a wide range of applications and cache-coherence protocols, we avoided the high overhead of

such detailed simulations by performing trace-driven simulations.

In a trace-driven simulation, a memory transaction consists of a processor-to-memory reference and its effect on the state of the memory system. Any transaction that causes a message to be sent out over the network contributes to the average request rate, average message size, and average memory latency. Each type of transaction is assigned a cost in terms of the number of messages that must be sent over the network (including both the requests and the responses), the latency encountered at the memory modules, and the total number of words (including routing information) transported through the network. Given a trace and a particular cache-coherence protocol, the cache and directory simulator determines the percentage of each transaction type in the trace. The percentage of the transaction type, multiplied by its cost, gives the contribution of the transaction to each of the three parameters listed above.

In addition to the cache-coherence strategy, other parameters affect the performance of the memory system. We chose values for these parameters (listed in Table 2) based on the technology used for contemporary multiprocessors. Although we chose a 256-kilobyte cache, the results of our analysis do not differ substantially for cache sizes from 256 kilobytes down to 16 kilobytes because the working sets for the applications are small when partitioned over a large number of processors. The effect of other parameters, including the cache-block size, has been explored in several studies (see

Eggers and Katz[9] and references therein).

The interconnection network model. The directory schemes that we analyze transmit messages over an interconnection network to maintain cache coherence. They distribute shared memory and associated directories over the processing nodes. Our analysis uses a packet-switched, buffered, multistage interconnection network that belongs to the general class of Omega networks. The network switches are pipelined so that a message header can leave a switch even while the rest of the message is still being serviced. A protocol message travels through n network switch stages to the destination node and takes M cycles for the memory access. The network is buffered and guarantees sequenced delivery of messages between any two nodes on the network.

Computation of the processor utilization is based on the analysis method that Patel[10] used. The network model yields the average latency T of a protocol message through the network with n stages, $k \times k$ size switches, and average memory delay M. We derive processor utilization U from a set of three equations:

$$U = \frac{1}{1 + mT}$$

$$\rho = UmB$$

$$T = n + B + M - 1 + \left(\frac{\rho B(1 - \frac{1}{k})}{2(1 - \rho)} \right) n$$

where m is the probability a message is generated on a given processor cycle, with corresponding network latency T. The channel utilization (ρ) is the product of the effective network request rate (Um) and the average message size B. The latency equation uses the packet-switched network model by Kruskal and Snir.[11] The first term in the equation ($n + B + M - 1$) gives the latency through an unloaded network. The second term gives the increase in latency due to network contention, which is the product of the contention delay through one switch and the number of stages. We verified the model in the context of our research by comparing its predictions to the performance of a packet-switched network simulator that transmitted messages generated by a Poisson process.

Table 2 shows the default network parameters we used in our analysis. While this article presents results for a packet-switched multistage network, it is possible to derive results for other types of networks by varying the network model used in the final stage of the analysis. In fact, we repeated our analysis for the direct, two-dimensional mesh network that we plan to use in our own machine. With the direct network model, the cache-coherence schemes showed the same relative behavior as they did with the network model described above. The ability to use the results from one set of directory simulations to derive statistics for a range of network or bus types displays the power of this modeling method.

Analysis of directory schemes

The graphs presented below plot various combinations of applications and cache-coherence schemes on the vertical axis and processor utilization on the horizontal axis. Since the data reference characteristics vary significantly between applications and trace gathering methods, we do not average results from the different traces. The results presented here concentrate on the Weather, Speech, and P-Thor applications. We discuss other applications when they exhibit significantly different behavior.

Are caches useful for shared data? Figure 3 shows the processor utilizations realized for the Weather, Speech, and P-Thor applications using each of the coherence schemes we evaluated. The long bar at the bottom of each graph gives the value for "no cache coherence." This number is derived by considering all addresses in each trace to be not shared. Processor utilization with no cache coherence gives, in a sense, the effect of the native hit/miss rate for the application. The number is artificial because it does not represent the behavior of a correctly operating system. However, the number does give an upper bound on the performance of any coherence scheme and allows us to focus on the component of processor utilization lost due to sharing between processors.

To assess the potential of shared data caching schemes in general, we compare the optimal (full-map) directory scheme to the scheme that caches only private data. For most applications (including the ones shown in Figure 3), the full-map directory yields significantly better processor utilization than the scheme that caches only private data. Generally good performance of the full-map scheme in 16 and 64 processor machines implies that caches are

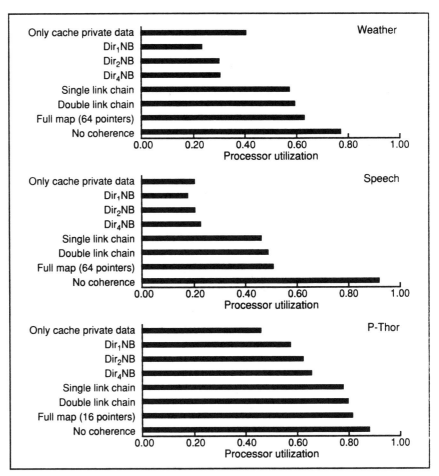

Figure 3. Comparison of coherence schemes.

useful for shared data, even when applications are not written or compiled specially for a system with directory-based cache coherence.

However, for two traces (Simple and MP3D), processor utilization for a full-map directory is worse than the utilization for the private data-cache scheme. Examining the network model shows the reason it is possible for private data caches to perform better than full-map directories: Even though the private cache scheme has a higher network message rate, it uses smaller message block sizes. In the model, network latency is proportional to the square of the message block size but is linearly dependent on the message rate.

The fact that for Simple and MP3D the private data-cache scheme performs better than the full-map directory scheme indicates that the average time between writes by different processors to each shared location is low. For these traces, the full-map directory scheme does not perform significantly better than the limited directory schemes.

Limited directory performance. How well do limited directories perform compared to the full-map directory scheme? The answer depends on the amount of shared data, the number of processors that access each shared data location, and the method of synchronization. The P-Thor application was written to minimize communication between processors by reducing the number of synchronization points and the number of processors that read each shared location. It is not surprising that all of the directory schemes perform well for this application.

On the other hand, four traces show significantly worse processor utilization for limited directories than for a full-map directory due to naive synchronization techniques (Weather, Simple, and SA-TSP) or widespread sharing of a large read-only data structure (Speech).

Chained directory performance. When applications use data structures that are widely shared and accessed frequently, a limited directory performs significantly

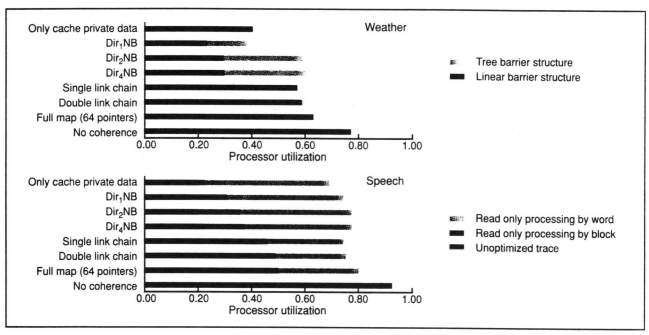

Figure 4. System-level optimizations.

worse than a full-map directory. However, Figure 3 shows that both singly and doubly linked directories perform almost as well as the full-map directory protocols. While the doubly linked scheme always performs slightly better than the singly linked scheme, the small increase in performance may not justify the additional resources needed for the doubly linked scheme. The difference between the schemes is small because the number of replacements as a percentage of total memory accesses is very small, even though we simulated direct-mapped caches.

In general, chained directory schemes yield higher utilization than limited directory protocols. However, chained directory protocols are more complex and have higher write latency than limited directory protocols. We are still investigating the ramifications of this trade-off.

Improving the performance of directories

The results presented above show that limited directory schemes suffer from data types that are both widely shared and frequently referenced. We use the Weather and Speech applications as case studies to demonstrate two methods for ameliorating the effects of this type of data. These meth-ods are examples of *system-level optimizations* because they involve contributions from several components of a multiprocessor system. In addition to improving the performance of limited directory schemes, the methods also enhance the performance of the other coherence schemes.

The Weather application uses barriers as the primary method of synchronization. In the straightforward implementation of barriers, each processor increments a barrier variable and then spin-locks on a barrier flag. The last processor to reach the synchronization point increments the barrier variable to its final value N and writes into the barrier flag, thereby releasing the spinning processors. The memory accesses from many processors spin-locking on a single location cause pointer thrashing (repeated evictions) in the limited directory.

A software solution, called a *combining tree*,[12] can alleviate this problem in directories. Instead of implementing barrier synchronizations with a single barrier variable and barrier flag, a balanced tree structure of nodes can be used for each. To demonstrate the benefits of this barrier implementation, we modified the postmortem scheduler to implement combining tree synchronization. The resulting trace was virtually identical to the original trace, except with respect to the distribution of synchronization address accesses. In the original trace, all of the synchroniza-tion addresses were accessed by all of the processors. In the combining-tree trace, almost all of the synchronization addresses were accessed primarily by one processor, with just one access by one other proces-sor.

The top graph in Figure 4 shows that the combining tree dramatically improves the performance of the limited directory schemes. The darker colored bars show the processor utilization of the application with linear barrier synchronization, and the lighter bars show the enhanced utiliza-tion when using the combining-tree struc-ture. The two- and four-pointer directories yield nearly the same processor utilization as the full-map scheme. The one pointer di-rectory suffers from sharing of other data between processors. However, this data sharing must exist only between processor pairs, because it does not affect the two-pointer directory. Thus, combining tree structures and limited directory schemes provides an efficient implementation of barrier synchronization.

The Speech application provides an example of both a different programming model and a different type of widely shared data. There are two primary data structures in the Speech application: an utterance (the sentence to be identified) and a dictionary (the algorithm's vocabulary). For the dura-tion of the application, these data struc-tures are only read, but they are shared by all the processors in the system. This type of data reference pattern causes pointer thrashing in limited directories.

Given the nature of the Speech application, it is fair to assume that all the read-only variables can be identified by the programmer. To assess the potential benefits of marking read-only data, we postprocessed the trace to find all the data locations that were only read for the duration of the trace. The read-only locations were then marked as private to prevent the cache and directory simulator from executing coherence transactions for this data. When these locations were identified on a block-by-block basis, the system showed moderate improvement for the limited directory schemes. However, when the postprocessor identified the read-only locations on a word-by-word basis and relocated the data to a special segment of memory, the improvement was more pronounced. The bottom graph in Figure 4 demonstrates the increase in processor utilization realized by specially processing read-only data. The darkest bars show the unoptimized performance of the Speech application; the lighter bars show the gains due to processing read-only data.

The boost in processor utilization due to read-only data detection on a word-by-word basis can be explained by the reduction of sharing due to cache blocks that contain unrelated data words accessed by different processors. The Mul-T runtime system ignored the boundary of cache blocks and allocated read-write data words in the same cache blocks as read-only data words. This data allocation policy prevented the block-by-block postprocessor from properly identifying read-only data words and lowered processor utilization by creating unnecessary shared data traffic in the network.

When multiprocessor algorithms and software are optimized for caches, large-scale cache-coherent systems realize their execution potential. In the case of the Weather and Speech applications, system-level optimizations resulted in processor utilizations between 0.6 and 0.8 for scalable cache-coherence protocols. Coordinating multiprocessor hardware and software requires some subset of programmer specifications, new language primitives, special compile-time analysis, support in the runtime system, specialization in the processor-to-cache interface, and additional states in the cache-coherence protocol. The modifications described in this article represent archetypes of systemwide efforts to improve multiprocessor performance.

This article has shown that, by using system-level optimizations, it is possible to build large-scale cache-coherent multiprocessors. Using processor utilization as a metric, we evaluated the performance of several cache-coherence protocols, including limited directories and chained directories. We compared protocols that are scalable in terms of their memory overhead to a protocol that cached only private data and to a nonscalable protocol (full-map). While the scheme that cached only private data performed fairly well, the shared data caching schemes performed better for the majority of the applications that we studied. Limited and chained directory schemes permitted the use of caches to significantly reduce the effective shared memory latency.

There is no hardware panacea for the cache-coherence problem. As with many other problems in computer architecture, good solutions balance hardware and software optimizations that combine to improve system performance. When we applied system-level optimizations to caching, we were able to improve the performance of systems with large numbers of processors.

Our work can be extended in several ways. The most straightforward extension would repeat our trace-driven evaluation using other network models.

Our research group at MIT is currently performing more detailed simulations of directory schemes, coupled with processor and network simulators, to get accurate multiprocessor performance statistics. Such simulations allow us to address the issue of hot spots, the impact of high-latency operations, and the effect of interrupting local cache accesses with external invalidation messages. We are also researching various methods for alleviating the effects of communication latency. These methods include using multithreaded processors with coherent caches, software emulation of directories, and coherence models other than sequential consistency. ∎

Acknowledgments

It is impossible to analyze a large range of applications, programming models, and architectures without becoming indebted to a host of collaborators.

Mathews Cherian laid the foundation for our analysis by writing both the postmortem scheduler with Kimming So at IBM and the cache and directory simulator. Pat Teller of New York University provided the Simple and Weather programs, and FFT was written at IBM. Harold Stone and Kimming So helped us obtain the IBM traces. Wolf-Dietrich Weber and Anoop Gupta provided us with the four VAX T-bit traces, which were generated using a system developed by Steve Goldschmidt at Stanford. David Kranz wrote the Mul-T compiler and the T-Mul-T trace generator and helped analyze the results from the Mul-T application. Kirk Johnson, who wrote and traced the Speech application, is responsible for the read-only data processing results. Gino Maa and Sue-Kyoung Lee wrote the packet switched network simulator that validated our network model.

Encore Computer Corporation provided the Multimax system that runs T-Mul-T. Digital Equipment Corporation and Harris Computer Systems provided the machines we used to manipulate gigabytes of trace data. We would also like to thank the rest of the Alewife group for putting up with our interminable trace-driven simulations.

The research reported in this article is funded by DARPA contract No. N00014-87-K-0825 and by grants from the Sloan Foundation and IBM.

References

1. J.R. Goodman, "Using Cache Memory to Reduce Processor-Memory Traffic," *Proc. 10th Ann. Symp. Computer Architecture*, June 1983, pp. 124-131.

2. L.M. Censier and P. Feautrier, "A New Solution to Coherence Problems in Multicache Systems," *IEEE Trans. Computers*, Vol. C-27, No. 12, Dec. 1978, pp. 1,112-1,118.

3. A. Agarwal et al., "An Evaluation of Directory Schemes for Cache Coherence," *Proc. 15th Int'l Symp. Computer Architecture*, CS Press, Los Alamitos, Calif. Order No. 861, June 1988, pp. 280-289.

4. D.V. James et al., "New Directions in Scalable Shared Memory Multiprocessor Architectures: Scalable Coherent Interface," *Computer*, June 1990, Vol. 23, No. 6, pp. 74-77.

5. L. Lamport, "How to Make a Multiprocessor Computer that Correctly Executes Multiprocess Programs," *IEEE Trans. Computers*, Vol. C-28, No. 9, Sept. 1979, pp. 690-691.

6. J. Archibald and J.-L. Baer, "Cache-Coherence Protocols: Evaluation Using a Multiprocessor Simulation Model," *ACM Trans. Computer Systems*, Vol. 4, No. 4, Nov. 1986, pp. 273-298.

7. D. Kranz, R. Halstead, and E. Mohr, "Mul-T: A High-Performance Parallel Lisp," *Proc. SIGPlan 89, Conf. Programming Languages Design and Implementation*, June 1989, pp. 81-90.

8. W.-D. Weber and A. Gupta, "Analysis of Cache Invalidation Patterns in Multiprocessors," *Third Int'l Conf. Architectural Support for Programming Languages and Operating Systems (ASPLOS III)*, CS Press, Los Alamitos, Calif. Order No. 1936, Apr. 1989, pp. 243-256.

9. S.J. Eggers and R.H. Katz, "The Effect of Sharing on the Cache and Bus Performance of Parallel Programs," *Third Int'l Conf. Architectural Support for Programming Languages and Operating Systems (ASPLOS III)*, CS Press, Los Alamitos, Calif. Order No. 1936, Apr. 1989, pp. 257-270.

10. J.H. Patel, "Analysis of Multiprocessors with Private Cache Memories," *IEEE Trans. Computers*, Vol. C-31, No. 4, Apr. 1982, pp. 296-304.

11. C.P. Kruskal and M. Snir, "The Performance of Multistage Interconnection Networks for Multiprocessors," *IEEE Trans. Computers*, Vol. C-32, No. 12, Dec. 1983 pp. 1,091-1,098.

12. P.-C. Yew, N.-F. Tzeng, and D.H. Lawrie, "Distributing Hot-Spot Addressing in Large-Scale Multiprocessors," *IEEE Trans. Computers*, Vol. C-36, No. 4, Apr. 1987, pp. 388-395.

David Chaiken is a member of the Laboratory for Computer Science at the Massachusetts Institute of Technology and a graduate student in the MIT Department of Electrical Engineering and Computer Science. His research involves computer architectures and programming models for parallel processing.

Chaiken received his BS in mathematics and chemistry from Brown University in 1986.

Craig Fields is an applications programmer for Project Athena at the Massachusetts Institute of Technology. He is also a member of the Alewife group in the institute's Laboratory for Computer Science. His research interests are parallel architectures and systems development.

Fields attended MIT until 1989.

Kiyoshi Kurihara, a systems engineer at IBM Japan, is a postgraduate studying in the Department of Electrical Engineering and Computer Science of the Massachusetts Institute of Technology under an MIT Overseas Study Program scholarship from the company. His research interests are computer architecture and system performance evaluation methodology. He is carrying out research work at MIT's Laboratory for Computer Science.

Kurihara received his bachelor of engineering degree from the University of Tokyo in 1981.

Anant Agarwal has been an assistant professor of electrical engineering and computer science in the Laboratory for Computer Science at the Massachusetts Institute of Technology since January 1988. His research interests include the design of scalable multiprocessor systems, VLSI processors, parallel processing software, and performance evaluation. He initiated MIT's Alewife project, which aims to design and implement a large-scale cache-coherent multiprocessor.

Agarwal received the BTech degree in electrical engineering from the Indian Institute of Technology, Madras, India, in 1982, and the MS and PhD degrees in electrical engineering from Stanford University in 1984 and 1987, respectively. He is a member of the IEEE Computer Society.

The authors can be contacted at the Laboratory for Computer Science, Massachusetts Institute of Technology, Cambridge, MA 02139.

The DASH Prototype: Logic Overhead and Performance

Daniel Lenoski, James Laudon, Truman Joe, David Nakahira, Luis Stevens, Anoop Gupta, and John Hennessy

Abstract—The fundamental premise behind the DASH project is that it is feasible to build large-scale shared-memory multiprocessors with hardware cache coherence. While paper studies and software simulators are useful for understanding many high-level design tradeoffs, prototypes are essential to ensure that no critical details are overlooked. A prototype provides convincing evidence of the feasibility of the design, allows one to accurately estimate both the hardware and the complexity cost of various features, and provides a platform for studying real workloads. A 48-processor prototype of the DASH multiprocessor is now operational. In this paper, we first examine the hardware overhead of directory-based cache coherence in the prototype. The data show that the overhead is only about 10–15%, which appears to be a small cost for the ease of programming offered by coherent caches and the potential for higher performance. We then discuss the performance of the system and show the speedups obtained by a variety of parallel applications running on the prototype. Using a sophisticated hardware performance monitor, we also characterize the effectiveness of coherent caches and the relationship between an application's reference behavior and its speedup. Finally, we present an evaluation of the optimizations incorporated in the DASH protocol in terms of their effectiveness on parallel applications and on atomic tests that stress the memory system.[1]

Index Terms— Directory-based cache coherence, implementation cost, multiprocessor, parallel architecture, performance analysis, shared-memory.

I. INTRODUCTION

FOR parallel architectures to achieve widespread usage it is important that they efficiently run a wide variety of applications without excessive programming difficulty. To maximize both high performance and wide applicability, we believe a parallel architecture should provide i) scalability to support hundreds to thousands of processors, ii) high-performance individual processors, and iii) a single shared address space.

Scalability allows a parallel architecture to leverage commodity microprocessors and small-scale multiprocessors to build larger-scale machines. These larger machines offer substantially higher performance, and can provide the impetus

Manuscript received December 4, 1991; revised July 20, 1992. This work was supported by DARPA Contract N00039-91-C-0138. D. Lenoski is supported by Tandem Computers Inc. A. Gupta is also supported by a Presidential Young Investigator Award.

The authors are with the Computer Systems Laboratory, Stanford University, Stanford University, CA 94305.

IEEE Log Number 9203540.

[1] Portions of the text in the abstract and Sections I through VI-B2, along with Figs. 1 through 5 and Tables I through III originally appeared in D. Lenoski *et al.* "The DASH Prototype: Implementation and Performance," in *Proc. 19th Int. Symp. Comput. Architecture*, pp. 92–103, Copyright 1992, Association for Computing Machinery, Inc. Reprinted with permission.

for programmers to port their sequential applications to parallel architectures. High performance processors are important to achieve both high total system performance and general applicability. A single address space greatly aids in programmability of a parallel machine by reducing the problems of data partitioning and dynamic load distribution, two of the toughest problems in programming parallel machines. The shared address space also provides better support for parallelizing compilers, standard operating systems, multiprogramming, and incremental tuning of parallel applications.

One important question that arises in the design of such large-scale single-address-space machines is whether or not to allow caching of shared writeable data. The advantage of caching is that it allows higher performance to be achieved by reducing memory latency; the disadvantage is the problem of cache coherence. While solutions to the cache coherence problem are well understood for small-scale multiprocessors, they are unfortunately not so clear for large-scale machines. In fact, no large-scale machine currently supports cache coherence, and it has so far not been clear whether it is feasible to do so, what the benefits are, and what the costs will be.

For the past several years, the DASH (Directory Architecture for SHared memory) project has been exploring the feasibility of building large-scale single-address-space machines with coherent caches. The key ideas are to distribute the main memory among the processing nodes to provide scalable memory bandwidth, and to use a distributed directory-based protocol to support cache coherence. To test our ideas, we have been constructing a prototype DASH machine. The final prototype is to consist of sixty-four 33 MHz MIPS R3000/R3010 processors, delivering up to 1600 MIPS and 600 scalar MFLOPS. A forty-eight processor prototype has recently begun working.

This paper examines the hardware overhead and performance of the prototype DASH system. We begin in Section II with a review of the DASH architecture and machine organization. Section III introduces the structure of the DASH prototype and the components that execute the directory-based coherence protocol. Section IV details the overhead of the directory logic exhibited in the prototype. Section V outlines the structure and function of the performance monitor logic incorporated into each DASH node. Section VI focuses on the performance of the DASH system. The system performance is given in terms of basic memory latency, the speedup on parallel applications, the reference behavior that leads to the observed speedup, and the effectiveness of the optimizations to the coherence protocol. We conclude in

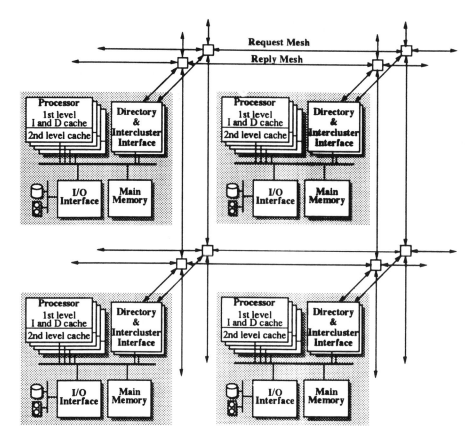

Fig. 1. Block diagram of a 2 × 2 DASH prototype.

Section VII with a summary of our experience with the DASH prototype.

II. The DASH Architecture

The DASH architecture has a two-level structure shown in Fig. 1. At the top level, the architecture consists of a set of processing nodes (clusters) connected through a mesh interconnection network. In turn, each processing node is a bus-based multiprocessor. Intra-cluster cache coherence is implemented using a snoopy bus-based protocol, while inter-cluster coherence is maintained through a distributed directory-based protocol.

The cluster functions as a high-performance processing node. A bus-based cache protocol is chosen for implementing small-scale shared-memory multiprocessors because the bus bandwidth is sufficient to support a small number of processors. The grouping of multiple processors on a bus within each cluster amortizes the cost of the directory logic and network interface among a number of processors. Furthermore, this grouping reduces the directory memory requirements by keeping track of cached lines at a cluster as opposed to processor level.

The directory-based protocol implements an invalidation-based coherence scheme. A memory location may be in one of three states: uncached, that is not cached by any processing node at all; shared, that is in an unmodified state in the caches of one or more nodes; or dirty, that is modified in the cache of some individual node. The directory keeps the summary information for each memory line, specifying the clusters that are caching it [9].

The DASH memory system can be logically broken into the four level hierarchy shown in Fig. 2. The level closest to the processor is the processor cache and is designed to match the speed of the processor. A request that cannot be serviced by the processor cache is sent to the second level in the hierarchy, the local cluster level. This level consists of other processors' caches within the requesting processor's cluster. If the data is locally cached, the request can be serviced within the cluster, otherwise the request is sent to the directory home level. The home level consists of the cluster that contains the directory and physical memory for a given memory address. For some accesses, the local and home cluster are the same and the second and third level access occur simultaneously. In general, however, the request will travel through the interconnect to the home cluster. The home cluster can usually satisfy the request, but if the directory entry is in the dirty state, or in the shared state when the requesting processor requires exclusive access, the fourth, remote cluster level, must be accessed. The remote cluster level responds directly to the local cluster level while also updating the directory level.

In addition to providing coherent caches to reduce memory latency, DASH supports several other techniques for hiding and tolerating memory latency. DASH supports the release consistency model [5], that helps hide latency by allowing buffering and pipelining among memory requests. DASH also supports software-controlled nonbinding prefetching to help hide latency of read operations [7]. Finally,

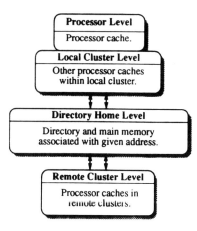

Fig. 2. Logical memory hierarchy of DASH.

DASH supports efficient spin locks in hardware and fetch-and-increment/decrement primitives to help reduce the overhead of synchronization. These optimizations will be discussed in more detail in Section VI-C.

III. THE DASH PROTOTYPE

To focus our effort on the novel aspects of the design and to speed the completion of a usable system, the base cluster hardware of the prototype is a commercially available bus-based multiprocessor. While there are some constraints imposed by the given hardware, the prototype satisfies our primary goals of scalable memory bandwidth and high performance.

The prototype system uses a Silicon Graphics POWER Station 4D/340 as the base cluster [2]. The 4D/340 system consists of four MIPS R3000 processors and R3010 floating-point coprocessors running at 33 MHz. Each R3000/R3010 combination can sustain execution rates of 25 VAX MIPS and 10 MFLOPS. Each CPU contains a 64 Kbyte instruction cache and a 64 Kbyte write-through data cache. The 64 Kbyte data cache interfaces to a 256 Kbyte second-level write-back cache. The interface consists of a read buffer and a 4 word deep write-buffer. Both the first and second level caches are direct-mapped and support 16 byte lines. The first level caches run synchronously to their associated 33 MHz processors while the second level caches run synchronous to the 16 MHz memory bus.

The second-level processor caches are responsible for bus snooping and maintaining coherence among the caches in the cluster. Coherence is maintained with a MESI (Illinois) protocol [14], and inclusion of the first-level cache by the second-level. The main advantage of using the Illinois protocol in DASH is the cache-to-cache transfers specified in this protocol. While they do little to reduce the latency for misses serviced by local memory, local cache-to-cache transfers can greatly reduce the penalty for remote memory misses. The set of processor caches effectively act as a cluster cache for remote memory. The memory bus (MPBUS) of the 4D/340 is a synchronous bus and consists of separate 32-bit address and 64-bit data buses. The MPBUS is pipelined and supports memory-to-cache and cache-to-cache transfers of 16 bytes

every 4 bus clocks with a latency of 6 bus clocks. This results in a maximum bandwidth of 64 Mbytes/s.

To use the 4D/340 in DASH, we have had to make minor modifications to the existing system boards and design a pair of new boards to support the directory memory and inter-cluster interface. The main modification to the existing boards is to add a bus retry signal that is used when a request requires service from a remote cluster. The central bus arbiter has also been modified to accept a mask from the directory which holds off a processor's retry until the remote request has been serviced. This effectively creates a split transaction bus protocol for requests requiring remote service. The new directory controller boards contain the directory memory, the intercluster coherence state machines and buffers, and a local section of the global interconnection network.

While the prototype could scale to support hundreds of processors, it is limited to a maximum configuration of 16 clusters and 64 processors. This limit was dictated primarily by the physical memory addressability of the 4D/340 system (256 Mbytes) which would severely limit the memory per processor in a larger system.

The directory logic in DASH is responsible for implementing the directory-based coherence protocol and interconnecting the clusters within the system. Pictures of the directory boards are shown in Fig. 3. The directory logic is split between the two boards along the lines of the logic used for outbound and inbound portions of inter-cluster transactions.

The DC board contains three major subsections. The first section is the directory controller (DC) itself, which includes the directory memory associated with the cachable main memory contained within the cluster. The DC logic initiates all out-bound network requests and replies. The second section is the performance monitor which can count and trace a variety of intra- and inter-cluster events. The third major section is the request and reply outbound network logic together with the X-dimension of the network itself. The second board is the RC board which also contains three major sections. The first section is the reply controller (RC) which tracks outstanding requests made by the local processors and receives and buffers replies from remote clusters using the remote access cache (RAC). The second section is the pseudo-CPU (PCPU), which is responsible for buffering incoming requests and issuing these requests onto the cluster bus. The PCPU mimics a CPU on this bus on behalf of remote processors except that responses from the bus are sent out by the directory controller. The final section is the inbound network logic and the Y-dimension of the mesh routing networks.

Directory memory is accessed on each bus transaction. The directory information is combined with the type of bus operation, the address, and the result of snooping on the caches to determine what network messages and bus controls the DC will generate. The directory memory organization is similar to the original directory scheme proposed by Censier and Feautrier [3]. Directory pointers are stored as a bit vector with 1 bit for each of the 16 clusters. While a full bit vector has limited scalability, it was chosen because it requires roughly the same amount of memory as a limited pointer directory given the size of the prototype, and it allows for more

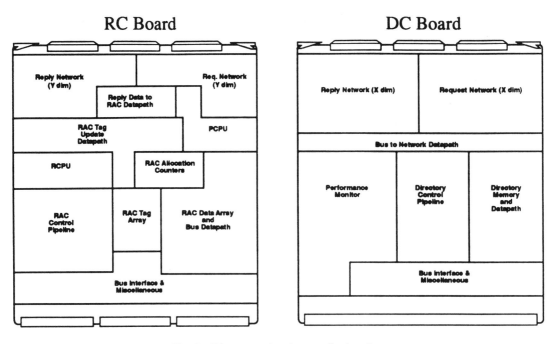

Fig. 3. Directory and reply controller boards.

direct measurements of the caching behavior of the machine. Each directory entry contains a single state bit that indicates whether the clusters have a shared or dirty copy of the data. The directory is implemented using DRAM technology, but performs all necessary actions within a single bus transaction.

The reply controller stores the state of on-going requests in the remote access cache (RAC). The RAC's primary role is the coordination of replies to inter-cluster transactions. This ranges from the simple buffering of reply data between the network and bus to the accumulation of invalidation acknowledgments and the enforcement of release consistency. The RAC is organized as a 128 Kbyte direct-mapped snoopy cache with 16 byte cache lines. One port of the RAC services the in-bound reply network while the other snoops on bus transactions. The RAC is lock-up free in that it can handle several outstanding remote requests from each of the local processors. RAC entries are allocated when a remote request is initiated by a local processor and persist until all inter-cluster transactions relative to that request have completed. The snoopy nature of the RAC naturally lends itself to merging requests made to the same cache block by different processors, and takes advantage of the cache-to-cache transfer protocol supported between the local processors. The snoopy structure also allows the RAC to supplement the function of the processor caches. This includes support for a dirty-sharing state for a cluster (normally the Illinois protocol would force a write-back, instead, in DASH the RAC takes the data in a dirty-shared state) and operations such as prefetch (the RAC holds the prefetched data).

As stated in the architecture section, the DASH coherence protocol does not rely on a particular interconnection network topology. However, for the architecture to be scalable, the network itself must provide scalable bandwidth. It should also provide low latency communication. The prototype system uses a pair of wormhole routed meshes to implement the interconnection network. One mesh handles request messages

while the other is dedicated to replies. The networks are based on variants of the mesh routing chips developed at Caltech where the datapaths have been extended from 8 to 16 bits [4]. Wormhole routing allows a cluster to forward a message after receiving only the first flit (flow unit) of the packet, greatly reducing the latency through each node (50 ns per hop). The bandwidth of each self-timed link is limited by the round trip delay of the request-acknowledge signals. In the prototype flits are transferred at approximately 30 MHz, resulting in a peak bandwidth of 120 Mbytes/s in and out of each cluster.

IV. GATE COUNT SUMMARY

One important result of building the DASH prototype is that it provides a realistic model of the cost of directory-based cache coherence. While some of these costs are tied to the specific prototype implementation (e.g., the full DRAM directory vector), they provide a complete picture of one system.

At a high level, the cost of the directory logic can be estimated by the fact that a DASH cluster includes six logic cards, four of which represent the base processing node and two of which are used for directory and inter-cluster coherence. This is a very conservative estimate, however, because Silicon Graphics' logic, in particular the MIPS processor chips and Silicon Graphics' gate arrays, are more highly integrated than the MSI PAL's and LSI FPGA's used in the directory logic.

Table I summarizes the logic for a DASH cluster at a more detailed level. The table gives the percent of logic for each section and the totals in terms of thousands of 2-input gates, kilobytes of static RAM, megabytes of dynamic RAM, and 16-pin IC equivalents. RAM bytes include all error detecting or correcting codes and cache tags. 16-pin IC equivalent is a measure of board area (0.36 sq. inch), assuming through-hole technology (i.e. DIP's and PGA's) was used throughout the

TABLE I
PERCENT OF ALL LOGIC IN A DASH CLUSTER

Section	Gates (thous.)	SRAM (KB)	DRAM (MB)	IC Equiv
Processors/Caches	69.3%	86.0%	0.0%	32.4%
Main Memory	3.3%	0.0%	75.8%	12.7%
IO Board	8.3%	0.0%	1.4%	13.5%
Directory Controller	4.4%	0.0%	12.0%	8.2%
Reply Controller	8.4%	7.3%	0.0%	12.0%
PCPU	0.5%	0.0%	0.0%	1.2%
Network Outbound	2.8%	0.7%	0.0%	4.3%
Network Inbound	1.1%	0.7%	0.0%	2.4%
Performance Mon.	1.8%	5.3%	10.8%	3.5%
Total	535	2420	83	2603

TABLE II
PERCENT OF CORE LOGIC IN A DASH CLUSTER

Section	Gates (thous.)	SRAM (KB)	DRAM (MB)	IC Equiv
Processors/Caches	70.8%	90.8%	0.0%	45.2%
Main Memory	3.9%	0.0%	86.3%	13.9%
IO Board	5.1%	0.0%	0.0%	10.3%
Directory Controller	5.2%	0.0%	13.7%	9.0%
Reply Controller	9.9%	7.7%	0.0%	13.1%
PCPU	0.6%	0.0%	0.0%	1.3%
Network Outbound	3.3%	0.8%	0.0%	4.7%
Network Inbound	1.3%	0.8%	0.0%	2.6%
Performance Mon.	0.0%	0.0%	0.0%	0.0%
Total	456	2292	73	2286

design. (Actually about 1/4 of the CPU logic is implemented in surface mount technology, but the IC Equivalent figures used here assume through-hole since all of the logic could have been designed in surface mount.) The number of 2-input gates is an estimate based on the number of gate-array 2-input gates needed to implement each function. For each type of logic used in the prototype the equivalent gate complexity was calculated as:

Custom VLSI — Estimate based on part documentation.

CMOS Gate Array — Actual gate count or estimate based on master-slice size and complexity.

PAL — Translation of 2-level minimized logic into equivalent gates.

PROM — Espresso minimized PROM files translated into 2-input gates. This includes the primary state machines in the DC and RC, but not the boot EPROM's for the CPU's.

TTL — Gates in equivalent gate array macros.

The numbers in Table I are somewhat distorted by the extra logic in the base Silicon Graphics' hardware and the directory boards that is not needed for normal operations. This includes i) the performance monitor logic on the directory board; ii) the diagnostic UART's and timers attached to each processor; iii) the Ethernet and VME bus interfaces on the Silicon Graphics' I/O board.[2] Table II shows the percentage of this core logic assuming the items mentioned above are removed.

As expected, only when measured in terms of IC equivalents (i.e., board area), is the cost of the directory logic approximately 33%. When measured in terms of logic gates the portion of the cluster dedicated to the directory is 20%, and the SRAM and DRAM portions are 13.9% and 13.7% respectively.

Note that in the above analysis, we do not account for the hardware cost of snooping on the local bus separately because these costs are very small. In particular, the processor's two-level cache structure does not require duplicate snooping tags, and the processor's bus interface accounts for only 3.2% of the gates in a cluster. Even if the second-level cache tags were duplicated, it would represent only 4.0% of a cluster's SRAM. In practice, we expect most future systems will use microprocessors with integrated first-level caches (e.g., MIPS R4000, DEC Alpha, etc.) and to incorporate an external second-level cache (without duplicate tags) to improve uniprocessor performance. Thus, the extra SRAM cost for snooping (e.g., extra state bits) is expected to be negligible.

[2] Each I/O board would still include a SCSI interface for disk interfacing.

Looking at the numbers in Table II in more detail also shows additional areas where the directory overhead might be improved. In particular, the prototype's simple bit vector directory grows in proportion to the number of clusters in the system, and in inverse proportion to cache line size. Thus, increasing cache line size from 16 to 32 or 64 bytes would reduce the directory DRAM overhead to 6.9% and 3.4% respectively, or it could allow the system to grow to 128 or 256 processors with the same 13.7% overhead. For larger systems, a more scalable directory structure [1], [8], [13] could be used to keep the directory overhead at or below the level in the prototype. The directory's overhead in SRAM could also be improved. The 128 KB remote access cache (RAC) is the primary use of SRAM in the directory. The size of the RAC could be significantly reduced if the processor caches were enhanced to be lockup-free, support a dirty-shared state, and track outstanding requests. With enhanced processor caches, the primary use of the RAC would be to collect invalidation acknowledgments, receive granted locks, and merge requests to the same memory line. This would allow a reduction in size by at least a factor of four, and result in an SRAM overhead of less than 2%. Likewise, a closer coupling of the base cluster logic and bus protocol to the inter-cluster protocol might reduce the directory logic overhead by as much as 25%. Thus, the prototype represents a conservative estimate of directory overhead. A more ideal DASH system would have a logic overhead of 18–25%, an SRAM overhead of 2–8% and a DRAM overhead 3–14%. This is still significant,[3] but when amortized over the cluster the overhead is reasonable.

The prototype logic distributions can also be extrapolated to consider other system organizations. For example, if the DASH cluster-based node was replaced by a uniprocessor node, the overhead for directory-based cache-coherence would be higher. Ignoring the potential growth in directory storage (that would need to track individual processor caches instead of clusters), the percent of directory logic in a uniprocessor node would grow to 44% (a 78% overhead). Thus, a system based on uniprocessor nodes would lose almost a factor of two in cost/performance relative to a uniprocessor or a small-scale multiprocessor.

Another possible system organization is one based on a general memory or messaging interconnect, but without support for global hardware cache coherence (e.g., the BBN TC2000 or Intel Touchstone). An optimistic assumption for such a system is that it would remove all of the directory DRAM and support, the RAC and its datapath, and 90% of the RC and DC control pipelines. Under these assumptions, the fraction of logic dedicated to the inter-cluster interface falls to 10% of a cluster, and the memory overhead becomes negligible. Thus, the cost of adding inter-cluster coherence to a large-scale, noncache coherent system is approximately 10%. If more than a 10% performance gain is realized by this addition, then the overall cost/performance of the system will improve. Our measurements on DASH indicate that caching improves performance by far more than 10%, and support for global cache coherence is well worth the extra cost.

Finally, by examining the required gates, memory bits and connectivity requirements, one can estimate how the DASH prototype might be integrated into a small number of VLSI chips. As examined in detail in [11], state-of-the-art VLSI technology could be used to integrate the prototype's cluster logic into seven VLSI chips plus memory to form a system with up to 512 clusters (2048 total processors) while maintaining a similar logic and memory overhead to that given in Table II.

V. Performance Monitor

One of the prime motivations for building the DASH prototype was to study real applications with large data sets running on a large ensemble of processors. The alternative, simulation, results in a real-time slow down in the range of 1000–100 000 [6]. Because many of the applications have an execution time measured in tens of minutes on actual hardware, simulation is prohibitively expensive. To enable more insight into these applications when running on the prototype, we have dedicated over 20% of the DC board to a hardware performance monitor. Integration of the performance monitor with the base directory logic allows noninvasive measurements of the complete system without extra test hardware. The performance hardware is controlled by software, and it provides low-level information on software reference characteristics and hardware resource utilizations. The monitor hardware can trace and count a variety of bus, directory and network events. Event selection is controlled by a software programmable Xilinx gate array (FPGA) [17]. This allows flexible event selection and sophisticated event preprocessing.

A block diagram of performance logic is shown in Fig. 4. It consists of three major blocks. First, the FPGA which selects and preprocesses events to be measured and controls the rest of the performance logic. Second, two banks of 16 K $\times$ 32 SRAM's and increment logic that count event occurrences. Third, a 2M $\times$ 36 trace DRAM which captures 36 or 72 bits of information on each bus transaction.

The counting SRAM's together with the FPGA support a wide variety of event counting. The two banks of SRAM are addressed by events selected by the FPGA. They can be used together to trace events that occur on a cycle by cycle basis, or the banks can be used independently to monitor twice as many events. By summing over all addresses with a particular address bit high or low the number of occurrences of that event can be determined. Likewise, the conjunction or disjunction of any set of events can be determined by summing over the appropriate address ranges. Another use of the count SRAM is as a histogram array. In this mode, certain events are used to start, stop and increment a counter inside the FPGA. The stop event also triggers the counter to be used as a SRAM address to increment.

The current use of the counting SRAM in the prototype increments the two banks of SRAM independently on each bus transaction. The address of the first bank is the directory controller's state machine PROM address. The resulting SRAM values give a complete distribution of bus transaction types and

---

[3] Approximately equal to the complexity of an entire processor with its caches.

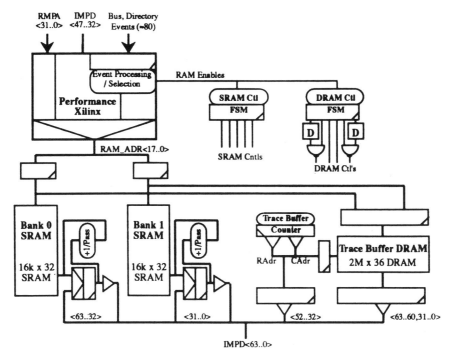

Fig. 4. Block diagram of performance monitor logic.

initiators, directory states, RAC states and local/remote status. From this data access type frequency, bus utilization, access locality, RAC performance, and remote caching statistics can be calculated. Indirectly, the output of the PROM's can be determined from the input address to calculate the frequency of network messages and network utilization. The second bank of SRAM is addressed with the local cache snoop results and histogram counters of remote latency. The snoop data allows one to determine the effectiveness of cache-to-cache sharing within the cluster. The remote latency histogram dedicates an internal counter to each CPU. An individual counter is reset until a processor is forced to retry for a remote access. When the processor is released the counter value is used to index the SRAM and increment a histogram bucket. The result is that a distribution of remote access latencies can be determined. Furthermore, when combined with the count of local bus cycles an estimate of processor utilization can be determined.

The other primary function of the performance monitor is a 2 M × 36 trace array. Again, which information is traced can vary based on programming of the FPGA, but the current use of the trace logic has two modes. In the first configuration, up to 2 M memory addresses together with the issuing processor number and read/write status are captured. The second mode can capture only 1 M addresses, but adds the directory controller's input PROM address and a bus idle count to each trace entry. With software assistance the tracer can be used to capture much longer traces with minimal distortion. The trace information can be used to do detailed analysis of reference behavior or as input to another memory simulator. The only restriction is that only bus references are captured, not references satisfied by the processor cache. If a complete address trace is desired, it can be generated by using only uncached memory spaces. Some distortion of the access

pattern may result, however, because the speed of memory will be substantially slower than normal, and will not include any of the effects of cache hits interspersed with cache misses.

VI. PROTOTYPE PERFORMANCE

This section examines the performance of the initial hardware prototype of DASH which includes 48 processors in twelve clusters. The first part summarizes the memory latencies measured on the prototype hardware. The second part describes the speedups obtained by parallel applications run on the actual machine. The third part discusses the effect of optimizations included in the coherence protocol.

A. Processor Issue Bandwidth and Latency

Although the coherent caches in DASH significantly reduce the number of remote accesses made by a processor, it is still essential to minimize the latency when misses do occur. Table III lists the processor bandwidth and latency for cache memory operations in DASH assuming no contention. (PClocks refer to processor clocks which are 30 ns in the prototype.) The delays are average for a 16 cluster DASH configuration and are based on hardware measurements. In the table, the best-case numbers assume stride-one access, with one cache miss every four references (cache lines are 16 bytes). The worst-case numbers assume stride-four accesses with no reuse of cache lines.

Table III presents data separately for reads and writes. For reads, the access latency is given by the last column of the table. The latency can vary by more than two orders of magnitude depending on where a read access is serviced in the memory hierarchy. The read bandwidth also varies considerably, from a high of 133 Mbytes/s from the primary cache to a meager 4 Mbytes/s if all of the data is dirty in a

TABLE III
CACHE OPERATION BANDWIDTH AND LATENCIES

Cache Operation	Best Case		Worst Case	
	MByte / Sec	PClock / Word	MByte / Sec	PClock / Word
Read from 1st-level Cache	133.3	1.0	133.3	1.0
Cache fill from 2nd-level cache	29.6	4.5	8.9	15.0
Cache fill from local bus	16.7	8.0	4.6	29.0
Cache fill from remote bus	5.1	26.0	1.3	101.0
Cache fill from dirty-remote bus	4.0	33.8	1.0	132.0
Write retired in 2nd-level cache	32.0	4.2	32.0	4.2
Write retired on local bus	18.3	7.3	8.0	16.7
Write retired on remote bus	5.3	25.3	1.5	88.7
Write retired on dirty remote bus	4.0	33.0	1.1	119.7

remote nonhome cluster. While, beyond a point, not much can be done about reducing the latency in large-scale machines, the bandwidth can be increased via pipelining, and it is for this reason we have provided nonblocking prefetch operations in DASH. The times given for store operations are the rate at which writes are retired from the write buffer into the second-level cache after acquiring ownership. Release consistency is assumed so that the processor need not wait for the write to retire, and invalidations do not affect write latency.

A more detailed break-down of the latency for local and remote cache misses is given in Fig. 5. The latency for a local miss that is serviced within the cluster is based entirely on the base SGI hardware (i.e., the hardware we have added to the SGI clusters does not slow the system down). In the prototype, a simple remote miss (i.e., a miss that is serviced by a remote home cluster) takes 3.5 times longer than a local miss. The final case illustrated in Fig. 5 represents the latency for fetching a location that is dirty in a cluster other than its home. In this case, an extra 1 μs of delay is incurred in forwarding the request to the dirty cluster. The DASH protocol supports the direct transfer of the dirty data between the dirty and requesting cluster, reducing latency by 20% over a simpler protocol that first causes a writeback to the home cluster and then replies to the requesting processor.

While latencies in the DASH prototype (when measured in microseconds) are far from optimal, we believe that the delays when measured in processor clocks are quite indicative of what we expect to see in future large-scale machines. The reason is that while state-of-the-art technology (with integration and optimization) would allow us to reduce the prototype's latencies by a factor of about three [11], state-of-the-art processor clock rates are also about three times the 33 MHz used in the prototype. As a result, we expect that exploiting cache and memory locality will continue to be important in future large scale machines, as will mechanisms that help hide or tolerate latency.

B. Parallel Application Performance

This subsection outlines the performance actually achieved on the prototype for a number of parallel applications. We begin by describing the software environment available on the prototype and how the measurements were made. We then present the speedup for ten parallel programs representing a variety of application domains. Four of these applications are studied more in-depth using data captured by the performance monitor.

1) Application Runtime Environment: The operating system running on the prototype DASH is a modified version of IRIX; a variant of UNIX System V.3 developed by Silicon Graphics. The applications for which we present results are coded in C and use the Argonne National Labs (ANL) parallel macros [12] to control synchronization and sharing.

Before giving the speedup results in the next subsection, we first state the assumptions used in measuring the speedups. The speedups were measured as the time for the uniprocessor to execute the parallel version of the application code (i.e., not all synchronization code is removed) divided by the time for the parallel application to run on a given number of processors. We timed the entire application for most of the applications. The four exceptions are Cholesky, Radiosity, LocusRoute, and VolRend. We discuss our decision to time only a portion of these applications later in this section.

For our measurements, each application process is attached to a processor for its lifetime, and we fully use one cluster before assigning processors to new clusters. Physical memory pages used by the application are allocated only from the clusters that are actively being used, as long as the physical memory in those clusters is enough. Thus, for an application running with 4 processes, all memory is allocated from the local cluster, and all misses cost about 30 clocks. However, with 8 processes, some misses may be to a remote cluster and cost over 100 clock cycles. Most of the programs allocate shared data randomly or in a round-robin fashion from the clusters being actively used, but some include explicit system calls to control memory allocation.[4] Finally, all applications were run under processor consistency mode, i.e., writes were not retired from the write-buffer until all invalidation acknowledgments had been received.

2) Application Speedups: Fig. 6 gives the speedup for ten parallel applications running on the hardware prototype using from 1 to 48 processors. The applications cover a variety of domains. There are some scientific applications (Barnes-Hut, FMM, and Water), several engineering applications (MP3D, PSIM4, Cholesky, and LocusRoute), two graphics applications (Radiosity and VolRend) and one kernel (matrix multiply).

[4] Currently all operating system code and data are allocated from cluster-0's memory. This causes cluster 0 to become a hot spot for OS misses, and causes some degradation in speedups. We are in the process of fixing this problem.

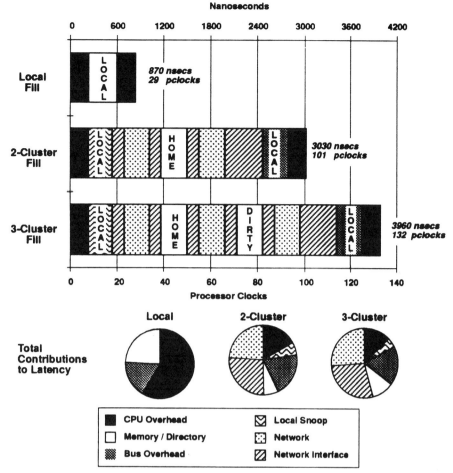

For clarity four processor clocks of bus overhead per bus access are not shown in the bar graphs, but are included in the total contributions breakdown.

Fig. 5. Cache fill latency in the DASH prototype.

Five of the programs (Barnes-Hut, Water, LocusRoute, MP3D and Cholesky) are applications taken from the SPLASH parallel benchmark suite [15]. The characteristics of the applications give some insight into why they achieve good or bad speedups. We begin with a quick overview of all ten applications and then go into detail on the performance for four of them.

Starting with the applications with the best speedup, Matmult is a blocked matrix multiply, which uses 88 x 88 blocks for a roughly 1000x1000 matrix. The size of the matrix is slightly modified with the number of processors to ensure an integral number of blocks per processor. Matmult gets almost perfect speedup and the overall performance with 48 processors is 363 double-precision MFLOPS. The second application is VolRend from the domain of computer graphics. It performs volume rendering for a 256x256x113 computer tomography dataset. Rendering is performed by ray tracing, casting one ray per pixel. An octree combined with early ray termination is used to reduce rendering time. VolRend is intended to be an interactive application. There is a fixed, large initialization overhead, which can be amortized over an arbitrary number of frames. Since the intention of VolRend is to allow real-time rendering and viewing of an image, we time a single frame in its entirety (including rendering and

copying the image to the frame buffer). VolRend achieved a speedup of over 45 on 48 processors for this frame. With 48 processors, DASH renders this image at approximately 2 frames per second.

The next application is the FMM code [16], which represents an n-body galactic simulation solved using the fast multipole method. The input consists of two Plummer-model clustered galaxies with 16 384 bodies each. The structure of the application and its data is complex, however, we see that caches work quite well and we get a speedup of over 40 with 48 processors. Immediately below is the Water code (the parallelized version of the MDG code from the Perfect Club benchmarks), a molecular dynamics code. We run it using 1728 water molecules and 45 time steps. We will discuss this application in detail later in this section.

The next application, Barnes-Hut [16] represents an n-body galactic simulation solved using the Barnes-Hut algorithm (an $O(N \log N)$ algorithm). The input consists of the same two Plummer-model clustered galaxies used for FMM, and again we see that although the structure of the program is complex, good speedups are obtained. We will discuss Barnes-Hut in detail later in this section. Below it is Radiosity [16], from the domain of computer graphics. It computes the

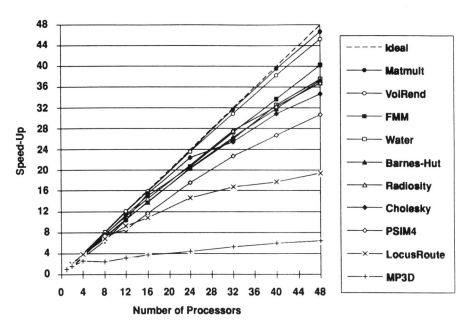

Fig. 6. Speedup of parallel applications run on the DASH prototype.

global illumination in a room given a set of surface patches and light sources using a variation of hierarchical n-body techniques. The particular problem instance solved starts with 364 surface patches, and ends with over 10 000 patches. Radiosity has a serial initialization portion consisting primarily of generating a large array of random numbers. We do not time the initialization, as it could be parallelized, but has not been in the current version. While the data structures used in Radiosity are a complex octree and a binary-space partition tree, the application achieves a speedup of 37 on 48 processors.

The next application is Cholesky. It performs factorization of sparse positive-definite matrices using supernodal techniques (data blocking techniques that enhance the performance of caches both for uniprocessors and multiprocessors). Here it is used to solve the BCSSTK33 problem from the Boeing-Harwell benchmark set, which contains 2.54 million nonzero matrix elements. The Cholesky numbers give speedups for the most important and most time-consuming phase of the computation, the numerical factorization. Runtimes for pre- and post-processing phases are not included because these phases have not yet been parallelized. Each phase is quite involved and would require a significant amount of parallelization effort. Parallelization of these phases is important and appears possible, but the required effort has simply not yet been expended. We note that much of the fall off in speedup for Cholesky is due to the trade-off between large data block sizes (which increase processor efficiency, but decrease available concurrency and cause load balancing problems) and small data block sizes. As we go to a large number of processors, we are forced to use smaller block sizes unless the problem size is scaled to unreasonably large sizes. With 48 processors, Cholesky achieves 190 MFLOPS. We feel that this is very good given the relatively low floating-point performance of the MIPS R3000 processors.

Next is PSIM4, an application from NASA, that is a particle-based simulator of a wind tunnel. PSIM4 is an enhanced version of the MP3D code, both in functionality and locality of memory accesses. The 48 processor run is done with over 300 000 particles and it achieves a speedup of over 31. In contrast, the older MP3D code achieves a speedup of under 7 with 48 processors simulating 40 000 particles. We discuss both PSIM4 and MP3D in detail later in this section. Finally, the LocusRoute application does global routing of standard cells using routed area to evaluate the quality of a given placement. The inner loop of LocusRoute is the routing of a given cell placement. LocusRoute exploits parallelism at two levels. First, multiple wires are routed simultaneously. Second, different routes for the same wire are evaluated in parallel. LocusRoute was run over a circuit consisting of 3817 wires and 20 routing channels. We ignore the serial initialization portion of LocusRoute, timing only the parallel routing. The serial initialization in LocusRoute consists of two portions: the reading of the design input file, and the data structure initialization. LocusRoute is intended to be the routing phase of a CAD tool, and the design would already be resident in memory. In addition, the data structure initialization could be parallelized, but this has not been done yet.

Overall, we see that most applications achieve good speedups, even though they have not been specially optimized for DASH. More than half the applications get over 36 times improvement on 48 processors and two of the applications get near-linear improvement.

3) Detailed Case Studies: To get a better understanding of the detailed reference behavior of some of the applications, we now examine the Water, Barnes-Hut, MP3D, and PSIM4 applications in more detail. These applications were chosen because they represent programs that achieved a range of good and bad speedups. Results are presented for only the parallel portions of the applications (with the exception of the speedup numbers). Statistics were ignored during the sequential initialization portion to avoid lowering the bus and network utilization.

TABLE IV
WATER MEMORY ACCESS CHARACTERISTICS

Execution Attribute	1 PE	2 PEs	4 PEs	8 PEs.	12 PEs	16 PEs	24 PEs	32 PEs	40 PEs	48 PEs
Speedup	1.00	1.98	3.85	7.13	10.42	13.95	20.27	26.05	32.58	37.57
Busy Pclks between Proc. Stalls	686.6	620.1	486.2	425.2	432.2	453.3	412.8	440.8	442.0	428.8
Est. Processor Utilization (%)	96.5	96.2	95.8	91.5	90.9	89.6	88.2	87.3	87.3	86.9
Cache Read (%)	60.9	67.9	62.6	60.7	58.0	54.7	58.4	56.2	58.1	58.9
Cache Read Exclusive (%)	3.9	2.8	15.6	20.9	23.9	25.3	23.8	24.9	24.0	23.5
Cache Lock (%)	17.6	14.6	10.8	9.2	9.1	10.0	9.0	9.5	9.0	8.9
Cache Unlock (%)	17.4	14.6	10.8	9.2	9.0	10.0	8.9	9.4	8.9	8.7
References to Local Memory (%)	99.9	99.6	99.9	56.0	37.1	29.0	20.5	16.5	12.6	11.3
Local Ref's satisfied Locally (%)	98.3	99.4	99.8	93.8	90.3	84.1	83.5	80.9	80.0	77.9
Remote Ref's satisfied Locally (%)	0.0	0.0	0.0	49.4	55.7	48.0	50.1	43.4	46.0	47.2
Remote Ref's satisfied in Home (%)	100.0	100.0	100.0	96.8	97.3	94.2	93.5	89.4	89.3	89.7
Measured Local Cache Fill (Pclks)	29.2	29.2	29.5	29.6	29.7	29.7	29.8	29.8	29.8	29.8
Unloaded Remote Cache Fill (Pclks)	101.0	101.0	101.0	103.3	104.9	109.5	111.5	116.5	117.4	116.9
Measured Remote Cache Fill (Pclks)	112.8	109.9	112.0	107.5	111.3	116.1	119.6	125.5	127.8	128.3
Bus Utilization (%)	4.9	6.9	11.9	16.1	16.7	17.7	19.1	19.8	19.6	19.8
Req. Net Bisection Util. (%)	0.6	0.8	0.8	1.6	1.9	4.6	5.4	6.4	6.5	6.5
Reply Net Bisection Util. (%)	0.5	0.7	0.7	2.0	2.2	5.2	5.8	6.4	6.3	6.4

a) Water: Water is a molecular dynamics code from the field of computational chemistry. The application computes the interaction between a set of water molecules over a series of time steps. For the problem size that we consider here, 1728 molecules, the algorithm is essentially $O(N^2)$ in that each molecule interacts with all other molecules in the system. As shown in Fig. 6, the Water application achieves good speedup on the DASH hardware.

Table IV gives a detailed memory reference profile of Water running on DASH as measured by the hardware performance monitor.[5] Table IV is broken into five sections: i) overall performance and processor utilization; ii) memory request distribution; iii) request locality; iv) memory latency characteristics and v) bus and network utilization.

The first section of the table gives the overall speedup and estimated processor utilization. Unfortunately, processor utilization cannot be measured directly from the bus, so what is given in the table assumes that the processor is doing active work whenever it is not waiting for a bus transaction to complete. This ignores stalls due to first-level cache misses satisfied by the second-level, TLB miss handling and floating-point interlocks.[6] Processor utilization (third row of table) and busy clocks between stalls (second row) give an indication of the level of cache locality in the application and its sensitivity to memory latency.

For Water, cache-locality is very high and the time between processor stalls indicates that Water is not highly sensitive to memory latency. The table shows a reduction in the busy clocks between stalls as the number of processors increases from 2 to 4 processors, but this levels off afterwards. The application computes the forces on molecules one at a time,

and incurs misses only between force computations. The amount of work done for each force computation is essentially independent of the number of processors, which explains why the number of busy clocks between stalls levels off.

The second section of Table IV gives a breakdown on the memory reference types. This breakdown indicates the type of accesses that cause bus transactions and whether synchronization references are significant. In Water, the percentage of synchronization references is fairly high. This is due in part to the high cache hit rates, and to the fact that every successful lock acquire and release reference the bus in the prototype. Given the percentage of locks and unlocks are very close, this data also indicates that lock contention is not a severe problem in Water.

The third section of Table IV gives a breakdown of cache fill locality. The first line indicates the fraction of all cache misses which refer to local memory (based on physical address). The next line shows the percentage of these local references which are satisfied locally. Note that a local memory reference may have to go to a remote cluster if the data is dirty in that cluster. The third line shows the percentage of remote references (based on physical address) that are satisfied locally. A remote reference may be satisfied locally if another processor's cache contains that data (using a cache-to-cache transfer) or if the RAC contains that data. The final line in this section shows the fraction of remote references (out of the remote references which are not satisfied locally) that are satisfied by the home cluster, that is, the home does not forward the request to another cluster where the data are dirty. As can be seen from Table IV, the Water application does not use any specific memory placement strategy—the fraction of references to local memory fall off in inverse proportion to the number of clusters. However, nearly 50% of remote references are satisfied locally for all the multiple-cluster runs. This good cluster locality agrees with simulations that indicate that Water should achieve over 50 times speedup on a 64 processor DASH [10].

The fourth section of Table IV shows the latencies for remote and local cache fills. Both unloaded and loaded latencies are given for remote fills. The latency figures are based on the

---

[5] The results given in the table are averaged over all active clusters. This implies some inaccuracies for the one and two processor runs due to the overhead of the idle processors running the UNIX scheduler and daemons (e.g., slightly lower processor utilization for 1 and 2 processors than for 4 processors).

[6] Since writes are buffered, they are not assumed to stall the processor directly. Instead, it is assumed that the processor can execute for 20 clocks before stalling. This delay is an estimate of the time for the processor to fill the other 3 words to the write-buffer (i.e. assuming 15% instructions are writes). In reality, the processor may not issue writes at this rate, or may stall earlier due to a first-level cache miss.

TABLE V
BARNES-HUT MEMORY ACCESS CHARACTERISTICS

Execution Attribute	1 PE	2 PEs	4 PEs	8 PEs.	12 PEs	16 PEs	24 PEs	32 PEs	40 PEs	48 PEs
Speedup	1.00	1.60	2.48	2.33	3.12	3.74	4.42	5.27	5.99	6.42
Busy Pclks between Proc. Stalls	82.5	46.1	43.6	44.2	38.6	49.7	56.0	58.9	61.5	84.5
Est. Processor Utilization (%)	73.8	67.5	62.0	34.6	24.8	27.2	26.5	26.2	26.4	32.1
Cache Read (%)	98.3	72.9	67.5	57.7	56.9	54.0	51.8	52.2	53.4	51.6
Cache Read Exclusive (%)	0.9	26.9	32.2	42.0	42.7	45.5	47.3	46.6	45.2	46.3
Cache Lock (%)	0.3	0.1	0.0	0.0	0.2	0.3	0.5	0.8	1.0	1.5
Cache Unlock (%)	0.3	0.1	0.0	0.0	0.0	0.0	0.0	0.0	0.0	0.0
References to Local Memory (%)	100.0	100.0	100.0	46.5	29.3	23.0	16.0	11.6	8.9	8.4
Local Ref's satisfied Locally (%)	99.8	99.9	100.0	79.3	74.7	67.9	62.3	63.3	66.1	59.3
Remote Ref's satisfied Locally (%)	0.0	0.0	0.0	30.8	18.9	17.1	12.9	10.0	8.1	10.4
Remote Ref's satisfied in Home (%)	100.0	100.0	100.0	99.3	89.0	80.5	71.6	71.0	73.3	63.1
Measured Local Cache Fill (Pclks)	29.4	30.8	37.0	37.2	38.1	36.6	36.0	35.7	35.2	34.1
Unloaded Remote Cache Fill (Pclks)	101.0	101.0	101.0	101.3	108.6	114.7	120.3	119.8	117.5	124.6
Measured Remote Cache Fill (Pclks)	109.5	117.5	130.4	138.7	160.9	172.2	186.8	191.3	192.7	201.6
Bus Utilization (%)	16.6	42.9	78.6	77.3	78.6	73.6	71.0	69.6	67.6	62.2
Req. Net Bisection Util. (%)	0.5	0.6	0.9	10.7	15.0	30.6	32.5	33.1	32.5	30.6
Reply Net Bisection Util. (%)	0.4	0.5	0.9	13.7	15.6	30.1	29.6	29.3	28.7	26.3

weighted average of remote and dirty-remote references. The remote reference latency figures indicate that Water does not heavily load the system; there is very little queueing. For 48 processors, less than 12 extra cycles are added due to queueing delays.

The final section of the table also shows that the memory system is not heavily loaded. With the low reference rate, both the bus and the request and reply networks have a low utilization. Bus utilization is measured directly by the performance monitor, while the network bisection utilizations are estimates assuming uniform network traffic. The bisection utilization is calculated by knowing the total number of network messages sent, assuming the half of the messages cross the midline of the mesh, and dividing by the bandwidth provided across the bisection. For Water, the bisection load is negligible.

b) Barnes-Hut: Barnes-Hut is a galactic N-body simulation solved using the hierarchical Barnes-Hut algorithm. This algorithm reduces the complexity of force computation among N bodies from $O(N^2)$ to $O(N \log N)$ by approximating groups of distant bodies by equivalent single points when possible. To do this, it recursively subdivides the computational domain to obtain a tree structured representation. The force on each body is computed by a partial depth-first traversal of the tree data structure which terminates at cells that are considered far enough away from the body. As a result, a body computes interactions directly with other bodies that are close to it, and with larger and larger cells as they get further away from it. The input for the runs in Table V consists of two Plummer-model clustered galaxies with 16 384 bodies each.

Barnes-Hut achieves a respectable 37.2 speedup on 48 processors. The processor utilization remains essentially constant as more processors are added up to 48 processors. Excellent cache locality is achieved despite the nonuniform and dynamically changing problem domain, because the nature of the tree traversals ensures that most of the interactions computed are between bodies in the same processor's partition.

c) MP3D: The MP3D application is a particle-based wind-tunnel simulator developed at NASA-Ames. In each time step, particles are moved according to their velocity vectors

and collisions are modeled. The results reported in Table VI correspond to a run with 40 000 particles and 300 time steps. The speedups are poor for MP3D because of frequent sharing of data that is actively being updated. While the particles are statically allocated to processors, the space cells (representing physical space in the wind tunnel) are referenced in a relatively random manner depending on the location of the particle being moved. Since each move operation also updates the corresponding space cell, as the number of processors increases, it becomes more and more likely that the space cell being referenced will be in remote-dirty state. Thus, as shown in Table VI cache hit rates fall (see busy clocks between processor stalls) and the average miss latencies go up.

The high miss rates together with low locality are the primary cause for the performance decrease that occurs when going from 4 to 8 processors. When all of the processors are within the same cluster, the miss latencies are 30 processor clocks. As soon as we go to two clusters (8 processors), there is a 50% chance that a space cell miss will be handled by a remote cluster, which takes over 100 clock cycles. Since the miss rates are high in MP3D, these larger miss latencies nullify the benefits of the extra processors. (As can be seen from Table VI, when we go to two clusters, the fraction of references to local memory goes down from 100% to 46%, and even the fraction of local references that are satisfied locally goes down from 100% to 79%.) Speedup when going from 8 to 12 processors is also poor because there is now a good possibility that a space cell cache miss will be satisfied by a dirty-remote cluster (132 versus 100 clock unloaded latency). Table VI shows this is occurring, with 10% of remote references for the 12 processor run being satisfied by a dirty-remote cluster. Thus, processor utilization falls further when going from 8 to 12 processors, and speedup is less than ideal. Interestingly enough, however, the busy time between processor stalls actually increases as more processors are added. This is not because the application is performing better, but instead because of load balancing problems. The processors spend more time spinning in their cache, waiting on barriers. This barrier time is counted as processor busy time by the performance monitor.

TABLE VI
MP3D MEMORY ACCESS CHARACTERISTICS

Execution Attribute	1 PE	2 PEs	4 PEs	8 PEs.	12 PEs	16 PEs	24 PEs	32 PEs	40 PEs	48 PEs
Speedup	1.00	1.96	3.81	7.29	10.59	13.82	20.42	26.33	31.84	37.24
Busy Pclks between Proc. Stalls	528.9	519.8	514.1	468.8	528.4	529.0	510.4	545.4	562.5	638.9
Est. Processor Utilization (%)	94.7	94.6	94.7	92.9	92.8	92.6	92.0	92.2	92.4	93.1
Cache Read (%)	91.8	93.8	95.3	94.3	93.6	93.4	93.6	92.7	92.5	91.7
Cache Read Exclusive (%)	4.2	3.9	3.3	4.4	5.0	5.1	4.8	5.4	5.5	6.0
Cache Lock (%)	2.0	1.1	0.7	0.7	0.8	0.8	0.9	1.1	1.2	1.4
Cache Unlock (%)	1.9	1.1	0.7	0.6	0.7	0.7	0.5	0.6	0.6	0.7
References to Local Memory (%)	99.1	99.5	99.5	50.5	33.6	25.7	17.6	12.7	10.6	8.7
Local Ref's satisfied Locally (%)	98.7	99.4	99.8	99.6	99.4	99.1	99.2	98.8	98.8	98.5
Remote Ref's satisfied Locally (%)	0.0	0.0	0.0	80.1	76.2	77.4	77.6	77.7	77.3	76.8
Remote Ref's satisfied in Home (%)	100.0	100.0	100.0	97.0	98.1	98.6	99.0	99.1	99.1	98.9
Measured Local Cache Fill (Pclks)	29.2	29.2	29.4	29.4	29.4	29.4	29.4	29.4	29.4	29.4
Unloaded Remote Cache Fill (Pclks)	101.0	101.0	101.0	103.9	102.6	102.4	102.1	102.2	102.2	102.5
Measured Remote Cache Fill (Pclks)	111.8	110.3	111.3	107.5	109.8	113.1	114.7	118.0	118.8	122.2
Bus Utilization (%)	5.2	6.9	10.1	11.5	11.1	11.2	11.5	11.1	11.0	10.2
Req. Net Bisection Util. (%)	0.6	0.6	0.6	0.8	0.8	1.7	1.7	1.8	1.8	1.7
Reply Net Bisection Util. (%)	0.5	0.5	0.5	0.9	1.1	2.2	2.4	2.3	2.3	2.2

TABLE VII
PSIM4 MEMORY ACCESS CHARACTERISTICS

Execution Attribute	1 PE	2 PEs	4 PEs	8 PEs.	12 PEs	16 PEs	24 PEs	32 PEs	40 PEs	48 PEs
Speedup	1.00	1.53	3.47	7.42	8.54	11.66	17.61	22.77	26.79	30.76
Busy Pclks between Proc. Stalls	166.5	180.4	191.9	217.5	252.2	281.9	315.8	397.2	413.7	432.1
Est. Processor Utilization (%)	80.6	82.9	82.0	88.8	84.5	86.9	88.9	91.1	91.5	92.1
Cache Read (%)	78.3	79.5	79.2	82.1	79.6	79.8	80.0	80.0	79.8	79.0
Cache Read Exclusive (%)	18.3	17.7	18.3	15.3	17.5	17.2	16.6	16.1	16.0	16.3
Cache Lock (%)	1.7	1.4	1.2	1.3	1.6	1.6	1.8	2.1	2.4	2.7
Cache Unlock (%)	1.7	1.4	1.2	1.3	1.3	1.4	1.5	1.7	1.8	2.0
References to Local Memory (%)	78.0	82.2	77.2	92.5	66.1	70.7	70.8	69.2	67.9	69.2
Local Ref's satisfied Locally (%)	99.7	99.8	99.9	99.9	99.8	99.9	99.9	99.9	99.8	99.9
Remote Ref's satisfied Locally (%)	1.0	1.5	0.0	48.0	24.4	24.7	37.2	44.6	49.2	51.3
Remote Ref's satisfied in Home (%)	100.0	100.0	100.0	100.0	98.0	97.8	98.6	98.1	98.0	98.2
Measured Local Cache Fill (Pclks)	29.2	29.4	30.0	29.9	30.1	29.9	29.8	29.6	29.6	29.6
Unloaded Remote Cache Fill (Pclks)	101.0	101.0	101.0	101.0	101.8	101.9	101.8	102.5	102.9	102.9
Measured Remote Cache Fill (Pclks)	104.3	105.1	107.6	109.4	114.5	114.1	116.4	120.0	121.4	124.3
Bus Utilization (%)	8.6	13.8	24.4	21.7	24.7	22.0	19.2	15.8	15.2	14.5
Req. Net Bisection Util. (%)	0.1	0.2	0.4	0.4	2.6	4.1	3.0	2.2	2.1	1.9
Reply Net Bisection Util. (%)	0.0	0.0	0.0	0.5	3.0	4.6	3.2	2.4	2.2	2.0

Looking at Table VI, it is also clear that MP3D puts a heavy load on the memory system. The load on the cluster bus is very high (up to 79%) when multiple clusters are used. The load on the network is not nearly as high (up to 33%). This heavy memory system load results in large queueing delays for remote references, increasing the latency by up to 63% for the 48 processor run (while the unloaded remote reference latency should have been 125 cycles, the measured remote latency was 202 cycles). The utilization data also confirms calculations, based on total bandwidth and uniform loading, that the cluster bus in the prototype limits memory system bandwidth more than the network. The bus utilization also indicates that, in the prototype, latency hiding techniques such as prefetching will not help applications like MP3D. A better solution is to restructure the application to achieve better locality of the space cells by not strictly tying particles to processors. This restructured MP3D is called PSIM4, and from Table VII we can see that this time the speedups are significantly better (more than 30-fold with 48 processors). PSIM4 provides a good example of how a poorly performing application can be restructured to achieve much better performance on DASH, and we discuss it next.

d) PSIM4: PSIM4 is an enhanced version of the MP3D code, both in terms of functionality and in terms of locality of memory accesses. The enhanced functionality includes modeling multiple types of gases and including molecular chemistry. To improve locality, PSIM4 uses spatial decomposition of simulated space to distribute work among processors. Thus, both particles and the space cells in a large spatial chunk are assigned to the same processor and the data allocated from its corresponding local memory.

While the results of PSIM4 are not directly comparable with MP3D (PSIM4 models the wind tunnel much more accurately and is solving a more realistic problem than MP3D), we can see from Table VII that the spatial decomposition of PSIM4 works quite well. The percentage of references to local memory does fall from 8 to 12 processors, but levels off at approximately 70% from 12 to 48 processors. In addition to this improved memory locality, PSIM4 is busy much longer between processor stalls than MP3D, mainly due to improved cache usage (some gains occur from performing more computation per particle to model the different molecule types and chemistry). The improved cache and memory locality results in very good speedups. The 48 processor run is done with over 300 000 particles running for 600 time steps and achieves a speedup of nearly 31, in contrast to the speedup of 6.4 for 48 processors for the old MP3D code.

4) Application Speedup Summary: Overall, a number of conclusions can be drawn from the speedup and reference statistics presented in previous sections. First, it is possible to get near linear speedup on DASH with a number of real applications. Applications with the best speedup have good cache locality, but even those with moderate miss rates (e.g., PSIM4) can achieve reasonable speedup.

In absolute terms, the number of busy clocks between bus accesses indicates that caching of shared data improves performance significantly. For example, earlier simulation work [10] with the Water application indicated that the reference rate to shared data is roughly one reference every 25 instructions. Even assuming that the number of processor instructions between stalls given in Table IV are optimistic by a factor of two, caches are satisfying 88% of the shared references in Water (i.e., there are at least 428/2/25 or 8.6 shared references for every miss). Thus, processor utilization without caching would be 26%[7]. Overall, this implies that caching of shared data improves performance by a factor of three, but as shown earlier only adds 10% to system's hardware cost.[8]

Even with caches, however, locality is still important. As shown by applications like MP3D, if locality is very low and the communication misses are high; speedup will be poor. However, for many applications the natural locality is enough (e.g., FMM, Barnes-Hut, VolRend, Water) that very good speedups can be achieved without algorithmic or programming contortions. Even in applications where natural locality is limited, DASH allows the programmer to focus on the few critical data structures that are causing loss in performance, rather than having to explicitly manage (replicate and place) all data objects in the program.

Looking at the system resource usage, the applications confirm that bus bandwidth is the primary limitation to overall memory system bandwidth in the prototype. Even without latency hiding techniques, MP3D was able to drive the buses to over 70% utilization. Oppositely, the network bisection had a much smaller loading (2–3 times less) and does not appear to be a major contributor to queueing. Finally, the loading on the request and reply networks appears to be well balanced.

C. Protocol Effectiveness

This section examines in detail how the protocol features and alternative memory operations provided in DASH improve system performance. Features of the base protocol optimizations are examined in the context of the parallel applications, while the alternative memory operations are studied with stand-alone atomic tests. The atomic tests allow the alternative operations to be studied in a more controlled environment where their effects can be easily decoupled from an application's ability to utilize the operation.

1) Base Protocol Features: While there are many facets of the base coherency protocol that could be examined in detail, this section focuses on three of the most important

and novel aspects of the DASH protocol: request forwarding, cache-to-cache sharing, and the use of the remote access cache. The protocol optimizations are examined on the four parallel applications that we have made performance monitor measurements on: Water, Barnes-Hut, MP3D, and PSIM4. The results in this section were derived from the reference statistics captured using the hardware performance monitor together with the measured latency of operations given in Section VI-A.

a) Request Forwarding: Request forwarding in DASH refers to the protocol's ability to forward remote requests from the home cluster to a third cluster that currently caches the requested memory block, and for the third cluster to respond directly to the cluster that originated the request. Two important uses of forwarding in DASH are the forwarding of memory requests to a dirty-remote cluster, and the forwarding of invalidations to clusters sharing a memory block. In both of these cases, the incoming memory request generates new outgoing request(s), and the destination cluster(s) reply directly to the cluster that originated the request. The primary advantage of forwarding is that it reduces the latency of these requests (usually by one cluster/network transaction, which is approximately 1 μs without contention). Fowarding also reduces hardware complexity by eliminating the need to buffer information about pending requests in the home. The home directory controller reacts to a request based on the current state of the directory, and when necessary, forwards responsibility for the request to the remote cluster(s) that should be able to complete it. The disadvantage of forwarding is that it requires a mechanism to avoid network deadlock[9] and complicates recovery from network errors. Forwarding can also lead to performance loss when requests are forwarded to dirty clusters that cannot satisfy the requests due to pending operations or changes in block ownership (the retry penalty is approximately 3 μs).

Table VIII summarizes the effectiveness of forwarding cache reads and read-exclusives to dirty-remote clusters for the benchmark applications using 48 processors. The improvement if the forward is successful is assumed to be 1 μs, while a retry has a cost of 3 μs. With these assumptions, Water and MP3D experience an improvement of approximately 11% in read fill times. Barnes-Hut and PSIM4 rarely fetch data from a dirty-remote cluster so neither of these see a large improvement from forwarding. Read-exclusive requests rarely need forwarding to a remote dirty cluster, and thus they see little benefit (two clusters writing a cache-line before reading it is usually the result of false sharing).

Table IX details the effect of forwarding write invalidation requests to shared-remote clusters. When release consistency is used, this type of forwarding is not as critical as dirty-remote forwarding because the receipt of invalidation acknowledgments can be overlapped with processor execution. When processor consistency is used, however, a read-exclusive request is not satisfied until all invalidations are received. Thus, in this case invalidation forwarding saves at least 1 μs

---

[7] This assumes the locality of shared references is the same as the locality seen for cache misses.

[8] The added costs for caching is conservative because we ignore any added costs in the uncached system that would be necessary to increase the bandwidth to main memory.

[9] Forwarding adds a dependency to the acceptance of incoming requests on the ability of the node to send outgoing requests. Without provisions to break this dependence, there could be deadlock due to buffer overflow of the PCPU's input FIFO that blocks a node's outgoing requests.

TABLE VIII
EFFECTIVENESS OF DIRTY-REMOTE FORWARDING

	Water	Barnes-Hut	PSIM4	MP3D
% Remote Reads, Dirty-Rem	51.2%	4.9%	6.0%	76.2%
Success Rate	100.0%	93.1%	99.7%	98.7%
Avg. Read Fill Improvement	**11.7%**	**1.0%**	**1.6%**	**10.7%**
% Remote Read-Ex's, Dirty-Rem	1.1%	5.3%	3.4%	5.1%
Success Rate	99.1%	99.4%	92.7%	82.6%
Avg. Read-Ex. Improvement	**0.3%**	**1.3%**	**0.7%**	**0.2%**

TABLE IX
EFFECTIVENESS OF INVALIDATION FORWARDING

	Water	Barnes-Hut	PSIM4	MP3D
% Read-Exclusive to Shared	76.4%	15.5%	1.5%	84.2%
Read-Ex Fill Improvement	**16.6%**	**3.9%**	**0.4%**	**11.8%**

TABLE X
EFFECTIVENESS OF LOCAL CACHE TO CACHE SHARING

	Water	Barnes-Hut	PSIM4	MP3D
Rem. Reads satisfied locally	24.9%	46.0%	11.6%	10.5%
Read savings from Snoop	14.4%	24.9%	5.7%	6.5%
Rem Read-Ex Satisfied Locally	0.04%	0.66%	1.41%	0.70%
Read-Ex savings from Snoop	-3.2%	-2.7%	-2.1%	-1.3%
Combined Read and Read-Ex	**9.9%**	**23.3%**	**4.3%**	**2.9%**

per write to a shared-remote location (again, one network and cluster hop).[10] Forwarding of invalidations has a significant effect in Water and MP3D (> 12%), but is unimportant for Barnes-Hut and PSIM4 where writes to shared variables are infrequent.

b) Local Cache to Cache Sharing: As illustrated in Fig. 5, all remote accesses are delayed in the originating cluster until the results of the local snoop are known. Performing this local snoop has the advantage that some remote cache and cache-lock requests are satisfied by a local cache-to-cache transfer and do not incur the latency of fetching the data from a remote home cluster. Of course, it has the disadvantage of increasing latency[11] for remote accesses not satisfied by a local transfer. Table X summarizes the measured gains from the local snoop on the 48 processor benchmark runs in terms of the percent improvement of remote memory latency. As with forwarding to dirty-remote clusters, reads benefit more than writes from the local sharing. The local snoop actually results in a performance loss for read-exclusive requests, but the overall effect is a decrease in remote latency because of local cache-to-cache sharing for read requests. This performance gain, together with the hardware simplifications that result from making all the network request generation timing the same (in local, home and dirty-remote clusters), imply that local cache sharing was well worth supporting in the prototype.

c) Remote Access Cache: Another design feature in DASH is the implementation of the reply controller's pending request buffer as a direct-map snoopy cache (RAC). While the RAC structure serves many purposes (e.g., enforcement of release consistency), it has two direct performance benefits. First, by serving as an additional cluster cache, the RAC supports cache-to-cache sharing and a cluster-level dirty-sharing cache state. Second, by merging outstanding requests, the RAC reduces the average latency for remote locations, and it can reduce hot-spot traffic. The disadvantage of the RAC arises from its cache structure which can cause conflicts for individual RAC entries. In these cases, the outstanding request must be satisfied before the new request can be initiated.

Table XI provides a summary of the performance impact of the RAC. The effectiveness of the RAC as a cluster cache is somewhat overstated in the table because for all requests that could be satisfied by either a local processor cache or the RAC, the RAC is given the credit (due to limits in the current performance monitor). This implies that the improvements from the cache sharing listed in Table X are understated, and that the savings given in the two tables can be added. The combined savings from the two types of cluster caching are significant. Cluster caches reduce the effective remote miss penalty by 6% in MP3D, by more than 20% in Water and PSIM4, and over 30% in Barnes-Hut. Merging of outstanding remote requests by the RAC has a much smaller impact on performance. While a number of requests are merged, they do not significantly reduce the fill time of the merged requests because latencies are not dramatically reduced. Thus, any benefits from merging are made indirectly through a reduction in hot-spot traffic.

2) Alternative Memory Operations: This section investigates the performance potential of the alternative memory operations such as prefetch, granting locks, Fetch&Op and update writes. While it would be desirable to present the effects of these operations on a variety of real benchmarks, such

---

[10]The data in Table IX also estimates the gain from release consistency over processor consistency in the prototype since the gain from release consistency is to allow a write to retire as soon as ownership is returned, even if invalidations are pending. The savings from release-consistency 1 μs as in forwarding, but this is compared with a nominal delay of 3 μs instead of 4 μs in the case of invalidation forwarding (implying gains are approximately 1/3 larger).

[11]The local cache snoop adds 2–4 processor clocks in the prototype.

TABLE XI
EFFECTIVENESS OF THE RAC

	Water	Barnes-Hut	PSIM4	MP3D
Rem Reads satisfied by RAC	32.6%	35.9%	51.9%	4.3%
RAC Read conflicts	0.00%	0.12%	0.32%	0.05%
Avg Read conflict penalty (Pclk)	45.2	21.4	23.1	51.9
Read savings from RAC	20.0%	21.4%	28.3%	3.4%
Rem Read-Ex satisfied by RAC	35.1%	1.0%	10.5%	4.7%
RAC Read-Ex conflicts	0.51%	0.11%	0.00%	0.01%
Avg Read-Ex cnflct. penalty (Pclk)	18.8	18.8	0.0	56.5
Read-Ex savings from RAC	23.2%	0.8%	8.2%	4.1%
Savings from RAC caching	**20.8%**	**20.3%**	**24.8%**	**3.7%**
Rem Reads merged by RAC	0.0%	0.1%	0.2%	0.1%
Avg Read merge fill time (Pclk)	85.2	80.5	86.1	89.1
Read savings from merging	0.0%	0.0%	0.1%	0.1%
Rem Read-Ex merged by RAC	0.3%	1.2%	0.9%	0.1%
Avg Read-Ex merge fill time (Pclk)	45.2	18.8	23.1	51.9
Read-Ex savings from merging	0.1%	0.2%	0.2%	0.0%
Savings from RAC merging	**0.0%**	**0.0%**	**0.1%**	**0.0%**
Total RAC/Merge Savings	**20.9%**	**20.3%**	**24.9%**	**3.8%**

optimized benchmarks are not readily available. Furthermore, if only these results were given, it would be difficult to distinguish the performance potential of the operations from the particular applications' ability to exploit them. Instead, this section quantifies the effectiveness of the alternative operations using small, atomic tests. These tests demonstrate how the operations would be commonly used and stress the individual operations heavily. In most cases, the results can be considered an upper bound on performance gain when using the operation in a real application. All of the atomic tests were run on the actual hardware, under a simple stand-alone multiprocessor monitor which is supplied with the SGI hardware.

a) Synchronization Operations: DASH provides four mechanisms for performing atomic read-modify-writes: uncached locks, invalidating locks, queued locks, and Fetch&Op. Uncached locks provide uncached test&set and clear operations, but spin waiting with uncached locks uses cluster and network resources. Invalidating locks are simple cached test&set locks. Unlocks, however, force waiting processors to rush for an contended lock when their cache copy is invalidated. Queued-locks use the directory state to avoid needlessly invalidating all waiting processors when a lock is released. Instead, a grant cluster is chosen at random from one of the nodes caching (spinning on) the lock, and this cluster is allowed to acquire the lock with a local cluster operation. Thus, the granted lock reduces both traffic and latency when a contended lock is released. Fetch&Op operations perform noncombining Fetch&Increment or Fetch&Decrement on uncached memory locations. These operations can be very useful because they are serialized only by the cycle time of local memory. For all of these operations, the atomic synchronization update is done at memory due to limitations of the base SGI hardware. While this precludes a processor from holding a lock in an exclusive state in its cache, which is ideal for locks with low contention and high processor affinity, memory updates are more efficient for contended locks or

locks with little processor affinity.

The test used to evaluate sychronization operations is the serialization time and network traffic when multiple processors update a simple counter variable. When using locks, the counter is kept in a cachable memory and protected by a spin lock. When Fetch&Inc is used, the Fetch&Inc location is updated in memory and no mutual exclusion is necessary. The test was run with the lock and counter variable in a cluster that was remote to all contending processors. Keeping these variables remote gives results that are more indicative of a large system.

To reduce latency for the counter in the lock case, the cache line with the count variable is brought into the cache in an exclusive state by writing to another variable in the same cache line. This eliminates the need to fetch the memory block twice (first to get a shared copy of the block to read the current value, and then to refetch to get an exclusive copy for the update). Likewise, the cache line with the counter is flushed back to memory after the mutual exclusion region is unlocked to avoid having the next incrementer fetch the data from a dirty-remote cache. These optimizations reduce the serialization by about 1 μs over simply leaving the counter variable uncached or in the updating processor's cache.

The left graph in Fig. 7 shows the time for one counter update when running the lock test with 1 to 44 processors spread across 1 to 11 clusters. The uniprocessor results show minimum time for the processor to execute one iteration of the loop which includes at least one remote memory fetch. The uncached lock case spins over the network waiting on the lock. Thus, as processors are added, the serialization actually decreases because the lock is sampled without waiting for an indication that lock is free. When going from 2 or 3 clusters, however, the advantage from sampling is lost because the excess memory traffic interferes with the execution of the critical section. For invalidating locks, latency is relatively constant except for the first increase when going from 1

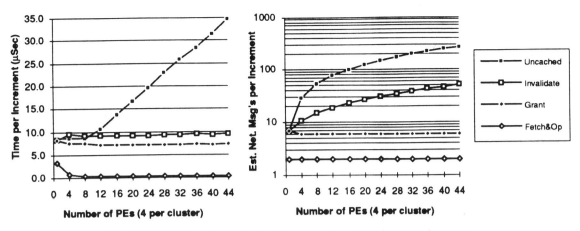

Fig. 7. Serialization time and network messages for an atomic counter increment.

to 4 processors. This increase results from the processor immediately acquiring the lock in the uniprocessor case, while receiving a locked copy of the lock from a locally spinning processor and waiting for a cache invalidation in the multiprocessor case. In contrast, the serialization of a granted lock decreases when going between 1 and 4 processors. This is because the lock grant takes place in parallel with the counter flush in the four processor case, while in the uniprocessor case, the processor is not ready to fetch the lock immediately after the unlock. For the Fetch&Inc case, serialization is low and throughput constantly increases. For the uniprocessor case, throughput is limited by the latency to remote memory. When using a single cluster, the requesting cluster's bus limits throughput. Above the three clusters throughput approaches the reply network outbound serialization limit in the home cluster.

Looking at Fig. 7, Fetch&Inc is obviously the best when it is applicable. For the more general case, the queue-based lock offers approximately 33% less latency for an unlock/lock pair than the invalidating unlock. Furthermore, one important feature not revealed directly by this test is the decrease in traffic when using queue-based locks. As shown in the right graph of Fig. 7 the amount of traffic per counter increment grows with the number of processors when using uncached or invalidating locks,[12] but is constant for granting locks and Fetch&Ops. Whether these latency or traffic reduction gains are important depends upon the frequency of synchronization and the amount of lock contention, but most applications will be adversely affected by added synchronization overhead or increased memory traffic.

b) Update Write: Update write operations allow the producer of data to communicate data to consuming processors without forcing the consuming processors to fetch the data from the producing processor's cache. Update writes are best suited to communicating small data items that the consumers have already cached. They are more appropriate for small data items because each word written, as opposed to each cache

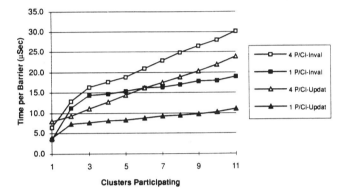

Fig. 8. Barrier synchronization with update writes and Fetch&Op variables.

line, generates a separate set of coherence messages. Likewise, update writes only deliver data to processors that are caching the block at the time of the write.

A useful application for update writes is in implementing the release from a barrier synchronization. Fig. 8 summarizes the timing of a single barrier while varying both the number of clusters (1 to 11) and number of processors per cluster (1 or 4). As in other tests, we assume that the variables for the barrier reside in a remote cluster. The implementation of the barrier uses a Fetch&Op variable to count the incoming processors, and a flag to release the waiting processors. In the case that the processors are all in one cluster, an invalidating write is actually superior to an update because the release flag becomes dirty in the local cluster. Beyond this degenerate case, however, update write reduces the barrier time by approximately 6 μs or about 20–40%.[13] Update writes also reduce serialization and traffic for release notification because the update is serialized only by the network send time. In the invalidation case, the refetch of the release flag is serialized by the first reader causing the dirty release flag to be written back to memory, and then by the other clusters serializing on the outbound reply network port in the home.

The barrier test is also useful in illustrating the power of the Fetch&Op variables. Shown in Fig. 9 is the time for the same

[12] Actual traffic growth for uncached locks can be unbounded since there is traffic generated during the entire time the critical region is held. The graph in Fig. 7 assumes these retries are limited to 3 per processor per iteration since each lock attempt takes approximately 3 μs and the critical region is held for approximately 9 microseconds.

[13] The 6 microsecond difference comes from the savings of reading the release flag from a processors second-level cache instead of the dirty-remote cache of the cluster that issued the write.

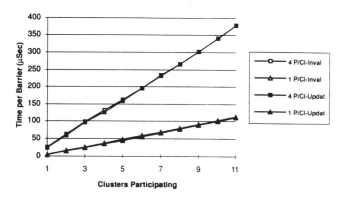

Fig. 9 Barrier synchronization without Fetch&Op variables.

barrier test when the Fetch&Op operations are replaced by a simple memory counter protected by an test&set lock (using simple invalidating unlocks). As expected from the atomic counter test (see Fig. 7), without the Fetch&Op variables, per processor serialization is greatly increased. The benefit of the update · write becomes lost in the large increase in the time to count the arrival of the processors at the barrier. By comparing Fig. 8 and Fig. 9 it is clear that Fetch&Op variables are key to efficient barrier synchronization, and that without Fetch&Op, barriers with a large fan-in would require some form of software gather tree to count the synchronizing processors.

c) Prefetch Tests: DASH supports software-controlled nonbinding prefetch operations which can either bring data closer to the issuing processor or send data to a set of specified clusters. Consumer prefetch operations bring a shared or exclusive copy of the requested memory block closer to the issuing processor. Producer prefetch sends a shared copy of the given block to the set of remote clusters specified as an input operand to the operation. Prefetches are software-controlled in the sense that application software issues an explicit operation to prefetch a given memory block. They are nonbinding in a sense that they only move data between coherent caches (into the RAC on the prototype). Thus, prefetched blocks are always kept coherent, and the value of a location is only bound when an actual load operation is issued. Not binding the value of the prefetch is important because it allows the user or compiler to aggressively prefetch data without a conservative dependency analysis and without affecting the memory consistency model. Prefetch operations can increase the amount of computation-communication and communication-communication overlap substantially because they replace blocking cache load operations with nonblocking operations. This overlap is especially useful when accessing a large data set that does not fit into cache or when accessing data generated by another processor. In the prototype, the prefetch operations have the effect of converting the penalty of a remote cache miss to that of a local miss. Thus, throughput can theoretically be increased from one cache line every 101 processor clocks to one block every 29 clocks (nearly a 3.5x improvement).

The first atomic test used to stress prefetch operations uses a varying number of processors that read blocks (128 bytes or 8 cache lines) of data from remote memory. This test models

a computation where at least one of the data structures is large and must always be fetched from memory. On each iteration, the processor picks a random remote cluster and reads a data block which is guaranteed to miss in the cache. When prefetching is enabled, the new block is prefetched while reading the previous block.

The results of the test are presented in Fig. 10 when using 1 to 48 processors fetching data from any of the active clusters (i.e. ones with enabled processors). The results are given in terms of number of processor clocks per cache line read, and the total megabytes per second read by all the processors. The code to read a block includes approximately 20 instructions. This instruction count corresponds with the measured time for the loop[14] which includes the 20 instructions plus one local (30 clock) or remote (100 clock) cache miss. Thus, prefetch results in a speedup of approximately 2.4 when the memory system is not saturated. As the number of processors increases beyond 12, the benefits of prefetching decrease because the memory system begins to saturate. In the prototype, this is due to saturation of the cluster buses (as opposed to the mesh network bisection) which are relatively slow (each cluster bus can sustain 20 Mbytes/s when doing remote references that require a total of 3 bus transactions per reference). Thus, on the prototype bandwidth limits throughput to approximately one prefetch every 20 instructions / cluster.

Another use of prefetch is in emulation of message-passing. To test the ability of prefetch to improve message-passing performance, a test was written to do simple one-way communications using a shared circular buffer. In the test, the sending processor checks for a free buffer in the message queue, and if available, writes a message into the buffer and increments the buffer full pointer. Similarly, the receiving processor polls the full pointer, reads each word of the message, and then increments the free buffer pointer. A large quantity of data is sent through the limited-size buffer, so throughput is determined by either the sender or receiver together with the latency to communicate that the message buffer has been filled or emptied.

Fig. 11 shows the throughput (in Mbytes/s) of running the message test with various optimizations and home clusters for the message queue. The test sends 64 000 64-byte messages, using a queue capable of holding 32 messages. The first version of the test uses the normal invalidating protocol (with release consistency) and achieves a throughput of 2.2–2.6 Mbytes/s. In this simple version, throughput is limited by the receiver who must fetch the data from the sending processor's cache. The first enhancement to the code uses writes with update coherence to store the incremented full and empty block pointers. This enhancement increases performance to 2.7–3.4 Mbytes/s because the receiver can read the updated buffer pointer from its cache, not the remote processor's cache. The third version of the test uses consumer prefetch for both the sender and receiver. The receiver prefetches all four blocks of the message as soon as it is notified that they are available, and the producer prefetches buffers exclusively when they are freed. Prefetch improves performance by a factor of 1.8–2.1

[14] When using a small number of processors (1 to 12).

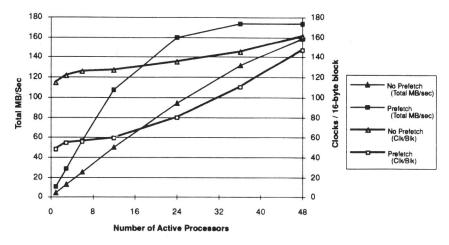

Fig. 10. Effectiveness of prefetch operations when doing block memory reads.

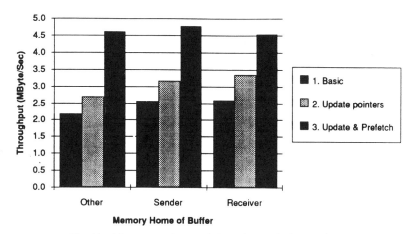

Fig. 11 Message passing emulation using prefetch operations.

to a rate of 4.6–4.8 Mbytes/s. This improvement comes from converting the four remote misses to read the message to a single remote cache miss and three local misses (the miss time for these remote misses are pipelined with the miss time for the first block). In this test, using producer-prefetch instead of consumer prefetch would add little because 3/4 of the remote miss latency has already been hidden, and forcing the producer to send the data to the consumer, in addition to its other tasks, makes the sender the bottleneck.

As shown by these tests, prefetch can successfully overlap a significant amount of interprocessor communication delay. Furthermore, even when remote latency cannot be completely hidden, prefetch allows misses to be pipelined, and greatly reducing the cost of communicating items that are larger than a single cache line. Overall, when memory bandwidth does not limit performance, we expect prefetch to be very useful in improving the performance of interprocessor communication.

3) Summary of Protocol Effectiveness: The parallel benchmark reference statistics and the atomic tests indicate that many of DASH's protocol optimizations can be quite effective. Forwarding requests to dirty-clusters reduces remote latency an average of 5%, and forwarding invalidations for write requests reduced ownership latency by 11%. Likewise, cache-to-cache sharing within a cluster reduces the average latency for remote memory by 27%.

The atomic tests of the alternative memory operations indicate that many of these operations are well-worth supporting. In particular, nonbinding prefetch can reduce effective memory latency by more than a factor of 2.5 and can improve message-passing throughput by a factor of 2. The latency gains from queue-based locks are more modest, but the significant reduction in traffic should make them very useful in applications with significant synchronization. Likewise, the low serialization of noncombining Fetch&Op accesses can be very useful in implementing common operations such as distributed loops and barriers. In contrast, the performance benefits of other alternative operations may not warrant the complexity they add to the memory system protocol. For example, the effectiveness of consumer prefetch operations may preclude the need for producer prefetch (unless multicast is supported in the network), and invalidating and uncached locks offer little compared with queue-based locks.

VII. CONCLUSIONS

This paper has outlined the architecture of DASH and our initial experience in building and using the prototype system. The goals of the DASH architecture are to support scalability to hundreds of processors, high-performance processing elements and a single address space. Key to these goals is a scalable directory-based cache coherence mechanism. The DASH prototype is an experimental system built to investigate the feasibility and performance of this architecture. It supports up to 64 RISC processors to achieve up to 1.6 GIPS and 600 MFLOPS of performance. The prototype utilizes a commercially available small-scale multiprocessor as a computing node, and interconnects the system by a pair of logic boards that implement the global coherence protocol and interconnection network.

The first result from building and using the prototype is that such systems are feasible. While the coherence protocol and hardware are not trivial, such systems can be built. Looking in more detail at the logic and memory costs exhibited by the prototype, we show that the logic overhead for supporting distributed shared memory (without coherence) is about 10%. Supporting scalable cache coherence adds another 10% in logic and 14% in memory overhead. Our experience also shows that using a small-scale multiprocessor as the base processing node, rather than a uniprocessor processing node, significantly reduces the per-processor overhead of supporting cache coherence.

Our second goal in building the prototype is to analyze the performance of the DASH architecture. Toward this goal we have added performance monitoring hardware to the directory logic in each cluster. This monitor uses a static RAM array with increment logic, and a large DRAM buffer to flexibly count and trace bus, directory and network events. This logic allows us to correlate application speedups to reference behavior, and to monitor hardware resource utilization.

We have begun to analyze the performance of the system in more detail. The first result has been to determine accurate memory system delays. In the prototype, memory access times for first-level cache, second-level cache, local memory, remote memory, and dirty-remote memory are 1:15:29:101:132 process clocks (30 ns) respectively. While the absolute delays can be improved, processor clock rates are also increasing. Thus, long latencies in terms of processor clocks are quite unavoidable, and the benefits from exploiting cache and memory locality will continue to be important for this class of systems.

The performance of several parallel applications has also been studied on the prototype. While not highly tuned for the prototype, over half of the applications achieve over 36-fold speedup on 48 processors. Many of these applications use complex and dynamically updated data structures, such as octrees, and the task of programming them on a noncache coherent machine would have been extremely difficult. The reference behavior of the applications indicates that best speedup is achieved if both cache and memory locality are high.

Finally, many of the optimizations in the DASH protocol appear to be effective. In particular, request forwarding and local cache-to-cache sharing can reduce remote latency by up to 25%. Prefetch operations can help overlap communication

traffic with other communication and computation, and low serialization operations such as Fetch&Op can be very useful in implementing common operations such as distributed loops and barriers.

Overall, our initial experience with the DASH prototype has been very positive. Scalable, directory-based coherence can be achieved with a modest hardware overhead and can deliver good performance on parallel applications.

ACKNOWLEDGMENT

We are especially grateful for the help we have received with applications. J. P. Singh helped with Barnes-Hut, FMM, Water, and Radiosity applications, E. Rothberg with MatMul and Cholesky applications, A. Erlichson with the PSIM4 application, and J. Nieh with the Volume Rendering application. D. Ofelt helped gather the application performance results.

REFERENCES

[1] A. Agarwal, B.-H. Lim, D. Kranz, and J. Kubiatowicz, "LimitLESS directories: A scalable cache coherence scheme," in *Proc. Fourth Int. Conf. Architectural Support Programming Languages and Oper. Syst.*, Apr. 1991, pp. 224–234.
[2] F. Baskett, T. Jermoluk, and D. Solomon, "The 4D-MP graphics superworkstation: Computing + graphics = 40 MIPS + 40 MFLOPS and 100,000 lighted polygons per second," in *Proc. Compcon Spring 88*, Feb. 1988, pp. 468–471.
[3] L. Censier and P. Feautrier, "A new solution to coherence problems in multicache systems," *IEEE Trans. Comput.*, vol. C-27, pp. 1112–1118, Dec. 1978.
[4] C. M. Flaig, "VLSI mesh routing systems," Tech. Rep. 5241:TR:87, California Institute of Technology, May 1987.
[5] K. Gharachorloo, D. Lenoski, J. Laudon, P. Gibbons, A. Gupta, and J. Hennessy, "Memory consistency and event ordering in scalable shared-memory multiprocessors," in *Proc. 17th Int. Symp. Comput. Architecture*, May 1990, pp. 15–26.
[6] S. Goldschmidt and H. Davis, "Tango introduction and tutorial," Tech. Rep. CSL-TR-90–410, Stanford Univ., 1990.
[7] A. Gupta, J. Hennessy, K. Gharachorloo, T. Mowry, and W.-D. Weber, "Comparative evaluation of latency reducing and tolerating techniques," in *Proc. 18th Int. Symp. Comput. Architecture*, May 1991, pp. 254–263.
[8] A. Gupta, W.-D. Weber, and T. Mowry, "Reducing memory and traffic requirements for scalable directory-based cache coherence schemes," in *Proc. 1990 Int. Conf. Parallel Processing*, Aug. 1990, pp. I:312–321.
[9] D. Lenoski, J. Laudon, K. Gharachorloo, A. Gupta, and J. Hennessy, "The directory-based cache coherence protocol for the DASH multiprocessor," in *Proc. 17th Int. Symp. Comput. Architecture*, May 1990.
[10] D. Lenoski, J. Laudon, K. Gharachorloo, W.-D. Weber, A. Gupta, J. Hennessy, M. Horowitz, and M. Lam, "The Stanford DASH Multiprocessor," *IEEE Comput. Mag.*, vol. 25, no. 3, Mar. 1992.
[11] D. Lenoski, "The design and analysis of DASH: A scalable shared-memory multiprocessor," Ph.D. dissertation, Stanford Univ., Dec. 1991.
[12] E. Lusk, R. Overbeek, J. Boyle, R. Butler, T. Disz, B. Glickfeld, J. Patterson, and R. Stevens, *Portable Programs for Parallel Processors*. New York: Holt, Rinehart and Winston, 1987.
[13] B. W. O'Krafka and A. R. Newton, "An empirical evaluation of two memory-efficient directory methods," in *Proc. 17th Int. Symp. Comput. Architecture*, May 1990, pp. 138–147.
[14] M. S. Papamarcos and J. H. Patel, "A low overhead coherence solution for multiprocessors with private cache memories," in *Proc. 11th Int. Symp. Comput. Architecture*, May 1984, pp. 348–354.
[15] J. P. Singh, W.-D. Weber, and A. Gupta, "SPLASH: Stanford parallel applications for shared memory," Tech. Rep. CSL-TR-91–469, Stanford Univ., 1991.
[16] J. P. Singh, C. Holt, T. Totsuka, A. Gupta, and J. Hennessy, "Load balancing and data locality in hierarchical N-body methods," Tech. Rep. CSL-TR-92–505, Stanford Univ., 1992.
[17] Xilinx, *The Programmable Gate Array Data Book*, 1991.

Daniel Lenoski (M'86) received the B.S.E.E. degree from the California Institute of Technology in 1983 and the M.S.E.E. degree from Stanford in 1985. He received his Ph.D. in electrical engineering from Stanford University in December 1991.

He is a senior staff engineer at Sun Microsystems working on high-performance processor and system design. His research efforts concentrated on the design and implementation of DASH, and other issues related to scalable multiprocessors. He also spent nine years at Tandem Computers where his work included the architectural definition and design of the CLX series of processors.

James Laudon received the B.S. degree in electrical engineering from the University of Wisconsin–Madison in 1987 and the M.S. degree in electrical engineering from Stanford University in 1988. He is a Ph.D. candidate in the Department of Electrical Engineering at Stanford University.

His research interests focus on multiprocessor architectures, with an emphasis on latency tolerating techniques.

Mr. Laudon is a member of the IEEE Computer Society and the Association for Computing Machinery.

Truman Joe received the B.S. degree in electrical and computer engineering from Rice University in 1987 and the M.S. degree in electrical engineering from Stanford University in 1989. He is a Ph.D. candidate in the Department of Electrical Engineering at Stanford University. His research interests are in the area of multiprocessor architecture with particular emphasis on high-performance memory systems.

Mr. Joe is a member of the Association for Computing Machinery, Eta Kappa Nu, and Tau Beta Pi.

David Nakahira received the B.A. degree in computer science from the University of California at Santa Cruz in 1984.

He is a staff research engineer in the Computer Systems Laboratory at Stanford University. His interests are in hardware design for large-scale multiprocessors. He worked in the computer industry for five years prior to joining Stanford's DASH project.

Luis Stevens received the Bachelor of Engineering degree in 1986, and the Civil Electronics Engineering degree in the area of computer systems in 1988, from the Universidad Tecnica Federico Santa Maria, Valparaiso, Chile. In 1990 he received the M.S.E.E. degree from Stanford University.

He is currently pursuing his Ph.D. in electrical engineering at Stanford University, doing research in the area of multiprocessor operating systems. He is also interested in distributed operating systems, compilers, and automatic control.

Anoop Gupta is an Assistant Professor of computer science at Stanford University. His primary interests are in the design of hardware and software for large-scale multiprocessors.

Prior to joining Stanford, he was on the research faculty of Carnegie Mellon University, where he received the Ph.D. in 1986.

Dr. Gupta was the recipient of a DEC faculty development from 1987–1989, and he received the NSF Presidential Young Investigatory Award in 1990. He currently holds the Robert Noyce faculty scholar chair in the School of Engineering at Stanford.

John Hennessy (F'91) is a Professor of Electrical Engineering and Computer Science at Stanford University. His current research interests are in exploiting parallelism at all levels to build higher performance computer systems.

Dr. Hennessy is the recipient of a 1984 Presidential Young Investigatory Award, and in 1987 was named the Willard and Inez K. Bell Professor of Electrical Engineering and Computer Science. He is a member of the National Academy of Engineering.

The KSR1: Experimentation and Modeling of Poststore

E. Rosti[1], E. Smirni, T.D. Wagner, A.W. Apon, L.W. Dowdy

Department of Computer Science
Vanderbilt University, Nashville, TN 37235
[erosti, esmirni, tdw, apon, lwd]@vuse.vanderbilt.edu

Abstract

Kendall Square Research introduced the KSR1 system in 1991. The architecture is based on a ring of rings of 64-bit microprocessors. It is a distributed, shared memory system and is scalable. The memory structure is unique and is the key to understanding the system. Different levels of caching eliminates physical memory addressing and leads to the ALLCACHE^{TM} scheme. Since requested data may be found in any of several caches, the initial access time is variable. Once pulled into the local (sub)cache, subsequent access times are fixed and minimal. Thus, the KSR1 is a Cache–Only Memory Architecture (COMA) system.

This paper describes experimentation and an analytic model of the KSR1. The focus is on the poststore programmer option. With the poststore option, the programmer can elect to broadcast the updated value of a variable to all processors that might have a copy. This may save time for threads on other processors, but delays the broadcasting thread and places additional traffic on the ring. The specific issue addressed is to determine under what conditions poststore is beneficial. The analytic model and the experimental observations are in good agreement. They indicate that the decision to use poststore depends both on the application and the current system load.

1. Introduction

Traditionally, the scalability of shared memory multiprocessors has been limited due to memory access path contention. However, the KSR1 system, recently developed by Kendall Square Research, demonstrates that scalable shared memory multiprocessors are feasible. From a measurement and modeling perspective, the KSR1 and its architectural paradigm deserve an in-depth analysis.

One novel feature of the KSR1 is its memory management scheme, ALLCACHE^{TM}. Each processor has its own local memory that is managed as a cache, and a valid copy of a data item must exist in the local cache of the processor in order to be accessed. Data items are not bound to any particular memory, but migrate dynamically to a processor when they are accessed. The entire memory is shared and the memory is viewed as a hierarchy of caches. Upon writing, a requesting processor writes the data item to its local cache and marks it as valid. All other copies of the item in other processor caches are marked as invalid. Prior to reading, a requesting processor must have a valid copy of the item in its local cache. If a valid copy of the item is not in the local cache of the requesting processor, then a valid copy is migrated from the local cache of another processor. Depending on which cache contains the requested data item at any particular time, the time required to perform this migration may vary. However, once a valid copy of the requested item is moved into the local cache, all subsequent accesses are to the local copy. Thus, the KSR1 has a Cache–Only Memory Architecture (COMA) [HLH92].

To take advantage of the architecture, programmers are provided with a *poststore* option. When a variable is updated by a write, using poststore will cause a valid copy of the variable to be sent to all caches which contain a copy of that variable. This will shorten the access time for any future reads on those other processors, since each will have a valid copy of the item in its local cache. Without poststore, whenever a future reader requests the variable, it must first pull a valid copy into its cache. Clearly, a tradeoff exists since using poststore will shorten the time for future reads, but lengthens the time for the write.

This paper presents an experimental and modeling study of the KSR1. The focus is on the poststore option. The stated goals and outline of this work are:

- to understand and describe the KSR1 architecture,
- to run controlled experiments on the KSR1, using a simple readers-and-writers workload, to observe performance with and without poststore,
- to construct and validate an analytic model of the system which could be used for predicting the general behavior of the KSR1 and for predicting the specific behavior of poststore, and
- to outline generalizations and summarize our findings.

The purpose of this paper is to study the effects of poststore for a particular reader/writer workload. The results show that relatively simple models accurately indicate the effects of poststore. Also, results show that poststore is more effective as the number of reader threads in one application increases, but becomes less effective as the total number of applications increases. Therefore, the effective use of poststore depends on both the programmer's application code as well as the system load.

[1] On leave from the Dipartimento di Scienze dell'Informazione - Università di Milano, Italy.

This work was partially supported by grant N. 92.01615.PF69 from the Italian CNR "Progetto Finalizzato Sistemi Informatici e Calcolo Parallelo – Sottoprogetto 3", and by sub-contract 19X-SL131V from the Oak Ridge National Laboratory managed by Martin Marietta Energy Systems, Inc. for the U.S. Department of Energy under contract no. DE-AC05-84OR21400.

"The KSR1: Experimentation and Modeling of Poststore," E. Rosti et al., *Proc. ACM SIGMETRICS '93*, ACM, New York, 1993, pp. 74–85. Copyright © 1993, Association for Computing Machinery, Inc. Reprinted with permission.

2. Architectural Overview of the KSR1

2.1. System Hardware

The general KSR architecture is a multiprocessor system composed of a hierarchy of rings. The lowest level, ring:0, consists of a 34 slot backplane connecting 32 processing cells (processing elements) and two cells responsible for routing to the next higher layer ring, ring:1. A fully populated ring:1 is composed of the interconnecting cells from 32 ring:0 rings. A fully configured KSR1 is composed of two layers containing 1024 processing cells along with two ring interconnecting cells on each ring:0. The general KSR architecture provides for a third layer which connects 32 ring:1 rings into a ring:2 layer. Figure 1 shows the hierarchical ring structure of the KSR multiprocessor.

This study deals with a KSR1 multiprocessor with a single ring:0 installed. The description that follows is of the general KSR architecture with specific attention given to the memory structure and management of a single ring:0.

Each processing cell is constructed from 12 custom CMOS chips:

- The Co-Execution Unit (CEU) fetches all instructions, controls data fetch and store, controls instruction flow, and does arithmetic required for address calculations.
- The Integer Processing Unit (IPU) executes integer arithmetic and logical instructions.
- The Floating Point Unit (FPU) executes floating point instructions.
- The eXternal Input/output Unit (XIU) performs DMA and programmed I/O.
- Four Cache Control Units (CCU) are the interface between the 0.5MB subcache and the 32MB local memory (referred to as the local cache).
- Four Cell Interconnect Units (CIU) are the interface between a processing cell and the ring:0 ring.

In one instruction cycle an instruction pair is executed. One member of the pair is an instruction for the CEU or XIU and the other member is an instruction for the FPU or IPU. The clock speed is 20 MHz. As in other superscalar processors, the KSR processor operates in a pipelined fashion with two pipelines, one for the FPU/IPU and one for the CEU/XIU. The pipelining and 20 MHz clock yield a peak 40 MFLOPS for each cell. Using shared data structures and optimized code, early implementations of a 1000 X 1000 double precision LINPACK running on a 32 processor system resulted in over 500 MFLOPS total capacity [Duni92].

Each processing cell also contains a 256KB data cache and a 256KB instruction cache. The on-board data and instruction caches are referred to as *subcaches*. A daughter board connected to each processing cell contains 32MB of memory referred to as *local cache*. The word size of the KSR is 64 bits and all functional units are based on 64 bit operands. All execute and control operations are register oriented. Each processor has 64 floating point registers, 32 integer registers, and 32 addressing registers. All registers are 64 bits wide. (The KSR1 implementation uses 40 bit addressing registers.)

In addition to the 32 processing cells, each ring:0 also contains 2 ALLCACHE Routing and Directory (ARD) cells.

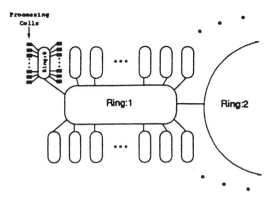

Figure 1: KSR hierarchy of rings.

One of the ARD cells is an uplink from the ring:0 to ring:1. The other ARD is a downlink from the ring:1 to ring:0. The ARDs participate in the transfer of data between ring:0s across ring:1.

All of the local caches, together with the interconnecting rings, make up the ALLCACHE memory system. Addressing in the KSR architecture is based on the translation of a Context Address (CA) into a System Virtual Address (SVA). Context addresses are composed of a segment and offset and are translated into System Virtual Addresses via fully associative hardware Segment Translation Tables (STTs) on each processor. There are two STTs, one for data and one for instructions. The System Virtual Address space consists of all of the local caches. The ALLCACHE memory system and the organization and management of System Virtual Address (SVA) space is the major difference between the KSR architecture and other architectures. When a processor references an SVA, a *search engine*, which is the collection of CIUs and the ARD on each ring:0 along with the ring interface, locates the SVA and moves its contents to the local cache of the referencing processor.

2.2. Memory Organization

ALLCACHE stores data in units of pages and subpages. Pages contain 16K bytes divided into 128 subpages of 128 bytes each. Each local cache can hold 2,048 pages. The memory system allocates storage in the local caches on the basis of pages and each page of SVA space is either entirely allocated in the caches or not allocated at all. The local caches share data in units of subpages. Whenever a page of SVA space is allocated in the system, there may be more than one copy present. This would be the case when several threads running on different processors are all referencing shared memory. It is possible that each local cache that has allocated a page may not contain a copy of all of the subpages in that page. That is, space in the local caches is allocated on a page basis, but data is transferred on a subpage basis. Each local cache maintains a cache directory in a 16-way set associative memory with 128 sets that maps physical pages in that cache to SVA pages. All of the pages of SVA space are divided into 128 equivalence classes, each associated with a cache directory set. Since there are 16 elements in each set in the cache directory, a cache can contain no more than 16 pages in the same equivalence class.

The subcaches are allocated on the basis of blocks (2K bytes) and data is moved into and out of the subcaches in subblocks of 64 bytes each. A two way set associative subcache directory maintains the mapping between subcache blocks and SVA pages with one descriptor for each block. The subcaches replace blocks as needed using a random replacement scheme.

In the cache directory of each cell, additional information is maintained that represents the *state* of each subpage in the local cache. There are four states that a subpage can be in:

- Exclusive owner: Indicates that this is the only valid copy of the subpage in all of the local caches (i.e., in the entire system). The contents can be read or modified.

- Atomic: Like exclusive, this is the only valid copy and the subpage can be modified. This state also provides a flag to allow synchronization by multiple processors. Thus, this state provides for locks.

- Read-Only: Indicates that there are two or more valid copies of this subpage among all of the local caches. The contents of this subpage cannot be modified until its state is changed to exclusive or atomic.

- Invalid: The contents of this subpage are not to be accessed (i.e., read or modified). Newly allocated pages set all subpage descriptors to invalid. This state is analogous to the setting of a "dirty bit."

The subcaches also maintain state information at the subblock level. The instruction subcache allows each subblock to be in either the invalid state or the read-only state. In addition to invalid and read-only, the data subcache allows a block to be in the exclusive owner state to allow for modification. The data subcache also maintains modification information for each subblock. The state of a subblock in the subcache is not allowed to be stronger than the state of the corresponding subpage in the local cache. Thus, it is not possible for a subblock's state to be exclusive in the subcache while read-only in the local cache.

When a processor references an SVA address it continues execution for two cycles, which is the latency of the subcache. If the address is not contained in the subcache, the processor is stalled and a request is presented to the CCUs to locate the subpage containing the requested address in the ALLCACHE memory. If the subpage containing the address is not present in the local cache (and in the state requested by the processor), then the CCUs make a request of the local CIUs to format a request message and place it on ring:0. The ring:0 communication interconnect is a slotted pipelined ring with a total bandwidth of 1GB. There are 13 slots on the ring:0 ring. Each message on the ring consists of a 16 byte header followed by one subpage (128 bytes) of data. As a request message passes each processing cell, the cell's CIU determines if the request can be satisfied from its local cache. If it can be satisfied, the request message is extracted from the ring and a response message is inserted. Also attached to each ring:0 is an ALLCACHE Router and Directory (ARD) cell that contains a directory of the entire ring:0 cache (i.e., all of the local caches). If the ARD determines that a request message cannot be satisfied on the local ring:0, it extracts the message and inserts a request on the

next higher ring in the hierarchy, ring:1. When the response message to the original request is inserted on the ring, the requesting processor copies the message and fills the original request from the local CCU. If a request message returns to the requesting processor unanswered, a hard page fault is generated and the subpage is brought in from the disk. The latency and total capacity of the ALLCACHE memory system hierarchy is shown in Table 1 [Kend91].

Table 1: Latencies and capacities

Location of subpage	Total capacity (MB)	Latency in cycles (5ns)
Local subcache	0.5	2
Local cache	32	18
Ring:0	1,024	175
Ring:1	34,816	600
Disk		400,000

The hardware management of the KSR memory system assures that the ALLCACHE memory is both *sequentially consistent* [Lamp79] and *strongly ordered* [DSG86]. The state of a subpage in local cache or a subblock in subcache is changed in response to requests from processing cells in the system. When a load instruction is issued, it can specify the state that the subblock should possess. A store instruction always requires that a subpage have an exclusive ownership state. Whenever a request for exclusive ownership is made, all copies of the subpage in other cells are marked as invalid. One distinction between the ALLCACHE memory and NUMA shared memory architectures is that no processor is the designated "home" of a subpage of memory. There can be multiple local caches that have allocated space for a subpage and the ownership travels around the rings as required, to satisfy state requests by the multiple processors.

One problem that floating ownership can cause is that as fetch requests are made, it is possible that the local cache of the processor issuing the request may have an invalid copy. There are two methods by which the inefficiencies created by this approach are moderated. First, whenever a copy of a subpage is sent across the ring to satisfy a request, any local cache that has a descriptor for the subpage (i.e., has allocated space) but does not have a valid copy, can pick up a read-only copy of the subpage if the cell is not too busy. This *automatic prefetching* is a function of the hardware. Second, there are two instructions, pcsp (prefetch subpage to cache) and pstsp (poststore subpage), that provide the programmer with some control over the locality of specific subpages. The prefetch instruction allows for the specification of the state that should be acquired when a subpage is fetched. The poststore instruction simply relinquishes exclusive ownership and broadcasts the contents of a subpage on the ring. All cells that have a descriptor for the subpage will take a copy from the ring if they are not too busy. If no advance copy is obtained by a cell, then a new request is issued whenever the cell requires a valid copy.

2.3. System Configuration

The KSR operating system is an implementation of OSF-1 and provides a standard UNIX interface. Built on top of the Mach threads of OSF-1 is a pthreads interface based on the IEEE POSIX draft standard, P1003.4a. The KSR pthreads interface includes extensions to enable an application to manage ring traffic and the geometry of thread placement for optimizing the performance of cooperating threads. The experiments described here were run using version R1.0.5 of the KSR OS. The system includes a fully configured ring:0 with 32 processing cells. The timings reported in the experimental section were collected using the two sub-microsecond timers on each cell, one which reports user time, the other system time.

3. Experimental Analysis

3.1. The Workload

In order to study the advantages and disadvantages of using poststore after an update, various workloads consisting of a parallel version of a readers/writers workload are constructed. Each workload performs the following steps:

- Initialization Phase
  1. A number of reader and writer threads are spawned, each bound to a specific processor.
  2. Each reader and writer reads a predetermined portion of a given data set. This ensures that a copy of the shared data set is in the local cache of each participating thread, and that no disk accesses will be required during the measurement phase.
- Measurement Phase
  1. Timing begins for each writer.
  2. Each writer updates its portion of the data set. Writing is done with or without poststore, depending on the experiment.
  3. Timing ends for each writer.
  4. Timing begins for each reader.
  5. Each reader sequentially reads its portion of the data set one time.
  6. Timing ends for each reader.

The emphasis of the experiments is to determine under which conditions the use of poststore is an advantage. If the writers broadcast their updates with poststore, then each reader should find a valid copy of the data in its local cache during the reading phase. If the updates are done without poststore, then no valid copy is available in the reader's local cache during the reading phase. In this case, every read is a cache miss and generates a request on the ring. Readers are allowed to read only after all the writers have finished. In all the experiments, readers and writers are implemented by distinct threads, and are mapped onto distinct processing cells, so that no two threads in the same application access the same local cache.

3.2. The Experiments

The parameters to be varied in the experiments are:
1. the amount of data requested per subpage access,
2. the amount of delay between accesses,
3. the read access pattern,
4. the number of writers,
5. the amount of data set sharing among readers, and
6. the number of concurrent reader/writer workloads.

Several experiments were run using different values for each of these parameters. Table 2 lists the experiments reported here with their parameter values. Three data set sizes were used: small (13K subpages), medium (52K subpages), and large (100K subpages). Different sizes test the effect of processing for longer periods of time. Each experiment was run for a varying number of readers.

Table 2: Experiment parameter values

Exp	Num Words	Delay	Access Pattern	Num Write	Shar	Num. Wklds
A	1/subpg	N	same	1	glob	1
B	all	N	same	1	glob	1
C	1/subpg	Y	same	1	glob	1
D	all	N	diff	1	glob	1
E	1/subblk	N	same	>1	glob	1
F	1/subblk	N	same	>1	priv	1
G	1/subpg	Y	same	1	glob	>1

Different access granularity levels affect the rate at which read requests are made to the ring. The access granularity may be one access per subpage, one access per subblock (i.e, two accesses per subpage), or the entire subpage. In the experiments reported, each read is a 64 bit word. Each subpage contains 16 words. When one word per subpage is read, without intervening processing, the rate at which requests for invalid pages are made is maximized. When one word per subblock is read, then the rate of ring requests decreases, since every other read is a local cache hit. When an entire subpage is read there will be one request to the ring (to acquire the subpage initially), one hit to the local cache (to get the first word of the second subblock), and fourteen hits to the subcache (to get the remaining 14 words of the subpage). The subcache and local cache latencies of 2 and 18 processor cycles, respectively, increase the time between requests to the ring. Experiments A and B show the effect of different access granularities.

When no additional time is used for processing (i.e., pure read requests), the single request to the ring outweighs the other delays since it is an order of magnitude greater than the local cache latency. The rate at which read requests are made to the ring may be slowed further by introducing a variable delay between read accesses to simulate data processing. Experiment C shows the effect of introducing delay between read accesses.

In Experiment D the access pattern is varied in order to study the effect of automatic prefetching. If many subpages are copied from the ring before they are requested, then the number of ring requests will be reduced. This has the effect of reducing total execution time.

Experiments E and F show the effects of multiple writers. With multiple writers, the data set is divided equally among the writers so that each writer has the valid copy of a distinct (private) portion of the data set. When multiple writers own different parts of a shared data set and multiple readers read different parts as well, the composition of read requests being placed on the ring changes and the read time per subpage changes. Readers may or not may not be allowed to share data sets. Two extremes are considered:

1. Full sharing, where each reader reads the entire data set. This is termed *global* readers.
2. No sharing, where the data set is divided equally into distinct portions among the readers, and each reader accesses only its portion. This is termed *private* readers.

Experiment E investigates the effects of multiple global readers. It is possible that a single writer could become the system bottleneck. Multiple writers can reduce this bottleneck effect. Also, it is possible for a reader to obtain a valid copy of a subpage through automatic prefetching because of a request made by another reader.

Experiment F shows the effect of multiple writers and private readers. With private readers, readers cannot take advantage of automatic prefetching since each reader is the only thread accessing the data for which it has put a request on the ring. With multiple writers and private readers, read requests are served by different writers at the same time, which reduces the demands on the writer process.

Since poststore reduces the execution time of the reader threads while increasing the execution time of writer threads, both thread types should be considered when making the decision of when to use poststore. It is expected that for a low reader-to-writer ratio the expense to the writers would dominate, indicating that poststore should not be used. Conversely, for a high reader-to-writer ratio, it is expected that the benefits to the readers would dominate, indicating that poststore should be used. Also, as the number of reader/writer workloads (i.e., heavyweight threads, multiprogramming level) changes, the relative benefit of poststore can be affected. Experiment G examines these issues.

3.3. The Results

The results of the 7 experiments are presented here. Except for Experiment G the performance metric used is the average access time per subpage by an average reader thread.

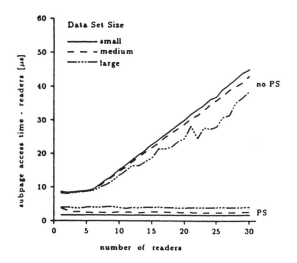

Figure 2: Granularity: 1 per subpage, Experiment A.

In Experiments A, B and C there is a single writer and progressively longer times between read requests. In each

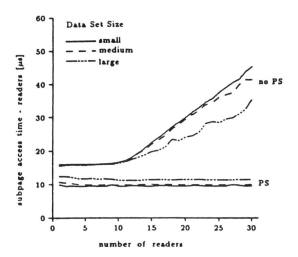

Figure 3: Granularity: entire subpage, Experiment B.

of these, the average read time per subpage is shown as the number of readers varies from 1 to 30. The results of Experiment A are shown in Figure 2. Experiment A has the highest rate of ring requests (one per subpage). Results are shown for the three data set sizes. When poststore is used, read time per subpage is constant, since every read is a hit in the local cache. With a larger data set, the average time to read a subpage increases because of the extra overhead incurred due to more subcache turnover. When no poststore is used, the average time to read a subpage increases as the number of readers increases. Regardless of the size of the data set, when more than six readers are executing, the time to read a subpage increases linearly due to delays at the cell of the writer thread which must handle all requests. Larger data sizes yield better performance because they allow for better exploitation of the pipelined execution, and the subcache turnover overhead is overlapped with the time the processor is waiting for the requested subpage. Furthermore, a longer global execution time favors automatic prefetching. This is because the longer readers execute, the more their executions are staggered from the initial synchronized start, increasing the probability that one reader will request a subpage that will be needed in the future by another reader.

In Experiment B every word in each subpage is read. The results are similar to those of Experiment A, as shown in Figure 3. Again, when no poststore is used, the average time to read a subpage increases as the number of readers increases. The increase becomes linear with the same slope as before but begins with a higher number of readers, since the request rate is smaller. The point where the curve reaches the asymptote is 11 readers, as Figure 3 shows. The absolute value of the average read time per subpage is larger than with Experiment A due to the extra accesses performed per subpage. However, when the system is not saturated, the difference between the average read time with poststore and the average read time without poststore is the same, and is equal to the measured ring latency.

Experiment C shows the effect of including a variable delay to represent processing time between each read, which

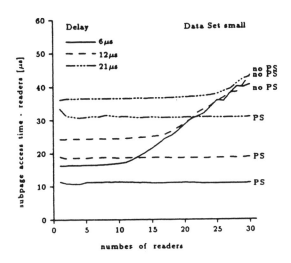

Figure 4: Readers with extra delay, Experiment C.

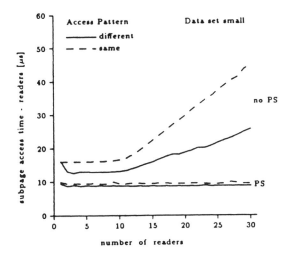

Figure 5: Access patterns, Experiment D.

further reduces the ring request rate. In this experiment, one word per subpage is read, so that with no poststore, every read generates a ring request. The curves in Figure 4 show the average read time per subpage for different delays between reads, as the number of readers increases from 1 to 30. The base case for a delay of $6\mu s$ yields the same performance as when an entire subpage is read and there is no delay between reads, as in Experiment B with the small data set. As the delay increases, the number of readers that it takes to saturate the system is larger. At saturation, the slope of the asymptote is the same as before for all curves, but the location of the saturation point is a function of the delay. Again, when the system is not saturated, the difference between the average read times with and without poststore is the same, and is equal to the measured ring latency. Experiment C shows that as the delay between reads increases, the ring latency and writer response time have less effect on total execution time.

Experiment D shows that performance improves if readers use different access patterns, as illustrated in Figure 5.

In this experiment there is one writer, readers are global, and the number of readers is varied from 1 to 30. Half of the readers read the entire data set sequentially forward, and half of the readers read the entire data set sequentially backward. Figure 5 shows that the slope of the saturation asymptote for the average read time without poststore is about 50% of the slope for the corresponding experiment where all readers use the same access pattern (Experiment B). The performance improvement is due to the automatic prefetching of subpages that have not yet been requested as they pass by on the ring. This effect of prefetching is noticeable from one to two readers. The read time drops because there is a high probability that subpages requested by the second reader are copied by the first reader also, and vice versa. This is an instance of "anomalous" behavior where performance improves as the workload increases. When both readers have read half of the data set, the probability of generating ring requests is very low. Additional readers do not give any advantage, since their read pattern is the same as one of the first two. As more reader threads are added, performance degrades less severely than in the other cases because during the second half of the execution the number of ring requests is reduced.

In Experiments E and F the number of readers varies from 1 to 29, and the number of writers varies from 29 down to 1, with the number of active threads fixed at 30. The results of Experiment E are shown in Figure 6. In this experiment, every reader reads the entire shared data set with the same reference pattern, and requests are satisfied by one writer at a time. At different times during execution, different writers supply the requested subpages. Because all readers tend to access similar parts of the data set at the same time, the trend is for a single writer at a time to be responding to reader requests. Thus, the expected improvement in execution time by spreading the requests among multiple writers is not realized. Figure 6 shows that average read time per subpage follows the same trend as in Experiment A, where there is a single writer and multiple global readers reading one word per subblock.

The results of Experiment F are shown in Figure 7. In this experiment, no two readers read the same piece of data, so no duplicated requests for the same subpage are seen on the ring. The data is distributed evenly among the writers. Thus, the readers segregate their read requests. Each reader will read data from a different set of writers, unlike Experiment E where each reader makes requests of each writer. When readers access distinct parts of the data set, the saturation behavior and the low load behavior are different. The slope of the asymptote is much steeper and occurs at a much higher number of readers due to the load balancing which occurs at the writers. The effect of many writers using poststore to a very few readers is also shown in this graph. With 29 writers and 1 reader the time to access a subpage is higher because not all poststore instructions were effective. The single reader was saturated with poststores from 29 writers and could not process all of the poststores.

The effectiveness of poststore is a tradeoff between the total time it takes the writer to update and poststore the data, and the reduction in read time for the readers. Figure 8

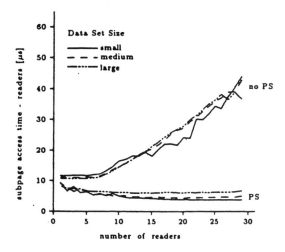

Figure 6: N global readers, $30 - N$ writers, Experiment E.

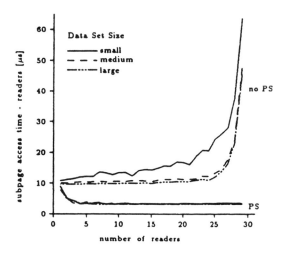

Figure 7: N private readers, $30 - N$ writers, Experiment F.

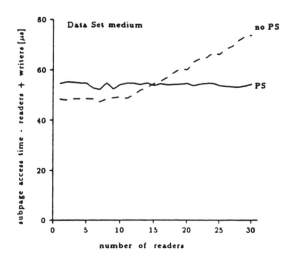

Figure 8: Combined access time, single reader/writer workload.

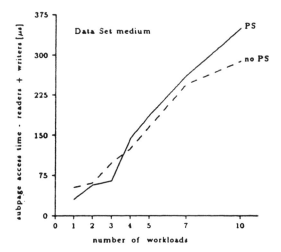

Figure 9: Combined access time, multiple reader/writer workloads, Experiment G.

shows the sum of average access time per subpage for readers and the average time to write a subpage for the writer as a function of the number of readers, for the medium data set. The data is taken from the Experiment B runs for both with and without poststore. When the number of readers is small, the additional time it takes the writer to poststore is not offset by the savings in average access time for the readers. However, as the number of readers increases, the average access time of the readers in the without poststore case increases, while the write time is always constant. After approximately 15 readers the savings in access time for the readers with poststore is greater than the extra time required for the writer to perform the poststore.

Experiment G illustrates a similar tradeoff as the number of workloads (i.e., reader/writer sets, heavyweight threads, multiprogramming level) increases. The data was collected by simultaneously executing multiple copies of the workload from Experiment C with 29 readers with a processing delay of $9\mu s$, and 1 writer. Figure 9 graphs the average over all workloads of the combined access time for the readers and

writers as the number of concurrently executing workloads increases. As the number of workloads increases (i.e., as the system load increases), the advantage of using poststore decreases. With 4 or more workloads, the average response time is lower without poststore. One possible reason is that retrieval of subpages from the ring can occur during the time that a thread is suspended due to context switching between workloads. When poststore is used, the time a thread is suspended (because it has been context switched with threads of other workloads) cannot be overlapped with data fetching. This tends to nullify the advantage of broadcasted updates. The higher the number of workloads, the more evident this effect becomes. In Figure 8 the advantage of poststore is more significant when there are more reader threads. The tradeoffs shown in Figure 8 and in Figure 9 explain why the decision of when to use poststore should be shared by the programmer and the system. As the system load increases, programmed poststores should be ignored by the system.

In general, the higher the rate at which non-local shared data is read, the greater the advantage of poststoring, especially when many other threads share that data. However, the number of threads which access the same data, and their access patterns, are other important factors to consider. When strict serialization of writes and reads cannot be ensured *a priori*, the use of poststore should be limited. When there are pending requests for a subpage for which a poststore has been issued, the poststore instruction is started but not completed, so no update broadcast is performed. This results in pure overhead for the writer.

4. Modeling and Validation

4.1. Detailed Model

In this section, analytical models of the system and the workloads presented in Section 3.2 are presented. The workloads modeled are the various applications of readers and writers with and without the use of poststore. The analytic model illustrates the processing which occurs in the subcaches, local caches, and the ring under the selected workloads. The following modeling assumptions are made:

1. Initial modeling will include only the effects of subcaches, local caches, and ring:0 traffic. However, the models could be extended to include disk accesses and ring:1 traffic.

2. No cache inconsistencies or synchronization occur among the reader/writer threads. Specifically, all writing completes before any reading occurs. The hardware guarantees cache consistency and the modeled workloads have no synchronization.

3. Access times for the subcache, local cache, and ring are exponentially distributed, with a mean given by the hardware specifications of the KSR1 (see Table 1).

4. Each processor may make a memory request to the subcache, local cache, or ring:0 based on probabilities which are determined by the specific workload running on the processor.

5. A request placed on the ring and the removal of a request may be effectively modeled probabilistically. That is, it is not necessary to track the exact path of every request on the ring and that modeling average path behavior is sufficient.

For the workloads modeled, each cell does some processing, followed by a memory request. When a memory request is made from a processor, the item may be located in either the subcache, the local cache, or the local cache of another processor. If the item is in the subcache, then it is transferred directly to the processor. If the item is found in the local cache, then it is transferred to the subcache, and then to the processor. If the item is not found locally in either the subcache or local cache of the processor, then a request is issued on ring:0 for the data item. When the response arrives, the data item is placed first in the local cache, then the subcache, then sent to the processor.

A Generalized Stochastic Petri Net (GSPN) [Moll82, MCB84] was selected to model the system. The detailed GSPN model includes a subnet for each of the 32 processing cells and subnets for the two ARDs which model the

ring propagation only. Each subnet models the cell's processing time, and subcache (sc), local cache (lc), and ring interactions. The subnets are connected together to form the complete ring:0.

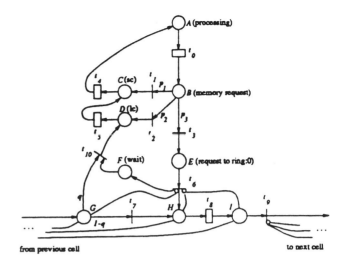

Figure 10: A subnet of one cell of the KSR1.

Figure 10 illustrates the detailed model of the subnet of one cell of the system. Places in each processor are labeled A through I. Transitions are numbered t_0 through t_{10} at each cell. The traffic on the ring is expressed by the number of occupied slots. Each cell has access to one slot, and this single slot is represented by the three places G, H, and I, in Figure 10. Inhibitor arcs on transition t_6 ensure that a cell can only place a message into an empty ring slot. Inhibitor arcs on transition t_9 from each of the places G, H, and I of the next cell ensure that a message on the ring will only be passed to the next cell if the slot for that cell is empty. Throughput on the ring at a processor can be measured as the throughput of transition t_8 at that processor. Throughput of a processor can be measured as the throughput of transition t_0, since all transactions at the processor must pass through that transition.

The subnet of a reader (i.e., a cell where the executing thread is a reader) operates as follows: Place A represents processing that occurs between memory requests. Transition t_0 is a timed transition which represents this processing time, and its rate depends on the volume of computation/processor cycles the reader is executing between two consecutive read requests. If a token is in place B, a memory request has been issued. After the memory request is issued, one of the immediate transitions t_1, t_2, or t_3 is fired with probability p_1, p_2, or p_3, respectively. If the requested item resides in the cell's subcache, t_1 fires. If the subpage containing the item resides in the cell's local cache, transition t_2 fires. If the subpage containing the item resides in the local cache of another cell, t_3 is fired. The firing probabilities of transitions t_1, t_2, and t_3 depend on the workload type. The modeling of automatic prefetching is approximated by adjusting the probabilities p_1, p_2, and p_3.

A token in place E represents a pending request to the ring. As soon as a slot becomes available, transition t_6 will fire, representing a request which is propagated on the ring. At the same time, the processor will go into a wait state, represented by place F, until the request is satisfied. Upon arrival of the response to place G, transition t_{10} is fired and the packet (i.e., the requested subpage) is received from the ring. The probabilities that a reader acquires the subpage from the ring or not are q and $1 - q$, respectively. Transitions t_4, t_5, and t_8 are timed transitions with firing times equal to the hardware latencies given by the manufacturer for the subcache, local cache, and the rate of ring propagation, respectively. Reader cells are initialized by placing a token in place A of each cell which represents an active reader process. This indicates that a read request is about to be made.

The subnet of a writer (i.e., a cell where the executing thread is a writer) operates similarly, except that the probabilities and transition rates are different. In each writer cell, q and $q - 1$ represent the probabilities that a writer does or does not own the subpage requested from the ring. Transitions t_0, t_4, and t_5 represent the total time for a writer to respond to a request. The probabilities p_1 and p_2 are zero for a writer thread, since no additional processing takes place, and the writer immediately issues a response on the ring as soon as a slot is available. Writer cells are initialized by placing a token in place F of each active writer thread, indicating that the writer is waiting to respond to a request.

The detailed model is a description of the interactions between threads and ring:0 of the KSR1. However, the detailed model contains 294 places and 358 transitions. Even a simple workload of 1 reader and 1 writer generates a reachability set containing over 800 states. Since the addition of each new active thread causes the number of states to increase exponentially, the model quickly becomes intractable with just a few active threads. Since this detailed model cannot be solved easily, simulation or an approximate model must be used. The latter option is chosen.

4.2. Approximate Load Dependent Model

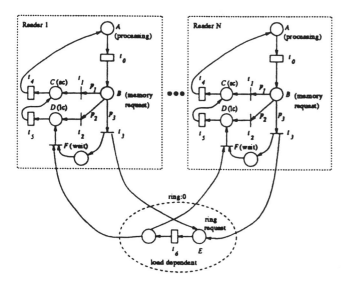

Figure 11: Load dependent GSPN model of ring:0.

The readers are modeled with the approximate load dependent model illustrated in Figure 11. In this model, transitions t_0 through t_5, and places A through F are as described for the detailed model. However, the ring delay (i.e., ring and writer activity) is modeled as a single load dependent server, and all processes interact through this single resource. Figure 12 illustrates the experimentally measured service rate of the ring and a single writer thread. Since the access rate increases linearly up through six readers, and flattens thereafter, an M/M/6 server is used in the approximate model.

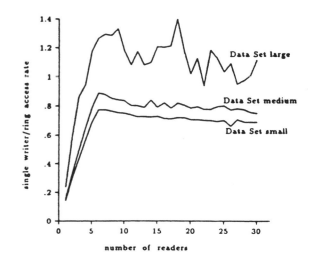

Figure 12: Service rate of the ring versus the number of active readers/threads.

If the assumption is made that a single thread executes at a time on each processing cell and each cell is statistically identical (i.e., single class), then the model can be reduced. The equivalent model shown in Figure 13 results after collapsing all subnets that represent the readers of the approximate load dependent model into a single subnet. This model is initialized by placing a number of tokens in place A equal to the number of readers. This model gives the same global performance metrics for the reader threads as the model in Figure 11. The response time measured with this model is the access time of a word.

The number of tokens in this model indicates the number of readers. As before, tokens in place A represent internal cell processing. Tokens pass to place B when processing is complete and a memory request is issued. Transitions t_1, t_2, and t_3 are immediate transitions, with the same functionality as that of the detailed model. A token in place C indicates that the requested word is in the subcache. A token in place D indicates that the word is in the local cache. A token in place E indicates that a fault to ring:0 has occurred. Transitions t_4, t_5, and t_6 are timed transitions. Transitions t_4 and t_5 are infinite servers, representing the subcache and local cache of each reader thread, again with rates equal to the hardware rates specified by the manufacturer for subcache and local cache access, respectively. Transition t_6 is an M/M/6 server, with a rate equal to the hardware rate specified by the manufacturer for ring:0 access. As more processes attempt to place messages on the ring, the server

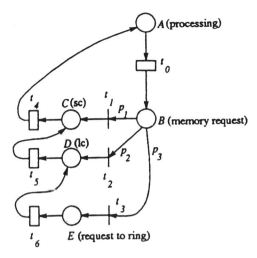

Figure 13: Reduced load dependent GSPN model for ring:0.

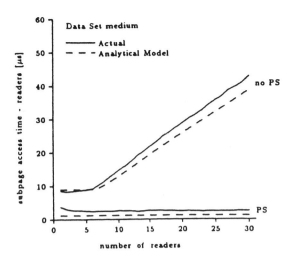

Figure 14: Model prediction for Experiment A.

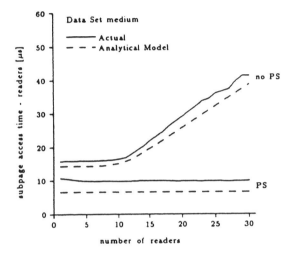

Figure 15: Model prediction for Experiment B.

becomes saturated and processes requests at a fixed maximum rate. As before, p_1, p_2, and p_3 depend on the modeled workload.

4.3. Theoretical Model/Experimental Comparisons

In this section, comparisons between the theoretical response time curves (dashed lines) and the experimentally observed response time curves (solid lines) of various workloads are presented. The theoretical results are based upon the reduced load dependent GSPN model. The model was programmed and solved using SPNP [CM91], an analytic GSPN solver. The service rate of t_0 is workload dependent and depends on the amount of delay or computation performed after each read. The granularity of access of the experimental workload is reflected in the transition probabilities p_1, p_2, and p_3. The size of the experimental workload affects both the amount of overlap of subcache overhead with processing and the effectiveness of pipelining. Experiments with different data sets yield different response time curves. However, the model does not incorporate any information about these types of overhead. The analytically predicted response times apply to the workload, regardless of the size of the data set. The medium data set is selected as representative and is used for comparisons to the theoretical model. The performance metric of interest is the average read time per subpage.

Figure 14 shows comparisons for Experiment A. For the average read time without poststore, the transition probabilities p_1, p_2, and p_3 are set to 0.0, 0.0, and 1.0, respectively (i.e., all reads generate a ring request). For the average read time with poststore, the transition probabilities are set to 0.0, 1.0, and 0.0 (i.e., all reads are a subcache miss, but a hit to the local cache). The model prediction is quite good. The analytical model overestimates performance by at most by 5μs (12.5%). In this case, the writer (i.e., the load dependent server) becomes the system bottleneck.

Figure 15 shows comparisons for Experiment B, where the global readers read the entire subpage. For the without poststore curve, the transition probabilities t_1, t_2, and t_3 are set to $\frac{14}{16}$, $\frac{1}{16}$, and $\frac{1}{16}$, since each subpage consists of two subblocks of 8 words each and as soon as a request is made to the ring, the subpage is moved to the local cache. For the with poststore curve, the transition probabilities are set to $\frac{14}{16}$, $\frac{2}{16}$, and $\frac{0}{16}$, since all read requests are satisfied in either the subcache or local cache. The theoretically predicted response time overestimates the experimental results by about 15%.

Similar comparisons between the analytic model and the experiments can be observed for Experiment C, as shown in Figure 16. (In the remaining figures, the with poststore curves do not provide any additional insight and have been deleted for clarity.) In Experiment C, delays of 6μs, 12μs, and 21μs are added after each read to simulate processing time. The rate for the timed transition t_0 is adjusted to account for this in the model. In this experiment, the rate of ring requests is the slowest (in contrast to Experiment A where the relative rate of generating a ring request is the highest possible). As before, the model predictions follow the trend of the experimental response time curves.

Figure 17 shows the predicted performance of the model

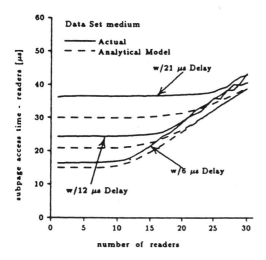

Figure 16: Model prediction for the "no poststore" case, Experiment C.

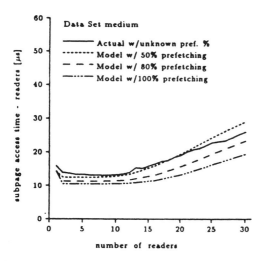

Figure 17: Model prediction for the "no poststore" case, Experiment D.

along with the actual performance of Experiment D. For Experiment D (i.e., in the single writer/multiple reader case where half of the readers read sequentially forward, from the beginning to the end, the other half read sequentially backwards), the performance improves (i.e., compared against Experiment B where all readers read in the same direction). Improvement results due to readers collecting subpages that they have not yet referenced but for which they have subpage descriptors. By adjusting the probabilities p_1, p_2, and p_3 it is possible to capture the effect of automatic prefetching of some percentage of the circulating subpages. The model indicates that the actual system is prefetching roughly 75% of the circulating subpages.

5. Generalizations

The model presented here may be generalized in a number of ways. These generalizations include such features as a more accurate load dependent server, a multiclass model, and less extreme workloads.

In Experiments A through D there is only one writer, with multiple readers which all behave similarly. This makes it possible to build a simple load dependent model of the readers on ring:0. The model reflects the readers' interactions with the "system", which is viewed as the combination of the ring and single writer, and is modeled as an M/M/6 server. The parameters of each model reflect the different behavior of the readers in each of the Experiments A through D. However, the simple load dependent model is not as accurate for Experiments E and F. Experiments E and F are different from the first four because there is more than one writer. In particular, when the readers are private, as in Experiment F, each reader is accessing data from a different writer at any one time.

Figure 18 shows the predicted performance using two different analytical models along with the actual performance for Experiment F. The first model is the one used in the previous section and uses a single M/M/6 server to model the ring/writer behavior. As seen, the model is a poor predictor for the case of multiple writers and private readers. The second model uses multiple M/M/6 servers, one for each writer. The behavior of this model is very close to that of the actual system. When there are 29 writers and 1 reader, the large number of writers (M/M/6 servers) can easily handle the number of requests from the single reader. Both the actual system curve and that from the analytic model are flat up to 25 readers (and 5 writers). If each writer behaves as an M/M/6 server, then there are equivalently 30 servers to handle the requests of the 25 readers. The system is behaving as an infinite server up until that point, since the number of readers is smaller than the total number of servers. For 26 readers there are 4 writers, with the number of total servers equal to 24. At that point, the read time per subpage begins to increase dramatically, since the number of readers is greater than the number of servers. With 29 readers and 1 writer, the writer is saturated, as in the earlier experiments.

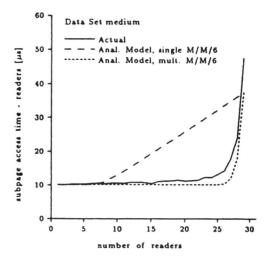

Figure 18: Model prediction for Experiment F.

The current model approximates the effect of automatic prefetching by adjusting the probabilities p_1, p_2, and p_3. A multiclass model could be used to show this effect more accurately by modeling each request as a separate class. Each reader would issue a ring request for a class of data not previously seen on the ring. Each reader would access future data on the ring with some probability dependent on other processor activity. The Petri net model would have a place for each class of data in the local cache and subcache. A more general model could also take into consideration subcache overhead and pipelining effects.

The current experimental workload was selected with the goal of illustrating the worst case behavior with and without the use of poststore. This workload is extreme in that all writing is completed before any reading starts, and the workload ensures that either all data is available in the local cache for each individual reader, or no data is available in the local cache for each individual reader at the time the reading occurs. Further work includes monitoring actual codes to acquire model parameters for the processing rates and the probabilities of memory requests of less extreme workloads.

6. Summary

The primary contributions of this paper are listed below, relative to the stated goals in the introduction.

- A description of the basic KSR1 architecture has been given. The key elements are: the ring of rings structure, the hierarchical (ALLCACHE) caching scheme, and the address resolution search engine. Attention is focused on the poststore option.

- Results from a suite of sensitivity analysis experiments have been reported. A simple readers/writers workload was used. Each experiment was run both with and without the poststore option. Performance sensitivity results were given with respect to: data granularity, reader delay, data access patterns, reader/writer ratio, data sharing, total system load, data set size, and number of readers.

- Analytic models, both a detailed model and an approximate model, have been constructed. Validation experiments indicate that the basic trends are accurately captured using relatively simple models.

The experimental results indicate where poststore is most effective. Figure 8 shows that as the number of reader threads increases, poststore is more advantageous. However, if the number of reader threads is small, poststore should not be used since the benefit to the readers does not offset the extra incurred overhead of the writers. Thus, the number of reader threads influences the decision of whether or not to use poststore, and this number is a parameter of the programmer's application code. Figure 9 shows that as the number of application workloads (i.e., the number of sets of reader/writer codes) increases, poststore becomes less advantageous. That is, as contention increases at the processing cells, poststore is not beneficial and should not be used. The system load is controlled by the operating system scheduler. Therefore, neither allowing a programmer to use poststore without knowledge of the system load, nor allowing the operating system to determine the use of poststore without knowledge of the application code, is advisable.

Using poststore is analogous to a sender-initiated transfer. Sender-initiated transfers are most beneficial under light load [ELZ86]. Using prefetch (i.e., another programmer option not addressed in this paper), or allowing the readers to pull in subpages as requested when poststore is not used, is analogous to a receiver-initiated transfer. Receiver-initiated transfers are most beneficial when the system load is heavy. Although applied here in a different context, the results in Figure 9 confirm these general findings.

As mentioned in Section 5, several improvements to the model are possible and other features of the KSR architecture warrant further study. The intent here was not to model all aspects of the KSR's memory or ring hardware. However, building on the basic understanding of the architecture, such a modeling effort would be useful. These modeling and experimentation efforts are continuing.

Acknowledgments

The helpful information, criticisms, and suggestions provided by Tom Dunigan, Rich Stirling, and Jim Rothnie have significantly improved this paper.

References

[CM91]   G. Ciardo and J. Muppala. *Manual for the SPNP Package, Version 3.1*. Department of Elec. Eng., Duke University, Sep. 1991.

[DSG86]   M. Dubois, C. Scheurich, and F. Griggs. Memory access buffering in multiprocessors. In *13th Intl. Symp. on Comp. Arch.*, pages 434–442, 1986.

[Duni92] T. Dunigan. Kendall Square multiprocessor: Early experiences and performance. Technical Report ORNL/TM-12065, Oak Ridge National Laboratory, April 1992.

[ELZ86]   D. Eager, E. Lazowska, and J. Zahorjan. A comparison of receiver-initiated and sender-initiated adaptive load sharing. *Performance Evaluation*, pages 53–68, Feb. 1986.

[HLH92]   E. Hagersten, A. Landin, and S. Haridi. DDM-a cache-only memory architecture. *IEEE Computer*, pages 45–54, Sep. 1992.

[Kend91] Kendall Square Research, Waltham, Ma. *KSR1 Principles of Operation*, Oct. 1991.

[Lamp79] L. Lamport. How to make a multiprocessor computer that correctly executes multiprocess programs. *IEEE Trans. on Computers*, pages 690–691, Sep. 1979.

[MCB84]   M. Marsan, G. Conte, and G. Balbo. A class of generalized stochastic Petri nets for the performance evaluation of multiprocessor systems. *ACM Trans. on Computer Systems*, pages 93–122, May 1984.

[Moll82] M. Molloy. Performance analysis using stochastic Petri nets. *IEEE Trans. on Computers*, pages 913–917, Sep. 1982.

DDM — A Cache-Only Memory Architecture

Erik Hagersten, Anders Landin, and Seif Haridi
Swedish Institute of Computer Science

Multiprocessors providing a shared memory view to the programmer are typically implemented as such — with a shared memory. We introduce an architecture with large caches to reduce latency and network load. Because all system memory resides in the caches, a minimum number of network accesses are needed. Still, it presents a shared-memory view to the programmer.

Single bus. Shared-memory systems based on a single bus have some tens of processors, each one with a local cache, and typically suffer from bus saturation. A cache-coherence protocol in each cache snoops the traffic on the common bus and prevents inconsistencies in cache contents.[1] Computers manufactured by Sequent and Encore use this kind of architecture. Because it provides a uniform access time to the whole shared memory, it is called a uniform memory architecture (UMA). The contention for the common memory and the common bus limits the scalability of UMAs.

Distributed. Computers such as the BBN Butterfly and the IBM RP3 use an architecture with distributed shared memory, known as a nonuniform memory architecture (NUMA). Each processor node contains a portion of the shared memory, so access times to different parts of the shared address space can vary. NUMAs often have networks other than a single bus, and the network delay can vary to different nodes. The earlier NUMAs did not have coherent caches and left the problem of maintaining coherence to the programmer. Today, researchers are striving toward coherent NUMAs with directory-based cache-coherence protocols.[2] By statically partitioning the work and data, programmers can optimize programs for NUMAs. A partitioning that enables processors to make most of their accesses to their part of the shared memory achieves a better scalability than is possible in UMAs.

Cache-only. In a cache-only memory architecture (COMA), the memory organization is similar to that of a NUMA in that each processor holds a portion of the address space. However, the partitioning of data among the memories does not have to be static, since all distributed memories are organized like large (second-level) caches. The task of such a memory is twofold. Besides being a large cache for the processor, it may also contain some data from the shared address space that the processor never has accessed — in other words, it is a cache and a virtual part of

A new architecture has the programming paradigm of shared-memory architectures but no physically shared memory. Caches attached to the processors contain all the system memory.

Reprinted from *Computer,* Vol. 25, No. 9, Sept. 1992, pp. 44–54.

0-8186-6522-X/95 $4.00 © 1992 IEEE

the shared memory. We call this intermediate form of memory *attraction memory*. A coherence protocol attracts the data used by a processor to its attraction memory. Comparable to a cache line, the coherence unit moved around by the protocol is called an *item*. On a memory reference, a virtual address is translated into an item identifier. The item identifier space is logically the same as the physical address space of typical machines, but there is no permanent mapping between an item identifier and a physical memory location. Instead, an item identifier corresponds to a location in an attraction memory, whose tag matches the item identifier. Actually, there are cases where multiple locations of different attraction memories could match.

A COMA provides a programming model identical to that of shared-memory architectures, but it does not require static distribution of execution and memory usage to run efficiently. Running an optimized NUMA program on a COMA results in a NUMA-like behavior, since the work spaces of the different processors migrate to their attraction memories. However, a UMA version of the same program would have a similar behavior, because the data are attracted to the using processor regardless of the address. A COMA also adapts to and performs well for programs with a more dynamic or semidynamic scheduling. The work space migrates according to its usage throughout the computation. Programs can be optimized for a COMA to take this property into account to achieve a better locality.

A COMA allows for dynamic data use without duplicating much memory, compared with an architecture in which a cached datum also occupies space in the shared memory. To avoid increasing the memory cost, the attraction memories should be implemented with ordinary memory components. Therefore, we view the COMA approach as a second-level, or higher level, cache technique. The accessing time to the attraction memory of a COMA is comparable to that to the memory of a cache-coherent NUMA. Figure 1 compares COMAs to other shared-memory architectures.

A new COMA. This article describes the basic ideas behind a new COMA. The architecture, called the Data Diffusion Machine (DDM),[3] relies on a hier-

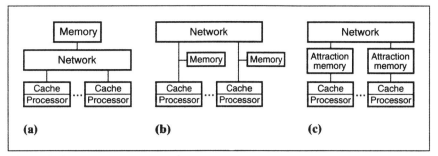

Figure 1. Shared-memory architectures compared with COMAs: (a) uniform memory architecture (UMA), (b) nonuniform memory architecture (NUMA), and (c) cache-only memory architecture (COMA).

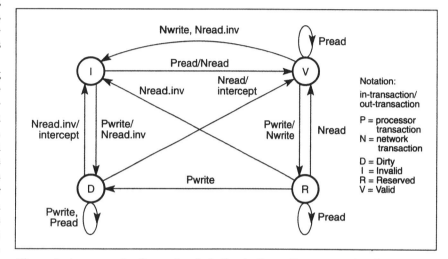

Figure 2. An example of a protocol similar to the write-once protocol.

archical network structure. We introduce the key ideas behind DDM by describing a small machine and its protocol. We also describe a large machine with hundreds of processors, overview the ongoing prototype project, and provide simulated performance figures.

Cache-coherence strategies

The problem of maintaining coherence among read-write data shared by different caches has been studied extensively. Either software or hardware can maintain coherence. We believe hardware coherence is needed in a COMA for efficiency, since the item must be small to prevent performance degradation by false sharing. (In false sharing, two processors accessing different parts of the same item conflict with each other, even though they do

not share any data.) We measured a speedup of 50 percent when false sharing was removed from the wind tunnel application, MP3D-Diff, reported in the "Simulated performance" section. Hardware-based schemes maintain coherence without involving software and can be implemented more efficiently. Examples of hardware-based protocols are snooping-cache protocols and directory-based protocols.

Snooping-cache protocols have a distributed implementation. Each cache is responsible for snooping traffic on the bus and taking actions to avoid an incoherence. An example of such a protocol is the write-once protocol introduced by Goodman and discussed by Stenström.[1] As Figure 2 shows, in that protocol, each cache line can be in one of four states: Invalid, Valid, Reserved, or Dirty. Many caches can have the same cache line in the state Valid at the same time, and may read it locally. When writing to a cache line in Valid, the line changes state to Reserved, and a write is sent on the common bus to the common memory. All other caches with lines in Valid snoop the write and invalidate their copies. At this point there is only one cached copy of the cache line containing the newly written value. The common memory now also contains the new value. If a cache already has the cache line in Reserved, it can perform a write locally without any transactions on the common bus. Its value now differs from that in the memory, and its state is therefore changed to Dirty. Any read requests from other caches to that cache line must now be intercepted to provide the new value (marked by "intercept" in Figure 2).

Snooping caches rely on broadcasting and are not suited for general interconnection networks: Unrestricted broadcasting would drastically reduce the available bandwidth, thereby obviating the advantage of general networks. Instead, directory-based schemes send messages directly between nodes.[1] A read request is sent to main memory, without any snooping. The main memory knows if the cache line is cached — and in which cache or caches — and whether it has been modified. If the line has been modified, the read request is passed on to the cache with a copy, which provides a copy for the requesting cache. On a write to a shared cache line, a write request sent to the main memory causes invalidation messages to all caches with copies to be sent. The caches respond with acknowledge messages. To achieve sequential consistency, all acknowledgments must be received before the write is performed.

The cache-coherence protocol for a COMA can adopt techniques used in other cache-coherence protocols and extend them with the functionality for finding a datum on a cache read miss and for handling replacement. A directory-based protocol could have a part of the directory information, the *directory home*, statically distributed in a NUMA fashion, while the data would be allowed to move freely. Retrieving the data on a read miss would then require one extra indirect access to the directory home to find where the item current-

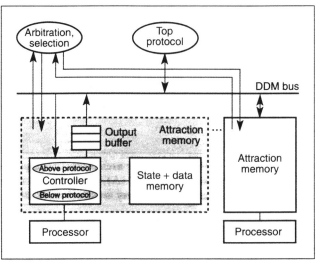

Figure 3. The architecture of a single-bus DDM. Below the attraction memories are the processors. On top of the bus are arbitration and selection.

ly resides. The access time, including this extra indirection, would be identical to that required for reading a dirty cache line not in a NUMA's home node. The directory home can also make sure that the last copy of an item is not lost.

Instead of the above strategy, DDM is based on a hierarchical snooping bus architecture and uses a hierarchical search algorithm for finding an item. The directory information in DDM is dynamically distributed in the hierarchy.

A minimal COMA

We introduce DDM by looking at the smallest instance of the architecture, which could be a COMA on its own or a subsystem of a larger COMA. A single bus connects the attraction memories of the minimal DDM. The distribution and coherence of data among the attraction memories are controlled by the snooping protocol *memory above*, and the interface between the processor and the attraction memory is defined by the protocol *memory below*. The protocol views a cache line of an attraction memory, here called an item, as one unit. The attraction memory stores one small state field per item. Figure 3 shows the node architecture in the single-bus DDM.

DDM uses an asynchronous split-transaction bus: The bus is released between a requesting transaction and its reply, for example, between a read re-

quest and its data reply. The delay between the request and its reply can be of arbitrary length, and there might be a large number of outstanding requests. The reply transaction will eventually appear on the bus as a different transaction. Unlike other buses, the DDM bus has a selection mechanism to make sure that at most one node is selected to service a request. This guarantees that each transaction on the bus does not produce more than one new transaction for the bus, a requirement necessary for deadlock avoidance.

Single-bus DDM protocol. We developed a new protocol, similar in many ways to the snooping-cache protocol, limiting broadcast requirements to a smaller subsystem and adding support for replacement.[4] The write coherence part of the protocol is the write-invalidate type: To keep data coherent, all copies of the item except the one to be updated are erased on a write. In a COMA with a small item size, the alternative approach, write update, could also be attractive: On a write, the new value is multicast to all "caches" with a shared copy of the item.

The protocol also handles the attraction of data (read) and replacement when a set in an attraction memory gets full. The snooping protocol defines a new state and a new transaction to send as a function of the transaction appearing on the bus, and the present state of the item in the attraction memory:

Protocol: old state × transaction → new state × new transaction

An item can be in one of seven states (the subsystem is the attraction memory):

- *Invalid.* This subsystem does not contain the item.
- *Exclusive.* This subsystem and no other contains the item.
- *Shared.* This subsystem and possibly other subsystems contain the item.
- *Reading.* This subsystem is waiting for a data value after having issued a read.

- *Waiting.* This subsystem is waiting to become Exclusive after having issued an erase.
- *Reading-and-Waiting.* This subsystem is waiting for a data value, later to become Exclusive.
- *Answering.* This subsystem has promised to answer a read request.

The first three states — Invalid, Exclusive, and Shared — correspond to the states Invalid, Reserved, and Valid in Goodman's write-once protocol. The state Dirty in that protocol — with the meaning that this is the only cached copy and its value differs from that in the memory — has no correspondence in a COMA. New states in the protocol are the transient states Reading, Waiting, Reading-and-Waiting, and Answering. Transient states are required because of the split-transaction bus and the need to remember outstanding requests.

The bus carries the following transactions:

- *Erase.* Erase all copies of this item.
- *Exclusive.* Acknowledge an erase request.
- *Read.* Read a copy of the item.
- *Data.* Carry the data in reply to an earlier read request.
- *Inject.* Carry the only copy of an item and look for a subsystem to move into — caused by a replacement.
- *Out.* Carry the item on its way out of the subsystem — caused by a replacement. It will terminate when another copy of the item is found.

A processor writing an item in Exclusive state or reading an item in Exclusive or Shared state proceeds without interruption. As Figure 4 shows, a read attempt of an item in Invalid will result in a Read request and a new state, Reading. The bus selection mechanism will select one attraction memory to service the request, eventually putting a Data transaction on the bus. The requesting attraction memory, now in Reading, will grab the Data transaction, change to Shared, and continue.

Processors are allowed to write only to items in Exclusive state. If the item is in Shared, all other copies have to be erased and an acknowledgment received before the writing is allowed. The attraction memory sends an Erase transaction and waits for the Exclusive ac-

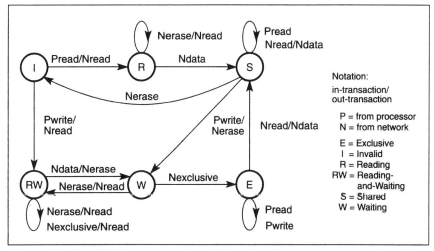

Figure 4. A simplified representation of the attraction memory protocol not including replacement.

knowledgment in the new state, Waiting. Many simultaneous attempts to write the same item will result in many attraction memories in Waiting, all with an outstanding Erase transaction in their output buffers. The first Erase to reach the bus is the winner of the write race.

All other transactions bound for the same item are removed from the small output buffers. Therefore, the buffers also have to snoop transactions. The output buffers can be limited to a depth of three, and deadlock can still be avoided with a special arbitration algorithm. The losing attraction memories in Waiting change state to Reading-and-Waiting, while one of them puts a read request in its output buffer. Eventually the top protocol of the bus replies with an Exclusive acknowledgment, telling the only attraction memory left in Waiting that it may now proceed. Writing to an item in the Invalid state results in a Read request and a new state, Reading-and-Waiting. Upon the Data reply, the state changes to Waiting and an Erase request is sent.

Replacement. Like ordinary caches, the attraction memory will run out of space, forcing some items to make room for more recently accessed ones. If the set where an item is supposed to reside is full, one item in the set is selected to be replaced. For example, the oldest item in Shared, of which there might be other copies, may be selected. Replacing an item in Shared generates an Out transaction. The space used by the item can now be reclaimed. If an Out transaction sees an attraction memory in

Shared, Reading, Waiting, or Reading-and-Waiting, it does nothing; otherwise it is converted to an Inject transaction by the top protocol. An Inject transaction can also be produced by replacing an item in Exclusive. The inject transaction is the last copy of an item trying to find a new home in a new attraction memory. In the single-bus implementation, it will do so first by choosing an empty space (Invalid state), and second by replacing an item in Shared state — in other words, it will decrease the amount of sharing. If the item identifier space, which corresponds to the physical address space of conventional architectures, is not made larger than the sum of the attraction memory sizes, it is possible to devise a simple scheme that guarantees a physical location for each item.

Often a program uses only a portion of a computer's physical address space. This is especially true of operating systems with a facility for eager reclaiming of unused work space. In DDM, the unused item space can be used to increase the degree of sharing by purging the unused items. The operating system might even change the degree of sharing dynamically.

The hierarchical DDM

So far, we have presented a cache-coherent single-bus multiprocessor without physically shared memory. Instead, the resources form huge second-level caches called attraction memories, minimizing the number of accesses to the

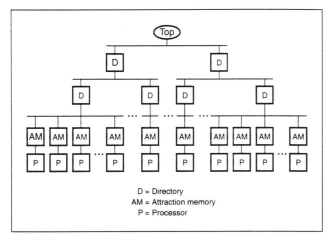

Figure 5. A hierarchical DDM with three levels.

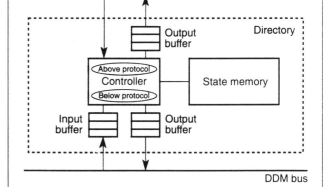

Figure 6. The architecture of a directory.

only shared resource left: the shared bus. Data can reside in any or many of the attraction memories. Data are automatically moved where needed.

To make the single-bus DDM a subsystem of a large hierarchical DDM, we replace the top with a directory, which interfaces between the bus and a higher level bus of the same type. Figure 5 shows the hierarchy.

The directory is a set-associative state memory that keeps information for all the items in the attraction memories below it, but contains no data. The directory can answer these questions: "Is this item below me?" and "Does this item exist outside my subsystem?" From the bus above, the directory's snooping protocol *directory above* behaves very much like the *memory above* protocol. From the bus below, its *directory below* protocol behaves like the *top protocol* for items in the Exclusive state. This makes operations on items local to a bus identical to those of the single-bus DDM. The directory passes through only transactions from below that cannot be completed inside its subsystem or transactions from above that need to be serviced by its subsystem. In that sense, the directory acts as a filter.

As Figure 6 shows, the directory has a small output buffer above it to store transactions waiting to be sent on the higher bus. Transactions for the lower bus are stored in another output buffer below, and transactions from the lower bus are stored in an input buffer. A directory reads from the input buffer when it has the time and space to do a lookup in its status memory. This is not part of the atomic snooping action of the bus.

The hierarchical DDM and its protocol have several similarities with architectures proposed by Wilson[5] and Goodman and Woest.[6] DDM is, however, different in its use of transient states in the protocol, its lack of physically shared memory, and its network (higher level caches) that stores only state information and no data.

Multilevel read. If the subsystems connected to the bus cannot satisfy a read request, the next higher directory retransmits the request on the next higher bus. The directory also changes the item's state to Reading, marking the outstanding request. Eventually, the request reaches a level in the hierarchy where a directory containing a copy of the item is selected to answer the request. The selected directory changes the item's state to Answering, marking an outstanding request from above, and retransmits the Read request on its lower bus. As Figure 7 shows, the transient states Reading and Answering in the directories mark the request's path through the hierarchy, like an unwound red read thread that shows the way through a maze, appearing in red in Figure 7.

A flow-control mechanism in the protocol prevents deadlock if too many processors try to unwind a read thread to the same set in a directory. When the request finally reaches an attraction memory with a copy of the item, its data reply simply follows the read thread back to the requesting node, changing all the states along the path to Shared.

Combined reads and broadcasts are simple to implement in DDM. If a Read request finds the read thread unwound for the requested item (Reading or Answering state), it simply terminates and waits for the Data reply that eventually will follow that path on its way back.

Multilevel write. An Erase from below to a directory with the item in Exclusive state results in an Exclusive acknowledgment being sent below. An Erase that cannot get its acknowledgment from the directory will work its way up the hierarchy, changing the directories' states to Waiting to mark the outstanding request. All subsystems of a bus carrying an Erase transaction will get their copies erased. The propagation of the Erase ends when it reaches a directory in Exclusive (or the top), and the acknowledgment is sent back along the path marked Waiting, changing the states to Exclusive.

A write race between any two processors in the hierarchical DDM has a solution similar to that of a single-bus DDM. The two Erase requests are propagated up the hierarchy. The first Erase transaction to reach the lowest bus common to both processors is the winner, as shown in Figure 8. The losing attraction memory (in Reading-and-Waiting) will restart a new write action automatically upon receipt of the erase.

Replacement in the hierarchical DDM. Replacement of a Shared item in the hierarchical DDM results in an Out transaction propagating up the hierarchy and terminating when it finds a subsystem in any of the following states: Shared, Reading, Waiting, or Answering. If the last copy of an item marked Shared is replaced, an Out transaction

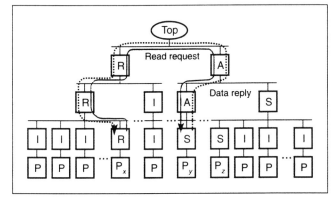

Figure 7. A read request from processor P_x has found its way to a copy of the item in the attraction memory of processor P_y. Its path is marked with states Reading (R) and Answering (A), which will guide the data reply back to P_x. (I indicates processors in the Invalid state, S processors in the Shared state.)

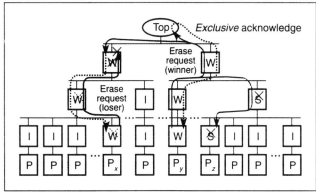

Figure 8. A write race between two processors P_x and P_y is resolved when the request originating from P_y reaches the top bus (the lowest bus common to both processors). The top can now send the acknowledgment, Exclusive, which follows the path marked with W's (processors in the Waiting state) back to the winning processor P_y. The Waiting states are changed to Exclusive by the acknowledgment. The Erase transaction will erase the data in P_x and P_z, forcing P_x to redo its write attempt.

that fails to terminate will reach a directory in Exclusive and turn into an Inject transaction. Replacing an item in Exclusive generates an Inject transaction that tries to find an empty space in a neighboring attraction memory. Inject transactions first try to find an empty space in the attraction memories of the local DDM bus, as in the single-bus DDM. Unlike in a single-bus DDM, an Inject failing to find an empty space on the local DDM bus will turn to a special bus, its home bus, determined by the item identifier. On the home bus, the Inject will force itself into an attraction memory, possibly by throwing out a foreigner or a Shared item. The item home space is equally divided between the bottommost buses, and therefore space is guaranteed on the home bus.

The preferred location in DDM is different from memory location in NUMAs in that an item seeks a home only at replacement after failing to find space elsewhere. When the item is not in its home place, other items can use its place. The home also differs from the NUMA approach in being a bus: Any attraction memory on that bus will do. The details of the directory protocols are available elsewhere.[4]

Replacement in a directory. Baer and Wang studied the multilevel inclusion property,[7] which has the following implications for our system: A directory at level $i + 1$ has to be a superset of the directories, or attraction memories, at level i. In other words, the size of a directory and its associativity (number of ways) must be B_i times that of the underlying level i, where B_i is the branch factor of the underlying level i, and size means the number of items:

Size: $Dir_{i+1} = B_i * Dir_i$
Associativity: $Dir_{i+1} = B_i * Dir_i$

Even if implementable, higher level memories would become expensive and slow if those properties were fulfilled for a large hierarchical system. However, the effects of the multilevel inclusion property are limited in DDM. It stores only state information in its directories and does not replicate data in the higher levels. Yet another way to limit the effect is to use "imperfect directories" with smaller sets (lower number of ways) than what is required for multilevel inclusion and to give the directories the ability to perform replacement, that is, to move all copies of an item out of their subsystem. We can keep the probability of replacement at a reasonable level by increasing the associativity moderately higher up in the hierarchy. A higher degree of sharing also helps to keep that probability low. A shared item occupies space in many attraction memories, but only one space in the directories above them. The implementation of directory replacement requires one extra state and two extra transactions.[4]

Other protocols. Our protocol gives the programmer a *sequentially consistent* system. It fulfills the strongest memory access model, but performance is degraded because the processor has to wait for the acknowledgment before it can perform the write. However, the acknowledgment is sent by the topmost node of the subsystem in which all copies of the item reside, instead of by each individual attraction memory with a copy. This not only reduces the remote delay, it also cuts down the number of system transactions. The writer might actually receive the acknowledgment before all copies are erased. Nevertheless, sequential consistency can be guaranteed.[8] The hierarchical structure can also efficiently support looser forms of consistency providing higher performance. We have designed a processor-consistent protocol[8] and a protocol combining processor consistency with an adaptive write update strategy.

Increasing the bandwidth

Although most memory accesses tend to be localized in the machine, the hierarchy's higher levels may nevertheless demand a higher bandwidth than the lower systems, creating a bottleneck. To take the load off the higher levels, we can use a smaller branch factor at the

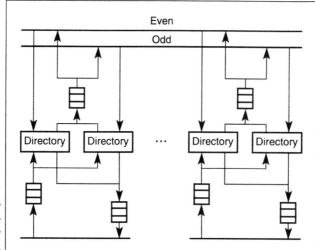

Figure 9. Increasing the bandwidth of a bus by splitting buses.

top of the hierarchy than lower down. This solution, however, increases the levels in the hierarchy, resulting in a longer remote access delay and an increased memory overhead. Instead, we can widen the higher levels of the hierarchy to produce a fat tree.[9] We split a directory into two directories half the original directory's size. The two directories deal with different address domains (even and odd). The communication with other directories is also split, which doubles the bandwidth. We can perform a split any number of times and at any level of the hierarchy. Figure 9 shows that regardless of the number of splits, the architecture is still hierarchical to each specific address.

Yet another solution is a heterogeneous network: We use the hierarchy with its advantages as far as possible and tie several hierarchies together at their tops by a general network with a directory-based protocol. This scheme requires some changes in the protocol to achieve the same consistency model.

The DDM prototype project

A prototype DDM design is near completion at the Swedish Institute of Computer Science. The hardware implementation of the processor and attraction memory is based on the system TP881V by Tadpole Technology, UK. Each such system has up to four Motorola MC88100 20-MHz processors, each one with two MC88200 16-Kbyte caches and memory management units; 8 or 32 Mbytes of DRAM; and interfaces for the SCSI bus, Ethernet, and terminals, all connected by the Motorola Mbus as shown in Figure 10.

We are developing a DDM node controller board to host a single-ported state memory. As Figure 10 shows, it will interface the TP881V node with the first-level DDM bus. The node controller snoops accesses between the processor caches and the memory of the TP881V according to the memory-below protocol, and also snoops the DDM bus according to the memory-above protocol. We have integrated the copy-back protocol of multiple processor caches into the protocol mechanisms. The node controller thus changes the memory's behavior into that of an attraction memory. Read accesses to the attraction memory take eight cycles per cache line, which is one more than in the original TP881V system. Write accesses to the attraction memory take 12 cycles compared with 10 cycles for the original system. A read/write mix of 3/1 to the attraction memory results in an access time to the attraction memory on the average 16 percent slower than that to the original TP881V memory.

As Table 1 shows, a remote read to a node on the same DDM bus takes 55 cycles at best, most of which are spent making Mbus transactions (a total of four accesses). Read accesses climbing one step up and down the hierarchy add about 45 extra cycles. Write accesses to shared state take at best 40 cycles for one level and 50 cycles for two levels.

The DDM bus is pipelined in four phases: transaction code, snoop, selection, and data. We designed our initial

Related activities

At the Swedish Institute of Computer Science, we are developing an operating system for the DDM prototype. This work is based on the Mach operating system from Carnegie Mellon University, which we modified to support DDM efficiently. Related activities involve a hardware prefetching scheme that dynamically prefetches items to the attraction memory; this is especially useful when a process is started or migrated. We are also experimenting with alternative protocols.[1]

A DDM emulator is currently under development at the University of Bristol.[2] The emulator runs on the Meiko transputer platform and models an architecture with a tree-shaped link-based structure, with transputers as directories. The transputers' four links permit a branch factor of three at each level. The transputers at the leaves execute the application. All references to global data are intercepted and handled in a DDM manner by software. The emulator's DDM protocol has a different representation suited for a link-based architecture structured like a tree, rather than for a bus-based architecture. The implementation has certain similarities to directory-based systems.

References

1. E. Hagersten, *Towards a Scalable Cache-Only Memory Architecture,* PhD thesis, SICS Dissertation Series 08, Swedish Institute of Computer Science, Kista, Sweden, 1992.

2. S. Raina and D.H.D. Warren, "Traffic Patterns in a Scalable Multiprocessor Through Transputer Emulation," *Proc. Hawaii Int'l Conf. System Sciences*, Vol. I, IEEE-CS Press, Los Alamitos, Calif., Order No. 2420, 1992, pp. 267-276.

bus conservatively, since pushing the bus speed is not a primary goal of this research. The prototype DDM bus operates at 20 MHz, with a 32-bit data bus and a 32-bit address bus. It provides a moderate bandwidth of about 80 Mbytes per second, which is enough for connecting up to eight nodes — that is, 32 processors. Still, the bandwidth has not been the limiting factor in our simulation studies. We can increase bus bandwidth many times by using other structures. The slotted ring bus proposed by Barosso and Dubois[10] has a bandwidth one order of magnitude higher.

For translations to item identifiers, DDM uses the normal procedures for translating virtual addresses to physical addresses, as implemented in standard memory management units. This means that an operating system has knowledge of physical pages.

Any attraction memory node can have a connected disk. Upon a page-in, the node first attracts all the data of an item page as being temporarily locked to its attraction memory. If the items of that page were not present in the machine earlier, they are "born" at this time through the protocol. Then the node copies (by direct memory access) the page from the disk to the attraction memory, unlocking the data at the same time. Page-out reverses the process, copying a dirty page back to the disk. The operating system can purge the items of unused pages for more sharing.

Memory overhead

It might seem that an implementation of DDM would require far more memory than alternative architectures. Extra memory is required for storing state bits and address keys for the set-associative attraction memories, as well as for the directories. We have calculated the extra bits needed if all items reside in only one copy (worst case). We assume an item size of 16 bytes — the cache line size of the Motorola MC88200.

A 32-processor DDM — that is, a one-level DDM with a maximum of eight two-way set-associative attraction memories — needs four bits of address tag per item, regardless of the attraction memory size. As we said earlier, the item space is not larger than the sum of the sizes of the attraction memories, so the size of each attraction memory is one eighth of the item space. Because each set in the attraction memory is divided two ways, 16 items can reside in the same set. In addition to the four bits needed to tell items apart, each item needs four bits of state. Thus, an item size of 128 bits gives an overhead of (4+4)/128 = 6 percent.

Adding another layer with eight eight-way set-associative directories brings the maximum number of processors to 256. The size of the directories is the sum of the sizes of the attraction memories in their subsystems. A directory entry consists of six bits for the address tag and four bits of state per item, using a calculation similar to the one above. The overhead in the attraction memories is larger than in the previous example because of the larger item space: seven bits of address tag and four bits of state. The total overhead per item is (6+4+7+4)/128 = 16 percent. A larger item size would, of course, decrease these overheads.

To minimize the memory overhead, we can use a different interpretation of the implicit state for different parts of the item space. In our initial implementation of DDM, the absence of an entry in a directory is interpreted as Invalid. The replacement algorithm introduces a home bus for an item. If an item is most often found in its home bus and nowhere else, the absence of an entry in a directory could instead be interpreted as Exclusive for items in its home subsystem, and as Invalid for items from outside. This would drastically reduce a directory's size. The technique would be practical only to a limited extent. Too small directories restrict the number of items moving out of their subsystems and thus limit sharing and migration, resulting in drawbacks similar to those of NUMAs.

Item space is slightly smaller than the sum of the attraction memories because of sharing in the system. This introduces a memory overhead not taken into account in the above calculations. However, in a COMA a "cached" item occupies only one space, while in other shared-memory architectures it requires two spaces: one in the cache and one in the shared memory.

Simulated performance

We used an execution-driven simulation environment that lets us study large programs running on many processors in a reasonable amount of time. We parameterized the DDM simulation

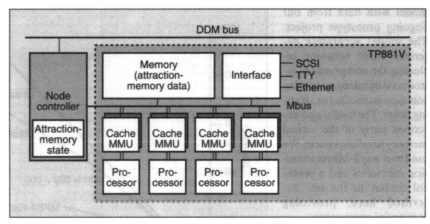

Figure 10. A node of the DDM prototype consisting of four processors sharing one attraction memory.

Table 1. Remote delay in a two-level DDM (best cases).

CPU Access	State in Attraction Memory	Delay, One Level (cycles)	Delay, Two Levels (cycles)
Read	Invalid	55	100
Write	Shared	40	50
Write	Invalid	80	130

model with data from our ongoing prototype project. The model accurately describes DDM behavior, including the compromises introduced by taking an existing commercial product as a starting point. The model also describes parts of the virtual memory handling system. We used two-way 1-Mbyte attraction memories and a protocol similar to the one described here, providing sequential consistency.

For a representation of applications from engineering and symbolic computing, we studied parallel execution of the Stanford Parallel Applications for Shared Memory (Splash),[11] the OR-parallel Prolog system Muse, and a matrix multiplication program. All programs were originally written for UMA architectures (Sequent Symmetry or Encore Multimax computers) and use static or dynamic scheduler algorithms. They adapt well to a COMA without any changes. All programs take on the order of one CPU minute to run sequentially, without any simulations,

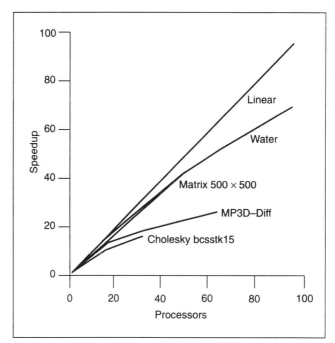

Figure 11. Speedup curves for some of the reported programs.

on a Sun Sparcstation. The speedups reported in Figure 11 and Table 2 are relative to the execution of a single DDM node with one processor, assuming a 100 percent hit rate in the attraction memory.

The Splash-Water program simulates the movements of water molecules. Its execution time is $O(m^2)$, where m is the number of molecules. Therefore, it is often simulated with a small working set. We used 192 molecules and a working set of 320 Kbytes. Each of the 96 processors in Figure 11 handles only two molecules. Most of the locality in the small working set can be exploited on the processor cache, and only about 44 percent of the transactions reaching the attraction memory will hit. A real-size working set would still have the same good locality and would benefit more from the large attraction memories to maintain the speedup. We tested this hypothesis with a single run with 384 molecules, as shown in Table 2.

The Splash-MP3D program is a wind tunnel simulator with which a good speedup is harder to achieve because of a high invalidation frequency resulting in a poor hit rate. The program is often run with the memory filled with data

Table 2. Statistics from DDM simulations. Hit rate statistics are for data only, except with Muse, where we used a unified I + D cache. The remote access rate is the percentage of the data accesses issued by a processor that create remote coherence traffic. An increased working set results in less load on the buses for Water and Cholesky.

	Water		MP3D	MP3D-Diff	Cholesky		Matrix	Muse
Input data	192 molecules	384 molecules	75,000 particles	75,000 particles	m14 (small)	m15 (large)	500×500	Pundit
Cold start included?	yes	yes	no	no	yes	yes	yes	no
DDM topology	2×8×4	2×8×4	2×8×2	2×8×2	2×8×2	2×8×2	8×4	4×4
Hit rate (data) percent								
D cache	99	99	86	92	96	89	92	98.5
Attraction memory	44	65	40	88	6	74	98	91
Remote access rate	0.6	0.4	8.4	1.0	3.8	2.8	0.16	0.20
Bus utilization percent								
Mbus	31	26	86	54	70	60	55	—
Lower DDM bus	39	30	88	24	80	66	—	—
Top DDM bus	25	20	66	13	70	49	4	—
Speedup per number of processors	52/64	53/64	6/32	19/32	10/32	17/32	29/32	—/16

structures representing particles, divided equally among the processors. The three-dimensional space is divided into space cells represented by data structures. MP3D runs in time phases and moves each particle once each phase. Moving a particle involves updating its state and also the state of the space cell where the molecule currently resides. All processors must write to all the space cells, resulting in a poor locality. In fact, 95 percent of the misses we found in DDM were due to this write-invalidate effect. We simulated 75,000 particles, a working set of 4 Mbytes.

MP3D-Diff is a rewritten version of the program that achieves a better hit rate. Particle distribution over processors is based on their current location in space. In other words, all particles in the same space cells are handled by the same processor. Updating of both particle state and space cell state is local to the processor. When a particle moves across a processor border, a new processor handles its data — the particle data diffuse to the new processor's attraction memory. The rewritten program has some 30 extra lines and requires a COMA to run well. In a COMA the particle data that occupy the major part of the physical memory are allowed to move freely among the attraction memories.

Splash-Cholesky factorizes a sparsely positive definite matrix. The matrix is divided into supernodes in a global task queue to be picked up by any worker — the scheduling is dynamic. We used the large input matrix bcsstk15 (m15), which occupies 800 Kbytes unfactored and 7.7 Mbytes factored. The nature of the Cholesky algorithm limits the available parallelism, which depends on the size of the input matrix. For comparison, Table 2 presents a run with the smaller matrix bcsstk14 (m14) of 420 Kbytes unfactored and 1.4 Mbytes factored.

The matrix multiplication program performs plain matrix multiplication on a 500×500 matrix using a blocked algorithm. The working set is about 3 Mbytes.

Muse is an OR-parallel Prolog system implemented in C at the Swedish Institute of Computer Science. Its input is the large natural language system Pundit from Unisys Paoli Research Center. An active working set of 2 Mbytes is touched during the execution. Muse distributes work dynamically and shows a good locality on a COMA. Because we ran Muse on an earlier version of the simulator, some of the statistics are not reported in Table 2.

Simulation shows that the COMA principle works well for programs originally written for UMA architectures and that the slow buses of our prototype can accommodate many processors. The overhead of the COMA explored in our hardware prototype is limited to 16 percent in the access time between the processor caches and the attraction memory. Memory overhead is 6 to 16 percent for 32 to 256 processors. ∎

Acknowledgments

The Swedish Institute of Computer Science is a nonprofit research foundation sponsored by the Swedish National Board for Technical Development (NUTEK), Swedish Telecom, Ericsson Group, ASEA Brown Boveri, IBM Sweden, Nobel Tech System AB, and the Swedish Defence Materiel Administration (FMV). Part of the work on DDM is being carried out within the ESPRIT project 2741 PEPMA.

We thank our many colleagues involved in or associated with the project, especially David H.D. Warren of the University of Bristol, who is a coinventor of DDM. Mikael Löfgren of the Swedish Institute of Computer Science wrote the DDM simulator, basing his work on "Abstract Execution," which was provided to us by James Larus of the University of Wisconsin.

References

1. P. Stenström, "A Survey of Cache Coherence for Multiprocessors," *Computer*, Vol. 23, No. 6, June 1990, pp. 12-24.

2. D. Lenoski et al., "The Directory-Based Cache Coherence Protocol for the DASH Multiprocessor," *Proc. 17th Ann. Int'l Symp. Computer Architecture*, IEEE-CS Press, Los Alamitos, Calif., Order No. 2047, 1990, pp. 148-159.

3. D.H.D. Warren and S. Haridi, "Data Diffusion Machine—A Scalable Shared Virtual Memory Multiprocessor," *Int'l Conf. Fifth Generation Computer Systems*, ICOT, Ohmsha, Ltd., Tokyo, 1988, pp. 943-952.

4. E. Hagersten, S. Haridi, and D.H.D. Warren, "The Cache-Coherence Protocol of the Data Diffusion Machine," in *Cache and Interconnect Architectures in Multiprocessors*, M. Dubois and S. Thakkar, eds., Kluwer Academic, Norwell, Mass., 1990, pp. 165-188.

5. A. Wilson, "Hierarchical Cache/Bus Architecture for Shared Memory Multiprocessor," Tech. Report ETR 86-006, Encore Computer Corp., Marlborough, Mass., 1986.

6. J.R. Goodman and P.J. Woest, "The Wisconsin Multicube: A New Large-Scale Cache-Coherent Multiprocessor," *Proc. 15th Ann. Int'l Symp. Computer Architecture*, IEEE-CS Press, Los Alamitos, Calif., Order No. 861, 1988, pp. 422-431.

7. J.-L. Baer and W.-H. Wang, "On the Inclusion Properties for Multi-Level Cache Hierarchies," *Proc. 15th Ann. Int'l Symp. Computer Architecture*, IEEE-CS Press, Los Alamitos, Calif., Order No. 861, 1988, pp. 73-80.

8. A. Landin, E. Hagersten, and S. Haridi. "Race-Free Interconnection Networks and Multiprocessor Consistency," *Proc. 18th Ann. Int'l Symp. Computer Architecture*, IEEE-CS Press, Los Alamitos, Calif., Order No. 2146, 1991, pp. 106-115.

9. C.E. Leiserson, "Fat Trees: Universal Networks for Hardware-Efficient Supercomputing," *IEEE Trans. Computers*, Vol. 34, No. 10, Oct. 1985, pp. 892-901.

10. L. Barroso and M. Dubois, "Cache Coherence on a Slotted Ring," *Proc. Int'l Conf. Parallel Processing*, IEEE-CS Press, Los Alamitos, Calif., Order No. 2355, 1991, pp. 230-237.

11. J.S. Singh, W.-D. Weber, and A. Gupta, *Splash: Stanford Parallel Applications for Shared Memory*, Tech. Report, CSL-TR-91-469, Computer Systems Laboratory, Stanford Univ., Stanford, Calif., 1991.

Erik Hagersten has led the Data Diffusion Machine Project at the Swedish Institute of Computer Science since 1988. He is a coinventor of the Data Diffusion Machine. His research interests include computer architectures, parallel processing, and simulation methods. From 1982 to 1988, he worked at the Ericsson Computer Science Lab on new architectures and at Ericsson Telecom on high-performance fault-tolerant processors. From 1984 to 1985, he was a visiting research engineer in the Dataflow Group at MIT.

Hagersten received his MS in electrical engineering in 1982 from the Royal Institute of Technology, Stockholm, where he is currently finishing off his PhD degree.

Anders Landin is a research staff member at the Swedish Institute of Computer Science, where he has been working with the DDM project since 1989. His research interests include computer architecture, parallel processing, memory systems for shared-memory multiprocessors, and VLSI systems and simulation.

Landin received his MS in computer science and engineering from Lund University, Sweden, in 1989. He is a PhD student at the Royal Institute of Technology, Stockholm.

Seif Haridi is leader of the Logic Programming and Parallel Systems Lab at the Swedish Institute of Computer Science. He is also an adjunct professor at the Royal Institute of Technology, Stockholm. His research interests include combining parallel logic programming, concurrent objects, and constraints, and multiprocessor architectures suitable for such programming paradigms. He is a coinventor of DDM. Before joining the Swedish Institute of Computer Science, he was at the IBM T.J. Watson Research Center.

Haridi received his BS from Cairo University and his PhD from the Royal Institute of Technology.

Readers can contact the authors at the Swedish Institute of Computer Science, Box 1263, 164 28 Kista, Sweden; e-mail {hag,landin,seif}@sics.se.

Comparative Performance Evaluation of Cache-Coherent NUMA and COMA Architectures

Per Stenström†, Truman Joe, and Anoop Gupta

Computer Systems Laboratory
Stanford University, CA 94305

Abstract

Two interesting variations of large-scale shared-memory machines that have recently emerged are *cache-coherent non-uniform-memory-access* machines (CC-NUMA) and *cache-only memory architectures* (COMA). They both have distributed main memory and use directory-based cache coherence. Unlike CC-NUMA, however, COMA machines automatically migrate and replicate data at the main-memory level in cache-line sized chunks. This paper compares the performance of these two classes of machines. We first present a qualitative model that shows that the relative performance is primarily determined by two factors: the relative magnitude of capacity misses versus coherence misses, and the granularity of data partitions in the application. We then present quantitative results using simulation studies for eight parallel applications (including all six applications from the SPLASH benchmark suite). We show that COMA's potential for performance improvement is limited to applications where data accesses by different processors are finely interleaved in memory space and, in addition, where capacity misses dominate over coherence misses. In other situations, for example where coherence misses dominate, COMA can actually perform worse than CC-NUMA due to increased miss latencies caused by its hierarchical directories. Finally, we propose a new architectural alternative, called COMA-F, that combines the advantages of both CC-NUMA and COMA.

1 Introduction

Large-scale multiprocessors with a single address-space and coherent caches offer a flexible and powerful computing environment. The single address space and coherent caches together ease the problem of data partitioning and dynamic load balancing. They also provide better support for parallelizing compilers, standard operating systems, and multiprogramming, thus enabling more flexible and effective use of the

† Per Stenström's address is Department of Computer Engineering, Lund University, P.O. Box 118, S-221 00 LUND, Sweden.

machine. Currently, many research groups are pursuing the design and construction of such multiprocessors [12, 1, 10]. As research has progressed in this area, two interesting variants have emerged, namely CC-NUMA (cache-coherent non-uniform memory access machines) and COMA (cache-only memory architectures). Examples of the CC-NUMA machines are the Stanford DASH multiprocessor [12] and the MIT Alewife machine [1], while examples of COMA machines are the Swedish Institute of Computer Science's Data Diffusion Machine (DDM) [10] and Kendall Square Research's KSR1 machine [4].

Common to both CC-NUMA and COMA machines are the features of distributed main memory, scalable interconnection network, and directory-based cache coherence. Distributed main memory and scalable interconnection networks are essential in providing the required scalable memory bandwidth, while directory-based schemes provide cache coherence without requiring broadcast and consuming only a small fraction of the system bandwidth. In contrast to CC-NUMA machines, however, in COMA the per-node main memory is converted into an enormous secondary/tertiary cache (called *attraction memory* (AM) by the DDM group) by adding tags to cache-line sized chunks in main memory. A consequence is that the location of a data item in the machine is totally decoupled from its physical address, and the data item is automatically migrated or replicated in main memory depending on the memory reference pattern.

The main advantage of the COMA machines is that they can reduce the average cache miss latency, since data are dynamically migrated and replicated at the main-memory level. However, there are also several disadvantages. First, allowing migration of data at the memory level requires a mechanism to locate the data on a miss. To avoid broadcasting such requests, current machines use a hierarchical directory structure, which increases the miss latency for global requests. Second, the coherence protocol is more complex because it needs to ensure that the last copy of a data item is not replaced in the attraction memory (main memory). Also, as compared to CC-NUMA, there is additional complexity in the design of the main-memory subsystem and in the interface to the disk subsystem.

Even though CC-NUMA and COMA machines are being built, so far no studies have been published that evaluate the performance benefits of one machine model over the other. Such a study is the focus of this paper. We note that the paper focuses on the relative performance of the two machines, and

"Comparative Performance Evaluation of Cache-Coherent NUMA and COMA Architectures," P. Stenström, T. Joe, and A. Gupta, *Proc. 19th Ann. Int'l Symp. Computer Architecture*, ACM, New York, 1992, pp. 80–91. Copyright © 1992, Association for Computing Machinery, Inc. Reprinted with permission.

not on the hardware complexity. We do so because without a good understanding of the performance benefits, it is difficult to argue about what hardware complexity is justified.

The organization of the rest of the paper is as follows. In the next section, we begin with detailed descriptions of CC-NUMA and COMA machines. Then in Section 3, we present a qualitative model that helps predict the relative performance of applications on CC-NUMA and COMA machines. Section 4 presents the architectural assumptions and our simulation environment. It also presents the eight benchmark applications used in our study, which include all six applications from the SPLASH benchmark suite [14]. The performance results are presented in Section 5. We show that COMA's potential for performance improvement is limited to applications where data accesses by different processors are interleaved at a fine spatial granularity and, in addition, where capacity misses dominate over coherence misses. We also show that for applications which access data at a coarse granularity, CC-NUMA can perform nearly as well as a COMA by exploiting page-level placement or migration. Furthermore, when coherence misses dominate, CC-NUMA often performs better than COMA. This is due to the extra latency introduced by the hierarchical directory structure in COMA. In Section 6, we present a new architectural alternative, called COMA-F (for COMA-FLAT), that is shown to perform better than both regular CC-NUMA and COMA. We finally conclude in Section 7.

2 CC-NUMA and COMA Machines

In this section we briefly present the organization of CC-NUMA and COMA machines based on the Stanford DASH multiprocessor [12] and the Swedish Institute of Computer Science's Data Diffusion Machine (DDM) [10]. We discuss the basic architecture and the coherence protocols, directory structure and interconnection network requirements, and finally the software model presented by the architectures.

2.1 CC-NUMA Architecture

A CC-NUMA machine consists of a number of processing nodes connected through a high-bandwidth low-latency interconnection network. Each processing node consists of a high-performance processor, the associated cache, and a portion of the global shared memory. Cache coherence is maintained by a directory-based, write-invalidate cache coherence protocol. To keep all caches consistent, each processing node has a directory memory corresponding to its portion of the shared physical memory. For each memory line (aligned memory block that has the same size as a cache line), the directory memory stores identities of remote nodes caching that line. Thus, using the directory, it is possible for a node writing a location to send point-to-point messages to invalidate remote copies of the corresponding cache line. Another important attribute of the directory-based protocol is that it does not depend on any specific interconnection network topology. Therefore, any scalable network, such as a mesh, a hypercube, or a multi-stage network, can be used to connect the processing nodes.

Handling a cache miss in a CC-NUMA machine requires knowledge about the *home node* for the corresponding physical address. The home node is the processing node from whose main memory the data is allocated. (It is usually determined by the high-order bits of the physical address.) If the local node and the home node are the same, a cache miss can be serviced by main memory in the local node. Otherwise, the miss is forwarded to the *remote* home node. If the home node has a clean copy, it returns the block to the requesting cache. (We call this a 2-hop miss since it requires two network traversals — one from the requesting node to the home node, and the other back.) Otherwise, the read request is forwarded to the node that has the dirty copy. This node returns the block to the requesting node and also writes back the block to the home node. (We call this a 3-hop miss, as it takes three network traversals before the data is returned to the requesting node.)

If the block is not exclusively owned by a processor that issues a write request, a read-exclusive request is sent to the home node. The home node returns ownership and multicasts invalidation requests to any other nodes that have a copy of the block. Acknowledgments are returned directly to the issuing node so as to indicate when the write operation has completed. A write request to a dirty block is forwarded (the same way as a read request) to the node containing the dirty copy, which then returns the data.

The Stanford DASH multiprocessor [12] is an example of a CC-NUMA machine. The prototype is to consist of 16 processing nodes, each with 4 processors, for a total of 64 processors. Each processor has a 64 Kbytes first-level and a 256 Kbytes second-level cache. The interconnection network is a wormhole routed 2-D mesh network. The memory access latencies for a cache hit, local memory access, 2-hop, and 3-hop read misses are approximately 1, 30, 100, and 135 processor clocks respectively.

The CC-NUMA software model allows processes to be attached to specific processors and for data to be allocated from any specific node's main memory. However, the granularity at which data can be moved between different node's main memories (transparently to the application) is page sized chunks. We note that the allocation and movement of data between nodes may be done explicitly via code written by the application programmer, or automatically by the operating system [3]. This is in contrast to the COMA machines where such migration and replication happens automatically at the granularity of cache blocks.

2.2 COMA Architecture

Like CC-NUMA, a COMA machine consists of a number of processing nodes connected by an interconnection network. Each processing node has a high-performance processor, a cache, and a portion of the global shared memory. The difference, however, is that the memory associated with each node is augmented to act as a large cache, denoted *attraction memory* (AM) using DDM terminology [10]. Consistency among cache blocks in the AMs is maintained using a write-invalidate protocol. The AMs allow transparent migration and replication of data items to nodes where they are referenced.

In a COMA machine, the AMs constitute the only memory in the system (other than the disk subsystem). A consequence is that the location of a memory block is totally decoupled from its physical address. This creates several problems. First, when a reference misses in the local AM, a mechanism is needed to trace a copy of that block in some other node's AM. Unlike CC-NUMA, there is no notion of a home node for a block. Second, some mechanism is needed to ensure that the last copy of a block (possibly the only valid copy) is not purged.

To address the above problems and to maintain cache and memory consistency, COMA machines use a *hierarchical directory scheme* and a corresponding hierarchical interconnection network (at least logically so[1]). Each directory maintains state information about all blocks stored in the subsystem below. The state of a block is either exclusive in exactly one node or shared in several nodes. Note that directories only contain state information to reduce memory overhead; data are not stored.

Upon a read miss, a read request locates the closest node that has a copy of that block by propagating up the hierarchy until a copy in state shared or exclusive is found. At that point, it propagates down the hierarchy to a node that has the copy. The node returns the block along the same path as the request. (A directory read-modify-write needs to be done at each intermediate directory along the path, both in the forward and return directions.) Because of the hierarchical directory structure, COMA machines can exploit *combining* [7]; if a directory receives a read request to a block that is already being fetched, it does not have to send the new request up the hierarchy. When the reply comes back, both requesters are supplied the data.

A write request to an unowned block propagates up the hierarchy until a directory indicates that the copy is exclusive. This directory, the root directory, multicasts invalidation requests to all subsystems having a copy of the block and returns an acknowledgement to the issuing processor.

As stated earlier, decoupling the home location of a block from its address raises the issue of replacement in the AMs. A shared block (i.e., one with multiple copies) that is being replaced is not so difficult to handle. The system simply has to realize that there exist other copies by going up the hierarchy. Handling an exclusive block (the only copy of a block, whether in clean or dirty state) is, however, more complex since it must be transferred to another attraction memory. This is done by letting it propagate up in the hierarchy until a directory finds an empty or a shared block in its subsystem that can host the block.

Examples of COMA machines include the Swedish Institute of Computer Science's DDM machine [10] and Kendall Square Research's KSR1 machine [4]. The processing nodes in DDM are also clusters with multiple processors, as in DASH. However, the interconnect is a hierarchy of buses, in contrast to the wormhole-routed grid in DASH. In KSR1, each processing node consists of only a single processor. The interconnect consists of a hierarchy of slotted ring networks.

In summary, by allowing individual memory blocks to be migrated and replicated in attraction memories, COMA machines have the potential of reducing the number of cache misses that need to be serviced remotely. However, because of the hierarchy in COMA, latency for remote misses is usually higher (except when combining is successful); this may offset the advantages of the higher hit rates. We study these tradeoffs qualitatively in the next section.

---

[1]Wallach and Dally are investigating a COMA implementation based on a hierarchy embedded in a 3-dimensional mesh network [16].

3 Qualitative Comparison

In this section, we qualitatively evaluate the advantages and disadvantages of the CC-NUMA and COMA models. In particular, we focus on application data access patterns that are expected to cause one model to perform better than the other. We show that the critical parameters are the relative magnitudes of different miss types in the cache, and the spatial granularity of access to shared data. We begin with a discussion of the types of misses observed in shared-memory parallel programs, and discuss the expected miss latencies for CC-NUMA and COMA machines.

3.1 Miss Types and Expected Latencies

Since both CC-NUMA and COMA have private coherent caches, presumably of the same size, the differences in performance stem primarily because of differences in the miss latencies. In shared-memory multiprocessors that use a write-invalidate cache coherence protocol, cache misses may be classified into four types: cold misses, capacity misses, conflict misses, and coherence misses.

A *cold miss* is the result of a block being accessed by the processor for the first time. A *capacity miss* is a miss due to the finite size of the processor cache and a *conflict miss* is due to the limited associativity of the cache. For our discussion below, we do not distinguish between conflict and capacity misses since CC-NUMA and COMA respond to them in the same way. We collectively refer to them as capacity misses. A *coherence miss* (or an invalidation miss) is a miss to a block that has been referenced before, but has been written by another processor since the last time it was referenced by this processor. Coherence misses include both *false sharing misses* as well as *true sharing misses* [15]. False sharing misses result from write references to data that are not shared but happen to reside in the same cache line. True sharing misses are coherence misses that would still exist even if the block size were one access unit. They represent true communication between the multiple processes in the application.

We now investigate how the two models respond to cache misses of different types. Beginning with cold misses, we expect the average miss penalty to be higher for COMA, assuming that data is distributed among the main memory modules in the same way. The reason is simply that cold misses that are not serviced locally have to traverse the directory and network hierarchy in COMA. The only reason for a shorter latency for COMA would be if combining worked particularly well for an application.

For coherence misses, we again expect COMA to have higher miss latencies as compared to CC-NUMA. The reason is that the data is guaranteed not to be in the local attraction memory for COMA, and therefore it will need to traverse the directory hierarchy.[2] In contrast to CC-NUMA, the latency for COMA can, of course, be shortened if combining is successful, or if the communication is localized in the hierarchy.

Finally, for capacity misses, we expect to see shorter miss latencies for COMA. Most such misses are expected to hit in the local attraction memory since it is extremely large and

---

[2]We assume one processor per node. If several processors share the same AM (or local memory), a coherence miss can sometimes be serviced locally.

organized as a cache. In contrast, in CC-NUMA, unless data referenced by a processor are carefully allocated to local main memory, there is a high likelihood that a capacity miss will have to be serviced by a remote node.

In summary, since there are some kinds of misses that are serviced with lower latency by COMA and others that are serviced with lower latency by CC-NUMA, the relative performance of an application on COMA or CC-NUMA will depend on what kinds of misses dominate.

3.2 Application Performance

In this subsection, we classify applications based on their data access patterns, and the resulting cache miss behavior, to evaluate the relative advantages and disadvantages of COMA and CC-NUMA. A summary of this classification is presented in Figure 1. As illustrations, we use many applications that we evaluate experimentally in Section 5.

On the left of the tree in Figure 1, we group all applications that exhibit low cache miss-rates. Linear algebra applications that can be blocked, for example, fall into this category [11]. Other applications where computation grows at a much faster rate than the data set size, e.g., the $O(N^2)$ algorithm used to compute interaction between molecules in the Water application [14], often also fall into this category. In such cases, since the data sets are quite small, capacity misses are few and the miss penalty has only a small impact on performance. Overall, for these applications that exhibit a low miss rate, CC-NUMA and COMA should perform about the same.

Looking at the right portion of the tree, for applications that exhibit moderate to high miss rates, we differentiate between applications where coherence misses dominate and those where capacity misses dominate. Focusing first on the former, we note that this class of applications is not that unusual. High coherence misses can arise because an application programmer (or compiler) may not have done a very good job of scheduling tasks or partitioning data, or because the cache line size is too large causing false sharing, or because solving the problem actually requires such communication to happen. Usually, all three factors are involved to varying degrees. In all of these cases, CC-NUMA is expected to do better than COMA because the remote misses take a shorter time to service. As we will show in Section 5, even when very small processor caches are used (thus increasing the magnitude of capacity misses), at least half of the applications in our study fall into this category.

The situation where COMA has a potential performance advantage is when the majority of cache misses are capacity misses. Almost all such misses get serviced by the local attraction memory in COMA, in contrast to CC-NUMA where they may have to go to a remote node. CC-NUMA can deliver good performance only if a majority of the capacity misses are serviced by local main memory.

We believe that it is possible for CC-NUMA machines to get high hit rates in local memory for many applications that access data in a "coarse-grained" manner. By coarse grained, we mean applications where large chunks of data (greater than page size) are primarily accessed by one process in the program for significant periods of time. For example, many scientific applications where large data arrays are statically partitioned among the processes fall into this class. A specific example is the Cholesky sparse factorization algorithm that we evaluate later in the paper. In the Cholesky application, contiguous columns with similar non-zero structure (called supernodes) are assigned to various processors. If the placement is done right for such applications, the local memory hit rates can be very high.

Even if the locus of accesses to these large data chunks changes from one process to another over time, automatic replication and migration algorithms implemented in the operating system (possibly with hardware support) can ensure high hit rates in local memory for CC-NUMA. In fact, we believe that an interesting way to think of a CC-NUMA machine is as a COMA machine where the line size for the main-memory cache is the page size, which is not unreasonable since main memory is very large, and where this main-memory cache is managed in software. The latter is also not an unreasonable policy decision because the very-large line size helps hide the overheads.

In applications where many small objects that are collocated on a page are accessed in an interleaved manner by processes, page-level placement/migration obviously can not ensure high local hit-rates. An example is the Barnes-Hut application for simulating the interaction of N-body problems (discussed in Section 5). In this application multiple bodies that are accessed by several processors reside on a single page and, as a result, page placement does not help CC-NUMA.

In summary, we expect the relative performance of CC-NUMA and COMA to be similar if the misses are few. When the miss rate is high, we expect CC-NUMA to perform better than COMA if coherence misses dominate; CC-NUMA to perform similar to COMA if the capacity misses dominate but the data usage is coarse grained; and finally, COMA to perform better than CC-NUMA if capacity misses dominate and data usage is fine grained.

4 Experimental Methodology

This section presents the simulation environment, the architectural models, and the benchmark applications we use to make a quantitative comparison between CC-NUMA and COMA.

4.1 Simulation Environment

We use a simulated multiprocessor environment to study the behavior of applications under CC-NUMA and COMA. The simulation environment consists of two parts: (i) a functional simulator that executes the parallel applications and (ii) the two architectural simulators.

The functional simulator is based on Tango [5]. The Tango system takes a parallel application program and interleaves the execution of its processes on a uniprocessor to simulate a multiprocessor. This is achieved by associating a virtual timer with each process of the application and by always running the process with the lowest virtual time first. By letting the architectural simulator update the virtual timers according to the access time of each memory reference, a correct interleaving of all memory references is maintained. The architectural simulator takes care of references to shared data; instruction fetches and private data references are assumed to always hit in the processor cache.

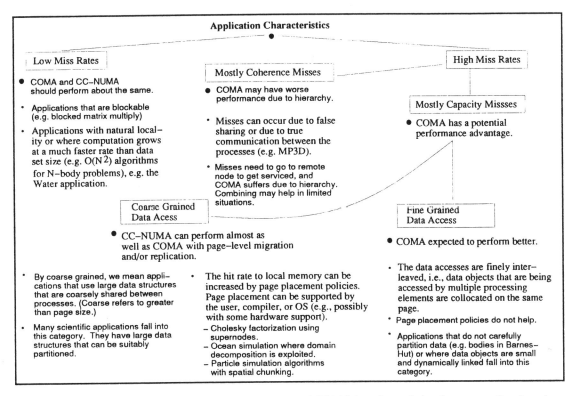

Application Characteristics

Low Miss Rates

- COMA and CC–NUMA should perform about the same.
- Applications that are blockable (e.g. blocked matrix multiply)
- Applications with natural locality or where computation grows at a much faster rate than data set size (e.g. $O(N^2)$ algorithms for N–body problems), e.g. the Water application.

Mostly Coherence Misses

- COMA may have worse performance due to hierarchy.
- Misses can occur due to false sharing or due to true communication between the processes (e.g. MP3D).
- Misses need to go to remote node to get serviced, and COMA suffers due to hierarchy. Combining may help in limited situations.

High Miss Rates

Mostly Capacity Misses

- COMA has a potential performance advantage.

Coarse Grained Data Acess

- CC–NUMA can perform almost as well as COMA with page–level migration and/or replication.

- By coarse grained, we mean applications that use large data structures that are coarsely shared between processes. (Coarse refers to greater than page size.)
- Many scientific applications fall into this category. They have large data structures that can be suitably partitioned.

- The hit rate to local memory can be increased by page placement policies. Page placement can be supported by the user, compiler, or OS (e.g., possibly with some hardware support).
  - Cholesky factorization using supernodes.
  - Ocean simulation where domain decomposition is exploited.
  - Particle simulation algorithms with spatial chunking.

Fine Grained Data Access

- COMA expected to perform better.

- The data accesses are finely interleaved, i.e., data objects that are being accessed by multiple processing elements are collocated on the same page.
- Page placement policies do not help.
- Applications that do not carefully partition data (e.g. bodies in Barnes–Hut) or where data objects are small and dynamically linked fall into this category.

Figure 1: Prediction of relative performance between CC-NUMA and COMA based on relative frequency of cache miss types and application data access pattern.

4.2 Architecture Simulators

Both architectures consist of a number of processing nodes connected via low-latency networks. In our simulations we assume a 16 processor configuration, with one processor per processing node. (Figure 2(a) shows the organization of the processing node.) We assume a cache line size of 16 bytes. In the default configurations, we use a processor cache size of 4 Kbytes, and in the case of COMA, infinite attraction memories. For COMA we assume a branching factor of 4, implying a two-level hierarchy.

The reasons for choosing this rather small default processor cache size are several. First, since the simulations are quite slow, the data sets used by our applications are smaller than what we may use on a real machine. As a result, if we were to use full-size caches (say 256 Kbytes), then for some of the applications all of the data would fit into the caches and we would not get any capacity misses. This would take away all of the advantages of the COMA model, and the results would obviously not be interesting. Second, by using very small cache sizes, we favor the COMA model, and our goal is to see whether there are situations where CC-NUMA can still do better. Third, 4 Kbytes is only the default, and we also present results for larger cache sizes. As for use of infinite attraction memories, our choice was motivated by the observation that the capacity miss-rates are expected to be extremely small for the attraction memories. As a result, the complexity of modeling finite sized attraction memories did not seem justified.

We now focus on the latency of cache misses in CC-NUMA and COMA. To do this in a consistent manner, we have defined a common set of primitive operations that are used to

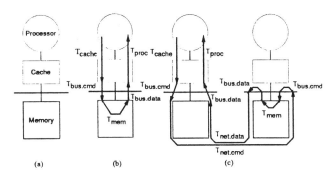

Figure 2: Node organization (a) and latency calculations for local and remote misses for CC-NUMA (b) and (c).

construct protocol transactions for both architectures. We can then choose latency values for these operations and use them to evaluate the latency of memory operations. In the following subsections, we describe reference latencies for the two architectures in terms of these primitive operations. Table 1, located at the end of this section, summarizes these primitive operations and lists the default latency numbers, assuming a processor clock rate of 100 MHz.

4.2.1 CC-NUMA Latencies

For CC-NUMA, a load request that hits in the cache incurs a latency of a cache access, T_{cache}. For misses, the processor is stalled for the full service latency of the load request.

In Figure 2(b) we depict the memory latency for a load

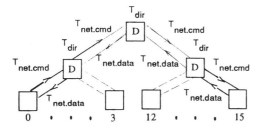

Figure 3: Latency model for global read requests in COMA.

request that hits in the local memory. The load first checks the cache (T_{cache}), it then arbitrates for the local bus and places the request onto the bus ($T_{bus.cmd}$), it then accesses memory (T_{mem}), the data is placed on the local bus ($T_{bus.data}$), and finally the cache loads data from the bus and restarts the processor (T_{proc}).[3] Similarly, in Figure 2(c) we show the latency for a load request to a shared block whose home is not the local node. $T_{net.cmd}$ is the network latency to send the load request to the home node, and $T_{net.data}$ is the network latency for the return data packet. If the block is dirty in a node other than the home node, an additional latency that consists of another network traversal and node memory access is needed.

Stores are handled according to the weakly ordered consistency model [6] by a write buffer which sits between the processor and the cache. Hence, the processor is not stalled on a store request. However, on a synchronization request, the processor is stalled until all pending invalidation acknowledgements have been received.

The default network latency numbers assume a 4×4 wormhole-routed synchronous mesh clocked at 100 MHz with 16-bit wide links.

4.2.2 COMA Latencies

For COMA, the processor cache hit latency is the same as CC-NUMA. The latency for a hit in the attraction memory is the same as a request serviced by local memory in CC-NUMA. For requests that need to go to a remote processing node, we illustrate the latency using a simple example. Figure 3 shows a request made by processor 0 and serviced by processor 15. The latency consists of a check in processor cache (T_{cache}); request issue on local bus ($T_{bus.cmd}$); check in local attraction memory (T_{mem}); traversal up through the hierarchy ($T_{net.cmd} + T_{dir}$ at each level); traversal down the hierarchy ($T_{net.cmd} + T_{dir}$ at each level); lookup in the memory of processor 15 ($T_{bus.cmd} + T_{mem} + T_{bus.data}$); traversal back up the hierarchy ($T_{net.data} + T_{dir}$ at each level); traversal down to the requesting node ($T_{net.data} + T_{dir}$ at each level); and finally back to the processor ($T_{bus.data} + T_{proc}$). Latency for other requests can be similarly derived. The protocol follows that used by DDM [10], assuming infinite write buffers and a weakly ordered consistency model. The effects of request combining in the hierarchy are also modeled in our simulator. However, we do not model contention at any of the buses or directories.

A hierarchical network with point-to-point links with a width of 32-bits and synchronous data transfers is assumed. Since a hierarchical layout makes it difficult to achieve high clock

---

[3]Note: The latency for $T_{bus.data}$ is only one bus cycle (2 pclocks) in Figure 2(b) because the return of data overlaps with the latency for processor restart T_{proc}.

Table 1: Default latencies for primitive operations in processor clock cycles (1 pclock $\approx$ 10 ns).

Primitive Operation	Parameter	Latency (pclocks)
Cache Access Time	T_{cache}	1
Cache Fill and Restart	T_{proc}	6
Local Bus Request Time	$T_{bus.cmd}$	4
Local Bus Reply Time	$T_{bus.data}$	2
Com. Net. Latency (CC-NUMA)	$T_{net.cmd}$	12
Data Net. Latency (CC-NUMA)	$T_{net.data}$	20
Com. Net. Latency (COMA)	$T_{net.cmd}$	4
Data Net. Latency (COMA)	$T_{net.data}$	12
Memory and AM	T_{mem}	20
Directory Update (rd-mod-wr)	T_{dir}	20

Table 2: Default latencies for various read operations.

Read Operation	Latency (pclocks)
Cache Hit	1
Fill from Local Node	33
2-hop Remote Fill (CC-NUMA)	71
3-hop Remote Fill (CC-NUMA)	109
1-level Remote Fill (COMA)	131
2-level Remote Fill (COMA)	243

rates (unlike a mesh), we assume that the links are clocked at 50 MHz yielding the latency numbers $T_{net.cmd} = 4$ and $T_{net.data} = 12$ pclocks, respectively.

In Table 2, we show the default latencies for read requests satisfied at various levels in the memory hierarchy, based on the default latencies for the primitive operations from Table 1. Note that these are just default latencies. We will present results for other architectural assumptions as well in Section 5.6.

4.3 Benchmark Programs

To understand the relative performance benefits of CC-NUMA and COMA we use a variety of scientific and engineering applications, including all six SPLASH benchmarks [14]. A summary of the eight applications that we use is given in Table 3.

The data sets used for our eight applications are as follows. MP3D was run with 10K particles for 10 time steps. PTHOR was run with the RISC circuit for 5000 time steps with incremental deadlock detection turned on. LocusRoute used the circuit Primary1.grin which has 1266 wires and a 481x18 cost array. Water was run with 288 molecules for 4 time steps. Cholesky was run using the matrix bcsstk14 from the Boeing-Harwell benchmark matrices, and it has 1806 equations and 61648 non-zeroes. LU was run on a 200×200 random matrix. Barnes-Hut [13] was run using 2048 bodies in a plummer distribution simulated for 10 time steps with a tolerance of 1.0. Finally, Ocean was run with a 98×98 grid with a convergence tolerance of 10^{-7} and w set to 1.15. Statistics acquisition is

Table 3: Benchmark programs.

Benchmark	Description
MP3D	Particle-based wind tunnel simulation
PTHOR	Distributed-time logic simulation
LocusRoute	VLSI standard cell router
Water	Molecular dynamics code: Water
Cholesky	Cholesky factorization of sparse matrix
LU	LU decomposition of dense matrix
Barnes-Hut	N-body problem solver O(NlogN)
Ocean	Ocean basin simulation

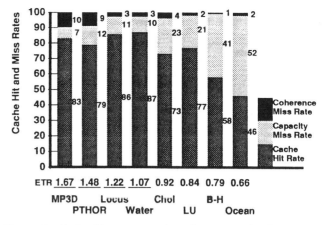

Figure 4: Cache hit-rate, capacity miss-rate, and coherence miss-rate assuming 4 Kbyte caches. ETR is the execution time for COMA divided by the execution time for CC-NUMA.

started when the parallel section of the application is entered (see SPLASH report [14]), because the initialization part is expected to be negligible for full-scale runs.

5 Quantitative Evaluation

In this section, we provide experimental results that show the advantages and disadvantages of CC-NUMA and COMA. We begin by investigating how the relative frequency of capacity and coherence misses impacts the relative performance of CC-NUMA and COMA. Then in Sections 5.2, 5.3, and 5.4, we explore how page migration and initial page placement can help CC-NUMA reduce the penalty of capacity misses, thus improving its performance. Finally, in Sections 5.5 and 5.6, we study how our results are affected by variations in architectural parameters.

5.1 Performance of CC-NUMA and COMA

Since performance of CC-NUMA and COMA machines is closely tied to the cache hit-rate achieved and the types of cache misses incurred, in Figure 4 we present relevant statistics. For each application, the bottom dark-gray section gives the cache hit-rate, the middle light-gray section gives the capacity miss-rate, and the top black section gives the coherence miss-rate. We do not show cold miss-rates separately because they are very small (0.9% for Cholesky, 0.26% for Locus-Route, and less than 0.1% for the remaining applications), and in Figure 4 they are lumped with capacity misses.

As can be seen from Figure 4, there is a large variation in the relative magnitude of capacity and coherence misses across the applications; for example, while coherence misses dominate in MP3D, capacity misses dominate in Ocean. To see how this impacts the relative performance of CC-NUMA and COMA, we also measured the *node hit-rate* for the applications, that is, the fraction of references that get serviced by the cache or the local memory. Although we do not present these data here directly, for COMA machines, the node hit-rate is essentially the cache hit-rate plus the capacity miss-rate, since all capacity misses are serviced by the local attraction memory. In contrast, for CC-NUMA, the node hit-rate is highly dependent on the way in which the data are distributed among the processing nodes. If we assume that the data pages are distributed randomly or in a round-robin manner (as default in this paper, we use the round-robin strategy), then node hit-rate

for CC-NUMA is expected to be the cache hit-rate plus the capacity miss-rate divided by the number of processors. Given that the number of processors is quite large, 16 in our case, the node hit-rate for CC-NUMA is approximately the same as the cache hit-rate. Thus the difference in the node hit-rate between COMA and CC-NUMA is roughly the middle light-gray section in Figure 4.

The question now becomes how the differences in node hit-rate and node miss penalty for CC-NUMA and COMA impact their relative performance. We use *execution time ratio* (ETR) of COMA to CC-NUMA as a measure of the relative performance. Thus ETR > 1 implies that CC-NUMA is performing better than COMA. In Figure 4, we show the ETR beneath the hit/miss rate bar for each application. As expected, for applications where the coherence miss-rate is a significant part of the overall miss-rate (MP3D, PTHOR, LocusRoute, and Water), COMA exhibits worse performance than CC-NUMA due to the higher node miss penalty incurred by COMA. For the other four applications (Cholesky, LU, Barnes-Hut, and Ocean), the capacity miss-rate dominates the overall miss-rate, and as expected, COMA shows better performance. We also observe that the overall swing in the relative performance is quite large; while CC-NUMA does 67% better than COMA for MP3D, COMA does 52% better than CC-NUMA for Ocean.

To study whether combining is playing an important role in the higher performance of COMA, we measured the percentage of node misses that get combined in the hierarchical directory structure. Combining turned out to be significant in one case only — in LU, 47% of all remote requests get combined. This is because the pivot column is read by all processors as soon as all modifications to it have been completed. Except for the LU application, combining was of little help in reducing the node miss penalty as incurred by the hierarchical directory structure in COMA — in Barnes-Hut, 6% of remote requests get combined, and for all remaining applications, less than 1% of remote requests get combined.

To summarize, we have shown that the relative frequency of capacity and coherence misses has a first order effect on the relative performance of CC-NUMA and COMA. We observed that four of the eight applications perform worse on COMA because of the coherence miss penalty associated with the hierarchical network. We also observed that request combining

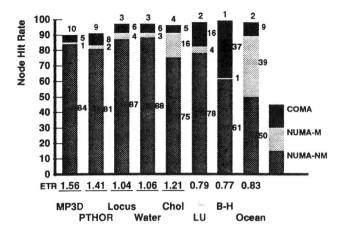

Figure 5: Node hit-rate for CC-NUMA with no migration (NUMA-NM), CC-NUMA with migration (NUMA-M), and COMA assuming 4 Kbytes pages. ETR is the execution time for COMA divided by the execution for NUMA-M.

Table 4: Node hit-rate and execution time for NUMA-M (with different page sizes) relative to NUMA-NM (with 4Kbyte pages).

Page Size	LU			Ocean		
	Node HR	Rel. Exec.	Mig. Count	Node HR	Rel. Exec.	Mig. Count
NUMA-NM	78	1.00	–	50	1.00	–
NUMA-M 4K	82	1.06	2.7K	89	0.79	6.6K
NUMA-M 2K	86	1.02	4.6K	93	0.68	6.6K
NUMA-M 1K	89	0.97	3.8K	96	0.64	4.7K
NUMA-M .5K	90	0.93	4.0K	96	0.66	7.8K
COMA	98	0.84	–	98	0.66	–

has only a small impact in hiding the higher network latency incurred by the hierarchy in COMA.

5.2 CC-NUMA: Page Migration

As stated in Section 3, if large chunks of data (greater than page size) are primarily accessed by one process in the program for significant periods of time, intelligent page migration and replication algorithms can help CC-NUMA reduce the penalty for capacity misses. In this subsection, we focus on the performance gains for CC-NUMA if the operating systems performed page migration. We consider a fairly aggressive competitive page migration algorithm proposed by Black et al. [2]. Note, our purpose here is to explore the performance potential of page migration rather than advocating the use of this particular page migration algorithm.

Our migration algorithm associates N counters with each page, given N processing nodes. A remote access to a page increments the corresponding counter and decrements some other randomly chosen counter. When a counter exceeds twice the migration cost (measured in units of remote access cost), the page is migrated to the corresponding node. We have estimated the software overhead of migration by examining the operating system code associated with page transfers. It includes invocation of the page management software (800 pclocks); invalidation of all TLB entries for the page ($300+40n$ pclocks, assuming n processors have TLB entries); and finally, migration of the page ($T_{mem}P/B$, where P is the page size and $B = 16$ is the block size). We also assume that the page is blocked from being accessed while it is being moved.

To see how well page migration manages to improve the node hit-rate for CC-NUMA, in Figure 5 we show the node hit-rate for CC-NUMA with no page migration (NUMA-NM), CC-NUMA with page migration (NUMA-M), and COMA assuming 4 Kbyte pages. The number on top of each bar represents the coherence miss-rate. We see that the node hit-rate improves significantly for Cholesky and Ocean for NUMA-M, since data usage in both applications is coarse grained. The Cholesky application works with groups of contiguous columns, called supernodes, that are often larger than a page. The Ocean ap-

plication works with arrays of data objects that are coarsely partitioned and assigned to each processor in chunks which are typically larger than 4 Kbytes.

Finally, to show the overall benefits of page migration, we present the execution time ratio (ETR) of COMA to NUMA-M beneath each bar in Figure 5. The four applications where previously NUMA-NM did better than COMA (MP3D, PTHOR, LocusRoute, and Water), NUMA-M continues to do better than COMA. The performance advantage is, however, slightly smaller now — in these applications the software overhead of migration is slightly larger than the benefits. However, for Cholesky, where previously NUMA-NM did worse than COMA (see Figure 4), NUMA-M does significantly better than COMA (ETR = 1.21). For Ocean, NUMA-M substantially decreases the performance advantage of COMA than before. For LU and Barnes-Hut the performance is essentially unchanged between NUMA-NM and NUMA-M. We speculate that one reason why the gains are small is that we have been using small data sets for our applications. To study the effects of larger data sets, we consider page size variations next.

5.3 Page Migration: Impact of Page Size

As stated in Section 4, the data set size we use for the applications is smaller than what we may use on real machines. Consequently, for applications that use coarse data partitioning, we expect data chunks to be larger for full-sized problems. For example, as matrix size is increased for LU, the columns will get larger. In this section, we indirectly study the performance gains from migration for larger data sets by instead considering smaller page sizes (512b, 1K, and 2K pages). Due to space limitations, we only present results for LU and Ocean. These two are among the three applications that are currently doing worse under COMA; the results for Barnes-Hut, the third application, are not expected to change with page size.

Table 4 shows the node hit-rate and the execution time relative to NUMA-NM (4 Kbyte pages) for various page sizes for LU and Ocean. We see that the node hit-rate increases as the page size is decreased. The explanation is that as the page size is decreased, the data partitions in these applications start becoming larger than the pages. As a result, pages are primarily referenced by only a single processor, and quickly migrate to that processor. In contrast, with larger pages there is false sharing with multiple processors referencing a page, and the migration algorithm can not satisfy all referencing processors. Responding to increasing node hit-rates, execution times go down as the page size is reduced. For 512 byte pages, the difference between the performance of NUMA-M and COMA is less than 10% for LU and none for Ocean.

For Ocean, it is interesting to note that the minimum execution time occurs for 1 Kbyte pages and not for 512 byte pages. The reason is simply the overhead due to page migrations. To understand this, we also show the number of migrations that occur for a given page size in Table 4. For Ocean, the number of migrations follows a U-shaped curve. For page sizes much larger than data objects, we have many migrations because of false sharing. For page sizes much smaller than data objects, we have many migrations because bringing each object closer takes multiple page migrations. For LU, it is interesting to note that the node hit-rates for NUMA-M never reach close to that achieved by COMA. The reason is that columns in the matrix do not occupy an integer number of pages. Since successive columns are assigned to different processors, the migration algorithm never succeeds in totally satisfying all processors. In contrast, COMA with its 32-byte memory blocks does very well in bringing data close to the processors.

To summarize, we see that for the scaled down problems used in this paper, migration with smaller page sizes is quite effective. In turn, the results also indicate that for full-sized problems, we are likely to be able to get good performance while using migration with regular sized pages. Of course, page migration is not expected to work for all applications. For applications such as Barnes-Hut, where data chunks are much smaller than the page size, the migration overheads are likely to exceed the benefits.

5.4 CC-NUMA: Benefits from Initial Placement

A disadvantage of using page migration algorithms is that they can require substantial hardware and software support. An alternative is to let the compiler/programmer spend some effort in partitioning the data set and in placing the pages so as to improve the local memory hit-rate. To study the benefits of initial placement, without doing the placement ourselves, we adopted the following scheme. We evaluated the performance of the applications using the same page migration algorithm as in the last subsection, but with only a single migration allowed for each page. In Table 5, we show the node hit-rate, the execution time ratio, and the number of migrations for LU and Ocean under this scheme (NUMA-I) with various page sizes. (The reasons for considering only LU and Ocean are the same as in the previous subsection.)

First, we note that the node hit-rate increases as the page size is reduced. This is what we expect since false sharing of pages is reduced. Second, execution time also drops as the page size goes down. Third, looking at the number of migrations, the general trend is that the migration count goes up as page size is decreased. The reason is that twice as many pages must be migrated when the page size is reduced by a factor of two.

Comparing the relative performance of NUMA-I and NUMA-M, we see that LU does significantly better with single migrations than with multiple migrations (see Table 4), in fact, even better than COMA with 512 byte pages. The reason is that we have significantly reduced the number of page migrations (e.g., down from 2.7K to 135 migrations for 4 Kbyte pages), thus reducing the software overhead of migration. When multiple migrations are allowed, a page in LU may thrash back-and-forth between the various processors that have columns allocated on that page, without really improving the overall hit-rate in local memory.

For Ocean, the performance for single versus multiple page migrations is essentially the same. Although the node hit-rate is lower when only a single migration per page is allowed, this is compensated by the fact that there are fewer page migrations and hence lower software overhead.

Table 5: Node hit-rate and execution time for CC-NUMA with single page migration (NUMA-I) relative to NUMA-NM for various page sizes.

Model	LU			Ocean		
	Node HR	Rel. Exec	Mig. Count	Node HR	Rel. Exec	Mig. Count
NUMA-NM	78	1.00	–	50	1.00	–
NUMA-I 4K	83	0.96	135	87	0.74	581
NUMA-I 2K	87	0.88	270	89	0.66	1091
NUMA-I 1K	90	0.87	511	95	0.62	2218
NUMA-I .5K	91	0.79	948	94	0.64	4250
COMA	98	0.84	–	98	0.66	–

In summary, we show that initial placement manages to eliminate most performance differences between CC-NUMA and COMA for LU and Ocean. (All other applications, with the exception of Barnes-Hut, already do quite well with CC-NUMA.) Of course, proper intial placement requires extra effort from the compiler/programmer, and this must be traded off against the higher implementation complexity of COMA. COMA, however, is expected to be more responsive to dynamically changing workloads (e.g., multiprogrammed workloads).

5.5 Impact of Cache Size Variations

All experiments so far have been based on 4 Kbyte caches. In this subsection we study how the relative frequency of capacity and coherence misses changes as the cache size is increased, while keeping the problem size fixed.

An important effect of increasing the cache size is that while the capacity misses go down, the coherence misses remain the same. As a result, with larger caches, we expect coherence misses to start dominating, thus making the relative performance of CC-NUMA better than COMA. In Table 6 we show this data for the four applications (Cholesky, LU, Barnes-Hut, and Ocean) that did worse on CC-NUMA than COMA in Section 5.1.

As the cache size is increased, we clearly see that the ca-

Table 6: Capacity miss-rate (on left) and execution time ratio of COMA versus NUMA-NM (on right) for various cache sizes. The bottom line of the Table shows the coherence miss-rate for the applications.

Cache Size	Cholesky	LU	B-H	Ocean
4 K	23/0.92	21/0.84	41/0.79	52/0.66
16 K	6/1.52	8/1.08	20/0.89	28/0.79
64 K	3/1.58	3/1.35	5/1.01	15/0.91
Coher. MR	4	2	1	2

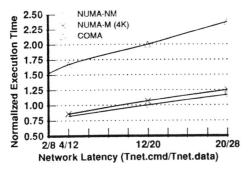

Figure 6: Network latency variation for MP3D.

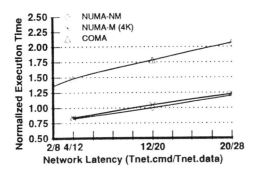

Figure 7: Network latency variation for PTHOR.

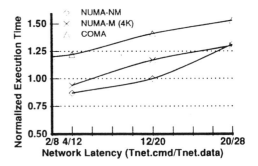

Figure 8: Network latency variation for LocusRoute.

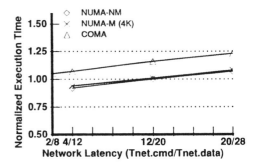

Figure 9: Network latency variation for Water.

pacity miss-rate is reduced and the coherence miss-rate starts to dominate. As expected, with larger caches the execution time ratio increases indicating that CC-NUMA is starting to perform better. As the data show, with 64 Kbyte caches, the performance of CC-NUMA (with no migration) is better for all applications except Ocean.

5.6 Impact of Network Latency Variations

We have seen that COMA's performance is limited primarily by the larger latency incurred by its hierarchical directory structure. In this subsection we explore how variations in the network latency and directory access times influence the relative performance. Due to space limitations, we only present results for MP3D, PTHOR, LocusRoute, and Water. By picking this set of applications that perform better on CC-NUMA, we wish to see if it is possible for COMA to perform better if a more aggressive network implementation is assumed. We will first study variations in network latency and then consider more aggressive directory implementations.

As default values for network latency, we have so far assumed a synchronous point-to-point hierarchy for COMA with latency numbers $T_{net.cmd} = 4$ and $T_{net.data} = 12$ pclocks. For CC-NUMA, we have assumed a synchronous mesh with default latency numbers $T_{net.cmd} = 12$ and $T_{net.data} = 20$ pclocks. In Figures 6–9 we show the relative performance of COMA, NUMA-M (with 4 Kbyte pages), and NUMA-NM under different network latency assumptions. All execution times are shown relative to NUMA-NM with default parameters. An important observation is that even if we consider a very aggressive point-to-point hierarchy for COMA ($T_{net.cmd} = 2$ and $T_{net.data} = 8$), default NUMA-NM outperforms COMA for MP3D, PTHOR, LocusRoute, and Water. We study variations

in directory access time for COMA next.

The directory access time is another important contributor to the node miss penalty associated with COMA. A directory access consists of a read-modify-write cycle in order to modify the state information. More specifically, the following basic actions and latencies are associated with a directory access, assuming 80ns DRAM-based directories and a 100 MHz processor clock rate: (i) arbitration among the multiple inputs into a directory (2 pclocks); (ii) directory DRAM access plus data buffering (10 pclocks); (iii) tag comparison and decision about next action (4 pclocks); (iv) directory DRAM update (6 pclocks); and (v) precharge before next directory access (8 pclocks). The busy time thus adds up to 30 pclocks. If the network load is low, the directory update and precharge operations can be overlapped by network transfers. We have partly taken this into account in our default directory access time by assuming $T_{dir} = 20$ pclocks. However, for applications with high coherence miss-rates, less overlap is expected. In Table 7 we show the execution time of COMA relative to CC-NUMA with default parameters, assuming less directory overlap ($T_{dir} = 28$ pclocks). We see that for applications with a significant coherence miss-rate, such as MP3D and PTHOR, less overlap can substantially degrade the performance of COMA.

One could reduce the node miss penalty for COMA by using faster (and more expensive) SRAM-based directories. In order to study the effect of faster directories, in Table 7 we show the performance of COMA (relative to CC-NUMA with default parameters), assuming directories built from 30ns SRAMs and where the update and precharge operations are completely overlapped by the network transfer ($T_{dir} = 12$ pclocks). We see that even for such an aggressive directory implementation, COMA performs worse than CC-NUMA for all four applications.

In summary, we note that even for more aggressive im-

Table 7: Execution time ratio of COMA to NUMA-NM as directory access time is varied.

T_{dir}	MP3D	PTHOR	Locus	Water
28	1.92	1.68	1.42	1.12
20	1.67	1.48	1.22	1.07
12	1.41	1.26	1.19	1.03

plementations of the hierarchical directory structure, COMA suffers from the higher network latency for applications with a significant coherence miss-rate.

6 COMA-F: A Flat COMA

We have seen that COMA's primary advantage is small capacity-miss penalties due to the large attraction memories, and its primary disadvantage is large coherence-miss penalties due to the hierarchical directory structure. The hierarchy is fundamental to COMA's coherence protocol because it helps locate copies of a memory block in the system. It also helps to support combining of requests. In contrast, CC-NUMA has an explicit home node for each memory block, and the directory at the home node keeps track of all copies of that memory block. Consequently, a copy of a memory block can be located without traversing any hierarchy, resulting in lower remote-miss latencies. In this section, we propose a new architecture called COMA-F (for COMA-FLAT) that provides the benefits of both COMA and CC-NUMA (low capacity-miss penalties and low coherence-miss penalties). To avoid confusion, we denote previously proposed COMA machines as COMA-H, for hierarchical COMA.

COMA-F has no hierarchy. However, like COMA-H, COMA-F supports migration and replication of cache blocks at the main-memory level by organizing its main memory as an attraction memory (i.e., there are tags associated with each memory block). In addition, like CC-NUMA, each memory block has a clear notion of a home node, and the directory memory there keeps track of all copies of that block. However, unlike CC-NUMA, the home node does not reserve its main memory for blocks for which it keeps directory entries (thus, blocks whose home is some other processing node can come and reside there). Below, we present an overview of the memory coherence protocol for COMA-F — the detailed protocol is described in [8].

We begin with the structure of the directory entries. Each entry contains a pointer to one of the copies denoted MASTER, and a list of other nodes having a copy of the block, called the sharing list. The state of a directory entry can either be SHARED or EXCLUSIVE. The state of an attraction-memory block can be one of INVALID, SHARED, MASTER-SHARED, or EXCLUSIVE. If a block is in MASTER-SHARED or EXCLUSIVE state, it implies that the directory entry considers the local node to be the MASTER. As for directory-memory overhead for COMA-F, we note that it should be possible to use limited-pointer directory schemes as proposed for CC-NUMA, but sparse directories are not expected to work well [9].

If a read request misses in the attraction memory, it is sent to the HOME node. The HOME forwards the read request to the MASTER node which responds with a copy of the data to the requesting node. The HOME also updates the sharing list. If the MASTER copy was in state EXCLUSIVE, the state of the directory entry is changed to SHARED and the block state in the MASTER node is changed to MASTER-SHARED. Note, in contrast to CC-NUMA, accessing a clean block in COMA-F may take three instead of two network traversals. Also in contrast to COMA-H, there is no hardware combining in COMA-F.

A read-exclusive request is also first sent to the HOME node. As before, the HOME node forwards the request to the MASTER node which responds with a copy of the block to the requesting node. In addition, the requesting node now becomes the new MASTER node and all other copies are invalidated. Acknowledgements are sent directly to the new MASTER node.

Since there is no physical memory backing up the attraction-memory cache blocks, replacements need special care in order to avoid replacing the last remaining copy. A node that initiates replacement of a SHARED block can simply discard it and then inform the HOME node to remove itself from the sharing list. However, if the state of the block is either EXCLUSIVE or MASTER-SHARED, then the initiating node is currently the MASTER node and it must send the replaced block to the HOME node. The HOME node must now nominate a new MASTER node. If there are other nodes with copies, an arbitrary node among them is nominated as the MASTER. If there are no other copies, then we need to get fresh space for the replaced block. While there are many different strategies possible, one reasonable strategy is to make a place for the replaced block in the HOME node itself. While this may cause another replacement, the chain of replacements is expected to be short.

We have investigated the performance of COMA-F using the protocol mentioned above, assuming infinite attraction memories. In Table 8, we present execution times for COMA-H and NUMA-NM relative to COMA-F, assuming 4 Kbyte pages and default latency numbers. As expected, COMA-F outperforms both COMA and NUMA-NM. Compared to COMA-H, COMA-F manages to reduce the coherence-miss penalty (as seen from performance of MP3D and PTHOR) and as compared to CC-NUMA, COMA-F manages to reduce the capacity-miss penalty (as seen from performance of LU, Barnes-Hut, and Ocean).

7 Conclusion

We have studied the relative performance of two different approaches to designing large-scale shared-memory multiprocessors, CC-NUMA and COMA. We have found that for applications with low miss rates, the two styles of machines achieve nearly identical performance. The performance differences arise as a result of the efficiency with which they handle cache misses. The COMA style handles capacity misses more efficiently than CC-NUMA. The replication and migration of small blocks of data at the main-memory level allows COMA to service a majority of such misses locally. The CC-NUMA style handles coherence misses more efficiently than COMA. The hierarchical directory structure that is needed by COMA results in a much larger latency than the flat structure in CC-NUMA. We have observed through simulation that the relative performance of these two machine models is easily predicted by the relative frequency of these two types of misses.

In contrast to COMA machines, CC-NUMA can replicate

Table 8: Execution time ratio of COMA-H and NUMA-NM relative to COMA-F.

	MP3D	PTHOR	Locus	Water	Chol	LU	B-H	Ocean
COMA-H	1.90	1.73	1.30	1.16	1.35	1.27	1.04	1.11
NUMA-NM	1.14	1.18	1.09	1.09	1.46	1.51	1.32	1.68

and migrate data at the main-memory level only in large page-sized chunks. However, we show that proper initial placement and smart migration of pages can still be quite effective for scientific applications that use coarse-grained data partitions. Overall, with page migration turned on, we show that CC-NUMA performs better than COMA or is competitive with COMA for seven of the eight benchmark applications that we evaluate.

Finally, by combining the notion of a home location for directory information with the feature of replication of cache-block sized chunks at the main-memory level, we have outlined a COMA-F architecture that does not rely on a hierarchical directory structure. Our preliminary results show that such an architecture can offer significant performance improvements. However, we believe it is still an open question whether the additional complexity and hardware overhead of COMA machines is justified by the expected performance gains; this question is especially critical for hierarchical COMA machines.

Acknowledgments

We would like to thank Ed Rothberg, Kourosh Gharachorloo, Rohit Chandra, John Hennessy, and Kunle Olukotun for discussions and helpful comments on earlier drafts of this paper. This work has been supported by DARPA contract N00039-91-C-0138. Per Stenström is supported by STU contract 9001797. Anoop Gupta is also supported by an NSF Presidential Young Investigator Award.

References

[1] Anant Agarwal, Beng-Hong Lim, David Kranz, and John Kubiatowicz. APRIL: A processor architecture for multiprocessing. In *Proceedings of the 17th Annual International Symposium on Computer Architecture*, pages 104–114, May 1990.

[2] David L. Black, Anoop Gupta, and Wolf-Dietrich Weber. Competitive management of distributed shared memory. In *Proceedings of Compcon 1989*, March 1989.

[3] William J. Bolosky, Michael L. Scott, Robert P. Fitzgerald, Robert J. Fowler, and Alan L. Cox. NUMA policies and their relation to memory architecture. In *Proceedings of the 4th International Conerfernce on Architectural Support for Programming Languages and Operating Systems*, pages 212–221, 1991.

[4] Henry Burkhardt III, Steven Frank, Bruce Knobe, and James Rothnie. Overview of the KSR1 Computer System. Technical Report KSR-TR-9202001, Kendall Square Research, Boston, February 1992.

[5] Helen Davis, Stephen R. Goldschmidt, and John L. Hennessy. Multiprocessor simulation and tracing using Tango. In *Proceedings of International Conference on Parallel Processing*, pages 99–107, 1991. Vol. II.

[6] Michel Dubois, Christoph Scheurich, and Faye Briggs. Memory access buffering in multiprocessors. In *Proceedings of the 13th Annual International Symposium on Computer Architecture*, pages 434–442, 1986.

[7] Alan Gottlieb, Ralph Grishman, C. Kruskal, Kevin McAuliffe, Larry Rudolph, and Mark Snir. The NYU Ultracomputer - Designing a MIMD, shared memory parallel machine. *IEEE Transactions on Computers*, 32(2):175–189, February 1983.

[8] Anoop Gupta, Truman Joe, and Per Stenström. Comparative performance evaluation of cache-coherent NUMA and COMA architectures. Technical report, Stanford University, March 1992.

[9] Anoop Gupta, Wolf-Dietrich Weber, and Todd Mowry. Reducing memory and traffic requirements for scalable directory-based cache coherence schemes. In *Proceedings of International Conference on Parallel Processing*, August 1990.

[10] Erik Hagersten, Seif Haridi, and David H.D. Warren. The cache-coherence protocol of the data diffusion machine. In Michel Dubois and Shreekant Thakkar, editors, *Cache and Interconnect Architectures in Multiprocessors*. Kluwer Academic Publishers, 1990.

[11] Monica S. Lam, Edward E. Rothberg, and Michael E. Wolf. The cache performance and optimizations of blocked algorithms. In *Proceedings of the 4th International Conerfernce on Architectural Support for Programming Languages and Operating Systems*, pages 63–74, 1991.

[12] Daniel E. Lenoski, James P. Laudon, Kourosh Gharachorloo, Anoop Gupta, and John L. Hennessy. The directory-based cache coherence protocol for the DASH multiprocessor. In *Proceedings of the 17th Annual International Symposium on Computer Architecture*, pages 148–159, 1990.

[13] Jaswinder P. Singh, Chris Holt, Takashi Totsuka, Anoop Gupta, and John L. Hennessy. Load balancing and data locality in parallel hierarchial N-body simulation. Technical Report CSL-TR-92-505, Stanford University, February 1992.

[14] Jaswinder P. Singh, Wolf-Dietrich Weber, and Anoop Gupta. SPLASH: Stanford parallel applications for shared-memory. Technical Report CSL-TR-91-469, Stanford University, April 1991.

[15] Joseph Torrellas, Monica S. Lam, and John L. Hennessy. Shared data placement optimizations to reduce multiprocessor cache miss rates. In *Proceedings of the International Conference on Parallel Processing*, pages 266–270, 1990. Vol. II.

[16] Deborah A. Wallach. A scalable hierarchial cache coherence protocol. Bachelor of Science Thesis, Massachuesetts Institute of Technology, May 1990.

Heterogeneous Distributed Shared Memory

Songnian Zhou, *Member, IEEE*, Michael Stumm, *Member, IEEE*, Kai Li, and David Wortman, *Member, IEEE*

Abstract—Heterogeneity in distributed systems is increasingly a fact of life, due to specialization of computing equipment. It is highly desirable to integrate heterogeneous hosts into a coherent computing environment to support distributed and parallel applications, so that the individual strengths of the different hosts can be exploited together. Distributed shared memory (DSM), a high-level, highly transparent model for interprocess communication in distributed systems, is a promising vehicle for achieving such an integration.

This paper studies the design, implementation, and performance of heterogeneous distributed shared memory (HDSM). As a practical research effort, we have developed a prototype HDSM system that integrates very different types of hosts, and have ported a number of applications to this system. Our experience shows that, despite a number of difficulties in data conversion, HDSM is indeed implementable with minimal loss in functional and performance transparency when compared to homogeneous DSM systems.

Index Terms—Data consistency, data sharing, distributed computer systems, distributed shared memory, heterogeneous computer systems, interprocess communication, parallel computation, performance evaluation, virtual memory systems.

I. INTRODUCTION

DISTRIBUTED shared memory (DSM) is a model for interprocess communication in distributed systems. In the DSM model, processes running on separate hosts can access a shared address space through normal load and store operations and other memory access instructions. The underlying DSM system provides its clients with a shared, coherent memory address space. Each client can access any memory location in the shared address space at any time and see the value last written by any client. The primary advantage of DSM is the simpler abstraction it provides to the application programmer, making it the focus of recent study and implementation efforts [10], [11], [15]–[18], [24], [3], [14], [25]. (See Stumm and Zhou [24] for an overview.) The abstraction is one the programmer already understands well, since the access protocol is consistent with the way sequential applications access data. The communication mechanism is entirely hidden from the application writer so that the programmer does not have to be conscious of data movement between processes, and complex data structures can be passed by reference, requiring no packing and unpacking.

In principle, the performance of applications that use DSM is expected to be worse than if they use message passing

directly, since message passing is a direct extension to the underlying communication mechanism of the system, and since DSM is typically implemented as a separate layer between the application and a message passing system. However, several implementations of DSM algorithms have demonstrated that DSM can be competitive to message passing in terms of performance for many applications [5], [18], [11]. For some existing applications, we have found that DSM can result in superior performance. This is possible for two reasons. First, for many DSM algorithms, data is moved between hosts in large blocks. Therefore, if the application exhibits a reasonable degree of locality in its data accesses, communication overhead is amortized over multiple memory accesses, reducing overall communication requirements. Second, many (distributed) parallel applications execute in phases, where each compute phase is preceded by a data exchange phase. The time needed for the data exchange phase is often dictated by the throughput of existing communication bottlenecks. In contrast, DSM algorithms typically move data on demand as they are being accessed, eliminating the data exchange phase, spreading the communication load over a longer period of time, and allowing for a greater degree of concurrency. One could argue that the above methods of accessing data could be programmed using messages, in effect imitating DSM in the individual applications. Such programming for communication, however, usually represents substantial effort in addition to that for the implementation of the application itself.

The most widely known algorithm for implementing DSM is due to Li [17], [18], which is well suited for a large class of algorithms. In Li's algorithm, known as SVM, the shared address space is partitioned into pages, and copies of these pages are distributed among the hosts, following a multiple-reader/single-writer (MRSW) protocol: Pages that are marked *read-only* can be replicated and may reside in the memory of several hosts, but a page being written to can reside only in the memory of one host.

One advantage of Li's algorithm is that it can easily be integrated into the virtual memory of the host operating system.[1] If a shared memory page is held locally at a host, it can be mapped into the application's virtual address space on that host and therefore be accessed using normal machine instructions for accessing memory. An access to a page not held locally triggers a page fault, passing control to a fault handler. The fault handler then communicates with the remote hosts in order to obtain a valid copy of the page before mapping it into the application's address space. Whenever

Manuscript received July 19, 1990; revised June 19, 1991.

S. Zhou, M. Stumm, and D. Wortman are with the Computer Systems Research Institute, University of Toronto, Toronto, Ont., Canada M5S 1A4.

K. Li is with the Department of Computer Science, Princeton University, Princeton, NJ.

IEEE Log Number 9202077.

[1] It is for this reason that Li called this algorithm and the concept it supports *Shared Virtual Memory* (SVM). In this paper, the more general term, DSM, will be used.

a page is migrated away from a host, it is removed from any local address space it has been mapped into. Similarly, whenever a host attempts to write to a page for which it does not have a local copy marked as *writable*, a page fault occurs and the local fault handler communicates with the other hosts (after having obtained a copy of the page, if necessary) to invalidate all other copies in the system, before marking the local copy as writable and allowing the faulted process to continue. This protocol is similar to the write-invalidate algorithms used for cache consistency in shared-memory multiprocessors, except that the basic unit on which operations occur is a page instead of a cache line. The DSM fault handlers communicate with DSM memory managers, one of which runs on each host. Each DSM memory manager manipulates local virtual page mapping tables according to the MRSW protocol, keeps track of the location of copies of each DSM page it manages, and passes pages to requesting page fault handlers. In this paper, we assume this protocol for supporting DSM.

For parallel and distributed application programming, distributed shared memory can hide communication complexity from the application when used on a homogeneous set of hosts. DSM in homogeneous systems achieves complete *functional transparency*, in the sense that a program written for a shared memory multiprocessor system can run on DSM without change. The fact that no physical memory is shared can be completely hidden from the applications programmer, as can the fact that, to transfer data, messages have to be passed between the hosts. On the other hand, *performance transparency* can only be achieved to a limited degree, since the physical location(s) of the data being accessed affect application performance, whereas in a uniform memory access (UMA) multiprocessor, the data access cost is not affected by its location in the shared memory. In the case of the MRSW protocol, if a page is not available on the local host when being accessed, it has to be brought in from another host, causing extra delay.

In this paper, we study how DSM can be extended to heterogeneous system environments, and to what degree the functional and performance transparency can be maintained. Heterogeneity exists in many (if not most) computing environments and is usually unavoidable because hardware and its software is often designed for a particular application domain. For example, supercomputers and multiprocessors are good at compute-intensive applications, but often poor at user interfaces and device I/O. Personal computers and workstations, on the other hand, usually have very good user interfaces. There exist many applications that require sophisticated user interfaces, dedicated I/O devices, as well as massive computing power. Examples of such applications can be found in CAD/CAM, artificial intelligence, interactive graphics, and interactive simulation. Hence, it is highly desirable to integrate heterogeneous machines into a coherent distributed system, and to share resources among them.

Heterogeneity in a distributed system comes in a number of forms. The hardware architectures of the machines may be different, including the instruction sets, the data representations, the hardware page sizes, and the number of processors on a host (i.e., uni- or multiprocessors). The operating systems, the system and application programming languages and their compilers, the types of distributed file systems, and the communications protocols may also differ.

A number of methods have been proposed to achieve heterogeneous system integration. (See Notkin *et al.* [22] for an overview.) For example, several remote procedure call (RPC) systems enable servers and application software running on hosts of different types to communicate [26], [1], [4], [12]. Such systems typically define a network standard data format for the procedure call and return messages that all hosts follow by converting between their local representations and this standard. Another method for heterogeneous system integration is to build a heterogeneous distributed file system [13], [9], [21], [2], [7]. Again, a file system access interface and data format is defined that all the hosts must follow to share files among them.

Heterogeneous distributed shared memory (HDSM) is useful for distributed and parallel applications to exploit resources available on multiple types of hosts at the same time. For instance, a CAM application controlling a manufacturing line in real time would be able to acquire data through I/O devices attached to a workstation and output results on its bit-mapped display, while doing most of the computation on compute servers. With HDSM, not only can workstations and compute servers be used simultaneously, but multiple compute servers can be used to increase the aggregate amount of computing power available to a single application. A similar effort to provide heterogeneous distributed shared memory is being undertaken by Bisiani and Forin [11] with their Agora system. However, they use a different DSM algorithm (one where the shared data is replicated on all hosts accessing the data). As discussed by Stumm and Zhou [24], we believe that the MRSW protocol performs better for a larger class of applications than the fully replicated algorithm used by Bisiani and Forin. Forin, Barrera, and Sanzi implemented a shared memory server on heterogeneous processors running the Mach operating system [11]. Their work addressed the issues of multiple VM page sizes, and the conversion of basic hardware data types, such as integer, in the context of Mach.

This paper studies the design, implementation, and performance of heterogeneous distributed shared memory. As a practical research effort, we have developed a prototype HDSM system with hosts that differ significantly. Our experience shows that, despite a number of difficulties in data conversion, HDSM can be implemented while retaining functional and performance transparency close to that of homogeneous DSM. Very good performance is obtained for a number of sample applications running on our prototype. In Section II, we discuss the problems that need to be addressed in order to achieve an HDSM system. Although some of the problems are very difficult, in Section III we show that it is possible to build an HDSM system supporting a wide range of applications, using our prototype system as an example. The performance characteristics of our system, as measured by its overhead and the performance of a number of applications running on it, are discussed in Section IV. Finally, concluding remarks are made in Section V.

II. Issues Related to Heterogeneity

Since with DSM, the components of a distributed application share memory directly, they are more tightly coupled than when data is shared through RPC or a distributed file system. For this reason, it is more difficult to extend DSM to a heterogeneous system environment. These difficulties are explained in this section. Our techniques for overcoming them will be discussed in the next section.

A. Data Conversion

Data items may be represented differently on various types of hosts due to differences in the machine architectures, the programming languages for the applications, and their compilers. For data types as simple as integers, the order of the bytes can be different. For floating point numbers, the lengths of the mantissa and exponent fields, as well as their positions can differ. For higher level structured data types (e.g., records, arrays), the alignment and order of the components in the data structure can differ between hosts. A simple example, depicted in Table I, presents two data types, an array of four characters and an integer, first in big-endian order and then in little-endian order [6]. This example illustrates the *type dependent* differences in data representation that can arise between hosts.

Sharing data among heterogeneous hosts means that the physical representation of the data will have to be converted when the data is transferred between hosts of different types. In the most general case, data conversion will not only incur run-time overhead, but also may be impossible due to nonequivalent data content (e.g., lost bits of precision in floating point numbers, and mismatch in their ranges of representation). This may represent a potential limitation to HDSM for some systems and applications. The question that needs to be addressed is whether, for a specific set of hosts and programming languages, data conversion can be performed for all or most data types to form a *useful* HDSM system (i.e., a system that supports a large collection of realistic applications).

B. Thread Management

As a means of supporting a shared address space, distributed shared memory usually goes hand in hand with a thread system that allows multiple threads to share the same address space. Such a combination makes programming of parallel applications particularly easy. In a heterogeneous system environment, the facilities for thread management, which includes thread creation, termination, scheduling and synchronization primitives, may all be different on different types of hosts, if they exist at all.

Migrating a thread from one host to another in a homogeneous DSM system is usually easy, since minimal context is kept for the threads. Typically, the per-thread stack is allocated in the shared address space, so the stack need not be moved explicitly. The descriptor, or Thread Control Block (TCB), constitutes a small amount of data that needs to be moved at migration time. In a heterogeneous DSM system, however, thread migration is much more difficult. The binary images of the program are different, so it is hard to identify "equivalent

TABLE I
Big-Endian and Little-Endian Byte Ordering

Byte	Big-Endian		Little-Endian	
	int	char array	int	char array
i	MSB	'J'	LSB	'J'
$i+1$		'O'		'O'
$i+2$		'H'		'H'
$i+3$	LSB	'N'	MSB	'N'

MSB = Most Significant Byte;   LSB = Least Significant Byte.

points of execution" in the binaries (i.e., the places in the different binary program images at which execution can be suspended and later resumed on another host of a different type such that the result of the execution is not affected). Similarly, the formats of the threads' stacks are likely to be different, due to architectural, language, and compiler differences; therefore, converting the stacks at migration time may be very difficult, if not impossible.

While it is clear that thread migration presents yet another limitation to HDSM, its significance is debatable for two reasons. First, in HDSM, threads can be created and started on remote hosts of any type, thus reducing the need for dynamic thread migration. Second, migration between hosts of the same type is still easy to achieve in HDSM, and, for many applications, this may be all that is required. For an application running on a workstation and a set of (homogeneous) compute servers, for instance, its threads can freely migrate between the compute servers to balance their load.

C. Page Sizes

The unit of data managed and transferred by DSM is a data block, which we call a *DSM page*. In a homogeneous DSM system, a DSM page has usually the same size as a native virtual memory (VM) page, so that the memory management hardware (MMU) can be used to trigger a DSM page fault. In a heterogeneous DSM system, the hosts may have different VM page sizes, presenting both complexity in the page coherency algorithm and opportunity in control of the granularity of data sharing.

D. Uniform File Access

A DSM system supporting an application running on a number of hosts benefits from the existence of a distributed file system that allows the threads to open files and perform I/O in a uniform way. While this is likely to be the case in a modern, homogeneous system, multiple incompatible distributed file systems may exist on heterogeneous hosts, due to the multiplicity of distributed file system protocols currently in existence. A uniform file access interface, encompassing both file names and file operations, should be provided to an HDSM application. One possibility is to choose one of the file systems as the standard and make the other(s) emulate it. It is also possible to define an independent file system structure, and make the native distributed file systems emulate it. Recent research on heterogeneous distributed file system is applicable here [7]. Since heterogeneous distributed file system is a research topic on its own, we will not address it any further in this paper.

E. Programming Languages

The system programming languages used on the heterogeneous hosts may be different. This implies that multiple (more-or-less) equivalent implementations of an HDSM system may have to be done in the various languages. However, applications running on HDSM should not be affected by the language(s) used to implement HDSM, as long as a functionally equivalent application interface is supported by HDSM on all the hosts. If a common application programming language is available on all the hosts, then the same program would be usable on the hosts (with recompilation). Otherwise, multiple (equivalent) implementations of an application would have to be written, increasing the difficulties in using HDSM substantially.

F. Interhost Communication

The realization of HDSM requires the existence of a common communication protocol between the different types of hosts involved. This requirement is not particular to HDSM, however, some common transport protocol must exist for the hosts to communicate in any case. The availability of the OSI and TCP/IP protocols on most systems makes the interhost communication increasingly feasible.

III. MERMAID: A PROTOTYPE

In the preceding section, we identified a number of issues that need to be addressed in order to build an HDSM system. Instead of studying these issues in the abstract, we have taken an experimental approach by designing and building an HDSM prototype, Mermaid, and by studying its performance. We discuss our experience in this section. Although the techniques we used to resolve the issues related to heterogeneity are in the context of Mermaid, we believe that most of them are generally applicable. For the use of Mermaid, please see [19].

A. System Overview

In selecting the types of hosts participating in Mermaid, we wanted to include machines that are sufficiently different, so that the difficult issues arising from heterogeneity can be studied. Based on suitability and availability, SunOS workstations and DEC Firefly multiprocessors were chosen. Sun-3 workstations are based on M68020 CPU's and run Sun's version of the UNIX operating system, SunOS. The system programming language is C. The Firefly, developed at DEC's System Research Center, is a small-scale multiprocessor workstation with up to 7 DEC CVAX processors [27]. Each processor has a direct-mapped 64 kilobyte cache. The caches are coherent, so that all processors within a single Firefly have a consistent view of shared memory. The operating system for the Firefly is Taos [20], an Ultrix with threads and inexpensive thread synchronization. The system programming language is

Modula-2+, an augmented version of Modula-2 [23]. Table II highlights the differences between the two types of machines.[2]

To focus on our research problems, we adopted a system architecture for Mermaid similar to that of the IVY system developed by Li [17] that uses a page-based MRSW consistency protocol, as described in Section I. It consists of three modules, as shown in Fig. 1. The *thread management module* provides operations for thread creation, termination, scheduling, as well as synchronization primitives. The *shared memory module* allocates and deallocates shared memory and handles page faults. It uses a page table for the shared address space to maintain data consistency, and performs data conversion at page transfer time, if necessary. The responsibility for managing the pages is assigned to the participating hosts in a round-robin fashion (named *fixed-distributed algorithm* by Li [18]). The above two modules are supported by the *remote operations module*, which implements a simple request-response protocol for communication between the hosts.

We chose to implement Mermaid at the user level, as a library package to be linked into application programs using DSM. Although a kernel-level implementation would be more efficient, the difference in performance is not expected to affect applications performance significantly, as evidenced by the low overhead of Mermaid which will be discussed in Section IV-A. More importantly, a user-level implementation has a number of advantages. First, it is more flexible and easier to implement; experimentation may be carried out without rebooting the hosts.

Second, several DSM packages can be provided to the applications on the same system. Our analysis of the performance of applications using different shared data algorithms showed that the correct choice of algorithm was often dictated by the memory access behavior of the application [24]. It is therefore desirable to provide multiple DSM systems employing different algorithms for applications to choose from. A user-level implementation makes this much easier.

Finally, a user-level DSM system is more portable, although some small changes to the operating system kernel are still needed for some systems. For example, Mermaid requires kernel support for setting the access permissions of memory pages from the user level, so that a memory access fault is generated if a nonresident page is accessed on a host. It was necessary to add a new system call to SunOS for this purpose (Taos provides such a call). A second change to the operating system kernel was to pass the address of the DSM page that has an access violation to its user-level fault handler. No other kernel changes were necessary for these two host types.

B. Basic Support

Programming Languages: As discussed in Section II-E, it is necessary to choose languages for implementing HDSM and for implementing applications running on HDSM. While it would be simpler to use a single language to implement HDSM, interfacing HDSM to the native operating systems is

---

[2]The hardware MMU page size on a CVAX is 512 bytes, but the VM implementation on the Firefly uses two MMU pages for one VM page of 1 kilobyte. On the Sun, both the hardware MMU page and the VM page have a size of 8 kilobytes.

TABLE II

HIGHLIGHTS OF THE HETEROGENEOUS FEATURES OF THE SUN AND FIREFLY

Attribute	Sun-3	Firefly
Processor	M68020	CVAX
Number of processors	1	4–6 (user usable) + 1 (I/O)
Byte order	Little-endian	Big-endian
Floating point	IEEE	VAX
VM page size	8 kilobytes	1 kilobyte
Operating system	SunOS 3.5	Taos
System language	C	Modula-2+
Application language	C	Modula-2+, C
Thread management	unavailable	available
Communication protocol	TCP/IP, UDP/IP, Sun RPC	UDP/IP subsets, FF RPC
File system	SUN NFS	RFS

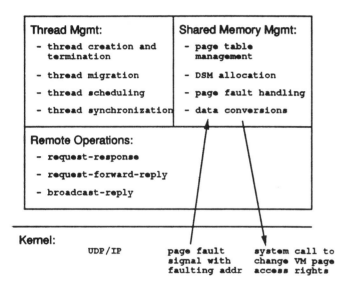

Fig. 1. Structure of the Mermaid system.

easier if the native system implementation languages are used. For Mermaid, we chose the latter approach by having a C implementation for the Sun, and a Modula-2+ implementation for the Firefly. As a result, most of the Mermaid functionalities had to be implemented twice, and, whenever changes are made to Mermaid, both implementations must be modified. Though certainly cumbersome, the modification process has been relatively straightforward.

The situation for application programs is quite different, since it is highly undesirable to force the user to implement an application in multiple languages. We therefore chose C as the common application language. We have ported to Mermaid a number of large, complex applications originally written in C for sequential machines, by only modifying the top-level logic to break the computation into parallel tasks, (without understanding the low-level algorithms employed by the application, which typically constitutes 80–95% of the code). This would have been impossible had multiple languages been required.

Communication Substrate: The distributed shared memory modules typically operate in a request-response mode. For instance, when a page fault occurs, the fault handler sends a

page request to the manager for this page, which either supplies the page, or forward the request to the owner on another host. The most suitable protocol for the remote operations module is therefore a request-response protocol, with forwarding and multicast capabilities. Multicast is used for write invalidation.

We implemented our own presentation layer protocol in the Remote Operations module following the above requirements, and use it to support all interactions between the memory and thread management modules running on different hosts. This presentation layer protocol is implemented using UDP/IP, a simple, datagram-based transport protocol. Our implementation was complicated by the fact that fragmentation in UDP/IP is not supported on the Fireflies, We did not use the RPC packages available on the Suns and Fireflies, since they are incompatible and do not meet our requirements with respect to functionality, i.e., broadcast and forwarding. Moreover, since data conversion is performed in HDSM, we need not incur the overhead of data marshalling and demarshalling at the RPC level.

Thread Support: Many well established operating systems, including SunOS, do not provide direct support for multiple threads that share a common address space. Mermaid therefore provides a simple thread module at the user level on the Sun. Since all threads in a Sun address space run within a single Unix process, the suspension of one thread by the operating system scheduler (e.g., for *synchronous* I/O) makes the other threads nonexecutable as well. This has not been a problem for the Mermaid applications we ported, since parallel applications often allocate only one thread on each processor. For the Firefly, a system-level thread package is available and is used by Mermaid. Mermaid threads in an address space may be created on one host and later moved to and started on other hosts of any type. Alternatively, threads may be created and started on remote hosts directly. However, no dynamic thread migration facility is provided in the current implementation of Mermaid.

Parallel executing threads need a way to synchronize. In principle, this could be supported by using atomic instructions on shared memory locations. In practice, however, this leads to an excessive movement of (large) DSM pages between the hosts involved. We therefore implemented a separate distributed synchronization facility that provides for more efficient P and V operations and events.

C. Data Conversion

When data is transferred from a machine of one type to a machine of another type, it must be converted before it is accessed on the destination machine. In Mermaid, the unit of data that is converted is a page, and the conversion is based on the type of data stored on the page. Our goals for data conversion were to minimize the amount of work the user has to do, to make the conversion method as general as possible, and to achieve good performance. We adopted a three-part conversion scheme for Mermaid. First, the types of data to be allocated in the shared memory are indicated in the memory allocation requests. Second, routines to convert the various types of data are automatically generated by utility software. Finally, a mechanism is built into Mermaid so that the appropriate conversion routine is invoked whenever a page is transferred. We discuss the three parts in more detail in the following sections.

1) Typed Data Allocation: The information about the layout of a page has to be passed to Mermaid so that appropriate conversion can be performed upon page transfer. For this purpose, we provide a special memory allocation subroutine similar to `malloc` in Unix that has an additional argument identifying the type of data being allocated, as shown in Fig. 2(b). When processing such a request, the memory management module of Mermaid records the range of the shared address space allocated for this request, and the data type, in the corresponding DSM page table entry or entries. There is no restriction as to the type or size of data that can be allocated; a structure may be larger than a page. For example, Fig. 2(a) depicts a user-defined structure, `sharedType`, that is allocated by the call in Fig. 2(b).

In principle, multiple types of data could be coallocated in the same page, but this makes keeping track of the data types complicated and the dynamic data conversion inefficient. We therefore made the restriction that a page contain data of one type only,[3] so that information with respect to only one data type needs to be kept in each HDSM page table entry, and only one conversion routine needs to be invoked (which may invoke other routines in turn, as will be discussed below). Multiple allocation requests for the same type of data may be satisfied, fully or partially, by the same page, given that there is space in the page.

Our requirement of allocating only one data type per page may result in more memory usage, since now several pages may be partially filled, rather than at most one. However, the number of pages wasted is limited by the number of distinct data types being allocated in the shared memory. For modern machines with a large main memory, this is typically not a serious problem. Also, as an optimization in our implementation, when a partially filled page is being transferred, only the part with valid data is transferred and converted (if necessary). Despite the increased memory usage,

segregating data by types may have the desirable side effect of reducing page contention for some applications, if unrelated data of different types no longer co-reside in a page.

2) Automatic Data Conversion: In addition to data type information, Mermaid also needs a corresponding conversion routine for each type. In Section II-A, we noted that data conversion may not be possible for some types due to differences in data content, size, or alignment. Here, we first assume that conversion is possible, and discuss a general framework for automatically generating the conversion routines. We then study the Mermaid case to expose its limitations.

Conversion Code Generation: In general, a hierarchy of conversion routines must be constructed that partially reflects the data type hierarchy defined in the application program. This hierarchy is partial, because only those types directly or indirectly allocated in the shared memory need conversion routines. For the basic data types defined by the language and supported by the hardware, such as `int`, `short`, `float`, and `double` in C, efficient conversion routines can be provided by the HDSM system itself.[4] For user-defined data types, a conversion routine is invoked that consists of a sequence of calls to lower level routines, mirroring the structure of the data type. If an element is of a basic type, then its HDSM routine is invoked directly. Otherwise, a routine composed for the element is invoked. Ultimately every data type is composed of basic types. Fig. 2(c) gives an example of the conversion code for user-defined, nested data types.

We have constructed a fully automatic conversion routine generator that processes the compiler output for a program and produces all the necessary conversion routines.[5] The conversion routines generated are structural, in that they only specify the names of the lower level routines and the order in which they should be invoked; the same source code may therefore be used on all machines, independent of which machine the routines are generated on. The machine-dependent basic conversion routines provided by HDSM ensure that the conversion is correct on each machine. A number of simple optimizations are made in our current implementation. For example, a single routine is called for an array of data elements, as shown in Fig. 2(c) for the structure `embeddedType`.

In addition to the conversion routines, the generator also generates a table matching the data types that are directly specified in the memory allocation routines to their corresponding conversion routines. This table is used by Mermaid at page transfer time to invoke the appropriate conversion routine.

Feasibility of Conversion: We now address the issue of the feasibility of data conversion. Three problems are involved: 1) the conversion of basic data types, 2) the handling of a data item crossing a page boundary, and 3) the handling of different ordering of fields in a record.

On both the Sun and the Firefly, the ASCII standard is used for characters (`char` in C); hence, no character conversion is needed. Conversion of integers (either the four-byte `int` or the two-byte `short`) is a matter of proper byte swapping.

---

[3] Note that the data type need not be a basic type provided by the programming language, but can be an application defined compound type.

[4] These are implemented as inline code for efficiency reasons.

[5] It was necessary to work with the compiler output since we were unable to obtain access to the source code or internal documentation for the C compilers on both machines.

```
struct embeddedType {
    double d;                    /* an 8-byte double precision floating number */
    char c[8];                   /* an array of eight ASCII characters */
};

struct sharedType {
    int *p;                      /* a (4-byte) pointer to an integer */
    float b;                     /* a 4-byte single precision floating number */
    struct embeddedType e[16];   /* an array of 16 records declared above */
};
```

(a)

```
ptr = (struct sharedType *) DSM_Alloc((sizeof(struct sharedType) * n, "sharedType");
```

(b)

```
conv_embeddedType(dst, src, numrecords)
  struct embeddedType dst[], src[];
  int numrecords;
{
  register struct embeddedType *dstp = dst, *srcp = src, *srcend = &src[numrecords-1];

  for (; srcp <= srcend; srcp++, dstp++) {
    conv_float64(dstp->d,srcp->d);
    conv_chars(dstp->c,srcp->c, 8);
  }
}

conv_sharedType(dst, src, numrecords)
  struct sharedType dst[], src[];
  int numrecords;
{
  register struct sharedType *dstp = dst, *srcp = src, *srcend = &src[numrecords-1];

  for (; srcp <= srcend; srcp++, dstp++) {
    conv_pointer(dstp->p,srcp->p);
    conv_float32(dstp->b,srcp->b);
    conv_embeddedType(dstp->e,srcp->e,16);
  }
}
```

(c)

Fig. 2. An example of data conversion. (a) Sample data structure with embedded substructure. (b) Sample allocation statement for the second structure in (a). (c) Data conversion routines generated for the structures in (a).

Conversion of floating point numbers is somewhat more complicated. While both the VAX and the IEEE formats of single precision floating point numbers (float in C) use 23 bits to represent a 24 bit mantissa, 7 bits to represent the exponent, and 1 bit for the sign, their layout is quite different. In the IEEE format, the bits in the mantissa are stored contiguously, while in the VAX format they are partitioned across bits 0–6 and 16–31. The bias used to represent the exponents differ by one in the two formats. Despite these differences, equivalent conversion is achievable, except for the following special cases. The IEEE format used on the Sun supports unnormalized numbers and special cases, such as infinity and NAN's (not a number), which are not supported by the VAX format on the Firefly. These cases can be detected with two additional comparison operations. The positions and lengths of the exponent and mantissa fields may be different (such is the case with IEEE and VAX), requiring bit manipulation operations.

The VAX and IEEE formats for representing double precision floating point numbers differ more significantly. The IEEE format uses an 11-bit exponent and a 52-bit mantissa, whereas the VAX uses an 8-bit exponent and a 55-bit mantissa. Therefore, the smaller exponent field and the smaller mantissa field of the two representations dictate the range of (floating point) numbers that can be correctly represented on both types of machines.

For pointers, conversion is necessary if the shared address space starts at different virtual addresses on different host types. The HDSM system on each host may obtain the starting address of the shared memory for each host type at initialization time by communicating with each other, without application intervention. Converting a pointer is then a simple matter of adding an offset to the value of the pointer. This is the scheme used in Mermaid.

In Mermaid, all the corresponding basic data types have the same sizes, but their alignment requirements may be different. For the double type, for instance, Sun requires only even-byte alignment, whereas Firefly (VAX) requires quad-byte alignment. Thus the size of a compound structure and the alignment of the elements in it may be different on the two machines. Our automatic conversion generator detects this problem and automatically generates a revised structure definition with dummy elements inserted to force data structure elements of interest to have the same alignment on both machines. The application program is then recompiled on both machines with the revised data structure definition and correct alignment of corresponding elements is achieved. This process will result in some wasted storage on the machine with the less strict alignment requirements but it is essential for the operation of HDSM.

In general, it is also possible for a data item to cross a page boundary. If the item is a compound structure, and none of its basic data items crosses the page boundary, then the partial structure on the page to be converted may be copied to a temporary buffer (with the missing part of the structure filled with some default values taken from a template), where the conversion may be performed in-place using the appropriate routine. The partial structure is then copied back to the appropriate location in the page. If, on the other hand, a basic data item crosses a page boundary, then the conversion will need the parts on both (neighboring) pages. One of these pages may be resident on another host, making it necessary for it to be transferred. For certain data types, page-based data conversion may not be possible. Consider, for example, an integer with its first two bytes at the end of one page, and its last two bytes at the beginning of the following page. If byte swapping is necessary in converting an integer, then transferring one of the two pages between hosts with different byte orders can result in the loss of half of the integer, since the two pages held by their owner(s) may end up having the *same* two bytes of the integer. Such a problem does not arise in Mermaid, since we ensure, by forced alignment, that no basic data items cross page boundaries.

A similar problem arises if compilers on different machines ordered the space allocated for the fields of a structure differently. Even if no basic data item crosses a page boundary, the same field in a structure may be located on different pages, depending on the type of machine(s) holding the data. Again, neighboring pages would be needed for conversion, and it is possible to lose some of the data items during conversion. For the C compilers on the Sun and the Firefly, this problem does not exist.

The `union` structure in C allows various formats for a compound data type. Unfortunately, C does not require a tag field to indicate the format being used, thus making automatic conversion of union structures impossible. In Mermaid, we require the user to add a tag field at the beginning of a union structure, and to set its value to indicate the interpretation of the rest of the structure. Such a requirement would not be necessary in more sensibly designed languages, such as Pascal and Modula-2.

3) Dynamic Conversion Mechanism: Once the conversion routines are generated as described above, they can be compiled and linked with the user program on each type of machine, without additional effort from the user. Upon page transfer, the remote machine type is checked, and, if different from the local one, the appropriate conversion routine is invoked. The conversion mechanism in Mermaid uses the data type information stored in the HDSM page table entries, and the table matching the data types to their corresponding conversion routines produced by the code generator described in Section III-C1.

In our current implementation, conversion is always done by the receiving machine. This is desirable for some cases, such as when a master thread distributes input data to multiple worker threads, because the conversion can be performed by the workers in parallel, rather than by the master sequentially. For other cases, such as when the master collects results from the workers, it is better to have the sending machine perform the conversion. Our primary motivation for the current scheme is simplicity and transparency. Since only two types of machine are involved, data is always converted from the foreign format to the native format, rather than using an intermediate, network standard format as in some RPC systems [9].

4) Limitations: A Summary: The data conversion problem is complex. Our experience indicates that our solution is sufficient for many practical applications in the context of Mermaid, and we believe that it is similar in complexity to the solution used by existing heterogeneous RPC schemes [26]. However, as pointed out above, our solution does have a number of limitations:

1) Some functional transparency is sacrificed by requiring the programmer to specify the type of data being allocated. This is usually only a small annoyance.

2) Floating point numbers can lose precision when being converted. Since an application does not have direct control over how many times a page is migrated between hosts of different types and hence converted, the numerical accuracy of results may become questionable. However, we do not consider this to be a practical problem for many environments; for example, in an environment consisting of workstations and computation servers, data is typically transferred once to the computation servers and then transferred back again at the end of the computation. The initial (floating point) data and final results are not likely to be in the extreme ranges, or nonnumbers. During the computation phase, data pages may be transferred among the (homogeneous) compute servers without conversion.

3) Entire pages are converted even though only a small portion of a page may be accessed before it is transferred away. However, we have found that the cost of page conversion to be small compared to the overall migration cost (to be discussed in Section IV-A). Applications that access only a few data items of a page between page migrations will perform poorly in both the homogeneous and heterogeneous cases when using a page-based MRSW algorithm. A DSM system based on the MRSW algorithm performs poorly with this type of access behavior in both the homogeneous and the heterogeneous cases.

4) An additional tag field is required in union structures in languages such as C and Modula-2; the value of the tag must be set by the application to indicate the interpretation of data in the structure.

5) The order of the fields within compound structures must be the same on each host.

6) A memory page may contain data of only one type, which may be a compound type containing multiple data items of other types.

Of the above limitations, the first three are "hard" in that they are limitations to our design. The fourth limitation is particular to the C language. The fifth is not a problem in any of the systems we know of, including the Sun and the Firefly. The last limitation is not necessary, but is desirable for efficiency.

D. Page Sizes

In a heterogeneous system with machines supporting different VM page sizes, choosing a size for the DSM page becomes an important issue. We may use the largest VM page size for DSM pages. Since VM page sizes are most likely powers of 2, multiple small VM pages fit exactly in one DSM page; hence, they can be treated as a group on page faults. The potential drawback of such a *largest page size* algorithm is that more data than necessary may be moved between hosts with smaller VM page sizes. In severe cases, *page thrashing* may occur, when data items in the same DSM page are being updated by multiple hosts at the same time, causing large numbers of page transfers among the hosts without much progress in the execution of the application. While page thrashing may occur with any DSM page size, it is more likely with larger DSM page sizes, due to increased *false sharing*, where nonoverlapping regions in the same page are shared and updated by threads on different hosts, causing repeated page transfers. False sharing should be contrasted to real sharing, in which a number of data items are shared and updated by multiple hosts. While performance degradation due to real sharing is hard to avoid, performance degradation due to false sharing can often be reduced by using smaller DSM pages.[6]

One way to reduce data contention is to use the smallest VM page size for the DSM pages. If a page fault occurs on a host with a larger page size, multiple DSM pages are moved to fill that (larger) page. If a fault occurs on a host with a small (DSM) page and no host with a large page size is sharing the data, then only this small (DSM) page needs to be obtained. We call this the *smallest page size* algorithm.[7]

Typically, if page thrashing does not occur, more DSM page faults occur on hosts with small VM page sizes, resulting in more fault handling overhead and (small) page transfers. Although intermediate DSM page sizes are possible, the above two algorithms represent the two extremes of the page size algorithms. We have implemented both algorithms in Mermaid, and the performance comparison between them will be discussed in Section IV-C2.

---

[6] False sharing can also be reduced by rearranging memory layout, so that data that would be falsely shared if placed on the same page is assigned to different pages.

[7] The actual algorithm must differentiate between many cases depending on the type of page fault (read or write), the page sizes of the requesting and the owner hosts, and how the page is currently being shared (what type of hosts have read/write accesses).

IV. Performance Evaluation

We have performed a number of experiments on our prototype Mermaid system in order to study the impacts of heterogeneity on the performance of distributed shared memory systems. Along the way, some performance aspects of distributed shared memory in general are also studied. In the following, we first discuss a number of overhead measurements, followed by the response time measurements of three Mermaid applications. We then assess the performance impact of DSM page size algorithms and page thrashing. All measurements were performed on Sun3/60 workstations and Fireflies. The measured hosts were idle during the experiments, except for the activities being studied. The results we observed were very stable (except for the page thrashing cases to be discussed in Section IV-C2). The Mermaid prototype is not fine-tuned to achieve optimal performance, since our goal is not to push the performance of HDSM to its limit, but to assess its practical value in terms of its performance and ability in supporting applications.

A. Overhead Assessment

Compared to physical shared memory, distributed shared memory has a number of additional overheads. Since data is no longer physically shared, DSM pages need to be moved between hosts upon page faults, typically over a slow, bit-serial network, such as the Ethernet. In a user-level implementation, the access rights of the DSM pages have to be set, and DSM page faults have to be passed to the user level. The allocation of shared memory, thread scheduling, and thread synchronization also introduce overhead, but they are relatively small compared to the communication overheads. Finally, for heterogeneous systems, the costs of data conversion and the page size algorithm must be added.

The basic costs of handling a page fault in Mermaid are shown in Table III. Included are the invocation of the user-level handler, the identification of page fault type (read or write), the HDSM page table processing, and the request message transmission time.[8] The delay in transferring the page over the network is not included. The values of a few milliseconds are considered to be quite small. The costs on the Fireflies are higher, due to the higher overhead of the page fault handling mechanism for access violation (about 4.5 ms or higher). The operating system kernel, the "nub," of Taos version 72.4 on the Fireflies, considers access violation fault to be a rare case.

Table IV shows the costs of transferring 8 kilobyte and 1 kilobyte pages between hosts. The higher cost when the Firefly is involved is partially due to user level message fragmentation and reassembly processing. The costs for 8 kilobyte transfers are only about three times that of 1 kilobyte transfers, due to the fixed portion of the cost of the message transport. Hence, in the absence of page thrashing, larger DSM pages incur fewer page faults and lower data transfer overhead.

---

[8] To collect the data for this and subsequent overhead measurements, the Mermaid system was slightly modified so that a large number of the same operation (e.g., 100 000) are performed in a sequence, and the total elapsed time measured.

TABLE III
Costs of Page Fault Handling (ms)

	Sun	Firefly
Read	1.98	6.80
Write	2.04	6.70

TABLE IV
Costs of Transferring a Page (ms)

to from	Sun	Firefly	Sun	Firefly
Sun	18	27	5.1	7.6
Firefly	25	33	7.3	6.7
page size	8 kilobyte		1 kilobyte	

TABLE V
Costs of Data Conversions (ms)

page data type	8 kilobyte page		1 kilobyte	
	Sun	Firefly	Sun	Firefly
`int`	5.01	7.75	0.63	1.00
`short`	6.53	10.0	0.82	1.15
`float`	9.72	13.9	1.22	1.68
`double`	11.6	29.0	1.46	3.63
user structure	6.61	21.6	0.67	2.15

The measured costs of converting a page of integers, shorts, floating point numbers (single and double precision), and the user-defined structure of Fig. 2(a) on a Sun3/60 and a Firefly are shown in Table V. In all of the cases except that of `double` on Fireflies, the conversion costs are substantially lower than those of page transfer. The cost of converting an 1 kilobyte page is approximately 1/8 of that for an 8 kilobyte page. It is interesting to note that the overhead for converting the user-defined structure with an embedded structure is not much larger than that for the basic types. We also measured several other user data structures and found their conversion costs to be comparable.

To consider the combined effects of the overhead costs discussed above, we show the end-to-end page fault delays for different types of hosts in Table VI. Three different scenarios are considered, depending on the locations of the host on which the thread triggering the page fault resides (Requester), the host acting as the manager for the page (Manager), and the host currently having ownership of the page (Owner). While the Requester and the Owner are always different (otherwise there would not be a page fault in the first place), the Requester and the Manager, or the Manager and the Owner may be the same host. The cost for (integer) data conversion is included when the Requester and Owner hosts are of different types. The measurements are based on the largest page size algorithm, so the values are for 8 kilobyte pages only. The costs for read and write page faults were found to be very similar. The HDSM page fault delay is comparable to that of a VM page fault involving a disk seek. The costs of page faults involving both the Sun and the Firefly are very comparable to the homogeneous case of Firefly, but higher than that of Sun, partly due to user-level message fragmentation and reassembly. As with traditional VM, if the HDSM fault rate is not excessive, the application's performance under distributed shared memory may be close to that under physical shared memory.

B. Evaluation of Application Performance

1) Three Sample Applications: While the cost measurements above are useful in assessing the performance penalty of distributed shared memory, the most direct measure of DSM performance is the execution times of applications. One of the

applications we implemented on Mermaid is a parallel version of matrix multiplication (MM) in which the computation of the rows in the result matrix is performed by a number of threads running simultaneously, each on a separate processor. The result matrix is divided into a number of groups of adjacent rows equal to the number of threads, and assigned to the threads. The result matrix is write-shared among the threads, whereas the two argument matrices are only read-shared, and can hence be replicated. At the end of the computation, pieces of the result matrix are transferred (implicitly) to the master thread, which creates and coordinates the activities of the slave threads, but performs no multiplication itself. Except where noted, the experiments discussed below use 512×512 matrices of `double`[9] numbers.

Another application we converted to run under Mermaid is a program that detects flaws in printed circuit boards (PCB). Two digital images (front- and back-lit) of a sample PCB are taken by a camera, digitized, and then transferred to a workstation to be stored as large matrices. The software then checks the geometric features on the board, such as conductors, wire holes, and spacing between them. If design rule violations are found, they are high-lighted in a third image, which is displayed on the workstation, so that a human decision may be made to rectify the problem. The amount of computation involved in the rule checking is substantial: on a Firefly, it takes about 11 min to process a 2 cm $\times$ 32 cm area using a sequential version of the software. Obviously, speeding up the execution would make the feedback on the manufacturing line more timely, reducing the number of boards that may have to be discarded. A suitable computing environment for on-line PCB inspection is a workstation with bit-mapped display, coupled with compute servers on which the checking software runs in parallel. We therefore used Mermaid as a prototype for such a system. Our version of the PCB software has a master thread that runs on a Sun, divides the board area into stripes, and creates threads on the Fireflies to check them.[10] All data including the raw and processed images, and the data structures containing the design rules and the flaw statistics are allocated in the DSM space, and are properly converted when transferred between the Sun master and the Firefly slave threads. For our measurements, an area of 2 cm $\times$ 32 cm is used.

A third application we used to study Mermaid performance is a partial differential equation solver that uses the Successive

---

[9] 64-bit, double precision floating point numbers.

[10] Small overlaps of the stripes are necessary so that features on the borders are checked properly.

TABLE VI
END-TO-END PAGE FAULT DELAYS FOR 8 KB PAGES (ms)

	Sun→Sun		Ffly→Sun		Sun→Ffly		Ffly→Ffly	
	R	W	R	W	R	W	R	W
R/M→O	26.4	26.7	47.7	48.3	56.3	47.8	46.5	46.4
R→M/O	29.6	27.9	50.9	51.6	58.6	59.4	49.6	49.1
R→M→O	31.7	31.3	54.7	55.5	61.9	61.3	54.4	53.6

R = Requester host;   M = Manager host;   O = Page Owner R/M:
R/M: Requester and Manager are on the same host.
M/O: Manager and Owner are on the same host.

Over-Relaxation method (SOR). Data is represented as a large two-dimensional matrix. With the boundary values fixed, the internal values are then iteratively updated to be the average of the values of their four neighbors, until they converge. While this application is again based on large matrices (so we can partition the computation along with the data by assigning groups of adjacent rows of the matrix to the threads on various Fireflies), its data access behavior is quite different from the above two applications. The threads update values in their regions asynchronously with each other. The entries in the matrix are updated many times, and, for each iteration, the neighboring entries in the neighboring rows are needed. Thus, page sharing occurs in every iteration, and the number of iterations generally grows with the size of the matrix. Furthermore, to reach a decision on global convergence, the local convergence condition of each thread needs to be recorded in a shared array, and is checked by all threads. Given the simple model of data sharing used in Mermaid, it is interesting to see if page thrashing can be avoided, and good speedup can be achieved. For the experiments described below, a matrix of 128×816 of `double` numbers is used.

2) Physical Versus Distributed Shared Memory: Since the Firefly is a multiprocessor, we are able to compare the performance of physical shared memory to that of distributed shared memory. The same number of threads are either allocated to the processors on the same Firefly or to multiple Fireflies, (with one thread on each). The speedups of MM for both cases are shown in Table VII, for up to a maximum number of four threads. The slightly worse performance for the distributed case is due mainly to the cost of transferring pages between the machines. As also observed with the PCB and SOR applications, the penalty for running in a distributed system depends on the costs of data distribution and replication and the costs of data consistency and less so on the costs of data conversion. The distribution and replication costs are determined by the underlying communication and data conversion costs, whereas data conversion costs also depend on the applications' data access behaviors.

3) Heterogeneous Versus Homogeneous Shared Memory: To assess the effect of heterogeneity, we measured the response times of the three sample applications with a number of threads running on one or multiple Fireflies, and the master thread running on a Sun3/60. This is a representative configuration of heterogeneous distributed shared memory that takes advantages of both the user-friendly programming environment on a workstation, and the computing power of the background server hosts. Compared to the similar case in which both

TABLE VII
SPEEDUPS OF MATRIX MULTIPLICATION WHEN
EXECUTED ON ONE OR MULTIPLE FIREFLIES

	number of processors			
	1	2	3	4
physical shared memory	1.00	1.98	3.00	3.97
distributed shared memory	0.97	1.91	2.87	3.32

the master and the slave threads run on Fireflies, very little performance difference is observed. In the first case, pages of the matrices are moved from the Sun to the Fireflies and the result matrix is then moved back to the Sun after the computation; all data movements are accompanied by appropriate data conversions. No data conversion is needed for the homogeneous case. This is further evidence that data conversion does not add significant overhead to HDSM.

4) Application Performance with HDSM: The speedup curves of the MM, PCB, and SOR applications running on Mermaid are shown in Figs. 3, 4, and 5. The speedups are computed with respect to a sequential execution on a Firefly. For all the data points, the master thread is located on a separate Sun3/60. One to four Fireflies are used, and the numbers of threads allocated to each are approximately balanced. Better performance was observed using the largest page size algorithm for MM and PCB, while for SOR the smallest page size algorithm produced the best results (to be discussed further in Section IV-C2). For MM, performance improvements are observed as more and more threads are added to the computation, up to 18, the maximum number of Firefly processors available, for a maximum speedup of 12.

For PCB, there are two additional limitations to speedup: First, the volume of data to be transferred is very high (about 5 megabytes for each image), incurring substantial synchronous delays to remote worker threads as parts of the images are faulted in from the master. Second, the overlapping areas of the images must be processed by two threads, and represent extra computation, which grows as more threads are used. Despite these limitations, good speedup (up to 10 using 14 threads on four Fireflies) were still observed. Hence, the checking can now be completed in 65 s on four Fireflies, instead of 11 min in the sequential case. In some cases, super-linear speedup was observed. This is due to a reduction in the VM working set, as the data is partitioned among more and more processors where CPU caching becomes more effective. This observation is analogous to one made by Li with respect to main memory and VM paging [17].

The performance of SOR is comparable to that of MM,

337

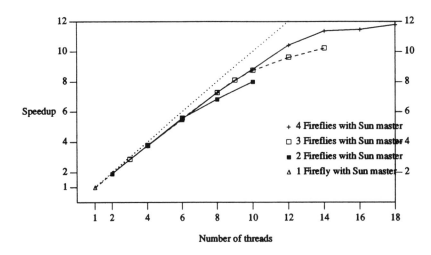

Fig. 3. Matrix multiplication with master on Sun and slaves on one to four Fireflies.

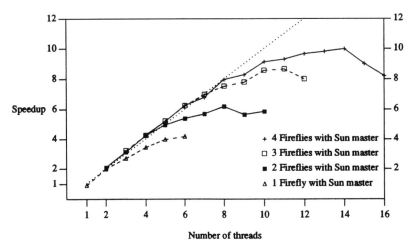

Fig. 4. PCB with master on Sun and slaves on one to four Fireflies.

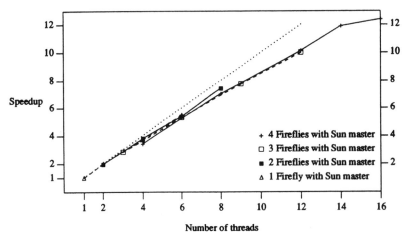

Fig. 5. SOR with master on Sun and slaves on one to four Fireflies.

despite the large numbers of iterations made by the threads, causing many page faults on the pages that are shared by threads running on different Fireflies. Thrashing does not usually happen, since an iteration for each thread takes 150 ms or more, whereas a fault on an 1 kilobyte page only takes

approximately 15 ms.

The same application has been studied in the Amber system at the University of Washington [8]. In Amber, an object-oriented approach is used for parallel application support. For the SOR application, the Amber implementation partitions the matrix into groups of rows called section objects, and stores one section object on each of the Fireflies. Multiple computation threads on each Firefly work on the local section object in parallel, and a separate communication thread on each Firefly sends the boundary rows of the section object to the neighboring Fireflies as the rows are updated. Thus, the potential of data contention in Mermaid is avoided in Amber, and the computing threads never have to stop for data. With the limited number of processors we have, however, our results are very comparable to those of Amber's on problems of similar sizes. (A 122×842 matrix was used with Amber.) Programming an application on Mermaid, on the other hand, is much simpler than on Amber, because communication is completely hidden in the shared memory system model.

It is interesting to note that physical shared memory is treated as a special case of distributed shared memory in Mermaid; the two types of memory are fully integrated throughout the heterogeneous system base, and the performance potential of such a system is well explored (in the sense that physical shared memory is used if present and distributed shared memory is used otherwise). Also, the number of machines involved does not affect the performance of any of the three applications much, as evidenced by the close clustering of the curves in Figs. 3, 4, and 5. The feasibility and performance potential of HDSM systems are therefore clearly demonstrated by these experiments, at least for certain classes of applications.

Besides the data sizes used in the above experiments, we also measured the performance of the three applications with several other data sizes to force the same DSM pages to be shared among multiple hosts. No significant changes to the speedup values were found from those presented above.

C. Effects of the Page Size Algorithms and Page Thrashing

To assess the effects of page thrashing due to data contention among threads, and to study the relationship between page size and thrashing, we conducted a number of experiments using two different implementations of matrix multiplication. The first, MM1, assigns large groups of rows of the result matrix to each thread,[11] the second, MM2, assigns rows to threads in a round-robin fashion. MM2 is expected to have more data contention on its DSM pages and is intended to represent the class of applications with this behavior. By using matrix multiplication for both, we are able to eliminate other factors affecting the performance of parallel applications, such as scalability and the size of data sets.

1) Effects of Page Size Algorithms and Locality: We compared the performance of MM1 using the largest page size algorithm to that using the smallest page size algorithm, and found that there is a small but definite degradation in performance when using smaller page sizes, due to an increased number of page faults on the Fireflies (see Fig. 6).

Since MM2 divides the result matrix into rows for the slave threads (4 kilobyte, or 512 `double` floats each), and since the smallest page size algorithm operates on 1 kilobyte pages, we expected the degradation of MM2 over MM1 using this smallest page size algorithm to be very small, which

[11]MM1 is the implementation of MM being used so far.

we verified experimentally (results not presented here). The degradation is slightly greater with 256×256 matrices of integers, where one DSM page of 1 kilobyte holds one row of the matrix (256 integers). Using integers instead of double precision floating point numbers, together with the smaller matrices, accentuates the importance of communication and locality.

2) Thrashing: The most likely case for thrashing is MM2 with the largest page size algorithm, where an 8 kilobyte page is shared by up to 8 threads running on several Fireflies. We ran MM2 with various numbers of threads on two or three Fireflies. The corresponding execution times we observed fluctuated greatly, even between consecutive runs of identical setup. Speedup relative to the sequential case was rarely observed, while execution times up to 10 times of that of the sequential case were measured. Examination of the detailed statistics of the numbers of page faults and transfers revealed that a large number of pages were being transferred between the Fireflies; the performance degradation and unpredictable fluctuations were clearly due to page thrashing.

From the above experiments, it may be concluded that if the locality in the application's data accesses is very good, large DSM page sizes may generate less overhead and better performance. If data in small ranges of the DSM space are updated by separate threads, however, performance may degrade greatly using large pages due to false sharing, and small page sizes are more likely to provide stable performance.

Our experience with a number of applications shows that small, seemingly minor changes to an implementation of an application may result in very different data sharing patterns and drastically different performance. MM1 versus MM2, using the largest page size algorithm, is such an example. For the SOR application, we initially implemented the algorithm so that each thread, during each iteration, updated the data elements in its portion of the matrix from top to bottom, thus sharing data with neighboring threads in every iteration. The resulting performance was unsatisfactory due to the frequent read–write sharing. We then changed the algorithm such that each thread updated the data elements in its portion of the matrix from top to bottom to top. Performance is improved substantially because the number of times the boundary rows are worked on is reduced by half, and the amount of computation in between such shared data zones is doubled. Consequently, data movement between machines and the possibility of data contention are reduced, and better speedups are observed (as shown in Fig. 5).

V. Concluding Remarks

In this paper, we discussed the main issues and solutions of building a DSM system on a network of heterogeneous machines. As a practical research effort, we designed and implemented an HDSM system, Mermaid, for a network of Sun workstations and Firefly multiprocessors, and we ported a number of applications to Mermaid. We conclude that heterogeneous DSM is indeed feasible. From a functional point of view, we showed that little transparency need be lost due to heterogeneity. The most important problem is data

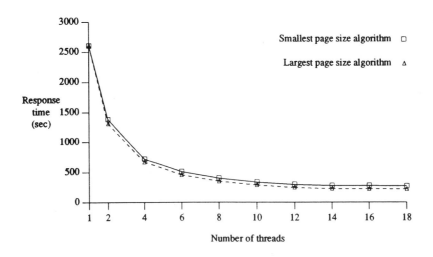

Fig. 6. Response times of MM1 using the largest (smallest) page size algorithms.

conversion. Our solution requires that the user specify the type of data being allocated in the HDSM space, which is usually natural to the programmer. For different representations of floating point numbers, equivalent data conversion may be impossible for extreme values. However, with the increasing use of the IEEE floating point standard, this may be considered to be a passing problem. We were able to easily integrate our HDSM system into the physical shared memory system on the Firefly, allowing the programmer to exploit both physical and distributed shared memory using one and the same mechanism.

From a performance point of view, we again showed that little transparency is lost due to heterogeneity; that is, our heterogeneous DSM implementation performs comparably to an equivalent homogeneous DSM system. Overall, we have found that the cost of data conversion does not substantially increase the cost of paging across the network. Other aspects of heterogeneity, such as accommodating different page sizes and user-level processing of messages, also do not contribute significantly to the DSM overhead. The presence of multiple VM page sizes on different types of machines presents applications with the opportunity of selecting the DSM page size according to their data access patterns; we noticed substantial performance gains in using suitable DSM page sizes.

Our measured performance results corroborate the results of other researchers in that distributed shared memory can be competitive to the direct use of message passing, for a reasonably large class of applications. In some cases, they actually outperform their message passing counterparts, even though the shared memory system is implemented in a layer on top of a message passing system.

Although our prototype Mermaid system integrates only two types of hosts, we believe that the techniques we developed to accommodate heterogeneity are easily extensible to more than two types of hosts, without significant additional overhead. For conversion of user-defined data types, the same conversion routines can be used on all machines since the routines only contain structural information. However, for the basic types, separate conversion routines need to be written for each (ordered) pair of machines, with a total of $N \times (N - 1)$ routines for each basic data type allocated in the HDSM space.

For the implementor of the HDSM system, this is a one-time only effort and is transparent to the application programmer. In contrast, defining a network standard data format would decrease the conversion coding effort, but increase the run-time conversion overhead.

ACKNOWLEDGMENT

T. McInnerny was responsible for most of the Mermaid implementation work, and conducted the measurements reported in this paper. M. Lalovic and S. Fink separately implemented two versions of the data conversion routine generator software. A. Yip performed an initial porting of the PCB software to Mermaid running on Suns. The SOR application is based on a parallel implementation for a Firefly by R. Unrau. Comments by the anonymous referees helped us to improve the presentation of this paper. Partial support for this work was generously provided by the Information Technology Research Center of Ontario and Digital Equipment Corporation.

REFERENCES

[1] "Network computing systems reference manual." Tech. rep., Apollo Computer Inc., Chelmsford, MA, 1987.
[2] E. Balkovich, S. Lerman, and R. P. Parmelee. "Computing in higher education: The Athena experience," *Commun. ACM*, vol. 28, no. 11, pp. 1214–1224, 1985.
[3] J. Bennet, J. Carter, and W. Zwaenepoel, "Munin: Distributed shared memory based on type-specific memory coherence," in *Proc. PPoPP*, Mar. 1990, pp. 168–176.
[4] B. N. Bershad, D. T. Ching, E. D. Lazowska, H. Sanislo, and M. Schwartz, "A remote procedure call facility for interconnecting heterogeneous computer systems," *IEEE Trans. Software Eng.*, vol. SE-13, no. 8, pp. 880–894, 1987.
[5] D. R. Cheriton, "Preliminary thoughts on problem-oriented shared memory: A decentralized approach to distributed systems," *ACM Oper. Syst. Rev.*, vol. 19, no. 4, Oct. 1985.
[6] D. Cohen, "On holy wars and a plea for peace," *IEEE Comput. Mag.*, vol. 14, no. 10, 1981.
[7] C. Pinkerton *et al.*, "A heterogeneous distributed file system," in *Proc. Tenth IEEE Int. Conf. Distributed Comput. Syst.*, 1990.
[8] J. Chase *et al.*, "The Amber system: Parallel programming on a network of multiprocessors," in *Proc. Twelfth ACM Symp. Oper. Syst. Principles*, 1989.
[9] R. Sandberg *et al.*, "Design and implementation of the Sun network filesystem," in *Proc. 1985 Summer USENIX Conf.*, 1985.

[10] B. D. Fleisch, "Mirage: A coherent distributed shared memory design," in *Proc. 12th ACM Symp. Oper. Syst. Principles*, Dec. 1989, pp. 211–223,

[11] A. Forin, J. Barrera, M. Young, and R. Rashid, "Design, implementation, and performance evaluation of a distributed shared memory server for Mach," in *Proc. 1989 Winter USENIX Conf.*, Jan. 1989.

[12] K. Geihs and U. Holberg, "Retrospective on DACNOS," *Commun. ACM*, vol. 33, no. 2, pp. 439–448, Apr. 1990.

[13] D. P. Geller, "The national software works: Access to distributed files and tools," in *Proc. ACM Nat. Conf.*, Oct. 1977, pp. 39–43,

[14] M. Kaashoek, A. Tanenbaum, S. Hummel, and H. Bal, "An efficient reliable broadcast protocol," *ACM Oper. Syst. Rev.*, vol. 23, no. 4, pp. 5–19, Oct. 1989.

[15] R.E. Kessler and M. Livny, "An analysis of distributed shared memory algorithms," in *Proc. 9th Int. Conf. Distributed Comput. Syst.*, June 1989.

[16] O. Krieger and M. Stumm, "An optimistic approach for consistent replicated data for mulitcomputers," in *Proc. 1990 HICSS*, 1990.

[17] K. Li, "Shared virtual memory on loosely coupled multiprocessors," Ph.D. dissertation, Dep. Comput. Sci., Yale Univ. 1986.

[18] K. Li and P. Hudak, "Memory coherence in shared virtual memory systems," *ACM Trans. Comput. Syst.*, vol. 7, no. 4, pp. 321–359, Nov. 1989.

[19] T. McInnerny, M. Stumm, and S. Zhou, "Mermaid user's guide and programmer's manual," Tech. rep., Computer Systems Research Institute, Univ. Toronto, Sept. 1990.

[20] P. R. McJones and G. F. Swart, "Evolving the UNIX system interface to support multithreaded programs," Tech. Rep. 21, Systems Research Center, Digital Equipment Corp., Sept. 1987.

[21] J. H. Moris, M. Satyanarayanan, D. S. H. Rosenthal M. H. Conner, J. H. Howard, and F. D. Smith, "Andrew: A distributed personal computing environment," *Commun. ACM*, vol. 29, no. 3, pp. 184–201, 1986.

[22] D. Notkin, N. Hutchinson, J. Sanislo, and M. Schwartz, "Heterogeneous computing environments: Report on the ACM SIGOPS workshop on accommodating heterogeneity," *Commun. ACM*, vol. 30, no. 2, pp. 142–162, Feb. 1987.

[23] P. Rovner, "Extending Modula-2 to build large integrated systems," *IEEE Software*, vol. 6, pp. 46–57, Nov. 1986.

[24] M. Stumm and S. Zhou, "Algorithms implementing distributed shared memory," *IEEE Comput. Mag.*, vol. 23, no. 5, May 1990.

[25] ———, "Fault tolerant distributed shared memory," in *Proc. IEEE Int. Conf. Parallel Distributed Comput.*, Dec 1990.

[26] "Networking on the Sun workstation," Tech. rep., Sun Microsystems Inc., Mt. View CA, 1985.

[27] C. P. Thacker, L. C. Stewart, and E. H. Satterthwaite, "Firefly: A multiprocessor workstation," *IEEE Trans. Comput.*, vol. 37, no. 8, pp. 909–920, Aug. 1988.

Songnian Zhou (S'83–M'87) received the B.S. degree from Northeastern University, Boston, MA, in 1982, and the M.S. and Ph.D. degrees in computer science from the University of California, Berkeley, in 1984 and in 1987, respectively.

Since 1987, he has been on the faculty of the Departments of Computer Science and Electrical Engineering at the University of Toronto, where he is currently an Associate Professor. He is a member of the Computer Systems Research Institute. His research interests include parallel computation, multiprocessor operating system, distributed systems, computer networks, and performance evaluation.

Dr. Zhou is a member of the IEEE Computer Society and the Association for Computing Machinery.

Michael Stumm (M'87) received the diploma in mathematics and the Ph.D. in computer science from the University of Zurich, Switzerland, in 1980 and 1984, respectively.

Since 1987, he has been on the faculty of the Departments of Electrical Engineering and Computer Science at the University of Toronto, where he is currently an Associate Professor. He is a member of the Computer Systems Research Institute. His research interests are in the area of computer systems.

Dr. Stumm is a member of the IEEE Computer Society and the Association for Computing Machinery.

Kai Li received the B.S. degree from Jilin University, China, in 1977, the M.S. degree from the Graduate School of the University of Science and Technology, China, in 1981, and the M.S. and Ph.D. degrees in computer science from Yale University in 1983 and 1986, respectively.

Since 1986, he has been on the faculty of the Department of Computer Science at Princeton University, where he is currently an Associate Professor. His research interests include parallel and distributed systems, parallel programming, and computer architecture.

Dr. Li is a member of the IEEE Computer Society and the Association for Computing Machinery.

David Wortman (S'65–M'70) received the B.S.E.E. degree from Yale University in 1961, and the M.Sc. and Ph.D. degrees in computer science from Stanford University in 1968 and 1972, respectively.

Since 1970 he has been on the faculty of the Department of Computer Science at the University of Toronto where he is currently a Professor. He is a member of the Computer Systems Research Institute at the University of Toronto where he pursues research in the areas of advanced compilation techniques, software engineering, and computer architecture. His most recent research has been on the design and implementation of high-performance concurrent and distributed compilers.

Dr. Wortman is a member of the IEEE, IFIP Working Group 2.4, the IEEE Computer Society and the Association for Computing Machinery.

Chapter 4
Performance of Message-Passing Multicomputers

In a message-passing multicomputer, multiple computers are connected by an interconnection network and operate under an integrated operating system. Each computer consists of a CPU, a local memory, and a switch connecting to the network. The system does not implement a shared-memory view, so the communication is achieved by passing messages explicitly over the network. The interconnection network may assume any topology, but hypercube and two-dimensional- (2D)-mesh topologies are most commonly used in multicomputer systems. Commercial examples are the Intel iPSC hypercube series and the Intel Paragon and n-cube multicomputers. A fat-tree interconnection has been used in the Connection Machine CM-5 multicomputer.

An important factor determining the efficiency of a message-passing multicomputer is the effectiveness with which data can be exchanged among its many processor nodes. This chapter gives general computing models and an analysis of hardware and software supporting a multicomputer system. The analysis is enhanced by examination and comparison of communication structures, message routing, interprocessor topology, and software/hardware protocols for message passing among commercially available multicomputers. In addition to its communication capabilities, a multicomputer has other special characteristics. First, a multicomputer system is able to support a large number of processors through connection with high-speed networks. Second, each processor node executes independently of all other processor nodes; synchronization among the nodes is supported by message passing. Finally, and most importantly, it is the programmer's duty to decompose the application and distribute the tasks among processors for the computation.

The papers we have selected discuss important design and performance issues of multicomputer systems. The first paper, by Athas and Seitz, overviews the system and architecture development of message-passing multicomputers and gives details on programming a multicomputer and on the effect of granularity on performance. The paper shows that a multicomputer system handles effectively medium- and large-grained parallel programs.

The next paper, by Bhuyan and Agrawal, presents a generalized hypercube (GH) structure based on a new mixed-radix number system. The paper shows that a variety of multidimensional structures can be obtained, based on how the total number of nodes is factorized. It presents a performance evaluation technique for a multicomputer when store-and-forward (packet) switching is followed for communication between the processors. The k-ary n-cube multicomputer, proposed in the next paper, by Dally, is a multidimensional torus that can be considered as a part of GH design, with k processors in each dimension and a constrained connection of links. However, the analysis given in Dally's paper is based on wormhole routing instead of store-and-forward routing. Wormhole routing is widely employed in multicomputers because the delay is independent of the distance between the source and the destination.

Wormhole routing works very well when the network traffic is low, but when network traffic is high, there is a lot of interference between the messages; then, as a result, wormhole routing performs poorly. The paper by Kim and Das gives an approximate analysis of wormhole routing in the hypercubes in the presence of such interference. Besides hypercubes, mesh interconnection networks are popular for implementing large-scale multiprocessors. A successful commercial implementation is the Intel Paragon. In the next paper, Adve and Vernon develop a detailed analytic performance of wormhole-routed mesh networks, considering both latency and contention. They develop an approximate-mean-value analysis with a closed queuing network model that is applicable to both message-passing and shared-memory work loads.

The paper by Johnsson and Ho analyzes four different communication problems in hypercubes and provides low-complexity solutions. The authors supplement their analytic results by doing some experiments on the Intel iPSC multicomputer. In the next paper, by Ahluwalia and Singhal, a discrete-time Markov chain model of the interprocessor communication network architecture of the CM-2 machine is developed to compute the message delay. Although CM-2 is a fine-grained single-instruction, multiple-data (SIMD) machine, the analytic model and results presented in the paper are applicable equally to the communication processors in any message-passing multicomputer system. Zhang takes an experimental approach in the next paper. A series of experiments and analyses on five types of hypercube and 2D-mesh topology multicomputers is presented. Also, a transputer system is introduced and its message-passing performance is reported.

Adaptive-routing protocols can route messages dynamically around network trouble spots such as component failures and communication bottlenecks. The next paper, by Gaughan and Yalamanchili, discusses a group of adaptive-routing protocols for a hypercube multicomputer. Besides Intel and n-cube multicomputers, other experimental message-passing architectures have been developed in recent years. The MIT J-Machine and the Connection Machine CM-5 are two such examples. The final paper, by Spertus et al., presents a comparative performance evaluation of these two machines.

Bibliography

Abraham, S., and K. Padmanabhan, "Performance of the Direct Binary n-Cube Network for Multiprocessors," *IEEE Trans. Computers*, Vol. 38, No. 7, July 1989, pp. 1000–1011.

Annaratone, M., C. Pommerell, and R. Ruhl, "Interprocessor Communication Speed and Performance in Distributed-Memory Parallel Processors," *Proc. 16th Ann. Int'l Symp. Computer Architecture*, IEEE CS Press, Los Alamitos, Calif., 1989, pp. 315–324.

Dally, W.J., and C.L. Seitz, "Deadlock-Free Message Routing in Multiprocessor Interconnection Networks," *IEEE Trans. Computers*, Vol. C-36, No. 5, May 1987, pp. 547–553.

Dunigan, T.H., "Performance of the Intel iPSC/860 and Ncube 6400 Hypercubes," *Int'l J. Supercomputing Applications*, 1992.

Fox, G., et al., *Solving Problems on Concurrent Processors*, Vol. 1 and Vol. 2, Prentice-Hall, Inc., Englewood Cliffs, N.J., 1990.

Hayes, J.P., and T. Mudge, "Hypercube Supercomputers," *Proc. IEEE*, Vol. 77, No. 12, Dec. 1989, pp. 1829–1841.

Leiserson, C.E., et al., "The Network Architecture of the Connection Machine CM-5," *Proc. 1992 ACM Symp. Parallel Algorithms and Architectures*, ACM, New York, N.Y., 1992.

Ni, L.M., and P.K. McKinley, "A Survey of Wormhole Routing Techniques in Direct Networks," *Computer*, Vol. 26, No. 2, Feb. 1993, pp. 62–76.

Preparata, F.P., and J. Vullemin, "The Cube-Connected Cycles: A Versatile Network for Parallel Computation," *Comm. ACM*, Vol. 24, No. 5, May 1981, pp. 300–309.

Reed, D.A., and R.M. Fujimoto, *Multicomputer Networks*, MIT Press, Cambridge, Mass., 1987.

Reed, D.A., and D.C. Grunwald, "The Performance of Multicomputer Interconnection Networks," *Computer*, Vol. 20, No. 6, June 1987, pp. 63–73.

Saad, Y., and M. Schultz, "Data Communication in Parallel Architectures," *Parallel Computing*, No. 11, 1989, pp. 131–150.

Samantham, M.R., and D.K. Pradhan, "The De Bruijn Multiprocessor Network: A Versatile Parallel Processing and Sorting Network for VLSI," *IEEE Trans. Computers*, Vol. 38, No. 4, Apr. 1989, pp. 567–581.

Sanguinetti, J., "Performance of a Message-Based Multiprocessor," *Computer*, Vol. 19, No. 9, Sept. 1986, pp. 47–55.

Seitz, C., "The Cosmic Cube," *Comm. ACM*, Vol. 28, No. 1, Jan. 1985, pp. 22–33.

Tanenbaum, A.S., *Computer Networks*, Prentice-Hall, Inc., Englewood Cliffs, N.J., 1981.

Wittie, L.D., "Communication Structures for Large Networks of Multicomputers," *IEEE Trans. Computers*, Vol. C-30, No. 4, Apr. 1981, pp. 264–273.

Multicomputers: Message-Passing Concurrent Computers

William C. Athas and Charles L. Seitz

California Institute of Technology

H ighly concurrent computers achieve remarkable performance on the broad class of computations that can be formulated and expressed as concurrent programs. This performance is scalable in the number of computing elements, open-ended with technology advances, and low in cost. Several highly concurrent or highly parallel systems are now commercially available, and innovative programmers are applying them successfully to a great variety of demanding computing problems.

This article provides a status report on the architecture and programming of a family of message-passing concurrent computers that have evolved out of the research of the DARPA-sponsored Submicron Systems Architecture Project in the Caltech Computer Science Department. These systems are organized as ensembles of small programmable computers, called nodes, connected by a message-passing network (see Figure 1). This multiple-computer structure has fittingly come to be known as a multicomputer.

First-generation multicomputers include the Cosmic Cube[1] and the well-known commercial hypercube multicom-

Attacking a large computing problem with a myriad of small programmable computers requires a combination of architecture, programming systems, and program formulation.

puters; more than one hundred of these machines are currently in use. Second-generation multicomputers with faster nodes and much faster message-passing networks appeared during the past year. Configurations of these systems with as few as 64 nodes exhibit performance comparable to that of conventional supercomputers on a wide variety of large computing problems.[2,3]

Multicomputer programming. The usual abstract unit in which a multicomputer computation is formulated, a *process,* is an instance of a program. Just as an electrical circuit might contain many instances of a certain type of component, and many types of components, a concurrent computation might contain many instances of one or more programs. The programs might be written in conventional programming notations, such as C, Fortran, Pascal, or Lisp, with a standard library of functions or subroutines that cause messages to be sent and received. Other functions that cause the creation and destruction of processes allow intermediate results to determine dynamically the distribution of a computation.

A process contains its own code and private variables, and coordinates its activities with other processes by sending and receiving messages. To support the process abstraction, each multicomputer node runs a multiprogramming operating system that allows multiple processes to coex-

Reprinted from *Computer,* Vol. 21, No. 8, Aug. 1988, pp. 9–24.

0-8186-6522-X/95 $4.00 © 1988 IEEE

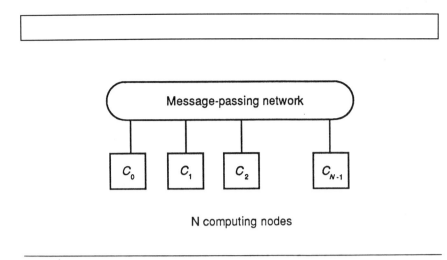

Figure 1. Programmer's model of a multicomputer.

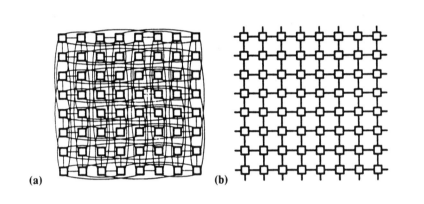

Figure 2. 64-node binary n-cube network (a), and two-dimensional mesh network (b).

ist within that node. Accordingly, the number of concurrent processes involved in a single computation can greatly exceed the number of nodes.

Physical architecture. Multiple-instruction, multiple-data parallel computers divide into two major types: shared-memory multiprocessors and message-passing multicomputers. We can uncover the reasons for many design choices used in multicomputers by comparing them with multiprocessors.

The logical structure of a shared-memory multiprocessor allows multiple processors to access memory in a single global address space. The aggregate demand on the global memory from a large number of processors dictates a number of memory elements comparable to the number of processors; hence, the shared global memory is a physically distributed memory that spans the global address space. Multiprocessors with large numbers of processors employ a switch network that allows any processor to connect to any memory. Some switch networks support a technique of combining references to, and operations on, the same storage location. Using a local or cache memory with each

processor can reduce the volume of accesses through the switch network; however, use of a cache for global variables requires a mechanism that allows the cache memories to discover when a global variable has changed.

In contrast, the message-passing multicomputer is both logically and physically a distributed-memory system. The processor in each node computer is tightly coupled to a memory that is physically separate and logically private from the memories of the other node computers. A global memory address does not exist; rather, each node has its own private memory address space. The fixed numbering of the nodes, $0, 1, \ldots, N - 1$, together with the unique numbering of the processes within each node, establishes globally unique identifiers for processes; hence, a global name space.

Interprocess communication in a multicomputer occurs by routing messages through a network such as a binary n-cube or mesh (see Figure 2). Regular networks simplify the routing. Their direct and bidirectional, as opposed to indirect,[4] structure allows process placement to exploit the locality of communications. The networks are also extensible, or scalable, to allow for systems with different numbers of nodes. The individual channels operate at rates comparable to the memory bandwidth of a node; the nodes cannot generate or absorb messages at a higher rate. The number of bits conveyed in parallel on a channel is typically less than the word length of the node memory, while messages are typically at least a few words long; hence, the message is serialized into a sequence of parallel-data units that we refer to as flow control units, or *flits*.

Latency issues. The *network latency* equals the time from when the head of a message enters the network at the source until the tail emerges at the destination. Since the flits move through the network in a pipeline fashion, the network latency equals the sum of two components:

- $T_p D$ is the time associated with forming the path through the network, where T_p is the delay of the individual routing nodes encountered on the path, and D is the number of nodes traversed, or the distance.
- L/B is the time required for a message of length L to pass through the channels of bandwidth B.

Multicomputer message-passing networks and multiprocessor switch networks have a similar function. The multicomputer network provides a complete $N \times N$ connection between N nodes. The multiprocessor network provides an $N \times M$ connection between N processors and M memories, where N and M have comparable magnitudes. Although multicomputer and multiprocessor networks are optimized somewhat differently for their different operating environments, the latest designs of both run up against the same physical electronic and packaging limitations. As we describe later, it is practical to build networks of tens of nodes in which the path formation component of the network latency equals one or two instruction times for a processor fabricated using comparable technology. However, networks with thousands of nodes are much more difficult to build and can exhibit latencies of tens of instruction times.

The performance of conventional instruction processors is quite sensitive to *memory-access latency*, the delay from when the processor emits an address to when the data is returned from memory. Interprocess communication in a multiprocessor occurs through the shared global memory. If the memory-access latency exceeds about one instruction time, the processor must idle until the storage cycle completes. Unless multiprocessor designers can discover methods to implement switch networks with lower latency or develop processors that are less sensitive to the memory-access latency, scaling multiprocessors into the range of thousands of nodes will be impractical.

Separate mechanisms that distinguish the different requirements for processor-to-memory communication and interprocess communication save the multicomputer from this scaling dilemma. Because the processor and memory are physically localized in a node, the processor-to-memory communication is not a problem. Interprocess message communication takes place in larger units and less frequently than memory accesses, and accordingly can exhibit a larger latency. Thus, no serious physical obstacles prevent scaling message-passing networks to support communication between thousands of nodes.

Multicomputers and multiprocessors are so logically similar that each can run programs written for the other. Programs written in a process model with message-passing are routinely run on multiprocessors simply by implementing the message-passing operations in the global shared

memory. Programs written in a process model with shared variables can be compiled to run on multicomputers by replacing assignments to shared variables with message-passing operations. The efficiency of this approach depends on how successfully the compiler can trace the data dependencies and manage the communications. Both multicomputers and multiprocessors can execute programs formulated for single-instruction, multiple-data message-passing parallel computers, such as the Connection Machine,[5] but such machines cannot efficiently execute programs that exploit the ability of multiple-instruction, multiple-data machines to run different programs on different processors.

Grain size. Although no single or perfect definition of grain size exists for multicomputers, the term loosely describes node size or complexity.[4] We refer to multicomputers whose nodes contain megabytes of memory as *medium-grain* machines, and to those whose nodes contain tens of kilobytes of memory as *fine-grain* machines.

Suppose we were to design a large-scale multicomputer with one gigabyte of primary storage. We might partition this storage into four-megabyte units for each of 256 nodes. We could package the integrated circuits for one node on a single circuit board or multichip carrier. Suitable programming environments for this medium-grain machine are directly compatible with programming environments hosted on workstations.

However, because multicomputers have few advantages over multiprocessors for small N, and because multiprocessors can simulate multicomputers more effectively than vice versa, consider the alternative of shifting N into a "niche" where multicom-

puters are still feasible but multiprocessors are not. For example, the same one gigabyte of storage might also be used for a fine-grain multicomputer with 32,768 nodes, each with 32 kilobytes of primary storage. This system could exhibit peak concurrency more than two orders of magnitude higher. A node would fit on a single very-large-scale-integration chip and would be extremely fast, given the advantage of processor-to-memory communication being localized to the chip.

Programming environments. A multicomputer includes one or more nodes with interfaces to a local area network, and/or one or more computers with interfaces to both the multicomputer's message-passing network and a local area network. Either of these configurations allows messages to be passed between processes in the multicomputer nodes and processes in network hosts, such as the user's workstation. Thus, multicomputers fit naturally into network computing environments and depend on the network hosts not only for preparing and compiling programs, but also for initiating and interacting with computations running on multicomputers.

The programming systems for medium-grain multicomputers have evolved through use for several years. Process code for an explicit concurrent formulation of a computing problem is written in familiar programming languages extended with a library of process-spawning and message-passing functions.

Our research group developed the Cosmic Environment and Reactive Kernel systems to support this multiple-process message-passing programming environment[6] on network hosts and medium-grain multicomputer nodes, respectively. The CE host runtime system consists of a set of daemon processes, utility programs, and libraries. It can serve as a stand-alone system for running message-passing programs on collections of network-connected Unix hosts. It can also handle the allocation of, and interfaces to, one or more multicomputers. When interfaced to a multicomputer, it supports uniform communication between host and node processes. The RK node operating system supports multiprogramming, message-driven process scheduling, storage management, and system calls for message-passing and other functions on each node.

CE and RK together provide uniform communication between processes

Figure 3. Intel iPSC/2 node (top) and vector accelerator (bottom).

independent of the multicomputer node or network host on which they happen to be located. These systems allow message-passing programs to be run not only on multicomputers, but also on shared-memory multiprocessors, across networks of workstations, and on sequential computers. A principle and a formal property of the entire CE/RK system—within the limits of the computation being deterministic and not exceeding available storage sizes—is that the results of a computation do not depend on the distribution of the processes.

Programming systems that support fine-grain concurrency are in their early stages of development. These systems are based on new programming languages that provide constructs for expressing fine-grain concurrency. Although many programming languages and language constructs have been proposed, two general approaches for expressing fine-grain concurrency have emerged.

One approach is based upon a static process structure in which the number of processes and their connectivity is known before the program executes. In Occam,[7] for example, all processes and channels for a computation are denoted in the source program. Each channel connects exactly two processes, and communication through the channel is synchronous; that is, the completion of the send action at one end of the channel is synchronized with the completion of the receive action at the other end. The Occam compiler performs an operation analogous to macro expansion on processes and channels, resulting in the static process structure.

The other general approach is based upon dynamic process structures in which processes are created and destroyed on demand. Message passing is accomplished by reference to the destination process rather than to a channel, and is asynchronous and buffered. Because references to processes can be communicated in messages, the connectivity of the process structure can vary as the computation proceeds. The Actor model[8] and programming notations, and the Cantor programming system,[9] which we describe later, exemplify this approach.

Medium-grain multicomputers

Between 1981 and 1985, members of our research group designed, built several copies of, and developed the system software for the Cosmic Cube,[1] an experimental message-passing concurrent computer that became the archetype of the first-generation multicomputers. Commercial multicomputers that use the same organization and programming methods—the Intel iPSC/1, Ametek S/14, and N-Cube/10—were introduced in 1985. The size of a single node in these systems ranges from seven chips (one custom VLSI chip with processor and communications, plus six RAM chips) in the N-Cube to two circuit boards (a regular node board plus a vector accelerator board) in the Intel iPSC/1 VX.

All of these systems use software-controlled routing on a binary n-cube network to connect $N = 2^n$ nodes; hence, they are sometimes called cubes or hypercubes. The number of nodes in a single system ranges from four (two-dimensional cube) to 1,024 (10-dimensional cube). The Floating Point Systems T-Series and other machines based on the Inmos transputer[7] are also multicomputers, but they employ a computational model based on the Occam programming language.

These first-generation multicomputers have proven to be reasonably "general-purpose" concurrent computers. They have been applied to a wide range of easily partitioned and distributed computing problems, such as matrix operations, differential equation solvers, finite element analysis, finite difference methods, distant- or local-field many-body problems, fast Fourier transforms, ray tracing, heuristic searches, circuit simulation, and distributed simulation of systems composed of loosely coupled physical processes. Hundreds of research papers and reports have been published on the concurrent formulations and results of these computations.

Current status. Multicomputers currently stand at the threshold of a second generation of medium-grain machines. The nodes of these systems employ the same 32-bit processor and megabit RAM technology used in personal computers and workstations. In comparison with first-generation machines, node performance and memory capacity have improved by nearly an order of magnitude within the same physical size simply by tracking the advances in single-chip processor and RAM technology. However, second-generation multicomputers are most distinguished by message-routing hardware that makes the topology of the message-passing network practically invisible to the programmer.

The message-routing hardware employs a blocking variant of cut-through routing that we call *wormhole* routing.[10-12] A message consists of a sequence of flits, in which the flit at the head of the message governs the route. As the head flit advances along the specified route, the remaining flits follow in a pipeline fashion. If the head encounters a channel already in use, it is blocked until the channel is freed; the flow control within the network blocks the trailing flits.

This form of routing and flow control has two important advantages over the store-and-forward packet cut-through routing used in first-generation machines. First, it avoids using storage bandwidth in the nodes through which messages are routed. To the designer of a multicomputer, the storage bandwidth of a node is a precious resource that should be spent on computing cycles rather than message routing. Second, this routing technique makes the message latency largely insensitive to the distance in the message-passing network. The network latency, $T_pD + L/B$, is dominated by the second term in the sum for all but very short messages. For example, in one implementation in which $T_p \approx 80$ nanoseconds and $B \approx 25$ megabytes per second, a 40-byte message that traverses five nodes would require 0.4 microsecond for path formation, but 1.6 microseconds to convey the message. Also, the fixed software overhead of system calls and context switching is much larger than the network latency.

Another improvement in message performance results from using lower-dimension and higher-radix versions of the k-ary n-cube network.[4] We can think of a k-ary n-cube—a family of torus networks with k^n nodes—as constructed in n dimensions with k periodic coordinates in each dimension. This family includes the binary (2-ary) n-cube (see Figure 2) network on one extreme and the k-element ring network (k-ary 1-cube) at the opposite extreme, and spans a range of wirability and average distance between pairs of nodes.

An analysis of the cost and performance of these networks must take into account that the more wirable networks can afford to assign more parallel wires, hence a higher bandwidth, to each channel. The optimization to minimize latency simply minimizes $T_pD + L/B$. High-dimension networks reduce the first term at the expense of the second, while low-

dimension networks reduce the second term at the expense of the first. An analysis[11] shows that a two-dimensional network minimizes latency for typical message lengths for $N \approx 256$.

The two-dimensional mesh (see Figure 2) is a variation on a k-ary 2-cube with the "end-around" cyclic connection eliminated. We prefer the mesh rather than the torus form of the cube because the mesh offers useful edge connectivity. Also, the mesh partitions into units that are still meshes, and the particular deadlock-free routing scheme used is simpler when the cyclic connection is eliminated.[10] Based on this reasoning, we expect that two-dimensional mesh networks will become the standard for second-generation machines.

Intel and Ametek recently introduced two early second-generation multicomputers. The Intel iPSC/2[2] is an upgraded Intel iPSC/1, with nodes based on the Intel 80386 processor and hardware wormhole message routing in the binary n-cube. Figure 3 shows an iPSC/2 node. The Ametek Series 2010[3] uses the Motorola 68020 as the node instruction processor, a microprogrammed second processor to manage the send and receive queues, and a two-dimensional wormhole routing mesh network. Figure 4 shows parts of two 4×4 submesh units of the Ametek Series 2010 and the way they are attached. Our research group developed the mesh routing chips[12]; MOSIS (Metal-Oxide Semiconductor Implementation Service) provided the fabrication. Both the iPSC/2 and the Series 2010 run the CE/RK programming environment.

In comparison with first-generation multicomputers, node performance has improved by nearly an order of magnitude, while the reduction in message latency for nonlocalized messages in the Series 2010 approaches three orders of magnitude. The relationship between communication and computing performance improved by two orders of magnitude. Faster communications extend the application span of multicomputers from easily partitioned and distributed problems to high-flux problems, such as searching, sorting, concurrent data structures,[11] graph problems, signal processing, image processing, and distributed simulation of systems composed of many tightly coupled physical processes. Making the message latency insensitive to message distance simplifies programming and allows more effective and less constrained dispersal of processes to achieve load balance.

Figure 4. Close-up of a region of the Ametek Series 2010 backplane.

Configurations. We can scale and configure medium-grain multicomputers in several ways. The number of nodes, N, is the most important scaling. Node memory size is another configuration choice. The preferred node memory size will likely approximate that in workstation computers, with nodes operating as virtual memory computers.

Although the first-generation systems are homogeneous—that is, the nodes are nominally identical—we can construct multicomputers equally well as heterogeneous systems with a variety of specialized nodes for different computations, so long as all the nodes employ the same communication protocols. One form of heterogeneous multicomputer system already exists in the installation of different accelerators on different nodes, such as an Intel iPSC/1 configured with floating-point vector accelerators on half of the machine and memory expansion on the other half. We can also install I/O device controllers—such as those for disks, displays, and communications—on individual nodes or around the edges of the mesh. With disk interfaces, second-generation multicomputers support their own file systems and can even act as high-performance file servers for a network.

Third-generation systems. To place these developments into a long-term per-

Table 1. Medium-grain multicomputer history and projections.

Generation Years	First 1983-87	Second 1988-92	Third 1993-97
Typical node			
MIPS	1	10	100
Mflops scalar	0.1	2	40
Mflops vector	10	40	200
memory (Mbytes)	0.5	4	32
Typical system			
N (nodes)	64	256	1,024
MIPS	64	2,560	100K
Mflops scalar	6.4	512	40K
Mflops vector	640	10K	200K
memory (Mbytes)	32	1K	32K
Communication latency (100-byte msg)			
neighbor (microseconds)	2,000	5	0.5
nonlocal (microseconds)	6,000	5	0.5

```
% peek
Cube Daemon version 7.2, up 2 days 8 hours on host sol

{               }  5d ipsc cube  , b:0000 [   mars iPSC d7]   5.4h
{CONCISE lena   }  5d ipsc cube  , b:0020 [   mars iPSC d7]   1.0h
{       TV wen-king}  6d ipsc cube  , b:0040 [neptune iPSC d7]   1.3h
{               }  3d cosmic cube, b:0000 [ venus fly trap ]   5.4h
{   orbits dian }  3d ghost cube , b:0000 [   mars :mimic ]  12.0m
{               }  3d ghost cube , b:0008 [ saturn :mimic ]   1.2d
{  tester jakov }  6d cosmic cube, b:0000 [  ceres 6-cube ]   6.4m
{  optic chuck  } 20n ginzu cube , b:0000 [  icarus ginzu d5]  20.0s
{               } 12n ginzu cube , b:0000 [ hermes ginzu d5]  12.0h


GROUP {optic chuck} TYPE reactive IDLE 0.0s

( -1    0)  optichost   3s  3r 0q  [icarus 5049] 20.0s
( -1   -1)  SERVER      3s  1r 0q  [icarus 5051] 16.0s
( -1   -2)  FILE MGR    0s  0r 0q  [icarus 5052] 16.0s
(--- ---)  CUBEIFC     5s  3r 0q  [ ceres 8327] 18.0s
```

Figure 5. Cosmic Environment display showing how multicomputers on a network are allocated in "space-sharing."

processor and communication performance together. Thus, we do not expect the relationship between communication and computing performance to change significantly in the further evolution of these architectures. The most important organizational improvements in the third generation will be in the instruction processors, both in their performance and in their ability to switch context more efficiently than processors designed for use in personal computers and workstations.

Table 1 summarizes our projections of the evolution of medium-grain multicomputers.

Medium-grain concurrent programming

In preparation for an example of programming medium-grain multicomputers using a process model, we will describe several of the essential features of the Cosmic Environment and Reactive Kernel systems.[6] We will illustrate the user-interface functions and example using the C programming language.

Process groups. The entire set of processes involved in a single computation is called a process group. A CE utility program establishes the process group and allocates the multicomputer nodes, and thereafter manages the entry of the host process into the process group, the messages between them, and the messages to and from any node processes.

Multicomputers are normally not time-shared, but space-shared. A CE utility displays how all the multicomputers on a network are allocated, as well as the user's own host processes (see Figure 5). In this example, the 128-node iPSC d7 is allocated with one user (wen-king) running a computation on a 6d ipsc cube (64 nodes), another user (lena) on a 5d ipsc cube (32 nodes), and the remaining 5-cube free. Of course, the user with 64 nodes cannot distinguish these 64 nodes from a separate 64-node multicomputer. The logical node numbers will be 0, 1, . . . , 63, regardless of their physical location in the multicomputer.

Space-sharing has proven most appropriate for multicomputers because it allows a user to select a number of nodes appropriate to the number of processes and the load-balancing characteristics of a particular computation. It also produces predictable runtimes and does not allow one user's processes to upset the load bal-

spective, we observe that in accordance with the technology development model in the DARPA Strategic Computing program, the first-generation machines used relatively unaggressive technology to establish the computational model, programming methods, and applications. The second-generation systems achieve much higher performance by a combination of organizational refinement and VLSI technology.

Since multicomputers are scalable in size and technology, we expect that a third generation can develop with little organizational change from the second generation, requiring only the application of VLSI technology advances. The use of VLSI with smaller-sized features will scale

ance of another process group.

The ghost cube in the display of Figure 5 is not a real multicomputer, but mimics one with a collection of 16 CE daemon processes distributed across a set of workstations on the local network. Using ghost cubes, sites that do not have regular access to a multicomputer have developed many multicomputer programs.

Process IDs, placement, and spawning. Every process within a process group has a unique identifier (ID), represented as an ordered pair: (node, pid). A value of the node parameter in the range $0 \ldots N-1$ designates a node process; otherwise, a host process. The pid part of the ID specifies a particular process within a node or within the host environment. The mynode, mypid, and nnode functions permit a process to determine its own ID and the number of nodes.

Processes in execution can freely spawn and kill other processes. The system's lowest-level process-spawning mechanisms give the programmer explicit control of process placement through the arguments of a dynamic process-creation function, spawn("filename", node, pid, "mode"). The node parameter determines process placement, and contrary to the usual practice in which the operating system assigns a pid, the pid is specified in the function. This scheme allows processes to build structures in which references to other processes are predetermined, rather than established by passing references in messages.

Process placement and IDs can also be decided dynamically during execution; other process-creation functions support this option. Functions also exist for creating a process in every node from the same "filename" specification. Fast process creation is crucial to the performance of many multicomputer computations. Accordingly, RK not only shares code segments for processes created from the same compiled program ("filename"), but also caches a copy of the initial data segment so that subsequent processes with the same "filename" specification can be created without accessing the file system.

Execution of spawn functions in host processes is how a computation that starts out as a process running on a host computer builds the process structure for a computation that runs on a multicomputer.

Once spawned, a process will not spontaneously migrate to another node; thus, it is most efficient to retain the physical

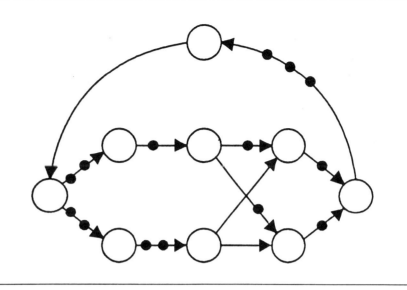

Figure 6. Example of a process-structure graph.

location of a process as a part of its unique ID. One of the implicit premises of multicomputer architectures is that costly communication mechanisms for dynamically binding computing resources to runable objects, as used in multiprocessors or in the dataflow model, are rarely necessary. It is instead sufficient for most problems to establish a binding of a process to a node that will persist for the life of the process. Although the CE/RK environment does not relocate processes, high-level programming systems that support dynamic relocation of processes are easily layered on top of the CE/RK environment.

Messages. A message is the logical unit of information exchange between processes. A message can be any number of bytes in length, from zero to any size that will fit in the memory of the nodes of the sending and receiving processes. Although message length or destination select different protocols for packetizing and routing messages, these differences are invisible to the application programmer.

Sending a message between processes requires that the sending process have reference to the receiving process. References are represented in message functions as IDs. The *process structure*—which we define as the set of processes within the process group, together with each

process's references to other processes—can be depicted as a directed graph with vertices representing processes and arcs representing references. We can also visualize the arcs as virtual communication channels, with messages traveling along the arcs (see Figure 6).

Messages are queued as necessary in the sending node, in transit, and in the receiving node. Accordingly, they have arbitrary delay from sender to receiver. However, message order is preserved between pairs of communicating processes; for example, if process A sends two messages in sequence to process B, they will arrive an arbitrary time later and in the same order as they were sent. Thus, we can think of the messages in Figure 6 as "traveling" at some arbitrary speed, but one message cannot pass another on a reference arc.

For the C-language user-interface routines to the CE/RK system, messages are sent and received from dynamically allocated storage accessed both by user processes and by the message system. Message buffers are blocks of memory with no presumed structure; thus, messages can convey arbitrary structures, such as simple variables, arrays, or user-defined types.

The xmalloc and xfree functions can allocate and free message space. These functions are semantically identical to the Unix malloc and free functions. When a

```c
#include <cube/cubedef.h>

typedef struct MESG MESG;            /* Message header structure.        */
struct MESG { int    pnode, ppid;    /* ID of the parent process.        */
              int    tbase      ;    /* Base for time-on-target tree.    */
              int    len        ;    /* Number of elements in the vector. */
              MESG   **type     ;} ; /* Type field for filtering message. */
#define BUF(v) ((double *)(v + 1))   /* Data follows MESG immediately.   */

unsigned int this_node, this_pid, node_cnt;

main( )
{    MESG *v;

     this_node = mynode( );          /* node number of this process.     */
     this_pid  =  mypid( );          /* pid number of this process.      */
     node_cnt  = nnodes( );          /* number of nodes in this machine. */
     v = (MESG *) xrecvb( );         /* Receive list from parent process. */
     mergesort(v);                   /* Sort the list.                   */
     xsend(v, v - >pnode, v - >ppid); /* Send list back to parent.        */

}

mergesort(v)
     MESG *v ;
{    unsigned k1, k2, i, new_node;
     MESG *v1, *v2, *vtemp;
     double *d, *s, *b1, *b2;

     if(v - >len <= 1) return;       /* len = 1 lists are already sorted. */
     k1 = ( v - >len + 1 ) / 2;      /* Break the list into two lists.   */
     k2 = ( v - >len      ) / 2;
     v1   = (MESG *) xmalloc(sizeof(MESG) + sizeof(double)*k1);
     v2   = (MESG *) xmalloc(sizeof(MESG) + sizeof(double)*k2);
     for(i = v1 - >len = k1, d = BUF(v1), s = BUF(v); i--; ) *d++ = *s++;
     for(i = v2 - >len = k2, d = BUF(v2)             ; i--; ) *d++ = *s++;

     new_node = this_node ^ v - >tbase;     /* Next node in the tree.     */
     v1 - >tbase = v2 - >tbase = v - >tbase << 1; /* New base for building */
                                            /* the time-on-target tree.   */
     if (v1 - >len > 20 && new_node < node_cnt )
     {                                      /* If list is long enough     */
         spawn("msort",new_node,this_pid," "); /* and next node exists,   */
         v1 - >pnode = this_node   ;        /* spawn a child process      */
         v1 - >ppid  = this_pid    ;        /* and send it a list.        */
         v1 - >type  = &v1         ;        /* The type field holds the   */
         xsend(v1,new_node,this_pid);       /* address of the msg ptr.    */
         v1 = 0;                            /* Msg ptr is set to nil.     */
     }
     else mergesort(v1);                    /* Sort v1 if can't split.    */

     mergesort(v2);                         /* Sort the second list.      */

     while(!v1) { vtemp = (MESG *) xrecvb( ); *vtemp - >type = vtemp; }

     for(b1 = BUF(v1), b2 = BUF(v2), d = BUF(v); k1 || k2; )   /* Merge.  */
     {   while(k1 && (!k2 || (k2 && b1 <= *b2))) { k1--; *d++ = *b1++; }
         while(k2 && (!k1 || (k1 && b2 <= *b1))) { k2--; *d++ = *b2++; }
     }
     xfree(v1); xfree(v2);
}
```

Figure 7. Program text for a mergesort process.

message has been built in a message block pointed to by p, its contents can be sent as a message by the function xsend(p, node, pid). The xsend function also deallocates the message space; that is, xsend(p, ...) resembles xfree(p), except that it also sends a message. Thus, there is no need for blocking or for feedback that the message has been sent; when the function returns, the message block is gone.

The function xrecvb can receive messages and return a pointer to a new message. This blocking function does not return until a message has arrived for the process. The execution of the xrecvb function is just like allocating a message buffer with xmalloc, except that the message received determines the contents and length of the block allocated. Once the message contents are no longer needed, the allocated space should be freed. Of course, xfree(p) can free the message space, but so can xsend(p, ...) if there is a message of the same length to send. Frequently in message-passing programs, as in a later example, a message is received, modified by a computation, and then sent on to another process.

If process A calls xrecvb when the next message in the node's receive queue is for process B, RK might save the state of process A and start running process B. The appearance of xrecvb in the code marks choice points for switching the execution to another process; in this sense the scheduling is reactive or message driven. So long as a process makes progress, RK does not necessarily force a context switch unless some exceptional system event occurs.

Portability. The C-language primitives described here are system primitives, and not necessarily those the user would find most convenient. We selected these functions for reasons of portability, and because we can easily and efficiently layer other message primitives on top of them. For example, the usual interface routines for Fortran are expressed in terms of the x primitives (such as xsend and xrecvb), but include message types and can exercise discretion in receiving messages by type and sender ID. The CE/RK environment also includes a sizable library of other functions, including many compatible with Unix functions of the same name, such as the C-language standard I/O package.

A multicomputer interprets the x functions by allocating storage and by sending and receiving messages. A multiprocessor

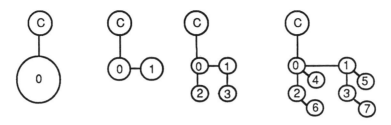

Figure 8. Sequence of building a time-on-target tree.

can interpret the same functions differently. The xmalloc and xfree functions allocate or free blocks in global shared memory. The xsend(p, node, pid) function passes ownership of the block pointed to by p to process (node, pid), and appends the pointer to the task queue of this process. The xrecvb function is the means by which a process can obtain a new task. This alternative operational interpretation allows CE/RK programs to run under native task systems on multiprocessors, and will also be a means of running the programs on future multicomputers that use multiprocessor nodes.

Programming example. Although we can use the functions in the low-level portable CE/RK environment as a compilation target for higher-level concurrent programming notations, the low-level environment is adequate for many purposes. This programming system has been used extensively in experiments with concurrent algorithms and in writing useful programs based on explicit concurrent formulations of computing problems typical of those in science and engineering. These application programs are based, for example, on concurrent adaptations of well-known sequential algorithms, on regular data-partitioning strategies, on the systolic algorithms developed for regular VLSI computational arrays, and on a wide variety of fundamental concurrent algorithms.

Our example uses the mergesort algorithm to sort a list of elements into ascending order. Briefly, we can describe mergesort as follows: A list of length 1 is already sorted and is returned. A list of length 2 or greater is split into two lists whose lengths differ at most by one. Mergesort is applied recursively to each of these lists. The resulting two sorted lists are then merged into a sorted list that is returned. List elements are compared only in the merge operation. Mergesort requires $O(n \log n)$ comparisons for a list of length n, a minimum for sorting algorithms based on performing comparisons.

Figure 7 illustrates the complete C program for our example. With the omission of the code in the shaded areas, the mergesort function within this program implements the sequential form of this algorithm. Lists are represented with a defined type MESG followed by a list of double-precision floating-point elements; the program could easily be modified for any other built-in C type. The MESG structure contains a member for the length of the list (len), and several members for control of data distribution in the concurrent program. Input to the mergesort function points to a MESG, and the function returns when the list is sorted.

The adaptation of this program to a multicomputer exploits the recursive divide-and-conquer strategy of the mergesort algorithm for distributing the computation across the nodes of the multicomputer. Because the algorithm's recursion is twofold, a straightforward mapping of mergesort recursive calls to processes would build a binary-tree process structure dynamically. However, it is somewhat more elegant and efficient to distribute the effort in a scheme in which a mergesort process recursively keeps half of the work and gives away the other half. As illustrated in Figure 8 by a sequence of snapshots of the process structure, this scheme also builds a tree of processes, but of a form that we refer to as a *time-on-target* tree. The area of the circle for each process is proportional to the length of the list it has to sort. We can systematically map this process structure onto $N = 2^n$ multicomputer nodes, as shown in the process labels.

The calling process, labeled C in Figure 8, invokes a sort by spawning the root mergesort process, labeled 0. The root mergesort process is nominally spawned in the same node as C (but potentially in any node). Process C then sends to process 0 a message in the format of the MESG structure followed by the list to be sorted. It includes in the members of the MESG structure its own ID (or some other ID to which the sorted list is to be returned), tbase equal to one, and the length of the message. Having handed off the sorting operation, process C can proceed concurrently with other computations until the sorted list is required, at which point it executes an xrecvb function.

The main function is an outer shell that allows the mergesort function to be used as a remote procedure. In the same fashion that C hands off the sort operation to the root mergesort process, the first shaded portion of the mergesort function hands off one of the two lists resulting from splitting the input list, but only if the list is long enough to justify it (v1 − >len > 20) and the multicomputer includes the target node (new_node < node_cnt). The distribution of the computation is inhibited when the individual sort operations are small or when all of the nodes are used. The new processes spawned are each identified in the MESG structure with a type in the form of a pointer to a v1 pointer. Returns from the recursive mergesort calls occur only after the computation has been completely distributed. The sorted lists from descendant processes can arrive in any order; thus, messages are

and programming. If a number of challenging problems can be solved, these machines might become the prevalent form of this architecture.

To understand some of the problems in the physical design and programming of such machines, members of our research group are developing a design and a programming system for a fine-grain multicomputer called Mosaic. Because medium-grain multicomputers can also host fine-grain computations, we have used medium-grain machines to develop fine-grain concurrent programs written in Cantor. We thus have a substantial collection of programs ready to run on Mosaic. Writing and instrumenting the execution of many diverse fine-grain Cantor programs was essential for establishing the requirements for the Mosaic design.

A stipulation of the Mosaic project has been that a node fit on a single chip. Our first attempt to design such a single-chip node resulted in the Mosaic A chip pictured in Figure 9. The bottom two-thirds of this chip is RAM—about the same fraction of the silicon complexity devoted to RAM in medium-grain nodes. The upper-left part of the chip includes a 16-bit instruction processor and program-controlled communication channels, and the upper right is ROM containing bootstrap and self-test programs. This processor ran at about six million instructions per second, and its four communication channels operated bit-serial at 2.5 megabytes per second.

The software-controlled routing is the most serious shortcoming in this design. It limits the effective channel bandwidth near the network bisection to about 0.25 megabyte per second, even if the nodes near the bisection spend all of their time routing messages. A machine with 1,024 nodes in a two-dimensional 32×32 mesh would have only 16 megabytes per second of bilateral message bandwidth across its network bisection to support 5,120 MIPS peak.

Our current node design, the Mosaic C, consists of a 14-MIPS 16-bit processor, 20-megabytes-per-second routing communication channels with $T_p = 50$ nanoseconds, and up to 16 kilobytes of RAM integrated onto a single VLSI chip using 1.2-micrometer complementary metal-oxide semiconductor technology. The major sections of this chip have been designed, fabricated separately through MOSIS, and shown to work correctly. We expect to build a full-size machine of 16,384 nodes in 1989, after assembling the

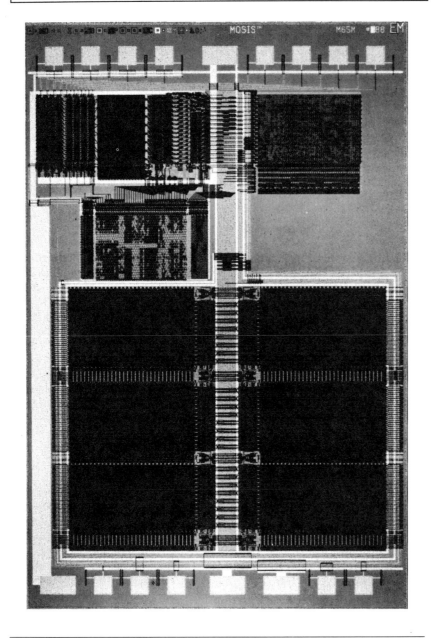

Figure 9. Photomicrograph of the Mosaic A single-chip node.

received and the pointers to them are stored into v1 pointers until the v1 pointer specific to this recursive call becomes non-0. Then the sorted v1 and v2 lists are merged and freed, and the mergesort function returns.

This programming paradigm of divide-and-conquer problems illustrates how a programmer can redesign a program or algorithm devised to run on a sequential computer so that, instead, it will distribute the computing to a collection of identical node processes. The mergesort algorithm performs a balanced splitting of a computing task, so that the computing load balances across the nodes of the multicomputer.

Fine-grain multicomputers

Fine-grain machines are the research frontier of multicomputer architectures

sections into a single chip and building some smaller prototypes. The peak performance of this experimental fine-grain system should be quite phenomenal—200,000 MIPS for the 16,384-node machine—and the system will serve as a testbed for the development of programming systems and applications.

A two-dimensional 128×128 network would be inadequate for this machine, so we will organize it as a three-dimensional $32 \times 32 \times 16$ mesh. The network bisection for the two-dimensional network would include 128 channels, in contrast with 512 channels for the three-dimensional network, and the longest path would be 255 nodes instead of 78. The execution bandwidth of the Mosaic will be reasonably well balanced with its 20,480-megabytes-per-second bilateral message bandwidth across the network bisection. The average latency for a 20-byte message to a randomly selected destination node will be about 35 instruction cycles.

Since the implementation of low-latency networks becomes increasingly difficult for large N, how small must the message latency be for the message networks in fine-grain multicomputers? If the program sequences that execute between message operations in the formulation of a concurrent computation are reduced to only tens of instructions (or even less, as they often are for fine-grain program objects), is it not necessary to reduce the message latencies in proportion? Since this scaling in latency would be motivated by the same factors that cause N to be scaled up, the construction of fine-grain systems would be physically very difficult, indeed. However, one of the ways multicomputers accommodate message latency is by maintaining multiple processes or program objects in each node. When a process attempts to receive a message not yet in the node's pool of received messages, it switches context to another process that does have a message available. Maintaining many processes per node is also important to achieving load balance statistically.

As we observed in connection with future medium-grain multicomputers, a reduction in context-switching time is increasingly important. The Mosaic C was designed as a two-context processor; it has two program counters and two partially overlapping register banks to switch in one clock cycle between system and user contexts. Operations to memory are only one clock cycle longer than operations to registers. Registers are used principally as pointers into data structures maintained

---

Cantor objects strictly observe the reactive property; they are normally at rest until a message arrives.

---

by the Cantor runtime system, and are not saved following an object execution.

Programming systems such as Cantor can also help manage the network resource. Direct networks exhibit paths of different lengths, so Cantor can place processes to balance the computing load and localize message traffic for communication-intensive computations. Relatively localized message traffic helps to reduce the message latency as well as the congestion in the communication network. The Cantor compiler can often extract the process structure from the program text—so it can map processes systematically—or employ heuristics to compute a static placement with good properties for balancing the multicomputer's communication and computing resources.

Fine-grain concurrent programming

For highly regular or symmetric computations, such as grid-point calculations or systolic algorithms, we can view a fine-grain multicomputer as a collection of thousands of small computers. A second approach for computations with more complex behavior views the fine-grain multicomputer as a single computer. A partition is established between the tasks required of the program writer and the capabilities provided by the programming system. The program writer must express the computation in a way that exposes all of the concurrency that the system can use in execution. The programming system has complete responsibility for managing system resources.

In our experiments with this second approach, we express computations in terms of fine-grain objects that communicate only by message-passing. The capabil-

---

ities of objects are comparable in many ways to the capabilities of the processes of the CE/RK system. The semantics of message-passing are identical, but references and object creation are handled more carefully. An object consists of a code area and a private memory area. We have observed that the private memory area of objects in fine-grain message-driven programs is usually quite small, often less than one hundred bytes.

Cantor. The Cantor programming environment consists of a compiler, runtime system, and other programming tools that together manage the concurrent resources of the fine-grain machine. Cantor[9] is a programming notation for writing message-driven programs using concurrent objects. Each object is an independent computing agent that interacts with other objects solely by message-passing. The semantics of an object program are a form of Actor semantics, as defined by Agha.[8] Each object consists of a set of private variables that persist between receiving messages, a list of variables that describe the expected contents of the next message, and a sequence of actions that describe how the object will react to the next message.

Cantor objects strictly observe the reactive property; they are normally at rest until a message arrives. An object's response is determined by the contents of the message, the current contents of the private variables, and a sequence of procedural statements that define the object's fundamental actions, including creating new objects and sending more messages. An object in Cantor must process a message in a bounded number of steps. In earlier versions of Cantor, the syntax enforced this property. The current syntax has been liberalized to permit objects to run indefinitely; however, objects capable of this type of behavior can permanently block a computation from making progress.

The composition of a node number and local object number produces a unique identifier for an object. The object identifier, part of the value domain of Cantor's semantics, is called a reference. Message-passing is based on the sending object's possessing a reference to a destination object. An object acquires a reference upon creating a new object, or might receive a reference in a message.

After the sending object completes the send action, the message exhibits arbitrary delay in traveling from sender to destination. Likewise, the action of creating a new object exhibits arbitrary delay. While the send action requires no value to be produced, creating a new object yields a reference value for the new object. Thus, the generation of the reference value is immediate and can be used in a computation before the object is instantiated. For an object to process a message, the object must be instantiated.

Flow analysis. In the implementation of Cantor, the decoupling between the reference to an object and the instance of an object permits speculation about references before an object is required by a program. When the reference to an object exists, but the object has not yet been built, we call the reference value a *future*. Generating futures prior to executing a program, called *future flow*, can improve load balancing and preserve locality among communicating objects.

The problem of future flow during compilation parallels the problem of constant propagation in optimizing compilers. Value propagation graphs are constructed to denote the dependencies between the execution points where values become defined and the execution points where values are used. By generating a future for each of the definition vertices and propagating the reference value through the other vertices, a subset of the reference values used by a program is generated as futures at compile time. We can represent these futures as vertices of graphs that

```
qlist (row,col : int, next : ref) ::
*[ case (cmd : sym) of                              % dispatch on message selector
   "check" : (rn,cn : int, caller : ref )           % check for conflict
            if rn = row or (cn − col) = abs (rn − row)   % if row or diagonal match then
               then send (false ) to caller         % reply false
               else if next = nil then send (true) to caller   % if no next then reply true
                        else send ("check",rn,cn,caller) to next   % else test next qlist element
                    fi
               fi
   "copy" : (caller : ref )                          % copy qlist
            if next = nil                            % if last element then copy and reply
               then send (qlist(row,col,nil )) to caller   % else forward copy request to next
               else send ("copy", self ) to next     % wait for copy list and add local copy
               [ (l : ref ) send (qlist(row,col,l)) to caller ]
            fi
]


queen (ql : ref, cn : int , out : ref ) ::           % ql — list of valid queen positions
                                                     % cn — column number
*[ (rn : int )                                       % receive test row number
   send ("check", rn, cn, self ) to ql               % check for conflict of (rn,cn) in ql
   [ (reply : bool )
     if reply                                        % if no conflict then copy ql
        then send ("copy", self ) to ql              % receive copy of ql
           [ (nql : ref )                            % add (rn,cn) to copy of ql
             nql = qlist(rn,cn,nql)                  % if last column
             if cn = 8 then send ("insert", nql) to out   % then enqueue result
                       else send (1) to queen(nql, cn + 1, out)   % else search next column
                       fi
           ]
     fi
   ]
   if rn < 8 then send (rn + 1) to self else exit fi  % if not last row
]                                                    % then search next row


make_q(out : ref ) ::
*[ (i : int) send (1) to queen(qlist(i,1,nil ),2,out)   % make initial set
           if i < 8 then send (i + 1) to self else exit fi   % of 8 queen objects
]
```

Figure 10. Concurrent eight-queens program.

show the connectivity and genealogy of objects.

The construction of the future graph is thwarted by data dependencies that cannot be resolved without running the program, and by nondeterminancy introduced by the message-passing semantics. A second type of flow analysis not obstructed by data dependencies and message nondeterminancy predicts how an object will be used based on its propensity to create new objects and send more messages. Based on the semantics of message-driven programs, concurrency is introduced only when an object sends more messages than it receives. The propensity to send more messages, called the *send factor* (*SF*), is defined as the maximum number of messages an object can send in response to processing a single message. The *new factor* (*NF*) is the maximum number of new objects the object can create in response to processing a message. *SF* and *NF* for each type of object can be calculated at compile time.

When creating a new object, for example, the object can generate concurrency ($SF > 1$), sustain concurrency ($SF = 1$), or reduce concurrency ($SF < 1$). If all objects for a program have $SF \leq 1$, then the program is sequential. *SF* and *NF* assist heuristic decisions about the placement of new objects. For example, if *SF* and *NF* are greater than one, then the new object should be placed on a distant node to prevent excessive congestion of messages and objects within a small patch of the host multicomputer.

An example. To illustrate Cantor as a notation for expressing concurrent programs, and to demonstrate message-driven programming, let us examine the "eight-queens" problem. The task is to place eight queen pieces on an 8×8 chessboard so that no queen is in jeopardy of capture. The queen game piece captures any other piece that lies along the same row, column, or diagonal.

The search for the problem's 92 solutions is highly concurrent. From the capture rule, there will be only one queen per row and column. A concurrent search can therefore be organized either by row or by column. Assuming a column-by-column search, a queen is placed in a row of column 1. The rows of column 2 are then searched to find a safe position for the second queen. After a safe position has been found, the rows of column 3 are searched to find a safe position for the third queen. Each subsequent column search involves

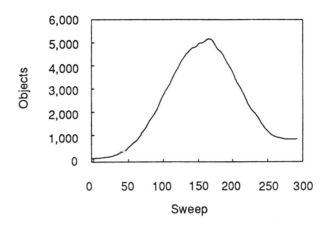

Figure 11. Object count for eight-queens ($N = \infty$).

checking the previous row and column pairs to be sure that the new position is safe. For the case where no safe row can be found, the partial solution is simply discarded.

A sequential search would involve backtracking once an impossible configuration is exposed. The backtracking step systematically removes the current emplacements of queens and then continues with a new placement. For the concurrent search, backtracking is not necessary, because all solutions are equally pursued. The only action taken in response to a detected impossible configuration is to discard the configuration.

The program fragment of Figure 10 performs the concurrent search. The names qlist, queen, and make_q denote object definitions and not objects. An object definition is a template for building an object; all objects result from object definitions. A program consists of a finite number of object definitions used to generate a possibly unbounded number of objects. The make_q object definition starts the concurrent search by creating eight new objects using the queen definition. Each of these objects searches for solutions starting with a different row number for column 1. The queen definition advances the search, column by column. The qlist definition maintains lists of partial solutions. The object definitions for starting the program and queueing the answers for display are not shown.

Performance analysis. The eight-queens program has been executed on sequential computers and such concurrent computers as the Cosmic Cube and Intel iPSC. The concurrent computers demonstrate the program's concurrency by exhibiting decreasing time to find the 92 solutions as more computing nodes are applied. These speedup curves are not themselves very revealing, so an alternate approach to studying the dynamics of the concurrency defines an abstract implementation for the execution environment and then measures the utilization of different resources.

Instrumented versions of the Cantor system allow a Cantor program to run under conditions ranging from infinite resources and zero latencies—the abstract implementation in which every opportunity for concurrency within a Cantor program is exploited—to specified numbers of nodes and message latencies. The only notable approximation in the measurements and analyses is that the processing of messages is assumed to be synchronized across all nodes. Each of these synchronized steps is called a *sweep*. Computations are organized into sweeps. For each sweep, every node that has one or more messages enqueued can process one message. All of the messages sent in response to processing a message are produced together. New objects are created initially as messages.

The instrumented execution of a program consists of a number of sweeps. For

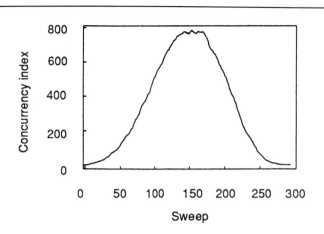

Figure 12. Concurrency index for eight-queens ($N = \infty$).

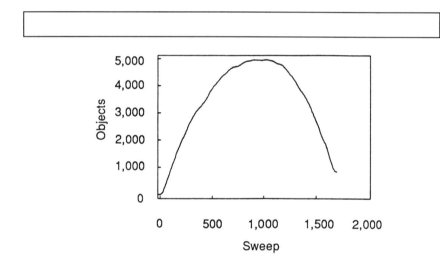

Figure 13. Object count for eight-queens ($N = 64$).

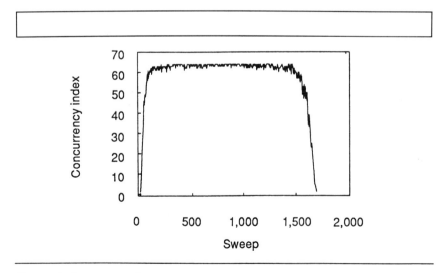

Figure 14. Concurrency index for eight-queens ($N = 64$).

each sweep the following data are tabulated:

- the total number of messages,
- the total number of active objects,
- the total number of objects, and
- the number of messages delivered this sweep.

An active object is defined as an object with one or more messages queued for it. The total number of object executions in a sweep, called the *concurrency index*, equals the number of active objects under the abstract implementation.

Figures 11 and 12 show the object count and concurrency index for the eight-queens program. The printing phase of the solutions was removed because it is entirely sequential. The program finds all 92 solutions in less than 300 sweeps. The cost for this performance is an immodest number of objects, peaking out at slightly over 5,000. Most of these objects, however, are purely transitory. The final object count, 830, includes the 92 solutions, requiring nine objects to represent each solution.

The abstract implementation represents a best case for the execution of the eight-queens program. A close similarity exists between message-driven programs and event-driven simulators, in which the only type of event is the processing of a message by an object. From this correspondence we expect any program that behaves poorly under the abstract implementation to perform poorly on any physically realizable implementation.

A variation on the abstract implementation fixes the number of nodes and evaluates program performance. Figures 13 and 14 show the object count and concurrency index graphs for the eight-queens program when the number of nodes is limited to 64. Because the mapping between objects and nodes is no longer one-to-one, a placement algorithm must assign objects to nodes. The algorithm attempts to balance the load of objects across the nodes by determining the node with the smallest object count and then placing the new object on this node.

The concurrency index graph for 64 nodes shows that nearly all nodes are utilized over a large interval of sweeps. By limiting the number of nodes to 64, the time to completion is increased by a factor of six. Because this program is deterministic (in the sense of performing exactly the same object executions on any execution), the area under the curves in Figures 12 and 14 is the same.

The placement algorithm used for Figures 13 and 14 required obtaining global information before placing a new object. Figure 15 compares the performance of three placement algorithms: the previous algorithm (o), a variation that uses the message count per node instead of the object count (m), and random placement (r). The figure plots the number of sweeps for each of the strategies against the number of nodes used to execute the program. The horizontal dashed line denotes the sweep count for the abstract implementation.

Random placement performs remarkably well and requires no global information. We can understand the performance of random placement by considering two cases. When the number of active objects is much smaller than the number of nodes, the probability that two or more objects are assigned to the same node is small. When the number of active objects is much greater than the number of nodes, then, by the weak law of large numbers, the probability that a node will be assigned an active object increases with the number of assignments made.

In our experiments with multicomputers over the past eight years, we have repeatedly underestimated their application span and overestimated the difficulty of writing programs. In fact, for certain applications the concurrent formulation for a problem has been simpler than the sequential formulation. Whether these machines will ever be considered general-purpose is debatable, but as message-passing performance improves relative to computing performance, the application span can only increase.

The next challenge for the architects of medium-grain multicomputers is to eliminate the software overhead of message-passing operations and to work with language and compiler developers to create programming environments that manage the system resources more completely.

Although we see the evolution of medium-grain multicomputers as a low-risk path, we are only cautiously optimistic about the practicality of fine-grain forms of the multicomputer architecture. However, it is clearly time to proceed to the full-scale experiment.□

Acknowledgments

The research described in this article was sponsored in part by the Defense Advanced Research Projects Agency, order number 6202, and monitored by the Office of Naval Research under contract number N00014-87-K-0745; and in part by grants from Intel Scientific Computers and Ametek Computer Research Division.

The architectures, designs, programming systems, and machines described in this article are the product of many years of effort by many creative, talented, and hard-working people, both in our Caltech Computer Science research group and in the industrial firms that have entered the multicomputer business. We wish to mention particularly the efforts of Wen-King Su, the designer and author of the Cosmic Environment system, and Jakov Seizovic, the author of the Reactive Kernel. We also wish to thank the MOSIS crew for their excellent service in fabricating message-routing chips and Mosaic elements.

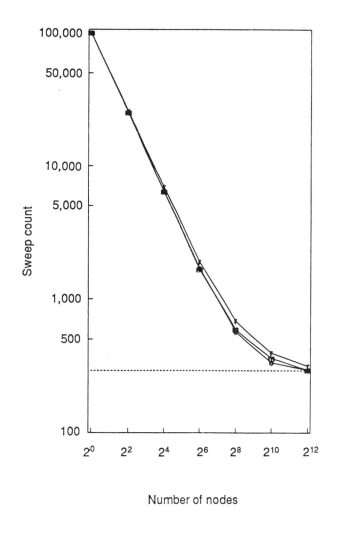

Figure 15. Comparison of message (m), object (o), and random placement (r).

References

1. C.L. Seitz, "The Cosmic Cube," *Comm. ACM,* Vol. 28, No. 1, Jan. 1985, pp. 22-33.

2. iPSC/2 brochures and application software reference material, Intel Scientific Computers, Beaverton, Ore., order number 280110-001.

3. Series 2010 brochures and application software reference material, Ametek Computer Research Division, Monrovia, Calif.

4. C.L. Seitz, "Concurrent VLSI Architectures," *IEEE Trans. Computers,* Vol. 33, No. 12, Dec. 1984, pp. 1247-1265.

5. W.D. Hillis, *The Connection Machine,* MIT Press, Cambridge, Mass., 1985.

6. C.L. Seitz, J. Seizovic, and W.-K. Su, "The

C Programmer's Abbreviated Guide to Multicomputer Programming," Caltech Computer Sci. Tech. Report 88-1, 1988.

7. Inmos, *The Occam Programming Manual,* Prentice-Hall, 1985.

8. G.A. Agha, *Actors: A Model of Concurrent Computation in Distributed Systems,* MIT Press, Cambridge, Mass., 1986.

9. W.C. Athas, "Fine-Grain Concurrent Computation," Caltech Computer Sci. Tech. Report, 5242:TR:87, 1987.

10. W.J. Dally and C.L. Seitz, "Deadlock-Free Message Routing in Multiprocessor Interconnection Networks," *IEEE Trans. Computers,* Vol. 36, No. 5, May 1987, pp. 547-553.

11. W.J. Dally, *A VLSI Architecture for Concurrent Data Structures,* Kluwer Academic Publishers, 1987.

12. C.M. Flaig, "VLSI Mesh Routing Systems," Caltech Computer Sci. Tech. Report, 5241:TR:87, 1987.

William C. Athas received his BS degree in Computer Science from the University of Utah, and his MS and PhD degrees in Computer Science from the California Institute of Technology. He is currently a Caltech research fellow in Computer Science and is engaged in research in VLSI architecture and design, and programming systems for fine-grain concurrent computers.

Readers may write to Seitz at the California Institute of Technology, Computer Science 256-80, Pasadena, CA 91125.

Charles L. Seitz received his BS, MS, and PhD degrees from the Massachusetts Institute of Technology. He is now a professor of Computer Science at the California Institute of Technology. His research and teaching are in VLSI architecture and design, concurrent computation, and self-timed systems.

Seitz received the MIT Goodwin Medal and the Leonard G. Abraham Award of the IEEE Communications Technology Group. His research in concurrent computing was selected by *Science Digest* as one of the top 100 innovations of 1985.

Generalized Hypercube and Hyperbus Structures for a Computer Network

LAXMI N. BHUYAN, MEMBER, IEEE, AND DHARMA P. AGRAWAL, SENIOR MEMBER, IEEE

Abstract — A general class of hypercube structures is presented in this paper for interconnecting a network of microcomputers in parallel and distributed environments. The interconnection is based on a mixed radix number system and the technique results in a variety of hypercube structures for a given number of processors N, depending on the desired diameter of the network. A cost optimal realization is obtained through a process of discrete optimization. The performance of such a structure is compared to that of other existing hypercube structures such as Boolean n-cube and nearest neighbor mesh computers.

The same mathematical framework is used in defining a corresponding bus oriented structure which requires only two I/O ports per processor. These two types of structures are extremely suitable for local area computer networks.

Index Terms — Distributed computers, hyperbus structures, hypercube structures, local area networks, multistage interconnection networks, parallel computers, topological optimization.

I. INTRODUCTION

SEVERAL structures have been proposed in the literature for interconnecting a large network of computers in parallel and distributed environments [2]–[12]. In this paper, we present a generalized hypercube structure and reveal some interesting properties of hypercubes. An interconnection structure in general should have a low number of links per node (degree of a node), a small internode distance (diameter), and a large number of alternate paths between a pair of nodes for fault tolerance. The distance between any two nodes is defined as the number of links traversed by a message, initiated from one node and sent to another via intermediate nodes. In a network of N nodes, the diameter is defined as $D = \max_m \{d_{ij} \mid 1 \leq i, j \leq N\}$, where $d_{ij} =$ distance between nodes i and j along the shortest path. Designing a network with a low message traffic density and good modularity is also desirable.

The Boolean n-cube computer [7] is an interconnection of $N = 2^n$ processors which may be thought of as placed at the corners of an n-dimensional cube with each edge of the cube having two processors. The degree of a node and the diameter of this type of structure are equal to $n = \log_2 N$. A loop structure with additional links is imbedded in this structure,

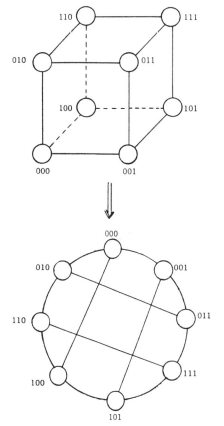

Fig. 1. A Boolean n-cube computer with $N = 8$.

and for $N = 8$, this is illustrated in Fig. 1. When the total number of nodes N equals W^D, W and D both being integers, the nodes can be arranged as a D-dimensional hypercube with W nodes in each dimension. If a node is connected to its two nearest neighbors in each dimension, a nearest neighbor mesh hypercube is obtained. The degree of a node in such a structure is $2D$ and the diameter is $WD/2$ for $W > 2$ [8]. There is also a loop structure associated with a nearest neighbor mesh as shown in Fig. 2 for a two-dimensional mesh with 9 nodes. We can also deduce that a bidirectional single loop structure [3] is equivalent to a nearest neighbor connection with dimension $D = 1$. This structure has a minimum number of links and a diameter of $N/2$. Any two nonadjacent faulty nodes will disconnect the loop. With the addition of an extra link to the loop structure the diameter is reduced to $0(\sqrt{N})$ [4]. On the other hand, a completely connected structure has $(N - 1)$ links per node with a distance of one between any two nodes. Any two nodes remain connected

Manuscript received March 24, 1983; revised October 12, 1983. A preliminary version of this paper was presented at the 9th Annual International Symposium on Computer Architecture, April 1982.

L. N. Bhuyan is with the Department of Electrical and Computer Engineering, University of Southwestern Louisiana, Lafayette, LA 70504.

D. P. Agrawal is with the Computer Systems Laboratory, Department of Electrical and Computer Engineering, North Carolina State University, P. O. Box 7911, Raleigh, NC 27650.

0-8186-6522-X/95 $4.00 © 1984 IEEE

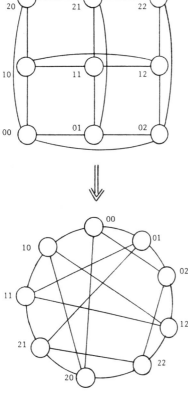

Fig. 2. A nearest neighbor mesh with $N = 3^2$.

generalized hypercube (GHC) and generalized hyperbus (GHB) structures. They possess the following characteristics:

1) The interconnection supports any number of nodes N. This is in contrast with the existing hypercube structures, where $N = W^D$ for some integer values of W and D.

2) The design is based on the allowable diameter of the network. If the diameter can be increased, a structure with a lower degree of a node can be obtained.

3) These structures are highly fault tolerant, they possess a small average message distance and a low traffic density.

4) The structures presented here are very general in nature. Single loop, Boolean n-cube, nearest neighbor mesh hypercube and fully connected systems can be considered as a part of this generalized structure.

5) The GHB structures have only two links per node, and hence require only two I/O ports per processor.

The paper is organized as follows. Section II describes a useful mixed radix number system used in [14], [15], the topology, the properties, and the routing and broadcasting algorithms of the GHC structures. Section III analyzes the GHC structures with respect to a cost parameter defined by (degree of a node) * (diameter). The section also outlines the procedure for obtaining an optimal GHC (OGHC) structure. Section IV considers the parameters like average distance, cost, traffic density, and fault tolerance, etc. to compare the performance of an OGHC to other hypercube structures. Section V obtains the equivalent m-cube multistage interconnection networks (MIN's) of the GHC structures. Section VI presents the GHB structures and derives the expressions for internode distances.

II. THE GENERALIZED HYPERCUBE (GHC) STRUCTURE

A. A Mixed Radix Number System

Let N be the total number of processors and be represented as a product of m_i's, $m_i > 1$ for $1 \leq i \leq r$.

$$N = m_r * m_{r-1} * \cdots * m_1.$$

Then, each processor X between 0 to $N - 1$ can be expressed as an r-tuple $(x_r x_{r-1} \cdots x_1)$ for $0 \leq x_i \leq (m_i - 1)$. Associated with each x_i is a weight w_i, such that $\sum_{i=1}^{r} x_i w_i = X$ and $w_i = \prod_{j=1}^{i-1} m_j = m_{i-1} * m_{i-2} * \cdots * m_1$ for all $1 \leq i \leq r$. Hence, $w_1 = 1$ always.

Example 1:

$$\text{Let} \quad N = 24 = 4 * 3 * 2.$$
$$m_1 = 2, \quad m_2 = 3, \quad m_3 = 4.$$
$$w_1 = 1, \quad w_2 = 2, \quad w_3 = 6.$$

Then, $X = (x_3 x_2 x_1)$, $0 \leq x_1 \leq 1$, $0 \leq x_2 \leq 2$, $0 \leq x_3 \leq 3$ for any X in the range 0–23. $0_{10} = (000)$, $23_{10} = (321)$ in this mixed radix system.

B. Description of the GHC Structure

Each processor $X = (x_r x_{r-1} \cdots x_{i+1} x_i x_{i-1} \cdots x_1)$ will be connected to processors $(x_r x_{r-1} \cdots x_{i+1} x_i' x_{i-1} \cdots x_1)$ for all $1 \leq i \leq r$, where x_i' takes all integer values between 0 to $(m_i - 1)$ except x_i itself. This type of interconnection will be

even if all other nodes fail. However, both the high cost of a large number of links and the multiport requirement of $0(N)$ limit the size of the network.

In a multicomputer environment, the average internode distance, message traffic density, and fault tolerance are very much dependent on the diameter and degree of a node. There is a tradeoff between the degree of a node and the diameter. A structure with a low degree of a node has a large diameter and a structure that has a low diameter usually possesses a large degree of a node. A single loop structure and a completely connected structure as described above represent the two extremes. The (diameter * degree of a node) is therefore a good criterion to measure the performance of a structure. The hypercube structures seem to offer a reasonable characteristic. One commonly noted disadvantage of the Boolean n-cube computer is that the number of I/O ports is $\log_2 N$. However, keeping in mind the simple routing, the low diameter, and the large ($\log_2 N$) number of disjoint paths, this topology seems extremely suitable for a local computer network. Moreover, with current advances in technology, the number of I/O ports per processor up to 1000 has become quite feasible [13]. Recently, a few structures have been proposed with better graph theoretic properties [9]–[12]. Their fault tolerance is basically limited by the fixed number of I/O ports per node. What we present here is a complete generalization of the hypercube and some interesting analyses of hypercube structures, where good fault tolerance is guaranteed. The present study should therefore be viewed in that context.

This paper presents two new hypercube structures, called

362

called the generalized hypercube (GHC) throughout this paper. In general, the total number of links (L) is greater than the total number of processors (N) in this GHC topology.

Example 2: For $N = 24$, any processor can be expressed in the mixed radix system between (000) and (321). Processor (000) is connected to processors (001), (010), (020), (100), (200), and (300). Processor (001) is connected to processors (000), (011), (021), (101), (201), and (301) and so on as shown in Fig. 3. For the sake of clarity, connection is not completed in the figure for the nodes shown by dotted lines. Imbedded in this structure is a loop structure arranged as (000) → (001) → (011) → (021) → (121) → (221) → (321) → (311) → (301) → (300) → (310) → (320) → (220) → (120) → (020) → (010) → (110) → (210) → (200) → (201) → (211) → (111) → (101) → (100) → (000) with 4 extra links per node.

The GHC structure consists of r-dimensions with m_i number of nodes in the ith dimension. A node in a particular axis is connected to all other nodes in the same axis. Accordingly, we make the following observations.

1) From any particular node $X = (x_r x_{r-1} \cdots x_{i+1} x_i x_{i-1} \cdots x_1)$, there are $(m_i - 1)$ number of links in the ith direction. Hence, for all i, $1 \leq i \leq r$, the total number of links per node or the degree of a node $\ell = \sum_{i=1}^{r} (m_i - 1)$.

2) Each link is connected to two processors. Hence, the total number of links in GHC structure $L = N/2 \cdot \sum_{i=1}^{r}(m_i - 1)$.

3) d_{xy} = distance between any two nodes x and y in terms of number of hops = Hamming distance between the nodes. Hamming distance between two nodes differing in their addresses in the ith coordinate only is unity and the total Hamming distance is the sum of the number of coordinates in which the addresses differ.

4) The addresses can differ at maximum in all the r-coordinates. Thus, the diameter of the structure = r.

C. Routing Procedure

A message is formatted at the source node with source address, destination address and a few tag bits. The source and destination addresses are specified in the binary equivalent of the mixed radix numbers. The ith digit of the address can take a maximum value of $(m_i - 1)$, and hence can be expressed in $\lceil \log_2 m_i \rceil$ binary bits, where $\lceil x \rceil$ is the smallest integer greater than or equal to x. As a result, any processor $0 \leq X \leq N - 1$ can be specified completely in $\sum_{i=1}^{r} \lceil \log_2 m_i \rceil$ binary bits. At each node, the destination address is compared to its own address, contained in a register. If the addresses match, the node accepts the message. If they do not, a digit by digit comparison takes place and the node transmits the message along the direction of the first differing digit. The process continues until the destination is reached. However, at each node the message goes through a certain delay, waiting for the particular link to be free.

Based on the above routing procedure, we can deduce the following.

1) If two nodes differ in their address by d coordinates (dimensions), then d is the shortest distance between these two nodes. A message can start from the source node along

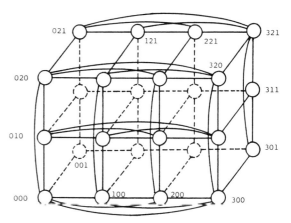

Fig. 3.   A 4 * 3 * 2 GHC-structure.

any one of these d coordinates and then follow the above routing procedure to reach the destination node. These paths, illustrated in Fig. 4(a), are disjoint and cover a distance d each. This observation is similar to the characteristics of a Boolean n-cube computer [16].

2) From any node $(x_r x_{r-1} \cdots x_i \cdots x_2 x_1)$, the message can go to an intermediate neighboring node and travel to the corresponding neighboring node of the destination $(y_r y_{r-1} \cdots y_i \cdots y_2 y_1)$. In the previous case, a message could start along a particular node in the ith coordinate only if the source and destination addresses differed in their ith coordinate. Note in Fig. 4(b), that a message can start along any of the nodes in the ith coordinate for $1 \leq i \leq r$ without depending on whether or not the source and destination addresses mismatch in their ith coordinate. Then the intermediate nodes encountered on a single path have their ith coordinate fixed at a particular digit. The paths are therefore disjoint. A suitable reference to the path generation process is [10]. Hence, there are ℓ alternate paths between any two nodes of the GHC structure where "ℓ" is the degree of a node.

3) For any number of faults less than "ℓ" in the system, the worst case distance between two connected nodes is $r + 1$. This is also clear from Fig. 4(b).

Alternate Routing Procedures: As mentioned above, there are d disjoint paths of equal length d between any two nodes separated by Hamming distance d. If the channels in one path are busy or faulty, a message can be routed in a different path with the same distance d. This is possible if the status of every link is updated at each node. In that case, the source node can route the message along an alternate path thus saving the delay in transmission. This process requires additional hardware and software and the path computation may be time consuming. If the link is busy another simple method is to route the message along the next digit of the first differing digit. For example, with $N = 24$, while routing from (001) to (221), instead of routing through (021) first, the message can be routed to (201) and then to (221), if the previous channel is busy.

D. Broadcasting

Any processor can send a message to all other processors in just r steps by using the following algorithms.

The structure is an r-dimensional hypercube with $(m_i - 1)$

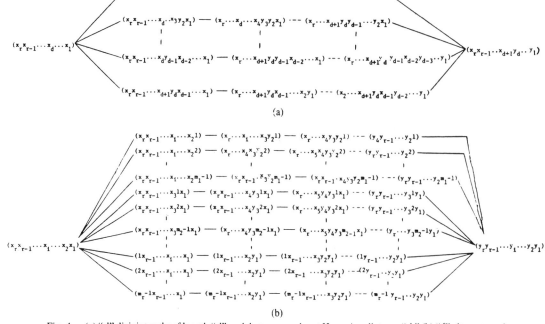

Fig. 4. (a) "d" disjoint paths of length "d" each between nodes at Hamming distance "d." (b) "ℓ" alternate paths between any source and destination.

numbers of links in the ith dimension. Each link in the machine is numbered, with the links in the ith dimension being numbered "i" for all $1 \le i \le r$. Let us assume node A $(00 \cdots 0)$ wishes to broadcast a message. To do so, it sends messages with a weight "i" in the links along the ith dimension. In the second step, all the receiving nodes reduce the weight by one and transmit the messages along all those dimensions whose numbers do not exceed the reduced weight. The process continues for r steps until all the nodes have received the message. It may be noted that r is the lower bound for the minimum number of steps required for broadcasting in a graph with a diameter of r.

Example 3: The structure for $N = 24$ is shown in Fig. 3. In the first step, nodes (001) will receive the message with a weight "1," nodes (010) and (020) will receive the message with weight "2," and nodes (100), (200), (300) will receive the message with weight "3." In the next step, all these nodes will reduce their weights by one and transmit the messages as shown below.

(001) → no transmission
(010) and (020) → (011) and (021) respectively with weight "1"
(100), (200) and (300) → (101), (201) and (301) respectively with weight "1," and
(110), (120), (210), (220), (310) and (320) with weight "2."

In the third and final step,

(110) → (111), (120) → (121), (210) → (211), (220) → (221), (310) → (311), (320) → (321) with weight "1."

The complete broadcasting is achieved in three steps, as shown in Fig. 5.

III. ANALYSIS OF GHC STRUCTURES

A. Structure Optimization

When an interconnection of N processors is desired with the constraint that the maximum distance between any two nodes along the shortest path or the diameter does not exceed r, N has to be expressed as a product of r quantities as $N = m_r * m_{r-1} * \cdots * m_1$. The number of links per node $= \sum_{i=1}^{r} (m_i - 1)$. In fact, there are several ways to factor N into r components. For example, 16 can be factored as $8 * 2$ or $4 * 4$. An optimized structure with diameter r is obtained when the total number of links in the structure is at the minimum.

Lemma 1: When $\sqrt[r]{N}$ is an integer, a cost optimal GHC with diameter "r" is obtained if $m_i = \sqrt[r]{N}$ for all $1 \le i \le r$.

Proof: Since the number of links per node "ℓ" is the same for all the nodes, a minimization of "ℓ" with respect to m_i's gives the desired result

$$m_1 = \frac{N}{m_r m_{r-1} \cdots m_2}$$

$$\ell = \sum_{i=2}^{r} (m_i - 1) + \left(\frac{N}{m_r m_{r-1} \cdots m_2} - 1 \right)$$

$$\frac{\partial \ell}{\partial m_r} = \frac{\partial \ell}{\partial m_{r-1}} = \frac{\partial \ell}{\partial m_2} = 0.$$

This results in $m_r = m_{r-1} = \cdots = m_2 = m_1 = \sqrt[r]{N}$. Q.E.D.

Since $\sqrt[r]{N}$ may not be an integer, all m_i's should lie as close to $\sqrt[r]{N}$ as possible. When $N = m^r$, the mathematics involved is simply a higher radix system, each x_i lying between 0 and $(m - 1)$ for all $1 \le i \le r$.

There is another aspect of the GHC structures. The number of links per node is different for different values of diameter

364

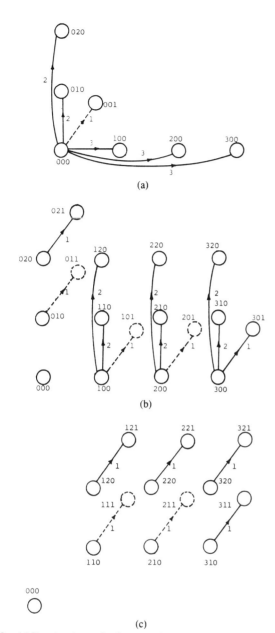

(a)

(b)

(c)

Fig. 5. (a) Broadcasting at the first step, (b) broadcasting at the second step, (c) broadcasting at the third step.

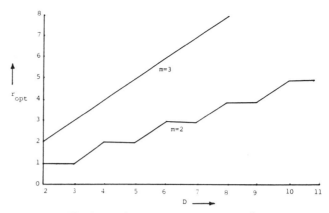

Fig. 6. r_{opt} for number of processors $= m^D$.

r. Again, for example, 16 can be expressed as $4 * 4$, $4 * 2 * 2$, $2 * 2 * 2 * 2$ with diameters 2, 3, and 4, respectively. As mentioned earlier, a structure with a lower degree of a node usually has a higher diameter. If a cost factor ξ is defined as the product of the diameter and the links per node, a discrete optimization of $r \sum_{i=1}^{r} (m_i - 1)$ with respect to r and subject to the constraint that $\prod_{i=1}^{r} m_i = N$ and integer values of m_i's, yields an optimized structure. As an example, the optimal values of r for processors equal to 2^D and 3^D, are plotted in Fig. 6. Because of the discrete optimization involved, it was not possible to derive a closed form solution for r_{opt}.

Conjecture 1: For N, a power of two, an absolute cost optimal GHC (OGHC) is obtained when $r = \lfloor \log_4 N \rfloor$, where $\lfloor x \rfloor$ is the largest integer smaller than or equal to x.

This deduction follows from Fig. 6. Up to $N = 2^3$, $r_{opt} = 1$ indicates a fully connected system. For $N = 2^4$, $r_{opt} = 2$

results in a two-dimensional GHC with 4 nodes in each dimension. For $N = 2^5$, there are 4 nodes in one dimension and 8 nodes in the other. For $N = 2^6$, $r_{opt} = 3$ and so on. Also, for N and m powers of two a GHC with m nodes in each dimension has a cost of $(m - 1) \log_m^2 N$ which has a local minimum at $m = 4$.

For N, a power of four, the degree of a node of an OGHC is $3 \log_4 N = 1.5 \log_2 N$. The diameter is $\log_4 N = 0.5 \log_2 N$. Hence, the cost $= 0.75 (\log_2^2 N)$. The cost of other structures [9]–[12] are proportional to $(\log_2 N)$ instead of $(\log_2^2 N)$. However, they do not possess as good a fault tolerance as the GHC structures do. For N, a power of 5, the cost is $0.742 \log_2^2 N$ when $m = 5$. However, only values of N which are powers of two are considered in conjecture 1 for later use in Section IV.

B. Internode Distance and Queueing Delay

Distance between any processor $X = (x_r x_{r-1} \cdots x_{i+1} x_i x_{i-1} \cdots x_2 x_1)$ and $X' = (x_r x_{r-1} \cdots x_{i+1} x_i', x_{i-1} \cdots x_2 x_1)$, $x_i' \varepsilon \{0, 1, 2, \cdots, m_i - 1\}$ and $x_i' \neq x_i$, is unity. In general, the distance between any two processors is equal to the Hamming distance between them; that is, in how many coordinates their addresses differ. The average internode distance plays a key role in determining the queueing delay in a computer network. For calculating the number of nodes at different distances, the node $(00 \cdots 0)$ can be assumed to be the source node without any loss in generality. There are $(m_i - 1)$ number of nodes which differ from the source node only in the ith dimension. Hence, $N_1 =$ total number of nodes differing by distance 1

$$= \sum_{i=1}^{r} (m_i - 1).$$

The nodes which have distance 2 from the source node must differ in their addresses by two coordinates i and j. In these two dimensions, $(m_i - 1)(m_j - 1)$ different combinations can occur. Again, these two dimensions are selected out of r such dimensions existing in the address space. Hence, the total number of nodes differing by the shortest distance 2,

$$N_2 = \sum (m_i - 1)(m_j - 1)$$

$$i, j \varepsilon \{1, 2, \cdots, r\} \quad \text{and} \quad i \neq j.$$

365

There are $\binom{r}{2}$ terms to be added in this summation. The same ideas can be extended to calculate the number of nodes differing by a Hamming distance d,

$$N_d = \sum (m_i - 1)(m_j - 1)(m_k - 1) \cdots d \quad \text{such terms}$$

$$i, j, k \cdots \varepsilon \{1, 2, \cdots, r\}$$
$$i \neq j \neq k \neq \cdots$$

and the summation includes $\binom{r}{d}$ such items.

A Boolean n-cube structure can be considered as a special case of GHC structures, where $m_i = 2$ for $1 \leqslant i \leqslant r$. As a result, $N = 2^r$ and $r = \log_2 N = n$.

$$\prod (m_i - 1) = 1 \quad \text{and} \quad N_d = \binom{n}{d} = \frac{n!}{d!(n - d)!}.$$

Once the number of nodes at a distance d is known, the average message distance is $\bar{d} = (\sum_{d=1}^{r} d N_d)/(N - 1)$.

To get an idea how the average message distance varies, let us consider the case when $N = m^r$. Also, as mentioned earlier, m_i's should be as close as possible to $\sqrt[r]{N}$ for an optimized structure with diameter r, and hence this should give approximate results for any N that can be factored into r-components.

When all m_i's are equal to m, the number of nodes at a distance d, $N_d = \binom{r}{d}(m - 1)^d$, and

$$\bar{d} = \left[\sum_{d=1}^{r} d \binom{r}{d} (m - 1)^d \right]/(N - 1)$$

$$= (m - 1) \left[\sum_{d=0}^{r} \binom{r}{d} \frac{\partial (m - 1)^d}{\partial (m - 1)} \right]/(N - 1)$$

$$= (m - 1) \frac{\partial}{\partial (m - 1)} \left[\sum_{d=0}^{r} \binom{r}{d} (m - 1)^d \right]/(N - 1)$$

$$= \left[(m - 1) \frac{\partial}{\partial (m - 1)} (m - 1 + 1)^r \right]/(N - 1)$$

$$= r \cdot (m - 1) \cdot m^{r-1}/(N - 1), \quad m = \sqrt[r]{N}.$$

Fig. 7 shows the variation of average message distance $(\bar{d})$ with respect to r for a few values of m. When $m = 2$, it is simply a Boolean n-cube structure. For an OGHC, $\bar{d} \cong 0.375 \log_2 N$.

The average message traffic density in a link of GHC structures is defined as

$$\rho = \frac{\text{Average message distance} * \text{number of nodes}}{\text{total number of links}}$$

$$= \frac{\bar{d} N}{\frac{N}{2} \sum_{i=1}^{r} (m_i - 1)} = \frac{2\bar{d}}{\sum_{i=1}^{r} (m_i - 1)}.$$

For $N = m^r$, $\rho = \dfrac{2\bar{d}}{r(m - 1)} = 0.5$ for an OGHC structure.

The GHC structures can be modeled as a communication net with the ith channel represented as an $M/M/1$ system with Poisson arrivals at a rate λ_i and exponential service time of mean $1/\mu c_i$ [17]. μ = average service rate and c_i =

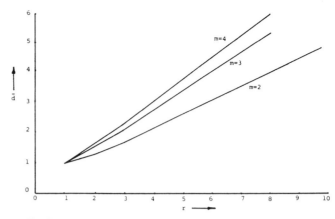

Fig. 7. Average message distance in GHC-structure with $N = m^r$.

capacity of the ith channel. Additionally, we assume the following.

1) Each node is equally likely to send a message to every other node in a fixed time period.

2) The routing is done as per the fixed routing algorithm described in Section II.

3) The load is evenly distributed, i.e., λ_i is the same for all i.

4) The capacity of each link in the network has been optimally assigned [17].

5) The cost per capacity per link is unity.

Under the above conditions, the delay of GHC structures is given by [17]

$$T = \frac{\bar{d} \left(\sum_{i=1}^{M} \sqrt{\frac{\lambda_i}{\lambda}} \right)^2}{\mu C (1 - \bar{d} \gamma)}$$

where

M = total number of directed links,
$\lambda = \sum_{i=1}^{M} \lambda_i = M \lambda_i$ because of assumption 3),
γ = the utilization factor, and
$C = \sum_{i=1}^{M} c_i$ = total capacity of the structure.

With N nodes and ℓ bidirectional links per node,

$$M = \left(\frac{N}{2} \right) \cdot 2\ell.$$

Hence,

$$T = \frac{\bar{d} \left(\frac{N}{2} \right) \cdot 2\ell}{\mu C (1 - \bar{d} \gamma)}.$$

With constants μ, C, and N, the above delay can be normalized as

$$T' = \frac{\bar{d} 2\ell}{(1 - \bar{d} \gamma)}.$$

The delay increases exponentially with increased utilization and saturates at a particular load, given by $\gamma_{\text{sat}} = 1/\bar{d}$. In a fully connected system, $\gamma_{\text{sat}} = 1$ since $\bar{d} = 1$, and hence the computer network performs very well under heavy load con-

366

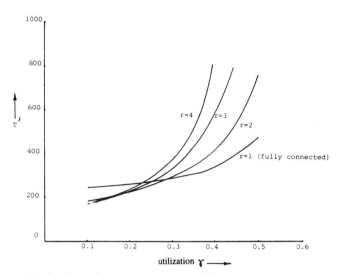

Fig. 8. Normalized queueing delay in GHC-structures with $N = 16$.

TABLE I
CHARACTERISTICS OF GHC STRUCTURES

N	Factors	Diameter r	Links per node ℓ	Cost Factor ξ	Average Message Distance $\bar{d}$	γ_{sat}
	2 * 2 * 2 * 2	4	4	16	2.13	0.47
	4 * 2 * 2	3	5	15	1.87	0.535
16	4 * 4	2	6	12	1.6	0.625
	16 (fully connected)	1	15	15	1	1
	3 * 2 * 2 * 2	4	5	20	2.26	0.442
	4 * 3 * 2	3	6	18	2.0	0.5
24	6 * 4	2	8	16	1.65	0.606
	24 (fully connected)	1	23	23	1	1

ditions. In general, the performance of the GHC structures will lie between a loop structure and a fully connected net. The average delay in different GHC structures for $N = 16$ is plotted in Fig. 8. As expected, the optimized structure with $N = 4 * 4$, performs well both in light load and heavy load conditions. Table I presents a summary of some relevant information for different GHC structures with $N = 16$ and 24.

IV. PERFORMANCE OF GHC STRUCTURES

In this section, the performance of the GHC structures will be compared to that of other hypercube structures. The number of nodes N will be assumed to be a power of two and the GHC considered here is the OGHC as obtained in Section III. The loop structure is a nearest neighbor mesh in one dimension, whereas a completely connected structure is a one-dimensional GHC. The Boolean n-cube computer, although it is a part of the GH and the nearest neighbor mesh, is a well known topology and will therefore be considered separately. The nearest neighbor mesh considered here is an optimal structure as described below.

Nearest Neighbor Mesh Hypercube Structures: If N can be expressed as a product of r-terms, a generalized nearest neighbor mesh hypercube is obtained when a node $(x_r x_{r-1} \cdots x_{i+1} x_i x_{i-1} \cdots x_2 x_1)$ is connected to $[x_r x_{r-1} \cdots x_{i+1}(x_i + 1)$ mod $m_i x_{i-1} \cdots x_2 x_1]$ and $[x_r x_{r-1} \cdots x_{i+1}(x_i - 1)$ mod $m_i x_{i-1} \cdots x_2 x_1]$ for all $1 \leq i \leq r$. Such a structure for $N = 4 * 3 * 2$ is shown in Fig. 9. The degree of a node is $2r$ when all the factors are greater than two. The diameter of such a structure is $\sum_{i=1}^{r} \lfloor m_i/2 \rfloor$. For a fixed value of N, there can be several ways to factor N into r components. The degree of a node being fixed at $2r$, an optimal structure is obtained when $\sum_{i=1}^{r} \lfloor m_i/2 \rfloor$ is minimum. For high values of m_i, the floor function can be neglected. The following lemma results.

Lemma 2: An optimal nearest neighbor mesh with some fixed r dimensions is obtained when $m_i \cong \sqrt[r]{N}$.

Again, for a fixed value of N, there can be several ways to design a nearest neighbor mesh. A discrete optimization of the product of the degree of a node and the diameter, for various values of r, will give rise to an optimal design. The

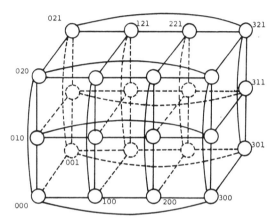

Fig. 9. A generalized nearest neighbor mesh hypercube with $N = 4 * 3 * 2$.

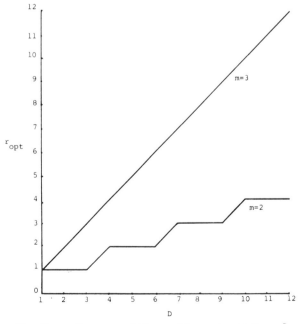

Fig. 10. r_{opt} for nearest neighbor mesh hypercube with $N = m^D$.

values of r_{opt} for N, powers of 2 and 3 are plotted in Fig. 10. For N, a power of two, an optimal structure is obtained when there are 8 nodes in each dimension, as can be seen from the computation.

Conjecture 2: For N, a power of two, an optimal nearest neighbor mesh hypercube is obtained when $r = \lceil \log_8 N \rceil$.

Throughout this section, such an optimal structure (8-cube) will be considered for performance comparison.

Average Message Distance ($\bar{d}$):

Loop:
$$\bar{d} = \frac{2\left(1 + 2 + 3 + \cdots + \frac{N-1}{2}\right)}{N-1}$$

$$= \frac{1}{4}(N+1) \quad \text{for} \quad N \quad \text{odd}$$

$$= \frac{2\left(1 + 2 + 3 + \cdots + \frac{N-2}{2}\right) + \frac{N}{2}}{N-1}$$

$$= \frac{1}{4}\frac{N(N-2)}{N-1} \quad \text{for} \quad N \quad \text{even}$$

$$\cong 0.25\,N \quad \text{for any} \quad N.$$

Boolean n-cube:
$$\bar{d} = \sum \binom{n}{d} d = \frac{n}{2} \cdot \frac{N}{N-1}$$

$$\cong 0.5 \log_2 N.$$

Nearest neighbor mesh:

With $N = W^r$, the maximum distance along each direction is $W/2$. The average distance along each dimension is $0.25\,W$ as in the case of a loop. For r dimensions, $\bar{d} \cong 0.25\,rW$. With an optimal design, $W = 8$ and $\bar{d} = 0.25 \times \log_8 N \times 8 = 0.667 \log_2 N$.

OGHC: $\bar{d} = 0.375 \log_2 N$.

Completely connected: $\bar{d} = 1$.

Cost:

The cost of a structure = degree of a node * diameter

Loop: Degree of a node = 2, Diameter = $0.5N$.
    Hence, cost = N.

Boolean n-cube: Degree of a node = Diameter = $\log_2 N$, cost = $\log_2^2 N$.

Nearest neighbor mesh: Degree of a node = $2 \log_8 N = 0.667 \log_2 N$
    Diameter = $r \cdot (W/2) = 4 \log_8 N = 1.333 \log_2 N$
    Cost = $0.889 \log_2^2 N$.

OGHC: Cost = $0.75 \log_2^2 N$.

Completely connected: Cost = $N - 1$.

Average message traffic density:

Average message traffic density $\rho = (\bar{d} \times N)/L$

Loop: Number of links $L = N$; hence $\rho = \bar{d} = 0.25N$

Boolean n-cube: $L = 0.5N \log_2 N$; $\rho = \bar{d}/0.5 \log_2 N = 1$

Nearest neighbor mesh: $L = r \cdot N = 0.334N \log_2 N$
    $\rho = \bar{d}/0.334 \log_2 N = 2$.

OGHC: $\rho = 0.5$.

Fault Tolerance: The fault tolerance of a structure is the connectivity or the number of node disjoint paths between any two nodes. The connectivity for a loop is 2; for a Boolean n-cube, it is $\log_2 N$; for a nearest neighbor mesh it is $2r$ [18], i.e., $0.667 \log_2 N$ here; for an OGHC it is $1.5 \log_2 N$ and for a completely connected structure it is $(N - 1)$.

V. m-CUBE INTERCONNECTION NETWORKS

An $N \times N$ multistage interconnection network (MIN) [19]–[21] is capable of connecting N number of processing elements (PE's) to N number of memory modules (MM's). Various MIN's described in the literature [19] employ 2-input 2-output switching elements (SE's). Here, we illustrate the use of GHC structures in designing $N \times N$ MIN's implemented with $m \times m$ SE's. We limit our discussions to only values of N and m which are powers of two.

An m-cube multicomputer is a GHC structure with m number of nodes in each dimension. When N is a power of m, there are m nodes in each of $r = \log_m N$ dimensions of the hypercube. When N is not a power of m, there will be $r - 1 = \lfloor \log_m N \rfloor$ dimensions with m nodes each and one dimension with $N/_m r - 1$ number of nodes. All the nodes in a dimension are connected to each other by dedicated links. A completely connected multicomputer corresponds to a crossbar [22] in a circuit switched multiprocessor. When an m-cube GHC is unfolded, an m-cube MIN results. By unfolding we mean that the ith stage of the MIN is connected as per the ith dimension of the GHC structure for $1 \le i \le r$. An m-cube MIN will consist of $\log_m N$ stages of N/m number of $m \times m$ crossbar modules at each stage when N is a power of m. When N is not a power of m, there will be $\lfloor \log_m N \rfloor$ stages of $m \times m$ crossbar modules followed by $N/_m r - 1 \times N/_m r - 1$ crossbar modules at the last stage. This also results by unfolding an m-cube GHC. The construction of a 32×32 4-cube MIN is illustrated in Fig. 11. When a Boolean n-cube structure with $m = 2$ is unfolded, a generalized cube interconnection network [20] results. Some recent studies [15], [23], [24] have shown that a 4-cube MIN gives optimal performance in terms of bandwidth and cost.

VI. GENERALIZED HYPERBUS (GHB) STRUCTURES

In the preceding section, N specifies the number of processors in the structure. If, however, it specifies the number of buses, a different configuration results. Then, each processor is connected to two adjoining buses, running in different dimensions of the generalized hypercube. Such a structure for $N = 3 * 2$ is shown in Fig. 12. These types of structures will be referred to as generalized hyperbus (GHB) structures. The number of processors P in a GHB structure will be greater than the number of buses N. The distance between two processors is specified by the number of buses a message has to travel from one processor to the other. Since GHB structures have fewer links than nodes, these structures will give rise to a high message traffic density in a bus, and hence will saturate rapidly. However, having only two I/O

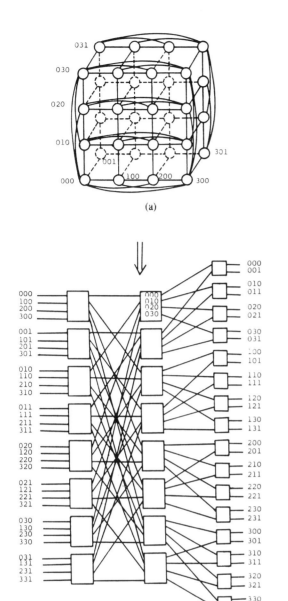

Fig. 11. (a) A 4 * 3 * 2 GHC structure, (b) a 32 × 32 4-cube network.

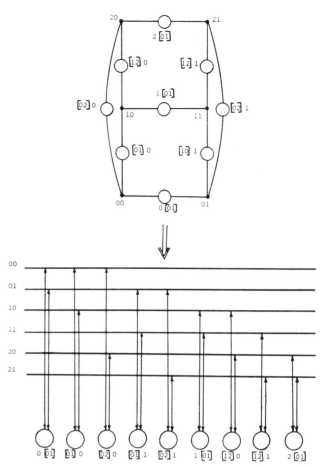

Fig. 12. A GHB structure with $N = 3 * 2$.

The GHB structures have the following features:
1) Each processor has only two I/O ports.
2) The number of processors connected to a bus is

$$p = \sum_{i=1}^{r} (m_i - 1).$$

3) Total number of processors in the system.

$$P = \frac{N}{2} \sum_{i=1}^{r} (m_i - 1).$$

4) Two processors can differ in their addresses in all the r-coordinates. Thus, the diameter of the structure $= r + 1$.

5) There are p bus disjoint paths between any two buses. A bus disjoint path also corresponds to a node disjoint path.

6) There are d disjoint paths of equal distance d between any two buses with a Hamming distance d.

7) A processor is disconnected if both the adjoining buses fail.

Internode Distance: Since the structure is symmetrical, let us consider 0^{r-1} [01] as the source node. 0^{r-1} means $000 \cdots$ up to $(r - 1)$ terms.

Nodes differing by unit distance:
1) When nodes have addresses $\{w0\}$ and $\{w1\}$, where w is a set of $(r - 1)$ terms $000 \cdots [0x_i] \cdots 0$ for all

ports per processor, the cost is very small as compared to the GHC structures.

The GHB structure consists of N buses with $N = m_r * m_{r-1} * \cdots * m_i * \cdots * m_2 * m_1$. A bus in the GHB structure is denoted by an r-tuple $(x_r x_{r-1} \cdots x_i \cdots x_2 x_1)$ for $0 \leq x_i \leq m_i - 1$ for $1 \leq i \leq r$. A processor will be denoted $(x_r x_{r-1} \cdots x_{i+1} [y_i z_i] x_{i-1} \cdots x_1)$, i.e., with x_i replaced by a 2-tuple $[y_i z_i]$ for $y_i, z_i \in \{0, 1, \cdots (m_i - 1)\}$. This means that the processor is connected to buses $(x_r x_{r-1} \cdots x_{i+1} y_i x_{i-1} \cdots x_1)$ and $(x_r x_r - 1 \cdots x_{i+1} z_i x_{i-1} \cdots x_1)$. $y_i, z_i \in \{0, 1, \cdots, (m_i - 1)\}$ and the ith position can vary between 1 and r. The Hamming distance between a pair $[y_i z_i]$ and some v_i is 0 if v_i is equal to y_i or z_i or $[y_i w_i]$ or $[w_i z_i]$ and equals 1, otherwise. Similarly, Hamming distance between x_i and v_i is 0 if $x_i = v_i$ and equals 1 if $x_i \neq v_i$. The actual distance between any two different processors = Hamming distance between them +1.

$1 \le x_i \le (m_i - 1)$ and $2 \le i \le r$. The number of such nodes $= 2 \sum_{i=2}^{r} (m_i - 1)$

2) When the nodes are of the form $\{0^{r-1}[0x_1]\}$ or $\{0^{r-1}[1x_1]\}$, $x_1 \ \varepsilon \ \{2, 3, \cdots (m_1 - 1)\}$. The number of such nodes $= 2(m_1 - 2)$. Hence, the total number of nodes with distance 1

$$N_1 = 2 \sum_{i=2}^{r} (m_i - 1) + 2(m_1 - 2).$$

When $N = m^r$, $N_1 = 2(r - 1)(m - 1) + 2(m - 2) = 2rm - 2r - 2$.

Nodes differing by distance d:

When $N = m_r * m_{r-1} * \cdots * m_1$, it is extremely difficult to derive closed form expressions for N_d. Let us consider $N = m^r$ with $m_i = m$, $1 \le i \le r$. There are several possibilities as discussed below.

1) Nodes of the form $\{w[0x_1]\}$ and $\{w[1x_1]\}$, where w is a $r - 1$ tuple differing from 0^{r-1} in $(d - 1)$ dimensions. For each $[0x_1]$ and $[1x_1]$ in the least significant digit (lsd), there are $\binom{r-1}{d-1}(m - 1)^{d-1}$ number of nodes and there are $(m - 1)$ such $[0x]$ and $(m - 2)$ such $[1x]$ in the lsd. Hence, number of nodes $= (2m - 3)\binom{r-1}{d-1}(m - 1)^{d-1}$.

2) Nodes of the form $\{w0\}$ or $\{w1\}$.

(a) When w contains one $[0x_i]$ in the ith dimension for $2 \le i \le r$. As a result of $[0x_i]$ in the ith dimension, the node must differ in its address by $(d - 1)$ places out of $(r - 2)$ dimensions. There are $(r - 1)$ values i can take and there are $(m - 1)$ different values for x_i. Hence, the number of nodes $= 2(r - 1)\binom{r-2}{d-1}(m - 1)^{d-1}(m - 1)$.

(b) When w contains $[yz]$, $y, z \ne 0$ in the ith dimension. There are $\binom{m-1}{2}$ such elements possible in one dimension and for each $[yz]$ there are $\binom{r-2}{d-2}(m - 1)^{d-2}$. Again, $[yz]$ can occupy $(r - 1)$ dimensions except lsd and the total number of nodes $= 2(r - 1)\binom{m-1}{2}\binom{r-2}{d-2}(m - 1)^{d-2}$.

3) Nodes of the form $\{wx\}$, $x \ \varepsilon \ \{2, 3, \cdots (m - 1)\}$.

(a) When w contains $[0y]$ in the ith dimension, for each x in the lsd, there can be $(m - 1)$ such $[0y]$ in a particular dimension. The number of nodes for each such $[0y] = \binom{r-2}{d-2}(m - 1)^{d-2}$. There are $(r - 1)$ dimensions and $(m - 1)$ number of $[0y]$ in each dimension; number of nodes for each $x = (r - 1)(m - 1)\binom{r-2}{d-2}(m - 1)^{d-2}$. Again, there can be $(m - 2)$ such x in the lsd. Hence, the total number of nodes $= (m - 2)(r - 1)(m - 1)\binom{r-2}{d-2}(m - 1)^{d-2}$.

(b) When w contains $[yz]$, $y, z \ne 0$ in the ith dimension, there can be $\binom{m-1}{2}$ such pairs in each dimension with each having $\binom{r-2}{d-3}(m - 1)^{d-3}$ nodes. For $(r - 1)$ such dimensions and $(m - 2)$ such x in the lsd, the total number of nodes $= (m - 2)(r - 1)\binom{m-1}{2}\binom{r-2}{d-3}(m - 1)^{d-3}$.

4) Nodes of the form $\{w[yz]\}$, $y, z \ \varepsilon \ \{2, 3, \cdots (m - 1)\}$. There are $\binom{m-2}{2}$ such pairs in the lsd. For each pair there will be $\binom{r-1}{d-1}(m - 1)^{d-2}$ nodes differing by distance d. Hence, the total number of nodes $= \binom{m-2}{2}\binom{r-1}{d-2}(m - 1)^{d-2}$.

The total number of nodes N_d differing by a distance d in the GHB structure will be the sum of all the nodes in the above four possibilities. The maximum possible distance $= r + 1$. The total number of nodes in GHB struc-

ture with $N = m^r$

$$P = 1/2 \cdot N \cdot r(m - 1).$$

Hence, the average message distance is

$$\bar{d} = 2 \left(\sum_{d=1}^{r+1} d N_d \right) / N \cdot r \cdot (m - 1).$$

The average message traffic density in a bus in GHB structure is

$$\rho = \frac{\bar{d} \cdot \dfrac{N}{2} \cdot \sum_{i=1}^{r} (m_i - 1)}{N} = 1/2 \cdot \bar{d} \sum_{i=1}^{r} (m_i - 1)$$

and when $N = m^r$, $\rho = 1/2 \cdot \bar{d} \cdot r(m - 1)$.

VII. Conclusion

Two types of hypercube structures, generalized hypercube (GHC) and generalized hyperbus (GHB) have been presented in this paper. The GHC structure has a low cost compared to other hypercube structures. Because of its high connectivity, the fault tolerance is quite good. It also has a low average message distance and a low traffic density in the links. These factors increase approximately as log N. In general, the performance of GHC structure lies between that of a loop and a completely connected structure. In a GHC design it is impossible to have degree of a node less than $\log_2 N$. The GHB structures are obtained when a node in the GHC is replaced by a bus and a link in GHC is replaced by a node. Hence, traffic density on a bus in a GHB structure may be quite high. However, the number of I/O ports per processor is fixed at two. A generalized spanning bus hypercube [8] can similarly be obtained when each node is connected to 'r' buses, each spanning a different dimension in the address space and m_i number of nodes sharing a bus in the ith direction. The nodes will have identical addresses except in their ith coordinate.

The study provides clean design methodologies for a computer network based on the desired diameter. It also reveals many interesting properties of the hypercubes.

Acknowledgment

The authors are thankful to R. Finkel and W. Leland of the University of Wisconsin, Madison for their constructive criticisms and helpful comments.

References

[1] L. N. Bhuyan and D. P. Agrawal, "A general class of processor interconnection strategies," in *Proc. 9th Annu. Int. Symp. on Comput. Arch.*, Austin, TX, Apr. 1982, pp. 90–98.
[2] G. A. Anderson and E. D. Jenson, "Computer interconnection structures: Taxonomy, characteristics and examples," *ACM Comput. Surveys*, vol. 7, pp. 197–213, Dec. 1975.
[3] M. T. Liu, "Distributed loop computer networks," in *Advances in Computers, Vol. 17.* New York: Academic, 1978.
[4] B. W. Arden and H. Lee, "Analysis of chordal ring network," *IEEE Trans. Comput.*, vol. C-30, pp. 291–295, Apr. 1981.

[5] D. P. Agrawal, T. Y. Feng, and C. L. Wu, "A survey of communication processor systems," in *Proc. COMPSAC,* Chicago, IL, pp. 668–673, Nov. 1978.

[6] A. M. Despain and D. A. Patterson, "X-tree: A tree structured multiprocessor computer architecture," in *Proc. 5th Symp. on Comput. Arch.,* Apr. 1978, pp. 144–151.

[7] H. Sullivan and T. R. Bashkow, "A large scale, homogeneous, fully distributed parallel machine I," in *Proc. 4th Symp. Comput. Arch.,* Mar. 1977, pp. 105–117.

[8] L. D. Wittie, "Communication structures for large networks of microcomputers," *IEEE Trans. Comput.,* vol. C-30, pp. 264–273, Apr. 1981.

[9] F. P. Preparata and J. Vullemin, "The cube connected cycles: A versatile network for parallel computation," *Commun. Ass. Comput. Mach.,* vol. 24, pp. 300–309, May 1981.

[10] D. K. Pradhan and S. M. Reddy, "A fault-tolerant communication architecture for distributed systems," *IEEE Trans. Comput.,* vol. C-31, pp. 863–870, Sept. 1982.

[11] H. S. Stone, "Parallel processing with the perfect shuffle," *IEEE Trans. Comput.,* vol. C-20, 1971, pp. 153–161, Feb. 1971.

[12] R. Finkel and M. H. Solomon, "The lens interconnection strategy," *IEEE Trans. Comput.,* vol. C-30, pp. 960–965, Dec. 1981.

[13] L. S. Haynes *et al.,* "A survey of highly parallel computing," *Computer,* vol. 15, pp. 9–24, Jan. 1982.

[14] D. H. Lawrie, "Memory-processor connection networks," Ph.D. dissertation, Univ. of Illinois, 1973.

[15] L. N. Bhuyan and D. P. Agrawal, "Design and performance of a general class of interconnection networks," in *Proc. 1982 Int. Conf. on Parallel Processing,* Bellaire, MI, Aug. 1982, pp. 2–9; see also, *IEEE Trans. Comput.,* vol. C-32, Dec. 1983.

[16] J. G. Kuhl, "Fault-diagnosis in computing networks," Univ. of Iowa, ECE Tech. Rep. R-80-1, Aug. 1980, 183 pages.

[17] L. Kleinrock, *Queueing Systems: Vol. II, Computer Applications.* New York: Wiley, 1976.

[18] K. Bhat, "On the properties of arbitrary hypercubes," *Computer and Mathematics with Applications,* to be published.

[19] T. Y. Feng, "A survey of interconnection networks," *Computer,* vol. 14, pp. 12–27, Dec. 1981.

[20] H. J. Siegel and R. J. McMillan, "The multistage cube: A versatile interconnection network," *Computer,* pp. 458–473, Dec. 1981.

[21] D. P. Agrawal, "Graph theoretic analysis and design of multistage interconnection networks," *IEEE Trans. Comput.,* vol. C-32, pp. 637–648, July 1983.

[22] W. A. Wulf and C. G. Bell, "C.mmp—A multiminiprocessor," in *Proc. AFIPS, Fall Joint Comput. Conf.,* Dec. 1972, pp. 765–777.

[23] R. J. McMillan, G. B. Adams, III, and H. J. Siegel, "Performance and implementation of 4×4 switching modes in an interconnection network for PASM," in *Proc. 1981 Int. Conf. on Parallel Processing,* Aug. 1981, pp. 229–233.

[24] L. N. Bhuyan and D. P. Agrawal, "VLSI performance of multistage interconnection networks using 4 * 4 switches," in *Proc. 3rd Int. Conf. on Distributed Computing Systems,* Oct. 1982, pp. 606–613.

Laxmi N. Bhuyan (S'81–M'83) received the M.Sc. degree in electrical engineering from Regional Engineering College, Rourkela, Sambalpur University, India, in 1979, and the Ph.D. degree in computer engineering from Wayne State University, Detroit, MI, in 1982.

During 1982–83, he taught at the University of Manitoba, Winnipeg, Canada. Since September 1983, he has been with the Department of Electrical and Computer Engineering, University of Southwestern Louisiana, Lafayette, as an Assistant Professor. His research interests include parallel and distributed computer architecture, VLSI layout, and multiprocessor performance evaluations.

Dr. Bhuyan is a member of the Association for Computing Machinery.

Dharma P. Agrawal (M'74–SM'79) was born in Balod, M.P., India, on April 12, 1945. He received the B.E. degree in electrical engineering from the Ravishankar University, Raipur, M.P., India, in 1966, the M.E. (Hons.) degree in electronics and communication engineering from the University of Roorkee, Roorkee, U.P., India in 1968, and the D.Sc. Tech. degree from Federal Institute of Technology, Lausanne, Switzerland in 1975.

He has been a member of the faculty in the M.N. Regional Engineering College, Alahabad, India, University of Roorkee, Roorkee, India, the Federal Institute of Technology, Lausanne, Switzerland, the University of Technology, Baghdad, Iraq; Southern Methodist University, Dallas, TX, and Wayne State University, Detroit, MI. Currently, he is with the North Carolina State University, Raleigh, NC, as an Associate Professor in the Department of Electrical and Computer Engineering. His research interests include parallel/distributed processing, computer architecture, computer arithmetic, fault tolerance, and information retrieval. He has served as a referee for various reputed journals and international conferences. He was a member of Program Committees for the COMPCON Fall of 1979, the Sixth IEEE Symposium on Computer Arithmetic, and Seventh Symposium on Computer Arithmetic held in Aarhus, Denmark in June 1983. Currently, he is a member and the Secretary of the Publications Board, IEEE Computer Society, and recently, he has been appointed as the Chairman of the Rules of Practice Committee of the PUBS Board. He served as the Treasurer of the IEEE-CS Technical Committee on Computer Architecture and has been named as the Program Chairman for the 13th International Symposium on Computer Architecture to be held in Ann Arbor in June, 1984. He is also a distinguished visitor of the IEEE Computer Society.

Dr. Agrawal is a member of the ACM, SIAM, and Sigma Xi. He is listed in *Who's Who in the Midwest,* the *1981 Outstanding Young Men of America,* and in the *Directory of World Researchers'* 1980's subjects published by the International Technical Information Institute, Tokyo, Japan.

Performance Analysis of *k*-ary *n*-cube Interconnection Networks

WILLIAM J. DALLY, MEMBER, IEEE

Abstract—VLSI communication networks are wire-limited. The cost of a network is not a function of the number of switches required, but rather a function of the wiring density required to construct the network. This paper analyzes communication networks of varying dimension under the assumption of constant wire bisection. Expressions for the latency, average case throughput, and hot-spot throughput of *k*-ary *n*-cube networks with constant bisection are derived that agree closely with experimental measurements. It is shown that low-dimensional networks (e.g., tori) have lower latency and higher hot-spot throughput than high-dimensional networks (e.g., binary *n*-cubes) with the same bisection width.

Index Terms—Communication networks, concurrent computing, interconnection networks, message-passing multiprocessors, parallel processing, VLSI.

I. INTRODUCTION

THE critical component of a concurrent computer is its communication network. Many algorithms are communication rather than processing limited. Fine-grain concurrent programs execute as few as ten instructions in response to a message [7]. To efficiently execute such programs the communication network must have a latency no greater than about ten instruction times, and a throughput sufficient to permit a large fraction of the nodes to transmit simultaneously. Low-latency communication is also critical to support code sharing and garbage collection across nodes.

As the grain size of concurrent computers continues to decrease, communication latency becomes a more important factor. The diameter of the machine grows, messages are sent more frequently, and fewer instructions are executed in response to each message. Low latency is more difficult to achieve in a fine-grain machine because the available wiring space grows more slowly than the expected traffic. Since the machine must be constructed in three dimensions, the bisection area grows only as $N^{2/3}$ while traffic grows at least as fast as N, the number of nodes.

Manuscript received September 3, 1987; revised March 28, 1988. This work was supported in part by the Defense Advanced Research Projects Agency under Contracts N000014-80-C-0622 and N00014-85-K-0124 and in part by a National Science Foundation Presidential Young Investigator Award with matching funds from General Electric Corporation. A preliminary version of this paper appeared in the Proceedings of the 1987 Stanford Conference on Advanced Research in VLSI [10].

The author is with the Artificial Intelligence Laboratory and the Laboratory for Computer Science, Massachusetts Institute of Technology, Cambridge, MA 02139.

IEEE Log Number 9034541.

VLSI systems are wire-limited. The cost of these systems is predominantly that of connecting devices, and the performance is limited by the delay of these interconnections. Thus, to achieve the required performance, the network must make efficient use of the available wire. The topology of the network must map into the three physical dimensions so that messages are not required to *double back* on themselves, and in a way that allows messages to use all of the available bandwidth along their path.

This paper considers the problem of constructing *wire-efficient* communication networks, networks that give the optimum performance for a given wire density. We compare networks holding wire bisection, the number of wires crossing a cut that evenly divides the machine, constant. Thus, we compare low-dimensional networks with wide communication channels against high-dimensional networks with narrow channels. We investigate the class of *k*-ary *n*-cube interconnection networks and show that low-dimensional networks outperform high-dimensional networks with the same bisection width.

The remainder of this paper describes the design of wire-efficient communication networks. Section II describes the assumptions on which this paper is based. The family of *k*-ary *n*-cube networks is described in Section II-A. We restrict our attention to *k*-ary *n*-cubes because it is the dimension of the network that is important, not the details of its topology. Section II-B introduces *wormhole routing* [20], a low-latency routing technique. Network cost is determined primarily by wire density which we will measure in terms of bisection width. Section II-C introduces the idea of *bisection width*, and discusses delay models for network channels. A performance model of these networks is derived in Section III. Expressions are given for network latency as a function of traffic that agree closely with experimental results. Under the assumption of constant wire density, it is shown that low-dimensional networks achieve lower latency and better hot-spot throughput than do high-dimensional networks.

II. PRELIMINARIES

A. k-ary n-cubes

Many different network topologies have been proposed for use in concurrent computers: trees [6], [15], [21], Benes networks [4], Batcher sorting networks [2], shuffle exchange networks [23], *Omega* networks [14], *indirect* binary *n*-cube or *flip* networks [3], [22], and direct binary *n*-cubes [19], [17], [24]. The binary *n*-cube is a special case of the family of *k*-

0-8186-6522-X/95 $4.00 © 1990 IEEE

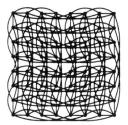

Fig. 1. A binary 6-cube embedded in the plane.

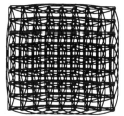

Fig. 2. A ternary 4-cube embedded in the plane.

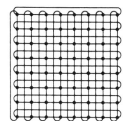

Fig. 3. An 8-ary 2-cube (torus).

ary n-cubes, cubes with n dimensions and k nodes in each dimension.

Most concurrent computers have been built using networks that are either k-ary n-cubes or are isomorphic to k-ary n-cubes: rings, meshes, tori, direct and indirect binary n-cubes, and Omega networks. Thus, in this paper we restrict our attention to k-ary n-cube networks. We refer to n as the *dimension* of the cube and k as the *radix*. Dimension, radix, and number of nodes are related by the equation

$$N = k^n, \ (k = \sqrt[n]{N}, \ n = \log_k N). \qquad (1)$$

It is the dimension of the network that is important, not the details of its topology.

A node in the k-ary n-cube can be identified by n-digit radix k address, $a_0, \cdots, a_{n-1}$. The ith digit of the address, a_i, represents the node's position in the ith dimension. Each node can forward messages to its upper neighbor in each dimension, i, with address $a_0, \cdots, a_i + 1 (\mathrm{mod}\, k), \cdots, a_{n-1}$.

In this paper, we assume that our k-ary n-cubes are unidirectional for simplicity. We will see that our results do not change appreciably for bidirectional networks. For an actual machine, however, there are many compelling reasons to make our networks bidirectional. Most importantly, bidirectional networks allow us to exploit locality of communication. If an object A sends a message to an object B, there is a high probability of B sending a message back to A. In a bidirectional network, a roundtrip from A to B can be made short by placing A and B close together. In a unidirectional network, a roundtrip will always involve completely circling the machine in at least one dimension.

Figs. 1–3 show three k-ary n-cube networks in order of decreasing dimension. Fig. 1 shows a binary 6-cube (64 nodes). A 3-ary 4-cube (81 nodes) is shown in Fig. 2. An 8-ary 2-cube (64 nodes), or torus, is shown in Fig. 3. Each line in Fig. 1 represents two communication channels, one in each direction, while each line in Figs. 2 and 3 represents a single communication channel.

B. Wormhole Routing

In this paper, we consider networks that use *wormhole* [20] rather than *store-and-forward* [25] routing. Instead of storing a packet completely in a node and then transmitting it to the next node, wormhole routing operates by advancing the head of a packet directly from incoming to outgoing channels. Only a few flow control digits (flits) are buffered at each node. A *flit* is the smallest unit of information that a queue or channel can accept or refuse.

As soon as a node examines the header flit(s) of a message, it selects the next channel on the route and begins forwarding flits down that channel. As flits are forwarded, the message becomes spread out across the channels between the source and destination. It is possible for the first flit of a message to arrive at the destination node before the last flit of the message has left the source. Because most flits contain no routing information, the flits in a message must remain in contiguous channels of the network and cannot be interleaved with the flits of other messages. When the header flit of a message is blocked, all of the flits of a message stop advancing and block the progress of any other message requiring the channels they occupy.

A method similar to wormhole routing, called *virtual cut-through*, is described in [13]. Virtual cut-through differs from wormhole routing in that it buffers messages when they block, removing them from the network. With wormhole routing, blocked messages remain in the network.

Fig. 4 illustrates the advantage of wormhole routing. There are two components of latency, distance and message aspect ratio. The distance D is the number of *hops* required to get from the source to the destination. The message aspect ratio (message length L normalized to the channel width W) is the number of channel cycles required to transmit the message across one channel. The top half of the figure shows store-and-forward routing. The message is entirely transmitted from node N_0 to node N_1, then from N_1 to N_2 and so on. With store-and-forward routing, latency is the product of D and L/W.

$$T_{\mathrm{SF}} = T_c \left(D \times \frac{L}{W} \right). \qquad (2)$$

The bottom half of Fig. 4 shows wormhole routing. As soon as a flit arrives at a node, it is forwarded to the next node. With wormhole routing, latency is reduced to the sum of D and L/W.

$$T_{\mathrm{WH}} = T_c \left(D + \frac{L}{W} \right). \qquad (3)$$

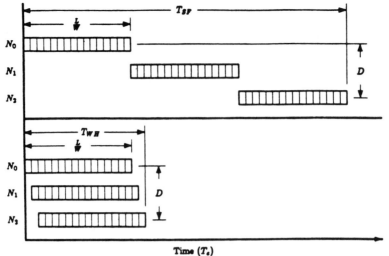

Fig. 4. Latency of store-and-forward routing (top) versus wormhole routing (bottom).

In both of these equations, T_c is the channel cycle time, the amount of time required to perform a transaction on a channel.

C. VLSI Complexity

VLSI computing systems [16] are wire-limited; the complexity of what can be constructed is limited by wire density, the speed at which a machine can run is limited by wire delay, and the majority of power consumed by a machine is used to drive wires. Thus, machines must be organized both logically and physically to keep wires short by exploiting locality wherever possible. The VLSI architect must organize a computing system so that its form (physical organization) fits its function (logical organization).

Networks have traditionally been analyzed under the assumption of constant channel bandwidth. Under this assumption each channel is one bit wide ($W = 1$) and has unit delay ($T_c = 1$). The constant bandwidth assumption favors networks with high dimensionality (e.g., binary n-cubes) over low-dimensional networks (e.g., tori). This assumption, however, is not consistent with the properties of VLSI technology. Networks with many dimensions require more and longer wires than do low-dimensional networks. Thus, high-dimensional networks cost more and run more slowly than low-dimensional networks. A realistic comparison of network topology must take both wire density and wire length into account.

To account for wire density, we will use bisection width [26] as a measure of network cost. The bisection width of a network is the minimum number of wires cut when the network is divided into two equal halves. Rather than comparing networks with constant channel width W, we will compare networks with constant bisection width. Thus, we will compare low-dimensional networks with large W with high-dimensional networks with small W.

The delay of a wire depends on its length l. For short wires, the delay t_s is limited by charging the capacitance of the wire and varies logarithmically with wire length.

$$t_s = \tau_{\text{inv}} e \log_e Kl \tag{4}$$

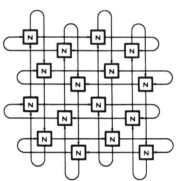

Fig. 5. A folded torus system.

where τ_{inv} is the inverter delay, and K is a constant depending on capacitance ratios. For long wires, delay t_l is limited by the speed of light.

$$t_l = \frac{l \sqrt{\epsilon_r}}{c}. \tag{5}$$

In this paper, we will consider three delay models: constant delay T_c independent of length, logarithmic delay $T_c \propto \log l$, and linear delay $T_c \propto l$. Our main result, that latency is minimized by low-dimensional networks, is supported by all three models.

III. PERFORMANCE ANALYSIS

In this section, we compare the performance of unidirectional k-ary n-cube interconnection networks using the following assumptions.

- Networks must be embedded into the plane. If a three-dimensional packaging technology becomes available, the comparison changes only slightly.
- Nodes are placed systematically by embedding $n/2$ logical dimensions in each of the two physical dimensions. We assume that both n and k are even integers. The long end-around connections shown in Fig. 3 can be avoided by folding the network as shown in Fig. 5.

- For networks with the same number of nodes, *wire density is held constant*. Each network is constructed with the same bisection width B, the total number of wires crossing the midpoint of the network. To keep the bisection width constant, we vary the width W of the communication channels. We normalize to the bisection width of a bit-serial ($W = 1$) binary n-cube.

- The networks use *wormhole* routing.

- Channel delay T_c is a function of wire length l. We begin by considering channel delay to be constant. Later, the comparison is performed for both logarithmic and linear wire delays; $T_c \propto \log l$ and $T_c \propto l$.

When k is even, the channels crossing the midpoint of the network are all in the highest dimension. For each of the $\sqrt{N}$ rows of the network, there are $k^{((n/2)-1)}$ of these channels in each direction for a total of $2\sqrt{N}k^{((n/2)-1)}$ channels. Thus, the bisection width B of a k-ary n-cube with W-bit wide communication channels is

$$B(k, n) = 2W\sqrt{N}k^{((n/2)-1)} = \frac{2WN}{k}. \quad (6)$$

For a binary n-cube, $k = 2$, the bisection width is $B(2, n) = WN$. We set B equal to N to normalize to a binary n-cube with unit width channels, $W = 1$. The channel width $W(k, n)$ of a k-ary n-cube with the same bisection width B follows from (6):

$$\frac{2W(k, n)N}{k} = N,$$

$$W(k, n) = \frac{k}{2}. \quad (7)$$

The peak wire density is greater than the bisection width in networks with $n > 2$ because the lower dimensions contribute to wire density. The maximum density, however, is bounded by

$$D_{\max} = 2W\sqrt{N}\sum_{i=0}^{\frac{n}{2}-1} k^i = k\sqrt{N}\sum_{i=0}^{\frac{n}{2}-1} k^i$$
$$= k\sqrt{N}\left(\frac{k^{n/2} - 1}{k - 1}\right)$$
$$= k\sqrt{N}\left(\frac{\sqrt{N} - 1}{k - 1}\right) < \left(\frac{k}{k - 1}\right)B. \quad (8)$$

A plot of wire density as a function of position for one row of a binary 20-cube is shown in Fig. 6. The density is very low at the edges of the cube and quite dense near the center. The peak density for the row is 1364 at position 341. Compare this density to the bisection width of the row, which is 1024. In contrast, a two-dimensional torus has a wire density of 1024 independent of position. One advantage of high-radix networks is that they have a very uniform wire density. They make full use of available area.

Each processing node connects to $2n$ channels (n input and n output) each of which is $k/2$ bits wide. Thus, the number

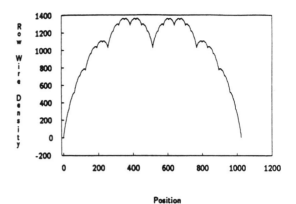

Fig. 6. Wire density versus position for one row of a binary 20-cube.

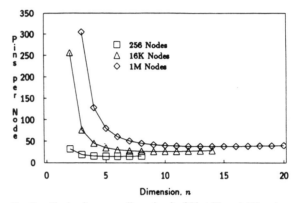

Fig. 7. Pin density versus dimension for 256, 16K, and 1M nodes.

of pins per processing node is

$$N_p = nk. \quad (9)$$

A plot of pin density as a function of dimension for $N = 256$, 16K, and 1M nodes[1] is shown in Fig. 7. Low-dimensional networks have the disadvantage of requiring many pins per processing node. A two-dimensional network with 1M nodes (not shown) requires 2048′ pins and is clearly unrealizable. However, the number of pins decreases very rapidly as the dimension n increases. Even for 1M nodes, a dimension 4 node has only 128 pins. All of the configurations that give low latency also give a reasonable pin count.

A. Latency

Latency T_l is the sum of the latency due to the network and the latency due to the processing node,

$$T_l = T_{\text{net}} + T_{\text{node}}. \quad (10)$$

In this paper, we are concerned only with T_{net}. Techniques to reduce T_{node} are described in [7] and [11].

If we select two processing nodes, P_i, P_j, at random, the average number of channels that must be traversed to send a message from P_i to P_j is given by

$$D = \left(\frac{k - 1}{2}\right)n. \quad (11)$$

[1] 1K=1024 and, 1M=1K×1K=1048576.

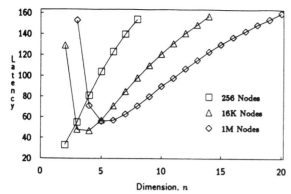

Fig. 8. Latency versus dimension for 256, 16K, and 1M nodes, constant delay.

The average latency of a k-ary n-cube is calculated by substituting (7) and (11) into (3)

$$T_{net} = T_c \left(\left(\frac{k-1}{2} \right) n + \frac{2L}{k} \right). \qquad (12)$$

Fig. 8 shows the average network latency T_{net} as a function of dimension n for k-ary n-cubes with 2^8 (256), 2^{14} (16K), and 2^{30} (1M) nodes.[2] The left most data point in this figure corresponds to a torus ($n = 2$) and the rightmost data point corresponds to a binary n-cube ($k = 2$). This figure assumes constant wire delay T_c and a message length L of 150 bits. This choice of message length was based on the analysis of a number of fine-grain concurrent programs [7]. Although constant wire delay is unrealistic, this figure illustrates that even ignoring the dependence of wire delay on wire length, low-dimensional networks achieve lower latency than high-dimensional networks.

The latency of the tori on the left side of Fig. 8 is limited almost entirely by distance. The latency of the binary n-cubes on the right side of the graph is limited almost entirely by aspect ratio. With bit serial channels, these cubes take 150 cycles to transmit their messages across a single channel.

In an application that exploits locality of communication, the distance between communicating objects is reduced. In such a situation, the latency of the low-dimensional networks, dominated by distance (the left side of Fig. 8) is reduced. High-dimensional networks, on the other hand, cannot take advantage of locality. Their latency, because it is dominated by message length, will remain high.

In applications that send short messages, the component of latency due to message length is reduced resulting in lower latency for high-dimensional networks (the right side of Fig. 8).

For the three cases shown in Fig. 8, minimum latencies are achieved for $n = 2$, 4, and 5, respectively. In general, the lowest latency is achieved when the component of latency due to distance D and the component due to message length L/W

[2] For the sake of comparison, we allow radix to take on noninteger values. For some of the dimensions considered, there is no integer radix k that gives the correct number of nodes. In fact, this limitation can be overcome by constructing a *mixed-radix cube* [5].

are approximately equal, $D \approx L/W$. The following assertion makes this statement more precise.

Assertion: Minimum latency T_{net} occurs at a dimension $n \leq n_x$, where n_x is the dimension for which $D = L/W$.

Proof: Differentiating (12) with respect to n gives

$$\frac{\partial T_{net}}{\partial n} = \frac{k - 1 - k \log k}{2} + \frac{2L \log^2 k}{k \log N}. \qquad (13)$$

For $n = n_x$, substituting $D = L/W$ into (7) and (11) gives

$$4L = nk(k-1) = \frac{k(k-1) \log N}{\log k}. \qquad (14)$$

Substituting into the derivative (13) gives

$$\left. \frac{\partial T_{net}}{\partial n} \right|_{n=n_x} = \frac{k - 1 - k \log k}{2} + \frac{(k-1) \log k}{2}$$
$$= \frac{k - 1 - \log k}{2}. \qquad (15)$$

For all $k \geq 2$, $(\partial T_{net}/\partial n)|_{n=n_x} \geq 0$. The derivative is monotonically increasing for $n \leq n_x$. Thus, the minimum latency $(\partial T_{net}/\partial n = 0)$ occurs for $n < n_x$. $\square$

Empirically, for all networks with $N < 2^{20}$ and integral valued k and n the minimum latency occurs when k and n are chosen so that $|D - (L/W)|$ is minimized.

The longest wire in the system becomes a bottleneck that determines the rate at which each channel operates, T_c. The length of this wire is given by

$$l = k^{(n/2)-1}. \qquad (16)$$

If the wires are sufficiently short, delay depends logarithmically on wire length. If the channels are longer, they become limited by the speed of light, and delay depends linearly on channel length. Substituting (16) into (4) and (5) gives

$$T_c \propto \begin{cases} 1 + \log_e l = 1 + \left(\dfrac{n}{2} - 1 \right) \log_e k & \text{logarithmic delay} \\ l = k^{(n/2)-1} & \text{linear delay.} \end{cases} \qquad (17)$$

We substitute (17) into (12) to get the network latency for these two cases:

$$T_l \propto \begin{cases} \left(1 + \left(\dfrac{n}{2} - 1 \right) \log_e k \right) \left(\left(\dfrac{k-1}{2} \right) n + \dfrac{2L}{k} \right) \\ \quad \text{logarithmic delay} \\ \left(k^{(n/2)-1} \right) \left(\left(\dfrac{k-1}{2} \right) n + \dfrac{2L}{k} \right) \\ \quad \text{linear delay.} \end{cases} \qquad (18)$$

Fig. 9 shows the average network latency as a function of dimension for k-ary n-cubes with 2^8 (256), 2^{14} (16K), and 2^{20} (1M) nodes, assuming logarithmic wire delay and a message length, L, of 150. Fig. 10 shows the same data assuming linear wire delays. In both figures, the leftmost data point corresponds to a torus ($n = 2$) and the rightmost data point corresponds to a binary n-cube ($k = 2$).

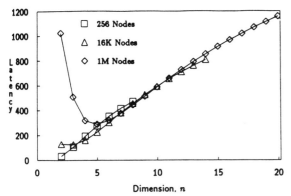

Fig. 9.   Latency versus dimension for 256, 16K, and 1M nodes, logarithmic delay.

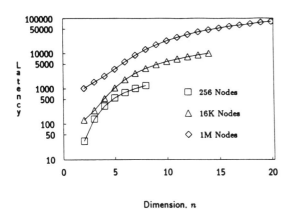

Fig. 10.   Latency versus dimension for 256, 16K, and 1M nodes, linear delay.

In the linear delay case, Fig. 10, a torus ($n = 2$) always gives the lowest latency. This is because a torus offers the highest bandwidth channels and the most direct physical route between two processing nodes. Under the linear delay assumption, latency is determined solely by bandwidth and by the physical distance traversed. There is no advantage in having long channels.

Under the logarithmic delay assumption, Fig. 9, a torus has the lowest latency for small networks ($N = 256$). For the larger networks, the lowest latency is achieved with slightly higher dimensions. With $N = 16K$, the lowest latency occurs when n is three.[3] With $N = 1M$, the lowest latency is achieved when n is 5. It is interesting that assuming constant wire delay does not change this result much. Recall that under the (unrealistic) constant wire delay assumption, Fig. 8, the minimum latencies are achieved with dimensions of 2, 4, and 5, respectively.

The results shown in Figs. 8–10 were derived by comparing networks under the assumption of constant wire cost to a binary n-cube with $W = 1$. For small networks it is possible to construct binary n-cubes with wider channels, and for large networks (e.g., 1M nodes) it may not be possible to construct a binary n-cube at all. The available wiring area grows as $N^{2/3}$ while the bisection width of a binary n-cube grows as N. In the case of small networks, the comparison

[3] In an actual machine, the dimension n would be restricted to be an even integer.

against binary n-cubes with wide channels can be performed by expressing message length in terms of the binary n-cube's channel width, in effect decreasing the message length for purposes of comparison. The net result is the same: lower dimensional networks give lower latency. Even if we perform the 256 node comparison against a binary n cube with $W=16$, the torus gives the lowest latency under the logarithmic delay model, and a dimension 3 network gives minimum latency under the constant delay model. For large networks, the available wire is less than assumed, so the effective message length should be increased, making low-dimensional networks look even more favorable.

In this comparison, we have assumed that only a single bit of information is in transit on each wire of the network at a given time. Under this assumption, the delay between nodes T_c is equal to the period of each node T_p. In a network with long wires, however, it is possible to have several bits in transit at once. In this case, the channel delay T_c is a function of wire length, while the channel period $T_p < T_c$ remains constant. Similarly, in a network with very short wires we may allow a bit to ripple through several channels before sending the next bit. In this case, $T_p > T_c$. Separating the coefficients T_c and T_p, (3) becomes

$$T_{\text{net}} = \left(T_c D + T_p \frac{L}{W} \right). \tag{19}$$

The net effect of allowing $T_c \neq T_p$ is the same as changing the length L by a factor of $\frac{T_p}{T_c}$ and does not change our results significantly.

When wire cost is considered, low-dimensional networks (e.g., tori) offer lower latency than high-dimensional networks (e.g., binary n-cubes). Tori outperform binary n-cubes because they better match form to function. The logical and physical graphs of the torus are identical; thus, messages always travel the minimum distance from source to destination. In a binary n-cube, on the other hand, the fit between form and function is not as good. A message in a binary n-cube embedded into the plane may have to traverse considerably more than the minimum distance between its source and destination.

B. Throughput

Throughput, another important metric of network performance, is defined as the total number of messages the network can handle per unit time. One method of estimating throughput is to calculate the capacity of a network, the total number of messages that can be in the network at once. Typically the maximum throughput of a network is some fraction of its capacity. The network capacity per node is the total bandwidth out of each node divided by the average number of channels traversed by each message. For k-ary n-cubes, the bandwidth out of each node is nW, and the average number of channels traversed is given by (11), so the network capacity per node Γ is given by

$$\Gamma \propto \frac{nW}{D} \propto \frac{n\left(\dfrac{k}{2}\right)}{\left(\dfrac{k-1}{2}\right)n} \approx 1. \tag{20}$$

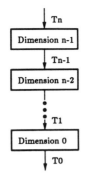

Fig. 11. Contention model for a network.

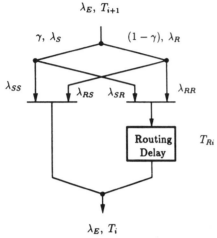

Fig. 12. Contention model for a single dimension.

The network capacity is independent of dimension. For a constant wire density, there is a constant network capacity.

Throughput will be less than capacity because contention causes some channels to block. This contention also increases network latency. To simplify the analysis of this contention, we make the following assumptions.

• Messages are routed using e-cube routing (in order of decreasing dimension) [8]. That is, a message at node $a_0, \cdots, a_{n-1}$ destined for nodes $b_0, \cdots, b_{n-1}$ is first routed in dimension $n-1$ until it reaches node $a_0, \cdots, a_{n-2}, b_{n-1}$. The message is then routed in dimension $n-2$ until it reaches node $a_0, \cdots, a_{n-3}, b_{n-2}, b_{n-1}$, and so on. As shown in Fig. 11, this assumption allows us to consider the contention in each dimension separately.

• The traffic from each node is generated by a Poisson process with arrival rate λ (bits/cycle).

• Message destinations are uniformly distributed and independent.

The arrival rate of λ(bits/cycle) corresponds to $\lambda_E = (\lambda/L)$(messages/cycles). At the destination, each flit is serviced as soon as it arrives, so the service time at the sink is $T_0 = L/W = 2L/k$. Starting with T_0 we will calculate the service time seen entering each preceding dimension.

For convenience, we will define the following quantities as illustrated in Fig. 12:

$\gamma = \dfrac{1}{k}$ probability that a message *skips* (does not route in) a dimension,

$\lambda_S = \gamma\lambda_E$ rate of traffic that skips the previous dimension, $i+1$, ($\frac{\text{messages}}{\text{cycle}}$),

$\lambda_R = (1-\gamma)\lambda_E$ rate of traffic that routes in the previous dimension, $i+1$, ($\frac{\text{messages}}{\text{cycle}}$),

$\lambda_{SS} = \gamma^2\lambda_E$ rate of traffic that skips both the previous dimension, $i+1$, and the current dimension i, ($\frac{\text{messages}}{\text{cycle}}$),

$\lambda_{SR} = \gamma(1-\gamma)\lambda_E$ rate of traffic that skips the previous dimension, $i+1$, and routes in the current dimension, i ($\frac{\text{messages}}{\text{cycle}}$),

$\lambda_{RS} = \gamma(1-\gamma)\lambda_E$ rate of traffic that routes in the previous dimension, $i+1$, and skips the current dimension i, ($\frac{\text{messages}}{\text{cycle}}$),

$\lambda_{RR} = (1-\gamma)^2\lambda_E$ rate of traffic that routes in both the previous dimension $i+1$, and the current dimension i, ($\frac{\text{messages}}{\text{cycle}}$).

$$(21)$$

Consider a single dimension i of the network as shown in Fig. 12. All messages incur a latency due to contention on entering the dimension. Those messages that are routed incur an additional latency T_{Ri} due to contention during routing. The rate λ_E message stream entering the dimension is composed of two components: a rate λ_S stream that skipped the previous $(i+1\text{st})$ dimension, and a rate λ_R stream that was routed in the previous dimension. These two streams are in turn split into components that will skip the ith dimension (λ_{SS} and λ_{RS}) and components that will be routed in the ith dimension (λ_{SR} and λ_{RR}). The entering latency seen by one component (say λ_{SS}) is given by multiplying the probability of a collision (in this case $\lambda_{RS}T_i$) by the expected latency due to a collision [in this case $(T_i/2)$]. The components that require routing must also add the latency due to contention during routing, T_{Ri}. Adding up the four components with appropriate weights gives the following equation for T_{i+1}.

$$T_{i+1} = T_i + (1-\gamma)T_{Ri} + \gamma(1-\gamma)^3\lambda_E(T_i + T_{Ri})^2 + \gamma^3(1-\gamma)\lambda_E T_i^2. \quad (22)$$

The first term of (22) is the latency seen entering the next dimension. The second term accounts for the routing latency T_{Ri} incurred by messages routing in this dimension (λ_{SR} and λ_{RR}). The entering latency due to contention when the two routing streams merge is given by the third term. The final term gives the entering latency for the messages that skip the dimension.

For large k, γ is small and the latency is approximated by $T_{i+1} \approx T_i + T_{Ri}$. For $k=2$ (binary n-cubes), $T_{Ri} = 0$; thus, $T_{i+1} = T_i + (\lambda_E T_i/8)$.

To calculate the routing latency T_{Ri} we use the model shown in Fig. 13. Messages enter the dimension with rate λ_R, route

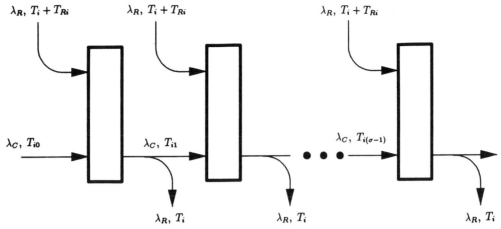

Fig. 13.   Contention model for routing latency.

through a number of stages, denoted by boxes, and exit the dimension. The latency due to contention in the stages sums to T_{Ri}. Given that a message is to be routed in a dimension, the expected number of channels traversed by the message is $(k/2)$, one entering channel and $\sigma = (k - 2)/2$ continuing channels. Thus, the *average* message rate on channels continuing in the dimension is $\lambda_C = \sigma \lambda_R$.

Using the average message rate to calculate latency is an approximation. The symmetry of the network assures that the traffic on physical channels is uniform. However, using virtual channels and *e*-cube routing [8] results in logical channels that form a spiral. Traffic on the *j*th channel on this spiral is given by $\lambda_{Cj} = (j - (i^2 + i)/2k)\lambda_R$. Using the uniform physical message rate results in a slightly pessimistic estimate of latency since contention for the physical channel occurs on flit boundaries while contention for the logical channel occurs on message boundaries.

To compute T_{Ri} we work backwards from the output. The service time in the last continuing channel in dimension *i* is $T_{i(\sigma-1)} = T_i$. Once we know the service time for the *j*th channel, T_{ij}, the additional service time due to contention at the $j - 1$st channel is given by multiplying the probability of a collision $\lambda_R T_{i0}$ by the expected waiting time for a collision $T_{i0}/2$. Repeating this calculation σ times gives us T_{i0}.

$$T_{i(j-1)} = T_{ij} + \frac{\lambda_R T_{i0}^2}{2},$$

$$T_{i0} = T_i + \frac{\sigma \lambda_R T_{i0}^2}{2} = T_i + \frac{\lambda_C T_{i0}^2}{2},$$

$$= \frac{1 - \sqrt{1 - 2\lambda_C T_i}}{\lambda_C}. \qquad (23)$$

Equation (23) is valid only when $\lambda_C < T_i/2$. If the message rate is higher than this limit, there is no steady-state solution and latency becomes infinite. There are two solutions to (23). Here we consider only the smaller of the two latencies. The larger solution corresponds to a state that is not encountered during normal operation of a network.

To calculate T_{Ri} we also need to consider the possibility of a collision on the entering channel.

$$T_{Ri} = T_{i0}\left(1 + \frac{\lambda_C T_{i0}}{2}\right) - T_i. \qquad (24)$$

If sufficient queueing is added to each network node, the service times do not increase, only the latency and (24) and (22) become

$$T_{Ri} = \left(\frac{T_i}{1 - \frac{\lambda_C T_0}{2}}\right)\left(1 + \frac{\lambda_C T_0}{2}\right) - T_i, \qquad (25)$$

$$T_{i+1} = T_i + (1 - \gamma)T_{Ri} + (\gamma(1 - \gamma)^3 + \gamma^3(1 - \gamma))\lambda_E T_0. \qquad (26)$$

To be effective, the total queueing between the source and destination should be greater than the expected increase in latency due to blocking. Two flits of queueing per stage are sufficient when $\lambda < 0.3$ and $L < 200$. Longer messages result in a longer service time T_0 and require additional queueing. The analysis here is pessimistic in that it assumes no queueing.

Using (22), we can determine 1) the maximum throughput of the network and 2) how network latency increases with traffic.

Figs. 14 and 15 show how latency increases as a function of applied traffic for 1K node and 4K node *k*-ary *n*-cubes. The vertical axis shows latency in cycles. The horizontal axis is traffic per node, λ, in bits/cycle. The figures compare measurements from a network simulator (points) to the latency predicted by (24) (lines). The simulation agrees with the prediction within a few percent until the network approaches saturation.

For 1K networks, a 32-ary 2-cube always gives the lowest latency. For 4K networks, a 16-ary 3-cube gives the lowest latency when $\lambda < 0.2$. Because latency increases more slowly for two-dimensional networks, a 64-ary 2-cube gives the lowest latency when $\lambda > 0.2$. At the left side of each graph ($\lambda = 0$), latency is given by (12). As traffic is applied to the

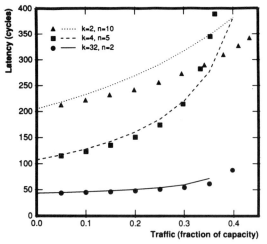

Fig. 14. Latency versus traffic (λ) for 1K node networks: 32-ary 2-cube, 4-ary 5-cube, and binary 10-cube, $L = 200$ bits. Solid line is predicted latency, points are measurements taken from a simulator.

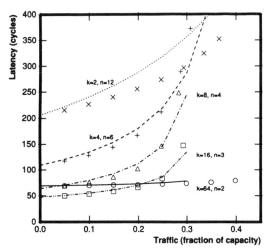

Fig. 15. Latency versus traffic (λ) for 4K node networks: 64-ary 2-cube, 16-ary 3-cube, 8-ary 4-cube, 4-ary 6-cube, and binary 12-cube, $L = 200$ bits. Solid line is predicted latency, points are measurements taken from a simulator.

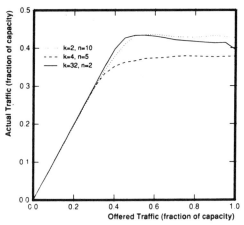

Fig. 16. Actual traffic versus attempted traffic for 1K node networks: 32-ary 2-cube, 4-ary 5-cube, and binary 10-cube, $L = 200$ bits.

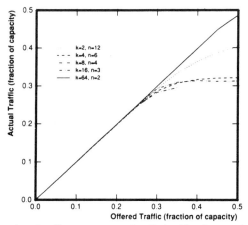

Fig. 17. Actual traffic versus attempted traffic for 4K node networks: 64-ary 2-cube, 16-ary 3-cube, 8-ary 4-cube, 4-ary 6-cube, and binary 12-cube, $L = 200$ bits.

TABLE I
MAXIMUM THROUGHPUT AS A FRACTION OF CAPACITY AND BLOCKING LATENCY IN CYCLES

Parameter	1K Nodes			4K Nodes				
Dimension	2	5	10	2	3	4	6	12
radix	32	4	2	64	16	8	4	2
Max Throughput	0.36	0.41	0.43	0.35	0.31	0.31	0.36	0.41
Latency $\lambda = 0.1$	46.1	128.	233.	70.7	55.2	79.9	135.	241.
Latency $\lambda = 0.2$	50.5	161.	269.	73.1	70.3	112.	181.	288.
Latency $\lambda = 0.3$	59.3	221.	317.	78.6	135.	245.	287.	357.

network, latency increases slowly due to contention in the network until saturation is reached. Saturation occurs when λ is between 0.3 and 0.5 depending on the network topology. Networks should be designed to operate on the flat portion of the curve ($\lambda < 0.25$).

When the network saturates, throughput levels off as shown in Figs. 16 and 17. These figures show how much traffic is delivered (vertical axis) when the nodes attempt to inject a given amount of traffic (horizontal axis). The curve is linear (actual = attempted) until saturation is reached. From this point on, actual traffic is constant. This plateau occurs because 1) the network is source queued, and 2) messages that encounter contention are blocked rather than aborted. In networks where contention is resolved by dropping messages, throughput usually decreases beyond saturation.

To find the maximum throughput of the network, the source service time T_0 is set equal to the reciprocal of the message rate, λ_E, and (22), (23), and (24) are solved for λ_E. At this

operating point the network can accept no more traffic. Messages are being offered as fast as the network can deliver them. The maximum throughput as a fraction of capacity for k-ary n-cubes with 1K and 4K nodes is tabulated in Table I. Also shown is the total latency for $L = 200$ bit messages at several message rates. The table shows that the additional latency due to blocking is significantly reduced as dimension is decreased.

In networks of constant bisection width, the latency of low-dimensional networks increases more slowly with applied traffic than the latency of high-dimensional networks. At $\lambda = 0.2$, the 32-ary 2-cube has $\approx \frac{1}{5}$ the latency of the binary 10-cube. At this point, the additional latency due to contention in the 32-ary 2-cube is $7T_c$ compared to $64T_c$ in the binary 10-cube.

Low-dimensional networks handle contention better because they use fewer channels of higher bandwidth and thus get better queueing performance. The shorter service times, L/W, of these networks results in both a lower probability of collision, and a lower expected waiting time in the event of a collision. Thus, the blocking latency at each node is reduced quadratically as k is increased. Low-dimensional networks require more hops, $D = (n(k-1)/2)$, and have a higher rate on continuing channels, λ_C. However, messages travel on the continuing channels more frequently than on the entering channels, thus most contention is with the lower rate channels. Having fewer channels of higher bandwidth also improves hot-spot throughput as described below.

C. Hot-Spot Throughput

In many situations traffic is not uniform, but rather is concentrated into *hot spots*. A *hot spot* is a pair of nodes that accounts for a disproportionately large portion of the total network traffic. As described by Pfister [18] for a shared-memory computer, hot-spot traffic can degrade performance of the entire network by causing congestion.

The *hot-spot throughput* of a network is the maximum rate at which messages can be sent from one specific node P_i to another specific node P_j. For a k-ary n-cube with deterministic routing, the hot-spot throughput, Θ_{HS}, is just the bandwidth of a single channel W. Thus, under the assumption of constant wire cost we have

$$\Theta_{HS} = W = k - 1. \tag{27}$$

Low-dimensional networks have greater channel bandwidth and thus have greater hot-spot throughput than do high-dimensional networks. Low-dimensional networks operate better under nonuniform loads because they do more resource sharing. In an interconnection network the resources are wires. In a high-dimensional network, wires are assigned to particular dimensions and cannot be shared between dimensions. For example, in a binary n-cube it is possible for a wire to be saturated while a physically adjacent wire assigned to a different dimension remains idle. In a torus all physically adjacent wires are combined into a single channel that is shared by all messages that must traverse the physical distance spanned by the channel.

IV. CONCLUSION

Under the assumption of constant wire bisection, low-dimensional networks with wide channels provide lower latency, less contention, and higher hot-spot throughput than higher-dimensional networks with narrow channels. Minimum network latency is achieved when the network radix k and dimension n are chosen to make the components of latency due to distance D and aspect ratio L/W approximately equal. The minimum latency occurs at a very low dimension, 2 for up to 1024 nodes.

Low-dimensional networks reduce contention because having a few high-bandwidth channels results in more resource sharing and thus better queueing performance than having many low-bandwidth channels. While network capacity and worst-case blocking latency are independent of dimension, low-dimensional networks have a higher maximum throughput and lower average blocking latency than do high-dimensional networks. Improved resource sharing also gives low-dimensional networks higher hot-spot throughput than high-dimensional networks.

The results of this paper have all been made under the assumption of constant channel delay, independent of channel length. The main result, that low-dimensional networks give minimum latency, however, does not change appreciably when logarithmic or linear delay models are considered. In choosing a delay model one must consider how the delay of a switching node compares to the delay of a wire. Current VLSI routing chips [9] have delays of tens of nanoseconds, enough time to drive several meters of wire. For such systems a constant delay model is adequate. As chips get faster and systems get larger, however, a linear delay model will more accurately reflect system performance.

Fat-tree networks have been shown to be universal in the sense that they can *efficiently* simulate any other network of the same volume [15]. However, the analysis of these networks has not considered latency. k-ary n-cubes with appropriately chosen radix and dimension are also universal in this sense. A detailed proof is beyond the scope of this paper. Intuitively, one cannot do any better than to fill each of the three physical dimensions with wires and place switches at every point of intersection. Any point-to-point network can be embedded into such a 3-D mesh with no more than a constant increase in wiring length.

This paper has considered only *direct* networks [19]. The results do not apply to *indirect* networks. The depth and the switch degree of an indirect network are analogous to the dimension and radix of a direct network. However, the bisection width of an indirect network is independent of switch degree. Because indirect networks do not exploit locality it is not possible to trade off diameter for bandwidth. When wire density is the limiting resource, a high-bandwidth direct network is preferrable to an indirect network.

The low-dimensional k-ary n-cube provides a very general communication media for digital systems. These networks have been developed primarily for message-passing concurrent computers. They could also be used in place of a bus or indirect network in a shared-memory concurrent computer, in place of a bus to connect the components of a sequential computer, or to connect subsystems of a special purpose digital system. With VLSI communication chips, the cost of implementing a network node is comparable to the cost of interfacing to a shared bus, and the performance of the network is considerably greater than the performance of a bus.

The networks described here have been demonstrated in the laboratory and incorporated into commercial multiprocessors. The Torus Routing Chip (TRC) is a VLSI chip designed to implement low-dimensional k-ary n-cube interconnection networks [9]. The TRC performs wormhole routing in arbitrary k-ary n-cube interconnection networks. A single TRC provides 8-bit data channels in two dimensions and can be cascaded to add more dimensions or wider data channels. A TRC network can deliver a 150-bit message in a 1024 node 32-ary 2-cube with an average latency of 7.5 μs, an order of magnitude better performance than would be achieved by a binary n-cube with bit-serial channels. A new routing chip, the Network Design Frame (NDF), improves the latency to ≈ 1 μs [12]. The Ametek 2010 uses a 16-ary 2-cube (without end around connections) for its interconnection network [1].

Now that the latency of communication networks has been reduced to a few microseconds, the latency of the processing nodes T_{node} dominates the overall latency. To efficiently make use of a low-latency communication network we need a processing node that interprets messages with very little overhead. The design of such a *message-driven processor* is currently underway [7], [11].

The real challenge in concurrent computing is software. The development of concurrent software is strongly influenced by available concurrent hardware. We hope that by providing machines with higher performance internode communication we will encourage concurrency to be exploited at a finer grain size in both system and application software.

ACKNOWLEDGMENT

I thank C. Seitz of Caltech for his many helpful suggestions during the early stages of this research.

REFERENCES

[1] Ametek Corporation, Ametek 2010 product announcement, 1987.
[2] K. E. Batcher, "Sorting networks and their applications," in *Proc. AFIPS FJCC*, vol. 32, 1968, pp. 307–314.
[3] K. E. Batcher, "The Flip network in STARAN," in *Proc. 1976 Int. Conf. Parallel Processing*, pp. 65–71.
[4] V. E. Benes, *Mathematical Theory of Connecting Networks and Telephone Traffic*. New York: Academic, 1965.
[5] L. N. Bhuyan and D. P. Agrawal, "Generalized hypercube and hyperbus structures for a computer network," *IEEE Trans. Comput.*, vol. C-33, no. 4, pp. 323–333, Apr. 1984.
[6] S. Browning, "The tree machine: A highly concurrent computing environment," Dep. Comput. Sci., California Instit. Technol., Rep. 3760, 1980.
[7] W. J. Dally, *A VLSI Architecture for Concurrent Data Structures*. Hingham, MA: Kluwer, 1987.
[8] W. J. Dally and C. L. Seitz, "Deadlock-free message routing in multiprocessor interconnection networks," *IEEE Trans. Comput.*, vol. C-36, no. 5, pp. 547–553, May 1987.
[9] ——, "The torus routing chip," *J. Distributed Syst.*, vol. 1, no. 3, pp. 187–196, 1986.
[10] W. J. Dally, "Wire efficient VLSI multiprocessor communication networks," in *Proc. Stanford Conf. Advanced Res. VLSI*, Losleben, Ed. Cambridge, MA: MIT Press, Mar. 1987, pp. 391–415.
[11] W. J. Dally et al., "Architecture of a message-driven processor," in *Proc. 14th ACM/IEEE Symp. Comput. Architecture*, June 1987, pp. 189–196.
[12] W. J. Dally and P. Song, "Design of a self-timed VLSI multicomputer communication controller," in *Proc. IEEE Int. Conf. Comput. Design*, 1987.
[13] P. Kermani and L. Kleinrock, "Virtual cut-through: A new computer communication switching technique," *Comput. Networks*, vol. 3, pp. 267–286, 1979.
[14] D. H. Lawrie, "Alignment and access of data in an array processor," *IEEE Trans. Comput.*, vol. C-24, no. 12, pp. 1145–1155, Dec. 1975.
[15] C. L. Leiserson, "Fat trees: Universal networks for hardware-efficient supercomputing," *IEEE Trans. Comput.*, vol. C-34, no. 10, pp. 892–901, Oct. 1985.
[16] C. A. Mead and L. A. Conway, *Introduction to VLSI Systems*. Reading, MA: Addison-Wesley, 1980.
[17] M. C. Pease, III, "The indirect binary n-cube microprocessor array," *IEEE Trans. Comput.*, vol. C-26, no. 5, pp. 458–473, May 1977.
[18] G. F. Pfister and V. A. Norton, "Hot spot contention and combining in multistage interconnection networks," *IEEE Trans. Comput.*, vol. C-34, no. 10, pp. 943–948, Oct. 1985.
[19] C. L. Seitz, "Concurrent VLSI architectures," *IEEE Trans. Comput.*, vol. C-33, no. 12, pp. 1247–1265, Dec. 1984.
[20] C. L. Seitz et al., "The hypercube communications chip," Dep. Comput. Sci., California Inst. Technol., Display File 5182:DF:85, Mar. 1985.
[21] C. H. Sequin, "Single chip computers, The new VLSI building block," in *Proc. Caltech Conf. VLSI*, C. L. Seitz, Ed., Jan. 1979, pp. 435–452.
[22] H. J. Siegel, "Interconnection network for SIMD machines," *IEEE Comput. Mag.*, vol. 12, no. 6, pp. 57–65, June 1979.
[23] H. S. Stone, "Parallel processing with the perfect shuffle," *IEEE Trans. Comput.*, vol. C-20, no. 2, pp. 153–161, Feb. 1971.
[24] H. Sullivan and T. R. Bashkow, "A large scale homogeneous machine," in *Proc. 4th Ann. Symp. Comput. Architecture*, 1977, pp. 105–124.
[25] A. S. Tanenbaum, *Computer Networks*. Englewood Cliffs, NJ: Prentice-Hall, 1981.
[26] C. D. Thompson, "A complexity theory of VLSI," Dep. Comput. Sci., Carnegie-Mellon Univ., Tech. Rep. CMU-CS-80-140, Aug. 1980.

William J. Dally (S'78–M'86) received the B.S. degree in electrical engineering from Virginia Polytechnic Institute, Blacksburg, in 1980, the M.S. degree in electrical engineering from Stanford University, Stanford, CA, in 1981, and the Ph.D. degree in computer science from Caltech in 1986.

From 1980 to 1982, he worked at Bell Telephone Laboratories where he contributed to the design of the BELLMAC-32 microprocessor. From 1982 to 1983 he worked as a consultant in the area of digital systems design. From 1983 to 1986 he was a Research Assistant and then a Research Fellow at Caltech. He is currently an Associate Professor of Computer Science at the Massachusetts Institute of Technology. His research interests include concurrent computing, computer architecture, computer-aided design, and VLSI design.

MODELING WORMHOLE ROUTING IN A HYPERCUBE*

Jong Kim
Real-Time Computing Laboratory
Dept. of Elec. Engr. and Comp. Sci.
The University of Michigan
Ann Arbor, Michigan 48109

Chita R. Das
Dept. of Elec. and Comp. Eng.
The Pennsylvania State University
University Park, PA 16802

Abstract

In this paper, we present an analytical model for the performance evaluation of asynchronous hypercubes. This analysis is aimed at modeling a deadlock free wormhole routing scheme prevalent on second generation hypercube systems. Probability of blocking and average message delay are the two performance measures discussed here. We start with the communication traffic to find the probability of blocking. The traffic analysis can capture any message destination distribution. Next, we find the average message delay that consists of two parts. The first part is the actual message transfer delay between any source and destination nodes. The second part of the delay is due to the blocking caused by wormhole routing scheme. The analysis is also extended to virtual cut-through routing and random wormhole routing techniques. The validity of the model is demonstrated by comparing analytical results with those from simulation.

1 Introduction

The growing demand for high processing power in various scientific and engineering applications has made multiprocessor architectures increasingly popular. This is exemplified by the proliferation of a variety of parallel machines with diverse design philosophies. This diversity in architectural design has created a need for developing performance models for multiprocessors not only to analyze the effectiveness of a design, but also to reduce the design space. In this paper, we present a performance model for a class of multiprocessors, known as hypercubes [1]-[3].

Hypercube machines have received increasing attention in recent years. Performance evaluation of hypercube systems has been investigated by several researchers [4]-[7]. These studies are concerned with the static analysis of the network topology. The performance measures used in these studies are mainly average message distance, average message delay, and degree of connection. These measures do not consider the actual communication protocol and hence do not reflect the true network delay. Abraham and Padmanabhan [8] have analyzed synchronous hypercubes considering probability of acceptance and network delay as performance measures. However, their work does not address multiple packet message delay.

Distributed memory architectures, such as the hypercube, generally use packet switching for communication. This communication method is not efficient in terms of average message delay. A second type of communication technique, known as the wormhole routing, has been proposed for hypercubes to reduce this communication delay [9, 10]. In this method, a message that consists of several packets travels along with the message header. If there is no blocked communication link between the source and destination nodes, the message is routed to the destination as in a circuit switching network. If the message header is blocked at some intermediate node, then all the links that hold packets (starting from the header to the last packet of the message) are blocked until the header can move forward. A variation of the wormhole routing is known as the virtual cut-through [11]. The node that causes blocking stores the complete message and clears the intermediate links in this approach. None of the previous works [4]-[8] has attempted to model wormhole routing on a hypercube. The communication delay of an architecture depends on the network structure and the communication protocol. It is therefore essential to analyze both the issues to predict the communication delay.

Dally has reported recently an evaluation technique for wormhole routing [12]. He analyzed the communication delay and throughput of a k-ary n-cube in-

*This research was supported in part by the National Science Foundation under grant CCR-8810131.

0-8186-6522-X/95 $4.00 © 1991 IEEE

terconnection network, where k and n represent the dimension and the number of processors in one dimension, respectively. Binary n-cube is a special case of the k-ary n-cube interconnection network. The communication delay of a k-ary n-cube is divided into two parts, namely; inter-dimension delay and intra-dimension delay. The intra-dimension delay of a binary n-cube is zero. A simple recursive expression for the communication delay has been derived under the assumption of uniform destination distribution. However, there is a large discrepancy between the analysis and simulation results with the increase in network traffic density. This is because of the very simplifying model that does not capture the probability of blocking on different channels accurately. Moreover, the validity of this model for other types of message destination distribution, like spherical [4], has not been studied.

In this paper, we present an evaluation technique for the communication analysis of asynchronous hypercubes. We model a deadlock free routing scheme for finding the average delay of a message in the network. The model is capable of handling any type of message destination distribution such as the uniform and spherical. The model first finds the traffic rate of each channel. Second, we find the message delay of each channel. This message delay is a function of the message length and traffic rate of the channel. The traffic rate and the message delay are used to find the probability of blocking for each channel. Probability of blocking is a parameter that affects the message delay in the network. Finally, we compute the average message delay of the network and analyze its variation with traffic density. The model is also extended to virtual cut-through and random wormhole routing schemes.

The rest of the paper is organized as follows. Section 2 describes the wormhole routing in hypercube systems. In section 3, we present an analytical model for finding the communication delay. Numerical results from analysis and simulation are analyzed in section 4. The last section summarizes the research contributions.

2 Principles of Operation

Node structure

Each hypercube node consists of a processing element (PE) and a communication controller (CC). The PE consists of a node processor and some local memory. The CC has a crossbar switch with $(n+1)$-inputs and $(n+1)$-outputs. The neighboring nodes are connected through n-input and n-output links. The local PE, attached to the CC, uses the other two lines. The structure of a node is shown in Figure 1. The CC can connect multiple inputs to multiple outputs simulta-

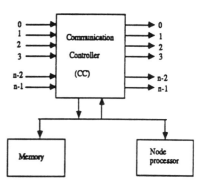

Figure 1: Hypercube Node Structure.

neously as long as there is no destination conflict. If multiple messages are to be delivered to the PE, the CC can accept all the messages concurrently.

Communication

The CC is responsible for all communication. It sends messages generated by the local PE over the network to the destination nodes. Each CC compares the destination address of a message with its own address. If they match, the message is delivered to the local PE. Otherwise, the CC chooses one of its neighboring nodes to transfer the message.

Message routing between a source and a destination is based on wormhole routing. The mechanism of wormhole routing is the following. A message consists of a series of flits — a flit is the basic communication unit. A head flit carrying the routing information advances from node to node towards the destination, while the remaining flits follow in a pipelined fashion. A message cannot be interleaved with any other message in wormhole routing since the regular flits do not have any routing capability. A head flit is blocked in an intermediate node, if it cannot find a free link (channel) to move ahead towards the destination. Consequently, the intermediate links that carry the remaining flits are blocked. This in turn blocks other messages. In a slightly different scheme, known as the virtual cut-through routing, the blocked message is queued at the intermediate node that holds the head flit. Hence, other messages can use the channels as soon as the blocked message is queued.

Selection of intermediate nodes (links) can be done at random in wormhole routing. This may result in deadlock in the network. Two deadlock-free routing schemes have been reported in the literature [10]. One is called the LR routing (also called e-routing) scheme and the second one is known as the virtual channel scheme. In the LR routing, the message is routed from source to destination by selecting intermediate nodes such that the address bits gradually match from the

MSB to LSB (left to right). Let the source and destination addresses be represented as $(s_0 \ldots s_{n-1})$ and $(d_0 \ldots d_{n-1})$ which differ in k-bit positions, for $k \leq n$. Then the source selects channel i such that the ith position is the first position from left (MSB) where the addresses differ. For example, in a 6-cube, if the source and destination nodes differ in bit positions $\{0, 2, 3, 5\}$, the source sends the message through channel 0, the next intermediate node transfers the message through channel 2, the third one through channel 3, and the last node sends to the destination using channel 5. LR routing scheme restricts the routing path between the source and the destination. In the virtual channel approach, a single channel is divided into two virtual channels and a cycle-free routing is employed. The LR routing is a simpler scheme compared to virtual channel. A virtual channel scheme is used in a structure where the LR-routing is impossible. For example, Dally and Seitz [10] have used the LR-routing for the inter-dimension routing and the virtual channel routing for the intra-dimension routing in the k-ary n-cube system.

3 Communication Analysis

The analysis is based on the following assumptions.

3.1 Assumptions

i) Messages generated by a processor (node) have a poisson distribution with a generation rate λ_g.

ii) The message length is exponentially distributed with average length $\bar{l}$.

iii) A PE can receive (consume) any number of messages (infinite nodal capacity).

iv) Deadlock-free routing (LR routing).

v) Each CC has a finite buffer.

The first two assumptions are common in any communication analysis to make the analysis tractable [11, 12]. The message generation rate, λ_g, of a node remains the same, if each CC has infinite buffer for outgoing messages. Otherwise, λ_g reduces when blocking in the network increases. Finite buffer capacity could result in retransmission, loss of message, or blocking as discussed in [11]. Since wormhole routing occupies channels until the message can move forward, it results in blocking. The throughput of the network decreases with more and more blocking. This is equivalent to a reduced generation rate. Here, we assume λ_n to be the reduced (adjusted) message generation rate of a node

in steady state. Assumption iii) implies that a PE can accept multiple messages simultaneously. There is no blocking of a terminating message at the destination node. Since random routing is susceptible to deadlock, we start with the deadlock-free LR routing scheme [8, 10, 13]. We have also extended the analysis for random routing taking deadlock into consideration. Messages generated by a node could travel k-hops, for $1 \leq k \leq n$, in an n-cube. We assume that nodes reachable using the same number of links (hops) have the same probability of receiving a message. Let P_k be the probability that a node generates a k-hop message to any of the $\binom{n}{k}$ nodes. The term P_k is useful in analyzing various patterns of message generation. For an n-cube with N nodes, $P_k = \frac{\binom{n}{k}}{N-1}$ implies uniform communication. Similarly, $P_k = \frac{1}{n}$ would give spherical communication [4].

3.2 Analysis

Traffic Analysis

The initial step of the analysis is to find the traffic on various channels connected to a node. Note that a CC has n-input channels and n-output channels (excluding the channels connected to the local processor). Now let us define various message rates at the input and output channels of a CC. Two types of messages arrive at a CC using the input channels. One is called a *terminating message*, since it is consumed by the local PE. It is denoted as λ_m. The second type is called a *transit message*, since it passes through the CC using one output channel. Let us represent the total transit message rate at a CC as λ_t. The local processor also generates messages at a rate λ_n (under steady-state). The transit and the generated messages use the output channels of the CC. Therefore, the total message rate at the output of a CC (over all the n output channels) is $\lambda_t + \lambda_n = \lambda_c$. The total message arrival rate at the input of a CC is the same as the total message departure rate at the output of the CC, in the steady state. λ_c represents the total message arrival rate (or departure rate) at a node.

Since messages are sent to the lowest channel that has a matching bit with the destination, each output channel has a different new message handling rate in LR routing. Moreover, transient messages arriving from other nodes never use lower channel numbers than the one they arrived from. It implies that each output channel has a different transient message arrival rate. Let $\lambda_{t,s}$ be the transit message arrival rate from other nodes at channel s of a CC. Similarly, $\lambda_{n,s}$ represents traffic generated by the source node for channel s.

We now give expressions for the traffic rates in addition to other useful relations with Lemmas. Proofs for these lemmas can be found in [15].

Lemma 1. The transient message arrival rate at channel s of a CC is given by

$$\lambda_{t,s} = \sum_{k=2}^{n} P_k \lambda_n \left[\sum_{j=m}^{M} \frac{\binom{s}{j-1}\binom{n-s-1}{k-j}}{\binom{n}{k}} \right] \qquad (1)$$

where $0 \leq s \leq (n-1)$, $m = \max(2, k-n+s+1)$, and $M = \min(s+1, k)$.

The following properties exist between λ_m, λ_t, λ_c, and λ_n.

Lemma 2. The parameters λ_c, λ_t, λ_m, and λ_n possess the following relations.

$$\lambda_m = \sum_{k=1}^{n} P_k \lambda_n = \lambda_n \qquad (2.a)$$

$$\lambda_t = \sum_{k=2}^{n} P_k (k-1) \lambda_n \qquad (2.b)$$

$$\lambda_c = \lambda_t + \lambda_m = \sum_{k=1}^{n} P_k k \lambda_n. \qquad (2.c)$$

The departure rate of messages from a node is the sum of the message generation rate λ_n and λ_t. We have derived expressions for λ_t and $\lambda_{t,s}$ in equations (2.b) and (1) respectively. The next step is to find the message generation rate for each channel.

Lemma 3. New messages for channel s are generated at a rate $\lambda_{n,s}$ by the local PE and is given by

$$\lambda_{n,s} = \sum_{k=1}^{n-s} P_k \lambda_n \frac{\binom{n-s-1}{k-1}}{\binom{n}{k}} \qquad (3)$$

where $0 \leq s \leq (n-1)$.

Now, it is possible to find the total traffic for each output channel of a CC. Let $\lambda_{c,s}$ be the total traffic rate for each channel in an n-cube.

Lemma 4. The message rate for each channel in an n-cube is the same regardless of its position, and is given as

$$\lambda_{c,s} = \lambda_n \cdot \frac{h_a}{n} = \frac{\lambda_c}{n} \qquad (4)$$

where h_a is the average message hops given as $\sum_{k=1}^{n} P_k \cdot k$, and λ_c is the total traffic at the output of a CC.

Delay Analysis

The probability that a channel is busy depends on the arrival rate and service rate of the channel. If a channel is occupied by other message(s), a newly arrived message waits until the channel is clear. Therefore, the probability of blocking is simply the probability that the channel is busy. The amount of time

a channel is occupied by a message depends on the message length (assumption ii) and average length of the message(s) that blocks it. Let $P_{b,s}$ be the probability of blocking for channel s. Now let us find the average length of a message that blocks an incoming message and results in blocking delay. Note that this would be different for different channels. For example, if a message is blocked at the last $(n-1)^{th}$ channel of a node, the average blocking in terms of message lengths is $d_{n-1} = \frac{1}{2}\bar{l}$. Since the average message length is $\bar{l}$, in an average, $\frac{1}{2}\bar{l}$ flits would block a message. If a message is blocked at the $(n-2)^{th}$ channel, then the average blocking length is given as $d_{n-2} = \frac{1}{2}[P_{t,n-2} \cdot \bar{l} + (1-P_{t,n-2})(\bar{l} + P_{b,n-1} \cdot H\{n-1|n-2\} \cdot d_{n-1})]$, where $P_{t,n-2}$ is the probability that the blocking message terminates after using the $(n-2)^{th}$ channel. $H\{n-1|n-2\}$ is the average number of hops the blocking message goes further after it uses channel $(n-2)$. In this case, $H\{n-1|n-2\}$ is 1 since $(n-1)$ is the last channel. The first term in the above expression represents the average length of the blocking message that terminates after using $(n-2)^{th}$ channel. The second term represents the length of blocking message when the blocking message at channel $(n-2)$ uses channel $(n-1)$ as the next route. Generalization of this for the average length of message(s) that blocks each channel is given in Lemma 5.

Lemma 5. The average length of messages involved in blocking for each channel is given as

$$d_s = \frac{1}{2}\left[\bar{l} + (1 - P_{t,s}) \sum_{j=s+1}^{n-1} P_{b,j} \cdot d_j \cdot H\{j|s\}\right] \qquad (5)$$

$$P_{t,s} = \sum_{k=0}^{s} P_{k+1} \frac{\binom{s}{k}}{\binom{n}{k+1}} \frac{1}{S(0)} \qquad (6)$$

$$H\{j|s\} = \sum_{m=0}^{n-j-1} \sum_{k=0}^{s} P_{m+k+2} \cdot \frac{\binom{n-j-1}{m}\binom{s}{k}}{\binom{n}{m+k+2}} \frac{(m+1)}{S(1)} \qquad (7)$$

where $S(j) = \sum_{m=j}^{n-s-1} \binom{n-s-1}{m} \sum_{k=0}^{s} P_{m+k+1} \frac{\binom{s}{k}}{\binom{n}{m+k+1}}$. The subscript s would be in the range $0 \leq s \leq (n-1)$.

The term $H\{j|s\}$ represents the average number of hops a blocking message travels when it takes channel j after channel s. The second term in equation (5) represents the contributions to blocking length by different channels for $s+1 \leq j \leq (n-1)$.

Now, we can find the average time a channel is occupied in terms of message lengths. Since the length a channel is occupied by a message is the same as the length the channel is blocked, the length a channel is occupied is twice the average length involved in blocking of a message, i.e., $2 \times d_s$ for each channel s. Let us find the total delay of a generated message when it uses channel s as the first route. We define it as D_s and write similar to equation (5) as

$$D_s = \bar{l} + (1 - \frac{P_1 \cdot \lambda_n}{n \cdot \lambda_{n,s}}) \times$$

$$\sum_{j=s+1}^{n-1} P_{b,j} \cdot d_j \frac{\sum_{m=0}^{n-j-1} P_{m+2}(m+1)\frac{\binom{n-j-1}{m}}{\binom{n}{m+2}}}{\sum_{m=0}^{n-s-1} P_{m+2}\frac{\binom{n-s-1}{m+1}}{\binom{n}{m+2}}} \quad (8)$$

where $\frac{P_1 \cdot \lambda_n}{n \cdot \lambda_{n,s}}$ represents the probability that a message terminates after it uses channel s. Subtracting this from 1 gives the probability that the message is not an one-hop message. The denominator represents the summation of all probabilities that the generated message is not an one-hop message and its first route is channel s. The numerator summation term represents the average number of hops the generated message travels when it takes a channel j after using channel s. A detailed description of equation (8) can be found in [15]. The second term in (8) is the message length that contributes to blocking delay at channel s and the first term $\underline{l}$ is the length of the actual message to be transmitted. Note that D_s can be approximated as $2 \times d_s$.

Probability of Blocking

Every blocked message waits until the blockage is cleared in wormhole routing. This implies that the channel (actually the CC) provides a queue for the blocked message. Since a blocked message could itself block other messages, a chained blocking is possible. In addition, a message accepted by the network is never lost due to blocking. Therefore, a channel behaves as an infinite queue as far as a blocked message is concerned, and we could model it as an M/M/1 queue. The service time of the channel s is thus $2 \cdot d_s$. Since the system utilization of an M/M/1 queue is $\frac{\lambda}{\mu}$ [14]. the probability of blocking of channel s is given by

$$P_{b,s} = 2 \cdot d_s \cdot t_u \cdot \lambda_{c,s} \quad (9)$$

where t_u is the time required to send a unit message a single hop.

Knowledge of $P_{b,s}$ is required to compute the adjusted message generation rate λ_n. Note that a channel (hence a CC) behaves as an infinite buffer for a transit message that is already accepted. However, the effect of blocking is different on the new message generation rate. It was assumed that a CC has a finite buffer (assumption v). This implies that if there is more traffic in the network, the probability that a channel would be busy ($P_{b,s}$) increases, which in turn reduces the acceptance of new messages. The steady-state message acceptance rate λ_n by a network is thus dependant on the probability of blocking. The relation between λ_n and λ_g for a channel s is expressed as

$$\lambda_n = (1 - P_{b,s})\lambda_g. \quad (10)$$

Equation (9) shows that $P_{b,s}$ is a function of blocking message d_s, i.e., the average message length that blocks a message in a channel. d_s is also a function of $P_{b,s}$ (equation 5). A closed-form solution of $P_{b,s}$ for each channel is very difficult to find due to this interdependency. Therefore, we compute $P_{b,s}$ and message delay for each channel iteratively using the following procedure.

Procedure for computing $P_{b,s}$ and D_s

Step 1: Let $P_{b,s}$ be $\bar{l} \cdot t_u \cdot \lambda_{c,s}$.

Step 2: Find d_s using equations (5)–(7).

Step 3: For all the channel s, do steps 4 and 5.

Step 4: Find the reduced message generation rate using equation (10).

Step 5: Find new $P_{b,s}$ using equation (9).

Step 6: If any one of the new $P_{b,s}$ deviates more than a given tolerance ξ, repeat steps 2 to 5.

Step 7: Calculate D_s for each channel using equation (8).

In a virtual cut-through network, the message is stored in an intermediate node if the communication link is blocked. Since the number of messages to be stored at a node due to blocking is theoretically unlimited, each node should have infinite buffer. The original message generation rate λ_g is not reduced for finite buffer capacity and $\lambda_n = \lambda_g$. This is also true for wormhole routing scheme with infinite buffer capacity at the CC. However, the probability of blocking is different. The probability of blocking for the wormhole routing with infinite buffer increases since d_s increases. The probability of blocking for the virtual cut-through remains the same since the message is queued in an intermediate node and does not occupy the channel, i.e., $P_b = \frac{h_a}{n}\lambda_g \cdot \bar{l}$ for any channel.

Average message delay

The delay that a message encounters depends on its entry channel. We can find average message delay for each channel from step 7 of the procedure to find $P_{b,s}$. We can then find the average message delay. Let t_{avg} be the average delay. Each channel has a different message arrival rate of generated messages, given as $\lambda_{n,s}$. Hence, a weighted average is more appropriate than a simple average of message delay for each channel. The fraction of the generated message that go to channel s is $\lambda_{n,s}/\lambda_n$. The weighted average message delay is thus

$$t_{avg} = (h_a - 1) \cdot t_u + \sum_{s=0}^{n-1} D_s * \frac{\lambda_{n,s}}{\lambda_n} \cdot t_u. \qquad (11)$$

The first term reflects the physical routing delay of a flit in the network. The second term represents the delay due to probability of blocking (delay of blocking message) and the transfer of the actual message $\bar{l}$. Note that equation (8) includes both blocking message and $\bar{l}$. This is defined as the length of the total message that is transferred in channel s.

3.3 Random routing

A disadvantage of LR routing scheme is that there is only one path between a source-destination pair. In contrast to LR routing, random routing provides multiple paths between any source-destination pair. Random routing, however, can result in deadlock. We analyze the probability of blocking and the message delay of random routing under the assumption that we have an efficient deadlock-avoidance or deadlock detection and removal scheme.

We know that the total traffic rate $\lambda_{c,s}$ for each channel is the same regardless of its position. The traffic rate of each channel under random routing is the same as that of the LR routing. The probability of blocking and the delay for each channel is thus the same regardless of its position. As discussed earlier, probability of blocking is a function of the message arrival rate and the message service time. Since the message arrival rate is $\frac{h_a}{n}\lambda_n$, the probability of blocking is $P_b = \frac{h_a}{n}\lambda_n \cdot t_{avg}$ for average message delay denoted t_{avg}.

The average message delay under random routing also consists of two parts. One is the delay due to actual message transfer and the other is the delay due to blocking in the network. The delay due to message length is $(\bar{l} + h_a - 1) \cdot t_u$, where h_a is the average number of hops between a source-destination pair. Hence, the average message delay is given by

$$t_{avg} = (\bar{l} + h_a - 1) \cdot t_u + P_b \cdot (h_a - 1) \cdot \frac{t_{avg}}{2}. \qquad (12)$$

The $P_b \cdot (h_a - 1)$ term represents the average number of blockings encountered by a $(h_a - 1)$-hops message. If we assume the CC has infinite buffer, then $\lambda_n = \lambda_g$.

Substituting P_b in equation (12) and solving for t_{avg}, we get

$$t_{avg} = \frac{n - \sqrt{n^2 - 2 \cdot n \cdot C_h \cdot (\bar{l} + h_a - 1) \cdot t_u}}{C_h} \qquad (13)$$

where C_h is $h_a(h_a - 1)\lambda_g$. For a finite buffer network, the traffic rate of the network is given by (10). Hence,

$$P_b = \frac{\lambda_g h_a t_{avg}}{n + \lambda_g h_a t_{avg}}. \qquad (14)$$

The average message delay for the finite buffer can be obtained using equations (12) and (14).

4 Results and Discussions

We have done extensive simulation to validate this analytical approach. Figure 2 shows the probability of blocking in a 10-cube system as a function of ρ, where $\rho = \lambda_g \cdot \bar{l}$. The message distribution is uniform, i.e, $P_k = \frac{\binom{n}{k}}{N-1}$. The solid lines (curves 1, 3, 5, and 7) show analytical results for wormhole routing with infinite buffer ($\lambda_n = (1 - P_b)\lambda_g$) and finite buffer. The dashed lines (curves 2, 4, 6, and 8) show the corresponding simulation results. Curves 1 and 3 show the probability of blocking of the highest channel and the lowest channel, respectively, for wormhole routing with infinite buffer. It is observed that P_b is different for the two channels and the difference increases with traffic intensity. Wormhole routing with finite buffer has less blocking than with infinite buffer. Wormhole routing with infinite buffer is seen to have the worst P_b. These observations do not necessarily mean that wormhole routing with finite buffer is better than others in all situations. Since we are analyzing only the communication delay, P_b is a performance measure. Figure 3 shows similar results for a 10-cube with spherical distribution of communication distance [4].

Figures 4 and 5 depict variation of average message delay (t_{avg}) as a function of ρ for the wormhole scheme with LR routing. The average message length $\bar{l}$ is 200 flits and the unit flit communication time $t_u = 1$ unit. The solid lines represent analytical results of wormhole routing with finite and infinite buffer and the dashed line represents the corresponding simulation results. The dotted lines represent analytical results of random routing with finite and infinite buffer. In all these cases, the analytical and simulation results match within 5%.

Figure 6 shows the comparison between our analytical result and Dally's analytical and simulation results [12]. This figure is based on the infinite buffer capacity and is extracted from Dally's result [12]. Since Dally's delay computation is based on simple average instead of weighted average as given in equation (11), we have modified equation (11) to $t_{avg} = (h_a - 1) \cdot t_u + \frac{1}{n}\sum_{s=0}^{n-1} D_s$. The dashed line represents our analytical result. In this figure, the delay is directly represented in terms of message length. Our analytical result is very close to the simulation result reported by Dally.

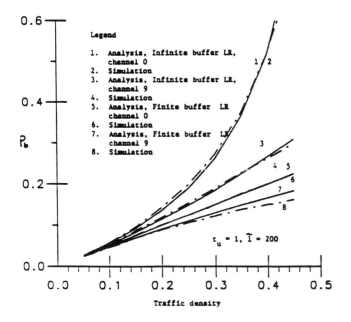

Figure 2: Probability of Blocking in a 10-cube (Uniform).

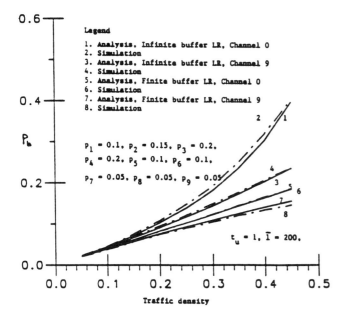

Figure 3: Probability of Blocking in a 10-cube (Spherical).

Figure 4: Average message delay in a 10-cube (Uniform).

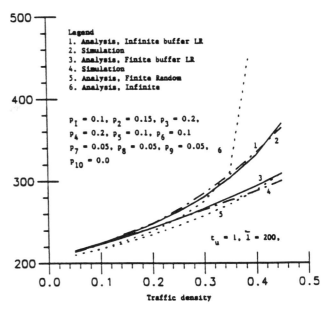

Figure 5: Average message delay in a 10-cube (Spherical).

5 Conclusions

We have presented an analytical model for predicting the performance of asynchronous hypercubes with a deadlock free wormhole routing scheme as the communication protocol. Probability of blocking and average message delay are used as the performance metrics here. Our analytical model, unlike most of the work presented before for hypercubes, has considered both the communication structure and the routing scheme in analyzing message delay. Analysis of wormhole was first reported by Dally [12]. However, the percentage of error between his analytical and the simulation results increases as the traffic density increases. The results from our model show close agreement with simulation results. Moreover, our model is general enough to capture any message destination distribution by suitably changing P_k.

References

[1] J. Rattner, "Concurrent processing: A New Direction in Scientific Computing," AFIPS Conf. Proc., Vol. 54, 1985 NCC, pp. 157–166.

[2] J. P. Hayes, T. Mudge, et. al., "Architecture of Hypercube Supercomputers," Intl. Conf. on Parallel Processing, Aug 1986, pp 653–660.

[3] Y. Saad and M. H. Schultz, "Topological Properties of Hypercube," IEEE Trans. on Computers, Vol. C-37, July 1988, pp. 867–872.

[4] D. A. Reed and D. C. Grunwald, "The Performance of Multicomputer Interconnection Networks," IEEE computer, June 1987, pp. 63–73.

[5] D. P. Agrawal, V. K. Janakiram, G. C. Pathak, "Evaluating the performance of multicomputer configurations," IEEE Computer, Vol. 19, 1986 May, pp. 23–37.

[6] L. N. Bhuyan and D. P. Agrawal, "Generalized Hypercube and Hyperbus Structures for a Computer Network," IEEE Trans. on Computers, Apr. 1984, pp. 323–333.

[7] L. D. Wittie, "Communications Structures for a Large Multicomputer System," IEEE Trans. on Computers, Vol. 30, 1981 Apr., pp. 264–273.

[8] S. Abraham and K. Padmanabhan, "Performance of the Direct Binary n-Cube Network for Multiprocessors," IEEE Trans. on Computers, Vol. 38, 1989 July, pp. 1000–1011.

[9] W. Athas and C. L. Seitz, "Multicomputers: Message-Passing Concurrent Computers," IEEE Computer, Aug. 1988, pp. 9–23.

[10] W. Dally and C. L. Seitz, "Deadlock-Free Message Routing in Multiprocessor Interconnection Networks," IEEE Trans. on Computers, Vol. 36, 1987 May, pp. 547–553.

[11] P. Kermani and L. Kleinrock, "Virtual Cut-Through: A New Computer Communication Switching Technique," Computer Networks, Mar. 1979, pp. 267–286.

[12] W. Dally, "Performance Analysis of k-ary n-cube Interconnection Networks," IEEE Trans. on Computers, Vol. 39, 1990 June, pp. 775–785.

[13] H. Sullivan and T. R. Bashkow, "A Large Scale Homogeneous Fully Distributed Parallel Machine: I," Proc. of 4th Annual Symposium on Computer Architecture, 1977, pp. 105–117.

[14] K. S. Trivedi, Probability and Statistics with Reliability, Queuing, and Computer Science Applications, Prentice-Hall, NJ, 1982.

[15] Jong Kim, Evaluation of Hypercube-Based Multiprocessor Systems, Ph.D. Thesis, The Pennsylvania State University, University Park, 1991.

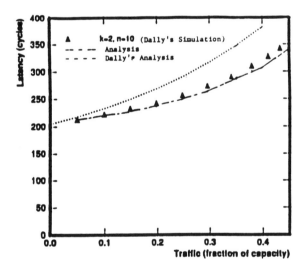

Figure 6: Comparison of average message delay in a 10-cube (Uniform). (Source: Performance Evaluation of k-ary n-cube, IEEE Trans. on Computers, 1990 June)

Performance Analysis of Mesh Interconnection Networks with Deterministic Routing

Vikram S. Adve, *Member, IEEE*, and Mary K. Vernon, *Member, IEEE*

Abstract—This paper develops detailed analytical performance models for k-ary n-cube networks with single-flit or infinite buffers, wormhole routing, and the nonadaptive deadlock-free routing scheme proposed by Dally and Seitz. In contrast to previous performance studies of such networks, the system is modeled as a *closed* queueing network that 1) includes the effects of blocking and pipelining of messages in the network, 2) allows for arbitrary source-destination probability distributions, and 3) explicitly models the virtual channels used in the deadlock-free routing algorithm.

The models are used to examine several performance issues for 2-D networks with shared-memory traffic. Some results obtained are: 1) when processors are allowed to have multiple outstanding requests, system performance is bandwidth-limited, and hence network performance does not *scale* well with increasing system size; 2) communication locality improves system efficiency, but a very high level of locality is needed in order for system performance to scale well; 3) in contrast to previous hot-spot studies for indirect networks that assume nonblocking processors, this study finds that significant tree-saturation *does not occur*, even in the presence of severe hot-spots in systems with up to four outstanding requests per processor; and 4) at some plausible system operating points, there is a perceptible difference in the efficiencies of processors at different locations in the mesh because of asymmetric loads on the virtual channels by the deadlock avoidance algorithm. These results should prove useful for engineering high-performance systems based on low-dimensional k-ary n-cube networks.

Index Terms—Approximate mean value analysis, closed queueing networks, finite buffers, hot-spots, multiprocessor interconnection networks, k-ary n-cube networks, mesh networks, near-neighbor communication, performance analysis, wormhole routing

I. INTRODUCTION

MULTIPROCESSOR mesh interconnection networks are 2-D networks, with the processors arranged at the nodes of a grid, and point-to-point links connecting each node to its neighbors. Mesh interconnection networks are a special case of k-ary n-cube networks in which the number of dimensions, n, is 2. Recent studies of k-ary n-cubes with *wormhole routing* (a low-latency pipelined routing scheme [9]) have shown that under reasonable assumptions, the optimal value for n is 2 or 3 [2], [8], [10]. Many existing and emerging multiprocessor systems use such low-dimensional

Manuscript received July 7, 1992; revised July 12, 1993. This work was supported by the National Science Foundation under Grant DCR–8451405, and by an IBM Graduate Fellowship.

V. S. Adve is with the Center for Research on Parallel Computation, Rice University, Houston, TX 77521.

M. K. Vernon is with the Department of Computer Sciences, University of Wisconsin, Madison, WI 53706.

IEEE Log Number 9215356.

direct networks to interconnect the processors, including the Intel Paragon, Cray T3D, Stanford Dash [14], MIT Alewife [1], MIT J-Machine [16], and CMU–Intel iWarp [5].

In this paper, we develop performance models to study k-ary n-cube networks with wormhole routing, with either single-flit or infinite network buffers. Our model for the single-flit buffer case includes the deadlock free routing algorithm of Dally and Seitz [9]. In contrast to previous analyses of these networks [2], [10], [11], the models we derive are *closed* queueing network models. Also in contrast to previous work, we 1) include the effects of blocking and pipelining of messages in the network, 2) allow for arbitrary source-destination probability distributions, and 3) explicitly model the virtual channels used in the deadlock avoidance algorithm. In the single-flit buffer model, the representation of message pipelining and blocking, and the asymmetric virtual channel loadings of the deadlock avoidance algorithm, require an approximate Mean Value Analysis (MVA) solution that is rather complex. These features, however, have a significant impact on system performance and are thus important to model. The model provides a further example that approximate Mean Value Analysis can be used for accurate performance prediction of highly complex systems with non-product-form queueing behavior.

We use the models to examine several performance issues for 2-D networks. We study network performance and scalability with processors that must block after each request, as well as with processors that can make multiple requests before blocking for responses. We compare the performance of three mesh network topologies: the unidirectional and bidirectional tori (meshes with end-around links connecting corresponding nodes on opposite edges) and the bidirectional mesh without end-around links. We first study the above issues under a uniform traffic pattern. We then examine the impact of communication locality on network performance and scalability, and discuss how the other conclusions obtained under uniform communication change in the presence of varying degrees of locality. We also study network performance when a communication hot-spot occurs, including the effect of a hot-spot on other traffic in the network. Finally, we analyze and explain a potentially important performance implication of the deadlock avoidance algorithm. Specifically, this algorithm produces asymmetric loads on the virtual channels sharing each physical network link. The performance analysis shows that this asymmetry can lead to a perceptible difference between the efficiencies of processors at different locations in the mesh.

The remainder of this paper is organized as follows. Section II describes the mesh network and key performance issues

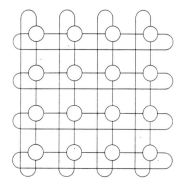

Fig. 1. Basic mesh topology.

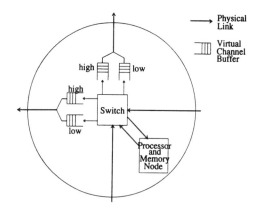

Fig. 2. A node in a unidirectional networks.

in more detail and states the assumptions about the system workload. Section III presents an overview of the models and gives the details for the new techniques developed. The models also use several previously developed Mean Value Analysis approximations; the complete set of equations is given in Appendix B. Section IV first presents the results of the model validations we performed by using simulation and then presents the performance analysis by using the analytical models. Section V contains the conclusions of our study.

II. SYSTEM DESCRIPTION

We describe the system and workload assumptions made in this study in Sections II-A through II-E. In Section II-F, we discuss several performance issues related to mesh networks that will be studied using the model.

A. Mesh Network Topologies

The basic topology of multiprocessor mesh interconnection networks is illustrated in Fig. 1. There are a number of variations on this basic topology. The connection between each pair of adjacent nodes may be *unidirectional* or *bidirectional*, with the latter usually being implemented as two unidirectional links. With the unidirectional topology, *end-around* connections that connect a node at one edge to the corresponding node at the opposite edge (as shown in Fig. 1) are necessary. A mesh with end-around connections is often called a *torus*. End-around connections may also be included in the bidirectional case to reduce the average number of hops that a message must travel in the network. A torus can be organized so that all links are of equal length, with each link being about twice as long as in the case without end-around connections [8].

B. Organization of a Node

A node in the system typically consists of one or more processors, some associated local memory, and a hardware switch that controls the routing of messages through the node (Fig. 2). When the node needs to send a message to another node, it queues the message in a local buffer (not shown in the figure). The message waits until the node-to-switch link (connecting the processor and memory to the local switch) becomes free, and then until space becomes available in the outgoing virtual channel buffer. (The message must compete for the channel buffer with messages from neighboring nodes that request the same buffer; we assume that the switch chooses among competing requests in first-come-first-serve

order.) Thereafter the message is forwarded down the link into the channel buffer in the pipelined manner of wormhole routing, which we describe next. We assume that the processor is not involved in transferring the message from the local buffer into the outgoing channel in the local switch.

C. Wormhole Routing

In *wormhole routing*, a switch begins forwarding a message as soon as the header is received and the required channel buffer in the next switch can accept one or more flits of this message. Thus, the flits of a message are transmitted from one switch to the next in a pipelined fashion and may occupy several channels along the path from source to destination. Only the header flit of a message contains routing information. If the header flit of a message is blocked because the required buffer in the next switch along its path is full, all of the flits in the message are blocked, and, therefore, so are the channels that they occupy. If more than one flit can be buffered at a node, flits behind the header can "catch up" until the available buffer space is filled. At this point, they block and can continue only after the header is unblocked. We assume this method of routing throughout the paper.

D. Deadlock Avoidance for Finite Buffers

In the ideal case, when buffer capacity is unlimited, deadlock cannot occur in the network and the wormhole routing scheme is equivalent to an optimized form[1] of the *virtual cut-through* routing algorithm defined for data communication networks [12]. In practice, buffer capacity in a node is limited and deadlock can occur in the networks with end-around connections because all of the buffers in a cycle could be filled, with no message able to make progress along that cycle.

Dally and Seitz have proposed a deterministic routing scheme that uses the concept of *virtual channels* to break cycles and prevent deadlock in the networks with end-around connections [9]. In this scheme, each physical link is shared by two virtual channels that are fed by separate buffers. As long as both virtual channels have messages to send, they alternate their flits on the physical link. If one of the buffers is empty or blocked, the other channel can transmit continuously, using

---

[1] The virtual cut-through algorithm specifies that if the header flit is blocked at a switch, the entire message has to be received before the message is forwarded. Instead, wormhole routing allows a partially received message to be forwarded as soon as its outgoing channel becomes available.

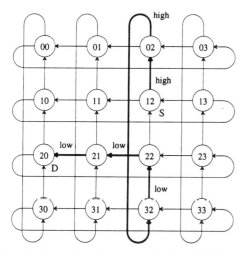

Fig. 3. Example for deadlock-free routing algorithm. Unidirectional 4 × 4 torus. Channels on path from $S = 12$ to $D = 20$.

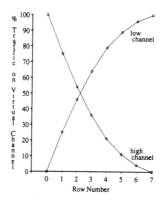

Fig. 4. Traffic on the high and low virtual channels along a column. Unidirectional 8 × 8 torus. Uniform traffic distribution.

the entire link bandwidth. When a message is blocked, all of the virtual channels occupied by the flits of that message are also blocked, and no other messages can use those channels.

The algorithm is illustrated in Fig. 3, and operates as follows. Each node in the k-ary n-cube is assigned an n-digit, base-k number that specifies the position of the node in the cube. Dimensions are numbered and messages are always routed in decreasing order of dimension. (For example, in Fig. 3, $d = 1$ for the columns, $d = 0$ for the rows, and routing is column first.) In each dimension d, $d = n-1, \cdots, 0$, a message is routed in that dimension until it reaches a node whose dth digit agrees with the dth digit of the destination node. The message is routed along the "high" virtual channel if the dth digit of the destination address is greater than the dth digit of the present node's address. Otherwise, it is routed along the "low" virtual channel. For example, in a unidirectional mesh network (as in Fig. 3), a message to a node with a higher row number is routed on the high virtual channel along the column until it crosses the link out of node on row 0 (shown at the edge of the network in the figure), and thereafter uses the low virtual channel on the column until it reaches the destination row.

The algorithm imposes a total order on the virtual channels that are used in each direction along any dimension of the network. Furthermore, the requirement that messages are routed in decreasing order of dimension implies that no cycles exist across dimensions. The algorithm is thus deadlock-free because it imposes a partial order on all virtual channels in the network.

The above deadlock-free routing scheme generates asymmetric loads on the virtual channels in the network *even when all processors have a uniform message destination probability distribution* (i.e., even when the loads on the physical links are balanced). Fig. 4 shows the fraction of total link traffic that uses each virtual channel for the links on a single column in a unidirectional 8 × 8 torus, assuming uniform message distribution. Note that all traffic on the link leaving the processor on row 0 uses the high virtual channel, and thus the buffer space of the low virtual channel is completely unused. In general, on a physical link near the "edge" row or column (after which traffic crosses over from the high to low channel,

or vice versa), the traffic tends to be concentrated on one of the two virtual channels. For links far away from the terminal row or column, the traffic is more evenly balanced on the two virtual channels. In parallel work, Bolding [4] has recently observed the same phenomenon and gives similar data as in Fig. 4, showing the buffer utilizations on the high and low channels for bidirectional and unidirectional topologies.

E. Workload Assumptions

We assume that all of the processors in the system execute subtasks of large multiple instruction, multiple data (MIMD) parallel programs.[2] Most previous studies of mesh networks, the hypercube, and other k-ary n-cubes, have assumed a message-passing workload [8], [10], [11]; but a number of recent shared-memory systems have also been based on mesh networks (Alewife [1], Dash [14], Cray T3D). Our model of the network is applicable to both types of workloads.

We allow a processor to have a maximum of N_{out} requests outstanding before it is required to block for a reply. (N_{out} is a parameter of the model.) For the model and results described in this paper, we assume that the rate of generation of requests is independent of how many requests are outstanding, until the maximum of N_{out} is reached. This assumption can accurately capture the behavior of systems in which each processor can switch between multiple contexts [1], [21], and should also be a reasonable model for many message-passing workloads. The assumption may be somewhat more approximate for processors that permit nonblocking memory operations (e.g., as with buffered writes, nonblocking caches, or prefetching), where the intervals between successive requests may depend in complex ways on the number of outstanding requests. Finally, as explained in Section III, a simple modification would allow the model to capture the behavior of hierarchical multiprocessors [14] containing multiple processors per node (by allowing the rate at which a node generates requests to be proportional to the number of additional requests it can make before blocking).

Our model does not restrict the communication patterns in the system. Each processor sends a message to each other processor with a specified probability, and these arbitrary probability distributions are inputs to the model. This permits

---

[2] We do not explicitly model synchronization events. Instead, we assume that these are reflected in the rate at which processors generate messages.

us to study the effect of nonuniform traffic patterns on system efficiency.

The workload and system parameters used in the study are defined in Section III.

F. Performance Issues for Mesh Networks

In Section IV, we use the model to study the performance as well as the scalability of mesh networks in varying configurations (various system sizes, buffer sizes, network topologies) and under different workloads (varying communication rates, single or multiple outstanding requests per processor, and uniform or nonuniform communication patterns). We begin by examing the performance and scalability of a *baseline* system: a bidirectional torus with a uniform communication workload and processors that must block after each request ($N_{out} = 1$). We then study a number of variations on this system to evaluate several issues that arise in the design of mesh networks. The issues we examine are as follows.

Channel Buffer Size: The buffer size per network link or channel is a design parameter that has significant cost and performance implications. In studying various network design issues, we compare network performance with single-flit buffers per virtual channel against the performance with infinite switch buffers. These are extreme cases that bound the performance of any particular finite buffer size, and show how much can be gained by increasing switch buffer sizes.

Multiple Outstanding Requests: Allowing a node to have more than one request outstanding has the potential to at least partially hide the latency of remote communication, but there is also potential for higher congestion in the network. We investigate how much improvement in absolute system efficiency is possible with multiple outstanding requests (due to overlapping communication with computation) and whether at some point network congestion cancels this gain. We also investigate how system scalability is affected by allowing multiple outstanding requests per processor.

Mesh Topology: There are performance and cost trade-offs between the three network topologies mentioned in Section I. In a k-ary n-cube network, the mean number of links that a message must traverse, assuming that all other nodes are equally likely to be the destination, is approximately $\frac{1}{4}n.k$, $\frac{1}{3}n.k$, and $\frac{1}{2}n.k$ for the bidirectional torus, the bidirectional mesh without end-around connections, and the unidirectional torus, respectively.

The extra links in the bidirectional networks imply a higher cost, however, and this must be accounted for to allow a fair comparison between the various topologies. When comparing these networks, we assume that the number of input and output *wires per switch* is fixed, which implies that the channels of the unidirectional network can be twice as wide as those in either of the bidirectional networks, offsetting the larger mean number of hops required. Furthermore, the bidirectional mesh without end-around connections, unlike the torus networks, does not require the deadlock-prevention algorithm of Dally and Seitz, because the fixed-dimension-first routing is sufficient to prevent cyclical dependencies between links in the network. To allow a fair comparison, we compare the torus networks with single-flit buffers per virtual channel

to nontorus mesh networks with two-flit buffers per physical link. This ensures that the buffer capacity per switch is equal for all three topologies.

Locality of Communication: A large class of scientific algorithms, called *continuum models* [19], involve a grid structure where a particular variable depends only on its nearest neighbors. Such problems can be mapped to the mesh network so that any processor requires mostly values calculated by its four neighboring nodes (or some set of nodes situated within at most a few hops). This would reduce network latency and contention compared with uniform communication. We investigate how near-neighbor communication locality affects system performance and scalability, and reevaluate the design issues discussed above under workloads exhibiting varying degrees of near-neighbor locality.

Communication Hot-Spots: It has been shown that communication hot-spots can seriously degrade the overall performance of indirect (e.g., multistage) interconnection networks with nonblocking processors. Furthermore, in such systems, hot-spots can cause buffers to fill up in large portions of the network, severely increasing the latency of unrelated (nonhot) network traffic as well, a phenomenon called *tree-saturation* [17]. We use our model to study the effect of communication hot-spots in mesh networks, with processors that block after a limited number of outstanding requests. We study the degradation in overall system performance due to a hot-spot, as well as the effect of a hot-spot on the latency of other traffic in the network.

Performance imbalance caused by the deadlock-avoidance algorithm: In Section II-D, we pointed out that the deadlock-free routing algorithm of Dally and Seitz generates asymmetric loads on the virtual channels in the network. The asymmetry does not necessarily imply that the processors near the edge are more adversely affected than the processors near the center of the mesh. The actual effect is complicated and requires careful reasoning about the pipelining effects of wormhole routing. A more detailed explanation of the asymmetry, and a quantitative analysis of its potential impact on performance, are given in Section IV-G.

III. THE MODEL

In order to study the design trade-offs outlined at the end of the previous section, we have created closed queueing network models of the k-ary n-cube network for each of two buffer sizes: finite buffers of size one flit, and infinite buffers. The parameters of the models are defined in Table I. N_{out} denotes the number of outstanding requests that each processor can have before it blocks. For the model and analyses in this paper, we assume that when a processor has less than N_{out} requests outstanding, it generates request messages with a mean interval of τ cycles between requests. A request message generated by processor i is directed to processor j, $j \neq i$ with probability F_{ij}. We allow two sizes of messages to be generated: L_{msg1} and L_{msg2}, with respective probabilities P_1 and P_2. These probabilities are the same for all processors. The sizes of the respective responses are L_{resp1} and L_{resp2}. For a shared-memory workload, the two request message types could represent memory *read* and *write* requests, and

TABLE I
MODEL INPUT PARAMETERS

Parameter	Description
N	Number of processors in the system
N_{out}	Maximum number of requests a processor can have outstanding before it must block for a reply
τ	Mean time between messages when less than N_{out} requests are outstanding
F_{ij}	Fraction of messages by processor i that are directed to processor j, $\sum_{j \neq i} F_{ij} = 1, i = 1, \cdots, N$
P_1, P_2	Probability that a message is type 1 (*msg 1*) or type 2 (*msg 2*), repsectively
L_i	Length of message of type $i \in msg\ 1,\ msg\ 2,\ resp\ 1,\ resp\ 2$
$D_{mem,r'},$ $D_{mem,w}$	Time to respectively read and write one word from a memory module

the reply types could represent *data* and *acknowledgment* responses, respectively. The network is assumed to operate synchronously. The values of τ, $D_{mem,r'}$, and $D_{mem,w}$ are assumed to be in units of switch cycles.

In our models, each processor forms a class of customers with its own destination probability distribution and with population equal to N_{out}. In other words, each possible message that a processor can have outstanding is modeled as a separate customer in the system. When there are $n < N_{out}$ requests outstanding, the remaining $N_{out} - n$ customers are served in first-come, first-served (FCFS) order at the processor,[3] as in [22]. Thus, each customer in the system repeatedly performs the following actions:

- *execute*—for an amount of time measured in switch cycles that is geometrically distributed, with mean τ,
- *visit a remote node and return to the processor*—(representing a remote memory access, or sending a message and receiving an acknowledgment),
- *queue at the processor*—to resume execution.

We develop the equations assuming that a remote processor is not interrupted when it receives an incoming message, which would be true for a shared-memory system. In this case, an incoming message requires only a memory access at the remote node. (The equations can easily be modified to reflect message processing by the node processor or message-handling coprocessors.)

We choose to develop approximate Mean Value Analysis models because of the previous success of this technique for analyzing other interconnection networks with features that violate separable model assumptions [20], [22]. Approximate Mean Value Analysis is based on estimating the mean round-trip time, or cycle time, for each class of customers in the queueing network, relative to some reference point. The processor serves as the reference point for the residence

[3] FCFS service at the processor is appropriate for systems such as those that maintain multiple contexts at each processor, because only one context executes at any time. An *infinite server* would be more accurate for hierarchical systems. The equations for queueing at the processor can easily be modified for this case.

time equations in our model. The mean round-trip time for a customer of class i is the sum of its mean residence times (queueing and service) in the local processor, in the network, and at the remote node, as shown below:

$$R[i] = r_{\text{proc}}[i] + r_{\text{network}}[i] + r_{\text{remote}}[i], \quad i = 1 \cdots N. \quad (1)$$

Each processor in the system has a distinct mean round-trip time, because of nonuniform virtual channel loads as well as possibly nonuniform communication patterns.

The mean round-trip time in the network is the weighted sum of the mean times for the message and the response, for each type of request, as shown below:

$$r_{\text{network}}[s] = \sum_{d \neq s} F_{sd} \big(P_1 (r_{\text{msg1},sd} + r_{\text{resp1},ds}) + P_2 (r_{\text{msg2},sd} + r_{\text{resp2},ds}) \big), \quad s = 1, \cdots, N, \quad (2)$$

where $r_{j,sd}$ is the mean time for a message of type j from node s to node d.

To calculate $r_{j,sd}$, we need to model the routing, pipelining, and blocking of messages in the network. These features require an approximate model solution. Our model for systems with infinite channel buffers is similar to the model developed for Banyan networks in [22]. Their equations assume that processor cycles are required to transfer a message into the network; we do not make this assumption. The only other difference is that we use a somewhat more accurate technique to estimate residence times at the processor for $N_{out} > 1$. This technique is also employed in our finite buffer model, and is discussed in Section III-C below. Otherwise, we do not give the model equations for the infinite buffer case.

For our model of wormhole routing with single-flit channel buffers, we have developed new approximations to estimate 1) the channel waiting and blocking times, 2) the customer queueing time at the processor, and 3) the mean queue length seen at the first outgoing link when multiple channels connect the processor to its switch. Below we present an overview of the model for networks with single-flit buffers, and then describe each of the three new approximations. Our notation is summarized in Appendix A, and the full set of model equations for the model with single-flit channel buffers is given in Appendix B. In Section IV, we discuss the results of validating the model and the results of analyses using the model. The validation studies show that the model is accurate over a wide range of input parameter values.

A. Overview of the Model with Single-Flit Buffers

Since messages in the mesh network can occupy several channels simultaneously, the mean message residence time, $r_{j,sd}$, is the sum of the following three terms:

1) the mean waiting time for the link from the node to its switch, $(w_{\text{node},sd|j})$,
2) the mean residence time for the *header* flit on each virtual channel c between s and d ($r_{j,c,sd}[1]$), and
3) the mean delay until the remaining flits of the message reach d (T_{catchup}):

$$r_{j,sd} = w_{\text{node},sd|j} + \sum_c r_{j,c,sd}[1] + T_{\text{catchup}},$$
$$j \in \{\text{msg1, msg2, resp1, resp2}\}, \quad (3)$$

where the summation is over virtual channels, c, on the path from s to d, including the channels out of the processor at s and into the processor at d.[4] Note that the above equation is similar in form to the equation used in [2] and [22]. One difference between our equation and the corresponding one in [2] is that we include the waiting time for the link that connects the processor to the switch, not just for the first switch buffer. A difference between our model and both [2], [22] is that T_{catchup} is not deterministic, because at each link, the flits may or may not have to alternate with flits on the link's other virtual channel. To compute T_{catchup}, we assume that the probability that a flit must share a link is approximately equal to the utilization of the link by messages on the other virtual channel mapped to the link. Appendix B contains the details.

Further development of the model equations requires new techniques for estimating $r_{j,c,sd}[1]$, r_{proc}, and the waiting time for the first network virtual channel when there are multiple channels from processor to switch. These approximations are motivated and outlined in Sections III-B through III-D, respectively. Section III-E concludes with a discussion of the model complexity.

B. Mean Channel Residence Time ($r_{j,c,sd}[k]$)

Let $r_{j,c,sd}[k]$ denote the average residence time of the kth flit of a type j message from s to d on channel c. The mean residence time for a header flit ($k = 1$) on channel c is itself the sum of three terms:

1) the average waiting time for the next channel on the path from s to d (this channel is denoted by $(c + 1)_{sd}$),
2) the average waiting time for a flit on the virtual channel that is multiplexed onto the same physical link as c (we denote this channel by $\bar{c}$, and approximate this term by $u_{\text{link},\bar{c}}$, the mean utilization of the link by messages on $\bar{c}$ (i.e., the fraction of time that the link is actually transmitting flits from $\bar{c}$)), and
3) the one cycle for transferring the flit to the next queue:

$$r_{j,c,sd}[1] = w_{(c+1)_{sd}|I} + u_{\text{link},\bar{c}} + 1, \qquad (4)$$

where a message from s to d enters $(c + 1)_{sd}$ via input port I. The possible input ports to a virtual channel are the virtual channels from neighboring switches or the channel from the processor at the current node. The waiting time for $(c + 1)_{sd}$ is a function of the input port, because the traffic on $(c + 1)_{sd}$ coming from the various input ports is asymmetric, in general.

For flits numbered k, $k > 1$, if d is k or more steps away from c, the mean residence time on c is estimated by the mean residence time of the header flit on channel $(c + k - 1)_{sd}$ (the channel $k - 1$ steps ahead on the path to d), plus waiting for a flit that might be on $\bar{c}$. Otherwise, the header flit has already reached the destination, and the residence time of the kth flit is one plus the mean waiting time for a flit on $\bar{c}$:

$$r_{j,c,sd}[k]$$
$$= \begin{cases} r_{(c+k-1)_{sd}}[1] + u_{\text{link},\bar{c}} & \begin{aligned} &d \text{ is } k \text{ or more steps} \\ &\text{away from channel } c \end{aligned} \quad (k>1). \\ 1 + u_{\text{link},\bar{c}} & \text{otherwise} \end{cases}$$
$$(5)$$

The key question for the model is how to calculate $w_{c|I}$, the waiting time for virtual channel c experienced by a header flit of a message that enters c via input port I. This waiting time is the sum of three terms:[5]

1) the mean residual residence time of a message in service at c that arrived via some other input port $i \neq I$, if any,
2) the mean residual residence time for the last flit of a message in service at c from port I, if any, and
3) the mean time to serve messages waiting to use c from other input ports (at most one per port):

$$w_{c|I} = \sum_{i \neq I} \sum_j \sum_{k=1}^{L_j} u_{j,c,i}[k] \left(\frac{1}{2} r_{j,c,i}[k] + \sum_{l=k+1}^{L_j} r_{j,c,i}[l] \right)$$
$$+ \sum_j \left(\frac{u_{j,c,I}[L_j]}{1 - \sum_{j'} \sum_{l=1}^{L_{j'}-1} u_{j',c,I}[l]} \times \frac{r_{j,c,I}[L_j]}{2} \right)$$
$$+ \sum_{i \neq I} \sum_j \left(u_{j,(c-1)_i}[1] \sum_{l=1}^{L_j} r_{j,c,i}[l] \right). \qquad (6)$$

The calculation of each of these terms is explained below:

1) The total residence time of a message at c is random with an unknown distribution. Rather than assume knowledge of this distribution to calculate the mean residual life of a message in service, we assume that the residence time of *each flit* of a message is deterministic, i.e., that its mean residual life is $r_{j,c,i}[k]/2$. We expect that this assumption will be good for low to moderate network traffic, and will introduce only small errors at higher loads, because a flit residence time is small compared with total message residence time. Thus, the mean residual residence time of an entire message (seen by an arrival on input port I) can be calculated by conditioning on the event that the arrival finds the kth flit of a type j message that arrived from input port i in service at channel c. The probability of this event is approximated by the average utilization of c by such a flit: $u_{j,c,i}[k]$. The mean residual life of the message in this case is $(\frac{1}{2} r_{j,c,i}[k] + \sum_{l=k+1}^{L_j} r_{j,c,i}[l])$. Summing over all flits $1 \leq k \leq L_j$ for all message types j, and all possible input ports $i \neq I$, gives the first term in the above equation.

2) Because of the pipelined routing scheme, if the tagged message arriving at c via input port I finds another message at c that also arrived via I, then it can find only the tail flit of that message occupying c, and *cannot find any other flit of the message*. Therefore, we approximate the second term by the ratio of time that channel c is occupied by a tail flit from I ($u_{j,c,I}[L_j]$) to the total time that channel c is *not occupied* by any other flits from I ($1 - \sum_{j'} \sum_{l=1}^{L_{j'}-1} u_{j',c,I}[l]$). The residual residence time in this case is just $r_{j,c,I}[L_j]/2$. Summing over j gives the second term.

[4] Henceforth, we use variables to denote the number of a virtual channel and ensure that the appropriate number or set of numbers in a summation is clear from the context.

[5] To denote a summation over all four types j, we write $\sum_j$ instead of $\sum_{j \in \{\text{msg1, msg2, resp1, resp2}\}}$.

3) The third term is the average waiting time for messages that are waiting on input ports other than i when a message arrives at input port I. We assume that these will be transmitted by channel c before the arriving message. For each input port $i \neq I$, the probability that a type j message is waiting to use c is approximated by the utilization of channel $(c-1)_i$ by header flits of type j messages *that will next use* c: $u_{j,(c-1)_i}[1]$. Multiplying by the total residence time of such a message and summing over $i \neq I$ and all message types j gives the third term.

The remaining unknowns in the above equations ($u_{j,c,i}[k]$, $u_{\text{link},\bar{c}}$) are calculated by using previously developed MVA techniques [20], [22], as described in Appendix B.

C. Processor Residence Times $(r_{\text{proc}}[i])$

The processor is modeled as an FCFS queueing center, where the service time is geometrically distributed with a mean value of τ cycles. In early model validation experiments, we found that the widely used Schweitzer [18] approximation for product-form networks is not sufficiently accurate for the processor queues, because the customer population for each processor, N_{out}, can be small. Furthermore, previously developed approximations such as Linearizer [6], which achieve greater accuracy by solving the equations at a few neighboring populations, introduce too much additional complexity into the model. Below we develop a new approximation for $r_{\text{proc}}[i]$ that is empirically accurate, yet requires very little additional computation when N_{out} is not large. The key idea is that we solve for $r_{\text{proc}}[i]$ recursively (i.e., similarly to exact MVA) without recursively solving for the residence times at other queues in the system for each customer population. Empirically, we found the new approximation to be considerably more accurate than the Schweitzer approximation. Furthermore, we note that the approximation is applicable to any multiclass queueing network where all of the demand at some queue comes from a small fraction of the customers in the network. As far as we are aware, this approach has not been previously reported in the literature.

Consider some processor i. Define $r_{\text{proc}}(i, n)$ to be the steady-state average residence time at processor i if there are n customers in its class. Thus, $r_{\text{proc}}[i] = r_{\text{proc}}(i, N_{\text{out}})$. Similarly, let $q_{\text{proc}}(i, n)$ and $u_{\text{proc}}(i, n)$ denote the mean queue length and the mean processor utilization at processor i with n customers in its class. $r_{\text{proc}}(i, n)$ is the sum of the mean service time (τ), the mean waiting time for customers found waiting in the queue, and the mean residual service time (res_{proc}) for the customer in service, if any. We estimate the mean queue length and processor utilization *seen by an arriving customer* by $q_{\text{proc}}(i, n-1)$ and $u_{\text{proc}}(i, n-1)$, respectively (just as in exact MVA), producing a recursion over $n = 1, \cdots, N_{\text{out}}$. The key to the approximation is that $q_{\text{proc}}(i, n-1)$ and $u_{\text{proc}}(i, n-1)$ are calculated by using the same values of $r_{\text{network}}[i]$ and $r_{\text{remote}}[i]$, for all $n = 1, \cdots, N_{\text{out}}$. (These values are available from the previous iteration in the numerical solution of the overall model.) Thus,

we have the following equations:

$$r_{\text{proc}}(i, n) = \tau + [q_{\text{proc}}(i, n-1) - u_{\text{proc}}(i, n-1)] \times \tau + u_{\text{proc}}(i, n-1) \times \text{res}_{\text{proc}}, \quad n > 1, \quad (14)$$

$$q_{\text{proc}}(i, n) = \frac{n \times r_{\text{proc}}(i, n)}{r_{\text{proc}}(i, n) + r_{\text{network}}[i] + r_{\text{remote}}[i]}, \quad n > 1, \quad (15)$$

$$u_{\text{proc}}(i, n) = \frac{n \times \tau}{r_{\text{proc}}(i, n) + r_{\text{network}}[i] + r_{\text{remote}}[i]}, \quad n \geq 1, \quad \text{and} \quad (16)$$

$$q_{\text{proc}}(i, 1) = u_{\text{proc}}(i, 1) = \frac{\tau}{\tau + r_{\text{network}}[i] + r_{\text{remote}}[i]}. \quad (17)$$

(The equations above are numbered to correspond to the complete set of equations in Appendix B.) The mean residual service time of a customer found in service, res_{proc}, has to be calculated as seen by the tail flit, not the header flit, because the customer is queued up at the processor only when its tail flit arrives. Conditioned on finding a customer in service, the mean residual service time seen by the head is τ, by the memoryless property of the geometric distribution. A returning message is of length L_{resp1} with probability P_1 and L_{resp2} with probability P_2. In one cycle, the probability that the customer in service at the processor does not complete service is $\gamma = 1 - (1/\tau)$. Therefore, the average residual service time seen by the tail flit is approximated by the following equation:

$$\text{res}_{\text{proc}} = (\tau - 1) \times (P_1 \gamma^{L_{\text{resp1}} - 1} + P_2 \gamma^{L_{\text{resp2}} - 1}). \quad (18)$$

Equations (14)–(18) are solved for each processor i separately, in order to calculate all of the $r_{\text{proc}}[i]$.

D. Waiting Time for First Virtual Channel with Multiple Processor-to-Switch Channels

In our mesh network analysis, we found the physical link that connects each processor to its associated switch to be a bottleneck under high loads, in the network with single-flit channel buffers. Therefore, we investigated the use of multiple physical links connecting the processor to the switch, one for each outgoing virtual channel from the switch to neighboring nodes. (In practice, only two to three physical processor-to-switch links should provide about the same performance, because almost all of the messages out of a processor are concentrated on a few outgoing virtual channels.) With this organization, when a message from the processor finds its link to the switch busy and later reaches the head of the queue for this link (where it must wait for the outgoing virtual channel buffer), it cannot find a message from any other input port occupying the channel; it can find only the tail flit from the preceding message. Furthermore, such an arriving message is more likely to find waiting messages at other input ports (which were blocked by the preceding message). These observations lead to a somewhat different expression for the waiting time for the outgoing channel (i.e., the first virtual channel along the path of the message) in the case of multiple processor-to-switch links.

Consider a tagged customer of class q, and let c denote the first virtual channel along its path. Define $w'_{c|q}$ to be the average time that this message has to wait before entering channel c. As in (6), $w'_{c|q}$ is the sum of three terms:

1) the mean waiting time for messages in service at c that arrived from input ports $i \neq$ PROC, if the tagged message found the processor-to-switch link idle (PROC denotes the input port used by messages arriving to c from the processor),

2) the mean waiting time for the tail flit of previous messages from PROC, if the tagged message found the processor-to-switch link busy, and

3) the mean waiting time for messages blocked at input ports $i \neq$ PROC that are waiting to use channel c:

$$
\begin{aligned}
w'_{c|q} = & \\
\sum_j \Bigg\{ & \sum_{i \neq \text{PROC}} \sum_{k=1}^{L_j} b'_{j,c,i|q}[k] \left(\frac{r_{j,c,i}[k]}{2} + \sum_{l=k+1}^{L_j} r_{j,c,i}[l] \right) \\
& + \left(\sum_{k=1}^{L_j} b_{\text{node},j,c|q}[k] \right) (r_{j,c|\text{PROC}}[L_j] - 1) \\
& + \sum_{i \neq \text{PROC}} \left(q'_{j,c,i|q} \sum_{k=1}^{L_j} r_{j,c,i}[k] \right) \Bigg\}.
\end{aligned}
\tag{24}
$$

The form of the first term for $w'_{c|q}$ is the same as the first term in (6), with $u_{j,c,i}[k]$ replaced by $b'_{j,c,i|q}[k]$. Here $b'_{j,c,i|q}[k]$ is the probability that a message of class q finds channel c busy serving the kth flit of a type j message that arrived via input port $i \neq$ PROC, $j \in \{\text{msg1, msg2, resp1, resp2}\}$. This is estimated as follows:

$$
\begin{aligned}
b'_{j,c,i|q}[k] = & \\
& \left(\frac{1 - \Pr\{\text{ processor-to-switch link is busy}\}}{\text{fraction of time } c \text{ not serving message coming from node}} \right) \\
& \quad \times u_{j,c,i}[k] \\
= & \left(\frac{1 - \sum_j \sum_{k=1}^{L_j} b_{\text{node},j,c|q}[k]}{1 - \sum_j \sum_{k=1}^{L_j} u_{j,c,\text{PROC}}[k]} \right) \times u_{j,c,i}[k],
\end{aligned}
\tag{25}
$$

where $b_{\text{node},j,c|q}[k]$ denotes the probability that a class q message finds the processor-to-switch link corresponding to outgoing channel c busy serving the kth flit of a type j message.

The second term in $w'_{c|q}$ is straightforward, because the probability that the processor-to-switch link for channel c is found busy with a message of type j is merely $\sum_k b_{\text{node}j,c|q}[k]$, and the tagged message must see all but one cycle of the residence time of the *last* flit of the message ahead of it.

For the third term, $q'_{j,c,i|q}$ is defined as the average number of messages of type j from $i \neq$ PROC found waiting to use c by the arriving class q message. The calculation of $q'_{j,c,i|q}$ requires another observation about the blocking phenomena in the mesh. A message following another message out of the node and into c is more likely than a random arrival at c to find a message on input port i already waiting for channel c. To account for this, we calculate the probability that a random message using c via $I =$ PROC blocks a type j message on incoming virtual channel i. (The latter message will then be waiting to use c when the following message from $I =$

PROC reaches the head of its queue for c.) Similarly, we consider messages from each $i' \neq$ PROC (and $i' \neq i$) blocking messages from i to c. Therefore, $q'_{j,c,i|q}$ is as follows:

$$
\begin{aligned}
q'_{j,c,i|q} = & \left\{ \sum_j \sum_{k=1}^{L_j} n_{\text{node},j,c|q}[k] \right\} \\
& \times \Pr\{ \text{ message from } I = \text{PROC blocks} \\
& \quad \text{a type } j \text{ message from } i \} \\
& + \sum_{\substack{i' \neq \text{PROC} \\ i' \neq i}} \left\{ \sum_j \sum_{k=1}^{L_j} b'_{j,c,i|q}[k] \right\} \\
& \times \Pr\{ \text{message from } i' \text{ blocks a} \\
& \quad \text{type } j \text{ message from } i \}.
\end{aligned}
\tag{26}
$$

We illustrate the calculation of one of these terms here. A key observation we make is that $\Pr\{\text{a message from } I = \text{PROC blocks a type } j \text{ message from } i\}$ is proportional to the relative number of messages to c that arrive from i and I, respectively, (counting only type j messages from i). But this relative number is exactly the ratio of the visit ratio of type j messages from i to c to the visit ratio of all message types from $I =$ PROC to c. This ratio of visit ratios, multiplied by the probability that a random message from i is blocked by a message from $I =$ PROC then gives us the probability that a random message from I to c blocks a message on i. Thus, define $V_{j,c,I}$ to be the sum of the visit ratios of customers of all classes as type j messages to channel c via input port i. Then, the following conditions exist:

$$
\begin{aligned}
& \Pr\{\text{message from } I = \text{PROC blocks a type } j \text{ message} \\
& \quad \text{from } i\} \\
& = \frac{V_{j,c,i}}{\sum_{j'} V_{j',c|I}} \left\{ \sum_j \sum_{k=1}^{L_j} u_{j,c,I}[k] + \sum_j u_{j,(c-1)}, [1] \right\},
\end{aligned}
$$

where the summations in the parentheses sum to the probability that a random message arriving to $\tilde{c}$ from i has to wait for a message from $I =$ PROC (which may be in service at c, or blocked on the processor-switch link to c).

The above discussion highlights the main points of this new heuristic used to calculate the waiting time for the first virtual channel. The complete equations are given with the rest of the model in Appendix B.

E. Complexity of the Models

The model for wormhole routing with single-flit buffers has $O[L_{\max} N^3]$ time complexity and $O[L_{\max} N^2]$ space complexity, where $L_{\max}$ is the length of the longest message type. As a result, the model with $L_{\max} = 11$ and $N = 64$ cannot practically be run on systems with fewer than 10 megabytes of main memory. Nevertheless, solving the model is still about 10 to 100 times faster than simulating the wormhole routing protocol under a statistical workload. Furthermore, the model allows us to explore various issues and design trade-offs under the realistic assumptions of arbitrary message sizes, and blocking due to finite buffers. For example, the effects

TABLE II
PARAMETER VALUES USED IN THE EXPERIMENTS

Symbol	Range of values	Symbol	Value	
			Bidirectional	Unidirectional
N	$16, 64, 144 - 1024$	L_{msg1}	3	2
N_{out}	$1 - 8$	L_{resp1}	9	5
τ	$20 - 200$	L_{msg2}	11	6
F_{nn}	$0\% - 100\%$	L_{resp2}	3	2
F_{hot}	$0\% - 20\%$	P_1, P_2	0.8, 0.2	0.8, 0.2
		$D_{mem,1} = D_{mem,2}$	4	4

of asymmetric channel loads and hot-spot traffic are a direct result of limited buffer space for the channels. Finally, the model with infinite buffers is highly efficient and can be used to explore many of the mesh network design trade-offs for larger systems.

IV. RESULTS

In this section, we describe the results of extensive analyses of 2-D networks using the above models. We assume a shared-memory workload for these experiments, as discussed below. We first present the ranges of input parameter values used in our study (Section IV-A), and the results of validation experiments (Section IV-B). In Section IV-C, we evaluate the performance and scalability of a baseline system that we use as a reference point for studying further network design issues. In Section IV-D, we study the impact of allowing multiple outstanding requests. In Section IV-E, we compare the alternative mesh topologies. In Section IV-F, we study the performance impact of near-neighbor workloads, and reevaluate the design issues studied in Sections IV-C through IV-E under such workloads. In Section IV-G, we study the degradation in system performance due to communication hot-spots. Finally, in Section IV-H, we analyze the imbalance in processor efficiencies caused by the asymmetric loads on the virtual channels in the deadlock prevention algorithm (see Section II-D).

A. Model Input Parameter Values and Performance Measures

The measures of system performance that we use are individual and average processor efficiency, defined as the fraction of time that a processor spends doing useful work, as shown below:

$$E[i] = \frac{N_{out} \times \tau}{R[i]} \leq 1, \quad \overline{E} = \frac{1}{N} \sum_{i=1}^{N} E[i].$$

Other measures that are obtained from the model equations include steady-state mean channel queue lengths and steady-state link utilizations. We validated the accuracy of several of these detailed measures as well.

The ranges of values used for the various model input parameters are given in Table II. Most of the experiments with finite-buffer systems focus on a 64-processor (8×8) mesh, whereas we use the infinite-buffer model to examine the performance impact of increasing system size for systems as large as 1024 processors (a 32×32 mesh). All processing times and memory access times are specified in units of switch cycles. In many of the graphs, processor efficiency is plotted

as a function of $1/\tau$, where $1/\tau$ intuitively measures the average communication rate (e.g., cache misses per cycle per processor). τ was varied from 20 to 200 cycles. Values of τ higher than 200 showed very little further improvement in processor efficiency (for our parameter settings). Also, because average remote access latencies are typically greater than 20 switch cycles in an 8×8 mesh, it is difficult to envisage programs that make requests faster than about 1 every 20 cycles executing with any reasonable efficiency on this or larger systems. Thus, we believe that the above range of τ should allow us to study the performance of a fairly wide range of programs.

Messages are assumed to consist of a header flit, plus address flits (type msg1), data flits (type resp1), address and data flits (type msg2), or acknowledgment flits (type resp2). These interpretations of the message contents and the associated message lengths in Table II are intended to represent a shared-memory workload. Message-passing programs could be expected to exchange larger messages between processes, though less frequently [8]. The models can be modified to study such workloads; however, that is beyond the scope of this paper. The message sizes also reflect the assumption that the channels in the unidirectional torus are twice as wide as in the bidirectional networks, with an equal number of wires per switch. Finally, we set $P_1 = 0.8$, $P_2 = 0.2$, and $D_{mem,r} = D_{mem,w} = 4$ for all experiments. We do not expect moderate changes in these parameters to significantly alter our results.

B. Validation of the Models Against Simulation

We used event-driven simulators to validate the analytical models, for both the single-flit and infinite buffer cases. The simulators use a statistical workload identical to that of the analytical models, but implement the wormhole routing of the flits and the deadlock-free routing algorithm exactly. We present representative results of the validations of the single-flit buffer model in Tables III and IV.

At low to moderate network loads, the average processor efficiency from the analytical model agrees closely with the value obtained by simulation (less than 3% error). Thus, our finite buffer model has accuracy similar to the very accurate, less complex models of the infinite buffer case; validations of the infinite buffer model gave results very similar to the model in the Willick Eager Multistage and are not shown here.

In cases of high network contention (e.g., with $N_{out} \geq 4$ and $\tau < 50$), the analytical single-flit buffer model tends to be somewhat optimistic. In these cases, some links are

TABLE III-A

COMPARISON OF OVERALL PERFORMANCE ESTIMATES WITH SIMULATION:
BIDIRECTIONAL 4 × 4 TORUS, SINGLE CHANNEL FROM PROCESSOR TO SWITCH

Parameters		Processor efficiency			Network residence time		
N_{out}	τ	Simulation	Analytical	% error	Simulation	Analytical	% error
1	5	12.37	12.01	−2.9%	22.62	24.70	9.2%
1	25	43.01	42.29	−1.7%	21.07	22.44	6.5%
1	100	76.54	76.02	−0.7%	19.59	20.15	2.8%
2	5	19.56	19.58	0.1%	31.05	33.18	6.8%
2	25	68.93	70.26	1.9%	24.90	26.55	6.6%
2	100	96.34	98.60	2.3%	20.21	20.69	2.4%
4	5	24.11	26.12	8.3%	60.81	57.29	−5.8%
4	25	91.48	98.30	7.4%	33.64	33.63	−0.0%
4	100	99.96	100.0	0.0%	20.44	20.75	1.5%
8	5	25.07	30.08	20.0%	136.79	112.53	−17.7%
8	25	99.56	100.0	0.4%	44.89	34.44	−23.3%
8	100	100.0	100.0	0.0%	20.43	20.76	1.61%

TABLE III-B

COMPARISON OF OVERALL PERFORMANCE ESTIMATES WITH SIMULATION:
BIDIRECTIONAL 8 × 8 TORUS, MULTIPLE CHANNELS FROM PROCESSOR TO SWITCH

Parameters		Processor efficiency			Network residence time		
N_{out}	τ	Simulation	Analytical	% error	Simulation	Analytical	% error
1	20	34.6	34.24	1.0%	32.98	33.54	1.7%
1	33.3	48.9	48.37	−1.1%	30.03	30.72	2.3%
1	50	60.4	59.92	0.8%	27.94	28.61	2.4%
1	100	76.9	76.50	0.5%	25.36	25.88	2.0%
4	20	44.8	49.54	10.5%	144.06	138.57	−3.8%
4	33.3	75.01	84.16	12.2%	105.88	90.55	−14.54%
4	50	97.8	100.0	2.25%	49.20	38.55	−21.6%
4	100	100.0	100.0	0.0%	27.61	27.35	−0.9%

TABLE IV

COMPARISON OF MAXIMUM AND MINIMUM PROCESSOR EFFICIENCY ESTIMATES WITH SIMULATION

Parameters		Maximum efficiency			Minimum efficiency			Maximum/Minimum efficiency		
N_{out}	τ	Simulation	Analysis	% error	Simulation	Analysis	% error	Simulation	Analysis	% error
1	25	37.78	38.92	3.0%	35.56	38.53	8.4%	1.062	1.010	−4.9%
1	40	50.39	52.55	4.3%	48.93	52.25	6.8%	1.030	1.005	−2.4%
1	100	73.90	76.13	3.0%	72.25	76.03	5.2%	1.023	1.001	−2.1%
4	25	63.76	68.62	7.6%	42.79	47.53	11.1%	1.490	1.444	−3.1%
4	40	88.36	96.00	8.6%	76.77	88.62	15.4%	1.151	1.080	−6.2%
4	100	99.96	100.0	0.0%	99.90	100.0	0.1%	1.001	1.000	−0.1%

nearly saturated, and the absolute value of the processor efficiency tends to be very low. The maximum error in average processor efficiency across all of our validation experiments was 20%, which is shown for $N = 16$, $\tau = 5$, and $N_{out} = 8$ in Table III-A. In all cases, the predicted efficiencies are qualitatively correct.

We also examined more detailed performance measures, including estimates of the individual asymmetric processor efficiencies. The maximum, minimum, and ratio of maximum to minimum processor efficiency predicted by the analytical model and simulation for the 8 × 8 torus are shown in Table IV. Again, agreement is very good, particularly for the max/min efficiency ratio. Note also that the ratio of the two efficiencies is always underestimated by the analytical model. Thus, the imbalance estimates, discussed in Section IV-H, are generally *conservative*.

C. Baseline System Performance

We choose as our "baseline system" (which we will use as a reference point for studying further network design issues),

the bidirectional torus with uniform traffic, and processors that block after each request (i.e., $N_{out} = 1$). In Fig. 5, the solid lines show the average processor efficiency as a function of request rate $(1/\tau)$ for the baseline system with single-flit channel buffers, and system sizes of 16 and 64 processors. The performance of this system is low at moderate or high request rates $(1/\tau > 0.03)$. The poor performance in this system is chiefly caused by the inherent latency of communication rather than by contention in the network. To show this, we also give the efficiency curves, assuming that there is no contention in the network (the dashed lines in Fig. 5). Comparing the two sets of curves, we see that the absolute loss in efficiency due to contention is about 5%–10%. Thus, the system performance is latency-limited rather than bandwidth-limited when processors block after each request.

Furthermore, because communication latency is the chief cause of low efficiency, *increasing buffer sizes per switch yields very little performance improvement for these system sizes*. In fact, for these systems, the average processor ef-

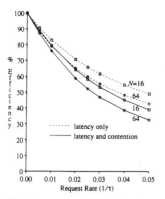

Fig. 5. Efficiency of baseline system. Bidirectional torus, single flit buffers, uniform traffic, $N_{out} = 1$.

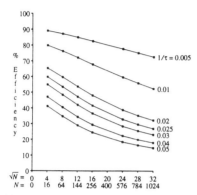

Fig. 6. Scalability of baseline system. Bidirectional torus, infinite buffers, uniform traffic, $N_{out} = 1$.

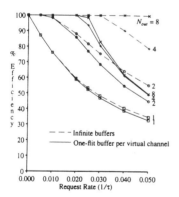

Fig. 7. Efficiency with multiple outstanding requests. Bidirectional torus, uniform traffic, $N = 64$.

ficiency with infinite channel buffers (shown in Fig. 6 and discussed below) is almost identical to the performance with single-flit channel buffers.

To examine how system performance scales with increasing system size, in Fig. 6, we plot the average processor efficiency as a function of mesh radix ($\sqrt{N}$) for different request rates ($1/\tau$) for the baseline system with infinite channel buffers. The figure shows that the performance of the baseline system scales well (i.e., average processor efficiency decreases slowly) with increasing system size, even though the absolute performance is low. These curves also show that the decrease in efficiency with increasing radix is primarily due to higher latency rather than to network contention. Specifically, the decrease in efficiency is close to linear, showing that it is

primarily due to the increasing number of hops that a message must travel, rather than an increase in the delay (due to contention) at each hop. We conjecture that a baseline system with small channel buffers will also show good scalability, based on the low network contention seen in all of the cases studied above. (The space complexity of our single-flit buffer model, and the time requirements of simulation, have prohibited us from testing this directly.)

D. Multiple Outstanding Requests

Since baseline system performance is chiefly limited by communication latency rather than contention, a plausible technique for improving processor efficiency is to allow processors to make multiple requests before blocking. The impact of multiple outstanding requests on system performance and scalability are as follows.

Fig. 7 shows how the performance of an 8×8 baseline system (i.e., a bidirectional torus, uniform traffic) with single-flit or infinite buffers improves as N_{out} increases from 1 to 8. The figure shows that for single-flit channel buffers (solid lines), hiding communication latency with small increases in N_{out} is clearly effective in improving average efficiency, but each additional increase in N_{out} brings diminishing returns because of increasing network contention. In fact, there is a threshold at $N_{out} = 4$ beyond which no appreciable improvement in performance is observed.

For the infinite buffer case (dashed lines), we find that increasing N_{out} up to 8 is worthwhile for this system size. In larger systems with infinite buffers (not shown here), we again found that beyond some threshold, increasing N_{out} brings little improvement; this threshold is about 8 and 4 for systems with 144 and 1024 processors, respectively. *In general, a few contexts per processor or a few prefetches are effective in improving efficiency, but there is a clear threshold at a small value of N_{out} beyond which no further improvement is observed because of increased network contention.* These results further support conclusions in previous papers that a few contexts per processor are sufficient in systems that are being prototyped today [1], [21].

The figure also shows that larger channel buffers become increasingly important as N_{out} is increased, because of the increasing contention. The performance difference between single-flit and infinite channel buffers is significant even for $N_{out} = 2$, and becomes quite large for $N_{out} \geq 4$.

Because of the increased contention, it is important to reevaluate the scalability of the network with multiple outstanding requests. In Fig. 8, we plot processor efficiency against mesh radix, $\sqrt{N}$, for $N_{out} = 4$, infinite channel buffers, and various values of $1/\tau$. In contrast with Fig. 6, efficiency drops sharply for moderate or high request rates ($1/\tau \geq 0.02$), because of increasing network contention. Thus, *the system with four outstanding requests does not scale well under uniform traffic, even with infinite channel buffers,* because network bandwidth in larger systems does not increase in proportion to the increased communication load. In the next several sections, we focus on systems with $N_{out} = 1$ and $N_{out} = 4$ when studying further network design trade-offs.

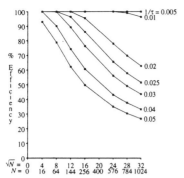

Fig. 8. Scalability with four outstanding requests. Bidirectional torus, uniform traffic, infinite buffers.

E. Alternate Mesh Network Topologies

We next compare the performance of the different network topologies under uniform communication. In this subsection, we use the term "mesh" specifically to refer to the network without end-around connections. Our first comparison is between the two bidirectional networks: the torus and the mesh. The average number of hops a message must travel assuming uniform traffic is about 33% larger without the end-around connections. On the other hand, as explained in Section II-F, the mesh does not require multiple virtual channels per physical link, as required by the deadlock prevention algorithm for the torus. We therefore use a buffer size of two flits per physical link in the mesh network, to ensure a fair comparison with the torus with a single-flit buffer per virtual channel.[6]

Fig. 9(a) plots processor efficiency versus request rate for one, two, and four outstanding requests for the two bidirectional topologies. The results are for an 8×8 system. For $N_{out} = 1$, there is only slight benefit to the end-around connections, because the higher number of hops in the mesh has only a small effect on latency, because of the pipelined routing of messages and the low contention per hop. For $N_{out} = 4$, however, the torus has up to 30% higher performance, because the higher network contention makes the higher number of hops in the mesh more significant. Thus, *end-around connections significantly improve performance with multiple outstanding requests*. This result should hold as well for larger systems (where the savings in hops for the torus increases) and larger buffer sizes (where network contention is still significant for $N_{out} = 4$, as shown in Section IV-D).

We next compare the bidirectional torus with the unidirectional torus. For the former, we use message lengths of $L_{msg1} = 4$, $L_{resp1} = 10$, $L_{msg2} = 12$, and $L_{resp2} = 4$, rather than 3, 9, 11, and 3 used in all other experiments. This allows us to halve these message lengths for the unidirectional torus, according to our assumption that its links are twice as wide as those in the bidirectional torus. Fig. 9(b) plots processor efficiency as a function of $1/\tau$ for $N_{out} = 1$, 2, and 4, for each topology. The results are similar to the comparison against the bidirectional mesh. In particular, *the bidirectional torus performs significantly better than the unidirectional torus with*

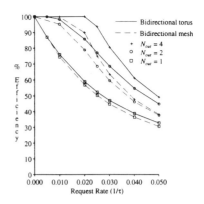

(a)

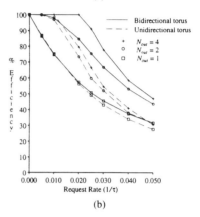

(b)

Fig. 9. Comparison of network topologies: 8×8 system, uniform traffic, single-flit buffers. (a) Bidirectional torus vs. mesh. (b) Bidirectional torus vs. unidirectional torus.

multiple outstanding requests. Thus, the extra number of hops in the unidirectional torus is not sufficiently offset by the wider channels. These results should hold approximately as system size increases, because the distance, as well as the bandwidth, scales at the same rate in both topologies.[7]

F. Nearest-Neighbor Workloads

The previous experiments assumed uniformly distributed internode communication, i.e., each node is equally likely to communicate with each other node. In this section, we investigate how near-neighbor communication locality affects system performance and our previous conclusions about system design trade-offs. We consider near-neighbor traffic patterns in which some fraction, F_{nn}, of the traffic generated by each processor is equally divided among its four nearest neighbors, whereas its remaining traffic is uniformly distributed to all nodes (including the four neighbors). The uniformly distributed traffic represents non-near-neighbor communication required by the near-neighbor application, as well as other activity on the system, such as operating system traffic.

Fig. 10(a) shows processor efficiency as a function of mesh radix, $\sqrt{N}$, for various values of F_{nn}, for $N_{out} = 1$. Curves are shown for two values of request rate, $1/\tau = 0.01$ and 0.04. In both cases, increasing locality of communication improves processor efficiency only gradually. Fig. 10(b) gives the results

---

[6] Since our single-flit-buffer analytical model does not extend to networks with two-flit buffers, we used simulation to estimate the performance in the mesh with two-flit buffers per link.

[7] Section IV-H, however, shows that performance imbalance between different parts of the system is higher with the unidirectional network, which may exacerbate the difference in performance at larger system sizes.

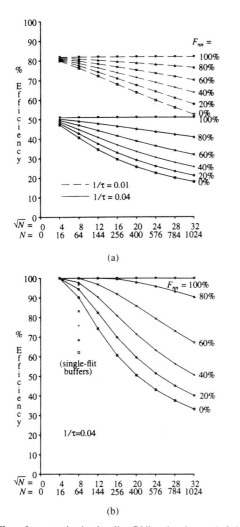

(a)

(b)

Fig. 10.   Effect of communication locality. Bidirectional torus, infinite buffers except single points in (b). (a) $N_{\text{out}} = 1$. (b) $N_{\text{out}} = 4$.

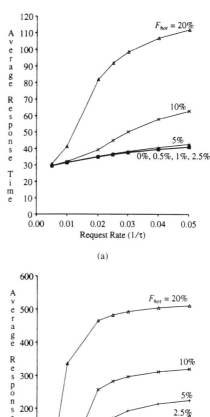

(a)

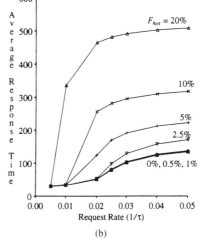

(b)

Fig. 11.   The effect of hot-spots on overall mean response times. Bidirectional 8×8 torus, single-flit buffers. (a) $N_{\text{out}} = 1$. (b) $N_{\text{out}} = 4$.

for $N_{\text{out}} = 4$ and $1/\tau = 0.04$. (At $1/\tau = 0.01$, the efficiency is close to 100% even with uniform traffic, as shown in Fig. 8.) In this case, efficiency improves substantially with increasing locality, because locality reduces contention as well as latency. For example, the 1024-processor system with $F_{\text{nn}} = 60\%$ shows more than twice the efficiency of the same system under uniform traffic.

Locality of communication influences many of the design issues that were examined in previous sections, assuming uniform traffic distribution. These must now be reevaluated.

The set of points for single-flit buffers in Fig. 10(b) shows mean processor efficiency for the 8×8 mesh with single-flit buffers and $N_{\text{out}} = 4$. We observe that as for uniform traffic, the infinite buffer case is significantly better than the single-flit buffer case even up to $F_{\text{nn}} = 70\%–80\%$.

The results for $1/\tau = 0.04$ in Fig. 10(a) and 10(b) show that the improvement when N_{out} goes from 1 to 4 is much stronger at higher levels of locality, for $N > 64$. Thus, *locality increases the benefit of multiple outstanding requests for large systems.* This is true because network contention is reduced for high values of F_{nn}, so that increasing N_{out} does not cause much higher contention; but it does improve performance by overlapping communication with computation.

We can also reevaluate how system performance scales when communication locality is present. Under uniform traffic, we concluded that the mesh network scales well when N_{out} is 1, but scales poorly for $N_{\text{out}} = 4$. In Fig. 10, we see that increasing locality has a positive effect on the scalability of the network (as expected); but, nevertheless, for $N_{\text{out}} = 4$, *system performance scales well only for $F_{\text{nn}} \geq 80\%$.* It may be unrealistic to expect such high levels of locality for real workloads.

Finally, the relative performance of the various mesh topologies may differ under near-neighbor workloads. In particular, we showed in Section IV-E that the bidirectional torus has a significant performance advantage over the unidirectional torus with multiple outstanding requests. The performance advantage of the bidirectional torus will increase in the presence of locality, because in the unidirectional torus, a round-trip message to a near-neighbor requires $\sqrt{N}$ hops as compared with two hops.

To summarize the results of this section, locality of communication improves system performance, particularly in large systems with multiple outstanding requests, and increases the benefit of multiple outstanding requests; but it only marginally improves the ability of the mesh to support larger system

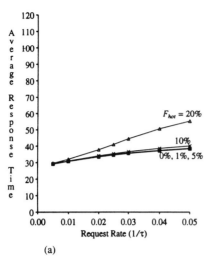
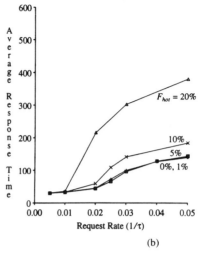

(a)   (b)

Fig. 12.   Overall mean response times under hot-spot traffic with multiple node-to-switch links. Bidirectional 8×8 torus, single-flit buffers. (a) $N_{out} = 1$. (b) $N_{out} = 4$.

sizes. In particular, the case of $N_{out} = 4$ does not scale well for $F_{nn} < 80\%$. Other conclusions of the experiments with uniform workloads are also not altered for workloads with communication locality.

G. Hot-Spot Effects

Hot-spots are a form of nonuniform communication that can strongly impact system performance. Hot-spots can arise, for example, when a number of processors make a significant fraction of their requests to a single memory module or to a single node in a multiprocessor. The issue has been studied by using open queueing models (i.e., assuming nonblocking processors) in the context of multistage interconnection networks [13], [17], [23].

We examine the effect of hot-spots in mesh networks by assigning some fraction, F_{hot}, of requests from each processor to a particular node in the system, while the remaining fraction $1 - F_{hot}$ is distributed uniformly across all processors. Fig. 11 plots the mean response time (sum of average network plus remote-node residence times) versus request rate, $1/\tau$, for various values of F_{hot} in a bidirectional 8×8 torus with single-flit buffers. For $N_{out} = 1$ (Fig. 11(a)), there is very little increase in mean round-trip time for $F_{hot} \leq 10\%$. For $N_{out} = 4$, however, much smaller fractions (about 2.5%) of hot traffic cause significant increases in mean round-trip time. (Note the larger range on the y-axis in Fig. 11(b).) This result indicates that *the effect of a hot-spot is very sensitive to N_{out}*. In particular, this suggests that open traffic models ($N_{out} = \infty$) may yield extremely pessimistic results.

The above hot-spot experiments assumed a single node-to-switch link, as in all previous experiments. This link in the hot node is a bottleneck in the system, and substantial queues build up at the link, because we have assumed unlimited buffer space for it. Hence, traffic in the rest of the network sees almost no contention. Using multiple links from node to switch (e.g., one node-to-switch link per outgoing virtual channel) alleviates this bottleneck. The average response times for this case are shown in Fig. 12.[8] The figure shows that the

average round-trip time has reduced considerably for the cases that showed non-negligible increases in response time due to hot-spots in Fig. 11. Although Fig. 12 assumes one link per outgoing channel, we would expect to see approximately the same performance if the eight processor-switch channels were multiplexed onto two or three physical links, because a very high fraction of the outgoing traffic at each node uses only two or three of the eight outgoing virtual channels. (Seven-eighths of the total traffic out of a node must go out first on the column, and is further restricted to only two or three of these four outgoing virtual channels by the deadlock-avoidance algorithm.)

When the bottleneck on the node-to-switch link in the hot node is alleviated, the switch-to-node link becomes the new bottleneck in the system. Now channel buffers on paths leading to this bottleneck link can get filled up, affecting messages to non-hot nodes as well. Hot-spot studies in indirect networks have shown that traffic to memory modules other than the hot module is slowed down as much as traffic to the hot module itself [17]. This phenomenon has been called *tree saturation*. To analyze the corresponding effect in mesh networks, we plot in Fig. 13 the average response time for messages to the hot processor (dashed lines) and to all other processors (solid lines), assuming multiple node-to-switch links.[9] For $N_{out} = 1$, we see that traffic to non-hot processors does not see significant increase in response time, even when F_{hot} is as high as 20%. For $N_{out} = 4$, mean response time to the non-hot processors actually decreases slightly when F_{hot} is increased from 0%–5%. In this case, contention at the hot node has significantly decreased overall network throughput, offsetting any tree-saturation effect.

---

[8] The curves for $N_{out} = 4$ and $F_{hot} = 10\%$ and 20% in Fig. 12(b) were

plotted by using data from simulations, because the analytical model did not converge in this case. (The results of the analytical models for lower values of F_{hot} were in good agreement with simulations.)

[9] Note that for $N_{out} = 4$, with uniform traffic ($F_{hot} = 0\%$) the round-trip time to the "hot" processor is actually lower than that to other processors. This is a direct result of the asymmetric loads on the virtual channels described in Section II-D and studied in Section IV-H. The hot processor chosen for these experiments (processor [2, 2]) is located at a point in the mesh where loads on the outgoing virtual channels are balanced.

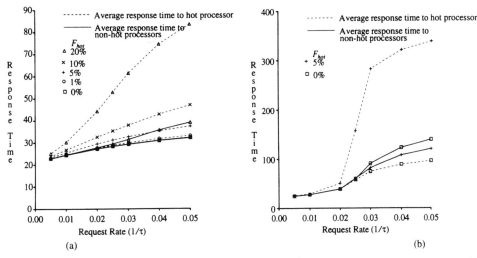

Fig. 13. The effect of hot-spots on mean response times to *non-hot* processors. Bidirectional 8×8 torus, single-flit buffers, multiple node-to-switch links.

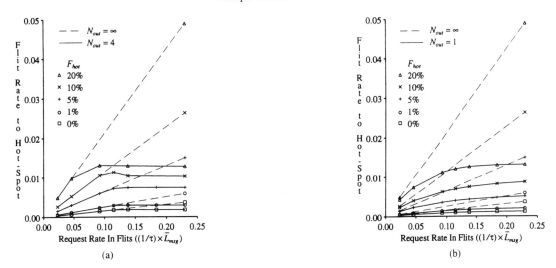

Fig. 14. Effective flit rate to hot node with blocking and nonblocking processors. Bidirectional 8×8 torus, single-flit buffers, multiple node-to-switch links.

The above results suggest that the presence of hot-spots in mesh networks does not significantly increase response times for non-hot traffic, in systems of this size. This is different from the conclusions of Pfister and Norton [17] for *systems of the same size* based on multistage interconnection networks. The principal reason for the difference in results is that Pfister and Norton assumed an open model, in which processors generate requests continuously without blocking for responses to return (i.e., $N_{out} = \infty$). To illustrate the effect of this assumption, Fig. 14 shows the actual request rate in flits per processor to the hot module for $N_{out} = \infty$ (dashed lines), as well as $N_{out} = 1$ and $N_{out} = 4$ (solid lines) as a function of the input rate (in flits), $(1/\tau) \times \overline{L}_{msg}$. The request rate to the hot module is significantly higher for $N_{out} = \infty$ than for finite values of N_{out}, and this would also be true for the multistage interconnection network.

The hot-spot experiments described in this section have focused on 64-processor systems. The degradation due to a hot-spot will become more severe with increasing system size. Finite-buffer models are necessary for realistic hot-spot studies, however, and we have been unable to use our analytical

finite-buffer model to study large systems quantitatively. (Simulating these systems is even more difficult.) Nevertheless, we believe that the results of this section provide insights that would be valuable in studying large systems. Qualitatively, we expect multiple node-to-switch links to significantly alleviate the effect of a hot-spot for larger systems as well. We also expect that larger systems with blocking processors (finite N_{out}) will be able to support much higher levels of hot-spot traffic without introducing tree-saturation than would be predicted using open system models (i.e., assuming that $N_{out} = \infty$).

H. Performance Imbalance Caused by the Deadlock-Free Routing Algorithm

The analyses of torus performance using the single-flit buffer analytical model show significant differences among processor efficiencies at different locations in the system, and these observations are corroborated by simulation (see Section IV-A). To illustrate the imbalance, Table V-A gives the efficiencies of the individual processors in the unidirectional 8×8 torus, ($N_{out} = 4$, $1/\tau = 0.02$) under *uniform* traffic,

TABLE V-A

EFFICIENCIES OF INDIVIDUAL PROCESSORS IN THE MESH: UNIDIRECTIONAL TORUS ($N_{out} = 4. 1/\tau = 0.02$)

	Col 0	1	2	3	4	5	6	7
Row 0	[91]	89	88	87	88	89	89	89
1	89	86	83	82	84	86	87	87
2	85	79	72	71	76	83	85	85
3	81	67	55	55	63	78	83	83
4	81	62	(46)	(46)	57	78	83	83
5	83	74	62	61	70	81	84	84
6	84	81	78	78	79	82	83	83
7	85	84	84	83	83	83	83	83

TABLE V-B

EFFICIENCIES OF INDIVIDUAL PROCESSORS IN THE MESH: BIDIRECTIONAL TORUS $N_{out} = 4. 1/\tau = 0.04$)

	Col 0	1	2	3	4	5	6	7
Row 0	(48)	52	57	60	60	59	55	49
1	52	55	60	62	63	61	58	53
2	59	61	64	66	66	65	63	60
3	64	65	67	[68]	[68]	67	66	64
4	64	65	67	[68]	[68]	67	66	65
5	60	62	64	65	65	65	63	60
6	53	57	61	62	62	61	58	54
7	49	53	58	60	60	58	55	49

Key: ○: Minimum efficiency value. □: Maximum efficiency value.

i.e., with equal loads on all physical links. The table shows that the processors near the corners have high efficiencies, whereas the ones near the center of the mesh have much lower efficiencies. Table V-B shows the processor efficiencies for the bidirectional 8×8 torus ($N_{out} = 4$, $1/\tau = 0.04$) under uniform traffic. Again, imbalance is observed; however, this time the processors near the corners have low efficiency. Note that these two cases represent operating points with moderate to high *average* processor efficiency (79% and 58%, respectively), yet also with significant performance imbalance across the system.

To quantify the performance imbalance at particular parameter settings, we use the ratio of the maximum processor efficiency to the minimum processor efficiency. Fig. 15 plots this ratio as a function of the request rate for the unidirectional and bidirectional 8×8 tori, for $N_{out} = 1$, 2, and 4. The figure shows that the imbalance becomes significant when network contention is moderately high, but includes cases that represent reasonable operating points (i.e., average efficiencies greater than 50%). For example, the 64-processor system with $N_{out} = 4$ has average efficiency greater than 50% at most request rates, as shown in Fig. 9(b); however, the imbalance is as high as 1.5 for the bidirectional torus and 4.0 for the unidirectional torus. Finally, comparing Fig. 15(a) and 15(b), we also see that the imbalance is much greater in the unidirectional torus than in the bidirectional torus.

The results described above suggest that the imbalance in system performance can be significant and needs to be considered during the design of the system. The imbalance in processor performance may have significant implications, for example, for parallel programs that synchronize via barriers. Whether the imbalance is significant for any particular system depends on several factors, including buffer size, message lengths, and request rate.

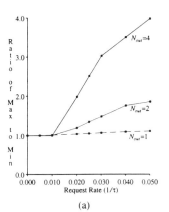

(a)

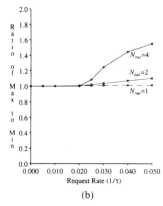

(b)

Fig. 15. Maximum performance imbalance. Single-flit buffers, uniform traffic. (a) Unidirectional 8×8 torus. (b) Bidirectional 8×8 torus.

Recent studies have shown that mesh networks *without end-around connections* also have significant, symmetric imbalances in processor performance, even under uniform communication [3], [7]. These imbalances occur because of unequal traffic requirements on the physical links, however, a situation which arises from edge effects due to the lack of end-around connections. In torus networks, physical link loads are balanced under uniform traffic; thus, the source of the observed imbalance in processor performance must be sought elsewhere.

A potential source of imbalance in torus networks is the asymmetric virtual channel loading by the deadlock-avoidance algorithm, described in Section II-D. In attempting to determine whether and how this asymmetry causes the imbalance, an obvious guess is that the round-trip communication by some nodes makes greater use of high-load virtual channels (i.e., channels that carry a high fraction of their links' traffic). However, this explanation cannot account for an observed peculiarity in the pattern of imbalance in the unidirectional case, namely, that *processors with poor performance are not necessarily located where greatest asymmetry in channel loading occurs.* In fact, channels near the edges have the greatest traffic asymmetry (Fig. 4), but processors near the edges have the best performance (Table V-A). To understand why the above explanation is invalid in general, note that for outgoing requests that use high-load channels, the responses will use low-load channels on the return trip (and vice versa) because of symmetries in the routing algorithm. (This is easiest to reason about for the unidirectional torus.) Some careful thought reveals that the differences between nodes that place somewhat greater load on balanced virtual channels versus nodes that place somewhat greater load on high- and low-load channels are not likely to account for the fairly large observed imbalance in processor efficiencies.

More careful consideration of message *pipelining and blocking* behavior reveals a different and potentially substantial impact of the asymmetric loads that can also explain the particular patterns of imbalance observed in Table V. Specifically, certain nodes' outgoing messages (both requests and responses *to* other nodes) experience relatively severe blocking because of high-load virtual channels after leaving the node. Such nodes will see significantly higher contention for their *node-to-switch link* because of the pipelining and blocking of messages. Because each processor is the heaviest user of its own node-to-switch link, increased contention on this link results in lower efficiency for the processor at such a node. Furthermore, in the unidirectional torus, it is the nodes near the center of the network whose outgoing messages experience most severe blocking because of high-load channels, whereas in the bidirectional torus it is the nodes near the edges. This leads to the different patterns of imbalance in the two cases.

To demonstrate the phenomenon quantitatively, consider the nodes on some fixed column (as in Fig. 4) of a mesh network. For the node on row i, define the following:

$R(c, i) \equiv$ mean residence time on outgoing virtual channel c for a message out of the node (i.e., for a message that was transferred over the node-to-switch link into the buffer for channel c),

$\overline{R}(i) \equiv$ average of $R(c, i)$, averaged over all outgoing channels c,

$W_{\mathrm{node}}(i) \equiv$ mean waiting time for the node-to-switch link at the node.

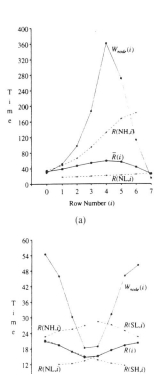

(a)

(b)

Fig. 16. Residence time on first virtual channel. Nodes on column 3; single-flit buffers, uniform traffic.

Fig. 16(a) plots $R(c, i)$, for $c =$ NH and NL, $\overline{R}(i)$, and $W_{\mathrm{node}}(i)$ as functions of i (row number) for column 3 of a unidirectional 8×8 torus (NH and NL denote the High and Low channels in the North direction). $\overline{R}(i)$ is higher near the middle of the column than near the edges, showing that outgoing messages from the nodes near the middle experience much more severe blocking, as described above. Now high $\overline{R}(i)$ also implies a high residence time on the node-to-switch link, and hence a high waiting time, $W_{\mathrm{node}}(i)$, just as shown in the figure. This leads to poorer performance for these nodes. For the bidirectional case, Fig. 16(b) plots $R(c, i)$ for $c \in \{$NH, NL, SH, SL$\}$, $\overline{R}(i)$, and $W_{\mathrm{node}}(i)$. In this case, $\overline{R}(i)$, and hence $W_{\mathrm{node}}(i)$, are higher near the edges of the torus, and thus the efficiency is lower.

Thus, the ultimate effect of high-load channels is the same in both networks: They cause more severe blocking for outgoing messages of some nodes, which produces much greater contention for the node-to-switch link at these nodes. However, the pattern of use of the high-load channels by outgoing messages is different in the two networks. In the bidirectional case, blocking of outgoing messages is more severe for nodes near the edges, because these nodes' outgoing messages make much greater use of high-load virtual channels compared to nodes near the center. For example, a node on row 7 in an 8×8 bidirectional network sends all of its outgoing messages on channels that carry 100% of their links' traffic (NL and SL), whereas the outgoing messages for a node on row 3 are mostly concentrated on channels with low to moderate load (NL and SH). In the unidirectional case, however, the nodes near the center, which have poor performance, make only slightly greater use of high-load virtual channels than do nodes near the edges. In these networks, it appears more significant that outgoing messages from nodes near the center travel from channels with a low to moderate load into channels with a high load, whereas for nodes near the edges the opposite is true. (Refer to Fig. 4.) The pipelined routing causes significantly greater blocking for the former than it does for the latter.

As the preceding discussion indicates, the precise explanation of the relationship between the asymmetric channel loadings and the performance imbalance is fairly subtle and nonintuitive. Formulating and validating the explanation required significant insight as well as analysis of detailed metrics obtained from the analytical model. Furthermore, the imbalance cannot be detected or analyzed by using models or simulations that ignore the virtual channel loadings or the finite switch buffers. Finally, note that the waiting times for the node-to-switch links, and hence the imbalance itself, might be reduced by the use of multiple physical node-to-switch links and/or multiple virtual node-to-switch channels.

V. CONCLUSION

We have developed accurate, approximate MVA models for k-ary n-cube interconnection networks with wormhole routing, with single-flit and infinite buffers at the switches. Interesting aspects of the model include the techniques used to estimate mean message blocking times, mean message queueing times at the processors, and the mean queue lengths seen at the first outgoing link when multiple channels connect each processor to its switch output channels. Many of the experimental results would not have been possible with simpler analytical models that do not represent the message blocking and details of the routing. The equations for channel waiting time, which form the foundation of the single-flit-buffer model, use recurrence relations to model the dependencies among flit blocking times within a single message, yet use random arrival instant assumptions to model interference by other messages. The models were shown to be quite accurate by extensive validations with simulation. We are not aware of any previous work that has used similar models of blocking in these networks. We believe the validation results are important evidence that approximate MVA is a viable technique for modeling complex systems.

We used the models to analyze various issues that arise in the design of 2-D (mesh) networks. These results (summarized below) should prove useful for engineering high-performance systems based on low-dimensional k-ary n-cube networks.

Some of our results confirm and quantify existing intuition about mesh interconnection networks. With processors that block on every request, we have shown that contention in the network is low, and the three network topologies (bidirectional and unidirectional torus and bidirectional mesh) show little difference in performance. Multiple outstanding requests can help increase performance, but can also cause increased contention. Thus, in this case, substantial performance gain is achievable by increasing buffer size.

We also gained new intuition from some of our results, including the following.

- Under uniform workloads, absolute performance is higher with multiple outstanding requests; but network performance does not scale well with increasing system size.
- Communication locality improves system performance, particularly for multiple outstanding requests, but at least 70%–80% of each processor's traffic must be directed to its nearest neighbors before the case of four outstanding requests scales well.
- With multiple outstanding requests, the bidirectional torus performs significantly better than do the other two topologies. Furthermore, it exhibits much lower performance imbalance (see below) due to the deadlock-free routing algorithm than does the unidirectional torus.
- Open system models can yield extremely pessimistic results in hot-spot studies. When processors block after making a few requests, only high fractions of hot-spot traffic cause significant performance degradation in 64-processor systems with single-flit buffers. Furthermore, traffic to the non-hot processors is not much affected by hot-spot traffic in these systems; i.e., tree-saturation is not observed.
- At some plausible operating points (i.e., in cases where average processor efficiency is reasonably high), there is a perceptible difference in the efficiencies of processors at different locations in the mesh. This imbalance is due to asymmetric loads on the virtual channels by the deadlock-avoidance algorithm.

A number of related issues for k-ary n-cube networks remain to be studied. The models developed in this paper can be used to study network performance for message-passing and hierarchical systems. The conclusions from the experiments need to be examined for 3-D networks. The result that a communication hot-spot does not significantly slow down other traffic in the system needs to be reexamined for larger systems. A related question that needs to be answered is what buffer sizes are required to approximate infinite buffer performance under various workload assumptions. For interconnection networks with pipelined routing in particular, however, modeling the performance with larger finite buffers is a difficult problem. (Previous analytical models of interconnection networks that allow finite buffer sizes are based on a decomposition approximation in which each queue is analyzed in isolation, thus *ignoring the dependencies between network stages* caused by the blocking and pipelining of messages. See, e.g., [15] and the references therein.) Finally, it would be worthwhile to develop a deadlock-free routing algorithm for the mesh network that does not lead to the imbalance in processor efficiencies that we have observed.

APPENDIX A
NOTATION USED IN THE MODEL

We use the following convention for integer subscripts in the model equations: i, s, d, and q denote node numbers. (In this usage, i always appears within brackets, i.e., "[i]"

and "(i, n)"). j denotes message type. k denotes flit number. c denotes a virtual channel. i, I denote input ports. (In this case, i always appears as a subscript, e.g., $r_{j,c,i}$.) The table below defines the variables used in the model equations.

The equations of the model are given in detail here. Throughout the development of the model, we call a message from s to d or a response from d to s a message of *class* s. Also, in a summation over all four types j, we write $\sum_j$ instead of $\sum_{j \in \text{msg1},\text{msg2},\text{resp1},\text{resp2}}$.

$$R[i] = r_{\text{proc}}[i] + r_{\text{network}}[i] + r_{\text{remote}}[i], \quad i = 1 \cdots N. \quad (1)$$

A. *Queueing in the Network*

$$r_{\text{network}}[s] = \sum_{d \neq s} F_{sd}(P_1(r_{\text{msg1},sd} + r_{\text{resp1},ds}) + P_2(r_{\text{msg2},sd} + r_{\text{resp2},ds})), \quad i = 1 \cdots N. \quad (2)$$

$$r_{j,sd} = w_{\text{node},sd|j} + \sum_c r_{j,c,sd}[1] + T_{\text{catchup},j,sd},$$
$$j \in \{\text{msg1, msg2, resp1, resp2}\}. \quad (3)$$

Term	Definition
	Terms common to the entire model
$R[i]$	Mean round-trip time for customer of class i.
$R_{network}[i], r_{proc}[i], r_{remote}[i]$	Mean residence time for a customer of class i in the network, at the processor, and at the remote node, respectively.
$r_{j,sd}$	Mean residence time in the network for a message of type j from s to d
$c \pm k)_{sd}$	The virtual channel that is k steps after (or before) virtual channel c on the path from s to d
$\bar{c}$	The virtual channel that shares the same physical link as c
	Queueing for the channels
$b_{node,j,s|q}[k], q_{node,j,s|q}$	For a message of class q arriving to the link from processor to switch at node s: respectively, the probability that the link is busy serving the kth flit of a request of type j, and the mean number of waiting requests of type j.
$r_{node,j,s}[k]$	Mean residence time for the kth flit of a request of type j, on the link from processor to switch at node s.
$D_{c,i|j}(s)$	Set $\{d|$ messages from s to d, or responses from d to s if j is a reply message, visit c via input port $i\}$.
$r_{j,c,I}[k], u_{j,c,I}[k]$	Respectively, the mean residence time of the kth flit of messages of type j on channel c, which arrive to c via input port I, and the mean utilization of channel c by such flits
$r_{j,c,sd}[k]$	Mean residence time on channel c of the kth flit of a message of type j from s to d
$u_{link,\bar{c}}$	Utilization of the physical link corresponding to channel c by messages on companion channel $\bar{c}$
$w_{node,s|q}$	Mean waiting time for the link from processor to switch at node s, for the header flit of a message of class q
$w_{c|I}$	Mean waiting time for channel c, for a message arriving to c via input port I
	Queueing for the processors
$q_{proc}(i, n), u_{proc}(i, n), r_{proc}(i, n)$	Steady state mean queue length, residence time, and utilization of processor i when there are n customers in class i
res_{proc}	Mean residual service time of a customer found in service by a message arriving to a processor, as seen by the tail flit of the message, conditioned on the header flit finding the processor busy
	Queueing at a remote node
$B_{mem,j,s|d}, Q_{mem,j,s|d}, W_{mem,j,s|d}$	For an arriving request from s at remote node d: respectively, the probability d is busy serving a request of type j', the mean number of waiting requests of type j, and the mean waiting time.
$res_{mem,j'|j}$	Mean residual service time of a request of type j at a remote node as seen by the tail flit of a type j' request, conditioned on the header flit finding the type j request in service
	Queueing for the first network virtual channel on a path, with multiple processor $\rightarrow$ switch channels
$b'_{j,c,i|q}[k], q'_{j,c,i|q}$	For a customer of class q arriving to channel c via input port i: respectively, the probability c is serving the kth flit of a request of type j, and the mean number of waiting requests of type j
$V_{j,c,I}$	Total visit ration of all customer classes to channel c as type j messages arriving via input port i
$w'_{c|q}$	Mean waiting time for channel c by a customer of class q, where c is the first network virtual channel on its path

where the sum is over all channels c on the path from s to d.

$$r_{j,c,sd}[k] = \begin{cases} w_{(c+1)_{sd}|I} + u_{\text{link},\bar{c}} + 1 & k = 1, \\ r_{(c+k-1)_{sd}}[1] + u_{\text{link},\bar{c}} & k > 1, d \text{ is } k \\ & \text{or more steps away} \\ & \text{from } c, \\ 1 + u_{\text{link},\bar{c}} & \text{otherwise.} \end{cases}$$
(4)

T_{catchup} is the length of the message minus 1 (for the header) plus the delay due to sharing the physical links with traffic on other virtual channels, summed over the links that the tail flit must traverse *after the header flit reaches the destination node*:

$$T_{\text{catchup},j,sd} = L_j - 1 + \sum_{c:cis < L_j \text{ hopsfrom} d} u_{\text{link},\bar{c}}.$$

The equation for the waiting time, $w_{c|I}$, is explained in Section III-B.

$$w_{c|I} = \sum_{i \neq I} \sum_j \sum_{k=1}^{L_j} u_{j,c,i}[k] \left(\frac{1}{2} r_{j,c,i}[k] + \sum_{I=k+1}^{L_j} r_{j,c,i}[l] \right)$$
$$+ \sum_j \left(\frac{u_{j,c,i}(L_j)}{1 - \sum_{j'} \sum_{l=1}^{L_{j'}-1} u_{j',c,I}[l]} \times \frac{r_{j,c,I}[L_j]}{2} \right)$$
$$+ \sum_{i \neq I} \sum_j \left(u_{j,(c-1)_i}[1] \sum_{l=1}^{L_j} r_{j,c,i}[l] \right).$$
(6)

$r_{j,c,i}[k]$, $u_{j,c,i}[k]$, and $u_{\text{link},c}$ remain to be calculated. These can be expressed in terms of $r_{j,c,sd}[k]$ in a straightforward manner. First, define $D_{c,i|j(s)} \equiv \{d|$ messages from s to d visit c via input port $i\}$. Then,

$$r_{j,c,I}[k] = \frac{\sum_{s=1}^N \sum_{d \in D_{c,i|j}(s)} F_{sd} P_j r_{j,c,sd}[k]}{\sum_{s=1}^N \sum_{d \in D_{c,i|j}(s)} F_{sd} P_j},$$
(7)

$$u_{j,c,i}[k] = \sum_{s=1}^N \sum_{d \in D_{c,i|j}(s)} \frac{N_{\text{out}} F_{sd} P_j r_{j,c,sd}[k]}{R[s]}.$$
(8)

$$u_{\text{link},c} = \sum_j \sum_{s=1}^N \sum_{d \in D_{c|j}(s)} \frac{N_{\text{out}} F_{sd} P_j L_j}{R[s]},$$
(9)

where $D_{c,|j}(s) \equiv \cup_i D_{c,i|j}(s)$.

B. Waiting Time for the Processor Link

The remaining term in (3), $w_{\text{node},sd|j}$, is calculated next. For request messages, $w_{\text{node},sd|j}$ is the average waiting time for the P-link at node s seen by a class s message ($w_{\text{node},s|s}$), and for reply messages $w_{\text{node},sd|j}$ is the average waiting time for the P-link at node s seen by a class d message ($w_{\text{nodes}|d}$). In general, $W_{\text{node},s|q}$ is calculated in a manner very similar to (6) for $W_{c|I}$. See (10) at the bottom of the preceding page.

The main differences from (6) for $W_{c|I}$ are as follows:
1) The second term in (6) is no longer required, and the first term does not have a summation over input ports. In both cases, the reason is that the buffer capacity for this link is unbounded.
2) The third term in (6) used the probability that there is a waiting request for each input port i. Now, however, we require an actual queue length, $q_{\text{node},j,s|q}$, denoting the average number of requests of type j waiting for the processor link in node s when a request of class q arrives. This can be calculated as follows:

$$q_{\text{node},j,s|q} =$$
$$\begin{cases} \sum_{d \neq s} \frac{(N_{\text{out}} - 1_{\{s=q\}}) F_{sd} P_j w_{\text{node},s|s}}{R[s]}, & j \in \{\text{msg1, msg2}\} \\ \sum_{s' \neq s} \frac{(N_{\text{out}} - 1_{\{s=q\}}) F_{s'q} P_j w_{\text{node},s'|q}}{R[s']}, & j \in \{\text{resp1, resp2}\} \end{cases}$$
(11)

where $1_{\{s=q\}}$ is 1 if $s = q$, and 0 otherwise. We can calculate $r_{\text{node},j,s}[k]$ and $b_{\text{node},j,s|q}[k]$ similarly:

$$b_{\text{node},j,s|q}[k]$$
$$= \begin{cases} \sum_{d \neq s} \frac{(N_{\text{out}} - 1_{s=q}) F_{sd} P_j}{R[s]}, & j \in \{\text{msg1, msg2}\} \\ \sum_{s' \neq s} \frac{(N_{\text{out}} - 1_{s'=q}) F_{s'q} P_j}{R[s']}. & j \in \{\text{resp1, resp2}\} \end{cases}$$
(12)

$$r_{\text{node},j,s}[k]$$
$$= \begin{cases} \frac{\sum_{d=1}^N F_{sd} P_j r_{j,\text{node},sd}[k]}{\sum_{d=1}^N F_{sd} P_j}, & j \in \{\text{msg1, msg2}\} \\ \frac{\sum_{s'=1}^N F_{s's} P_j r_{j\text{node},s'p}[k]}{\sum_{s'=1}^N F_{s'p} P_j}, & j \in \{\text{resp1, resp2}\}. \end{cases}$$
(13)

C. Queueing at the Processor

As defined in Appendix A, $r_{\text{proc}}(i, n)$ is the average residence time at the processor for a customer of class i when there are n customers in its class. Hence, $r_{\text{proc}}[i] = r_{\text{proc}}(i, N_{\text{out}})$ by definition. $r_{\text{proc}}(i, n)$ is calculated by recursion on n:

$$r_{\text{proc}}(i, n) = [q_{\text{proc}}(i, n-1) - u_{\text{proc}}(i, n-1)] \times \tau$$
$$+ u_{\text{proc}}(i, n-1) \times \text{res}_{\text{proc}}, \quad n > 1, \quad (14)$$

$$q_{\text{proc}}(i, n) = \frac{n \times r_{\text{proc}}(i, n)}{r_{\text{proc}}(i, n) + r_{\text{network}}[i] + r_{\text{remote}}[i]}, \quad (15)$$

$$u_{\text{proc}}(i, n) = \frac{n \times \tau}{r_{\text{proc}}(i, n) + r_{\text{network}}[i] + r_{\text{remote}}[i]}, \quad (16)$$

and

$$q_{\text{proc}}(i, 1) = u_{\text{proc}}(i, 1) = \frac{\tau}{\tau + r_{\text{network}}[i] + r_{\text{remote}}[i]}, \quad (17)$$

$$\text{res}_{\text{proc}} = (\tau - 1) \times (P_1 \gamma^{L_{\text{resp1}}-1} + P_2 \gamma^{L_{\text{resp2}}-1}),$$
$$\gamma = 1 - (1/\tau). \quad (18)$$

$$w_{\text{node},s|q} = \sum_j \left\{ \sum_{k=1}^{L_j} \left\{ b_{\text{node}j,s|q}[k] \left(\frac{r_{\text{node},j,s}[k]}{2} + \sum_{l=k+1}^{L_j} r_{\text{node},j,s}[l] \right) \right\} + q_{\text{node},j,s|q} \sum_{l=1}^{L_j} r_{\text{node},j,s}[l] \right\}. \quad (10)$$

D. Residence Time at the Remote Node

The equations for the residence time at the remote node are developed assuming that the request is serviced at the memory of the remote node without interrupting the remote processor (we denote r_{remote} as r_{mem} here). For example, in a shared-memory system, remote memory accesses could be of this type, with msg1, msg2, resp1, and resp2 corresponding to *read, write, data* and *acknowledgment* messages, respectively. The time to access one word is $D_{\text{mem},1}$ for a read request and $D_{\text{mem},2}$ for a write request. We assume that a request is queued for a memory module only when its last flit is received at the node. We also assume that the memory at each node is interleaved, and, to simplify the analysis, that all accesses read or write the first byte from the first module, the second byte from the second module, and so on. This implies that $D_{\text{mem},1}$ ($D_{\text{mem},2}$) cycles after a read (write) request begins service, the next memory request can begin service. Further, for a read request, the response (data message) is queued up to be transmitted as soon as the first word of data is read out from the first memory module, with subsequent words being transmitted one per cycle. An acknowledgment in response to a write request is queued when the last byte has been written, i.e., after L_{msg2} cycles. We do not limit the number of requests that can simultaneously be queued up for a given module.

The method for calculating the mean residence time at memory is the same as that in [22]:

$$r_{\text{mem}}[s] = \sum_d \sum_{j \in \{1,2\}} F_{sd} P_j (D_{\text{mem},j} + w_{\text{mem},j,s|d}), \quad (19)$$

$$w_{\text{mem},j,s|d} = \sum_{j' \in \{1,2\}} \left\{ q_{\text{mem},j',s|d} D_{\text{mem},j'} + b_{\text{mem},j',s|d} \text{res}_{\text{mem}j'j} \right\} \quad (20)$$

$$q_{\text{mem},j',s'|d} = \sum_{s \neq d} (N_{\text{out}} - 1_{\{s = s'\}}) F_{sd} P_{j'} \frac{w_{\text{mem},j',s|d}}{R[s]}. \quad (21)$$

$$b_{\text{mem},j',s'|d} = \sum_{s \neq d} (N_{\text{out}} - 1_{\{s = s'\}}) F_{sd} P_{j'} \frac{D_{\text{mem},j'}}{R[s]}. \quad (22)$$

Finally, just as in the processor queueing equations, the residual life of a memory request in service has to be calculated as seen by the tail flit rather than as seen by the head. Defining $\text{res}_{\text{mem},j'|j}$ to be the residual service time of a type $j' \in \{1,2\}$ request as seen by the tail flit of a message of type $j \in \{\text{msg1, msg2}\}$, we have the following equation:

$$\text{res}_{\text{mem},j'|j} = (D_{\text{mem},j'} - L_j + 1) \times \frac{(D_{\text{mem},j'} - L_j)}{(2 \times D_{\text{mem},j'})}. \quad (23)$$

E. Waiting Time for the First Virtual Channel in the Network, with Multiple Processor-Switch Channels

The equations of the model described so far have been the same for single or multiple processor $\rightarrow$ switch channels. The only exception is (10) for $w_{\text{node},s|q}$, which now would be denoted by $w_{\text{node},c|q}$, and must be calculated separately for each outgoing channel c from node s. Similarly, $q_{\text{node},j,c|q}$, $b_{\text{node},j,c|q}[k]$, and $r_{\text{node},j,c}[k]$ have to be calculated separately for each c; however, in all cases, the equations remain essentially the same.

The waiting time for the buffer in the first switch is the only part that needs to be calculated somewhat differently, as described in Section III-E. The equations are as follows:

$$w'_{c|q} = \sum_j \left\{ \sum_{i \neq \text{PROC}} \sum_{k=1}^{L_j} b'_{j,c,i|q}[k] \left(\frac{r_{j,c,i}[k]}{2} + \sum_{l=k+1}^{L_j} r_{j,c,i}[l] \right) \right.$$
$$+ \left(\sum_{k=1}^{L_j} b_{\text{node},j,c|q}[k] \right) (r_{j,c|\text{PROC}}[L_j] - 1)$$
$$\left. + \sum_{i \neq \text{PROC}} \left(q'_{j,c,i|q} \sum_{k=1}^{L_j} r_{j,c,i}[k] \right) \right\}. \quad (24)$$

The first term in (24) has been explained in Section III-E, and the remaining two terms are similar to the second and third terms in (6). Then, as explained in Section III-E, $b'_{j,c,i|q}[k]$ is calculated as follows:

$$b'_{j,c,i|q}[k] = \left\{ \frac{1 - \sum_j \sum_{k=1}^{L_j} b_{\text{node},j,c|q}[k]}{1 - \sum_j \sum_{k=1}^{L_j} u_{j,c,\text{PROC}}[k]} \right\} \times u_{j,c,i}[k] \quad (25)$$

Finally, the equation for $q'_{j,c,i|q}$ is as follows:

$$q'_{j,c,i|q} = \left\{ \sum_j \sum_{k=1}^{L_j} b_{\text{node},j,c|q}[k] \right\} \times$$
$$\frac{V_{j,c,i}}{\sum_{j'} V_{j',c,\text{PROC}}} \times$$
$$\left\{ \sum_j \sum_{k=1}^{L_j} u_{j,c,\text{PROC}}[k] + \sum_j u_{j,(c-1)_{\text{PROC}}}[1] \right\}$$
$$+ \sum_{\substack{i' \neq \text{PROC} \\ i' \neq i}} \left\{ \sum_j \sum_{k=1}^{L_j} b'_{j,c,i|q}[k] \right\}$$
$$\times \frac{V_{j,c,i}}{\sum_{\substack{i' \neq \text{PROC} \\ i' \neq i}} \sum_{j'} V_{j',c|i'}}$$
$$\times \sum_{\substack{i' \neq \text{PROC} \\ i' \neq i}} \sum_j \sum_{k=1}^{L_j} u_{j,c,i'}[k]. \quad (26)$$

The first line of (26) corresponds to waiting for messages that were blocked on input port $i \neq \text{PROC}$ by the preceding message on the processor-to-switch link, when the processor-to-switch link is found busy. When it is found idle, but channel c is busy serving a message that arrived from input port $i' \neq i, i' \neq \text{PROC}$, the tagged message also has to wait for messages on input port i that were blocked by the message occupying c. This is the second line of (26).

This completes the equations for the case with multiple processor switch channels, and the description of the model.

ACKNOWLEDGMENT

We thank A. Mukherjee and D. Eager for valuable discussions during the development of the model. We also thank S. Adve, A. Agarwal, D. Eager, M. Hill, S. Owicki, G. Sohi, and an anonymous referee for valuable comments on earlier drafts of this paper.

REFERENCES

[1] A. Agarwal, B. Lim, D. Kranz, and J. Kubiatowicz, "APRIL: A processor architecture for multiprocessing," *17th Ann. Int. Symp. Comput. Architecture,* May 1990, pp. 104–114.

[2] A. Agarwal, "Limits on interconnection network performance," *IEEE Trans. Parallel Distrib. Syst.* vol. 2, pp. 398–421, Oct. 1991.

[3] K. Bolding and L. Snyder, "Mesh and torus choatic routing," *Advanced Research in VLSI and Parallel Systems: Proceedings of the Brown/MIT Conference,* 1992, pp. 333–347.

[4] K. Bolding, "Non-uniformities introduced by virtual channel deadlock prevention," Tech. Rep. 92–07–07, Dept. of Comput. Sci. and Eng., Univ. of Washington, 1992.

[5] S. Borkar, "iWarp: An integrated solution to high-speed parallel computation," *Proc. Supercomputing '88,* Nov. 1988.

[6] K. M. Chandy and D. Neuse, "Linearizer: A heuristic algorithm for queueing network models of computer systems," *Communic. ACM 25,* pp. 126–134, 1982.

[7] S. Chittor and R. Enbody, "Performance degradation in large wormhole-routed interprocessor communication networks," *Proc. 1990 Int. Conf. Parallel Processing,* 1990, pp. I-424–I-428.

[8] W. J. Dally, "A VLSI Architecture for Concurrent Data Structures," Ph.D. dissertation, Cal. Inst. of Tech., 1986.

[9] W. J. Dally and C. L. Seitz, "Deadlock-free message routing in multiprocessor interconnection networks," *IEEE Trans. Comput.,* vol. C-36, no. 5, pp. 547–553, May 1987.

[10] W. J. Dally, "Performance analysis of k-ary n-cube interconnection networks," *IEEE Trans. Comput.,* vol. 39, pp. 775–785, June 1990.

[11] E. Gelenbe, "Performance analysis of the connection machine," *Proc. ACM SIGMETRICS Conf. Measurement and Modeling of Comput. Syst.,* vol. 18, pp. 183–191, May 1990.

[12] P. Kermai and L. Kleinrock, "Virtual cut-through: A new computer communication switching technique," *Computer Networks* vol. 3, pp. 267–286, Oct. 1979.

[13] G. Lee, C. P. Kruskal, and D. J. Kuck, "The effectiveness of combining in shared-memory parallel computers in the presence of 'hotspots'," *Proc. Int. Conf. Parallel Processing,* 1986, pp. 35–41.

[14] D. Lenoski, J. Laudon, K. Gharachorloo, W. Weber, A. Gupta, J. Henessy, M. Horowitz, and M. Lam, "The Stanford DASH multiprocessor," *IEEE Comput.* vol. 25, pp. 63–79, Mar. 1992.

[15] T. Lin and L. Kleinrock, "Performance analysis of finite-buffered multistage interconnection networks with a general traffic pattern," *Proc. 1991 ACM SIGMETRICS Int. Conf. Measurement Modeling Comput. Syst.,* San Diego, CA, May 21–24, 1991.

[16] M. D. Noakes, D. A. Wallach, and W. J. Dally, "The J-machine multicomputer: An architectural evaluation," *20th Ann. Int. Symp. Comput. Architecture,* May 1993, pp. 224–235.

[17] G. F. Pfister and V. A. Norton, "'Hot spot' contention and combining in multistage interconnection networks," *IEEE Trans. Comput.* vol. C-34, no. 10, Oct. 1985.

[18] P. Schweitzer, "Approximate analysis of multiclass closed networks of queues," *Int. Conf. Stochastic Control and Optimization,* 1979.

[19] H. S. Stone, *High Performance Computer Architecture.* Reading, MA: Addison-Wesley, 1987.

[20] M. K. Vernon, E. D. Lazowska, and J. Zahorjan, "An accurate and efficient performance analysis technique for multiprocessor snooping cache-consistency protocols," *Proc. 15th Int. Symp. Comput. Architecture,* June 1988.

[21] W. Weber and A. Gupta, "Exploring the benefits of multiple hardware contexts in a multiprocessor achitecture: Preliminary results," *16th Ann. Int. Symp. Comput. Architecture,* May 1989, pp. 273–280.

[22] D. L. Willick and D. L. Eager, "An analytic model of multistage interconnection networks," *Proc. ACM SIGMETRICS Conf. Measurement Modeling Comput. Syst.,* May 1990, pp. 192–202.

[23] P. Yew, N. Tzeng, and D. H. Lawrie, "Distributing hot-spot addressing in large-scale multiprocessor," *IEEE Trans. Comput.,* vol. C-36, Apr. 1987.

V.S. Adve (S'87–M'87–S'88–M'89–S'89–M'92) received the B.Tech. degree in electrical engineering from the Indian Institute of Technology, Bombay, in 1987, and the M.S. and Ph.D. degrees in computer science from the University of Wisconsin—Madison in 1989 and 1993, respectively.

He is a Research Scientist at the Center for Research on Parallel Computation at Rice University, Houston, TX. His research interests lie in the design and performance evaluation of hardware and software for parallel computer systems. His current research is focused on techniques for parallel program performance prediction, and on techniques and tools for the interactive performance evaluation and tuning of automatically parallelized programs.

Dr. Adve is a member of the IEEE Computer Society and ACM.

M.K. Vernon (S'82–M'92) received the B.S. degree with departmental honors in chemistry in 1975, and the M.S. and Ph.D. degrees in computer science in 1979 and 1983, respectively, from the University of California at Los Angeles.

In August 1983, she joined the Department of Computer Science, University of Wisconsin, Madison, WI, where she is currently an Associate Professor. Her research interests include techniques for parallel system performance analysis, and parallel architectures and systems.

Dr. Vernon received a National Science Foundation (NSF) Presidential Young Investigator Award in 1985 and an NSF Faculty Award for Women in Science and Engineering in 1991. She is currently on the Editorial Board of the IEEE Transactions on Software Engineering. She has served on the Computer Science Advisory Board of the Computer Measurement Group, the Board of Directors of ACM SIGMETRICS, and several NSF advisory committees, including the Advisory Committee for the Computing and information Science and Engineering Directorate and the 1993 NSF Blue Ribbon Panel on High Performance Computing. She is a member of ACM, the IEEE Computer Society, and the IFIP Working Group 7.3 on Information Processing System Modeling, Measurement, and Evaluation.

Optimum Broadcasting and Personalized Communication in Hypercubes

S. LENNART JOHNSSON MEMBER, IEEE, AND CHING-TIEN HO

Abstract—Effective utilization of communication resources is crucial for good overall performance in highly concurrent systems. In this paper, we address four different communication problems in Boolean n-cube configured multiprocessors: 1) one-to-all broadcasting: distribution of common data from a single source to all other nodes; 2) one-to-all personalized communication: a single node sending unique data to all other nodes; 3) all-to-all broadcasting: distribution of common data from each node to all other nodes; and 4) all-to-all personalized communication: each node sending a unique piece of information to every other node. Three new communication graphs for the Boolean n-cube are proposed for the routing, and scheduling disciplines provably optimum within a small constant factor are proposed. One of the new communication graphs consists of n edge-disjoint spanning binomial trees and offers optimal communication for case 1; a speedup with a factor of n over the spanning binomial tree for large data volumes. The other two new communication graphs are a balanced spanning tree and a graph composed of n rotated spanning binomial trees. With appropriate scheduling and concurrent communication on all ports of every processor, routings based on these two communication graphs offer a speedup of up to $n/2$, $n/2$, and $O(\sqrt{n})$ over the routings based on the spanning binomial tree for cases 2, 3, and 4, respectively. All three new spanning graphs offer optimal communication times for cases 2, 3, and 4 and concurrent communication on all ports of every processor. The graph consisting of n edge-disjoint spanning trees offers graceful degradation of performance under faulty conditions. Timing models and complexity analysis have been verified by experiments on a Boolean cube configured multiprocessor.

Index Terms—Balanced trees, Boolean cubes, broadcasting, binomial trees, multicast, personalized communication, routing.

I. INTRODUCTION

IN THIS paper, we investigate *broadcasting* and *personalized communication* on Boolean n-cube configured ensemble architectures. In *broadcasting,* a data set is copied from one node to all other nodes, or a subset thereof. In *personalized communication,* a node sends a unique data set to all other nodes, or a subset thereof. We consider broadcasting from a single source to all other nodes, *one-to-all broadcasting,* and concurrent broadcasting from all nodes to all other nodes, or *all-to-all broadcasting.* Broadcasting is used in a variety of linear algebra algorithms [10], [17], [19]

Manuscript received January 23, 1987; revised January 15, 1988. This work was supported in part by the Office of Naval Research under Contracts N00014-84-K-0043 and N00014-86-K-0564. This work was presented in part at the 1986 International Conference on Parallel Processing.

S. L. Johnsson is with the Department of Computer Science and Electrical Engineering, Yale University, New Haven, CT 06520 on leave at the Thinking Machine Corporation, Cambridge, MA 02142.

C.-T. Ho is with the Department of Computer Science, Yale University, New Haven, CT 06520.

IEEE Log Number 8928027.

such as matrix–vector multiplication, matrix–matrix multiplication, LU-factorization, and Householder transformations. It is also used in database queries and transitive closure algorithms [4]. The reverse of the broadcasting operation is *reduction,* in which the data set is reduced by applying operators such as addition/subtraction or max/min.

For personalized communication, we consider *one-to-all personalized communication* and *all-to-all personalized communication.* Fundamentally, the difference between broadcasting and personalized communication is that in the latter no replication/reduction of data takes place. The bandwidth requirement is highest at the root and is reduced monotonically towards the leaves. Personalized communication is used, for instance in transposing a matrix, and the conversion between different data structures [17], [22]. Matrix transposition is useful in the solution of tridiagonal systems on Boolean cubes for certain combinations of machine characteristics [20], [23] and for matrix–vector and matrix–matrix [21] multiplications.

For single-source broadcasting and personalized communication, a *one-to-all communication graph* is required. Graphs of minimum height have minimum propagation time which is the overriding concern for small data volumes, or a high overhead for each communication action. For large data volumes, it is important to use the bandwidth of a Boolean cube effectively, in particular, if each processor is able to communicate on all its ports concurrently. We propose three new spanning graphs for Boolean n-cubes of $N = 2^n$ nodes: one consisting of n edge-disjoint binomial tree (nESBT); one that consists of n rotated spanning binomial trees (nRSBT); and one *balanced tree* (SBnT), i.e., a tree with fan-out n at the root and approximately N/n nodes in each subtree. We prove some of the critical topological properties of the new one-to-all communication graphs and compare them to Hamiltonian paths and binomial tree embeddings. For each of the communications we consider, we prove the lower bounds in Table I.

We generalize the one-to-all communication to all-to-all communications and study the interleaving of communications from different sources by defining *all-to-all communication graphs* as the union of *one-to-all communication graphs.* We define scheduling disciplines for the four different communications as follows: 1) *one-to-all broadcasting;* 2) *one-to-all personalized communication,* 3) *all-to-all broadcasting,* and 4) *all-to-all personalized communication.* We show that for communication restricted to one port at a time, our spanning binomial tree scheduling results in communication times within a factor of two of the best known lower bounds for communications 2, 3, and 4. For case 1, the

TABLE I
TABLE I
LOWER BOUNDS FOR SOME BOOLEAN CUBE COMMUNICATIONS

Comm. model	Communication task	Lower bound
one-port	One-to-all broadcasting	$\max((M + n - 1)t_c, n\tau)$
	One-to-all personalized comm.	$\max((N - 1)Mt_c, n\tau)$
	All-to-all broadcasting	$\max((N - 1)Mt_c, n\tau)$
	All-to-all personalized comm.	$\max(\frac{nNM}{2}t_c, n\tau)$
n-port	One-to-all broadcasting	$\max((\frac{M}{n} + n - 1)t_c, n\tau)$
	One-to-all personalized comm.	$\max(\frac{(N-1)M}{n}t_c, n\tau)$
	All-to-all broadcasting	$\max(\frac{(N-1)M}{n}t_c, n\tau)$
	All-to-all personalized comm.	$\max(\frac{NM}{2}t_c, n\tau)$

scheduling we define for the n edge-disjoint spanning binomial trees completes within a factor of four of the best known lower bound, also for concurrent communication on all ports. For concurrent communication and *one-to-all personalized communication,* the schedules for both the n edge-disjoint and the rotated binomial trees are of optimal order, as are the schedules for the balanced graph. These graphs also yield *all-to-all* communication within a factor of two of the lower bound for arbitrary cube sizes and data volumes, except for the nESBT graph which allows optimum scheduling within a factor of 2 only asymptotically, Table XVI.

Communication in Boolean cubes has recently received significant interest due to the success of the Caltech Cosmic Cube project [30] and commercially available Boolean cube configured concurrent processors (from Intel, NCUBE [12], and Ametek, and cube-like architectures from Floating-Point Systems [11] and Thinking Machines Corporation [13]). Embedding of complete binary trees is treated in [33], [17], [29], [6], and [3]. Wu [33] also discusses the embedding of k-ary trees. Embedding of arbitrary binary trees is discussed in [3] and improved in [2]. Efficient routing using randomization for arbitrary permutations has been suggested by Valiant *et al.* [32]. Our algorithms attain a speedup of up to a factor of n for case 1 with *one-port* and *n-port* communication, and cases 2 and 4 with *n-port* communication over the best previously known algorithms [28]. For case 3 and *n-port* communication, the improvement is by a constant factor. Communication on hypercubes has also been studied independently by Fox and Furmanski [8] and Stout and Wager [31]. For case 1, the best algorithm in [8] is about a factor of two slower than the best algorithm presented here and in [14]. The best algorithm in [31] requires one less routing cycle. The nRSBT routing [24] for cases 2, 3, and 4 with *n-port* communication was discovered independently by Stout. However, the SBnT routing [14] described here performs better, or as well as the nRSBT routing. The nESBT routing degrades gracefully under faulty conditions. The analysis is compared to experimental data.

The outline of the paper is as follows. Notations, definitions, and general graph properties used throughout the paper are introduced in Section II. In Section III, one-to-all communication graphs are defined and characterized. Scheduling disciplines and associated complexity estimates are given in Section IV for *one-to-all broadcasting,* in Section V for *one-to-all personalized communication,* in Section VI for *all-to-all broadcasting,* and in Section VII for *all-to-all personalized communication.* Section VIII presents implementation results

for some of the communication algorithms on the Intel iPSC. Conclusion follows in Section IX.

II. PRELIMINARIES

In the following, node i has address $(i_{n-1}i_{n-2} \cdots i_0)$, and node s has address $(s_{n-1}s_{n-2} \cdots s_0)$. The bitwise Exclusive-OR operation is denoted $\oplus$, and throughout the paper $i \oplus s = c = (c_{n-1}c_{n-2} \cdots c_0)$ where $c_m = i_m \oplus s_m$. c is the *relative address* of node i with respect to node s. Address bits are numbered from 0 through $n - 1$ with the lowest order bit being the 0th bit. The mth bit corresponds to the mth dimension in a Boolean space. Caligraphic letters are used for sets. The set of *node* addresses is $\mathfrak{N} \equiv \{0, 1, \cdots, N - 1\}$, and the set of dimensions is $\mathfrak{D} \equiv \{0, 1, \cdots, n - 1\}$. $|\mathcal{S}|$ is used to denote the cardinality of a set $\mathcal{S}$. d or m is used to denote an arbitrary dimension, $d, m \in \mathfrak{D}$.

Definition 1: The *Hamming* distance between a pair of binary numbers, or nodes, i and j is $Hamming(i, j) = \sum_{m=0}^{n-1} (i_m \oplus j_m)$.

Definition 2: A *Boolean n-cube* is graph $B = (\mathcal{V}, \mathcal{E}^B)$ such that $\mathcal{V} = \mathfrak{N}$ and $\mathcal{E}^B = \{(i, j)| i \oplus j = 2^m, \forall m \in \mathfrak{D}, \forall i, j \in \mathfrak{N}\}$. An edge (i, j) such that $i \oplus j = 2^m$ is in dimension m, and nodes i and j are connected through the mth *port*.

An *edge* (i, j) is *directed* from node i to node j, and of unit length, i.e., $Hamming(i, j) = 1$. It is a $0 \rightarrow 1$ edge if the bit that differs in i and j is zero in i; otherwise, it is a $1 \rightarrow 0$ edge. In a directed graph, all edges are directed. A node with no edges directed to it is a *root (source)* node, and a node with no edges directed away from it is a *leaf (sink)* node. A node that is neither a leaf node nor a root node is an *internal* node. If (i, j) is a directed edge, then node i is the *parent* of node j, and j is a *child* of i.

Lemma 1 [18], [29]: A Boolean n-cube has $N = 2^n$ nodes, diameter n, $\binom{n}{x}$ nodes at Hamming distance x from a given node, and n edge-disjoint paths between any pair of nodes i and j. Of these n paths, $Hamming(i, j)$ are length $Hamming(i, j)$ and $n - Hamming(i, j)$ paths are of length $Hamming(i, j) + 2$. Every node has n edges directed to it and n edges directed away from it. The total number of (directed) communication links is nN.

Definition 3: With *rotation of a node* we mean a right cyclic rotation of its address, $Ro(i) = (i_0i_{n-1} \cdots i_2i_1)$. With *rotation of a graph* $G(\mathcal{V}, \mathcal{E})$ we mean a graph $Ro(G(\mathcal{V}, \mathcal{E})) = G(Ro(\mathcal{V}), Ro(\mathcal{E}))$, where $Ro(\mathcal{V}) = \{Ro(i)|\forall i \in \mathcal{V}\}$ and $Ro(\mathcal{E}) = \{(Ro(i), Ro(j))|\forall (i, j) \in \mathcal{E}\}$. Moreover, Ro^{-1} is left rotation and $Ro^k = Ro \circ Ro^{k-1}$ for all k.

The right rotation operation is also known as an *unshuffle* operation and the left rotation as a *shuffle* operation.

Definition 4: With *reflection of a node* we mean a bit-reversal of its address, $\text{Re}(i) = (i_0 i_1 \cdots i_{n-2} i_{n-1})$. With *reflection of a graph* $G(\mathcal{V}, \mathcal{E})$ we mean a graph $\text{Re}(G(\mathcal{V}, \mathcal{E})) = G(\text{Re}(\mathcal{V}), \text{Re}(\mathcal{E}))$, where $\text{Re}(\mathcal{V}) = \{\text{Re}(i) | \forall\, i \in \mathcal{V}\}$ and $\text{Re}(\mathcal{E}) = \{(\text{Re}(i), \text{Re}(j)) | \forall\, (i, j) \in \mathcal{E}\}$.

Definition 5: With *translation of a node* i by s we mean a bitwise Exclusive-OR of the addresses, $\text{Tr}(s, i) = c$. With *translation of a graph* $G(\mathcal{V}, \mathcal{E})$ with respect to node s, we mean a graph $\text{Tr}(s, G(\mathcal{V}, \mathcal{E})) = G(\text{Tr}(s, \mathcal{V}), \text{Tr}(s, \mathcal{E}))$, where $\text{Tr}(s, \mathcal{V}) = \{\text{Tr}(s, i) | \forall\, i \in \mathcal{V}\}$ and $\text{Tr}(s, \mathcal{E}) = \{(\text{Tr}(s, i), \text{Tr}(s, j)) | \forall\, (i, j) \in \mathcal{E}\}$.

Lemma 2: Rotations, reflections, and translations of a graph preserve the Hamming distance between nodes. The *rotation* operation Ro^k maps every edge in dimension d to dimension $(d - k) \bmod n$, the *reflection* operation maps every edge in dimension d to dimension $n - 1 - d$, and the *translation* operation preserves the dimension of every edge. *Rotation* and *reflection* preserve the direction of every edge. *Translation* reverses the direction of all edges in the dimensions for which $s_m = 1$, $m \in \mathcal{D}$.

Corollary 1: The topology of a graph remains unchanged under *rotation, reflection,* and *translation.*

Definition 6: For binary number i the *period* of i, $P(i) = \min_{m > 0} \text{Ro}^m(i) = i$. A binary number i is *cyclic* if $P(i) < n$; and *noncyclic,* otherwise. A *cyclic node* is a node with cyclic *relative* address.

The period of the number (011011) is 3. A cyclic node is defined only when the source node is given. Node (001000) is cyclic with respect the the source node (000001).

Definition 7: A *spanning tree* $T^{\text{id}}(s)$ rooted at node s of a Boolean cube is a tree containing all the nodes of the Boolean cube. id is used to identify different spanning trees. $T^{\text{id}}(s) = \text{Tr}(s, T^{\text{id}}(0))$.

Definition 8: For the Boolean n-cube a *one-to-all communication graph, o-graph,* with source node s is a connected, directed graph $G^{\text{id}}(s) = \text{Tr}(s, G^{\text{id}}(0))$ where $G^{\text{id}}(0)$ is either a spanning tree, $G^{\text{id}}(0) = T^{\text{id}}(0)$, or a composition of n distinctly rotated spanning trees, $G^{\text{id}}(0) = \bigcup_{d \in \mathcal{D}} \text{Ro}^d(T^{\text{id}'}(0))$. The weight of every edge in an *o-graph* is 1 if the graph is a tree; and $1/n$, otherwise. id$'$ identifies the generating spanning tree for the *o-graph.*

The weight $1/n$ is introduced to account for the data to be communicated being split into n peices for an *o-graph* composed of n spanning trees. There exist n paths from the root to any other node. If no two edges $\text{Ro}^\alpha(T^{\text{id}'}(0))$ and $\text{Ro}^\beta(T^{\text{id}'}(0))$ are mapped to the same cube edge $\forall \alpha, \beta \in \mathcal{D}, \alpha \neq \beta$, then the paths of the *o-graph* are *edge-disjoint* and there is no contention problem.

The root of a spanning tree has *level* 0. The node i in a spanning tree has a level which is one more than the level of its parent. The height h of a tree is the largest level of all the nodes.

Definition 9: For an *o-graph* G^{id}, the total weight of the edges in dimension d between levels l and $l + 1$ is denoted $e^{\text{id}}(d, l)$, and the total weight of edges in dimension d is $E^{\text{id}}(d)$.

Lemma 3: Given an *o-graph* $G^{\text{id}}(s) = \text{Tr}(s, G^{\text{id}}(0))$ where $G^{\text{id}}(0) = \bigcup_{d \in \mathcal{D}} \text{Ro}^d(T^{\text{id}'}(0))$, then $E^{\text{id}}(d) = (N - 1)/n$ and $e^{\text{id}}(d, l) = (1/n) \sum_{d \in \mathcal{D}} e^{\text{id}'}(d, l)$.

Proof: The lemma follows from Definition 9 and the rotation property in Lemma 2. ∎

We define three basic spanning trees: a *Hamiltonian* path T^H, a *spanning binomial tree* T^{SBT}, and a *spanning balanced n-tree* T^{SBnT}. These trees are used to form composition graphs that provide multiple paths (not necessarily edge-disjoint) to all other nodes.

For the definition/implementation of *o-graph* we use distributed algorithms that for any node compute the addresses of its set of children nodes, if any, and the address of the parent node, except for the root node. A node has one parent and a set of children nodes for each spanning tree used for the composition.

Definition 10: The *children*$^{\text{id}}(i, s, k)$ function generates the set of children addresses of node i in the kth spanning tree of $G^{\text{id}}(s)$. The *parent*$^{\text{id}}(i, s, k)$ function generates the address of the parent of node i in the kth spanning tree of $G^{\text{id}}(s)$. For the G^{id} being a spanning tree we omit the last parameter.

Definition 11: A *greedy spanning tree* rooted at node s of a Boolean n-cube is a spanning tree such that $\forall\, i \in \mathfrak{N}$, the level of node i is $Hamming(i, s)$. A *greedy o-graph* of a Boolean n-cube is a composition of greed spanning trees.

Lemma 4: A greedy *o-graph* contains only $0 \rightarrow 1$ edges "relative" to the root.

Lemma 5: A spanning tree is greedy iff $|\{i | Hamming(i, s) = l\}| = \binom{n}{l}$. A greedy *o-graph* is acyclic and of minimal height.

Corollary 2: If $G^{\text{id}}(0) = \bigcup_{d \in \mathcal{D}} \text{Ro}^d(T^{\text{id}}(0))$, and T^{id} is greedy, then $e^{\text{id}}(d, l) = (1/n)\binom{n}{l+1}$.

Lemma 5 follows from Definition 11 and Lemma 1. Corollary 2 follows from Lemmas 3 and 5.

Note that an *o-graph* of minimum height is not necessarily a greedy *o-graph*. In all-to-all personalized communication, only greedy *o-graphs* have scheduling disciplines that accomplish minimal data transfer time.

Definition 12: In *one-port* communication, a processor can only send *and* receive on one of its ports at any given time. The port on which a processor sends and receives can be different. In *n-port* communication, a processor can communicate on all its ports concurrently.

We also assume that there is an overhead, startup time τ, associated with each communication of B elements, each of which requires a transfer time t_c. B_{opt} denotes an optimal packet size. For the analysis, it is convenient to assume that communication takes place during distinct time intervals. The duration of a *routing cycle* is $\tau + B t_c$. Routing cycles are labeled from 0.

For *broadcasting*, the data are replicated $|children^{\text{id}}(i, s, k)|$ times in node i for spanning tree k of the *o-graph* $G^{\text{id}}(s)$. With *n-port* communication, and negligible time for replication, all ports are scheduled concurrently. With *one-port* communication, the order of communications on different ports is important.

In *personalized communication*, the source node sends a unique message to every other node. An internal node needs to receive and forward all the data for every node of the subtree of which it is a root. The ordering of data for a port is important for the communication time both for *one-port* and *n-port* communication.

The *scheduling discipline* defines the communication order for each port, and the order between ports for every nonleaf node. We assume the same data independent scheduling discipline for every node. The scheduling disciplines are completely specified later.

Definition 13: In a *reverse-breadth-first* scheduling discipline for *one-to-all personalized communication* based on an *o-graph* of height h, the root sends out the data for the nodes at level $h - p$ during the pth cycle, $0 \le p < h$. The data received by an internal node are propagated to the next level during the next cycle, if the data are not destined for the node itself. In a *postorder* [1] scheduling discipline, each node sends out the entire data set to each of its children nodes before accepting its own data.

The analysis of the complexity of the one-to-all personalized communication is considerably simplified for *n-port* communication and *reverse-breadth-first* scheduling if the root dominates the communication (in sending out the data). The following lemma characterizes the spanning trees for which the "root-dominant" property exists.

Lemma 6: Given a spanning tree, let $\phi^{id}(i, x)$ be the number of nodes at distance x from node i in the subtree rooted at node i. If for any child of the root, say node i, we have $\phi^{id}(i, x) \ge \phi^{id}(j, x)$ for any child node j of node i for all x, then the data transfer time of *n-port* one-to-all personalized communication based on *reverse-breadth-first* ordering is dominated by the data transfer over the edges from the root.

Proof: The lemma follows from the fact that with *reverse-breadth-first* scheduling, the propagation time for the internal nodes is at most the same as the transmission time for the root during each routing cycle. ∎

Definition 14: An *all-to-all communication graph, a-graph*, $G^{id}(*) = \cup_{s \in \mathfrak{N}} G^{id}(s)$.

The quantities $v^{id}(d, l)$ and $u^{id}(d, l)$ defined next are useful in deriving the time complexity of *all-to-all personalized communication* for the *a-graph*.

Definition 15: Define $v^{id}(d, l)$ of an *o-graph* as the total weight of all edges within all subtrees rooted at level $l + 1$ of all spanning trees with subtree roots connected to a parent node through an edge in dimension d, inclusive of the edge to the parent node. Let $S_d^{id} = \{j | j \in \mathcal{V}, (i, j) \in \mathcal{E}^{id} \text{ and } i \oplus j = 2^d\}$. Define $u^{id}(d, l)$ to be the total weight of edges terminating on all nodes k such that k is descendent of j at distance l, $\forall j \in S_d^{id}$.

Lemma 7: $v^{id}(d, l) = u^{id}(d, l) = \sum_{x=l}^{h-1} e^{id}(d, x) = 1/n \sum_{x=l}^{h-1} \sum_{d \in \mathfrak{D}} e^{id'}(d, x)$, $\forall l \in [0, h - 1]$, $d \in \mathfrak{D}$ for an *o-graph* $G^{id}(0) = \cup_{d \in \mathfrak{D}} \text{Ro}^d(T^{id'}(0))$, where h is the height of $T^{id'}$.

Proof: From the n distinct rotations and Lemma 2, it follows that $v^{id}(d, l) = 1/n \times$ (the sum of the number of nodes at levels x, $l + 1 \le x \le h$) of $T^{id'}$. Similarly, $u^{id}(d, l) = 1/n \times$ (the sum of the number of nodes at levels x, $l + 1 \le x \le h$) of $T^{id'}$. By Lemma 3, $e^{id}(d, l) = 1/n \times$ (the number of edges between levels l and $l + 1$) of $T^{id'} = 1/n \sum_{d \in \mathfrak{D}} e^{id'}(d, l)$. ∎

Corollary 3: If an *o-graph* $G^{id}(0) = \cup_{d \in \mathfrak{D}} \text{Ro}^d(T^{id'}(0))$ and $T^{id'}$ is greedy, then $v^{id}(d, l) = u^{id}(d, l) = 1/n \sum_{i=l+1}^{n} \binom{n}{i}$.

Proof: The corollary follows from Lemma 7 and Corollary 2. ∎

Lemma 8: For an *a-graph* $G^{id}(*)$, the total weight of communication graph edges mapped to every cube edge in dimension d is $E^{id}(d)$. The total weight of communication graph edges between levels l and $l + 1$ in dimension d is $e^{id}(d, l)$.

Proof: Since $G^{id}(*) = \cup_{s \in \mathfrak{N}} G^{id}(s) = \cup_{s \in \mathfrak{N}} \text{Tr}(s, G^{id}(0))$, every *o-graph* edge is mapped to a distinct cube edge in the same dimension through N distinct Exclusive-OR operations. Hence, the total weight of *a-graph* edges mapped to every cube edge in dimension d is $E^{id}(d)$. The bitwise Exclusive-OR operation preserves the topology of a spanning tree, and hence the number of edges at a given distance from the source node. ∎

III. Spanning Graphs

A. Three Spanning Trees

1) A Hamiltonian Path: A Hamiltonian path H originating at node 0 is defined by traversing the nodes of the Boolean cube in a *binary-reflected* Gray code [27] order with starting address equal to 0. Let the n-bit code of 2^n integers be $Gray(n)$. Two definitions of the code that are convenient to use are the following.

Definition 16: The *binary-reflected Gray code* on n bits is defined recursively as follows. Let $Gray(n) = (\hat{G}_0, \hat{G}_1, \cdots, \hat{G}_{2^n-2}, \hat{G}_{2^n-1})$.

Then $Gray(n + 1) = (0\hat{G}_0, 0\hat{G}_1, \cdots, 0\hat{G}_{2^n-2}, 0\hat{G}_{2^n-1}, 1\hat{G}_{2^n-1}, 1\hat{G}_{2^n-2}, \cdots, 1\hat{G}_1, 1\hat{G}_0)$, or alternatively, $Gray(n + 1) = (\hat{G}_0 0, \hat{G}_0 1, \hat{G}_1 1, \hat{G}_1 0, \hat{G}_2 0, \hat{G}_2 1, \cdots, \hat{G}_{2^n-1} 1, \hat{G}_{2^n-1} 0)$.

The following alternative definition is also useful for distributed routing algorithms. Let $T(n) = (t_0, t_1, \cdots, t_{2^n-2})$ be the sequence of dimensions on which a transition takes place in proceeding from integer 0 to integer $2^n - 1$ in the n-bit Gray code with the most significant bit labeled $n - 1$.

Definition 17: Then the *binary-reflected Gray code* can be defined through the recursion

$$T(n) = (T(n-1), n-1, T(n-1)), \qquad T(1) = 0.$$

Note that t_i is also the lowest order dimension with a 0-bit in the binary encoding of i. Let the binary encoding of $i = (i_{n-1} i_{n-2} \cdots i_0)$ and the Gray code encoding be $\hat{G}_i = (g_{n-1} g_{n-2} \cdots g_0)$. Then the conversions between binary and Gray code encoding are defined by $g_m = i_m \oplus i_{m+1}$, and conversely $i_m = g_{m+1} \oplus g_{m+2} \oplus \cdots \oplus g_{n-1}$.

2) A Spanning Binomial Tree: A 0-level binomial tree has one node. An n-level binomial tree is constructed out of two $(n - 1)$-level binomial trees by adding one edge between the roots of the two trees and by making either root the new root [1], [7]. The familiar spanning tree rooted in node 0 of a Boolean n-cube generated by complementing leading zeros of the binary encoding of a processor address i [9], [17], [26], [28], [29] is indeed a *spanning binomial tree* (SBT).

Definition 18: The spanning binomial tree rooted at node s,

$T^{\text{SBT}}(s)$, is defined as follows. Let p be such that $c_p = 1$ and $c_m = 0, \forall m \in \{p + 1, p + 2, \cdots, n - 1\} \equiv \mathfrak{M}^{\text{SBT}}(c)$ and let $p = -1$ if $c = 0$. The set $\mathfrak{M}^{\text{SBT}}(c)$ is the set of leading zeros of c. Then,

$$\text{children}^{\text{SBT}}(i, s) = \{(i_{n-1} i_{n-2} \cdots \bar{i}_m \cdots i_0)\},$$

$$\forall m \in \mathfrak{M}^{\text{SBT}}(c),$$

$$\text{parent}^{\text{SBT}}(i, s) = \begin{cases} \phi, & i = s; \\ (i_{n-1} i_{n-2} \cdots \bar{i}_p \cdots i_0), & i \neq s. \end{cases}$$

It is easy to verify that the parent and children functions are consistent, i.e., that node j is a child of node i iff node i is the parent of node j. Fig. 1 shows the $T^{\text{SBT}}(0)$ for a 4-cube.

Definition 19: Subtree k of the $T^{\text{SBT}}(s)$ consists of all nodes such that $c_k = 1$ and $c_m = 0, \forall m \in \{0, 1, \cdots, k - 1\}$.

Lemma 9: There are 2^{n-k-1} nodes in subtree k, and the maximum degree of any node at level l in subtree k is $n - k - l, 0 < l \leq n - k$.

Lemma 10: Let $\phi^{\text{SBT}}(i, s, x)$ be the number of nodes at distance x from node i in the subtree rooted at node i of the SBT rooted at node s. Then, $\phi^{\text{SBT}}(i, s, x) \geq \phi^{\text{SBT}}(j, s, x)$, if $j \in \text{children}^{\text{SBT}}(i, s)$.

Proof: From the definition of the SBT, the subtree rooted at node j is a connected subgraph of the subtree rooted at node i. ∎

3) A Spanning Balanced n-Tree and a Spanning Balanced Graph: In the *spanning balanced n-tree* [15], the node set is divided into n sets of nodes with approximately an equal number of nodes. Each such set forms a subtree of the source node. The maximum number of elements that needs to traverse any edge directed away from the source node is minimized for personalized communication.

Definition 20: Let $\mathcal{K}(i, s) = \{k_1, k_2, \cdots, k_m | 0 \leq k_1 < k_2 < \cdots < k_m < n\}$ be such that $\text{Ro}^\alpha(c) = \text{Ro}^\beta(c), \forall \alpha, \beta \in \mathcal{K}(i, s)$, and $\text{Ro}^\alpha(c) < \text{Ro}^\gamma(c), \forall \alpha \in \mathcal{K}(i, s), \gamma \notin \mathcal{K}(i, s)$. Then $\text{base}^{\text{SBnT}}(i, s) = k_1$.

For example, $\text{base}^{\text{SBnT}}((011100), 0) = 2$ and $\text{base}^{\text{SBnT}}((110100), (000010)) = 1$. Note that $|\mathcal{K}(i, s)| = n/P(c)$ where $P(c)$ is the period of c. The value of the base equals the minimum number of right rotations that minimized the value of c. For noncyclic nodes $|\mathcal{K}(i, s)| = 1$, but for a cyclic node c, $P(c) < n$ and $|\mathcal{K}(i, s)| > 1$. The notion of $\text{base}^{\text{SBnT}}$ is similar to the notion of the distinguished node used in [25] in that $\text{base}^{\text{SBnT}} = 0$ distinguishes a node from a generator set (necklace). To simplify the notation, we omit the subscript on k in the following.

Definition 21: Subtree k of the *spanning balanced n-tree* rooted at node s consists of all nodes $i \neq s$ such that $\text{base}^{\text{SBnT}}(i, s) = k$.

Note that all nodes in subtree k have $c_k = 1$, but not all with $c_k = 1$ are in the kth subtree.

Definition 22: Let $\text{base}^{\text{SBnT}}(i, s) = k$. For $c = 0$ let $p = -1$, else if $c = (00 \cdots 01_k 0 \cdots 0)$, then $p = k$, else let p be the first bit cyclically to the right of bit k that is equal to 1 in c, i.e., $c_p = 1$, and $c_m = 0, \forall m \in \{(p + 1) \bmod n, (p + 2) \bmod n, \cdots, (k - 1) \bmod n\} \equiv \mathfrak{M}^{\text{SBnT}}(i, s)$ with $k = n$ if c

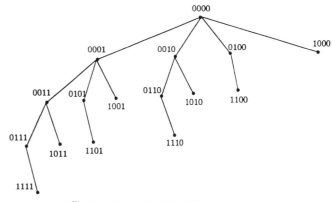

Fig. 1   A spanning binomial tree in a 4-cube.

$= 0$. The spanning tree $T^{\text{SBnT}}(s)$ is defined through

$$\text{children}^{\text{SBnT}}(i, s)$$

$$= \begin{cases} \{(i_{n-1} i_{n-2} \cdots \bar{i}_m \cdots i_0)\}, & \\ \quad \forall m \in \mathfrak{M}^{\text{SBnT}}(i, s), & \text{if } c = 0; \\ \{q_m = (i_{n-1} i_{n-2} \cdots \bar{i}_m \cdots i_0)\}, & \\ \quad \forall m \in \mathfrak{M}^{\text{SBnT}}(i, s) \text{ and } \text{base}^{\text{SBnT}}(q_m, s) & \\ \quad = \text{base}^{\text{SBnT}}(i, s), & \text{if } c \neq 0. \end{cases}$$

$$\text{parent}^{\text{SBnT}}(i, s) = \begin{cases} \phi, & \text{if } c = 0; \\ (i_{n-1} i_{n-2} \cdots \bar{i}_p \cdots i_0), & \text{otherwise.} \end{cases}$$

The $\text{parent}^{\text{SBnT}}$ function preserves the base, since for any node i with base k, c_p is the highest order bit of $\text{Ro}^k(c)$. Complementing this bit cannot change the base. It is also readily seen that the $\text{parent}^{\text{SBnT}}$ and $\text{children}^{\text{SBnT}}$ functions are consistent.

Theorem 1: The $\text{parent}^{\text{SBnT}}(i, s)$ function defines a spanning tree rooted at node s.

Proof: For every node i the $\text{parent}^{\text{SBnT}}(i, s)$ function generates a path to node s. Hence, the graph is connected. Moreover, the parent node of a node at distance l from node s is at distance $l - 1$ from node s, and each node only has one parent node. Hence, the graph is a spanning tree. ∎

Fig. 2 shows a spanning balanced 5-tree in a 5-cube.

Lemma 11: The SBnT is a greedy spanning tree.

Proof: From the definition of the $\text{parent}^{\text{SBnT}}(i, s)$ function, it follows that the distance from node i to node s is $\text{Hamming}(i, s)$. ∎

Lemma 12 [15]: Let $\phi^{\text{SBnT}}(i, s, x)$ be the number of nodes at distance x from node i in the subtree rooted at node i of the SBnT rooted at node s. Then, $\phi^{\text{SBnT}}(i, s, x) \geq \phi^{\text{SBnT}}(j, s, x)$, if $j \in \text{children}^{\text{SBnT}}(i, s)$.

Theorem 2: Excluding node $(\bar{s}_{n-1} \bar{s}_{n-2} \cdots \bar{s}_0)$, all the subtrees of the root of the SBnT are isomorphic, if n is a prime number. Furthermore, the kth subtree can be derived by $(k - j) \bmod n$ left rotation steps of each node of the jth subtree.

Proof: For n a prime number there are no cyclic nodes, except nodes with relative addresses $(00 \cdots 0)$ and $(11 \cdots 1)$. For all other nodes $|\mathcal{K}(i, s)| = 1$, and each generator set has n members. Any subtree has the same number of nodes as any other subtree at every level. It follows from the definition of

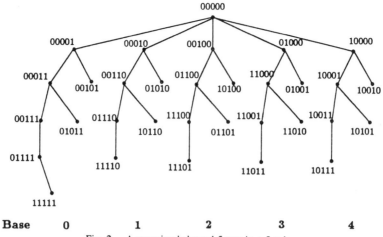

Fig. 2. A spanning balanced 5-tree in a 5-cube.

base_SBnT that if $j \in$ children_SBnT(i, s), then Ro$^k(j) \in$ children_SBnT (Ro$^k(i), s) \forall k \in \mathfrak{D}$. ∎

If n is not a prime number, then some subtrees of the root of the SBnT will contain more nodes than others. It can be shown that the number of nodes in a subtree is of $O(\frac{N}{n})$ [15]. The imbalance is illustrated in Table II. This imbalance is important for personalized communication. The number of elements transferred over the edges can be perfectly balanced in the sense that the maximum at any level is minimized by allowing multiple paths to cyclic nodes. With multiple paths to cyclic nodes, the graph is no longer a tree. We call the SBnT so modified a *spanning balanced graph* (SBG). The SBG can be defined as a composition of n distinctly rotated SBnT's as follows.

Definition 23: Define $G^{SBG}(0) = \bigcup_{d \in \mathfrak{D}} \text{Ro}^d(T^{SBnT}(0))$ and $G^{SBG}(s) = \text{Tr}(s, G^{SBG}(0))$. The number of different paths to a node i in an SBG rooted at node s is $n/P(i \oplus s)$ where $P(i)$ is the period of i.

B. Spanning Graphs Composed of n Spanning Trees

1) n Rotated Hamiltonian Paths:

Definition 24: The graph $G^{nRH}(s) = \text{Tr}(s, G^{nRH}(0))$, and $G^{nRH}(0) = \bigcup_{d \in \mathfrak{D}} \text{Ro}^d(T^H(0))$.

The paths generated through n distinct rotations of the $G^H(s)$ path are not edge-disjoint, for $n > 2$. For instance, the edge $(2, 6)$ is used in two paths of the graph $G^{3RH}(0)$, and these paths are part of every graph $G^{nRH}(0)$ for $n > 3$.

Lemma 13: Path Ro$^k(T^H(s))$ and path Ro$^m(T^H(s))$ share $2^{n-\alpha-1} + 2^{n-\beta-1} - 2$ directed edges, where $\alpha = (k - m)$ mod n and $\beta = (m - k)$ mod n.

Each of the n cube edges $((00 \cdots 01_d 0 \cdots 0), (00 \cdots 01_{(d+1)\bmod n} 1_d 0 \cdots 0))$, $\forall d \in \mathfrak{D}$ are shared by $n - 1$ paths for $s = 0$. Fig. 3 shows the graph $G^{3H}(0)$. The fact that the paths are not edge-joint limits the potential for pipelining.

Lemma 14: In graph $G^{nRH}(s)$, the edges between nodes at distance l and distance $l + 1$ from the source node are edge-disjoint for $l \in \mathfrak{N}$.

Proof: By construction the edges are in different dimensions. ∎

Note that even though the n rotated Hamiltonian paths are not edge-disjoint it is possible to have edge-disjoint embeddings of several Hamiltonian paths generated in other ways.

TABLE II
A COMPARISON OF SUBTREE SIZES OF SBT AND SBnT. THE LAST COLUMN CONTAINS THE RATIO OF SBnT(max) *to* $(N - 1)/n$

n	SBT(max)	SBnT(max)	SBnT(min)	$(N - 1)/n$	factor
2	2	2	1	1.50	1.33
3	4	3	2	2.33	1.29
4	8	5	3	3.75	1.33
5	16	7	6	6.20	1.13
6	32	13	9	10.50	1.24
7	64	19	18	18.14	1.05
8	128	35	30	31.88	1.10
9	256	59	56	56.78	1.04
10	512	107	99	102.30	1.05
11	1024	187	186	186.09	1.00
12	2048	351	335	341.25	1.03
13	4096	631	630	630.08	1.00
14	8192	1181	1161	1170.21	1.01
15	16384	2191	2182	2184.47	1.00
16	32768	4115	4080	4095.94	1.00
17	65536	7711	7710	7710.06	1.00
18	131072	14601	14532	14563.50	1.00
19	262144	27595	27594	27594.05	1.00
20	524288	52487	52377	52428.75	1.00

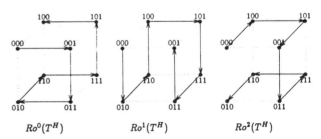

| $\text{Ro}^0(T^H)$ | $\text{Ro}^1(T^H)$ | $\text{Ro}^2(T^H)$ |

Fig. 3. Three rotated binary-reflected Gray code paths in a 3-cube.

Indeed, there exist n undirected edge-disjoint Hamiltonian cycles in a $2n$-cube [34]–[36]. Fig. 4 shows two of the four directed Hamiltonian cycles. The other two cycles are of a reversed direction.

2) n Rotated Spanning Binomial Trees:

Definition 25: The graph $G^{nRSBT}(s) = \text{Tr}(s, G^{nRSBT}(0))$, and $G^{nRSBT}(0) = \bigcup_{d \in \mathfrak{D}} \text{Ro}^d(T^{SBT}(0))$.

Fig. 5 shows the nRSBT graph of a 3-cube. In general, a cube edge (i, j) is part of several rotated SBT's. The number on each cube edge in the figure shows the sum of the weights of the graph edges mapped onto it.

Lemma 15: For any node in the graph $G^{nRSBT}(0)$, except the root, the weight of the incoming cube edge in dimension d is

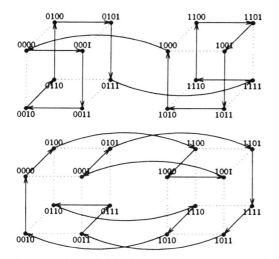

Fig. 4. Four directed edge-disjoint Hamiltonian cycles in a 4-cube. Only two cycles are shown. The other two are of a reversed direction.

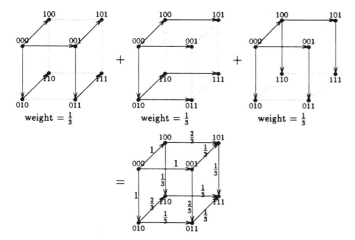

Fig. 5. Three rotated spanning binomial trees as an *o-graph* in a 3-cube.

$(p + 1)/n$, where p is the number of consecutive 0-bits immediately to the left of bit d.

Proof: A node in the SBT graph has an incoming edge in dimension d if the bit in dimension d is the highest order bit that is one. In the nRSBT graph, the number of incoming

in $\text{Ro}^m(G^{\text{SBT}}(0))$ for $m = \{d + 1, d + 2, \cdots, d + p + 1\}$ i.e., in these $p + 1$ SBT's, bit d is the last bit complemented in reaching node j. ∎

For instance, node (011001) has an incoming cube edge in dimension 0 with weight 1/2, an incoming edge in dimension 3 weighted 1/6, and an incoming edge in dimension 4 weighted 1/3.

Corollary 4: The sum of the weights of incoming edges is 1 for every node, except the source node.

Proof: From Lemma 15, the weight of an incoming edge is equal to the number of dimensions between the dimension considered and the next higher dimension with a 1-bit. ∎

Lemma 16: In any dimension, the edges of the nRSBT graph are only mapped to half of the cube edges.

Proof: Rotation does not change the direction of edges. ∎

3) n Edge-Disjoint Spanning Binomial Trees: The nESBT (n edge-disjoint spanning binomial trees) graph is composed of n SBT's with one tree rooted at each of the nodes adjacent to the source node. The SBT's are rotated such that the source node of the nESBT graph is in the smallest subtree of each SBT. The nESBT graph is then obtained by reversing the edges from the roots of the SBT's to the source node.

Definition 26: The nESBT graph $G^{\text{nESBT}}(s) = \text{Tr}(s, G^{\text{nESBT}}(0))$, where $G^{\text{nESBT}}(0) = \cup_{d \in \mathfrak{D}} T^{\text{SBT}}d(0)$, and $T^{\text{SBT}}d(0) = \text{Tr}(2^d, \text{Ro}^{n-d-1}(T^{\text{SBT}}(0)))$ (with the root being node 0 instead of node 2^d).

Fig. 6 shows an nESBT graph in a 3-cube. The nESBT graph is not a tree, and contains cycles. Every node appears in every subtree of the source node. The height of the nESBT graph is $n + 1$, since the source node is adjacent to all the roots of the SBT's used in the definition of the nESBT graph. The number of distinct edges in the n SBT's is $n(N - 1)$. An alternative definition of G^{nESBT} is through the functions children^{nESBT} and parent^{nESBT} below.

Definition 27: For a given k, let p be such that $c_p = 1$ and $c_m = 0, \forall m \in \{(p + 1) \bmod n, (p + 2) \bmod n, \cdots, (k - 1) \bmod n\}$. For $c = (00 \cdots 01_k 0 \cdots 0)$, $p = k$. Then $\mathfrak{M}^{\text{nESBT}}(i, s, k) = \{(p + 1) \bmod n, (p + 2) \bmod n, \cdots, (k - 1) \bmod n\}$. The children and parent of node i in the kth spanning tree, $T^{\text{SBT}}k(s)$, are

$$\text{children}^{\text{nESBT}}(i, s, k) = \begin{cases} \{(i_{n-1}i_{n-2} \cdots \bar{i}_k \cdots i_0)\}, & \text{if } c = 0; \\ \{(i_{n-1}i_{n-2} \cdots \bar{i}_m \cdots i_0)\}, \forall m \in \mathfrak{M}^{\text{nESBT}}(i, s, k) \cup \{k\}, & \text{if } c_k = 1, p \neq k; \\ \{(i_{n-1}i_{n-2} \cdots \bar{i}_m \cdots i_0)\}, \forall m \in \mathfrak{M}^{\text{nESBT}}(i, s, k), & \text{if } c_k = 1, p = k; \\ \phi, & \text{if } c_k = 0, c \neq 0. \end{cases}$$

$$\text{parent}^{\text{nESBT}}(i, s, k) = \begin{cases} \phi, & \text{if } c = 0; \\ (i_{n-1}i_{n-2} \cdots \bar{i}_k \cdots i_0), & \text{if } c_k = 0, c \neq 0; \\ (i_{n-1}i_{n-2} \cdots \bar{i}_p \cdots i_0), & \text{if } c_k = 1. \end{cases}$$

edges (i, j) to node j is equal to the number of graphs $\text{Ro}^m(G^{\text{SBT}}(0))$, $m \in \mathfrak{D}$ such that there exists an edge (i^m, j^m), where $i = \text{Ro}^m i^m$ and $j = \text{Ro}^m j^m$. Such an edge occurs

Dimension p is the first dimension to the right of dimension k, cyclically, which has a bit equal to one. All nodes with $c_k = 0$, except node s, are leaf nodes of the kth subtree (or kth

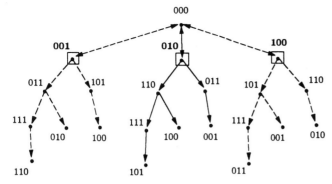

Fig. 6. Subtrees of an nESBT viewed as SBT's.

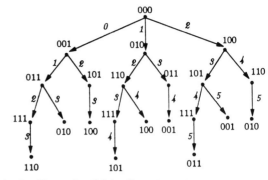

Fig. 7. Three edge-disjoint directed spanning trees in a 3-cube.

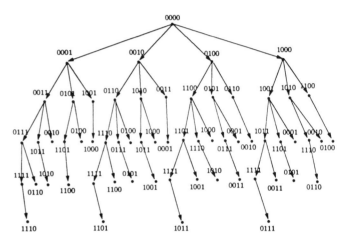

Fig. 8. Four edge-disjoint directed spanning trees in a 4-cube.

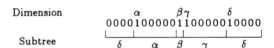

Fig. 9. Scheduling of broadcasting operations for a node with nESBT routing.

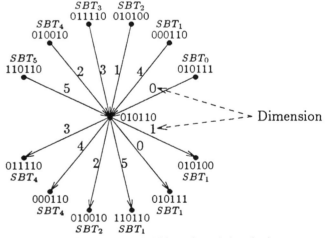

Fig. 10. Parents and children of a node in a 6-cube.

spanning tree). Conversely, all nodes with $c_k = 1$ are internal nodes of the kth subtree. The exceptional connection to node 0 is handled by the conditions on p. The first case defines the children for the source node, the second defines the set of children nodes of internal nodes of the kth subtree, except the node at level 1. The third case handles the node at level 1, and the last case handles the leaf nodes. Figs. 7 and 12 show that the three subtrees (spanning trees) of a 3ESBT graph are edge-disjoint. The lables on the edges will be used later. Fig. 8 shows a 4ESBT graph with source node 0. Every 1-bit in the node address divides the outgoing edges into distinct sets. The set of 0-bits to the right of 1-bit defines children nodes for a spanning subtree with the same index as the dimension of the 1-bit, Fig. 9.

Theorem 3: The n subtrees of the nESBT graph are edge-disjoint.

Proof: We only need to prove that for an arbitrary node the address of its parent node in each of the n subtrees is obtained by complementing a distinct bit.

From the definition of the children$^{\text{nESBT}}(i, s, k)$ [or parent$^{\text{nESBT}}(i, s, k)$] function, it is clear that a node is a leaf node of the kth subtree iff $c_k = 0$, with the exception of node s. If a node is a leaf node in a particular subtree, then its parent address in that subtree is obtained by complementing the corresponding bit in its address (bit k for the kth subtree). If a node is an internal node of the kth subtree, then the corresponding bit is 1, and the parent address is obtained by complementing the first bit cyclically to the right of the kth address bit that is equal to 1. Hence, the addresses of the parent nodes for all the subtrees of which the node is an internal node are also obtained by complementing distinct bits. ∎

Fig. 10 shows the parent and children of one node in a 6-cube. The numbers on the edgs are the dimensions through which the node connects to its parents or children nodes in different subtrees. The labels on the nodes denote the subtree to which the parent and children nodes belong.

Corollary 5: There exists an edge-disjoint embedding of n spanning binomial trees in an n-cube.

Corollary 6: The nESBT graph for a Boolean n-cube is a directed graph, such that all directed cube edges, except those incident on the source node, appear precisely once in the nESBT graph.

Proof: Follows from Theorem 3. ∎

Corollary 7: The in-degree and the out-degree of any node

in an nESBT graph is n, with the exception that the source has in-degree 0 and all the neighbors of the source have out-degree $n - 1$.

Theorem 4: The height of the nESBT graph is minimal among all possible configurations of n edge-disjoint spanning trees.

TABLE III
SOME TOPOLOGICAL CHARACTERISTICS OF SOME *o-graphs*

Graph	$E(d)$	$e(d,l)$	$v(d,l)$	$u(d,l)$
G^H	2^{n-d-1}	0, $d \neq t_l$ or 1, o.w.	0, $d \neq t_l$ or $N-l-1$, o.w.	$\frac{N}{2^{d+1}} - \left\lceil \frac{l-2^d+1}{2^{d+1}} \right\rceil$
G^{nRH}	$\frac{N-1}{n}$	$\frac{1}{n}$	$\frac{1}{n}(N-l-1)$	$\frac{1}{n}(N-l-1)$
G^{SBT}	2^d	$\binom{d}{l}$	$\binom{d}{l}2^{n-d-1}$	$\binom{n-d-1}{l}2^d$
G^{nRSBT}	$\frac{N-1}{n}$	$\frac{1}{n}\binom{n}{l+1}$	$\frac{1}{n}\sum_{i=l+1}^{n}\binom{n}{i}$	$\frac{1}{n}\sum_{i=l+1}^{n}\binom{n}{i}$
G^{nESBT}	$\frac{N-1}{n}$	1, $l=0$; $n-1$, $l=1$; $\frac{1}{n}\binom{n}{l}$, $l \geq 2$	$N-1$, $l=0$; $N-2$, $l=1$; $\frac{1}{n}\sum_{i=l}^{n}\binom{n}{i}$, $l \geq 1$	$\frac{1}{n}\sum_{i=l+1}^{n}\binom{n}{i}$
G^{SBG}	$\frac{N-1}{n}$	$\frac{1}{n}\binom{n}{l+1}$	$\frac{1}{n}\sum_{i=l+1}^{n}\binom{n}{i}$	$\frac{1}{n}\sum_{i=l+1}^{n}\binom{n}{i}$

Proof: To prove that with n edge-disjoint spanning trees, the height $n + 1$ is minimal, we prove that n disjoint spanning trees with height n is impossible. The total number of directed edges in an n-cube is nN, but those n directed edges incident on the source node are not used. Each spanning tree has $N - 1$ edges. Hence, every eligible edge is used by the n edge-disjoint spanning trees. It follows that the edges directed out from the node with address $(\bar{s}_{n-1}\bar{s}_{n-2} \cdots \bar{s}_0)$ also must be used, and since this node is at distance n from the source node, the theorem follows. ∎

Lemma 17: The number of nodes at level l of a subtree of the nESBT graph is

$$
\begin{cases}
\binom{n-1}{l-1} + \binom{n-1}{l-2} = \binom{n}{l-1}, \\
\qquad \text{for } n+1 \geq l \geq 1, \; l \neq 2; \\
1, \qquad \text{for } l = 0; \\
n-1, \qquad \text{for } l = 2.
\end{cases}
$$

Proof: Follows directly from the definition. ∎

Lemma 18: Let $\phi^{nESBT}(i, s, x)$ be the number of nodes at distance x from node i in the subtree rooted at node i of the nESBT rooted at node s. Then, $\phi^{nESBT}(i, s, x) \geq \phi^{nESBT}(j, s, x)$, if $j \in \text{children}^{nESBT}(i, s)$.

Proof: By Definition 26, each subtree of the nESBT is an SBT with the smallest subtree removed. The lemma can be shown by Lemmas 10, 17, and 9. ∎

C. Summary of Topological Properties of the Communication Graphs

The topological characteristics used for the complexity analysis are summarized in Table III.

With respect to the entry for the SBT graph in Table III note that $\binom{x}{y} = 0$ if $x < y$. Moreover,

$$
\max_{d} v^{SBT}(d, l) = v^{SBT}(\min(2l, n-1), l) =
\begin{cases}
\binom{2l}{l} 2^{n-2l-1}, & \text{if } l \in \left\{ 0, \cdots, \left\lfloor \frac{n-1}{2} \right\rfloor \right\}; \\
\binom{n-1}{l}, & \text{if } l \in \left\{ \left\lfloor \frac{n+1}{2} \right\rfloor, \cdots, n-1 \right\}.
\end{cases}
$$

The entries in Table III for the SBG graph can be proved by Lemmas 3 and 11 and Corollaries 2 and 3. The characteristics for the nRH graph can be proved from Definition 24 and Lemmas 3 and 7, and the entries for the nRSBT graph proved using Definition 25, Corollaries 2, 3, and the fact that T^{SBT} is greedy. The nESBT properties can be proved using Definition 26 and Lemmas 3, 7, and 17.

IV. ONE-TO-ALL BROADCASTING

Lemma 19: A lower bound for *one-to-all broadcasting* with *one-port* communication is $\max((M + n - 1)t_c, n\tau)$, and $\max((\lceil M/n \rceil + n - 1)t_c, n\tau)$ for *n-port* communication.

Proof: The height of any *o-graph* is at least n. The root needs a time of Mt_c (or $\lceil M/n \rceil t_c$) to send out the data. An additional delay of at least $(n - 1)t_c$ is required to reach the node at maximum distance from the root. ∎

With $M = 1$ a tight lower bound is $n(t_c + \tau)$ both for *one-port* and *n-port* communication. This bound is realized by SBT routing and appropriate scheduling. In fact, it can be shown that with $M = 1$ and *one-port* communication, any routing for broadcasting that yields the lower bound is topologically equivalent to the graph G^{SBT}. With *n-port* communication any *o-graph* of height n can realize the lower bound communication for $M = 1$. The scheduling discipline we propose for the graph G^{nESBT} yields the lowest communication complexity of the broadcasting algorithms we consider, both for *one-port* and *n-port* communication, except $B_{opt} = M$ for *one-port* communication and $B_{opt} = M/n$ for *n-port* communication. For these two cases, our scheduling for the graph G^{nESBT} is inferior only by 1 routing cycle. With $1 < M \leq n$ and *n-port* communication, our scheduling for the graph G^{nRSBT} yields the lower bound, $n(t_c + \tau)$.

A. The Time Complexity of One-to-All Broadcasting

Table IV summarizes the routing algorithms and scheduling disciplines we have analyzed. The estimated communication times are summarized in Table V. For an *o-graph* composed of n spanning trees, the data set M is divided into n approximately equal size subsets, and each such subset communicated by one of the spanning subtrees. If the trees are not edge-disjoint, we assume no pipelining.

TABLE IV
SCHEDULING DISCIPLINES FOR ONE-TO-ALL BROADCASTING

Comm.	Routing	Scheduling discipline
one-port	H	Pipeline.
	SBT	All data for a port at once. Tallest remaining subtree first.
	nRSBT	All data for the tallest remaining subtree of the spanning trees $0, 1, \ldots, p$ at once during routing cycle $p < n$, and all data for the tallest remaining subtrees of all spanning trees during cycles $n \le p < 2n - 1$. For the source $B = \frac{p+1}{n}M$ for $p < n$, and $B = \frac{2n-p-1}{n}M$ for $n \le p < 2n - 1$.
	nESBT	The source node sends to spanning trees $0, 1, \ldots, n - 1$ cyclically, i.e., pipeline among n spanning trees. The internal nodes always propagate (replicate) to the tallest subtree of the same spanning tree first.
n-port	SBT	Pipelining for each subtree, subtrees concurrently.
	nRSBT	All data at once for the tallest remaining subtree of every spanning tree. (The subtrees of each spanning tree are treated sequentially, and spanning trees concurrently.)
	nESBT	Pipelining for each subtree; subtrees and spanning trees concurrently.

TABLE V
THE COMPLEXITY OF ONE-TO-ALL BROADCASTING

Comm.	Routing	T	B_{opt}	T_{min}
one-port	H	$(M + (N - 2)B)t_c + (\lceil \frac{M}{B} \rceil + N - 2)\tau$	$\sqrt{\frac{M\tau}{(N-2)t_c}}$	$(\sqrt{Mt_c} + \sqrt{(N-2)\tau})^2$
	SBT	$Mnt_c + \lceil \frac{M}{B} \rceil n\tau$	M	$n(Mt_c + \tau)$
	nRSBT	$nMt_c + (2\sum_{i=1}^{n-1}\lceil \frac{M_i}{nB} \rceil + \lceil \frac{M}{B} \rceil)\tau$	M	$nMt_c + (2n - 1)\tau$
	nESBT	$(M + nB)t_c + (\lceil \frac{M}{B} \rceil + n)\tau$	$\sqrt{\frac{M\tau}{nt_c}}$	$(\sqrt{Mt_c} + \sqrt{n\tau})^2$
n-port	SBT	$(M + (n - 1)B)t_c + (\lceil \frac{M}{B} \rceil + n - 1)\tau$	$\sqrt{\frac{M\tau}{(n-1)t_c}}$	$(\sqrt{Mt_c} + \sqrt{(n-1)\tau})^2$
	nRSBT	$Mt_c + \lceil \frac{M}{nB} \rceil n\tau$	$\frac{M}{n}$	$Mt_c + n\tau$
	nESBT	$(\frac{M}{n} + nB)t_c + (\lceil \frac{M}{Bn} \rceil + n)\tau$	$\frac{1}{n}\sqrt{\frac{M\tau}{t_c}}$	$(\sqrt{\frac{Mt_c}{n}} + \sqrt{n\tau})^2$

For the graph G^{nRH}, the n paths are not edge-disjoint. But, all edges at a given distance from the source are mapped to different cube edges. Sending the entire data set M/n for each path concurrently is contention free. The data transfer time is an order of N/n higher than that of the H routing with pipelining. For nRSBT routing, the number of elements traversing every edge from the root is the same as in the SBT routing, and the transmission time is bounded from below by nMt_c with *one-port* communication. This time is an order of n higher than the lower bound.

Theorem 5: For a fixed packet size, the number of routing cycles to broadcast n packets by nRSBT routing is bounded from below by $2n - 1$ for *one-port* and n for *n-port* communication.

Proof: For *one-port (n-port)* communication, the root needs n (1) cycles to send out n packets, and the last packet has a latency of $n - 1$ cycles for a fixed packet size. ∎

With *one-port* communication, our scheduling discipline for the nRSBT routing completes in $2n - 1$ routing cycles for a packet size $B \ge M$. With *n-port* communication the scheduling of the data for each SBT used in the nRSBT graph is made as in the case of *one-port* communication for a single SBT. Since the SBT's are rotated, all ports of the root are used in every routing cycle until the last packet leaves the root. Data for the mth SBT is sent across dimension $(m + p)$ mod n during cycle p. There is no edge-conflict for this nonpipe-

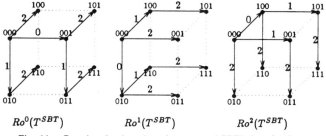

$Ro^0(T^{SBT})$ $Ro^1(T^{SBT})$ $Ro^2(T^{SBT})$

Fig. 11. Broadcasting based on three rotated SBT's in a 3-cube.

lined routing. Fig. 11 shows the routing of the three distinctly rotated SBT's in a 3-cube. The labels on the edges represent the routing cycle.

The number of routing cycles to broadcast n packets by nESBT routing is bounded from below by $2n$ for *one-port* and $n + 1$ for *n-port* communication, since the height of the graph is $n + 1$. The scheduling discipline for *one-port* communication and nESBT routing is defined by labeling the edges of the nESBT graph. The labels define the routing cycles during which the first packet arrives through that graph edge. We first define the edge label in the 0th spanning tree of the nESBT graph. Edges in dimension m are labeled m, except that the labels of the edges to the leaf nodes are labeled n. The labels of the edges in the kth spanning tree are defined by adding k to the label of the corresponding edges in the 0th spanning tree.

Fig. 7 shows an nESBT graph for a 3-cube labeled by the

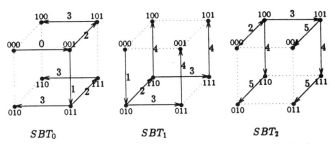

Fig. 12. Scheduling in an nESBT graph with *one-port* communication.

TABLE VI
NUMBER OF CYCLES PER DISTINCT PACKET (LEFT) AND PROPAGATION
DELAY (RIGHT)

Routing	# of cyc. per pkt.		Propagation delay
	one-port	*n-port*	*one- & n-port*
H	1	1	$N - 1$
SBT	n	1	n
nRSBT	n	1	n
nESBT	1	$\frac{1}{n}$	$n + 1$

algorithm above. Fig. 12 shows a different view of the labels of the three composed spanning trees.

Theorem 6: For the nESBT graph, the scheduling discipline defined by the labeling scheme allows conflict-free *one-port* communication.

Proof: It follows from the labeling scheme that edges in dimension m are labeled m (mod n). Also, for each spanning tree, the label of the outgoing edges of any node is greater than the label of the incoming edge. ∎

The largest label of all the input edges is $2n - 1$. Broadcasting the first n packets (one packet per subtree) can be done in $2n$ cycles. The complexity for *one-port* nESBT routing follows directly from the definition of the scheduling discipline, and the proof of it being contention free. For *n-port* communication, it is easy to determine the time of arrival of messages. The path length between nodes s and i in the kth spanning tree is equal to

$$\begin{cases} \|c\|, & \text{if } c_k = 1; \\ \|c\| + 2, & \text{if } c_k = 0, \end{cases}$$

where $\|c\|$ is the number of 1-bits in c. The input ports of node i that correspond to bits that are equal to 1 in the binary encoding of c receive the first element during the $(\|c\| - 1)$th routing cycle. The other input ports receive the first element during the $(\|c\| + 1)$th cycle.

B. Summary of One-to-All Broadcasting

In general, the data set to be broadcast is divided into a number of distinct packets. If the *o-graph* is a spanning tree, then every packet needs to be sent on every port of the root. The number of routing cycles required by the root to complete the communication of each distinct packet is summarized on the left of Table VI and the maximum propagation delay is summarized on the right.

In the nRSBT routing, every packet needs to be routed on every port because of the edge sharing. Note, that broadcasting by Hamiltonian path routing may be faster than by SBT routing depending on the values of M, t_c, τ and N. With *n-port* communication, the source can send out n distinct packets every cycle in the nESBT routing since the spanning trees are edge-disjoint, but only n packets every n cycles for the nRSBT routing.

For *n-port* communication, the data transmission time is reduced by a factor of approximately n for an arbitrary packet size in the SBT, nRSBT, and nESBT routings and the schedulings defined in Table IV. Optimizing the packet size makes the number of routing cyles proportional to the height of the *o-graph*. The data transmission times for the optimum packet sizes and *n-port* communication are approximately a

factor of n less than the transmission times for *one-port* communication with optimized buffer and an *o-graph* for which the root has degree n.

The nESBT routing always offers a reduction in bandwidth requirement for individual communication links by a factor of approximately n over the SBT and nRSBT routings. The nESBT routing offers a speedup of up to n over SBT and nRSBT routings for sufficiently large values of M, both for *one-port* and *n-port* communication. Communication complexities of broadcasting based on the H, SBT, and nRSBT algorithms are compared to that based on the nESBT in Table VII.

V. ONE-TO-ALL PERSONALIZED COMMUNICATION

In personalized communication, no replication of information takes place during distribution, nor is there any reduction during the reverse operation; the root has M elements for every node.

Lemma 20: The data transmission time for *one-to-all personalized communication* is bounded from below by $(N - 1)Mt_c$ for *one-port* communication, and by $((N - 1)M/n)t_c$ for *n-port* communication. A lower bound for the total time is max $((N - 1)Mt_c, n\tau)$, and max $(((N - 1)M/n)t_c, n\tau)$, respectively.

Proof: The root needs to send out $(N-1)/M$ elements. ∎

In SBT routing for personalized communication the maximum number of nodes connected to the root through one of its edges is $NM/2$, and a data transmission time of the order given in the lemma is not achievable for *n-port* communication. In an SBnT graph, all edges of the root connect subtrees of approximately equal size. For the SBG, nRSBT, and nESBT graphs, all outgoing (cube) edges of the root transmit the same amount of data, $(N - 1)M/n$.

A. The Time Complexity of Personalized Communication

The general strategy for personalized communications is to schedule the data for the most remote nodes first. With *n-port* communication the ordering between ports is irrelevant, and a *reverse-breadth-first* ordering for each port of each node is the scheduling discipline. For *one-port* communication the scheduling disciplines depend on the *o-graph*, Table VIII.

Lemma 21: Scheduling nodes by complementing their binary addresses results in port communications in a binary-reflected Gray code order for *one-port* SBT routing.

Note that for *one-port* communication, scheduling the tallest remaining subtree first for each node recursively has the same complexity as the suggested discipline, but if certain

TABLE VII
RELATIVE COMPLEXITIES OF ONE-TO-ALL BROADCASTING

Communication model	Routing	One packet	$B = B_{opt}$, $\tau \gg M t_c$	$B = B_{opt}$, $n^2\tau \ll M t_c$
one-port	H/nESBT	$\frac{N-1}{n+1}$	$\frac{N-2}{n}$	1
	SBT/nESBT	$\frac{n}{n+1}$	≈ 1	n
	nRSBT/nESBT	$\frac{n}{n+1}$	≈ 2	n
n-port	H/nESBT	$\frac{N-1}{n+1}$	$\frac{N-2}{n}$	n
	SBT,nRSBT/nESBT	$\frac{n}{n+1}$	≈ 1	n

TABLE VIII
SCHEDULING DISCIPLINES FOR ONE-TO-ALL PERSONALIZED
COMMUNICATION

Comm.	Routing	Scheduling discipline
one-port	H	Order nodes by decreased distance, pipeline.
	SBT	Order nodes by complementing their binary addresses.
	nESBT	All data for the tallest remaining subtree for each spanning tree.
	nRSBT	All data for the tallest remaining subtree of the spanning trees $0, 1, \ldots, p$ at once during routing cycle $p < n$, and all data for the tallest remaining subtrees of all spanning trees during cycles $n \le p < 2n - 1$. For the source $B = N(1 - \frac{1}{2^{p+1}})\frac{M}{n}$ for $p < n$, and $B = N(\frac{1}{2^{p+1-n}} - \frac{1}{N})\frac{M}{n}$ for $n \le p < 2n - 1$.
	SBG	Order nodes by decreasing distance for each subtree. Order subtrees cyclically.
n-port	All	Order nodes in *reverse-breadth-first* order. All subtrees (spanning trees) are scheduled concurrently.

overlap between communications on different ports is possible, as on the Intel iPSC, then the discipline we adopt yields a lower time complexity if $M \ge B$.

B. Summary of One-to-All Personalized Communication

Tables IX and X summarize the communication complexities of personalized communication. For the SBT routing and *one-port* communication, our scheduling discipline yields a time complexity within a factor of two of the lower bound, providing the packet size is sufficiently large. The data transmission time of the nRSBT scheduling discipline is the same as the lower bound, $M(N - 1)t_c$; however, the minimum number of routing cycles is $2n - 1$. For the SBG routing and $B \ge (N - 1)M/n$, the root needs to perform only one communication per subtree, and completes the communication in time $T = (N - 1)Mt_c + n\tau$. But, an additional $n - 1$ routing cycles are needed to complete the communication. An upper bound on the time for personalized communication with unbounded packet size is $T = N(1 + (2 \log n)/n)Mt_c + (2n - 1)\tau$ for SBG routing [15]. The number of routing cycles is almost twice that of the SBT personalized communication and the total transfer time is higher by a lower order term. With a packet size of $(N - 1)M/n$, the number of routing cycles is approximately $2n$ for SBT, nESBT, nRSBT, and SBG communication. With *one-port* communication and a packet size $B \le M$, the complexities of SBT, nRSBT, SBG, and H communications are approximately the same.

With *n-port* communication and *reverse-breadth-first* scheduling, the data transmission time of the SBT, nESBT, nRSBT, and SBG routings are all dominated by the root by Lemmas 6, 10, 12, and 18. The number of element transfers is approximately the same for all ports of the root except for the SBT communication. The number of routing cycles and the transmission time of the nESBT, SBG, and nRSBT communications are lower than that of the SBT by a factor of $1/2n$ for a packet size $B \le M$. With a sufficiently large packet size all communications yield a minimum of n routing cycles, with the exception of the nESBT, which requires one more cycle. The optimum packet size for the nESBT, nRSBT, and SBG communications is $\sqrt{2/\pi}NM/n^{3/2}$, compared to $NM/\sqrt{2\pi(n-1)}$ for the SBT. The nRSBT routing is never of a lower complexity than the SBG routing, and of a higher complexity if n does not divide M. With $(M \bmod n) = k \ne 0$ a combination of *reflections* and *rotations* minimizes the maximum number of elements that need to be transferred over any cube edge. For k even $k/2$ distinct rotations should be used, and for every rotated graph a reflected graph is also used. For k even and optimally rotated SBT's the maximum number of elements transferred over a cube edge is $(N - 1)2^{(n/k)-1}/(2^{n/k} - 1)$ and for optimally reflected and rotated SBT's it is $(N - 1)(2^{(2n/k)-1} + 1)/(2^{2n/k} - 1)$.

VI. ALL-TO-ALL BROADCASTING

A. Time Bounds and Scheduling Disciplines

Theorem 7: A lower bound for all-to-all broadcasting is $\max((N - 1)Mt_c, n\tau)$ for *one-port* communication and $\max((N - 1)M/n)t_c, n\tau)$ for *n-port* communication.

Proof: Each node receives M elements from every other node, i.e., each node receives $(N - 1)M$ elements. Hence, for *one-port* communication a lower bound for the data

TABLE IX
THE COMPLEXITY OF ONE-TO-ALL PERSONALIZED COMMUNICATION

Comm.	Routing	T
one-port	H	$(N-1)Mt_c + \max(\lceil\frac{(N-1)M}{B}\rceil, N-1)\tau$
	SBT	$(N-1)Mt_c + \sum_{i=0}^{n-1}\lceil\frac{2^i M}{B}\rceil\tau$
	nESBT	$\frac{n+1}{n}(N-1)Mt_c + (n\lceil\frac{(N-1)M}{nB}\rceil + \sum_{i=0}^{n-1}\lceil\frac{2^i M}{nB}\rceil)\tau$
	nRSBT	$(N-1)Mt_c + (\sum_{i=1}^{n-1}\lceil\frac{(N-2^i)M}{nB}\rceil + \sum_{i=1}^{n}\lceil\frac{(2^i-1)M}{nB}\rceil)\tau$
n-port	SBT	$\frac{NM}{2}t_c + \sum_{i=0}^{n-1}\lceil\binom{n-1}{i}\frac{M}{B}\rceil\tau$
	nESBT	$\frac{(N-1)M}{n}t_c + (\lceil\frac{M}{nB}\rceil + \lceil\frac{(n-1)M}{nB}\rceil + \sum_{i=2}^{n}\lceil\frac{M}{nB}\binom{n}{i}\rceil)\tau$
	nRSBT	$\frac{(N-1)M}{n}t_c + \sum_{i=0}^{n-1}\lceil\binom{n}{i}\frac{M}{nB}\rceil\tau$
	SBG	$\frac{(N-1)M}{n}t_c + \sum_{i=0}^{n-1}\lceil\binom{n}{i}\frac{M}{nB}\rceil\tau$

TABLE X
THE OPTIMUM COMPLEXITY OF ONE-TO-ALL PERSONALIZED COMMUNICATION

Comm.	Routing	B_{opt}	T_{min}
one-port	H	M	$(N-1)Mt_c + (N-1)\tau$
	SBT	$\frac{NM}{2}$	$(N-1)Mt_c + n\tau$
	nESBT	$\frac{(N-1)M}{n}$	$\frac{n+1}{n}(N-1)Mt_c + 2n\tau$
	nRSBT	$\frac{(N-1)M}{n}$	$(N-1)Mt_c + (2n-1)\tau$
	SBG	$\frac{(N-1)M}{n}$	$\le N(1+\frac{2\log n}{n})Mt_c + (2n-1)\tau$
n-port	SBT	$\frac{NM}{\sqrt{2\pi(n-1)}}$	$\frac{NM}{2}t_c + n\tau$
	nESBT	$\sqrt{\frac{2}{\pi}}\frac{NM}{n^{3/2}}$	$\frac{(N-1)M}{n}t_c + (n+1)\tau$
	nRSBT	$\sqrt{\frac{2}{\pi}}\frac{NM}{n^{3/2}}$	$\frac{(N-1)M}{n}t_c + n\tau$
	SBG	$\sqrt{\frac{2}{\pi}}\frac{NM}{n^{3/2}}$	$\frac{(N-1)M}{n}t_c + n\tau$

TABLE XI
SCHEDULING DISCIPLINE FOR ALL-TO-ALL BROADCASTING

Comm.	Scheduling discipline
one-port	1. For each spanning tree of the *a-graph*, the labels of the outgoing edges of any node are greater than the label of the incoming edge.
	2. All the edges with the same label in the *o-graph* are in the same dimension.
n-port	All data sent at once, spanning trees concurrently.

transfer time is $(N-1)Mt_c$, and with *n-port* communication the time is bounded by $((N-1)M/n)t_c$. ∎

Lemma 22: The data transfer time for *one-port* communication is minimized if one dimension is routed per cycle, and all nodes use the same scheduling discipline.

Proof: The number of elements transferred on every edge in the dimension subject to routing is the same, since the communication graphs for the different sources are translations of each other. ∎

For *one-port* all-to-all broadcasting it remains to define a scheduling discipline that minimizes the number of startups, preserving the minimum data transfer time. This can be accomplished implicitly by labeling the edges of the *o-graph* generating the *a-graph*. The label on the edge corresponds to the cycle during which the data are transferred across that edge. The rules are summarized in Table XI, which also gives the scheduling discipline for the *n-port* case. Rule 1 is obvious. Rule 2 is a sufficient condition satisfying the *one-port* communication constraint. The labeling scheme is the same as the one used in the *one-port one-to-all personalized communication* based on the nESBT graph. The number of

startups required for the broadcasting is equal to the maximum label plus 1 (the least label being 0). For a spanning tree of height h, the minimax label is at least $h - 1$ by rule 1.

For the H path, we label the ith edge in the path i. The maximum label is $N - 2$, which is a minimax label. For the SBT graph labeling edges in dimension i by i satisfies both rules. The maximum label is $n - 1$, which is also a minimax label. For an *a-graph* based on the nESBT, nRSBT or SBG graphs, we first define the edge label in the 0th spanning tree of each such graph. Edges in dimension i are labeled i, except for the nESBT graph for which the labels of the edges to the leaf nodes (all in dimension 0) is n. The 0th subtree of the nESBT graph is equal to an n level SBT with the smallest subtree deleted. Hence, the minimax label is n for the 0th spanning tree of the nESBT graph. For the nESBT and nRSBT graphs, the labels of the edges in subtree j are defined by adding j to the label of the corresponding edges in subtree 0. The minimax label for the entire graph is equal to the minimax label of subtree 0 plus $n - 1$. For the SBG graph, all the n composed SBnT's are labeled in the same way. By Theorem 2, it can be shown that the minimax label of the rotated SBnT

$R^d(G^{\text{SBnT}})$, $d \in \mathfrak{D}$, is $2n - 2$ if $d = 1$; and $2n - 3$, otherwise. The minimax label of the nESBT, nRSBT, and SBG are $2n - 1$, $2n - 2$, and $2n - 2$, respectively. The labeling of the nESBT graph defined here is the same as the labeling for *one-port* one-to-all broadcasting, Fig. 12. The amount of data transferred during cycle i is equal to $M/n \times$ (number of edges labeled i). The maximum packet size and the number of startups can be derived easily from the labels of the edges.

Lemma 23: A lower bound for data transmission time of all-to-all broadcasting based on $G^{\text{id}}(*)$ and "any" scheduling discipline is

$$\max_{\forall d \in \mathfrak{D}} E^{\text{id}}(d) M t_c.$$

Proof: $E^{\text{id}}(d)M$ elements need to be sent across every cube edge in dimension d. ∎

Theorem 8: The communication time for all-to-all broadcasting based on $G^{\text{id}}(*)$ of height h, *n-port* communication and the defined scheduling discipline requires a time of

$$T = \sum_{l=0}^{h-1} \left(M t_c \times \max_{\forall d \in \mathfrak{D}} e^{\text{id}}(d, l) + \left\lceil \frac{M}{B} \times \max_{\forall d \in \mathfrak{D}} e^{\text{id}}(d, l) \right\rceil \tau \right).$$

If $B \geq \max_{0 \leq l \leq h-1, \forall d \in \mathfrak{D}} (M \times e^{\text{id}}(d, l))$ then

$$T = \left(\sum_{l=0}^{h-1} \max_{\forall d \in \mathfrak{D}} e^{\text{id}}(d, l) \right) M t_c + h\tau.$$

Proof: Each node broadcasts its data set M according to its own *o-graph*. During the lth routing cycle all nodes at level $l + 1$ of each *o-graph* receive messages sent out from the roots during the 0th routing cycle. By Lemma 8, the amount of data contending for a communication link in dimension d is $M \times e^{\text{id}}(d, l)$. ∎

Theorem 7 gives a lower bound for the communication time for any routing and scheduling discipline, and Lemma 23 gives a lower bound expressed in terms of an *a-graph*. Theorem 8 gives an upper bound. Next we give complexity estimates for some *a-graphs,* and show that broadcasting based on $G^{\text{SBT}}(*)$ with the scheduling disciplines in Table XI is optimum within a factor of 2 for *one-port* communication, and that the schedulings of the $G^{\text{SBG}}(*)$ and $G^{\text{nRSBT}}(*)$ graphs are optimum within a factor of 2 for *n-port* communication.

Corollary 8: For a given *a-graph* satisfying $e^{\text{id}}(x, l) = e^{\text{id}}(y, l)$, $\forall x, y \in \mathfrak{D}$, and $0 \leq l < h$, the communication time for *all-to-all broadcasting* based on the graph $G^{\text{id}}(*)$ of height h and *n-port* communication and the scheduling disciplines of Table XI is

$$T = \frac{(N-1)M}{n} t_c + h\tau, \quad \text{if } B \geq \max_{0 \leq l < h} (M \times e^{\text{id}}(d, l)).$$

Proof: The corollary follows from Theorem 8. ∎

From Table III and Corollary 8, the nRH, nRSBT, nESBT, and the SBG routings all yield the lower bound for the data transfer time with *n-port* communication. In fact, following Corollary 8, we have the following corollary.

Corollary 9: For $G^{\text{id}}(*)$ with $G^{\text{id}}(0)$ composed of n distinctly rotated spanning trees, the data transfer time for all-to-all broadcasting is minimun with *n-port* communication and the defined scheduling.

Routing according to a greedy *o-graph,* while it is a necessary condition for the *all-to-all personalized communication* to attain the minimum data transfer time, is not necessary for the *all-to-all broadcasting.* The nRSBT and the SBG both with minimum height also attain the minimum number of startups.

B. The Complexity of All-to-All Broadcasting

Tables XII and XIII summarize the complexity of all-to-all broadcasting.

The *one-port* $G^H(*)$ routing is employed in the matrix multiplication algorithm by Dekel [5], [21]. Messages with different source nodes are routed through different H paths. Messages are exchanged along a sequence of dimensions such as 0, 1, 0, 2, 0, 1, 0, 3, $\cdots$, etc. The SBT communication amounts to a single exchange per dimension [28].

With *one-port* communication SBT routing for all-to-all broadcasting is optimum within a factor of two. The H, nESBT, nRSBT, and SBG routings all have the minimum data transfer time. The number of startups is $(N - 1)$, $2n$, $2n - 1$ and $2n - 1$, respectively, with a packet size of $M(N - 2)/n$, $M(N - 1)/n$, and $M(N - 1)/n$, respectively. With a packet size of order MN/n, the number of startups for SBT, nESBT, nRSBT, and SBG routings are all comparable. Note that if the packet size is smaller than the data set to be broadcast, then the SBT routing is of the same complexity as the H routing. But, if $B \geq MN/2$ then $T_{\min} = (N - 1)M t_c + n\tau$, which is optimum within a factor of 2. The startup time is reduced by a factor of $(N - 1)/n$ compared to the H routing.

With *n-port* communication the nRH, nESBT, nRSBT, and SBG routings achieve the lower bound transmission time for a sufficiently large packet size. Both the nRSBT and SBG routings also attain the minimum number of startups n with the same packet size $B \geq \sqrt{2/\pi} NM/n^{3/2}$. The nESBT routing has one more startup. The nRH routing, although optimum for data transfer time, has $N - 1$ startups. The SBT routing yields a slow-down of approximately $n/2$ for the data transfer time compared to the lower bound routing.

VII. ALL-TO-ALL PERSONALIZED COMMUNICATION

A. Time Bounds

Theorem 9: A lower bound for *one-port* all-to-all personalized communication is $\max ((nNM/2)t_c, n\tau)$. The packet size must be at least $NM/2$ to attain this lower bound.

Proof: The bandwidth requirement for distributing personalized data from one node is

$$\sum_{i=0}^{n} i \binom{n}{i} M = \frac{nNM}{2}.$$

The total bandwidth requirement is $nN^2M/2$. During each cycle only N edges of the n-cube can communicate in the case of *one-port* communication; $nNM/2$ is the minimum number of element transfers in sequence. The number of startups is at

TABLE XII
THE COMPLEXITY OF ALL-TO-ALL BROADCASTING

Comm.	Routing	T
one-port	H	$(N-1)Mt_c + \lceil\frac{M}{B}\rceil(N-1)\tau$
	SBT	$(N-1)Mt_c + \sum_{i=0}^{n-1}\lceil\frac{2^iM}{B}\rceil\tau$
	nRSBT	$(N-1)Mt_c + (\sum_{i=0}^{n-1}\lceil\frac{(2^{i+1}-1)M}{nB}\rceil + \sum_{i=n}^{2n-2}\lceil\frac{(N-2^{i-n+1})M}{nB}\rceil)\tau$
	nESBT	$(N-1)Mt_c + (\sum_{i=0}^{n-1}\lceil\frac{2^iM}{nB}\rceil + \sum_{i=n}^{2n-1}\lceil\frac{(N-1-2^{i-n})M}{nB}\rceil)\tau$
n-port	nRH	$\frac{(N-1)M}{n}t_c + \lceil\frac{M}{nB}\rceil(N-1)\tau$
	SBT	$\frac{NM}{2}t_c + \sum_{i=0}^{n-1}\lceil\binom{n-1}{i}\frac{M}{B}\rceil\tau$
	nRSBT	$\frac{(N-1)M}{n}t_c + \sum_{i=1}^{n}\lceil\binom{n}{i}\frac{M}{nB}\rceil\tau$
	nESBT	$\frac{(N-1)M}{n}t_c + (\sum_{i=2}^{n}\lceil\binom{n}{i}\frac{M}{nB}\rceil + \lceil\frac{M}{nB}\rceil + \lceil\frac{(n-1)M}{nB}\rceil)\tau$
	SBG	$\frac{(N-1)M}{n}t_c + \sum_{i=1}^{n}\lceil\binom{n}{i}\frac{M}{nB}\rceil\tau$

TABLE XIII
THE OPTIMUM COMPLEXITY OF ALL-TO-ALL BROADCASTING

Comm.	Routing	B_{opt}	T_{min}
one-port	H	M	$(N-1)Mt_c + (N-1)\tau$
	SBT	$\frac{NM}{2}$	$(N-1)Mt_c + n\tau$
	nRSBT	$\frac{(N-1)M}{n}$	$(N-1)Mt_c + (2n-1)\tau$
	nESBT	$\frac{(N-2)M}{n}$	$(N-1)Mt_c + 2n\tau$
	SBG	$\frac{(N-1)M}{n}$	$(N-1)Mt_c + (2n-1)\tau$
n-port	nRH	$\frac{M}{n}$	$\frac{(N-1)M}{n}t_c + (N-1)\tau$
	SBT	$\frac{NM}{\sqrt{2\pi(n-1)}}$	$\frac{NM}{2}t_c + n\tau$
	nRSBT	$\sqrt{\frac{2}{\pi}}\frac{NM}{n^{3/2}}$	$\frac{(N-1)M}{n}t_c + n\tau$
	nESBT	$\sqrt{\frac{2}{\pi}}\frac{NM}{n^{3/2}}$	$\frac{(N-1)M}{n}t_c + (n+1)\tau$
	SBG	$\sqrt{\frac{2}{\pi}}\frac{NM}{n^{3/2}}$	$\frac{(N-1)M}{n}t_c + n\tau$

least n. The maximum packet size can be derived by dividing the total bandwidth requirement $nN^2M/2$ by the number of cycles n, and the number of directed edges that can be used in each routing cycle N. ∎

Theorem 10: A lower bound for *n-port* all-to-all personalized communication is max $((NM/2)t_c, n\tau)$. The packet size must be at least $NM/(2n)$ to attain this lower bound.

Proof: From Theorem 9 the total bandwidth requirement is $nN^2M/2$. During each routing cycle nN directed edges can communicate concurrently. The maximum packet size is derived by dividing the total bandwidth requirement by the number of cycles n and the total number of links nN. ∎

Theorem 11: The time for *n-port* all-to-all personalized communication based on $G^{\mathrm{id}}(*)$ of height h and *postorder* scheduling is

$$T = \sum_{l=0}^{h-1}\left(Mt_c \times \max_{\forall d \in \mathfrak{D}} v^{\mathrm{id}}(d, l) + \left\lceil \frac{M}{B} \times \max_{\forall d \in \mathfrak{D}} v^{\mathrm{id}}(d, l)\right\rceil \tau\right).$$

If $B \geq \max_{0\leq l\leq h-1,\ \forall d\in \mathfrak{D}}(M \times v^{\mathrm{id}}(d, l))$ then

$$T = \left(\sum_{l=0}^{h-1} \max_{\forall d \in \mathfrak{D}} v^{\mathrm{id}}(d, l)\right) Mt_c + h\tau.$$

Proof: For each $G^{\mathrm{id}}(s)$, the total amount of data transmitted across all edges in dimension d during routing cycle l is $v^{\mathrm{id}}(d, l) \times M$, $0 \leq l \leq h - 1$. For $G^{\mathrm{id}}(*) = \bigcup_{s\in\mathfrak{R}}\mathrm{Tr}(s, G^{\mathrm{id}}(0))$, each *a-graph* edge is mapped to N distinct cube edges with N distinct Exclusive-OR operations on both endpoints. The amount of data transmitted across each cube edge in dimension d during routing cycle l is $v^{\mathrm{id}}(d, l) \times M$. ∎

Theorem 12: The time for *n-port* all-to-all personalized communication based on $G^{\mathrm{id}}(*)$ of height h and *reverse-breadth-first* scheduling is

$$T = \sum_{l=0}^{h-1}\left(Mt_c \times \max_{\forall d \in \mathfrak{D}} u^{\mathrm{id}}(d, l) + \left\lceil \frac{M}{B} \times \max_{\forall d \in \mathfrak{D}} u^{\mathrm{id}}(d, l)\right\rceil \tau\right).$$

If $B \geq \max_{0\leq l\leq h-1,\ \forall d\in \mathfrak{D}}(M \times u^{\mathrm{id}}(d, l))$ then

$$T = \left(\sum_{l=0}^{h-1} \max_{\forall d \in \mathfrak{D}} u^{\mathrm{id}}(d, l)\right) Mt_c + h\tau.$$

Proof: Similar to the proof of Theorem 11. ∎

Theorem 13: The all-to-all personalized communication based on N translated *o-graphs* will attain the lower bound for the data transfer time iff the *o-graph* is greedy.

Proof: The bandwidth requirement for each node is

$$\sum_{l=0}^{h-1}\sum_{d=0}^{n-1} v^{\mathrm{id}}(d, l) = \sum_{l=0}^{h-1}\sum_{d=0}^{n-1} u^{\mathrm{id}}(d, l)$$

$$= \sum_{l=1}^{h} l \times (\text{the number of nodes at level } l).$$

Hence, nongreedy *o-graphs* require more data transfer than greedy *o-graphs*. ∎

Theorem 14: All-to-all personalized *n-port* communication based on $G^{\mathrm{id}}(*)$ where $G^{\mathrm{id}}(0) = \bigcup_{d\in\mathfrak{D}} \mathrm{Ro}^d(T^{\mathrm{id}\prime}(0))$ and $T^{\mathrm{id}\prime}(0)$ is greedy, can attain both the minimum data transmission time, $(NM/2)t_c$, and the minimum number of startups, n, for $B \geq (N - 1)M/n$ both for *postorder* and *reverse-breadth-first* schedulings.

Proof: From Theorem 11 and Corollary 3, the data transfer time is

$$\sum_{l=0}^{n-1}\sum_{i=l+1}^{n} \frac{M}{n}\binom{n}{i} t_c = \frac{NM}{2} t_c.$$

For the *postorder* scheduling, the packet size $(N - 1)M/n$ occurs during routing cycle 0. Similarly, the *reverse-breadth-first* scheduling discipline can be shown to be optimum, and has the same value of the maximum packet size. It occurs during the last routing cycle. ∎

TABLE XIV
THE COMPLEXITY OF ALL-TO-ALL PERSONALIZED COMMUNICATION

Comm.	Routing	T
one-port	H	$\frac{(N-1)NM}{2}t_c + \sum_{i=1}^{N-1}\lceil\frac{iM}{B}\rceil\tau$
	SBT	$\frac{nNM}{2}t_c + \lceil\frac{NM}{2B}\rceil n\tau$
	nRSBT	$\frac{nNM}{2}t_c + (\sum_{i=0}^{n-1}\lceil\frac{(i+1)NM}{2nB}\rceil + \sum_{i=n}^{i=2n-2}\lceil\frac{(2n-i-1)NM}{2nB}\rceil)\tau$
	nESBT	$(\frac{nN}{2}+N-2)Mt_c + (\sum_{i=0}^{n-1}\lceil(\frac{(i+2)N}{2}-1)\frac{M}{nB}\rceil + \sum_{i=1}^{n}\lceil(\frac{iN}{2}-1)\frac{M}{nB}\rceil)\tau$
	SBG	$\approx \frac{nNM}{2}t_c + \max(2n-1, \frac{nNM}{2B})\tau$
n-port	nRH	$\frac{(N-1)NM}{2n}t_c + \sum_{i=1}^{N-1}\lceil\frac{iM}{nB}\rceil\tau$
	SBT	$(\sum_{l=0}^{\lfloor\frac{n-1}{2}\rfloor}\binom{2l}{l}2^{n-2l-1} + \sum_{l=\lfloor\frac{n+1}{2}\rfloor}^{n-1}\binom{n-1}{l})Mt_c$ $+ (\sum_{l=0}^{\lfloor\frac{n-1}{2}\rfloor}\lceil\binom{2l}{l}\frac{2^{n-2l-1}M}{B}\rceil + \sum_{l=\lfloor\frac{n+1}{2}\rfloor}^{n-1}\lceil\binom{n-1}{l}\frac{M}{B}\rceil)\tau$
	nRSBT	$\frac{NM}{2}t_c + \lceil\frac{NM}{2nB}\rceil n\tau$
	nESBT	$(\frac{N}{2}+\frac{N-2}{n})Mt_c + (\sum_{i=2}^{n}\lceil\sum_{j=i}^{n}\binom{n}{j}\frac{M}{nB}\rceil + \lceil\frac{(N-2)M}{nB}\rceil + \lceil\frac{(N-1)M}{nB}\rceil)\tau$
	SBG	$\frac{NM}{2}t_c + \sum_{i=1}^{n}\lceil\sum_{j=i}^{n}\binom{n}{j}\frac{M}{nB}\rceil\tau$

TABLE XV
THE OPTIMUM COMPLEXITY OF ALL-TO-ALL PERSONALIZED COMMUNICATION

Comm.	Routing	B_{opt}	T_{min}
one-port	H	$(N-1)M$	$\frac{(N-1)NM}{2}t_c + (N-1)\tau$
	SBT	$\frac{NM}{2}$	$\frac{nNM}{2}t_c + n\tau$
	nRSBT	$\frac{NM}{2}$	$\frac{nNM}{2}t_c + (2n-1)\tau$
	nESBT	$\frac{M}{n}(\frac{N(n-1)}{2}-1)$	$(\frac{nN}{2}+N-2)Mt_c + 2n\tau$
	SBG	$\frac{NM}{2}$	$\frac{nNM}{2}t_c + (2n-1)\tau$
n-port	nRH	$\frac{(N-1)M}{n}$	$\frac{(N-1)NM}{2n}t_c + (N-1)\tau$
	SBT	$\frac{NM}{2}$	$O(\sqrt{n})NMt_c + n\tau$
	nRSBT	$\frac{NM}{2n}$	$\frac{NM}{2}t_c + n\tau$
	nESBT	$\frac{(N-1)M}{n}$	$(\frac{N}{2}+\frac{N-2}{n})Mt_c + (n+1)\tau$
	SBG	$\frac{(N-1)M}{n}$	$\frac{NM}{2}t_c + n\tau$

Corollary 10: All-to-all personalized *n-port* communication based on $G^{nRSBT}(*)$ and $G^{SBG}(*)$ can attain the time $(NM/2)t_c + n\tau$, which is within a factor of 2 of the lower bound.

Notice that in *one-port* communication the data transfer time is always optimal if the routing is based on N translated greedy *o-graphs* and appropriate scheduling. But, not all greedy *o-graphs* have the same number of startups. Only the SBT graph allows a minimum of n startups for sufficiently large packet size. The minimum number of startups can be decided by the same labeling rules as were used in all-to-all broadcasting. The minimum number of startups is the same as for the all-to-all broadcasting. The difference is that the amount of data transferred during cycle i is equal to the sum of weighted subtree sizes with the root of each subtree connected through an edge labeled i to its parent.

B. The Complexity of All-to-All Personalized Communication

Tables XIV and XV summarize the complexity estimates.

With *one-port* communication and H routing, both the data transfer time and the startup times are off by a factor of N/n compared to the optimum for *one-port* communication. The complexity for *n-port* communication and nRH routing holds for both the *postorder* and *reverse-breadth-first* schedulings. The routing fully utilizes the cube bandwidth; however, much of the data transfer is not through the shortest path, i.e, nongreedy.

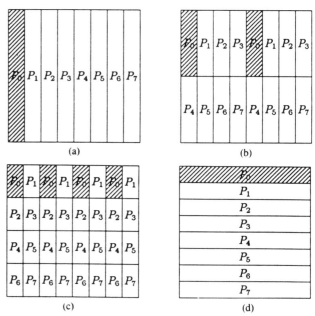

Fig. 13. All-to-all personalized communication in a 3-cube based on SBT's.

Fig. 13 shows all-to-all personalized communication on a 3-cube based on eight SBT's. The shaded area represents the portion of the data residing in processor 0 (denoted P_0). The task is to exchange the jth block of data of processor i with the ith block of processor j for any two distinct processors i and j.

If initially processor i owns the ith block column as in Fig. 13(a) then on completion of the all-to-all personalized communication processor i contains the ith block row as in Fig. 13(d).

Lemma 24: All-to-all personalized *one-port* communication based on $G^{SBT}(*)$ can be accomplished in time $(nNM/2)t_c + n\tau$, which is within a factor of 2 of the lower bound.

Proof: During the routing cycle 0, $NM/2$ data are exchanged along the lowest dimension. Then, the procedure is applied recursively with data set doubling for each cycle of the recursion and the dimension of the cube decreasing by 1. Let $T(i, M)$ be the time required by the stated personalized all-to-all routing algorithm with initially M data per node in an i-cube. Clearly, $T(n, M) = 2^{n-1}Mt_c + \tau + T(n - 1, 2M)$ and $T(1, M) = Mt_c + \tau$. Hence, $T(n, M) = (nNM/2)t_c + n\tau$. ∎

In the case of *n-port* communication, we can find the communication complexity from the previously derived formula. The interesting quantity for *postorder* scheduling is $\sum_{l=0}^{n-1} \max v^{id}(d, l)$.

$$\sum_{l=0}^{n-1} \max_d v^{SBT}(d, l) = \sum_{l=0}^{\lfloor (n-1)/2 \rfloor} \binom{2l}{l} 2^{n-2l-1}$$
$$+ \sum_{l=\lfloor (n+1)/2 \rfloor}^{n-1} \binom{n-1}{l}$$

which is of $O(\sqrt{n}N)$. Since $u^{SBT}(d, l) = v^{SBT}(n - d - 1, l)$, Table III, the *reverse-breadth-first* scheduling yields the same result.

The maximum packet size for nRSBT communication can be reduced from $(N - 1)M/n$ to $NM/(2n)$ by using a scheduling such that each SBT used in composing the nRSBT graph is the same as the scheduling for the SBT graph in *one-port one-to-all personalized communication*. The n SBT's are scheduled concurrently. Note that the same scheme, if applied to all-to-all broadcasting, will increase the maximum packet size from $\sqrt{2/\pi}NM/n^{3/2}$ to $NM/(2n)$. The time for nESBT communication is obtained from Theorems 11 and 12.

C. Summary of All-to-All Personalized Communication

With *one-port* communication, the SBT, nRSBT, SBG, and nESBT routings with *postorder* and *reverse-breadth-first* schedulings for all-to-all personalized communication are optimum within constant factors, Table XV. The SBT has the lowest complexity with a sufficiently large packet size. Only greedy *o-graphs* attain the optimum data transfer time. In fact, the optimum data transfer time can always be attained for the greedy *o-graphs* with appropriate scheduling. The number of startups is equal to the maximum edge label plus one for a graph labeling such that edges in the same dimension carry the same label, and outgoing edges always carry a higher label than incoming edges for the spanning trees making up the *o-graph*. Both the nRSBT and the SBG routings attain the optimum data transfer. The nESBT and H routings have a data transfer time that exceeds the lower bound by a factor of $(n + 2)/n$, and N/n. The number of routing cycles for the SBT communication is at least n, for the nRSBT and SBG

communications it is $2n - 1$ and for the nESBT communication it is $2n$.

With *n-port* communication, the nESBT, nRSBT, and SBG routings are optimum within a constant factor of ≈ 2 for *postorder* and *reverse-breadth-first* schedulings. Both the nESBT and nRH are nongreedy, but the extra distance of the edges from the root of the nESBT is constant. The SBT routing, although greedy, does not evenly utilize edges in the same dimension, and hence is nonoptimum. The data transfer time for the nESBT, the SBT, and the nRH routings are a factor of $n + 2/n$, $\sqrt{n}$, and N/n higher than the optimum time.

VIII. EXPERIMENTAL RESULTS

Some of the communication algorithms presented here have been implemented on an Intel iPSC1 [16] with 128 nodes, connected as a seven-dimensional Boolean cube. It has a message passing programming model. Up to 16k bytes, an *external packet*, can be passed in each communicaton; however, the operating system subdivides messages into *internal packets* of size 1k bytes. There is a communication overhead (startup time) associated with each packet. For an external packet we recorded a startup time averaging 8 ms. For internal packets the startup time was approximately 6 ms (at the time our programs were tested). Interprocessor communication channels are 10 Mbit Ethernet channels. Although there are seven ports per processor, the storage bandwidth can only support 2–3 ports concurrently. However, we have effectively been unable to realize this potential with the available operating system. The concurrency in communication on different ports of the same processor amounts to an overlap of about 20 percent.

For *one-to-all broadcasting* the communication time increases almost linearly for external packet sizes below 1k bytes, Fig. 14. Fig. 15 shows the measured time of the SBT and nESBT communications for an external packet size of 1k bytes and for cube dimensions ranging from 2 to 6. As predicted, measured speedup is approximately n.

For *one-to-all personalized communication* based on SBT routing we schedule port communications in a *binary-reflected* Gray code order to take advantage of the partial overlap in communication on different ports. In the SBG routing, the root determines which node belongs to which subtree. If n is a prime number, the subtrees are isomorphic [excluding node $(\bar{s}_{n-1}\bar{s}_{n-2} \cdots \bar{s}_0)$] and the root only needs to keep one table of length $\approx N/n$ with each entry of size n bits. The order of the entries corresponds to the transmission order for each port. The table entries point to the messages transmitted over port 0. The pointers for the other ports are obtained by (right) cyclic shifts of the table entries. A one step cyclic rotation is used for port 1, two steps for port 2, etc. For n not a prime number there are also other cyclic nodes. The period $P(i)$ for each table entry needs to be found, and the message divided into $P(i)$ pieces. Our implementation uses a single path to every node (SBnT).

Internal nodes can either route according to the destination address if it is included, or use tables. If the destination is included, then a node first checks if it is the destination.

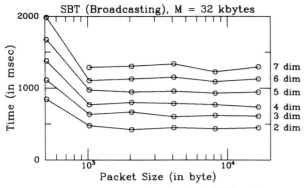

Fig. 14. One-to-all broadcasting for the SBT routing.

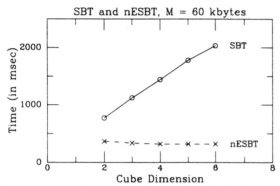

Fig. 15. One-to-all broadcasting for the SBT and nESBT routings.

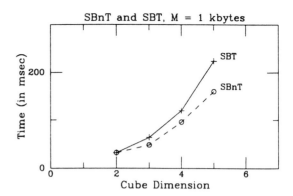

Fig. 16. One-to-all personalized communication for the SBnT and SBT routings.

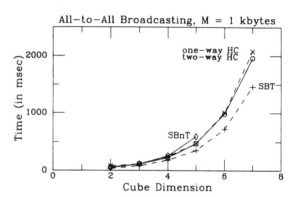

Fig. 17. All-to-all broadcasting on the Intel iPSC.

Otherwise, the output port is determined by finding the base from base^{SBnT} ((myaddress) $\oplus$ (source)) and then finding the first bit that is equal to 1 in ((myaddress) $\oplus$ (destination)) to the left (cyclically) of the bit corresponding to the base. If tables are used instead of a destination field, then for *postorder* scheduling it suffices that each internal node keeps a count for each port. Since the number of ports used in each subtree is at most $n - 3$ and the number of nodes in the entire subtree is approximately N/n, bound on the table size in each node is n^2 bits. A *reverse-breadth-first* scheduling can be implemented by internal nodes keeping a table of how many nodes there are at a given level in each of its subtrees. The table has at most n^2 entries. An upper bound for the number of nodes in a subtree at any level is $N/n^{3/2}$, and the total table size in a node is at most n^3 bits. Hence, without a more sophisticated encoding the *postorder* scheduling discipline requires less table space. It is used for the measurements presented in Fig. 16.

With *one-port* one-to-all personalized communication the expected time for SBT routing and SBG routing is the same for $B = M$. The observed advantage of the SBG over the SBT routing is due to the fact that the SBG can take better advantage of the overlap between communication on different ports. In the SBT case, even though messages were communicated over different ports in a binary-reflected Gray code order, the nodes adjacent to the root may not be finished with retransmitting the last packet received when a new packet arrives, in practice. In the SBG, a subtree receives a packet once every n cycles, and full advantage of the 20 percent overlap in communication actions is taken.

For *all-to-all broadcasting* the execution times are ex-

pected to be of the same order for all forms of all-to-all broadcasting on the Intel iPSC with $B = M$. The results of implementing the SBT, SBG, and two H routings are shown in Fig. 17.

We have also implemented the *all-to-all personalized communication* based on the SBT graph on the iPSC. The result is presented in [22].

IX. SUMMARY AND CONCLUSION

We have presented three new communication graphs for Boolean cubes and defined scheduling disciplines for 1) one-to-all broadcasting, 2) one-to-all personalized communication, 3) all-to-all broadcasting, and 4) all-to-all personalized communication, so that the communication tasks are completed within a small constant factor of the best known lower bounds. For each case we considered two communication models: communication restricted to one-port at-a-time for each processor; and concurrent communication on all ports of every processor. One of the new communication graphs consists of n edge-disjoint spanning binomial trees. Another is a balanced tree. Each subtree of the root of the balanced n-tree we define has approximately N/n nodes.

For communication restricted to *one-port at-a-time*, the nESBT routing is optimum for case 1 within a factor of 4 of the best known lower bound, a speedup of up to n over the SBT routing. For cases 2, 3, and 4, the SBT routings with appropriate scheduling are shown to be optimum within a factor of 2. The nESBT, nRSBT, and SBG routings are all optimum within a factor of 4. For *concurrent communication on all ports,* the nESBT routing is optimum within a

TABLE XVI
TIME COMPLEXITY OF COMMUNICATION ALGORITHMS. THE LAST
COLUMN SHOWS THE CONSTANT FACTORS AS COMPARED TO THE BEST
KNOWN LOWER BOUNDS

Comm.	Data distribution	Assumption	Routing	B_{opt}	T_{min}	Factor
one-port	One-to-all	$M = 1$	SBT	1	$n(t_c + \tau)$	1
	Broadcasting	$M > 1$	nESBT	$\sqrt{\frac{M\tau}{nt_c}}$	$(\sqrt{Mt_c} + \sqrt{n\tau})^2$	4
	One-to-all P.C.	$M \geq 1$	SBT	$\frac{NM}{2}$	$(N-1)Mt_c + n\tau$	2
	All-to-all B.	$M \geq 1$	SBT	$\frac{NM}{2}$	$(N-1)Mt_c + n\tau$	2
	All-to-all P.C.	$M \geq 1$	SBT	$\frac{NM}{2}$	$\frac{nNM}{2}t_c + n\tau$	2
n-port	One-to-all	$M \leq n$	nRSBT	1	$n(t_c + \tau)$	1
	Broadcasting	$M > n$	nESBT	$\frac{1}{n}\sqrt{\frac{M\tau}{t_c}}$	$(\sqrt{\frac{Mt_c}{n}} + \sqrt{n\tau})^2$	4
	One-to-all	$M \geq n$	nESBT	$\sqrt{\frac{2}{\pi}\frac{NM}{n^{3/2}}}$	$\frac{(N-1)M}{n}t_c + (n+1)\tau$	$\frac{2(n+1)}{n}$
	Personalized comm.	$M \geq 1, M \geq n$	SBG, nRSBT	$\sqrt{\frac{2}{\pi}\frac{NM}{n^{3/2}}}$	$\frac{(N-1)M}{n}t_c + n\tau$	2
	All-to-all	$M \geq n$	nESBT	$\sqrt{\frac{2}{\pi}\frac{NM}{n^{3/2}}}$	$\frac{(N-1)M}{n}t_c + (n+1)\tau$	$\frac{2(n+1)}{n}$
	Broadcasting	$M \geq 1, M \geq n$	SBG, nRSBT	$\sqrt{\frac{2}{\pi}\frac{NM}{n^{3/2}}}$	$\frac{(N-1)M}{n}t_c + n\tau$	2
	All-to-all	$M \geq n$	nESBT	$\frac{(N-1)M}{n}$	$(\frac{N}{2} + \frac{N-2}{n})Mt_c + (n+1)\tau$	$\frac{2(n+2)}{n}$
	Personalized comm..	$M \geq 1$	SBG	$\frac{(N-1)M}{n}$	$\frac{NM}{n}t_c + n\tau$	2
		$M \geq n$	nRSBT	$\frac{NM}{2n}$	$\frac{NM}{2}t_c + n\tau$	2

factor of 4 for case 1, a speedup of up to n over the SBT routing. For cases 2, 3, and 4, the nRSBT and SBG routings are optimum within a factor of 2. The nESBT routing is optimum within a factor of ≈ 2. The speedup of the data transmission time for the three routings over the SBT routing is $n/2$, $n/2$, and $O(\sqrt{N})$ for cases 2, 3, and 4 respectively. Table XVI summarizes the results.[1]

The SBG routing has the additional property that the order of the time complexity holds for any data volume, while this is not true for the routings using n paths to every node, such as the nESBT and nRSBT routings. The nESBT routing offers n edge-disjoint paths between the source and any destination node, and hence inherently has a good degree of fault tolerance with respect to communication links.

Routing for the four communication operations can also be based on two-rooted complete binary trees (TCBT) [3], [6]. Communication algorithms based on the TCBT may yield performance comparable to the algorithms presented here for *one-port* communication. For some such scheduling algorithms see [24].

The packet size is very important for the communication complexity. With *one-port* communication and a packet size less or equal to the data set to be communicated to every node, all considered routings have approximately the same complexity for one-to-all personalized communication and all-to-all broadcasting.

Experimental results on the Intel iPSC/d7 confirm the timing model and complexity analysis. The generic communications have been applied to matrix multiplication [21], matrix transpostion [22], and tridiagonal system solvers [23].

ACKNOWLEDGMENT

The authors would like to thank Q. Stout for his helpful comment on the lower bound in Lemma 20; A. Wagner for pointing out [34] and giving the construction of n (undirected) edge-disjoint Hamiltonian cycles in a $2n$-cube based on [34]; and referee D for making many helpful observations and suggestions that significantly improved the presentation.

REFERENCES

[1] A. V. Aho, J. E. Hopcroft, and J. D. Ullman, *The Design and Analysis of Computer Algorithms.* Reading, MA: Addision-Wesley, 1974.
[2] S. N. Bhatt, F. R. K. Chung, F. T. Leighton, and A. L. Rosenberg, "Optimal simulations of tree machines," in *Proc. 27th IEEE Symp. Foundations Comput. Sci.*, 1986, pp. 274–282.
[3] S. N. Bhatt and I. I. F. Ipsen, "How to embed trees in hypercubes," Tech. Rep. YALEU/CSD/RR-443, Dept. Comput. Sci., Yale Univ., Dec. 1985.
[4] S. A. Browning, "The tree machine: A highly concurrent computing environment," Tech. Rep. 1980:TR:3760, Comput. Sci., California Instit. Technol., Jan. 1980.
[5] E. Dekel, D. Nassimi, and S. Sahni, "Parallel matrix and graph algorithms," *SIAM J. Comput.*, vol. 10, pp. 657–673, 1981.
[6] S. R. Deshpande and R. M. Jenevin, "Scaleability of a binary tree on a hypercube," in *Proc. Int. Conf. Parallel Processing*, 1986, pp. 661–668.
[7] M. J. Fischer, *Efficiency of Equivalence Algorithms.* New York: Plenum, 1972, pp. 153–167.
[8] G. C. Fox and W. Furmanski, "Optimal communication algorithms on hypercube," Tech. Rep. CCCP-314, California Instit. Technol., July 1986.
[9] G. C. Fox and D. Jefferson, "Concurrent processor load balancing as a statistical physics problem," Tech. Rep. CCCP-172, California Instit. Technol., May 1985.
[10] D. Gannon and J. Van Rosendale, "On the impact of communication complexity in the design of parallel numerical algorithms," *IEEE Trans. Comput.*, vol. C-33, pp. 1180–1194, Dec. 1984.
[11] J. L. Gustafson, S. Hawkinson, and K. Scott, "The architecture of a homogeneous vector supercomputer," in *Proc. 1986 Int. Conf. Parallel Processing*, 1986, pp. 649–652.
[12] J. P. Hayes, T. N. Mudge, Q. F. Stout, S. Colley, and J. Palmer, "Architecture of a hypercube supercomputer, in *Proc. 1986 Int. Conf. Parallel Processing*, 1986, 653–660.
[13] W. D. Hillis, *The Connection Machine.* Cambridge, MA: MIT Press, 1985.
[14] C. T. Ho and S. L. Johnsson, "Distributed routing algorithms for broadcasting and personalized communication in hypercubes," in *Proc. 1986 Int. Conf. Parallel Processing*, 1986, pp. 640–648. Tech. Rep. YALEU/DCS/RR-483, May 1986.
[15] ——, "Spanning balanced trees in Boolean cubes," Tech. Rep. YALEU/DCS/RR-508, Dept. Comput. Sci., Yale Univ., Jan. 1987.

---

[1] For the nESBT routing, T_{min} is valid only if $1 \leq B_{opt} \leq M$ for *one-port* and $1 \leq B_{opt} \leq M/n$ for *n-port* communication.

[16] *Intel iPSC System Overview,* Intel Corp., Jan. 1986. *SIAM J. Sci. Stat. Comput.,* to be published.

[17] S. L. Johnsson, "Communication efficient basic linear algebra computations on hypercube architectures," *J. Parallel Distrib. Comput.,* vol. 4, pp. 133–172, Apr. 1987. Rep. YALEU/DCS/RR-361, Jan. 1985.

[18] ——, "Ensemble architectures and their algorithms: An overview," in *Proceedings* of the *IMA Workshop Numerical Algorithms Par. Comput. Architectures,* H. Schultz Ed., Berlin, Germany:Springer-Verlag, 1987. YALE/DCS/RR-580. Revision of YALEU/DCS/RR-367, Feb. 1985.

[19] ——, "Odd-even cyclic reduction on ensemble architectures and the solution tridiagonal systems of equations," Tech. Rep. YALE/DCS/RR-339, Dep. Comput. Sci., Yale Univ., Oct. 1984.

[20] ——, "Solving tridiagonal systems on ensemble architectures," *SIAM J. Sci. Stat. Comp.,* vol. 8, pp. 354–392, May 1987; Rep. YALEU/DCS/RR-436, Nov. 1985.

[21] S. L. Johnsson and C. T. Ho, "Algorithms for multiplying matrices of arbitrary shapes using shared memory primitives on a Boolean cube," Tech. Rep. YALEU/DCS/RR-569, Dep. Comput. Sci., Yale Univ., Oct. 1987. Revision of YALEU/DCS/RR-530. Presented at the ARMY Workshop on Medium Scale Parallel Processors, Stanford Univ., Jan. 1986.

[22] ——, Matrix transposition on Boolean n-cube configured ensemble architectures," *SIAM J. Matrix Anal. Appl.,* vol. 9, pp. 415–454, July 1988. YALE/DCS/RR-572. rev. ed. YALEU/DCS/RR-494 Nov. 1986, to be published.

[23] ——, "Multiple tridiagonal systems, the alternating direction method, and Boolean cube configured multiprocessors," Tech. Rep. YALEU/DCS/RR-532, Yale Univ., June 1987. *SIAM J. Sci. Stat. Comput.,* to be published.

[24] ——, "Spanning graphs for optimum broadcasting and personalized communication in hypercubes," Tech. Rep. YALEU/DCS/RR-500, Dep. Comput. Sci., Yale Univ., Nov. 1986.

[25] F. T. Leighton, *Complexity Issues in VLSI: Optimal Layouts for the Shuffle-Exchange Graph and Other Networks.* Cambridge, MA: MIT Press, 1983.

[26] O. A. McBryan and E. F. Van de Velde, "Hypercube algorithms and implementations," *SIAM J. Scientif. Statist. Comput.,* vol. 8, pp. s227–s287, Mar. 1987.

[27] E. M. Reingold, J. Nievergelt, and N. Deo, *Combinatorial Algorithms.* Englewood Cliffs, NJ: Prentice-Hall, 1977.

[28] Y. Saad and M. H. Schultz, "Data communication in hypercubes," Tech. Rep. YALEU/DCS/RR-428, Dep. Comput. Sci., Yale Univ., Oct. 1985.

[29] ——, "Topological properties of hypercubes," Tech. Rep. YALEU/DCS/RR-389, Dep. Comput. Sci., Yale Univ., June 1985.

[30] C. L. Seitz, "The cosmic cube," *Commun. ACM,* vol. 28, pp. 22–33, 1985.

[31] Q. F. Stout and B. Wager, "Passing messages in link-bound hypercubes," in *Proc. 1986 Hypercube Conf.,* SIAM, 1987.

[32] L. Valiant and G. J. Brebner, "Universal schemes for parallel communication," in *Proc. 13th ACM Symp. Theory of Computat.,* ACM, 1981, pp. 263–277.

[33] A. Y. Wu, "Embedding of tree networks in hypercubes," *J. Parallel Distrib. Comput.,* vol. 2, pp. 238–249, 1985.

[34] J. Aubert and B. Schneider, "Decomposition de la somme cartesienne d'un cycle et de l'union de deux cycles hamiltoniens en cycles hamiltoniens," *Discrete Math.,* vol. 38, pp. 7–16, 1982.

[35] M. Foregger, "Hamiltonian decompositions of products of cycles," *Discrete Math.,* vol. 24, pp. 251–260, 1978.

[36] A. S. Wagner, personal communication, 1988.

S. Lennart Johnsson (M'87) received the M.S. and Ph.D. degrees from Chalmers Institute of Technology, Gothenburg, Sweden, in 1967 and 1970, respectively.

He is director of Computational Sciences at Thinking Machines Corporation, and an Associate Professor of Computer Science and Electrical Engineering, Yale University, New Haven, CT. From 1970 to 1979 he was affiliated with the Central Research and Development Laboratories of ASEA AB, Sweden, first as a staff member and later as manager of Systems Engineering. He initiated and lead the development of large computer-based real-time computer systems for electric utilities, intelligent controllers, and mathematical software. From 1979 to 1983, he was a Senior Research Associate in computer science at the California Institute of Technology, where he taught VLSI design and started a course in scientific computing on parallel architectures. Since 1983 he has been with Yale University, where he has continued to teach courses on parallel algorithms and architectures. His current research interests include architecture, algorithms and software for high-performance parallel computers for the computational sciences, particularly the design of communication systems, graph embeddings, and the automatic mapping of data and control structures to parallel architectures, linear algebra, and fluid and solid mechanics applications. He has lead the development of scientific software for the Connection Machine at Thinking Machines Corporation since 1986. He has authored or co-authored over 50 publications in the areas of VLSI architecture and parallel scientific computing, and is an editor of the *Journal of Parallel and Distributed Computing.*

Dr. Johnsson is a co-recipient of the 1986 Outstanding Paper Award of the International Conference of Parallel Processing, and he is a recipient of the John Ericson medal. He is a member of SIAM and ACM.

Ching-Tien Ho was born in Taiwan, on April 9, 1957. He received the B.S. degree in electrical engineering from National Taiwan University, Taiwan, in 1979 and the M.S. and M.Phil. degrees in computer science from Yale University, New Haven, CT, in 1985 and 1986, respectively.

He is currently pursuing a Ph.D. degree in computer science at Yale University, New Haven, CT. He has co-authored more than 10 papers. His primary research interests include routing algorithms for interconnection networks, graph embeddings, parallel algorithms and architectures.

Mr. Ho is a co-recipient of the 1986 Outstanding Paper Award of the International Conference on Parallel Processing. He is a student member of ACM and SIAM.

432

Performance Analysis of the Communication Architecture of the Connection Machine

Anup K. Ahluwalia and Mukesh Singhal

Abstract— The Connection Machine CM-2 exhibits massive parallelism and can support several forms of interprocessor communications. In this paper, we analyze the performance of the interprocessor communication architecture of the CM-2. A discrete-time Markov chain model of the network architecture of the CM-2 is developed to compute the message delay introduced by the network architecture. Due to "synchronous time-division multiplexing" nature of the operation of the communication network, it is amenable to a discrete-time Markov chain modeling. Besides response time, the analysis yields formulas for several other related performance measures. These formulas indicate how the performance of the communication network of the CM-2 degrades with the message arrival rate and other parameters of the network architecture. Since the communication delays affect the interprocess communication in an application running on the CM-2, the knowledge of the sensitivity of the delays with the parameters can be a useful aid in designing a high performance parallel system. To keep the analysis tractable, we made some simplifying assumptions. Due to the largeness of the Markov model, an approximate Markov model is used that requires the use of "fixed-point iteration" to solve it. Validation of the analytical results against a simulation study reveals that the analysis presented in this paper predicts the performance of the communication network with high accuracy.

Index Terms— Connection Machine, discrete-time Markov chain, high performance computing, interprocessor communication, massively parallel machines, performance modeling and analysis, simulation.

I. Introduction

IN the last several years, parallel and distributed processing architectures have proliferated, evolving from research concepts and paper designs to, in many cases, commercially-available products. Consequently, potential users are now confronted with a myriad of choices in parallel machine architectures. Examples include the Connection Machine CM-2 from Thinking Machines Corporation [7], Goodyear's Massively Parallel Processor [1], BBN's Butterfly [3], and Intel's iPSC Hypercube [16].

Despite the proliferation of these parallel machines, our understanding of parallelism and how to exploit it remains limited. While the hardware design and manufacturing technology have progressed to a point where it has become relatively easy to produce such machines, the techniques for designing and developing software to control and program them have not evolved as quickly. As a result, there exists a

Manuscript received December 3, 1991; revised July 21, 1992.
The authors are with the Department of Computer and Information Science, The Ohio State University, Columbus, OH 43210.
IEEE Log Number 9203548.

Reprinted from *IEEE Trans. Parallel and Distributed Systems,* Vol. 3, No. 6, Nov. 1992, pp. 728–738. Copyright © 1992 by The Institute of Electrical and Electronics Engineers, Inc.

gap which inhibits researchers and users from fully exploiting the capabilities of these machines.

The lack of effective parallel processing software and tools reflects the critical problems associated with translating the concept of parallelism into effective use in parallel processing systems. The problems arise from the lack of a coherent design methodology for parallel algorithms and a lack of understanding of the relationship between parallel processing architectures and the algorithms designed to execute on them [22]. To date, much research has been directed toward the development of techniques for describing and partitioning parallel algorithms and assigning them to the elements of a particular parallel processing architecture [15], [18]. However, hardly any work has been done in the area of performance modeling of the communication architecture of these massively parallel machines. The communication architecture is a very important component of these machines and can have a significant impact on the performance of parallel applications running on these machines. Accurate modeling of the timing delays in the communication architectures is important for restructuring a parallel application on a parallel machine and also for engineering new architectures.

The goal of this paper is to model the performance of the communication architecture of a massively parallel machine. To ensure that our analysis remains focused, we restrict ourselves to a fine-grained SIMD machine, the Thinking Machine Corporation's Connection Machine CM-2 [7], [13]. The CM exhibits massive parallelism and can support several forms of interprocessor communications. We model and analyze the performance of the communication architecture of the CM-2. A discrete-time Markov model of the network architecture is developed to compute the message delay introduced by the routing algorithm and the network architecture.

Related Work

Recently, two studies [11], [22] have focused on the performance of the router network of the CM-2. Gelenbe [11] modeled a router node as an M/D/1 queue to compute message waiting time at a router. Though this simple model provides a reasonable approximation to the performance, it may not be accurate when load is high because this model neglects blocking when buffers are full at a router node. It assumes infinite buffer capacity at routers. Upton and Tripathi [22] provide an interesting qualitative analysis of the performance of the CM-2 using the notion of "local sphere of computation." However, no analytic expression for the performance is given.

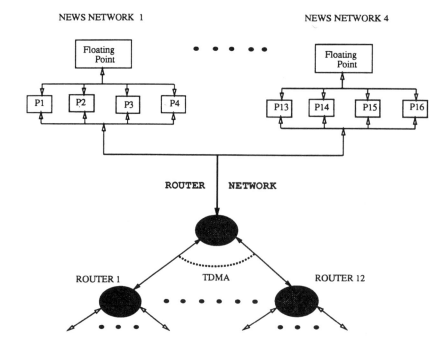

NEWS NETWORK 1   NEWS NETWORK 4

Fig. 1. A router cluster in the Connection Machine.

The rest of the paper is organized as follows: The next section provides an overview of the CM-2, detailing its processor/memory organization and the communication network. In Section III, we develop a performance model of the communication network of the CM-2. In Section IV, we compare the results of a simulation study and the analysis of our model of the CM-2. Finally, Section V summarizes the conclusions and discusses areas for further research.

II. THE CONNECTION MACHINE ARCHITECTURE

The Connection Machine CM-2 is a massively parallel, fine-grain "single-instruction multiple-data-stream" processor capable of providing extremely high speed processing [7], [19]. The CM-2 has 65 536 (64 K) single-bit processors each with up to 128K bytes of memory. In CM-200 configuration, which is an upgraded version of CM-2 with 10 MHz clock and WTL3164 FPU's, it is capable of providing a peak performance of 40 Gflops (in a chained multiply-add). The CM-2, which typically has a 7 MHz clock, can provide a sustained performance of 14 Gflops [17]. The 64K processors may be divided into four parts, thereby, allowing four users to independently access a quarter machine.

The latest model of the Connection Machine, CM-5, is a coarse-grain "multiple-instruction multiple-data-stream" processor and consists of thousands of processing nodes each of which can fetch, interpret, and execute its own instruction stream, calculate memory address, and perform interprocessor communication [8]. Each processing node can have up to 32 Mbytes of memory and can deliver up to 128 Mips/Mflops.

A. Router Network

The fundamental element of the router network is a router (also referred to as a "router node") which handles messages for 16 physical processors. The 64K processors are divided into groups of 16 processors. Each group of 16 processors, called a *router cluster*, is connected to a router node. A schematic diagram of a router cluster is shown in Fig. 1. The 16 processors in a router cluster are arranged in four equal size groups. The four processors in a group communicate via a nearest-neighbor grid interconnection, called the NEWS (North-East-West-South) network, wherein the data are passed to or from one of the four neighboring processors. Another principal form of communication between processors is via the *router network*, which allows arbitrary-length messages to be sent from any processor to any other [14]. The router network is unique and distinguishes the CM-2 from other parallel processors.

The 4096 routers are wired in as a Boolean 12-cube [2]. Every router has 12 bidirectional physical channels which connect it, along a different dimension of the 12-cube, to another router. The address of routers within the network depends on their relative position within the 12-cube. The 4096 routers have addresses 0 through 4095. A router with address i is directly connected to the router with address j if and only if $|i - j| = 2^k$ for some positive integer k. In this case, we say that the routers are connected along the kth dimension. An edge of the 12-cube pointing along the kth dimension connects two routers whose addresses differ by 2^k; That is, they differ in the kth bit of the address. Because any two 12-bit addresses differ by no more than 12 bits, any router of the 12 cube can be reached from any other by traveling over no more than 12 edges.

B. Routing Algorithm

The routing algorithm used by the router network consists of repeating cycles called the *petit* cycles. Each *petit* cycle is divided into 12 dimension cycles (also called *slots*), one for each dimension of the router. During a *petit* cycle, messages

434

are moved across each of the 12 dimensions in sequence. A message is delivered to a neighboring router within a single *petit* cycle, unless it is delayed due to a slot contention (only one message can move along each dimension during a *petit* cycle). (A *slot contention* occurs when several messages want to move in the same dimension cycle concurrently.) The operation of the router network can be divided into five categories: *injection, delivery, forwarding, buffering,* and *referral* [13].

Injection: The 16 processors that a router serves can send messages over the network by the process of injection. A message injection can be initiated by a router at the beginning of each *petit* cycle. The number of (injected) messages accepted by a router during a *petit* cycle depends on the number of buffers that are free at the beginning of the *petit* cycle. A router accepts no more messages than it has free buffers, and in no case it accepts more than four messages in a single *petit* cycle.

Buffering: A message is queued at a router if it can not be sent in the current petit cycle due to slot contention. The number of buffers at a router is the degree of the hypercube—12 in this case.

Forwarding: In *forwarding,* a message is transmitted from one router to another. The destination address of a message is specified relative to the address of router at which the message currently resides. If the address is 000000100100, then the message must move across two dimensions to reach its destination. During kth dimension cycle in a petit cycle, each router chooses a message to be sent across the physical link corresponding to dimension k. A router makes this choice by looking at the kth bit of all the messages in its buffer. Any message with a 1 in the kth bit needs to move along the kth dimension. If there are several messages with the kth bit set, the one that has been at the router the longest gets the priority. When a message is sent along the kth dimension, its kth address bit is reset to maintain address relativity.

Delivery: Each message is checked for a zero router address at the end of a *petit* cycle. A message with zero address has arrived at its destination router and is delivered to the destination processor (to one of the 16 processors in its router cluster).

Referral: Since a router has limited buffer capacity, a mechanism is needed to deal with a buffer overflow. A buffer overflow occurs at a router in a dimension cycle when 1) all the buffers are full in the beginning of the dimension cycle, 2) none of the buffered messages wants to move in the current dimension cycle, and 3) a message is being received in the dimension cycle. Buffer overflow problem is solved by a mechanism called the *referral* which works in the following manner: When a router's buffers are full in the beginning of a dimension cycle and no message wants to move in the current dimension cycle, then the router forces the lowest priority message (i.e., the message that arrived last) to go along the current dimension. Thus, a referred message *may* be misrouted, but it contains the address of its intended destination and is eventually delivered to its destination router (may be in the same petit cycle).

III. PERFORMANCE MODELING

A. Overview

In this paper, we focus on communication slowdown due to the exchange of messages between processors. Note that the time spent by the processors in waiting for messages to arrive from other processors constitutes a source of reductions in the processing power of the machine.

A message entering the router network via some router can reach its destination router in just one *petit* cycle or less if none of the slots which the message requires as it progresses through the network are already occupied. However, messages can be delayed due to contention. When a message can not move in the current slot due to contention, it may still move in subsequent slots in the same petit cycle if some additional bits in its address are set. Otherwise, it must wait for the next opportunity to move along this dimension, which comes a full *petit* cycle later. Thus, a message may be delayed for several petit cycle and slot contention can significantly delay a message. In this section, we present an analytical method for evaluating the delay introduced by the router network. The method is based on a Markovian analysis of the router network.

B. Queueing Model of the Router Network

A queueing model for a router node is shown in Fig. 2. This figure shows the Connection Machine's router network from the perspective of a single router node. Messages generated by the processors in the router cluster are queued up (Local queue) at the router before they are injected into the router network at the beginning of a *petit* cycle.

A router node is represented by a queue, called the router queue, whose capacity is equal to the degree of the network. A router queue is connected to 12 other router queues, each of which represents a router in one of the 12 possible dimensions through which a message in the buffer can pass.

Let λ be the arrival rate of messages from the 16 processors in a router cluster, which are destined to processors in different router clusters. Since message arrival process is a superimposition of several independent message sources, it is reasonable to assume that the arrival process is Poisson [23].

We next present a Markov chain model of a router node. Since modeling of entire router network is extremely complex, we model a single router node.

C. A Discrete-Time Markov Chain Model

Since the state of a router buffer may change after every dimension cycle (a discrete interval), we model the router by a discrete-time Markov chain (DTMC) [23]. In this section, we develop a DTMC model of a router and compute the transition probability matrix and the steady state probabilities of the Markov chain.

Fig. 3 depicts a DTMC of the buffer of a router node. A state of the Markov chain is represented by a tuple (i, j) where i is the dimension cycle within a *petit* cycle and j is the number of messages in the buffer of the router at the beginning of the slot i. A row of the transition probability matrix corresponds to a current state and a column corresponds to a potential next state.

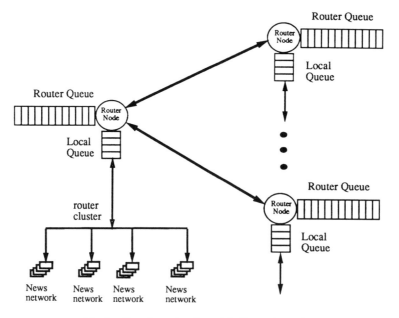

Fig. 2.   Queueing network model of a router node.

DIMENSION CYCLE

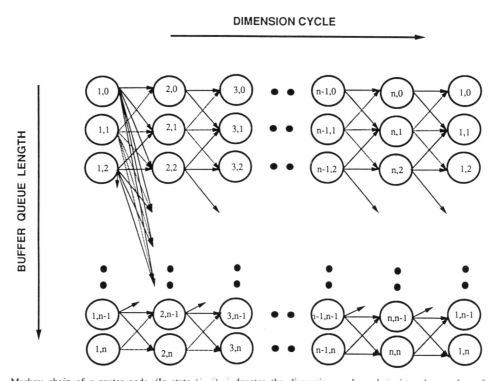

Fig. 3.   Markov chain of a router node. (In state (i, j), i denotes the dimension cycle and j gives the number of messages in the router buffer.)

The entry at row (i, j) and column (k, l) of the matrix gives the probability that the system makes a transition from state (k, l) to state (i, j). Since the router network is a hypercube of degree 12, there are $12 * (12 + 1) = 156$ possible states. The size of the transition probability matrix is $156 * 156$. We denote the transition probability matrix by M_T.

All messages are serviced in TDMA fashion, hence, from slot i a router network can only go to slot $(i+1)$ (with a wrap around). Thus, from state $(i, *)$, the next transition must be to a state $(i + 1, *)$. Apart from the states where injection is happening, state transitions can occur from a state (i, j) to

only at most 3 other states—$(i + 1, j - 1)$, $(i + 1, j)$, and $(i + 1, j + 1)$. Thus, M_T is highly sparse. We now compute the probabilities of sending and receiving messages in a state which are needed to compute M_T. We assume that a message is destined from a router to any of its neighboring routers with equal probability. Thus, given a message in the router queue, the probability that it is sent out in a dimension cycle, denoted by P_R, is given by $1/n$, where n is the degree of the network. The probability that a given message is not sent during a dimension cycle is $1 - P_R$.

We assume routing behavior of messages is independent. In

state (i, j), there are j messages in the router queue. Hence, the probability that no message is sent in state (i, j), denoted by $NOGIVE_j$, is given by the following equation:

$$NOGIVE_j = [(1 - P_R)^j]. \tag{1}$$

Hence, for any state (i, j) the probability that a message is sent during dimension cycle, denoted by $GIVE_j$, is given by

$$GIVE_j = 1 - NOGIVE_j = [1 - (1 - P_R)^j]. \tag{2}$$

Let the average queue length at a router buffer be $\overline{Q}$. We assume that a router sees the average behavior of the routers which can send messages to this router. Thus, the probability of a router not receiving a message from another router during a dimension cycle in state (i, j), denoted by $NOTAKE$, is given by

$$NOTAKE = [(1 - P_R)^{\overline{Q}}]. \tag{3}$$

Note that $\overline{Q}$ may not be an integer. Since the value of $\overline{Q}$ is not known, we solve the DTMC using the "fixed-point iteration" technique [12]. The probability of receiving a message in state (i, j), denoted by $TAKE$, is given by

$$TAKE = 1 - NOTAKE = [1 - (1 - P_R)^{\overline{Q}}]. \tag{4}$$

Let A_j denote the probability that a message is sent but no message is received in state (i, j) in the current dimension cycle. Then

$$A_j = GIVE_j * NOTAKE. \tag{5}$$

Let B_j denote the probability that a no message is sent but a message is received in state (i, j) in the current dimension cycle. Then

$$B_j = NOGIVE_j * TAKE. \tag{6}$$

Let C_j denote the probability that either 1) no message is received nor sent or 2) a message is received and a message is sent in the current dimension cycle in state (i, j). Then

$$C_j = (1 - A_j - B_j). \tag{7}$$

1) Computation of Transition Probability Matrix: Based on if injection is happening, how many buffers are full, and if a referral is happening, we categorize the states of the Markov chain into the following five cases. This categorization is convenient because the states in a case exhibit similar behavior and thus, permit us to write their transition probabilities in general form.

Case 0: This case represents states when injection is happening at the beginning of the *petit* cycle and all the $n(= 12)$ buffers are empty. There is only one state $(1,0)$ which falls into this category. From this state, the system can transit to one of the 6 possible states—(2,0), (2,1), (2,2), (2,3), (2,4), and (2,5). The state transition probabilities are computed below:

$$
\begin{aligned}
p_{(1,0)(2,0)} &= P_0 * NOTAKE \\
p_{(1,0)(2,1)} &= P_1 * NOTAKE + P_0 * TAKE \\
p_{(1,0)(2,2)} &= P_2 * NOTAKE + P_1 * TAKE \\
p_{(1,0)(2,3)} &= P_3 * NOTAKE + P_2 * TAKE \\
p_{(1,0)(2,4)} &= (1 - P_0 - P_1 - P_2 - P_3) * NOTAKE \\
&\quad + P_3 * TAKE \\
p_{(1,0)(2,5)} &= (1 - P_0 - P_1 - P_2 - P_3) * TAKE.
\end{aligned}
$$

Case 1: This case represents the states when injection is happening at the beginning of the *petit* cycle and not all the $(n = 12)$ buffers are empty. Case 1 consists of 12 states represented by $(1, j) \, \forall j, \, 1 \leq j \leq 12$. Transition probabilities are

$$
\begin{aligned}
p_{(1,j)(2,j-1)} &= P_0 * A_j \\
p_{(1,j)(2,j)} &= P_0 * C_j + P_1 * A_j \\
p_{(1,j)(2,j+1)} &= P_0 * B_j + P_1 * C_j + P_2 * A_j \\
p_{(1,j)(2,j+2)} &= P_1 * B_j + P_2 * C_j + P_3 * A_j \\
p_{(1,j)(2,j+3)} &= P_2 * B_j + P_3 * C_j + (1 - P_0 - P_1 - P_2 - P_3) * A_j \\
p_{(1,j)(2,j+4)} &= P_3 * B_j + (1 - P_0 - P_1 - P_2 - P_3) * A_j \\
p_{(1,j)(2,j+5)} &= (1 - P_0 - P_1 - P_2 - P_3) * B_j.
\end{aligned}
$$

Case 2: This case represents states when injection is not taking place (i.e., $i > 1$) and all the $(n = 12)$ buffers are empty. In this case, we have 11 states represented by $(i, 0) \, \forall i$, $2 \leq i \leq 12$. Transition probabilities are

$$
\begin{aligned}
p_{(i,0)(i+1,0)} &= NOGIVE_0 * NOTAKE \\
p_{(i,1)(i+1,1)} &= 1 - (NOGIVE_1 * NOTAKE).
\end{aligned}
$$

Case 3: This case represents all the states when injection is not happening and all the buffers are full (i.e., a referral happens). In this case, we have 11 states represented by $(i, 12) \, \forall i, \, 2 \leq i \leq 12$. Transition probabilities are:

$$
\begin{aligned}
p_{(i,12)(i+1,12)} &= TAKE \\
p_{(i,12)(i+1,11)} &= NOTAKE.
\end{aligned}
$$

Case 4: This case covers all the remaining states. This case has 121 states $(degree-1*degree-1)$ represented by $(i, j) \, \forall i$, $2 \leq i \leq 12$ and $\forall j, \, 1 \leq j \leq 11$. Transition probabilities are:

$$
\begin{aligned}
p_{(i,j)(i+1,j-1)} &= A_j \\
p_{(i,j)(i+1,j)} &= C_j \\
p_{(i,j)(i+1,j+1)} &= B_j.
\end{aligned}
$$

2) Steady-State Probabilities: Let $\pi_{(i,j)}$ denote the steady state probability of being in state (i, j). Clearly,

$$\sum_{\forall i, \forall j} \pi_{i,j} = 1. \tag{8}$$

If the steady state probability vector is denoted by Π, then we can obtain the steady state probability vector from the following equation: (Recall that M_T is the transition probability matrix.)

$$\Pi * M_T = \Pi. \tag{9}$$

Since entries of M_T are functions of $\overline{Q}$ and $\overline{Q}$ in turn is a function of Π (and hence of M_T), a fixed-point iteration [12] is required to solve the problem.

D. Computation of Performance Measures

We now derive expressions for the performance measures in terms of the steady state probabilities of the Markov chain. The performance measures are derived in time units of a dimension cycle.

Throughput: The throughput, Λ, is defined as the number of messages transferred per unit of time at a router node. It is the sum of the steady state probabilities of the states in which messages can be sent by a router node, weighted by the probability of sending a message in that state. Note that when the buffer is full, states $(i, 12)$, the probability of sending a message is 1. Hence,

$$\Lambda = \sum_{i=1}^{12} \sum_{j=0}^{11} (GIVE_j * \pi_{(i,j)}) + \sum_{i=1}^{12} \pi_{(i,12)}. \qquad (10)$$

First and second terms give the throughput when the buffer is not full and when it is completely full, respectively. The throughput due to referral, denoted by Λ_{ref}, is defined as the number of messages referred per unit of time at a router node. It is the sum of the steady state probabilities of the states in which buffer is completely full, weighted by the probability that a message is referred. Hence,

$$\Lambda_{ref} = \sum_{i=1}^{12} (1 - P_R)^{12} * \pi_{(i,12)}. \qquad (11)$$

The Average Queue Length: The average queue length, $\overline{Q}$, is the expected number of messages in the buffer at a router and is given by the following expression:

$$\overline{Q} = \sum_{i=1}^{12} \sum_{j=0}^{12} (j * \pi_{(i,j)}). \qquad (12)$$

The Probability of Referral: The probability of referral, P_{ref}, is the probability that a message is referred at a router (it is the fraction of messages referred) and is given by the following expression:

$$P_{ref} = \frac{\Lambda_{ref}}{\Lambda}. \qquad (13)$$

The Average Number of Hops Due to Referral: The average number of hops due to referral, $HOPS_{ref}$, is the average number of extra hops taken by a message due to referral. When a message is referred, it typically requires 2 extra hops to reach its destination (one hop to misroute the message and the another to correct it). A message has a risk of being referred with probability P_{ref} at every router node it traverses. The probability of referral is independent at each of those router nodes. Hence, the average number of times a message is referred is: the average number of hops taken by a message $* P_{ref}$. Since messages are destined to all the router nodes with equal probability, the average number of hops taken by a message is equal to the average distance between any two router nodes and is given by the following expression:

$$\frac{\sum_{i=1}^{12} i * {}^{12}C_i}{2^{12} - 1} \qquad (14)$$

Therefore, $HOPS_{ref}$ is given by

$$HOPS_{ref} = \frac{\sum_{i=1}^{12} i * {}^{12}C_i}{2^{12} - 1} * P_{ref} * 2. \qquad (15)$$

The Average Number of Hops: The average number of hops, HOPS, is a sum of two components. First component is the average number of hops a message takes provided there is no

referral, and second component is the average number of extra hops due to referral, $HOPS_{ref}$. Thus,

$$HOPS = \frac{\sum_{i=1}^{12} i * {}^{12}C_i}{2^{12} - 1} + HOPS_{ref}. \qquad (16)$$

Response Time: The response time, R, is defined as the total time spent by a message in the router network—from submission to the local queue at the source router till arrival at the destination router. It is the sum of wait time in the local queue of the router before injection and the time spent in the network after *injection.*

According to Little's Law, the average time spent by a message at a router node is $\overline{Q}/\Lambda$. Thus, the average time spent by a message in the system is $HOPS * \frac{\overline{Q}}{\Lambda}$. Since the waiting time for messages arriving at the local queue is uniformly distributed between 0 and the duration of the petit cycle, T, the expected waiting time at the local queue before injection is given by $T/2$. Therefore,

$$R = (HOPS * \frac{\overline{Q}}{\Lambda}) + T/2. \qquad (17)$$

IV. NUMERICAL RESULTS AND VALIDATION

We numerically solved the analytic model for the performance measures and validated its results against a simulation study. We computed values for the performance measures for several numerical examples. We wrote and ran a discrete-event based simulation [10] of "the router network and the routing algorithm" of the CM-2 described in Section II. We compared the results obtained from the simulation experiments with the results computed analytically.

A. Input Parameters

The system model has the following four input parameters:

- *Degree of the Network* (n): We restricted the degree of the router network to 8. Due to the following reasons, it was not feasible to simulate the router networks of higher degrees: First, when the number of nodes in the router network approaches a thousand, the memory requirements of data structures and associated queues in the simulator become too large to be supported by a UNIX machine due to memory limitations. (The memory requirement of the program for analytic solution was within 40 Kbytes.) Second, when the number of nodes is high, the simulation runs extremely slowly because of high bookkeeping overhead. (We observed that simulation time increases exponentially with the degree of the router network.) When $n = 8$, a simulation run required about 4 h of CPU time (on a 20 Mips processor) to achieve 80 000 message deliveries across the router network. (Whereas, a run of analytic solution terminates in 8 to 12 iterations and takes about 20 s of CPU time on the same machine.)
- *Arrival Rate* (λ): It is the rate at which messages arrive at a router from the 16 processors in the router cluster. Arrival rate is varied from 0.4 to 0.8 to study various loading conditions.
- *Dimension Cycle* (τ): It is equal to 1 time unit. ($\tau = 1$.)

438

- *Petit Cycle* (T): It is equal to $n * \tau$ time units.

B. Analytic Results

Since derivation of transition probabilities requires the knowledge of the mean buffer queue length, $\overline{Q}$, which is an unknown, we used an iterative procedure, called the "fixed-point iteration" [5], [20], [9] to obtain the steady state probabilities of the Markov chain. Fixed-point iteration is a quite accurate and cost effective technique to analyze queueing networks when the exact analysis is numerically intractable. Fixed-point iteration has been previously used in the analysis of concurrent programs [12], availability modeling [21], and stochastic Petri Net modeling [6].

We used the fixed-point iteration to solve our model in the following manner: We started with an initial value of $\overline{Q}$ and obtained steady state probabilities of the Markov chain (from (1)–(9) and equations in Section III-C1). Using these values, we computed new value of $\overline{Q}$ [from (12)] and repeated the procedure until the queue length converged within 1% of its value. After having determined the steady state probabilities, we computed the performance measures from the expressions derived in Section III-D. In an iterative solution method, we must discuss the existence, uniqueness, and convergence of the solution. We found that the analytic solution converged in 8 to 12 iterations in all the cases considered in this paper. We iterated with various initial values of $\overline{Q}$ and found that the solution converges to the identical values. We also iterated on the throughput at a router node (10) and found that the solution converged to the same values (as those obtained by iterating on queue length). Thus, empirical evidence suggests that a solution exists to the fixed-point problem and it is unique and the convergence is rapid. However, theoretical issues remain to be investigated.

C. Simulation Experiments

The simulation program, written in SIMPAS [4], faithfully mimicked the operation of the communication architecture and mechanisms of the CM-2. From arrival of a message at the local queue to its delivery at the destination router, it simulated the behavior of the routing algorithm of the router network in the CM-2. Only two assumptions, namely, Poisson message arrival and equiprobable destination of messages, were made about the application running on the CM-2. As mentioned before, these two assumptions are quite reasonable. No assumption was made regarding the communication mechanisms of the CM-2.

However, the analysis presented in Section III made additional assumptions to make the analysis tractable, which were not made in the simulation model. For example, in the analytic solution, a single router node has been analyzed in isolation (instead of the entire router network). Whereas the entire router network has been simulated in the simulation model. Second, in the analytic solution, we determine the probability of a message arrival at a router node in a dimension cycle by assuming the average behavior at the preceding router nodes [see (3) and (4)]. Whereas in the simulation, a message arrival at a router depends upon currently prevailing conditions at the preceding routers. Third, in the analytic solution, routing of a message at a router node is determined by assuming that branching probability of a message is equal for any of its neighboring routers. Whereas in simulation, this is determined by actual address information contained in the message. Clearly, the analysis of the router network of the CM-2 is approximate due to the above assumptions.

Thus, the simulation model is more realistic than the analytic model and captures the behavior of the CM-2 communication architecture much more faithfully. Therefore, we can assess the accuracy of the analytic model by validating it against simulation results.

To identify a steady state in the simulation, we observed statistics in steps of 5000 delivered messages (across the router network) and started collecting statistics only after the steady state was reached. This allowed us to weed out transients. In simulation experiments, a steady state was normally reached after 20 000 messages had been delivered. Simulation experiments required total of 40 000, 60 000, and 80 000 message deliveries (higher for higher degree of the router network). To increase our confidence, we computed 95% confidence interval for the performance measures. Tables I–VI report values the mid-points as well as 95% confidence intervals of the performance measures.

D. Validation of Results

In this section, we compare results of the performance measures obtained from the analytical model with the simulation model. We plot the performance measures (throughput, average queue length, response time, average hop length, and the probability of referral) for various values of arrival rate, λ, and degree of the router network, n.

1) Results on Throughput: Table I shows analytical and simulation results (with % error) on throughput for various arrival rates and degrees of the router network. Results of the analysis are within 3% of the simulation results. As expected, the throughput increases as we increase the arrival rate. The throughput is not linear with respect to the arrival rate, λ, because injection limits the number of messages that can enter the router network. We also observe that the throughput changes only marginally as the degree of the router network increases (for same λ).

2) Results on Average Queue Length: Table II shows analytical and simulation results (with % error) on the average queue length for various arrival rates and degrees of the router network.

Results of the analysis are within 8% of the simulation results. We observe that the average queue length increases as we increase the arrival rate. This is because as λ is increased, the expected number of messages injected also increases.

3) Results on the Probability of Referral: Table III shows analytical and simulation results (with % error) on the probability of referral for various arrival rates and degrees of the router network.

We observe that the probability of a message being referred increases as we increase the arrival rate. This is because the average queue length increases as we increase the arrival rate,

TABLE I
RESULTS ON THROUGHPUT (IN UNITS OF MESSAGES/τ). DEGREE OF ROUTER n VARIED FROM 5 TO 8; MESSAGE ARRIVAL RATE λ VARIED FROM 0.4/τ TO 0.8/τ

n = 5				n = 6			
Arrival Rate	Analysis	Simulation	Error Percent	Arrival Rate	Analysis	Simulation	Error Percent
0.4	0.72	0.74±.01	−2.78	0.4	0.72	0.72±.01	0.00
0.5	0.74	0.75±.01	−1.35	0.5	0.73	0.74±.01	−1.37
0.6	0.75	0.76±.01	−1.33	0.6	0.74	0.75±.01	−1.35
0.7	0.76	0.77±.01	−1.32	0.7	0.75	0.77±.01	−2.67
0.8	0.76	0.78±.01	−2.63	0.8	0.76	0.77±.01	−1.32
n = 7				n = 8			
Arrival Rate	Analysis	Simulation	Error Percent	Arrival Rate	Analysis	Simulation	Error Percent
0.4	0.72	0.73±.01	−1.39	0.4	0.72	0.74±.01	−2.78
0.5	0.73	0.74±.01	−1.37	0.5	0.73	0.75±.01	−2.74
0.6	0.74	0.75±.01	−1.35	0.6	0.74	0.76±.01	−2.70
0.7	0.75	0.76±.01	−1.33	0.7	0.75	0.77±.01	−2.67
0.8	0.75	0.76±.01	−1.33	0.8	0.75	0.77±.01	−2.67

TABLE II
RESULTS ON THE AVERAGE QUEUE LENGTH (IN UNIT OF MESSAGES). DEGREE OF ROUTER
n VARIED FROM 5 TO 8; MESSAGE ARRIVAL RATE λ VARIED FROM 0.4/τ TO 0.8/τ

n = 5				n = 6			
Arrival Rate	Analysis	Simulation	Error Percent	Arrival Rate	Analysis	Simulation	Error Percent
0.4	4.12	3.95±.06	4.13	0.4	5.06	5.22±.07	−3.16
0.5	4.18	4.23±.06	−1.20	0.5	5.12	5.41±.07	−5.66
0.6	4.22	4.34±.06	−2.84	0.6	5.16	5.48±.07	−6.20
0.7	4.26	4.41±.06	−3.52	0.7	5.20	5.52±.07	−6.15
0.8	4.28	4.45±.06	−3.97	0.8	5.22	5.55±.07	−6.32
n = 7				n = 8			
Arrival Rate	Analysis	Simulation	Error Percent	Arrival Rate	Analysis	Simulation	Error Percent
0.4	6.00	6.41±.08	−6.83	0.4	6.95	7.47±.09	−7.48
0.5	6.07	6.52±.08	−7.41	0.5	7.02	7.56±.09	−7.69
0.6	6.11	6.57±.08	−7.53	0.6	7.06	7.60±.09	−7.65
0.7	6.14	6.59±.08	−7.33	0.7	7.09	7.61±.09	−7.33
0.8	6.17	6.61±.08	−7.13	0.8	7.12	7.62±.09	−7.02

TABLE III
RESULTS ON THE PROBABILITY OF REFERRAL (THE FRACTION OF MESSAGES REFERRED). DEGREE
OF ROUTER n VARIED FROM 5 TO 8; MESSAGE ARRIVAL RATE λ VARIED FROM 0.4/τ TO 0.8/τ

n = 5				n = 6			
Arrival Rate	Analysis	Simulation	Error Percent	Arrival Rate	Analysis	Simulation	Error Percent
0.4	0.18	0.17±.003	5.56	0.4	0.17	0.16±.003	5.88
0.5	0.19	0.18±.003	5.26	0.5	0.18	0.17±.003	5.56
0.6	0.19	0.18±.003	5.26	0.6	0.19	0.18±.003	5.26
0.7	0.20	0.19±.003	5.00	0.7	0.19	0.19±.004	0.00
0.8	0.20	0.20±.004	0.00	0.8	0.20	0.19±.004	5.00
n = 7				n = 8			
Arrival Rate	Analysis	Simulation	Error Percent	Arrival Rate	Analysis	Simulation	Error Percent
0.4	0.17	0.16±.003	5.88	0.4	0.17	0.18±.003	−5.88
0.5	0.18	0.17±.003	5.56	0.5	0.17	0.18±.003	−5.88
0.6	0.18	0.18±.003	0.00	0.6	0.18	0.19±.003	−5.56
0.7	0.19	0.19±.003	0.00	0.7	0.18	0.19±.004	−5.56
0.8	0.19	0.19±.004	0.00	0.8	0.19	0.19±.004	0.00

increasing the likelihood that all the buffers are full at a router, thereby increasing referrals. The results from the analysis are within 6% of the simulation results.

4) Results on the Average Number of Hops due to Referral: Table IV shows analytical and simulation results (with % error)

on the average number of hops due to referral for various arrival rates and degrees of the router network.

Results demonstrate that the average number of hops due to referral increases as the arrival rate increases. This is because the probability of referral increases as we increase the arrival

TABLE IV

RESULTS ON THE AVERAGE NUMBER OF HOPS DUE TO REFERRAL. DEGREE OF ROUTER
n VARIED FROM 5 TO 8; MESSAGE ARRIVAL RATE λ VARIED FROM $0.4/\tau$ TO $0.8/\tau$

$n = 5$				$n = 6$			
Arrival Rate	Analysis	Simulation	Error Percent	Arrival Rate	Analysis	Simulation	Error Percent
0.4	0.92	0.86±0.16	6.52	0.4	1.06	1.04±.019	1.89
0.5	0.96	0.90±.017	6.25	0.5	1.11	1.08±.021	2.70
0.6	0.99	0.90±.017	9.09	0.6	1.14	1.18±.024	−3.51
0.7	1.02	0.92±.017	9.80	0.7	1.17	1.23±.024	−5.13
0.8	1.04	0.96±.017	7.69	0.8	1.19	1.28±.025	−7.56
$n = 7$				$n = 8$			
Arrival Rate	Analysis	Simulation	Error Percent	Arrival Rate	Analysis	Simulation	Error Percent
0.4	1.20	1.30±.023	−8.33	0.4	1.34	1.39±.025	−3.73
0.5	1.25	1.33±.023	−6.40	0.5	1.40	1.44±.025	−2.86
0.6	1.29	1.38±.025	−6.98	0.6	1.44	1.49±.027	−3.47
0.7	1.32	1.40±.027	−6.06	0.7	1.47	1.54±.027	−4.76
0.8	1.35	1.42±.028	−5.19	0.8	1.50	1.58±.028	−5.33

TABLE V

RESULTS ON THE AVERAGE NUMBER OF HOPS. DEGREE OF ROUTER n VARIED FROM 5 TO 8; MESSAGE ARRIVAL RATE λ VARIED FROM $0.4/\tau$ TO $0.8/\tau$

$n = 5$				$n = 6$			
Arrival Rate	Analysis	Simulation	Error Percent	Arrival Rate	Analysis	Simulation	Error Percent
0.4	3.50	3.24±.06	7.43	0.4	4.11	3.92±.07	4.62
0.5	3.54	3.29±.06	7.06	0.5	4.16	4.13±.07	0.72
0.6	3.57	3.37±.06	5.60	0.6	4.19	4.22±.07	−0.72
0.7	3.60	3.43±.06	4.72	0.7	4.22	4.28±.07	−1.42
0.8	3.62	3.47±.06	4.14	0.8	4.24	4.33±.07	−2.12
$n = 7$				$n = 8$			
Arrival Rate	Analysis	Simulation	Error Percent	Arrival Rate	Analysis	Simulation	Error Percent
0.4	4.73	4.84±.08	−2.33	0.4	5.35	5.76±.09	−7.66
0.5	4.78	5.05±.08	−5.65	0.5	5.41	5.83±.09	−7.76
0.6	4.82	5.13±.08	−6.43	0.6	5.46	5.87±.09	−7.51
0.7	4.85	5.17±.08	−6.60	0.7	5.49	5.91±.09	−7.65
0.8	4.88	5.21±.08	−6.76	0.8	5.51	5.93±.09	−7.62

TABLE VI

RESULTS ON THE RESPONSE TIME (IN UNITS OF τ). DEGREE OF ROUTER n VARIED FROM 5 TO 8; MESSAGE ARRIVAL RATE λ VARIED FROM $0.4/\tau$ TO $0.8/\tau$

$n = 5$				$n = 6$			
Arrival Rate	Analysis	Simulation	Error Percent	Arrival Rate	Analysis	Simulation	Error Percent
0.4	22.50	20.88±.21	7.20	0.4	31.79	30.21±.45	4.97
0.5	22.62	21.07±.27	6.85	0.5	31.96	30.48±.43	4.63
0.6	22.71	21.14±.26	6.91	0.6	32.07	31.23±.47	2.62
0.7	22.78	21.60±.29	5.18	0.7	32.16	31.60±.46	1.74
0.8	22.83	21.95±.33	3.85	0.8	32.23	32.09±.49	0.43
$n = 7$				$n = 8$			
Arrival Rate	Analysis	Simulation	Error Percent	Arrival Rate	Analysis	Simulation	Error Percent
0.4	42.83	40.95±.57	4.39	0.4	55.63	54.56±.80	1.92
0.5	43.04	42.57±.60	1.09	0.5	55.89	56.49±.85	−1.07
0.6	43.19	43.33±.64	−0.32	0.6	56.07	57.44±.84	−2.44
0.7	43.30	43.71±.61	−0.95	0.7	56.21	58.05±.85	−3.27
0.8	43.39	44.14±.68	−1.73	0.8	56.31	58.17±.87	−3.30

rate, thereby, increasing the average number of hops due to referrals. The results of the analysis are within 8% of the simulation results.

5) Results on the Average Number of Hops: Table V shows analytical and simulation results (with % error) on the average number of hops for various arrival rates and degrees of the router network. We observe that the average number of hops taken by a message increases as we increase the arrival rate. This is because the average number of hops due to referral increases as we increase the arrival rate. The results of the

441

analysis are within 8% of the simulation results.

6) Results on Response Time: Table VI shows analytical and simulation results (with % error) on the response time for various arrival rates and degrees of the router network.

The results show that the response time increases with both the arrival rate and the degree. This is mainly due to the following two reasons: First, as λ is increased, the average queue length at routers increases. Consequently, a message waits for a longer period of time before it is routed to the next router node. Second, the average number of hops taken by a message increases as the arrival rate (and the degree) increases and hence, the response time increases as we increase the arrival rate (and the degree). The results of the analysis, for most cases, are within 5% of the simulation results.

V. Concluding Remarks

We modeled the performance of the Connection Machine CM-2, with special emphasis on estimating the performance of its interprocessor communication architecture. We analyzed the performance of the router network of the CM-2 to compute message delay introduced by the router network and various other performance measures of the network architecture.

We developed an analytical model of the router network using a DTMC. Since operation of the router network is synchronous time-division multiplexing (TDM) in nature, it is amenable to DTMC modeling. In our analysis, we computed six performance measures, namely, throughput, average queue length, probability of referral, average number of hops due to referral, average number of hops, and response time. The analysis yielded formulae for these performance measures as a function of the degree of the router network and message arrival rate. These formulae indicate how the performance of the router network of the CM-2 degrades with the message arrival rate and with other parameters of the router network architecture. Since the router delays affect the interprocessor communication in an application running on the CM-2, knowledge of the sensitivity of the delays with parameters can be a useful aid in designing a high-performance parallel system.

To make the analysis tractable, we made some simplifying assumptions. Since the value of the mean buffer queue length, $\overline{Q}$, was not known, we solved the Markov chain model using the "fixed-point iteration" technique. We ran several simulation experiments of the router network for various values of the system parameters to validate the analysis. We found that the analysis presented in this paper estimates the performance of the router network with high accuracy. Due to implementation limitations, we could simulate router networks of only degree up to 8. Nonetheless, we are confident that the analysis will predict the performance of higher degree router networks with the same good accuracy because the error due to "isolated router analysis" (which is the main source of error) should diminish when the number of routers becomes large.

Main observations from the study are: 1) The average queue length, response time, the probability of referral, and the average number of hops due to referral all increase with increasing λ. 2) For fixed arrival rate, λ, throughput and the probability of referral are pretty much independent of the

degree of the router network. A comparison of Tables IV and V reveals that the referrals account for about 25% of the number of hops travelled by a message. Therefore, the referral is a simple and inexpensive, yet an effective mechanism to handle blocking and deadlock problems in the router network. Also, the injection is a reasonable mechanism for flow control in the router network. Future research should focus on allocation of program modules of a parallel application to the processors of the CM-2 (clusters and NEWS network) so as to exploit the locality of communication pattern to maximize the performance.

Acknowledgment

The authors are greatly indebted to the anonymous referees and the guest editors of the special issue for making several suggestions to improve the paper. Ashwani Gahlot of Ohio State helped in developing the simulator.

References

[1] K. Batcher, "Architecture of a massively parallel processor," in *Proc. 7th Annu. Symp. Comput. Architecture*, France, May 1980.
[2] L. N. Bhuyan and D. P. Agrawal, "Generalized hypercube and hypercube structures for a computer network," *IEEE Trans. Comput.*, pp. 323–333, Apr. 1984.
[3] BBN Laboratories, "Butterfly parallel processor overview," BBN, Cambridge, MA, Dec. 1985.
[4] R. Bryant, "SIMPAS—A simulation language based on PASCAL," Tech. Rep. 390, Dep. Comput. Sci., Univ. Wisconsin, Madison, June 1980.
[5] G. Ciardo and K. S. Trivedi, "Solution of large GSPN models," in *Numerical Solution of Markov Chains*, W. J. Stewart, Ed. New York: Marcel Dekker, 1991, pp. 565–595.
[6] H. Choi and K. S. Trivedi, "Approximate performance models of polling systems using stochastic Petri nets," in *Proc. IEEE Infocom 92, 11th Annu. Joint Conf. IEEE Computer and Communication Societies*, Florence, Italy, May 1992.
[7] "Connection machine model CM-2 technical summary," Thinking Machines Tech. Rep. HA87-4, Thinking Machines Corp., Cambridge, MA, Apr. 1987.
[8] "Connection Machine CM-5 technical summary," Thinking Machines Corp. Tech. Rep., Thinking Machines Corp., Cambridge, MA, Oct. 1991.
[9] E. de Souza e Silva, S. S. Lavenberg, and R. R. Muntz, "A perspective on iterative methods for the approximate analysis of closed queueing networks," in *Mathematical Computer Performance and Reliability*, G. Iazeolla, P. J. Courtois, and A. Hordijk, Eds. Amsterdam: Elsevier Science Publishers B. V. (North-Holland), 1984, pp. 225–244.
[10] M. R. Garzia, R. F. Garzia, and B. P. Ziegler, "Discrete-event simulation," *IEEE Spectrum*, Dec. 1986.
[11] E. Glenebe, "Performance analysis of the Connection Machine," Rapport de recherche no. 89-9, Sept. 1989. (Also in *ACM SIGMETRICS*, 1990).
[12] P. Heidelberger and K. S. Trivedi, "Analytic queueing models for programs with internal concurrency," *IEEE Trans. Comput.*, pp. 73–82, Jan. 1983.
[13] W. D. Hillis, *The Connection Machine*. Cambridge, MA: M.I.T. Press, 1985.
[14] ——, "The Connection Machine: A computer architecture based on cellular automata," *Physica*, vol. 10, pp. 213–238, 1984.
[15] Indurkhya *et al.*, "Optimal partitioning of randomly generated distributed programs," *IEEE Trans. Software Eng.*, pp. 483–495, Mar. 1986.
[16] Intel Corp., "iPSC system overview," Oct. 1985.
[17] J. Myczkowski and G. Steele, "Seismic modeling at 14 Gigaflops on the Connection Machine," in *Proc. Supercomput.'91*, Nov. 18–22, 1991, pp. 316–326.
[18] Reed, L. Adams, and M. Patrick, "Stencil and problem partitioning: Their influence on performance of multiple processor systems," *IEEE Trans. Comput.* vol. C-36, no. 7, 1987.
[19] L. Tucker and G. Robertson, "Architecture and application of the Connection Machine." *IEEE Comput. Mag.*, pp. 26–38, Aug. 1988.
[20] I. Mitrani, "Fixed-point approximations for distributed systems," in *Mathematical Computer Performance and Reliability*, G. Iazeolla, P.

J. Courtois, and A. Hordijk, Eds. Amsterdam: North-Holland, 1984, pp. 245–258.

[21] L. A. Tomek and K. S. Trivedi, "Fixed point iteration in availability modeling," *Informatik-Fachberichte*, vol. 91: Fehlertolerierende Rechensysteme, M. Dal Cin, Ed. Berlin, Germany: Springer-Verlag, 1991.

[22] R. A. Upton and S. K. Tripathi, "On the performance evaluation of fine-grained SIMD computer architecture: An analysis of the Connection Machine," in *High Performance Computer Systems*, E. Gelenbe, Ed. Amsterdam: Elsevier Science, North-Holland, 1988.

[23] K. S. Trivedi, *Probability and Statistics with Reliability, Queuing, and Computer Science Applications*. Englewood Cliffs, NJ: Prentice-Hall, 1982.

Anup K. Ahluwalia was born in New Delhi, India. He received the M.S. degree in computer and information science from The Ohio State University, Columbus, in 1991. He also received the B.S. in computer and information science from The Ohio State University.

His research interests include performance analysis and computer architecture. Currently he is working as a Senior Consultant with AGS Information Services, Inc., a subsidiary of NYNEX.

Mukesh Singhal was born in India on May 8, 1959. He received Bachelor of Engineering degree in electronics and communication engineering with high distinction from University of Roorkee, Roorkee, India, in 1980. He joined the Department of Computer Science, University of Maryland, College Park, in January 1981, where he received the Ph.D. degree in May 1986.

Since 1986, he has been on the faculty of Computer and Information Science at The Ohio State University, Columbus, where he is currently an Associate Professor. His current research interests include distributed systems, distributed databases, and performance modeling. He has published in IEEE COMPUTER, IEEE TRANSACTIONS ON COMPUTERS, IEEE TRANSACTIONS ON SOFTWARE ENGINEERING, IEEE TRANSACTIONS ON KNOWLEDGE AND DATA ENGINEERING, IEEE TRANSACTIONS ON PARALLEL AND DISTRIBUTED SYSTEMS, *Performance Evaluation*, and *Distributed Computing*. He is co-authoring a book titled *Advanced Concepts in Operating Systems* (New York: McGraw-Hill, to be published). He served as a co-guest editor of a special issue of IEEE COMPUTER on Distributed Computing Systems.

System Effects of Interprocessor Communication Latency in Multicomputers

An important factor in the efficiency of a distributed-memory multicomputer is the effectiveness with which data can be exchanged among its many nodes. A series of experiments and analyses on five types of hypercube and grid-topology multicomputers helped to evaluate interprocessor communication performance. Examination and comparison of system communication speed, message routing, interprocessor connectivity, and software/hardware protocols for passing messages among the five multicomputers enhanced the analysis.

Xiaodong Zhang

University of Texas at San Antonio

Parallel processing applies a simple idea: A computing job can be divided into several tasks that may be executed in parallel. Over the last 10 years designers implemented this concept using distributed-memory multicomputers in a variety of forms in different applications. This experience shows that parallel processing does not reach its anticipated speed when a large number of processors are used in solving problems.[1,2] The communications of common-state information among processors cause a major degradation of the performance (speed).

The literature[3-5] records efforts to measure and evaluate the interprocessor communication performance on the Intel hypercube and the Ncube multicomputers. In addition, Saad and Schultz[6] present several efficient algorithms for data communication on a hypercube multicomputer.

This article takes a wider view, studying various system effects of interprocessor performance, including communication speed, message routing, interprocessor connectivity, and message-passing software hardware protocols. Both analytical and experimental results offer a clear and comprehensive understanding of the various effects, which is important for the effective use of a distributed-memory multicomputer.

Five multicomputer architectures

In a distributed-memory multiprocessor system, or multicomputer, each processor has its own local memory, and tasks on separate processors coordinate their activities by sending messages through an interconnection network. However, many recent commercial distributed-memory systems vary in computing power, number of processors, type of processors, and network interconnection topology, as well as communication hardware and software.

The hypercube is one example of a distributed-memory, message-passing multicomputer. In a hypercube network 2^n processors are consecutively numbered 0 through $2^n - 1$. Each processor connects to all of the other processors, whose binary representation differs from its own by exactly one bit. This arrangement results in a network that is connected densely enough to support efficient communication between arbitrary processors. Another virtue of the hypercube network is its flexibility: Many other interconnection topologies, such as rings and trees, can be embedded in the hypercube. The dimension n of a hypercube with 2^n nodes determines the maximum number of hops needed to send messages between two nodes. Some system parameters of the five studied multicomputers are:

Reprinted from *IEEE Micro*, Vol. 11, No. 2, Apr. 1991, pp. 12–15 and 52–55. Copyright © 1991 by The Institute of Electrical and Electronics Engineers, Inc. All rights reserved.

- **Intel iPSC/1.** The iPSC/1, one of the first commercially available hypercube computers, may support up to 128 nodes. Each node includes an 8-MHz Intel 80286 processor and 512 Kbytes of local memory. The node operating system supports message-routing asynchronous communications and multitasking within each node.[8]
- **Intel iPSC/2.** This second-generation hypercube features a 4-million-instructions-per-second Intel 80386 node processor, which is four times faster than the 286. Each node can access up to 16 Mbytes of local memory, whereas the iPSC/1 accesses 0.5 Mbytes. The NX/2 operating system supports the new message-passing protocols in the iPSC/2 besides providing a normal system environment in each node.[9]
- **Ncube/10.** This first-generation hypercube system supports up to 1,024 processors. The 32-bit, custom-chip node processor operates at a 7-MHz clock rate and contains 128 Kbytes of local memory. Since the processor includes communication channels, the number of chips per node on the Ncube is relatively low. The Axis operating system supports the transmission of messages between arbitrary nodes of the Ncube/10.[3,10]
- **Ametek 2010.** The Ametek 2010 multicomputer system is based on a 2D grid topology. Each node includes a 25-MHz Motorola 68020 processor and up to 8 Mbytes of local memory.
- **Topology 1000.** This parallel system is a transputer-based variable topology board. The interprocessor network of this Topologix system can be reconfigured. The processor in each node of the network uses the 32-bit, 20-MHz Inmos T800 transputer and up to 16 Mbytes of local memory per processor node.[11-13] The transputer's links are based upon point-to-point interprocessor communication, which eliminates bus contention when messages are transferred. Logix OS is the distributed Unix-compatible operating system supported on the Topology 1000. The Trollius operating system developed at the Cornell Theory Center forms the basis of the Logix OS.

Table 1 summarizes the five types of architectures.

Interprocessor communication

Communication efficiency, one of the most important factors to be considered when designing a multicomputer architecture, often becomes one of the main obstacles to increased performance of parallel algorithms on distributed systems. When a message passes between a pair of nodes in a network, it may be routed through a connected circuit in a number of hops. In addition, intermediate processors may be interrupted to store and then forward the message, or the message may be directly transferred by communication-processing data links through a connected circuit. Thus, the communication speed of the interprocessor network depends on the communication-routing protocols, processor speed, data link speed, and topology of the network.

A comparison of the various effects of different routing models, different interprocessor connections, and other factors to the performance of interprocessor communication on the five types of distributed memory architectures follows.

Communication models. Consider the store-and-forward mechanism[14] used as a typical communication model for first-generation multicomputers such as the iPSC/1, Ncube/10, and Ametek/14. In this communication model, messages pass indirectly between a pair of nodes that are not directly connected via other connected nodes. Each node in the communication path temporarily stores the message in its memory. The processor on each node in that path interrupts work on a task to forward the stored message either to its neighbor or the destination node. Thus, while messages move between a pair of nodes across the network, memory bandwidth and computing cycles in the intermediate nodes are consumed.

The communication latency of this model is also very sensitive to the distance a message must be passed, or it is linearly proportional to the number of hops of the communication. We can express the communication latency of the store-and-forward model as:

$$T_{lat1} = T_{d1} H \qquad (1)$$

where $T_{d1} = K/B_1$, which is the time for a message of size K (bytes) to pass through the channel of bandwidth B_1 (bytes/s) in one hop. H equals the distance in the number of hops,

| Table 1. Architecture overviews. | | | | | |
Features	iPSC/1	iPSC/2	Ncube/10	Ametek 2010	Topology 1000
Node CPU	Intel 286	Intel 386	Custom 32-bit	Motorola 68020	Inmos T800
Clock rate (MHz)	8	16	7	25	20
Node operating system	Axis 3.0	NX/2	Axis 2.3	R Kernel	Logix OS
Node memory (bytes)	512K	Up to 16M	128K	8M	Up to 16M
Data rate (Mbytes/s)	1.25	4	0.875	20	5

and we can view T_{d1} as the routing delay of each node.

Kermani and Kleinrock[14] and Athas and Seitz[15] called the basic routing model used in second-generation multicomputers (for example, the iPSC/2 and Ametek 2010) wormhole routing. Instead of storing a packet completely in a node and then transmitting it to the next node, wormhole routing operates by advancing the head of a packet directly from incoming to outgoing channels. Only a few flow-control digits are buffered at each node. These digits, or flits, are the smallest units of information that a queue or channel can accept or refuse. A message consists of a sequence of flits, in which the flit at the head of the message governs the route, and the remaining flits follow in pipeline fashion. Besides avoiding the use of storage bandwidth in the nodes through which messages are routed, wormhole routing and its flow control also reduce the message latency caused by distance in the network. Therefore, the data transfer rate becomes the limiting factor for message-passing speed.

We can express the communication latency of the wormhole model as:

$$T_{lat2} = T_{d2}H + (K/B_2) \qquad (2)$$

where $T_{d2} = K_b/B_2$ is the routing delay in each node for sending the packet head in K_b (bytes) to pass through the channels of bandwidth B (bytes/s). K/B_2 is the time required to transmit the whole packet K (bytes) continuously through the wormhole channels of bandwidth B_2 (bytes/s), and H is the communication distance. The ratio between Equations 1 and 2 is a quantitative comparison of the two models:

$$R = \frac{T_{lat1}}{T_{lat2}} = \left(\frac{B_2}{B_1}\right)\frac{KH}{K_bH + K} \qquad (3)$$

The size of the packet head K_b is trivial in comparison with the size of the whole packet K. For example, the packet head size in the Ametek 2010 is only 2 bytes. Therefore the ratio R in Equation 3 may be expressed as:

$$R \approx (B_2/B_1)H \qquad (4)$$

This equation indicates that the wormhole model reduces the communication latency up to $B_2/B_1 \times H$ times over the store-and-forward model. In this case, we assumed the message size K and the communication distance H to be the same in both communication architectures, and the bandwidth of the second-generation multicomputer B_2 to be higher than the one of the first-generation B_1.

Even if the data bandwidth of the two models were the same, $B_1 = B_2$, the communication latency would be reduced to H times in the wormhole model. For example, the first-generation hypercube Intel iPSC/1 uses the store-and-forward

model; its data bandwidth is 1.25 Mbytes/s. The second-generation hypercube Intel iPSC/2 uses the wormhole model; its data bandwidth is 4 Mbytes/s. If we substitute $B_1 = 1.25$, $B_2 = 4$, and $H = 5$ for a 32-node hypercube in Equation 4, we obtain $R \approx 16$. This ratio indicates that a 32-node iPSC/2 hypercube may reduce the communication latency time up to 16 times over a 32-node iPSC/1 hypercube.

Hardware implementation. The communication mechanisms based on the store-and-forward technique used in the Intel iPSC/1 and Ncube/10 are typical first-generation message-passing protocols on a distributed-memory multiprocessing system. The processor on each node in that path participates in handling communications, stopping other processing tasks during message-passing periods.

The iPSC/1 and the Ncube/10 consume the local memory bandwidth and computing cycles in the routing nodes while accumulating a latency of several hundred microseconds per hop. Thus, the computing speed and bandwidth in each processor mainly determine the store-and-forward communication speed. The higher the clock rate of each processor, the lower the latency in communication will be, since the processor more speedily accomplishes the store-and-forward operation. The experiment's results discussed in the next section show the low efficiency of the store-and-forward techniques on the Intel iPSC/1 and Ncube/10.

We can implement the wormhole model differently on a multicomputer. The hardware structures on the iPSC/2 and Ametek 2010 are two typical implementations for the wormhole routing model on a interconnecting network.

The wormhole routing model greatly reduces communication latency.

The direct-connect router, a hardware-controlled message-passing system in the Intel iPSC/2, forms the basis of the communication system. Think of the router as a switching network. When one node wants to communicate with another, the sending node closes a series of switches and establishes the communication path. Then, messages proceed at the full hardware speed of 4 Mbytes/s. Only the sending and destination processors participate in the communication; the other processors in the routing path continue with their normal activities. Since it takes only a few microseconds per node to build the path, the additional overhead for multihop communications is insignificant. In addition, the hardware routes messages independently, and the iPSC/2 communication latency is significantly reduced over that in the iPSC/1.

The Ametek 2010 communication network is the most efficient one among the five multiprocessing architectures. The message network consists of a 2D grid of custom mesh routing chips. Message packets advance directly from one of these chips to another in a blocking variant of cut-through routing of the wormhole routing. At the 20-MHz rate, the 8-bit-wide channels yield a communication bandwidth of 20 Mbytes/s per channel. Thus, the network quickly establishes a connection circuit between two remote nodes, and the mesh routing chips transfer messages in a byte-serial fashion in one operation.

The Topology 1000 implements the store-and-forward technique differently. The communication system is tied into each transputer at a very low level. The transputer employs a hardware scheduler to schedule the communication of messages. Therefore, setting up a communication takes just a few microseconds.

On the other hand, the transputer implements synchronized message passing. Both sender and receiver must be ready before a communication can take place. This coordination occurs at the lowest level of the communication protocol and results in the absence of problems with data overruns or buffer overflows. In addition, the store operation acts the same as it does in the iPSC/1 and Ncube/10, storing the message in the local memory of the routing node. However, each processor is only responsible for initiating the forward operation. Then the DMA data link carries out the message transfer without further interruption of the processor.

The DMA data links on the Topology 1000 operate at a maximum unidirectional rate of 1.75 Mbytes/s or a bidirectional rate of 2.5 Mbytes/s. Four links per transputer produce a 10-Mbyte/s rate. The basic idea of this model is to use *excess* parallelism to hide the latency in the data transfer. For very short messages, a low transfer rate is possible because most of the time spent in the communication occurs in the processor cycles upon initializing a data transfer. However, the communication can take advantage of a large message transfer when the processor's initialization time is trivial (compared with the data transfer time used by the DMA data links).

Experimental results on a Topology 1000 with the DMA data links show improvement in communication efficiency. The communication speed of the Topology 1000 is much higher than on the Intel iPSC/1 and Ncube/10, although all three multiprocessing systems use general store-and-forward techniques.

Comparing the two topologies. The Ncube and both iPSC systems use the hypercube interconnection topology. The Ametek 2010 uses a 2D grid as the interprocessor connecting topology. We can compare these two network topologies in terms of the communication efficiency.

We can make a hypercube of arbitrary dimension by using a linear arrangement with connecting wires. We obtain the cube of each dimension by replicating the one in the next-

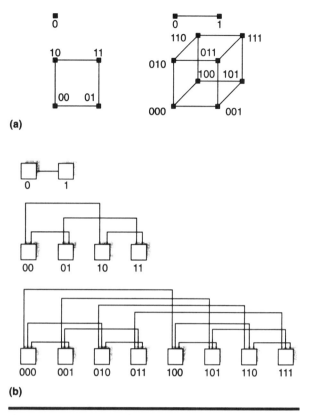

(a)

(b)

Figure 1. Construction of a hypercube.

lower dimension and then connecting corresponding nodes. For example, directly connecting two nodes labeled 0 and 1 between the two nodes gives us a one-dimensional hypercube (2^1). We make a 2D hypercube by duplicating the bisection, or the 1D hypercube, by directly connecting the corresponding node of each bisection together. Adding a high-order bit to the node number sets it to 0 for the lower order bisection and 1 for the other. We construct the higher dimensional hypercube by further connecting the bisections of the hypercube. As Figure 1a shows, each processor in a hypercube connects to all other processors whose binary tags differ by exactly one bit. We can make a hypercube of arbitrary dimension by using a linear arrangement with connecting wires, as shown in Figure 1b.

We can make a channel that physically links two directly connected nodes from a bundle of wires consisting of data bits and any necessary control bits. We need $N/2$ channels across the bisection to construct a hypercube, where N is number of nodes in the hypercube. However, using the same method to construct a 2D grid requires $O\sqrt{N}$ channels across the bisection, where N is the number of nodes in the 2D grid. We can determine the maximum distance between a pair of nodes in a hypercube if we know the dimension of the hypercube, or $\log_2(N)$. The same factor in a 2D grid is $O(\sqrt{N})$, which increases faster than $\log_2(N)$.

Recall that the communication latency is dependent on the channel width, distance (number of hops), and size of the message. The network latency in the wormhole model precisely equals the time it takes the head of a message to enter the network at the source and the tail to emerge at the destination:

$$T_{lat} = t_d H + (K/B) \qquad (5)$$

Here, T_d is the delay of the individual routing nodes encountered on the path, H is the number of hops needed in passing messages, and K/B is the time required for a message of size K to pass through the channels of bandwidth B.

In lower dimensional hypercube topology, the number of hops increases, but so does the channel width. The optimization to minimize latency simply minimizes Equation 5. In this equation, higher dimensional networks reduce the first term at the expense of the second, while lower dimensional networks reduce the second term at the expense of the first. The 2D grid has $O(\sqrt{N})$ times more wires per channel for a fixed number N of nodes than an equivalent N-node topology. The following numerical comparisons indicate the advantage of lower latency in the 2D grid network. Assume the routing delay T_d in both the hypercube and 2D grid networks is identical. We can express the time needed to send a message with K bytes between a pair of nodes in the maximum distance $\log_2(N)$ in the hypercube with N nodes as:

$$T_{cube} = T_d \log_2(N) + (K/B) \qquad (6)$$

We express the same timing factor in the 2D grid network of N nodes to send a K-size message differently, since the bandwidth in each channel is $O(\sqrt{N})$ times wider, and the maximum distance $O(\sqrt{N})$ is also a faster-increasing function:

$$T_{grid} = T_d O(\sqrt{N}) + \frac{K}{O(\sqrt{N})B} \qquad (7)$$

We derive the ratio of T_{cube}/T_{grid} by

$$R = O(\sqrt{N}) \frac{T_d \log(N) + T_c}{T_d N + T_c} \qquad (8)$$

where $T_c = K/B$.

The second term K/B of Equation 5 dominates the network latency for all but very short messages in the second-generation multicomputers. For example, in one implementation conducted by the California Institute of Technology,[16] the routing delay in one node T_d was 80 nanoseconds. Even the fast bandwidth of the Ametek 2010—B = 20 Mbytes/s needed to transfer a 160-byte message—would take 8 microseconds, which is 100 times longer than T_d. When K is reasonably large, T_d may be ignored, and the ratio R of Equation 8 is $O(\sqrt{N})$. That is, the communication latency in a 2D grid network may be reduced up to $O(\sqrt{N})$ times over a hypercube network.

In summary, given a constant bisection width, the 2D grid network produces lower latency and higher throughput than a higher dimensional hypercube. Mainly, fewer channels contribute to the bisection, which permits each channel to be made wider. On the other hand, the throughput is bounded by allowing more channels crossing the bisection in a higher dimensional hypercube.

A transputer is a good candidate for constructing a 2D grid network.

The Topology 1000 provides hardware reconfigurability of the network topology under software control through the use of the Inmos C004 link crossbar adapter. Thus, a user can define an interprocessor communication topology, and the hardware and software can implement it. Since each transputer has four links to connect with other transputers in the network, a transputer becomes a good candidate for constructing a 2D grid network. We can achieve full connectivity or high connectivity in a lower dimensional topology with a small number of nodes and construct a 4D hypercube by connecting 16 transputers properly.

However, we cannot build higher dimensional hypercubes out of transputers exclusively since they are limited to four links per node, and hypercubes of five or more dimensions require five or more links per node. Such topologies are possible with the addition of hardware link switches such as the Inmos C004 crossbar adapter used in the Topologix system. Performance losses occur with the use of such switches, however.

The experiment

A distributed-memory multicomputer is a collection of processors or nodes connected by a communication network. Thus, the basic communication timing test for distributed-memory multicomputers requires measurement of the time

Table 2. Alphas and betas (in microseconds/byte) for one-hop communication.		
Multiprocessor	α	β
iPSC/1	893	1.51
iPSC/2	349	2.30×10^{-1}
Ncube/10	447	2.40
Ametek 2010	168	1.01×10^{-1}
Topology 1000	215	1.02×10^{-1}

required to transmit a message packet from one node to its nearest neighbor. This test, also known as an echo test, directs a test node to send a message to an echo node that is directly connected to the test node. The echo node receives the message and sends it back to the test node. We can express the interprocessor communication time required to transmit a message between two directly connected nodes as:

$$T_{comm} = \alpha + \beta K$$

where K is the number of bytes contained in the message. Here, α equals the overhead or the start-up time for sending a packet in microseconds, and β equals the bandwidth of the communication channel (microseconds/byte). The experiment used different sizes of message packets and a least square fit to approximate α and β. Table 2 reproduced from Zhang and Beguelin[17] lists the αs and βs of the five types of multicomputers.

Since multiple-hop communications occur more often in most applications on a multiprocessor system, the one-hop communication measurements do not let us sufficiently evaluate the performance of the interprocessor communication. For this reason, we[17] constructed a comprehensive experiment to measure the overall communication performance on a multiprocessor system for a given topology network.

In the experiment, a test node sent n messages to and received n messages from all nodes in the network. We measured the time it took for a test node to send a message to every node in the network and return. We repeated this process m times and continued the whole process until every node had become the test node. We obtained the average communication time in the network from the p timing measures, where p is number of processors in the network. We chose the message size from a minimum of 1 byte to a maximum of 8 Kbytes. The communication distances in this experiment range from a minimum zero hop (a node to itself) to a maximum H_{max} hops. $H_{max} = n$, for an n-dimensional hypercube topology, and $H_{max} = O(\sqrt{N})$, for an N-node 2D grid topology.

Figure 2 charts the average communication time for different message sizes on different types of multiprocessors. The iPSC 1, iPSC 2, and Topology 1000 have a hypercube topology, and the Ametek 2010 has 2D grid topology. The results of the experiment showed that communication timing differences are very close to the results predicted earlier by the latency models. For example, Equation 4 predicted the iPSC 1 and iPSC 2 communication latency ratio for a 16-node system to be 12.8. The experiment's results in Figure 2 also show that the timing ratio was more than 10.

To show that the communication latency of the wormhole model exhibits little sensitivity to message distance, we conducted another experiment on the five types of multicomputers. In this experiment we fixed the message size, let the communication time become the function of the distance, and set the number of hops as H. We ran this experiment with message-packet sizes of 1 Kbytes to 8 Kbytes and used the average timing value from eight runs as the

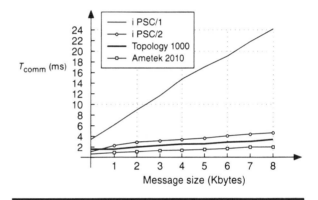

Figure 2. Average multihop communication time on the Intel, Topologix, and Ametek multiprocessors.

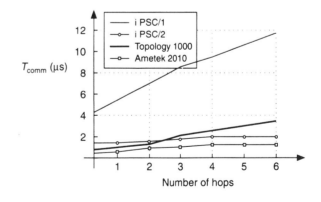

Figure 3. Average communication time with different hops on the same multiprocessors.

measure to cover a wide range of message sizes. Figure 3 describes this timing function based on the experimental data.

The experiment's results clearly show the performance difference of the interprocessor communication between the first-generation multicomputer systems and the second-generation distributed multiprocessor systems. The traditional store-and-forward technique for interprocessor communication greatly limits the communication speed among the processors. In addition, the processors of the first-generation multiprocessing systems are not very powerful, which is another major reason communication proceeds slowly in these systems.

To transfer a message in a store-and-forward network, such as the iPSC 1 or the Ncube 10, the processor must move each byte of data through its own memory, thus consuming both storage bandwidth and computing cycles in the routing nodes. The Intel iPSC/2 uses more powerful processors and, more importantly, uses direct switches as the interprocessor connections. Thus, the communication performance is greatly improved over that of the iPSC 1 and the Ncube 10.

The Topology 1000's high-performance interprocessor communication occurs especially when the number of processors in the network is not very large and the message size is not too small. The four links of each transputer, which may create more hops and a low number of direct connections for a large number of transputer networks, limit the inter-transputer connectivity. The DMA data links in the multiple-transputer system play an important role in transferring data at high speeds. However, as the graph in Figure 3 shows, the communication latency of the Topology 1000 is more sensitive than are the iPSC 2 and Ametek 2010 when the number of hops increases. The Topology 1000 uses the store-and-forward model, after all. We obtained the timing results from a 16-node hypercube network on both the iPSC system and the Topology 1000. Finally, the point-to-point communication established on the Ametek 2010, which contains a powerful mesh routing chip on each node, produces the best interprocessor communication performance among the five multiprocessor architectures.

THE WORMHOLE ROUTING MODEL greatly reduces communication latency and is no longer sensitive to the distance involved in passing messages. In addition, the high-data bandwidth and high-speed nodes of the second-generation multicomputers such as the iPSC 2 and Ametek 2010 increase communication speed. The Topology 1000 interprocessor communication may perform at a rate similar to that of the iPSC 2 and Ametek 2010 on a medium-size network since the system takes advantage of the high-speed transputer data links. The 2D grid topology is a more efficient structure than a higher dimensional hypercube topology in terms of reducing communication latency, as long as the routing delay in each node is small, such as the one in the second-generation multicomputers. 🔟

Acknowledgments

The National Science Foundation under grants CCR-9008991 and CCR-9047481 partially supported this research.

References

1. C. Moler, "Matrix Computation on Distributed-Memory Multiprocessors," *SIAM Proc. Hypercube Multiprocessors*, Soc. Industrial and Applied Mathematics, Philadelphia, 1986, pp. 181-195.
2. X. Zhang, R. Byrd, and R. Schnabel, "Solving Nonlinear Block-Bordered Circuit Equations on Hypercube Multicomputers," *Proc. Fourth Conf. Hypercubes, Concurrent Computers, and Applications,* Vol. I, 1989, pp. 701-707.
3. A. Beguelin and D. Vasicek, "Communication Between Nodes of a Hypercube," *SIAM Proc. Hypercube Multiprocessors*, 1987, pp. 162-168.
4. D.A. Reed and R.M. Fujimoto, *Multicomputer Network: Message-Based Parallel Processing,* MIT Press, Cambridge, Mass., 1987.
5. D.C. Grunwald and D.A. Reed, "Benchmarking Hypercube Hardware and Software," *SIAM Proc. Hypercube Multiprocessors,* 1987, pp. 169-175.
6. Y. Saad and M.H. Schultz, "Data Communication in Hypercubes," *J. Parallel Distributed Computing,* Vol. 6, 1989, pp. 115-135.
7. C.L. Seitz, "The Cosmic Cube," *Comm. ACM,* Vol. 28, No. 1, 1985, pp. 22-33.
8. *iPSC User's Guide,* No. 17455-3, Intel Corp., Portland, Ore., 1985.
9. P. Pierce, "The NX/2 Operating System," *Proc. Third Conf. Hypercube Concurrent Computers and Applications,* ACM Press, 1988, pp. 384-390.
10. *Ncube Handbook, Version 1.1,* Ncube Corp., Beaverton, Ore., 1986.
11. *The Transputer Data Book,* Inmos Corp., Bristol, UK, 1989.
12. *The Transputer Application's Notebook: Architecture and Software,* Inmos Corp., 1989.
13. *The Transputer Application's Notebook: Systems and Performance,* Inmos Corp., 1989.
14. A.S. Tanenbaum, *Computer Network,* Prentice-Hall, Inc., Englewood Cliffs, N.J., 1981.

15. P. Kermani and L. Kleinrock, "Virtual Cut-Through: A New Computer Communication Switching Technique," *Computer Networks,* Vol. 13, 1979, pp. 267-286.

16. W.C. Athas and C.L. Seitz, "Multicomputers: Message-Passing Concurrent Computers," *Computer,* Vol. 21, No. 8, 1988, pp. 9-24.

17. X. Zhang and A. Beguelin, "Interprocessor Communication Performance on Different Types of Multicomputers," *Intelligent Distributed Processing,* R. Ammar, ed., ACTA Press, Anaheim, Calif., 1989, pp. 73-76.

Xiaodong Zhang is an assistant professor of computer science at the University of Texas at San Antonio and holds a visiting faculty position at the Center for Research on Parallel Computation at Rice University. Earlier, he had worked as a member of the technical staff for Topologix Inc., Denver. His research interests lie primarily in the areas of parallel and distributed computation, parallel system performance evaluation and VLSI simulation, and numerical analysis of nonlinear equations and optimization problems.

Zhang received the BS degree in electrical engineering from Beijing Polytechnic University and the MS and PhD degrees in computer science from the University of Colorado at Boulder. He is a member of the IEEE Computer Society, the Association of Computing Machinery, and the Society for Industrial and Applied Mathematics.

Address questions concerning this article to the author at the Division of Mathematics and Computer Science, University of Texas at San Antonio, San Antonio, TX 78285-0664; or via Internet at zhang@ringer.cs.utsa.edu.

Adaptive Routing Protocols for Hypercube Interconnection Networks

Patrick T. Gaughan and Sudhakar Yalamanchili

Georgia Institute of Technology

Multipath networks and adaptive routing protocols dynamically adapt to network conditions such as communication bottlenecks, thus lifting a major impediment to the development of massively parallel architectures.

T he motivation for adaptive routing protocols stems from several sources. Interprocessor communication is potentially the dominant component of performance in multiprocessor architectures. This has been responsible for developments in routing algorithms,[1,2] hardware routers,[1] and interconnection networks.[3] Researchers have used these developments to address network latency and bandwidth utilization issues for current-generation parallel architectures. However, in advancing to the use of large-scale parallel architectures, we foresee a number of issues that encourage the use of adaptive routing protocols.

First, large-scale parallel architectures will necessarily resort to physically distributed memory to provide scalable memory bandwidth. Efficient implementation of shared- and distributed-memory computing models will require efficient use of high-bandwidth interprocessor communication resilient to failures and bottlenecks. Protocols that always route messages along a static, fixed path make poor use of bandwidth, blocking when alternative paths are available. They are particularly susceptible to component failures.

Adaptive routing protocols can use alternative paths between communicating processors, making more efficient use of network bandwidth and providing resilience to failures. The latter property is particularly important for large-scale architectures, since expanding system size can increase the probability of encountering a faulty network component. For these reasons, we believe multipath networks in conjunction with adaptive routing protocols will become the rule rather than the exception in massively parallel architectures.

One such class of multipath networks is the family of binary *n*-cubes. These networks form a subset of a much larger class that includes *k*-ary *n*-cube, hyperrectangular, and generalized hypercube interconnection networks. We use the term

Reprinted from *Computer,* Vol. 26, No. 5, May 1993, pp. 12–23.
0-8186-6522-X/95 $4.00 © 1993 IEEE

hypercube interconnection networks (HINs) to include all of these classes, referring to specific classes when necessary.

HINs are powerful generalizations of the binary n-cube. Adaptive routing protocols studied to date for HINs have been largely limited to the binary n-cube and the k-ary n-cube (for $n = 2$) networks. However, the rich interconnection topology and implementation constraints such as wiring complexity, layout, and chip pin count make some HINs more desirable than binary n-cubes for large-scale parallel architectures.

For example, the increased bandwidth utilization afforded by adaptive routing protocols can enable a lower dimensional HIN (and therefore lower cost) to provide the necessary communication performance. This, in fact, has a direct impact on the size, weight, and power considerations of the physical network.

As parallel architectures become larger and faster, packaging and physical constraints are assuming more important roles. Thus, other classes of HINs such as k-ary n-cube and hyperrectangular networks are receiving increasing attention.

In this article, we propose a taxonomy for characterizing adaptive routing protocols for HINs. The taxonomy is based on classes of routing decisions common to any HIN. We use this taxonomy to discuss existing and proposed protocols. Rather than an exhaustive enumeration of related research, the protocols we selected for discussion are intended to be representative of the classes defined by the taxonomy.

These protocols are candidates for use in massively parallel architectures configured with HINs. Therefore, we are particularly concerned with how well their performance "scales" with system size. To provide some insight into their behavior in very large HINs, we conclude this article with the results of simulation studies of representative protocols.

Hypercube interconnection networks

Consider the interconnection of N processors in an HIN.[3] Let a distinct factorization of N be

Common adaptive routing terminology

Completely or *fully adaptive* — A protocol capable of using all paths in its domain (for example, profitable paths for a profitable protocol). If it is restricted to a subset of these paths, it is said to be partially adaptive.

Free link — A link that is nonfaulty and is available for use in constructing a path.

Misrouted or *derouted message* — A message routed over a link that is not profitable. (Also called nonminimal routing.)

Optimal or *minimal path* — A path that contains the minimum number of links from a source to a destination when all links in the network are free. An optimal path contains only profitable links.

Path — A series of links through a network connecting intermediate nodes over which a message is transmitted from a source node to a destination node.

Physical link or *physical channel* — A hardware bus connecting two nodes over which data can be transmitted. Links may be unidirectional or bidirectional.

Profitable link — A link at a source or intermediate node over which a message moves closer to the destination node.

Routing header or *routing tag* — A portion of the message used by the routing protocol to direct the message from the source to the destination node. (A routing header used in circuit switching is also called a circuit probe.)

Shortest path — A path that contains the minimum number of links from a source to a destination when constrained by the presence of busy and faulty links within the network.

Virtual link or *virtual channel* — A logical entity associated with a physical link used to distinguish multiple data streams traversing the same physical channel. Multiple virtual links are time-multiplexed across a physical channel.

$$N = b_d \times b_{d-1} \times b_{d-2} \times \ldots \times b_1 = \prod_{i=1}^{d} b_i \quad (1)$$

Each processor can now be represented in a mixed radix number system with a d-digit address

$$r_d, r_{d-1}, r_{d-2}, \ldots, r_1 \quad (2)$$

where digit r_i is in base b_i, d is the number of dimensions in the configuration, and b_i is the number of processors in dimension i. Different HINs can now be described based on constraints on the values of d, b_i, and the interconnection of processors within a dimension.

Generalized HINs: Each processor is connected to every other processor whose address differs in exactly one digit; that is, $\forall i$, $r_d, r_{d-1}, \ldots, r_i, \ldots, r_1$ is connected to processor $r_d, r_{d-1}, \ldots, r_i', \ldots, r_1$, where $0 \le r_t' \le b_i - 1$ and $r_i \ne r_i'$.

Hyperrectangular interconnection networks: Each processor is connected to

every other processor whose address differs in exactly one digit by ± 1 modulo the dimension radix; that is, $\forall i$, $r_d, r_{d-1}, \ldots, r_i, \ldots, r_1$ is connected to processor $r_d, r_{d-1}, \ldots, ((r_i \pm 1) \bmod b_i), \ldots, r_1$.

k-ary n-cube interconnection networks: For all i, $b_i = k$, and each processor is connected to every other processor whose address differs in exactly one digit by ± 1 modulo k; that is, $\forall i$, $r_d, r_{d-1}, \ldots, r_i, \ldots, r_1$ is connected to processor $r_d, r_{d-1}, \ldots, ((r_i \pm 1) \bmod k), \ldots, r_1$.

The well-known binary hypercubes represent a subset of generalized hypercubes where the number of processors in each dimension is limited to two; that is, $b_i = 2$, $\forall i$. It follows from the definition above that, for a given number of processors, there are potentially many different interconnection schemes within each class — each defined by a distinct factorization of N.

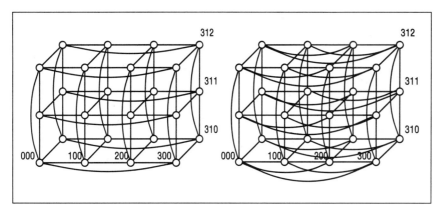

Figure 1. A (4, 3, 2) hyperrectangular and generalized hypercube.

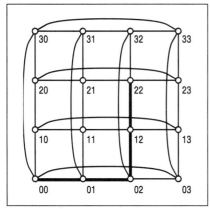

Figure 2. A fixed-path route in a 4-ary 2-cube.

We will refer to such a hypercube as a $(b_d, b_{d-1}, \ldots, b_1)$ hypercube. For example, Figure 1 shows a $(4, 3, 2)$ hyperrectangular hypercube and generalized hypercubes with 24 processors. In the former case, processors within a dimension form a ring; in the latter case, processors form a completely connected subgraph. (Bhuyan and Agrawal discuss some combinatorial properties of specific classes of HINs.[3])

For a *fixed path* or oblivious routing protocol, the path a message takes is determined solely by the source-desti-nation pair without regard to network state. An adaptive protocol uses the network state to make routing decisions. In either case, routing proceeds as a traversal of a sequence of dimensions. Consider fixed-path routing on a 4-ary 2-cube. Figure 2 shows a fixed route from node 00 to node 22 in a 4-ary 2-cube. The route the message takes is

$$00 \rightarrow 01 \rightarrow 02 \rightarrow 12 \rightarrow 22.$$

Note that the first two links taken by the message eliminate the difference in the first dimension — 02 and 22 have the same digit in the first dimension. When the difference in the address of the current node and that of the desti-nation node is 0 in dimension i, we say the message has *traversed* dimension i. Once all dimensions are successfully traversed, the message is at the destina-tion node.

Communication considerations

In interprocessor communication where several links must be traversed, several issues involving data transmis-sion mechanisms and routing require-ments must be addressed.

Communication mechanisms. In gen-eral, we can identify three mechanisms for interprocessor communication in parallel architectures; they are packet switching, circuit switching, and virtual cut-through routing.

Packet-switching mechanisms behave in a store-and-forward manner, analo-gous to the mail service. Packet-switched methods are generally advantageous when messages are short and/or infre-quent. Minimum message latency is pro-portional to the product of the number of hops and the message length.

Circuit-switching methods behave like telephone systems where a path from the source to the destination is initially established and the circuit is held until the entire message is transmitted. Cir-cuit switching can use physical circuits, where each physical link is reserved for the duration of the message, or virtual circuits, where only virtual links are reserved. We refer to the virtual-circuit variant as pipelined circuit switching, since it pipelines data through the net-work in a manner similar to wormhole routing.

Pipelined circuit switching is similar to wormhole routing except that the data does not follow the header imme-diately, but waits until a circuit acknowl-edgment has been received at the source node. Flow control mechanisms will dif-fer depending on whether physical or virtual circuits are used. Circuit-switched mechanisms generally are most effec-tive when messages are long and/or in-frequent. Minimum message latency is proportional to the sum of the message length and some constant (> 1) multiple of the path length.

Virtual cut-through routing attempts to combine the benefits of packet switch-ing and circuit switching. The message

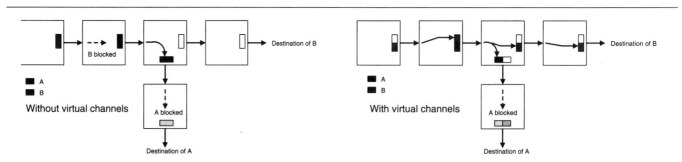

Figure 3. Increased throughput with virtual channels: routing without virtual channels (left) and with virtual channels (right).

is broken into small parcels called *flow control digits*, or *flits*,[1] that are pipelined through the network. As soon as enough routing information becomes available at an intermediate node and the output link is free, forwarding of flits begins even before the entire message is received. If no output link is free, flits are buffered at intermediate nodes. If the buffers are large enough to hold the entire message, the message is buffered at the blocked intermediate node and no links are held. If the buffers are not large enough, the message will be buffered across several intermediate nodes, holding the links between them.

At heavy loads, virtual cut-through routing tends to behave like packet-switching protocols; at light loads, it behaves more like circuit-switching protocols.[4] *Wormhole* routing is a special case of virtual cut-through, where the buffers at the intermediate nodes are the size of a message header. Minimum latency is proportional to the sum of the message length and the path length.

The *communication mechanism* (that is, the packet, circuit, or virtual cut-through) can be separated from the determination of a source-destination path. The routing decisions have little to do with the particular mechanism involved. Thus, in general, an adaptive routing protocol can be used for packet, circuit, or virtual cut-through communication (within the limitations discussed below).

Virtual channels. A virtual channel is a logical entity associated with a physical link used to distinguish multiple data streams traversing the same physical channel. Virtual channels are multiplexed over the physical channel in a demand-driven manner, with bandwidth allocated to each virtual channel as needed.

Virtual channels can be used for deadlock avoidance by imposing routing restrictions on them to break cyclic dependencies in the network.[1,5] Virtual channels can also be useful in increasing network throughput by reducing physical-link idle time.[6]

Increased sharing of network resources provides a dramatic increase in network throughput. Consider the situation shown in Figure 3, where message A is blocked at node *n*. On the left side of Figure 3, message B must block because message A has reserved the physical link. On the right side of Figure 3,

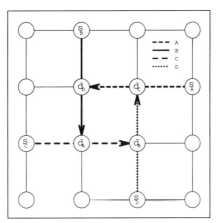

Figure 4. A deadlocked message pattern.

virtual links allow message B to continue toward its destination.

Consider the case where virtual channels are not used in wormhole-routed or circuit-switched networks. When a routing header blocks, all physical links in the path are idle until the header can advance. When virtual channels are used, other messages can use these physical links while the blocked header waits. When virtual channels are used, all virtual channels must be idle for the physical link to be idle.

Deadlock and livelock. While routing in the presence of traffic, some messages inevitably will be in a situation where they cannot route profitably. If the routing protocol opts to wait for the required resources (that is, links or buffer space) to become available, deadlock can occur. Deadlock results from cyclic dependencies within the network. All routing protocols must have some method of dealing with deadlock.

One of the most popular methods of deadlock avoidance is the imposition of a routing restriction on the protocol

that makes it provably deadlock free by preventing the occurrence of cyclic dependencies.[1,5,7,8] Other methods include structured buffer pools (for packet switching), priority schemes, and abort/retry mechanisms.

Messages do not have to wait for busy resources, but can misroute in hope of finding another path to the destination. This behavior can lead to another situation known as livelock. Livelock occurs when a message circulates endlessly in the network, never reaching its destination. Protocols that misroute in this fashion must have some method of dealing with livelock. Livelock is particularly a problem for packet-switched and large-buffer virtual cut-through. Circuit-switched and wormhole-routed networks rarely have problems with livelock, since routing restrictions placed to avoid deadlock usually limit the freedom to misroute.

Deadlock occurs in a network where cyclic dependencies can develop among network resources. Consider the situation in Figure 4. Four wormhole-routed messages, A, B, C, and D, are waiting for links held by another message. Since none will advance until the required links are released, the messages are deadlocked. Similar examples can be constructed for packet-switched and circuit-switched networks. Deadlock is a serious problem that must be addressed by all routing protocols.

Taxonomy

In this section, we introduce a taxonomy of adaptive routing protocols that refines an earlier classification scheme[9] and is illustrated in Figure 5.

Consider a circuit-switched network where a probe attempts to establish a

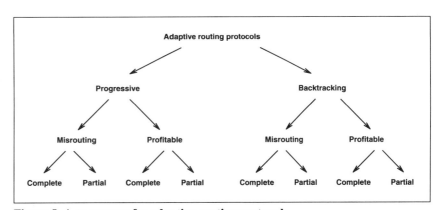

Figure 5. A taxonomy for adaptive routing protocols.

source-destination path. In the absence of bottlenecks and failures, the probe will follow a fixed path and will behave exactly as it would under an oblivious protocol. Adaptive routing differs from oblivious routing in the routing decisions made in the presence of bottlenecks and failures.

At the first level, protocols are classified as *backtracking* or *progressive*. Progressive protocols move "forward" and have only limited ability to backtrack. Backtracking protocols systematically search the network, backtracking as needed, using history information to ensure that no path is searched more than once.

At the second level the protocols are classified as *misrouting* or *profitable*.[4] The distinction here is based on the set of links that are candidates for routing at each intermediate node. A profitable protocol only considers profitable links as viable candidates for routing at each node. A misrouting protocol can use both profitable and nonprofitable links at each node.

At the lowest level, protocols can be either completely adaptive or partially adaptive. A completely adaptive protocol can use all paths in its class. For example, a profitable protocol that is completely adaptive is not deterred by routing restrictions from establishing any profitable path. A backtracking protocol that is completely adaptive is also called *exhaustive*.

Due to routing restrictions to avoid deadlock, some protocols are only partially adaptive. This taxonomy is based on the classes of routing decisions and, as such, is independent of the specific interconnection topology.

Misrouting protocols are based on an optimistic view of the state of the network; taking an unprofitable link is likely to bring the probe to another set of free profitable links that will allow further progress to the destination. Conversely, profitable protocols hold a conservative view — routing only over links known to be guaranteed to move toward the destination.

If deadlock avoidance techniques are used, profitable protocols can be guaranteed to eventually find a path in a fault-free network. Purely misrouting protocols may suffer from livelock. On the other hand, profitable protocols are less resilient in the presence of static faults. Every faulty link severs communications between at least one pair of

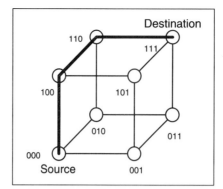

Figure 6. An *e*-cube route from 000 to 111 in a binary 3-cube.

processors: that pair connected by the link. Several faulty links can separate large parts of the network. The ability to use unprofitable links gives misrouting protocols more flexibility and greatly increases the number of possible paths between nodes.

While circuit- and packet-switched mechanisms can be employed by any of the classes of routing protocols, some virtual cut-through routing cannot. If buffers can contain the entire message, virtual cut-through routing can be considered equivalent to packet switching so far as adaptive routing is concerned.

Small buffer schemes, such as wormhole routing, are incompatible with backtracking protocols, since the pipelined nature of the dataflow makes it infeasible to backtrack across links. Thus, we would restrict wormhole routing protocols to be progressive. Furthermore, since misrouting can cause cycles in the data path that can lead to deadlock, we would also restrict wormhole and small-buffer virtual cut-through protocols to be profitable or to have some other means of dealing with deadlock (for example, routing restrictions).

Examples

This discussion of representative adaptive routing protocols in each class is based on a circuit-switched model of communication where a probe initially sets up a path. Adaptive routing decisions are made during path setup. The discussion is also applicable to packet-switched communications and, within the limitations pointed out, to virtual cut-through.

Oblivious protocols. *e*-cube is an oblivious protocol proposed for binary hy-

percubes as a deadlock-free routing protocol. Dally and Sietz[1] extended its functionality to *k*-ary *n*-cubes by introducing virtual channels and virtual-channel assignment rules. In a binary *n*-cube, only one virtual link is required in each direction across a bidirectional link. In a *k*-ary *n*-cube, two virtual channels are required in each direction.

e-cube routes traverse one dimension at a time in fixed order — from the highest indexed dimension to the lowest. If the link needed to traverse a dimension is busy, the protocol buffers the probe and waits for the link to become available, holding the links it has already acquired. Since *e*-cube is deadlock-free, the busy link will eventually become free unless it is permanently faulty.

Figure 6 shows an example *e*-cube route, with 000 the source and 111 the destination. The path shown is the only path that can be established with this source-destination pair. Other oblivious protocols are possible and generally share the advantages of simplicity and deadlock freedom, while not making use of all the bandwidth available between each source-destination pair.

Progressive protocols. The main philosophical difference between progressive and backtracking protocols is in the routing decision at an intermediate node when no profitable link is free. Progressive protocols will wait, abort, or misroute, preferring to move forward rather than back up and start over at a previous node. Backtracking protocols work on the premise that it is better to be searching for other paths than to be waiting for one to become available.

Profitable protocols are advantageous because they realize minimal-length paths, make it easier to prove deadlock freedom, and are free from livelock. Misrouting protocols are advantageous because they potentially explore a greater number of paths from source to destination than do purely profitable protocols. This class is perhaps the largest in the taxonomy and, therefore, precludes exhaustive discussion. (Among those we don't discuss is Ngai's framework for adaptive routing. Ngai proposed and analyzed a misrouting, progressive protocol that uses virtual cut-through.[4] This protocol is innovative in that it provides deadlock freedom with (relatively) large-buffer virtual cut-through and misrouting by introducing a message priority scheme. This work and that of others share many characteristics by virtue of their membership in the class of progressive protocols.)

Inter- and intradimensional routing. Young and Yalamanchili[9] studied adaptive circuit-switched routing in the richly connected generalized hypercube architecture. Three adaptive routing protocols were proposed for this architecture: *interdimensional routing, intradimensional routing,* and *intra/interdimensional routing.* These protocols are all partially adaptive, misrouting, and progressive.

Intradimensional routing transmits the probe one dimension at a time. When the link needed to traverse a dimension is not available, the probe is misrouted over another link in the same dimension.

Let a message be routed from source node $\sigma = (s_0, s_1, \ldots, s_{n-1})$ to destination node $\delta = (d_0, d_1, \ldots, d_{n-1})$. At some intermediate node, $\nu = (d_0, d_1, \ldots, d_{j-1}, s_j, \ldots, s_{n-1})$ the probe encounters a busy link — the needed link in dimension j. Intradimensional routing will route the probe to a new node $\nu' = (d_0, d_1, \ldots, d_{j-1}, \alpha_j, \ldots, s_{n-1})$ where $\alpha_j \neq s_j \neq d_j$. While it is not purely profitable, this type of misrouting does not take the probe further from the destination; ν and ν' are equally distant from δ due to the topology of the generalized hypercube.

To avoid unnecessarily long paths, a time-out interval defines when path setup is aborted, and transmission is retried later. This time-out interval is typically set to 10 times the time it takes to cross one link (that is, a maximum path length of 10). This abort/retry mechanism avoids deadlock, while the time-out interval precludes livelock.

Interdimensional routing also attempts to traverse dimensions one at a time in the same order as *e*-cube. If the required profitable link is busy, the probe is misrouted over a link in another dimension. Again, let a message be routed from σ to δ, passing through intermediate node $\nu = (d_0, d_1, \ldots, d_{j-1}, s_j, \ldots, s_{n-1})$ where it encounters a busy link. In this case, the probe will be routed to $\nu' = (d_0, d_1, \ldots, d_{j-1}, s_j, d_j, s_{j+2}, \ldots, s_{n-1})$. To avoid cycles, a probe is restricted to visiting a node only once. Again, a time-out interval aborts path setup and schedules a retransmission later.

Intra/interdimensional routing com-

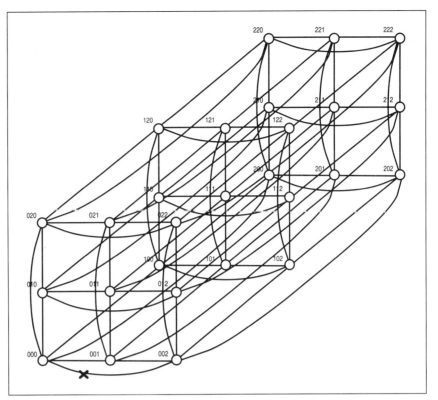

Figure 7. A (3, 3, 3) generalized hypercube with one busy link.

bines the two protocols in an attempt to get the best features from each. Again, the protocol attempts to traverse dimensions in the same order as *e*-cube. If the profitable link is unavailable, the protocol will attempt to perform intradimensional misrouting. If this fails, interdimensional misrouting is attempted.

To demonstrate the behavior of these protocols, consider the following example for a (3, 3, 3) generalized hypercube (see Figure 7). Suppose the source node is 000 and the destination is 212. The *e*-cube protocol would traverse the path $000 \rightarrow 002 \rightarrow 012 \rightarrow 212$. In the absence of traffic or faults, all protocols will use the same path.

Suppose the link $000 \leftrightarrow 002$ is busy or faulty. The three protocols will trace the following paths:

Intradimensional: $000 \rightarrow 001 \rightarrow 002 \rightarrow 012 \rightarrow 212$
Interdimensional: $000 \rightarrow 020 \rightarrow 022 \rightarrow 012 \rightarrow 212$
Intra/interdimensional: $000 \rightarrow 001 \rightarrow 002 \rightarrow 012 \rightarrow 212$

Intra/interdimensional routing will only differ from intradimensional routing when intradimensional routing cannot route the probe. Suppose link 001 $\leftrightarrow$ 002 were also busy or faulty. Then intradimensional routing could not route

the probe and we would have

Intra/interdimensional: $000 \rightarrow 001 \rightarrow 021 \rightarrow 022 \rightarrow 012 \rightarrow 212$

Turn model. Glass and Ni developed an innovative view of the routing restrictions required to prevent deadlock.[8] To avoid deadlock, cyclic dependencies must not exist within the network. They show that by disallowing certain combinations of turns allowed in routing, these cyclic dependencies cannot occur. This observation gave rise to several partially adaptive, misrouting, progressive protocols for *k*-ary 2-cubes.

The most adaptive of these is the *negative-first* protocol. In a two-dimensional mesh, this protocol disallows turns from positive to negative directions (that is, north to west and east to south, as in Figure 8). From these restrictions, it is clear that the probe can only route in a negative direction (that is, to the south

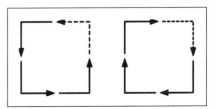

Figure 8. Disallowed turns for negative-first routing.

457

or west) if it begins in a negative direction. Hence, the name negative-first.

Figure 9 shows some examples of negative-first routed paths. Variants of this protocol were also shown to be deadlock-free for n-dimensional meshes and for k-ary n-cubes when the wraparound channel is used only on the first hop of a route.

Algorithm A1. Algorithm A1 is a partially adaptive, misrouting, progressive protocol for routing in binary hypercubes that Chen and Shin proposed.[10] Chen and Shin proved that A1 will successfully route a message in an n-dimensional binary hypercube if the network contains up to $n - 1$ faulty or busy links. In the presence of greater than $n - 1$ faulty links, the algorithm has a high probability of finding a path. Further, with a relatively high probability, this path will be the shortest path that exists in the presence of the faulty links.

A1 requires a routing header considerably more complex than an e-cube routing header. The routing header is a three-tuple $(k, [c_1, c_2, \ldots, c_k], [d_1, \ldots, d_n])$ where k is the number of dimensions to be traversed to reach the destination (requiring $\log_2 n$ bits), $[c_1, \ldots, c_k]$ is an ordered list of those dimensions (requiring $n \log_2 n$ bits at most), and $[d_1, \ldots, d_n]$ is a bit vector of dimensions that have been used for misrouting.

At each node, A1 will attempt to send the message over a profitable link. If no profitable links are available, A1 will send the message over a nonprofitable link after recording the state of the busy profitable links in the bit vector $[d_1, \ldots, d_n]$. Thus, misrouting occurs at most once across each dimension. A1 seeks to make progress toward the destination at all times and will only return over the link it arrived on if there are no other alternatives.

Idle. Grunwald and Reed proposed a completely adaptive, profitable, progressive protocol called Idle.[2] Idle traverses profitable links in a fixed order, as does e-cube, until it encounters a busy link. In such a case, Idle examines the next profitable link in its order and takes that one if possible. Idle will continue to

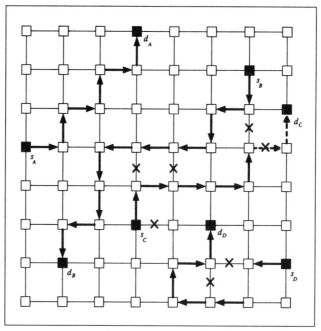

Figure 9. Negative-first paths.

progress toward its destination as long as profitable links are available. If all profitable links are unavailable, Idle must block or tear down the path and retry.

Idle requires no extra status bits in its routing header; its header is identical to that for e-cube. If the protocol requires probes to block indefinitely, Idle can deadlock. The method used to prevent deadlock in Grunwald and Reed involved simply aborting and retrying whenever it could not route.

Figure 10 shows an example Idle route, with 000 the source and 111 the destination. Since link $100 \rightarrow 110$ is busy, Idle routes to 101 and then to 111.

Duato's protocol. Duato[5] states a general theorem defining a criterion for deadlock freedom and then uses the theorem to propose a fully adaptive, profitable, progressive protocol. Called Duato's protocol (DP), the theorem states that by separating virtual channels on a link into restricted and unrestricted partitions, fully adaptive routing can be performed and yet be deadlock-free.

In essence, Duato's theorem allows the creation of hybrid protocols that operate over these distinct channel partitions. Duato proposed this in the context of binary hypercubes, which are easily extended to k-ary n-cubes.

DP uses two virtual channels per physical channel for an e-cube[1] routing subfunction (a routing function over a subset of channels) and the remaining virtual

channels for an Idle[2] routing subfunction. The combined protocol attempts to route using Idle first. If it cannot route using Idle, e-cube routing is performed. If that fails, the protocol blocks. Duato's theorem guarantees that this protocol is deadlock-free. DP requires no extra status bits in its routing header — its header is identical to that for e-cube.

The routing example for Idle will also work for DP, which is completely adaptive. The routing restrictions that provide deadlock freedom are on virtual links. While it cannot use all profitable virtual paths, DP can use all profitable physical paths.

Backtracking protocols. Backtracking protocols search the network for a path in a depth-first manner. Neither deadlock nor livelock is a problem with backtracking protocols because they do not block holding resources and they can use history information to avoid searching the same path repeatedly.

Most backtracking protocols proposed to date use the routing header to store history information. This significantly increases the size of the header over progressive protocols and, consequently, increases the time required to route the probe through the network.

This is particularly a problem for misrouting backtracking protocols, since the number of links traversed during path setup can be very high. To overcome this problem, the history information can be distributed throughout the nodes of the network, reducing the header size to that of e-cube with the addition of one bit.[11]

At a node in the network, for each link we associate a history bit vector h that has as many bits as the node has channels. This history vector is associated with the circuit probe that came in on that channel. As each candidate outgoing channel is searched, the corresponding bit is set to "remember" that channel has been searched. Each node also has a history bit vector h_r for the node itself, since the node (not a channel) may be the source of the probe.

Exhaustive profitable backtracking. Exhaustive profitable backtracking

(EPB) performs a straightforward depth-first search of the network using only profitable links.[2] It is guaranteed to find a minimal path if one exists. With the history information distributed throughout the nodes, the probe consists of a vector of dimension offsets and a backtrack flag. This protocol is completely adaptive, profitable, and backtracking.

k-family. Although the exhaustive backtracking protocol does not repeatedly search the same paths, it can visit a specific link or node several times. This can lead to unnecessary backtracking and longer setup times. The k-family routing paradigm is a family of partially adaptive, profitable, backtracking protocols proposed for binary hypercubes that use a heuristic to help minimize redundancy in the search for a path.[2]

Originally proposed at the Jet Pro-

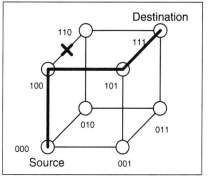

Figure 10. An Idle route from 000 to 111 in a binary 3-cube.

pulsion Laboratory, k-family protocols are two-phased, using a heuristic search in the first phase and an exhaustive search in the second. Each protocol is distinguished by a parameter k that determines when the heuristic is used and when exhaustive backtracking is used. When the probe is at a distance from the

destination greater than k, the heuristic is used; when the distance is less than or equal to k, an exhaustive profitable search is used. If $k = 1$, the protocol is a strictly heuristic search — the search is only exhaustive for the last link in the path. As k grows to the distance between the source and destination, the search becomes more and more exhaustive.

A k protocol makes use of a *history mask* contained in the circuit probe. At each level in the search tree, the cumulative history mask of the ancestor nodes determines which links might be explored. The history mask records all the dimensions explored at each link and all dimensions explored at all ancestor nodes. The heuristic limits exploration to dimensions not marked in the history mask. In this manner, the search tree in the "Backtracking examples" sidebar is

Backtracking examples

To illustrate backtracking protocols, we present the network shown in Figure A. We will examine routing from 000 to 111 for exhaustive profitable backtracking (EPB), k-family with $k = 1$, exhaustive misrouting backtracking (EMB), and two-phase backtracking-1 (TPB-1). Backtracking protocols "search" the network for a path to the destination node much as a backtracking algorithm might search a tree. The vertices and edges of the search tree are the nodes and links of the network.

Figure A shows the search tree for a profitable backtracking protocol routing a message from node 000 to node 111 in a binary 3-cube. EPB will perform a depth-first search of the tree (left to right). Each path from the root node to a leaf node corresponds to a path from the source node (000) to the destination node (111) in the network. In Figure A, links 011 ↔ 111 and 101 ↔ 111 are busy. In routing from 000 to 111, the EPB probe would visit the following nodes in sequence:

000 → 001 → 011 → 001 → 101 → 001 → 000 → 010 → 011 → 010 → 110 → 111.

The final circuit the probe established would be

000 → 010 → 110 → 111.

Notice that the probe had to backtrack all the way back to the source node and visited node 011 twice. The k-family

probe would visit the following node sequence:

000 → 001 → 011 → 001 → 101 → 001 → 000 → 010 → 110 → 111.

The resulting circuit would be the same as EPB. Note that the k-family protocol pruned the second visit to 011 because the history mask passed to 010 from the source indicated that dimension 0 had already been searched. For EMB and TPB-1 the probe's search would proceed as follows:

000 → 001 → 011 → 010 → 110 → 111.

In this case, the final circuit would be

000 → 001 → 011 → 010 → 110 → 111.

In this case, since misrouting occurs at a node only one hop from the destination, TPB-1 behaves identically to EMB. If it were not possible to route at node 010, EMB would be free to misroute again, but TPB-1 would have to backtrack. The final circuits established by the profitable protocols will always be the minimal length. The circuits established by the misrouting protocols can be much longer.

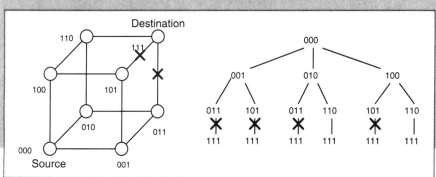

Figure A. Search tree for a profitable backtracking protocol.

459

Table 1. Estimates of probe size.

Protocol	Hypercube Interconnection Networks	Class	Probe Size (Bits)
e-cube	Any	Oblivious	$\sum_{i=1}^{n}\log_2 b_i$
Intra	Generalized	Misrouting progressive	$\sum_{i=1}^{n}\log_2 b_i + 4$
Inter	Generalized	Misrouting progressive	$\sum_{i=1}^{n}\log_2 b_i + \log_2 n + 4$
Intra/Inter	Generalized	Misrouting progressive	$\sum_{i=1}^{n}\log_2 b_i + 2\log_2 n + 4$
Negative-first	k-ary n-cubes	Misrouting progressive	$\sum_{i=1}^{n}\log_2 b_i$
A1	Binary	Misrouting progressive	$(n+1)\log_2 n + n$
Idle	Any	Profitable progressive	$\sum_{i=1}^{n}\log_2 b_i$
Duato's protocol	Any	Profitable progressive	$\sum_{i=1}^{n}\log_2 b_i$
Exhaustive profitable backtracking	Any	Profitable backtracking	$\sum_{i=1}^{n}\log_2 b_i + 1$
k-family	Binary	Profitable backtracking	$2n + 1$
Exhaustive misrouting backtracking	Any	Misrouting backtracking	$\sum_{i=1}^{n}\log_2 b_i + 1$
Two-phase backtracking-u	Any	Misrouting backtracking	$\sum_{i=1}^{n}\log_2 b_i + 1$

pruned of links that are likely to lead into areas of the network that have been searched already.

Exhaustive misrouting backtracking. The exhaustive misrouting backtracking (EMB) protocol does a depth-first search of the network using both profitable and unprofitable links. It uses the "best first" heuristic, taking profitable links over unprofitable ones. Although, on the average, the established circuits are longer than a purely profitable protocol, EMB's probability of finding a path is greater.

The drawback of this algorithm is that it cannot detect that a message is undeliverable until it searches every path it can reach in the network. In the worst case, a single probe can tie up large amounts of network resources searching in vain for a nonexistent path. The protocol is just "too optimistic." To make this protocol valuable for very large networks, some bounds must be set on its freedom to misroute.

Two-phase misrouting backtracking. To curb the optimism of EMB, we make a partially adaptive two-phase protocol analogous to the k-family protocol where

the probe is free to misroute only if it is within a certain distance u of its destination. The first phase of two-phase backtracking (TPB-u) performs an exhaustive profitable search when the probe is at a distance greater than u from the destination. When TPB-u is within u of the destination, it enters the second phase, where it performs an exhaustive misrouting search. A TPB-u probe can switch phases several times during a single route.

Implementation considerations

These protocols present major hardware/software implementation issues. How complex is the routing algorithm? Will the hardware cost or the intranode routing delay nullify the gains made by the added routing flexibility? These difficult questions have not been fully answered and are the focus of ongoing research efforts. The routing header requirements constitute one initial measure for comparison.

Different protocols have different routing header requirements. The size

of the routing probe contributes to communications overhead and should be minimized. Table 1 shows estimates for the probe size. In the table, n is the number of dimensions of the network, and b_i is the radix of the ith dimension.

We can develop some insights into the complexity of these protocols by examining the amount of information used by the routing algorithm to determine where the probe will go. For e-cube, the information is the destination address (routing header) and the status of the virtual link it needs to traverse next. For Idle and DP, the required information is the destination address and the status of all virtual links on profitable channels.

For backtracking protocols, we also add the history mask. This is only a rough estimate of complexity, since there are certainly methods for reducing the information. For example, the history mask of a backtracking protocol can be ORed with channel status bits to reduce the routing complexity to that of a progressive protocol. Also, physical channel selection can be a function of the number of virtual channels reserved on a physical link rather than the status of the individual virtual links themselves.

Simulations

We conducted simulation studies to evaluate the performance of representative progressive and backtracking protocols compared to the oblivious protocol *e*-cube. The simulator is a program that performs a time-step simulation of the network operation at the flit level.

A processor *s* was allowed to communicate to other processors in the neighborhood defined by $\{d : \|s \quad d\|_\infty \leq 4\}$. Destinations were picked uniformly through this neighborhood. We thought this would be a more realistic traffic distribution than the networkwide uniform traffic assumption.

We ran each simulation 30,000 flit times, discarding information occurring during a 10,000 flit-time warmup period. In an average run, 320,000 flits were moved through the network. The 95 percent confidence intervals for latency and throughput were within 2 percent of their respective means.

We chose to examine DP and TPB-2 performance versus that of *e*-cube. In

Adding an extra pair of virtual channels per physical channel dramatically increases throughput for *e*-cube.

addition, we wished to demonstrate the added performance obtained through the use of virtual channels.

We simulated these protocols on 16-ary 2-cubes for message sizes of 16 and 64 flits. For each protocol, we wanted to use the "natural" implementation. For instance, if a protocol can be implemented using wormhole routing, the added overhead of pipelined circuit switching will result in an unnecessarily low performance evaluation.

We implemented DP and *e*-cube using wormhole routing and TPB-2 with pipelined circuit switching. All physical links were implemented with four virtu-

al channels per direction. Since *e*-cube is only defined on two virtual channels, we implemented *e*-cube in two different ways.

In the first method, *e*-cube simply uses the two lowest indexed channels and does not use the others — the classic *e*-cube implementation. In the second method, we partitioned the four virtual channels into two sets of two virtual channels each. In this way, we can obtain the additional throughput discussed in Dally.[6]

Figure 11 shows the latency-throughput characteristics of these protocols. Our first observation is that adding an extra pair of virtual channels per physical channel dramatically increases throughput for *e*-cube. Its peak throughput nearly doubles.

In the case where message length $L = 16$, we see that the added overhead of pipelined circuit switching does not justify the use of TPB-2 over *e*-cube using four virtual channels. However, in the case where $L = 64$, the added adaptability of TPB-2 gives increased performance for large network loads. In both cases, DP combines the low overhead of worm-

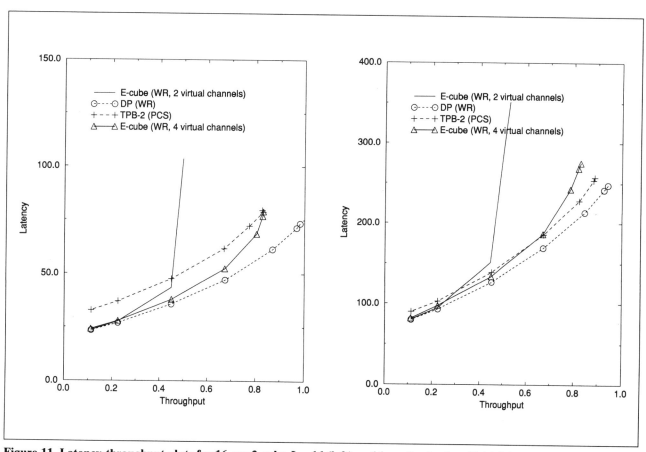

Figure 11. Latency-throughput plots for 16-ary 2-cube *L* = 16 (left) or 16-ary 2-cube *L* = 64 (right).

hole routing and the flexibility of adaptive routing to get the best performance overall.

These results reflect several emerging trends. The use of virtual channels is gaining acceptance as a powerful mechanism for high-performance interprocessor communication. They are expanding the performance range of oblivious protocols across larger networks and higher network loads.

In applications that require larger message sizes (> 64 flits), backtracking protocols are beneficial at higher network loads. In addition, because backtracking protocols can regress and try alternate paths from earlier nodes, there is reason to believe they are better candidates for fault-tolerant routing.

For performance, however, wormhole routing has the edge. In particular, the partitioning of virtual channels and the use of protocols satisfying the relaxed constraints proposed by Duato realize performance over a wide range that appears very difficult to improve on.

Related research

Several related research efforts toward the efficient use of network resources are not covered in this article. These efforts are closely related to adaptive routing, both influencing and being influenced by adaptive routing protocols. They generally can be implemented in addition to the adaptive routing protocols.

Tamir and Turner[12] propose an algorithm for dynamically reconfiguring existing circuits in a network. When a requested path cannot be set up, an existing circuit (for example, least recently used) at the intermediate node where conflict for an outgoing channel is detected is torn down. Then, if possible, it is rerouted along another path and the new path is provided the released resources.

This technique represents a relatively more "heavy handed" approach to dealing with busy links. In a sense, this technique is independent of the techniques described here — techniques that are uniformly applied only during path setup. However, once established, a circuit exists as long as it is needed. We can envisage an implementation employing both techniques — adaptive protocols to set up a path and reconfiguration when one cannot be found.

The use of *virtual networks* has emerged as a powerful paradigm.[7] The primary motivation for this paradigm is to provide deadlock-free, wormhole routing. Dally and Seitz[1] show that the deadlock-free routing problem in the physical network can be transformed into a nonrestricted routing problem in acyclic virtual networks. The virtual networks are then realized on the physical network. This is done to ensure that cyclic dependencies cannot occur and deadlock freedom is assured. Duato provided a powerful extension to this paradigm and eliminated the necessity to restrict routing to acyclic virtual networks. This opens the doors to new classes of protocols that are known deductively to be deadlock-free by virtue of satisfying the relaxed constraints that Duato specified.

Communication bottlenecks will become one of the major impediments to massively parallel computing. Multipath networks and adaptive routing protocols will be the rule rather than the exception in massively parallel architectures.

Research will focus on the simulation studies of new protocols in parallel with the development of analytic models and hardware support.

We foresee at least two trends in the study of such protocols. The first is the notion of optimism/conservatism in the behavior of these protocols. We have already seen how such concepts affect performance.[9,11] Quantifying these concepts and studying their relationships to network topology, workload, and performance will be a direction for future research.

In addition, attention will focus on the implementation of these routing protocols. As the networks become faster and demands on routing speed increase, the effect of intranode routing delay will increase. While the protocols themselves exploit the network topologies, the complexity of their implementations must not preclude their use. ∎

Acknowledgment

This research was supported in part by a grant from Digital Equipment Corporation under the Digital Faculty Program.

References

1. W.J. Dally and C.L. Sietz, "Deadlock-Free Message Routing in Multiprocessor Interconnection Networks," *IEEE Trans. Computers*, Vol. C-36, No. 5, May 1987, pp. 547-553.

2. D. Grunwald and D. Reed, "Analysis of Backtracking Routing in Binary Hypercube Computers," Tech. Report UIUC-DCS-R-89-1486, Dept. of Computer Science, Univ. of Illinois at Urbana-Champaign, Feb. 1989.

3. L.N. Bhuyan and D.P. Agrawal, "Generalized Hypercube and Hyperbus Structures for a Computer Network," *IEEE Trans. Computers*, Vol. C-33, No. 4, Apr. 1984, pp. 323-333.

4. J.Y. Ngai, "A Framework for Adaptive Routing in Multicomputer Networks," PhD thesis, California Inst. of Tech., 1990.

5. J. Duato, "Deadlock-Free Adaptive Routing Algorithms for Multicomputers: Evaluation of a New Algorithm," *Proc. Third IEEE Symp. Parallel and Distributed Processing*, IEEE CS Press, Los Alamitos, Calif., Order No. 2310, 1991, pp. 840-847.

6. W.J. Dally, "Virtual-Channel Flow Control," *IEEE Trans. Parallel and Distributed Systems*, Vol. 3, No. 2, Mar. 1992, pp. 194-205.

7. D.H. Linder and J.C. Harden, "An Adaptive and Fault-Tolerant Wormhole Routing Strategy for *k*-ary *n*-cubes," *IEEE Trans. Computers*, Vol. C-40, No. 1, Jan. 1991, pp. 2-12.

8. C.J. Glass and L.M. Ni, "The Turn Model for Adaptive Routing," *Proc. 19th Int'l Symp. Computer Architecture*, IEEE CS Press, Los Alamitos, Calif., Order No. 2940, 1992, pp. 278-287.

9. S.D. Young and S. Yalamanchili, "Adaptive Routing in Generalized Hypercube Architectures," *Proc. Third IEEE Symp. Parallel Distributed Processing*, IEEE CS Press, Los Alamitos, Calif., Order No. 2310, 1991, pp. 564-571.

10. M.S. Chen and K.G. Shin, "Adaptive Fault-Tolerant Routing in Hypercube Multicomputers," *IEEE Trans. Computers*, Vol. 39, No. 12, Dec. 1990, pp. 1,406-1,416.

11. P. Gaughan and S. Yalamanchili, "Performance Evaluation of Adaptive Routing Protocols in HINs," Tech. Report GIT/CSRL-92/01, Georgia Inst. of Tech., Jan. 1992.

12. Y. Tamir and Y.F. Turner, "High-Performance Adaptive Routing in Multicomputers Using Dynamic Virtual Circuits," *Proc. Sixth Distributed-Memory Computing Conf.*, IEEE CS Press, Los Alamitos, Calif., Order No. 2290, 1991, pp. 404-411.

Sudhakar Yalamanchili joined the faculty of the Georgia Institute of Technology in 1989 and is currently an associate professor in the School of Electrical Engineering. His research interests are in the design and analysis of multiprocessor interconnection networks, distributed simulation, and multiprocessor modeling and simulation.

Yalamanchili received a BE degree in electronics from Bangalore University, India, in 1978, and MS and PhD degrees in electrical and computer engineering from the University of Texas at Austin in 1980 and 1984. He is a senior member of IEEE, and a member of the IEEE Computer Society, ACM, the Society for Computer Simulation, and the American Institute for Astronautics nd Avionics.

Patrick T. Gaughan is a research assistant in the Computer Systems Research Laboratory at the Georgia Institute of Technology, where he is pursuing a PhD in electrical and computer engineering. His research interests include design and analysis of high-performance multiprocessor interconnection networks, parallel architectures and algorithms for computer vision, and fine-grained parallel computation.

Gaughan received BS and MS degrees in electrical and computer engineering from New Mexico State University in 1989 and 1990.

Readers can contact the authors at the Computer Systems Research Laboratory, School of Electrical Engineering, Georgia Institute of Technology, Atlanta, GA 30332-0250. Their electronic mail addresses are {pgaughan, sudha}@eecom.gatech.edu.

Evaluation of Mechanisms for Fine-Grained Parallel Programs in the J-Machine and the CM-5

Ellen Spertus[†], Seth Copen Goldstein[‡], Klaus Erik Schauser[‡], Thorsten von Eicken[‡], David E. Culler[‡], William J. Dally[†]

†MIT Artifical Intelligence Laboratory
545 Technology Square
Cambridge, MA 02139
{ellens,billd}@ai.mit.edu

‡Computer Science Division — EECS
University of California
Berkeley, CA 94720
tam@cs.berkeley.edu

Abstract

This paper uses an abstract machine approach to compare the mechanisms of two parallel machines: the J-Machine and the CM-5. High-level parallel programs are translated by a single optimizing compiler to a fine-grained abstract parallel machine, TAM. A final compilation step is unique to each machine and optimizes for specifics of the architecture. By determining the cost of the primitives and weighting them by their dynamic frequency in parallel programs, we quantify the effectiveness of the following mechanisms individually and in combination. Efficient processor/network coupling proves valuable. Message dispatch is found to be less valuable without atomic operations that allow the scheduling levels to cooperate. Multiple hardware contexts are of small value when the contexts cooperate and the compiler can partition the register set. Tagged memory provides little gain. Finally, the performance of the overall system is strongly influenced by the performance of the memory system and the frequency of control operations.

Keywords: *Parallel Processing, Performance Analysis, Compilation.*

1 Introduction

Several experimental parallel architectures have been developed in recent years to demonstrate novel hardware mechanisms that may enhance the performance of programs written in emerging parallel languages. For example, Monsoon focuses on Id90, the J-Machine on CST, Alewife on Mul-T, the CM-5 on Fortran90, and Dash and KSR-1 on extensions to C and Fortran. All of these architectures provide a family of mechanisms that collectively support the requirements of the parallel language, are universal enough to support any of the other language paradigms, and are real enough to be constrained by the traditional technology

forces. Thus, it would seem that the time has come for parallel architecture research to begin the shift from "big new ideas" to careful quantitative analysis of the effectiveness of various mechanisms. In this paper, we seek to evaluate the set of mechanisms in the MIT J-Machine with respect to the implicitly parallel language Id90 and draw a quantitative comparison with the CM-5.

At the current state of parallel computing, a completely satisfactory quantitative analysis of mechanisms is difficult to achieve because there is no well-established body of machine-independent software reflected in a standard set of benchmarks. There is not even a consensus on the programming languages of choice. Where benchmarks exist, they have been developed specifically for the machine that they are intended to evaluate [14, 9] or specifically avoid emerging languages and the novel mechanisms which could bring them within practical reach [3]. It is also difficult to obtain high-quality compilers for such new languages on more than one machine, yet it is well understood that the architectural support can only be evaluated in the context of sophisticated compilation, rather than direct execution of high-level constructs. Finally, the machines reflect substantially varying engineering budgets and designer capabilities, which should be factored out of the evaluation of the architectural contribution. Simply comparing execution times gives only a crude and noisy calibration, failing to isolate the reasons for the differences.

The method of analysis employed in this paper is as follows. We consider two recent parallel machines: the J-Machine, developed at MIT as a study in universal mechanisms for fine-grained parallelism, and the CM-5, developed at Thinking Machines Corp. as a commercial product supporting data-parallel programs. We take as a basis for comparison a powerful machine-independent parallel language, Id90, which was not the primary target for either architecture, but for which a high-quality compilation sys-

Reprinted from *Proc. 20th Ann. Int'l Symp. Computer Architecture,* IEEE CS Press, Los Alamitos, Calif., 1993, pp. 302–313.

0-8186-6522-X/95 $4.00 © 1993 IEEE

tem exists. The compiler performs a variety of high-level optimizations in translating the language down to code for a simple abstract machine, TAM [6, 13]. The TAM code is identical for the two machines, controlling for effects of high-level optimizations. The translator from TAM code to machine language, however, employs a variety of machine-specific optimizations reflecting the most advantageous use of the available mechanisms. The performance of isolated mechanisms is reflected in the cost of the individual TAM primitives on the machine. The overall effectiveness of the family of mechanisms is determined by weighting each of the primitives by its frequency in a suite of programs. The J-Machine essentially provides direct hardware support for every aspect of TAM; however, TAM does not use all the mechanisms in the machine. The CM-5 provides a variety of mechanisms for data-parallel programming, which are not useful to TAM. What remains is a very reasonable baseline machine, essentially a collection of workstation-class processors on a dedicated network. Thus, we can compare a sophisticated set of mechanisms against a familiar baseline architecture with respect to the dynamic load presented by Id90 programs compiled to TAM.

Section 2 describes the two architectures under study and explains the salient aspects of TAM. TAM-level dynamic instruction frequencies are produced for a variety of programs to serve as a basis for comparison. Section 3 corrects for a set of architectural and engineering factors that have a significant impact on execution time for the two machines, but for which conventional wisdom (and hindsight) applies. The remaining sections deal with architectural aspects that are unique to parallel computing. Section 4 examines the impact of the processor/network coupling on message-passing cost. Section 5 looks at three mechanisms related to asynchronous message arrival that interact with dynamic scheduling. Section 6 considers the utility of tagged memory words and Section 7 ties together our observations. Two important lessons arise from the study. First, novel mechanisms do not substitute for solid engineering of the processor pipeline and storage hierarchy. Second, mechanisms should not be evaluated in isolation, but in how they work together in the compilation framework for the programming language.

2   Background

2.1   CM-5

The CM-5 [16] is a massively-parallel MIMD computer based on the Sparc processor, interconnected in two identical disjoint "hypertree" networks. Each node consists of a 33 MHz Sparc RISC processor chip-set (including FPU, MMU and 64 KByte cache), 8 MBytes of local DRAM memory and a network interface to the hypertrees and broadcast/scan/prefix control networks. (The node may also contain vector units with additional memory, but we will not address the vector capability.) The network interface consists of a pair of memory-mapped FIFO queues for each of the two data networks. Messages are limited to a maximum of five 32-bit words in length. Message delivery is reliable, but no guarantee is made on ordering. The study uses a 128-node CM-5, although machines of 1024 nodes are currently in the field.

2.2   J-Machine

The J-Machine is a massively-parallel MIMD computer based on the Message-Driven Processor (MDP) interconnected by a 3-D mesh network. The MDP is a single-chip processing node composed of a 16 MHz 32-bit integer unit, a 4K by 36-bit static memory, a closely integrated network interface, a packet router, and an ECC DRAM controller. The on-chip memory is augmented with a 256K by 36-bit off-chip memory. The 36-bit words include 4-bit tags, which indicate data types such as booleans, integers, and user-defined types. Two special tag values *future* and *cfuture* cause a trap when accessed. The MDP has three separate priority levels: background, 0, and 1, each of which has a complete context, consisting of an instruction pointer, four address registers, four general-purpose registers, and other special-purpose registers. A 512-node J-Machine has been built, and a 1024-node machine is planned.

The MDP implements a prioritized scheduler in hardware. When a message arrives at its destination node, it is automatically written into a message queue, consisting of a fixed-size ring buffer in on-chip memory. Background execution is interrupted by priority 0 message reception, which in turn may be interrupted by priority 1 message reception.

2.3   TAM

TAM defines a fine-grained parallel execution model used as a compilation target for Id90. Although it grew out of work on dataflow, it defines a simple model of self-scheduling threads that can be implemented on any machine. The key ways in which TAM differs from "thread packages" are that TAM threads are even lighter weight, the scheduling is integrated with aspects of compilation, such as register allocation, and there is no external scheduler.

A TAM program consists of a collection of *code-blocks*, which typically represent functions or loops in the source program. Each code-block consists of a collection of *threads*, which correspond roughly to basic blocks. Two instructions appear in the same thread only if they can be statically ordered and if no operation whose latency is unbounded occurs between them.

The TAM execution model centers on the *activation frame*, which is the analog of a stack frame for parallel calls. To invoke a code-block, a frame is allocated on a processor and initialized, and arguments are sent to the frame. Initialization consists of setting the values of *synchronization counters* stored within the frame. A thread is allowed to run only when all its antecedents have been executed. To detect the completion of antecedents, a synchronization counter is associated with each thread. The counter is omitted for threads that have only one antecedent, *i.e.*, *unsynchronizing* threads. For each frame, a stack of instruction pointers, called the *continuation vector* (CV), holds the list of threads that are ready to run. The arguments to the code-block, results from subordinate calls, and responses to global heap accesses are received by *inlets*. Inlets are compiler-generated message handlers that copy the arguments into the frame and enable computation dependent on the message. In order to process requests from the network quickly, inlets are small and run at a higher priority than threads.

Maintaining the thread queue in the frames provides a natural two-level scheduling hierarchy. When a frame is scheduled, the *remote* continuation vector (RCV) is copied into the *local* continuation vector (LCV), from which enabled threads are executed until the LCV is empty. The set of threads that run during this time is called a *quantum*. Each processor maintains a queue of *ready* frames with non-empty CVs. A new frame is activated from the queue when a quantum completes.

Global data structures in TAM provide synchronization on a per-element basis to support I-structure and M-structure semantics [10]. In particular, reads of empty elements are deferred until the corresponding write occurs. Accesses to the data structures are split-phase and are performed via special instructions: `ifetch` reads an element by sending a message to the processor containing the data which returns the value to an inlet, `istore` writes a value to an element, resuming any deferred readers, and `ialloc` and `ifree` allocate and deallocate I-structures.

In the current implementation of TAM, instructions are primarily three address, where the operands are constants, registers, or frame locations. TAM registers and frame slots are statically typed into integers, floats, various pointers, and generals. Generals are sufficiently large to contain any TAM type but do not identify the type. Correct compilation ensures that the producer and consumer of a general agree on the type of the contained value. No fixed limit is placed on the number of TAM registers, although the compiler tries to use them as efficiently as possible. The translator from TAM to a target machine is responsible for mapping TAM registers to physical registers or spill areas.

The key issues presented by TAM are the parallel call, dynamic synchronization of computation with asynchronous responses from both remote requests and calls, split-phase remote operations, and the overlap of computation with communication.

2.4 Mapping to the machines

The basic mapping of TAM to the two machines is relatively straightforward. Program code is placed on every processor, but a given code-block invocation takes place on a single processor. Because the compiler may pull loops out into separate code-blocks, these can be spread across the machine to implement parallel loops [7]. The memory on each processor is divided into two areas. One holds small arrays and activation frames. The other holds large arrays, which are spread across all the processors such that logically consecutive elements are on different processors. Memory is managed explicitly through library routines.

The J-Machine implementation of TAM [15] makes direct use of the hardware support for different priority levels. Threads run at the background priority level, allowing them to be quickly interrupted by messages arriving in the priority 0 queue. (Priority 1 is currently not used.) Because each priority level has its own register set, inlets do not interfere with thread execution. An address register is set aside in each register set to hold the frame pointer. Threads use an additional general-purpose register to hold the address of the top of the LCV. Two general-purpose registers are used as temporaries to hold memory operands and to implement complex TAM instructions. The remaining general-purpose register is used to hold one TAM register. All other TAM registers are mapped to the base of on-chip memory, a region that can be addressed easily. Frames are stored in main memory.

A similar approach is followed on the Sparc with inlets using a new register window. However, due to the tight coupling between threads and inlets, it proves to be more efficient to simply partition a single window. The CM-5 implementation [8] uses 32 registers divided into three classes: *global registers* which hold frequently-used values, *TAM registers* which are preserved for the duration of a quantum, and *inlet registers*, used during inlet execution and to pass information from threads to inlets. The CM-5 translator attempts to keep as many TAM variables as possible in the TAM registers and spills the rest into the frame.

2.5 Benchmarks

The empirical basis for comparison is provided by six benchmark programs described below. TAM-level dynamic instruction distributions are collected by running an instrumented version of the program on the CM-5. The translator inserts in-line code to record roughly a hundred specific statistics on each processor, which are combined at the end of the program.[1] These are grouped into the basic

---

[1] The Benchmark programs, raw data, and tools to process the data can be retrieved by anonymous FTP from ftp.cs.berkeley.edu under /ucb/TAM/isca93.tar.Z.

instruction categories in Figure 1. *ALU* includes integer and floating-point arithmetic, *messages* includes instructions executed to handle messages, *heap* includes global I-structure and M-structure accesses, and *control* represents all control-flow instructions including moves to initialize synchronization counters.

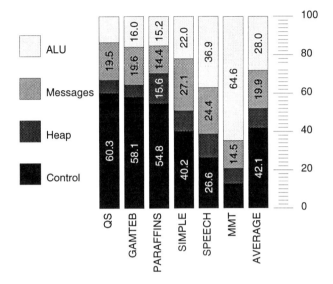

Figure 1: *Dynamic instruction mix statistics for the benchmark programs. The final column shows the arithmetic mean of the distributions.*

Six benchmark programs ranging from 50 to 1,100 lines are used. *QS* is a simple quick-sort using accumulation lists. The input is a list of random numbers. *Gamteb* is a Monte Carlo neutron transport code [4]. It is highly recursive with many conditionals. *Paraffins* [2] enumerates the distinct isomers of paraffins. *Simple* is a hydrodynamics and heat conduction code widely used as an application benchmark, rewritten in Id90 [5, 1]. *Speech* determines cepstral coefficients for speech processing. *MMT* is a simple matrix operation test using 4x4 blocks; two double precision identity matrices are created, multiplied, and subtracted from a third.

The programs toward the left of Figure 1 represent fine-grained parallelism. Notice that they are control intensive and make frequent remote references, as opposed to the blocked matrix multiply which is dominated by arithmetic. We will focus primarily on the two largest programs, Gamteb and Simple.

The Id90 implementations of these programs take about twice as long on a single processor as implementations in standard languages like C or Fortran [6]. Some of this overhead (mostly seen in the amount of control in Figure 1) is recouped in the parallel implementation.

3 Baseline Architectural Issues

By relating the dynamic statistics to the cost of the implementation of each TAM primitive we can obtain an estimate of how time is spent on each machine and isolate the contribution of specific mechanisms. However, there are several significant engineering differences between the study machines including cycle time, pipelining, floating point support, caches, and message size. These differences are determined primarily by circumstances under which the machines were developed and do not reflect significant architectural characteristics. The J-Machine was developed by a small academic team and many tradeoffs were made in favor of reduced design time at the expense of absolute performance. The CM-5 was developed by a relatively small company with significant time-to-market pressures. However, it was able to exploit the sizable investment in the Cypress Sparc chip set. To understand the impact of the novel mechanisms in detail, we first compensate for these differences. In particular we adjust the cycle time, floating point performance, and memory system of the J-Machine to reflect advances in technology and engineering that have occurred since it was implemented.

In this section we develop hypothetical versions of the two machines, called J′-Machine and CM-5′, with similar engineering characteristics. The predicted performance breakdown of the two real and two hypothetical machines on our benchmark programs is shown in Figure 2 and explained below. The metric used is cycles per TAM instruction (CPT). The bars show the contribution to the CPT resulting from each class of TAM instruction. Three new segments have been introduced to highlight important implementation issues. The *memory* system segment at the top indicates the penalty introduced due to cache misses. Since the J-Machine manages the movement between SRAM and DRAM explicitly, there is no direct penalty. The *operands* segment reflects the memory access penalty in bringing data into registers for ALU instructions. The *atomicity* segment at the bottom accounts for overhead in ensuring certain operations are atomic. The *heap* bar has been split into three distinct implementation components.

Our main task in the paper is to show how the cost coefficients are determined for each category, and specifically how the novel mechanisms in the J-Machine contribute toward reducing each cost. In this section we address the top two segments, because these have to do with conventional processor efficiency. The remaining sections examine the lower segments, which involve issues that are unique to fine-grained parallelism. The factors that we normalize are the following.

Cycle time and pipelining: The Cypress Sparc processor in the CM-5 has a cycle time of 30 ns and has a four-stage pipeline, while the MDP in the J-Machine has a

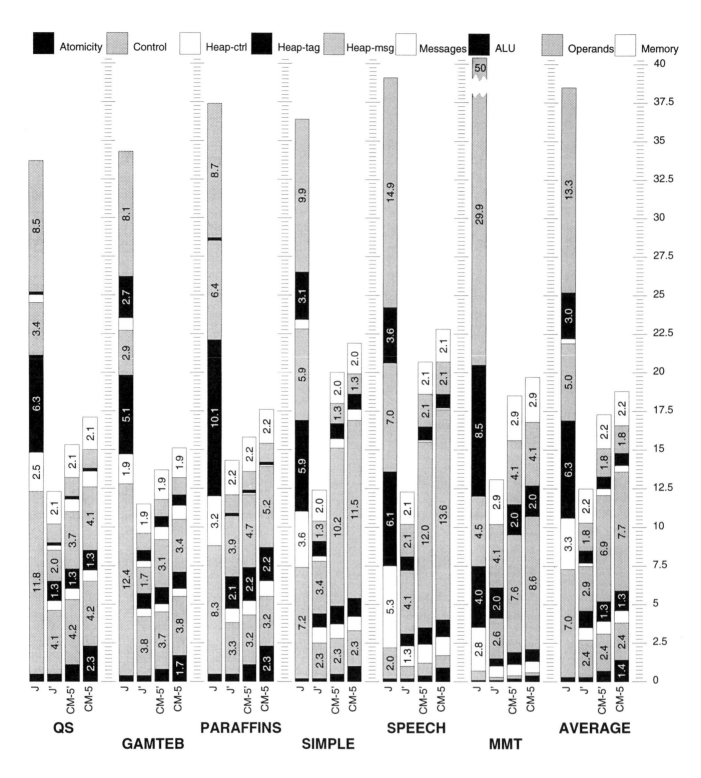

Figure 2: *Relative performance of the J-Machine, the CM-5 and their hypothetical variations on the sample dynamic instruction mix. The variations are used in the study to compensate for differences in engineering which do not offer any new architectural insight. Since the J-Machine does not have a cache, the memory penalty is factored into the other segments.*

cycle time of 62.5 ns and is unpipelined. Since the novel mechanisms of the J-Machine do not fundamentally impact cycle time or pipelining, we ignore these differences. We scale DRAM access time accordingly and measure it in terms of processor cycles. We also assume the MDP has the same control pipeline as the Sparc; in particular, we introduce annulling branches and branch delay slots into the MDP.

Networks and load balancing: In the analysis, we assume the performance characteristics of the network to be identical in the two machines and to affect each processor in a similar way. Similarly, we assume idle time resulting from inadequate parallelism or improper load balancing to affect the two machines equally.

Floating point arithmetic: On the Sparc, floating point operations run on a co-processor and take roughly seven cycles, unless overlapped with integer execution. The MDP has no built-in floating-point hardware, so software routines, typically taking 12–28 cycles, are used. For this analysis, we assume that the J'-Machine has the same floating point support as the Sparc. For all arithmetic-logic operations, operands in the frame must be brought into registers by explicit load instructions (2 cycles for 32-bit operands, 3 cycles for 64-bit), and results must be stored back (3 cycles for 32-bit, 4 cycles for 64-bit).

Storage hierarchy: Both machines have a 3-level memory hierarchy — registers, SRAM, and DRAM. However, the two faster levels differ significantly. The MDP has eight general-purpose or address registers for each of three priority levels. The Sparc has overlapping register windows of 32 registers each. The MDP has on-chip SRAM mapped into the bottom of the address space. One additional cycle is required to read the on-chip SRAM and 6 for off-chip DRAM, which we treat as 2 and 12, respectively, since we have doubled the MDP's clock rate. The Sparc has off-chip SRAM organized as a 64 Kbyte direct-mapped unified data and instruction cache. Cache hits causes a one-cycle processor stall, while refills from DRAM take 20 cycles. We assume that the J'-Machine has as many registers and the same memory system as the Sparc. A cache miss rate of 5% is used.

Message size: The TAM send and receive instructions do not place a limit on the number of words transferred. Although most messages are small, arguments to a code-block may involve a few tens of data elements. On the J-Machine, these can be delivered in a single message to a single inlet. The CM-5 limits the message size to five 32-bit words; thus, large messages are broken into smaller messages which are each sent to different inlets (to handle possible reordering of the smaller messages), incurring additional overhead. The CM-5' is assumed to be able to send larger packets, 16 words, which is sufficient to hold the biggest message generated in our benchmarks.

Polling: Due to the current implementation of the network interface in the CM-5 the two data networks must be polled separately, which doubles the cost of polls. In the future both data networks will be polled simultaneously, which is what we assume for the CM-5'.

Correcting for the memory system and lack of floating point results in a significant improvement of the J'-Machine performance. Observe this improvement affects all the categories in Figure 2. After the correction, the time spent in arithmetic operations and memory access is nearly identical on the two machines. More interestingly, adding a cache and registers results in a more uniform memory system and increases processor state which not only speeds up ALU operations but allows for significant optimizations of all TAM instructions. This is particularly noticeable in how similar the cost of control becomes between the J'-Machine and the CM-5'.

The message, control, and heap components are the remaining factors and demonstrate significant differences between the machines. These are examined in detail below to explain precisely how these costs arise.

4 Processor/Network Coupling

This section examines the cost of sending and receiving messages and relates it to architectural features in the two machines. The J-Machine provides extensive message support with an intimate coupling between the processor and network, whereas the CM-5 has a memory-mapped network interface connected to the MBUS on each node.

4.1 TAM requirements

The *messages* segment in Figure 2 reflects the cost of passing arguments and return values for function calls, and of initializing loop constants and forwarding iteration variables for parallel loops. In TAM a message is formed and issued with the send instruction, which sends a number of data values to an inlet of a potentially remote frame. The message is received by a receive instruction in the destination inlet which extracts the data from the message and stores it into the frame. The adjacent segment of the *heap* segment reflects the cost of the message component of global data structure accesses, represented by ifetch and istore instructions. Note that a heap fetch requires two messages, a request to the node containing the accessed element and a response with the data.

4.2 Hardware support

On the J-Machine, the SEND instruction appends one or two 32-bit values to the message currently being composed. The first word of the message contains the destination address, and a bit in the SEND instruction indicates the end of the message and completes its injection into the network. Overflow of the output buffer causes a fault. The CM-5 operates similarly with two exceptions: the message data must be stored into the outgoing fixed length FIFO queue of the memory-mapped network interface, and the network interface status register must be checked after each message to verify its successful injection. If the network is backed-up, the CM-5 network interface simply discards additional messages, and the program must retry the SEND until the status register indicates success.

Hardware support for message reception differs substantially on the two machines. The J-Machine implements asynchronous message reception by directly storing messages into an on-chip queue and dispatching to the code indicated by the first word of the message at the head of the queue, *i.e.*, the inlet. The inlet may load the message data one word at a time into registers from there. On the CM-5 message arrival is detected by software polling. When a message has arrived, software loads the first word of the message into a register and dispatches on it. The message data is received through additional loads from the network interface.

While an asynchronous message reception model appears most natural on the J-Machine, an alternate synchronous implementation is also possible: the message dispatch mechanism can be kept generally disabled except for short periods during which the network is essentially polled. This approach maintains the advantage of fast hardware dispatch but lets the compiler control when the computation can be interrupted by inlets. This will be shown to be a useful property in the following section. Similarly, an asynchronous message reception model can be implemented on the CM-5 using interrupts: on message arrival the network interface signals an interrupt, causing the Sparc to trap to the kernel. The kernel forwards the interrupt to the user process by creating a stack frame for the inlet and returning to it.

4.3 Implementation costs

Table 1 shows the cost of sending and receiving a message using synchronous and asynchronous reception on both machines. The start-up cost for sending a message to a remote processor is 3.5 times as high on the CM-5' as on the J'-Machine, mainly due to the status register check. The per-word cost is twice as high on the CM-5', due to the cost of stores across the MBUS. Periodic polling is required in the synchronous reception models. The start-up cost for receiving a message includes the dispatch and the return to the interrupted computation. It is roughly twice as high on the CM-5' with synchronous reception. However, the extremely high receive start-up cost for the asynchronous reception on the CM-5' shows that the user-level interrupt which comes with the hardware dispatch is a

dramatic improvement. The 100 cycles for the kernel trap on the CM-5' is an approximation and assumes that, on average, two to three messages are received back-to-back per interrupt. Notice that the asynchronous model also increases the cost of local messages, in that local messages must be atomic with respect to remote messages. A remote ifetch involves two messages (request and reply), and a remote istore involves a single message.

Given the high message cost on the CM-5', it is advantageous to treat local messages as a special case in software if their frequency is non-negligible, *i.e.*, to exploit send to local frames and ifetch and istore to local structures. The required destination check costs two cycles per message. The rightmost section of Table 1 shows the resulting costs for local messages. This optimization was tried on the J-Machine and found to hurt performance, so the general SEND mechanism is used for all messages. Local messages on the CM-5' are cheaper than on the J'-Machine because the data does not need to be moved in and out of the network interface. The local ifetch and istore entries show that optimizing for local messages can enable further optimizations: the access portion of the ifetch is performed directly in the thread and if the data is present the threads which use it can be enabled cheaply, as discussed in Section 6.

4.4 Discussion

The implementation costs highlight three key points: network access cost is far higher on the CM-5' than on the J'-Machine, receiving is more expensive than sending on both machines, and optimizing for local messages can be valuable. On Simple, where 93% of the messages are remote, the CM-5' spends three times as much time on messages as the J'-Machine. However, on Gamteb where 30% of the messages are local the CM-5' spends only twice as much time.

The high network interface access cost on the CM-5' is due to the node architecture which connects the network interface chip to the MBUS. As a result, all loads and stores take 7 cycles each (8 cycles for double-word loads or stores). Further, checking the status register after every send accounts for 1/3 of the send cost. On the other hand, the J-Machine effectively connects the network interface to the ALU bus. The J-Machine faults if the outgoing send buffers overflow, so, while a fault handler is necessary to retry, the check is free. Asynchronous message reception is prohibitively expensive on the CM-5' due to poor support for user-level interrupts in the Sparc.

Several factors cause message reception to be more expensive than sending. Sending is synchronous to the computation whereas reception is logically asynchronous. Thus values to be sent are typically available in registers, whereas values received must be stored in memory until the waiting

TAM operation	Cycles					
	J'-Machine All Messages		CM-5'			
			Remote Messages		Local Messages	
	sync.	async.	sync.	async.	sync.	async.
Send N-word message	$7+N$	$7+N$	$25+4\lceil\frac{N}{2}\rceil$	$25+4\lceil\frac{N}{2}\rceil$	$2+N$	$4+N$
Receive N-word message	$5+7\lceil\frac{N}{2}\rceil$	$5+7\lceil\frac{N}{2}\rceil$	$13+12\lceil\frac{N}{2}\rceil$	$\approx 100+12\lceil\frac{N}{2}\rceil$	$2+4\lceil\frac{N}{2}\rceil$	$4+4\lceil\frac{N}{2}\rceil$
Poll	4	—	9	—	—	—
Ifetch message	24	24	93	≈ 190	16 or 4[†]	18 or 4[†]
Istore message	15	15	60	≈ 160	2 or 0[†]	4 or 2[†]

†: Cost when the element is present for an `ifetch`, or empty for an `istore`.

Table 1: *Local cost for sending and receiving messages.*

computation can be scheduled.[2] Reception involves a dispatch, while sending does not. Finally, stores to the CM-5' network interface can take advantage of the write buffer, while loads see the full latency. On the MDP, the send buffer can be written to at the rate of two words per cycle through the SEND instruction, while reading a word from the message queue takes 3 normalized cycles, the same as any on-chip memory access.

An intimate processor/network coupling reduces the cost of actual message transmission, but we must also account for the cost of dynamic scheduling introduced by messages, since they must be integrated with the rest of the program. Optimizing for local messages raised this issue, which the following sections address in more detail.

5 Dynamic Scheduling and Control Cost

This section examines the cost of control and shows how it is influenced by a combination of hardware mechanisms: prioritized scheduling and dispatch, multiple contexts, and atomic operations. While in a more conventional setting, we would be concerned only with the costs of jumps and branches, in the context of fine-grained parallel programs, the flow of control in the program is closely tied to the asynchronous arrival of messages, so we must also be concerned with the costs of dynamic scheduling and synchronization.

5.1 TAM requirements

The bottom three segments in Figure 2 show the relative cost of control. In TAM control is realized with the fork, switch, post, and swap instructions. Basic control flow is described by the fork instruction, which attempts to enable a thread in the current frame, and switch, which is a conditional fork to one of two threads. If a thread is synchronizing, it has an associated synchronization counter in the frame. Fork will decrement the counter and, if the counter becomes zero, enable the thread. When a fork

___

[2]Moving computation into the inlet, as in a message-driven model, does not help because it replaces memory accesses for storing message data with memory accesses for retrieving local operands.

succeeds then the thread address is pushed onto the LCV, the structure that holds the list of threads that are ready to run for the current frame. At the end of every thread is a stop instruction, which pops the next enabled thread and transfers control to it.

In addition, threads can be enabled from inlets by a post instruction. Whereas fork enables a thread for the currently running frame, post enables a thread for the frame associated with the message, whether it is currently running, idle, or ready. A post of a synchronizing thread requires decrementing the synchronization counter, just as fork does. If the post enables the thread, then it must check the state of the frame. If the frame is idle, it is made ready and placed on the frame queue. Finally, the swap instruction schedules the next frame from the ready queue.

Observe that inlets and threads cooperate in determining the flow of computation, but inlets may preempt threads to handle incoming messages. The two levels of scheduling share the synchronization counters, the continuation vector, and the frame ready queue. Thus, the implementation must guarantee that either thread and frame scheduling operations (*e.g.*, fork, stop, and swap) are atomic with respect to post instructions or that threads and inlets use distinct resources.

5.2 Hardware support

Recall that the J-Machine provides distinct priority levels for threads and inlets with separate register sets, and upon message arrival the hardware dispatches to the inlet, unless interrupts have been explicitly disabled. Since there are no read-modify-write operations on memory, disabling interrupts becomes the primary means of ensuring atomicity. The CM-5 has a single user level, uses a single register set, and, as described in the previous section, uses a synchronous model for receiving messages.

5.3 Implementation

The implementation of the fork, stop, and swap instructions is basically the same on both machines. The translator specializes most forks into fall throughs and branches, which eliminates the corresponding stop at the end of the thread. The remaining forks translate into a push onto the LCV. A pointer to the top of the LCV is kept in a register. The top portion of Table 2 shows the cost of the specific code sequences, depending on the position of the fork in the thread and whether the destination thread is synchronizing. Taking the dynamic frequencies of these cases into account, the average cost of a fork is about 8 cycles on both the CM-5′ and J′-Machine. Nonetheless, forks account for roughly half of the cost of control operations. Both machines implement synchronization counters as locations in the frame which must be initialized to the entry count of their associated thread. This incurs the cost of a memory write.

The instruction sequence executed for post depends on whether or not the target thread is synchronizing and on the state of the frame. When the frame is idle or ready, the CV pointer is contained in the frame, not a register. Also, if the frame is idle it must be placed on the ready queue. However, if the thread is being posted to the running frame, it can simply be pushed onto the LCV, like a fork. On the J′-Machine, the cost of a post to a running frame is higher because the register holding the pointer to the top of the LCV is stored in the low-priority (thread) context, causing a slight penalty for high-priority (inlet) code access. Similarly, determining if the post is for the running frame incurs the cost of accessing the other register context.

5.4 CM-5: Compiler-controlled message reception

The CM-5 translator inserts polls into the threads to allow for message reception. The poll incurs a cost of 9 cycles; however, by placing the polls in the appropriate places, it ensures that fork, stop, and swap run atomically relative to post. Eliminating the cost of polling by implementing an interrupt-based approach on the CM-5 is impractical for fine-grained parallelism. This is due to the high cost of an interrupt, about the same as 10 polls.

The cost of a post is reduced further in inlets that handle an ifetch response. If the element being fetched is local and present (see Section 6), the response inlet is inlined into the thread. This eliminates all the inlet overhead and as a result turns the post into a fork. The result is that the average post instruction takes between 9 and 13 cycles depending on the application program.

5.5 J-Machine: Asynchronous message reception

The J-Machine supports two-level scheduling directly, with threads interrupted by the automatic dispatch to an inlet. The challenge with this approach is ensuring that the fork, switch, and swap instructions run atomically.

TAM operation	J′′ cycles	J′ cycles	CM-5′ cycles
Fork a thread			
Fall through	0	0	0
Branch to thread			
unsynchronizing	1	1	1
successful sync.	4	4	4
unsuccessful sync.	13	13	13
Push thread onto CV			
unsynchronizing	5	5	5
successful sync.	10	10	10
unsuccessful sync.	7	7	7
Switch one of two threads	fork+2	fork+2	fork+2
Stop (pop thread from CV)	5	5	5
Poll	0	4	9
Initialize sync. counter	4	4	4
Post a thread from inlet			
Idle frame			
unsynchronizing	19	19	19
successful sync.	24	24	23
unsuccessful sync.	11	7	7
Ready frame			
unsynchronizing	15	15	14
successful sync.	20	20	19
unsuccessful sync.	11	7	7
Running frame			
unsynchronizing	31	10	8
successful sync.	31	15	12
unsuccessful sync.	27	7	7

Table 2: *Cost of TAM synchronization and scheduling instructions. J′′-Machine represents the asynchronous J′-Machine, discussed in Section 5.5. For most operations, several different versions reflect the various compiler optimizations or runtime conditions, such as whether a fork can be combined with a stop into a branch, whether the target thread is synchronizing, and whether the synchronization was successful or not.*

The first approach we adopted was to restrict the use of shared resources, i.e., the synchronization counters and CV pointers. In this approach, each inlet contains code to check whether the inlet frame is the same as the currently-running frame. If so, the synchronization counter and the thread address are pushed onto a special stack which does not interfere with thread execution. When the CV is empty, these posts are processed. Message interrupts are disabled when the special stack is being cleared. Swapping frames is made atomic by explicitly disabling interrupts.

This approach had the advantage of leaving interrupts disabled a minimal amount of time, shortening the waiting time of incoming messages, meaning that requests are serviced more quickly and the queue is less likely to overflow.

However, the cost of a `post` to a running frame (including the subsequent processing) was considered unacceptably high, as shown in Table 2. The cost of an unsuccessful `post` is also higher since the status of the frame must be checked before the synchronization counter is decremented and tested.

By leaving interrupts disabled for a significant proportion of thread execution, the J-Machine can almost be thought of as using polling instead of being fully message-driven. Setting or resetting the interrupt flag on the MDP takes two one-cycle instructions, which makes the J-Machine "poll" instruction 4 cycles.

5.6 Discussion

Control in fine-grained parallel programs involves the integration of asynchronous events with the control flow internal to the computation. In TAM, the two are closely related as the compiler generates the code for both scheduling levels. With this kind of coupling, the compiler can partition the available registers by convention; hardware partitioning into distinct contexts can restrict how registers can be used and can prevent certain optimizations.

The close relationship between the two levels also requires that asynchronous scheduling be complemented by efficient atomic operations on shared resources. Polling for messages avoids this issue and is acceptable for fine-grained parallelism. For instance, in our benchmark programs, polling accounts, on average, for 4% of execution time. It may, however, constitute unnecessary overhead for coarser-grained computation.

In hindsight, it appears that instead of focusing resources on multiple register contexts, it would be more advantageous to provide support for atomicity and fine-grained control operations, like `fork`, which contribute as much as 40% to the cost of running a program.

6 Heap access cost

The I-structure memory model used in TAM requires split-phase access to synchronizing data structures in the global heap. Implementing this memory model has multiple facets: (i) to access a remote heap location involves generating a request message, (ii) to perform synchronization on memory *elements*, each is augmented by a few tag bits which must be checked and updated on every access, and (iii) remote and suspended accesses must be delivered to the computation when they complete. The costs of the first and third parts were described in Sections 4 and 5, respectively. This section focuses on the middle portion and considers whether J-Machine hardware support for tags is beneficial.

6.1 Requirements

In TAM, the heap consists of 64-bit elements, each with a small tag. The tag indicates whether the element is empty, holds data, points to a list of waiting (deferred) readers, or holds a thunk which must be evaluated to yield the data value. The exact state transitions follow Id90 I-structure semantics and permit synchronization on a per-element basis. The discussion in this section focuses on I-structures, but it applies equally to other global heap structures (*e.g.*, M-structures). Three issues arise in implementing I-structure operations: representing the presence bits, checking and updating their state on every access, and maintaining the lists of deferred readers.

6.2 Hardware support

The J-Machine provides tagged memory in hardware to support dynamic typing and dynamic synchronization. Each 32-bit memory word is augmented with 4 tag bits, and instructions may trap on certain tag values. TAM does not require dynamic typing, so it cannot demonstrate the benefit of this use of tags. (A significant component of the high-level compilation process from Id90 to TAM is type inference and resolution of overloading to eliminate the need for dynamic typing.) Tags are used to support the I-structure state transitions, without binding the specific semantics of I-structures in hardware.

6.3 Implementation

On the J-Machine, each I-structure element uses two words and one four-bit tag which will trap on access to futures (empty locations), transferring control to a handler that enqueues deferred reads in a linked list, the head of which is stored in the structure element. Each link in the list holds the node, inlet, and frame information necessary to satisfy the read when a write occurs. When an I-structure is allocated each element's tag must be set to empty, which requires one store per element.

On the CM-5, the tags are stored in a memory area disjoint from the data area. One tag byte is allocated for each 8-byte I-structure element, which allows 8 tags to be cleared at once. All I-structure accesses must explicitly check the tag byte before reading or writing the data. Deferred reads are handled similarly as on the J-Machine.

6.4 Discussion

Table 3 shows the costs of I-structure heap accesses in detail. The simple case of reading a present data element is where hardware tags exhibit some advantage. On the CM-5, the tag check is half of the access cost in this case. With tags, the trap occurs on deferred reads and all stores. Without tags, these cases require only a branch. So the deciding factor is the frequency of the simple case. We find that this differs radically on different programs. On Simple

TAM operation	Cycles	
	J'-Machine	CM-5'
I-fetch		
Data present	6	9
Defer	48	41
I-store		
Cell empty	14	15
Deferred readers	17	22
I-structure allocate (N words)		
Local/remote policy	—	7
Allocate	18	18
Clear tags	$5N$	$.75N$

Table 3: *Access to data structures with synchronization on a per-element basis. The costs shown reflect the memory access including checking and updating the tags. I-structure allocation includes initializing all tags to empty.*

there are more than seven ifetches per istore, and only 3% of the ifetches are deferred. On Gamteb, there are only 1.6 ifetches per istore, and 24% of the ifetches are deferred.

The other difference between the two implementations is the often neglected time to allocate an I-structure, which includes initializing all tags to empty. On the J-Machine, each element must be set separately to the future-tagged value denoting an empty unrequested element. On the CM-5, the tags of eight elements can be initialized using a single store-double instruction.

Returning to the cost breakdown in Figure 2 we see that the cost of actually accessing the heap is only a fraction of the total cost. Once the cost of the message component and the control component are included, it becomes apparent that the primary factor in determining the utility of the hardware mechanisms supporting the global heap is the ratio of local to remote accesses. On remote access, the message handling overhead diminishes the impact of fast tag checking. While treating the local access specially in software reduces both the message and control overhead, it incurs the cost of the tag check. However, when at least 30% of accesses are local, the reduction in control overhead balances the difference in cost of sending messages on the CM-5'.

7 Summary

We have compared the performance of the J-Machine, a recent experimental architecture with several novel mechanisms that support fine-grained parallelism, and the CM-5, a recent commercial architecture using conventional Sparc processors, on fine-grained parallel programs written in Id90. A complete quantitative comparison in this regime is very difficult because there are so many variables that can influence performance and there is little consensus on what constitutes a representative workload. We follow a method of analysis similar to the Abstract Machine Characterization Model used to evaluate a wide range of conventional machines and benchmarks [12]. We normalize for software effects, including programming language, programming style, and high-level compiler optimizations by using a common low-level representation of each program in terms of a Threaded Abstract Machine. Machine-specific optimizations are realized in compiling the TAM code to each machine. Examination of the generated code yields the cost for each TAM primitive. An instrumented version of the program is run to produce roughly a hundred dynamic statistics. These are combined with the machine cost coefficients to obtain the average cycles per TAM instruction.

We look forward to a much broader set of studies following a similar methodology using additional machines and additional language frameworks. Clearly it should be possible to evaluate proposals such as *T [11] in this framework. Although other parallel language implementations may differ from TAM in many ways, the primary ingredients are likely to be similar: message exchange, remote references, synchronization, control flow, and dynamic scheduling. We do anticipate that the granularity of parallelism will have a significant impact on the evaluation. Coarser grained models will not stress the message handling and dynamic scheduling as heavily.

In this comparison we found that traditional architectural issues, such as the average memory access time and the floating point performance had a substantial impact on the performance of the experimental architecture. After correcting for these factors, the fast message send and receive are a clear gain, accounting for as much as a 50% improvement in some programs. Treating local messages as a special case in software compensated for larger message overhead in many programs because it also reduced the control overhead of dynamic scheduling; however, the resulting system is more sensitive to variations in the remote reference frequency. The fast message dispatch mechanism was of modest value in the absence of adequate atomic operations on resources that are shared between the primary computation and the message handlers which operate on its behalf. Multiple disjoint register sets were not of particular value, since code was generated for the different scheduling levels from a single program. The compiler could simply partition the register file, which allows a tight integration of the two levels. The utility of tagged memory was undercut by the high cost of initialization.

Our measurements suggest some directions in the design of parallel computers:

- The network interface should be integrated with the processor register file or cache.

- Fast dispatch to user-level message handlers significantly reduces communication overhead. However, careful attention must be paid to atomicity and sharing between the message handlers and the on-going computation.

- Fine-grained parallel programs are control intensive. When the communication and memory requirements are adequately addressed, this stands out as the primary avenue for further advancement.

- While individual mechanisms need to be efficient in isolation, the interactions among the mechanisms must be carefully considered.

The general observation is that in evaluating novel architectures it is essential to carry the implementation of programming languages to completion, as that is the only way to perceive the completeness and the synergy between the various mechanisms and to determine the relative importance of each component.

Acknowledgments

We are grateful to the anonymous referees for their valuable comments. We would also like to thank Fred Chong, Richard Lethin, and Nate Osgood for their comments on earlier versions of this paper. Computational support at Berkeley was provided by the NSF Infrastructure Grant number CDA-8722788. Funding at MIT was provided in part by the Defense Advanced Research Projects Agency under contracts N00014-87K-0825, F19628-92-C-0045, and N00014-91-J-1698 and in part by a National Science Foundation Presidential Young Investigator Award, Grant MIP-8657531, with matching funds from General Electric Corporation, IBM Corporation, and AT&T. Ellen Spertus is supported by a NSF Graduate Fellowship. Seth Copen Goldstein is supported by an AT&T Graduate Fellowship. Klaus Erik Schauser is supported by an IBM Graduate Fellowship. Thorsten von Eicken is supported by the Semiconductor Research Corporation. David Culler is supported by an NSF Presidential Faculty Fellowship CCR-9253705 and LLNL Grant UCB-ERL-92/172.

References

[1] Arvind and K. Ekanadham. Future Scientific Programming on Parallel Machines. *Journal of Parallel and Distributed Computing*, 5(5):460–493, October 1988.

[2] Arvind, S. K. Heller, and R. S. Nikhil. Programming Generality and Parallel Computers. In *Proc. of the Fourth Int. Symp. on Biological and Artificial Intelligence Systems*, pages 255–286. ESCOM (Leider), Trento, Italy, September 1988.

[3] D. H. Bailey et al. The NAS Parallel Benchmarks — Summary and Preliminary Results. In *Proc. Supercomputing '91*, November 1991.

[4] P. J. Burns, M. Christon, R. Schweitzer, O. M. Lubeck, H. J. Wasserman, M. L. Simmons, and D. V. Pryor. Vectorization of Monte-Carlo Particle Transport: An Architectural Study using the LANL Benchmark "Gamteb". In *Proc. Supercomputing '89*. IEEE Computer Society and ACM SIGARCH, New York, NY, November 1989.

[5] W. P. Crowley, C. P. Hendrickson, and T. E. Rudy. The SIMPLE code. Technical Report UCID 17715, Lawrence Livermore Laboratory, February 1978.

[6] D. Culler, A. Sah, K. Schauser, T. von Eicken, and J. Wawrzynek. Fine-grain Parallelism with Minimal Hardware Support: A Compiler-Controlled Threaded Abstract Machine. In *Proc. of 4th Int. Conf. on Architectural Support for Programming Languages and Operating Systems*, Santa-Clara, CA, April 1991. (Also available as Technical Report UCB/CSD 91/591, CS Div., University of California at Berkeley).

[7] D. E. Culler. Managing Parallelism and Resources in Scientific Dataflow Programs. Technical Report 446, MIT Lab for Comp. Sci., March 1990. (PhD Thesis, Dept. of EECS, MIT).

[8] S. C. Goldstein. Implementation of a Threaded Abstract Machine on Sequential and Multiprocessors. Master's thesis, Computer Science Division — EECS, U.C. Berkeley, 1993. (In preparation, to appear as UCB/CSD Technical Report).

[9] J. Gustafson, G. Montry, and Benner R. Development of Parallel Methods for a 1024-Processor Hypercube. *SIAM Journal on Scientific and Statistical Computing*, 9, 1988.

[10] R. S. Nikhil. ID Language Reference Manual Version 90.1. Technical Report CSG Memo 284-2, MIT Lab for Comp. Sci., 545 Tech. Square, Cambridge, MA, 1991.

[11] R. S. Nikhil, G. M. Papadopoulos, and Arvind. *T: A Killer Micro for A Brave New World. Technical Report CSG Memo 325, MIT Lab for Comp. Sci., 545 Tech. Square, Cambridge, MA, January 1991.

[12] R. H. Saavedra-Barrera and A. J. Smith. Benchmarking and The Abstract Machine Characterization Model. Technical Report UCB/CSD 90/607, U.C. Berkeley, Computer Science Div., November 1990.

[13] K. E. Schauser, D. Culler, and T. von Eicken. Compiler-controlled Multithreading for Lenient Parallel Languages. In *Proceedings of the 1991 Conference on Functional Programming Languages and Computer Architecture*, Cambridge, MA, August 1991. (Also available as Technical Report UCB/CSD 91/640, CS Div., University of California at Berkeley).

[14] J. P. Singh, W.-D. Weber, and A. Gupta. SPLASH: Stanford Parallel Applications for Shared-Memory. Technical Report CSL-TR-91-469, Stanford University, 1991.

[15] E. Spertus. Execution of Dataflow Programs on General-Purpose Hardware. Master's thesis, Department of EECS, Massachusetts Institute of Technology, 545 Tech. Square, Cambridge, MA, August 1992. To be expanded and released as MIT AI Lab Technical Report 1380.

[16] Thinking Machines Corporation, Cambridge, MA. *The Connection Machine CM-5 Technical Summary*, January 1992.

Author Index

About the Authors

Laxmi N. Bhuyan

Laxmi N. Bhuyan is a professor in the Computer Science Department at Texas A&M University, College Station. He has been chosen as a Haliburton Professor and a Fellow of the Texas Engineering Experiment Station. Previously, he was with the Center for Advanced Computer Studies at the University of Southwestern Louisiana, Lafayette. His research interests are computer architecture, parallel and distributed computing, and performance evaluation.

He currently serves as an editor for the *Parallel Computing* journal and as the area editor for systems architecture for *Computer* magazine. He is Program Committee Chair for the First International Symposium on High-Performance Computer Architecture (HPCA), being held in Raleigh, North Carolina, in 1995.

Bhuyan received the MSc degree in electrical engineering from Sambalpur University, India, in 1979 and the PhD degree in computer engineering from Wayne State University, Detroit, Michigan, in 1982. He is an ACM Lecturer and was a distinguished visitor of the IEEE Computer Society.

Xiaodong Zhang

Xiaodong Zhang is an associate professor of computer science and director of the High-Performance Computing and Software Laboratory at the University of Texas at San Antonio. In 1993, he received the Distinguished Research Achievement Award from the University. He has held research and visiting faculty positions at Rice University, Houston, Texas, and Texas A&M University, College Station. His research interests are parallel and distributed computation, parallel-system performance evaluation, and scientific computing. His research has been continually supported by numerous federal and private funding agencies and industries.

He currently serves on the editorial board of the *Parallel Computing* journal.

Zhang received the BS degree in electrical engineering from Beijing Polytechnic University, China, in 1982 and the MS and PhD degrees in computer science from the University of Colorado, Boulder, in 1985 and 1989, respectively. He is an ACM National Lecturer, a member of ACM and SIAM, and a senior member of the IEEE Computer Society.

Other titles from
IEEE Computer Society Press

Multidatabase Systems:
An Advanced Solution for Global Information Sharing
edited by A. R. Hurson, M. W. Bright, and S. H. Pakzad

Begins with an introduction defining multidatabase systems and provides a background on their evolution. Subsequent chapters examine the motivations for and major objectives of multidatabase systems, the environment and range of solutions for global information-sharing systems, the issues specific to multidatabase systems, and different approaches to designing a multidatabase system. The book focuses on the application of multidatabase systems to integrate data from preexisting, heterogeneous local databases in a distributed environment. These applications present global users with transparent methods enabling them to use the total information in the system.

Sections: Introduction, Global Information-Sharing Environment, Multidatabase Issues, Multidatabase Design Choices, Multidatabase Projects, The Future of Multidatabases.

400 pages. 1993. Hardcover. ISBN 0-8186-4422-2. Catalog # 4422-01 — $62.00 Members $50.00

The Cache Coherence Problem in Shared-Memory Multiprocessors: Hardware Solutions
edited by Milo Tomasevic and Veljko Milutinovic

Provides insight into the nature of the cache coherence problem and the wide variety of proposed hardware solutions available today. The chapters discuss the shared-memory multiprocessor environment, the cache coherence problem and solutions, and directory cache coherence schemes. Other chapters examine scalable schemes for large multiprocessor systems and evaluate different hardware coherence solutions.

Sections: Introductory Issues, Memory Reference Characteristics in Parallel Programs, Directory Cache Coherence Protocols, Snoopy Cache-Coherence Protocols, Coherence in Multilevel Cache Hierarchies, Cache Coherence Schemes in Large-Scale Multiprocessors, Evaluation of Hardware Cache Coherence Schemes.

448 pages. 1993. Hardcover. ISBN 0-8186-4092-8. Catalog # 4092-01 — $62.00 Members $50.00

Codes for Detecting and Correcting Unidirectional Errors
edited by Mario Blaum

Presents state-of-the-art theory and practice for codes that correct or detect unidirectional errors. The text begins with a selection of four papers providing an introduction to the field, including applications. Its also features key papers demonstrating the best results in each subject related to unidirectional errors.

Sections: Unidirectional Errors, Codes for Detecting Unidirectional Errors, Codes for Correcting Unidirectional Errors, Codes for Correcting *t*-Symmetric Errors and Detecting All Unidirectional Errors, Codes for Correcting and Detecting Combinations of Symmetric and Unidirectional Errors, Codes for Detecting and/or Correcting Unidirectional Burst Errors, Codes for Detecting and/or Correcting Unidirectional Byte Errors.

224 pages. 1993. Hardcover. ISBN 0-8186-4182-7. Catalog # 4182-03 — $44.00 Members $35.00

Decision Fusion
by Belur V. Dasarathy

Provides a historical sketch of sensor fusion and presents new research carried out by the author in the past few years. The book begins with a brief overview of sensor fusion and delineates the role of decision fusion within this broader field. The subsequent chapters detail the advances made in decision fusion. It discusses nearly 80 studies focusing on fusion at the decision levels. Following this are reprints of 25 papers considered milestones in the development of this field. The book concludes with a bibliography of more than 500 entries covering the field of sensor fusion.

Sections: Fusion Field Overview, Decision Fusion Under Parallel Configuration, Decision Fusion Under Serial Configuration, Decision Fusion Under Parallel-Serial Configuration, Decision Fusion Survey, Selected Studies, Bibliography.

300 pages. 1993. Hardcover. ISBN 0-8186-4452-4. Catalog # 4452-01 — $55.00 Members $44.00

 IEEE COMPUTER SOCIETY PRESS

▼   **To order call toll-free: 1-800-CS-BOOKS**   ▼

▼   **Fax: (714) 821-4641**   ▼   **E-Mail: cs.books@computer.org**   ▼

10662 Los Vaqueros Circle   Los Alamitos, CA   90720-1264   Phone: (714) 821-8380